W9-BRV-108

CYCLING FRANCE

Sally Dillon
Neil Irvine
Catherine Palmer
Katherine Widing

LONELY PLANET PUBLICATIONS
Melbourne • Oakland • London • Paris

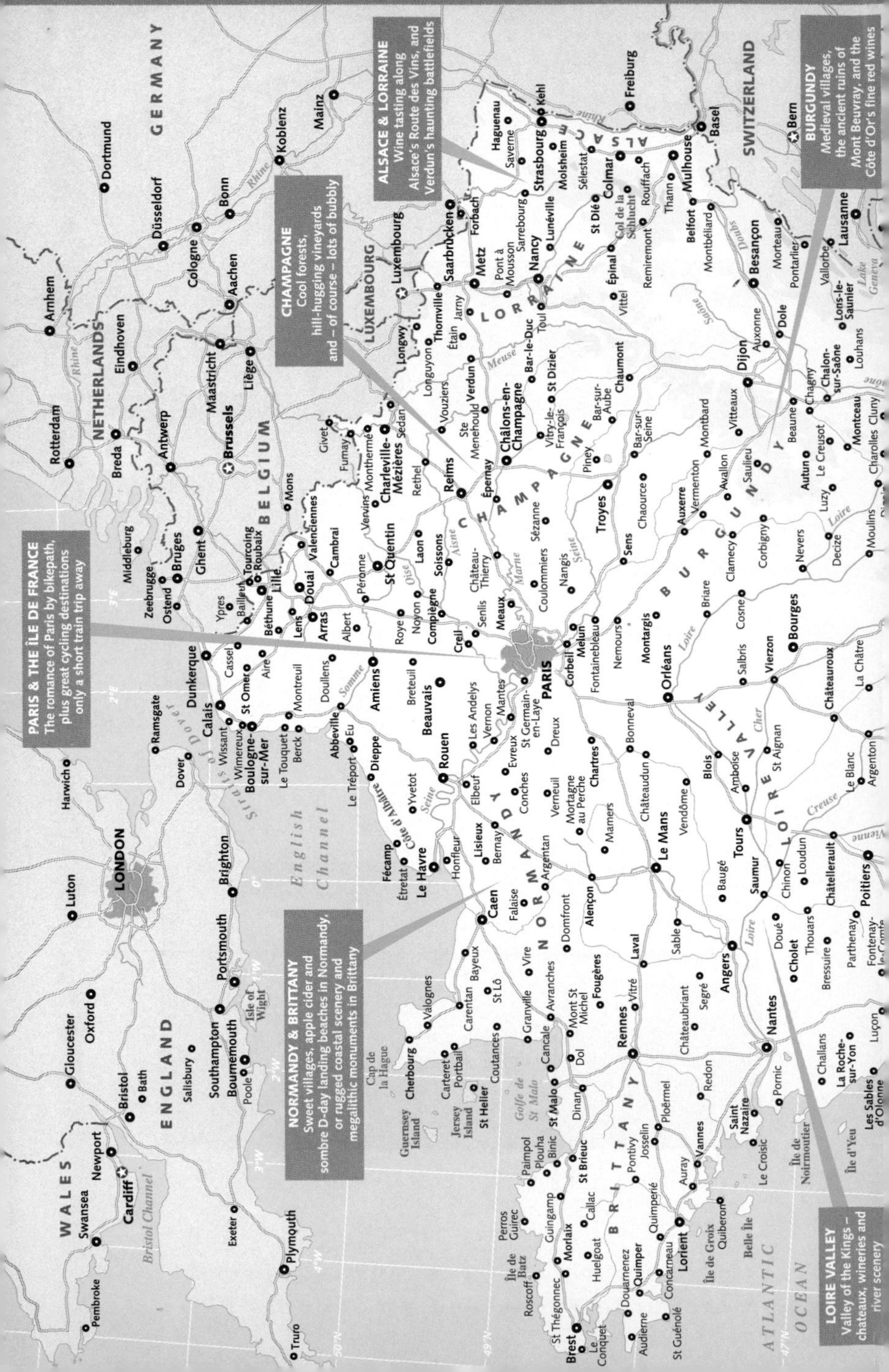

PARIS & THE ÎLE DE FRANCE
The romance of Paris by bikepath, plus great cycling destinations only a short train trip away
CHAMPAGNE
Cool forests, hill-hugging vineyards and – of course – lots of bubbly
ALSACE & LORRAINE
Wine tasting along Alsace's Route des Vins, and Verdun's haunting battlefields
BURGUNDY
Medieval villages, the ancient ruins of Mont Beuvray, and the Côte d'Or's fine red wines
NORMANDY & BRITTANY
Sweet villages, apple cider and sombre D-day landing beaches in Normandy, or rugged coastal scenery and megalithic monuments in Brittany
LOIRE VALLEY
Valley of the Kings – chateaux, wineries and river scenery
WALES
ENGLAND
LONDON
NETHERLANDS
BELGIUM
LUXEMBOURG
GERMANY
SWITZERLAND
NORMANDY
BRITTANY
CHAMPAGNE
LORRAINE
ALSACE
BURGUNDY
LOIRE VALLEY
English Channel
Strait of Dover
Bristol Channel
ATLANTIC OCEAN
Golfe de St Malo
PARIS
Brussels
Luxembourg
Bern
Cardiff
Swansea
Pembroke
Newport
Bristol
Bath
Gloucester
Oxford
Luton
Harwich
Salisbury
Southampton
Portsmouth
Bournemouth
Poole
Brighton
Dover
Ramsgate
Exeter
Plymouth
Truro
Isle of Wight
Rotterdam
Breda
Antwerp
Eindhoven
Arnhem
Middleburg
Zeebrugge
Bruges
Ostend
Ghent
Maastricht
Liège
Aachen
Cologne
Düsseldorf
Dortmund
Bonn
Koblenz
Mainz
Mons
Ypres
Tourcoing
Roubaix
Lille
Dunkerque
Calais
Boulogne-sur-Mer
Wissant
Wimereux
St Omer
Cassel
Aire
Béthune
Lens
Douai
Arras
Valenciennes
Cambrai
Le Touquet
Berck
Montreuil
Abbeville
Eu
Le Tréport
Dieppe
Doullens
Amiens
Albert
Péronne
St Quentin
Laon
Soissons
Noyon
Compiègne
Roye
Breteuil
Beauvais
Creil
Senlis
Meaux
Rouen
Fécamp
Étretat
Le Havre
Honfleur
Yvetot
Elbeuf
Les Andelys
Vernon
Mantes
Evreux
St Germain-en-Laye
Dreux
Conches
Lisieux
Bernay
Caen
Bayeux
Falaise
Argentan
Cherbourg
Valognes
Carentan
St Lô
Coutances
Granville
Avranches
Mont St Michel
Vire
Domfront
Alençon
Mortagne au Perche
Verneuil
Mamers
Chartres
Châteaudun
Bonneval
Le Mans
Laval
Fougères
Rennes
Vitré
St Malo
Dinan
Dol
Cancale
St Brieuc
Binic
Plouha
Paimpol
Guingamp
Perros Guirec
Morlaix
Roscoff
Île de Batz
Huelgoat
Callac
Brest
St Thégonnec
Le Conquet
Douarnenez
Quimper
Audierne
Concarneau
Quimperlé
Lorient
Île de Groix
Quiberon
Belle Île
Auray
Vannes
Pontivy
Josselin
Ploërmel
Redon
Châteaubriant
St Guénolé
Saint Nazaire
Le Croisic
Pornic
Nantes
Île de Noirmoutier
Île d'Yeu
Challans
La Roche-sur-Yon
Les Sables d'Olonne
Luçon
Angers
Segré
Sable
Cholet
Doué
Saumur
Chinon
Loudun
Thouars
Bressuire
Parthenay
Poitiers
Châtellerault
Fontenay-le-Comte
Tours
Baugé
Vendôme
Blois
Amboise
St Aignan
Le Blanc
Argenton
Châteauroux
La Châtre
Vierzon
Bourges
Orléans
Salbris
Montargis
Nemours
Fontainebleau
Melun
Corbeil
Sens
Briare
Cosne
Gien
Clamecy
Auxerre
Vermenton
Avallon
Chaource
Troyes
Nangis
Coulommiers
Château-Thierry
Sézanne
Épernay
Reims
Rethel
Charleville-Mézières
Sedan
Monthermé
Fumay
Givet
Vervins
Châlons-en-Champagne
Ste Menehould
Vouziers
Verdun
Bar-le-Duc
St Dizier
Vitry-le-François
Bar-sur-Aube
Bar-sur-Seine
Chaumont
Piney
Montbard
Vitteaux
Saulieu
Dijon
Auxonne
Dole
Beaune
Chagny
Autun
Le Creusot
Chalon-sur-Saône
Louhans
Montceau
Cluny
Charolles
Luzy
Corbigny
Nevers
Decize
Moulins
Besançon
Morteau
Pontarlier
Vallorbe
Lons-le-Saunier
Lausanne
Lake Geneva
Longwy
Longuyon
Étain
Jarny
Thionville
Metz
Pont à Mousson
Toul
Nancy
Lunéville
Saarbrücken
Forbach
Sarrebourg
Saverne
Haguenau
Strasbourg
Kehl
Molsheim
Sélestat
Colmar
St Dié
Épinal
Vittel
Col de la Schlucht
Remiremont
Rouffach
Thann
Mulhouse
Belfort
Montbéliard
Basel
Freiburg
Rhine
Seine
Loire
Somme
Oise
Aisne
Marne
Meuse
Saône
Doubs
Cher
Creuse
Vienne
Côte d'Albâtre
Cap de la Hague
Guernsey Island
Jersey Island
St Helier
Carteret
Portbail
50°N
49°N
48°N
47°N
4°W
3°W
2°W
1°W
0°
2°E
3°E

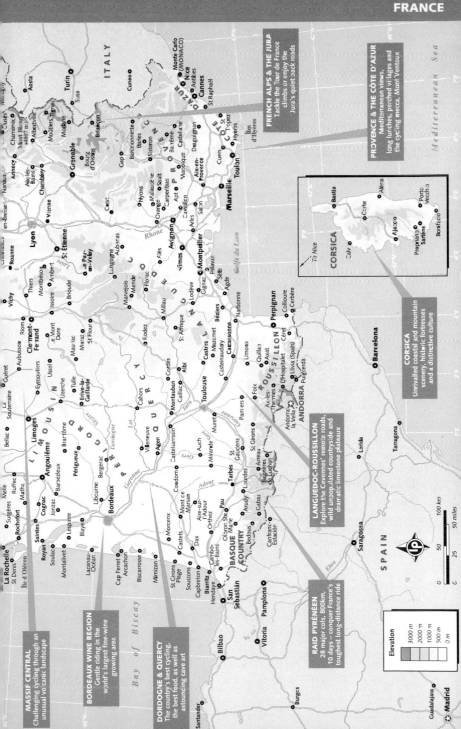

FRANCE

FRENCH ALPS & THE JURA
Tackle the Tour de France climbs or enjoy the Jura's quiet back roads

PROVENCE & THE CÔTE D'AZUR
Mediterranean views, long lunches, perched villages and the cycling mecca, Mont Ventoux

CORSICA
Unrivalled coastal and mountain scenery, historic fortresses and a distinctive culture

LANGUEDOC-ROUSSILLON
Explore the Cévennes' remote roads, wild unpopulated countryside and dramatic limestone plateaux

RAID PYRÉNÉEN
28 major cols, 800km, 10 days – conquer France's toughest long-distance ride

DORDOGNE & QUERCY
The country's best cycling, the best food, as well as astounding cave art

BORDEAUX WINE REGION
Gentle riding in the world's largest fine-wine growing area

MASSIF CENTRAL
Challenging cycling through an unusual volcanic landscape

CORSICA

To Nice

Elevation
3000 m
2000 m
1000 m
500 m
0 m

0   50   100 km
0   25   50 miles

Cycling France
1st edition – February 2001

Published by
Lonely Planet Publications Pty Ltd ABN 36 005 607 983
90 Maribyrnong St, Footscray, Victoria 3011, Australia

Lonely Planet Offices
Australia Locked Bag 1, Footscray, Victoria 3011
USA 150 Linden St, Oakland, CA 94607
UK 10a Spring Place, London NW5 3BH
France 1 rue du Dahomey, 75011 Paris

Photographs
Many of the images in this guide are available for licensing from
Lonely Planet Images (e lpi@lonelyplanet.com.au)

Main front cover photograph
Mont Lazère, Languedoc-Roussillon (Neil Irvine)

Small front cover photograph
Road sign, south-west France (Sally Dillon)

Back cover photographs (from left to right)
Cycling up to the Col de Jouels, Pyrenees (Neil Irvine)
Cyclist on Mont Ventoux, Provence (Neil Irvine)
Woman riding a bicycle with the obligatory baguette (John Elk III)

ISBN 1 86450 036 0

Printed by SNP Offset Sdn Bhd
Printed in Malaysia

Although the authors and Lonely Planet try to make the information as accurate as possible, we accept no responsibility for any loss, injury or inconvenience sustained by anyone using this book.

Contents

2 Contents

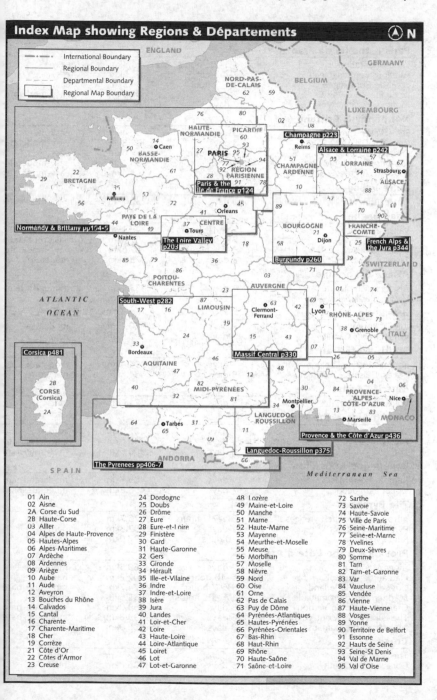

Index Map showing Regions & Départements

01 Ain	24 Dordogne	48 Lozère	72 Sarthe
02 Aisne	25 Doubs	49 Maine-et-Loire	73 Savoie
2A Corse du Sud	26 Drôme	50 Manche	74 Haute-Savoie
2B Haute-Corse	27 Eure	51 Marne	75 Ville de Paris
03 Allier	28 Eure-et-Loire	52 Haute-Marne	76 Seine-Maritime
04 Alpes de Haute-Provence	29 Finistère	53 Mayenne	77 Seine-et-Marne
05 Hautes-Alpes	30 Gard	54 Meurthe-et-Moselle	78 Yvelines
06 Alpes-Maritimes	31 Haute-Garonne	55 Meuse	79 Deux-Sèvres
07 Ardèche	32 Gers	56 Morbihan	80 Somme
08 Ardennes	33 Gironde	57 Moselle	81 Tarn
09 Ariège	34 Hérault	58 Nièvre	82 Tarn-et-Garonne
10 Aube	35 Ille-et-Vilaine	59 Nord	83 Var
11 Aude	36 Indre	60 Oise	84 Vaucluse
12 Aveyron	37 Indre-et-Loire	61 Orne	85 Vendée
13 Bouches du Rhône	38 Isère	62 Pas de Calais	86 Vienne
14 Calvados	39 Jura	63 Puy de Dôme	87 Haute-Vienne
15 Cantal	40 Landes	64 Pyrénées-Atlantiques	88 Vosges
16 Charente	41 Loir-et-Cher	65 Hautes-Pyrénées	89 Yonne
17 Charente-Maritime	42 Loire	66 Pyrénées-Orientales	90 Territoire de Belfort
18 Cher	43 Haute-Loire	67 Bas-Rhin	91 Essonne
19 Corrèze	44 Loire-Atlantique	68 Haut-Rhin	92 Hauts de Seine
21 Côte d'Or	45 Loiret	69 Rhône	93 Seine-St Denis
22 Côtes d'Armor	46 Lot	70 Haute-Saône	94 Val de Marne
23 Creuse	47 Lot-et-Garonne	71 Saône-et-Loire	95 Val d'Oise

The Rides	Duration	Distance	Standard
Paris & the Île de France			
Paris Orientation	1½–2½ hours	11.4km	easy
Fabulous Fontainebleau	2–4 hours	42.5km	easy
Forêt de Compiègne	1½–3 hours	34.3km	easy
Île de France Diversity	2 days	90.3km	easy-moderate
Monet's Passions	2 days	64.7km	easy
Normandy & Brittany			
Seine Valley Circuit	2½–4½ hours	50.4km	easy-moderate
Calvados Classique	3 days	132.8km	easy-moderate
D-day Beaches	3–5½ hours	57.0km	easy
Northern Brittany Majesty	4 days	195.1km	easy-moderate
Southern Brittany Contrasts	6 days	254.4km	easy-moderate
Loire Valley			
Chateau Explorer	5 days	232.7km	easy-moderate
Champagne			
Vallée de la Marne	2½–4½ hours	46.3km	easy-moderate
Montagne de Reims	2½–5 hours	52.8km	easy-moderate
Côte des Blancs	3–5½ hours	57.5km	easy-moderate
Taste of Southern Champagne	3 days	173.8km	moderate
Alsace & Lorraine			
Alsatian Wine Route	4 days	233.1km	moderate-hard
Verdun Battlefields	1½–3 hours	25.0km	easy
Burgundy			
Classic Burgundy	7 days	360.0km	moderate
Wine Lover's Circuit	3 days	127.0km	easy
South-West France			
Bordeaux Wine Explorer	6 days	294.4km	moderate
Caves, Cuisine & Chateaux	9 days	454.8km	moderate
Massif Central			
Volcans d'Auvergne	3 days	171.0km	hard
French Alps & the Jura			
Vercors Contrasts	3 days	202.0km	hard
High Cols of the Tour de France	4 days	245.0km	hard-very hard
The Jura	6 days	300.6km	moderate-hard
Languedoc-Roussillon			
Remote Cévennes	5 days	405.7km	moderate-hard
Upper Languedoc	7 days	458.8km	moderate-hard
The Pyrenees			
Introduction to the Pyrenees	3½–7½ hours	75.7km	moderate
Pyrenean Foothills	2 days	92.8km	hard
Raid Pyrénéen	10 days	827.0km	very hard
Provence & the Côte d'Azur			
Alpes Maritime	2 days	69.5km	moderate
Plateau de Caussols	5–10 hours	102.2km	hard
Côte d'Azur Hinterland	3½–7 hours	74.7km	moderate-hard
Mediterranean Promenade	1¾–3½ hours	32.5km	easy
Grand Canyon du Verdon	3 days	159.0km	moderate-hard
The Luberon & Mont Ventoux	6 days	339.8km	moderate-hard
Majesty of the Romans	3 days	206.9km	moderate
Corsica			
The Scented Isle	5 days	222.9km	hard
Corsica – the South	5 days	226.0km	hard

Features	Page

The Authors

Katherine Widing

Katherine began cycling when she was five years old, riding her bike to school in Melbourne, Australia. France is the country that inspired her to take up international bicycle touring. There was always 'so much to eat, so little time'. Eventually, she realised she could satisfy her culinary desires for picnic lunches and three-course dinners by working up a substantial appetite by cycling. It also allowed her to travel at a pace she enjoyed, observing, meeting people, and inhaling the sights, sounds and smells of France.

Since then she has cycle toured in several European countries. Her first book, *Cycling the Netherlands, Belgium & Luxembourg*, was co-authored with her husband, Jerry. She is a freelance travel writer and has been the travel book editor for *Transitions Abroad* magazine since 1991. She currently lives in Seattle, Washington. When not on the road, she works at Wide World Books & Maps, a travel bookshop, allowing her to travel vicariously through customers' adventures. *Cycling France* is her first Lonely Planet adventure.

Sally Dillon

Sally spent her university years in Brisbane saving for overseas holidays. After five months aboard the Australian tall ship *Young Endeavour* in 1992, Sally was looking for other adventures and discovered cycling. A year in New Zealand introduced the thrills of mountain biking and touring in the rain, and it wasn't long before she was honeymooning on the back of a tandem.

These days Sally lives with her husband, Peter Hines, and eight and a half bikes (counting the unicycle) in Melbourne, Australia, which they escape as often as possible for cycling tours in search of decent hills, quiet country roads, bakeries, wineries and beaches. A member of the Melbourne Bicycle Touring Club, Sally is also president of the Tandem Club of Australia and a committed cycle commuter.

Sally worked as a radio journalist, public relations practitioner and academic before joining Lonely Planet as an editor and, in 1999, an author.

Catherine Palmer

Born in Adelaide, South Australia, Catherine has made pedalling around France something of a life's work. Having lived in France for 18 months, she gained, in 1997, a PhD in Anthropology from the University of Adelaide, for which she examined the making of French identity through the Tour de France. Her work on the subject can be found in a range of academic and other publications. Before her incarnation as a roving cycle tourist for Lonely Planet, Catherine worked as a researcher, a university lecturer and an ethnographer.

Neil Irvine

Neil has been an unashamed Francophile ever since his first cycle tour in France in 1987. After founding *Australian Cyclist* magazine in 1989 (he was editor until 1998), he made further cycle touring visits to France with his features editor and wife, Alethea.

Since 1987 he has twice completed the Raid Pyrénéen, a 790km, 28-pass traverse of the French Pyrenees, and has ridden the 1200km Paris-Brest-Paris randonnée three times. Neil has also toured extensively – by road bike, mountain bike and tandem – in Australia, North America, Europe and (as a Lonely Planet author) New Zealand. His interests include involvement in lobbying for better cycling conditions at local, state and national level, and a love of the challenges of distance and mountains. Lately his riding has been more gentle, with a child-seat on the back, as he introduces his young son, Alexander, to the pleasures of cycling.

FROM THE AUTHORS

Katherine Widing A warm *merci beaucoup* to all the wonderful French people and cyclists I met en route. An enormous merci to tourist office staff throughout France for their valuable assistance.

Many thanks to Sally Dillon, Neil Irvine and Catherine Palmer, a great team of authors, *encore une fois* to Sally in her second role as editor, and to Darren Elder, the grand overseer of the project, for your patience, advice and answers to endless questions. Thanks also to Vincent and Babeth Vallet, Benoit and Anne Bruder, Rose Burke, Holly Smith, Mary Schafer, Miles Roddis, Sandra Bardwell, the terrific staff of the bicycle-friendly Port Royal Hotel in Paris, Marine Doisy at Roue Libre, Joseph in Lisieux, and to the manufacturers of Kevlar tyres (which allowed me to cycle France for months without a single flat tyre).

Special thanks to my husband Jerry, for his tolerance and support, and to Abigail Hookway for enthusiastic pedalling. I would like to dedicate the Paris chapter to my mother, a brave and resourceful woman who, after surviving WWII in Poland, spent three months in the 'City of Lights' awaiting passage to Australia.

Sally Dillon Being involved from this book's inception to the day it went to the printer has been made rewarding by the help and support of my friends, family and work colleagues.

Special thanks to Darren Elder for all his guidance throughout; to Katherine Widing for her committment; and to Associate Publisher Sue Galley for sending me to France. To Ali Smith and Damien Basa, *milles mercis* for helping with route research and providing a welcoming home base in France. Thanks also to Vincent and Babeth Vallet for their hospitality and putting up with weird queries.

In preparing for the trip, Frederique Robert and Veronique Wanis helped me brush up on my French; Don Macrea, Neil Irvine, Clare Walder, Wayne & Vanessa Goldsmith, and Heather Margetts shared their French favourite places; and Paul & Charlie Farren lent me their precious books. Jean-Bernard Carillet and the other staff in the Lonely Planet Paris office gave a friendly welcome and valuable advice before I hit the road, while author Miles Roddis helped with some Massif Central information.

To fellow cycle tourists Steffan Jacobs and Markus Eckardt; Markus Holub and 'the seven Germans'; and Mark and Alexandra of Switzerland – thanks for your company (and spare parts). Gary Humphries provided a tent in an emergency; Guy Brooks and Nicky Dawson reminded me what it's like to be holidaying in Corsica; and my husband, Peter, made three weeks on that beautiful island memorable.

Thanks also to the Hines family for the use of the Straddie shed; the Dillons for moral support; and my friends from the Tandem Club of Australia, the Brisbane Bicycle Touring Association and the Melbourne Bicycle Touring Club for continuing to make cycling fun.

Catherine Palmer A number of people helped make these wheels turn, and special thanks are due to the following: Martin Pruimers for his encyclopaedic knowledge of Paris-Roubaix, Jérôme Gonin and his little red Peugeot for his hair-raising help in negotiating the freight section of Roissy Charles de Gaulle airport, the staff of tourist offices in Auxerre and Pont-en-Royans, as well as the many fellow cycle tourists encountered along the way. Bonne route, bon courage to you all. Thanks also to Neil and Sally, and to Katherine – leader of the pack – Widing for dinner in Paris and for co-ordinating this particular Tour de France. Darren Elder deserves special thanks for his editorial savvy. Above all, I am grateful to David Johnson for his unfailing support throughout 1800km of pedalling (and the rest), for carrying the heavy stuff, and for knowing his left from his right.

Neil Irvine It would not have been possible for me to undertake this project without the tremendous support of my wife, Alethea, of my parents, Bob and Dulcie, and of Alethea's parents, Bill and Mary, who all kept the household and two-year-old Alexander under control while I was absent and during the long writing/correcting process.

Special thanks to Mary Morison – who is in no way the cliché mother-in-law – for using her excellent conversational French to assist with detailed research. And to Janet Flanagan of Pyrenean Pursuits Guesthouse for fielding, and patiently answering, all manner of strange questions from a stranger.

Thanks are also due to Graeme & Sue Lothringer for putting up with my dragging the chain along the Pyrenees and to the staff at Bicycle New South Wales for allowing me to monopolise their equipment.

Maps & Profiles

Most rides described in this book have an accompanying map that shows the route, services provided in towns en route as well as any attractions and possible side trips. These maps are oriented left to right in the direction of travel; a north point is located in the top right corner of each map. The maps are intended to stand alone but could be used together with one of the commercial maps recommended in the Planning section for each ride.

We provide a profile, or elevation chart, when there is a significant level of climbing and/or descending on a day's ride; most of the time these charts are included on the corresponding map but where space does not permit they accompany the text for that day. These charts are approximate and should be used as a guide only.

MAP LEGEND

Note: not all symbols displayed below appear in this book

CUE SHEET SYMBOLS

↑ Continue Straight	↰ Left Turn	✳ Point of Interest	⯗ Traffic Lights
↱ Right Turn	↖ Veer Left	▲ Mountain/Hill Climb	◆ Roundabout (Traffic Circle)
↗ Veer Right	↩ Return Trip	⚠ Caution or Hazard	●● Side Trip
		■■ Alternative Route

RIDE MAP SYMBOLS

Airfield	Hotel, Motel, B&B	**CITY MAP SYMBOLS**
Airport	Information	Church
Bike Shop	Point of Interest on ride	Embassy
Cafe, Takeaway Food	Point of Interest	Hospital
Camping	Restaurant	Museum
Hostel, Gîte d'étape	Store, Supermarket	Post Office

ROUTES & TRANSPORT

Freeway, Tunnel	Train Line, Train Station	**CYCLING ROUTES**
D254 Highway, Route Number	Fast Track TGV	Main Route
Major Road	Underground Train	Alternative Route
Street, Minor Road	Metro	Side Trip
Unsealed Road	Cable Car, Chairlift	Previous/Next Day
Lane	Ferry	Bikepath, Track
		Direction of Travel

HYDROGRAPHIC FEATURES

Coastline	Lake	**GEOGRAPHIC FEATURES**
Major River or Canal	Rapids or Lock	Cave
Minor River or Canal	Sand bar	Mountain
		Pass, Saddle

AREA FEATURES

Building	Glacier	**BOUNDARIES**
Cemetery	National/Regional Park	International
		Regional

POPULATION

✪ CAPITAL National Capital	● LARGE Medium City	Town Town on ride
◉ CAPITAL State Capital	● Town or Village Town	Urban Area

9

Cue Sheets

Route directions in this book are given in a series of brief 'cues', which tell you at what kilometre mark to change direction and point out features en route. The cues are placed on the route map, most of the time with a profile, or elevation chart. Together these provide all the primary directions for each route in one convenient reference. The only other thing you need is a cycle computer.

To make the cue sheets as brief as we can, yet still relatively simple to understand, we've developed a series of symbols (see the Map Legend on p9) and the following rule:

Once your route is following a particular road, continue on that road until the cue sheet tells you otherwise.

Follow the road first mentioned in the cue sheet even though it may cross a highway, shrink to a lane, change name (we generally only include the first name, and sometimes the last), wind, duck and climb its way across the country. Rely on us to tell you when to turn off it.

Because the cue sheets rely on an accurate odometer reading we suggest you disconnect your cycle computer (pop it out of the housing or turn the magnet away from the fork-mounted sensor) whenever you deviate from the route.

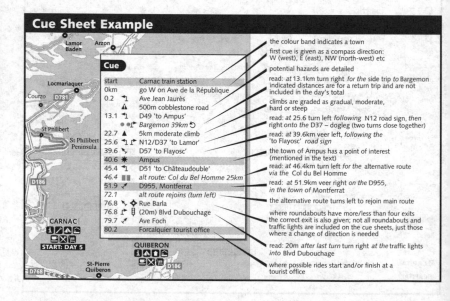

Cue Sheet Example

the colour band indicates a town

first cue is given as a compass direction: W (west), E (east), NW (north-west) etc

potential hazards are detailed

read: *at* 13.1km turn right *for the* side trip *to* Bargemon indicated distances are for a return trip and are not included in the day's total

climbs are graded as gradual, moderate, hard or steep

read: *at* 25.6 turn left *following* N12 road sign, *then* right *onto the* D37 – dogleg (two turns close together)

read: *at* 39.6km veer left, *following the* 'to Flayosc' *road sign*

the town of Ampus has a point of interest (mentioned in the text)

read: *at* 46.4km turn left *for the* alternative route *via the* Col du Bel Homme

read: *at* 51.9km veer right *on the* D955, *in the town of* Montferrat

the alternative route turns left to rejoin main route

where roundabouts have more/less than four exits the correct exit is also given; not all roundabouts and traffic lights are included on the cue sheets, just those where a change of direction is needed

read: 20m *after last turn* turn right *at the* traffic lights *into* Blvd Dubouchage

where possible rides start and/or finish at a tourist office

Cue

start		Carnac train station
0km		go W on Ave de la République
0.2	⤴	Ave Jean Jaurès
	⚠	500m cobblestone road
13.1	⤴	D49 'to Ampus'
	● ⟳	*Bargemon 39km* ↺
22.7	▲	5km moderate climb
25.6	⤴ ⤵	N12/D37 'to Lamor'
39.6	⤶	D57 'to Flayosc'
40.6	✳	Ampus
45.4	⤴	D51 'to Châteaudouble'
46.4	▮▮	*alt route: Col du Bel Homme 25km*
51.9	⤶	D955, Montferrat
72.1		*alt route rejoins (turn left)*
76.8	⤶ ⬡	Rue Barla
76.8	⤷ 🏛	(20m) Blvd Dubouchage
79.7	⤴	Ave Foch
80.2		Forcalquier tourist office

Foreword

HOW TO USE A LONELY PLANET GUIDEBOOK

The best way to use a Lonely Planet guidebook is any way you choose. At Lonely Planet we believe the most memorable travel experiences are often those that are unexpected, and the finest discoveries are those you make yourself. Guidebooks are not intended to be used as if they provide a detailed set of infallible instructions!

Contents All Lonely Planet guidebooks follow roughly the same format, including the cycling guides. The Facts about the Destination chapters give background information ranging from history to weather. Facts for the Cyclist gives practical information on the destination. Health & Safety covers medical advice and road rules. Basic bicycle maintenance is addressed in Your Bicycle. Getting There & Away gives a brief starting point for researching travel to/from the destination. Getting Around gives an overview of the transport options when you arrive.

The peculiar demands of each destination determine how subsequent chapters are broken up, but some things remain constant. We always start each ride with background and getting to/from the ride information. Each day's ride is summarised and the highlights en route detailed in the text, and locations noted on the map and cue sheets. A selection of the best sights and places to stay and eat in each start and end town are also detailed.

Heading Hierarchy Lonely Planet headings are used in a strict hierarchical structure that can be visualised as a set of Russian dolls. Each heading (and its following text) is encompassed by any preceding heading that is higher on the hierarchical ladder.

Entry Points We do not assume guidebooks will be read from beginning to end, but that people will dip into them. The traditional entry points are the list of contents and the index. In addition, the cycling guides also have a table of rides and a map index illustrating the regional chapter break-up.

There is also a colour map that shows highlights. These highlights are dealt with in greater detail in the Facts for the Cyclist chapter, along with planning questions and suggested itineraries. Each chapter covering a geographical region also begins with a map showing all the rides for that region. Once you find something of interest turn to the index or table of rides.

ABOUT LONELY PLANET GUIDEBOOKS

The process of creating new editions begins with the letters, postcards and emails received from travellers. This correspondence often includes suggestions, criticisms and comments about the current editions. Interesting excerpts are immediately passed on via newsletters and the Web site, and everything goes to our authors to be verified when they're researching on the road. We're keen to get more feedback from organisations or individuals who represent communities visited by travellers.

Lonely Planet gathers information for everyone who's curious about the planet – and especially for those who explore it first-hand. Through guidebooks, phrasebooks, activity guides, maps, literature, newsletters, image library, TV series and Web site we act as an information exchange for a worldwide community of travellers.

Research Authors aim to gather sufficient practical information to enable travellers to make informed choices and to make the mechanics of a journey run smoothly. They also research historical and cultural background to help enrich the travel experience and allow travellers to understand and respond appropriately to cultural and environmental issues.

Authors don't stay in every hotel because that would mean spending a couple of weeks in each medium-sized city and, no, they don't eat at every restaurant because that would mean stretching belts beyond capacity. They do visit hotels and restaurants to check standards and prices, but feedback based on readers' direct experiences can be very helpful.

Many of our authors work undercover, others aren't so secretive. None of them accept freebies in exchange for positive write-ups. And none of our guidebooks contain any advertising.

Production Authors submit their raw manuscripts and maps to offices in Australia, USA, UK or France. Editors and cartographers – all experienced travellers themselves – then begin the process of assembling the pieces. When the book finally hits the shops, some things are already out of date, we start getting feedback from readers and the process begins again...

WARNING & REQUEST

Things change – prices go up, schedules change, good places go bad and bad places go bankrupt – nothing stays the same. So, if you find things better or worse, recently opened or long since closed, please tell us and help make the next edition even more accurate and useful. We genuinely value all the feedback we receive. A well-travelled team reads and acknowledges every letter, postcard and email and ensures that every morsel of information finds its way to the appropriate authors, editors and cartographers for verification.

Everyone who writes to us will find their name in the next edition of the appropriate guidebook. They will also receive the latest issue of *Planet Talk*, our quarterly printed newsletter, or *Comet*, our monthly email newsletter. Subscriptions to both newsletters are free. The very best contributions will be rewarded with a free guidebook.

Excerpts from your correspondence may appear in new editions of Lonely Planet guidebooks, the Lonely Planet Web site, *Planet Talk* or *Comet*, so please let us know if you *don't* want your letter published or your name acknowledged.

Send all correspondence to the Lonely Planet office closest to you:

Australia: Locked Bag 1, Footscray, Victoria 3011
USA: 150 Linden St, Oakland, CA 94607
UK: 10A Spring Place, London NW5 3BH
France: 1 rue du Dahomey, 75011 Paris

Or email us at: e talk2us@lonelyplanet.com.au

For news, views and updates see our Web site: www.lonelyplanet.com

Introduction

How can a cyclist resist France? From the saddle, the holiday possibilities are endless. Whether neophyte or veteran cyclist, the terrain of France caters to all levels of fitness and experience. Freed from the restrictions of tour buses and schedules, you can choose your own pace and become intimate with the land.

The vast network of quiet back roads in France provides idyllic cycling through the countryside. Look over your handlebars at picturesque towns, expansive vineyards and bountiful farmlands. Ride through cool forests, alongside tranquil canals and magnificent rivers. Visit the coast with its quaint fishing villages, sandy beaches and rugged sea cliffs. And, for those seeking a challenge, France offers demanding alpine climbs, spectacular gorge traverses and plenty of off-road mountain-biking adventures.

France is not limited to gorgeous scenery and diverse landscapes. Explore megalithic sites and medieval towns; visit castles, abbeys, cathedrals, museums and wine cellars; join traditional festival celebrations; or soak up the convivial atmosphere of the ubiquitous French cafe.

Cycling in France stimulates the senses. Imagine weaving through brilliant fields of

yellow sunflowers; inhaling the scent of lavender or freshly baked croissants; or listening to cow bells echoing in the mountains. And, for the ravenous cyclist, France tantalises the taste buds. Breakfast on hot chocolate and croissants; picnic on the simple delights of crusty bread and farm-produced cheese and olives for lunch; and reward yourself with an outstanding meal at the day's end. France's incredible variety of mouthwatering pastries, superb cheeses, diverse regional specialties and some of the world's best wines are, without a doubt, some of the greatest daily rewards.

France offers the cyclist so many choices that in this book we have tried to make the task easier for you. We have mapped and detailed a selection of the best rides in the country, ranging from a few hours to several days, to suit all ability levels. We offer a wealth of suggestions to help smooth your trip: tips on transporting your bike; inside knowledge on the best places to stay, taste wine and sample regional cooking en route; and advice on fixing your bike and staying healthy on tour.

This is the country where the bicycle was born and developed, and where everyone loves the bicycle and welcomes cyclists. Here the bicycle is affectionately known as *la petite reine* (the little queen, meaning queen of the road). And here is the home of the world's most famous cycle race, the *Tour de France*, which captures cyclists' imaginations everywhere for three weeks in July. Join the French as they use *la petite reine* to cycle to work, ride on country back roads or shop for a baguette. Wave to a fellow cyclist and offer the salutation *'bonne route!'* as you enjoy the fellowship of the road.

Facts about France

HISTORY

15,000–13,000 BC – Prehistoric art begins with Cro-Magnon people, evidenced by cave paintings at Lascaux cave in Périgord.

4000–2400 BC – Megalithic monuments are erected in Carnac and vicinity, Brittany.

1500–500 BC – Celtic Gauls move into what is now known as France.

300 BC – Celtic tribe, the Parisii, settle on Île de la Cité (Paris).

125 BC – Romans colonise southern Gaul (the area which is today Provence).

58–51 BC – Julius Caesar conquers Gaul, which remains under Roman rule until the 5th century.

2nd century AD – Christianity is introduced to Roman Gaul.

486–511 – Clovis the Frank defeats Roman armies from the east and establishes the Merovingian dynasty, which remains in power until 751.

496 – Clovis the Frank converts to Christianity.

732 – Charles Martel defeats the Moors at Poitiers, ensuring France does not fall under Muslim rule as has Spain.

751 – Pepin is crowned first Carolingian king of the Franks.

800 – Charlemagne (Charles Martel's grandson) is crowned Holy Roman Emperor. He extends the power and boundaries of the kingdom and inspires a period of cultural revival.

9th century – Scandinavian Vikings (Norsemen) raid France's western coast, eventually settling in the lower Seine valley and forming the duchy of Normandy early in the 10th century.

987 – Hugh Capet is elected first king of France, thus beginning the Capetian dynasty, which is to last the next 800 years.

1066 – William the Conquerer, Duke of Normandy, conquers England.

1095 – Pope Urban II preaches the first crusade at Clermont.

1120 – Birth of the Gothic style of architecture sees the building of St Denis and other major Gothic cathedrals such as Chartres, Reims and Amiens over the next couple of centuries.

1152 – Eleanor of Aquitaine divorces Louis VII of France and marries Henry Plantagenet of Anjou (later Henry II of England) and her substantial holding of France comes under the control of the English crown.

1309 – French-born Pope Clement V flees political turmoil in Rome and moves the seat of the papacy to Avignon, where it remains until 1377.

1337 – The Hundred Years War between England and France begins.

1348–49 – The bubonic plague, the 'Black Death', kills about one-third of the population.

1415 – The French are defeated at Agincourt and the dukes of Burgundy ally with the English.

1429 – Joan of Arc (Jeanne d'Arc) defeats the English at Orléans. Charles VII crowned King at Reims.

1431 – Joan of Arc is burnt at the stake by the English at Rouen.

1453 – France defeats England, thus ending the Hundred Years War, with only Calais remaining in English hands.

early 16th century – Renaissance (French for 'rebirth') arrives in France during the reign of François I.

1536 – John Calvin's *Institution of the Christian Religion* is published.

1562 – Wars of Religion between Protestants (Huguenots) and Catholics begin.

1572 – St Bartholomew's Day Massacre of 3000 Huguenots occurs in Paris.

1589 – Henri III is assassinated, and Henri IV becomes the first Bourbon king of France.

1598 – Edict of Nantes grants Huguenots religious toleration, thus ending the Wars of Religion.

1610 – Louis XIII takes the throne; much of the control is under his ruthless chief minister Cardinal Richelieu.

1618–48 – The Thirty Years War, involving France, Austria, Denmark, Spain, Sweden and the German states, begins as a war over religion but turns into a power struggle between the states.

1643 – Louis XIV, Le Roi Soleil (the Sun King), ascends the throne at the age of five and rules until 1715. He seeks to project the power of the French monarchy, gaining territory through costly wars and nearly bankrupting the treasury.

17th century – The Age of Enlightenment begins and philosophers such as Voltaire, Rousseau, Diderot and Montesquieu inspire a new generation of thinkers.

1756–63 – The Seven Years War is fought, and France loses most of its colonies to England.

1774 – Louis XVI and his queen, Marie Antoinette, take the throne.

1789 – The Bastille is stormed by the masses, and a constitutional monarchy established.

1792 – The monarchy is abolished and the First Republic established.

1793 – Louis XVI and Marie-Antoinette are guillotined at place de la Révolution (known today as place de la Concorde). The Reign of Terror under the radical Jacobin party begins.

1794 – The Jacobins are overthrown and the Reign of Terror ends only after thousands of people all over France have been killed.

1804 – Napoleon Bonaparte is crowned Emperor of France, and the First Empire is established.

1805–12 – Napoleon institutes several important reforms to France, among which he reorganises the judicial system and introduces a new education system. His armies conquer most of Europe.

1814 – Napoleon is defeated, abdicates and is exiled to the island of Elba. The House of Bourbon, and its head Louis XVIII (Louis XVI's brother), is restored to the French throne.

1815 – Napoleon escapes from Elba to southern France, gathers a large army and heads north, only to be defeated at Waterloo (Belgium). He is again exiled, this time to the remote South Atlantic island of St Helena, where he dies in 1821.

1830 – Louis-Philippe comes to the throne for what is known as the July Monarchy.

1848 – Louis-Philippe is overthrown. The Second Republic begins with the election of Napoleon Bonaparte's nephew, Louis-Napoleon.

1851 – Louis-Napoleon leads a coup d'etat, after which he is proclaimed Emperor Napoleon III.

1852 – The Second Empire begins and France enjoys significant economic growth.

1870 – Franco-Prussian War is fought. France cedes Alsace-Lorraine to Germany. Napoleon III is defeated and overthrown. The Third Republic begins, ushering in the glittering *belle époque* (beautiful age) with Art Nouveau architecture, impressionism, and advances in science and engineering, including the first metro line.

1889 – The World Exhibition is held in Paris and Gustave Eiffel builds the Eiffel Tower (much maligned at the time) as its showpiece. Centennial of the French Revolution.

1894–1906 – The Dreyfus Affair follows the alleged treason of a Jewish army officer. Authors such as Zola become involved. Eventually, Dreyfus is vindicated, discrediting both the army and the Catholic Church.

1903 – First Tour de France is held.

1914–18 – France regains Alsace-Lorraine during WWI.

1919 – The Treaty of Versailles is signed, officially ending the war.

1918–39 – France, Paris in particular, is seen as a centre of the avant-garde, attracting writers such as Ernest Hemingway, Gertrude Stein and F Scott Fitzgerald, and artistic movements such as cubism and surrealism.

1939–45 – WWII is fought.

1944 – D-day, the Allies land on the Normandy beaches and liberate France.

1946 – Fourth Republic begins. Women get the right to vote. First Cannes Film Festival is held.

1958 – Fifth Republic forms (and continues to this day) under the leadership of President Charles de Gaulle.

1960 – First French atomic bomb tests are held in the Sahara Desert.

1969 – Georges Pompidou replaces de Gaulle as president.

1970 – Charles de Gaulle dies.

1976 – Supersonic Concorde flies trans-Atlantic for the first time.

1981 – Socialist François Mitterrand is elected and becomes the longest-serving president in French history.

1985 – Breton Bernard Hinault wins his fifth Tour de France, and becomes the last Frenchman to win the Tour in the 20th century.

1986 – American Greg LeMond becomes the first non-European to win the Tour de France.

1994 – The Channel Tunnel opens, linking France and England.

1996 – François Mitterrand dies.

1998 – France hosts and wins the Football World Cup.

1999 – Two sets of prices are displayed in France: the franc and the euro. Brutal storms batter northern France; the Château de Versailles parklands are severely damaged.

2000 – France wins the European Football Championship, becoming the only country to hold the world and European titles at the same time.

History of Cycling in France

The Bicycle is Born While France, England and Germany argue over who invented the bicycle, it can't be denied that French ingenuity played an instrumental role in the development of the bicycle: *le vélo*.

In 1816, German Karl von Drais developed a swift-walking machine (*Draisienne*, or swift-walker). Over the next 50-odd years, people continued to tinker with wooden tricycles and quadricycles. Real bicycle history, however, was made in 1861 in the workshop of Pierre Michaux, a carriage repairer and perambulator maker, when an old swift-walker was brought in for repair. Pierre and his 14-year-old son, Ernest, thought of putting pedal-cranks on the front wheel. Improvements continued, and the pair made two experimental bicycles. Michaux et Compagnie, the first bicycle factory, was born. In 1862 it produced 142 bicycles known as *vélocipèdes*, or boneshakers (because of the rough ride on the cobbled streets). In 1865 they churned out about 400 of the machines.

Michaux's success continued, and in 1866–67 his company introduced a new model with a larger front wheel (his first bikes had a front-wheel diameter of 80cm). Michaux exhibited this new model at the 1867 World Exhibition in Paris and received numerous orders, including one from Napoleon III.

Eugene Meyer, in 1869, built the first wheels with steel rims and tensionable spokes, enabling larger wheels to be built.

Let the Racing Begin By the 1867 World Exhibition the bicycle craze was in full swing. The first formal pedal bicycle race was sponsored by Napoleon III at the Parc de St Cloud in Paris on 31 May 1868. The 2km track-course was won in 3 minutes, 50 seconds by Englishman James Moore.

The following year, the first bicycle club in France, *Véloce Club de Paris*, was formed and organised bicycle races and events. On 1 April 1869 the world's first successful cycling magazine, *Le Vélocipède Illustré*, was launched.

Michaux, took early retirement and sold his factory in April 1869 to the Olivier brothers, who formed the Compagnie Parisienne des Vélocipèdes and a cycling school. In 1870 they boasted production of 200 machines a day, built by 500 employees.

On 7 November 1869, the first major road race in France was held, co-sponsored by *Le Vélocipède Illustré* and the Compagnie Parisienne des Vélocipèdes. The 123km (76 mile) race went from Paris to Rouen with entrants numbering about 100 men and a dozen women. The winner was again James Moore, in 10 hours 45 minutes, and the women's winner, riding as 'Miss America', came in 29th, with a time of 17 hours.

France was more accepting of female cyclists than many other countries. In 1868 the first women's bicycle race was held at Paris' Hippodrome du Parc Bordelais. Clearly, women were allowed to enter races but, even as late as 1887, a woman still had to get her husband's permission to join a bicycle club!

A Flurry of Innovations In the years 1870–71, during the Franco-Prussian War, bicycle manufacturing came to a standstill in France and moved to England. Here, thanks to Meyer's invention of tensionable spokes, the high-wheeler bicycle (otherwise known as an 'ordinary', 'penny farthing' or, once introduced to France, *'le grand bi'*) and tricycle were invented, followed by the safety bicycle. On this invention the cyclist sat upright to pedal between two equally sized wheels with a chain drive mechanism connected to (usually) the rear wheel. This machine revolutionised cycling and set trends in production and marketing. After the war, St Étienne (in the Massif Central), an arms manufacturing centre, became an important city for bicycle manufacturing.

During the 1880s, Frenchman Charles Terront captured cycling attention and became known as France's first sports 'star'.

He came from a working-class background and began his riding career by hiring and competing on wooden vélocipèdes. He then raced seriously on high-wheelers and successfully converted to safety bikes when they arrived. He won races in Europe and the USA and rode from St Petersburg (Russia) to Paris in 14 days, 7 hours.

In 1891 Édouard Michelin repaired a bicycle with a Dunlop pneumatic tyre; these air-filled tyres offered speed, stability and comfort, not to mention decreasing the weight of the bicycle. Michelin realised a cyclist's dream by designing and perfecting an inflatable and *detachable* tyre.

The invention was a case of perfect timing for Édouard and his brother André (the marketing genius of the two), and they recruited Charles Terront to ride a bicycle fitted with their new tyres in the first Paris-Brest-Paris race on 6 September 1891. The 1200km (660 mile) event was created by Pierre Giffard, editor-in-chief of Parisian newspaper *Petit Journal*. He created and heavily advertised the race to prove the bicycle's reliability (see also the boxed text 'Paris-Brest-Paris' in the Randonnées chapter). Charles Terront won the race in 71 hours, 18 minutes, and was paid

MUSÉE DE LA PUBLICITÉ, PARIS

The late 19th century brought parks and halls where people could learn the new art of cycling – in safety. (Lucien Baylac 1894)

to attribute his victory to the simplicity of the Michelin tyres to remove and repair. This wasn't quite true – his bike had a nightmarish system of screws holding the tyres onto the rims, and it took Michelin mechanics 40 minutes to repair his tubes!

The following year the Michelin brothers organised a race from Paris to Clermont-Ferrand (the location of their factory). As a marketing tool, the sly brothers scattered the roadway with nails, unknown to the racers, to prove how quickly and easily their tyres could be changed.

French Love Affair with the Bicycle

The enhanced status of cycling, and the fact that bicycles were becoming more affordable and liberating, attracted people from all classes. Improvements continued, and the bicycle started to look very much like it does today. Clubs formed, clothing specific to cycling was designed, races were organised and the French company Peugeot designed a bicycle for the French army. The French were enamoured with cycling.

Long-distance races continued to grow in popularity, with the Paris-Brussels starting in 1893, and both the first Paris-Roubaix and Paris-Tours in 1896 (see also the boxed text 'Mud, Mayhem & Cobblestones' in the Paris & the Île de France chapter). In 1903, Henri Desgranges, of the newspaper *L'Auto* (subtitled *L'Automobile Cyclisme*) launched the 'greatest bike race in the world'. On July 1, from a small cafe on the outskirts of Paris 60 cyclists set off on the first Tour de France (see the Tour de France chapter).

The bicycle was a part of French society and was used for recreation, competition and utilitarian tasks. In WWI the French deployed bicycle troops in France and Belgium, and bicycles were also used for relaying messages. WWII did not see the same use of the bicycle and, as with other recreational activities at this time, cycling declined in popularity.

The Bicycle in France Today

The French continue to use the bicycle for recreation, and competitive cycling is a passion, with hundreds of clubs and races throughout the country. More recently, mountain biking (*vélo tout terrain*, or VTT) has become popular. VTT centres have been opened, thousands of kilometres of mountain bike tracks developed, and rides and competitive events

Vélocio – Patron Saint

Paul de Vivie (1853–1930) was better known by the nom de plume Vélocio, and is considered the patron saint of cyclotourism. He brought together cycle tourists through his magazine *Le Cycliste*, published in St Étienne from 1888. He was a passionate cyclotourist and known for his advice on technique, diet, exercise and hygiene. Vélocio and other early cycle tourists experimented with many different gearing systems, helping in the development of the derailleur bicycle. He is best remembered for his *Seven Commandments* for the cyclist, such as 'Eat lightly and frequently: eat before you're hungry, drink before you're thirsty' and 'Never pedal to show how good you are'.

Vélocio, with his beloved touring bike, 1929.

organised (see the boxed text 'Mountain Biking' in the Facts for the Cyclist chapter).

Today 47% of French people own a bicycle and France has more than 5000 bike shops. However, the French love their cars and, except for within small towns and more recently Paris, they do not typically commute by bicycle. Increased pollution and traffic congestion are causing this slowly to change. Efforts have been made in

Paris, Bordeaux, Grenoble, St Malo and various other cities to create bikepaths.

History of Cycle Touring in France

Cycle touring came early to France and the first touring club, Le Touring Club de France (TCF), was created in 1890. Although later disbanded, it lead the way, in 1923, for the formation of the Fédération Française des Sociétés de Cyclotourisme (FFSC). In 1945 the FFSC was reborn as the present-day Fédération Française de Cyclotourisme (FFCT). Today the FFCT claims to be the most important organisation of its sort in the world, with more than 115,000 members (20% of whom are women, and including 20,000 under 18 years) in 3100 clubs and an annual budget of 30 million francs. It runs a cycle touring school, organises large touring events in France and abroad, and publicises weekend tours run by its member clubs. See also the National Cycling Organisations section in the Facts for the Cyclist Chapter.

GEOGRAPHY

France covers 551,000 sq km and is the largest country in Europe after Russia and the Ukraine. It is shaped like a hexagon bordered by either mountains or water except for the relatively flat north-east frontier (abutting Germany, Luxembourg and Belgium), from where France has been invaded repeatedly.

France's 3200km coastline is remarkably diverse, ranging from the white chalk cliffs of Normandy and the treacherous promontories of Brittany to the fine-sand beaches along the Atlantic. The Mediterranean coast tends to have pebbly and even rocky beaches, though beaches in Languedoc and some in Roussillon are sandy.

France is drained by five major river systems. The Seine passes through Paris on its way from Burgundy to the English Channel. The longest river in the country, the Loire, stretches for 1020km from the Massif Central to the Atlantic. The Rhine, which flows into the North Sea, forms the eastern border of Alsace for about 200km. Its tributaries include the Moselle and the Meuse. Farther south, the Rhône links Lake Geneva and the Alps with the Mediterranean, and is joined by the Saône at Lyon. The Garonne system, which includes the Tarn, Lot and Dordogne Rivers, drains the Pyrenees and the rest of the south-west before emptying into the Atlantic.

GEOLOGY

A significant proportion of France is covered by mountains, many of them among the most spectacular in Europe.

The French Alps, which include Mont Blanc (4807m), Europe's highest peak, run along France's eastern border from Lake Geneva (Lac Léman) to the Côte d'Azur. There is permanent snow cover above 2800m. The Jura Range, gentle limestone mountains north of the Alps that peak at just over 1700m, stretches along the Swiss frontier north of Lake Geneva. The Pyrenees run along France's entire 450km border with Spain, from the Atlantic to the Mediterranean. Though the loftiest peak is only 3404m high (Pico d'Aneto, in Spain), the Pyrenees can be almost as rugged as the Alps.

The Alps, the Jura and the Pyrenees, though spectacular, are young ranges in comparison with France's ancient massifs, formed between 225 and 345 million years ago. The most spectacular is the Massif Central, a huge region in the middle of France whose 91,000 sq km cover a sixth of the entire country. It is perhaps best known for its chain of extinct volcanoes, such as the Puy de Dôme (1465m; see the boxed text 'Puy de Dôme & Le Tour' in the Massif Central chapter).

France's other ancient massifs, worn down over the ages, include the Vosges, a forested upland in the country's north-east corner between Alsace and Lorraine; the Ardennes, most of which lies in Belgium and Germany and whose French part is on the northern edge of Champagne; and the Massif Armoricain, which stretches westward from Normandy and forms the backbone of Brittany and Normandy.

CLIMATE

In general, France has a temperate climate, with mild winters, except in mountainous areas and Alsace.

The Atlantic has a profound impact on the north-west, particularly Brittany, whose weather is characterised by high humidity and lots of rain (200 days a year compared to the national average of 164). The area is also subject to persistent and sometimes violent westerly winds.

France's north-east, especially Alsace, has a continental climate, with fairly hot summers and winters cold enough for snow to stay on the ground for weeks at a time.

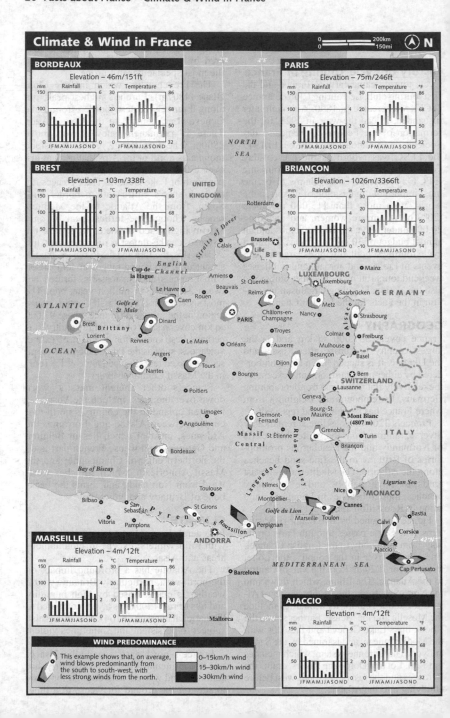

Climate & Wind in France

0 200km
0 150mi

N

BORDEAUX
Elevation – 46m/151ft
Rainfall — Temperature

PARIS
Elevation – 75m/246ft
Rainfall — Temperature

BREST
Elevation – 103m/338ft
Rainfall — Temperature

BRIANÇON
Elevation – 1026m/3366ft
Rainfall — Temperature

MARSEILLE
Elevation – 4m/12ft
Rainfall — Temperature

AJACCIO
Elevation – 4m/12ft
Rainfall — Temperature

WIND PREDOMINANCE
This example shows that, on average, wind blows predominantly from the south to south-west, with less strong winds from the north.

0–15km/h wind
15–30km/h wind
>30km/h wind

The wettest months in Alsace are June and July, when storms are common.

Midway between Brittany and Alsace – and affected by the climates of both – is the Paris basin. The region records the nation's lowest annual precipitation (about 575mm), but rainfall patterns are erratic: you're just as likely to be caught in a heavy spring or autumn downpour as in a sudden summer cloudburst. Paris' average yearly temperature is 12°C, but the mercury sometimes drops below zero in January and can climb to the mid-30s or higher in August.

The southern coastal plains are subject to a Mediterranean climate as far inland as the southern Alps, the Massif Central and the eastern Pyrenees. For hot summers and mild winters, visit the south of France.

The south is also the region of the Mistral, a cold, dry wind that blows south down the Rhône Valley for about 100 days a year. Most relentless (and fierce) in spring, it is sometimes blamed for making people ill-tempered or even driving them mad. Another dominant wind in the south is the Tramontane, a cold, dry wind from the north-west which blows through Languedoc and Rousillon. It almost synchronises with the Mistral, gaining or losing strength within hours of its counterpart.

The plains of the north and west of France are subject to prevailing winds from the south-west. Brittany, jutting to the west, gets westerly blasts right off the Atlantic. A little farther south, the dominant wind along the Atlantic coast is from the north-west.

Although not as strong, the Traverse, a westerly wind, influences the Massif Central. In summer it brings storms and humid weather, while in winter this cold wind is often accompanied by snow. This area is also subject to winds from the north and the south. This same wind affects the northern Alps and the Jura from the north-west.

The Bise, a wind from the north or north-east, influences the north-east quarter of the country, particularly in winter, when it brings periods of cold, dry weather.

ECOLOGY & ENVIRONMENT

The Office National des Forêts (ONF) manages most of the forests in France. However, these are not protected reserves. French ecologists charge that the ONF runs them less to ensure the survival of their ecosystems than to bring in revenue from timber sales.

Summer forest fires are an annual hazard. Great tracts of land are burned each year, often because of careless day-trippers or, as is sometimes the case in the Maures and Esterel Ranges in the Côte d'Azur, intentionally set alight to get licences to build on the damaged lands. France's northern forests, particularly in the Vosges, have been affected by acid rain.

Wetlands – productive ecosystems that are essential for the survival of many species of birds, reptiles, fish and amphibians – are also shrinking. More than two million hectares – 3% of French territory – are considered important wetlands, but only 4% is protected.

Energy

France may not have as many nuclear power stations as the USA, but while the US ceased building new ones more than a decade ago, the French program – the world's most ambitious – is still going strong. Since the late 1980s, the state-owned electricity company, Électricité de France (EDF), has produced about three-quarters of the country's electricity with nuclear power. Most of France's nuclear reactors are on main rivers or near the coast. France has also tried to export nuclear technology to developing countries. Nuclear waste, an increasingly important issue, is dumped on Normandy's Cotentin Peninsula.

EDF also controls France's hydroelectric program. Damming rivers to produce electricity has created huge recreational lakes but has destroyed the traditional habitats of many animals. High-voltage power lines are a blight on much of the countryside and electrocute at least 1000 birds of prey each year. The EDF has announced that new lines will run underground where possible.

In 1992 the French government finally agreed to suspend nuclear testing on the Polynesian island of Mururoa and a nearby atoll. The tests, begun in 1964, were carried out above-ground for a decade before being continued underground. Protesters claimed the tests had disastrous effects on the health of the Mururoa islanders, causing increased rates of birth defects and leukaemia, and had disrupted the atoll's food chain. In July 1985 French agents blew up the Greenpeace ship *Rainbow Warrior* in Auckland harbour (New Zealand) to try to derail the organisation's campaign against the tests. One person on board was killed. However, in 1995, President Jacques Chirac decided to conduct one last series of tests on Mururoa Atoll before supporting a worldwide test ban treaty. This round of tests concluded in January 1996, and France and the UK signed the treaty in April 1998.

FLORA & FAUNA

France is blessed with a rich variety of flora and fauna. However, many fragile species are having a hard time surviving in the face of urbanisation, intensive agriculture, the draining of wetlands, hunting, pollution, the encroachment of industries and the expansion of the tourism infrastructure. As France has precious few established nature reserves, the long-term future of much of the fauna, in particular, appears bleak.

France is home to 113 species of mammals (more than any other country in Europe), 363 species of birds, 30 of amphibians, 36 of reptiles and 72 of fish. About 14 million hectares of forest – mostly beech, oak and pine – cover about 20% of France. There are 4200 species of plants and flowers.

Endangered Species

At least three kinds of mammals have disappeared in modern times, and the Pyrenean ibex, Corsican deer, and about 10 species of bats are currently on the endangered list. A quarter of the fish species is also in trouble. Wolves are believed to be extinct, but some reports indicate a couple of them may still roam the Massif Central. River otters, once abundant, have fallen victim to trappers.

The once-common brown bear disappeared from the Alps in the mid-1930s, when about 300 of the animals still lived in the Pyrenees. Today, that number has dwindled to 15. Many birds, including vultures and storks, have all but disappeared from the skies, and Bonnelli's eagle is down to about two dozen pairs from 670 only 20 years ago.

Some animals still live in the wild thanks to reintroduction programs in national and regional parks. Storks are being bred in Alsace; vultures have been reintroduced in Languedoc; and beavers, once nearly wiped out, are prospering in the Armorique Regional Park in Brittany and in the Rhône Valley. Alpine creatures such as the chamois (a mountain antelope) and the larger bouquetin (a type of ibex) were widely hunted until several national parks were established.

France has 1.7 million hunters, many of whom head to the forests and woodlands with their dogs as soon as the five-month season opens at the end of September. To safeguard the passage of migratory birds, the Brussels Directive was introduced in 1979 to protect wild birds, their eggs, nests and habitats; it applies to all member states of the EU.

The French government signed the directive but didn't make its provisions part of French law, so birds that can safely fly over other countries may still be shot as they cross France. As a result, environmentalists have in the past rented entire mountain passes on birds' flight paths to keep hunters away.

National & Regional Parks

About 0.7% of France's land is within a *parc national* (national park), and another 7% within a *parc naturel régional* (regional park). There are also nearly 100 small *réserves naturelles* (nature reserves) and a few private reserves set up by environmental groups. The proportion of protected land is low relative to France's size.

The national parks, which are uninhabited, are under the direct control of the government and are fully protected by legislation: dogs, vehicles and hunting are banned and camping is restricted. However, the parks themselves are relatively small (all are under 1000 sq km), and the ecosystems they are supposed to protect spill into what are called 'peripheral zones', populated areas around the parks in which tourism and other economic activities are permitted.

France has six national parks, all of them in the mountains except for the Parc National de Port-Cros, which covers the Île de Port-Cros and surrounding waters off the Côte d'Azur. Most national parkland is in the Alps, where the Vanoise, Écrins and Mercantour parks are hugely popular with nature lovers and hikers in summer. The Parc National des Pyrénées runs for 100km along the Spanish border and is a favourite with rock climbers. The wild Parc National des Cévennes, which has a few inhabitants in its central zone, is on the border of the Massif Central and Languedoc.

The country's almost three dozen regional parks and its nature reserves, most of which were established both to improve (or at least maintain) local ecosystems and to encourage economic development and tourism, all support human populations and are locally managed. The regional parks are mainly in areas with diminishing human populations that are facing severe economic problems, such as the Massif Central and parts of Corsica. Some of the regional parks visited on cycle tours in this book are Parc Régional du Morvan (Burgundy), Parc Naturel Régional des Ballons des Vosges (Alsace), Parc Naturel Régional du Verdon (Provence), Parc Naturel Régional de la Montagne de Reims (Champagne) and Parc National Régional de la Corse (Corsica).

GOVERNMENT & POLITICS

France has had 11 constitutions since 1789. The present one, instituted by de Gaulle in 1958, is known as the Fifth Republic and gives considerable power to the French president. The 577 Assemblée Nationale members are directly elected in single-member constituencies for five-year terms. The 321 members of the rather powerless Sénat serve for nine years and are indirectly elected. The French president is chosen by direct election for a seven-year term. The voting age is 18.

France is one of the five permanent members of the UN Security Council. It withdrew from NATO's joint military command in 1966 and has maintained an independent arsenal of nuclear weapons since 1960.

France has long been a highly centralised state. For administration, the country has, since 1790, been divided into units of about 6100 sq km called *départements* (departments). There are 96 departments in France – the mainland and Corsica – and another five in overseas territories, including: Guadeloupe, Martinique, French Guiana, Réunion and St Pierre et Miquelon. The island of Mayotte, off the Mozambique coast, has quasi-departmental status.

In addition, France has three overseas territories: French Polynesia, New Caledonia, and the Wallis and Futuna islands. France also claims a sizeable chunk of Antarctica. All overseas departments and territories are known as DOM TOM *(Départements et Territoires d'Outre-Mer).*

ECONOMY

France's economy may not be the powerhouse of Europe, but French financial leaders have enough clout to determine the shape of the European Monetary Union.

EMU, as it is known, was the driving force behind much of Europe's financial direction in the last half of the 1990s.

For the traveller the most important consequence will be that many of Europe's banknotes and bills will disappear in 2003, when the euro (€) becomes the standard European Union currency.

The French state still owns much of France and has been slow to privatise industry. Pragmatism has had something to do with the Socialists now opting for more privatisation. France continually wrestles with a budget deficit, and in the late 1990s it was feared that France would not be eligible to join the EMU in the first group. Selling off state assets was one way to meet the EMU's membership criteria.

The French economy is growing at about the EU average. This sluggish rise in annual gross domestic product – predicted at just under 3% in 1999 – will keep France's relatively high unemployment at around 12%, a figure that has not budged in years.

France is one of the world's most industrialised nations, with 40% of the workforce employed in the industrial sector. About 50% of GNP (gross national product) comes from industrial production. However, coordination between academic research and companies that might turn good ideas into products is poor, and the country has fewer large corporations than other similar size industrialised nations.

France is also the EU's largest agricultural producer and exporter, especially in wheat, barley, maize (corn) and cheese. The country is to a great extent self-sufficient in food except for tropical products such as bananas and coffee. Nearly one in 10 workers nationwide is engaged in agricultural production. Despite this, the agricultural sector is the weakest part of the economy, largely because many of the holdings are too small and low-tech for efficient production.

POPULATION & PEOPLE

France has a population of 58.3 million, more than 20% of whom live in the greater metropolitan area of Paris. The number of people living in rural and mountain areas has been declining since the 1950s.

For much of the last two centuries, France has had a considerably lower rate of population growth than its neighbours. On the other hand, over that period the country has accepted more immigrants than any other European nation, including significant numbers of political refugees. During the late 1950s and early 60s, as the French colonial empire collapsed, more than one million French settlers returned to France from Algeria, Morocco, Tunisia and Indochina.

Although 80% of French people say they are Catholic and most have been baptised, very few attend church. France has between four and five million nominally Muslim residents, who make up the country's second-largest religious group. Most came from North Africa during the 1950s and 60s. Protestants number about one million. About 75,000 French Jews were killed during the Holocaust in WWII. The country's Jewish community now numbers 650,000.

ARTS
Painting
An extraordinary flowering of artistic talent took place in France during the late 19th and early 20th centuries. The impressionists, who dealt with colour as a property of light (rather than of objects) and endeavoured to capture the ever-changing aspects of reflected light, included Édouard Manet, Claude Monet, Edgar Degas, Camille Pissarro and Pierre-Auguste Renoir.

They were followed by a diverse but equally creative group of artists known as the postimpressionists, among whose ranks were Paul Cézanne, Paul Gauguin and Georges Seurat. A little later, the Fauves (literally, 'wild beasts'), the most famous of whom was Henri Matisse, became known for their radical use of vibrant colour.

In the years before WWI Pablo Picasso, who was living in Paris, and Georges Braque pioneered cubism, a school of art which concentrated on the analysis of form through abstract and geometric representation.

WWII ended Paris' role as the world's artistic capital. Many artists left France, and though some returned after the war, the city never regained its old art magnetism.

Sculpture
At the end of the 11th century, sculptors began to decorate the portals, capitals, altars and fonts of Romanesque churches. Two centuries later, sculpture had spread from the central portal to the whole facade. In the 14th century, Dutchman Claus Sluter, working at the court of Burgundy, introduced a vigorous realism with his sculptures.

Sculpture was increasingly commissioned for the tombs of the nobility. In Renaissance France, Pierre Bontemps decorated the tomb of François I at St Denis. The baroque style is best exemplified by Guillaume Coustou's *Horses of Marly* at the entrance to the ave des Champs Élysées.

In the 19th century, public memorial statues came to replace sculpted tombs, such as François Rude's bas relief on the Arc de Triomphe. At the end of the 19th century, Auguste Rodin revitalised sculpture with works such as *The Kiss* and *The Thinker*.

One of the most important French sculptors of the early 20th century was Aristide Maillol, whose voluptuous female nudes show his attachment to formal analysis. After WWII one of the most influential sculptors to emerge was César Baldaccini (known as César). He used iron and scrap metal to create imaginary insects and animals. His best-known work is the little statue handed to actors at the Césars, the French cinema awards equivalent to Hollywood's Oscars.

Music
French music is often associated with accordions and *chansonniers* (cabaret singers) such as Édith Piaf. But they're only part of a much larger and more complex picture. At many points in history France has been at the centre of musical culture in Europe.

In the 17th and 18th centuries, French baroque music greatly influenced European music. Composers such as François Couperin (1668–1733), noted for his harpsichord studies, and Jean Phillipe Rameau (1683–1764), a key figure in the development of modern harmony, were two major contributors.

France's two greatest classical composers of the 19th century were Hector Berlioz, the founder of modern orchestration, and César Franck. Berlioz's operas and symphonies and Franck's organ compositions sparked a musical renaissance in France that produced such greats as Gabriel Fauré and the impressionists Claude Debase and Maurice Ravel.

Jazz hit Paris in the 1920s and has remained popular ever since. France's contribution to the world of jazz includes the violinist Stéfane Grappelli and, in the 1950s, Claude Luter and his Dixieland Band.

Popular music has come a long way since the *yéyé* (imitative rock) of the 1960s sung by Johnny Halliday, though you might not think so listening to middle-of-the-roaders Vanessa Paradis and Patrick Bruel. Watch out for rappers MC Solaar, Reg'lyss and I Am from Marseille. Evergreen balladeers–folk singers include Francis Cabrel and Julien Clerc. Some people like the new-age space music of Jean-Michel Jarre; others say his name fits his sound.

France's most recent claim to fame has been *sono mondial* (world music) – from Algerian *raï* (Cheb Khaled, Zahouania) and Senegalese *mbalax* (Youssou N'Dour) to West Indian *zouk* (Kassav, Zouk Machine). The chants of Les Nouvelles Polyphonies Corse, from Corsica, are also very popular.

Architecture of France

Prehistoric

The earliest monuments made by humans in France were stone megaliths erected during the Neolithic period from about 4000 to 2400 BC. Mainly found in Brittany, particularly around Carnac, there are others in northern Languedoc and on Corsica.

Gallo-Roman

The Romans constructed a large number of public works from the 1st century BC. They also established regular street grids in many towns. Southern France – especially Provence and the coastal plains of Languedoc – is the place to find France's *gallo-romain* legacy, including the Pont du Gard aqueduct between Nîmes and Avignon, the amphitheatres at Nîmes and Arles, the theatre at Orange, the Maison Carrée in Nîmes and the public buildings in Vaison-la-Romaine.

Romanesque

A religious revival in the 11th century led to the construction of a large number of Romanesque churches. Such buildings typically have round arches, heavy walls, few windows and a lack of ornamentation that borders on the austere. Chateaux built during this era tend to be massive, heavily fortified structures. This style remained popular until the mid-12th century.

KELLI HAMBLET

Inside, Fontevraud Abbey's Romanesque church boasts the finest cupola nave in France.

Gothic

The Gothic style, originating in the mid-12th century in northern France, is characterised by ribbed vaults carved with great precision, pointed arches, slender verticals, refined decoration and large stained-glass windows.

Cathedrals built in the early Gothic style, which lasted until about 1230, were majestic but lacked lightness and airiness. As the stained-glass windows could not support the roof, thick stone buttresses were placed between them. The discovery that adding outer piers (flying buttresses) could carry the thrust and allow the other buttresses to be made less bulky created a lighter building and helped lift the style to its greatest achievements between 1230 and 1300.

During this period, French architecture dominated the European scene for the first time. Gothic masterpieces such as the cathedral at Chartres and its successors at Reims and Amiens were decorated with ornate tracery (delicate stone rib-work on stained-glass windows) and huge, colourful rose windows.

In the 14th century, the Rayonnant (Radiant) Gothic style – named for the radiating tracery of the rose windows – developed, with interiors becoming even lighter thanks to broader

continued on page 26

Literature
To get a feel for France and its literature of the 19th century, you might pick up a translation of any novel by Victor Hugo *(Les Misérables* or *The Hunchback of Notre Dame)*, Stendahl *(The Red and the Black)*, Honoré de Balzac *(Old Goriot)*, Émile Zola *(Germinal)* or Gustave Flaubert *(A Sentimental Education* or *Madame Bovary)*.

After WWII, existentialism, a significant literary movement, emerged. Based on the philosophy that people are self-creating, it placed total moral responsibility on individuals to give meaning to their existence. The most prominent figures in the movement – Jean-Paul Sartre *(Being and Nothingness)*, Simone de Beauvoir, and Albert Camus *(The Plague)* – stressed the importance of the

Architecture of France

windows and more translucent stained glass. One of the most influential Rayonnant buildings was Paris' Ste Chapelle.

By the 15th century, decorative extravagance led to Flamboyant Gothic, so named because its wavy stone carving resembled flames. Examples include Rouen cathedral's Tour de Beurre and the Strasbourg cathedral spire.

KELLI HAMBLET

The Gothic Cathédrale Notre Dame at Reims, begun in 1211, is famous for its magnificent rose window, ornate tracery and intricate statues.

Renaissance
The Renaissance began in Italy in the early 15th century and set out to realise a 'rebirth' of classical Greek and Roman culture. It first impacted on France at the end of the 15th century.

The French Renaissance is divided into two periods: early Renaissance and Mannerism. During the first period, a variety of classical components and decorative motifs (columns, tunnel vaults, round arches, domes etc) were blended with the rich decoration of Flamboyant Gothic, best exemplified by the Loire Valley's Château de Chambord. The transition from late Gothic to Renaissance can be seen most clearly in the Château de Blois, whose Flamboyant section was built only 15 years before its early Renaissance wing. Mannerism began around 1530, when François I hired Italian architects to design and decorate his new chateau at Fontainebleau.

Over the next few decades, French architects took over from their Italian colleagues. Because French Renaissance architecture was very much the province of the aristocracy and designed by imported artists, the middle classes – resentful French artisans among them – remained loyal to the indigenous Gothic style, and Gothic churches continued to be built throughout the 16th century. The Mannerist style lasted until the early 17th century.

Baroque
The baroque period (end 16th century to the late 18th century) integrated painting, sculpture and classical architecture to create structures and interiors of great subtlety, refinement and elegance. Baroque elements are particularly in evidence in Château de Versailles' lavish interiors, such as the Galerie des Glaces (Hall of Mirrors).

Neoclassicism
Neoclassical architecture emerged in about 1740, along with a renewed interest in classical forms. It was a search for order, reason and serenity and adopted the forms and conventions

writer's political commitment. De Beauvoir, author of the ground-breaking study *The Second Sex*, has had a profound influence on feminist thinking.

In the late 1950s, some younger novelists began to experiment with the novel in an attempt to show different aspects of reality. Critics began to speak of the *nouveau roman* (new novel), referring to the works of Alain Robbe-Grillet, Nathalie Sarraute, Michel Butor and Claude Simon among others. Although these writers did not form a school, they all rejected the traditional novel with its conventions of plot, linear narrative and identifiable characters. Other authors who enjoy a wide following are Marguerite Duras, Françoise Sagan, Patrick Modiano, Pascal Quignard and Denis Tillinac.

Architecture of France

of Graeco-Roman antiquity: columns, simple geometric forms and traditional ornamentation. France's greatest 18th-century neoclassical architect was Jacques-Germain Soufflot, who designed the Panthéon in Paris. But neoclassicism really came into its own under Napoleon, who used it extensively for monumental architecture. Well-known Paris sights designed during the First Empire (1804–14) include the Arc de Triomphe, La Madeleine, the Arc du Carrousel at the Louvre, the Assemblée Nationale and the Bourse.

Art Nouveau

Art Nouveau emerged in Europe and the USA in the second half of the 19th century. It is characterised by sinuous curves and flowing, asymmetrical forms reminiscent of tendrilous vines, water lilies and the flowering boughs of trees. It was influenced by the arrival of *objets d'art* from Japan, and its name comes from a Paris gallery that featured works in the new style.

Art Nouveau combined materials, including iron, brick, glass and ceramics, in ways never seen before. France's major Art Nouveau centres were Nancy and Paris; the latter is still graced by Hector Guimard's noodle-like metro entrances. Also in Paris are some fine Art Nouveau interiors in the Musée d'Orsay, an Art Nouveau glass roof over the Grand Palais and, on rue Pavée in the Marais, a synagogue designed by Guimard.

Contemporary Architecture

France's most celebrated architect last century was Le Corbusier (1887–1965). A radical modernist, he tried to adapt buildings to their functions in industrialised society without ignoring the human element. His chapel at Ronchamp (1955), in eastern France, is one of the most important works of modern architecture in France.

France's leaders have long sought to immortalise themselves by erecting huge public edifices in Paris. Most recently, the late President Georges Pompidou commissioned the Centre Beaubourg (1977) and his successor, Giscard d'Estaing, transformed a derelict train station into the glorious Musée d'Orsay.

Since the early 1980s, Paris has seen the construction of IM Pei's glass pyramid at the entrance to the Louvre; the Opéra-Bastille; the Grande Arche in the La Défense business district; the science museum and park at La Villette; Parc André Citroën in the 15e *arrondissement* (15th district); and the controversial new Bibliothèque Nationale (National Library).

It's thought the design of the Renaissance Château de Chambord was begun by Leonardo da Vinci.

KELLI HAMBLET

See the Books section in the Facts for the Cyclist chapter for titles backgrounding France's literature.

Cinema

Think of cinema in France and you think of the Cannes Film Festival – one of the western film industry's main annual events, where the coveted Palme d'Or is awarded to French and foreign films.

The industry has always attracted artists, intellectuals and theorists. Some of the most innovative and influential film makers of the 1920s and 30s were Jean Vigo, Marcel Pagnol and Jean Renoir.

After WWII, a new generation of directors burst onto the scene with experimental films that abandoned such constraints as temporal continuity and traditional narrative. Known as the *nouvelle vague* (new wave), this genre includes many disparate directors such as Jean-Luc Godard, François Truffaut, Claude Chabrol, Alain Resnais, Agnès Varda and Eric Rohmer, whose main tenet was that a film should be the conception of the film maker not the product of a studio or a producer.

Despite the onslaught of American films in Europe, France is still producing commercially viable (albeit subsidised) films. Contemporary directors of note include Bertrand Blier *(Trop Belle pour Toi)*, Jean-Jacques Beineix *(Betty Blue)* and Jacques Rivette *(Jeanne la Pucelle)*.

Dance

Ballet was brought to France in the late 16th century by Catherine de Médecis and by the end of the 18th century it had developed into a fully fledged art form. In the early 19th century, romantic ballets such as *Giselle* and *La Sylphide* were more popular than opera in Paris.

France lost its pre-eminent position in dance during the 20th century, though Roland Petit managed to shake French ballet out of its lethargy between 1945 and 1955. Another important figure was Maurice Béjart, who shocked the public in 1955 with his *Ballet sur la Symphonie d'un Homme Seul* danced in black.

Today French dance seems to be moving in a new, more personal, direction with performers such as Caroline Marcadé and Maguy Martin and choreographers such as Odile Duboc and Jean-Claude Gallotta.

LANGUAGE

Around 122 million people worldwide speak French as their first language, and various forms of creole are used in Haiti and French Guiana, and Cajun French is spoken in parts of Louisiana. French is the national language, but pockets of France have their own language: Breton (Brittany), Basque (south-west), Catalan (around Perpignan) and Corsican (Corsica).

The French tend to assume that all human beings should speak French; it was the international language of culture and diplomacy until WWI. Your best bet is always to approach people politely in French, even if the only words you know are *'Pardon, Madame/Mademoiselle/Monsieur, parlez-vous anglais?'* ('Excuse me madam/miss/sir, do you speak English?'). See also the Language section at the back of the book.

LE TOUR
DE FRANCE

It is impossible to grasp the greatness and grandeur of the Tour de France in words alone. If riding your bicycle through the countryside on a fine summer's day were equivalent to a child's drawing of a wild flower, then the Tour de France is a Sistine Chapel fresco painted by Michelangelo.

Le Dauphiné Libéré, 12 June 1995

It is often said that you can raise the price of bread, you can add taxes, you can do almost anything you want in July, because the French only care about who's wearing the yellow jersey in the Tour de France. A veritable national monument, the annual return of the Tour certainly captures the attention of a nation. Almost nothing stops the Tour, except, of course, the two world wars, which led to its cancellation from 1915–18 and 1940–46. Here and gone in less than a minute for many spectators, the Tour de France is the only sporting event in the world that can be glimpsed from one's own door step, and for the estimated 3.5 million people who line the roads to watch the Tour each day in France, the race provides a three week splurge of athletic bravado, triumph, joy, suffering and despair. For 21 days in July, Tour fans follow the triumphs and tragedies of *'les hommes du juillet'*.

Known as 'La Grande Boucle' – the Big Lap – the Tour circumnavigates France, covering nearly 4000km in just three weeks. For the riders in the Tour, however, seeing France by bicycle challenges the limits of both physical and mental endurance. Road rash, saddle sores, broken bones, penile numbness, boils the size of golf balls, weeping blisters and fatigue-induced hallucinations become simply occupational hazards for those who sit on their bikes for eight hours a day. As one rider mused:

…when the legs and the spirit starts to wobble, the thought seeps through. Quit. Go home. But you don't. It's the Tour de France. So you learn to suffer. After all, this isn't soccer. You can't pass the bike off.

The Tour de France is the cyclist's Everest, Wimbledon or four-minute mile, and to conquer cycling's toughest challenge guarantees enduring public veneration.

A RACE IS BORN

First staged in 1903, the Tour de France was the brainchild of newspaper editor Henri Desgrange, and his chief cycling correspondent, Géo Lefèvre. Searching for a money spinner to boost the circulation of their newly established newspaper, *L'Auto* (now *L'Equipe*), the race was announced by Desgrange in a florid editorial that claimed:

…with the same broad and powerful swing of the hand which Zola gave to his labourer in The Earth, L'Auto, a newspaper of ideas and action, is going to fling across France those reckless and uncouth sowers of energy who are the great professional riders of the road. From Paris to the blue waves of the Mediterranean, from Marseille to Bordeaux, passing along roseate and dreamy roads, sleeping under the sun, across

TITLE PAGE:
Spaniard Roberto Heras leads eventual victor, Lance Armstrong (USA), up on alpine pass in the 2000 Tour.

the calm of the fields of the Vendée, following the Loire, which flows on still and silent, our men are going to race madly, unflaggingly.

'Le Tour de France', the greatest cycling test in the world – a month long race. Paris to Lyon. Marseille to Toulouse. Bordeaux to Nantes. Nantes to Ville d'Avray. 20,000FF in prizes. Leaving 1 June, arriving in Paris, 5 July at the Parc des Princes.

Despite widespread publicity, the Tour de France had a difficult birth. Even Desgrange contemplated cancelling the event when, in May of 1903, only 12 riders had signed up. As few riders could afford to be away from home for 35 days, Desgrange reduced the duration of the Tour to 21 days – the length it remains to this day.

The inaugural Tour de France proved to be an overwhelming success. Seventy-eight riders started (60 finished) and the circulation of L'Auto rose from 80,000 to 300,000. The second Tour, however, was a disaster. Treachery and sabotage were rampant, with crowds of hooligans blocking the road, beating up riders and only allowing their favourites through. Nails were strewn on the road, puncturing the riders' tyres and even Desgrange's car as he attempted to regain control of the race. Shots were fired at some of the riders to force them to quit and several disguised themselves as waiters to escape at night. Given these circumstances, it was perhaps not surprising when Desgrange declared that the race of 1904 meant the end of the Tour de France. He wrote in L'Auto:

The inaugural Tour de France is announced by Desgrange in his newspaper, L'Auto, to help boost its circulation.

It is finished … and the second edition, I'm afraid, has been killed by success, by the blind passions it has unleashed, by the injuries and filthy suspicions caused by the ignorant and the wicked.

Persuaded by Lefèvre to let the race continue, Desgrange made several changes that have helped shape the race in its contemporary form. The length of the stages was shortened (some of the early stages were nearly 500km long), the route was enlarged to include excursions into Alsace (then under German rule) and the overall length of the course grew to 2975km. Desgrange had obviously found the right formula for the Tour: in 1905, 60 riders signed on for the race; today, a limit is set but many more want to participate (some consider their year wasted if they do not get a start).

The Tour de France has evolved from these humble origins into a sporting spectacle on a scale that has few rivals. It is now the world's richest bike race, with a total of 12 million francs prize money on offer, of which the overall winner receives a purse of 2.2 million francs.

Tour Cycliste Féminin

As a microcosm of French life, it is entirely consistent that the Tour de France is, in many ways, incredibly sexist. It is only very recently that the race has even allowed female spectators in the official areas. The American rider, Jonathan Boyer, remembers his sister having to disguise herself as a man, complete with false beard, so as to watch him finish the race in Paris in the early 1980s. The Tour is largely an all-male affair; the riders are men, as are the team managers, mechanics and most of the team *soigneurs* (trainers), photographers and journalists who cover the race. Indeed, a popular French expression translates as 'salt in coffee', which refers to the fact that, each morning, all the women in France are crying into their coffee as they follow the exploits of their husbands, boyfriends, fathers or brothers who are competing in the race.

Some progress, however, has been made with the staging of the Tour Cycliste Féminin. Raced over a shorter course (there are usually only 12 stages and international rules limit women to racing shorter distances than men), the women's Tour begins the day the men's race ends in Paris. Despite the Tour de France receiving significantly more media attention and sponsorship money (the women race for a 25th of what the men earn), the Tour Cycliste Féminin has evolved into a race no less challenging or spectacular than the better known men's race, routinely including stages over the very toughest climbs of the Alps and the Pyrenees.

The idea of a women's Tour de France was first put forward in 1955, although it wasn't until 1984, the same year women's cycling was first contested as an Olympic sport in Los Angeles, that the idea became a reality. With only 35 starters, the race was won by American rider Maryanne Martin. The race was then re-routed as the Tour of the European Community, before being renamed and remarketed as the Tour Cycliste Féminin in 1992.

As in men's cycling, women's cycling has produced athletes who are in a class of their own. The exploits of the superb Italian climber Fabiana Luperini, nicknamed 'la Pirata', after that other great Italian climber, Marco Pantani, and the return to form of Dutch champion Leontien van Moorsel have both made for some exciting racing.

However, the grand dame of women's cycling and the most successful rider in the Tour Cycliste Féminin is Frenchwoman Jeannie Longo. Born in the alpine town of Annecy, Longo took up cycling at 20 years of age. Always an athlete, she began cycling in 1979 so she could compete in the 1980 world championships, which were to be held right in her backyard, in Sallanches (Haute-Savoie). Full of determination, at age 21, she didn't win, but one year later she stood on the podium with a silver medal around her neck. Her career has so far spanned two decades, and she has established herself as one of France's (and one of the world's) great athletes in a sport typically dominated by men. Her list of achievements is long: in addition to setting the hour record five times (in 2000, she reset the standard-bike record at 44.767km), 'La Longo' has been world champion 12 times, and she has a sensational record at the Olympic Games – at Barcelona in 1992, she won a silver medal in the road race, following that up with a gold medal in the same event at Atlanta in 1996, and a bronze medal in the time trial in Sydney in 2000.

Jeannie Longo has won the Tour Cycliste Féminin three times.

Tough qualifying standards must be met if a cyclist is to secure a place in this moving hall of fame. Twenty or so teams, each consisting of nine riders, contest the Tour de France. Currently, the top 12 teams in the world rankings as of 1 January, plus the previous year's winning team, and all the remaining French teams in the top 20 receive automatic entry to the Tour. Three other teams are awarded wild card entries. Following the drugs scandal of 1998, riders are now also expected to meet several 'moral obligations' relating to the fight against doping.

THE MODERN TOUR

The modern Tour de France is no doubt a far cry from the race first envisaged by Desgrange. The riders who start each year are far outnumbered by the 2000 reporters and photographers, 264 team officials, mechanics and masseurs, 745 chauffeurs and technical assistants, 20 judges, 263 race officials and 1300 sponsor publicists. The Tour has grown to such a scale that it now has its own bank (the only branch allowed to open on Bastille Day – July 14), its own hospital, weather station, hairdresser, local produce stalls and bakery.

The scale and size of the Tour de France needs to be seen to be believed. Perhaps the most striking aspect of the Tour is the way in which it takes over the towns and villages it visits. To quote Jean-Marie Leblanc, the current Directeur Général du Tour, 'we close towns for a living'. In each stage town, common garden areas are transformed into the Village Départ; car and furniture show rooms become the *salle de presse* (media room); and soccer pitches and rugby grounds are turned into helicopter landing pads. Press cars park haphazardly on the footpaths and technical vehicles scream through the streets. Roads are closed off and traffic is diverted as the riders race towards the finish line. For a 1991 stage finish at Alpe d'Huez, the church was converted into the press room. Nôtre Dame des Neiges is probably the only church where, for one day of the year at least, there were ashtrays in the nave, a bar in the vestry and where, as local opinion has it, an organist was asked to leave because he was disturbing the journalists' concentration.

The peloton stops for a water break on their way to Luxembourg during stage three of the 1947 Tour de France.

Selling the Spectacle

Financial involvement touches every aspect of the Tour de France, so much so that cynics label it the 'Tour de Franc'. However, with an overall budget estimated at 250 million francs, the Tour is necessarily – and unashamedly – commercial. Reportedly bringing in 100 million francs, not a centime of profit comes from admission fees to this *fête populaire*. Rather, the most significant financial offerings are made by corporate giants such as Coca-Cola, Nike and the French banking empire Crédit Lyonnais. The sale of television rights and contributions from those towns hosting a stage start or finish help make up the total Tour budget.

The Tour itself is a product, so competition for sponsor association is fierce. The arrivals and departures are timed by Festina. Its results are computed by IBM. Supermarché Champion rewards the best climber. Even cycling's most revered prize, *le maillot jaune* – the yellow jersey of the overall leader/winner – is named, not after some heroic effort, but after the colour of the newspaper that first sponsored the race. It is with good reason that more and more sponsors are slapping their names upon the Tour de France, for it commands – after the Olympic Games and soccer's World Cup – the highest viewing figures of any sporting event.

Of course, the increasing involvement of non-French corporations and sponsors in the staging of the Tour invites the question: just how French is the Tour de France? With riders coming from Australia, Canada, Colombia, Mexico, New Zealand, the United States and all over Europe, with stage starts in Andorra, Belgium, Britain, Germany, Ireland, Italy, Luxembourg, the Netherlands, Spain and Switzerland, and with the main sponsors coming predominantly from the United States, the Tour hardly seems the embodiment of *French* national character. Indeed, Leblanc can imagine a time when the race will begin in New York – of all places.

La Caravane Publicitaire

One of the most bizarre, and shamelessly commercial, aspects of the Tour de France is the publicity caravan; a garish cavalcade of corporate excess that precedes the riders, tantalising the fans standing roadside with their

A rider launches an attack (right) in front of onlookers of this early edition of the Tour – today, the crowd is entertained for hours prior to the riders' arrival by the publicity caravan and hundreds o team and official cars.

bounty of tacky consumer goods. Resembling a giant Christmas pageant, *la caravane* represents a surreal consumer world. Featuring vehicles designed as huge cereal boxes, cans of vegetables, telephones, ice-cream cones, rockets, corn cobs, giant hot dogs, roof-top profiteroles and computer floppy disks – you name it – the publicity caravan is a sight to behold. Although not the financial mainstay that it was when first introduced 60 years ago, it still contributes significantly to the revenue of the Tour. With nearly 500 vehicles, each paying an estimated 20,000FF per day to participate, the caravan represents a major source of income for the race organisation.

For those standing roadside, the caravan is central to the total Tour experience. During a flat stage, the race can take only a minute or two to pass any given point, so it is the caravan that whiles away the hours for the thousands of supporters who line the route. While it seems a small distraction for those who may have waited for anything up to three days for the race to arrive, vehicles in the caravan provide spectators with plastic bags of trinkets and other giveaways advertising their product or company. When it is all over, a paper trail of litter and sweet wrappers, of publicity pamphlets and discarded product samples, marks the passage of la caravane.

How the Race is Won

The nuances of the Tour de France can be confusing, particularly for first-time spectators. Basically, the race consists of 20 stages and a prologue – a short, individual time trial that determines which rider will wear the yellow jersey for the following day (the first official day of racing). After that the Tour 'formula' usually consists of 11 'flat' stages, where the flashy sprinters provide thrills and spills in their furious race to the finish line. As well, it has three 'mountain' and four 'high mountain' stages, where the goats who thrive on back-breaking, lung-busting climbs dance away from the pack as the race heads for the hills. The two individual time trials – 'the race of truth' – require riders to compete against the clock in the purest test of strength, stamina and endurance.

The Tour de France is often described as a race within a race. Each day's stage is a competition in itself. For some it is merely the prestige of winning a stage, while others are chasing the *le maillot jaune* (the yellow jersey), which is awarded to the rider who has the lowest cumulative time at the end of each day. The ultimate prize is to be wearing this jersey after the final stage. Thus, an individual stage win is not as important as to securing overall victory as are consistency and the time gained over the rest of the field. After three weeks of racing, this can be a matter of seconds. In 1989, a mere eight seconds separated first and second place. After racing more than 3800km over 21 days, Greg LeMond claimed victory over the much fancied and enigmatic Parisian Laurent Fignon by a miniscule eight seconds. Of course, not every rider can be a winner and, at the back of the field, you'll find the ignobly named *lanterne rouge*. The very last rider in the race is so named because he was traditionally given a red lantern to find his way home, long after the other riders had reached Paris.

To identify their wearers from the blur of the fast moving peloton, the Tour de France has three distinctive jerseys. Le maillot jaune is worn by the race leader, while *le maillot vert* (the green or 'points' jersey) is worn by the most consistent daily finisher on placings rather than time. *Le maillot á pois* (the red and white polka dot jersey) is worn by the 'king of the mountains', the rider who wins the most points for being first over each 'mountain'. Each jersey is prestigious in its own right, and the battle rages for the right to wear these coveted shirts each day, adding to the drama and excitement of the greatest bike race in the world.

Convicts of the Road

Despite the relentless commercialisation of the Tour de France, it is rarely seen as diminishing the Tour's status as a race of unsurpassed sporting excellence. Nor has it compromised the tales of bravery and heroism that are as much a part of the race as the caravane publicitaire. Despite its stature as a *gigantisme*, the scale of the Tour de France never dwarfs the action of the race. It has never lost the essence of courage, endurance, pride and determination first displayed in 1903. Indeed, when you see the riders, their faces scarlet with effort, with sweat and mucus running down their chins, you realise the 'world's greatest bike race' showcases some of the world's greatest athletes.

The phrase, *les forçats de la route* (the convicts of the road) was first introduced in 1924 to capture the heroism and gritty determination of the very greatest riders in the Tour de France. While the list of 'Tour greats' is too long to include here, some of the people who have shaped the history of the Tour de France include Frenchmen Jacques Anquetil and Bernard Hinault, Belgian Eddy Merckx, and Spaniard Miguel Indurain, who have each won the Tour de France a record five times. The list also includes Greg LeMond, who, having won the Tour in 1986, looked set to win again the following year when he was shot by his brother-in-law in a hunting accident. Despite having a body full of lead pellets, LeMond overcame the odds to win the race in 1989 and 1990.

In addition to these champions, the Tour also has a colourful history of also-rans; riders who are celebrated for their close calls and near misses, rather than their victories. Raymond Poulidor is perhaps cycling's most famous near miss (see the 'Puy de Dôme & Le Tour' boxed text in the Massif Central chapter). Then there was Abdel Kader Zaaf – the 'Lion of Chebli' – who was included in a North African team racing in the 1950s. During one very long stage across the baking hot fields of Provence, he was refreshed by glasses of *rosé*, supplied by the spectators. Not surprisingly, Zaaf fell asleep. When he awoke, he set off in the wrong direction and was eventually disqualified from the race. The Dutch rider Wim van Est, competing in the 1951 Tour, fell 70 feet over the edge of the Col de l'Aubisque in the Pyrenees. Miraculously,

Cheers! The convicts of the road during a relaxed moment of the 1930 Tour de France.

van Est survived. When he had recovered from his numerous injuries, he was featured in a newspaper advertisement for the Swiss watch company Pontiac. The copy read, 'I fell seventy feet. My heart missed a beat, but my Pontiac never stopped ticking'.

National Politics & Local Life

The Tour de France is also a brilliant showcase of local life in France, as tiny villages get behind the race in a show of regional pride and identity. Intricate flower arrangements painstakingly assembled by townsfolk welcome the Tour in Avranches; in Livarot, a gigantic wheel of cheese, prominently displayed alongside the finish line, draws attention to Normandy's dairy industry. Commemorative bottles of wine are used to mark the passage of the Tour through Villard-de-Lans, and art work on T-shirts, coffee mugs, cigarette lighters, cuff-links, refrigerator magnets and postcards, among other things, are all used to highlight the passage of the Tour through the various regions of France.

Perhaps the most remarkable display of local life being touched by the Tour de France is the custom of the *bon de sortie*, which allows a local rider to ride, unchallenged, ahead of the peloton when the race passes through his home town. The *régional*, as the local boy is known, usually has time for a quick hello, or perhaps half a glass of champagne with assorted relatives and friends, before being swept up by the following peloton. Similarly, when the peloton passes a village in which a wedding is taking place, it is customary for the *maillot jaune* to kiss the bride and groom; his actions are believed to bring good luck to the newlyweds.

Certainly a grand celebration of French life, the Tour de France also has a darker side. Its use of public roads, and the massive media coverage that it attracts, makes the Tour an especially vulnerable target for protest groups, and the extent to which it is appropriated for political ends is certainly remarkable. In 1982, striking steel workers in the town of Denain blocked the road and forced the Tour to cancel a stage. In 1990, the third stage from Poitiers to Nantes was seized by militant sheep farmers who, angry at the quota system for mutton imports from Eastern Europe, poured boiling oil onto the road the Tour was to travel along.

But it is the actions of pro-Basque terrorist wing Euzkadi Ta Askatasuna (ETA) that are perhaps the most dramatic expressions of discontent. Its members sometimes overrun the road when the Tour heads south to the French-Spanish border. In other instances, Basque nationalists have stormed stage villages and refused to let the race start. However, the most spectacular instance of terrorism in the Tour de France occurred at the start of the 1992 edition in San Sebastian – the capital of the Basque region – when ETA members placed an incendiary device under the car of leading English-speaking cycling commentator Phil Liggett. More recently, in 1997, Spanish police detonated a 6kg bomb placed in a rubbish bin outside a bank in Pamplona, also in Basque country.

Don't be deterred by these sorts of isolated terrorist actions. For most, the Tour de France is a magnificent spectacle, and the achievements of the riders surpass all of the other elements that make up this three-week festival of French life. It's the greatest show on earth.

Facts for the Cyclist

HIGHLIGHTS

France has so many outstanding features, it is hard to know where to begin and end. Cycling here is more than just enjoying quiet country roads: it's about strolling through markets buying gourmet picnic ingredients, stopping to explore a museum or historic church, or spending a few hours off the bike walking through a national park. After months of travelling on two wheels, the authors have decided on some of their favourite cycling highlights.

See the Table of Rides towards the beginning of this book for page numbers of rides featuring the highlights detailed here:

Coastal Scenery

The warm Mediterranean laps France's southern shores, and riding the Grande Corniche is the place for bird's-eye views over the playground of the rich, the Côte d'Azur. Across the water, the island of Corsica is fringed with popular family beaches to the east, and a ruggedly beautiful coastline of cliffs and coves to the west; cycling the winding road through the shattered red cliffs of the Calenche is breathtaking.

Hundreds of kilometres of bikepaths lace the pine forests lining France's Atlantic coast in the South-West, where quaint, century-old *villas balnèares* (seaside holiday houses) provide an atmosphere of times-past among the new surfer culture. Farther north, the Channel beaches in Normandy are remembered for the bloodshed of D-day, and Brittany's rugged coastline is epitomised along the Côte d'Émeraude (Emerald Coast).

Climbs & Descents

The ups and downs of mountain cycling offer demanding climbs, unparalleled views and exhilarating descents. The high cols of the French Alps typify this, and the ultimate challenge is yours, ascending the classic Tour de France climb, the Alpe d'Huez – 13km of leg-breaking beauty and cycling history. Also synonymous with the Tour, the Col du Tourmalet in the Pyrenees and Mont Ventoux in Provence are both classic long, hard climbs.

In the western Pyrenees, the Col Bagargui is a steep, twisting climb on a narrow, deserted road. After a strenuous ascent from the east, the western side of Col de Marie-Blanque offers one of the fastest, most thrilling descents in the Raid Pyrénéen.

In Corsica the long climb through the Gorges de la Restonica parallels a tempting icy stream and promises a hurtling descent on the return journey. The volcanic folds of the Massif Central provide challenges at every turn, including the Tour de France quad-killing special of the Puy de Dôme and the long, hard climb to sweeping views at the Pas de Peyrol, below Puy Mary.

Chateaux

Frequent reminders of the opulent streak of French royalty are the magnificent chateaux. The grandeur of the Île de France's Château de Chantilly is striking – if you cycle alongside, it appears to float on water.

In the Dordogne, Castelnaud has everything you'd expect from a cliff-top castle: walls up to 2m thick, a superb panorama of the meandering Dordogne, and views of the fortified chateaux that dot the nearby hilltops.

And *la crème de la crème* are the Loire Valley chateaux, including Blois, Chenonceau, Chaumont, Cheverny, Azay-le-Rideau and Lângeais.

Fortresses & Walled Towns

France's long history of strife has left the country with a rich legacy of fortified towns. Many are perched on cliff-top promontories and beckon the cyclist on the long climb towards them. The sheer white walls of Corsica's Bonifacio loom spectacularly over the water atop an undercut limestone cliff.

Cycling towards Brittany's St Malo, the walled town enclosed by its sturdy ramparts and the sea, can't fail to impress. Domme, in the Dordogne, is one of France's best-preserved *bastide* (medieval fortified towns), and provides spectacular views from its hill-top eyrie.

In Provence, impressive Avignon acquired its fortifications as the Papal seat in the 14th century. The Basque walled town of St Jean-Pied de Port in the Pyrenees is on the pilgrim trail to Santiago de Compostela, and fairy-tale Carcassonne in Languedoc is a splendid 'fake': its ramparts date only from the 19th century.

Forests & Regional Parks
Many Île de France forests are the old hunting grounds of kings; the immense Forêt de Fontainebleau, with *routes forestières*, many closed to cars, is an interesting green space, while the Forêt de Compiègne offers quiet cycling on paved bicycle paths.

France's regional parks offer varied scenery, from Corsica's Parc National Régional de la Corse with its wild terrain to the Massif Central's Parc Naturel Régional des Volcans showing off its volcanic past. Languedoc's Parc Naturel Régional du Haut Languedoc preserves a landscape dotted with small villages that hardly seems to have changed in a century, and the Jura's majestic Route des Sapins travels through thick, hundred-year-old forest.

Gardens
France is studded with stunning gardens. Artist Claude Monet created his famous gardens at Giverny in Normandy, where a stroll among the plants immerses you into several of his paintings. Château Villandry in the Loire Valley has the world's most famous vegetable garden, where green fingers have created formal geometric patterns with seasonal produce. Meanwhile, the Parc du Château in Vieux Nice on the Côte d'Azur is a cool, peaceful refuge from a bustling city.

Picture-Postcard Villages
France is dotted with charming villages, where centuries-old houses hung with colourful flower boxes line narrow cobbled lanes. For a glimpse of the distinctively quirky Quercynoise architecture, visit Carennac in the South-West; and, for the traditional, quaint half-timbered houses of Normandy, Beuvron-en-Auge is a must. Brittany's Josselin sits on the Canal Nantes à Brest, the sheer walls of its chateau rising up from beside the canal, the village tucked cosily behind the chateau.

In Burgundy, stroll through the quiet, cobblestoned streets of Noyers-sur-Serein, contained within the loop of the Serein River, and in Provence, Peille typifies the region's perched villages, with streets so narrow two pedestrians can barely pass.

In the Pyrenees, Arreau nestles at the foot of the Col d'Aspin, its flowered historic centre straddling two rivers.

Spectacular Views
You may be out of breath when you take in these views, but they're worth the effort! In Normandy, the imposing vestiges of Château Gaillard, high above the Seine, is a magnificent vantage point overlooking the river and Les Andelys. Drink in the celebrated champagne vineyards of the Marne Valley from above Hautvillers. Admire the religious sanctuary of Rocamadour as pilgrims have done for centuries in the Dordogne. Take your mind off the climb to Corsica's Col de Bavella with the sight of the jagged granite needles of the Aiguilles de Bavella.

Gasp at the Pic du Midi de Bigorre and other Pyrenean summits from Col d'Aspin, and breathe fresh air on Mont Aigoual in the Cévennes while surveying the bare *causses* (limestone plateaux) and the isolated Parc National des Cévennes from its weather observatory. The French Alps offer the raw beauty of Gorges de la Bourne, so steep that it shuts out the sky, and the towering peaks and valleys of the High Cols. Or enter a different world and cycle the Alsace's Grand Ballon, with its lunar-like landscape.

SUGGESTED ITINERARIES
France is a large and diverse country. Getting around can be time-consuming, particularly on the trains, many of which do not have provision to carry bicycles except in a bike bag, thus limiting your options (see the Getting Around chapter). If you are spending only one or two weeks in France, limit your cycling to one or two adjacent areas.

See the Table of Rides early in this book for page numbers of rides.

One Week
Those flying into Paris could start with the day rides Fabulous Fontainebleau, Forêt de Compiègne or Monet's Passions. Add one of the three-day rides, Calvados Classique in Normandy or, for wine buffs, either the Taste of Southern Champagne or the Wine Lover's Circuit in Burgundy. If you want to do just one ride, the Chateau Explorer is a five-day tour through the Loire Valley. Those arriving in Nice could begin with the two-day Alpes

Maritime circuit, offering Côte d'Azur variety. Move on to Provence and the three-day Majesty of the Romans ride.

Two Weeks

From Paris, head to the Loire Valley for the Chateau Explorer, and combine this with either the Southern Brittany Contrasts or the Classic Burgundy route.

In the south, couple the Côte d'Azur's Alpes Maritime circuit with the Luberon & Mont Ventoux ride through Provence. Add to this a taste of the Alps with Vercors Contrasts, or fly or catch the ferry to Corsica for the Scented Isle ride.

One Month

Begin with some day rides from Paris. In Brittany enjoy the Northern Brittany Majesty ride. Head back to Paris and to Burgundy for the Classic Burgundy ride and then to Provence for the Luberon & Mont Ventoux ride. Complete the month with the Cave Art, Cuisine & Chateaux ride through the Dordogne and Lot *départements* (departments: administrative division), or swing back through the Loire to ride the Chateau Explorer.

Two Months

Acclimatise with a couple of day rides out of Paris. The Calvados Classique offers gentle riding through Normandy. Then, the Classic Burgundy ride provides a taste of Burgundy's wine region; travel farther east for more wine country on the Alsatian Wine Route. For a challenge, add a ride in the Alps (Vercors Contrasts or High Cols of the Tour de France).

Head back to sea level and spend a few days on the Côte d'Azur by doing the Mediterranean Promenade day ride and two days on the Alpes Maritime circuit. Take a side trip to Corsica for The Scented Isle ride, then return to the mainland, to Provence, for the Luberon & Mont Ventoux ride.

If you want to see more wine country, head west and cycle the Bordeaux Wine Explorer or, if mountains are your thing, choose the rides out of Foix for a good Introduction to the Pyrenees. The Cave Art, Cuisine & Chateaux ride through the Dordogne and Lot departments makes a fine ending to this Grand Tour de France.

PLANNING
When to Cycle

Considering the variety of terrain, and France's regional climatic differences, deciding when to cycle largely depends on where you will be cycling. As a rule of thumb, the weather is best between April and October. July and August have the best weather, with their long, warm days, and are also the time for cycling events (see the boxed text) and the festival season (see Public Holidays & Special Events later in this chapter). However, August, the best month in most places weather-wise, sees the unavoidable crowds of summer holiday-makers, especially on the coast. July is less crowded than August. Farther inland and at higher altitudes, it's likely to be less crowded.

May, June, September and October are excellent choices. Temperatures are pleasant, accommodation and places of interest are less crowded and price breaks on lodgings and airline tickets are often available. It is an ideal time to cycle in Provence, Corsica and the south, where it can become extremely hot in July and August. Beach areas are quieter and more relaxed, although some attractions may be closed. Check camping grounds' opening dates, as many open only from mid-May to mid-September.

Spring is probably the most unpredictable season, but the best time for early blooms and blossoms. This season has stretches of glorious weather, yet winter-like relapses are not uncommon. When planning spring travel, consider that Easter is popular for domestic tourism and often crowded. Typically, it is too early to cycle in the higher altitudes, which may have snow on the ground and many passes still closed.

Autumn is another good season to cycle, with pleasant (yet shorter) days, stable weather and the grape harvest. In places like the Dordogne (see the South-West France chapter), the autumn colours are spectacular.

Winter can be cold and damp, though it is possible to cycle in areas such as Provence, the Côte d'Azur, the Loire, Île de France, Champagne, Normandy and parts of Burgundy. Be prepared with cold- and wet-weather gear, and bear in mind that days are shorter. The Alps, Pyrenees, and other mountainous areas are out of the question for cycle touring during winter.

Cycling Events

Throughout the year, on any given weekend, you are bound to find some sort of cycling event, whether it be a national race or a local club tour. The Fédération Française de Cyclotourisme (FFCT) includes an enormous list of country-wide events in its 100pp magazine, *Où irons-nous?*. It lists randonnées, brevets, audax rides, mountain bike (VTT) events and club information. The FFC (Fédération Française de Cyclisme) Web site 🖳 www.ffc.fr lists race information. Bike shops usually publicise local events and races.

Most activities occur in the warmer months, from around May to September. One of the best organised rides open to visiting cycle tourists is the FFCT's Semaine Fédérale Internationale de Cyclotourisme, which attracts more than 12,000 participants. Now in its 63rd year, each year finds it in a different location: Crest (2001) and Quimper (2002); see the Useful Organisations section in this chapter for FFCT contact details.

Below is a selection of French cycling events. More area-specific events can be found in the 'In Brief' table of the regional chapters of this book.

When	Event	When	Event
Jan	Festival du Voyage à Vélo*, Cyclo-Camping International association's annual gathering	Jun–Jul	Cyclo-Montagnardes series*, five annual FFCT rides to French summits
Mar	Paris-Nice, the 'Race to the Sun' professional race	Jul	Tour de France
Mar–Oct	Paris Citybike rides*, see the boxed text 'Cycling in the City' in the Paris & the Île de France chapter	Jul	Memorial Fabio Casartelli ride* series, see the boxed text 'Mort Pour Le Tour' in the Provence chapter
Apr	La Journée du Piéton et du Vélo*, Paris's Pedestrian and Cyclist's Day, held first Sunday of Spring	early Aug	Tour VTT, the mountain bike 'Tour de France'
Easter	numerous FFCT regional rides*	early Aug	Semaine Fédérale Internationale de Cyclotourisme*, the FFCT's annual week-long tour
Apr/May	Paris-Roubaix race, see the boxed text 'Paris-Roubaix' in the Paris & the Île de France chapter	Aug	Paris-Brest-Paris*, 1200km randonnée, see the Randonnées chapter
May	Trophée des Grimpeurs (Climber's Trophy) professional race, held Ascension Day	Sep	Grand Prix des Nations professional time trial, location varies
Jun	La Fête du Vélo*, national cycling festival, held first weekend of June	early Oct	Paris-Tours professional race

* public participation is invited at these events

Always take into account Sunday and public holidays. Although attractions may remain open, small villages can shut down and food shops (even restaurants) will more than likely be closed.

Maps

France has two major mapping companies: Michelin and IGN (Institut Géographique National).

A great trip-planning resource is the Michelin map No 989 *France* (1: 1,000,000; 25FF). However, this red jacketed map is inadequate for cycling navigation. Michelin's larger scale, yellow jacketed maps (1:200,000) work well as a supplement to those in this book. These maps come in two sheet sizes: small (14FF for each of the 39 sheets), marked with two-digit identification numbers, Nos 51–90; and large (32FF),

Cycle-Touring Map

A good planning resource is the IGN map No 906 *France: VTT & Randonnées Cyclos* (1:1,000,000; 29FF). It outlines hundreds of permanent *randonnées* (tours), of between 100km and 1000km, that have been recommended by Féderation Française de Cyclotourisme (FFCT) affiliated clubs on the basis of their tourist appeal and regional character. The clubs responsible for each tour will supply – for a small fee – a ride kit. Contact the FFCT for details (see Useful Organisations in this chapter).

The map also shows the starting point for 43 Office National des Forêt mountain-bike rides. All the Fédération Française de Cyclisme (FFC) mountain bike centres are marked.

Regional parks are also shown, and the park office address, phone and fax numbers are listed.

identified by three-digit numbers, Nos 230–246. The latter cover the country in 17 sheets, roughly corresponding to each of France's administrative regions. The new Michelin Alentours series (35FF) is useful for cycling in the environs of cities. These 1:150,000 maps cover 75km around the principal city in the region and have an index and city maps. At the time of writing *Bordeaux*, *Nancy*, *Nantes*, *Poitiers*, *Rouen* and *Strasbourg* were available.

IGN covers France with 16 1:250,000 scale maps (29FF) and 74 1:100,000 scale maps (29FF), but neither series has the clarity of the Michelin series. For map aficionados, or serious mountain bikers, IGN covers all of France with 2200 1:25,000-scale maps, known as the Blue series or Top 25 series (46FF). IGN also publishes a key map listing hundreds of permanent *randonnées* (long-distance routes) and VTT (mountain bike) circuits, with contact details; see the boxed text 'VTT & Randonnées Cyclos Map'. Other IGN cycling maps include *90 Circuits Cyclos en Île de France* and regional *cyclocartes* (58FF) such as *La Drôme à Vélo* and *Le Calvados à Bicyclette*.

Maps are available at Maisons de la Presse (large newsagencies) found all over France, tourist offices, bookshops and even from some newspaper kiosks. In Paris, for a full selection of IGN maps, visit the Espace IGN (☎ 01 43 98 80 00, 🖳 www.ign.fr) at 107 rue La Boétie (8e, metro Franklin D Roosevelt).

What to Bring

Clothing The most important thing to keep in mind is that everything you pack, you carry! Evaluate each item by asking, 'Do I really need this?' You need virtually the same amount of gear whether you are touring for two weeks or two months.

Padded bicycle shorts are a must and are designed to be worn without underwear to prevent chafing. If you prefer the look of regular shorts, an option is 'double shorts' – ordinary-looking shorts with a lightweight padded lining sewn in. For cooler weather, take Lycra or thermal tights to pull over your padded bicycle shorts; rain pants can be a blessing.

For the most practical use of your garments, layer. In cooler weather start with a lightweight cycling, polypropylene or fine wool top, followed by an insulating layer such as a thin synthetic fleece jacket, then a rain jacket. Many lightweight rain jackets are water resistant, rather than waterproof, and work in drizzle but not a downpour; they're often not made of breathable fabric. The most well-known breathable and waterproof fabric is Gore-Tex. Whenever choosing rain gear choose a neon (or fluorescent) colour for greatest visibility. The same is true of all cycling clothing. French drivers are cognisant of cyclists, but every bit of visibility helps.

Cycling exposes you to the sun for long periods. Consider wearing a long-sleeved top made of something light and breathable such as Coolmax, Capilene or even silk. Cotton is cool and a natural fibre, but takes a long time to dry.

Sunglasses are essential, not only to prevent glare from the sun, but also to stop your eyes from drying out in the wind. Glasses also protect your eyes from insects and dust.

Wear cycling gloves: the padded palms reduce the impact of jarring on your hands, which can lead to nerve damage. They also prevent sunburn and protect your hands if you fall.

In cold weather you may want full-finger cycling gloves (either thin polypropylene gloves that can be worn under cycling gloves, or more wind- and rain-resistant ones). To keep your feet warm, take thermal socks, or light wool socks, which dry quickly and stay warm when wet; cotton socks are uncomfortable and cold when wet. Several types of booties can be put over your shoes for warmth and waterproofing. If your ears get cold, take a head band or wear a close-fitting beanie under your helmet.

Cycling shoes help you pedal more efficiently. They have stiff soles that transfer the power from your pedal stroke directly to the pedal. Spongy soled running shoes are inefficient, may leave your feet sore and can ultimately cause knee problems. (See the Your Bicycle chapter for more on shoes and pedals.)

The clothing you wear in the evening and days off your bike largely depends on where you stay and eat. If you are in France to 'eat', as many of us are, and intend to eat out at restaurants, carry some smart casual clothes that pack easily and don't wrinkle. Also take a pair of casual shoes or sandals, and consider packing walking shoes. Campers need to take adequate clothing for cool nights.

Some other useful items are a day pack, a bandanna or scarf, a hat, swimming costume and a sarong (which can act as a towel, sheet, picnic blanket, shawl, skirt or discreet on-the-beach changing aid).

Bicycle Even France's tiny back roads are generally sealed and well surfaced, making them suitable for any type of bike. If taking a road bike into the mountains, consider adding some lower gears for the hills. The hassles with getting bikes on trains could make a folding bike a good investment. See the Your Bicycle chapter for more tips on choosing a steed.

Equipment See the Health & Safety chapter for the basic equipment requirements under French law.

To make the most of the rides in this guide, you will need a bicycle computer. It allows you to keep track of distance and – depending on the model – will have functions such as speed, clock, elapsed time and average speed. A compass is another handy item, and is useful for finding the start direction of the rides.

Camping Equipment If you intend camping, the bare minimum equipment is a tent, insulated mat and a sleeping bag. Beyond that, the weight of each item enters the equation. How self-sufficient are you going to be? If you intend to eat mostly in restaurants, take only basic picnic items, saving the weight of cooking and cleaning supplies you carry. Begin with the basics; if you need more, it is not difficult to find camping supply shops en route.

Buying Locally France has more than 5000 bike shops, so one is rarely far away. They range from the chains of mega-sports stores to regular bicycle shops; most small towns will at least have a combination bicycle, motor bike and lawn mower shop. Peugeot car dealerships will often have a bicycle sales and repairs section, and will

What's in a Name?

In France, you can often get some idea of a town's location by its name. Town names can often be rather lengthy to accommodate a descriptive suffix. You can be sure that Soulac-sur-Mer is a town on the seaside (*mer*, 'sea'), while you'll have to climb up to St-Laurent du Mont (*mont*, 'mount'). Milly-la-Forêt is in the forest (*forêt*, 'forest') and St-Gatien des Bois is in the woods (*bois*, 'woods').

The prepositions *sur* (on), *sous* (under) and *en* (in) play a huge role in town names. Auvers-sur-Oise means Auvers is on the Oise River, and Belval-sous-Châtillon is a dependent of the town of Châtillon. When reading signs or maps, sur is often abbreviated as s/ and sous as s/s. Beuvron-en-Auge is in the Auge area, and Châlons-en-Champagne is in Champagne.

The French have a habit of naming more than one town with the same name, thus the suffix will distinguish them. In Brittany you'll find, for example, Belle Île-en-Mer (Beautiful Island in the Sea) on the coast, and inland, Belle Île-en-Terre (*terre*, 'land').

Locals will often refer to a town only by its root name, eg, Tarascon-sur-Ariège in the Pyrenees will be known, and possibly even signed, only as Tarascon. Where this applies, we have followed the local example, though maps will usually list the full name.

often hire bikes. The selection of bikes and equipment in shops varies from fully stocked to basic parts.

Independent bicycle shops thrive in this country where people are avid cyclists. However, some of the big chain stores can provide a one-stop shop for visiting cyclists. One of the best-known chain stores is Decathlon, which has 190 stores throughout the country, including several in Paris. This general sports store has an excellent bicycle department, helpful staff and a good selection of bicycles, accessories and clothing. Go Sport has shops in Paris and throughout France; its bicycle

department is well stocked. Both these chains sell *housses*, the bags needed to transport bikes on TGV trains (see the boxed text 'What is une housse?' in the Getting Around chapter).

The France-wide Bouticycle network links 160 bicycle shops that provide a good range of bicycles, touring equipment, accessories and clothing. The franchise's motto is '*Comment imaginer la vie sans vélo?*' (How can you imagine life without a bicycle?).

Each of these companies' catalogues list a wide range of products. Shop locations can be found on their web sites:

Equipment Check List

This list is a general guide to the things you might take on a bike tour. Your list will vary depending on the kind of cycling you want to do, whether you're roughing it in a tent or planning on luxury accommodation, and on the time of year. Don't forget to take on board enough water and food to see you safely between towns.

Bike Clothing
- ☐ cycling gloves
- ☐ cycling shoes and socks
- ☐ cycling tights or leg-warmers
- ☐ helmet and visor
- ☐ long-sleeved shirt or cycling jersey
- ☐ padded cycling shorts (knicks)
- ☐ sunglasses
- ☐ thermal undershirt and arm-warmers
- ☐ T-shirt or short-sleeved cycling jersey
- ☐ visibility vest
- ☐ waterproof jacket & pants
- ☐ windproof jacket or vest

Off-Bike Clothing
- ☐ change of clothing
- ☐ spare shoes or sandals
- ☐ swimming costume
- ☐ sunhat
- ☐ fleece jacket
- ☐ thermal underwear
- ☐ underwear and spare socks
- ☐ warm hat and gloves

Equipment
- ☐ bike lights (rear and front) with spare batteries (see torch)
- ☐ elastic cord
- ☐ camera and spare film

- ☐ cycle computer
- ☐ day-pack
- ☐ first-aid kit* and toiletries
- ☐ sewing/mending kit (for everything)
- ☐ panniers and waterproof liners
- ☐ pocket knife (with corkscrew)
- ☐ sleeping sheet
- ☐ small handlebar bag and/or map case
- ☐ small towel
- ☐ tool kit, pump and spares*
- ☐ torch (flashlight) with spare batteries and globe – some double as (front) bike lights
- ☐ water containers
- ☐ water purification tablets, iodine or filter

Camping
- ☐ cooking, eating and drinking utensils
- ☐ clothesline
- ☐ dishwashing items
- ☐ portable stove and fuel
- ☐ insulating mat
- ☐ matches or lighter and candle
- ☐ sleeping bag
- ☐ tent
- ☐ toilet paper and toilet trowel

* see the 'First-Aid Kit' boxed text in the Health & Safety chapter; 'Spares & Tool Kit' boxed text in the Your Bicycle chapter.

Bouticycle (🖳 www.bouticycle.com) Huge (148pp) paper catalogue, with locations and services listed online.
Decathlon (🖳 www.decathlon.com) Extensive paper catalogue; online in French and English.
Go Sport (🖳 www.go-sport.fr) Paper catalogue, plus basic online version.

Bicycles, parts, accessories and clothing tend to be a combination of French-made and imported. Road bikes cost as little as 1299FF; high-end models may be priced at 8999FF. For a decent hybrid or mountain bike, prices range from 2999FF to 10,999FF, but are available as cheaply as 1499FF. Helmets are readily available and prices range from as low as 100FF to 749FF. Panniers in France tend to be the very basic, saddle bag version, which cost from 199FF; it's best to bring some from home. Prices for jerseys and padded cycling shorts (knicks) range from 99FF to 349FF.

Shops with camping equipment and outdoor gear can be found all over France. General sports stores (including Decathlon and Go Sport) often have a camping or hiking section. Many camping grounds have a shop selling basic camping supplies.

A note on camping fuel: make sure your stove is compatible with the fuel canisters available in Europe. Camping GAZ brand is the most widespread. If you are using an MSR (Mountain Safety Research) or another brand of gasoline-type stove, white gas or shellite (*essence blanche*) is sold as Coleman gas. However, this is not easily found outside Paris, even in large towns, so stock up before leaving the capital. Methylated spirits (denatured alcohol; *alcool à brûler*) – the fuel used in Trangia-type stoves – is available in supermarkets.

A good camping supply store in Paris is Aux Vieux Campeur (☎ 01 53 10 48 48, fax 01 46 34 14 16, 🖳 www.au-vieux-campeur .fr), 48 rue des Écoles (5e). It also has shops in Lyon and Sallaches (near Chamonix, Savoie). You can *not* carry fuel on planes.

Hiring Locally Bicycle hire is quite common in France. A basic *vélo de ville* (city bike), *vélo tout chemin* (VTC; hybrid bike) or *vélo tout terrain* (VTT; mountain bike) can be hired from many bicycle shops, some youth hostels and bicycle hire companies (most often in tourist areas or areas where cycling is popular). Hiring a road

bike is less likely. A few train stations still hire out bicycles, though at the time of writing, they were generally of poor quality and not well maintained. However, as part of a commitment to improve conditions for cyclists, in September 1999 the SNCF said it would improve station bicycle rental.

Throughout the tours in this book we indicate bike shops and hire places en route. Daily rates range from 70FF to 120FF, and weekly rates from 300FF to 500FF. A hefty deposit of at least 1000FF is usually required, often in the form of a credit card, although some places will accept travellers cheques or cash. Ask for, at the very least, a pump and a lock; see the Language chapter for tips.

Most places will provide some sort of basic lock, but it is a good idea to take your own. Almost no places hire panniers, and many bikes do not have a rear rack. Be prepared for this by bringing a day pack; in case the bike does have a rack, carry some elastic cords (bungee or occy straps). For longer rides, hire a bicycle with a rack in advance and bring your own panniers. Helmets for adults and children are only sometimes available for hire, so consider bringing your own; see also the boxed text 'Bicycle Touring with Children' later in this chapter.

TOURIST OFFICES
Local Tourist Offices
Every city, town, village and hamlet seems to have either an *office de tourisme* (a tourist office run by some unit of local government) or a *syndicat d'initiative* (a tourist office run by an organisation of local merchants). Both are excellent resources and can usually provide a map at the very least. Some will also change foreign currency, especially when banks are closed, though the rate is rarely very good.

Services at tourist offices vary. Many will make local hotel reservations, usually for a small fee. They will provide lists of local lodgings, such as hotels, B&Bs and camping grounds, and many sell local maps and guides. If there are cycling routes in the area, offerings vary from a free photocopied sheet to a packet or booklet of rides, which can be purchased.

At towns or villages without tourist offices, the *mairie* or *hôtel de ville* (both 'town hall') may be able to help. Don't be surprised if the person behind the desk speaks only French. See the Language chapter for lists of useful phrases; don't forget *merci* (thank you) and a smile, and you'll get the basic information you need.

Details on tourist offices appear under Information at the beginning of each city, town or area listing in the regional chapters.

Tourist Offices Abroad

French government tourist offices (usually called Maisons de la France) can provide every imaginable sort of tourist information on Paris and the rest of the country. Be specific when contacting these offices or you will simply receive a general packet of brochures. Indicate you are interested in cycling and mention any particular activities and specific regions you'd like to know more about.

The Maison de la France head office has an incredible Web site (see Internet Resources later in this chapter). Their office is in Paris at 8 ave de l'Opéra (☎ 01 42 96 10 23, fax 01 42 86 80 52).

Other Maisons de la France include:

Australia (☎ 02-9231 5244, fax 9221 8682, e ifrance@internetezy.com.au) 25 Bligh St, 22nd floor, Sydney, NSW 2000
Canada (☎ 514-288 4264, fax 845 4868, e mfrance@mtl.net) 1981 McGill College Ave, Suite 490, Montreal, Que H3A 2W9
Germany (☎ 069-580 13 1, fax 745 55 6, e maison_de_la_France@t-online.de) Westendstrasse 47, D-60325 Frankfurt
Ireland (☎ 01-679 0813, fax 679 0814, e frenchtouristoffice@tinet.ie) 10 Suffolk St, Dublin 2
Japan (☎ 03-3582 6965, fax 3505 2873) Landic 2, Akasaka Bldg, 10–9 Akasaka 2-chome, Minato-Ku, Tokyo 107
Netherlands (☎ 0900-112 2332, fax 020-620 3339, e informatie@fransverkeersbureau.nl) Prinsengracht 670, 1017 KX Amsterdam
South Africa (☎ 011-880 8062, fax 770 1666, e mdfsa@frenchdoor.co.za) Oxford Manor, 1st floor, 196 Oxford Road, Illovo, Johannesburg, 2196
UK (☎ 020-7399 3500, fax 7493 6594, e piccadilly@mdlf.demon.co.uk) 178 Piccadilly, London W1V 0AL
USA *New York*: (☎ 212-838 7800, fax 838 7855, e info@francetourism.com) 444 Madison Ave, 16th floor, New York, NY 10022-6903
Los Angeles: (☎ 310-271 6665, fax 276 2835, e fgto@gte.net) 9454 Wiltshire Blvd, Suite 715, Beverly Hills, CA 90212-2967

VISAS & DOCUMENTS
Passport & Visas

By law, everyone in France, including tourists, must carry some sort of ID at all times. For foreigners, this means a passport (if you don't want to carry your passport for security reasons a photocopy should do, although you may be required to report to a police station later to verify your identity) or, for citizens of the European Union (EU), a national ID card.

Tourist Visas No entry requirements or restrictions apply to nationals of the EU. Citizens of Australia, the USA, Canada, New Zealand and Israel do not need visas to visit France as tourists for up to three months. Except for people from a handful of other European countries, everyone else must have a visa.

Among those who need visas are South Africans. Visa fees depend on the current exchange rate, but a transit visa should cost about US$10, a 30-day visa around US$26, and a single/multiple entry visa of up to three months about US$32. You will need your passport (valid for three months beyond the date of your departure from France), a return ticket, proof of sufficient funds to support yourself, proof of pre-arranged accommodation (possibly), two passport-size photos and the visa fee in cash.

If all the forms are in order, your visa will be issued on the spot. You can also apply for a French visa after arriving in Europe – the fee is the same, but you may not need to produce a return ticket. If you enter France overland, your visa may not be checked at the border, but major problems can arise if you don't have one later (eg, at the airport as you leave the country). Even at airports the official may just glance at your passport and hand it back without stamping the date of entry. It's a good idea to keep the plane, train or ferry ticket you arrived with to prove your date of entry.

Visa Extensions Tourist visas *cannot* be extended except in emergencies (eg, medical problems). If you're in Paris and have an urgent problem, call the Préfecture de Police (☎ 01 53 71 51 68) for guidance.

If you don't need a visa to visit France, you'll almost certainly qualify for another automatic three-month stay if you exit and then re-enter France. The fewer recent French entry stamps you have in your passport, the easier this is likely to be. If you needed a visa the first time around, one way to extend your stay is to go to a French consulate in a neighbouring country and apply for another one there.

Onward Tickets

Non-EU residents are required to have an onward or return ticket. Their passports also need to be valid for six months, or more for some countries, from their date of arrival into France.

Travel Insurance

A travel insurance policy to cover theft, loss and medical problems is a good idea. Some policies offer lower and higher medical-expense options; the higher ones are chiefly for countries such as the USA, which have extremely high medical costs. A wide variety of policies is available, so check the small print. Most cover loss of baggage, sickness, accidental injury or death, and cancellation costs in the event that your trip is cancelled due to accident, illness or death, concerning yourself or another family member. Check whether the policy covers theft and damage to your bicycle.

Some policies specifically exclude 'dangerous activities', which can include scuba diving, motorcycling, even hiking, so check carefully what it says about cycling and any other activities you may consider in France.

Consider a policy which pays doctors or hospitals directly rather than your having to pay on the spot and claim later. If you have to claim later, keep all documentation. Some policies ask you to call back (reverse charges) to a centre in your home country where your problem is assessed immediately. Ensure the policy covers ambulances or an emergency flight home.

Other Documents

Bring your drivers licence in case you hire a car or motorbike. Many non-European driving licences are valid in France, but it's still a good idea to bring along an International Driving Permit.

A Hostelling International (HI) card is necessary at official *auberges de jeunesse* (youth hostels), and it may also get small discounts at other hostels and for some local activities. Buy it before you leave home or at most official French hostels. Membership costs 70/100FF for over-26-year-olds/ families. An International Student Identity Card (ISIC) can be useful for obtaining discounts, especially at museums.

For campers, the Camping Card International (CCI; formerly the Camping Carnet) can be used instead of a passport when checking into a camping ground. Many camping grounds offer a small discount if you sign in with one. CCIs are issued by many automobile associations, camping federations and, sometimes, on the spot at camping grounds.

Copies

Photocopy all important documents (passport data page and visa page, credit cards, travel insurance policy, air/bus/train tickets, driving licence etc) before you leave home. Leave one copy with someone at home and keep another with you, separate from the originals. Add some emergency money, say 250FF in cash, to this separate stash. Also write down the serial numbers of your travellers cheques (cross them off as you cash them); the telephone numbers needed to report lost and stolen credit cards and travellers cheques; and your bike's and camera's serial numbers.

It's also a good idea to store details of your vital travel documents in Lonely Planet's free online Travel Vault in case you lose the photocopies or can't be bothered with them. Your password-protected Travel Vault is accessible online anywhere in the world – create it at ⌨ www.ekno.lonelypl anet.com.

If you do lose your passport, notify the police immediately to get a statement, and contact your nearest consulate.

EMBASSIES & CONSULATES
French Embassies & Consulates

French embassies abroad include (consulates in italics):

Australia (☎ 02-6216 0100, fax 6216 0127)
   6 Perth Ave, Yarralumla, ACT 2600.
   Consulates: Melbourne, Sydney
Canada (☎ 613-789 1795, fax 562 3735)
   42 Sussex Drive, Ottawa, Ont K1M 2C9.
   Consulates: Montreal, Toronto
Germany (☎ 030-206 3900 0, fax 206 3900 0)
   Kochstrasse 6–7, D-10969 Berlin.
   Consulates: Berlin, Munich

Ireland (☎ 01-260 1666, fax 283 0178) 36
Ailesbury Rd, Ballsbridge, Dublin 4
Japan (☎ 03-5420 8800, fax 5420 8847) 11/44
Chome Minami Azabu – Minato-Ku, Tokyo
106. *Consulates*: Tokyo, Osaka
Netherlands (☎ 070-312 5800, fax 312 5854)
Smidsplein 1, 2514 BT The Hague. *Consulate*: Amsterdam
New Zealand (☎ 04-384 2555, fax 384-2577)
34–42 Manners St, Wellington
South Africa *April to January*: (☎ 12-429 7000
ext 7008, fax 429 7029) 807 George Ave,
Arcadia Pretoria 0083.
Febrary to March: (☎ 21-422 1338, fax 426
1996) 78 Queen Victoria St, 8001 Cape
Town. *Consulate*: Johannesburg
UK (☎ 020-7201 1000, fax 7201 1004) 58
Knightsbridge, London SW1X 7JT.
Visas: (☎ 020-7838 2051, or ☎ 0891-887733
for visa information) 6A Cromwell Place,
London SW7 2EW. *Consulate*: London
USA (☎ 202-944 6000, fax 944 6166) 4101
Reservoir Rd NW, Washington, DC 20007.
Consulates: Atlanta, Boston, Chicago,
Houston, Los Angeles, Miami, New Orleans,
New York, San Francisco

Embassies & Consulates in France

All foreign embassies are in Paris. Canada,
Germany, Japan, the UK and the USA also
have consulates in other major cities (listed
in italics). To find an embassy or consulate
not listed here, consult the *Pages Jaunes*
(Yellow Pages; look under Ambassades et
Consulats).

Australia (☎ 01 40 59 33 00; metro Bir
Hakeim) 4 rue Jean Rey, 15e
Canada (☎ 01 44 43 29 00; metro Alma Marceau
or Franklin D Roosevelt) 35 ave Montaigne,
8e. *Consulates*: Strasbourg, Toulouse
Germany (☎ 01 53 83 45 00; metro Franklin D
Roosevelt) 13 ave Franklin D Roosevelt, 8e.
Consulates: Paris, Strasbourg
Ireland (☎ 01 44 17 67 00; metro Argentine)
4 rue Rude, 16e, between ave de la Grande
Armée and ave Foch
Japan (☎ 01 48 88 62 00; metro Courcelles) 7
ave Hoche, 8e. *Consulate*: Marseille
Netherlands (☎ 01 40 62 33 00; metro Doroc
or St François Xavier) 7–9 rue Eblé, 7e
New Zealand (☎ 01 45 00 24 11; metro Victor
Hugo) 7ter rue Léonard de Vinci, 16e, one
block south of ave Foch
South Africa (☎ 01 53 59 23 23; metro Invalides)
59 quai d'Orsay, 7e, near the American Church
UK (☎ 01 44 51 31 00; metro Concorde or
Madeleine) 35 rue du Faubourg St-Honoré,
8e. *Consulates*: Paris, Bordeaux, Lille, Lyon,
Marseille

USA (☎ 01 43 12 22 22, fax 01 42 66 97 83;
metro Concorde or Champs Élysées) 2 ave
Gabriel, 1er. *Consulates*: Paris, Marseille,
Nice, Strasbourg

CUSTOMS

The usual allowances apply to duty-free
goods purchased at airports or on ferries
outside the EU: tobacco (200 cigarettes, 50
cigars, or 250g of loose tobacco), alcohol
(1L of strong liquor or 2L of less than 22%
alcohol by volume, plus 2L of wine), coffee
(500g or 200g of extracts) and perfume
(50g of perfume and 0.25L of toilet water).

Do not confuse these with duty-paid items
(including alcohol and tobacco) bought at
normal shops and supermarkets in another
EU country and brought into France, where
certain goods might be more expensive.
Then the allowances are more than generous:
800 cigarettes, 200 cigars, or 1kg of loose tobacco; 10L of spirits (more than 22% alcohol by volume), 20L of fortified wine or
aperitif, 90L of wine or 110L of beer.

MONEY
Currency

The national currency is the French franc,
abbreviated in this book to 'FF'. One franc
is divided into 100 centimes.

French coins come in denominations of
5, 10, 20 and 50 centimes (0.50FF) and 1FF,
2FF, 5FF, 10FF and 20FF. Keep a supply of
coins for using in laundrettes and buying
small items.

Banknotes are issued in denominations of
20FF, 50FF, 100FF, 200FF and 500FF. It
can be difficult to get change for a 500FF
bill.

The euro – the new currency for 11 European Union (EU) countries – is legal tender
in France, but can only be used for credit
cards until notes and coins are issued in
January 2002. The French franc will cease
to be legal tender in July 2002.

Euro coins will come in 1, 2, 5, 10, 20 and
50 cent (€0.5) pieces, plus €1 and €2.
Banknotes will come in denominations of
€5, €10, €20, €50, €100, €200 and €500.

Exchange Rates

The currencies in the table below, as well as
many other European currencies, are all
readily exchanged in France. Check up-to-
date exchange rates at 🖳 www.x-rates.com.

country	unit	€	franc
Australia	A$1	0.64	4.16
Canada	C$1	0.74	4.84
euro	€1	–	6.55
Germany	DM1	0.51	3.35
Ireland	IR£1	1.27	8.32
Japan	¥100	1.03	6.78
Netherlands	f1	0.45	2.97
New Zealand	NZ$1	0.50	3.33
South Africa	R1	0.15	1.00
UK	UK£1	1.65	10.82
USA	US$1	1.11	7.25

Exchanging Money

Banks, exchange bureaus and post offices (not all have exchange facilities) often give a better rate for travellers cheques than for cash. Major train stations and large hotels also have exchange facilities, which usually operate in the evening, on weekends and during holidays, but the rates are usually poor.

Cash In general, foreign currency is not a very good way to carry money. Not only can it be stolen, but in France you don't get an optimal exchange rate. The Banque de France rate, for instance, is usually about 2.5% higher for travellers cheques, which more than makes up for the 1% commission usually involved in buying travellers cheques.

However, carry around 600FF in low-denomination notes of US dollars to make it easier to change a small sum of money when an inferior rate is on offer or you need just a few francs (eg, at the end of your stay).

Because of problems with counterfeiting, it may be difficult to change US$100 notes; even most Banque de France branches refuse to accept them.

Travellers Cheques This is one of the safest ways to carry money. Except at exchange bureaus, and the Banque de France, you have to pay a commission of 16FF to 35FF to cash travellers cheques. A percentage fee may apply for large sums. American Express offices do not charge a commission on their own travellers cheques. See also the Copies section earlier.

ATMs ATMs are known in French as DABs (*distributeurs automatiques de billets;* often shortened to *distributeurs*) or *points d'argent*. ATM cards give direct access to your cash reserves back home at a superior exchange rate. Most ATMs will also give cash

advances through Visa or MasterCard, functioning as a sort of debit card attached to your bank account. This method of getting an advance usually incurs the lowest fees.

Some non-US ATMs won't accept PIN codes with more than four digits – ask your bank how to handle this. Plenty of ATMs in France are linked to the international Cirrus and Maestro networks.

Credit Cards Overall, the most convenient way to take money is by using a credit or debit card, both to pay for things and to get cash advances. Visa (Carte Bleue) is the most widely accepted, followed by MasterCard (Access or Eurocard). American Express cards are not very useful except at upmarket establishments. In general, all three cards can be used to pay for travel by train.

Some small family-run hotels, B&Bs and small restaurants may not accept credit cards. Take note that you may not be able to replace a lost or stolen Visa or Master-Card until you get home. It is a good idea to carry two different credit cards.

Cash Advances Carefully check the fees charged by your bank for getting cash advances against your Visa or MasterCard account while overseas; they can be high. Your bank may also charge up to 1.5% of each foreign transaction as a currency conversion fee. In France, many banks charge a commission of 30FF or more.

Cash advances are available at American Express offices to enrolled credit card holders.

International Transfers Telegraphic transfers can be quite slow. Specify the name of the bank and the name and address of the branch where you'd like to pick it up.

The easiest way to transfer money is through Moneygram (serving Thomas Cook) or Western Union. Fees vary from

US$50 to US$68 per US$1000, depending on the company used, and originating country of transfer.

Banque de France France's central bank offers the best exchange rates in the country. It does not accept Eurocheques or provide credit card cash advances. Most branches exchange in the morning only.

Post Offices Many post offices perform exchange transactions. The commission for travellers cheques is 1.2% (minimum 16FF). Post offices accept banknotes in a variety of currencies as well as travellers cheques issued by American Express (either US dollars or French francs) or Visa (in French francs only).

Exchange Bureaus In large cities, *bureaux de change* at airports, train stations, and major tourist centres are open longer hours and, with the exception of those at train stations, most give better rates than the banks. Check for hidden charges and verify the amount you will receive ahead of the transaction.

Security

Be aware of your documents and money at all times. Carry them in a money pouch or belt concealed under your clothes. While cycling you may wish to take this off and keep it in your handlebar bag, but as soon as you stop in a city or town, or leave your bicycle, put it on!

Costs

Individual travel styles will dictate your budget. Two people travelling together can greatly reduce hotel costs. Single room rates are not much lower than doubles, and are sometimes not available.

If you are camping, tent sites cost between 15FF and 25FF plus a similar additional charge per adult (very basic municipal camping grounds are often cheaper). However, in July and August, rates at large camping resorts can skyrocket to more than 150FF for a site for two people. Staying in hostels (or *gîtes d'étape* – walkers, horse riders or cyclists hostels) will cost 41FF to 72FF per night. Showerless, toiletless rooms in budget hotels come as low as 120/150FF for singles/doubles, while rooms with facilities in a moderate hotel begin at 200/220FF. Hotel

prices in Paris will be at least 25% higher, although food prices only increase minimally.

With the plethora of food shops and markets in France, picnics are a money-saver and a great way to sample local cuisine. Most restaurants offer a fixed two- or three-course meal *(menu)* for about 70FF, which is better value than ordering dishes separately. A decent bottle of wine with a restaurant meal costs 50FF or more. Instead of buying bottled water with your meal ask for *une carafe d'eau* (carafe of water), which will be *gratuit* (free) most of the time. A typical hotel breakfast (usually additional to the room price) is 20FF to 40FF. Other approximate prices are:

item	cost
baguette	5FF
round of camembert	10FF
apple	1.50FF
double scoop of ice cream	12FF
petit café (short black coffee)	5FF
café au lait (large milky coffee)	20FF
glass of wine in a bar	5FF
chateau entry (adult/child)	35/25FF
museum entry (adult/child)	25/15FF
good-quality bicycle tube	35FF

Taking the train will cost about 70FF to 80FF an hour, and bus about 60FF an hour. Transporting your bike on the train is free in some circumstances (see the boxed text 'What is une Housse' in the Getting Around chapter), but often buses charge between 10FF and 20FF per bicycle.

Tipping & Bargaining

French law requires that restaurant, cafe and hotel bills include the service charge (usually 10% to 15%), so a *pourboire* (tip) is neither necessary nor expected in most cases. However, most people leave a few francs in restaurants, unless the service was bad. They rarely tip in cafes and bars when they've just had a coffee or a drink.

In taxis, the usual tip is 2FF no matter what the fare, with the maximum about 5FF. People in France rarely bargain, except at flea markets.

Taxes & Refunds

France's VAT is 20.6% on most goods except food, medicine and books, for which it's 5.5%; it goes as high as 33% on such items as watches, cameras and video cassettes. Prices that include VAT are often marked TTC (*toutes taxes comprises*, 'all taxes included').

Non-EU residents can get a refund of most of the VAT (TVA in French), provided: they're aged over 15, spend less than six months in France, purchase goods (not more than 10 of the same item) worth at least 1200FF (tax included) at a single shop; and the shop offers *vente en détaxe* (duty-free sales).

Present a passport at the time of purchase and ask for a *bordereau de détaxe* (export sales invoice). Some shops may refund 14% of the purchase price rather than the full 17.1% entitlement to cover the time and expense involved in the refund procedure. They'll explain what you have to do as you leave France.

Instant Refunds If you're flying out of Orly or Roissy Charles de Gaulle airports, certain stores can arrange for you to receive your refund as you're leaving the country. You must make such arrangements at the time of purchase, when the seller can explain the steps involved in getting the refund.

POST & COMMUNICATIONS
Post
Postal services in France are fast and reliable. Post offices are recognisable by their yellow 'La Poste' sign; older branches may also be marked with the letters PTT, the abbreviation of *Postes, Télégraphes, Téléphones*.

Postcards and letters up to 20g cost 3FF within France and the EU; 3.80FF to most of the remainder of Europe as well as Africa; 4.40FF to the USA, Canada and the Middle East; and 5.20FF to Australasia.

Sea-mail services have been discontinued, so sending packages overseas can be expensive. The most economical way is *économique* (discount) air mail.

A new service appearing in post offices throughout the country is Internet access (see Email & Internet Access later this chapter).

To receive mail in France, poste restante is available at all French post offices. It costs 3FF or 4FF to pick up each piece. Poste restante mail is held alphabetically by last name, so make sure that your *nom de famille* (surname or family name) is written first, in capital letters. For example, to have

mail sent to the main post office in Rouen, have it addressed as:

SMITH, John
Poste Restante
Recette Principale
76000 Rouen
FRANCE

Poste restante mail not addressed to a particular branch is sent to each city's main post office.

Another option for receiving mail (not parcels) in France is care of an American Express Office. If you don't have an American Express card or at least one American Express travellers cheque, there's a 5FF charge. They hold mail for 30 days before returning it to the sender.

Telephone
The country code for France is ☎ 33. France is divided into five regional dialling areas: Paris region ☎ 01, north-west ☎ 02, north-east ☎ 03, south-east (including Corsica) ☎ 04 and south-west ☎ 05.

To call France from abroad, dial your country's international access code, then ☎ 33, then omit the 0 at the beginning of the 10-digit local number. Within France dial the entire 10 digit number, ie, include the initial 0.

To call someone outside France, dial the international access code ☎ 00, the country code, the area code (without the initial zero if there is one) and the local number. International Direct Dial (IDD) calls to almost anywhere in the world can be placed from public telephones. Country codes are usually posted in public phone booths.

Emergency calls – SAMU (24-hour ambulance) ☎ 15, police ☎ 17, fire ☎ 18 – are free. So are directory inquiries; dial ☎ 12 for domestic numbers, and dial ☎ 00 33 12 and the country code for international numbers.

Country Direct numbers and *numéros verts* (toll-free numbers – literally, 'green numbers' – which have 10 digits and begin with ☎ 0800), can be dialled from public telephones without inserting a télécarte or coins. The prefix ☎ 08, when followed by two digits other than zero, denotes a premium service, usually information lines, for which the company offering the service can charge ridiculously high rates. For example, the SNCF information line (☎ 08 36 35 35 35) costs 2.23FF per minute, even when you're on hold.

Mobile phone (cell phone) numbers are preceded by the ☎ 06 code.

In France, long beeps mean the phone's ringing, short beeps mean it's busy.

Télécartes Almost all public telephones in France require a *télécarte* (phonecard), which can be bought at post offices, *tabacs* (tobacconists), supermarket check-out counters, SNCF ticket windows, Paris metro stations, and anywhere displaying a blue sticker *'télécarte en vente ici'* (phonecards sold here). Cards worth 50/120 calling units cost 49/98FF.

Phonecards A wide range of local and international phonecards is also on the market. Lonely Planet's eKno Communication Card is aimed specifically at independent travellers and provides budget international calls, a range of messaging services, free email and travel information – for local calls, you're usually better off with a local card.

You can join eKno online at ⌨ www.ekno .lonelyplanet.com, or by phone from France by dialling ☎ 0800 91 26 77.

Minitel Minitel is a useful telephone-connected, computerised information service, though it can be expensive to use. Minitel numbers consist of four digits and a string of letters (eg, 3615 RATP). Home users pay a per-minute access fee, however, consulting the *annuaire* (directory) is free. Most of the Minitels in post offices are also free for directory inquiries (though some take a 1FF or 2FF coin), and many let you access pay-as-you-go online services.

Fax

Faxes *(télécopies* or *téléfaxes)*, are commonplace in France. Most hotels, hostels and camping grounds have fax machines, making it a convenient way to make reservations. Many will allow you to send and receive faxes. You can also send faxes from some post offices, cybercafes and 'mail' shops (such as Mail Boxes etc.), which are starting to pop up in France. It costs about 15FF within France, 30FF to the EU, 45FF to the USA and 50FF to Australia to send a one-page fax.

Email & Internet Access

Email and the Internet is gaining popularity in France. Cybercafes have been slow to appear, but are on the increase in both cities and small towns. Internet services are also available at some hostels, bars, libraries, universities and tourist offices. In this book, places with Internet access are listed under Information in each town. However, check with the tourist office en route as new ones are constantly opening. Also check ⌨ www.netca feguide.com for an up-to-date list.

A new Internet service called Cyberposte (⌨ www.cyberposte.com) is currently being set up at 1000 post offices throughout France. To use Cyberposte, you will have to buy a rechargeable card for 50FF. This includes one hour of Internet use; recharges cost 30FF per hour. France Telecom sponsors 'Internet stations' around France, including ones in Paris, Montpellier and Grenoble. These are not cybercafes but high tech centres where people can surf the Internet, send emails and take free beginners courses on how to use the Internet.

Internet access rates vary, but the usual rates are 40FF to 50FF per hour. Some cybercafes require a minimum half-hour use.

The cheapest way to have email access while traveling is to get a free, Web-based email account such as Lonely Planet's eKno (⌨ www.ekno.lonelyplanet.com), Hotmail (⌨ www.hotmail.com) or Yahoo! (⌨ www .yahoo.com). This allows you to access your mail from cybercafes and other facilities anywhere in the world using any net-connected machine running a standard web browser.

INTERNET RESOURCES

The World Wide Web is a rich resource for travellers. You can research your trip, hunt bargain air fares, book hotels, check weather conditions or chat with locals and other travellers about the best places to visit (or avoid!).

Useful Web sites in English include:

Lonely Planet (⌨ www.lonelyplanet.com) There's no better place to start your Web explorations: includes summaries on France, postcards from other travellers and the Thorn Tree bulletin board, where you can ask questions before you go or dispense advice when you get back. You can also find travel news and updates to many of our most popular guidebooks, and the sub-WWWay section links you to the most useful travel resources elsewhere on the Web.

French Government Tourism Office (🖳 www .francetourism.com) Official French government tourist office site: comprehensive and diverse, full of all types of travel details and information.

Maison de la France (🖳 www.franceguide.com) The official tourism site with all manner of information about travel in France.

Guide Web (🖳 www.guideweb.com) Details on accommodation, crafts, museums, regional products and leisure activities in the south-east.

Paris Tourist Office (🖳 www.paris-touristoffice .com) Find out what's on, where to stay and eat, and the latest news about the nation's capital.

Real France (🖳 www.realfrance.com) Get the 'inside' information on arts and crafts, nature, leisure, food, restaurants, wine, museums, sights, events, hotels, guesthouses and chateaux.

BOOKS

There are so many excellent books on France that it's hard to choose just a few to recommend.

Lonely Planet

The thorough Lonely Planet *France* is an ideal supplement to the information provided in this book. Regional, city and activity guides include: *Paris* and *Paris Condensed* (pocket guide), *Provence & the Côte d'Azur*, *The Loire*, *South-West France*, *Corsica* and *Walking in France*.

If you're not a French speaker – or even if you are – slip the *French phrasebook* into your handlebar bag. It has a range of terms for just about every situation you're likely to come across, and has a great section on eating to help make the most of every morsel.

Cycling

The Fédération Française de Cyclotourisme (FFCT) publishes, through Éditions Franck Mercier, a series of 17 cycle touring books, *La France à Vélo* (118FF) covering most of the country. Each loose-leaf book describes, in French, about 90 tours of one to seven days, each with a basic map and brief listings of lodging, places to eat, bike shops and sights. The books are available direct from the FFCT, or newsagents and tourist offices will stock their local title. See the Useful Organisations section for FFCT contact details.

For information on regional titles check Books under the Information sections in each rides chapter. See also the Maps & Books section in the Randonnées chapter.

See the boxed text 'Mountain Biking' later in this chapter for books on off-road trails.

Although now out of print, *Fat Man on a Bicycle: A Discovery of France*, by Tom Vernon, makes light-hearted reading as this BBC commentator cycles through France from north to south.

General

Michelin's *guides verts* (green guides; 69FF each), which cover all of France in 24 regional volumes – most of which are available in English – are full of historical, architectural and touring information.

A variety of excellent works on French history is available. A handy one for a good overview is *Traveller's History of France*, by Ian Cole, offering an introduction to French history and cross-referencing the historical importance of sites, towns and monuments for the traveller. Some other informative historical reads include *The Age of the Cathedrals*, by Georges Duby, an authoritative study of the relations between art and society in medieval France; *The Sun King*, by Nancy Mitford, a classic work on Louis XIV and the country he ruled from Versailles; and *A History of Modern France*, by Alfred Cobban, a readable, three-volume history from Louis XIV to 1962.

To get an insight into the French and their culture look for intelligent, humorous *The French*, by Theodore Zeldin, or *France Today*, by John Ardagh, a good introduction to the politics and people of modern-day France. Also by John Ardagh, the *Cultural Atlas of France* is a superb illustrated synopsis of French culture and history.

For nature lovers, *Wild France*, edited by Douglas Botting, gives an overview of France's wilderness areas, and does a good job on flora and fauna. If you can understand French, the Office National des Forêts (🖳 www.onf.fr) sells several titles covering the forests of France, including flora, fauna etc.

Food & Wine

There is no lack of books on this subject to whet your appetite. Foodies should look at Lonely Planet's *World Food France*, a full-colour pocket-sized encyclopedia on the country's culture of eating and drinking, complete with two-way dictionaries and a comprehensive menu reader.

The undisputed classic, first published in 1958, is *The Food of France*, by Waverley Root, an absolutely superb region-by-region introduction to French cuisine.

Feast your eyes and tempt your taste buds on Dorling Kindersley's full-colour *French Cheese* describing more than 350 cheeses. And wine lovers should take a look at either Christopher Fielden's *Traveller's Wine Guide to France*, which covers the wine regions, vineyards, wineries and tasting, or Dorling Kindersley's *French Wines*.

French Literature

For suggested reading, see Literature in the Facts about France chapter. Most of the writers mentioned have been translated into English. For a good introduction to French literature try *France: Traveller's Literary Companion*, by John Edmundson, featuring more than 120 extracts from novels, poems and short stories alongside cultural notes and reading lists.

Literature & Travelogues by Foreign Writers

France has long attracted writers from all over the world. Some celebrated titles include *Tropic of Capricorn* and *Tropic of Cancer*, by Henry Miller, both steamy 1930s novels set in Paris. Ernest Hemingway's *A Moveable Feast* portrays bohemian life in Paris between the two world wars. *The Autobiography of Alice B Toklas* is an autobiographical account of Gertrude Stein's years in Paris, and her friendships with artists such as Picasso.

MFK Fisher, an American who moved to France as a young woman, has written several books, include *Long Ago in France*, describing her three years in Dijon, and *Two Towns in Provence*. *Flaubert's Parrot*, by Julian Barnes, is a highly entertaining novel that pays witty homage to the great French writer.

Recently, the name synonymous with the south of France is English transplant, Peter Mayle. *A Year in Provence, Toujours Provence* and, his latest, *Encore Provence* have become best-selling accounts of life in Provence.

Traveler's Tales France is a collection of writings, capturing the personality of France through accounts both on and off the beaten track.

Pictorial Books

The beauty of France is evident in numerous photographic essays. *France*, photographed by Colin Baxter, is a stunning representation of the country. The photographic series by Thames and Hudson began with *The Most Beautiful Villages of France* and now includes gorgeous books on the *Most Beautiful Villages of...*, showcasing *Brittany, Dordogne, Burgundy* and *Provence* in separate volumes.

NEWSPAPERS & MAGAZINES

French France's main daily newspapers are *Le Figaro* (right wing; aimed at professionals, businesspeople and the bourgeoisie), *Le Monde* (centre-left; very popular with businesspeople, professionals and intellectuals), *Le Parisien* (centre; middle-class, easy to read if your French is basic), *France Soir* (right; working and middle-class), *Libération* (left; popular with students and intellectuals) and *L'Humanité* (communist; working-class). *L'Équipe* is a daily devoted exclusively to sport.

English In cities and important towns, larger newsagents and those at train stations usually carry the informative, intelligent *International Herald Tribune* (10FF), published jointly by the *New York Times* and the *Washington Post*. Issued daily (except Sunday), it is edited in Paris and has very good coverage of French news.

Other English-language papers available in France include the *Guardian*, the *Financial Times*, the *Times* and *USA Today*. The *European* weekly newspaper is also readily available, as are *Newsweek*, *Time* and the *Economist*.

Cycling Several monthly cycling magazines are available (all written only in French). Magazines covering all types of cycling include *Cyclo Passion* (28FF), *Le Cycle* (34FF), *Top Vélo* (28FF) and *Vélo Magazine* (26FF). *VTT Magazine* (28FF) is a monthly magazine devoted to mountain biking. Most are available from newsagents and news stands.

The FFCT magazine *Cyclotourisme* focuses on touring news and FFCT events and is published 11 times a year, in French. Subscriptions cost 150FF for members and 295FF for nonmembers (see Useful Organisations).

RADIO & TV

You can pick up a mixture of the BBC World Service and BBC for Europe on 648 kHz AM. The Voice of America (VOA) is on 1197 kHz AM, but reception is often poor.

In Paris, an hour of Radio France Internationale (RFI) news is broadcast in English every day at 3 pm on 738 kHz AM. Radio Netherlands often has programming in English on 1512 kHz AM.

France Info broadcasts the news headlines in French every few minutes on 105.5 MHz FM in Paris.

Upmarket hotels often offer cable and satellite TV access to CNN, BBC Prime, Sky and other networks. Canal+ (pronounced ka-**nahl** ploose), a French subscription TV station available in many mid-range hotels, sometimes shows nondubbed English movies.

A variety of weekend-to-weekend TV listings are sold at all newsstands. Foreign movies that haven't been dubbed and are shown with subtitles are marked 'VO' or 'v.o.' *(version originale)*.

Cable TV offers two sports channels, ESPN and EuroSport.

WEATHER FORECASTS

If you understand French, you can find out the *météo* (weather forecast) by calling the national forecast (☎ 08 36 70 12 34) or regional forecasts (☎ 08 36 68 00 00). For more localised departmental forecasts, dial ☎ 08 36 68 02 plus the two digit departmental number (eg, ☎ 08 36 68 02 75 for Paris). Ask the tourist office or a local for the department number, or look at the car number plates, which end in the two-digit number of the department (see the map at the start of this guide). Each call costs five télécarte units or 2.23FF per minute. In popular walking areas, tourist offices often display the weather forecast for the next 72 hours. In the mountains, refuge wardens should be *au fait* with conditions.

You can also go to the nearest post office and dial 3615 Météo on the Minitel, then enter the departmental code when requested to get weather forecasts.

One of the simplest methods to check the weather, other than look at the sky, is the newspaper. The Météo section is usually on the back page or close to it; you can look at the universal symbols, and check the predicted high and low temperatures.

PHOTOGRAPHY & VIDEO

Film & Equipment

Colour-print film produced by Kodak and Fuji is widely available in supermarkets, photo shops and FNAC stores (entertainment megastores). At FNAC, a 36 exposure roll of Kodacolor costs 39/48FF for 100/400 ASA. One-hour developing is widely available.

For slides *(diapositives)*, count on paying at least 52FF for a 36 exposure roll of 100 or 200 ASA Ektachrome film, or 75FF for a 400 ASA roll; developing costs 28/32FF for 24/36 exposures.

Photography is rarely forbidden, except in museums and art galleries. Of course, taking snapshots of military installations is not appreciated in any country. When photographing people, it is basic courtesy to ask permission. If you don't know any French, smile while pointing at your camera and they'll get the picture – as, most likely, will you.

For a guide to taking the best pictures of your holiday, look through Lonely Planet's *Travel Photography: A Guide to Taking Better Pictures*, written by renowned travel photographer Richard I'Anson.

Video

Today's video cameras are small and light enough for a cyclist to carry. Properly used, a video camera can give a great record of your holiday. Carry batteries, charger, plugs, transformer and correct format tapes. Follow the same rules regarding people's sensitivities as for still photography.

Airport Security

Your camera and film will have to go through the X-ray machine at all airports. The claims that the machines are film-safe may no longer be true. Concerns about international terrorism means a new type of machine, which can fog film, is being used at more than 50 international airports to scan luggage, and in some cases to scan hand luggage.

After the first X-ray scan these machines automatically rescan suspicious objects at a higher intensity. The silver halide coating on film and its metal casing may trigger this high-intensity scan, which can ruin unprocessed film.

This means you should never pack unprocessed film in checked luggage. Ask for hand inspections if possible (*Pouvez-vous s'il-vous-plait ne pas passer mes pellicules photos aux rayons X?* – Could you please not put my films through the x-ray?).

TIME
France uses the 24-hour clock, with the hours separated from the minutes by a lower-case letter 'h'. Thus, 15h30 is 3.30 pm, 21h50 is 9.50 pm and 00h30 is 12.30 am.

France is one hour ahead of (ie, later than) GMT/UTC. During daylight-saving (or summer) time, which runs from the last Sunday in March to the last Sunday in October, France is two hours ahead of GMT/UTC.

ELECTRICITY
France and Monaco run on 220V at 50Hz AC. Andorra has a combination of 220V and 125V, both at 50Hz. Carry the correct transformers for any appliances you pack.

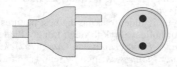

French plugs have two round prongs.

WEIGHTS & MEASURES
France uses the metric system, which was invented by the French Academy of Sciences after the Revolution. A conversion chart is inside the back cover of this book.

LAUNDRY
Doing laundry while on the road in France is pretty straightforward. A *laverie libre-service* is an unstaffed, self-service laundrette. French laundrettes are not cheap. They usually charge 18FF to 25FF for a 6kg machine and 3/5FF for five/10 minutes of drying. Some laundrettes offer self-service *nettoyage à sec* (dry cleaning) for about 60FF per 6kg. Carry lots of change: 2FF pieces are handy for the *séchoirs* (dryers) and the *lessive* (laundry powder) dispenser.

WOMEN CYCLISTS
Attitudes to Women Cyclists
France is not a difficult country for women travellers, and the same rings true for women cyclists. A woman cycling on her own will find French cyclists (and the French, in general) pleasant and helpful, but probably surprised to come across a woman travelling alone on a loaded touring bike through France. (Three of the authors of this book are women, who all travelled in France as solo cyclists.)

Safety Precautions
The French seem to have given relatively little thought to sexual harassment *(harcèlement sexuel)*, and many men (and some women) still think that to stare suavely at a passing woman is to pay her a flattering compliment.

Physical attack is very unlikely but, of course, it does happen. As in any country, the best way to avoid being assaulted is to use common sense; be conscious of your surroundings and aware of situations that could be potentially dangerous, such as deserted streets, lonely beaches and dark corners of large train stations. Try to arrive in towns well before dark, and don't walk alone late at night. Using the metros until late is generally OK, as stations are rarely deserted, but there are a few to avoid; locals will tell you which ones.

France's national rape-crisis hotline (☎ 0800 05 95 95) can be reached toll-free from any telephone without using a phonecard. It is staffed by volunteers Monday to Friday from 10 am to 6 pm. In an emergency, call the police (☎ 17), who will take you to the hospital.

Organisations
France's women's liberation movement flourished along with its counterparts in other western countries in the late 1960s and early 70s, but by the mid-80s was pretty moribund. For reasons that have more to do with French society than anything else, few women's groups function as the kind of supportive social institutions that have been formed in the USA, UK and Australia.

The women-only Maison des Femmes (☎ 01 43 43 41 13; metro Reuilly Diderot) at 163 rue Charenton (12e) is the main meeting place for women of all ages and nationalities. It is staffed on Wednesday from 4 to 7 pm and on Saturday from 3 to 6 pm.

GAY & LESBIAN CYCLISTS
France is one of Europe's most liberal countries when it comes to homosexuality, in part because of the long French tradition of public tolerance towards groups of people

Tandeming in France

With all the hype about the French and romance, you'd expect to see lots of Gallic couples cycling *à deux*. However, relatively few French cyclists ride tandems (*tandem* also in French) – the French Tandem Club, Tandem Club de France: Amicale Cyclo Tandemiste, has only around 812 members.

While this means tandem tourists are likely to be quite an attraction, bicycles built for two will also face some difficulties in finding parts and in getting around the country.

Spare Parts

Bring a good supply of tandem-specific spares and get a hold of the Tandem Club de France's annual member directory, which lists tandem-friendly bike shops. The directory also includes all members' names and contact details and is sent free to members. Membership costs 150/120FF joint/single and also includes four issues of the club's 28pp newsletter *Duocipède* and a rides calendar. Contact the club at Tandem Club de France ACT, 5 rue du Président Fruchon, 36200 Saint Marcel. Club members Vincent (& Elizabeth) Vallet (✉ vvallet@wanadoo.fr) are happy to be contacts for the club (you can write in English).

Tandem Rides

The Tandem Club de France runs several rides a year (extra fee). These are listed in the rides calendar and on an 'unofficial' Web page for the club 💻 perso.wanadoo.fr/tandem.

Travelling to & Around France

Most airlines require that you box your bike for domestic and international flights. However, finding tandem-sized boxes isn't always easy, and is impossible if you're riding to the airport. Try to make a special arrangement with the airline *in advance*.

If you are planning on using trains to get around France, you'll have to plan carefully to travel on those with luggage carriages. Tandems can't be taken on the TGV or transported by the SNCF's freight service (see the Getting Around chapter). Using a folding tandem such as the Tandem Two'sDay (see 💻 www.bikefriday.com) or fitting S&S couplings to allow your tandem to be pulled apart for packing may be the solution.

Sally Dillon

who choose not to live by conventional social codes. In addition to the large gay and lesbian communities in Paris, a thriving gay centre since the late 1970s, active communities exist in Cannes, Lyon, Marseille, Nice, Toulouse and many other provincial cities. France's lesbian scene is much less public than its gay counterpart and is centred mainly on women's cafes and bars.

Gay Pride marches are held in Paris, Marseille, Montpellier, Nantes, Rennes and other cities each year in June. For details, contact Paris' Centre Gai et Lesbien (see following).

Organisations

Most of France's major gay organisations are based in Paris, including Centre Gai et Lesbien (✆ 01 43 57 21 47; metro Ledru Rollin) 3 rue Keller, 11e. Écoute Gaie is a hotline (✆ 01 44 93 01 02) for gays and lesbians, and there's also Act Up Paris (✆ 01 48 06 13 89 for a recording, 💻 www.actupp.org; metro Voltaire) at 45 rue Sedaine, 11e. *Guide Gai Pied*, a predominantly male, French and English-language annual guide to France, has a Web site 💻 www.gaipied.fr; another good resource is 💻 www.france.qrd.org, a 'queer resources directory' for gay and lesbian travellers.

CYCLISTS WITH A DISABILITY

France is not particularly well-equipped for *handicapés* (people with disabilities): kerb ramps are few and far between, older public facilities and budget hotels often lack lifts, cobblestone streets are a nightmare to navigate in a wheelchair, and the Paris metro is hopeless to access. But physically

Mountain Biking

France is a nation of competitive and passionate cyclists, and a country with an incredible variety of terrains, so it comes as no surprise that the French have embraced mountain biking. From the late 1980s, when it was first imported from the USA, the sport has grown in popularity. The French now dominate competitive mountain biking. Nicolas Vouilloz is the king of the French downhill racers, winning five straight world championship gold medals (1995–99), while Anne-Caroline Chausson is the Queen, winning four (1996–99). In the cross-country events the French are not quite as dominant, but riders like Laurence Leboucher (1998 world champion) and Miguel Martinez (1997–98 under-23 mens world champion) head a rich talent pool.

The French are also organising increasing numbers of events (more than 1300 annually). The largest of these is the annual Tour VTT (Mountain Bike Tour de France), the longest mountain bike stage race in the world, held in early August.

Originally the mountain bike was known as *le vélo de montagne* (literally, mountain bike), but now it is more commonly referred to as *vélo tout terrain*, or VTT (all terrain bike). When mountain biking began, most bikes were imported, but today many are made in France.

Miguel Martinez in action.

SPORT: THE LIBRARY/TOM MORAN

Mountain-Bike Centres

The Fédération Française de Cyclisme (FFC) has set up a network of VTT centres around the country. Each offers a network of at least 100km of safe, marked routes and supply tourist information (including maps and route guides), bike-washing facilities and, usually, accommodation and food services. They also offer skills training, and often will hire bikes to groups of more than 20. Many are listed on the FFC Web site 🖳 www.ffc.fr.

Where to Ride

France has about 20,000km of FFC-designated VTT trails of varying standards of difficulty. These routes are signed with markers indicating the circuit ID number, the level of difficulty and the direction to follow. The starting point of these trails is listed on the IGN map No 906 *France: VTT & Randonnées Cyclos* (1:1,000,000); see Maps in this chapter.

Mountain bikers can also consider riding on the *Grande Randonnée* (GR) long-distance trails found all over France. IGN map No 903 *France – Grande Randonnée* (1:1,000,000; 29FF) shows these trails. Various topoguides give an idea of the routes, some of which are more suitable for mountain biking than others. Each GR route is marked with red-and-white horizontal stripes. These are primarily hiking trails, so give priority to walkers.

Routes in this book are designed for touring. However, wherever possible, mountain biking opportunities within a reasonable distance of the route are indicated. In this case, the ride information sections detail where to get the necessary maps, information and bike hire. Good regions to mountain bike include the Massif Central and the Pyrenees. Tourist offices and bike shops may have information on mountain biking in their area. VTT rental prices usually range from 80FF to 120FF per day, with a deposit of 1000FF or more.

Mountain Biking Books

The Office National des Forêts (ONF) has mapped and described a series of 65 VTT routes in its *VTT Évasion* series (35FF). Each booklet details a one- to four-hour ride in French, using universally understood symbols. They list places of interest and include a fold-out map. See Useful Organisations in this chapter for ONF contact details.

Didier Richard publishes a series of regional mountain biking books, each of which details, in French, 20 to 36 routes, accompanied by topographic maps (30FF).

challenged people who would like to visit France can overcome these problems. Most hotels with two or more stars are equipped with lifts, and Michelin's *Guide Rouge* hotel and restaurant guide indicates places with lifts and facilities for disabled people.

In recent years the SNCF has made efforts to make its trains more accessible to people with physical disabilities. A traveller in a wheelchair *(fauteuil roulant)* can travel in the wheelchair in both TGV and regular trains, provided they make a reservation by phone or at a train station at least a few hours before departure. Details are available in SNCF's booklet *Guide du Voyageur à Mobilité Réduite*. You can also contact SNCF Accessibilité on ☎ 08 00 15 47 53.

Some publications of interest are: *Paris & Île de France pour Tous*, available from the Paris tourist office (60FF), *Gîtes Accessibles aux Personnes Handicapés* (60FF), a guide to *gîtes ruraux* (rural self-contained accommodation) and *chambres d'hôtes* (B&Bs) with disabled access, published by Gîtes de France (see Gîtes and Chambres d'Hôtes under Accommodation in this chapter). *Access in Paris* is a 245-page guide to Paris for the disabled; it's published by Quiller Press (☎ 020-7499 6529), 46 Lilliue Rd, SW6 London.

SENIOR CYCLISTS
People aged over 60 are entitled to discounts in France on public transport, and entry into places such as museums, galleries and public theatres, provided they show proof of their age. In some cases they might need a special pass.

The SNCF issues the Carte Senior to those over 60, which gives reductions of 20% to 50% on train tickets. It costs 140FF for a card valid for purchasing four train tickets, or 285FF for a card valid for one year.

CYCLING WITH CHILDREN
France is an ideal country to travel in with children. Health problems are not a major issue and many attractions and activities cater for children.

Children are well received in French hotels and restaurants, and camping grounds often have play areas and other facilities for children. Many hostels have family rooms. Check with tourist offices and hotels for baby-sitting services *(garde d'enfants)*.

Supermarkets stock all the child care products you can buy at home, but opening hours may be quite different, so plan accordingly (see Business Hours later in this chapter).

Many of the tours in this book rated as easy or easy-moderate are suitable for children. Select routes that will suit the child's ability, have interesting activities or sights for children and allow for frequent breaks during the day. Keep plenty of snacks and water on hand. Try to use the 'D' *(Départementale)* roads wherever possible, as these are the quiet backroads and more fun for children.

Many bike hire outlets have children's seats and, sometimes, helmets for hire. In tourist areas where cycling is one of the main activities, such as the central Atlantic Coast, trailers and kids bikes are also likely to be available.

Lonely Planet's *Travel with Children*, by Maureen Wheeler, is a good source of information.

DANGERS & ANNOYANCES
Racism
The rise in support for the extreme right-wing National Front in recent years reflects the growing racial intolerance in France, particularly against North African Muslims and, to a somewhat lesser extent, blacks from sub-Saharan Africa and France's former colonies and territories in the Caribbean.

In many parts of France, especially in the south (eg, Provence and the Côte d'Azur), places of entertainment such as bars and discotheques are, for all intents and purposes, segregated: owners and their bouncers make it abundantly clear who is 'invited'.

Hunting
The hunting season usually runs from the end of September to the end of February. If you see signs reading *chasseurs* or *chasse gardé* strung up or tacked to trees, you might want to think twice about wandering into the area, especially if you're wearing anything that might make you resemble a deer.

Smoking
The French are heavy smokers. Laws banning smoking in public places do exist, but no-one pays much attention to them. In restaurants, diners will often smoke in the nonsmoking sections of restaurants – and the waiter will happily bring them an ashtray.

USEFUL ORGANISATIONS
National Cycling Organisations

The Fédération Française de Cyclotourisme (FFCT; ☎ 01 44 16 88 88, fax 01 44 16 88 99, 🖳 www.ffct.org; metro Corvisart), 8 rue Jean-Marie Jégo (13e), 200m north of rue Bobillot, governs cycle touring and VTT touring. It acts as a liaison among France's 3100 cycling clubs and administers *brevets* (rides where a certificate must be stamped along the way), randonnées and *diagonales* (series of nine routes cutting diagonally across each corner of France; see the Randonnées chapter). FFCT-organised bicycle trips are open to people visiting France. Write for a packet of free general information in English; however, they cannot answer specific queries. If you visit the Paris office there are usually people who can offer advice. They sell cycling guides (see Cycling under Books earlier in this chapter) and maps, plus some cycle clothing. Individual membership costs 383FF annually (which includes a cut-price subscription to the FFCT magazine *Cyclotourisme* and an annual calendar of rides around the country).

Each region in France has its own FFCT *ligue* (league), listed in the information section of each chapter. FFCT-affiliated clubs run weekend rides almost year-round. Anyone can join these club rides for a small fee, usually 20FF per person, which includes sandwiches, coffee, chocolate and fruit juice every 30km. If you're in France and want to join an FFCT ride, they're all listed in the FFCT magazine *Où irons nous?*, sent to members.

Bicycle Touring with Children

Children can travel by bicycle from the time they can support their head and a helmet, at around eight months. There are some small, lightweight, cute-looking helmets around, such as the L'il Bell Shell. To carry an infant to toddler requires a child seat or trailer. Child seats are more common for everyday riding, and are cheaper, easier to move as a unit with the bike, and let you touch and talk to your child while moving.

Disadvantages, especially over long distances, can include exposure to weather, the tendency of a sleeping child to loll, and losing luggage capacity at the rear. The best makes, such as the Rhode Gear Limo, include extra moulding to protect the child in case of a fall, have footrests and restraints, recline to let the child sleep and fit very securely and conveniently onto a bike.

With a capacity of up to 50kg (versus around 18kg for a child seat), trailers can accommodate two bigger children and luggage. They give better, though not always total, protection from sun and rain and let children sleep comfortably. Look for a trailer that is lightweight, foldable, conspicuous (brightly coloured, with flag) and that tracks and handles well. It's also handy to be able to swap the trailer between bikes so adults can alternate towing and riding beside the trailer. Child trailers tend to be preferred for serious touring, but may be illegal in some places, for example, Western Australia. Trailers or seats are treated as additional luggage items when flying.

Be sure that the bike to which you attach a child seat or trailer is sturdy and low-geared, to withstand – and help you withstand – the extra weight and stresses.

From the age of about four, children can move on to a 'trailer-bike' (effectively a child's bike, minus a front wheel, which hitches to an adult's bike) or to a tandem (initially as 'stoker', as the back seat is called, with 'kiddy cranks', crank extenders) – this lets them assist with the pedalling effort. The tandem can be a long-term solution, keeping you and your child together and letting you compensate if the child tires.

Be careful of children rushing into touring on a solo bike before they can sustain the effort and concentration required. Once they are ready and keen to ride solo, at about age 10 to 12, they will need a good quality touring bike, properly fitted (A$300, US$200, UK£30 and up). The British publication *Encycleopedia*, by Alan Davidson et al, is a good guide to quality trailers, trailer-bikes and tandems available from manufacturers around the world.

Bike touring with children requires a new attitude as well as new equipment. Be sensitive to their needs – especially when they're too young to communicate them fully. In a seat or trailer, they're not expending energy and need to be dressed accordingly. Take care to keep them dry, at the right temperature and protected from the sun.

The Fédération Française de Cyclisme (FFC; ☎ 01 49 35 69 00, fax 01 48 94 09 97, Ⓔ info@ffc.fr, ▣ www.ffc.fr), 5 rue de Rome, 93561 Rosny-sous-Bois, is the governing body of all racing disciplines, including road, criteria, track, VTT and BMX. Their Web site has a race calendar and licence information (in French). Organise a racing licence from your country's racing federation before leaving home.

The Audax Club Parisien (☎ 01 48 46 56 84, ▣ www.audax-club-parisien.com), 32 rue Moissan, 93130 Noisy-le-Sec, is dedicated to running the long-distance, noncompetitive rides known as randonnées. See the Randonnées chapter for more details.

One of the main advocacy groups for cycling in France is Mouvement de Défense de la Bicyclette (MBD; ☎ 01 43 20 26 02, fax 01 43 35 14 06, Ⓔ mbdidf@club-internet.fr, ▣ perso.club-internet.fr/mdbidf/), 32 rue Raymond Losserand (14e). As well as promoting the use of bicycle transportation, they organise rides in Paris. Another is Fédération des Usagers de la Bicyclette (FUBICY; ☎ 03 88 75 71 90, fax 03 88 22 56 07, Ⓔ FUBICY@sdv.fr, ▣ perso.club-internet. fr/dugas95/fubicy /index.html), 4 rue Brûlée, Strasbourg, which promotes the bicycle as a pollution-free means of transport.

Cyclo-Camping International (☎ 01 47 97 62 18, Ⓔ cci@club-internet.fr, ▣ perso .club-internet.fr/cci/index.htm) is an association of French cyclists, with 500 members, who tour internationally. Their office

Bicycle Touring with Children

Keep their energy and interest up. When you stop, a child travelling in a seat or trailer will be ready for action, so always reserve some energy for parenting. This means more stops, including at places like playgrounds. Older children will have their own interests and should be involved in planning a tour.

Before setting off on a major journey, try some day trips to check your set-up and introduce your child to cycling.

Children need to be taken into account in deciding each day's route – traffic and distances need to be moderate, and facilities and points of interest adequate. Given the extra weight of children and their daily needs, you may find it easier to leave behind the camping gear and opt for indoor accommodation or day trips from a base or series of bases. The very fit and adventurous may not need to compromise to ride with children, but those who do will still find it worthwhile. As with other activities, children bring a new perspective and pleasure to cycle touring. They tend to love it.

Alethea Morison

PAUL FARREN COLLECTION

in Paris, at 25 rue Ramus, is staffed by volunteers, only on the second and fourth Tuesday of the month. The members are willing to exchange advice and consult with cycle tourists.

Other Organisations

The Office National des Forêts in Paris (☎ 01 40 19 58 47, fax 01 40 19 78 13, ℮ infoonf@onf.fr, ⌨ www.onf.fr; metro Nation), at 2 ave de St Mandé, has maps, books and forest information. They also have offices in major centres throughout the country and publish a series of guides for mountain bikers (see the boxed text 'Mountain Biking' earlier in this chapter); titles are listed on the Web site.

France has 37 Regional Nature Parks. The head office is in Paris (☎ 01 44 90 86 20, fax 01 45 22 70 88, ℮ info@parcs-naturels-region aux.tm.fr), 4 rue de Stockholm (8e). Their Web site ⌨ www.parcs-naturels-regionaux .tm.fr lists all the parks and has loads of information. Each park has a *maison du parc*, a park information office, with displays, presentations and brochures.

LEGAL MATTERS

The French police can pretty much search anyone they want to at any time – whether or not there is probable cause.

If asked a question, police are likely to be helpful. If the police stop you for any reason, be polite and remain calm.

French police are very strict about security, especially at airports. They're serious when they warn that unattended luggage and suspicious objects will be summarily blown up.

As elsewhere in the EU, the laws are very tough when it comes to drinking and driving – or riding. The acceptable blood-alcohol limit is 0.05%, and drivers or cyclists exceeding this amount face fines of up to 30,000FF plus up to two years in jail. Licences can also be immediately suspended.

The fine for littering is about 1000FF.

Importing or exporting drugs can lead to a 10- to 30-year jail sentence. The fine for possession of drugs for personal use can be as high as 500,000FF.

BUSINESS HOURS

Business hours in France are not cut and dried. Most places have a midday break from noon or 1 pm to 2 or 3 pm, whether it be an office, bank or shop. At times hours will be posted as 'nonstop', meaning they do not close for lunch. Most tourist attractions remain open at midday during July and August.

Throughout this book, hours are indicated if they differ considerably from the norm:

Banks Open Monday to Friday from 9 or 10am to 5 or 5.30pm, with the typical midday break. Crédit Agricole branches generally open these hours from Tuesday to Saturday. The Banque de France often opens only on weekday mornings for currency exchange.

Bicycle Shops Open Tuesday to Saturday from 9 am to noon and 2 to 7 pm. Some shops also open Monday from 2 to 7 pm.

Museums and Attractions Open from 9 or 10 am to 5 or 6 pm; many close for lunch. Outside the high season in major tourist areas they usually close on either Monday or Tuesday.

Small Businesses Open daily, except Sunday and often Monday. Hours are usually from 9 or 10 am to 6.30 or 7 pm, with the ubiquitous lunch break.

Supermarkets and Hypermarkets Open Monday to Saturday, from 8 or 9 am to 7 or 8 pm, and a few on Sunday morning.

Small Food Shops Hours vary. They are mostly closed on Sunday morning and/or afternoon and on Monday.

Restaurants Open for lunch from just before noon until 2 pm, and dinner from 7 pm until 9 or 10 pm (later in larger cities). Brasseries, bars and cafes do not generally close during the day.

Tourist Offices Open from 9 or 10 am to noon and 2 to 6.30 or 7 pm, seven days a week in summer. In winter closing times are slightly earlier and offices are usually closed Sunday.

In July and August, lots of businesses shut for their annual holidays, for anywhere from a week to a month. The sign on the door will read *'Fermeture Annuelle'* (annual closure).

PUBLIC HOLIDAYS & SPECIAL EVENTS

Jours fériés (public holidays) observed in France are:

1 January *Jour de l'An* (New Year's Day)
late March/April *Pâques* & *Lundi de Pâques* (Easter Sunday & Easter Monday)
1 May *Fête du Travail* (May Day)
8 May *Victoire 1945* – celebrates the Allied victory in Europe that ended WWII
May *L'Ascension* (Ascension Thursday) – celebrated on the 40th day after Easter
mid-May to mid-June *Pentecôte* & *Lundi de Pentecôte* (Pentecost/Whit Sunday & Whit Monday) – celebrated on the 7th Sunday after Easter

14 July *Fête Nationale* (Bastille Day/National Day)
15 August *L'Assomption* (Assumption Day)
1 November *La Toussaint* (All Saints' Day)
11 November *Le onze novembre* (Remembrance Day) – celebrates the armistice of WWI
25 December *Noël* (Christmas)

Days that *aren't* public holidays in France are: Shrove Tuesday (Mardi Gras; the first day of Lent); Maundy (or Holy) Thursday *(jeudi saint)* and Good Friday *(vendredi saint)* just before Easter; and Boxing Day (26 December). However, Good Friday and Boxing Day are holidays in Alsace.

Most museums and shops – but not cinemas, restaurants or most *boulangeries* (bakeries) – are closed on public holidays. When a holiday falls on a Tuesday or a Thursday, the French have a custom of making a *pont* (bridge) to the nearest weekend by taking off Monday or Friday as well. The doors of banks are a good place to look for announcements of upcoming long weekends.

France's national day, 14 July, commemorates the day in 1789 when defiant Parisians stormed the Bastille prison, thus beginning the French Revolution. Often called Bastille Day by English speakers, it is celebrated with great gusto in most of the country, and in many cities and towns it can seem as if every person and their poodle is out on the streets. The day ends with a fireworks display.

Most French cities have at least one major music, dance, theatre, cinema or art festival each year. On Midsummer's day, June 21, many large towns hold a *Fête de la Musique* (Midsummer Music Festival). Some villages hold *foires* (fairs) and *fêtes* (festivals) to honour anything from a local saint to the year's garlic crop. In this book, annual regional events are listed under Special Events in the 'In Summary' box at the start of each regional chapter and in many city and town listings; for precise details about dates, which change from year to year, contact the local tourist office. The largest festivals make it difficult to find accommodation, so reserve in advance. For a list and information on festivals and events in France, check the Web site ⌨ www.viafrance.com.

CYCLING ROUTES
Route Descriptions

This guide covers the best areas for cycle touring on roads that France has to offer. The rides do not traverse the country from north to south or east to west, but offer a selection of the distinct routes through the wonderful and varied regions of France. Rides vary from one to 10 days. This allows the visitor to choose one or more short routes (by hiring a bicycle) as part of a noncycling itinerary, select a few routes in a couple of regions, or link several rides by cycling or taking public transport (discussed for each ride) for an extended bicycle tour. Rides accommodate both the novice and the experienced cyclist.

In most cases, the rides have been designed to make carrying camping gear and food optional. Each ride is broken into a set number of days, with accommodation and food options available at each day's destination. In some cases alternative destinations are offered.

Ride Difficulty

Each ride is graded according to its difficulty in terms of distance, terrain, road surface and navigation. The grade appears in the Table of Rides at the beginning of the book and at the start of each ride.

Grading is unavoidably subjective and is intended as a guide only; the degree of difficulty of a particular ride may vary according to the weather, the weight in your panniers, whether children are cycling, pre-trip training or how tired and hungry you are.

Easy These rides involve no more than a few hours riding each day, over *mostly* flat terrain with good, sealed surfaces. They are navigationally straightforward and are suitable for children over 10 years of age.

Moderate These rides present a moderate challenge to someone of average fitness; they are likely to include some hills, three to five hours of riding, and may involve some unsealed roads and/or complex navigation.

Hard These are for fit riders who want a challenge, and involve long daily distances and/or challenging climbs, may negotiate rough and remote roads, and present navigational challenges.

Times & Distances

Each ride is divided into stages, and we suggest that a day be spent on each stage. In some cases the distance for a particular stage is relatively short, but the attractions en route, or nearby, warrant spending extra time – distance junkies may decide to condense two stages into one day.

The directions for each day's ride are given in terms of distance (in kilometres) from the starting point (specified on the cue sheets).

A suggested riding time has been given for each day's ride. Because individual riding speed varies, these should be used as a guide only. They only take into account actual riding time – not time taken for rest stops, taking photographs, eating or visiting a museum – and are generally based on an average riding speed of between 10km/h and 20km/h.

Cue Sheets & Elevation Charts
See the Foreword for descriptions of how to use these.

ACTIVITIES
France's varied geography and climate make it a superb place for a wide range of outdoor pursuits. Some hostels, such as those run by the Fédération Unie des Auberges de Jeunesse (FUAJ; see Hostels in the Accommodation section of this chapter), offer week-long sports *stages* (training courses). Lonely Planet's *France* guide has more in-depth information about arranging some of these activities from overseas.

Walking
If you are combining walking with cycling, pick up a copy of Lonely Planet's *Walking in France*. The book offers a good selection of walks from one to 15 days, in a country crisscrossed by a staggering 120,000km of *sentiers balisés* (marked walking paths).

Probably the best-known trails are the *sentiers de grande randonnée* (long-distance footpaths), known as GR trails. You are likely to come across the red-and-white striped GR track indicators on trees, rocks, walls or posts as you cycle the quiet backroads and forests.

Other trails include the *grandes randonnées de pays* (GRP) trails, whose markings are yellow and red; and *sentiers de promenade randonnée* (PR), walking paths whose trail markings are yellow. Many *chemins de halage*, towpaths built in the days when canal barges were pulled by animals from the shore, are open to walkers (and cyclists). Shorter day walks and circuits are often known as *sentiers de petites randonnées* or *sentiers de pays*.

The Fédération Française de la Randonnée Pédestre (FFRP; ☎ 01 45 45 31 02, fax 01 43 95 68 07; metro Pernety), has an information centre in Paris at 64 rue de Gergovie 14e, and is the publisher of most major topoguides.

Swimming
France has lovely beaches along all of its coasts – the English Channel, the Atlantic and the Mediterranean (including the coast of Corsica) – as well as on lakes such as Lac d'Annecy and Lake Geneva. The fine, sandy beaches along the family-oriented Atlantic coast (eg, near Bordeaux) are much less crowded than their pebbly counterparts on the Côte d'Azur. Corsica is crowded only during July and August. Beaches along the Channel and in southern Brittany are cooler than those farther south. The public is free to use any beach not marked as private in France.

Topless bathing for women is pretty much the norm in France – if other people are doing it, you can assume it's OK.

Surfing & Windsurfing
The best surfing in France is on the Atlantic coast around Biarritz and Lacanau-Océan, where waves can reach 4m. Windsurfing is popular wherever there's water and a breeze, and renting equipment is often possible on lakes.

Rafting & Canoeing
White-water rafting, canoeing and kayaking are practised on many French rivers, including those that flow from the Massif Central (eg, the Dordogne River) and the Alps. Farther south, the Gorges du Verdon are popular for white-water rafting. Canoe and kayak enthusiasts tend to favour the Gorges du Tarn.

Canal Boating
One of the most relaxing ways to see France is to rent a houseboat for a leisurely cruise along canals and navigable rivers, whose slow-moving and often tree-lined channels pass through some of the most beautiful countryside in Europe. Changes in altitude are taken care of by a system of *écluses* (locks), where you can often hop ashore to meet the lock-keeper. See Boat in the Getting Around chapter for details of rental companies.

Fishing

Fishing in France requires not only the purchase of a licence, but familiarity with all sorts of stock conservation rules that differ from region to region and even from river to river. Depending on the area, the rules can cover the fishing season or even fishing days, permissible fishing equipment and catch size; ask a local tackle shop.

Spas & Thalassotherapy

For more than a century, the French have been keen fans of *thermalisme* (water cures), and visitors with ailments ranging from rheumatism to serious internal disorders flock to hot spring resorts.

Once only the domain of the wealthy, spa centres now offer fitness packages intended to appeal to a broad range of people of all ages. Many of the resorts are in the volcanic Massif Central, but others are found along the shore of Lake Geneva and in the Pyrenees.

A salty variant of thermalisme is *thalassothérapie* (sea-water therapy). Centres dot the Côte d'Azur, the Atlantic Coast and the Brittany coast.

ACCOMMODATION

France has accommodation of every sort and for every budget. For details, contact the nearest tourist office. They usually charge a small fee to make reservations.

In many parts of France, local authorities impose a *taxe de séjour* (tourist tax) on each visitor. The prices charged at camping grounds, hotels, hostels and B&Bs may, therefore, be as much as 1FF to 7FF per person higher than the posted rates. Some areas only levy this tax in summer, from around 1 June.

Advance reservations are a good way to avoid the hassle of searching for a place to stay each time you pull into a new town, especially as cyclists rarely arrive in the morning. During periods of heavy domestic or foreign tourism (around Easter, Christmas to New Year and in July and August), having a reservation can mean the difference between finding a room in your price range and cycling to the next town.

If you are running late, call to let the proprietor know you are on a bicycle so they don't give away your room; let them know also if you need to cancel.

Some places will have a secure garage for your bike; others will squeeze your bike into a wine cellar or may let you take your bike into your room. Paris is the only place you're likely to run across hotel owners who won't accept bicycles, but always check first.

Camping

France has thousands of camping grounds. Each one's facilities and amenities determine how many stars it has (usually two to four), which, along with location and seasonal demand, influence the prices. Some of the huge ones have swimming pools, tennis courts and small theatres. The smaller camping grounds, often municipal ones, might only have basic facilities, but are quieter, less expensive and often in gorgeous settings.

Children up to about the age of 12 enjoy significant discounts. Few camping grounds are in the city centre, so you may have to cycle up to 5km to get there. In some rural towns they are within 1km or 2km of the centre, and some are even closer, in a park or recreation area. Many close for at least a few months in winter, and some only open in summer. Hostels sometimes let travellers pitch tents in the back garden.

Camping à la ferme (camping on the farm) is coordinated by Gîtes de France (see Gîtes later in this section), publisher of the annual guide *Camping à la Ferme* (60FF). The sites – of which there are more than 1100 all over the country – are in lovely rural settings, usually at least a few kilometres from a town, so stock up on food for the night.

For details on camping grounds not mentioned in the text, inquire at a local tourist office. If you'll be doing lots of camping, pick up a copy of Michelin's *Camping-Caravanning France* (72FF), which lists 3500 camping grounds, or the FFCC's comprehensive *Les 11,100 Camping-Caravaning en France* (76FF).

In July and especially August, when most camping grounds are completely packed, and you arrive late in the day, they will generally find a spot for a small tent, especially if they see you have arrived by bicycle. Camping ground offices are often closed for most of the day – the best times to call for reservations are in the morning (before 10 or 11 am) and in the late afternoon or early evening.

If you'll be doing an overnight walk, remember that camping is generally permitted only at designated camp sites. Pitching your tent anywhere else (eg, in a road or trailside meadow), known as *camping sauvage* in French, is usually illegal, though it's often tolerated to varying degrees. Except in Corsica, you probably won't have any problems if you're not on private land, have only a small tent, are discreet, stay only one or two nights, take the tent down during the day, do not light a campfire, and are at least 1500m from a camping ground (or, in a national park, at least an hour's walk from a road).

The largest listing of camping grounds on the Internet is ⌨ www.campingfrance.com. Chains of commercial camping grounds (usually of the huge variety) include Campotel (☎ 0800 973 040, ⌨ www.campotel.com), Airotel France (⌨ www.airotel.com), and Capéole (⌨ www.campeoles.fr).

Refuges

A *refuge* (mountain hut or shelter; pronounced reh-**fuuzh**) is a very basic dorm room established and operated by national park authorities, the Club Alpin Français or other private organisations along trails in uninhabited mountainous areas that are frequented by hikers and mountain climbers. *Refuges*, some of which are open year-round, are generally marked on hiking and climbing maps.

In general, *refuges* are equipped with bunks (usually wall-to-wall), mattresses and blankets but not sheets, which you have to bring yourself or (sometimes) rent for 15FF to 20FF. Overnight charges average between 50FF to 70FF a night per person; given how much space you get, *refuges* are more expensive per square metre than most luxury hotels. Meals, prepared by the *gardien* (attendant), are sometimes available. Most *refuges* are equipped with a telephone – often it's a good idea to call ahead and make a reservation.

For details on *refuges*, contact a tourist office near where you'll be cycling or hiking or consult the *Guide des Refuges et Gîtes des Alpes*, published by the Grenoble-based Glénat, which covers the Alps; or, for the Pyrenees, *Hébergement en Montagne*, published by the St Girons-based Éditions Randonnées Pyrénéennes. Both should be available in French bookshops or Maisons de la Presse.

Hostels

Official hostels in France are known as *auberges de jeunesse*. The Fédération Unie des Auberges de Jeunesse (FUAJ; ⌨ www.fuaj.org) and Ligue Française pour les Auberges de la Jeunesse (LFAJ) both require Hostelling International cards (see the Visas & Documents section earlier). Unofficial hostels and hostels in the group Union des Centres de Rencontres Internationales de France (UCRIF; ⓔ ucrif@aol.com) do not require HI cards, but may offer a small discount if you have one.

In university towns, you may also find *foyers* (pronounced fwa-**yei**), student dormitories converted for use by travellers during the summer school holidays. In certain cities and towns, young workers are accommodated in dormitories called either *foyers de jeunes travailleurs* or *travailleuses*. Despite the names, most are now co-ed. These places, which often take *passagers* and *passagères* (male and female short-term guests) when they have space, are relatively unknown to most travellers and very frequently have space available when other hostels are full. Information on hostels and foyers not mentioned in the text is available from local tourist offices.

In Paris, expect to pay 90FF to 120FF a night for a hostel bed, including breakfast. In the provinces, a bunk in the single-sex dorm room generally costs somewhere from 50FF to 70FF, which does not include a sometimes-optional continental breakfast (around 20FF). Most auberges de jeunesse, and some hostels and foyers, have kitchen facilities of one sort or another. Hostels require that you either bring a sleeping sheet or rent one for 13FF to 16FF per stay.

Not all hostels and foyers accept telephone reservations and, if they do, will usually only hold a place for a few hours. In July and August, when swarms of summer backpackers descend on France, it's an excellent idea to arrive in town early, or call ahead to tell them you are cycling.

Gîtes

The term gîte covers a wide range of accommodation in rural areas, from B&Bs to rental country cottages. Gîte means 'resting place'. The Fédération Nationale des Gîtes de France (☎ 01 49 70 75 75, fax 01 42 81 28 53, ⌨ www.gites-de-france.fr; metro Trinité) at 59 rue St Lazare, 75009 Paris, oversees all the gîtes in France.

Each department has a Gîtes de France *antenne* (branch) that publishes a brochure listing the local gîtes (branch addresses are listed on the Web site). Details on how to find or contact the nearest Gîtes de France office are available at any local tourist office, which may also be able to supply a brochure. Some associations are listed in the regional chapters.

Some branches may be able to handle English-language bookings through their *service de réservation*. Otherwise, you need to contact the owner yourself. During holiday periods, it is necessary to reserve rural accommodation in some areas well in advance. Most owners will ask for deposits.

Chambres d'Hôtes (or B&Bs)

A chambre d'hôte, a B&B (bed and breakfast), is a room in a private house rented to travellers by the night. Breakfast is included. France has about 15,000 chambres d'hôtes. They are an excellent way to meet local people and stay in a family home. Some serve evening meals, that is, *table d'hôte*, for an additional charge. A complete listing can be found in the Gîte de France book, *Chambres et Tables d'Hotes* (120FF; see Gîtes, earlier).

Gîtes d'Étape & de Séjour

Gîtes d'Étape and *de Séjour* are in less remote areas than *refuges*, often in villages and rural settings. Gîtes Panda are environmentally aware and lie within a Parc Naturel Regional.

They cost around 70FF per person and are listed in *Gîtes d'Étape et de Séjour* (60FF), published annually by Gîtes de France. They offer dormitory-style accommodation (some supply sheets), and many have hot showers, a common room and cooking facilities. Some hosts offer meals. They cater to walkers and cyclists, are particularly well suited to families, and are often booked by groups (call ahead to make sure there is room). Reservations must be made directly with the owner. Tourist offices usually have information on local gîtes d'étape et de séjour.

Rando'Plume (☎ 05 62 90 09 92, fax 05 62 90 09 91) is a separate chain of more than 100 gîtes specialising in outdoor and adventure holidays.

Throughout the book, we categorise gîtes d'étape as a hostel alternative, and on maps the hostel symbol may refer to them as well.

Gîtes Ruraux

A *gîte rural* – of which France has 35,000 – is a holiday cottage (or part of a house) in a village or on a farm. Amenities always include a kitchenette and bathroom facilities. There is a minimum rental period – often one week, but sometimes only a few days. The list can be found in the book *Nouveaux Gîtes Ruraux* (120FF).

Hotels

Most French hotels have between one and four stars; the fanciest places have four. Most hotels offer a *petit déjeuner* (breakfast), usually consisting of a croissant, French rolls, butter, jam and either coffee or hot chocolate. Some now offer a buffet, which may include juice, cheese, yoghurt, fruit and perhaps cereal. The charge is usually 20FF to 40FF per person, a bit more than you would pay at a cafe. Some places in heavily touristed areas increase their high-season profits by requiring that guests take breakfast. Some hotels insist you pay for *demi-pension* (half-board, ie, breakfast and either lunch or dinner). You will be told this at check-in, but if unsure, ask.

Lower-priced or budget hotels often have doubles that cost less than two hostel beds, ie, up to 170FF (240FF in Paris). Most are equipped with a washbasin (and, usually, a bidet) but lack private bathroom or toilet. Almost all these places also have more expensive rooms equipped with shower or bath, toilet and other amenities. Most doubles, which generally cost only marginally more than singles, have only one double bed, though some places have rooms with twin beds. Taking a shower in the hall bathroom is sometimes free but is usually *payant*, which means there's a charge of 10FF to 25FF per person; often you need a *jeton*, a special coin to operate the shower for a designated time.

Hotels with double rooms equipped with showers and toilets charge from 170FF to about 350FF. Around 4000 hotels – many of them family-run places in the countryside, by the sea or in the mountains – belong to Logis de France, an excellent organisation whose affiliated establishments meet strict standards of service and amenities. They generally offer very good value. The Fédération Nationale des Logis de France (☎ 01 45 84 70 00, fax 01 45 83 59 66, 🖳 www.logis-de-france.fr) based at 83 ave d'Italie, 75013 Paris, issues an annual guide, with maps.

FOOD

One of the best reasons to cycle in France is that you get to eat as much of the country's fabulous food as you want. You owe it to yourself to enjoy the wonderful cuisine France has to offer.

Eating is of prime importance to the French. They may rush some things in life, but never a meal. The French spend an incredible amount of time contemplating, preparing, discussing and ultimately eating a meal. They live to eat!

There is so much to say about French cuisine that it could take up the rest of this book. Rather than do that, take a look at one of the culinary guides and phrasebooks described in the Books section of this chapter, or read the informative Food & Wine guide in Lonely Planet's *France* guide.

Local Food

French cuisine owes a lot to the variety and freshness of its ingredients. France is blessed with a tremendous diversity of climate and terrain, the result being a range of regional products to satisfy any craving, from the olive oil, garlic and tomatoes from the south to the butter, cream, and apples of the north. In between you can find anything from *truffes* (truffles) in the Périgord, to *choucroute* (sauerkraut) in Alsace, freshwater fish in lakes and rivers, and abundant seafood and saltwater fish along the coastlines. And a reminder by Charles de Gaulle of the huge selection of French regional cheese in his statement 'Un pays qui compte 350 sortes de fromage, c'est ingouvernable' (A country with 350 types of cheese is ungovernable).

Dishes are often named after their region of origin. Something on a menu that is *à la normande* will have a sauce made with cream, cheese and possibly Calvados (apple brandy); something described as *bourguignonne* will have a rich red wine sauce; *provençale* denotes a sauce made with tomatoes, olive oil and garlic; and *dijonnaise* will have a mustard base.

The list of regional dishes is enormous. Some worth seeking are Languedoc's cassoulet (a hearty stew of white beans and pork) and *confit de canard* (preserved duck), Provence's bouillabaisse (a fish soup made with fish, seafood onions, tomatoes, saffron and herbs), *œufs en meurette* (eggs poached in a rich red wine sauce) found in Lyon and Burgundy, buttery crepes from Brittany and the prizes of Périgord, *pâté de foie gras* (goose liver pâté) and truffles.

Where to Eat   One of the most difficult things about eating in restaurants or brasseries in France is choosing one. You can spend hours perusing the menus and prices that are posted outside. Restaurants will usually specialise in a particular type of food: regional, traditional or ethnic (such as North African, Middle Eastern, Thai or Vietnamese). Brasseries serve a more standard fare but unlike restaurants, which close between lunch and dinner, they remain open.

There are two options for selecting your meal: *á la carte*, ordering each dish separately off the *carte* (menu), which can be pricey; for better value, choose a multicourse set meal known in France as a *menu, menu à prix fixe* or *menu du jour* (menu of the day). Throughout this book we italicise *menu* to distinguish it from the English word menu. A good three-course *menu* can cost as little as 70FF; usually a choice of differently priced menus will be offered.

Vegetarians are not well-catered-for in France. From time to time you may come across a vegetarian restaurant, but only in major cities. Most *menus* will have at least a couple of vegetarian entrees (starters or first course). A good option is a *saladerie*, a restaurant that serves *salades composées* (mixed salads), but read carefully as many salads include meat or fish. Salads are also often featured on brasserie menus, as are vegetarian quiches and omelettes. Another option is the crêperie, which specialises in crepes – ultra-thin pancakes folded or rolled over a filling. In some parts of France, the word *crêpe* is used only to refer to the sweet crepes made with *farine de froment* (regular wheat flour), whereas savoury crepes, often made with *farine de sarrasin* (buckwheat flour) and filled with cheese, mushrooms and the like, are called *galettes*.

For a cup of coffee and a snack, but more for atmosphere, head to a cafe. The French look upon the cafe as a place to read, write, meet friends, or simply watch the world go by. Most will serve a baguette filled with cheese or pâté, or a croque monsieur. Salons de Thé (tearooms) are trendy and somewhat pricey establishments that usually offer quiches, salads, cakes, tarts, pies and pastries in addition to tea and coffee.

Self-Catering

Shopping for food in France is a treat. One of the highlights of a cyclist's day can be sitting down to a gourmet *pique-nique*.

Begin in one of the country's 36,000 *boulangeries* (bakeries) and pick up a baguette. Move on to the *fromagerie* (cheese shop), which will have an enormous selection. The *charcuterie* (delicatessen) offers sliced meats, prepared salads, pâtés, terrines and other delights; some also sell cheese. The *marchand de légumes et de fruits* sells vegetables and fruit. And for dessert, visit the 'to die for' *pâtisserie* (pastry shop) or the *confiserie* (sweet shop) selling amazing, high-quality chocolates and other sweets.

Other shops include the *boucherie* (butcher) and the *poissonnerie* (fish shop). A small grocery store, often found in towns and villages, is the *alimentation générale* or the *épicerie* (literally 'spice shop'). Of course, there are always the *supermarchés* (supermarkets), some found in the basement of a department store, and the even bigger *hypermarchés* (hypermarkets), the latter usually on the outskirts of town.

Almost every city, town and village in France has a weekly market *(marché)*, feasts for the stomach and for the eyes. They are a tapestry of colour, with seasonal fruit and vegetables cascading down artistic displays, fresh fish shimmering on beds of ice, a patchwork of brilliant flowers, and a multitude of local cheeses, olives, herbs, dried fruits and other comestibles. They are also a place for local 'flavour' – a meeting place for friends.

DRINKS
Nonalcoholic Drinks

All tap water in France is safe to drink, so there is no need to buy expensive bottled water. Tap water that is not drinkable (eg, at most public fountains or in some streams) will usually be signed *'eau non potable'*. If you would like tap water with your meal, ask for *une carafe d'eau* (a jug of water). Otherwise you'll be paying for *eau de source* (mineral water), which comes *plate* (flat or noncarbonated) or *gazeuse* (fizzy or carbonated).

Soft drinks are expensive in France. A refreshing drink is *sirop* (fruit syrup), including flavours such as *cassis* (blackberry), *grenadine* (pomegranate), *menthe* (mint) and *citron* (lemon). It's served either *à l'eau* (mixed with water), with *soda* (carbonated water) or Perrier. A *citron pressé* is a freshly squeezed lemon juice, and a glass of freshly squeezed orange juice is an *orange pressée*. The French are not particularly fond of drinking very cold things. If you would like your drink with ice cubes, ask for *des glaçons*.

Coffee comes in various shapes and sizes. A small, black espresso is called *un café noir*, or *un petit café*, or you can ask for a *grand* (large) version. *Un café crème* is espresso with steamed milk or cream. *Un café au lait* is lots of hot milk with a little coffee served in a large cup or, sometimes, a bowl; *un café américain* is a coffee with extra hot water. Decaffeinated coffee is *un café décaféiné* or *un déca*. *Thé* (tea), *tisane* (herbal infusion) and *chocolat chaud* (hot chocolate) are widely available.

Sports Drinks Sports drinks, such as Gatorade and PowerAde, are not widely available in France, except in the sports chain stores and Bouticycle shops. If you have a drink of choice that comes in powder form, bring it with you.

Alcoholic Drinks

There are dozens of wine-producing regions throughout France, and they make for superb cycling. Tours of the wine regions included in this book are: Alsace, Burgundy, Champagne, the Loire, Bordeaux, Languedoc, and Provence; in Normandy the Cider Route is taken in.

Wine can be purchased in shops as cheaply as 12FF, but something better can be bought for 35FF to 60FF. The French always drink wine with meals. In restaurants, you can order *une bouteille* (a bottle) of *rouge* (red), *blanc* (white) or rosé. It is possible to order *une demi-bouteille* (a half-bottle) or *un pichet* (small jug). Try to sample local wines

Study, Swirl, Sniff, Sip, Swallow

The art of wine tasting is a complex process that takes years to fully appreciate. For many people tasting new wine, it's enough to just concentrate on a new wine for the first few minutes – think about its aromas and flavours and decide what you like. However, if you want to get a bit more technical, here's a rough guide:

1. **Colour** Look through the wine towards a source of light. Then tilt the glass slightly and look through it towards a pale background. You're looking for clarity and colour. Clarity is obvious, but colour is more complex. A young red wine is purple-red and the colour softens with age to become more orange-red.

2. **Smell** Swirl the wine around and smell in one inhalation. Close your eyes and concentrate: what do you smell? Eleven main groups of smells are associated with wine, ranging from fruits to plants, herbs and spices, and even toast or cigar box, so if asked what you are smelling, use your imagination. Swirl the wine around and smell it again; the agitation will release a different range of bouquets and will oxygenate the wine, which is especially necessary to give red wine its best taste.

3. **Taste** Take a sip, swill it around in your mouth and then (here's the tough part) draw in some air to bring out the flavour. The first rule of thumb is pleasure. After that, it gets more complex, with different parts of the tongue detecting different tastes. Check the wine is not too acidic, and that the tastes are balanced. Again, all sorts of words are used to characterise the palate of wine: young wines may taste fresh and fruity; older red wines may have chocolaty, ripe berry tastes; and you'll be able to taste the wood in wine matured in oak barrels. If you're drinking with someone who knows more about wine than you do, don't be afraid to ask questions. Wine makers, especially, are always happy to initiate newcomers into their passion. After tasting, swallow the wine. Better wines often leave a long aftertaste.

in restaurants, or when shopping. For an explanation of the French labelling and quality control systems, see the boxed texts 'Reading a Wine Label' and 'The ABC of AOC' in the South-West chapter.

Before a meal, the French like an aperitif. Pastis, one of a range of aperitifs, is a refreshing aniseed-flavoured drink which turns cloudy when mixed with water and is a particular favourite in southern France. Two popular brand names are Pernod and Ricard. Another is *kir* (white wine sweetened with cassis), *kir royale* (champagne with cassis). In Normandy, *pommeau* and Calvados, both apple-based, are popular.

In bars and cafes, beer is usually served very cold and by the *demi* (about 330mL). It' usually cheaper *à la pression* (on draught/tap) than in a bottle, but prices vary widely depending upon the establishment. At a decent but modest, sort of place, count on paying 12FF to 16FF for a demi of draught.

Health & Safety

Keeping healthy on your travels depends on your predeparture preparations, your daily health care and diet while on the road, and how you handle any medical problem that develops. Few touring cyclists experience anything more than a bit of soreness, fatigue and chafing, although there is potential for more serious problems. The sections that follow aren't intended to alarm, but they are worth a skim before you go.

Before You Go

HEALTH INSURANCE
Make sure that you have adequate health insurance. For details, see Travel Insurance in the Visas & Documents section in the Facts for the Cyclist chapter.

IMMUNISATIONS
You don't need any vaccinations to visit France. However, it's always wise to keep up-to-date with routine vaccinations such as diphtheria, polio and tetanus – boosters are necessary every 10 years and protection is highly recommended.

FIRST AID
It's a good idea at any time to know the appropriate responses in the event of a major accident or illness, and it's especially important if you are intending to ride off-road in a remote area. Consider learning basic first aid through a recognised course before you go, and carrying a first-aid manual and small medical kit.

Although detailed first-aid instruction is outside the scope of this guidebook, some basic points are listed in the section on Traumatic Injuries later in this chapter. Undoubtedly the best advice is to avoid an accident in the first place. The Safety on the Ride section at the end of this chapter contains tips for safe on-road and off-road riding, as well as information on how to summon help should a major accident or illness occur.

PHYSICAL FITNESS
Most of the rides in this book are designed for someone with a moderate degree of cycling

---

First-Aid Kit

A possible kit could include:

First-Aid Supplies
- [ ] sticking plasters (Band Aids)
- [ ] bandages & safety pins
- [ ] elastic support bandage for knees, ankles etc
- [ ] gauze swabs
- [ ] nonadhesive dressings
- [ ] small pair of scissors
- [ ] sterile alcohol wipes
- [ ] butterfly closure strips
- [ ] latex gloves
- [ ] syringes & needles – for removing gravel from road-rash wounds
- [ ] thermometer (note that mercury thermometers are prohibited by airlines)
- [ ] tweezers

Medications
- [ ] antidiarrhoea, antinausea drugs and oral rehydration salts
- [ ] antifungal cream or powder – for fungal skin infections and thrush
- [ ] antihistamines – for allergies, eg, hay fever; to ease the itch from insect bites or stings; and to prevent motion sickness
- [ ] antiseptic powder or solution (eg, povidone-iodine) and antiseptic wipes for cuts and grazes
- [ ] nappy rash cream
- [ ] calamine lotion, sting relief spray or aloe vera – to ease irritation from sunburn and insect bites or stings
- [ ] cold and flu tablets, throat lozenges and nasal decongestant
- [ ] painkillers (eg, aspirin or paracetamol/ acetaminophen in the USA) – for pain and fever
- [ ] laxatives

Miscellaneous
- [ ] insect repellent, sunscreen, lip balm and eye drops
- [ ] water purification tablets or iodine

Getting Fit for Touring

Ideally, a training program should be tailored to your objectives, specific needs, fitness level and health. However, if you have no idea how to prepare for your cycling holiday these guidelines will help you get the fitness you need to enjoy it more. Things to think about include:

Foundation You will need general kilometres in your legs before you start to expose them to any intensive cycling. Always start out with easy rides – even a few kilometres to the shops – and give yourself plenty of time to build towards your objective.

Tailoring Once you have the general condition to start preparing for your trip, work out how to tailor your training rides to the type of tour you are planning. Someone preparing for a three-week ride will require a different approach to someone building fitness for a one-day or weekend ride. Some aspects to think about are the ride length (distance and days), terrain, climate and weight to be carried in panniers. If your trip involves carrying 20kg in panniers, incorporate this weight into some training rides, especially some of the longer ones. If you are going to be touring in mountainous areas, choose a hilly training route.

Recovery You usually adapt to a training program during recovery time, so it's important to do the right things between rides. Recovery can take many forms, but the simple ones are best. These include getting quality sleep, eating an adequate diet to refuel the system, doing recovery rides between hard days (using low gears to avoid pushing yourself), stretching and enjoying a relaxing bath. Other forms include recovery massage, spas and yoga.

If you have no cycling background this program will help you get fit for your cycling holiday. If you are doing an easy ride (each ride in this book is rated; see Cycling Routes in the Facts for the Cyclist chapter), aim to at least complete Week 4; for moderate rides, complete Week 6; and complete the program if you are doing a hard ride. Experienced cycle tourists may start at Week 3, while those who regularly ride up to four days a week could start at Week 5.

Don't treat this as a punishing training schedule: try cycling to work or to the shops, join a local touring club or get a group of friends together to turn weekend rides into social events.

	Monday	Tuesday	Wednesday	Thursday	Friday	Saturday	Sunday
Week 1	10km*	–	10km*	–	10km*	–	10km*
Week 2	–	15km*	–	15km*	–	20km*	–
Week 3	20km*	–	20km†	25km*	–	25km*	20km†
Week 4	–	30km*	–	35km*	30km†	30km*	–
Week 5	30km*	–	40km†	–	35km*	–	40km†
Week 6	30km*	–	40km†	–	–	60km*	40km†
Week 7	30km*	–	40km†	–	30km†	70km*	30km*
Week 8	–	60km*	30km†	–	40km†	–	90km*

* steady pace (allows you to carry out a conversation without losing your breath) on flat or undulating terrain
† solid pace (allows you to talk in short sentences only) on undulating roads with some longer hills

The training program shown here is only a guide. Ultimately it is important to listen to your body and slow down if the ride is getting too hard. Take extra recovery days and cut back distances when you feel this way. Don't panic if you don't complete every ride, every week; the most important thing is to ride regularly and gradually increase the length of your rides as you get fitter.

For those with no exercise background, be sure to see your doctor and get a clearance to begin exercising at these rates. This is especially important for those over 35 years of age with no exercise history and those with a cardiac or respiratory condition of any nature.

Kevin Tabotta

fitness. As a general rule, however, the fitter you are, the more you'll enjoy riding. It pays to spend time preparing yourself physically before you set out, rather than let a sore backside and aching muscles draw your attention from some of the world's finest cycle touring countryside.

Depending on your existing level of fitness, you should start training a couple of months before your trip. Try to ride at least three times a week, starting with easy rides (even 5km to work, if you're not already cycling regularly) and gradually building up to longer distances. Once you have a good base of regular riding behind you, include hills in your training (you'll appreciate hill fitness in parts of France) and familiarise yourself with the gearing on your bike. Before you go you should have done at least one 60km to 70km ride with loaded panniers.

As you train, you'll discover how to adjust your bike to increase your comfort – as well as any mechanical problems.

Staying Healthy

The best way to have a lousy holiday (especially if you're relying on self-propulsion) is to become ill. Heed the following simple advice and the only thing you're likely to suffer from is that rewarding tiredness at the end of a full day.

Reduce the chances of contracting an illness by washing your hands frequently, particularly after working on your bike and before handling or eating food.

HYDRATION

You may not notice how much water you're losing as you ride, because it evaporates in the breeze. However, don't underestimate the amount of fluid you need to replace – particularly in warmer weather. The magic figure is supposedly 1L per hour, though many cyclists have trouble consuming this much – remembering to drink enough can be harder than it sounds. Sipping little and often is the key; try to drink a mouthful every 10 minutes or so and don't wait until you get thirsty. Water 'backpacks' can be great for fluid regulation since virtually no physical or mental effort is required to drink. Keep drinking before and after the day's ride to replenish fluid.

Use the colour of your urine as a rough guide to whether you are drinking enough. Small amounts of dark urine suggest you need to increase your fluid intake. Passing reasonable quantities of light yellow urine indicates that you've got the balance about right. Other signs of dehydration include headache and fatigue. For more information on the effects of dehydration, see Dehydration & Heat Exhaustion later in this chapter.

Water

Tap water is almost always safe to drink in France, though you should check for 'eau non potable' (undrinkable water) signs in places such as public toilets. However, the intestinal parasite *Giardia lamblia* has been found in water from lakes, rivers, streams and drinking fountains. Giardia is not common but, to be certain, water from these sources should be purified before drinking. For more information on giardiasis, see Infectious Diseases later in this chapter.

The simplest way of purifying water is to boil it thoroughly. Vigorous boiling for five minutes should do the job.

Simple filtering will not remove all dangerous organisms, so if you can't boil water treat it chemically. Chlorine tablets will kill many pathogens, but not giardia. Iodine is very effective in purifying water and is available in tablet and liquid form, but follow the directions carefully and remember that too much iodine can be harmful. Flavoured powder will disguise the taste of treated water and is a good thing to carry if you are spending time away from town water supplies.

Sports Drinks

Commercial sports drinks such as Gatorade and PowerAde are an excellent way to satisfy your hydration needs, electrolyte replacement and energy demands in one. On endurance rides especially, it can be difficult to keep eating solid fuels day in, day out, but sports drinks can supplement these energy demands and allow you to vary your solid fuel intake a little for variety. The bonus is that those all-important body salts lost through perspiration get re-stocked. Make sure you drink plenty of water as well; if you have two water bottles on your bike (and you should), it's a good idea to fill one with sports drink and the other with plain water.

If using a powdered sports drink, don't mix it too strong (follow the instructions) because, in addition to being too sweet, too many carbohydrates can actually impair your body's ability to absorb the water and carbohydrates properly.

NUTRITION

One of the great things about bike touring is that it requires lots of energy, which means you can eat more of France's fabulous food. Depending on your activity levels, it's not hard to put away huge servings of food and be hungry a few hours after.

Because you're putting such demands on your body, it's important to eat well – not just lots. As usual, you should eat a bal-anced diet from a wide variety of foods. This is easy in France, with so much fresh food widely available (see Food in the Facts for the Cyclist chapter).

The main part of your diet should be carbohydrates rather than proteins or fats. While some protein (for tissue maintenance and repair) and fat (for vitamins, long-term energy and warmth) is essential, carbohydrates provide the most efficient fuel. They are easily digested into simple sugars, which are then used in energy production. Less-refined foods like pasta, rice, bread, fruits and vegetables are all high in carbohydrates.

Eating simple carbohydrates (sugars, such as lollies or sweets) gives you almost immediate energy – great for when you

---

Avoiding the Bonk

The bonk, in a cycling context, is not a pleasant experience; it's that light-headed, can't-put-power-to-the-pedals weak feeling that engulfs you (usually quite quickly) when your body runs out of fuel.

If you experience it the best move is to stop and refuel immediately. It can be quite serious and risky to your health if it's not addressed as soon as symptoms occur. It won't take long before you are ready to get going again (although most likely at a slower pace), but you'll also be more tired the next day so try to avoid it.

The best way to do this is to maintain your fuel intake while riding. Cycling for hours burns considerable body energy, and replacing it is something that needs to be tailored to each individual's tastes. The touring cyclist needs to target foods that have a high carbohydrate source. Foods that contain some fat are not a problem occasionally, as cycling at low intensity (when you're able to ride and talk without losing your breath) will usually trigger the body to draw on fat stores before stored carbohydrates.

Good on-bike cycling foods include:

- bananas (in particular) and other fruits
- bread with jam or honey
- breakfast and muesli bars
- rice-based snacks
- prepackaged high carbohydrate sports bars (eg, PowerBar)
- sports drinks

During lunch stops (or for breakfast) you can try such things as spaghetti, cereal, creamed rice, pancakes, baked beans, sandwiches and rolls.

It's important not to get uptight about the food you eat. As a rule of thumb, base all your meals around carbohydrates of some sort, but don't be afraid to also indulge in local culinary delights.

DON HATCHER

need a top-up (see the boxed text 'Avoiding the Bonk'); however, because they are quickly metabolised, you may get a sugar 'high' then a 'low'. For cycling it is far better to base your diet around complex carbohydrates, which take longer to process and provide 'slow-release' energy over a longer period. (But don't miss the opportunity to indulge guiltlessly in pastries and that delicious cheese every now and then ...)

Cycle Food: A Guide to Satisfying Your Inner Tube, by Lauren Hefferon, is a handy reference for nutrition and health advice with practical recipes.

Day-to-Day Needs

Eat a substantial breakfast – wholegrain cereal or bread is best, if you can find them in France – and fruit or juice for vitamins. You're unlikely to get cooked breakfasts in hotels or hostels, but if you're camping and cooking your own, include carbohydrates (such as porridge, toast or potatoes). Try to avoid foods high in fat (such as croissants), which take longer to digest.

Bread is the easiest food for lunch, topped with ingredients like cheese, peanut butter, salami and fresh salad vegetables. If you're in a town, filled baguettes make for a satisfying meal (*frites* – chips – or pizza, with their high fat content, will feel like a lump in your stomach if you continue straight away).

Keep topping up your energy during the ride. See the boxed text 'Avoiding the Bonk' for tips.

Try to eat a high carbohydrate meal in the evening. If you're eating out, Italian or Asian restaurants tend to offer more carbohydrate-based meals.

Rice, pasta and potatoes are good staples if you're self-catering. Team them with fresh vegetables and ingredients such as instant soup, canned beans, fish or bacon. Remember that even though you're limited in terms of what you can carry on a bike, it's possible – with some imagination and preparation – to eat delicious as well as nutritious camp meals.

AVOIDING CYCLING AILMENTS
Saddle Sores & Blisters

While you're more likely to get a sore bum if you're out of condition, riding long distances does take its toll on your behind. To minimise the impact, always wear clean, preferably padded bike shorts (also known as 'knicks'). Brief, unfitted shorts can chafe, as can underwear (see Clothing under What to Bring in the Facts for the Cyclist chapter). Shower as soon as you stop and put on clean, preferably nonsynthetic, clothes. Moisturising or emollient creams or baby nappy rash cream also help guard against chafing – apply liberally around the crotch area before riding. For information on correctly adjusting your bike seat, see the Your Bicycle chapter.

If you do suffer from chafing, wash and dry the area and carefully apply a barrier (moisturising) cream.

You probably won't get blisters unless you do a very long ride with no physical preparation. Wearing gloves and correctly fitted shoes will reduce the likelihood of blisters on your hands and feet. If you know you're susceptible to blisters in a particular spot, cover the area with medical adhesive tape before riding.

Knee Pain

Knee pain is common among cyclists who pedal in too high a gear. While it may *seem* faster to turn the pedals slowly in a high gear, it's actually more efficient (and better for your knees) to 'spin' the pedals – that is, use a low enough gear so you can pedal quickly with little resistance. For touring, the ideal cadence (the number of pedal strokes per minute) ranges from 70 to 90. Try to maintain this cadence even when you're climbing.

It's a good idea to stretch before and after riding, and to go easy when you first start each day. This reduces your chances of injury and helps your muscles to work more efficiently.

You can also get sore knees if your saddle is too low, or if your shoe cleats (for use with clipless pedals) are incorrectly positioned. Both are discussed in greater detail in the Your Bicycle chapter.

Numbness & Backache

Pain in the hands, neck and shoulders is a common complaint, particularly on longer riding days. It's generally caused by leaning too much on your hands. Apart from discomfort, you can temporarily damage the nerves and experience numbness or mild

Stretching

Stretching is important when stepping up your exercise levels: it improves muscle flexibility, which allows freer movement in the joints; and prevents the rigidity developing in muscles that occurs through prolonged cycling activity.

Ideally, you should stretch for 10 minutes before and after riding and for longer periods (15 to 30 minutes) every second day. Stretching prepares muscles for the task ahead, and limits the stress on muscles and joints during exercise. It can reduce post-exercise stiffness (decreasing the recovery time between rides) and reduce the chance of injury during cycling.

You should follow a few basic guidelines:

- before stretching, warm up for five to 10 minutes by going for a gentle bike ride, jog or brisk walk
- ensure you follow correct technique for each stretch
- hold a stretch for 15 to 30 seconds
- stretch to the point of discomfort, not pain
- breathe freely (ie, don't hold your breath) and try to relax your body whenever you are stretching
- don't 'bounce' the stretch; gradually ease into a full stretch
- repeat each stretch three times (on both sides, when required)

Do not stretch when you have an injury to a muscle, ligament or tendon (allow it to heal fully), as it can lead to further injury and/or hinder recovery. Warming up the muscles increases blood flow to the area, making it easier to stretch and reducing the likelihood of injury.

The main muscle groups for the cyclist to stretch are: quadriceps, calves, hamstrings, lower back and neck. Use the following stretches as a starting point, adding extra stretches that are already part of your routine or if you feel 'tight' in other areas (eg, add shoulder rolls if your shoulders feel sore after a day's cycling).

Quadriceps

Facing a wall with your feet slightly apart, grip one foot with your hand and pull it towards the buttocks. Ensure the back and hips are square. To get a better stretch, push the hip forward. You should never feel pain at the knee joint. Hold the stretch, before lowering the leg and repeating the stretch with the other leg.

Calf

Stand facing a wall, placing one foot about 30cm in front of the other. Keep the heels flat on the ground and bend the front leg slowly toward the wall – the stretch should be in the upper-calf area of the back leg. Keep the back straight and bend your elbows to allow your body to move forward during the stretch. Hold the stretch; relax and repeat the stretch with the other leg.

Stretching

Hamstrings

Sit with one leg extended and the other leg bent with the bottom of the foot against the inside of the extended leg. Slide your arms down the extended leg – bending from the waist – until you feel a pull in the hamstring area. Hold it for 15 seconds, before returning to the start position. Keep the toes pointed up; avoid hunching the back.

Lower-Back Roll

Lie on your back (on a towel or sleeping mat) and bring both knees up towards the shoulders until you feel a stretch in the lower back. Hold the stretch for 30 seconds; relax.

'Cat Stretch' Hunch

Another stretch for the lower back. Move to the ground on all fours (hands shoulder-width apart; legs slightly apart), lift the hips and lower back towards the sky until you feel a stretch. Hold it for 15 seconds; return to start position.

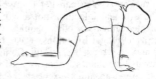

'Cat Stretch' Arch

One more stretch for the lower back. With hands and knees in the same position as for the Cat Stretch above, roll the hips and lower back toward the ground until you feel a stretch. Hold it for 15 seconds; return to start position.

Neck

Gently and smoothly stretch your neck each of the four ways: forward, back and side to side. Do each stretch separately. (Do not rotate the head in a full circle.) For the side stretches, use your hand to pull the head very gently in the direction of the stretch.

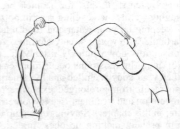

paralysis of the hands. Prevent it by wearing padded gloves, cycling with less weight on your hands and changing your hand position frequently (if you have flat handlebars, fit bar ends to provide more hand positions).

When seated your weight should be fairly evenly distributed through your hands and seat. If you're carrying too much weight on your hands there are two ways of adjusting your bike to rectify this: either by raising the height of your handlebars or, if you are stretched out too much, fitting a smaller stem (talk to your local bike shop). For more guidance on adjusting your bicycle for greater comfort, see the Your Bicycle chapter.

Fungal Infections
Warm, sweaty bodies are ideal environments for fungal growth, and physical activity, combined with inadequate washing of your body and/or clothes, can lead to fungal infections. The most common are athlete's foot (tinea) between the toes or fingers, and infections on the scalp, in the groin or on the body (ringworm). You can get ringworm (which is a fungal infection, not a worm) from infected animals or other people.

To prevent fungal infections, wash frequently and dry yourself carefully. Change out of sweaty bike clothes as soon as possible.

If you do get an infection, wash the infected area at least daily with a disinfectant or medicated soap and water, and rinse and dry well. Apply an antifungal cream or powder like tolnaftate. Expose the infected area to air or sunlight as much as possible, avoid artificial fibres and wash all towels and underwear in hot water, change them often and let them dry in the sun.

Staying Warm
Except on extremely hot days, put on another layer of clothing when you stop cycling – even if it's just for a quick break. Staying warm when cycling is as important as keeping up your water and food intake. Particularly in wet or sweaty clothing, your body cools down quickly after you stop working. Muscle strains occur more easily when your body is chilled and hypothermia can result from prolonged exposure (for prevention and treatment, see Hypothermia later in this chapter). Staying rugged up will help prevent picking up chest infections, colds and the flu.

It's not advisable to cycle at high altitude during winter; however, you can get caught suddenly in bad weather at any time of year, especially in the mountains. No matter when you go, always be prepared with warm clothing and a waterproof layer. Protect yourself from the wind on long downhill stretches – even stuffing a few sheets of newspaper under your shirt cuts the chill considerably.

Medical Problems & Treatment

ENVIRONMENTAL HAZARDS
Sun
You can get sunburnt quite quickly, even on cool or cloudy days, especially during spring and summer and at higher altitudes.

Take sun protection seriously – unless you want to be fried and increase your chances of heatstroke and skin cancer:

- Cover yourself wherever possible: wear a long-sleeved top with a collar, and a peaked helmet cover – you may want to go the extra step and add a 'legionnaire's flap' to your helmet to protect the back of your neck and ears. Make sure your shirt is sunproof: very thin or loosely woven fabrics still let sun through. Some fabrics are designed to offer high sun protection.
- Use high protection sunscreen (30+ or higher). Choose a water-resistant 'sports' sunscreen and reapply every few hours as you sweat it off. Don't forget to protect your neck, ears, hands, and feet if wearing sandals. Zinc cream is good for sensitive noses, lips and ears.
- Wear good sunglasses; they will also protect you from wind, dust and insects and are essential protection against sticks and flying objects if you're mountain biking.
- Sit in the shade during rest breaks.
- Wear a wide-brimmed hat when off the bike.

Mild sunburn can be treated with calamine lotion, aloe vera or sting-relief spray.

Heat
Treat heat with respect. France is temperate but can get very hot in the south in summer, so don't set yourself a demanding touring schedule as soon as your arrive; take things lightly until you acclimatise.

Dehydration & Heat Exhaustion Dehydration is a potentially dangerous and easily preventable condition caused by excessive fluid loss. Sweating and inadequate fluid intake are common causes of dehydration in cyclists, but others include diarrhoea, vomiting and high fever – see Diarrhoea later in this chapter for details on appropriate treatment in these circumstances.

The first symptoms are weakness, thirst and passing small amounts of very concentrated urine. This may progress to drowsiness, dizziness or fainting when standing up and, finally, coma.

It's easy to forget how much fluid you are losing via perspiration while you are cycling, particularly if a strong breeze is drying your skin quickly. Make sure you drink sufficient liquids (see Hydration earlier in this chapter). Refrain from drinking too many caffeinated drinks such as coffee, tea and some soft drinks (which act as a diuretic, causing your body to lose water through urination) throughout the day; don't use them as a water replacement.

Dehydration and salt deficiency can cause heat exhaustion. Salt deficiency is characterised by fatigue, lethargy, headaches, giddiness and muscle cramps; salt tablets may help, but adding extra salt to your food is probably sufficient.

If one of your party suffers from heat exhaustion, lie the casualty down in a shady spot and encourage them to drink slowly but frequently. If possible, seek medical advice.

Heatstroke This serious and occasionally fatal condition can occur if the body's heat-regulating mechanism breaks down and the body temperature rises to dangerous levels. Continuous periods of exposure to high temperatures and insufficient fluids can leave you vulnerable to heatstroke.

The symptoms are feeling unwell, not sweating very much (or at all) and a high body temperature (39°C to 41°C or 102°F to 106°F). Where sweating has ceased, the skin becomes flushed and red. Severe, throbbing headaches and lack of coordination will also occur, and the sufferer may be confused or aggressive. Eventually the victim will become delirious or convulse.

Hospitalisation is essential, but in the interim get the casualty out of the sun, remove their clothing, cover them with a wet sheet or towel and then fan continuously. Give them plenty of fluids (cool water), if conscious.

Cold
Hypothermia This is a real danger in France's mountains because of the changeable weather.

Hypothermia occurs when the body loses heat faster than it can produce it and the core temperature of the body falls. It is surprisingly easy to progress from very cold to dangerously cold due to a combination of wind, wet clothing, fatigue and hunger, even if the air temperature is above freezing.

Symptoms of hypothermia are exhaustion, numb skin (particularly toes and fingers), shivering, slurred speech, irrational or violent behaviour, lethargy, stumbling, dizzy spells, muscle cramps and powerful bursts of energy. Irrationality may take the form of sufferers claiming they are warm and trying to take off their clothes.

To prevent hypothermia, dress in layers (see Clothing under What to Bring in the Facts for the Cyclist chapter). A strong, waterproof outer layer is essential. Protect yourself against wind, particularly for long descents. Eat plenty of high-energy food when it's cold; it's important to keep drinking too – even though you may not feel like it.

To treat mild hypothermia, first get the person out of the wind and/or rain, remove wet clothing and replace it with dry, warm clothing. Give them hot liquids – not alcohol – and some high-kilojoule, easily digestible food. Do not rub victims: instead, allow them to slowly warm themselves. This should be enough to treat the early stages of hypothermia; however, medical treatment should still be sought, urgently if the hypothermia is severe. Early recognition and treatment of mild hypothermia is the only way to prevent severe hypothermia, which is a critical condition.

Hay Fever
If you suffer from hay fever, bring your usual treatment, as the pollen count in the Loire Valley and southern France (Périgord, Quercy, Provence and Corsica) is very high in May and June.

INFECTIOUS DISEASES
Diarrhoea
Simple things like a change of water, food or climate can cause a mild bout of diarrhoea, but a few rushed toilet trips with no other symptoms are not indicative of a

major problem. More serious diarrhoea is caused by infectious agents transmitted by faecal contamination of food or water, by using contaminated utensils or directly from one person's hand to another. Paying particular attention to personal hygiene, drinking purified water and taking care of what you eat are important measures to take to avoid getting diarrhoea while touring.

Dehydration is the main danger with any diarrhoea, particularly in children or the elderly, as it can occur quickly. Under all circumstances, the most important thing is to replace fluids (at least equal to the volume being lost). Urine is the best guide to this – if you have small amounts of dark-coloured urine, you need to drink more. Weak black tea with a little sugar, soda water, or soft drinks allowed to go flat and diluted 50% with clean water are all good. With severe diarrhoea it's better to use a re-hydrating solution to replace lost minerals and salts. Commercially available oral re-hydration salts should be added to boiled or bottled water. In an emergency, make a solution of six teaspoons of sugar and a half teaspoon of salt in a litre of boiled or bottled water. Keep drinking small amounts often. Stick to a bland diet as you recover.

Gut-paralysing drugs such as diphenoxylate or loperamide can be used to bring relief from the symptoms, although they do not actually cure the problem. Only use these drugs if you do not have access to toilets, that is, if you *must* travel. These drugs are not recommended for children under 12 years of age, or if you have a high fever or are severely dehydrated.

Seek medical advice if you pass blood or mucus, are feverish or suffer persistent or severe diarrhoea.

Another cause of persistent diarrhoea in travellers is giardiasis.

Giardiasis

This intestinal disorder is contracted by drinking water contaminated with the Giardia parasite. The symptoms are stomach cramps, nausea, a bloated stomach, watery and foul-smelling diarrhoea, and frequent gas. Giardiasis can appear several weeks after you have been exposed to the parasite. The symptoms may disappear for a few days and then return; this can go on for several weeks. Seek medical advice if you think you have giardiasis but, where this is not possible, tinidazole or metronidazole are the recommended drugs. Treatment is a 2g single dose of tinidazole or 250mg of metronidazole three times daily for five to 10 days.

Rabies

Rabies is a fatal viral infection, but is rare in France. It is contracted by being bitten by an infected animal, which could be a dog, pig, cat, fox or bat: their salvia is infectious. Once symptoms have appeared, death is inevitable, but the onset of symptoms can be prevented by a course of injections with the rabies vaccine, which you will need irrespective of whether or not you have been immunised previously.

Tetanus

This disease is caused by a germ that lives in soil and in the faeces of horses and other animals. It enters the body via breaks in the skin. The first symptom may be discomfort in swallowing, or stiffening of the jaw and neck; this is followed by painful convulsions of the jaw and whole body. The disease can be fatal. It can be prevented by vaccination.

BITES & STINGS
Dogs & Pigs

You're bound to encounter barking dogs while riding in France, and some are likely to be untethered. In regions such as Corsica

---

Pharmacies

French pharmacies are easily recognisable by a green cross. *Pharmaciens* (pharmacists) can often suggest treatments for minor ailments and can administer basic first aid.

French pharmacies coordinate their days and hours of closure so that a town or district isn't left without a place to buy medication. Details on the nearest *pharmacie de garde* (pharmacy on weekend/night duty), will be posted on the door of any pharmacy.

If you are prescribed medication, make sure you understand the dosage, and how often and when you should take it. It's a good idea to ask for a copy of the *ordonnance* (prescription) for your records.

and the Pyrenees you're also likely to come across pigs by the side of the road, emboldened by tourists feeding them. As rabies exists in France (see Infectious Diseases), all dogs and pigs should be regarded as dangerous, and preventative action taken to avoid them. Ride through their territory quickly and, for dogs, try shouting an assertive *'Coucher!'* (Lie Down!). A squirt from the water bottle or tap with the bike pump may provide added deterrent if the animal won't take the hint – though use the pump as a last resort, especially if the owner is in sight.

Bees & Wasps

These are usually painful rather than dangerous. However, anyone allergic to these can suffer severe breathing difficulties and will need medical care.

Calamine lotion or a commercial sting relief spray will ease discomfort, and ice packs will reduce the pain and swelling. Antihistamines can also help.

Snakes

A bite by any of the adders or vipers in France is unlikely to be fatal. Even so, if bitten, wrap the bitten limb tightly, as you would for a sprained ankle, and immobilise it with a splint. Keep the victim still and seek medical assistance; it will help if you can describe the offending reptile. Tourniquets and sucking out the poison are now totally discredited treatments.

WOMEN'S HEALTH

Cycle touring is not hazardous to your health, but women's health issues are relevant wherever you go, and can be a bit more tricky to cope with when you are on the road.

If you experience low energy and/or abdominal or back pain during menstruation, it may be best to undertake less strenuous rides or schedule a rest day or two at this time.

Gynaecological Problems

If you have a vaginal discharge that is not normal for you with or without any other symptoms, you've probably got an infection.

- If you've had thrush (vaginal candidiasis) before and think you have it again, it's worth self-treating for this (see the following section).
- If not, get medical advice, as you will need a laboratory test and an appropriate course of treatment.

- It's best not to self-medicate with antibiotics because there are many causes of vaginal discharge, which can only be differentiated with a laboratory test.

Thrush (Vaginal Candidiasis) Symptoms of this common yeast infection are itching and discomfort in the genital area, often in association with thick white vaginal discharge (said to resemble cottage cheese). Many factors, including diet, pregnancy, medications and hot climatic conditions can trigger this infection.

You can help prevent thrush by wearing cotton underwear off the bike and loose-fitting bicycle shorts; maintaining good personal hygiene is particularly important when wearing cycling knicks. It's a good idea to wash regularly, but don't use soap, which can increase the chance of thrush occurring. Washing gently with a solution of 1tspn salt dissolved in 1L warm water can relieve the itching. If you have thrush a single dose of an antifungal pessary (vaginal tablet), such as 500mg of clotrimazole is an effective treatment. Alternatively, you can use an antifungal cream inserted high in the vagina (on a tampon). A vaginal acidifying gel may help prevent recurrences.

If you're stuck in a remote area without medication, you could use natural yoghurt (applied directly to the vulva or on a tampon and inserted in the vagina) to soothe and help restore the normal balance of organisms in the vagina.

Avoid yeasty products such as bread and beer, and eat yoghurt made with acidophilus culture.

Urinary Tract Infection

Cystitis, or inflammation of the bladder, is a common condition in women. Symptoms include burning when urinating and having to urinate urgently and frequently. Blood can sometimes be passed in urine.

If you think you have cystitis:

- Drink plenty of fluids to help flush the infection out; citrus fruit juice or cranberry juice can help relieve symptoms.
- Take a nonprescription cystitis remedy to help relieve the discomfort. Alternatively, add a teaspoon of bicarbonate of soda to one glass of water when symptoms first appear.
- If there's no improvement after 24 hours despite these measures, seek medical advice because a course of antibiotics may be needed.

TRAUMATIC INJURIES

Although we give guidance on basic first-aid procedures here remember that, unless you're an experienced first aider and confident in what you're doing, it's possible to do more harm than good. Always seek medical help if it is available, but if you are far from any help, follow these guidelines.

Cuts & Other Wounds

Here's what to do if you suffer a fall while riding and end up with road-rash (grazing) and a few minor cuts. If you're riding in a hot, humid climate or intend continuing on your way, there's likely to be a high risk of infection, so the wound needs to be cleaned and dressed. Carry a few antiseptic wipes in your first-aid kit to use as an immediate measure, especially if no clean water is available. Small wounds can be cleaned with an antiseptic wipe (only wipe across

---

Bleeding Wounds

Most cuts will stop bleeding on their own, but if a blood vessel of any size has been cut it may continue bleeding for some time. Wounds to the head, hands and at joint creases tend to be particularly bloody.

To stop bleeding from a wound:

• Wear gloves if you are dealing with a wound on another person.
• Lie the casualty down if possible.
• Raise the injured limb above the level of the casualty's heart.
• Use your fingers or the palm of your hand to apply direct pressure to the wound, preferably over a sterile dressing or clean pad.
• Apply steady pressure for at least five minutes before looking to see if the bleeding has stopped.
• Put a sterile dressing over the original pad (don't move this) and bandage it in place.
• Check the bandage regularly in case bleeding restarts.

Never use a tourniquet to stop bleeding as this may cause gangrene – the only situation in which this may be appropriate is if the limb has been amputated.

---

the wound once with each). Deep or dirty wounds need to be cleaned thoroughly:

• Clean your hands before you start.
• Wear gloves if you are cleaning somebody else's wound.
• Use bottled or boiled water (allowed to cool) or an antiseptic solution like povidone-iodine
• Use plenty of water – pour it on the wound from a container.
• Embedded dirt and other particles can be removed with tweezers or flushed out using a syringe to squirt water (you can get more pressure if you use a needle as well) – this is especially effective for removing gravel.
• Dry wounds heal best, so avoid using antiseptic creams that keep the wound moist; instead apply antiseptic powder or spray.
• Dry the wound with clean gauze before applying a dressing – alternatively, any clean material will do as long as it's not fluffy (avoid cotton wool), because it will stick.

Any break in the skin makes you vulnerable to tetanus infection – if you didn't have a tetanus injection before you left, get one now

A dressing will protect the wound from dirt, dust and flies. Alternatively, if the wound is small and you are confident you can keep it clean, leave it uncovered. Change the dressing regularly (once a day to start with), especially if the wound is oozing, and watch for signs of infection.

If you have any swelling around the wound, raising the affected limb can help the swelling settle and the wound to heal.

It's best to seek medical advice for any wound that fails to heal after a week or so

Major Accident

Crashing or being hit by an inattentive driver in a motor vehicle is always possible when cycling. When a major accident does occur what you do is determined to some extent by the circumstances you are in and how readily available medical care is. However, remember that emergency services may be different from what you're used to at home And, as anywhere, if you are outside a major town they may be much slower at responding to a call, so you need to be prepared to do at least an initial assessment and to ensure that the casualty comes to no further harm. First of all, check for danger to yourself. If the casualty is on the road ensure oncoming traffic is stopped or diverted around you. A basic plan of action is:

* Keep calm and think through what you need to do and when.
* Get medical help urgently; send someone to phone ☎ 15.
* Carefully look over the casualty in the position in which you found them (unless this is hazardous for some reason, eg, on a cliff edge).
* Call out to the casualty to see if there is any response.
* Check for pulse (at the wrist or on the side of the neck), breathing and major blood loss.
* If necessary (ie, no breathing or no pulse), and you know how, start resuscitation.
* Check the casualty for injuries, moving them as little as possible; ask them where they have pain if they are conscious.
* Don't move the casualty if a spinal injury is possible.
* Take immediate steps to control any obvious bleeding by applying direct pressure to the wound.
* Make the casualty as comfortable as possible and reassure them.
* Keep the casualty warm by insulating them from cold or wet ground (use whatever you have to hand, such as a sleeping bag).

Safety on the Ride

ROAD RULES
French road rules, are outlined in the 'Code de la Route' (Road Code). The code is essentially for motor vehicles, but there is a section that relates to cyclists. General rules are:

* Ride on the right side of the road.
* Ride in single file, and always keep to the extreme right, unless you are turning left or passing.
* Obey all traffic lights and road signs, and use hand signals to indicate turns.
* Never ride the wrong way down a one-way street.
* Always yield to pedestrians.
* Do not ride on the footpath unless there is road construction or cobblestones, in which case you must ride slowly and give priority to pedestrians.
* Keep a suitable distance from parked cars.

For a list of commonly seen road signs, see the Language chapter.

Priorité à Droite (Priority to the Right)
The most confusing (and dangerous) traffic law in France is the notorious 'priority to the right' rule, under which any car entering an intersection (including a T-junction) from a road on your right has right-of-way no matter how small the road it's coming from. Basically, this means cyclists must yield to all vehicles approaching from the right, unless the traffic on your right has a stop or yield sign or you are on a priority road.

A yellow diamond edged with white indicates a priority (usually major) road; adjoining (small) roads are marked with stop and give-way signs. However, still watch for traffic entering from your right, in case they ignore the rules.

Rond Points (Roundabouts)
Roundabouts (traffic circles) are probably the least 'bicycle-friendly' thing you'll encounter on French roads. French road engineers love them; they're everywhere.

At most larger roundabouts, priorité à droite has been suspended so the cars already in the roundabout have right of way. This circumstance is indicated by signs reading either *'vous n'avez pas la priorité'* (you do not have right of way) or *'cédez le passage'* (give way), or by yield signs displaying a circle made out of three curved arrows.

As a cyclist, use extreme caution. Enter the roundabout and move left to allow enough room for cars to exit (if you are not taking the first exit). When you approach your exit indicate with a right hand turn signal to let cars know you are exiting.

Road Use
Cyclists may use all roads except autoroutes ('A' roads) or roads parallelled by a compulsory bike path. A round blue sign with a white bicycle symbol indicates a *piste cyclable* (bicycle path). You are obliged to use it, especially if it is signed with the word *obligatoire* (compulsory). The end of a piste cyclable is indicated by the same sign, with a red line through it.

In Paris and other large cities, you will often see a bus lane with the bicycle sign, or the bicycle symbol painted on the roadway; if this is the case, the bus lane doubles as a bike lane. If there is no indication for bicycles, the bus lane is restricted to buses and taxis only.

BICYCLE EQUIPMENT

French law mandates that bicycles must have two functioning brakes, a bell (audible for 50m), a red reflector on the back and yellow ones on the pedals. After sunset and when visibility is poor, cyclists must turn on a white light at the front and a red one at the rear.

The name and address of the bicycle's owner are supposed to appear on a metal plate which should be attached to the front of the bike.

Tips for Better Cycling

These tips on riding technique are designed to help you ride more safely, comfortably and efficiently:

- Ride in bike lanes if they exist.
- Ride about 1m from the edge of the kerb or from parked cars; riding too close to the road edge makes you less visible and more vulnerable to rough surfaces or car doors being opened without warning.
- Stay alert: especially on busy, narrow, winding and hilly roads it's essential to constantly scan ahead and anticipate the movements of other vehicles, cyclists, pedestrians or animals. Keep an eye out for potholes and other hazards as well.
- Keep your upper body relaxed, even when you are climbing.
- Ride a straight line and don't weave across the road when you reach for your water bottle or when climbing.
- To negotiate rough surfaces and bumps, take your weight off the saddle and let your legs absorb the shock, with the pedals level (in the three and nine o'clock positions).

At Night

- Only ride at night if your bike is equipped with a front and rear light; consider also using a reflective vest and/or reflective ankle bands.

Braking

- Apply front and rear brakes evenly.
- When your bike is fully loaded you'll find that you can apply the front brake quite hard and the extra weight will prevent you doing an 'endo' (flipping over the handlebars).
- In wet weather gently apply the brakes occasionally to dry the brake pads.

Climbing

- When climbing out of the saddle, keep the bike steady; rock the handlebars from side to side as little as possible.
- Change down to your low gears to keep your legs 'spinning'.

Cornering

- Loaded bikes are prone to sliding on corners; approach corners slowly and don't lean into the corner as hard as you normally would.
- If traffic permits, take a straight path across corners; hit the corner wide, cut across the apex and ride out of it wide – but never cross the dividing line on the road.
- Apply the brakes before the corner, not while cornering (especially if it's wet).

Descending

- Stay relaxed, don't cramp up and let your body go with the bike.
- A loaded bike is more likely to wobble and be harder to control at speed, so take it easy.
- Pump the brakes to shed speed rather than applying constant pressure; this avoids overheating the rims, which can cause your tyre to blow.

Helmets & Visible Clothing

Although helmets are not compulsory in France, we recommend you wear one. Make sure it fits properly: it should sit squarely on your head with the front low on your brow to protect your forehead. It should be snug, but not tight, once it has been fastened, and there should be no slack in the straps. If it has been in a crash, replace it.

Whether it is day or night, it is always a good idea to wear brightly coloured clothing, and at night garments with reflective strips.

Tips for Better Cycling

Gravel Roads

- Avoid patches of deep gravel (often on the road's edge); if you can't, ride hard, as you do if driving a car through mud.
- Look ahead to plan your course; avoid sudden turning and take it slowly on descents.
- Brake in a straight line using your rear brake and place your weight over the front wheel if you need to use that brake.
- On loose gravel, loosen your toe-clip straps or clipless pedals so you can put your foot down quickly.

Group Riding

- If you're riding in a group, keep your actions predictable and let others know, with a hand signal or shout, before you brake, turn, dodge potholes etc.
- Ride beside, in front or behind fellow cyclists. Don't overlap wheels; if either of you moves sideways suddenly it's likely both of you will fall.
- Ride in single file on busy, narrow or winding roads.

'TRAINER WHEELS' WISH I'D THOUGHT OF THEM AGES AGO!

DON HATCHER

In Traffic

- Obey the rules of the road, and signal if you are turning.
- Look at the wheels to see if a car at a T-junction or joining the road is actually moving or not.
- Scan for trouble: look inside the back windows of parked cars for movement – that person inside may open the door on you.
- Look drivers in the eye; make sure they've seen you.
- Learn to bunny hop your bike (yes, it can be done with a fully loaded touring bike; just not as well) – it'll save you hitting potholes and other hazards.

In the Wet

- Be aware that you'll take longer to slow down with wet rims; exercise appropriate caution.
- When descending apply the brakes lightly to keep the rims free of grit/water etc and allow for quicker stopping.
- Don't climb out of the saddle (unless you want a change); shift down a gear or two and climb seated.

On Bikepaths

- Use a bell or call out to warn others of your approach on bikepaths.

Do not hesitate to use your bell or voice to make your presence felt.

RIDING OFF-ROAD

Some mountain bike (VTT) rides are suggested in Things to See & Do sections under town headings throughout the book. Although most rides are not far from civilisation, you should always remember one of the first rules about VTT riding: never go alone. It's not uncommon for people to go missing, either through injury or after losing their way. It's best, if possible, to go in a small group – four is usually considered the minimum number. This way, if someone in the group has an accident or is taken ill, one person can stay with the casualty and the others can go for help.

Always tell someone where you are going and when you intend to be back – and make sure they know that you're back! Take warm clothing, matches and enough food and water in case of emergency. Carry enough tools with you so that you can undertake any emergency bicycle repairs (see the Your Bicycle chapter for advice on a basic tool kit).

Carry a map and take note of your surroundings as you ride (terrain, landmarks, intersections and so on) so if you do get lost, you're more likely to find your way again. If you get really lost, stay calm and stop. Try to work out where you are or how to retrace your route. If you can't, or it's getting dark, find a nearby open area, put on warm clothes and find or make a shelter. Light a fire for warmth and assist searchers by making as many obvious signs as you can (such as creating smoke, displaying brightly coloured items, or making symbols out of wood or rocks).

EMERGENCY PROCEDURE

If you or one of your group has an accident (even a minor one), or falls ill during your travels, you'll need to decide on the best course of action, which isn't always easy. Obviously, you will need to consider your individual circumstances, including where you are and whether you have some means of direct communication with emergency

services, such as a mobile phone (cell phone). Some basic guidelines are:

- Use your first-aid knowledge and experience, as well as the information in this guide if necessary, to make a medical assessment of the situation.
- For groups of several people, the accepted procedure is to leave one person with the casualty, together with as much equipment, food and water as you can sensibly spare, and for the rest of the group to go for help.
- If there are only two of you, the situation is more tricky; you will have to make an individual judgement of the best course of action.
- If you leave someone, mark their position carefully on the map (take it with you); you should also make sure they can be easily found by marking the position with something conspicuous, such as bright clothing or a large stone cross on the ground. Leave the person with warm clothes, shelter, food, water, matches and a torch (flashlight).
- Try attracting attention by using a whistle or torch, lighting a smoky fire (use damp wood or green leaves) or waving bright clothing; shouting is tiring and not very effective.

The uncertainties associated with emergency rescue in remote wilderness areas should make it clear how important careful planning and safety precautions are, especially if you are travelling in a small group.

Emergency Numbers

The following toll-free emergency numbers can be dialled from any public phone without inserting a *télécarte* (phonecard) or coins:

SAMU medical treatment/ ambulance	☎ 15
Police	☎ 17
Fire	☎ 18

SAMU, Service d'Aide Médicale d'Urgence (Emergency Medical Aid Service), is a 24-hour service. There is usually someone on duty who speaks English.

If there is an accident, give the dispatcher all the details, including where you are, how many people are injured, and the injuries.

YOUR
BICYCLE

Fundamental to any cycle tour you plan is the bicycle. In this chapter we look at choosing a bicycle and accessories, setting it up for your needs, learning basic maintenance, and loading and carrying your gear. In short, everything you need to gear up and get going.

CHOOSING & SETTING UP A BICYCLE

The ideal bike for cycle touring is (strangely enough) a touring bike. These bikes look similar to road bikes but generally have relaxed frame geometry for comfort and predictable steering; fittings (eyelets and brazed-on bosses) to mount panniers and mudguards; wider rims and tyres; strong wheels (at least 36 spokes) to carry the extra load; and gearing capable of riding up a wall (triple chainrings and a wide-range freewheel to match). If you want to buy a touring bike, most tend to be custom-built these days, but Cannondale (🖳 www.cannondale.com) and Trek (🖳 www.trekbikes.com) both offer a range of models.

Of course you can tour on any bike you choose, but few will match the advantages of the workhorse touring bike.

Mountain bikes are a slight compromise by comparison, but are very popular for touring. A mountain bike already has the gearing needed for touring and offers a more upright, comfortable position on the bike. And with a change of tyres (to those with semi-slick tread) you'll be able to reduce the rolling resistance and travel at higher speeds with less effort.

Hybrid, or cross, bikes are similar to mountain bikes (and therefore offer similar advantages and disadvantages), although they typically already come equipped with semi-slick tyres.

Racing bikes are less appropriate: their tighter frame geometry is less comfortable on rough roads and long rides. It is also difficult to fit wider tyres, mudguards, racks and panniers to a road bike. Perhaps more significantly, most racing bikes have a distinct lack of low gears.

Tyres Unless you know you'll be on good, sealed roads the whole time, it's probably safest to choose a tyre with some tread. If you have 700c or 27-inch wheels, opt for a tyre that's 28–35mm wide. If touring on a mountain bike, the first thing to do is get rid of the knobby tyres – too much rolling resistance. Instead, fit 1–1½ inch semi-slick tyres or, if riding unpaved roads or off-road occasionally, a combination pattern tyre (slick centre and knobs on the outside).

To protect your tubes, consider buying tyres reinforced with Kevlar, a tightly woven synthetic fibre very resistant to sharp objects. Although more expensive, Kevlar-belted tyres are worth it.

Pedals Cycling efficiency is vastly improved by using toe clips, and even more so with clipless pedals and cleated shoes. Mountain bike or touring shoes are best – the cleats are recessed and the soles are flexible enough to comfortably walk in.

 Fold & Go Bikes

Another option is a folding bike. Manufacturers include: Brompton (🖳 www.phoenixcycles.com), Bike Friday (🖳 www.bikefriday.com), Slingshot (🖳 www.slingshotbikes.com), Birdie (🖳 www.whooper.demon.co.uk) and Moulton (🖳 www.alexmoulton.co.uk). All make high-quality touring bikes that fold up to allow hassle-free train, plane or bus transfers. The Moulton, Birdie, Brompton and Slingshot come with suspension and the Bike Friday's case doubles as a trailer for your luggage when touring.

Touring Bike

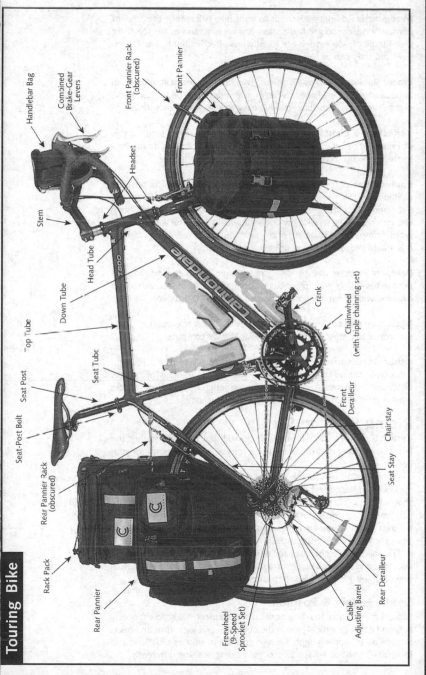

Handlebar Bag

Combined
Brake-Gear
Levers

Front Pannier Rack
(obscured)

Front Pannier

Stem

Headset

Head Tube

Down Tube

Top Tube

Seat Tube

Seat Post

Seat-Post Bolt

Rear Pannier Rack
(obscured)

Rack Pack

Rear Pannier

Freewheel
(9-Speed
Sprocket Set)

Cable
Adjusting Barrel

Rear Derailleur

Seat Stay

Chainstay

Front
Derailleur

Crank

Chainwheel
(with triple chainring set)

Mudguards Adding mudguards to your bike will reduce the amount of muddy water and grit that sprays you when it rains or the roads are wet. Plastic clip-on models are slightly less effective but not as expensive, and they can be less hassle.

Water Bottles & Cages Fit at least two bottle cages to your bike – in isolated areas you may need to carry more water than this. Water 'backpacks', such as a Camelbak, make it easy to keep your fluids up.

Reflectors & Lights If riding at night, add reflectors and lights so you can see, and others can see you. A small headlight can also double as a torch (flashlight). Flashing tail-lights are cheap and effective.

Pannier Racks It's worth buying good pannier racks. The best are aluminium racks made by Blackburn. They're also the most expensive, but come with a lifetime guarantee. Front racks come in low-mounting and mountain bike styles. Low-mounting racks carry the weight lower, which improves the handling of the bike, but if you're touring off-road it is a better idea to carry your gear a bit higher.

Panniers Panniers (see pp104-6) range from cheap-and-nasty to expensive top-quality waterproof bags. Get panniers that fit securely to your rack and watch that the pockets don't swing into your spokes.

Cycle Computer Directions for rides in this book rely upon accurate distance readings, so you'll need a reliable cycle computer.

Other Accessories A good pump is essential. Make sure it fits your valve type (see p94). Some clip on to your bicycle frame, while others fit 'inside' the frame. Also carry a lock. Although heavy, U- or D-locks are the most secure; cable locks can be more versatile.

Riding Position Set Up

Cycling is meant to be a pleasurable pursuit, but that isn't likely if the bike you're riding isn't the correct size for you and isn't set up for your needs.

In this section we assume your bike shop did a good job of providing you with the correct size bike (if you're borrowing a bike get a bike shop to check it is the correct size for you) and concentrate on setting you up in your ideal position and showing you how to tweak the comfort factor. If you are concerned that your bike frame is too big or small for your needs get a second opinion from another bike shop.

The following techniques for determining correct fit are based on averages and may not work for your body type. If you are an unusual size or shape get your bike shop to create your riding position.

Saddle Height & Position

Saddles are essential to riding position and comfort. If a saddle is poorly adjusted it can be a royal pain in the derriere – and legs, arms and back. In addition to saddle height, it is also possible to alter a saddle's tilt and its fore/aft position – each affects your riding position differently.

Saddle Tilt Saddles are designed to be level to the ground, taking most of the weight off your arms and back. However, since triathletes started dropping the nose of their saddles in the mid-1980s many other cyclists have followed suit without knowing why. For some body types, a slight tilt of the nose might be necessary. Be aware, however, that forward tilt will place extra strain on your arms and back. If it is tilted too far forward, chances are your saddle is too high.

Fore/Aft Position The default setting for fore/aft saddle position will allow you to run a plumb bob from the centre of your forward pedal axle to the protrusion of your knee (that bit of bone just under your knee cap).

re/Aft Position: To eck it, sit on your bike ith the pedals in the ree and nine o'clock sitions. Check the ignment with a plumb b (a weight on the d of a piece of string).

Saddle Height The simplest method of roughly determining the correct saddle height is the straight leg method. Sit on your bike wearing your cycling shoes. Line one crank up with the seat-tube and place your heel on the pedal. Adjust the saddle height until your leg is almost straight, but not straining. When you've fixed the height of your saddle pedal the cranks backwards (do it next to a wall so you can balance yourself). If you are rocking from side to side, lower the saddle slightly. Otherwise keep raising the saddle (slightly) until on the verge of rocking.

The most accurate way of determining saddle height is the Hodges Method. Developed by US cycling coach Mark Hodges after studying the position of dozens of racing cyclists, the method is also applicable to touring cyclists.

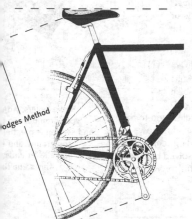

odges Method

Standing barefoot with your back against a wall and your feet 15cm apart, get a friend to measure from the greater trochanter (the bump of your hip) to the floor passing over your knee and ankle joints. Measure each leg (in mm) three times and average the figure. Multiply the average figure by 0.96.

Now add the thickness of your shoe sole and your cleats (if they aren't recessed). This total is the distance you need from the centre of your pedal axle to the top of your saddle. It is the optimum position for your body to pedal efficiently and should not be exceeded; however, people with small feet for their size should lower the saddle height slightly. The inverse applies for people with disproportionately large feet.

If you need to raise your saddle significantly do it over a few weeks so your muscles can adapt gradually. (Never raise your saddle above the maximum extension line marked on your seat post.)

Handlebars & Brake Levers

Racing cyclists lower their handlebars to cheat the wind and get a better aerodynamic position. While this might be tempting on windy days it doesn't make for comfortable touring. Ideally, the bars should be no higher than the saddle (even on mountain bikes) and certainly no lower than 75mm below it.

Pedals

For comfort and the best transference of power, the ball of your foot should be aligned over the centre of the pedal axle (see right).

If using clipless pedals consider the amount of lateral movement available. Our feet have a natural angle that they prefer when we walk, run or cycle. If they are unable to achieve this position the knee joint's alignment will be affected and serious injury may result. Most clipless pedal systems now have some rotational freedom (called 'float') built in to allow for this, but it is still important to adjust the cleats to each foot's natural angle.

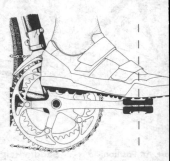

Comfort Considerations

Now that you have your optimum position on the bike, there are several components that you can adjust to increase the comfort factor.

Pedal Alignment: Th ball of your foot shou be over the centre the pedal axle f comfort and the be transfer of powe

Handlebars come in a variety of types and sizes. People with small hands may find shallow drop bars more comfortable. Handlebars also come in a variety of widths, so if they're too wide or narrow change them.

With mountain bike handlebars you really only have one hand position, so add a pair of bar-ends. On drop bars the ends should be parallel to the ground. If they're pointed up it probably means you need a longer stem; pointed down probably means you need a shorter stem.

On mountain bikes the **brake levers** should be adjusted to ensure your wrist is straight – it's the position your hand naturally sits in. For drop bars the bottom of the lever should end on the same line as the end section.

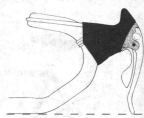

Getting the right **saddle** for you is one of the key considerations for enjoyable cycling. Everybody's sit bones are shaped and spaced differently, meaning a saddle that suits your best friend might be agony for you. A good bike shop will allow you to keep changing a new (undamaged) saddle until you get one that's perfect. Women's saddles tend to have a shorter nose and a wider seat, and men's are long and narrow.

Brake Levers: Adju your drop bars so th end section is parallel the ground and th brake lever ends this same lin

If you feel too stretched out or cramped when riding, chances are you need a different length **stem** – the problem isn't solved by moving your saddle forward/aft. Get a bike shop to assess this for you.

 Record Your Position

When you've created your ideal position, mark each part's position (scratch a line with a sharp tool like a scribe or use tape) and record it, so you can recreate it if hiring a bike or when reassembling your bike after travel. The inside back cover of this book has a place to record all this vital data.

MAINTAINING YOUR BICYCLE

If you're new to cycling or haven't previously maintained your bike, this section is for you. It won't teach you how to be a top-notch mechanic, but it will help you maintain your bike in good working order and show you how to fix the most common touring problems.

If you go mountain biking it is crucial you carry spares and a tool kit and know how to maintain your bike, because if anything goes wrong it's likely you'll be miles from anywhere when trouble strikes and face a long walk home.

If you want to know more about maintaining your bike there are dozens of books available (*Richard's Bicycle Book*, by Richard Ballantine, is a classic; if you want to know absolutely everything get *Barnett's Manual for Bicycle Maintenance* or *Sutherland's Handbook*) or inquire at your bike shop about courses in your area.

Predeparture & Daily Inspections

Before heading off on tour get your bike serviced by a bike shop or do it yourself. On tour, check over your bike every day or so (see the boxed text 'Pre-Departure & Post-Ride Checks' on p97).

Spares & Tool Kit

Touring cyclists need to be self-sufficient and should carry some spares and, at least, a basic tool kit. How many spares/tools you will need depends on the country you are touring in – in France, bike shops are common and the towns are not too spread out so you should get by with the following.

Multi-tools (see right) are very handy and a great way to save space and weight, and there are dozens of different ones on the market. Before you buy a multi-tool though, check each of the tools is usable – a chain breaker, for example, needs to have a good handle for leverage otherwise it is useless.

Adjustable spanners are often handy, but the trade-off is that they can easily burr bolts if not used correctly – be careful when using them.

The bare minimum:
☐ pump – ensure it has the correct valve fitting for your tyres (see p94)
☐ water bottles (2)
☐ spare tubes (2)
☐ tyre levers (2)
☐ chain lube and a rag
☐ puncture repair kit (check the glue is OK)
☐ Allen keys to fit your bike
☐ small Phillips screwdriver
☐ small flat screwdriver
☐ spare brake pads
☐ spare screws and bolts (for pannier racks, seat post etc) and chain links (2)

For those who know what they're doing:
☐ spoke key
☐ spare spokes and nipples (8)
☐ tools to remove freewheel
☐ chain breaker
☐ pliers
☐ spare chain links (HyperGlide chain rivet if you have a Shimano chain)
☐ spare rear brake and rear gear cables

Always handy to take along:
☐ roll of electrical/gaffer tape
☐ nylon ties (10) – various lengths/sizes
☐ hand cleaner (store it in a film canister)

Fixing a Flat

Flats happen. And if you're a believer in Murphy's Law then the likely scenario is that you'll suffer a flat just as you're rushing to the next town to catch a train or beat the setting sun.

Don't worry – this isn't a big drama. If you're prepared and know what you're doing you can be up and on your way in five minutes flat.

Being prepared means carrying a spare tube, a pump and at least two tyre levers. If you're not carrying a spare tube, of course, you can stop and fix the puncture then and there, but it's unlikely you'll catch that train and you could end up doing all this in the dark. There will be days when you have the time to fix a puncture on the side of the road, but not always. Carry at least two spare tubes.

1 Take the wheel off the bike. Remove the valve cap and unscrew the locknut (hex nut at base; see Valve Types) on Presta valves. Deflate the tyre completely, if it isn't already.

2 Make sure the tyre and tube are loose on the rim – moisture and the pressure of the inflated tube often makes the tyre and tube fuse with the rim.

3 If the tyre is really loose you should be able to remove it with your hands. Otherwise you'll need to lift one side of the tyre over the rim with the tyre levers. Pushing the tyre away from the lever as you insert it should ensure you don't pinch the tube and puncture it again.

4 When you have one side of the tyre off, you'll be able to remove the tube. Before inserting the replacement tube, carefully inspect the tyre (inside and out); you're looking for what caused the puncture. If you find anything embedded in the tyre, remove it. Also check that the rim tape is still in

 Valve Types

The two most common valve types are Presta (sometimes called French) and Schraeder (American). To inflate a Presta valve, first unscrew the round nut at the top (and do it up again after you're done); depress it to deflate. To deflate Schraeder valves depress the pin (inside the top). Ensure your pump is set up for the valve type on your bike.

Unscrew

Locknut

Presta Schraeder

place and no spoke nipples (see pp102–3) protrude through it.

5 Time to put the new tube in. Start by partially pumping up the tube (this helps prevent it twisting or being pinched) and insert the valve in the hole in the rim. Tuck the rest of the tube in under the tyre, making sure you don't twist it. Make sure the valve is straight – most Presta valves come with a locknut to help achieve this.

6 Work the tyre back onto the rim with your fingers. If this isn't possible, and again, according to Murphy's Law, it frequently isn't, you might need to use your tyre levers for the last 20–30cm. If you need to use the levers, make sure you don't pinch the new tube, otherwise it's back to Step 1. All you need to do now is pump up the tyre and put the wheel back on the bike. Don't forget to fix the pucture that night.

ixing the Puncture

 fix the puncture you'll need a repair kit, which usually comes with glue, patches, sandpaper nd, sometimes, chalk. (Always check the glue in your puncture repair kit hasn't dried up efore heading off on tour.) The only other thing you'll need is clean hands.

 The first step is to find the puncture. Inflate the tube and hold it up to your ear. If you can ear the puncture, mark it with the chalk; otherwise immerse it in water and watch for air

ubbles. Once you find the puncture, mark it,
over it with your finger and continue looking –
st in case there are more.

 Dry the tube and lightly roughen the area
ound the hole with the sandpaper. Sand an area
rger than the patch.

 Follow the instructions for the glue you have.
enerally you spread an even layer of glue over
e area of the tube to be patched and allow it to
y until it is tacky.

 Patches also come with their own instructions
 some will be just a piece of rubber and others will come lined with foil (remove the foil on
e underside but don't touch the exposed area). Press the patch firmly onto the area over
e hole and hold it for 2–3 minutes. If you want, remove the excess glue from around the
atch or dust it with chalk or simply let it dry.

 Leave the glue to set for 10–20 minutes. Inflate the tube and check the patch has worked.

Chains

Chains are dirty, greasy and all too often the most neglected piece of equipment on a bike. There are about 120 or so links in a chain and each has a simple but precise arrangement of bushes, bearings and plates. Over time all chains stretch, but if dirt gets between the bushes and bearings this 'ageing' will happen prematurely and will likely damage the teeth of your chainrings, sprockets and derailleur guide pulleys.

To prevent this, chains should be cleaned and lubed frequently (see your bike shop for the best products to use).

No matter how well you look after a chain it should be replaced regularly – about every 5000–8000km. Seek the advice of a bike shop to ensure you are buying the correct type for your drivetrain (the moving parts that combine to drive the bicycle: chain, freewheel, derailleurs, chainwheel and bottom bracket).

If you do enough cycling you'll need to replace a chain (or fix a broken chain), so here's how to use that funky-looking tool, the chain breaker.

1 Remove the chain from the chainrings – it'll make the whole process easier. Place the chain in the chain breaker (on the outer slots; it braces the link plates as the rivet is driven out) and line the pin of the chain breaker up with the rivet.

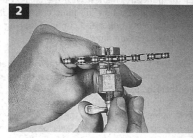

2 Wind the handle until the rivet is clear of the inner link but still held by the outer link plate.

3 Flex the chain to 'break' it. If it won't, you'll need to push the rivet out some more, but not completely – if you push it all the way out, you'll have to remove two links and replace them with two spare links. If you're removing links, you'll need to remove a male and female link (ie, two links).

4 Rejoining the chain is the reverse. If you turn the chain around when putting it on you will still have the rivet facing you. Otherwise it will be facing away from you and you'll need to change to the other side of the bike and work through the spokes.

Join the chain up by hand and place it in the breaker. Now drive the rivet in firmly, making sure it is properly lined up with the hole of the outer link plate. Stop when the rivet is almost in place.

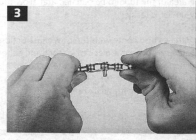

5 Move the chain to the spreaders (inner slots) of the chain breaker. Finish by winding the rivet into position carefully (check that the head of the rivet is raised the same distance above the link plate as the rivets beside it). If you've managed to get it in perfectly and the link isn't 'stiff', well done!

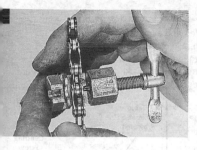

Otherwise, move the chain to the spreaders on the chain breaker and gently work the chain laterally until the link is no longer stiff.

If this doesn't work (and with some chain breakers it won't), take the chain out of the tool and place a screwdriver or Allen key between the outer plates of the stiff link and carefully lever the plates both ways. If you're too forceful you'll really break the chain, but if you're subtle it will free the link up and you'll be on your way.

 Chain Options

Check your chain, if you have a Shimano HyperGlide chain you'll need a special Hyper-Glide chain rivet to rejoin the chain. This will be supplied with your new chain, but carry a spare.

Another option is to fit a universal link to your chain. This link uses a special clip to join the chain – like the chains of old. You'll still need a chain breaker to fix a broken chain or take out spare links.

Pre Departure & Post-Ride Checks

Each day before you get on your bike and each evening after you've stopped riding, give your bike a quick once-over. Following these checks will ensure you're properly maintaining your bike and will help identify any problems before they become disasters. Go to the nearest bike shop if you don't know how to fix any problem.

Pre-Departure Check List

- brakes – are they stopping you? If not, adjust them.
- chain – if it was squeaking yesterday, it needs lube.
- panniers – are they all secured and fastened?
- cycle computer – reset your trip distance at the start.
- gears – are they changing properly? If not, adjust them.
- tyres – check your tyre pressure is correct (see the tyre's side wall for the maximum psi); inflate, if necessary.

Post-Ride Check List

- pannier racks – check all bolts/screws are tightened; do a visual check of each rack (the welds, in particular) looking for small cracks.
- headset – when stationary, apply the front brake and rock the bike gently; if there is any movement or noise, chances are the headset is loose.
- wheels – visually check the tyres for sidewall cuts/wear and any embedded objects; check the wheels are still true and no spokes are broken.
- wrench test – wrench (pull) on the saddle (if it moves, tighten the seat-post bolt and/or the seat-clamp bolt, underneath); wrench laterally on a crank (if it moves, check the bottom bracket).

Brakes

Adjusting the brakes of your bike is not complicated and even though your bike shop will use several tools to do the job, all you really need is a pair of pliers, a spanner or Allen key, and (sometimes) a friend.

Check three things before you start: the wheels are true (not buckled), the braking surface of the rims is smooth (no dirt, dents or rough patches) and the cables are not frayed.

Begin by checking that the pads strike the rim correctly: flush on the braking surface of the rim (see right and p99) and parallel to the ground.

Calliper Brakes

It's likely that you'll be able to make any minor adjustments to calliper brakes by winding the cable adjusting barrel out. If it doesn't allow enough movement you'll need to adjust the cable anchor bolt:

1 Undo the cable anchor bolt – not completely, just so the cable is free to move – and turn the cable adjusting barrel all the way in.

2 Get your friend to hold the callipers in the desired position, about 2–3mm away from the rim. Using a pair of pliers, pull the cable through until it is taut.

3 Before you tighten the cable anchor bolt again, check to see if the brake lever is in its normal position (not slack as if somebody was applying it) – sometimes they jam open. Also, ensure the brake quick-release (use it when you're removing your wheel or in an emergency to open the callipers if your wheel is badly buckled) is closed.

4 Tighten the cable anchor bolt again. Make any fine-tuning to the brakes by winding the cable adjusting barrel out.

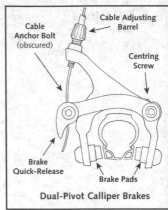

Cable
Anchor Bolt
(obscured)

Cable Adjusting
Barrel

Centring
Screw

Brake
Quick-Release

Brake Pads

Dual-Pivot Calliper Brakes

 Brake Cables

If your brakes are particularly hard to apply, you may need to replace the cables. Moisture can cause the cable and housing (outer casing) to bond or stick. If this happens it's often possible to prolong the life of a cable by removing it from the housing and applying a coating of grease (or chain lube) to it.

If you do need to replace the cable, take your bike to a bike shop and get the staff to fit and/or supply the new cable. Cables come in two sizes – rear (long) and front (short) – various thicknesses and with different types of nipples.

Cantilever Brakes

These days most touring bikes have cantilever rather than calliper brakes. The newest generation of cantilever brakes (V-brakes) are more powerful and better suited to stopping bikes with heavy loads.

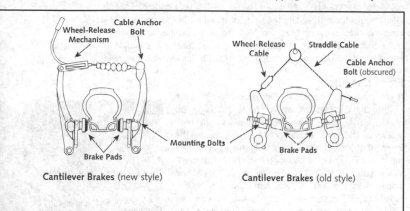

Cantilever Brakes (new style)

Cantilever Brakes (old style)

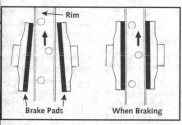

Cantilever Brake Toe-In: This is how the brake pads should strike the rim (from above) with correct toe-in.

On cantilever brakes ensure the leading edge of the brake pad hits the rim first (see left). This is called toe-in; it makes the brakes more efficient and prevents squealing. To adjust the toe-in on cantilever brakes, loosen the brake pad's mounting bolt (using a 10mm spanner and 5mm Allen key). Wiggle the brake pad into position and tighten the bolt again.

If you only need to make a minor adjustment to the distance of the pads from the rim, chances are you will be able to do it by winding the cable adjusting barrel out (located near the brake lever on mountain bikes and hybrids). If this won't do you'll need to adjust the cable anchor bolt.

1 Undo the cable anchor bolt (not completely, just so the cable is free to move) and turn the cable adjusting barrel all the way in. Depending on the style of your brakes, you may need a 10mm spanner (older bikes) or a 5mm Allen key.

2 Hold the cantilevers in the desired position (get assistance from a friend if you need to), positioning the brake pads 2–3mm away from the rim. Using a pair of pliers, pull the cable through until it is taut.

3 Before you tighten the cable anchor bolt again, check to see if the brake lever is in its normal position (not slack as if somebody was applying it) – sometimes they jam open.

4 Tighten the cable anchor bolt again. Make any fine-tuning to the brakes by winding the cable adjusting barrel out.

Gears

If the gears on your bike start playing up – the chain falls off the chainrings, it shifts slowly or not at all – it's bound to cause frustration and could damage your bike. All it takes to prevent this is a couple of simple adjustments: the first, setting the limits of travel for both derailleurs, will keep the chain on your drivetrain, and the second will ensure smooth, quick shifts from your rear derailleur. Each will take just a couple of minutes and the only tool you need is a small Phillips or flat screwdriver.

Front Derailleur

If you can't get the chain to shift onto one chainring or the chain comes off when you're shifting, you need to make some minor adjustments to the limit screws on the front derailleur. Two screws control the limits of the front derailleur's left and right movement, which governs how far the chain can shift. When you shift gears the chain is physically pushed sideways by the plates (outer and inner) of the derailleur cage. The screws are usually side by side (see photo No 1) on the top of the front derailleur. The left-hand screw (as you sit on the bike) adjusts the inside limit and the one on the right adjusts the outside limit.

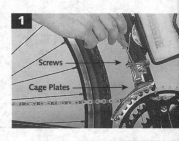

Screws
Cage Plates

Front Derailleur: Befo
making any adjustmen
remove any build-up
grit from the scre
(especially underneat
by wiping them with
rag and applying a qu
spray (or drop)
chain lub

After you make each of the following adjustments, pedal the drivetrain with your hand and change gears to ensure you've set the limit correctly. If you're satisfied, test it under strain by going for a short ride.

Outer Limits Change the gears to position the chain on the largest chainring and the smallest rear sprocket. Set the outer cage plate as close to the chain as you can without it touching. Adjust the right-hand limit screw to achieve this.

Inner Limits Position the chain on the smallest chainring and the largest rear sprocket. For chainwheels with three chainrings, position the inner cage plate between 1–2mm from the chain. If you have a chainwheel with two chainrings, position the inner cage plate as close to the chain as you can without it touching.

Rear Derailleur

If the limit screws aren't set correctly on the rear derailleur the consequences can be dire. If the chain slips off the largest sprocket it can jam between the sprocket and the spokes and could then snap the chain, break or damage spokes or even break the frame.

The limit screws are located at the back of the derailleur (see photo No 2). The top screw (marked 'H' on the derailleur) sets the derailleur's limit of travel on the smallest sprocket's (the highest gear) side of the freewheel. The bottom screw ('L') adjusts the derailleur's travel towards the largest sprocket (lowest gear).

Outer Limits Position the chain on the smallest sprocket and largest chainring (see photo No 3). The derailleur's top guide pulley (the one

Guide
Pulleys

closest to the sprockets) should be in line with the smallest sprocket; adjust the top screw ('H') to ensure it is.

Inner Limits Position the chain on the largest rear sprocket and the smallest chainring (see photo No 4). This time the guide pulley needs to be lined up with the largest sprocket; do this by adjusting the bottom screw ('L'). Make sure the chain can't move any further towards the wheel than the largest sprocket.

Cable Adjusting Barrel

If your gears are bouncing up and down your freewheel in a constant click and chatter, you need to adjust the tension of the cable to the rear derailleur. This can be achieved in a variety of ways, depending on your gear system.

The main cable adjusting barrel is on your rear derailleur (see photo No 5). Secondary cable adjusting barrels can also be found near the gear levers (newer Shimano combined brake-gear STI levers) or on the downtube of your frame (older Shimano STI levers and Campagnolo Ergopower gear systems) of some bikes. Intended for racing cyclists, they allow for fine tuning of the gears' operation while on the move.

Raise the rear wheel off the ground – have a friend hold it up by the saddle, hang it from a tree or turn the bike upside down – so you can pedal the drivetrain with your hand.

To reset your derailleur, shift gears to position the chain on the second smallest sprocket and middle chainring (see photo No 6). As you turn the crank with your hand, tighten the cable by winding the rear derailleur's cable adjusting barrel anti-clockwise. Just before the chain starts to make a noise as if to shift onto the third sprocket, stop winding.

Now pedal the drivetrain and change the gears up and down the freewheel. If things still aren't right you may find that you need to tweak the cable tension slightly: turn the cable adjusting barrel anti-clockwise if shifts to larger sprockets are slow, and clockwise if shifts to smaller sprockets hesitate.

Replacing a Spoke

Even the best purpose-made touring wheels occasionally break spokes. When this happens the wheel, which relies on the even pull of each spoke, is likely to become buckled. When it is not buckled, it is considered true.

If you've forgotten to pack spokes or you grabbed the wrong size, you can still get yourself out of a pickle if you have a spoke key. Wheels are very flexible and you can get it roughly true – enough to take you to the next bike shop – even if two or three spokes are broken.

If you break a spoke on the front wheel it is a relatively simple thing to replace the spoke and retrue the wheel. The same applies if a broken spoke is on the non-drive side (opposite side to the rear derailleur) of the rear wheel. The complication comes when you break a spoke on the drive side of the rear wheel (the most common case). In order to replace it you need to remove the freewheel, a relatively simple job in itself but one that requires a few more tools and the know-how.

If you don't have that know-how fear not, because it is possible to retrue the wheel without replacing that spoke *and* without damaging the wheel – see Truing a Wheel (below).

1 Remove the wheel from the bike. It's probably a good idea to remove the tyre and tube as well (though not essential), just to make sure the nipple is seated properly in the rim and not likely to cause a puncture.

2 Remove the broken spoke but leave the nipple in the rim (if it's not damaged; otherwise replace it). Now you need to thread the new spoke. Start by threading it through the vacant hole on the hub flange. Next lace the new spoke through the other spokes. Spokes are offset on the rim; every second one is on the same side and, generally, every fourth is laced through the other spokes the same way.

Spoke Key

3 With the spoke key, tighten the nipple until the spoke is about as taut as the other spokes on this side of the rim. Spoke nipples have four flat sides – to adjust them you'll need the correct size spoke key. Spoke keys come in two types: those made to fit one spoke gauge or several. If you have the latter, trial each size on a nipple until you find the perfect fit.

Truing a Wheel

Truing a wheel is an art form and, like all art forms, it is not something mastered overnight. If you can, practise with an old wheel before leaving home. If that's not possible – and you're on the side of the road as you read this – following these guidelines will get you back in the saddle until you can get to the next bike shop.

1 Start by turning the bike upside-down, so the wheels can turn freely. Check the tension of all the spokes on the wheel: do this by

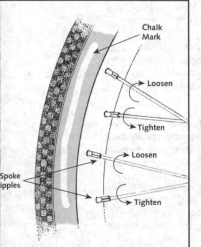

squeezing each pair of spokes on each side. Tighten those spokes that seem loose and loosen those that seem too tight. Note, though, the spokes on the drive side of the rear wheel (on the same side as the freewheel) are deliberately tighter than the non-drive side.

2 Rotate the wheel a couple of times to get an idea of the job at hand. If the wheel won't rotate, let the brakes off (see pp98–9).

3 Using the chalk from your puncture repair kit, mark all the 'bumps'. Keep the chalk in the same position (brace the chalk against the pannier rack or bike's frame) and let the bumps in the wheel 'hit' the chalk.

4 In order to get the bumps out you'll need a constant point of reference – to gauge if the bumps are being removed. Often, if it is not a severe buckle, you can use a brake pad. Position the brake pad about 2–3mm from the rim (on the side with the biggest buckle).

5 With your spoke key, loosen those spokes on the same side as the bump within the longest chalked area, and tighten those on the opposite side of the rim. The spokes at the start and the finish of the chalked area should only be tightened/loosened by a quarter-turn; apply a half-turn to those in between.

6 Rotate the wheel again; if you're doing it correctly the buckle should not be as great. Continue this process of tightening and loosening spokes until the bump is as near to gone as you can get it – as the bump is removed turn the nipples less (one-eighth of a turn on the ends and a quarter-turn in between). Experienced exponents can remove buckles entirely, but if you can get it almost out (1mm here or there) you've done well.

7 If the wheel has more than one bump, move onto the second-longest chalk mark next. As each bump is removed you might find it affects the previous bump slightly. In this case, remove the previous chalk mark and repeat Steps 4–6. Continue to do this until all the buckles are removed.

Don't forget to readjust the brakes.

If you've trued the wheel without replacing the broken spokes, have them replaced at the next bike shop.

Chalk Mark

Loosen

Tighten

Loosen

Spoke Nipples

Tighten

LOADING YOUR BICYCLE

If you've ever been to Asia and seen a bike loaded with boxes piled 2m high or carrying four, five or six people, plus a chicken or two, you'll realise that there are more ways to carry your gear than would otherwise seem. More realistic options for you come from a combination of front and rear panniers, a handlebar bag or trailer.

'Credit-card tourists', who are intent on travelling lighter, further and faster and who are happy to stay in hotels or hostels, can get by with a handlebar bag and/or rear panniers (see top right). The downside to this configuration is poor bike-handling; the steering feels particularly 'airy'. It's possible to adopt the 'lighter, further, faster' principle and still camp, but it means frugal packing.

If you want to be more self-sufficient or you're carrying 20kg or more, you'll probably find it easier (and your bike will handle better) with front and rear panniers. The tried-and-tested configuration that works best for a touring bike is to use four panniers: two low-mounting front panniers with two high-mounting rear panniers (see bottom right). The only other thing you might want to add is a small handlebar bag for this book, snacks, sunblock, money, camera etc.

Pannier configuration; the four-pannier system is the best way of carrying your gear and having a bike that handles well; packing light saves weight but the compromise can be poor bike handling

This combination, with a few light but bulky items on the rear rack (eg, tent, sleeping mat etc), allows you to carry a large load and still have predictable and manageable bike-handling.

If you're riding a mountain bike and riding off-road you'll probably want high-mounting front panniers to give you more clearance.

Packing Your Gear

It's frequently said that, in packing for a cycle tour, you should lay out everything you need to take and then leave half of it behind. The skill is in knowing which half to leave behind. Almost as much skill is needed in organising the gear in your panniers. Here are some tried and tested tips.

Compartmentalise Pack similar items into nylon drawstring bags (stuff sacks), to make them easier to find again (eg, underwear in one, cycling clothes in another, and even dinner food separated from breakfast food). Using different coloured stuff sacks makes choosing the right one easier.

Waterproof Even if your panniers are completely waterproof, and especially if they're not, it pays to put everything inside heavy-duty plastic bags. Check bags for holes during the trip; replace them or patch the holes with tape.

Reduce Flood Damage If your panniers are not waterproof and they pool water, you can reduce problems by putting things that are unaffected by water, say a pair of thongs, at the bottom of the bag. This keeps the other stuff above 'flood level'. Try using seam sealant on the bags' seams beforehand, too.

Load Consistently Put things in the same place each time you pack to avoid having to unpack every bag just to find one item.

Balance the Load Distribute weight evenly – generally around 60% in the rear and 40% in the front panniers – and keep it as low as possible by using low-mounting front panniers and packing heavy items first. Side-to-side balancing is just as critical.

Group Gear Pack things used at the same time in the same pannier. Night/camp things like your mat, sleeping bag and pyjamas, which you don't need during the day, could all be in the bag most difficult to access – likely to be on the same side as the side of the road you are riding on, since you will probably lean that side of the bike against a tree, pole or roadside barrier.

Put all clothing in one pannier, if possible, sorted into separate bags of cycling clothes, 'civilian' clothes, underwear, wet weather gear and dirty clothes. Keep a windproof jacket handy on top for descents.

In the Front Food and eating utensils are convenient to have in a front pannier along with a camping stove. Toiletry items, towel, first-aid kit, reading material, torch and sundry items can go in the other front bag.

In the Pockets or Bar Bag Easily accessible pockets on panniers or on your cycling shirt are useful for items likely to be needed frequently or urgently during the day, such as snacks, tool kit, sun hat or sunscreen. A handlebar bag is good for these items if your panniers don't have pockets, but remember that weight on the handlebars upsets a bike's handling.

Keep Space Spare Remember to leave some spare space for food and, if using a camping stove, for the fuel canister. Be mindful when

Another Option – Trailers

Luggage trailers are gaining in popularity and some innovative designs are now on the market. By spreading the load onto more wheels they relieve the bike and can improve rolling resistance. Their extra capacity is a boon for travelling on a tandem or with a young family. They can be combined with racks and panniers, but the hitch (point it connects with the bike) of some trailers may interfere with your panniers, so check first.

PETER HINES

Two-wheeled trailers are free standing and can take very heavy loads, including babies and toddlers. Often brightly coloured, they give a strong signal to car drivers who tend to give you a wide berth. However, their relatively wide track can catch a lot of wind and makes them ungainly on rough, narrow roads or trails.

Single-wheeled trailers such as the BOB Yak share the load with the bike's rear wheel. They track well and can be used on very rough trails and may be the easiest option for full-suspension bikes. The load capacity of these units is somewhere between that of a bike with a rear rack only and a fully loaded (four panniers plus rack-top luggage) touring bike.

packing foods that are squashable or sensitive to heat and protect or insulate them – unless you're working on a gourmet pasta sauce recipe that includes socks.

Prevent 'Internal Bleeding' Act on the premise that anything that can spill will, and transfer it to a reliable container, preferably within a watertight bag. Take care, too, in packing hard or sharp objects (tools, utensils or anything with hooks) that could rub or puncture other items, including the panniers. Knives or tools with folding working parts are desirable.

Fragile Goods Valuables and delicate equipment such as cameras are best carried in a handlebar bag, which can be easily removed when you stop. Alternatively, carry these items in a 'bum bag', which will accompany you automatically.

Rack Top Strap your tent lengthways on top of the rear rack with elastic cord looped diagonally across from front to rear and back again, and maybe across to anchor the rear end. Be sure the cord is well-tensioned and secure – deny its kamikaze impulses to plunge into the back wheel, jamming the freewheel mechanism, or worse.

What to Look for in Panniers

Panniers remain the popular choice for touring luggage. They offer flexibility, in that one, two or four can be used depending on the load to be carried and they allow luggage to be arranged for easy access.

Many people initially buy just a rear rack and panniers, and it is wise to buy the best quality you can afford at this stage. These bags will accompany you on all of your tours as well as for day-to-day shopping and commuting trips for years to come.

The attachment system should be secure, but simple to operate. That big bump you hit at 50km/h can launch a poorly designed pannier and your precious luggage.

The stiffness of the pannier backing is another concern – if it can flex far enough to reach the spokes of the wheel the result can be catastrophic. Good rack design can also help avoid this.

The fabric of the panniers should be strong and abrasion- and water-resistant. You can now buy roll-top panniers, made from laminated fabrics, that are completely waterproof. Bear in mind that these bags are only waterproof until they develop even the smallest hole, so be prepared to check them and apply patches occasionally. Canvas bags shed water well, but should be used in conjunction with a liner bag to keep things dry. Cordura is a heavy nylon fabric with excellent abrasion resistance. The fabric itself is initially waterproof, but water tends to find the seams, so using a liner bag is a good idea once again.

Pockets and compartments can help to organise your load, but the multitude of seams increase the challenge of keeping the contents dry in the wet. A couple of exterior pockets are great for sunscreen, snacks and loose change that you need throughout the day. Carrying front panniers as well as rear ones allows more opportunities to divide and organise gear.

When fitting rear panniers check for heel strike. Long feet, long cranks and short chainstays will all make it harder to get the bags and your body to fit.

Getting There & Away

AIR

Air France and numerous other airlines link Paris, and several regional airports, with every part of the globe. Many airlines offer direct flights from the USA, Canada and parts of Australasia. However, connections will more than likely be necessary during most long-haul flights. Very few direct flights go to Corsica from abroad.

Airports

For information on public transport links and cycling options between Paris' two air ports, Orly and Roissy Charles de Gaulle, see Getting There & Away in the Paris & the Île de France chapter.

Buying Tickets

If you are planning to fly with your bicycle, simply buying the cheapest ticket may not be the best option. Check each airline's bicycle policy: how much will they charge for your bicycle, and how do they require you to pack it? (See the boxed text 'Cycle friendly Airlines'.) Also consider how many connections you will have to make en route (the less the better).

Return (round-trip) tickets are usually cheaper than two one-way tickets. In some cases, the return fare may actually be less than a one-way ticket. The cheapest tickets often come with restrictions: minimum and/or maximum stays, advance reservation requirements, mandatory Saturday overnight stay, non-refundable conditions and so on.

Round-the-world (RTW) tickets make visiting several continents easy. For Australasians, they are often no more expensive than an ordinary return fare. Prices start at about UK£1000, A$1900 or US$1500. The initial departure date usually determines the fare. They're usually valid for a year.

The best way to find a cheap ticket is to shop around. Start early. Check the total fare, the stopovers allowed (or required), the duration of the journey, the period of validity, cancellation penalties and any other restrictions. The Internet allows you to shop online; many airlines offer great deals. You may decide it's worthwhile to pay a bit more than the rock-bottom fare to

book through a travel agent with whom you are familiar. Such established firms include:

Council Travel (US-based)
  🖳 www.counciltravel.com
Nouvelles Frontières (French-based)
  🖳 www.newfrontiers.com
Travel CUTS (Canadian-based)
  🖳 www.travelcuts.com
USIT (Irish-based)
  🖳 www.usit.ie
Wasteels (French- and Belgian-based)
  🖳 www.voyages-wasteels.fr
STA Travel (worldwide)
  🖳 www.sta-travel.com

Children, depending on their age, are eligible for discounted fares. Youth and senior fares may also be available.

Use the fares quoted in this book as a guide only. They are based on the rates advertised by airlines and travel agents as we went to press.

Cyclists with Special Needs

If you have any special needs – require vegetarian meals, are travelling with a baby, or need any other special assistance – let the airline know as soon as possible. Reconfirm this at least 72 hours in advance and at check in.

The UK

Several carriers operate from London and other British regional airports. A straightforward and fully flexible London-Paris ticket with British Airways, British Midland or Air France can cost as little as UK£64 to UK£74 return. Cheap tickets can be found on Easy Jet (🖳 www.easyjet.com), with fares from Luton to Nice as low as UK£39 each way. Carriers also fly to Bordeaux, Lyon, Marseille and Toulouse. Several airlines offer scheduled flights to Corsica (Bastia or Ajaccio) with one change en route.

Continental Europe

Return discount fares to Paris include Berlin (DM266), Madrid (38,000pta), and Rome (L590,000). The only direct flights to Corsica (Ajaccio) leave from Brussels: Belgian airline Sabena (Bfr15,000) has a regular service; Nouvelles Frontières has

Packing for Air Travel

We've all heard the horror stories about smashed/lost luggage when flying, but a more real threat to cycle tourists is arriving in a country for a two-week tour and finding their bike with broken wheels or in little bits spread out around the baggage carousel. Fixing a damaged bike could take days, and the delay and frustration could ruin your holiday.

How do you avoid this? Err on the side of caution and box your bike. Trust airline baggage handlers if you want (we're told some people actually do) and give your bike to them 'as is' – turn the handlebars 90°, remove the pedals, cover the chain with a rag or bag (to protect other people's baggage) and deflate your tyres (partially, not all the way) – but is it worth the risk? If you want to take that risk do it on your homeward flight, when you can get your favourite bike shop to fix any damage any time.

Some airlines sell bike boxes at the airport, but most bike shops give them away. Fitting your bike into a box requires a few simple steps and only takes about 15 minutes:

1 Loosen the stem bolt and turn the handlebars 90°; loosen the clamp bolt(s) and twist the handlebars as pictured.

2 Remove the pedals (use a 15mm spanner, turning each the opposite way to how you pedal), wheels and seat post and saddle (don't forget to mark its height before removing it).

3 Undo the rear derailleur bolt and tape it to the inside of the chainstay. There's no need to undo the derailleur cable. You can remove the chain (it will make reassembly easier) but it isn't necessary.

4 Cut up some spare cardboard and tape it beneath the chainwheel to prevent the teeth from penetrating the floor of the box and being damaged.

5 Remove the quick-release skewers from the wheels and wrap a rag (or two) around the cluster so it won't get damaged or damage anything else.

If you run your tyres at very high pressure (above 100psi), you should partially deflate them – on most bikes this won't be necessary.

6 Place the frame in the box, so it rests on the chainwheel and forks – you might want to place another couple of layers of cardboard underneath the forks.

Most boxes will be too short to allow the front pannier racks to remain on the bike; if so, remove them. The rear rack should fit while still on the bike but may require the seat stay bolts to be undone and pushed forward.

Packing for Air Travel

Side View

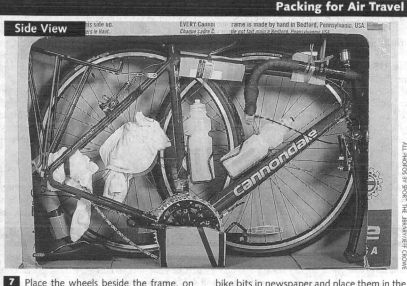

ALL PHOTOS BY SPORT: THE LIBRARY/JEFF CROWE

7 Place the wheels beside the frame, on the side opposite the chainwheel. Keep the wheels and frame separate by inserting a piece of cardboard between them and tying the wheels to the frame (to stop them moving around and scratching the frame).

8 Slot the saddle and seatpost, your helmet, tools and any other bits and pieces (eg, tent, sleeping bag) into the vacant areas. Wrap the skewers, chain and other loose bike bits in newspaper and place them in the box. Add cardboard or newspaper packing to any areas where metal is resting on metal.

9 Seal the box with tape and write your name, address and flight details on several sides.

Now all you need to do is strap your panniers together and either take them with you as carry-on luggage or check them in.

Top View

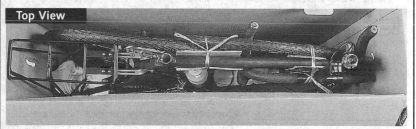

Bike Bags

If you're planning on travelling between regions via train, plane or bus then consider taking a bike bag *(housse)*. The simplest form of zippered bike bag has no padding built into it, is made of Cordura or nylon, and can be rolled up and put on your rear pannier rack and unfurled when you need to travel again.

Some of the smaller ones require you to remove both wheels, the front pannier racks, pedals and seatpost to fit inside the bag. However, these make for (relatively) easy and inconspicuous train, plane or bus transfers so the extra effort is worthwhile.

direct flights only in summer; flights from other European cities usually go via Nice. The cheapest fares are available in early spring and late autumn.

The USA & Canada

The flight options across the North Atlantic, the world's busiest long-haul air corridor, are bewildering. Major newspapers such as the *New York Times*, *LA Times*, *Chicago Tribune* and *San Francisco Chronicle* have weekly travel sections which list scores of travel agents' ads. Council Travel (☎ 800-226 8624) and STA Travel (☎ 800-777 0112) have offices in major cities nationwide.

A New York–Paris return fare should cost from US$248 to US$328 in low season or from US$550 to US$700 in high season.

Equivalent fares from the west coast are US$100 to US$200 higher.

In Canada, Travel CUTS (☎ 1888-838 CUTS) has offices in all major cities. Also scan the budget travel agents' ads in the Toronto *Globe & Mail*, the *Toronto Star* and the *Vancouver Province*.

A Montreal-Paris return ticket should start at about C$529 in low season, and in high season from C$1021; add about C$200 to C$300 for fares from Vancouver and Calgary.

No direct flights go from North America to Corsica.

Australia & New Zealand

STA Travel and Flight Centres International are major dealers in cheap air fares. The Saturday travel sections in major newspapers

---

Cycle-Friendly Airlines

Not too many airlines will carry a bike free of charge these days – at least according to their official policy. Most airlines regard the bike as part of your checked luggage. Carriers working the routes to France from Europe, Asia and Australia usually allow 20kg of checked luggage (excluding carry-on), so the weight of your bike and bags shouldn't exceed this. If you're over the limit, technically you're liable for excess-baggage charges.

Carriers flying routes to France from or through North America use a different system. Passengers are generally allowed two pieces of luggage, each of which must not exceed 32kg. Excess baggage fees are charged for additional pieces, rather than for excess weight. On some airlines a bike may be counted as one of your two pieces; others charge a set fee for carrying a bike, which may then be carried in addition to your two other pieces. Check whether these fees are paid for the whole journey, each way or per leg.

Some airlines require you to box your bike, while others accept soft covers, or just ask that you turn the handlebars, remove the pedals and cover the chain. Check this policy before getting to the airport; only a few airlines sell sturdy boxes at the check-in counter.

When we looked into the policies of different carriers, we found that not only does the story sometimes change depending on who you talk to – and how familiar they are with the company's policy – but the official line is not necessarily adhered to at the check-in counter. If a company representative or agent reassures you that your bike travels for free, ask them to annotate your passenger file to that effect. If your flight is not too crowded, the check-in staff are often lenient with the excess charges, particularly with items such as bikes.

The times when you are most likely to incur excess baggage charges are on full flights and, of course, if you inconvenience the check-in staff. If you suspect you may be over the limit, increase your chances of avoiding charges by checking in early, being well organised and being friendly and polite – a smile and a 'merci' can go a long way!

DON HATCHER

have many ads offering cheap fares to Europe. However, they are usually low-season fares on obscure airlines with strict conditions attached.

Airlines such as Thai, Qantas and Singapore have fares to Paris from about A$1700 (low season) to A$2600 (high season). Frequent promotional fares come up, so it pays to check. Flights to/from Perth are a couple of hundred dollars cheaper. Qantas also flies direct to Bordeaux, and to Corsica (Ajaccio) via Paris.

STA Travel and Flight Centres International also have offices in New Zealand. The cheapest fares to Europe are routed through Asia. Low-season fares (via Bangkok) start at about NZ$2249 return. Via the USA, fares in the low season start at NZ$3149 return.

South Africa
Return fares to Paris start at around R3400 on Swiss Air or R3950 on South Africa Airways from Capetown. Fares are often a bit cheaper from Johannesburg.

LAND
Paris, France's main rail and road hub, is linked with every part of Europe. Travel from northern Europe to other parts of France sometimes involves switching train stations in Paris. For details of train passes such as Eurail see the Getting Around chapter.

The UK
Bus The best way to get yourself and your bike across the Channel to France (and to northern Italy, northern Spain and Switzerland) is by using European Bike Express (☎ 01642-251440, fax 232209, 🖳 www .bike-express.co.uk).

It transports bikes in special trailers, and cyclists travel in a comfortable bus. All you need to do is buy your ticket and turn your handlebars! The service collects passengers from several pick-up points in England. It operates four routes, with numerous drop-off points throughout France, between May and September. France is divided into three zones from north to south; the further south you go, the more expensive the fare. A return ticket to Zone 1 (north) costs UK£149; Zone 2 (centre) UK£159; and Zone 3 (south) is UK£169. Cyclists' Touring Club (CTC) members get a UK£10 reduction, and children pay UK£25 less. These fares can be

> ### Warning
> The information in this chapter is particularly vulnerable to change: prices for international travel are volatile, routes are introduced and cancelled, schedules change, special deals come and go, and rules and visa requirements are amended.
>
> You should check directly with the airline or a travel agent to make sure you understand the conditions of your ticket. The details given in this chapter should be regarded as pointers and are not a substitute for your own careful, up-to-date research.

conveniently combined between two zones, for drop off in one and pick up in another.

Train The highly civilised Eurostar (English information line in France ☎ 08 36 35 35 39, UK 0990-186186; 🖳 www.eurostar.com) passenger train service through the Channel Tunnel operates between London's Waterloo Station and Paris' Gare du Nord. The journey takes about three hours, with frequent daily services. Passport and customs checks are usually done before boarding.

The regular 2nd-class fare on Eurostar's London-Paris service costs approximately UK£109 (1100FF) one way. More restrictive *sourire* (excursion) tickets are available, as well as fares for children and people aged under 25. Special deals are often on offer – contact Eurostar for the latest information.

In London, Eurostar tickets are available from some travel agents; many mainline train stations; and from the SNCF-owned Rail Europe (☎ 0990-300003), 179 Piccadilly, which also sells other SNCF tickets (SNCF is France's national rail service). In France, ticketing is handled by the SNCF.

Not all Eurostar trains will accept bicycles as checked baggage. On the Esprit service (☎ 08705-850850) trains with luggage carriages carry checked bicycles for a UK£25 fee. However, there is no guarantee that your bicycle will travel on the same train as you do. It's best to use a bike bag *(housse)*, which you carry onto the carriage, just as you would on a TGV (see the boxed text 'What is une Housse?' in the Getting Around chapter).

Eurotunnel (UK ☎ 01303-288680, France ☎ 08 36 35 35 39; 🖥 www.eurotunnel.com) services operate from near Folkestone to Coquelles, just west of Calais; the trip takes 35 minutes. Bicycles are carried on several services each day in specially adapted trailers. A maximum of six bicycles can be carried on any departure, so book at least 48 hours in advance. It costs UK£15 (single or return), including the bicycle.

Continental Europe

Bus The bus services to/from France are not particularly bicycle-friendly.

The major bus companies, such as Eurolines (UK ☎ 01582-404511, France ☎ 01 49 72 51 51; 🖥 www.eurolines.co.uk) and Busabout (UK ☎ 020-7950 1661, 🖥 www.busabout.com) won't carry bicycles.

Train Rail services link France with every country in Europe; schedules are available from major train stations in France and abroad. For details on the SNCF, see Train in the Getting Around chapter.

As with planes, rules for taking bikes on international trains differ from country to country, service to service and – seemingly – from conductor to conductor. In some cases, you may need to remove the wheels, pedals, turn your handlebars and carry your bicycle in a bike bag (storing it in a luggage area of the carriage). On other trains, you will have to check your bicycle, which will be loaded in a luggage car. There is also the possibility that you will have to check your bicycle, and it will not be transported on the same train as you, but will arrive within the next day or two. Verify the rules in advance (see the boxed texts 'May I take my Bike on *this* Train?' and 'What is une Housse?' in the Getting Around chapter).

Very few trains between Paris and major European cities will allow you to put your bicycle in the *fourgon* (luggage van):

from	to	price	duration
nightly:			
Paris Nord	Brussels	248FF	5 hrs
Paris Nord	Amsterdam	403FF	8½ hrs
Paris Est	Stuttgart	452FF	8 hrs
daily (summer only):			
Paris Austerlitz	Irun, Spain	409FF	7 hrs
Paris Est	Basel, Swit	298FF	6 hrs

Each of these runs has a corresponding return service to Paris. A fee is charged for bicycles carried on these trains, and you must load and unload the bicycle yourself with the train conductor attending.

The Thalys high-speed train service links Paris-Nord with Brussels-Midi (355FF, 1½ hours, 15 per day), Amsterdam CS (479FF, 4½ hours, four per day) and Cologne's Hauptbahnhof (443FF, four hours, six per day). Bicycle rules for the TGV apply (see the boxed text 'What is une Housse?' in the Getting Around chapter).

SEA

Reservations and tickets for ferry travel are available from most travel agencies in France and other destination or departure countries. The prices given below are for standard one-way tickets for foot passengers; return fares generally cost less than two one-way tickets. Children aged from four to 15 travel for half to two-thirds of an adult fare. Bikes travel for free with most carriers; otherwise the charge is around UK£5 (50FF) per bike.

Departure Tax

Passengers crossing the Channel or coming from Italy do not pay separate departure or port taxes; these are included in the fares. In Corsica, at least, a variable port tax is charged; the price is usually included in the ticket price.

The UK

Fares vary widely according to seasonal demand, and tickets can cost almost three times as much in July and August as in winter. To take advantage of promotional fares you may have to reserve 24 hours or more in advance. Some companies (eg, Hoverspeed, Brittany Ferries and Condor) have pricing policies that make it more expensive to buy a ticket in pounds than in francs. Some discounts are available for students (eg, on SeaFrance) and young people (eg, on Brittany Ferries), at least for tickets bought in France.

Eurailpasses are *not* valid for ferry travel between England and France.

Several ferry companies operate from ports in England across the Channel to ports in northern France, Normandy and Brittany:

Brittany Ferries (UK ☎ 0990-360360, France ☎ 08 03 82 88 28; ☐ www.brittany-ferries.com) Services between: Plymouth-Roscoff; Poole-Cherbourg; Portsmouth-Ouistreham (Caen) and Portsmouth St Malo. Prices vary according to the season and crossing: adult foot passenger fares range from UK£19 to UK£36 one way; bicycle cost UK£5 one way or free in low season.

Condor Ferries (UK ☎ 01305-761551, France ☎ 02 99 20 03 00; ☐ www.condorferries.co.uk) Services from Weymouth to St Malo from May to October. The adult foot passenger fare is UK£27; bicycles travel free, but must be booked in advance.

Hoverspeed (UK ☎ 01304 240241, France ☎ 08 00 90 17 77; ☐ www.hoverspeed.co.uk) The fastest channel crossing (Dover-Calais); other services are Folkestone-Boulogne-sur-Mer and Newhaven-Dieppe. Bicycles free on standard fares.

P&O European Ferries (UK ☎ 0990-80555, France ☎ 08 03 01 30 13; ☐ www.poef.com) Two services: Portsmouth-Cherbourg and Portsmouth-Le Havre. Fares for both cost from UK£18 to UK£32 one way; bicycles cost UK£5 (free from October to March).

Stena Line (UK ☎ 0990-980980, France ☎ 01 44 51 00 51; ☐ www.postena.com) Operates from Dover to Calais. Fares cost from UK£24 for foot passengers for a five-day return; bicycles are free. Ferries run about every 45 minutes.

SeaFrance Sealink (UK ☎ 0990-711711, France ☎ 03 21 34 55 00; ☐ www.seafrance.co.uk) Runs from Dover to Calais. Foot passengers pay UK£15 one way; bicycles travel free.

Ireland

Eurailpass holders pay 50% of the relevant fare for crossings with Irish ferries (if you book ahead).

Irish Ferries (Ireland ☎ 01-661 0551, France ☎ 01 44 94 20 40; ☐ www.irish-ferries.ie) Irish Ferries links Rosslare with Cherbourg and Roscoff. Two or three ferries a week sail from September to March; ferries leave every second day during the rest of the year. Pedestrians pay between IR£35 and IR£70 one way (plus IR£5 per person in Irish taxes); bicycles cost from IR£15 to IR£20 in summer (free in low season).

Brittany Ferries (UK ☎ 0990-360360, France ☎ 08 03 82 88 28; ☐ www.brittany-ferries.com) Cork to Roscoff services run from April to early October only. Prices vary according to the season: adult foot passenger fares cost from IR£34 to IR£65 one way; bicycles cost from IR£15 to IR£20 one way (free in low season).

Italy

A variety of ferry companies ply the waters between Corsica and Italy. For details of ferries from mainland France, see the Corsica chapter.

Fares for a single adult one-way ticket between Italy and Corsica range from 96FF to 200FF, depending on the time of year and destination. An additional arrival tax of 30FF is charged, along with a port tax, which ranges from 20FF to 72FF per person, depending on the port. A further tax, similar to the passenger tax is charged for each accompanied car.

It is essential that reservations be made well in advance for ferry travel during the summer, especially from mid-July to early September. The following companies all have offices in Bastia, Corsica:

Corsica Ferries (☎ 04 95 32 95 95, fax 04 95 32 14 71; ☐ www.corsicaferries.com) Services from Savona to Livorno to Bastia and from Savona to Île Rousse in summer. Bicycles travel free.

Corsica Marittima (☎ 04 95 54 66 95, fax 04 95 32 69 09; ☐ www.corsica-marittima.com) A fast service from Genoa and Livorno to Bastia between April and September. Bicycles travel free.

Moby Lines (☎ 04 95 34 84 94, ☐ www.mobylines.it) Links Genoa, Livorno and Piombino with Bastia, and Bonifacio with Santa Teresa di Galluria (Sardinia) from May through September. Bicycles travel free.

Société Nationale Corse Méditerranéenne (☎ 04 95 29 66 99, fax 04 95 26 66 77, ☐ www.sncm.fr) SNCM runs a service from mid-April to September from Marseille or Toulon to Porto Torres on the Italian island of Sardinia. SNCM also links the Corsican ports of Ajaccio and Propriano with Porto Torres during about the same period, but the service only runs two to five times a month. It charges 95FF per bike, and a per kilogram charge for trailers.

The USA, Canada & Elsewhere

The days of earning your passage on a freighter to Europe have well and truly passed, and long-distance passenger ships disappeared with the advent of cheap air travel.

However, it's still possible to travel as a passenger on a cargo ship. Such vessels typically take five to 12 passengers and charge about US$100 per person a day. Details are available from Travltips Cruise and Freighter Travel Association (USA ☎ 800-872 8584, ☐ www.travltips.com) and The Cruise People (UK ☎ 0800-526 313, Canada ☎ 416-444 2410; ☐ members.aol .com/CruiseAZ/home.htm).

Bicycle Tour Companies

France is a popular choice for organised cycle tours. Many companies throughout the world offer tours of varying lengths, standards and accommodation levels. Most have Web sites and will send you enticing full-colour brochures. Prices vary from company to company, often depending on accommodation and meals, so shop around.

The USA & Canada

Backroads (☎ 800-462 2848, fax 510-527 1444, 🖳 www.backroads.com), 801 Cedar St, Berkeley, CA 94710, offers six- to nine-day tours in Provence, the Loire, Brittany & Normandy, Burgundy, and the South-West.

Europeds (☎ 800-321 9552, fax 831-655 4501, 🖳 www.europeds.com), 761 Lighthouse Ave, Monterey, CA 93940, runs a dozen or so seven- to nine-day tours, some of which cover Burgundy, Provence, the Dordogne and Alsace.

Erickson Cycle Tours (☎ 888-972 0140, fax 206-527 0701, 🖳 www.ecycletours.com), 6119 Brooklyn Ave NE, Seattle, WA 98115, designs challenging 16-day tours of the Alps, Provence, Dordogne or the Pyrenees for tandemists (single bikes also welcome).

Van Gogh Tours (☎ 800-435 6192, fax 781-729 0929, 🖳 www.vangoghtours.com), PO Box 57, Winchester, MA 01890, offers both guided (Loire, Brittany & Normandy, Burgundy) and self-guided (Loire, Atlantic Coast, Languedoc) tours of varying lengths.

Randonnée Tours (☎ 800-465 6488, fax 204-474 1888, 🖳 www.randonneetours.com), 249 Bell Ave, Winnipeg, MB R3L 0J2, specialises in self-guided tour packages. Well-organised eight-day tours go to the Loire, Provence, the Dordogne and Burgundy.

The UK

Bike Tours (☎ 01225-310859, fax 480132, 🖳 www.biketours.co.uk), 82 Walcot St, Bath, Somerset BA1 5BD, offers tours with either a hotel or a camping option. Tours are available to the Loire, Bordeaux area, Burgundy, Brittany/Normandy and Dordogne.

The Cyclists' Touring Club (CTC; ☎ 01483-417217, fax 426994, 🖳 www.ctc.org.uk), Cotterell House, 69 Meadrow, Godalming, Surrey GU7 3HS, offers tours (usually 15 to 17 days) run by volunteer members through places such as Burgundy, Provence and Gascony.

The Chain Gang Cycle Tours (☎ 0171-323 1730, fax 0171-323 1731), 4th Floor, 24 Foley St, London W1P 7LA, offers one-week tours to the Dordogne, and the Bordeaux wine area in small groups (up to 10 participants).

France

Fédération Française de Cyclotourisme (FFCT) France's national bike touring association (see Useful Organisations in the Facts for the Cyclist chapter) offers tours in France and overseas, aimed primarily at the domestic market, though international participants are welcome. Tours vary from three to 10 days; gradings vary; some are designed for mountain bikes and others for touring bikes. Tours are outlined in the annual *Séjours et Voyages en France et à l'étranger* magazine.

France Randonnée (☎ 02 99 67 42 21, fax 02 99 67 42 23), 9 rue des Portes Mordelaises, 35000 Rennes, offers guided and self-guided tours to Alsace, Brittany, Burgundy and Champagne of three days to one week.

Breton Bikes (☎ 02 96 24 86 72, 🖳 www.bretonbikes.com), 14 Grande Rue, 22570, is based in France and specialises in cycle-camping tours in Brittany, plus women's only tours.

La Bicyclette Gourmande (☎ 03 89 49 28 67, fax 03 89 49 27 39, 🖳 www.bicyclettegourmande), 53 rue de Pfaffenheim, 68420 Gueberschwihr (Alsace) offers guided and self-guided tours concentrating on the culinary pleasures of Alsace, Burgundy, Normandy and Provence.

Departmental Tours Many French departments operate supported bicycle tours; ask the tourist office listed in Information Sources in each chapter for information.

Getting Around

France's domestic transport network, much of it state-owned and subsidised, tends to be monopolistic: the SNCF takes care of virtually all inter-departmental land transport; the SNCM handles most ferry services to Corsica; and short-haul bus companies are either run by the *département* (administrative region) or grouped so each local company handles different destinations.

AIR
Domestic Air Services
Carriers with domestic networks include Air France, Air Liberté, AOM, Air Littoral, Corsair (run by the Nouvelles Frontières travel agency), Corse Méditerranée, Flandre Air and Proteus. The government assigns routes and sets prices to avoid 'excessive competition', though the market is slowly being liberalised.

Travel on the TGV (high-speed train) between some cities (eg, Paris and Lyon) is faster and easier than by air.

Any French travel agent can make bookings for domestic flights and supply details on the complicated fare system. Outside France, Air France representatives sell tickets for many domestic flights.

Discounts are available for children, young people, students, couples, families, seniors and, on many flights, everyone else, depending on restrictions and when you fly.

One-way/return adult air fares on Air France (☎ 08 02 80 28 02, ☐ www.airfrance.com) include Paris-Ajaccio/Bastia 1056FF/1450FF; Paris-Bordeaux 1070FF/750FF, which is inexplicably cheaper for a return fare; Paris-Nice 1125FF/1180FF; and Marseille-Strasbourg 1105FF/1050FF. It is often cheaper to buy a return ticket than a one-way fare. An 8FF departure tax is added to all tickets.

Air Passes
Air France offers a Euro Pass for air travel within France. Each coupon costs 750FF; you must purchase between three and nine. The pass is economical if you are taking a lot of one-way domestic flights, as these tend to be very expensive and are rarely discounted.

Carrying Your Bicycle
On most flights, each passenger is allowed one carry-on bag and 23kg of checked luggage. Excess baggage costs 10FF per kilogram. For further details on bicycles see the boxed text 'Cycle Friendly Airlines' in the Getting There & Away chapter.

To/From the Airport
For information on public transport links and cycling options between Paris' two airports, Orly and Roissy Charles de Gaulle, see Getting There & Away in the Paris & the Île de France chapter.

BUS
Because French transport policy is biased in favour of the state-owned rail system, the country has extremely limited inter-regional bus services. However, buses are used quite extensively for short-distance travel within departments, especially in rural areas with relatively few train lines (eg, Brittany and Normandy). Over the years, certain uneconomical rail lines have been replaced by SNCF buses and these are free for people with rail passes; they don't carry bikes.

Costs
Expect to pay between 40FF and 60FF per hour of bus travel for adult tickets. Some companies will take the bicycle *gratuit* (free); others will charge a small fee, such as 16FF per bicycle.

Carrying Your Bicycle
If a service takes bicycles the process is usually easy; the bicycle is simply put in *la soute* (the luggage storage bay) under the bus. Try to avoid travelling at peak times, as most bus companies will tell you that the bicycle will only be put on the bus *'selon disponibilité'* (depending on (space) availability). Buses will only be able to take a maximum of two bicycles, and some only one. On occasion, if the back door and the aisle are wide enough, and the bus is not crowded, it may be possible to put a bicycle inside the bus if the storage bay is full. Be early, have your panniers off and, if you can, buy your ticket ahead of time.

TRAIN

France's superb rail network, operated by the state-owned SNCF (Société Nationale des Chemins de Fer), reaches almost every part of the country. Many towns not on the SNCF train and bus network are linked with nearby railheads by intra-departmental bus lines. SNCF information offices and ticket windows can advise you on how to get from any French train station to any other, irrespective of how many *correspondances* (transfers) it takes.

The free booklet *Guide du Train et du Vélo* (available at most train stations) is full of indispensable information about travelling by train with your bike, including four pages of 'bicycle friendly' rail schedules.

The SNCF creates a veneer of being bicycle-friendly by allowing you to take your bike, for free, on any train, as long as it is in a bicycle bag. However, this is often easier said than done; see the boxed text 'What is une Housse?' for the restrictions this imposes on touring cyclists.

France's most important train lines radiate from Paris like the spokes of a wheel, making rail travel between provincial towns on different spokes infrequent and rather slow. In some cases you have to transit through Paris (or another regional hub).

The pride and joy of the SNCF is the world renowned TGV *(train à grande vitesse)*, whose name – pronounced teh-zheh-veh – means 'high-speed train'. TGV (and other high-speed) services include:

SNCF Railways & Ferries

ENGLAND
London Dover Channel Tunnel Calais
Portsmouth Folkestone Dunkerque Ghent,
Newhaven Boulogne Gare Antwerp, Brussels
Poole Calais- LILLE BELGIUM GERMANY
Weymouth Frétun Brussels,
Plymouth Antwerp, Amsterdam
Arras Liège, Cologne, Hamburg, Copenhagen
ENGLISH CHANNEL TGV NORD LUXEMBOURG
Departs from Gare du Nord Luxembourg, Koblenz
Le Dieppe Amiens St Quentin Frankfurt, Mannheim,
Havre Berlin Prague
Cherbourg Beauvais Laon Verdun Metz
Guernsey Diélette ROUEN Charles de REIMS NANCY
Channel Bayeux Gaulle Épernay Châlons-en-
Islands Sark Airport Champagne Strasbourg
Jersey Carteret Ouistreham Chantilly PARIS
Roscoff Granville Caen Évreux Disneyland Karlsruhe,
Brest Paris Stuttgart
St Malo Alençon Chartres Massy Troyes Épinal Munich, Vienna
Quimper Fontainebleau Chaumont Mulhouse
RENNES Le Mans Orléans Laroche- BASEL
Lorient TGV ATLANTIQUE Migennes Montbard Besançon Zürich,
Departs from Gare Montparnasse Blois Auxerre DIJON Milan
Angers Tours Beaune Bern
NANTES Chinon Bourges Autun SWITZERLAND
ATLANTIC Nevers Lausanne,
OCEAN Poitiers TGV SUD-EST Milan, Rome
Les Sables Departs from Gare de Lyon Mâcon Geneva Évian
d'Olonne Niort Montluçon Vichy Chamonix
La Rochelle Annecy
Limoges Clermont- Bourg St
Angoulême Ferrand LYON Chambéry Maurice
Périgueux St Étienne Grenoble ITALY
BORDEAUX Brive-la- Valence Turin, Milan,
Bergerac Gaillarde Aurillac Rome
Arcachon Gap Turin
Cahors Rodez Mende Digne-
Bay of Mont de Orange les-Bains Genoa
Biscay Marsan Albi Avignon Ventimiglia
Biarritz Montauban Nîmes Aix-en- Nice Monaco
Santander Irun Bayonne Pau Auch TOULOUSE Mazamet Montpellier Provence Cannes Genoa, Florence,
Bilbao Tarbes Béziers Sète Rome, Greece
San Sebastián, Burgos, Lourdes Carcassonne Narbonne MARSEILLE Corsica
Pamplona, Saragossa, Can Franc Foix Toulon
Madrid, Lisbon Perpignan MEDITERRANEAN SEA
SPAIN Saragossa ANDORRA Puigcerdà Port-Bou Corsica
Barcelona, Valencia Tanger Tunis Sardinia Corsica Sardinia

Rosslare
Cork & Rosslare

0 150km
0 100mi N

- - - TGV, fast track section
——— TGV
——— Normal SNCF track

TGV Sud-Est Links Paris' Gare de Lyon with Lyon and the south-east, including Dijon, Geneva, the Alps, Avignon, Marseille, Nice and Perpignan.

TGV Atlantique Links Paris' Gare Montparnasse with Brittany (Rennes, Quimper, Brest), Nantes, the Loire Valley, La Rochelle, Bordeaux, the French Basque Country and Toulouse.

TGV Nord Links Paris' Gare du Nord with Arras, Lille and Calais.

Eurostar Links Paris' Gare du Nord with Lille, Calais-Fréthun and, via the Channel Tunnel, London Waterloo (three hours), Ashford and other British cities (see The UK under Land in the Getting There & Away chapter).

Thalys Links Paris' Gare du Nord with Brussels-Midi, Amsterdam and Cologne's Hauptbahnhof (see Continental Europe under Land in the Getting There & Away chapter).

A train that is not a TGV is often referred to as a *corail* or *classique* and regional trains are often known as TERs (Transport Express Régional).

Costs & Reservations

Most French trains, including the TGV, have both 1st- and 2nd-class sections. Overnight trains are usually equipped with *couchettes* (sleeping berths), for which you must reserve and pay an additional fee.

For 2nd-class travel, count on paying from 50FF to 60FF per 100km for cross-country trips and from 70FF to 100FF per 100km for short hops. Round trips cost twice as much as one-way. Travel in 1st class is 50% more expensive than 2nd class. Children aged under four travel for free; those aged from four to 11 pay 50% of the adult fare. A range of other discounts is available, including:

Reduced Price Tickets Discounts of 25% on one-way or return travel within France are available to young people aged from 12 to under 26; one to four adults travelling with a child aged four to 11; and over 60-year-olds. Two people travelling together are eligible for the discount on return travel only.

What is une Housse?

Une housse is literally a covering. In the case of a bicycle, it is a bike bag – your key to unrestricted, hassle-free travel on French trains, particularly the TGVs and coralls.

The SNCF advertises that you can take your bicycle for free on *any* train in France. Sounds good doesn't it? However, TGVs, which are replacing trains on ever-increasing numbers of services, only accept bicycles packed in a housse. The bike bag must measure no more than 90cm by 120cm, the maximum size of the luggage stacks in the TGVs and corail trains.

To get a bike into a housse you need to remove the wheels, pedals, saddle (sometimes), turn the handlebars 90° and zip the bike in each time you take the train.

This is all very fine for racing or unloaded bikes. However, bicycles set up for touring are likely to have front and rear racks, and fenders, making them longer than the 120cm allowed, even without wheels. You'll probably have to take off the racks and fenders to make the bicycle fit into a housse, which can be very time consuming.

If your bicycle is in a housse, you can simply load it into the end-of-carriage luggage racks and don't have to rely on trains having a *fourgon* (luggage carriage) or being designated as a bicycle-carrying service. The same restrictions apply to the international Thalys and Eurostar trains, although on some Eurostar trains you may have to check in your bicycle.

If you don't want to carry a housse or disassemble your bike, you need to plan on taking trains with a fourgon, which are few and far between. A better option is to tour on a folding bicycle (see the Your Bicycle chapter).

In France, housses are sold at major sports stores, though they don't fit large frame bicycles, and can't accommodate front racks. One author on this guide improvised with a cheap tarpaulin sealed with packing tape.

Découverte Séjour Anyone can get a 25% reduction for return travel within France if they are travelling at least 200km and are spending Saturday night at their destination.

Découverte G30 et G8 These fares give discounts of between 40% and 60% for tickets booked on a specific train well in advance. See the *Guide Découverte G30 et G8* (available at ticket windows) for details.

Reservations can be made via telephone, Minitel, the SNCF's Web site (see the boxed text 'How to Find Rail Information'), at any SNCF ticketing office or by using train station ticket machines. Don't forget to specify *non-fumeur* (non-smoking) or *fumeur* (smoking).

To collect your tickets, go to a ticket counter with your reference number. Reservations can be changed for no charge up to one hour *after* your scheduled departure time, but only if you are at your departure station.

Tickets can be purchased on board the train, but prohibitive tariffs (90FF plus) apply: if you find yourself aboard a train without a ticket it's a good idea to search out the *contrôleur* (ticket inspector or conductor) to inform them of your circumstance.

Validating Your Ticket

Before boarding the train you must validate your ticket by time-stamping it in a *composteur*, orange posts situated somewhere between the ticket windows and the tracks.

If you forget to validate your ticket before boarding, find a conductor to punch it for you (if you wait for your 'crime' to be discovered, you're likely to be fined). Keep your ticket and reservation card with you until the end of the journey.

Train Passes for Non-Europeans

Several types of rail passes are available to Non-European residents:

Eurailpass This popular pass is valid for travel in France and other European countries. The standard version entitles you to unlimited rail travel over a period of 15 or 21 days or one, two or three months. Other versions exist, including ones for several adults travelling together. Youth fares are available to under 26-year-olds.

One month of unlimited travel with the regular adult Eurailpass costs US$890, and with the Eurail Youthpass US$623. Where applicable, Eurailpass holders must pay reservation fees and couchette charges.

Europass This pass lets you travel in certain European countries for between five and 15 consecutive or non-consecutive days over a two-month period. Regular adult fares, good for 1st-class passage within France, Germany, Italy, Spain and Switzerland, range from US$348 for five days to US$728 for 15 days (15% less for two adults travelling together). The Netherlands, Belgium, Luxembourg, Portugal, Austria, Hungary and Greece can be added for a modest surcharge. The Europass Youth is available to people under 26.

France Railpass People who are not residents of France are entitled to this pass, allowing unlimited travel on the SNCF system for three to nine days over one month. In 2nd class, the three-day version costs US$180 (US$146 each for two people travelling together); each additional day of travel costs US$30. Versions including car rental are also available.

People under 26 are eligible for the France Rail Youthpass. This costs US$164 for four days of train travel over two months; additional days (up to a maximum of 10) cost US$20.

How to Find Rail Information

From 7 am to 10 pm every day, you can get schedule and fare information and make reservations via the SNCF's domestic and international services in several languages (2.23FF per minute):

English	☎ 08 36 35 35 39
French	☎ 08 36 35 35 35
German	☎ 08 36 35 35 36
Italian	☎ 08 36 35 35 38
Spanish	☎ 08 36 35 35 37

Internet

Eurostar	🖥 www.raileurope.com
Rail Europe	🖥 www.raileurope.com
SNCF	🖥 www.sncf.fr
TER	🖥 ter.sncf.fr
Thalys	🖥 www.thalys.com

Train Passes for Residents of Europe

These are available to anyone, provided they have been resident in Europe for at least six months. However, you cannot purchase a pass for use in your country of residence. In France, the passes are sold at most train stations. Holders of these passes get discounts on the Eurostar and Thalys, but must pay all SNCF reservation fees and supplements.

Euro Domino Flexipass This comes in various versions for travel within one of

the 29 participating countries. It gives three to eight non-consecutive days of midnight-to-midnight travel over a period of one month. The pass also allows 25% off tickets for travel from the place where it was purchased to the border of the country in which the holder will be travelling to next.

Euro Domino France This version is good for travel on the SNCF. The adult version costs from UK£105 to UK£220 for three to eight days in 2nd class. A youth version exists for people under 26.

Reading Train Timetables

SNCF's pocket-sized *horaires* (schedules) are available for free at stations. They can be a bit complicated to read, but are essential to decipher which trains will take your bike in *le fourgon* (the luggage carriage) if you are not carrying your bike in a *housse* (bicycle bag).

Through a complicated system of footnote references and symbols, these timetables explain everything about the trains servicing a particular line. Of the 40 or so trains listed on the schedule, only a few may be running on the day you'd like to travel, and only one (if you're lucky) will take bicycles in the luggage carriage.

Where possible throughout the rides, trains that take bicycles in the luggage carriage are indicated (see Getting to/from the Ride). You can always ask for help at the information office or, in small stations, at the ticket window. For planning from home, the *Thomas Cook European Timetable* (125FF in France, more overseas) is updated monthly, but has no bicycle information.

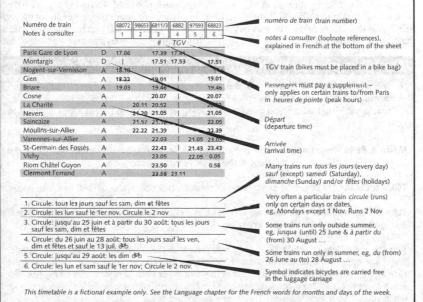

Numéro de train		68072	98653	6811/3	6882	97593	68823
Notes à consulter		1	2	3	4	5	6
				#	TGV		
Paris Gare de Lyon	D	17.06		17.39	17.41		
Montargis	D			17.51	17.53		17.51
Nogent-sur-Vernisson	A	18.10					
Gien	A	18.22	19.01				19.01
Briare	A	19.03	19.46				19.46
Cosne	A		20.07				20.07
La Charité	A		20.11	20.52			20.52
Nevers	A		21.20	21.05			21.05
Saincaize	A		21.57	21.10			22.05
Moulins-sur-Allier	A		22.22	21.39			22.39
Varennes-sur-Allier	A			22.03	21.05	23.05	
St-Germain des Fossés	A			22.43	21.43	23.43	
Vichy	A			23.05	22.05	0.05	
Riom Châtel Guyon	A			23.50		0.58	
Clermont Ferrand	A			23.58	23.11		

numéro de train (train number)

notes á consulter (footnote references), explained in French at the bottom of the sheet

TGV train (bikes must be placed in a bike bag)

Passengers must pay a supplement – only applies on certain trains to/from Paris in *heures de pointe* (peak hours)

Départ (departure time)

Arrivée (arrival time)

Many trains run *tous les jours* (every day) *sauf* (except) *samedi* (Saturday), *dimanche* (Sunday) and/or *fêtes* (holidays)

1. Circule: tous les jours sauf les sam, dim et fêtes
2. Circule: les lun sauf le 1er nov. Circule le 2 nov
3. Circule: jusqu'au 25 juin et à partir du 30 août: tous les jours sauf les sam, dim et fêtes
4. Circule: du 26 juin au 28 août: tous les jours sauf les ven, dim et fêtes et sauf le 13 juil. ᴓᴓ
5. Circule: jusqu'au 29 août: les dim ᴓᴓ
6. Circule: les lun et sam sauf le 1er nov; Circule le 2 nov.

Very often a particular train *circule* (runs) only on certain days or dates, eg, Mondays except 1 Nov. Runs 2 Nov

Some trains run only outside summer, eg, *jusqua* (until) 25 June & *à partir du* (from) 30 August ...

Some trains run only in summer, eg, *du* (from) 26 June *au* (to) 28 August ...

Symbol indicates bicycles are carried free in the luggage carriage

This timetable is a fictional example only. See the Language chapter for the French words for months and days of the week.

Inter Rail Pass With this pass you can travel in 29 European countries organised into eight zones; France is in Zone E, grouped with the Netherlands, Belgium and Luxembourg. Passes exist for varying combinations of time periods and zones and discounts exist for under-25-year-olds. For 22 days of unlimited 2nd-class travel in one zone, the cost is 1836FF. The pass gives 50% off travel from your home country to your zone(s) and between non-adjacent zones.

Carrying Your Bicycle

SERNAM (☎ 08 03 84 58 45, seven days a week) is the SNCF's official baggage service. It is the only way to send your bicycle unaccompanied by train. SERNAM centres are open Monday to Friday from 9 am and 6 pm; larger centres are also open Saturday from 9 am to 1 pm.

An important consideration when using SERNAM is timing, both for reserving transport and planning your touring schedule. Your bicycle does not travel with you on the train, but is transported by SERNAM truck. SERNAM guarantees delivery of the bicycle within 48 hours, but they do not work on Saturday and Sunday. Check on public holidays, as this will also affect your timing.

Just like anything to do with the SNCF, SERNAM has lots of rules. You can pay for the freight service by:

- Purchasing your rail ticket and, at the same time, indicating that you intend to use SERNAM to send your bicycle. You will then pay for both your ticket and the bicycle's transport and receive what looks like two tickets. One is the actual passenger ticket, the other is the *bon d'échange*, the coupon for your bicycle, which is your SERNAM reference.
- Purchasing your passenger ticket and calling SERNAM separately to pay for your bicycle's transport over the phone with a credit card (only).

You also have several options for pick-up and delivery of your bicycle (the first two are available only to people catching the train themselves):

- Use SERNAM's door-to-door service. SERNAM will pick up and deliver from/to houses, hotels, offices and 350 French train stations at a cost of 295FF per bicycle (irrespective of the distance).
- Drop off and pick up your bike at one of 102 SERNAM centres. This costs 195FF per bicycle, again regardless of distance.
- If you are not travelling by train and wish to use SERNAM, you can ship your bike for a cost of 350FF anywhere in the country.

You must phone SERNAM at least two days in advance of your rail journey to set up your bicycle's transport. If you have already paid to transport your bicycle and have the *bon*

May I Take my Bike on *this* Train?

Navigating the many rules and regulations that govern getting bikes on French trains is often as complicated as solving a puzzle.

To help solve that puzzle you need a basic knowledge of the different types of trains in France:

Metro & RERs These trains operate in Paris and the Île de France; for details see the boxed text 'Cycling in the City' in the Paris & the Île de France chapter.

TGVs & Corails These accept bicycles on all services, but only when packed in a bike bag.

TERs & 'Trains' Those regional train services designated by a bicycle logo in the small blue and white *horaires* (timetables) carry bikes.

And the *contrôleur* (conductor) of TERs and 'trains' is the other key to solving the puzzle. Some will approach cyclists with a smile, others see bicycles as annoyances. Whatever the case arrive early, validate your ticket, greet the contrôleur with *bonjour* and a smile. Ask *'Où est le fourgon?'* (Where is the luggage carriage?); they should unlock the carriage and wait while you lift your bicycle inside. Throw in a *merci* and enjoy the ride.

d'échange, you will be asked for the reference number, the six digit computer code found in the bottom right hand corner of this voucher. Otherwise, arrange this over the phone.

SERNAM place your bicycle in a huge cardboard box the width of your handlebars. The bike is automatically insured for loss or damage for 2600FF, and extra insurance is available on request.

SERNAM will not take tandems; unless you can disguise children's trailers or recumbents as luggage, they're unlikely to carry them.

Left-Luggage

If you want to explore a city on foot, and are not staying overnight, you may be able to leave your bicycle and panniers at the station.

Most larger SNCF stations have both a *consigne manuelle* (left-luggage office), where you pay 30FF per bag or 35FF per bicycle for 24 hours, and a *consigne automatique*, a 72-hour computerised luggage locker that will issue you with a lock code in exchange for 15FF, 20FF or 30FF, depending on the size. At smaller stations you can usually check your bag with the clerk at the ticket window (30FF). Check when the left-luggage facilities close; some almost keep banking hours.

CAR

Driving a car can be expensive, and cars are often inconvenient in city centres or anywhere else where parking and traffic are a problem.

Essence (petrol or gasoline), also known as *carburant* (fuel), is expensive in France. At the time of writing, *sans plomb* (unleaded) petrol cost around 6.40FF a litre (US$4 per US gallon). Tolls are charged for travel on almost all autoroutes and many bridges.

In France all drivers must carry a national ID card or passport; a valid driver's permit or licence *(permis de conduire)*; car ownership papers *(carte grise*, or grey card); and proof of insurance *(carte verte*, or green card).

In Paris, the Automobile Club de l'Île de France (☎ 01 40 55 43 00, 🖳 www.autocl ubs-associes.tm.fr or 🖳 www.automobilecl ub.org; metro Argentine) at 14 ave de la Grande Armée (17e) sells insurance and can supply basic maps and itinerary suggestions.

Types of Roads

France, along with Belgium, has the densest highway network in Europe. The four types of intercity roads are:

Autoroutes Multi-lane divided motorways/ highways (usually subject to tolls), whose alphanumeric designations begin with A, eg, A1. Marked by blue symbols showing a divided highway receding into the distance, they often have *aires de repos* (rest areas), some with restaurants and pricey petrol stations. Bicycles are *not* allowed on autoroutes.

Routes Nationales Main highways whose names begin with N (or, on older maps and signs, RN). The newer ones are wide, well-signposted and lavishly equipped with reflectors. In most cases, these are busy roads and, although suitable for cycling, are best avoided.

Routes Départementales Quiet secondary and tertiary local roads whose names begin with D; they make cycling in France a 'D'ream.

Routes Communales Minor rural roads whose names sometimes begin with C. They are maintained by the smallest unit of local government, the commune. Although quiet and pleasant for cycling, they are often farm roads and are frequently unsigned.

Car Rental

Given the expenses involved in driving across France (fuel costs and tolls), it may make sense to rent a car after you arrive in the region you'd like to explore. Airport tariffs may be higher than the rates charged in town. *Kilométrage illimité* means unlimited kilometres. Most rental companies require drivers be aged over 21 (or, in some cases, over 23) and have had a driver's licence for at least one year.

The multinational rental agencies, such as Hertz, Avis, Budget and Europe's largest, Europcar, are outrageously expensive if you walk into one of their offices and hire a car on the spot – up to 900FF a day for the smallest car with unlimited kilometres. However, pre-booked and prepaid promotional rates can be very reasonable. For instance, weekly rates for Europe, as advertised in the USA, can be less than a quarter of the rate in France.

For rentals that are not arranged in advance, domestic companies (Rent-a-Car Système, Grand Garage Jean Jaurès) and some of the student travel agencies (eg, USIT) have the best rates. The largest French company is ADA Location de Véhicules.

Because you'll probably have to leave a deposit for the insurance excess and perhaps the petrol in the tank, many companies *require* that you have a credit card.

BOAT
Canal boats can be a good way to get around some parts of France; many canals are lined with bikepaths. For a booklet listing boat rental companies, contact the Syndicat National des Loueurs de Bateaux de Plaisance (☎ 01 44 37 04 00, fax 01 45 77 21 88; metro Javel) at Port de Javel, 75015 Paris. For rental from abroad, Crown Blue Lines offers canal boat rental in Brittany, Alsace, Languedoc and the Camargue area of Provence and along the Canal du Midi in the Toulouse area. In the UK, contact Crown Travel (☎ 01603-630513, fax 664298), 8 Ber St, Norwich, NR1 3EJ.

Much of the passenger traffic between mainland France and Corsica is handled by the Société Nationale Maritime Corse Méditerranée (SNCM; see the Corsica chapter).

LOCAL TRANSPORT
France's cities and larger towns generally have excellent public transport systems, including metros (underground railways) in Paris, Lyon, Marseille, Lille and Toulouse, and ultra-modern trams in such cities as Paris, Nantes, Strasbourg and Grenoble. Details on routes, fares, tourist passes etc are usually available at tourist offices and bus information counters.

French taxis are rather expensive, especially outside the major cities. All large and medium-sized train stations – and many small ones – have a taxi stand (rank) out front. There may be a surcharge of 5FF to get picked up at a train station or airport and a fee of 6FF per bag. Bikes can be loaded into *breaks* (station wagons), which should only cost 6FF extra.

ORGANISED TOURS
Some bicycle tours are organised by French companies, of which the national touring association, the Fédération Française de Cyclotourisme (FFCT), is the most well known. See the boxed text 'Bicycle Tour Companies' in the Getting There & Away chapter for details of organised tours in France.

Paris & the Île de France

A 300m-high iron tower, world famous museums, historic monuments, elegant avenues, magnificent churches, romantic quay-side strolls and sidewalk cafes epitomize Paris. Whatever the time of year, whether for a short or long stay, first or fifth visit, Paris offers something for everyone. But something that people don't typically envisage when they think of Paris is cycling.

Most people think of Paris as a city for walking. True enough, but the city's 130km network of bikepaths, intense encouragement by the Paris *mairie* (town hall) and city-wide cycling programs make central Paris one of the most cycle-friendly cities in Europe.

The 12,000-sq-km region surrounding Paris is known as the Île de France (literally, 'Island of France') and boasts some of the country's most magnificent chateaux and cathedrals. This wooded region forms Paris' green belt and is known as the 'lungs of Paris'.

Although densely populated, and crisscrossed by a web of heavily trafficked roads, the Île de France offers quiet back roads and surprisingly good cycling. Once beyond Paris, by way of a short bike ride or train trip, the villages, forests and peaceful, undulating terrain sprinkled with magnificent architectural delights seem far from the capital's frenetic energy.

HISTORY

Paris was founded towards the end of the 3rd-century BC on what is now Île de la Cité by a tribe of Celtic Gauls known as the Parisii. Julius Caesar's legions took control in 52 BC, and the settlement became a Roman town. It remained so until the Franks took over in the 5th century, making the city the capital of their kingdom and naming it Paris.

Paris prospered during the Middle Ages. In the 12th century, construction began on the cathedral of Notre Dame and the Right Bank was settled. As a centre of religion and learning, the Sorbonne opened in 1253; the beautiful Ste Chapelle was consecrated in 1248; building of the fortress of the Louvre began in around 1200; and expansion began into the Île de France.

In Brief

Highlights
- exploring **Paris** on two wheels
- the **Château de Chantilly**
- the **Forêt de Fontainebleau**
- **Monet's house & garden** at Giverny

Terrain
Gentle river valleys, flat plains and rolling hills; huge forested tracts

FFCT Contact
Ligue Île de France, 15 rue d'Avron, 93330 Neuilly-sur-Marne

Cycling Events
- **Paris-Roubaix** (first Sunday after Easter) Compiègne
- **Fête du Vélo** (first weekend in June) Paris
- **Tour de France** (3rd or 4th Sunday in July) Paris – finishes on the Champs Élysées
- **Open des Nations** track cycling meet (October) Paris

Special Events
- **Paris International Marathon** (mid-April)
- **French Open Tennis** (late May)
- **Paris Air Show** (mid-June 2001; every two years)
- **Bastille Day** (14 July) Paris
- **Festival d'Île de France** music festivals and concerts (September to mid-October)

Gourmet Specialities
- brie (cheese), such as brie de Meaux
- *gâteau Paris-Brest*
- *potage St Germain* (thick green pea soup)

In 1337, the Hundred Years War began, resulting in French defeat and English control of Paris in 1420. However, in 1429 Jean d'Arc (Joan of Arc) rallied the French troops to defeat the English at Orléans. The

English were eventually expelled from France in 1453.

The Renaissance of the early 16th century, and the Enlightenment about 100 years later, brought Paris to the forefront as a centre of culture and ideas. In the Île de France, Fontainebleau was redesigned by François I in Renaissance style in 1528.

Louis XIV, known as *le Roi Soleil* (the Sun King), ascended to the throne in 1643. His most tangible legacy is the palace at Versailles. The excesses of Louis XVI and his queen, Marie-Antoinette, led to an uprising of Parisians on 14 July 1789 and the storming of the Bastille prison, the act that started the French Revolution, only to be followed by a guillotine-happy Paris and the Reign of Terror.

In the early 1800s Napoleon Bonaparte crowned himself emperor and vowed to make Paris and France prosper. His legacy in modern Paris includes such monuments as the neoclassical Arc de Triomphe.

Napoleon III came to power in 1851, and in 17 years, he oversaw Baron Haussman's transformation of the city, introducing wide boulevards, sculptured parks and a modern sewer system. In 1889, Paris' famous Eiffel Tower was erected for the World Exhibition. Paris was seen as one of the great cultural cities of the world and ushered in the glittering *belle époque* (beautiful age), with its famed Art Nouveau architecture, a barrage of advances in the arts and sciences and a city of free-thinking individuals patronising fashionable salons.

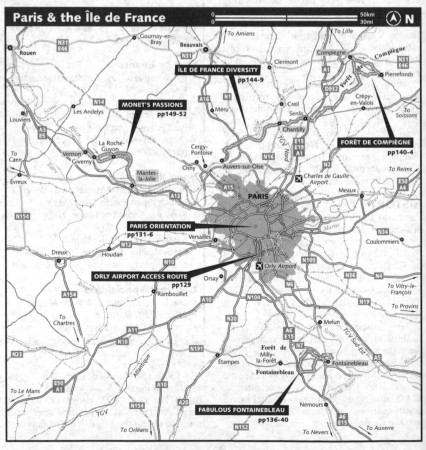

Parc de St Cloud

Designed by Le Nôtre, the beautiful 440 hectare Parc de St Cloud (pronounced clue) retains most of its original layout. High above the Seine, the terraces have lovely views of Paris. In this park, in 1868, the first bicycle race in France took place, a 2km track course, won by Englishman James Moore. The park's chateau was destroyed by fire in 1870.

The excesses of that era were cut short by the Nazi occupation of 1940, and Paris remained under Germany's thumb until 25 August 1944. After the war, Paris regained its cultural and creative position, which it retains to this day.

NATURAL HISTORY

Paris and the Île de France are in the geological area called the Paris Basin. For the small area covered by the basin, it is a quite a mixed bag. Much of it is made up of forests, primarily of oak, beech, pine, chestnut and birch. The rivers of the Île de France, the Aube, the Marne, the Oise and the Seine provide fertile alluvial valleys for farming, as do the limestone plateaux that dot the region. In the south-east, pockets of limestone and sandstone in the Forêt de Fontainebleau have formed unusual outcrops and gorges.

Much of the area is arable land, and agriculture plays an important role. Wheat fields sprawl around the south-west, east and north, while market gardens can be found closer in to Paris, especially to the north. The eastern Brie region, bordering Champagne, is mainly limestone, lending itself to wheat and vegetable farming, plus production of the well-known cheese, brie.

Many of the forests used to be royal hunting grounds, so it is not unusual to see deer, and from time to time wild boar, as well as red squirrels darting through the forest. Bird life is also abundant; look for woodpeckers, robins, blackbirds, the ubiquitous pigeons and, near water, kingfishers.

Lily-of-the-valley, columbines and violets peek through the ground in spring, while heather arrives later in the season. Blackberries ripen in the autumn, also the time when colourful fungi appear.

CLIMATE

The weather in Paris and the Île de France is typified by a continental climate; warm summers and cool winters, neither of which are particularly extreme. Occasionally summer days reach the upper 30s, especially in August, the month that records the highest average rainfall (64mm). Winters are relatively mild. See the climate charts in the Facts about France chapter for more details.

The Île de France region records the nation's lowest annual precipitation (about 575mm), but rainfall patterns are erratic; you are just as likely to be caught in a spring or autumn downpour as in a sudden summer cloudburst.

The northerly position of Paris and the Île de France means summer days are long and light; the downside to this are early sunsets in winter.

Paris

The city of Paris is quite small: approximately 9.5km (north to south) by 11km (west to east), not including the Bois de Vincennes and the Bois de Boulogne, the two huge parks which bound Paris on the east and west.

There is so much to see and do in Paris, that if you can only spend a few days, try to avoid Monday and Tuesday, as many museums and some shops are closed. Sunday is a great day; many museums are free or cheaper, though this can often make them crowded, and some roads are reserved for cyclists and pedestrians.

INFORMATION

Paris is divided into 20 *arrondissements* (districts) that spiral outwards from the city centre. Paris addresses always include the arrondissement as streets with the same name exist in different districts. In this chapter, arrondissement numbers are listed after the street names using French notation: *1er* for *premier* (1st), *4e* for *quatrième* (4th) and so on. This chapter also lists the closest metro station with the phone number.

Maps & Books

Lonely Planet produces a range of Paris products: the durable, plastic-coated *Paris City Map*, which is indexed, easy to use and includes a metro map; *Paris*, a complete guide; and *Paris Condensed*, which slips comfortably into a pocket or pannier.

The Paris mairie (🖳 www.paris-france .org, metro Hôtel de Ville), 4 rue de Lobau (4e), has the free *Mini Paris à Vélo* map, which marks every bikepath and lane and lists bike shops, rental locations and other information.

Another free bicycle map is *130km pour Vivre Paris à Vélo*. It indicates the bikepaths on a very simple map, and lists bike shops and rental locations. The map can also be found at some bike shops and the Paris tourist office at 127 ave des Champs Élysées.

Bookshops Le Sportsman (☎ 01 45 79 38 93, metro Émile Zola), 7bis rue Henri Duchêne (15e), is a 'sport' bookshop run by Michel Merejkowsky, a keen cycle tourist and author. It has a huge cycling section, but only opens Friday from 11 am to 8 pm and Monday from 2 pm to 7 pm; call beforehand.

Information Sources

Paris' main tourist office (☎ 08 36 68 31 12, fax 01 49 52 53 00, 🖳 www.paris-touristof fice.com, metro Georges V) is at 127 ave des Champs Élysées (8e). It is closed only on 1 May and Christmas Day.

It has branches at Gare de Lyon (closed Sunday) and the Eiffel Tower (open from 11 am to 6 pm daily from May to September).

There are exchange bureaus (open daily from 6 am to 11 pm) at both Roissy Charles de Gaulle and Orly airports. And each of Paris' six major train stations have exchange bureaus and ATMs. Banks are located everywhere across the city.

The main post office (☎ 01 40 28 20 00, metro Sentier or Les Halles), 52 rue du Louvre, is open 24 hours.

Bike Shops & Rentals

There are about 50 bike shops in central Paris alone (most are closed on Sunday or Monday).

Rental prices tend to be a little higher than in the rest of the country (70FF to 150FF per day) and demand a deposit of up to 2000FF. Most rental locations open on weekends.

Chains Decathlon (🖳 www.decathlon .com) and Go Sport (🖳 www.go-sport.fr) have several shops in Paris. They offer sales

and repairs, but not rental bikes. Bike shops and rental locations in Paris include:

Decathlon Les Trois Quartiers (☎ 01 55 35 97 55, metro Madeleine), 17 blvd de la Madeleine (1er).
Go Sport Rivoli (☎ 01 55 34 34 03, metro Pont Neuf or Châtelet), 10 rue Boucher (1er).
Roue Libre (☎ 01 53 46 43 77, metro Les Halles), 95bis rue Rambuteau (1er). Rentals (Paris and environs), guided tours (see the Citybike section in the 'Cycling in the City' boxed text).
Au Réparateur de Bicyclettes (☎ 01 48 04 51 19, metro Châtelet-les-Halles), 44 blvd de Sébastopol (3e). Sales, repairs, rentals.
Paris à Vélo, c'est sympa! (☎ 01 48 87 60 01, metro Bastille), 37 blvd Bourdon (4e). Sales, rentals, guided tours.
Gepetto et Vélos (☎ 01 43 37 59 22, metro Censier-Daubenton), 46 rue Daubenton (5e). Sales, repairs, rentals.
La Maison du Vélo (☎ 01 42 81 24 72, metro Gare du Nord), 11 rue Fénelon (10e). Sales, repairs, rentals.
Rando-Cycles (☎ 01 40 01 03 08, metro Porte de Vincennes), 1 rue Fernand-Foureau (12e). Sales, repairs. Good selection of touring gear.
Cycles Archambaud (☎ 01 43 20 60 07, metro Montparnasse-Bienvenüe), 23 blvd Edgar-Quinet (14e). Sales, repairs.
Paris Cycles (☎ 01 47 47 22 37). Two locations in Bois de Boulogne (16e). Rentals from mid-April to mid-October; Wednesday and weekends the rest of the year.

THINGS TO SEE & DO

See the Paris Orientation ride (pp131–6) for ideas on things to see and do in Paris.

PLACES TO STAY

Many hotels in Paris aren't bicycle friendly, usually because of architectural constraints such as narrow stairs and corridors, no lift, and rooms too small to store a bicycle. But every lodging listed here *is* bicycle friendly.

Camping

The *Camping du Bois de Boulogne* (☎ 01 45 24 30 00; fax 01 42 24 42 95; allée du Bord de l'Eau, 16e), at the western edge of the Bois de Boulogne along the Seine, has sites for two people with tent from 75FF to 86FF. It has 800 tent sites, is open year round, and is very crowded in summer.

Hostels

Of the four official youth hostels in Paris, only two will accept bicycles: the *Auberge de Jeunesse Le d'Artagnan* (☎ 01 40 32 34 56; fax 01 40 32 34 55; e d_artagnan _yh@csi.com; 80 rue Vitruve, 20e; metro Porte de Bagnolet), on the eastern edge of Paris, and *Auberge de Jeunesse Léo Lagrange* (☎ 01 41 27 26 90; fax 01 42 70 52 63; e 106002.1300@compuserve.com; 107 rue Martre; metro Mairie de Clichy), northwest, in Clichy. Both cost 100FF per night, including breakfast and sheets.

The *Auberge Internationale des Jeunes* (☎ 01 47 00 62 00; fax 01 47 00 33 16; e aij@aijparis.com; 10 rue Trousseau, 11e; metro Ledru Rollin) has dorm beds for 91FF, including breakfast. Get there early to secure a room.

On the Left Bank, in the Latin Quarter, the *Centre International BVJ Paris-Quartier Latin* (☎ 01 43 29 34 80; fax 01 53 00 90 91; 44 rue des Bernardins, 5e; metro Maubert Mutualité) charges 120FF, including breakfast, for a dorm bunk. Single rooms cost 130FF.

Hotels
Paris has a huge selection of budget hotels.

Right Bank The central Marais/Bastille area is handy to Gare de Lyon and Gare d'Austerlitz, and a short ride to Gare de l'Est and Gare du Nord.

Hôtel Central Bastille (☎ 01 47 00 31 51; fax 01 47 00 77 29; 16 rue de la Roquette, 11e; metro Bastille), just east of place de la Bastille, has singles/doubles with shower and toilet from 250/350FF. Bikes are stored on the first floor.

Hôtel Castex (☎ 01 42 72 31 52; fax 01 42 72 57 91; e info@castexhotel.com; 5 rue Castex, 4e; metro Bastille), is a charming family-run hotel, and one of the best in the Marais. Rooms with shower and toilet start at 260/340FF; book six weeks in advance.

Few hotels near the Gare de l'Est and Gare du Nord accommodate bicycles. Close to Gare de l'Est is the pleasant *Grand Hôtel de Paris* (☎ 01 46 07 40 56; fax 01 42 05 99 18; 72 blvd de Strasbourg, 10e; metro Gare de l'Est), where rooms with shower and toilet cost 300/350FF. Bikes are kept in your rooms (ask for one on the first or second floor), as the lift is too small for bikes.

Left Bank The lively Latin Quarter is a good choice for lodging, and is convenient

if you are cycling to/from Orly airport. It's also close to Gare d'Austerlitz, Gare de Lyon and Gare Montparnasse.

The *Port Royal Hôtel* (☎ 01 43 31 70 06; fax 43 31 33 67; 8 blvd de Port Royal, 5e; metro Gobelins) is a (better than) one-star family-run hotel where pretty rooms with washbasin cost 222/299FF. Hall showers cost 15FF. There is a little garden courtyard for your bike; credit cards are not accepted; book early.

Hôtel Gay Lussac (☎ 01 43 54 23 96; fax 01 40 51 79 49; 29 rue Gay Lussac, 5e; metro Luxembourg) is family-run and has spacious rooms from 200FF. Doubles with shower and toilet cost 300FF. Bikes can either be kept on the landing or in your room; credit cards are not accepted.

The *Hôtel Résidence Monge* (☎ 01 43 26 87 90; fax 01 43 54 47 25; e hotelmonge @gofornet.com; 55 rue Monge, 5e; metro place Monge) has rooms with shower and toilet from 370/450FF.

PLACES TO EAT
Self-Catering
Paris' neighbourhood food markets offer the freshest and best-quality fruits, vegetables, cheeses, prepared salads etc at the lowest prices in town. The *marchés découverts* (open-air markets) – 60 of which pop up in public squares around the city two or three times a week – are open from 7 am to 1 pm. About a dozen *marchés couverts* (covered markets) are scattered around town. To find out market times and places, ask at your hotel or at the tourist office. The bottom of *rue Mouffetard* is magically transformed every morning except Monday into one of Paris' liveliest, most colourful (and oldest) markets.

Supermarkets in Paris tend to be small. In the Marais (metro St Paul, 4e) there are three supermarkets on rue St Antoine: *Monoprix* at No 71, *Supermarché G20* at No 117, *Franprix* at No 133, and numerous food shops in between. The 5e arrondissement has a *Franprix* (82 rue Mouffetard, metro Censier Daubenton) and a *Shopi* (34 rue Monge, metro place Monge).

If you're looking for a large, well-stocked supermarket, try the *Inno* (metro Montparnasse-Bienvenüe, 14e) across from Tour Montparnasse. Innumerable food shops can be found throughout the city.

Restaurants

Except for touristy areas, most of the city's thousands of restaurants are pretty good value for money – at least by Parisian standards. It still pays to check the posted *menus* (set meals) outside and see how popular it is with locals.

The **Marais** (metro Bastille, 3e & 4e) is known for its kosher and kosher-style restaurants on rue des Rosiers (many close Friday evening, Saturday and Jewish holidays).

Slightly east of the Marais is **place de la Bastille**, where lively *brasseries* and *restaurants* cluster around the busy roundabout (traffic circle).

For village ambience, and a huge selection of eateries, head to **rue Mouffetard** (metro place Monge, 5e). You'll find everything, including Greek, Mexican, Spanish, Thai and, of course, traditional French cuisine. Just off rue Mouffetard is tiny **rue du Pot-de-Feu**, popular with locals and tourists, and where almost every restaurant has outdoor seating.

The northern part of the **Latin Quarter**, especially around rue de la Huchette, is a collection of poor-quality tourist restaurants, mainly serving Greek, North African and Middle Eastern cuisines. Much better food in this area can be found by wandering slightly west into the 6e arrondissement, where **rue St André des Arts** is lined with restaurants. There are lots of options down the side streets between Église St Sulpice and Église St Germain des Prés.

The **Montparnasse** area, a little east of the train station, around blvd Montparnasse, has some good eating opportunities.

For light and healthy fare, *Le Paradis du Fruit* is a chain of eight restaurants/*salons de fruit* scattered throughout Paris.

And, what cyclist can resist an ice cream? Go to the best: *Berthillon* (☎ 01 43 54 31 61, 31 rue St Louis en l'Île, metro Pont Marie, 4e), on Île St Louis, reputed to serve the best ice cream in Paris. The takeaway counter is open from 10 am to 8 pm (closed Monday, Tuesday and school holidays).

GETTING THERE & AWAY
Air

General airport information, terminal maps and the facilities at both Paris airports can be found on the Aéroports de Paris Web site 🖥 www.adp.fr.

Orly Airport Sixteen kilometres south of central Paris, Orly Airport (☎ 01 49 75 15 15) has two terminals: Ouest (domestic flights) and Sud (some international flights). A free overhead rail line (bikes allowed) links the terminals, as does a more convenient footpath.

Taxis aren't a bad option from Orly if you're staying on the south side of Paris. Request a station wagon *(un break)*; a charge of 6FF applies for the bicycle and each piece of luggage. The usual tip is 2FF, no matter what the fare, with the maximum about 5FF. The following are the transport options linking Orly with Paris for passengers with bikes. All services run about every 20 to 30 minutes, between 6 and 7 am and 10.30 and 11 pm. Purchase tickets on board buses unless detailed otherwise.

Air France Bus No 1 (☎ 01 41 56 89 00; 45FF, bikes free; 35 to 45 minutes) To/from Gare Montparnasse (15e) and Aérogare des Invalides (8e). Bikes are stored under the bus; if it's full you must wait for the next bus.

Orlyval (57FF, bikes free; 30 minutes) Links the airport with Paris via RER line B. Buy your ticket in the terminal, then go to the upper level, where the automated shuttle train connects Orly's two terminals with the Antony RER station on RER line B to Paris. To get to Antony from Paris, take Line B4 towards St Rémy-les-Chevreuse, then connect to Orlyval.

Orlyrail (32.50FF, bikes free; 40 minutes) Links the airport with Paris by RER line C. Take the Aéroports de Paris (ADP) shuttle bus *(navette)* to Pont de Rungis-Aéroport de Orly RER station, and connect on RER line C to Paris. To get to Orly from Paris, take a train on the RER C2 line coded ROMI or MONA towards Pont de Rungis or Massy-Palaiseau, then connect on the ADP shuttle bus.

Roissy Charles de Gaulle Airport

About 30km north-east of the city, Roissy Charles de Gaulle airport (☎ 01 48 62 22 80) is used by most international carriers and some charter companies. It's big, confusing and has several terminals and two train stations, so allow plenty of time. Free shuttle buses link the terminals and the train stations. Bikes are allowed on the shuttles but only in the back section. It is often a tight squeeze; they are often full, so you may need to wait for more than one.

Five transport choices are available between Roissy Charles de Gaulle Airport and

Boulangers abound in Paris.

Roue Libre's free Citybike tours introduce cyclists to Paris.

Cool your heels outside the Louvre's glass pyramid.

See it all by bike!

The classic Parisian touch.

Monet's house and gardens in Giverny inspired many of his works.

Every town in France has a market and speciality shops selling all the ingredients a cyclist could need for a gourmet picnic: bread and wine are the basic picnic ingredients...then add vegetables for a salad, marinated olives and salami, and choose sweet pastries or soft cheese for dessert. Delicious!

Riding to/from Orly Airport

Traffic on this ride is hectic. Most of the route is straight, along the busy N7 (which changes its name several times), so catch public transport if you have to get to the airport during peak hours.

Orly Airport to Place d'Italie
1–1½ hours, 12km

Take the lift on level 0 in the Orly Sud terminal to level -1. Follow the signs to bus No 285, passing the post office. Go out the doors and carry your bike down the stairs to the bikepath (on your left).

Head north to Paris on the bikepath. At 2.5km the path ends, and for the next 1.1km, the N7 resembles a freeway; use the footpath and cross carefully where required. At 3.6km, begin riding on the road. Use the bus lane, and keep as far right as possible. On the right is the cemetery, Cimitière Parisien de Thiais. The rest of the route continues straight except a slight veer to the right at blvd Maxime Gorki.

At Porte d'Italie, cross over the Péripherique and enter central Paris. In about 600m, a bike lane begins. Place d'Italie is a huge roundabout. From here it is 1km to blvd Port Royal, and about 5km to Île de la Cité.

Place d'Italie to Orly Airport
1–1½ hours, 12km

The start point at place d'Italie is on the south side of the roundabout. The theatre complex, Graumont Grand Écran is on the right. Begin on the bike lane heading south. At Porte d'Italie, cross over the Péripherique. The route continues straight for about 8km, except a veer to the left at blvd Maxime Gorki. At 9.3km, there is a sign for the bikepath to the airport. Go down the stairs and under the N7 to the other side. At the top of the stairs (do a 180° turn), continue south to the airport on the bikepath.

At the airport, carry your bike up the stairs, go through the doors and past the post office. Use the lift to go to level 0 of the Orly Sud terminal.

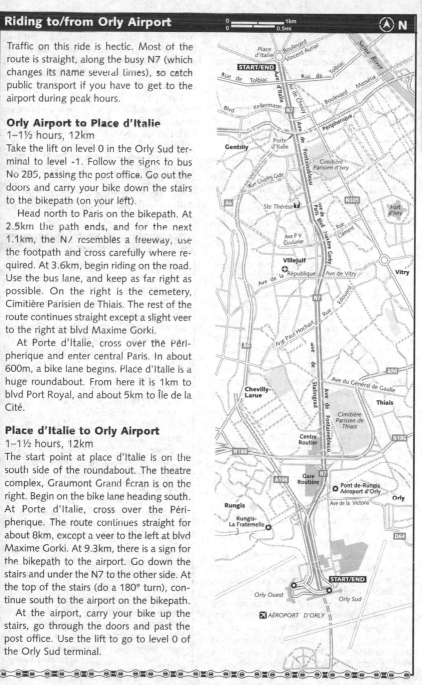

Paris; the regular RATP bus is not an option with a bike.

The easiest way to/from Paris is Roissy-rail; however, there are certain stations in Paris where you may not enter/exit with a bicycle (see the Bikes on Paris' Trains section in the 'Cycling in the City' boxed text).

The following services run every 20 to 30 minutes between 6 and 7 am and 10.30 and 11 pm. Purchase tickets on board buses.

Roissyrail (49FF, bikes free; 35 minutes to Gare du Nord) Links Paris's RER line B stations with both of the airport's train stations. From Terminal 1, take the free shuttle to the train station. From Terminal 2, take the lift directly down to the station, and go one more level down to the platforms. A rail attendant will need to open the gate, then either take the lift or use the escalator to reach the platform level. To get to the airport from Paris, take any B train, whose four letter destination code begins with E (eg, EIRE), then head up to Terminal 2, or take the shuttle to Terminal 1.

Air France Bus No 2 (☎ 01 41 56 89 00; 60FF, bikes free; 35 to 50 minutes) Links the airport with two Right Bank locations: the end of ave Carnot nearest the Arc de Triomphe and the Palais des Congrès de Paris at Porte Maillot (17e). Bikes go in the luggage storage under the bus; if it's full you need to wait for the next bus.

Air France Bus No 4 (☎ 01 41 56 89 00; 70FF, bikes free; 45 to 55 minutes) Links the airport to Gare de Lyon (12e) and Gare Montparnasse (15e).

Roissybus (☎ 01 48 04 18 24 or RATP ☎ 08 36 68 77 14; 48FF, bikes free; 45 minutes) This RATP-run bus links the airport with place d'Opéra (2e); bikes are carried at the driver's discretion in the corridor.

Airport to Airport Air France bus No 3 (☎ 01 41 56 89 00) connects the two airports every 20 to 30 minutes from 6 am to 11 pm (75FF, bikes free, 50 to 60 minutes).

Bus

Unfortunately, if you have your bike with you, buses are not a viable option for getting to Paris from international destinations. Neither Eurolines nor Busabout accept bikes. For passenger-only information, see Bus under Continental Europe in the Getting There & Away chapter.

From the UK, European Bike Express is an excellent bus service for cyclists (see Bus under The UK in the Getting There & Away chapter).

Train

Arriving in Paris by train, with your bicycle, means that you've fathomed the first step in transporting your bike on French trains (see the Train section in the Getting Around chapter).

You will arrive at one of Paris' six major train stations, each of which handles passenger traffic to different parts of France and Europe. SNCF train information for mainline services is available on ☎ 08 36 35 35 35 (in French) and ☎ 08 36 35 35 39 (in English) and for suburban services on ☎ 01 53 90 20 20.

The six Paris train stations and destinations served, both within France and internationally, are:

Paris, all to Myself!

It quickly becomes evident to anyone trying to put their bike on a long-distance train in France, that the SNCF has a vendetta against 'non-morning' people. The one train per day that might take bikes typically runs at the most inconvenient time, usually early morning.

Not being a morning person, that annoyed me. Most of the trains I needed to catch left around 7 am, which meant leaving my Paris hotel by 6 am. But after doing this a few times, I realised as I sleepily attached my panniers and rode off, these early starts were, in fact, a bonus as the streets of Paris were empty.

There was no traffic at 6 am, except the occasional delivery truck. The streets were all *mine* as I whizzed unobstructed down bike lanes, and arrived at the station earlier than anticipated. Sunrise over the Seine was gorgeous, the smells emanating from ubiquitous *boulangeries* were intoxicating, the deserted streets took on a different charm, and the uncrowded sights of Paris were magical.

The SNCF had converted me! While in Paris, I found myself getting up for a dawn ride, ready to grasp the city in its early morning splendour: the Eiffel Tower with no crowds, the quiet quays of the Seine, and the chance to ride around the normally frenetic Arc de Triomphe!

Katherine Widing

Gare d'Austerlitz (13e) Loire Valley, south-western France, Languedoc, Roussillon, Pyrenees, Spain, Portugal.

Gare de l'Est (10e) Champagne, Alsace, Lorraine, Luxembourg, parts of Switzerland, southern Germany and points further east.

Gare de Lyon (12e) Areas south-east of Paris, including Burgundy, Provence, the Côte d'Azur, the Alps, parts of Switzerland, Italy and beyond.

Gare Montparnasse (15e) Parts of southern Normandy, Brittany, places between Paris and Brittany (Chartres, Angers, Nantes, Tours) and TGVs to parts of south-western France.

Gare du Nord (10e) Northern France, UK, Belgium, the Netherlands, northern Germany, Scandinavia, Moscow etc, and Eurostar to London.

Gare St Lazare (8e) Normandy.

Paris Orientation

Duration	1½–2½ hours
Distance	11.4km
Difficulty	easy
Start/End	Eiffel Tower

This sightseeing tour of Paris traverses the city mostly on bikepaths along the Seine. The route takes in many of the major monuments, museums and churches that make Paris famous. Although there is not time to visit each one, the route gives a sense of geography and could even be broken into several sightseeing trips.

The ride can be done year-round; on Sunday much of the area beside the Seine is closed to vehicular traffic. The route has been designed as a loop which cyclists can start/end at any point for convenience.

THE RIDE

At the (described) starting point of the ride, the **Eiffel Tower** (☎ 01 44 11 23 23) and the grassy area, the **Champ de Mars**, are on the right. To the left, across the Pont d'Iéna and the **River Seine**, the **Palais de Chaillot** houses four museums.

Begin in the bike lane on quai Branly. At Pont de l'Alma, the bike lane continues straight, but you turn left. It is easier to go straight through the intersection and then cross the road to get onto the bridge. At the start of the bridge, on the right, the sign **Visite des Égouts de Paris'** marks the entry to Paris' sewers (*égouts*), which can be toured (☎ 01 47 05 10 29).

At the other end of the bridge, a quick 2km detour on the bike lanes straight up ave Marceau leads to the **Arc de Triomphe** (☎ 01 43 80 31 31), at the end of the bustling **ave des Champs Élysées**. The main route turns right onto cours Albert 1er and the lovely tree-lined bicycle path along the Seine.

On cours Albert 1er, the gravel areas on the right, next to the Seine River, are a favourite spot with locals for a game of *boules* (a type of bowls). Pass the dazzling belle époque bridge, **Pont Alexandre III**, to the right.

Turn left immediately after Pont de la Concorde, carefully cross the road, then turn right onto what looks like a footpath (actually a bikepath) and follow the bike signs. **Place de la Concorde** is at the south-eastern end of the **ave des Champs Élysées**. Check out the crazy traffic before continuing on the bikepath, shared with *piétons* (pedestrians). It travels along the side of the **Jardin des Tuileries** (Tuileries Gardens) where the **Musée de l'Orangerie** (☎ 01 42 97 48 16) houses Monet's *Water Lilies* and other impressionist works.

At the Pont Royal traffic lights, cross the road and continue cycling in the shared bus/bike lane on the other side. In 400m the **Musée du Louvre** is on the left, with the famous IM Pei **glass pyramid** at the entrance. (Across from the Musée du Louvre is the underground shopping mall **Carrousel du Louvre**, the centrepiece being a fabulous **inverted glass pyramid**, also by Pei.)

Turn right onto the oldest bridge in Paris, **Pont Neuf** (literally, 'New Bridge'), which leads onto the island, **Île de la Cité**. In just under 300m get into the left lane to turn left, following the bike lane onto quai des Orfèvres. Reaching Pont St Michel, **Ste Chapelle** (☎ 01 53 73 78 51), famed for its

PARIS & THE ÎLE DE FRANCE

Paris Orientation

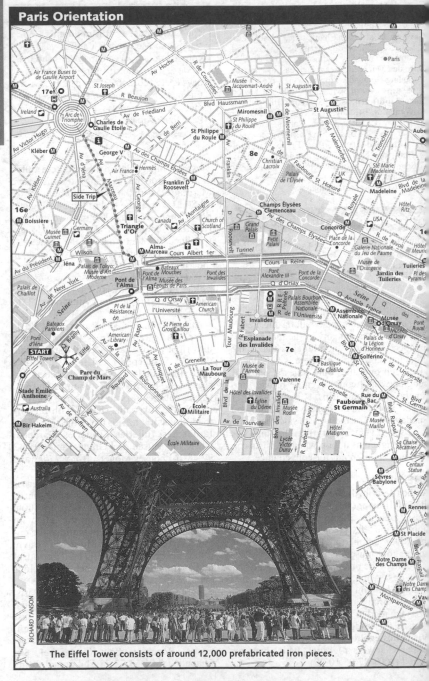

The Eiffel Tower consists of around 12,000 prefabricated iron pieces.

RICHARD I'ANSON

luminescent 13th-century stained glass, is just to the left in the Palais de Justice.

At Pont St Michel the route continues straight to place du Parvis Notre Dame, where the magnificent Gothic facade of **Notre Dame** (☎ 01 42 34 56 10) towers above. Before the cathedral, follow the bike signs to the left to land directly in front of the **Crypte Archéologique** (☎ 01 43 29 83 51), with remains from the Gallo-Roman period. Pont St Louis leads onto **Île St Louis**, a Parisian village unto itself.

At the end of the bridge, the bike lane disappears for a while, but it's quiet cycling

Cycling in the City

Paris has more than 130km of bikepaths, with more planned. The main ones run north to south and east to west. The *Mini Paris à Vélo* map is a must (see Maps & Books earlier in this chapter).

Drivers are aware of cyclists in the city, but always be on your guard. If there is a bikepath, you are obliged to use it (or risk a 250FF fine).

There are numerous parking spaces for *deux roues* (literally, two wheels), a term that refers to both bicycles and motorbikes. These are indicated by a blue and white 'deux roues' sign. However, Parisians lock their bikes to anything immovable. Always use two locks, remove panniers, computers etc and never leave your bike on the street overnight.

Sunday is for Cycling

Sunday is a terrific day for cycling in Paris. Not only is there generally less traffic, but the Paris *mairie* (town hall) has instituted 'traffic free' roads in several *arrondissements* (districts), so cyclists and pedestrians can enjoy those areas unencumbered by motorised vehicles.

On the Right Bank, these are the quays along the Seine from quai des Tuileries to quai Henri IV and along Canal St Martin, Bassin de la Villette and Canal de l'Ourcq. On the Left Bank the quays from quai Anatole France to quai Branly and rue Mouffetard are closed. The quays along both sides of the Seine are only closed Sundays from April to November, but the others are closed every Sunday year round from 10 am to 5 pm.

Citybike

On the last Saturday of every month (from March to October) hundreds of cyclists take over the streets of Paris. This is Citybike, a free event, run by Roue Libre, one of the most happening bicycle organisations in Paris. The idea behind it all is to encourage people to discover Paris by bicycle, learn about the bike lanes, see the sights from a different perspective, and become comfortable using a bicycle in the city.

The day starts at 9 am with a welcome breakfast of coffee, tea and pastries. (This *is* France!). At 10 am, the two-hour ride begins, when cyclists are led by Roue Libre employees and volunteers. The ride takes a different route each month.

To find out more, contact Roue Libre (☎ 01 53 46 43 77, metro Les Halles), 95bis rue Rambuteau (1er).

Bikes on Paris' Trains

Two types of suburban trains operate in Paris: the metro and the RER. The rules for the metro are simple: you can't travel on it with a bike, except on line No 1 (La Défense to Château de Vincennes) on Sunday until 4.30 pm. Louvre and La Défense-Grande Arche stations are not equipped for bikes and should be avoided.

Bikes are allowed (free) on the four RER lines all weekend and outside weekday peak times (6.30 to 9 am and 4.30 to 7 pm). Always ride in the carriages marked with the bicycle logo (usually the first or last carriages). Passengers with bikes cannot enter/exit RER stations at: Aubur (RER line A), Châtelet-Les-Halles (A, B & D), Cité Universitaire (B), Charles de Gaulle-Étoile (A), Denfert-Rochereau (B), La Défense-Grande Arche (A), Luxembourg (B), Nation (A), Port Royal (B) and St Michel-Notre Dame (B).

along the quays. Stop for an ice cream at **Berthillon** (see Places to Eat).

At **Pont de la Tournelle**, for a 2km side trip continue on quai de Béthune and turn left on Pont de Sully. Take the bikepath on blvd Henri IV to place de la Bastille, site of the infamous prison, **La Bastille**. The prison was stormed on 14 July 1789 and demolished shortly thereafter. Now a busy roundabout, the site is commemorated by the **Colonne de Juillet**. The **Marais**, just west of place de la Bastille, has several museums and an interesting Jewish neighbourhood. Don't miss the stately **Place des Vosges**, the **Musée Picasso**

Cycling in the City

Other Cycling Ideas

The two huge parks, the **Bois de Boulogne** (west) and the **Bois de Vincennes** (east), allow Parisians to enjoy green spaces and recreational activities. Both parks have several kilometres of bikepaths and have bike-hire facilities. The parks tend to be more crowded on weekends.

The towpaths along the **Canal St Martin** (10e) and the **Canal de l'Ourcq** (19e) offer peaceful cycling. To ride along them, start at place de La Bastille (see the Paris Orientation Ride) and take the bikepath on blvd Richard Lenoir to Canal St Martin (closed to motorised traffic on Sunday). The 4.5km canal, with its nine locks and pretty bridges, was built under Napoleon between 1805 and 1825 to link the Seine to the 108km Canal de l'Ourcq.

At the end of Canal St Martin, go under the railway tracks, through the busy intersection at place de la Bataille de Stalingrad (look for the Rotonde de la Villette on the left) and continue along the Bassin de la Villette, which becomes the Canal de l'Ourcq. The **Parc de la Villette** is 2km further on. At the northern end of the 30 hectare park, the **Cité des Sciences et de l'Industrie** (☎ 01 40 05 12 12) has high-tech exhibits and the superb **Cité des Enfants** for kids. Next door, the **Géode**, a 36m-high mirrored sphere, houses a theatre showing high-resolution 70mm films. The next portion of the canal becomes industrialised, passing alongside a cement factory and railway yards, but beyond this are several kilometres of towpath, used only by cyclists, walkers and in-line skaters. Return to Paris by retracing your steps.

Organised Cycle Tours

Several companies offer guided bike tours of Paris. Reservations are recommended and, for some tours, essential.

Roue Libre (☎ 01 53 46 43 77, metro Les Halles), 95bis rue Rambuteau (1er), has 10 theme tours (105FF to 165FF) departing at 10 am and 2 pm daily, plus an early morning and an evening tour and, on Saturday mornings, a market tour.

Paris à Vélo, c'est sympa! (☎ 01 48 87 60 01, metro Bastille), 37 blvd Bourdon (4e), has seven tours of Paris and two of the Île de France (150FF to 195FF). They operate daily from May through September, and weekends the rest of the year.

Bullfrog Bike Tours (☎ 06 09 98 08 60, 🖳 www.bullf rogbikes.com) runs two tours (120FF) daily from 1 May to 20 August at 11 am and 3.30 pm (20 August to 15 September, 11 am only) in the Champs de Mars across from the Eiffel Tower (look for the Bullfrog flag). Night tours are run from Sunday to Thursday at 9 pm.

Escapade Nature (☎ 01 53 17 03 18, fax 01 43 45

Signs and maps denote the car-free Sunday routes.

57 19, 🖳 www.novomundi.com/escapade-nature/) runs city tours (80FF to 160FF) at 11 am and 3 pm, but heads further afield with one-day outings to the Île de France on Sunday. The meeting point is place du Châtelet.

(☎ 01 42 71 25 21) and the **Mémorial du Martyr Juif Inconnu** (Memorial to the Unknown Jewish Martyr; ☎ 01 42 77 44 72).

Otherwise, at the bridge, turn right to return to the Left Bank. From the middle of the bridge is a superb view of Notre Dame. Turn right onto quai de la Tournelle and continue until blvd St Michel.

A side trip, left along blvd St Michel leads, through the **Latin Quarter**, home of Paris' most famous university, La Sorbonne, and on to the Jardin de Luxembourg (Luxembourg Gardens). It passes the **Musée National du Moyen Age** (Museum of the Middle Ages; ☎ 01 53 73 78 00) at the intersection with blvd St Germain, where the superb 15th-century tapestries *La Dame à la Licorne* (The Unicorn Lady) hang.

On the main route, soon after Pont Royal, the **Musée d'Orsay** (☎ 01 45 49 11 11) is a spectacular museum in a renovated train station. Its collections include impressionist, postimpressionist and Art Nouveau works. Continuing on quai d'Orsay, the **Assemblée Nationale**, the lower house of the French parliament, comes into view on the left.

At **Pont Alexandre III**, on the left is the **Hôtel des Invalides**, originally built as housing for disabled war veterans. The building with the golden dome, **Église du Dôme**, houses Napoleon's tomb. To the south-east of the hôtel is the **Musée Rodin** (☎ 01 47 05 01 34), with sculptures by Rodin and Claudel displayed both inside the museum and in the serene gardens.

Continue on the bike lane on quai d'Orsay to quai Branly and back to the Eiffel Tower.

Île de France

The region surrounding Paris is known as the Île de France (Island of France) because it lies between four rivers: the Aube, Marne, Oise and Seine. It was from this relatively small area that, beginning in around 1100, the kingdom of France began to expand.

Today, the region's exceptional sights – the cathedrals of St Denis, Chartres, Beauvais and Senlis; the chateaux of Versailles, Fontainebleau and Chantilly; and Euro Disneyland – and its woodland areas, such as the forests of Fontainebleau and Chantilly, make it especially popular with day-trippers.

INFORMATION

The handy Espace du Tourisme Île de France (☎ 01 44 50 19 98, fax 01 44 50 19 99, 🖳 www.paris-ile-de-france.com, metro Palais-Royal-Musée du Louvre, 1er), is in the lower level of the Carrousel du Louvre shopping mall in Paris.

Yvelines, the western department of the Île de France, has a free booklet of 12 cycling circuits, *Randonnées à Vélo en Yvelines* (in French). The booklet is available from the Espace du Tourisme Île de France, or any of the tourist offices in Yvelines.

Maps & Books

Michelin map No 237 *Île de France* (1:200,000) is a good planning and touring map of the entire area; Michelin map No 106 *Environs de Paris* (1:100,000) covers most of the Île de France in twice the detail.

IGN's cycling map, *90 Circuits Cyclos en Île de France* (1:100,000), shows 90 circuits in the Île de France.

Fontainebleau is a mountain biker's mecca and several guide books are available. In the ONF VTT Évasion series Nos 6 & 7 of the *Seine et Marne: 77* guides have rides in the forest, as does *VTT: Île de France Sud-Est*, by Jean-Jacques Reynier.

GETTING THERE & AWAY

The Île de France is served by an excellent rail network with frequent services; all trains take bicycles (except during weekday peak periods of 6.30 to 9 am and 4.30 to 7 pm).

Fabulous Fontainebleau

Duration	2–4 hours
Distance	42.5km
Difficulty	easy
Start/End	Fontainebleau

Nature lovers, culture buffs and art enthusiasts will all be satisfied by this ride. Visit the grand chateau; ride through the Forêt de Fontainebleau, crossed by walking and cycling paths; and stop in the village of Barbizon, home of the Barbizon School of Art. A side trip leads to a bizarre modern sculpture.

The ride can be done year round, but be conscious of available daylight hours in winter. There is so much to see that an overnight stay in Fontainebleau is advised f the forest is your focus, weekdays are less crowded; if the chateau is your main interest, it is closed on Tuesday.

GETTING TO/FROM THE RIDE

Fontainebleau is only about 100km from Auxerre, the start of the Classic Burgundy ride (Burgundy chapter), though you have to go through Paris to get there by train.

About 25 SNCF commuter trains link Paris' Gare de Lyon with Fontainebleau-Avon (47FF, 40 to 60 minutes); in off-peak periods, about one train runs per hour. All trains take bikes but, be careful, some carriages (out of Paris) terminate in Melun. The last train to Paris leaves Fontainebleau Avon at about 9.45 pm (about 10.30 pm on Sunday and holidays).

The train station is about 3km from the tourist office on ave de Valvine. To ride to the tourist office, turn left onto ave de Valvine, which becomes ave Franklin Roosevelt. At 1km, veer left onto rue Aristide Briand. At 1.8km go through place de l'Étape and continue on rue Grande until the post office, where you veer slightly right onto rue Dénecourt. At place du Général de Gaulle, turn right. The tourist office is 100m further on the right.

THE RIDE
Fontainebleau

The stylish town of Fontainebleau is known for its elegant Renaissance chateau, one of the most beautifully ornamented and lavishly furnished in France.

The original chateau was built in the early 12th century, but was reconstructed under François I (ruled 1515–47), whose superb artisans blended Italian and French styles in ornate decorations. The latter half of the 16th century saw the chateau enlarged yet again, and later Louis XIV hired Le Nôtre to redesign the gardens. In WWII, the chateau served as a German headquarters.

Information The tourist office (☎ 01 60 74 99 99, fax 01 60 74 80 22, ☐ www .fontainebleau.org), 4 rue Royale, is open daily year round. Bikes can be hired here for 100FF to 120FF a day.

The ONF office (☎ 01 60 74 93 50) for the Forêt de Fontainebleau is at located at 217bis rue Grande. The Banque de France is at 192 rue Grande.

Cycles La Petite Reine (☎ 01 60 74 57 57, fax 01 60 74 57 50), 32 rue des Sablons, hires bikes for 80/100FF weekdays/weekends (closed Monday). In the warmer months, M Mulot (☎ 01 64 22 36 14), at the train station, hires bikes for 120FF per day. Call to ensure he's there.

Things to See & Do In the enormous 1900-room **chateau** (☎ 01 60 71 50 70) you can visit the magnificent rooms of the **Grands Appartements** (State Apartments); the **Musée Napoléon 1er**, a museum of Napoleon memorabilia; and the **Musée Chinois** (Chinese Museum), filled with objects from east Asia. Entry to the **gardens** and **grounds**, including the Jardin de Diane, Jardin Français, Étang de Carp (Carp Pond) and the Grand Canal, is free. Bikes are not allowed in the formal garden area close to the chateau, but can be ridden in the Parc de Palais and around the Grand Canal.

Places to Stay & Eat The pleasant *Hôtel La Carpe d'Or (☎ 01 64 22 28 64, fax 01 64 22 39 95, 7 rue d'Avon)* has singles/doubles with shower and toilet from 190/290FF. Friendly and well situated, the *Hôtel de la Chancellerie (☎ 01 64 22 21 70, fax 01 64 22 64 43, 1 rue de la Chancellerie)* has comfortable rooms with shower and toilet for 240/280FF. Right across from the chateau, the *Hôtel Richelieu (☎ 01 64 22 26 46, fax 01 64 23 40 17, 4 rue Richelieu)* maintains Logis de France standards. Rooms with shower and toilet start from 260/300FF.

On Tuesday, Friday and Sunday the *market* sets up on place du Marché. Along rue Grande are *boulangeries*, *patisseries* and *assorted food shops*, plus, at No 58, the *Prisunic* supermarket. Near the train station, the *Champion* supermarket is at 36 ave Franklin Roosevelt.

There are plenty of places to eat serving a variety of cuisines in Fontainebleau. Restaurants, brasseries and cafes can be found on *rue Grande* and *rue de France*. Admire the chateau from the terrace of the *Restaurant le Bacchus* at the Hôtel Richelieu, where *menus* cost 85/125FF.

Fabulous Fontainebleau
2–4 hours, 42.5km

It's easy cycling along the forest's network of *routes forestières* (forest roads; RFs on

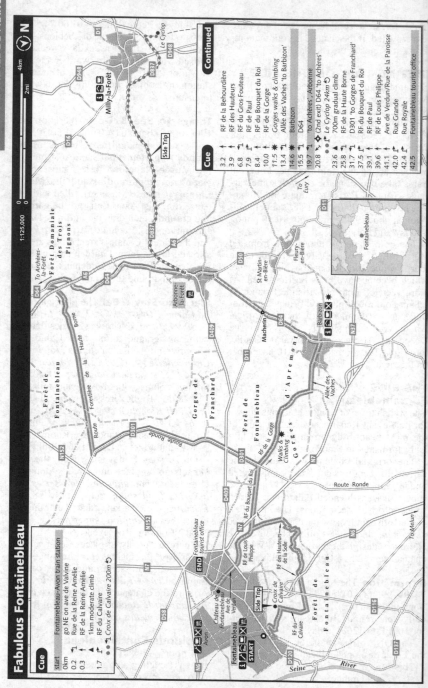

Fabulous Fontainebleau

Cue

start		Fontainebleau–Avon train station
0km		go NE on ave de Valvine
0.2	↱	Rue de la Reine Amélie
0.3	◄	RF de la Reine Amélie
		1km moderate climb
1.7	↱	RF du Calvaire
	●●● ↱	Croix de Calvaire 200m ↻

Cue

3.2	←	RF de la Behourdière
3.9	←	RF des Hauteurs
6.8	↱	RF du Gros Fouteau
7.9	↲	RF de Paul
8.4	↱	RF du Bouquet du Roi
10.0	↱	RF de la Gorge
11.5	✳	Gorges walks & climbing
13.4	✳	Allée des Vaches 'to Barbizon'
14.6	✳	Barbizon
15.5	◇	'to Achères', Arbonne
19.7	◇ ↲	(2nd exit) D64 'to Achères'
20.8	●●●	Le Cyclop 24km ↻
23.6	◄	700m gradual climb
25.8	◄	RF de la Haute Borne
31.7	↱	D301 'to Gorges de Franchard'
37.5	↲	RF du Bouquet du Roi
39.1	←	RF de Paul
39.6	←	RF de Louis Philippe
41.1	↱	Ave de Verdun/Rue de la Paroisse
42.0	↲	Rue Grande
42.4	↱	Rue Royale
42.5		Fontainebleau tourist office

naps), with only two discernible inclines. To picnic in the forest, pick up supplies in Fontainebleau before you leave.

The 250-sq-km forest surrounding the town has been a favourite royal hunting ground for centuries. It is one of the loveliest wooded tracts in the Île de France, boasting oaks, beeches, birches and planted pines, as well as interesting rock formations and gorges which attract rock climbers. Many car-free roads and trails – including parts of the GR1 and GR11 – crisscross the area, which is also popular with walkers, cyclists and equestrians.

The ride starts with an easy climb. At the top, a short detour left leads to the **Croix de Calvaire** and **viewpoint** over the town. Ride through the forest and, soon after crossing the N6, along the Route Forestières des Hauteurs de la Solle with **views** to the right. Similar views can be seen from the terrace of the pricey restaurant, *Auberge du Mont Chauvet* (☎ 01 64 22 92 30), closed Tuesday. *Menus* start at 150FF, and salads cost between 42FF and 72FF.

The gate at Route Forestière de Paul is to keep out cars, not cyclists and walkers. Carefully cross the busy N7 and continue on Route Forestière du Bouquet du Roi, another gated, car-free road.

About 1.5km after crossing the D301 there are parking areas (and entry points for several walks and climbs) for the **Gorges d'Apremont**.

The pretty village of **Barbizon** invites a stop. It was here in the mid-1800s that the Barbizon School of landscape artists was formed. The artists were the first to paint outdoors; two of the most notable were Théodore Rousseau and François Millet.

Walk your bike, as **Grande Rue**, the main street, is one way. It's lined with small galleries, *cafes*, *restaurants* and *hotels*, some quite expensive, as Barbizon is a favourite spot for Parisian day-trippers. The tourist office is at No 47. Visit the museum **Maison-Atelier de Théodore Rousseau** (☎ 01 60 66 22 38) next door. L'Auberge Ganne, at No 92, houses the **Musée de l'École de Barbizon** (Museum of the Barbizon School; ☎ 01 60 66 22 27; closed Tuesday).

At the roundabout (20.8km) just after Arbonne-la-Forêt, detour to **Milly-la-Forêt** (see Side Trip), or continue on the shady D64 into the Forêt Domaniale des Trois Pignons and the second climb of the day. Look carefully for Route Forestière de la Haute Borne (25.8km), a wonderful 6km stretch of car-free road heading east through the forest. It begins on the left opposite a parking area, just under the A6 freeway, and is gated to prevent car traffic.

The D301 is also known as **Route Ronde**. Centuries old, it was one of the first roads in the forest, created by Henri IV in a semi-circle around the chateau. Pass the parking area for the **Gorges de Franchard**, a great spot for **hiking**.

Retrace the outward ride along the shaded, car-free Route Forestière du Bouquet du Roi. Cross the N7 (which in late afternoon can be very busy) to the Route Forestière de Paul and continue straight on the unsigned Route Forestière de Louis Philippe into Fontainebleau, past the **chateau** (see the Fontainebleau Things to See & Do section) to the tourist office.

Side Trip: Milly-la-Forêt & Le Cyclop
1–2 hours, 24km

The charming village of **Milly-la-Forêt** surrounds the magnificent covered **wooden market hall**, built in 1479, almost entirely of chestnut. Artist Jean Cocteau lived in Milly and his work decorates the 12th-century **Chapelle St-Blaise des Simples**. The tourist office (☎ 01 64 98 83 17, fax 01 64 98 94 80) is at 60 rue Jean Cocteau (closed Wednesday and Sunday afternoons).

Just 2km outside Milly-la-Forêt is one of the most bizarre pieces of art in France, or for that matter, the world. **Le Cyclop** is a 22.5m-high, glistening cyclopean head. Made with 300 tonnes of steel, it is zigzagged by stairs and footbridges to enable the visitor to explore sculptor Jean Tinguely's contemporary monster. Begun in 1969 with the help of 15 artists, whose work can be viewed inside, it took 10 years to complete. Check the Web site 🖳 www.art-public.com/cyclop for more information or ask at the Milly-la-Forêt tourist office. It costs 35FF to enter (open May to October, Friday through Sunday from 11 am to 5 pm).

To reach Milly and Le Cyclop, at the roundabout after Arbonne-la-Forêt, turn right (1st exit) on the D837 and continue straight until Milly-la-Forêt. To go to Le Cyclop, stay on the D837 at the intersection before Milly. Shortly after the roundabout intersecting the D948, turn right at the sign for Le Cyclop. To go to Milly-la Forêt from Le Cyclop, retrace your steps, but at the roundabout, turn right on the D948 and ride the 1km into Milly.

Forêt de Compiègne

Duration	1½–3 hours
Distance	34.3km
Difficulty	easy
Start/End	Compiègne

The 220-sq-km Forêt de Compiègne, ideal for both cycling and walking, is one of the great green escapes for Parisians on weekends. Beeches, oaks, elms and pines cover this former royal hunting ground, stretching south-east from Compiègne to the pretty town of Pierrefonds.

The forest played a part in both world wars and in the north of the forest is the *Clairière de l'Armistice* (Armistice Clearing; see Side Trip).

PLANNING
Combine this and the Île de France Diversity rides for a three-day tour.

When to Ride
Weekdays are less crowded than weekends, and autumn – when the forest is awash with a colourful cloak of leaves – is an ideal time to ride.

Maps
The IGN *Forêts de Compiègne et de Laigue* (1:25,000) shows the area in good detail. The Compiègne tourist office has a free (and very simple) map of all the area's bikepaths.

GETTING TO/FROM THE RIDE
This ride could follow any of the northern Champagne rides – Vallée de la Marne, Montagne de Reims or Côte des Blancs – which start and end in Épernay, around a 100km ride from Compiègne. However, train connections from Champagne are easier through Paris. The Île de France Diversity ride detailed later in this chapter also starts in Compiègne.

Although Compiègne borders the Île de France, none of the commuter SNCF trains go that far. Fortunately, the SNCF recognises the Forêt de Compiègne is a popula cycling destination and three or four train a day (in each direction) take bicycles.

About a dozen trains daily leave fo Compiègne from Paris' Gare du Nord (69FF, one to 1¼ hours). At the time o writing, the last train to Paris that took bikes left at 5.35 pm.

The train station is on place de la Gare the tourist office is 700m away. Exit the sta tion and go right on place de la Gare, then turn left at place 54e Rgt d'Infanterie, cross ing the Oise on Pont Solférino. Continue straight along on rue Solférino until place de l'Hôtel de Ville. The tourist office is or the left.

THE RIDE
Compiègne
A country retreat for French rulers since Merovingian times, Compiègne's popularity reached its height in the mid-19th century under Napoleon III.

One of the world's most gruelling cycling races, the Paris-Roubaix, does not begin ir Paris, as the name suggests, but here in Compiègne.

Information The tourist office (☎ 03 44 40 01 00, fax 03 44 40 23 28, 🖳 www.mairie-co mpiegne.fr), in the Hôtel de Ville on place de l'Hôtel de Ville, is open daily (closed Sunday from November to mid-April). Pick up the English pamphlets *Compiègne: A City of Art* and *The Forest of Compiègne*. It also sells *Guide Pédestre: Forêt de Compiègne* (10FF), which details seven hiking circuits.

A couple of banks can be found on rue Magenta: the Banque Nationale de Paris at No 1, and the Société Générale at No 2. The Banque de France is at 2 rue du Dahomey across from the chateau.

Cycles Coquerel (☎ 03 44 40 15 24) is at 7 rue Hippolyte-Bottier. For bike hire, AB Cyclette (☎ 06 85 08 12 80, fax 03 44 40 03 45), 24 rue d'Ulm, is pricey at 130FF/day. On weekends, bicycles can be hired (☎ 06 07 54 99 26) at the Carrefour Royal.

Things to See & Do On place Hôtel de Ville, the facade of the 15th-century, Flamboyant Gothic **Hôtel de Ville**, is eye-catching. The huge **statue of Joan of Arc**

opposite remembers the saint's capture in Compiègne in 1430. Around the corner, on rue St Corneille, are the vestiges of the 14th-century **cloisters** of the Benedictine St Corneille Abbey.

After the forest, the main attraction is the old royal palace on place Général de Gaulle. Known as the **Musée National du Château de Compiègne** (☎ 03 44 38 47 00), the chateau complex dates back to 1752 and

Paris-Roubaix: Mud, Mayhem & Cobblestones

Forming the backbone of the 10-race world cup of professional cycle racing is a series of six one-day races known as the 'classics': Milan–San Remo (Italy), Tour of Flanders (Belgium), Liège-Bastogne-Liège (Belgium) and Paris-Roubaix are all held in spring, while Paris-Tours and the Tour of Lombardy (Italy) are held in autumn. The classics date back to the turn of the 19th century, when the roads were unsealed, the bikes were basic and the racing was very, very tough.

Paris-Roubaix is perhaps the quintessential classic. Usually held the first Sunday after Easter, the 270km or so route of 'La Pascale' across northern France is designed to provide the ultimate test in strength, skill and endurance. Using roads once trodden by Napoleon's armies and then ravaged by the bombs of two world wars, l'Enfer du Nord (literally, 'Hell of the North'), as the race is popularly known, includes around two dozen sections of *pavé* (cobblestone) road.

In a race at breakneck speed, usually less than half of the 180-odd starters reach the finish on the Roubaix velodrome. Negotiating the pavé requires phenomenal strength and steely concentration to simply remain upright, let alone finish. The former Dutch professional cyclist Theo de Rooy recalls his experiences of the Hell of the North, '…it's a pile of shit this race. It's a whole pile of shit. You haven't even got the time to piss. You ride and you piss in your pants. It's a whole pile of shit.' When asked whether he would do it again, de Rooy replied, 'Of course! It's the most beautiful race in the world.'

Despite technological innovations such as the introduction of front-suspension forks and thick cyclo-cross style tyres, the very best riders still fall foul of the pavé. The enduring image of the race is of mud-stained cyclists clutching bent wheels and broken bicycles, while team cars (banked up bumper to bumper on the narrow roads) try to cut through the crowds to reach their stricken riders, their race now effectively over.

Despite its name, the race does not actually start in Paris, but in the neighbouring town of Compiègne. Believed to capture the essential virtues of the people of the north of France, Paris-Roubaix has come to embody the qualities of tenacity, gritty determination and the capacity to endure hardships that go with living in a region beset by high unemployment, economic stagnation and crippling winters.

The brainchild of wealthy Roubaix industrialists, the first event was held in 1896 as a way of attracting interest to the area. The 45 professionals and six amateur riders racing to the town's new velodrome were competing for 1000FF in prize money, which was won by Josef Fischer, a German who finished 36 minutes ahead of the field.

Belgian Roger de Vlaeminck is considered the master of Paris-Roubaix, having raced it 14 times between 1969 and 1982 and finishing in the top seven on 13 occasions, with four victories. Others whose names are inextricably linked with the event include Belgian Eddy Merckx (three victories), Italian Francesco Moser (three), Irishman Sean Kelly (two) and the persistent Frenchman Gilbert Duclos-Lassalle who contested Paris-Roubaix 14 times before eventually claiming victory in 1991 (and again in 1992).

The worst stretches of road are at Troisvilles (after about 100km), although the Arenberg Forest near Valenciennes (after about 160km) is a traditional black spot, with its long sections of pavé and big crowds. (It's possible to tackle the pavé as a 'tourist' in a separate event – see the Randonnées chapter for details.) It's somewhat ironic, and part of the magic of the race, that despite massive technological innovations in cycling, the greatest riders can be humbled by something as anachronistic as a cobblestone. For this very reason, Paris-Roubaix remains one of the most exciting and unpredictable of races.

comprises the beautifully furnished Royal Apartments and the Musée du Second Empire. Also on the grounds is the **Musée de la Voiture** (Car Museum) which, as well as a collection of historic carriages and early cars, has a section devoted to the evolution of the bicycle, from the Draisienne to turn-of-the-20th-century machines (all close Tuesday).

Places to Stay The *Camping de l'Hippodrome (☎ 03 44 20 28 58, ave du Baron Roger de Soultrait)* charges 8.40FF for a site, and 9FF per adult. It is across from Carrefour Royal (open from mid-March to mid-November).

The *Hôtel du Lion d'Or (☎ 03 44 23 32 17, fax 03 44 86 06 23, 4 rue de Général Leclerc)* has basic singles/doubles with washbasin for 140/150FF, and rooms with shower and toilet for 165/180FF. The charming and cosy *Hôtel de France (☎ 03 44 40 02 74, fax 03 44 40 48 37, 17 rue Eugène Floquet)* has simple rooms with washbasin from 140/170FF (more with shower and toilet). Overlooking the Oise River, the *Hôtel de Flandre (☎ 03 44 83 24 40, fax 03 44 90 02 75, 16 quai de la République)* has spacious rooms with shower and toilet from 240FF.

Places to Eat Place du Change hosts a *market* on Wednesday and Saturday mornings. The *Monoprix* supermarket is central, at 37 rue Solférino.

Just south of place de l'Hôtel de Ville, on rue Jean Legendre, are a couple of good *brasseries*. Around the corner, on tiny rue St Martin, is a cluster of *restaurants*, including *Le Bouchon (☎ 03 44 40 05 32)* at No 5, with starters from 40FF and interesting mains from 60FF. Across the street at No 2ter, is *Crêperie-Saladerie La Bolée (☎ 03 44 40 80 88)*, where salads start at 39FF, and crepes at 18FF (closed Monday).

Restaurant Le Stromboli (☎ 03 44 40 06 21, 2 rue des Lombards) has an outdoor eating area in a secluded courtyard between half-timbered houses. Pizzas start at 37FF, salads at 37FF and main courses at 56FF (closed Sunday, and for lunch on Saturday and Monday).

Restaurant Nouvelle Étoile (☎ 03 44 20 39 44, 17 place du Change) specialises in Chinese, Thai and Vietnamese food. Appetisers begin at 22FF, mains at 38FF, and *menus* range from 79FF to 120FF.

Forêt de Compiègne
1½–3 hours, 34.3km
Effortless cycling is the order of the day. The trip is peaceful and easy: a paved, signed bicycle path on flat terrain is interspersed with small detours to appealing villages.

The forest's bikepath begins 2km out of town, at the Carrefour Royal (Royal Crossroads), to the left of the information board. The path crosses a few busy roads.

The first detour, left on the D602, is to the village of **Vieux Moulin**. At the foot of a hill, this was originally a woodcutters village. The adorable **church** was rebuilt by Napoleon III in 1860. A small *alimentation générale* (general store) is at 17 rue St Jean (closed Tuesday afternoon and Wednesday).

Back on the main route, in the small town of **Pierrefonds**, the immense, fairy-tale **chateau** dominates. Built in the 14th century, it fell into ruins and was purchased in 1813 by Napoleon I for just under 3000FF! It was restored by Viollet-le-Duc under Napoleon III. Guided tours run daily (☎ 03 44 42 80 77).

Mountain bikers can head to the tourist office (☎ 03 44 42 81 44, fax 03 44 42 37 73, 🖳 perso.wanadoo.fr/ot.pierrefonds), rue Louis d'Orléans on the way to the chateau via rue Michelet, for a pamphlet, *L'Encerclement du Château de Pierrefonds* (in French), detailing a 30km ride.

To get back onto the bikepath, continue on rue du Beaudon. The right turn is easy to miss: look for the small sign 'Sente de Point de Vue'. Take a minute to climb to this **viewpoint** for an absolutely fabulous view of the chateau.

On the way back to Compiègne, the bikepath tips the edge of the village of **St Jean-aux-Bois**. A 1km detour leads through the tiny village to the serene 13th-century **church** and monastic buildings dating from the 12th century.

On the main route, rejoin the road at the Carrefour Royal for the last 2km. In front of the chateau is a section of cobblestones, your chance to get a feel for the Paris-Roubaix race.

Side Trip: Clairière de l'Armistice
1–1½ hours, 13.2km return
East of Compiègne, in the north of the forest, is the **Clairière de l'Armistice** (Armistice Clearing). Here, in a railway carriage, the

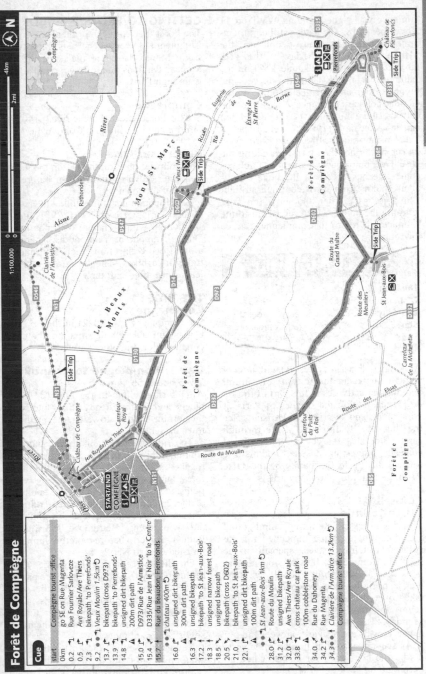

Forêt de Compiègne

Cue	
0km	Compiègne tourist office
	go SE on Rue Magenta
0.2	Rue Fournier Sarloveze
0.5	Ave Royale/Ave Thiers
2.3	bikepath 'to Pierrefonds'
9.2	*Vieux Moulin 1.5km* ↻
13.7	bikepath (cross D973)
13.9	bikepath 'to Pierrefonds'
14.8	unsigned dirt bikepath
	200m dirt path
15.0	D973/Rue de l'Armistice
15.4	D335/Rue Jean le Noir 'to le Centre'
15.7	Rue du Beaudon, Pierrefonds
	chateau 400m ↻
16.0	unsigned dirt bikepath
	300m dirt path
16.3	unsigned bikepath
17.2	bikepath 'to St Jean-aux-Bois'
18.3	unsigned narrow forest road
18.5	unsigned bikepath
20.5	bikepath (cross D602)
21.0	bikepath 'to St Jean-aux-Bois'
22.1	unsigned dirt bikepath
	100m dirt path
	St Jean-aux-Bois 1km ↻
28.0	Route du Moulin
31.2	unsigned bikepath
32.0	Ave Thiers/Ave Royale
33.8	cross chateau car park
	100m cobblestone road
34.0	Rue du Dahomey
34.2	Rue Magenta
34.3	*Clairière de l'Armistice 13.2km* ↻
	Compiègne tourist office

armistice was signed, ending WWI on 11 November 1918. The date is still commemorated annually by many people on 'the 11th hour of the 11th day of the 11th month'. In WWII, on 22 June 1940, in the same carriage, the Germans forced the French to sign an armistice recognising the German conquest of France. A replica of the carriage and a museum (☎ 03 44 85 14 18) can be visited daily (10FF), except Tuesday.

From the tourist office head north-west on rue Solférino, then turn right along the Oise River onto cours Guynemer, which becomes the busy N31. At the huge roundabout 4.3km from town continue straight ('to Soissons'). After another 500m veer left onto the quieter D546 for 1.7km to the entrance. To return to Compiègne, retrace the route.

Île de France Diversity

Duration	2 days
Distance	90.3km
Difficulty	easy-moderate
Start	Compiègne
End	Auvers-sur-Oise

Although only a short ride, you will quickly come to appreciate the diversity of cultural and outdoor activities in this part of the Île de France. Within the reaches of Paris, it will come as no surprise that Parisians flee the 'big city' to this area. Ride through serene forests, marvel at magnificent chateaux, interesting museums and historic towns, and cycle the banks of the Oise River, an inspiration to many artists.

PLANNING
When to Ride
This ride is best in late spring, summer and autumn. Autumn is recommended for the colourful canopy of leaves, especially in the Forêt de Compiègne. It is a good idea to book accommodation in Chantilly in summer, especially June, when horse racing takes over the town. Several of the museums in Auvers-sur-Oise are closed on Monday. The area's proximity to Paris means crowds are heaviest on weekends.

As accommodation is limited in Auvers, it's best to book early, or plan to catch an evening train back to Paris.

GETTING TO/FROM THE RIDE
The Forêt de Compiègne ride also starts in Compiègne. Auvers-sur-Oise is about 40km from Mantes-la-Jolie, the start of the Monet's Passions ride following; rail access is through Paris.

Compiègne
See the Forêt de Compiègne ride (p140) for information on getting to Compiègne.

Auvers-sur-Oise
The train station is on the D4 on the left as you enter Auvers, about 300m before the centre of the town.

SNCF commuter trains link Auvers-sur-Oise to Paris' Gare du Nord (29FF, one to 1¼ hours), with a change of trains in St-Ouen l'Aumône or Valmondois. There are at least two connections each hour and all trains take bikes. The last train to Paris leaves just after 8.30 pm.

THE RIDE
Compiègne
See Compiègne (pp140–2) in the Forêt de Compiègne ride for information about accommodation and other services.

Day 1: Compiègne to Chantilly
2½–5 hours, 55.4km
After a short climb in the Forêt de Compiègne and another steady climb into Néry, the terrain flattens towards the medieval town of Senlis.

The ride begins on bikepaths and then continues through the forest on quiet, shady roads. A short, steep climb leads out of the forest and the trees are replaced by wheat fields. Explore the temple, theatre and baths of the 2nd-century **Gallo-Roman ruins** of Champlieu (15.3km). Cruise downhill into the twin towns, Béthisy-St Martin and Béthisy-St Pierre before a pretty climb on a forested road to Néry.

On the left entering Bray, the **13th-century Priory** (La Prieuré) is now a private residence. On leaving Barbery, the small farm road on the right is easy to miss; don't take the D134 by accident. After turning onto the D330, the spire of the cathedral of Senlis comes into view.

Navigating Senlis (43.7km) is tricky. At the roundabout (with the deer statue in the centre), go left on ave du Général Leclerc (not rue de la République). Curve past Église St Pierre on the right to rue du Chancellier. At place du Parvis, where the tourist office (☎ 03 44 53 06 40, fax 03 77 53 29 80; closed Tuesday) is opposite the cathedral, turn right again onto rue de Villevert.

The appeal of medieval Senlis comes from its winding cobblestone streets, Gallo-Roman ramparts and lovely old houses. It is like stepping back in time, which is why Senlis is often used as a film set. Visit the magnificent 12th-century Gothic **Cathédrale de Notre Dame**. All of the several **museums** in town, including the **Musée d'Art de Archéologie** (☎ 03 44 53 00 80) in the former bishop's palace, are closed all day Tuesday and Wednesday morning. The tourist office brochure 'Ville Royale' details four walking tours (in English).

At 46.6km wind down rue de la Vallée, through a gorgeous shady lane and to the pretty houses of Avilly-St Léonard. Right after Avilly, enter the Forêt de Chantilly. Lose the serenity when you hit the D924A, but after 1km the **Château de Chantilly** (see the Chantilly Things to See & Do section) is an incredible sight.

Chantilly

Chantilly stretches along two busy main streets: ave du Maréchal Joffre and rue du Connétable, meeting almost at a right angle at place Omer Vallon. The chateau is about 1.5km south-east of the main part of town. Other than the chateau, Chantilly is known as a horse-racing and training centre, and for the Forêt de Chantilly (to the south and east of the town).

Information The tourist office (☎ 03 44 57 08 58, fax 03 44 57 74 64), 60 ave du Maréchal Joffre, is open daily from April to September, and closed Sunday the rest of the year. For information on the forest, the ONF (☎ 03 44 57 03 88) is at 1 route de l'Aigle.

Several banks are on ave du Maréchal Joffre, including the Société Générale at No 1 and Banque Nationale de Paris at No 8.

Chantilly doesn't have a bike shop; however, Chantilly Motos (☎ 03 44 58 54 15), 16 place Omer Vallon, may be able to help. Orry Cycles Évasion (☎ 03 44 58 04 03), 5 rue Neuve, is in Orry-la-Ville, about 10km south-east. Bikes can be hired there for 90FF a day.

Things to See & Do The chateau (☎ 03 44 62 62 62) consists of two attached buildings, the Renaissance-style Grand Chateau, demolished during the Revolution and rebuilt in the 1870s, and the Petit Chateau, built around 1560 for Anne de Montmorency.

The Grand Chateau contains the **Musée Condé**, the most remarkable works found in a room called the Sanctuaire. In the Petit Chateau are the Appartements des Princes (Princes' Apartments), the highlight being the **Cabinet des Livres**, a repository of 700 manuscripts and more than 12,000 other volumes, including a Gutenberg Bible.

The grounds are a combination of formal gardens and park. In the mid-17th century Le Nôtre laid out the **Jardin Français**, the **Jardin Anglais** was begun in 1817, and the **Jardin Anglo-Chinois** (Anglo-Chinese Garden) was created in the 1770s. Great views can be had from the **Aérophile**, the world's largest hot air balloon. The **Hydrophile**, an electric boat glides along the Grand Canal.

Horse lovers will want to visit the **Musée Vivant du Cheval** (Living Horse Museum) in the chateau's stables, the Grandes Écuries (☎ 03 44 57 40 40).

On Sunday at 3 pm, from June to September, the ONF offers **guided forest tours**.

Places to Stay The closest camping ground, *Campix* (*☎ 03 44 56 08 48, fax 03 44 56 28 75, e campix@aol.com, Chemin de la Carrière),* is in St-Leu d'Esserent, 5km north-west of Chantilly. It costs 30FF to pitch a tent, and 25FF per adult.

The *Hôtel La Calèche (☎ 03 44 57 02 55, fax 03 44 57 77 93, 3 ave du Maréchal Joffre)* has spotless, renovated rooms with shower and toilet for 240FF. Just a few doors away, all of the rooms at the *Hôtel d'Angleterre (☎ 03 44 58 78 18, 9 place Omer Vallon)* have shower and toilet and cost 220FF.

Auberge Le Vertugadin (☎ 03 44 57 03 19, fax 03 44 57 92 31, 44 rue du Connétable) has plain rooms with shower for 250FF. The hotel reception keeps restaurant hours (it is closed until 7 pm). Book ahead.

Places to Eat On Wednesday and Saturday morning, the *market* sets up in place Omer Vallon. Also in the square is an *Atac* supermarket, while a *Franprix* supermarket is at 128 rue du Connétable.

Day 1: Compiègne to Chantilly

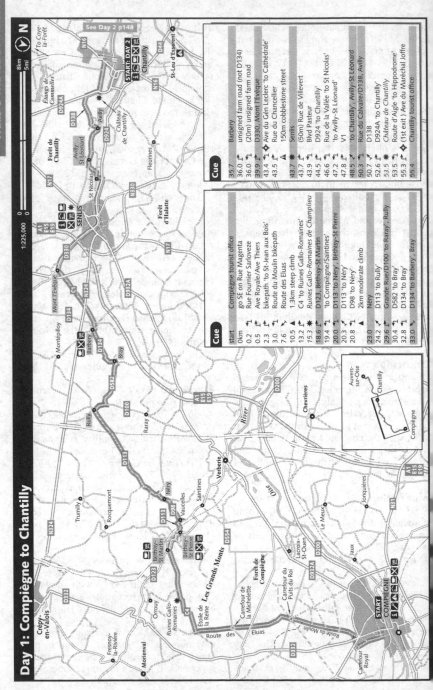

See Day 2 p148

Cue

start	Compiègne tourist office
0km	go SE on Rue Magenta
0.2	Rue Fournier Sarloveze
0.5	Ave Royale/Ave Thiers
2.3	bikepath 'to St-Jean aux Bois'
3.0	Route du Moulin bikepath
7.6	Route des Eluas
10.5	1.3km steep climb
13.2	C4 'to Ruines Gallo-Romaines'
15.3	Ruines Gallo-Romaines de Champlieu
18.6	D123, Béthisy-St Martin
19.4	'to Compiègne/Saintines'
20.0	D113 'to Néry', Béthisy-St Pierre
20.3	D113 'to Néry'
20.8	D98 'to Néry'
	2km moderate climb
23.0	Néry
24.2	D113 'to Rully'
29.6	Grande Rue/D100 'to Raray', Rully
30.4	D582 'to Bray'
32.8	D134 'to Bray'
33.0	D134 'to Barbery', Bray

Cue

35.7	Barbery
36.0	unsigned farm road (not D134)
36.0	(20m) unsigned farm road
39.9	D330, Mont l'Evêque
43.4	Ave du Gén Leclerc 'to Cathédrale'
43.5	Rue du Chancellier
	150m cobblestone street
43.7	Senlis
43.7	(50m) Rue de Villevert
43.9	Blvd Pasteur
44.5	D924 'to Chantilly'
46.6	Rue de la Vallée 'to St Nicolas'
47.2	'to Avilly-St Léonard'
47.8	V1
48.5	to Chantilly', Avilly-St Léonard
50.3	Rue du Calvaire/D138, Avilly
50.7	D138
52.6	D924A 'to Chantilly'
53.5	Château de Chantilly
55.3	Route d'Aigle 'to Hippodrome'
	(1st exit) Ave du Maréchal Joffre
55.4	Chantilly tourist office

1:225,000

8km / 5mi

0

Auvers-sur-Oise

Chantilly

Compiègne

Crêperie La Cour Pavée (☎ *03 44 57 23 41, 136 rue du Connétable*) serves crepes from 27FF in a lovely garden courtyard; it also offers salads from 55FF and grilled meat dishes from 78FF. For Chinese food, the *Chateau Mandarin* (☎ *03 44 57 00 29, 62 rue du Connétable*) has a *menu* at 73FF, and main courses in the 40FF to 68FF range.

The *Hôtel-Brasserie La Calèche* has *menus* from 80FF. The restaurant at *Auberge Le Vertugadin* has interesting *menus* from 98FF, but expensive main courses (from 100FF). See Places to Stay for both.

Day 2: Chantilly to Auvers-sur-Oise
2–4 hours, 34.9km

Although only a short day, this route passes lots of attractions: the Abbaye de Royaumont, the town of l'Isle-Adam and, for lovers of van Gogh, Auvers-sur-Oise. Cycling is easy, except for one massively ugly overpass between Beaumont and l'Isle-Adam, and a short, steep hill after l'Isle-Adam.

After Chantilly, the route passes the entrance on the right to **Les Fontaines**, a huge private park. In Gouvieux watch carefully for rue Colliau, where you turn left; continuing straight leads to the town centre. Just before the T-junction (4.8km) is a small all-purpose shop selling bikes.

At 10.3km, the lovely Cistercian **Abbaye de Royaumont** (☎ 01 30 35 59 00, 🖥 www .royaumont.com), founded in 1228, is 1km to the left. Stroll through the peaceful grounds and visit the church ruins and abbey buildings (28FF).

The D922Z is a quieter alternative to the D922 it parallels. At 14.4km, follow the sign to Noisy-sur-Oise rather than the one to Beaumont which leads to the D922.

Entering Beaumont-sur-Oise, follow the signs to Église St Laurent, a medieval church. Continue to the town centre and turn left onto rue Prince Albert 1er, where you will have to walk your bike down the pedestrianised main street. **Église St Laurent** is about 50m off to the right from rue Prince Albert 1er (18.6km). For a **panorama** over the valley, turn right (off the route) at place Gabriel Peri and ride 100m to the **chateau ruins**. Otherwise continue on rue de la Libération which becomes the D922.

At 21.4km, begin a 400m ride over the A16 and the N1 freeways. Ride carefully through the roundabouts and on the busy D922. The road quietens about 1km later along the edge of the Forêt de l'Isle-Adam.

Heading into l'Isle-Adam, detour to the **Pavillion Chinois**, an intricate pagoda in a lovely park. **L'Isle-Adam** is best described as 'green'. Nestled between the Oise River and the Forêt de l'Isle-Adam, it is a town of parks, gardens and lakes. At 25.3km, stop at **allée Le Nôtre** and walk through the **gardens**, laid out by none other than Le Nôtre.

Visit the 16th-century church, **Église St Martin**, and the **Musée Louis Senlecq**, an art and history museum at 46 Grande Rue (closed Tuesday). The **forest**, former hunting ground of the Princes de Conti, is crisscrossed by walking, cycling and equestrian paths and, unfortunately, the N184.

Leave town and cross two bridges over the Oise to Parmain (26.4km). The **Château de Conti**, 100m before town, is not the original, which was razed during the Revolution.

Climb on the forested road until La Naze; from there it's downhill to Auvers. Stop at the replica of the van Gogh painting (34.2km; see the Auvers Things to See & Do section).

Auvers-sur-Oise

This charming town, on the right bank of the peaceful Oise River, today looks very much like it did a century ago. It's not hard to see why it became a favourite spot for artists. The town attracted painters such as Pissarro, Cézanne, Corot, Daubigny and Morisot. The one who left the greatest 'impression', Vincent van Gogh, is the one who perhaps spent the shortest time here – the last 70 days of his life.

Information The tourist office (☎ 01 30 36 10 06, fax 01 34 48 08 47, 🖥 www.au vers-sur-oise.com) is in Manoir des Colombières on rue de la Sansonne.

A Société Générale bank is at 17 rue Générale de Gaulle. There is no bike shop in Auvers-sur-Oise.

Things to See & Do This tiny town has a mind-boggling list of attractions. Van Gogh fans should begin at **Maison de van Gogh** (☎ 01 30 36 60 60), place de la Mairie, actually the inn, Auberge Ravoux, where the artist spent the last weeks of his life.

The church, **Église Notre Dame**, depicted in van Gogh's well-known painting, *Church*

PARIS & THE ÎLE DE FRANCE

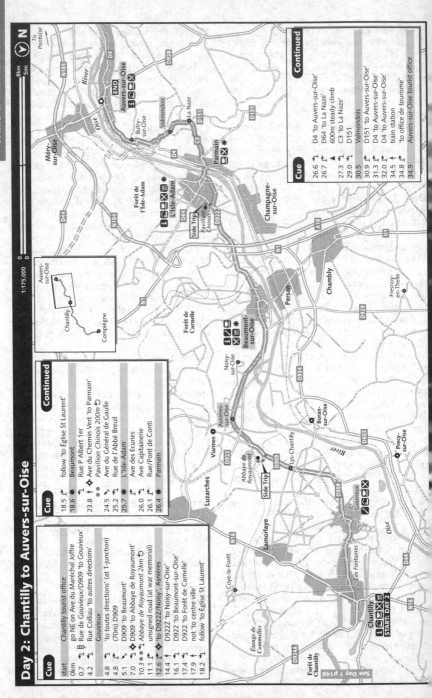

Day 2: Chantilly to Auvers-sur-Oise

Cue		
start		Chantilly tourist office
0km		go NE on Ave du Maréchal Joffre
0.7	⌐⌐	Rue de Gouvieux/D909 'to Gouvieux'
4.2	⌐	Rue Colliau 'to autres directions'
		Gouvieux
4.8	⌐	'to toutes directions' (at T-junction)
4.8	⌐	(70m) D909
5.1	⌐	D909 'to Beaumont'
7.0	◇	D909 'to Abbaye de Royaumont'
10.3	● ◇	Abbaye de Royaumont 2km ⟲
11.1	⌐	unsigned road (at war memorial)
12.6	⌐	to D922Z/Noisy', Asnières
14.4	⌐	D922Z 'to Noisy-sur-Oise'
16.1	⌐	D922 'to Beaumont-sur-Oise'
17.4	⌐	D922 'to Forêt de Carnelle'
17.9	⌐	not 'to centre ville'
18.2	⌐	follow 'to Église St Laurent'

Cue			Continued
18.5	⌐	follow 'to Église St Laurent'
18.6	*	Beaumont
		Rue P Albert 1er
23.8	● ◇	Ave du Chemin Vert 'to Parmain'
		Pavillion Chinois 200m ⟲
24.5	⌐	Ave du Général de Gaulle
25.2	⌐	Rue de l'Abbé Breuil
25.7	*	L'Isle-Adam
		Ave des Ecuries
26.0	⌐	Ave Capitainerie
26.1	⌐	Rue/Pont de Conti
26.4	*	Parmain

Cue			Continued
26.6	⌐	D4 'to Auvers-sur-Oise'
26.7	⌐	D64 'to La Naze'
	◄	600m steady climb
27.3	⌐	C3 'to La Naze'
29.0	⌐	D151
30.5		Valmondois
30.9	⌐	D151 'to Auvers-sur-Oise'
31.3	⌐	D4 'to Auvers-sur-Oise'
32.0	⌐	D4 'to Auvers-sur-Oise'
34.5		train station
34.8		'to office de tourisme'
34.9		Auvers-sur-Oise tourist office

at Auvers, is on rue Émile Bernard. A climb up the hill past the church leads to the **cemetery** where Vincent and his brother Théo are buried in simple ivy-covered graves against the north wall.

Sprinkled throughout town are replicas of paintings on the sites of the depicted scenes. The tourist office has a brochure listing these paintings and their locations. On the ride route (34.2km), there's a replica of a van Gogh painting, on the spot where the artist painted the river scene.

Above the tourist office, the **Musée Daubigny** (☎ 01 30 36 80 20) houses a collection of 19th-century works. **L'Atelier de Daubigny** (☎ 01 34 48 03 03), 61 rue Daubigny, is the studio and house of the artist, the walls of which are decorated with murals by Daubigny, Corot and others.

The 17th-century **Château d'Auvers** (☎ 01 34 48 48 48, 🖳 www.chateau-au vers.fr), rue de Léry, has an audio-visual illustrating Impressionist life.

Known as the 'green muse', absinthe is represented through a collection of artefacts and posters at the **Musée de l'Absinthe** (☎ 01 30 36 83 26), 44 rue Callé.

Places to Stay & Eat Auvers has no camping ground or hotels, but at the time of research, had two *chambres d'hôtes*. Check with the tourist office or the Web site for current listings.

For a unique van Gogh experience, have a meal at the *Auberge Ravoux*. The gastronomic delights are an expensive adventure (more than Vincent would have paid). Lunch and dinner – served daily, except Sunday evening and Monday – will cost 145FF for two courses, or 185FF for three. For something less extravagant, several *restaurants* and *cafes* line the streets of Auvers, particularly *rue du Général de Gaulle*.

Monet's Passions

Duration	2 days
Distance	64.7km
Difficulty	easy
Start/End	Mantes-la-Jolie

For anyone whose passion is Monet, this ride is a must. Meander along the Seine, visiting the pretty town of Vétheuil, where Monet once lived, and the chateau of La Roche-Guyon. Calmness reigns at Monet's gardens in Giverny, just around the corner from Vernon, a charming Norman town.

Days 1 and 2 can squeezed into a one-day ride or done on their own, as trains connect Paris with both Mantes-la-Jolie and Vernon.

PLANNING
When to Ride

Giverny's attractions are only open from early April to late October. Monet's Gardens are magnificent any time during these months, but particularly so in spring when the wisteria is in bloom, and early summer when the scent of roses is overpowering.

GETTING TO/FROM THE RIDE

Vernon makes a lovely overnight stop and is the start of the Seine Valley Circuit day ride in the Normandy & Brittany chapter. It is around 100km from Honfleur, the start of the Calvados Classique ride in the Normandy & Brittany chapter.

Mantes-la-Jolie

The train station is on place de la Gare. Get out at Mantes-la-Jolie, *not* Mantes-la-Ville.

Two or three SNCF commuter trains link Paris St Lazare (53FF, 45 to 60 minutes) to Mantes-la-Jolie every hour; all take bikes. The last train back to Paris is shortly after 11 pm. Trains also run to and from Vernon.

Vernon

The Vernon train station is 1km from the tourist office.

From Paris St Lazare to Vernon (66FF, 50 to 60 minutes), about eight direct trains run every day: two in the morning and about two an hour between 4 and 7 pm (less on weekends). Otherwise change trains in Mantes-la-Jolie; only three take bikes.

From Vernon to Paris (66FF, 50 to 60 minutes), two direct trains travel each hour between 6 and 9 am (less on weekends), and about one runs every two hours until about 8.30 pm. Otherwise, change trains in Mantes-la-Jolie. A couple of connections between 7 and 8.30 am allow bikes, as do a couple between 5 and 7 pm.

Frequent trains go between Vernon and Le Havre, the closest train station to Honfleur (127FF, two hours, eight a day), though none carry bikes outside a bike bag.

THE RIDE
Mantes-la-Jolie

The bustling town of Mantes-la-Jolie has almost become a suburb of Paris. It has a few accommodation options but, due to its proximity, Paris is a better option as an overnight stop.

The tourist office (☎ 01 34 77 10 30, fax 01 30 98 61 49) is on the way out of town, at 5 place Jean XXIII, a small square on rue Thiers. It's tucked in front of the massive 12th-century church, **Collégiale Notre-Dame**, which has a fabulous rose window and a nave just a fraction shorter than that of Notre-Dame in Paris. Other than this church and the **Tour St Maclou**, the only vestige of an 11th-century church, there is not much to see in the town.

There's a Banque de France at 1 place Aristide Briand and a Crédit Agricole at 23 ave de la République. The bike shop is part of the Intersport shop (☎ 01 30 98 17 00) at 41 rue Nationale.

Day 1: Mantes-la-Jolie to Vernon

1½–3 hours, 31.2km

Enjoy easy cycling, for the most part, with the Seine and the Epte Rivers at your side. There is a quick climb after La Roche-Guyon and a lovely descent as you leave the Île de France and glide into Normandy.

Cross the Seine on Pont Neuf (New Bridge). The remains of the **Vieux Pont** (Old Bridge) are on the right. It's one of the oldest bridges in France, dating back to the 11th century.

The pretty village of Vétheuil was home for Monet for five years. Turn left onto the D913 and immediately in front of you is the **church** featured in some of Monet's paintings of the town.

Cruise alongside the Seine to La Roche-Guyon (17.5km). Perched above the chalk cliffs flanking the Seine, the crumbling 12th-century **keep** dominates the scene. Right below is the **Château de La Roche-Guyon** (☎ 01 34 79 74 42), begun in the 14th century. The castle is open daily.

Climb out of La Roche-Guyon, and the route leaves the Île de France (Val de l'Oise department) to enter Normandy (Eure department). You know you've arrived in Normandy when, at 22km, you see the sign *Cidre: goûter à la ferme* – **cider tasting** on the farm. A 5km detour in the direction of Bois-Jérôme offers a taste.

Step into Monet's former home, the **Musée Claude Monet** (26.1km; ☎ 02 32 51 28 21), in Giverny. Next to the pink-and-green house is the **Clos Normand**, the gardens Monet designed. The **Jardin d'Eau** (Water Garden), fed by the Epte River, has the famous water-lily ponds and Japanese bridge draped with wisteria. The brightly painted house contains reproductions of Monet's work (open April to October; closed Monday). A little further down the road, at 99 rue Claude Monet, the **Musée d'Art Américain** (☎ 02 32 51 94 65) contains works of many American impressionist painters (open April to October).

Take the **bikepath** to Vernonnet, and cross the Seine to enter Vernon.

Vernon

On the banks of the Seine, between the forests of Vernon and Bizy, it comes as no surprise that this town's name is said to have come from the words *vert* (green) and *nom* (name). This pleasant place, often overlooked by people heading to Giverny, is well worth a visit.

Information The tourist office (☎ 02 32 51 39 60, fax 02 32 51 86 55, 🖳 www.giverny .org/vernon/ot/index.htm), is at 36 rue Carnot (closed Monday and, in winter, Sunday).

Several banks are around place Évreux, including the Société Générale. The Banque Nationale de Paris is at 6 place de Paris.

Cycling is one of the easiest ways to get to Giverny and, as a result, bike shops and rental places thrive in Vernon. Martin Cycles (☎ 02 32 21 24 08), at 84 rue Carnot, has rental bikes for 100/300FF a day/week. Across from the station, the brasserie Les Amis de Monet (☎ 02 32 51 55 16) hires bikes for 88FF/day.

The bar L'Estaminet (☎ 02 32 21 10 88) at 46 route des Andelys in the tiny village of Pressagny-l'Orgueilleux, doubles as a cybercafe. It is 5km north-west of Vernon on the D313 on the way to Les Andelys.

Things to See & Do The tourist office, housed in one of Vernon's oldest buildings, **Le Temps Jadis**, which dates to the 15th century, is a sight in itself. Next door is

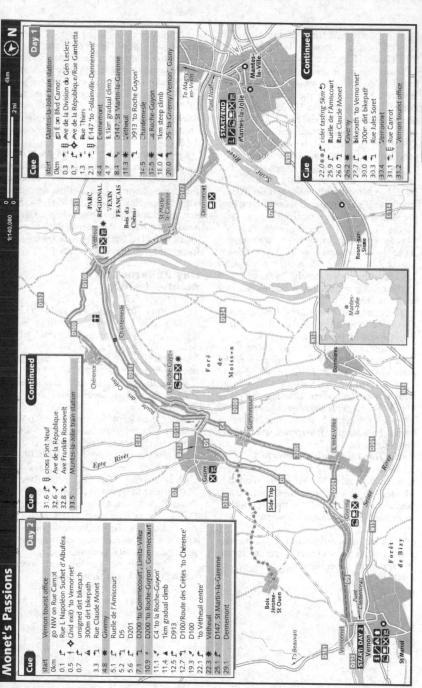

Monet's Passions

1:140,000 ⊕ N 2mi 4km

Day 1

Cue	
start	Mantes-la-Jolie train station
0km	E on Blvd Carnot
0.3	Ave de la Division du Gén Leclerc
0.7	Ave de la République/Rue Gambetta
1.3	Rue Thiers
2.1	E147 'to ollainville-Dennemont'
4.4	Dennemont
4.7	1km gradual climb
8.1	D147, St Martin-la-Garenne
11.3	Vétheuil
	D913 'to Roche Guyon'
14.5	Chantemesle
17.5	La Roche-Guyon
18.0	1km steep climb
20.0	D5 'to Giverny/Vernon', Gasny

Continued

Cue	
22.0	cider tasting 5km
25.9	Ruelle de l'Amiscourt
26.0	Rue Claude Monet
26.2	Giverny
27.7	bikepath 'to Vernonnet'
30.0	300m dirt bikepath
30.3	Rue Jules Soret
30.4	Vernonnet
31.1	Rue Carrot
31.2	Vernon tourist office

Day 2

Cue	
start	Vernon tourist office
0km	go NW on Rue Carnot
0.1	Rue L Napoleon Suchet d'Albuféra
0.5	(2nd exit) to Vernonnet'
0.7	unsigned dirt bikepath
	300m dirt bikepath
3.3	Rue Claude Monet
4.8	Giverny
5.1	Ruelle de l'Amiscourt
5.2	D5
5.6	D201
7.1	D200 'to Gommecourt', Limitz-Villez
10.9	D200 'to Roche-Guyon', Gommecourt
11.1	C4 'to la Roche-Guyon'
11.4	1km gradual climb
12.5	D913
12.7	D100/Route des Crêtes 'to Chérence'
19.3	D100
22.1	'to Vétheuil centre'
22.3	Vétheuil
25.1	D147, St Martin-la-Garenne
29.1	Dennemont

Continued

Cue	
31.6	cross Pont Neuf
32.6	Ave de la République
32.8	Ave Franklin Roosevelt
33.5	Mantes-la-Jolie train station

Vernon's **Collégiale Notre-Dame**, begun in the 12th century. Opposite is the **Hôtel de Ville** (Town Hall), constructed in 1895.

Vernon has some great examples of traditional Norman **half-timbered houses**: the best can be found on rue Carnot and rue Potard. Off rue Carnot, at 12 rue du Pont, the **Musée Poulain** (☎ 02 32 21 28 17) is housed in a 15th-century half-timbered mansion. It has a few Monets, and works by other Impressionists, but its specialty is animal art.

On the western edge of Vernon is the 18th-century **Château de Bizy** (☎ 02 32 51 00 82). Adorned with pools and fountains, the chateau's extensive grounds merge into the surrounding forest of Bizy.

Places to Stay To camp in Vernon, the *Auberge de Jeunesse* (☎ 02 32 51 66 48, fax 02 32 21 23 41, 28 ave Île de France) has space for 10 tents in the back yard, and charges 27FF per person. A bed in the hostel costs 48FF.

There are a few *chambres d'hôtes* in the area. Check with the tourist office; prices begin at 250FF per room.

Vernon has only two hotels. Oozing ambience, the gorgeous, half-timbered *Hôtel d'Évreux* (☎ 02 32 21 16 12, fax 02 32 21 32 73, 11 place d'Évreux) has only 12 rooms, all with shower and toilet; doubles cost from 290FF. The larger *Hôtel Normandy* (☎ 02 32 51 97 97, fax 02 32 21 01 66, 1 ave Mendès-France) has comfortable rooms, with shower and toilet, from 350FF.

The *Hôtel du Haut Marais* (☎ 03 32 71 22 50, fax 02 32 71 22 51, 2 route de Rouen) is about 2km out of Vernon, on the road to St Marcel. Doubles with shower and toilet begin at 240FF (closed for the second half of February, and Sundays in winter).

Places to Eat A *market* is held Wednesday and Saturday mornings at place de Gaulle. A *Monoprix* supermarket is at 1 rue aux Huilliers.

For pizzas and Italian food, *Pizza del Teatro (34 rue d'Albuféra)* serves a good selection. For crepes, choose from *Crêperie des Roses (37 rue de Bizy)*, near the station, or *Crêperie du Vexin (21 rue aux Huilliers)*.

About 1km from the centre, *Restaurant Le Havre (☎ 02 32 51 43 83, 80 ave de Rouen)* serves good-value Norman *menus* from 65FF and has a terrace overlooking the Seine.

Les Fleurs (☎ 02 32 51 16 80, 71 rue Carnot) offers casual dining in the bistro, with 78FF *menus* including 1/4L of wine, and more elaborate meals in the restaurant, where *menus* cost from 125FF (closed Sunday, and Monday evening). For a splurge, head to *Le Relais Normand*, the restaurant in the Hôtel d'Évreux, where *menus* cost from 130FF to 180FF.

Day 2: Vernon to Mantes-la-Jolie

1½–3 hours, 33.5km

The return to Mantes-la-Jolie takes a slightly different route, climbing to the route des Crêtes for grand views of the Seine from above La Roche-Guyon. Then it's downhill to Vétheuil and an easy ride to Mantes-la-Jolie.

Cross the Seine and take the **bikepath** from Vernonnet to **Giverny** (see Day 1 for details).

After the sleepy towns of Limitz-Villez and Gommecourt the route begins a short climb to the **route des Crêtes**. At 14km walk towards the river for a **lookout** over the keep of the Château de La Roche-Guyon (see Day 1) and the Seine River.

Continue to **Vétheuil** (22.3km) and wind through the streets to the central square (see Day 1). Cross Pont Neuf, watching for traffic at the large intersection immediately after the bridge, and continue onto rue August Goust, which becomes rue Nationale. Pass the **Tour St Maclou** and continue through town to the train station.

Normandy & Brittany

Normandy and Brittany sit side by side in north-western France. The sea dominates both, but other than sharing a similar climate the two provinces are vastly different. Normandy's varied shore includes rugged seascapes, sophisticated resorts and sombre landing beaches flowing into gentle hills and rich farmlands, while Brittany offers wild coastlines, white sandy beaches and savage cliffs.

Brittany sets itself apart from the rest of France with its strong sense of identity, evident in its Celtic traditions and language. Cycling through the two regions offers a range of sights as varied as prehistoric monuments and medieval towns, picturesque ports and serene canals, solid chateaux and magnificent cathedrals, with gastronomic delights all the way.

Normandy

Cycling through quintessential Normandy reveals a verdant, pastoral landscape. Plump cows graze on lush pastures interspersed with apple orchards and dotted with picture-perfect half-timbered houses. Beyond this image there are coastal stretches of chalky cliffs to the east, D-day landing beaches to the west, and seaside resorts in between. In the south-west the *Suisse Normande* (Norman Switzerland) is without its own Matterhorn, but instead boasts forests, gorges and hills, surrounding the Orne river valley.

Among these peaceful settings are Normandy's cities, towns and attractions, including the celebrated island abbey of Mont St Michel, the picturesque port of Honfleur, Bayeux, home of the famous 11th-century tapestry, and the ruins of Château Gaillard.

Normandy's distinctive light has inspired Impressionist artists. Claude Monet painted *Impression: Soleil Levant* (Impression: Sunrise) at Le Havre and settled in Giverny, where he created his famous gardens, while Eugène Boudin's palette was inspired by Honfleur and its environs.

Gourmets and gourmands alike will take pleasure in the Norman table – sumptuous meals laden with cream, cheese and rich

In Brief

Highlights

- haunting **D-day beaches**
- all the **apple cider** you can drink
- the approach to **Mont St Michel**
- **megalithic sites**

Terrain

Normandy's woodlands and pastures are cut by low valleys and rolling hills (more pronounced in the south); Brittany has low-lying plains and gentle uplands, with hills in the north-west and central-south.

FFCT Contacts

- **Ligue Haute-Normandie**, 6 Clos Tiger, 27170 Beaumontel
- **Ligue Basse-Normandie**, 20 rue du Beau Site, 14250 Tilly-sur-Seulles
- **Ligue Bretagne**, Ferme de la Bouderie, 35440 Dingé

Cycling Events

- **Paris-Brest-Paris** (August 2003 – held every four years)
- **Tour de Normandie** (late March)
- **Tour d'Armorique** (April–May) Brittany
- **Grand Prix de Plouay** (late August) Brittany

Special Events

- **Fêtes Médiévales** (first weekend in July) Bayeux
- **Festival de Jazz** (late July) Vannes
- **Festival de Cornouaille** (late July) Quimper
- **Fête des Remparts** (late September) Dinan

Gourmet Specialities

- Normandy's apple drinks and cheeses (livarot, pont l'évêque and pavé d'auge)
- Brittany's fish, seafood and oysters
- *far breton* (custard dessert with prunes)

sauces, and apple delights both edible and drinkable.

HISTORY

Normandy's history begins in the 9th century with invasions by Scandinavian Vikings. In 911 Charles the Simple of France and Viking chief Hrölfr agreed to make the Rouen region home to these Norsemen (or Normans), hence the area's name.

Norse stock produced great soldiers. The most famous, the Duke of Normandy, crossed the English Channel in 1066 with 6000 soldiers and crushed the English in the Battle of Hastings. The duke, better known as William the Conqueror, was crowned king of England, and his story is told by the Bayeux Tapestry.

In the Hundred Years War (1337–1453), Normandy switched between French and English rule until 1450, when the French gained permanent control. During the war English troops captured a young woman, Joan of Arc, who, in 1431 at age 19, was burned at the stake in Rouen.

In the 16th century Normandy, a Protestant stronghold, was the scene of much fighting between Catholics and Huguenots.

During WWII, 6 June 1944, better known as D-day, saw the landing of 45,000 Allied troops on the beaches north of Bayeux. The Battle of Normandy followed, and after several months and 100,000 deaths, German resistance was finally broken. The area still bears the memory and the scars of that battle.

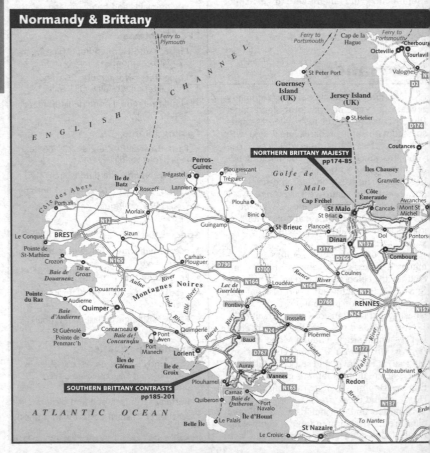

NATURAL HISTORY

The eastern part of Normandy is ideal for farming and grazing. North of the Seine it is a vast plateau ending at the coast with chalky white cliffs. Central Normandy is an area known as the *bocage* (farmlands subdivided by hedges and trees) – a mixture of woodlands and pasturelands cut by low, humid valleys and rolling hills. These hills become more pronounced to the south in the Suisse Normande. Western Normandy and the Cotentin Peninsula bordering Brittany is part of the granite Massif Armoricain, evident in the peninsula's rugged coastline.

Normandy is home to three regional nature parks. The Parc Naturel Régional de Brotonne straddles the Seine. It is carpeted in bluebells in springtime and deer, boar and hare are abundant. The Parc Naturel Régional Normandie-Maine in the south crosses into the Pays de Loire, and the Cotentin Peninsula is home to the Parc Naturel Régional des Marais du Cotentin et du Bessin, a marsh area where migratory birds stop over.

CLIMATE

Normandy is blessed with a mild maritime climate, with few temperature extremes. Summer begins in mid-June with temperatures in the mid- to upper-20s. These temperatures sometimes last through September and into early October, when the weather cools and rain settles in. Winters have infrequent frosts and are usually snow-free but rainy.

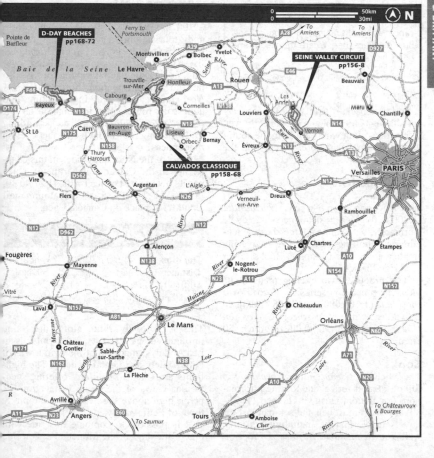

NORMANDY & BRITTANY

'Le Normand'

Jacques Anquetil (1934–87), born in Mont St Aignan, Normandy, was a true Normand; he loved to eat (no matter what the time of year, no matter what the race). He was the first man to win the Tour de France five times. Not only that, he won the Grand Prix des Nations a record nine times, six of which were in a row. His impressive *palmarès* (list of results) includes being a two-time winner of the Giro d'Italia (Tour of Italy) and the first Frenchman to ever win the race (in 1960). He was also the first man to win, over several years, the triple crown of three-week stage races: the Giro d'Italia, Tour de France and Vuelta ã Espana (Tour of Spain).

Anquetil's professional career spanned from 1953 to 1969. Tragically, he died of cancer at 53. His memory lives on in Paris' Bois de Vincennes, where the velodrome bears his name.

Spring, especially April and May, is pleasant although still cool and sporadically wet.

The prevailing winds are from the southwest and west, felt more strongly on the coast than inland.

INFORMATION
Maps
The Michelin map No 231 *Normandie* (1:200,000) gives the detail needed to cycle Normandy, but is quite a large sheet. Michelin also publishes several maps covering smaller areas – see Maps & Books under each ride for details.

IGN produces two cycling maps in its *plein air* (open air) series: *Le Calvados à Bicyclette* (1:100,000) details 58 circuits in Calvados, while *Itinéraires Cyclos en Haute-Normandie* (1:200,000) outlines 50 circuits.

Books
The Michelin *Green Guide: Normandy* is full of good historical and touring information. For fiction, Gustave Flaubert (1821–80) was born in Rouen and set many of his novels in Normandy, including his most well known *Madame Bovary. A Place in*

Normandy, by Nicholas Kilmer, offers a sense of Norman life.

The FFCT *(Fédération Française de Cyclotourisme)* publishes *La France à Vélo: Normandie* (118FF; see Books in the Facts for the Cyclist chapter). For mountain bikers, the ONF *VTT Évasion* series has rides in three forests in Normandy (see the 'Mountain Biking' boxed text in the Facts for the Cyclist chapter).

Information Sources
Administratively the five *départements* (departments; administrative divisions) of Normandy are divided into two regions: Haute-Normandie (Upper Normandy) covers Seine-Maritime and Eure; and Basse-Normandie (Lower Normandy) covers Calvados, Orne and Manche.

The Normandy tourist office (☎ 02 32 33 79 00, fax 02 32 31 19 04, ☐ www.normandy-tourism.org) is at 14 rue Charles Corbeau, Évreux. Its booklet *Active Normandy* lists (in English) organised walking, cycling, horse riding and kayaking trips. It also has the map/information sheet *Randonnées Normandie*, with walking, cycling and equestrian routes, plus information on GR (*Grande Randonnée*; long-distance walking trail) walking routes and permanent cycling randonnées.

Most of the Normandy rides in this chapter are in the Calvados department, which has its own tourist office (☎ 02 31 27 90 30, fax 02 31 27 90 35, ☐ calvatour@mail.cpod.fr) at place du Canada, Caen.

Seine Valley Circuit

Duration	2½–4½ hours
Distance	50.4km
Difficulty	easy-moderate
Start/End	Vernon

This is a lovely route along the Seine through villages, forests and farmlands to Les Andelys (made up of the twin towns of Petit Andely and Grand Andely). The highlights are Château Gaillard, offering spectacular views of the Seine valley from its perch high above the Seine, and the pretty town of Petit Andely.

It is possible to combine this ride with one of the days of the Monet's Passion ride

NORMANDY & BRITTANY

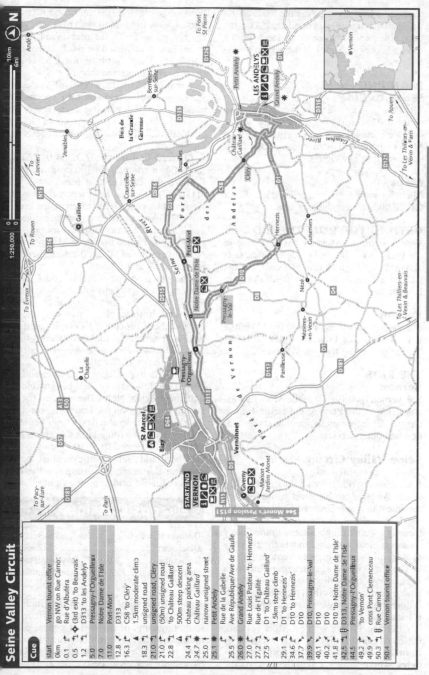

Seine Valley Circuit

Cue		
start		Vernon tourist office
0km		go NW on Rue Carnot
0.1	↰	Rue d'Albuféra
0.5	↱ ◇	(3rd exit) 'to Beauvais'
1.2	↱	D313 'to les Andelys'
5.0		Pressagny-l'Orgueilleux
7.0		Notre Dame de l'Isle
11.0		Port-Mort
12.8	↙	D313
16.3	↰	C58 to Cléry
		1.5km moderate climb
18.3	↓	unsigned road
21.0	↰	unsigned road, Cléry
21.0	↱	(50m) unsigned road
22.8	↰	'to Château Gaillard'
		500m steep descent
24.4		château parking area
24.7	✱	Château Gaillard
25.0	↑	narrow unsigned street
25.1		Petit Andely
25.5	↗	Rue de la Gabelle
		Ave République/Ave de Gaulle
26.0		Grand Andely
27.0	↰	Rue Louis Pasteur 'to Hennezis'
27.2	↱	Rue de l'Égalité
27.5	↰	D1 'to Château Gaillard'
		1.5km steep climb
29.1	↱	D1 'to Hennezis'
34.6	↰	D10 'to Hennezis'
37.7	↘	D10
39.9	↱	D10, Pressagny-le-Val
40.1		D10
40.2	↱	D10
41.8	↱	D10 'to Notre Dame de l'Isle'
42.5	⊞ ↱	D313, Notre Dame de l'Isle
44.5		Pressagny-l'Orgueilleux
49.2	↱	'to Vernon'
49.9	↰	cross Pont Clemenceau
50.3	↱	Rue Carnot
50.4		Vernon tourist office

to create a two-day trip (see the Paris & the Île de France chapter). Or, add a 10km (return) side trip from Vernon to see Monet's former home (see Day 1 of the Monet's Passions ride).

PLANNING
When to Ride
The best time to ride is between April and October. This works out particularly well if you are combining the ride with a visit to Monet's home in Giverny (only open from early April to late October).

Maps
Michelin map No 55 *Caen, Rouen, Paris* (1:200,000) covers the ride area.

GETTING TO/FROM THE RIDE
Vernon is on the Monet's Passions ride in the Paris & the Île de France chapter. It is about 100km from Honfleur, the start of the Calvados Classique ride detailed later in this chapter.

Vernon
See the Monet's Passions ride (p149) in the Paris & the Île de France chapter for information on getting to/from Vernon.

THE RIDE
Vernon
See Vernon (pp149–52) in the Monet's Passions ride in the Paris & the Île de France chapter for information about accommodation and other services.

Seine Valley Circuit
2½–4½ hours, 50.4km
It's a leisurely ride through the Seine valley to Les Andelys, with a short climb through the forest to reach Château Gaillard. Leaving Les Andelys on the return to Vernon, there is a quick climb almost immediately outside Grand Andely, and then it's easy cycling all the way back to Vernon.

The first village after leaving Vernon is Pressagny-l'Orgueilleux (5km; 44.5km), whose name is bigger than the village itself. It does, however, have a bar and cybercafe, L'Estaminet.

After the village of Port-Mort (11km), the route climbs slightly as it veers away from the Seine and enters the **Forêt des Andelys**, where there's a 3km descent. At the

bottom, just before the roundabout (traffic circle), look for a small road off to the right. Do not go as far as the roundabout, as bicycles are not allowed on the busy road beyond. The short climb on the C58 is on a quiet road through the forest.

The road 'to Château Gaillard' is steep: a 15% downhill grade leads to spectacular **views** from the parking area above the chateau. Before winding down to the chateau, walk the **trails** for more superb vantage points.

Château Gaillard (☎ 02 32 54 04 16) is a fantastic medieval fortification built by Richard the Lionheart in less than a year (1196–97) to check the French advance on Rouen. It was eventually taken by the French in 1203, who entered through the latrines. In 1603, Henri IV ordered its demolition. The ruins can be visited from mid-March to mid-November (closed all day Tuesday, Wednesday morning and 1 May).

The steep, narrow chemin de Château Gaillard leads into Petit Andely, on the banks of the Seine. The pretty town displays **half-timbered houses** along rue Grande and around the 13th-century church, **Église St Saveur**. The helpful tourist office (☎ 02 32 54 41 93), 24 rue Philippe-Auguste, is 100m south of rue de la Gabelle.

Ave de la République leads to Grand Andely. The 16th-century Flamboyant and Renaissance **Église Notre Dame** is on the left as you turn right on rue Louis Pasteur. Over the Gambon River the next climb begins.

The rest of the route back to Vernon is either flat or downhill, with views of the Gambon and Seine valleys. Just before crossing the Seine to Vernon are the remnants of an **old bridge** on the right.

Calvados Classique

Duration	3 days
Distance	132.8km
Difficulty	easy-moderate
Start/End	Honfleur

This is Normandy at its best. Beginning in the attractive port town of Honfleur, the route hugs one of the region's most prestigious stretches of coastline, then turns inland to the Pays d'Auge. This is classic Normandy – cows, cheese, cider and cuisine

– in an unforgettable setting of rolling hills, orchards and rustic villages. Along the way, take in parts of *La Route du Cidre* (The Cider Route), interesting chateaux and Lisieux, home of the last saint to be canonised.

PLANNING
When to Ride
Normandy's mild climate means this ride can be done any time from April through October. The coastal resorts are most crowded on summer weekends (May through September), while all of August is busy. Reserve accommodation at these times.

For a few weeks in April and May the landscape of the Pays d'Auge is transformed by the mass of white-blossomed apple trees. In September the trees are laden with fruit, harvest begins, the crowds have thinned and the weather remains pleasant.

Maps
Michelin map No 54 *Cherbourg, Caen, Rouen* (1:200,000) is a good, clear map of the area.

Information Sources
The Cambremer (Day 2) tourist office (☎ 02 31 63 08 87, fax 02 31 63 08 21), rue Pasteur, is the area's main tourist office and the best contact for Route du Cidre information.

GETTING TO/FROM THE RIDE
Honfleur is around 100km from Vernon, the start of the Seine Valley Circuit detailed earlier in this chapter. This ride could also be linked with the D-day Beaches ride (detailed later in this chapter), which begins at Bayeux, about 75km from Honfleur.

Honfleur is reached by bus or bike from Le Havre (at the end of the line from Paris). Another option is to begin the ride on Day 3, in Lisieux, which has train connections from Paris and Caen.

Although it is only 22km from Le Havre to Honfleur, it is an ugly, industrial ride. The bus is a pleasant, quick and easy option.

Le Havre
Train Direct trains from Paris' St Lazare to Le Havre (168FF, two hours, 10 a day) stop in Rouen. From Paris, only the daily 9.15 am train takes bikes, and from Le Havre back to Paris, only the 2 pm train allows bikes without a bike bag.

Boat P&O European Ferries links Le Havre with Portsmouth, England. The terminal is on ave Lucien Corbeaux, about 1km south-west of the train and bus stations. For ferry information and prices, see the Sea section in the Getting There & Away chapter.

Honfleur
Bus After reaching Le Havre, buses provide the only public transport to Honfleur. Le Havre's bus station is across the road from the train station. Honfleur's bus station (☎ 02 31 89 28 41) is south east of the Vieux Bassin, on rue des Vases.

Caen-based Bus Verts du Calvados (☎ 02 31 44 77 44) runs five buses a day from Le Havre to Honfleur. From Le Havre the most convenient connection is the 1.10 pm on Monday to Saturday (42FF, 30 minutes, line No 50 to Lisieux), and the 2.30 pm on Sunday and holidays (42FF, 30 minutes, line No 20 to Caen). From Honfleur the most convenient connection to Le Havre's 2 pm train to Paris, Monday through Saturday, is at 12.03 pm (42FF, 30 minutes, line No 20), and at 12.40 pm on Sunday and holidays (42FF, 30 minutes, line No 20 or 50).

From Honfleur, Bus Verts also has services to Caen (69FF, or 86FF for the express, 1½ to two hours, 15 a day, line No 20) and Lisieux (42FF, one hour, four or five a day, line No 50).

Bus Restrictions Most Bus Verts buses will take bicycles for free, subject to space availability. Bikes are transported in *la soute* (luggage-storage bin), under the bus. You may have to wait for the next bus if there's no room.

Bicycle If you're determined to ride from Le Havre, go south to the lock, Écluse François 1er, cross the Grand Canal Le Havre and continue through the more industrial area along the Seine until the Pont de Normandie (the massive bridge across the Seine). Cross the bridge and head west to Honfleur.

Lisieux
Train Frequent trains from Paris' St Lazare (149FF, 1¾ hours, nine a day) serve Lisieux, but none of the weekday trains, in either direction, take bikes outside a bike bag. Weekend and public holiday travellers

are in luck; one train a day from Paris to Lisieux, the 10.10 am, takes bikes. Heading back to Paris, the 5.15 pm allows bikes.

About a dozen trains a day operate between Caen and Lisieux (45FF, 30 minutes). On weekdays, five TER trains take bikes in each direction, and on weekends only three take bikes.

THE RIDE
Honfleur

At the mouth of the Seine, the pretty port of Honfleur escaped damage during WWII, leaving intact much of the traditional architecture that gives the town its charm. In 1608 Samuel de Champlain set sail from here and founded Quebec (Canada). In 1681 Cavelier de la Salle left to explore what is now the USA and claimed Louisiana, naming it after King Louis XIV.

Born in Honfleur, artist Eugène Boudin (1824–1898) and composer Erik Satie (1866–1925) are honoured by museums here.

Information The tourist office (☎ 02 31 89 23 30, fax 02 31 89 31 82) is at place Arthur Boudin (closed Sunday from Easter to October, and open Sunday and holidays from 10 am to 1 pm outside that period).

The Crédit Agricole is at 26 rue du Dauphin, with a Banque Nationale de Paris a few doors away (both closed Monday). The post office, at 7 cours Albert-Manuel, is the only place to log on in Honfleur.

There are no bike shops in Honfleur, but the Fina service station (☎ 02 31 89 91 73), cours Jean de Vienne, hires bikes daily/weekly for 90/350FF. The closest bike shops are in Deauville, including Cycles La Deauvillaise (☎ 02 31 88 56 33) at 11 quai de la Marine.

Things to See & Do Honfleur is made for wandering. Begin on quai Ste Catherine and quai St Étienne, admiring the skinny, slate-hung **16th- and 18th-century houses** reflecting in the water of the **Vieux Bassin** (old harbour), the focal point of Honfleur. Explore the winding back streets and discover the town's sights and galleries. **Église Ste Catherine** is a unique wooden church built by ship carpenters in the late 15th and early 16th centuries. Opposite is **Clocher Ste Catherine** (☎ 02 31 89 54 00), the church's freestanding wooden bell tower.

Among Honfleur's museums are the **Musée Eugène Boudin** (☎ 02 31 89 54 00) on rue de l'Homme at place Erik Satie filled with the work of Boudin and othe impressionists. The **Musée de la Marine** (☎ 02 31 89 14 12), quai St Étienne, is a small maritime museum. The newest museum, **Maisons Satie** (☎ 02 31 89 11 11), a 67 blvd Charles V, pays homage to the composer of the same name.

The closest **beach** is 1km away, but is spoiled by the views of oil refineries. The beaches improve towards Trouville.

Places to Stay The *Camping du Phare* (☎ 02 31 89 10 26, blvd Charles V) is abou 500m north-west of the Vieux Bassin. I charges 28FF per person and 35FF for the site (open April to September).

Honfleur is not a cheap place to stay and becomes particularly crowded on weekends when visitors arrive from Paris, so it's bes to reserve. There's no youth hostel. However, a good option is to stay in one of the 15 *chambres d'hôtes* (B&Bs), with singles doubles from 150/180FF, plus about 25FF for breakfast. A list is available from the tourist office.

The tiny *Bar de la Salle des Fêtes* (☎ 02 31 89 19 69, 8 place Albert Sorel) charges 160FF (including breakfast) for one of its four double rooms. The well-maintained quiet *Hôtel Les Loges* (☎ 02 31 89 38 26 18 rue Brûlée) has rooms with a shower and toilet from 300FF. The pleasant *Hôte du Dauphin* (☎ 02 31 89 15 53, fax 02 3 89 92 06, e hotel.dudauphin@wanadoo.fr 10 place Berthelot) is almost next door and has rooms with shower and toilet fo 350/400FF.

For a splurge head to *Hôtel le Cheva Blanc* (☎ 02 31 81 65 00, fax 02 31 89 52 80, e LeCheval.Blanc@wanadoo.fr, 2 qua des Passagers), a gorgeous 15th-century hotel overlooking the port, each room with a view. Prices (including breakfast) fo rooms with shower and toilet start from 472/494FF.

Places to Eat The Saturday morning *market* is held outside the church at place Ste Catherine. On Wednesday mornings, a *bio (organic) market* is held at place S Léonard. The *Champion* supermarket is a 54 rue de la République and the excellen

Cycle the causeway to Normandy's Mont St Michel abbey at dawn.

Visit the war cemetery at Bayeux.

Drink in the glorious reflections of Honfleur in the Vieux Bassin.

Stock up with picnic ingredients from a Honfleur bakery.

See where apple cider is made.

Spring flowers brighten the Loire's wheat fields.

Picnic in style outside Château de Azay-le-Rideau.

Loire limestone is a beautiful building material.

Cosy restaurants are only ever a bike ride away.

You can spend hours exploring the Château de Villandry's immaculate vegetable garden.

Cidre, Calvados or Pommeau?

Cidre, calvados or pommeau? That is the question. These three words form an essential part of the Norman vocabulary. Normandy is apple country; a region that produces no wine. But rest assured – the Normans have three apple-based drinks to compensate.

Refreshing *cidre* (cider), either *doux* (sweet) or *brut* (dry), made from fermented apple juice, is the perfect accompaniment to the rich, creamy local cuisine and ubiquitous crepes. Calvados, a

Pont l'Éveque has long been famous for its cider production, immortalised here in a postcard.

distilled spirit, is best described as an apple brandy. Pommeau is Normandy's very own aperitif. Made from a mixture of cider and calvados, it is drunk chilled.

Along the Route du Cidre, and other parts of Normandy, cider producers offer *dégustations* (tastings). Farms displaying the sign 'Cru de Cambremer' usually offer tours of their cellars and presses.

Many dishes in Normandy have cream sauces and are also either flamed with calvados or prepared with cider. A dessert staple is *tarte aux pommes* (apple pie) with cream.

In Normandy, calvados may be offered at the end of the meal, either straight or as *café calva* (coffee with calvados). Traditionally, a shot of calvados is taken between courses and is known as *le trou Normand* (the Norman hole). Many restaurants offer le trou Normand in the form of an apple sorbet doused in calvados. Either way, calvados is said to aid digestion, thus helping make room for the next luscious course.

boulangerie-pâtisserie (bakery and pastry shop) **La Paneterie** is at No 22 (closed Monday).

Seafood is Honfleur's specialty. **Restaurants** line the Vieux Bassin, place Ste Catherine and place Arthur Boudin. For a traditional Norman meal, the cosy **La Tortue** (☎ 02 31 89 04 93, *36 rue de l'Homme de Bois*) has *menus* (set meals) from 99FF. The atmospheric **La Cidrerie** (☎ 02 31 89 59 85, *26 place Hamelin*) has a huge array of savoury and sweet crepes (from 20FF), plus a good selection of cider, pommeau and calvados.

Day 1: Honfleur to Beuvron-en-Auge

2–4 hours, 44.6km

Enjoy gentle cycling along the coast, and then through the undulating pastoral areas of the Pays d'Auge. There are two moderate

climbs, one as the route turns inland after Villers-sur-Mer, and another shortly after Dozulé.

The ride begins at the **Lieutenance**, the remains of the 16th-century house of the King's lieutenant, the Governor of Honfleur, at the north end of the Vieux Bassin. Glimpses of Le Havre's industry mar the sea views until Cricquebœuf – with its pretty 12th-century church (7.7km) – and the small seaside town of Villerville.

The **route de la Corniche** provides a steep descent into Trouville-sur-Mer. The turn is easy to miss – look for the sign '*sentier*' (path) for walkers.

Separated from Deauville by the Touques River, **Trouville-sur-Mer** began as a fishing village and then became popular in the mid-19th century with artists and writers. The more charming of the two towns, it has some stately **villas** lining the route de la

NORMANDY & BRITTANY

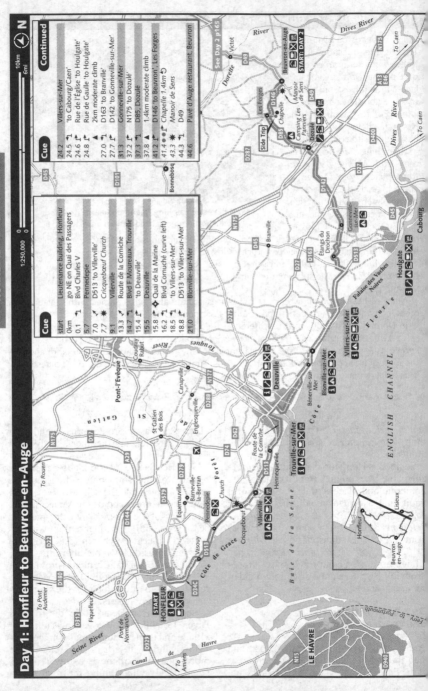

Day 1: Honfleur to Beuvron-en-Auge

1:250,000

N

Cue		
start		Lieutenance building, Honfleur
0km	↑	go NE on Quai des Passagers
0.1	↱	Blvd Charles V
5.7	↰	Pennedepie
7.0	↱	D513 'to Villerville'
7.7	✳	Cricqueboeuf Church
9.1	↱	Villerville
13.3	↱	Route de la Corniche
14.7	↱	Blvd F Moureaux, Trouville
15.4	↰	'to Deauville'
15.5	↱	Deauville
15.8	◇	Quai de la Marine
16.2	↰	Blvd Cornuché (curve left)
18.5	↱	'to Villers-sur-Mer'
18.8	↱	D513 'to Villers-sur-Mer'
21.0		Blonville-sur-Mer

Cue		Continued
24.2		Villers-sur-Mer
24.5	↱	'to Cabourg/Caen'
24.6	↱	Rue de l'Église 'to Houlgate'
24.8	↰	Rue de Gaulle 'to Houlgate'
	◀	2km moderate climb
27.0	↱	D163 'to Branville'
27.7	↱	D142 'to Gonneville-sur-Mer'
31.3		Gonneville-sur-Mer
37.2	↱	N175 to Dozulé
37.3	↱	D85, Dozulé
37.8	◀	1.4km moderate climb
41.2		D146 'to Beuvron', Les Forges
41.4	●↑↰	Chapelle 1.4km ⟲
43.3	✳	Manoir de Sens
44.3	↰	D49
44.6		Pavé d'Auge restaurant, Beuvron

Corniche and the beach promenade.
Deauville (15.5km), created soon after, has
an air of chic. Both have white sand
beaches, *promenades des planches* (board-
walks) and casinos.

After the Deauville roundabouts on the
busy D513 , the route takes the quieter road
alongside the beach. The area from Trouville to Cabourg, lined with fashionable seaside homes, is known as the **Côte Fleurie**. It
is also referred to as Paris' 21st *arrondissement* (district), because of the number of
Parisians who flock here.

Villers-sur-Mer sits on a lovely beach and
backs onto wooded hills. On the climb out
of town the coast gives way to the lush pastures and rolling hills of the **Pays d'Auge**.
The rather plain town of Dozulé (37.3km)
can be used as an alternative overnight stop
f accommodation in Beuvron is unavail-
ble. Most things are on Grande Rue. The
hotel-restaurant *Hostellerie Normande*
(☎ *02 31 79 20 18, fax 02 31 39 65 02)*, at
No 98, has rooms with hand basins for
60FF; its *menus* start at 68FF. Across the
road, at No 79, the bar-hotel *Le Rustique*
(☎ *02 31 79 25 99)* has doubles without
lower from 130FF. The bike shop, Cycles
Pascal Eudes (☎ 02 31 79 13 30) is at No 76.
The closest *camping ground* to Beuvron-
n-Auge is 2.3km out of Dozulé.

At Les Forges are the first signs for **La
Route du Cidre**, a signposted circuit
through the top cider-producing region of
the Pays d'Auge.

The tiny 17th-century **Chapelle St Michel**
(Chapelle de Clermont) in its secluded set-
ing, and the views over the Dives and Vie
alleys, make a pleasant side trip before the
downhill run into Beuvron-en-Auge.

Just before town, stop at the 16th-century
Manoir de Sens (43.3km; see Places to Stay
under Beuvron), a superb half-timbered
manor house that is also a working farm,
producing cider and calvados for sale.

Beuvron-en-Auge

This gorgeous village has every right to be
called 'one of the 100 most beautiful villages in France'. Basically a small street of
well-preserved, 16th-century half-timbered
houses with lace curtains and colourful window boxes gathered around the main
square, the village is one photo opportunity
after another.

There is no tourist office, but some
brochures are kept in a fixture hanging on
the wall next to the Pavé d'Auge restaurant
in the village centre. There is no bank; bring
cash if you are staying at one of the chambres d'hôtes.

Things to See & Do Stroll up and down
the main street taking in the ambience of the
village houses, particularly the manor at the
south end of the village; look at the carvings
on its wooden beams. Visit the pretty little
17th-century **church** and some of the **shops**
selling local cider and cheeses.

In the centre square is the **old covered
market**, which was destroyed twice, in 1845
and 1959. In 1975 it was meticulously restored with traditional methods and today
houses a restaurant (see Places to Eat).

Each year, in late October, Beuvron hosts
a **cider market/festival** in the town square.

Places to Stay The closest camping
ground is the *camping à la ferme* (farm
camping) *Camping Les Panniers (☎ 02 31
65 12 90, route de Beuvron/the D85)*, on the
route 5km before Beuvron. It costs 9FF per
adult and 9FF for the site.

It is essential to pre-book lodging in Beuvron. The village has three charming *chambres d'hôtes*, each with two rooms. Prices
start at 250FF per room, including breakfast. *Marie-Thérèse Duval (☎ 02 31 79 23
79)* is next to the church; *Monique Hamelin
(☎ 02 31 39 00 62)* is on the square; and
Jacques Marie (☎ 02 31 79 23 01) is on
route de Gerrots.

The only hotel in Beuvron, the three-
roomed *Auberge La Boule d'Or (☎ 02 31 79
78 78, fax 02 31 39 61 50)*, is on the square.
To secure a room in this quaint 18th-century
hotel, book a couple of months in advance.
Doubles with shower cost 320FF, including
breakfast.

For a Normandy experience, stay at the
*Manoir de Sens (☎ 02 31 79 23 05, fax 02
31 79 45 20)*, with rooms ranging from
350FF to 650FF, including breakfast. It is
on the route, 1.3km before Beuvron.

Places to Eat Beuvron has a small *alimentation générale* (grocery store) and a
great bakery, *Au Bon Pain*, specialising in
pain au cidre, a cider-flavoured bread with
apple chunks.

The *Auberge La Boule d'Or* has interesting *menus* from 99FF to 175FF and *Restaurant La Forge (☎ 02 31 79 29 74),* across the square, has 78FF to 135FF *menus* (closed Wednesday). The creperie *La Colomb'Auge (☎ 02 31 39 02 65)* has crepes from 15FF and salads from 36FF.

If your budget permits, *Le Pavé d'Auge* restaurant *(☎ 02 31 79 26 71)* in the covered market offers Norman cuisine (dinner only) at its finest, with *menus* from 140FF. Reservations are recommended (closed Monday, and also Tuesday from September to April).

Day 2: Beuvron-en-Auge to Lisieux
2½–4½ hours, 46.3km

Continuing through the rolling pastures and apple orchards of the Pays d'Auge, spend some time following the **Route du Cidre**. The day begins and ends with two vastly different Normandy-style chateaux. There are a few hills, but nothing too strenuous. When planning, remember that most cider producers close for lunch between noon and 2 pm.

A little further on the right after Victot is an old **manor house** (4.6km), the restoration of which started in June 1999. At 5.2km, a short side trip leads to the cider producer, **M Dupont**, where you can taste and buy cider, pommeau and calvados, and tour the premises.

The main route passes the moated walls of the medieval **Château de Crèvecœur** (☎ 02 31 63 02 45; closed Tuesday and in winter). The walls protect a chateau, chapel and farm buildings dating from the 11th century, plus half-timbered buildings housing museums and exhibits.

The climb from Crèvecœur-en-Auge to Cambremer has three more cider producers. Pleasant Cambremer (15.5km) is in the heart of apple country and has **half-timbered houses** and a Romanesque **church**.

Rejoin the Route du Cidre at Cambremer, passing a few more producers before leaving the official route at the turn-off to La Boissière.

The turn (33.4km) after Le Mesnil-Eudes onto the unsigned farm road is a hard right; the small road almost looks like a driveway, and begins with a short incline.

With its moat and turreted towers the 'little' **Château de St-Germain de Livet (☎ 02 31 31 00 03; 39.9km)** looks like a fairy-tale

image. It's worth touring this unusual chateau, which has a 16th-century wing patterned with gorgeous chequered brickwork, and an adjoining 15th-century half-timbered structure around an Italian-style courtyard.

Lisieux
Lisieux is the capital of the Pays d'Auge, and for centuries was the principal town of the region. Today it has a religious feel, and is best known for its enormous Basilique Ste Thérèse, destination of religious pilgrimages.

The town was damaged in 1944, losing many of its timber-framed houses. Some old architecture remains, allowing glimpses of what the town was like before WWII.

Information Because of the huge numbers of visiting pilgrims, Lisieux is well prepared for tourists. The main tourist office (☎ 02 31 48 18 10, fax 02 31 48 18 11) is at 11 rue d'Alençon (closed Sunday in winter). A second office is at place Mitterrand (closed Sunday year-round). In summer the tourist office has a small booth at the basilica.

Three banks can be found on place Mitterrand, plus a couple more on rue Pont Mortain.

Lisieux has two bike shops. Cycles Billette (☎/fax 02 31 31 45 00) at 20 rue au Char hires VTCs (hybrids) and mountain bikes (VTTs) daily/weekly for 80/450FF. Cycles Camus (☎ 02 31 32 06 30) is located at 44 blvd Ste Anne.

Things to See & Do The huge, ornate **Basilique Ste Thérèse**, modelled after Sacré Cœur in Paris, stands atop a hill in the south of Lisieux. Thérèse Martin (1873–1897) grew up in Lisieux and devoted her short life to the Carmelite order. She died just before her 25th birthday and was canonised in 1925. The basilica, one of the largest 20th-century churches, was begun in 1929 and consecrated in 1954.

Overshadowed by the basilica, in the centre of Lisieux is the 12th-century Gothic church, **Cathédrale St Pierre**. Adjacent to the church is the peaceful **Jardin de l'Évêché** (Bishop's Garden).

Examples of old Lisieux **architecture** can be seen on rue Henri Chéron. The **Musée d'Art et d'Histoire** (Museum of Art and History; ☎ 02 31 62 07 70) on blvd Pasteur is open from 2 to 6 pm, except Tuesday.

Day 2: Beuvron-en-Auge to Lisieux

NORMANDY & BRITTANY

Cue	
start	Pavé d'Auge restaurant, Beuvron
0km	go S on D49
1.7	D49 'to Victot-Pontfol'
3.7	Victot
4.6	Manor House
5.2	D15 'to Carrefour St Jean'
	M Dupont 4km
7.3	N13 'to Chateau de Crèvecœur'
10.0	Chateau de Crèvecœur
10.6	D101 'to Cambremer', Crèvecœur
10.8	2km moderate climb
13.9	(30), St-Laurent du Mont
14.0	(30m) D101 'to Cambremer'
15.5	Cambremer
15.5	D101
15.5	(2km) D101
15.6	500m moderate climb
17.5	C1 to Grandouet
18.0	C1
19.6	C1
19.9	D85A
21.8	D151 'to La Boissière'
23.4	D59 'to La Boissière'
24.4	N13 'to Lisieux, La Boissière'
25.9	D103 'to La Corne'
26.3	Chemin du Moulin/D103A
28.8	D511 'to St-Julien-le-Faucon'
29.8	D136A 'to St-Pierre des Ifs'
	1km gradual climb
33.3	D135, Le Mesnil-Eudes
33.4	unsigned farm road
35.2	unsigned farm road
36.1	unsigned road
39.6	D263A 'to Lisieux & Chateau'
39.9	Chateau de St-Germain de Livet
41.9	D579 'to Lisieux'
42.8	St-Martin de la Lieue
46.2	'to 'toutes directions'
46.3	Lisieux tourist office

On Wednesdays in July and August, Lisieux comes alive with **Les Mercredis de l'Été**. From 4 to 8 pm a market with crafts, food and local products is held in place Mitterrand, followed by evening concerts.

Places to Stay The *Camping de la Vallée (☎ 02 31 62 00 40, 9 rue de la Vallée)* is 2km north of Lisieux. It charges 11FF per adult and 5.25FF per site (open from April to mid-October).

To ensure all the pilgrims and visitors have a bed for the night, Lisieux has plenty of places to stay. Backing onto the Bishop's Garden, the *Hôtel des Arts (☎ 02 31 62 00 02, fax 02 31 32 23 36, 26 rue Condorcet)* has a friendly owner. Singles/doubles with shower and toilet begin at 175/190FF.

The quiet *Hôtel St Louis (☎ 02 31 62 06 50, 4 rue St Jacques)* has rooms with hand basin and toilet for 190FF (hall showers 20FF), and rooms with shower and toilet from 265FF. The *La Coupe d'Or (☎ 02 31 31 16 84, fax 02 31 31 35 60, 49 rue Pont Mortain)* has rooms with shower and toilet from 199/250FF.

Places to Eat The weekly *market* is held on Saturday morning at place de la République. A *Champion* supermarket is at 5 rue Mathurins.

The *Brasserie Le Français (☎ 02 31 31 01 66, 3 place Mitterrand)* has a range of snacks, salads, omelettes and crepes from 20FF.

The restaurant in *La Coupe d'Or* hotel serves *menus* from 68FF to 170FF. With a cosy atmosphere in a 15th-century half-timbered building, *Les Mille et Une Crêpes (☎ 02 31 62 46 88, 16 rue Henri Chéron)* serves a good variety of crepes (closed Wednesday and throughout autumn). Next door, *Au Vieux Normand (☎ 02 31 62 03 35, 14 rue Henri Chéron)* serves local cuisine with *menus* from 58FF (closed Monday). Full of ambience, *Le France (☎ 02 31 62 03 37, 5 rue de Char)* serves traditional meals with *menus* from 85FF to 210FF (closed Monday).

Day 3: Lisieux to Honfleur
2–4 hours, 41.9km
The first half of the ride is flat, as the route hugs the pretty valley of the Touques River. The second half of the ride leaves the valley to head through the hilly St Gatien forest to Honfleur. Still in apple country, the route passes some distilleries, interesting museums and a manor house.

The first short side trip of the day is on the D159 to the **Église de Ouilly-le-Vicomte** dating back to the 10th century, making it one of the oldest churches in Normandy.

At Coquainvilliers (6.2km), a tiny detour on the D270 leads to the **Calvados Boulard Distillery** (☎ 02 31 48 24 01) at the Moulin de la Foulonnerie. An interesting guided tour goes through the distillery, with its superb **copper stills**, and concludes with a tasting of its excellent cider, pommeau and calvados.

The side trip on the D264 to the **Château du Breuil** (☎ 02 31 65 60 00) offers another chance for a tour and taste in the distillery. The 17th-century chateau is not open to the public, but the serene, wooded 28-hectare grounds make a lovely picnic spot.

The **lake** and **Centre de Loisirs** (Leisure Centre; ☎ 02 31 64 23 93), 2km before Pont-l'Évêque, offers boating, windsurfing, mini-golf and *camping* facilities. Across the road is the **Château de Betteville** and the **Musée de la Belle Époque de L'Automobile** (Museum of the Golden Age of the Automobile; ☎ 02 31 65 05 02), a vintage car museum that also exhibits motorcycles and horse-drawn carriages.

After severe damage in WWII, **Pont-l'Évêque** still has some buildings worth noting. At the town entrance is a fine street of half-timbered houses, the most notable being Les Vikings (16.6km). Across from the tourist office (☎ 02 31 64 12 77), at 16bis rue St Michel, is a fabulous half-timbered building, now a pharmacy. The **Église St Michel** was built in the 13th and 15th centuries. The town's main claim to fame is the cheese of the same name, made here since the 13th century.

Outside Pont-l'Évêque, the **Musée de Calvados et des Métiers Anciens** (Museum of Calvados and Ancient Trades; ☎ 02 31 64 12 87) is next to the **Père Magloire distillery**. Caution is required as the N177 goes under the A132 freeway and exiting traffic merges on the right.

The 13th- to 15th-century **Manoir des Évêques de Lisieux** (Manor of the Bishops of Lisieux) is also known as the Manoir de Canapville (☎ 02 31 65 24 75). It is one of the best preserved manors in Normandy and

Day 3: Lisieux to Honfleur

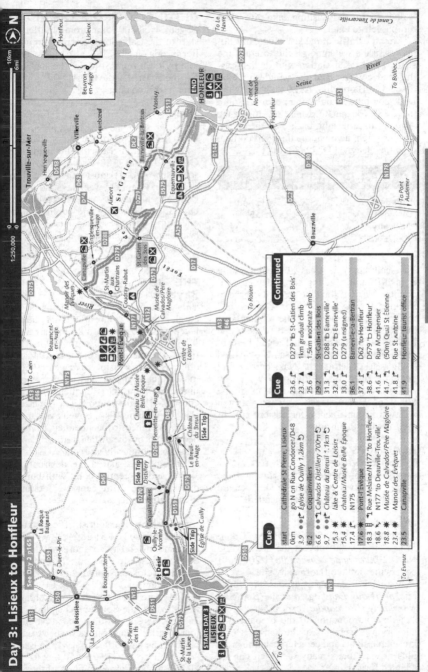

NORMANDY & BRITTANY

Cue

start	Cathédrale St Pierre, Lisieux
0km	go N on Rue Condorce/D-8
3.9	Église de Ouilly 1.2km
6.2	Coquainvilliers
6.6	Calvados Distillery 700m
9.7	Château du Breuil 1.1km
15.3	lake & Centre de Loisirs
15.4	chateau//Musée Belle Époque
17.4	Pont-l'Évêque
17.6	Rue Melaine/N177 'to Honfleur'
18.3	N177 'to Deauville-Trouville'
18.8	Musée de Calvados/Père Magloire
23.4	Manoir des Evêques
23.5	Canapville

Cue — Continued

23.6	D279 'to St-Gatien des Bois'
23.7	1km gradual climb
25.6	1.5km moderate climb
29.2	St-Gatien des Bois
31.3	D288 'to Earneville'
32.4	D279 'to Earneville'
33.0	D279 (unsgned)
36.1	Barneville-la-Bertran
37.4	D62 'to Honfleur'
38.6	D579 'to Honfleur'
41.6	Rue Montpensier
41.7	(50m) Quai St Étienne
41.8	Rue St Antoine
41.9	Honfleur Tourist office

is open for tours. If visiting, take care when turning left to enter.

After the traffic of the last couple of kilometres, it's a welcome respite to enter the shady **Fôret de St-Gatien** with its hamlets, thatched cottages and the wonderful 3km descent to Barneville. At 29.2km cross the D74, continue straight, then turn left onto the D288 (do not turn here to Honfleur). After 1km, turn right, back onto the D279, and turn right again at the thatched cottage onto the unsigned D279 (33km).

D-day Beaches

Duration	3–5½ hours
Distance	57km
Difficulty	easy
Start/End	Bayeux

Physically this ride is easy, but emotionally it is difficult. Cycling through peaceful countryside and along the coast, it is hard to imagine the ravages of war. Cemeteries, memorials, museums and the remnants of bunkers are constant reminders of the tragic loss of lives, the battle that raged here in 1944 and the effort of thousands of Allied soldiers to penetrate the Nazi barrier and begin the liberation of Europe.

This ride only covers a section of the 80km of D-day beaches, which stretch westward from Caen to the eastern side of the Cotentin Peninsula.

PLANNING
When to Ride
There is a lot to see on this ride and the longer days between April to October are ideal. An early start is recommended.

Maps & Books
Michelin map No 54 *Cherbourg, Caen, Rouen* (1:200,000) covers the area, while No 102 *Bataille de Normandie* (1:200,000) covers the Battle of Normandy site.

Available from tourist offices, the booklet *The D-day Landings and the Battle of Normandy: Normandie Terre Liberté* is an excellent introduction to the preparations and troop movements of the battle. It lists museums, sights and cemeteries in the area, plus driving tours, many of which can be adapted for cycling.

GETTING TO/FROM THE RIDE
Bayeux is about 75km from Honfleur, the start of the Calvados Classique circuit earlier in this chapter. It is also easily accessible by train from St Malo, the start of the Northern Brittany Majesty ride detailed later in this chapter.

Train
The train station is on place de la Gare about 1.5km south of the tourist office.

Trains to/from Bayeux link with Paris Gare St Lazare (188FF, two to 2½ hours, seven to 10 a day), most requiring a change of train in Caen. On weekdays, no trains to Paris accept bicycles unless in a bike bag. On Saturday, Sunday and public holidays, one train a day takes bikes in each direction (via Lisieux and changing in Caen).

It's a three-hour trip to St Malo (127FF, two a day, both take bikes).

THE RIDE
Bayeux
This attractive town, known for its cathedral, museums and nearby D-day beaches is a popular tourist base for this area.

The settlement dates to Gallo-Roman times, but the years 1066 and 1944 stand out in Bayeux's history. The year 1066 saw the conquest of England by the Normans under William the Conqueror, an event chronicled in the magnificent Bayeux tapestry. On 7 June 1944, Bayeux was the first town in France to be liberated from Nazi occupation by the Allied forces. Two fine museums honour these events.

Bayeux was spared the destruction of WWII and its central core, with buildings dating to the 15th century, retains the town's atmosphere.

Information The tourist office (☎ 02 31 51 28 28, fax 02 31 51 28 29, ⌨ www.cpod .com/monoweb/bayeux-tourisme) is at Pont St Jean, just off the northern end of rue Larcher (closed Sunday outside June to mid-September).

Banks are open Tuesday to Saturday. On rue St Malo, the Société Générale is at No 26, and the Caisse d'Épargne at No 59; the tourist office changes money when banks are closed. The post office is at 14 rue Larcher.

Tandem (☎ 02 31 92 03 50, fax 02 31 92 20 44), a bike shop 2km north of the centre n blvd Winston-Churchill, near the camping ground, hires bikes daily/weekly for 0/310FF. For more convenient day hire, the Family Home hostel (see Places to Stay) s in the centre and hires bikes for 60FF.

For Internet use, Bar Le Petit Rouen ☎ 02 31 21 10 10, ℮ hector@mail.cpod.fr) s at 14 rue de Petit Rouen.

hings to See & Do Bayeux beckons; put our bike aside and explore the town on oot. Begin with the **Bayeux Tapestry**, a 0m-long strip of embroidered linen deicting the events of the Norman invasion n 58 action-packed panels. Probably the ost precious medieval document in existnce, it is housed in its own museum, the **Musée de la Tapisserie de Bayeux** (☎ 02 31 1 25 50) on rue de Nesmond.

The spectacular **Cathédrale Notre Dame**, ainly Norman Gothic architecture, had Roanesque beginnings in the late 11th cenry. The central tower was added in the 15th entury, and the copper dome in the 1860s. he creepy crypt dates from the 11th century.

Set the scene for the D-day Beaches ride. isit the **Mémorial du Général de Gaulle**

(☎ 02 31 92 45 55), 10 rue Bourbesneur (open daily mid-March to mid-November), the **Musée Mémorial 1944 Bataille de Normandie** (☎ 02 31 92 93 41), on blvd Fabien-Ware, and the **Bayeux Commonwealth Cemetery**, a few hundred metres west.

Bayeux lace and porcelain, plus 15th- to 19th-century paintings, are displayed at **Musée Baron Gérard** (☎ 02 31 92 14 21), next to the cathedral. For a closer look at Norman lacemaking, head to **Conservatoire de la Dentelle** (Lace Conservatory; ☎ 02 31 92 73 80), at 6 rue Lambert-Leforestier.

Unscathed by WWII, the streets are rich in **old houses**. Walk along rue St Malo, rue des Cuisiniers and rue Franche. Quai de l'Aure offers a view of the **water mill** and river. The Bayeux tourist brochure lists the most notable houses.

Les Fêtes Médiévales, a huge medieval festival, is on the first weekend in July.

Places to Stay The *Camping Municipal de Bayeux (☎ 02 31 92 08 43, blvd d'Eindhoven)* is about 2km north of the town centre. It charges 17.10FF per adult and 10FF per site (open mid-March to mid-November).

D-day & the Battle of Normandy

WWII's D-day landings, codenamed Operation Overlord, were the largest military operation in history. Early on the morning of 6 June 1944, swarms of landing craft – part of a flotilla of almost 7000 boats – hit the beaches, and tens of thousands of soldiers from the USA, UK, Canada and elsewhere began pouring onto French soil.

Most of the 135,000 Allied troops stormed ashore along 80km of beach north of Bayeux, codenamed (from west to east) Utah and Omaha (in the US sector), and Gold, Juno and Sword (in the British and Canadian sectors).

AUSTRALIAN WAR MEMORIAL (P02018.233)

Normandy, France. British soldiers crouch on the beach immediately after the D-day landing.

The landings on D-day, called Jour J In French, were followed by the Battle of Normandy, which led to the liberation of Europe from Nazi occupation. In the 76 days of fighting, the Allies suffered 210,000 casualties, including 37,000 deaths. German casualties are believed to be around 200,000; another 200,000 German soldiers were taken prisoner.

D-day and the Battle of Normandy are honoured and explained in museums in Caen, Bayeux and Arromanches. Many villages near the D-day beaches and the battle area have small museums with war memorabilia collected by local people.

A lovely old residence in the centre of Bayeux, the **Family Home** youth hostel (☎ 02 31 92 15 22, fax 02 31 92 55 72, 39 rue du Général de Dais) offers beds for 95/105FF (member/nonmembers). A private room with toilet and shower costs 115FF. Prices include breakfast.

The tourist office has a list of **chambres d'hôtes** in the area. Prices (including breakfast) start at around 180FF.

Between the station and the cathedral are several bike-friendly hotels. The **Relais des Cèdres** (☎ 02 31 21 98 07, 1 blvd Sadi-Carnot) is in an old mansion. Doubles cost 150/250FF with washbasin and toilet/shower and toilet. The **Hôtel Le Bayeux** (☎ 02 31 92 70 08, fax 02 31 21 15 74, 9 rue Tardif) has spotless rooms, all with shower and toilet, from 180FF per double.

Opposite the cathedral, **Hôtel Notre Dame** (☎ 02 31 92 87 24, 02 31 92 67 11, 44 rue des Cuisiniers) has doubles without/with shower for 160/260FF. On weekends and in summer guests must eat at the restaurant.

The central **Au Bon Coin** (☎ 02 31 92 06 57, 81 rue St Jean) has rooms without/with shower for 140/200FF.

Places to Eat Bayeux has two outdoor **markets**: one on Wednesday morning on rue St Jean, the other on Saturday morning at place St Patrice. Along rue St Jean and rue St Malo are numerous **boulangeries** and **charcuteries** (delicatessens). All the supermarkets – **Leclerc, Intermarché, Stoc** and **Champion** – are strategically placed on the ring road around Bayeux.

The **Family Home** youth hostel serves dinner for 65FF. The **Hôtel Notre Dame** has an excellent and reasonably priced restaurant specialising in Norman cuisine, with **menus** from 95FF (closed Monday from December to March).

The pedestrianised rue St Jean has numerous **bars**, **cafes** and **restaurants**. **Le Fringale** (☎ 02 31 21 34 40, 43 rue St Jean) has **menus** from 55FF (closed Tuesday evening and all Wednesday).

For traditional Norman cuisine try **Le Petit Normand** (☎ 02 31 22 88 66, 35 rue Larcher) with **menus** from 58FF to 128FF (closed Thursday from November to mid April). Cosy **Le Printanier** (☎ 02 31 92 03 01, place aux Pommes) serves fine Norman cuisine and has **menus** from 97FF to 195FF.

Try **Le Domesday** (☎ 02 31 22 01 21, 20 rue Larcher) for Italian food: crepes from 20FF; pizzas from 40FF; and **menus** at 54FF and 95FF (closed Wednesday).

D-day Beaches
3–5½ hours, 57km

The mellow pastoral lands north of Bayeux and the gentle coastline, with just a few ups and downs, ensure easy cycling. However much of the day should be taken slowly to grasp the significance of the sites, as they're charged with the memories of war and death.

The route leaves Bayeux to the west to avoid the town's one-way street network. Bayeux's street names are a constant reminder of war and military figures. The **Monument de la Libération**, on the roundabout at rue St Patrice and blvd du 6 Juin, commemorates D-day and General de Gaulle's visit to Bayeux.

Shortly after the roundabout, the route passes the **Botanic Gardens**, and the 18th century **Château de Sully**, now a hotel.

The **memorial** (5.1km) in Sully honours the town's fallen citizens. From here, it' tree-lined roads, farms and tiny villages. The short climb after Russy's **memoria** (13.5km) is the worst of the day.

The turn just before Colleville-sur-Mer is easy to miss, as there's only a small sign indicating the one-way road 'to Plage d'Omaha' (Omaha Beach). The serene ride on the small, forested road leads to **Omaha Beach** the site of one of D-day's fiercest battles.

Pass a **monument** on the right as you climb to the **American Military Cemetery** (☎ 02 31 51 62 00), a huge expanse of lawn on a cliff overlooking Omaha Beach. White marble crosses and Stars of David speak of the catastrophic loss of lives. The cemetery contains the graves of 9386 American soldiers and a memorial to 1557 others whose remains were never found.

Port-en-Bessin (30.4km) is a fishing town tucked in a hollow between coastal cliffs. The main part of town lines the boat filled harbour. To the east is a **17th-century tower** erected by Vauban.

On the approach to Longues-sur-Mer (36.2km), the magnificent spires of the Bayeux Cathedral are visible on the right. A side trip to the bluff, Le Chaos, takes in the **Batterie Allemande**. View mammoth German artillery pieces designed to hit targets

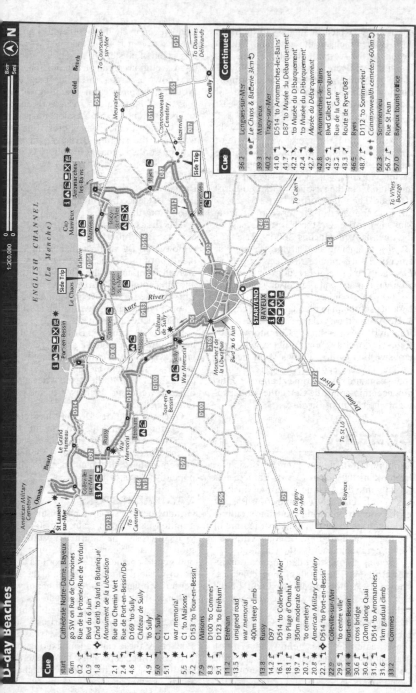

NORMANDY & BRITTANY

D-day Beaches

Cue		
0km	▲	Cathédrale Notre-Dame, Bayeux
0.2	↱	go SW on Rue de Chamoines
0.9	↱	Rue de la Poterie/Rue de Verdun
1.8	◇	(2nd exit) 'to Jardin Botanique'
	✳	Monument de la Libération
2.1	↱	Rue du Chemin Vert
2.4	↱	Rue de Port-en-Bessin/D6
4.6	↱	D169 'to Sully'
		Château de Sully
4.9	↱	'to Sully'
5.0	↱	C1, Sully
5.1	✳	war memorial'
5.5	↱	C1 'to Maisons'
7.2	↱	D153 'Tour-en-Bessin'
7.9		Maisons
8.3	↱	D100 'to Commes'
9.1	↱	D123 'to Etreham'
11.2		Etreham
13.5	✳	unsigned road
	✳	war memorial
	▲	400m steep climb
13.8		Russy
14.2	↱	D97
16.1	↱	D514 'to Colleville-sur-Mer'
18.1	↱	'to Plage d'Omaha'
19.7	▲	350m moderate climb
20.7	↱	'to cemetery'
20.8	◇	American Military Cemetery
22.1	↱	D514 'to Port-en-Bessin'
		Colleville-sur-Mer
22.9	↱	'to centre ville'
29.9		Port-en-Bessin
30.4	↱	cross bridge
30.6	↱	(20m) along Quai
31.5	↱	D514 'to Arromanches'
31.6	▲	1km gradual climb
33.2		Commes

Cue		Continued
36.2		Longues-sur-Mer
39.3	••↱	Le Chaos & Batterie 3km↺
40.2		Manvieux
41.0	↱	D514 'to Arromanches-les-Bains'
41.7	↱	D87 'to Musée du Débarquement'
42.2	↱	'to Musée du Débarquement'
42.4		'to Musée du Débarquement'
42.7	✳	Musée du Débarquement
42.8		Arromanches-les-Bains
42.9	↱	Blvd Gilbert Longuet
43.2	↱	Rue de la Gare
43.3	↱	Route de Ryes/D87
46.5		Ryes
48.7	↱	D112 'to Sommervieu'
	••↱	Commonwealth cemetery 600m↺
52.3	↱	Sommervieu
56.7	↱	Rue St Jean
57.0		Bayeux tourist office

20km away (which in June 1944 included both Gold Beach, to the east, and Omaha Beach, to the west). Parts of the film *The Longest Day* were filmed here. From the bluff, the **Mulberry Harbour** – an enormous floating harbour towed from England for the D-day invasion – can be seen to the east at Arromanches-les-Bains.

Arromanches-les-Bains (42.8km), with its narrow, winding streets, was the site of landing operations in June 1944. The informative **Musée du Débarquement** (Invasion Museum; ☎ 02 31 22 34 31) at place du 6 Juin faces the vestiges of the Mulberry Harbour. The tourist office (☎ 02 31 21 47 56) is to the west of the museum at 2 rue Maréchal Joffre. Up the hill to the east of the town is **Arromanches 360** (☎ 02 31 22 30 30), at chemin de Calvaire, a circular cinema. Its 18-minute film *Le Prix de la Liberté* (The Price of Freedom) is a mix of archival footage and present-day pictures.

The pedestrianised rue Maréchal Joffre continues through to blvd Gilbert Lonnguet.

Between the villages of Ryes and Bazenville is a small **Commonwealth Cemetery**, a truly moving place, with epitaphs written by the families of the dead.

The D112 becomes the D12, which changes name several times before eventually becoming route de Corseulles and leading to the centre of Bayeux.

Brittany

Brittany (Bretagne in French, Breizh in Breton), in the north-west of France, juts proudly into the Atlantic. Its corner position has kept it relatively isolated from the rest of the country, allowing the Breton culture and language to remain a distinct feature of the region, and aligning Bretons with their Celtic neighbours across the Channel.

There is no question that the sea dominates Brittany. The 1100km-long coastline, known as Armor (meaning 'Land of the Sea'), varies: from the wild west, beaten by Atlantic blasts, to the calmer stretches of the English Channel and the Gulf of Morbihan. The sea is a source of livelihood for those catching the renowned Breton seafood. It also nurtures tourism; the mild climate and fabulous shores draw crowds of beach lovers.

However, cycle through Brittany and yo will discover it is more than just seascapes It is a land of mysterious megaliths, medieva towns, religious art and traditions. The inter ior, known as Argoat (meaning 'Land of th Woods'), inspires calm pedalling throug forests and farms, along rivers and canals.

The Bretons have a passion for cyclin and Tour de France stages often find the way into the region. Brittany's favourit cycling son is Bernard Hinault.

HISTORY

Brittany was first inhabited by Neolithi tribes, evidenced by menhirs and dolmer throughout the region.

The first Celts appeared around the 6t century BC. Julius Caesar conquered th region in 56 BC and it remained in Roma hands until the 5th century AD. More Cel arrived from across the Channel in the 5t and 6th centuries. The region was graduall Christianised by Celtic missionaries, afte whom many Breton towns, such as St Ma and St Brieuc, are named.

In the 9th century, Brittany's nationa hero Nominoë revolted against French rul taking control of Rennes and Nantes. Bri tany was contested by England and Franc throughout the Middle Ages. After a seri of royal weddings, Brittany became part France in 1532.

Over the centuries Brittany has retaine a separate regional identity. In the 196(there was a strong movement in support an independent Breton state. Although th movement has faded, many people still ho hope of independence.

NATURAL HISTORY

Brittany occupies a good part of the ancier granite Massif Armoricain, and 300 milli(years of erosion have turned most of the r gion into an expanse of low-lying plai and gentle uplands. The exceptions are th north-western Monts d'Arrée and the south central Montagnes Noires, neither of whic fall into the category of mountains as th name suggests – they are more like hills.

The classic image of Brittany is rugged coastline and rocky seascape Pockets of these can be found along the e tire coastline, especially the westernmo peninsulas, mingling with stretches sandy beaches and sheltered inlets.

The Badger

At the age of 15, Bernard Hinault's parents gave him his first bicycle for passing a high school exam. He was only allowed to ride the few kilometres from their Breton farm to Yffiniac, from where he caught the bus the extra 10km to school. After some nagging, he was eventually allowed to ride the whole distance, and one of France's greatest sporting heroes was created.

Only two years later, on 2 May 1971, Bernard surprised his family by entering and winning his first race, the local Prix de Plouguenoual. That year he won 12 more junior races, and the following year he won the Premier Pas de Dunlop (French national junior championship).

In 1975, Hinault began his career as a professional cyclist, and the rest is history. He dominated the world cycling scene and raced professionally until 1986, winning the Tour de France five times, Giro d'Italia (Tour of Italy) three times and amassing over 250 career wins.

In 1983, tendonitis threatened his career, but he overcame it to win the Tour again in 1985. In 1986, his career in its twilight, Hinault declared he would ride the Tour one last time, to repay team-mate Greg LeMond, his 'prodige' from the year previous, and help him win his first Tour. However, mid-way through the Tour Hinault changed his mind and an epic battle between the two ensued. LeMond prevailed and went on to win the race another two times; Hinault retired, but returned to the Tour some years later as race director.

A formidable and obstinate opponent, Hinault was known as Le Blaireau (The Badger), after the tenacious and aggressive animal he hunted when he was young.

Breton forests are oak and beech. In the south-east the wetlands, marshes and islands of the Parc Naturel Régional de Briére are a birdwatcher's delight. The Parc Naturel Régional d'Armorique, in the west, encompasses both the landscape of the Monts d'Arrée and the maritime features of the Crozon peninsula and the islands off the coast to the west.

CLIMATE

Brittany has a deserved reputation for being wet, recording France's highest annual precipitation. Although the average is 200 days a year of rain, don't despair, as even in the wettest months from January to May, rainy spells usually only last for a few days. On the bright side, Brittany does enjoy an extremely mild, maritime climate.

Summer temperatures hover around the mid-20s, but it is not unusual to have several days climbing into the low 30s, especially on the more protected southern coast and inland.

The winds coming straight off the Atlantic can be a cyclist's nightmare. Westerly winds dominate and winds from the north-west and south-west can be unrelenting.

INFORMATION
Maps & Books

Michelin map No 230 *Bretagne* (1:200,000) covers the entire province. It provides good coverage for cycling, but some farm roads are not included. Michelin also publishes several maps covering smaller areas – see Maps & Books under each ride for details.

The Michelin *Green Guide: Brittany* has a wealth of information on the history, sights and background of the region. *The Most Beautiful Villages of Brittany* is a gorgeous photographic collection of Breton villages, some of which are visited on the rides in this chapter. *The Oysters of Locmariaquer* by Eleanor Clark is set in Locmariaquer, famous for its oysters. Not just about the townspeople and oysters, the book delves into the historical background, myths and legends of Brittany.

The Fédération Française de Cyclotourisme (FFCT) publishes *La France à Vélo: Bretagne* (118FF), which details rides of varying lengths throughout Brittany (see Books in the Facts for the Cyclist chapter). *Balades à Vélo en Loire-Atlantique*, published by the Loire-Atlantique Tourist Office (☎ 02 51 72 95 30, fax 02 40 20 44 54) in Nantes, describes 23 rides in the Loire-Atlantique, the south-eastern department of Brittany.

Information Sources

The Brittany regional tourist office (☎ 02 99 36 15 15, fax 02 99 28 44 40, ▯ www.brittanytourism.com), 1 rue Raoul

Ponchon, Rennes, serves the entire province. It publishes the excellent booklet *Vélo-VTT en Bretagne,* which suggests itineraries for road and VTT tours, and details a host of cycling information.

Each department has its own tourist office. The Northern Brittany Majesty ride travels through the departments of Ille-et-Vilaine (☎ 02 99 78 47 47, fax 02 99 78 33 24, 🖳 www.bretagne35.com) and, for a short stretch, Côtes d'Armor (☎ 02 96 62 72 00, fax 02 96 33 59 10). The Southern Brittany Contrasts ride loops through the department of Morbihan (☎ 02 97 54 06 56, fax 02 97 42 71 02).

As well as the FFCT, Brittany has a government cycling body which organises events within the region, the Comité Régional de Bretagne Cyclisme, (☎ 02 96 94 03 29, fax 02 96 78 80 47), 1 rue du Vau Louis, 22001 St Brieuc.

Language

The west of Brittany is known as Basse Bretagne (Lower Brittany), and the eastern portion as Haute Bretagne (Upper Brittany). Breton customs and language are most evident in Basse Bretagne, while Haute Bretagne has retained little of the Breton culture and only French is spoken.

The indigenous language of Brittany, Breton (Brezhoneg), is a Celtic language related to Cornish and Welsh and, more distantly, to Irish and Scottish Gaelic. Breton can sometimes still be heard in western Brittany, especially around Cornouaille, the southwestern tip, where as many as 600,000 people have some degree of fluency.

After the Revolution the new government made a concerted effort to suppress the Breton language and replace it with French. Even 20 years ago, if schoolchildren spoke Breton in the classroom they were punished. Things have changed, and about 20 privately subsidised schools now teach Breton. Recently a new radio station, Radio Kerne (90.4 Mhz), hit the airwaves. It plays traditional Celtic music and broadcasts only in Breton.

Place Names

In west Brittany, most town names are displayed in both French and Breton, and shops, hotels and restaurants often have Breton names. Wherever possible we have indicated the Breton name in brackets in the text.

Some Breton words you may come across, especially in place names (the spelling may vary), are:

Breton	French	English
avon, aven	rivière	river
bae	baie	bay
bihan	petit	little
enez	île	island
fest-noz	fête de nuit	night festival
gall	français	French
hir	long	long
iliz	église	church
kêr*	village	town, village
koad, coat	forêt	forest
kromm	courbé	curved
maen, mein	pierre	stone
menez	montagne	mountain
mor	mer	sea
plou, plo, ple**	paroisse	parish
raz	détroit	strait
roz	coteau	hill, hillside
tuchenn	tertre	hillock, mound
ti, ty	maison	house

* short for 'kêriadenn'
** used only as a prefix in place names

Festivals

The Festival de Cornouaille, a showcase for traditional Breton music, costume and culture, is held in Quimper every July between the third and fourth Sundays. After the traditional festival, classical music concerts are staged at different venues around the town.

Each year Lorient draws visitors from a host of Celtic regions for the Festival Interceltique, a ten-day celebration of Celtic music, literature and dance in early August.

Northern Brittany Majesty

Duration	4 days
Distance	195.1km
Difficulty	easy-moderate
Start/End	St Malo

This ride showcases the splendour of this corner of Brittany, dipping into Normandy to marvel at the island abbey of Mont St Michel. The four overnight stops are treats in themselves, combining rural landscapes with seascapes to make this ride truly majestic.

Set off from the walled city of St Malo and ride alongside the Rance River to the medieval town of Dinan. The next two days on the country back roads of Brittany lead to Combourg, dominated by its chateau, and then the spectacular abbey of Mont St Michel. The last day is 'beach day', contrasting expansive bay vistas with the craggy Côte d'Émeraude (Emerald Coast).

PLANNING
When to Ride

The ideal time to visit this area is from May to late September. These are the least rainy months, but bear in mind that Brittany swells with crowds of beach-worshipping tourists in summer, particularly in August. Summer thunderstorms are no surprise.

This part of the Brittany coast experiences massive tidal variations. The tide times are posted in tourist offices, some hotels and in the newspaper. The high tides *(grandes marées)* at Mont St Michel and along the coast are phenomenal, advancing at a rapid rate. The sight of Mont St Michel surrounded by water at high tide is exceptional, so allow enough time to take this in.

Maps

Michelin map No 59 *St-Brieuc, St-Malo, Rennes* (1:200,000) covers the ride area.

GETTING TO/FROM THE RIDE

Trains link St Malo with Bayeux, the start of the D-day Beaches ride detailed earlier in this chapter. Trains also connect to Vannes, the start of the Southern Brittany Contrasts ride detailed later in this chapter.

St Malo

Train The train station is 1.5km east of the old city, along the bikepath on ave Louis Martin.

The direct service to/from Paris' Gare Montparnasse (290FF, 4½ hours, one a day) in July and August takes bikes.

The rest of the year you have to first get from Paris to Rennes (241FF, three hours), but only one train a week takes bikes outside a bike bag; from Rennes on a Sunday and from Paris, a Friday. A dozen TGV trains (283FF, two hours) will take bikes in bags between Paris and Rennes. From Rennes to St Malo it's easy (69FF, one hour, nine a day, all take bikes).

Between Bayeux and St Malo, two trains a day travel via Dol-de-Bretagne (127FF, three hours, both take bikes). To get to Vannes, go to Rennes, then connect to Vannes via Redon (96FF, 1½ hours, 10 to 12 a day, two take bikes).

Ferry St Malo is linked to several UK destinations by sea. Hydrofoils and catamarans depart from the Gare Maritime de la Bourse. Car ferries leave from the Gare Maritime du Naye. Both are south of the walled city.

Brittany Ferries links St Malo with Portsmouth. From May to October, Condor Ferries has services to/from Weymouth. Condor also has a service to the Channel Islands, as does Émeraude Lines. See the Sea section in the Getting There & Away chapter for details.

THE RIDE
St Malo

Gateway to the northern Brittany coast, St Malo is on the beautiful Côte d'Émeraude, lined with beaches, peninsulas and rugged promontories.

Settlement began in the 6th century, but St Malo was fortified in the 12th century with the building of the ramparts. Go through the gateway of Porte St Vincent to the walled town of St Malo. Originally an island, it is now connected to the mainland by a causeway. *Intra muros* (inside the walls), the old city is a world apart. WWII left 80% of St Malo in ruins, but it was carefully rebuilt in a 17th- and 18th-century architectural style.

Jacques Cartier sailed from here to explore Canada. Writer and statesman François Chateaubriand found inspiration here.

Information The tourist office (☎ 02 99 56 64 48, fax 02 99 40 93 13, 🖳 www.ville-saint-malo.fr) is on Esplanade St Vincent just outside the walled city. Ask for the free St Malo bikepath map, *Vélo Cité Saint Malo*, and the *Saint Malo: Plan de Ville* (city map).

Several banks are near the train station on blvd de la République. Within the walls, Banque de France, at 7 rue d'Asfeld, only exchanges money weekday mornings, and the Banque de Bretagne branch is at place Chateaubriand. The post office is at 4 place des Frères Lammenais. Many shops offer exchange with no commission, but their rates are often poor.

The closest bike shop is in Paramé: Cycles Nicole (☎ 02 99 56 11 06), 11 rue Robert Schuman, hires bikes for 50/280FF daily/weekly. A little further out, Cycles Le Goallec (☎ 02 99 81 39 65), 9 rue de la Saulie, runs rides on Sunday mornings.

To send email, visit the printer Cop Imprim (☎ 02 23 18 08 08, e copimprim @wanadoo.fr), 39 blvd des Talards (near the train station).

Things to See & Do The **ramparts** afford fabulous views over the Channel, the old city and the port. Fortunately they were spared the destruction of WWII and are mostly original. Visit the **chateau** at Porte St Vincent. The **Musée de la Ville** (☎ 02 99 40 71 57), housed in the keep, focuses on the history of the city and the surrounding area.

Almost in the centre of the old city is **Cathédrale St Vincent**, begun in the 11th century. Don't miss the beautiful stained-glass windows.

St Malo has two **aquariums**: the Petit Aquarium Intra-Muros (☎ 02 99 56 94 77) next to place Vauban, and the Grand Aquarium St Malo (☎ 02 99 21 19 00) on ave du Général Patton, 4km south of the old city.

At low tide walk to the **Île du Grand Bé**, the island where François Chateaubriand is buried. Be aware of the quick incoming tides, lest you should be stranded there.

Places to Stay St Malo has plenty of accommodation. Reserve in July and August.

The *Camping Municipal La Cité D'Aleth* (☎ 02 99 81 60 91) is at the western tip of the St Servan peninsula. The fabulous views make it the most attractive of the several campgrounds in the area. It costs 21FF per person and 28FF per site (open year-round).

The *Auberge de Jeunesse* (☎ 02 99 40 29 80, fax 02 99 40 29 02, 37 ave du Père Umbricht), in Paramé, has dorm-beds for 72FF, including breakfast.

Inside the city walls are several reasonably priced hotels. The *Hôtel Le Victoria* (☎ 02 99 56 34 01, fax 02 99 40 32 78, 4 rue des Orbettes) has rooms from 167/185FF without/with shower. The *Hôtel du Commerce* (☎ 02 99 56 18 00, fax 02 99 56 04 68,

11 rue St Thomas) has rooms from 170/240FF without/with shower. The friendly, stylish *Hôtel du Louvre* (☎ 02 99 40 86 62, fax 02 99 40 86 93, e lelouvre@aol.com, 2 rue des Marins) has spacious rooms priced between 200FF and 350FF, all with shower and toilet. Across from the chateau at place Chateaubriand, the grand *Hôtel de l'Univers* (☎ 02 99 40 89 52, fax 02 99 40 07 27, 🖳 www.st-malo.com/hotel-de-lunivers) charges from 240/270FF for singles/doubles with shower and toilet.

Outside the city walls there are several hotels between the station and Grande Plage.

Places to Eat *Markets* are held next to La Halle au Blé between rue des Cordiers and rue de la Herse on Tuesday and Friday. A *Marché Plus* supermarket is at 9 rue St Vincent (downstairs). For a selection of small *food shops* head to rue de l'Orme.

The seafood in St Malo is great, and the walled town has no lack of choices. Rue Jacques Cartier is lined with *seafood restaurants* where *menus* begin at 75FF. Place Chateaubriand has several *brasseries* and *cafes* and the *restaurant* at the Hôtel de l'Univers has *menus* from 75FF. Rue de Dinan has several *creperies*, and there is a variety of *restaurants* and *glaciers* (ice-cream shops) in the vicinity of Marché aux Légumes and place de la Poissonnerie.

Day 1: St Malo to Dinan
2–3 hours, 31.3km

This short ride allows enough time to explore Dinan. Getting out of St Malo requires careful navigation. Following the Rance River, it's effortless cycling on the gently undulating route, but you'll need a burst of energy to get up the steep hill just before Dinan.

The route leaves St Malo to the south. The free *Plan de Ville* from the tourist office would be a handy reference. The first part of the ride skirts the Bassin Vauban and the Bassin Bouvet before crossing the river on the Barrage de la Rance.

The traffic on the Barrage de la Rance is heavy; the **barrage** (dam) is 750m long, and in the centre is **Usine Marémotrice de la Rance** (☎ 02 99 16 37 14), the hydroelectric power station, which uses St Malo's extraordinarily high tides to generate electricity. It is open daily and runs tours by appointment on weekdays.

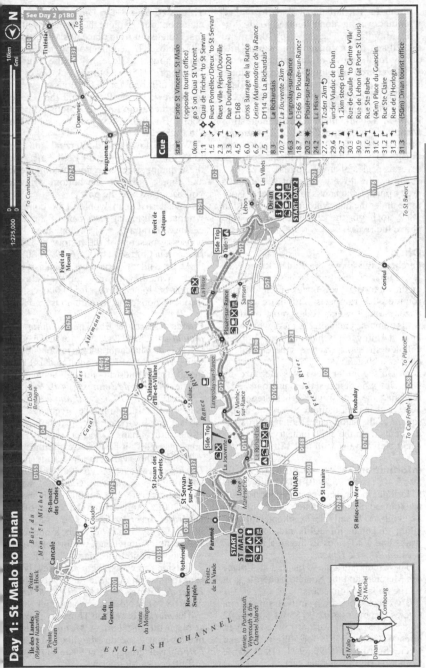

From La Richardais (8.3km) to Dinan, it's quiet cycling along forested roads dotted with villages. The side trip (10.7km) to the village of **La Jouvente** is worthwhile purely for the views of the Rance River.

The **church** at Plouër-sur-Rance dates from the 18th century. After La Hisse (24.2km) fine **views** of the Rance Valley extend to the left. Off the route a short distance is Taden, a small village with the interesting **Manoir de la Grand-Cour**, a 14th-century turreted manor house. Continue through the village to view the Taden Plain, home of several species of aquatic birds.

Enjoy the lovely descent to Dinan's pretty **port** on the banks of the Rance. Continue under the huge **viaduct**, inaugurated in 1852, to begin the climb to Dinan, 75m above the river.

Dinan

Perched high above the Rance River Valley, Dinan is Brittany's best preserved medieval town. It was once completely surrounded by ramparts and more than a dozen stone towers. Today most of these walls remain, enclosing a medieval fairyland of 15th-century half-timbered houses, cobbled streets, attractive squares and, of course, a chateau.

Dinan's popular hero was Bernard du Guesclin, who defeated the English in 1357, releasing the city from English siege. His heart rests in the Basilique St Saveur, on the square of the same name. Dinan's prosperity stems from the cloth industry that flourished between the 15th and 18th centuries.

Information The tourist office (☎ 02 96 39 75 40, fax 02 96 39 01 64) is at 6 rue de l'Horloge, in the 16th-century Hôtel Kératry (closed Sunday outside June through September). It sells an excellent map and guide to Dinan for 20FF and a guide to walks and VTT rides in the area, *Randonnées en Pays de Dinan*.

The Crédit Agricole is located at 4 place des Merciers and the Société Générale is at 13 rue de la Ferronnerie.

Two bike shops are near the train station. Cycles Gauthier (☎ 02 96 85 07 60, fax 02 96 85 08 95), to the west at 15 rue Deroyer, hires VTCs and VTTs for 50FF a day, and Cycles Scardin (☎ 02 96 39 21 94), at 30 rue Carnot, is slightly further east.

Things to See & Do Dinan is best appreciated on foot. Explore the streets and alleys that radiate out from **place des Merciers**, itself enclosed by a collection of gabled, timbered houses. Close by is the **Tour de l'Horloge**, a 15th-century clock tower that can be climbed for a fabulous view. For good **views** of the Rance and the viaduct, head to the **Jardin Anglais** (English Garden) behind Basilique St Saveur, or east to **Tour Ste Catherine**.

Wander down **rue du Jerzual** and continue on the steep **rue du Petit Port**. Both these quaint streets are lined with galleries and shops; going to the bottom will take you back down to the **port**.

A visit to Dinan wouldn't be complete without walking at least part of the 13th-century **ramparts**. The chateau's keep houses a museum of the history of Dinan, **Musée du Château** (☎ 02 96 39 45 20).

At the end of September, Dinan reverts back to medieval times for the **Fête des Remparts**. Joined by up to 40,000 visitors, the locals don medieval garb, joust and feast.

Places to Stay & Eat The *Camping Municipal* (☎ 02 96 39 11 96, fax 02 96 85 06 97, 103 rue* Chateaubriand) is just outside the walls. It costs 13FF per adult and 14FF for the site (open mid-May through September).

The *Auberge de Jeunesse* (☎ 02 96 39 10 83, fax 02 96 39 10 62, ✉ dinan@fuaj.org) is in an old mill, Moulin de Méen, at Vallée de la Fontaine des Eaux, just before the climb into Dinan. A bed costs 48FF, and breakfast 19FF; it has a few camping spots.

Within the walls the pleasant *Hôtel Duchesse Anne* (☎ 02 96 39 09 43, fax 02 96 85 09 76, 10 place du Guesclin*), with a bar and creperie, has doubles with shower from 200FF. Across from the tourist office, the *Hôtel Arvor* (☎ 02 96 39 21 22, fax 02 96 39 83 09, 5 rue Pavie*) is a converted 18th-century convent. Comfortable rooms with shower and toilet start at 280FF.

Outside the walls, there are a few hotels near the station on place du 11 Novembre. *Hôtel de France* (☎ 02 96 39 22 56, fax 02 96 39 08 96*), at No 7, has rooms from 180FF.

The *market* is held on Thursday morning at place du Guesclin. A *Monoprix* supermarket is at 7 rue du Marchix and a small *EPI Service* grocery is at 9 rue de l'Apport (off place des Merciers).

On rue Ste Claire, around the corner from the tourist office, *Le Saigon*, at No 12, serves Asian food. *Taj Mahal*, at No 9, has Indian specialties and *Le Cantorbery*, at No 6, French cuisine. Two good bets serving traditional food on rue de Haute Voie are *Le Pélican* (☎ 02 96 39 47 05), at No 3, with *menus* from 60FF (closed Monday), and *Le Jacobin* (☎ 02 96 39 25 66), at No 11, with *menus* from 80FF (closed Tuesday). Down by the port, *restaurants* line rue du Quai.

Day 2: Dinan to Combourg
3–5½ hours, 54.8km

The route begins with serene cycling alongside the Canal d'Ille et Rance, then meanders through farmlands, crossing the canal several times. The only real climb is to the hilltop town of Hédé (37.2km). From here it's downhill past a set of locks and through forest and quiet countryside to Combourg.

Leave St Malo's walled city, descending through place St Louis and the streets, heading out to the village of Léhon (1.3km). The village entrance is marked with a small sign, 'Le Bourg' (the village), on the first house on the left (after 30m of cobblestones). At the river, veer left onto the *halage* (towpath) alongside the **Canal d'Ille et Rance**, which offers peaceful cycling for the next 4km, passing a couple of **locks** (*écluses*). Soon after the second lock, leave the river and turn onto the unsigned farm road with a large farm on the left. Continue to the village of Calorguen and onto the bustling town of Evran.

Leave Evran (14.7km) and cross the canal. Take a look at the **lock** and **lock house** adorned with flowers – it's clearly a loved lock! Watch carefully for the turn to the right onto the first road after the lock.

Château La Bourbansais (☎ 02 99 69 40 07) is a short side trip from Pleugueneuc (21.3km). The turreted chateau, surrounded by gardens, was built in the 16th century, and enlarged in the 18th. The interior has 18th-century furnishings and its **zoo** has animals from five continents. The complex is open daily from April to September and afternoons only (2 to 6 pm) the rest of the year. Admission to the chateau is 55FF, to the zoo 55FF, and a combination ticket 68FF. The grounds make a lovely picnic spot.

From Pleugueneuc, it's a straight run on the N137 to Tinténiac. The maps get a little confusing around here, as N137 is also the name used for the large road to the right of the route.

Tinténiac (30.9km) is on the banks of the Canal d'Ille et Rance. The route passes the town's interesting **church**; after the church, go left to reach the **canal** and the **Musée de l'Outil et des Métiers** (Museum of Tools and Trades; ☎ 02 99 68 02 03), 5 quai de la Donac, which shows the work of trades people such as coopers (barrel makers) and blacksmiths. Tinténiac is on the Paris-Brest-Paris route (see 'The Paris-Brest-Paris Experience' boxed text in the Randonnées chapter).

It's a pleasant climb to Hédé along a forested road, past the lake and into the centre of the attractive, lofty town. From the main square, it's just 70m to the left to see the **ruins** of the 13th-century castle and the **view** over the valley.

Leave Hédé and, just after the cemetery on the left (37.9km), descend to the canal. From the bridge you can see **11 locks** built to compensate for the 27m drop in water level.

The sight of the imposing **chateau** welcomes you to Combourg.

Combourg
Dominated by its chateau, this medieval fortress is a stunning sight. It was built between the 11th and 15th centuries and its picturesque setting is completed with the Lac Tranquille (Tranquil Lake). In the 18th century the chateau was home to Romantic writer François-René de Chateaubriand, who wrote, '*C'est dans les bois de Combourg que je suis devenu ce que je suis.*' ('It was in the woods of Combourg that I became what I am.')

Information The tourist office (☎ 02 99 73 13 93, fax 02 99 73 52 39, 🖳 www .combourg.org), 23 place Albert Parent, is inside La Maison de La Lanterne, a restored 16th-century house (closed Sunday in winter). It sells *Les Sentiers du Pays Gallo* (20FF), a booklet with walks and VTT circuits in the area between Antrain (to the north-east) and Mont St Michel.

Crédit Mutuel is at 30 rue Notre Dame, and the Banque Populaire at 3 place St Guilden.

The town's two bicycle shops are just a few doors apart. Cycles Lefrançois (☎ 02 99 73 01 43) is at 10 rue Notre Dame and

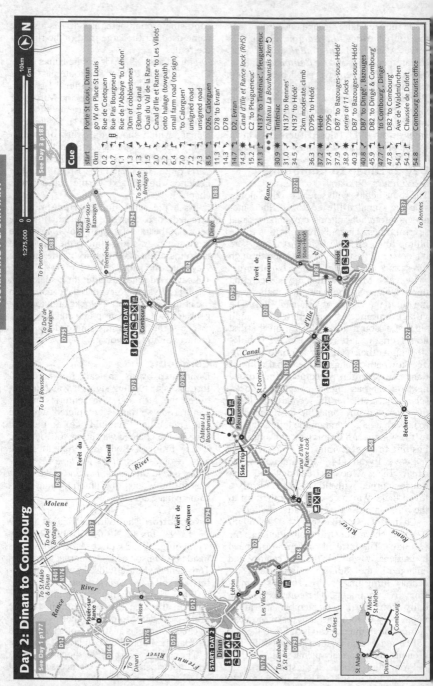

Day 2: Dinan to Combourg

NORMANDY & BRITTANY

Cue		
start		Porte St Louis, Dinan
0km		go W on Place St Louis
0.2		Rue de Coetquen
0.7		Rue Pas Bourgneuf
1.1		Rue de l'Abbaye 'to Léhon'
1.3		30m of cobblestones
1.3		(30m) to canal
1.5		Quai du Val de la Rance
2.0		Canal d'Ille et Rance 'to Les Villots' onto halage (towpath)
2.2		small farm road (no sign)
6.4		'to Calorguen'
7.0		unsigned road
7.2		unsigned road
7.3		D26, Calorguen
8.5		D78 'to Evran'
11.3		D78
13.3		D2, Evran
14.7		Canal d'Ille et Rance lock (RHS)
14.9		C2 'to Pleugueneuc'
15.2		N137 'to Tinténiac', Pleugueneuc
21.3		Château La Bourbansais 2km ↻
30.9		Tinténiac
31.0		N137 'to Rennes'
34.5		N137 'to Hédé'
36.3		2km moderate climb
37.2		D795 'to Hédé'
37.4		Hédé
37.9		D87 'to Bazouges-sous-Hédé'
38.9		series of 11 locks
40.3		D87 'to Bazouges-sous-Hédé'
40.8		D87 'to Dingé', Bazouges
45.9		D82 'to Dingé & Combourg'
47.7		'to Combourg', Dingé
47.8		D82 'to Combourg'
54.1		Ave de Waldmünchen
54.2		Chaussée de Dufort
54.8		Combourg tourist office

Cycles Quévert (☎ 02 99 73 06 93) is at No 42. Neither offers bicycle hire.

Bar de la Tour (☎ 02 99 73 33 04), 8 rue Chateaubriand, has internet access.

Things to See & Do The **Château de Combourg** (☎ 02 99 73 22 95) can be toured in the afternoon. Memorabilia of Chateaubriand is displayed in the chateau and the author's bedroom, in the tower, can be visited. The **chateau grounds** are open to visitors all day.

Lac Tranquille provides a lovely setting for an evening stroll. For walks further afield, pick up the two **walking itineraries** offered free by the tourist office.

Places to Stay The *Camping Municipal Le Vieux Châtel* (☎ 02 99 73 07 03) is on the banks of Lac Tranquille. It costs 14.60FF per adult, and 8.90FF per tent.

The two hotels with the best location are on place Chateaubriand, below the chateau. *Hôtel du Château* (☎ 02 99 73 00 38, fax 02 99 73 25 79, 1 place Chateaubriand) has rooms, with shower and toilet, from 260FF. Across the square, *Hôtel du Lac* (☎ 02 99 73 05 65, fax 02 99 73 23 34, 2 place Chateaubriand) is better value, with rooms from 200FF (closed February). About 200m further (along the street leading into town), the *Hôtel Le Romantic* (☎ 02 99 73 05 52, 12 place des Déportés) has rooms from 170FF (hall shower and toilet).

Places to Eat A lively *market* is held on Monday morning at place Albert-Parent. *Food shops* abound on rue Chateaubriand and around place Albert-Parent. *Charcuterie Destouches*, 22 rue Chateaubriand, has great salads and cheeses. An *8 á Huit* supermarket is at 36 rue Notre Dame and a big *Super U* is on ave des Érables as you leave town for Mont St Michel.

A couple of *creperies* are on rue Chateaubriand, another is on rue des Princes around the corner. Rue des Princes also has a *pizzeria*, as does the Hôtel Le Romantic.

For a restaurant with a cosy atmosphere, try *L'Écrivain* (☎ 02 99 73 01 61, 1 place St Gilduin), where *menus* start at 78FF (closed Wednesday evening and Thursday). Both the *Hôtel du Château* and *Hôtel du Lac* have restaurants, the latter being more affordable, with *menus* from 85FF.

Day 3: Combourg to Mont St Michel
2–4 hours, 44.5km
The lack of sightseeing en route is more than made up for by the overnight stop at Mont St Michel. From Combourg it's leisurely cycling as the route rolls through farms and villages to Bazouges-la-Pérouse, an artists' village, and down towards the coast.

A small farm road leads to Noyal-sous-Bazouges (10.5km), with a few gentle ups and downs through the Breton farmlands. The quiet hamlet's church steeple heralds the settlement from more than a kilometre away. From the church, head north on the D87, which is unsigned until after the town.

After the solitary **menhir** (13.7km) past Les Trois Croix, it's an easy hill into Bazouges-la-Pérouse. At the entrance, the **Parc de Bellevue**, a small park of interesting sculptures, is a good introduction to the 'art town'.

Bazouges-la-Pérouse is a lovely town set on a spur. In summer its population grows, not from tourists, but because the artists move in. Many shops have been turned into **galleries** and **studios**.

Cycle into the cool, shady **Forêt de Ville-Cartier** (21.5km) and come out the other end for superb views of Mont St Michel, sublimely silhouetted on the horizon. The D91 becomes the D83 for a short distance before Vieux-Viel; glide down past the church, and follow the Couesnon River to skirt busy Pontorson, thriving on its position as gateway to Mont St Michel. Pontorson and Mont St Michel are both in Normandy, the boundary marked by the Couesnon River.

There is heavy traffic all the way to Mont St Michel. A pleasant alternative is the road through Moidrey, but careful navigation is required. At 35.7km, the D312 is unsigned (don't take the D75 by accident!); make a hard left, almost a U-turn, then head north.

After Moidrey, fine views of **Mont St Michel** appear. From Beauvoir, it is 4km to the magnificent monument – the final 2km on the causeway.

Mont St Michel
Words can't describe Mont St Michel. Whether it's your first or fifth visit, whether it's sunny or misty, day or night, it's awesome. Riding on the causeway towards the

Mont at dawn, before the tourists arrive, is breathtaking, and the night illuminations of the abbey are stunning.

In 708 the Archangel Michael appeared to the bishop of Avranches and instructed him to build an oratory on the island. In 966 Richard I, Duke of Normandy, gave Mont St Michel to the Benedictines, who turned it into an important centre of learning, and in the 11th century replaced the oratory with an abbey. Further enhancements over the centuries resulted in today's magnificent Gothic abbey, which was named in honour of the Archangel.

Mont St Michel is also famous for its extraordinary high tides – the highest in Europe. The difference in the water level between low and high tides can reach 15m. However, the causeway is never under water, so you won't get stranded.

Information The Mont St Michel tourist office (☎ 02 33 60 14 30, fax 02 33 60 06 75, e ot.Mont.Saint.Michel@wanadoo.fr) is up the stairs to the left as you enter Porte de l'Avancée, the only opening in the ramparts (closed Sunday from September to Easter).

The Pontorson tourist office (☎ 02 33 60 20 65, fax 02 33 60 85 67), place de l'Église, is open Monday to Saturday all year.

It is possible to change money in Mont St Michel, but better rates can be found in Pontorson at the CIN bank, 98 rue Couesnon.

The bike shop, Videloup (☎ 02 33 60 11 40), at 1bis rue Couesnon in Pontorson, is on your right as you turn onto the D19 (34.1km). Bikes can be hired from the camping ground (see Places to Stay) near Mont St Michel for 100FF a day.

Things to See & Do With the enormous amount of visitors, it's no wonder that Mont St Michel is crowded during the day. Early morning and early evening are the ideal times to have a 'quiet' time to explore.

Around the base are the ancient ramparts and the 15th- and 16th-century buildings that house the 72 people who live here. The Mont's single, narrow and very steep street, **Grande Rue** is lined with restaurants, a few hotels and souvenir shops. It leads to the abbey and **views** of the bay.

Allow time to visit the **Abbey** (☎ 02 33 60 14 14): the church, the cloister, the refectory and other rooms, plus the gardens.

The island has two museums: **Musée Grévin** (☎ 02 33 60 14 09) is a wax museum, while the **Musée Maritime** (☎ 02 33 60 14 09) has information on the tides and the bay. The **Archéoscope** is a 20-minute multimedia presentation of the Mont's history.

Places to Stay The closest camping ground is the *Camping du Mont St Michel* (☎ 02 33 60 09 33, fax 02 33 68 22 09), behind the Hotel-Motel Vert complex, before the start of the causeway. It costs 22FF per adult and 35FF for the site (open mid-February to mid-November).

A hostel, *Centre Duguesclin* (☎ 02 33 60 18 65, fax 02 33 60 25 81, 21 rue Général Patton), is in Pontorson, on the way into town at 34.3km. It charges 41FF per night and 19FF for breakfast (open from June through September).

Hotel options for cyclists are limited on the Mont – only two have room for bikes. It can also be a struggle to get a bike through the crowds. The first option on Grande Rue is *Les Terrasses Poulard* (☎ 02 33 60 14 09, fax 02 33 60 37 31), a charming hotel with rooms from 350FF to 900FF, all with shower and toilet. Further up Grande Rue, small *Hôtel le St-Michel* (☎/fax 02 33 60 14 37) has rooms with shower from 200FF to 350FF.

On the mainland, at the start of the causeway, hotels and restaurants cluster. The *Hotel-Motel Vert* (☎ 02 33 60 09 33, fax 02 33 68 22 09) has double bungalows, with shower and toilet, next to the camping ground for between 200FF and 240FF (bikes can be taken inside). Double hotel rooms cost between 250FF and 310FF, but bikes must be kept outside.

In Pontorson, *Hôtel La Tour Brette* (☎ 02 33 60 10 69, fax 02 33 48 59 66, 8 rue Couesnon) is good value. Rooms with shower and toilet cost 220FF in summer (closed Wednesday from mid-September to June).

Places to Eat The *supermarket* nearest the Mont is on the D976 in front of the Hotel-Motel Vert (closed mid-November to mid-February). In Pontorson an *8 à Huit* supermarket is at 3 rue Couesnon.

Huge, fluffy omelettes are the specialty on the Mont, as is seafood (particularly local mussels and oysters) and *pré salé lamb* (lamb raised on the salt marshes). Several *restaurants* line Grande Rue:

Day 3: Combourg to Mont St Michel

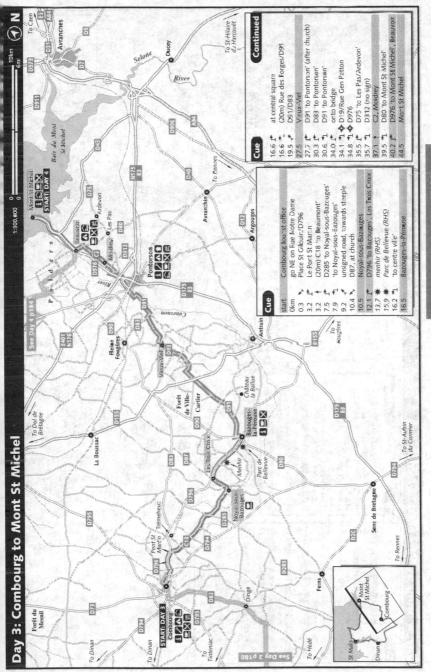

Cue		
start		Combourg tourist office
0km	↗	go NE on Rue Notre Dame
0.3	↰	Place St Gilduin·D796
3.2	↰	Le Pont St Martin
3.2	↱	(20m) C18 'to Beaumont'
7.5	↱	D285 'to Noyal-sous-Bazouges'
7.9	↰	'to Noyal-sous-Bazouges'
9.2	↱	unsigned road, towards steeple
10.4	↰	D87, at church
10.5		Noyal-sous-Bazouges
12.1	↱	D796 'to Bazouges'·Les Trois Croix
13.7	✳	menhir (RHS)
15.9	✳✳	Parc de Bellevue (RHS)
16.2	↰	'to centre ville'
16.5		Bazouges-la-Pérouse

Cue		Continued
16.6	↰	at central square
16.6	↱	(20m) Rue des Forges/D91
19.5	↱	D91/D83
27.5		Vieux-Viel
27.7	↰	D91 'to Pontorson' (after church)
30.3	↰	D83 'to Pontorson'
30.6	↱	D91 'to Pontorson'
34.0		or to bridge
34.1	◆◆	D19/Rue Gen Patton
34.8	◆◆	D976
35.5	↱	D75 'Les Pas/Ardevon'
35.7	↰	D312 (no sign)
37.1	↱	C2, Moidrey
39.5	↱	D80 'to Mont St Michel'
40.2	↰	D976 'to Mont St Michel · Beauvoir
44.5		Mont St Michel

NORMANDY & BRITTANY

Day 4: Mont St Michel to St Malo

Cue		
start		Mont St Michel
0km		go S on D976
4.3	↰	to 'Les Polders', Beauvoir
4.5	↱	after crossing bridge
6.4	↰	farm road 'to Teisserenc & Bort'
8.3	↰	unsigned farm road
9.2	↱	at board with Quatre Salines map
10.8	↰	unsigned farm road
11.8		Quatre Salines
12.2	↰	D797
17.4	↱	D797 'to Cherrueix', St Broladre
23.1	✸	windmills (RHS)
27.2	✸	Le Vivier-sur-Mer
33.3	✸	St-Benoît des Ondes
37.0	↰	tiny road 'to La Coudre'
37.6	↱	D76, La Coudre
39.0	↰	C15 to Cancale-Le Port'
39.8	✸	Oyster Museum
41.1	✸	Cancale
41.3	◈	Rue du Port 'to centre ville'
	▲	500m steep climb

Cue		Continued
41.7		main tourist office (LHS)
41.8		Place de la République
41.9		'toutes directions' (E of square)
42.3		Rue de Duguesclin
43.0		D201
46.0	↱	D201 'to St Malo par la Côte'
	●↻	Pointe du Grouin 1km ↻
51.0	✸	Fort du Guesclin
58.5	↰	Place Canada, Rothéneuf
58.5	↰	Rochers Sculptés 1km ↻
58.5	↱	(20m) D201/Ave Kennedy
61.4	↱	Blvd Chateaubriand/Chaus Sillon
64.5		Porte St Vincent, St Malo

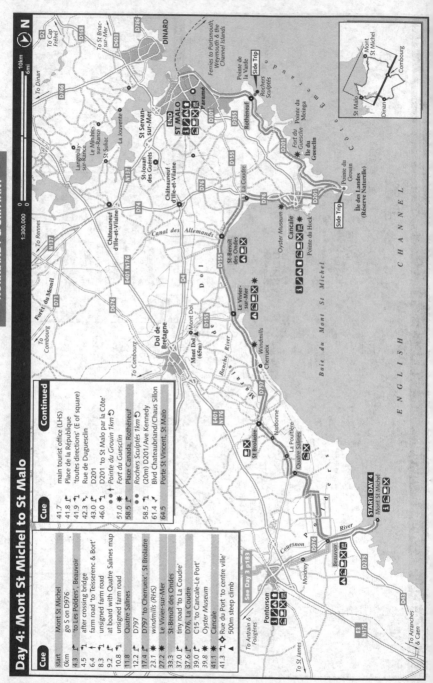

menus start at around 80FF. Quality and price improves as you walk up the street. An excellent choice is the **Restaurant Le St-Michel**, with the same owners as the hotel; it has *menus* from 88FF to 134FF.

Pontorson has several restaurants along rue Couesnon. The **Hôtel La Tour Brette** restaurant has *menus* from 59FF to 140FF.

Day 4: Mont St Michel to St Malo

3½–6½ hours, 64.5km
The route along the Bay of Mont St Michel is flat until just before Cancale. Then the spectacular Côte Émeraude begins and the road to St Malo is undulating. The only steep climb is a short one through Cancale. The riding is easy, but if you want to linger on the beaches (watch the tides) or explore the Côte Émeraude, Cancale makes a great overnight stop.

After leaving Beauvoir, cross the Couesnon River. The route winds through the **polders**, a flat area of reclaimed land, the sandy soil now covered with farms of onions, garlic, carrots and potatoes. Plenty of farms sell vegetables, especially *ail* (garlic). None of the farm roads are signed until the tiny Quatre Salines (11.8km).

The ride turns a little inland at this point, but heads to the coast after St Broladre. The bases of long-forgotten **windmills** indicate the past use of the area's blustery coastal winds. Turn around occasionally to see Mont St Michel in the background. Ahead the views extend to Pointe du Grouin.

The coast is lined with **mussel farms**, and roadside stalls sell mussels, as well as oysters from Cancale. At Le Vivier-sur-Mer (27.2km), contact Maison de la Baie (☎ 02 99 48 84 38, fax 02 99 48 80 93) for interesting, four-hour bay **walking tours**.

At St-Benoît des Ondes, the road begins to climb. Soon after the chateau (now a hotel) perched on the cliff, look for the tiny coastal road to La Coudre to the right (37km). The first **viewpoint** affords a fabulous panorama over the entire bay and one of the last views of Mont St Michel.

Descend into Cancale, looking down on the bay and the Port de la Houle. Cancale is world-famous for its oysters and from here at low tide you can see the **oyster beds**. On the right is **La Ferme Marine** (☎ 02 99 89 69 99), an oyster museum (only guided tour in English is at 2 pm in summer).

If you're an oyster lover, Cancale is the place to be! Its port area is lined with **restaurants** offering oysters brought in from only a few hundred metres away. The tourist office maintains a small annexe at the port in summer, but its main office (☎ 02 99 89 63 72, fax 02 99 89 75 08) is in 'upper' Cancale at 44 rue de Port. There are plenty of **museums**, **attractions** and **walks** around Cancale, and no lack of accommodation: **camping grounds**, a great **hostel** and **hotels**.

In 'upper' Cancale, navigate the one-way streets by turning right at place de la République. Go around the square behind the church, then follow the road around to rue de Duguesclin. Turn right onto the D201. After Cancale, continue straight (when the route heads left) to reach the rocky headland of **Pointe du Grouin**, offering an amazing panorama of the Bay of Mont St Michel, the Normandy coast, Cap Fréhel and, in the distance, the Iles of Chausey. **Île des Landes**, the island just off the coast, is a bird sanctuary, home to cormorants, gulls and oystercatchers.

The coastal route to St Malo takes in secluded bays, beaches and superb coastal scenery. Stop at Anse du Guesclin, a bay with a sandy beach and the island fortress, **Fort du Guesclin** (51km). The many small roads off the D201 reach **beaches** and **sand dunes**, such as Les Dunes du Port and Les Dunes des Chevrets.

From Rothéneuf, an interesting if not bizarre side trip is the **Rochers Sculptés** (☎ 02 99 56 97 64): rock sculptures carved over 25 years from 1870 by Abbé Fouré, a hermit. To get there follow the signs from place du Canada.

Entering St Malo, ride along the **Grande Plage** to reach Porte St Vincent.

Southern Brittany Contrasts

Duration	6 days
Distance	254.4km
Difficulty	easy-moderate
Start/End	Vannes

This ride through the magical department of Morbihan begins in the lively medieval town of Vannes, then heads for the hills through rolling countryside that has seen the Tour de France pass through more than once. From Josselin, cycle the former towpath along the Canal Nantes à Brest, reserved today for cyclists and walkers. The water theme continues as the ride follows the Blavet River and turns south to Carnac and its vicinity, strewn with megalithic sites dating back to the Neolithic period. Gentle riding along the Golfe du Morbihan, lined with quaint villages and dotted with tiny islands, concludes the ride in Vannes.

PLANNING
When to Ride
Weatherwise this area can be comfortably cycled from April until October, but the operational times of facilities on the coast, a mecca for summer holiday-makers, are centred around the heaviest tourist times.

Outside July and August, several ferries cut services or do not operate, and attractions reduce their hours or close. Camping grounds are typically open from May or June through mid-September. Hotels are open most of the year, offering better deals outside July and August. Steer clear of August, when the crowds are heaviest; optimum months are June, July and September.

Maps & Books
The Michelin map No 63 *Vannes, La Baule, Angers* (1:200,000) is ideal.

GETTING TO/FROM THE RIDE
Train services via Rennes connect this ride with the Northern Brittany Majesty ride, which starts in St Malo.

Vannes
Train The train station is about 1km north of the old city, at place de la Gare.

All trains to/from Paris' Gare Montparnasse are TGVs (324FF, 3½ hours, six a day). Only one train, on Friday afternoon, will take unbagged bikes from Paris (289FF, 4½ hours). The same service from Vannes is on Sunday afternoon.

Reach Rennes (96FF, 1½ hours, 10 to 12 a day, two take bikes) via Redon, then connect to St Malo.

THE RIDE
Vannes
The history of Vannes (Gwened) dates to pre-Roman times, when it was the capital of the Veneti, a Gallic tribe of intrepid sailors who were eventually conquered by Julius Caesar in the 1st century BC. In the 9th century, the Breton hero Nominoë united Brittany and Vannes became its capital. The union of Brittany with France was signed here in 1532.

Today the protected port town is the gateway to the Golfe du Morbihan. The old town, enclosed by ramparts, has a lively well-preserved medieval quarter, made all the more charming by its mostly pedestrianised streets.

Information The tourist office (☎ 02 97 47 24 34, fax 02 97 47 29 49, 🖳 www .vannes-bretagne-sud.com), 1 rue Thiers, is in a lovely 17th-century house down by the port (closed Sunday outside June to September). *Canton d'Elven: Itineraires en VTT* (2FF), a map of four bike routes around the area of Elven, north of Vannes, is available here.

The Banque de France, at 55 ave Victor Hugo, is open weekday mornings. There are also banks at place de la République, and along rue Thiers.

Cycles P LeMellec (☎ 02 97 63 00 24, fax 02 97 63 80 05), La Madeleine (51te rue Jean Gougaud), hires VTCs and VTT daily/weekly for 70/350FF. Closer to the station, on blvd de la Paix, are two more bike shops: MBK (☎ 02 97 47 27 13) at No 47 and, across the road at No 50, Le Penvei (☎ 02 97 47 29 21).

The cybercafe and bar 7 Seven (☎ 02 97 54 04 72, 🖂 seven@wanadoo.fr) is at 1 place du Général de Gaulle.

Things to See & Do To appreciate the ambience of Vannes, wander the streets and stroll along sections of the **ramparts**, which have a great view of the manicured gardens set in the former moat. The tourist office sells a pamphlet in English, *Vannes: Town of Art & History* (2FF), that deals with the major sights of the old city.

The huge **Cathédrale St Pierre**, originally built in the 13th century, has been remodelled several times over the centuries. Poke around some of the quaint streets and squares, such as **rue St Guenhaël, rue des Halles, place des Lices** (site of medieval tournaments) and **rue St Vincent**, which leads to **place Gambetta** down at the port

Opposite the Cathédrale St Pierre is La Cohue, a market and law court in the 13th century. Today it houses the **Musée de la Cohue** (☎ 02 97 47 35 86), which displays local Morbihan exhibits, and the **Musée des Beaux-Arts**. The **Musée d'Archéologie** (☎ 02 97 42 59 80), in the 15th-century Château Gaillard at 2 rue Noë, has artefacts from the megalithic sites of Carnac and Locmariaquer.

For music lovers, Vannes hosts a four-day **Festival de Jazz** in late July/early August. **Free concerts** are also held each Wednesday evening in July and August, sometimes featuring traditional Breton music.

Places to Stay The *Camping de Conleau* (☎ 02 97 63 13 88, fax 02 97 40 38 82, ave du Maréchal Juin) is about 3km south of the tourist office, on the gulf. It charges 24FF per adult and 43FF for a tent site (open from April through September).

There's an *Auberge de Jeunesse* (☎ 02 97 66 94 25, fax 02 97 66 94 15, route de Moustérian) in Séné, about 4km south-east of place Gambetta, on the east side of the harbour. It is open all year and charges 70FF with breakfast.

Convenient to the train station, the comfortable *Le Richemont* (☎ 02 97 47 12 95, fax 02 97 54 92 79, 26 place de la Gare) has rooms without/with shower for 160/220FF. Between the station and the port is the plain three-star *Hôtel Manche Océan* (☎ 02 97 47 26 46, fax 02 97 47 30 86, 31 rue du Colonel Maury). Rooms with shower and toilet cost from 295FF.

Down by the harbour, the *Hôtel Le Marina* (☎ 02 97 47 22 81, fax 02 97 47 00 34, 4 place Gambetta) has singles/doubles for 170/190FF (more with shower and toilet).

Places to Eat The huge *market* is on Wednesday and Saturday morning at place du Poids Public. The supermarkets are *Monoprix* (1 place Joseph Le Brix) and *Stoc* (19 rue du Méné). *La Hûche á Pains* (23 place des Lices) has delicious Breton pastries such as *far Breton* and *kouign amman*. Several *food shops* can be found on rue St Vincent.

Place Gambetta is surrounded by *bars* and *cafes*. Adjacent is the brasserie *Le Sinagot* (☎ 02 97 54 19 17, Porte St Vincent), with tasty-looking *menus* from 69FF

to 135FF. Several *restaurants* line rue des Halles. One of note is the *Breizh Caffé* (☎ 02 97 54 37 41, 13 rue des Halles), which serves Breton fare; the 89FF *menu tradition* has a selection of specialties. For some of the best crepes in Brittany, *La Cave St-Gwenael* (☎ 02 97 47 47 94, 23 rue St Guenhaël), next to the Cathédrale, has a *menu* for 50FF, plus a huge selection of galettes and crepes; try their Breton cider.

Day 1: Vannes to Josselin
2½–5 hours, 49.8km

Morbihan is well known for its coast, but Day 1 showcases the department's variety, quickly leaving the coast behind for quiet forest and pretty rural landscape. The route has a series of moderate climbs (only one hefty climb before Plumelec) and exhilarating descents.

The first 3km is on the busy D126, with a bikepath for part of the way. For picnic supplies, the huge *Intermarché* supermarket is on the right in St Avé (Senteve).

The route turns left (11.2km) without entering St Nolff; continuing straight down the hill allows you to see this pretty town. The main route passes through St Amand (15.1km) with its **18th-century church**.

A glorious 4km descent through lovely forest ends in tiny Cadoudal (28km), then the climb to Plumelec passes a viewpoint giving a **panorama** of the valley. You are riding Tour de France territory; the Tour passed through **Plumelec** (30.8km) in 1997 and 1998.

If you are lucky enough to be in Plumelec in the spring or summer, the town will be adorned with flowers. Watch carefully for the turn to Billio off rue de Folguet (the sign is tiny); it's a gorgeous descent on a small back road.

In the sleepy village of Guéhenno, the church cemetery has a **calvaire** (calvary) dating from 1550. This intricate piece was damaged during the Revolution and somewhat poorly restored in the 19th century. Behind the calvaire is a small ossuary.

The D123 provides 7km of idyllic country cycling through forest and farms where you're unlikely to meet more than a couple of cars. It passes the **Manoir de la May**, a small, run-down 16th-century chateau, which may finally be undergoing a slated six-million-franc restoration.

NORMANDY & BRITTANY

NORMANDY & BRITTANY

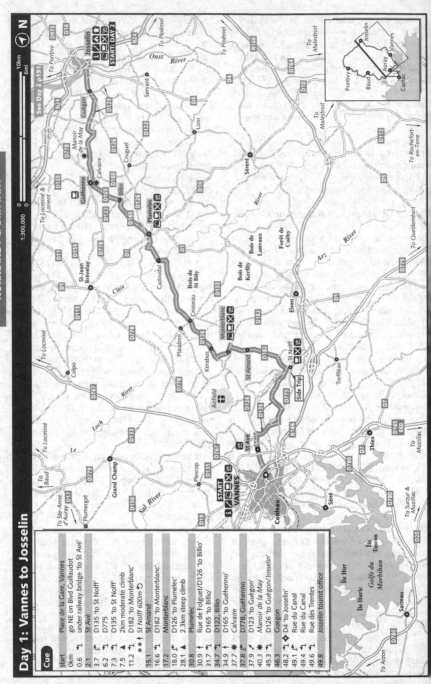

Day 1: Vannes to Josselin

Cue		
start		Place de la Gare, Vannes
0km	↱	go NE on Blvd Guillaudot
0.6	↰	under railway bridge 'to St Avé'
2.1		St Avé
3.7	↱	D135 'to St Nolff'
6.2	↱	D775
7.3	↰	D135 'to St Nolff'
7.5	▲	2km moderate climb
11.2	↰	D182 'to Monterblanc'
	●●↑	St Nolff 600m ↻
15.1		St Amand
16.6	↱	D182 'to Monterblanc'
17.2		Monterblanc
18.0	↰	D126 'to Plumelec'
28.1	▲	2.3km steep climb
30.8		Plumelec
30.9	↱	Rue de Folguet/D126 'to Billio'
31.7	↱	D165 'to Billio'
34.7		D122, Billio
34.9	✳	D165 'to Guéhenno'
37.7	✳	Calvaire
37.8	↱	D778, Guéhenno
37.9	↱	D123 'to Guégon'
40.3	✳	Manoir de la May
45.3	↱	D126 'to Guégon/Josselin'
46.3		Guégon
48.2	◇	D4 'to Josselin'
49.1	↱	Rue du Canal
49.4	↰	Rue du Canal
49.6	↱	Rue des Trentes
49.8		Josselin tourist office

After Guègon, it's downhill into Josselin with a fabulous view of the **chateau**. Cross the Oust River and ride alongside the chateau following the road around to the left.

Josselin

Josselin is the epitome of the word picturesque. Nestled in the Oust Valley, the town hides behind its turreted, fairy-tale chateau rising from beside the river. Centered on place Notre Dame and the basilica, Josselin is a mass of steep cobbled streets filled with 16th-century half-timbered houses.

Information The tourist office (☎ 02 97 22 36 43, fax 02 97 22 20 44, e o.t.josselin @wanadoo.fr) is tucked away on place de la Congrégation. From November to March it's closed Saturday afternoon, all day Sunday and Monday morning.

A Banque de Bretagne is at 8 rue Olivier de Clisson. A few doors along, a Caisse d'Épargne is at No 14.

Cycles Yves Roblin (☎ 02 97 22 28 02), at place de la Duchesse Anne, is the only bike shop in town. VTTs can be hired daily/weekly for 110/390FF from Garage Renault de Texier (☎ 02 97 22 22 55, fax 02 97 22 26 52) at 2 place St Nicolas. Photocopies of local VTT routes are free with hire.

Things to See & Do The Château de Josselin (☎ 02 97 22 36 45) is a two-for-one deal. From the river you see a simple, sheer facade and four of the original 12th-century towers, while the inward facade is busy flamboyant Gothic style. The chateau was owned by Olivier de Clisson, and for centuries the Rohan family, a great power in this area of Brittany.

The castle's stables house **Le Musée de Poupées** (☎ 02 97 22 36 45), displaying the Rohan collection of more than 500 dolls from around the world. The dolls date back to the 17th century.

The **Basilique Notre Dame de Roncier**, parts of which are from the 13th century, is on place Notre Dame. Fabulous gargoyles and other creatures adorn the exterior. Inside is the mausoleum of Olivier de Clisson and his wife Marguerite de Rohan.

The **pardon** de Notre Dame du Roncier (see the boxed text on the right) is held on 8 September.

(see the boxed text on the right)

Pardon en Breton

To most, the word *pardon* in French means 'excuse me'. In Brittany, the word *pardon* refers to a religious tradition; a church ceremony and a procession (or pilgrimage) paying homage to the local saint on their saint's day. The procession offers a chance to see traditional Breton costumes. Most churches and communities have a pardon.

One of the largest is at Ste-Anne d'Auray on 26 July. Pardons are listed in the text for the towns on the Southern Brittany Contrasts route.

Places to Stay The *Camping Bas de la Lande* (☎ 02 97 22 22 20, fax 02 97 73 93 85) is about 1.5km west of Josselin on the Canal Nantes à Brest. It costs 20FF per person and 18FF for a tent site in July and August, a little less during the other months (open May to September).

There is no hostel in Josselin, but there is a *gîte d'étape (lodging, usually in a remote area, ☎ 02 97 22 21 69, fax 02 97 75 69 12, Écluse de Josselin)* on the canal. It charges 50FF per person and 10FF for showers (open year-round).

On the square across from the basilica, the charming *Hôtel de France (☎ 02 97 22 23 06, fax 02 97 22 35 78, 6 place Notre Dame)* has rooms with shower/shower and toilet from 200/230FF (closed Sunday evening and Monday out of season). Superbly sited on the river with great views of the chateau, the *Hôtel du Château (☎ 02 97 22 20 11, fax 02 97 22 54 09, 1 rue du Générale de Gaulle)* charges 230/320FF for rooms with shower/shower and toilet (closed February).

Places to Eat Josselin's *market* is on Saturday from 8.30 am to 1 pm, stretching from place des Remparts along rue Olivier de Clisson and rue Georges Le Berd to place de la Résistance. A small grocery, *Alimentation au Verger,* is at 3 rue Beaumanoir. A sparsely stocked *Spar* supermarket is at 1 rue Georges LeBerd.

You don't have to walk far to find a *creperie* in Josselin; there are four scattered around the town, including one on place Notre Dame.

The *Restaurant La Duchesse Anne* (☎ 02 97 22 22 37, place de la Duchesse Anne) has *menus* from 60FF. The elegant *Hôtel de France* restaurant offers fine dining for reasonable prices: *menus* range from 81FF to 205FF. The *Hôtel du Château* restaurant has a chateau view and *menus* ranging from 85FF to 160FF.

Day 2: Josselin to Pontivy

2½–5 hours, 48.4km

If you enjoy quiet, car-free cycling, then today's your day. The quiet, tree-lined *halage* (towpath) along the Canal Nantes à Brest is 'your road' from start to finish, shared only with cyclists, walkers and maybe an equestrian. Only the sounds of birds and rushing water break the silence. Look for the muskrats and otters that live in the canal.

The route is flat, apart from an ever-so-gentle incline after Rohan, where the locks are at their tightest. Then it's smooth 'downhill' sailing into Pontivy. The towpath is made of hard packed dirt and gravel the entire way (and can become muddy after rain).

The route passes several **écluses**, each named and numbered and most with a **lock house**. In the old days each house was occupied by a lock keeper, who regulated the lock for the constant boat traffic. The locks are still maintained, but today's keepers look after three or four locks, travelling between each one by bicycle or moped, which means the towpaths are maintained. Lace curtains and well-tended gardens show which houses are inhabited.

Cross the stone bridge over the canal (7.4km) at Bocneuf-la-Rivière and continue on the other side of the canal until the two bridges at 15km. Cross back to reach Écluse 45: Griffet (15.3km).

At Écluse 50: Timadeuc (21.5km), a short side trip up the hill leads to the **Abbaye de Timadeuc**, a Trappist monastery founded in 1841, in a forest setting. Unfortunately the abbey can't be visited, but there is an audio-visual presentation and a shop selling cheese, biscuits and fruit jellies made at the monastery.

The town of Rohan (24.8km) was the birthplace of the Rohan family, but it hardly has the grandeur of Josselin or Pontivy, where the famous family built their chateaux.

At Écluse 55: Coëtprat, cross again to a favourite fishing spot for trout, pike and perch. The red-and-white markings are for walkers on the GR37.

Within 1km the locks (Écluse 57 to 78), looking like a **staircase**, come thick and fast, and a slight incline is discernible. After 4km, the path flattens as it travels through a gorgeous wooded area. From Écluse 87: Le Couëdic, cross the canal for the last time and it's a breeze into Pontivy. Leave the canal 10m after Écluse 107: Le Ponteau. Cross the road and head to the tourist office.

Pontivy

Pontivy was founded in the 7th century by the monk Ivy, who built a *pont* (bridge) over the Blavet River. From the 12th century, the town was associated with the Rohan family, who built the chateaux in Pontivy and Josselin.

Pontivy was reshaped under Napoleon. He initiated construction of the Canal Nantes á Brest and realised the strategic position of the town, halfway between the ports of Nantes and Brest. Developed into a

Canal Nantes à Brest

Originally, the idea to build the Canal Nantes à Brest came at a time when British warships were dominating Brittany's coast. As a military strategy, Napoleon Bonaparte decided to build a safe inland waterway linking the important seaports of Nantes and Brest, thus avoiding the sea. The Blavet River was also canalised, allowing a connection with Lorient.

Construction took several years and the canal was opened for navigation in 1836, well after Napoleon's death. It was no longer of military interest, but was successfully used to transport coal and cargo.

The different elevations along the canal required the building of locks (*écluses*). The locks, using a system of chambers, gates and valves, raise and lower the water level. The greatest concentration of locks can be found between Josselin and Pontivy. In the 18km section before Pontivy, the 51 locks resemble a staircase.

Nowadays the canal is not used for cargo and some sections are no longer navigable. For the most part the canal is used by pleasure craft and kayaks and the old towpaths are enjoyed by cyclists and pedestrians.

NORMANDY & BRITTANY

Day 2: Josselin to Pontivy

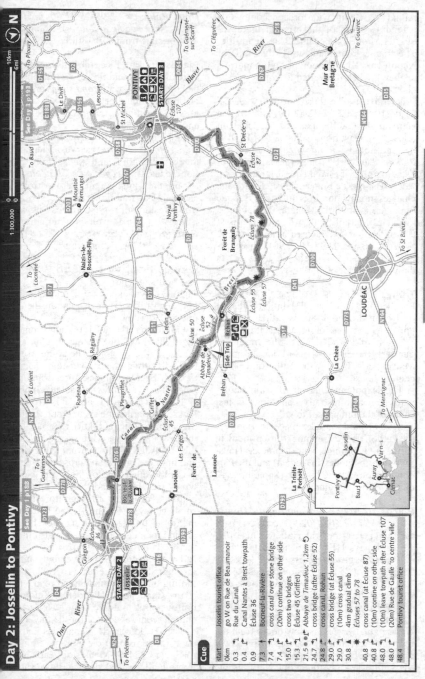

Cue

start	Josselin tourist office
0km	go W on Rue de Beaumanoir
0.3	Rue du Canal
0.4	Canal Nantes à Brest towpath
0.9	Écluse 36
7.3	Bocneuf-la-Rivière
7.4	cross canal over stone bridge
7.4	(20m) continue on other side
15.0	cross two bridges
15.3	Écluse 45 (Griffet)
21.5	Abbaye de Timadeuc 1.2km ⟳
24.7	cross bridge (after Écluse 52)
24.8	cross canal, Rohan
29.0	cross bridge (at Écluse 55)
29.0	(10m) cross canal
30.8	4km gradual climb
	Écluses 57 to 78
40.8	cross canal (at Écluse 87)
40.8	(10m) contine on other side
48.0	(10m) leave towpath after Écluse 107
48.0	(20m) Rue de Gaulle 'to centre ville'
48.4	Pontivy tourist office

military base, with wide, orderly boulevards extending south of the original medieval quarter, Pontivy became Napoléonville. The name remained until the fall of Napoléon III (Napoléon Bonaparte's nephew), when it reverted to Pontivy.

Information The tourist office (☎ 02 97 25 04 10, fax 02 97 27 87 09) is at 61 rue Général de Gaulle, next to the chateau (closed Sunday from October to May). It has the booklet *Randonnée au Pays des Rohan*, detailing 37 routes for walkers, cyclists (mainly VTT) and equestrians.

The Banque de France, 83 rue Nationale, changes money mornings only. The Banque Populaire is at 75 rue Général de Gaulle.

Cycles Martail (☎ 02 97 25 05 02) is at 97 rue Nationale. Cycles Lamouric (☎ 02 97 25 03 46, fax 02 97 25 39 90) is less central at 1 rue Clémentel, but hires VTTs daily/weekly for 60/350FF.

Things to See & Do The **Château de Pontivy** (☎ 02 97 25 12 93), built by Jean II de Rohan around 1480, is rather squatty, unlike its slender sibling at Josselin.

South of the chateau is the **medieval quarter**. Rue du Fil, rue du Pont and place Martray are lined with 16th- and 17th-century houses.

The **Napoléon Quarter** of wide boulevards and administrative buildings is just south of the old part of town.

Several **pardons** take place in Pontivy: the Pardon de Ste Tréphine (third Sunday in July), the Pardon de Notre Dame de Houssaye (fourth Sunday in August) and the Pardon de Notre Dame de Joie (September 12 or the following Sunday).

Places to Stay The *Camping du Douric* (☎ 02 97 27 92 20 or 02 97 25 09 51) is to the right across the bridge after Écluse 107. An adult pays 11FF and a site costs 11FF.

The *Auberge de Jeunesse* (☎ 02 97 25 58 27, fax 02 97 25 76 48) is on Île des Récollets, an island in the Blavet River. Beds cost 51FF a night (68FF with breakfast).

The pleasant *Hôtel du Porhoet* (☎ 02 97 25 34 88, fax 02 97 25 57 17, 41 rue Général de Gaulle) is a few doors from the tourist office. Singles/doubles with shower are 210/240FF. Further south, 1.5km from the centre across from Pont Neuf, is the

Hôtel Robic (☎ 02 97 25 11 80, fax 02 97 25 74 10, 2 rue Jean-Jaurès). Rooms with shower start from 130/180FF.

Places to Eat Place du Martray hosts a vegetable, fruit and flower **market** on Monday morning. Several *food shops* are on rue Nationale, including a **Comod** supermarket at No 31 and an **Intermarché** supermarket and *bakery* at No 68.

Le Vietnamien (☎ 02 97 27 92 10, 14 rue Général de Gaulle) serves Vietnamese meals from 40FF and *menus* from 54FF. For crepes, try **Crêperie Le Château**, at No 54 on the same street, across from the chateau. For traditional cuisine, the *Hôtel Robic* restaurant is good value, with *menu* from 59FF. In the old quarter, the cosy *Restaurant Martray* (☎ 02 97 25 68 64, 3 rue du Pont) has *menus* from 78FF.

Day 3: Pontivy to Baud
2–4 hours, 40.1km

The next two stages are neither strenuous nor long. It is possible to combine them into one 86.2km day.

Follow the Blavet River south from Pontivy. This lush, picturesque Breton valley offers idyllic cycling. The route uses the towpath along the Blavet and meanders through Breton villages, forests and farmlands. There are a few moderate climbs.

The Blavet is not a canal: it is a river with locks. Soon after the second one, Écluse 3 Signanou St Michel (4km), the route leaves the towpath. There is a dirt path either side of the bridge (4.2km); walk your bike up and onto the bridge and cross the Blavet.

On the other side of the river, the route winds past farms and through tiny Breton hamlets, dropping through forest into small valley at 8.1km. At the bottom is **memorial bridge** honouring French underground members and parachutists killed by the Nazis on 18 June 1944.

The route crosses the river and continues through Talvern-Nénez (15.1km) before turning onto a tiny undulating road, ending at the **Chapelle St Nicodème**. Sitting in hollow, this rather large 16th-century church seems oversized for the tiny hamlet.

The D1 goes to St-Nicolas des Eaux, but the route turns onto the more pleasant farm road, the C124. **St-Nicolas des Eaux** is a delightful village nestled in the Blavet valley. It

Day 3: Pontivy to Baud

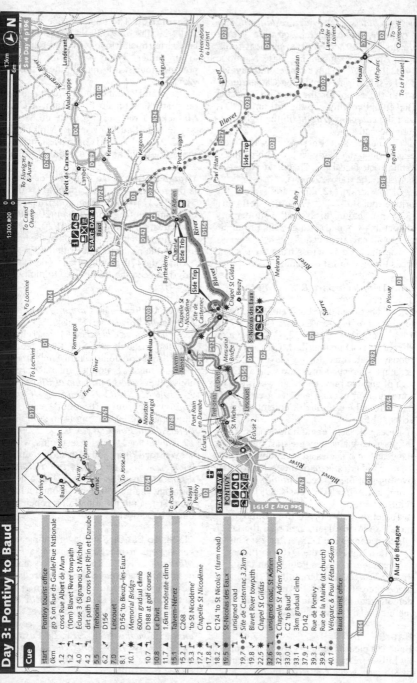

Cue		
start		Pontivy tourist office
0km	↑	go S on Rue de Gaulle/Rue Nationale
1.2	←	cross Rue Albert de Mun
1.2	←	(10m) Blavet River towpath
4.0	←	Écluse 3 (Signanou St Michel)
4.2	←	dirt path to cross Pont Rhin et Danube
5.5		Trehonin
6.2	↗	D156
7.0		Lescouet
8.1	↖	D156 'to Bieuzy-les-Eaux'
10.1	✳	Memorial Bridge
10.7	◀	600m gradual climb
10.8	←	D188 at golf course
11.7	◀	1.6km moderate climb
15.1		Talvern-Nénez
15.2	↙	C268
15.3	↙	'to St Nicodeme'
17.2	✳	Chapelle St Nicodeme
17.8	↙	D1
18.2	←	C124 'to St Nicolas' (farm road)
19.5	✳	St-Nicolas des Eaux
19.7	●↱	Site de Castennac 3.2km ↺
19.8	↗	Blavet River towpath
22.5	←	Chapel St Gildas
32.6	↙	unsigned road, St Adrien
32.8	●●↱	Chapelle St Adrien 700m ↺
33.0	↱	C2 'to Baud'
33.1	◀	3km gradual climb
37.9	←	D142
39.3	↙	Rue de Pontivy
39.8	↱	Rue de la Marie (at church)
40.1	●●	Véloparc & Poul Fétan 56km ↺
		Baud tourist office

has two *hotels*, each with a *restaurant*, and a *creperie*, but no general food store. Blavet Loisirs (☎ 02 97 51 92 93) runs **boat tours** from April to October. The Base Nautique (☎ 02 97 51 87 71) hires **canoes and kayaks**.

The side trip to the **Site de Castennec** is worth the effort for the views. Cross the Blavet and continue up the hill on the D1, past the *camping ground* on the right. Return the same way.

The next 12km are superb as the river cuts through the shady valley with its interesting rock faces; the **Chapel St Gildas** is built into the rock (22.5km).

At St Adrien (32.6km), don't cross the bridge but turn left. Another left turn (32.8km) detours to a small 15th-century **chapel** in a wooded setting, with a fountain and small calvaire outside.

The small C2 is across from the bar and leads through forest to Baud.

Side Trip: Véloparc & Poul Fétan
3–5 hours, 56km

Located between the Scorff and Blavet Valleys, the 50-hectare **Véloparc** (☎ 02 97 33 15 15, fax 02 97 33 05 22, ⌨ www.veloparc.com), at Domaine de Ménéhouarne in Plouay, is devoted to the bicycle. On the grounds is a **bicycle museum** with a collection of antique bicycles and a wealth of information on cycling and its greats (open daily from June through September; entry costs 30FF).

Rides, classes, excursions and cycling events are organised by the staff throughout the year and bicycles are available for hire. To take full advantage of the Véloparc, stay overnight at the 37-bed *Rando'plume gîte*. Dorm accommodation costs 80FF a night (high season).

To get to the Véloparc from Baud, cycle the D3 to Pont Augan, then take the D327, which becomes the D23. After 2km on the D23, turn right onto the D102 to Plouay.

The side trip passes **Poul Fétan** (☎ 02 97 39 72 82), a recreated traditional Breton village where townsfolk in period costume demonstrate 19th-century trades and farming methods. Entry costs 25FF.

Baud

Baud is a pleasant country town surrounded by hills, forests and farmlands. The church of St Pierre is the centre of town.

Information The tourist office (☎ 02 97 51 02 29, fax 02 97 39 07 22) is on rue de la Mairie (open Monday to Saturday, May to September). The Hôtel de Ville next door provides tourist information the rest of the year.

Banks in Baud include a Crédit Agricole on place Champ de Foires and a Crédit Mutuel de Bretagne at 3 place du Marché.

The bike shop, Espace Motoculture (☎ 02 97 39 10 56), is on place Champ de Foires, not too far from the tourist office.

Things to See & Do Baud's pride and joy is the recently opened **Cartopole** (☎ 02 97 51 15 14, ⌨ www.cartopole.org), a postcard museum housing more than 20,000 old postcards, 90% from before 1920. The museum gives an interesting look at the history of both the postcard and Brittany.

Since the 17th century, Baud's best known lady has been the **Vénus de Quinipily** (see Day 4).

Places to Stay The *Camping Municipal L'Orée du Bois* (☎ 02 97 51 02 29, fax 02 97 39 07 22, ave Corbel de Squirio) charges 8FF for an adult and 8FF for a tent site (open from mid-June to mid-September).

Baud has two hotels. In a lovely old house, the *Auberge du Cheval Blanc* (☎ 02 97 51 00 85, fax 02 97 51 15 26, 16 rue de Pontivy) has only 10 rooms, each with shower and toilet, costing from 200FF. The *Relais de la Forêt* (☎/fax 02 97 51 02 77, 19 rue de la Mairie) has rooms without shower for 170FF, and with shower and toilet for 250FF. The Robics run a *chambre d'hôte* (☎/fax 02 97 51 08 02) on a nearby farm and charge 240FF per room, including breakfast. Call for directions (open April through October).

Places to Eat On Saturday morning a *market* is held at place du Marché; a *Proxi Market* is at No 6. Rue de Pontivy and rue de la Mairie have *bakeries* and *charcuteries*.

You can't miss the bright green exterior of the creperie *Au Citron Vert* (☎ 02 97 51 03 62, 41 rue St Yves), which serves crepes from 18FF. Both the hotels have *restaurants* with *menus* from 79FF. *La Pastorelle* (☎ 02 97 39 07 84, 6bis rue de Pontivy) serves pizza and pasta from 40FF and meat dishes from 70FF.

Day 4: Baud to Carnac
2–4 hours, 46.1km

Head back to the coast, leaving the hills of 'inland' Morbihan behind. There is only one climb at the start of the day and then it's downhill for most of the way to Carnac, flattening out as the route nears the coast.

The first stop of the day is the **Vénus de Quinipily**. This 2.2m-high statue of the goddess is now displayed in the lush gardens of the chateau of Quinipily (destroyed during the Revolution). It seems the Vénus dates back to Roman or Egyptian times and has been worshipped for centuries. Twice thrown into the Blavet River by clergy concerned about pagan worshippers, the Vénus was finally rescued and brought here in the late 17th century. The park is open daily; entry costs 10FF.

Be very careful that you make the correct turn at 3.2km; the road is unsigned – don't be tempted to turn at the small road 250m earlier. Take the correct road and in 200m, cross railway tracks. Continue up the hill to Guérégarh (6.3km; not on Michelin maps). Kerantallec, a cluster of three houses, is 800m off the route to the right.

From Lambal, the road has the gentlest of downhill gradients; coast all the way to Landévant (Landevan). At the four-way intersection (20.1km; at the hotel, **Relais des Voyageurs**), signs appear for three directions, except the turn to the left to Landaul!

On the left, just before entering Carnac, pass the megalithic site (see the boxed text on the right), part of the **Alignments of Kermario**. The route also passes the **Musée de Préhistoire** on the left.

Side Trip: Quiberon Peninsula & Belle Île
2–4 hours, 40km

It's a 40km round trip to Quiberon but the overall distance of the side trip depends on how much of Belle Île you want to see. Allow a full day to take the ferry and do a part of the island or consider staying overnight on Belle Île.

The town of Quiberon (Kiberen) lies at the end of the 15km-long peninsula south-west of Carnac. It is a popular seaside town surrounded by sandy beaches. On the windy, west side of the peninsula, the rocky Côte Sauvage (Wild Coast) has some spectacular seascapes, but is unsafe for swimming. From

The Megaliths of Carnac

Megalithic culture arose during the Neolithic period between 4500 and 2000 BC, created by people whose lives were based on agriculture and herding – a radical change from the hunting and gathering of the earlier Palaeolithic era.

The most enduring monuments left by this culture include: *menhirs*, stones between 1m and 20m high, weighing between two and 200 tonnes and planted upright in the ground (in Breton, *men* means stone and *hir* means long); *dolmens* (*dol* meaning table), stone burial chambers, standing on their own or accessed by a narrow passage, often engraved with symmetrical designs; and *tumuli*, earth mounds which covered the dolmens. The most spectacularly decorated dolmens and one of the largest tumuli are on the island of Gavrinis, in the Golfe du Morbihan.

The concentration of menhirs and dolmens around Carnac has made this region famous. The wealth of sites ranges from solitary menhirs to *alignements*, parallel lines of menhirs running for several kilometres and capped by a *cromlech*, a semicircle of stones. Their purpose has not been deciphered, though theories abound. Solitary rocks have been interpreted as everything from phallic symbols to signposts for burial grounds, while it has been suggested that alignments have astronomical and religious significance.

Quiberon it's possible to catch a ferry to the appropriately named Belle Île, Brittany's largest island (at about 20km long and 9km wide). The island is known for its natural rock formations.

To ride to Quiberon, take the D781 to Plouharnel, then turn left onto the D768, an incredibly busy road, but the only option. In summer and on weekends the traffic can be bumper-to-bumper, so the best time to ride is very early morning. About halfway down the peninsula, take the D186 to leave the main road and follow the coastal route along the Côte Sauvage and around the southern tip of the peninsula to Quiberon.

NORMANDY & BRITTANY

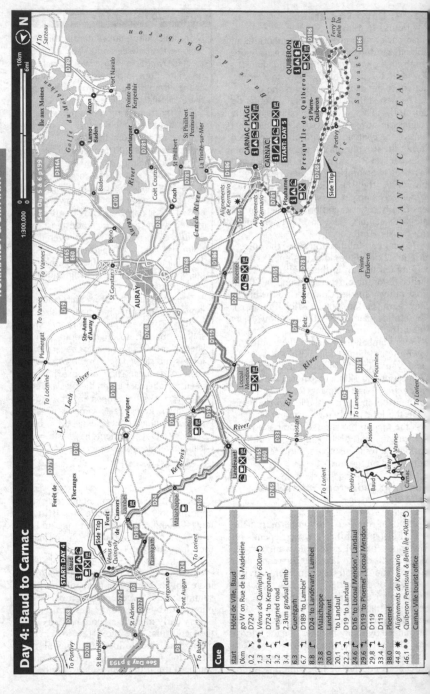

NORMANDY & BRITTANY

Day 4: Baud to Carnac

Cue		
start	Hôtel de Ville, Baud	
0km	go W on Rue de la Madeleine	
0.2	D724	
1.3	Vénus de Quinipily 600m ↻	
2.4	D724 to Kergonan'	
3.2	unsigned road	
3.4	2.3km gradual climb	
6.3	Guérégan	
6.7	D189 'to Lambel'	
8.8	D24 'to Landévant', Lambel	
13.8	Malachappe	
20.0	Landévant	
20.1	'to Landaul'	
22.3	D19 'to Landaul'	
24.6	D16 'to Locoal Mendon', Landaul	
29.6	D119 'to Ploemel', Locoal Mendon	
29.8	D119	
33.4	D119	
38.0	Ploemel	
44.8	Alignements de Kermario	
46.1	Quiberon Peninsula & Belle Île 40km ↻	
	Carnac Ville tourist office	

Quiberon's tourist office (☎ 02 97 50 07 4, fax 02 97 30 58 22) is at 14 rue de Verun. The town has *camping facilities*, a *ostel* and several *hotels*. Ferries to Belle e, operated by MN (☎ 02 97 50 06 90, ☐ www.mn-les-iles.com), run all year with p to six sailings a day, more in summer and n weekends. The trip takes 45 minutes. The eturn fare is 110FF, plus 50FF for a bicycle.

Belle Île is incredibly popular and teams ith tourists in the summer. Its compact ize and interesting terrain make it great for ycling. Its tourist office (☎ 02 97 31 81 93, ax 02 97 31 5617, ☐ www.belle-ile-en-mer com) is in Le Palais, the main village, on uai Bonnelle. The island has a plethora of *amping grounds* and *hotels*, a *hostel* and ome *chambres d'hôtes*. Le Palais has two ike shops.

Carnac

arnac (Garnag) has some of the world's reatest megalithic monuments. North of the wn is a feast of megalithic sites: thousands f menhirs, several dolmens and two tumuli.

The town is made of two parts. Carnac ille is an attractive old village and Carnac lage, along the sheltered bay of Quiberon, a modern seaside resort with a 2km-long andy beach (Grand Plage).

Carnac Ville and Carnac Plage are 1.5km part. They're linked by ave de la Poste and ve de l'Atlantique, which run south from arnac Ville to blvd de la Plage along the eachfront; all have bike lanes. Place de Église is Carnac Ville's centre. Busy ave des ruides is the Carnac Plage's main street.

Information Carnac has two very helpful nd efficient tourist offices. The ride finhes at the annexe (☎ 02 97 52 13 52, fax 02 7 52 86 10, ☐ www.ot-carnac.fr) on place e l'Église, next to the church. On Sunday, is only open from 10 am to 1 pm. The ain tourist office (with the same contact etails) is in Carnac Plage at 74 ave des ruides. The free map *La Côte des Mégahes: Plan de Carnac, La Trinité, Plouharl* is useful.

Most banks are in Carnac Ville. On rue St ornély, a Crédit Mutuel de Bretagne is at o 27, and a Caisse d'Épargne at No 36. In arnac Plage, a Crédit Industriel de l'Ouest at 42 ave des Druides. In low season, any banks only open from 9 am to noon.

Carnac Ville has two bike shops: Cycles Lorcy (☎ 02 97 52 09 73), at 6 rue de Courdiec, and Cycles Berest (☎ 02 97 52 88 92), at 2bis ave des Salines. Both hire bikes for 60FF a day. Carnac Plage doesn't have any bike shops, but has six places which hire bikes. Le Randonneur (☎ 02 97 52 02 55), charges 70FF a day.

For the Internet, head to La Maison Casa House (☎ 02 97 52 64 45), at 2 rue St Cornély, in Carnac Ville.

Things to See & Do In Carnac Ville the **Musée de Préhistoire** (☎ 02 97 52 22 04), at 10 place de la Chapelle, provides a good introduction to the megalithic sites. **Eglise St Cornély**, next to the tourist office, is dedicated to the patron saint of horned beasts. The *pardon* of St Cornély is held the second Sunday in September. The **Tumulus St Michel** burial ground dates to 5000 BC and is 200m north-east of place de l'Église, at the end of rue du Tumulus.

One of the best ways to explore the **megalithic sites** is by bike. With the map from the tourist office, create your own tour. When you're done, the **beaches** beckon. The **Alignements du Ménec** (1100 menhirs in 11 lines) are the closest to Carnac Ville. The very impressive **Alignements de Kermario** (1029 menhirs in 10 lines) has a viewing platform that gives another perspective. At the western end of the **Alignements de Kerlescan** (555 menhirs in 13 lines) is a cromlech of 39 stones.

Some others to visit are the **Géant de Manio**, a huge dolmen, and the nearby **Quadrilatère**, an unusual group of menhirs in a square. In the grounds of Château Kercado is the **Tumulus de Kercado**, which dates from 3800 BC and was the burial ground of a Neolithic Chieftan.

It's fun to search for some of the area's individual dolmens and menhirs, but finding some of them requires wandering down overgrown forest paths.

Places to Stay Carnac is surrounded by about 20 camping grounds, ranging from basic to luxurious. Most are open from April or May until September or October. *Camping Nicolas* (☎ 02 97 52 95 42, fax 02 97 52 22 28, blvd Légenèse), in Carnac Plage, charges 24FF per adult and 33FF per site. The huge, four-star *Camping La*

NORMANDY & BRITTANY

Grande Metarie (☎ 02 97 52 24 01, fax 02 97 52 83 58, route Alignements de Kermario) is like a holiday village, with amenities such as swimming pool, tennis courts, *restaurant* and horse riding. It charges 30FF per adult and a hefty 128FF per site (open from April to mid-September).

The large hotels in Carnac tend to be costly. The hotels listed are small and more reasonably priced; reserve for July and August. In Carnac Ville, the charming little *Chez Nous (☎ 02 97 52 07 28, 5 place de la Chapelle)* has rooms with shower and toilet from 200FF (230FF in high season); a small fridge is available for guest use (open from Easter through October). *Le Râtelier (☎ 02 97 52 05 04, fax 02 97 52 76 11, 4 chemin de Douet)* is a pretty inn in a secluded part of Carnac Ville. Rooms with shower start at 230FF (250FF in summer).

In Carnac Plage, tiny *La Frégate (☎ 02 97 52 97 90, 14 allée des Alignements)*, around the corner from the tourist office, has rooms from 170FF (open Easter to September). The *Hôtel Ho-Ty (☎ 02 97 52 11 12, fax 02 97 52 80 03, 15 ave de Kermario)* has rooms from 200FF. On the water, *Les Rochers (☎ 02 97 52 10 09, fax 02 97 52 75 34, 6 blvd de la Base Nautique)* has rooms with shower and toilet from 295FF.

Places to Eat Carnac Ville's amazing, huge *market* on Wednesday and Sunday morning (north-east of the Musée de Préhistoire) sells seafood, baked goods and local produce. Carnac Ville has a *Casino* supermarket *(ave des Salines)*. Carnac Plage has a *Marché U (68 ave des Druides)* beside the tourist office and a *Super U (188 ave des Druides)*.

In Carnac Ville, *La Brigantine (☎ 02 97 52 17 72, 3 rue Colary)* has superb seafood and fish *menus* from 65FF. The restaurant in *Le Râtelier* serves local specialities and seafood, with *menus* from 95FF to 225FF. *Chez Yannick (☎ 02 97 52 08 67, 8 rue du Tumulus)* serves crepes, salads and seafood outside. In Carnac Plage, ave des Druides has many *restaurants, pizzerias* and *creperies*.

Day 5: Carnac to Auray
2–4 hours, 39.1km

This level route follows the coast to the pretty town of Locmariaquer, site of some of the region's most important megalithic monuments, and then heads north to Auray.

It's easy cycling on bike lanes for most of the way from Carnac Ville, via Carnac Plage to the picturesque port of La Trinité-sur-Mer (An Drinded), a name synonymous with yachting throughout France. From the **Pont de Kerisper**, across the Crach River, there are great **views** of the town and the estuary.

The coast road *(Route Cotière)* on the **St Philibert Peninsula** follows the Crach River on the west side, then passes oyster beds along the east side.

The quaint town of Locmariaquer, famous for oysters and megaliths, is on a peninsula at the western entrance to the Golfe du Morbihan. Before entering the town proper, visit the **Sites des Mégalithes** (20.1km); it's open daily from April to October. For information contact the Locmariaquer tourist office (☎ 02 97 57 33 05, fax 02 97 57 44 30), which is next to the *mairie* (town hall) at 1 rue de la Victoire.

The Sites des Mégalithes has two of the region's largest monuments. The **Table des Marchands** is a huge 30m-long dolmen and the **Grand Menhir Brisé** (350 tons) once stood 20m high. This impressive menhir, now lying broken on its side, makes you wonder how it ever stood upright, or was even moved! The **Tumulus d'Er-Grah** is also on the site.

Several other megalithic sites are free and not fenced on the peninsula around Locmariaquer. The tourist office has a map of their locations, plus information on the four small *hotels* and four *camping grounds* in the vicinity. In July and August an hourly boat, Vedette 'Lez V' (☎ 02 97 57 99 25), crosses the peninsula from Locmariaquer to Port Navalo.

From Locmariaquer, the route follows the **Circuit des Mégalithes** to two more dolmens. On the beach, facing the Baie de Quiberon, is the **Dolmen des Pierre Plate**. This is a worthwhile stop; carry a torch (flashlight). A menhir indicates the dolmen's entrance and inside the 24m-long chamber are interesting engravings.

To reach the **Dolmen de Kerlud**, turn left (24.4km) onto route de Kerlud. Continue 600m to the tiny hamlet of Kerlud and veer right down a small street that dead ends after 100m. The dolmen is between the two last houses. Backtrack to return to the route.

In Auray, it's a circuitous route to the tourist office via one-way streets.

Days 5 & 6: Carnac – Auray – Vannes

1:290,000

0   10km
0   6mi

Ⓝ N

NORMANDY & BRITTANY

Cue — Day 6

start		Auray tourist office
0km	↰	go E on Rue du Lait
0.2	↱	Ave Wilson
0.6	↰	Rue du Sablen
0.9	↱	Pont de St Goustan
1.0	↱	Quai Neuf 'to Vannes/Bono'
1.7	↰	Rue St Fiacre
1.8	↱	Rue de la Terre Rouge
2.0	↱	D101
5.7	●●↰	Tumulus de Kerneurs 1km ↻
8.5	↰	'to Baden/Larmor Baden'
9.7		D316, Baden
14.2	↰	D316, Baden
	●●	Boat to Tumulus de C 1.2km ↻
17.4	↰	D316A 'to Île aux Moines'
18.9	↰	'to Penmem'
	●●	Île aux Moines 22...km ↻
19.2	↰	minor road (no sign)
19.2		(20m) minor road (no sign)
20.1		unsigned road, Penmem
21.1	◇↱	D101 'to Arradon/Vannes'
30.7	↱	Rue Thiers
30.9		Vannes tourist office

Cue — Day 5

start		Carnac Ville tourist office
0km		go S from Place de l'Église
0.1	↱	Rue de la Poste 'to Les Plages'
1.6	↰	Blvd de la Plage 'Carnac Plage'
3.3		Ave d'Orient/D' 86
6.3		La Trinité-sur-Mer
7.1	↰	'to Auray/Locmariaquer'
8.5	↱	D28/Route Côtière 'to St Philibert'
13.9	↰	D28, St Philibert
15.0	↰	D781 'to Locmariaquer'
15.7	↰	(1st exit) D781
19.4	↰	Voie des Mégalithes
20.0	✱↱	C106 to Sites des Mégalithes'
20.1	✱	Sites des Mégalithes
20.4	↱	D781
20.7		unsigned road, Locmariaquer
20.7	↱	(20m) 'to Circuit des Mégalithes'
21.9	✱	Circuit des Mégalithes
23.2	✱	Dolmen des Pierres Plates
23.2	●●↰	'to Locmariaquer/Dolmen de Kerlud'
24.4	●●↰	Dolmen de Kerlud -. 4km ↻
25.7	↱	D781
26.1	↰	'to Le Roch Dü/La Rivière d'Auray'
27.7		unsigned road, Coët Courzo
28.7	↰	D781
30.1	◇↱	D28 'to Auray'
37.0	↰	D28 'to Auray'
38.3	↱	Place de la République/Rue Barré
38.9	↰	Rue de l'Église
39.0	↰	Rue du Lait
39.1		Auray tourist office

Auray

Auray is on the banks of the Loch River. The upper town is centred on place de le République and is a bustling commercial centre. On the river banks is the old quarter, St Goustan, undeniably one of the most picturesque ports in France. St Goustan (Auray), with easy access to the gulf, was a thriving port in its day. In 1776 Benjamin Franklin docked in Auray, after sailing across the Atlantic.

Information The tourist office (☎ 02 97 24 09 75, fax 02 97 50 80 75, e officetourismeauray@wanadoo.fr) is in the beautiful 17th-century Chapelle de la Congrégation at 20 rue du Lait. They have a packet of VTC circuit maps, Le Loch á Vélo, with three rides in the area (10FF); all three rides take in Ste-Anne d'Auray (see Things to See & Do).

On place de la République, Banque Populaire de Bretagne is at No 47, and Banque Nationale de Paris is at No 29. Around the corner, at 1 rue Barré, is a Crédit Agricole.

Cycles Fouché (☎ 02 97 24 08 33), 9 rue Ludovic-Castel, hires bikes for 60FF a day.

Things to See & Do On the way to the tourist office, you will pass the huge 17th-century church, **Église St Gildas**. In upper Auray, between place Notre Dame and rue du Belzic, there are some charming squares and streets of **16th-century houses**.

Auray's *pièce de la résistance* is without a doubt the **St Goustan** quarter; walk down rue du Château to get there. Perfect 15th- and 16th-century dwellings cluster around the harbourside at place St Sauveur, and up the steep cobbled streets to Église St Sauveur. At the water's edge, the schooner **Goélette St Sauveur** is now a museum (☎ 02 97 56 63 38) with information on the history of St Goustan.

For fabulous views over St Goustan, **Promenade du Loch** is a must.

Ste-Anne d'Auray is 8km north of Auray. The town, a centre for pilgrimages, is the site of the biggest **pardon** in Brittany, on 26 July.

Places to Stay The *Camping les Pommiers* (☎ 02 97 24 01 48, fax 02 97 50 85 53, Branhoc) is on the Day 6 route. At the D101 (2km) turn left; the camping ground is 100m further on. The charge per adult is 22FF, plus 36FF for a tent (open from Easter to October).

Hôtel Le Celtic (☎ 02 97 24 05 37, fax 02 97 50 89 79, 38 rue Clémenceau) has rooms from 150FF to 290FF. The charming *Hôtel Le Cadoudal* (☎ 02 97 24 14 65, fax 02 97 50 78 51, place Notre Dame) has rooms fo between 170FF and 250FF. The newer motel-style *Le Branhoc* (☎ 02 97 56 41 55 fax 02 97 56 41 35, 5 route de Bono) is 2km from Auray and has rooms starting from 290FF.

Places to Eat The Monday morning *market* is at place de la République next to Église St Gildas. A *Monoprix* supermarke is at 11 ave Maréchal Foch.

The spot to eat is St Goustan; lively plac St Sauveur is bordered by *restaurants* many serving excellent seafood. Most hav outside seating and, on a warm night, th harbour setting can't be beaten. An excellen choice to sample Breton seafood, *Le Chasse-Marée* (☎ 02 97 56 50 46, 11 plac St Sauveur) serves seafood platters and fish with *beurre rouge*, a creamy red wine sauce In upper Auray, a couple of cosy *creperie* are on rue Belzic and there are *restaurant* on place de la République.

Day 6: Auray to Vannes

2–3 hours, 30.9km

Day 6 offers a taste of the **Golfe du Morbihan**. It follows the coast to Vannes, visiting two islands en route (see Side Trips). Th route is flat, except for a few slight incline at the start of the day and a few bumps o Île aux Moines.

Working around the ferry schedules t visit both islands requires planning, particu larly because the boat to Île Gavrinis doe not run between noon and 2 pm.

The route bypasses Bono, a small por town to the left. To go to the **Tumulus d Kernours** (5.7km), turn right on the C20 and head downhill to the park, thickl shaded with pine trees. The tumulus is no immediately obvious – walk about 50r through the park. Carry a torch to guide yo through the corridor to the burial chambe Backtrack to the main route.

Larmor Baden is an attractive little por town on the Golfe du Morbihan. It has couple of *hotels*, a *camping ground* and few *restaurants*. *Charcuterie Le Bohelle*

as delicious salads and other picnic supplies; across the road is a **boulangerie**. Head
to the port to see a megalithic wonder (see
Side Trip 1).

At 18.9km, continue straight to cycle
round **Île aux Moines** (see Side Trip 2).
From Penmern, the route to Vannes is
straightforward; the D101 has a bike lane
for the last 3km into town.

Side Trip: Boat to Tumulus de Gavrinis

½–2 hours (visit), 1.2km (to boat; return)
The tiny **Île Gavrinis**, dating back to 4000
BC, is thought by some people to be the
most important megalithic site in Brittany.
The tumulus is 6m high and 50m in width.
The setting, and the fact that every stone
in the passage and burial chamber is decorated with engravings, makes Gavrinis truly
remarkable.

Continue straight at Larmor Baden, then
turn right after 300m to reach the town's
port – the departure point for **gulf day
cruises** with Vedettes Blanches Armor
☎ 02 97 57 15 27) and **boat trips** to the island of Gavrinis.

From June through September boats
☎/fax 02 97 57 19 38) run daily to Gavrinis
every half hour between 10 and 11.30 am,
and 2 and 5.30 pm. Booking is essential in
July and August. In April and May, the
boats run on weekends and public holidays,
and in October they run afternoons daily
except Tuesday. The boat ride, including a
guided tour of Gavrinis and the tumulus,
costs 56FF and takes about an hour. Bikes
can be left in the corridor of the ticket office – ask first. The 10-minute crossing
gives you a chance to view the gulf and
other islands.

Side Trip: Île aux Moines

*4–5 hours, 2.2km (to boat; return), plus
20km on island*
You can cycle as much or as little of **Île aux
Moines** (Izenah) as you choose, but about
20km will give you a good look around. The
cross-shaped granite island has only a handful of cars and is set up for cycling, with
three routes designated by different coloured
road markings. Simply follow the dots; **Circuit du Trec'h** (yellow), **Circuit de Brouhel**
(red) and **Circuit de Penhap** (blue). They all
start in Le Bourg, the island's village, 1km
from the port. To return to Le Bourg, for all
routes, follow the green arrows. If you only
have time for one route, the Circuit de Penhap leads to the southern tip through lanes of
charming houses and thatched cottages, past
dolmens and small calvaires, with gorgeous
views of the gulf and surrounding islands.

The tourist office (☎ 02 97 26 32 45), at
the port, is open Easter to September. The
camping ground *Le Vieux Moulin (☎ 02 97
26 30 68, fax 02 97 26 38 27)* is open mid-
June to September. There are two hotels on
the island: *Hôtel de l'Isle (☎ 02 97 26 32 50,
fax 02 97 26 39 54, Le Bourg)* has six rooms
at 230FF; and *Hôtel San Francisco (☎ 02 97
26 31 52, fax 02 97 26 35 59, Le Port)* has
eight rooms from 350FF (closed November
through March). Reservations are essential.

Begin with a 1.1km ride (cycle 1km then
turn left to reach Port Blanc) to catch the
year-round boat to the cycling paradise.
Izenah Croisières (☎ 02 97 26 31 45 or ☎ 02
97 57 23 24, fax 02 97 26 31 01) runs boats
to the island every 30 minutes from 7 am to
7.30 pm (10 pm in July and August). Return
tickets for the five-minute crossing cost 21FF,
plus 20FF per bike. The ticket price includes
a pamphlet with a very basic island map.

NORMANDY & BRITTANY

The Loire Valley

The Loire Valley – the 'playground of kings', 'garden of France', 'cradle of the Renaissance' and 'land of arts and letters' – has a reputation that draws flocks of visitors, many on bikes. Visiting the Loire on two wheels frees you from the tour bus scene – you can visit chateaux at your own pace and discover some of the region's other faces along quiet back roads. And what better way to end a day touring than with a fine meal in a chateau hotel or to picnic, with wine, crunchy bread, fresh goats cheese and vine ripened tomatoes in a camping ground across the river from a floodlit chateau?

HISTORY

From the 15th to the 18th century the Loire Valley was a favourite place of kings and noblefolk, who spent fortunes to create a vast neighbourhood of chateaux.

The area's earliest chateaux were medieval *châteaux forts* (fortresses), some constructed in the 9th century to defend against marauding Vikings. These structures were built on high ground and, once stone came into wide use in the 11th century, were often outfitted with massive walls topped with battlements, fortified keeps and loopholes (arrow slits), and surrounded by moats spanned by drawbridges.

As the threat of invasion diminished – and the cannon, introduced in the mid-15th century, made castles almost useless for defence – the architecture of new chateaux and renovations began to reflect priorities of aesthetics and comfort. Under the influence of the Renaissance at the end of the 15th century, the defensive structures developed into whimsical, decorative features, prominent at Azay-le-Rideau, Chambord and Chenonceau. Instead of being built on isolated hilltops, the Renaissance chateaux were placed near water or in a valley and harmonised with their surroundings. Most 17th- and 18th-century chateaux, in contrast, are grand country houses, built in the neoclassical style and set amid formal gardens.

CLIMATE

It's said that from the Loire, south, the climate becomes warmer and sunnier. Summer maximum temperatures average about

In Brief

Highlights
- seeing the **chateaux** at your own pace

- visiting elegant **Saumur** and medieval **Loches**

- exploring some of the **Loire's lovely tributaries**

Terrain
Flat along the Loire, but the riverside cliffs give way to rolling hills inland.

FFCT Contacts
- **Ligue Pays de la Loire**, 6 allée des Tilleuls, 49360 Toutelemonde

- **Ligue Orléanais**, 4 rue Pasteur, 45380 La Chapelle St-Mesmin

Cycling Events
- **FFCT Tour d'Indre-et-Loire** (mid-September) loop from Chinon via Amboise

- **Fête du Vélo** (3rd Sunday in June) Saumur region

Special Events
- **Concours de Voltige** horse-riding event (early June) Saumur

- **Festival de Théâtre Musical** opera festival (mid-July) Loches

- **À La Cour du Roy François** sound & light show (summer) Château d'Amboise

- **Marché Rabelais** fair and market (first weekend in August) Chinon

Gourmet Specialities
- *chêvre* (goats cheese)

- *champignons de paris* (button mushrooms) and white asparagus

- *tarte tatin* (caramelised apple tart)

- rich reds from Chinon and Bourgueil, light and fruity Saumur-Champigny, sparkling Saumur Brut and the Touraine's white Vouvray and Montlouis

23°C. In winter minimum averages only drop to around 7°C. The area often experiences frosts in March and April. Winds are predominantly from the west.

INFORMATION
Maps

The incredible network of tiny, often unsigned, roads in the Loire can complicate navigation. The Michelin map *Vallée des Rois* (Valley of the Kings; 1:200,000) covers the Loire Valley, but the boxed chateau names obscure portions of roads.

To extend the tour in this chapter, the excellent, free map *Val de Loire-Berry: 200 cycle tours* (1:200,000) clearly marks routes, labels attractions, suggests overnight stops and includes street plans of the region's major towns. It's available from the Centre-Val de Loire regional tourist office (☎ 02 38 70 32 74, fax 02 38 70 33 80, 🖳 www .loirevalleytourism.com), 9 rue St-Pierre Lentin, 45041 Orléans Cedex 1.

Books

Lonely Planet's *The Loire* guide is packed with all the practical details you need to extend a stay in the region. The Michelin green guide *Châteaux of the Loire* gives historical and architectural background.

Les Plus Belles Promenades à Vélo en Anjou (49FF), the Fédération Français de Cyclotourisme's (FFCT) *La France à Vélo: Pays de Loire* and *La France à Vélo: Centre, Berry, Bourbonnais* describe, in French, a series of rides in the area. For those on mountain bikes, the Office National des Forêts (ONF) publishes *Central Loire: Guide VTT – Évasion* (see Books in the Facts for the Cyclist chapter for details of the ONF and FFCT books).

Tourist shops sell many coffee-table books and chateau guides; *The Chateaux of the Loire*, with text by Pierre Miguel and photos by Jean-Baptiste Leroux, is available outside France.

In *A Wine & Food Guide to the Loire*, Jacqueline Friedich describes the products of the Loire's five wine regions and local food traditions.

For a literary insight into the Touraine, Rabelais' *Gargantua & Pantagruel* borrows settings from the towns of Seuilly and Lerné, on the route.

Information Sources

The region known collectively as the 'Loire Valley' takes in two regions and numerous *départements* (departments; administrative regions), each with its own tourist office (see the 'So What is the Loire Valley?' boxed text). This ride goes through three departments, each with its own Comité Départemental du Cyclo-tourisme to help cyclists:

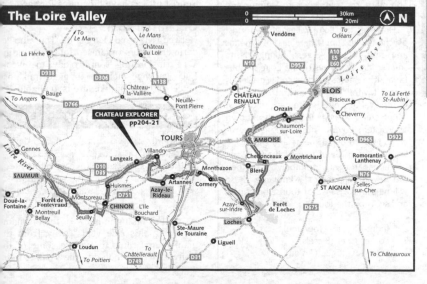

The Loire Valley

THE LOIRE VALLEY

Departmental

Maine-et-Loire (☎ 02 41 23 51 51, fax 02 41 88 35 77, e anjou.cdt@wanadoo.fr) BP 2147, Angers Cedex

Indre-et-Loire (☎ 02 47 31 47 48, fax 02 47 31 42 76, ☐ www.tourism-touraine.com) BP 3217, Tours Cedex

Loir-et-Cher (☎ 02 54 78 55 50, fax 02 54 74 81 79, ☐ www.chambordcountry.com) BP 149, 41005 Blois Cedex

The Indre-et-Loire's brochure *Loisirs & Randonnées: Nature & Leisure* includes maps and descriptions of eight cycle tours and mountain bike excursions (18km to 120km). The accompanying brochure *Randonnées Cyclotourisme et VTT: Touraine* lists bike hire and repair outlets. Anjou's *Randos dans les Pays de la Loire* just lists contact details of bike hire outlets and accommodation.

Gîtes (self-contained accommodation) and *chambres d'hôtes* (B&Bs) are listed at ☐ www.loire-valley-holidays.com; many of

---

Warning

Swimming is banned in the Loire because the fast eddies around its moving sandbanks are dangerous and unpredictable. Avoid walking on the sandbanks; they could actually be made of *sables mouvants* (quicksand).

Hayfever and asthma sufferers should bring their medication as many cyclists have reported the vast wheat fields triggered their allergies.

---

them allow bookings online. Or order th *Pays de la Loire* and *Centre-Val de Loire* guides (small charge; see Gîtes under Ac commodation in the Facts for the Cyclis chapter).

Cycle Tourism

Many businesses promote themselves a cyclist-friendly through two programs: *Véle Bleu, Vélo Vert* (Blue Bike, Green Bike) i the Pays de la Loire region and *Vélotel Vélocamp* in Centre-Val de Loire. They pro vide maps and descriptions of local cyclin; circuits, which could be used to plan a tou – especially a family holiday – based in on town. They also offer bike storage and hire technical advice and sometimes car storage Tourist offices have brochures for each.

Organised Tours

Between May and October the Touraine de partment offers organised tours, includin; VTT trips, lasting from two days to a week Each package includes luggage transpor hotels and meals; bike hire is available.

So What is the Loire Valley?

The Loire Valley is a world-famous tourist attraction, but administratively it doesn't exist. The valley takes its name from one of the world's great rivers, the 1020km Loire, which flows north-west from its source in the Massif Central towards Orléans, abruptly turns south-west to Saumur and then flows west to the Atlantic at Nantes.

However, the 'Loire Valley' of the tourist psyche begins somewhere east of Orléans and ends around Angers, taking in the smaller, pretty valleys of the Loire's tributaries, the Indre, Vienne and Cher. This places it within two administrative regions: Centre-Val de Loire to the east, and, past Montsoreau, Pays de la Loire (also known as Western Loire). These regions are divided into 10 departments and the 'Loire Valley' runs through four of them. Many of the departments commonly go by their pre-Revolution names – knowing these will help make sense of tourist brochures and signs on the tour:

Indre-et-Loire (Touraine)
Loir-et-Cher (Blesois)
Loire Atlantique (Anjou)

Chateau Explorer

Duration	5 days
Distance	232.7km
Difficulty	easy-moderate
Start	Saumur
End	Blois

As well as taking in many of the big-nam chateaux, this ride veers away from th main tourist route to explore some of th Loire's lovely tributaries, the Vienne, Indr and Cher.

These side routes are generally hillier, as the flat ground by the Loire is monopolised by busy, straight roads. However, the extra effort is rewarded by calm stretches through lovely oak woods and fields of wheat, corn, sunflowers and grapevines, and allows glimpses of traditional village life in farming communities away from the ubiquitous tourist brawl.

PLANNING
When to Ride
Although some cyclists brave the road from March, the weather can be cold and wet, and many of the attractions remain closed until Easter. April and May, when the Loire wears its colourful spring cloak, can also have variable weather and cool nights. June is ideal to beat the crowds and to enjoy warm, generally fine weather.

As well as being crowded in July and August, the weather is hot and most crops have been harvested, leaving expanses of stubble.

September (early autumn) is usually mild and ideal for cycling; visitors have a good chance of catching a traditional grape harvest procession. October is a good time to visit and appreciate the autumn colours.

GETTING TO/FROM THE RIDE
This ride could be linked with the Southern Brittany Contrasts ride in the Normandy & Brittany chapter by catching a train through Nantes to Vannes.

Only 1½ hours from Paris, the Loire is easy to get to by train – unless you have a bike that doesn't fit into the regulation-sized *housse* (bike bag). The SNCF has replaced most regular trains to the region with restrictive TGVs (see the 'What is une Housse' boxed text in the Getting Around chapter).

Between 26 June and 28 August one train a day carries bikes in each direction; outside this period it's only possible to carry a bike without a bike bag to the Loire on Friday, and from the Loire on Sunday. If you're relying on train transport you might have to ship your bike through SERNAM (see Train in the Getting Around chapter), or hire a bike in Saumur (bring panniers).

Transport is slightly easier from outside France. From Britain, the European Bike Express service (see Bus under Continental Europe in the Getting There & Away chapter) charges UK£149 (return) to take a passenger and bike to Tours or Orléans, from where trains link to Saumur and Blois.

Saumur
The Saumur train station is 1.5km north of the city centre.

Trains reach Saumur from Tour's St-Pierre des Corps station (56FF, 19 minutes, six a day, two take bikes), Nantes (98FF, one hour, about 15 direct a day, one takes bikes, if changing at St-Pierre des Corps two take bikes) and Paris, via St-Pierre des Corps (233FF, one hour, around 12 a day, none carry bikes outside July and August). The once-weekly (daily in July and August) service that takes bikes from Paris is via Angers.

Blois
Blois train station is at the western terminus of ave Dr Jean Laigret.

Trains run to Paris (123FF, 1½ hours, 10 a day, none carry bikes outside July and August), St-Pierre des Corps (51FF, 38 minutes, around 30 a day, plenty take bikes) and Nantes (159FF, 1½ hours, three to six a day, none take bikes). Dozens of TER services run daily to Orléans (52FF, 30 minutes, five to 10 take bikes). The once-weekly service (daily in July and August) that takes bikes to Paris is via Angers.

For those who've left cars at the start, note that only two trains daily carry bikes between St-Pierre des Corps and Saumur.

THE RIDE
Saumur
Known as '*la perle d'Anjou*' (the pearl of Anjou), the bleached, bourgeois Saumur is, indeed, one of the Loire's jewels. Its many fine slate-roofed buildings are carved out of the area's soft *tuffeau* (tufa), a limestone, which becomes paler with age and lends itself to intricate carving. Cobbled pedestrian streets form a lively shopping and social precinct at the base of the multiturreted fortified chateau. Home to the Cadre Noir riding school and historically a famous cavalry regiment, Saumur also has a rich past as a one-time Protestant stronghold and international centre of learning.

Information The large Saumur tourist office (☎ 02 41 40 20 60, fax 02 41 40 20 69, e off.tourisme.saumur@interliger.fr) is in the 16th-century neoclassical theatre by the

THE LOIRE VALLEY

river on place de la Bilange. Its friendly, helpful staff will make hotel reservations for 5/10FF in/outside the Saumur region.

Crédit Lyonnais is at 11 rue Beaurepaire. The post office is on place Dupetit-Thouars.

Peugeot Cycles (☎ 02 41 67 36 86), 19 ave Général de Gaulle (on Île d'Offard), stocks basic supplies and does repairs (closed Sunday and Monday).

Good quality hybrid and mountain bikes with racks and locks can be hired at Camping Île d'Offard (see Places to Stay) for 70F/375F per day/week; kids' bikes and child seats are available.

Things to See & Do On the third Sunday of June, thousands of bikes take over the roads along the Loire in the annual **Fête du Vèlo**. Between 8 am and 6 pm, 75.5km of the levee roads on both sides of the river are closed to motor traffic. The tourist office has details.

The **Château de Saumur** (☎ 02 41 40 24 40) was built in the 12th century as a dungeon during the reign of the Plantagenets. I' was converted into a fortress in the 13th century, and later became a country residence. The chateau offers good views over the town and is on Day 1 of the ride.

It's a busy, 4km ride along D960 to the **Dolmen de Bagneux** (☎ 02 41 50 23 02), a prehistoric burial chamber made of 15 rock slabs weighing more than 500 tonnes in total

From April to September the **École Nationale d'Équitation et Cadre Noir** (☎ 02 41 53 50 60), route de Marson, St Hilaire-S Florent, allows tours.

The **Maison du Vin** (☎ 02 41 51 16 40) at 25 rue Beaurepaire, introduces visitors to the region's wines and offers tastings.

Chateau Tips

Chateau Accommodation

For some, a cycling tour of the Loire Valley won't be complete without staying in a chateau (or two). While chateau hotels haven't been listed in this chapter (as they're usually away from alternative accommodation and dining options), they're easy to find. Expect to pay from around 500FF per night for a double.

Bienvenue au Château (🖳 www.bienvenue-au-chateau.com) is an association of Loire chateau owners who offer chambre d'hôte accommodation in their fabulous homes. The annual, free catalogue is available from larger and regional tourist offices, and is online.

Tourist offices can usually provide brochures of chateau hotels in their area. Another option is to browse the Gîtes de France guide *Chambres d'Hôtes Prestige et Gîtes de Charme*, which details 500 B&Bs in chateaux and manors (see Accommodation in the Facts for the Cyclist chapter). Several hotels and restaurants in the upmarket Relais & Château chain are also along the route; see the *Relais & Château* annual guide or the Web site 🖳 www.relaischateaux.fr for details.

Avoiding Chateau Burnout

If your prime motivation for touring in the Loire Valley is to see its magnificent chateaux, plan carefully to avoid the ABC (Another Bloody Chateau) syndrome. Each chateau tour packs in so much magnificent architecture, furnishing, artwork and history that it's best to visit only two a day.

Tours may be run in English only once or twice a day, so phone ahead or ask a tourist office for the time. Chateau grounds make magnificent picnic settings and are often open until nightfall (even if the chateau has closed).

Chateau Pass

The pass 'La clé des temps' (🖳 www.monuments-france.fr) gives entry to 10 government-owned chateaux and 15 monuments for 130FF. On this route it will save only 9FF off the combined admission prices for Chambord, Chaumont, Azay-le-Rideau and Fontevraud, but the saving increases if you visit other chateaux and monuments during your holiday. The pass is available at participating sites.

In the town of St Hilaire-St Florent, 2.5km north-east of Saumur, many wineries offer tours and tastings of their *méthode traditionelle* sparkling wine; **Rouvet-Ladubay** (☎ 02 41 83 83 82), rue Jean Ackerman, also has a contemporary art museum.

Places to Stay The Vélo Bleu, Vélo Vert-affiliated *Camping Île d'Offard* (☎ 02 41 40 30 00, fax 02 41 67 37 81) is on the island in the middle of the Loire. Some sites have million dollar views over the river to the chateau; charges are 26FF per person and 13.50FF for the site (high season). Four person bungalows cost 2000FF per week.

On the same site, the sometimes noisy *Centre International de Séjour*, charges 32.5/106FF per person for B&B (room without/with shower). Some rooms have exceptional views. Guests can use the communal kitchen and pool (in summer).

La Bouère Salée (☎ 02 41 67 38 85, fax 02 41 51 12 52) offers B&B year-round in an enormous 1850s farmhouse. Musty but quaint rooms cost 250FF/320FF for a single/double. The tufa stables are being converted into a two-bedroom gîte.

Across from the train station, the *Hôtel Le Nouveau Terminus* (☎ 02 41 67 31 01, fax 02 41 67 34 03, 15 ave David d'Angers) charges 220/250FF for a room with shower.

The *Hôtel Central* (☎ 02 41 51 05 78, fax 02 41 38 35 36, 23 rue Daillé) has doubles starting at 280FF (with shower) and a buffet breakfast for 39FF.

Places to Eat The main food *market* runs from 7 am to 7 pm Saturday in place de la Bilange; ask the tourist office about the others, held Wednesday to Sunday.

The *Bricomarché* supermarket (rue de Rouen) is a few kilometres north-east of town. Saumurois queue for bread and *patisseries* (pastries) at *Guy Boré Boulanger Patissier* (56 rue St Nicolas). Opposite, *La Maison des Produits Régionaux* is the place to prepare a gourmet picnic; a rubbery bust of local wine maker and film star Gérard Depardieu may still be in the window among bottles of his Chateau Tigné. Cheeses are beautifully displayed at *R Asselin* (18 rue du puits neuf). Several cheap *crêperies* and *pizzerias* line rue St Nicolas.

The *Auberge Reine de Sicile* (☎ 02 41 67 30 48, 71 rue Waldeck-Rousseau), beside

the only historic home not bombed on Île d'Offard in WWII, is known for its gastronomic food, with *menus* (set meals) at 110FF or 200FF (closed Sunday night).

Auberge St Pierre (☎ 02 41 51 26 25, 6 place St Pierre) serves traditional food in a 15th-century half-timbered inn and an outside eating area. *Menus* cost between 55FF and 150FF.

Day 1: Saumur to Chinon
2–4 hours, 36.7km

Today's ride links two impressive chateaux and Europe's largest remaining monastic city, with delightful pastoral scenery in between. Sweeping downhills through quiet woods alternate with calming scenes of tiny, stone walled villages among waving fields of sunflowers and wheat. Many vineyards offer **wine tasting** (ask the Saumur tourist office for the brochure *Saumur Champigny: Guide du Vignoble*). In the cliffs, look for signs of modern-day **cave dwellers** (see 'The Troglodytes' boxed text overleaf).

Negotiating Saumur's maze of streets is tricky; from the tourist office, head away from the river, turning left at the end of the block. Pass the intricately carved machicolations and tiny towers of the **Hôtel de Ville**, dating from 1508, and turn right, following signs to the chateau. These are easy to miss at place St Pierre, where you shouldn't go under the arch.

From the end of this street it's a stiff climb to the **chateau** entry (see Things to See & Do under Saumur) and the narrow, cliff-top rue des Moulins, lined with ruined windmills (*moulins*); one is next to the **panoramic lookout** (1.5km).

The route enters Fontevraud through the large forest once attached to the town's abbey. The **Abbaye Royale** (15.1km; ☎ 02 41 51 71 41), a sprawling complex of glaringly white tufa, is well worth visiting. Founded in 1101, the abbey was unique in that it consisted of separate communities of priests, nuns, laypeople, invalids and lepers, overseen by a woman. The royal or noble abbesses brought power and wealth to the abbey, but frequent unrest among the priests. The guided tour is excellent.

At the abbey, turn left to visit the villages of Montsoreau and Candes-St Martin (see Side Trip). Otherwise, follow the abbey

THE LOIRE VALLEY

THE LOIRE VALLEY

Day 1: Saumur to Chinon

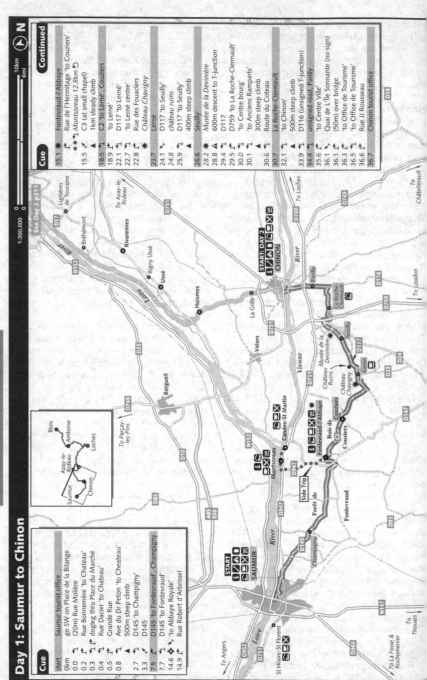

Cue		
start		Saumur tourist office
0km		go SW on Place de la Bilange
0.0	↰	(20m) Rue Molière
0.2	↱	Rue Bonnemère 'to Chateau'
0.3	↱↰	dogleg thru Place du Marché
0.4	↰	Rue Dacier 'to Chateau'
0.5		Grande Rue
0.8	↱	Ave du Dr Peton 'to Cheateau'
		500m steep climb
2.7	↰	D145 'to Champigny'
3.3	↱	D145
7.5	↰	D145 'to Fontevraud', Champigny
7.7	↱	D145 'to Fontevraud'
14.6	◆↰	'to Abbaye Royale'
14.9	↰	Rue Robert d'Arbrissel

Cue		Continued
15.1	✳	Fontevraud-l'Abbaye
		Rue de l'Hermitage 'to Couziers'
15.5	●↰↺	Montsoreau 12.8km ↺
15.5	↙	C3 (at small chapel)
	◀	1km steady climb
18.5	↱	C2 'to Lerné', Couziers
18.9	↱	'to Lerné'
22.1	↰	D117 'to Lerné'
22.7	↰	'to Lerné centre'
22.8	↱	Rue des Fouaciers
	✳	Château Chavigny
23.7		Lerné
24.1	↱	D117 'to Seuilly'
24.8		chateau ruins
25.9	↰	D117 'to Seuilly'
	◀	400m steep climb
26.6		Seuilly
28.2	✳	Musée de la Devinière
28.8	↙	600m descent to T-junction
29.4	↰	D117
29.5	↱	D759 'to La Roche-Clermault'
30.0	↱	'to Centre bourg'
30.1	↰	'to Anciens Ramparts'
		300m steep climb
30.6		Route du Coteau
30.7		La Roche-Clermault
32.1	↰	'to Chinon'
		500m steep climb
33.9	↱	D116 (unsigned T-junction)
34.4		unsigned road, Parilly
35.6	↱	'to Centre Ville'
36.1	↰	Quai de L'Ile Sonnante (no sign)
36.1	↱	(50m) over bridge
36.3	↱	'to Office de Tourisme'
36.5	↰	'to Office de Tourisme'
36.6	↰	Rue JJ Rousseau
36.7		Chinon tourist office

walls to the right onto the undulating back road to Chinon. The route darts into Lerné, passing the small, elegant **Château de Chavigny** (☎ 02 47 95 94 30; visit by appointment), and travels along rue des Fouaciers past 16th-century tufa houses. (*Fouaciers* were bakers of a variety of unleavened bread, *fouace*.)

It's easy to miss the turn into Seuilly, at 25.9km, about 1km after some chateau ruins. On the far side of the village the route passes **La Devinière** (28.2km; ☎/fax 02 47 95 91 18), the farmhouse where 16th-century writer François Rabelais is said to have been born and raised. It's now a museum to Rabelais, famous for his ribald satires such as *Gargantua*, set around Chinon. Admission is 23/15FF.

From La Roche-Clermault (30.7km) it's mostly downhill to Chinon, entered through a graceful avenue of plane trees.

Side Trip: Montsoreau & Candes-St Martin

½–1 hour, 12.8km return

On the confluence of the Loire and the Vienne Rivers, these neighbouring towns are deservedly classified as one of France's *Plus Beaux* (Most Beautiful) villages, with their flower-strewn paths and cobbled streets lined with 15th-, 16th- and 17th-century houses. Access is via one of the busier roads in the area, the D947. At the T-junction with the riverside D751, turn left to see some fine **troglodyte houses** hewn into the cliffs.

To the right, the Renaissance **Château de Montsoreau** (☎ 02 41 51 70 25) lacks interesting furnishing and interior decorations but offers a good view. Admission costs 29/17FF adult/child. Further along, Candes-St Martin's 12th- and 13th-century **collegiate church** was fortified in the 15th century and has a spectacularly carved portal and soaring Angevin vaulting.

Chinon

Chinon's massive, 400m-long castle looms over the town's medieval quarter, where the uneven, cobblestone streets lined with ancient houses are wonderful to explore. Some of the houses are built of decaying tufa stone, others are half-timbered and brick; the contrast between the triangular, black slate roofs and the whitish-tan tufa gives the town its distinctive appearance.

The Troglodytes

While the kings of France were building self-glorifying edifices in the Loire Valley, many of their subjects were going underground. Quarrying tonnes of soft *tuffeau* (tufa), a limestone, to build the chateaux left gaping holes which, with a little ingenuity, were turned into homes.

Selling the stone paid for the cost of digging and the peasant farmer had a new home at little expense. The caves were cool in summer, required less heating than conventional homes in winter and provided shelters for animals from cold, thieves and wolves. The soft stone made catering for a growing family simple: when a new child was born the parents simply dug space for another bed.

Some settlements have been dated back to the 13th century and, at the turn of the 20th century, 5% of French people still lived in troglodyte dwellings. Most were dug into the riverside cliffs, but the Loire is one of the few places in France that also has *troglodytisme de plaine*, where houses are below the surface. Farming communities dug entire villages around a central, sunken courtyard, with radiating caves for homes, wine cellars, walnut presses, hemp-drying ovens and mangers below, and crops above to help absorb rainwater.

Today many kilometres of caves have been converted to wine cellars and mushroom farms or abandoned. Once the homes of the poor, some are being taken over by city dwellers willing to spend large amounts of money to convert them to comfortable holiday houses.

At least two 17th-century troglodyte hamlets south-west of Saumur (both about 15km from Saumur, off the D177) are open to the public and are furnished with old farming implements and objects from daily life early in the 20th century. **La Fosse** (☎ 02 41 59 00 32) still housed three families at the turn of the 20th century (admission costs 25/15FF adults/children). **Rochemenier** (☎ 02 41 59 18 15) dates back to the 13th century and included about 250 underground rooms (admission costs 24/13FF).

Information The tourist office (☎ 02 47 93 17 85, fax 02 47 93 93 05) is on place d'Hofheim (closes at 6 pm and on Sunday from mid-September to mid-June). The friendly staff have the Vélotel cycling routes brochure *Val de Loire – Touraine.* The Crédit Agricole is at 2 place Hôtel de Ville. The post office is at 80 quai Jeanne d'Arc.

Espace ICM (☎ 02 47 93 01 07), on the way out of town on the route de Tours, sells and repairs bikes (closed Sunday, and Monday morning). Bike hire is available at Hôtel Agnès Sorel (see Places to Stay) for 90/350FF a day/week; children's bikes, child carriers and helmets are also available. The manager can do simple repairs.

Internet access is available at L'Astrol@be (☎ 02 47 98 01 00), 26 rue Rabelais.

Things to See & Do On the first weekend in August, musicians, dancers and locals don period costume for the **Marché Rabelais**, where crafts and local products are sold. On the third weekend of August, wines and traditional food products are sold at the **Marché à l'Ancienne**, a re-creation of a 19th-century farmers' market.

On a rocky spur high above the Vienne River is the huge, mostly ruined medieval fortress of the **Château de Chinon** (☎ 02 47 93 13 45), illuminated on summer nights. It consists of three parts separated by waterless moats: in the Château du Milieu (the Middle Castle), Joan of Arc picked out Charles VII from a crowd and convinced him to go to Reims to be crowned. The chateau is on the Day 2 route.

The kitsch **Musée Animé du Vin** (☎ 02 47 93 25 63), 12 rue Voltaire, has life-sized mechanical figures that demonstrate how wine and wine barrels are made.

The **municipal pool** (☎ 02 47 93 08 45) is next to the camping ground.

Places to Stay The riverside, partly shaded *Camping de l'Île Auger* (☎ 02 47 93 08 35, fax 02 47 93 53 33) is across the Vienne from the town centre. Fees are 11.10FF for a site and 10.70FF per adult (open mid-March to mid-October).

The friendly *Auberge de Jeunesse* (☎ 02 47 93 10 48, fax 02 47 98 44 98, rue Descartes) charges 48FF for a bed in a basic dorm. You must check-in before 6 pm (closed Sunday to new arrivals).

The Vélotel *Hôtel Agnès Sorel* (☎ 02 47 93 04 37, fax 02 47 93 06 37, 4 quai Pasteur) has six pretty rooms, starting from 180FF (hall-shower and toilet). The 38FF breakfast consists of enough pastries and bread to keep a cyclist happy.

Right in the heart of the medieval town, the pleasant three-star *Hôtel de France* (☎ 02 47 93 33 91, fax 02 47 98 37 03, 47–49 place Général de Gaulle) occupies a 16th-century building and has comfortable doubles with shower from 450FF, including breakfast.

Places to Eat An *outdoor market* is held at the northern end of place Général de Gaulle on weekend mornings. Nearby, *Charcuterie-Traiteur N Rémy (4 rue Voltaire)* has delicious prepared foods (closed Sunday afternoon and Monday). Place Jeanne d'Arc hosts a *food market* all day Thursday. The *Super U (digue St-Lazare)* is on the way into town (closed Sunday afternoon).

Crêperie-Pizzeria Jeanne de France (☎ 02 47 93 20 12, 12 place Général de Gaulle) is a good choice for pizzas (35FF to 60FF), *galettes* (savoury crepes) and salads. *La Saladerie* (☎ 02 47 93 99 93, 5 rue Rabelais), which closed Monday, has meal-sized salads (about 45FF) and other dishes (50FF to 63FF).

La Maison Rouge (☎ 02 47 98 43 65, 38 rue Voltaire) is recommended as an excellent place to try regional food and wine; its generous *menus* cost 79FF to 129FF (closed on Monday outside July and August).

Day 2: Chinon to Azay-le-Rideau

2½–5 hours, 49.3km

One of the best days cycling in the tour, today's route passes three of the valley's most famous chateaux and explores some of the Loire's tributaries on tiny roads seemingly made for cycling. Many of the waterside roads run along the tops of levees built to protect the nearby towns from flooding; the languid Loire can turn into a torrent when swollen by winter rains. Here the river is its most typical – broad, studded with sandbanks and lined with thick vegetation. By the road are some typical brown-tiled farm homes.

Leave Chinon by retracing yesterday's route to the quai and slogging up the hill

Day 2: Chinon to Azay-le-Rideau

THE LOIRE VALLEY

N

10km
5mi

1:300,000

Cue		
0km		Chinon tourist office
0.0	↰	go W on Imp des Caves Vasl'n
		(20m) Rue JJ Rousseau
0.1	↰	Place Général de Gaulle
C.3	↱	Quai Jear d'Arc
0.8	◀	D751 to "Chateau"
		1.4km steep climb
2.4	◀	D16 'to H Jismes'
3.8	◈	(2nd exit) D16 'to Huismes'
9.2	↱	'to Rigny-Ussé'
9.5		Huismes
10.0	↱	'to Rigny-Ussé'
10.5	↰	D7 'to Bourgueil'
10.6	◀↱	Route du Pont 'to L'île St-Mart'n'
13.2	↱	Rue d'île St-Martin/D16
13.3		Ile St-Martin
15.2	↱↰	Château Ussé 2.7km ↰
22.0		Bréhémont
26.6	●↰↗	Château de Langeais 3km ↰
27.9		La Chapelle-aux-Naux
		650m cobblestone section
33.7	◀	'to Villandry'
34.1	↰	'to Villandry'
34.3	↱	at stone cross
35.0	↰	
36.4	●↰↱	'to Druye', Villandry ◯
		Château de Villandry 400m ◯
		600m hard climb
36.5	◀	'to Vallères'
39.5	↱	
43.3	◀	D39 'to Azay-le-Rideau', Vallères
43.7	↱	'to Azay-le-Rideau'
48.6	◈	(2nd exit) 'to Azay Chateau'
49.3		Azay-le-Rideau tourist office

See Day 3 p214

START: DAY 2
CHINON

START: DAY 3
Azay-le-Rideau

Side Trip
Château Ussé

Side Trip

Side Trip

See Day 1 p208

To Angers

To Saumur

To Tc Saumur

To Châtellerault

To rChâtellerault

To Ste-Meure
de Touraine

Blois
Amboise
Loches
Azay-le-
Chinon Rideau
Saumur

below the **chateau** (1.6km; see Things to See & Do under Chinon). At Huismes (9.5km) the route drops onto the riverflat and, ignoring the signs to Rigny-Ussé, crosses the Indre to travel along the strip of land between the Loire and the Indre. The turrets of **Château Ussé**, known as the Sleeping Beauty Castle for its role in inspiring Perrault's fairy tale, rise above the fields. The side trip to the chateau is unforgettable for its stunning approach.

However, the entry fee (59FF/19FF for adults/children) for this chateau (☎/fax 02 47 95 54 05) is one of the steepest in the Loire and many visitors are disappointed with the run-down interior.

From the turn-off to Ussé (15.2km) the route sits high on the riverside dike. At the intersection with the D57 (26.6km) it's possible to turn left to Langeais. The 15th-century **Château de Lângeais** (☎ 02 47 96 72 60) has a rich decor and a collection of Gothic and Renaissance tapestries, despite its stern exterior. The marriage of Charles VIII and Anne de Bretagne was celebrated here in 1491, sealing the fate of Brittany. Admission costs 40/20FF.

At 33.3km the route turns south along the Cher River to Villandry. The short section of cobbles is best handled by riding on the dirt edges or by walking. The 16th-century **Château de Villandry** (☎ 02 47 50 02 09), the last of the large chateaux built along the Loire during the Renaissance, is best known for the geometric beauty of its formal *potagers* (kitchen gardens). The Ornamental Gardens, symbolising aspects of love, are best seen from the belvedere inside the chateau. Combined admission to the chateau and gardens costs 45/38FF, and garden alone 32/26FF.

From Villandry the route climbs into rolling farmland, before 12km gliding down a long hill into Azay-le-Rideau.

Azay-le-Rideau

Built by the Indre River, this pretty village has been settled since Gallo-Roman times. In the 12th century a chateau was built to defend the Indre between Tours and Chinon. Razed by Charles VII in 1418 after a petty insult, the town was reconstructed in the mid-15th century. Today Azay exists for the most part to service tourists. However, at night the town has a gentle charm, its cob-

bled streets lined with 15th-, 16th- and 17th-century tufa stone houses.

Information The tourist office (☎ 02 47 45 44 40, fax 02 47 45 31 46, @ otsi.azay .le.rideau@wanadoo.fr) is in place de l'Europe. The Crédit Agricole is at 9 rue Carnot (closed Monday, Wednesday morning and Sunday). LeProvost cycles (☎/fax 02 47 45 40 94) is at 13 rue Carnot; it has VTTs for hire for 65/290FF a day/week (closed Monday and Sunday, except from June to August, when it opens on Sunday and Monday morning).

Things to See & Do The prime attraction, **Château de Azay-le-Rideau** (☎ 02 47 45 42 04) is on an island in the middle of the Indre. Built between 1518 and 1523 for French treasurer Gilles Berthelot, it's one of the country's most beautiful Renaissance chateaux. The evocative audiocassette tour makes sense of the complex architectural elements, but the summer evening *son et lumière* (sound and light show) hardly warrants the entry fee.

Art galleries and winemakers' **caves** (cellars) jostle for space on Azay's main streets and the collective **Caveau de Vignerons** is opposite the tourist office on place de la République.

Canoes and **kayaks** can be hired in summer; ask at the tourist office. The municipal **pool** and **tennis courts** are next to the camping ground.

Places to Stay The pleasant, shaded, three-star *Camping du Sabot* (☎ 02 47 45 42 72) is by the Indre; cyclists pay 24FF each (closed November to March).

Hôtel Le Balzac (☎ 02 47 45 42 08, fax 02 47 45 29 87, 4–6 ave Adélaïde Riché) has adequate but musty rooms with shower and bidet for 180/220FF single/double (closed January and on Monday in the low season).

You can't go past the charming Vélotel *Hôtel de Biencourt* (☎ 02 47 45 20 75, fax 02 47 45 91 73, 7 rue Balzac), in 18th- and 19th-century tufa buildings in the heart of the old town. Pretty, if floral, rooms with shower and hall toilet cost 210FF.

For stylish and peaceful B&B in an 18th- and 19th-century farmhouse, try *Le Plessis* (☎ 02 47 45 48 24, @ p.lepage@wanadoo .fr), 800m east of the chateau (follow rue de

Chateau out of town and look for the 'Chambre d'Hôte' sign to the left. Four en suite bedrooms share kitchen, laundry and lounge with fireplace; they cost from 300FF to 400FF a double.

Places to Eat The main *market* is held on Saturday morning in place de la République; place de la Nationale hosts a smaller one Wednesday morning. The *Stoc* supermarket is about 1km out of town up the steep D751 (closed Monday and Sunday mornings). In town, the small *grocery* opposite Hôtel Le Balzac, on ave Adélaïde Riché, stays open into the night (closed Sunday afternoon).

Several fairly ordinary tourist restaurants are along rue Balzac. The rustic *La Ridelloise* (☎ 02 47 45 46 53, *34–35 rue Nationale*) is a better choice, with *menus* from 68FF to 148FF (open lunch only mid-November to mid-March).

The place locals go to splurge is the *Restaurant l'Aigle d'Or* (☎ 02 47 45 24 58, *10 ave Adélaïde Riché*), which serves excellent *menus* of local specialties from 150FF. Book ahead (closed Sunday evening and Monday).

Day 3: Azay-le Rideau to Loches

2½–6 hours, 57.7km

Travel through the heart of the Touraine to discover the landscape that inspired Rabelais and, later, Balzac. The route criss-crosses the Indre as it flows through woods and past small wooden fishing platforms. Market gardens grow in the rich alluvial soil; in places, ancient *lavoirs* (wash houses) remain, along with ruined watermills. Away from the river the route is hilly; look for storage sheds or houses burrowed into the cliffs (see 'The Troglodytes' boxed text earlier in this chapter).

Leave Azay past the chateau gates to travel on the Indre's north bank, passing rough-hewn sandstone houses with well-tended gardens, and some **troglodyte houses** (2.6km). It's possible to detour briefly into Saché at 6.2km to visit the small 19th-century **Château de Saché** (☎/fax 02 47 26 86 50). It was a favourite retreat of one of France's most prolific writers, Honoré de Balzac (1799–1850), and now displays his manuscripts, letters, first editions, portraits and small bedroom. Admission costs

23/15FF for adults/children. Another former Saché resident, American sculptor Alexander Calder, left one of his colourful **stabiles** (a giant mobile, on a base) in the square outside the *mairie* (town hall). To get to the chateau and town, turn right onto the C9 and follow the signs.

At 9.9km it's worth turning right onto the D17 towards Pont de Ruan, where the **Moulins de Balzac**, a pair of wooden water mills, paddle gently on a wide green meander of the Indre; the scene has changed little from Balzac's description more than a century ago.

From Artannes (11.4km) the route, along the D17, is busier. However, the river, dawdling through woods, remains a pleasant companion. On the outskirts of Montbazon, it's a steep 700m climb for those who can't resist looking at the much-signposted, elegant **Château d'Artigny** (19.8km) – a hotel and restaurant built in the old style at the start of the 20th century. At Montbazon (21.9km) the route leads under the town's fortified gate, with the ruins of its chateau on the rocky hill to the right, and climbs into a vast sea of wheat on the plateau.

Cormery (33.3km) was the Touraine's most important wheat market until the 19th century. The town was also the site of the huge **Benedictine Abbey St Paul**, founded in 791. The monastery declined in the 17th and 18th centuries and was sacked during the Revolution; today many town buildings incorporate elements of the ruins. The tourist office (☎ 02 47 43 30 84) runs excellent guided tours of the abbey and town. To explore the abbey, detour left into town, crossing the bridge to see the huge waterwheels. The small lane to the tourist office is to the right just before the bridge.

On the way out of town a patisserie sells Cormery's famous **macaroons** (first baked by the monks). For a lovely riverside **picnic spot**, turn left at 37.4km onto the D83 to Courçay, site of the distinctive 12th-century **Église St Urbain** (St Urbain Church), with a rough-hewn, rounded spire.

The route crosses to the Indre's north bank at Chambourg-sur-Indre (48.4km). Just past Isle Auger it's possible to duck down a side track to see the two remaining perfectly arched spans of a **Gallo-Roman bridge** (52.2km).

Ride into Loches towards the 15th-century **Porte des Cordeliers**, where a bridge has

Day 3: Azay-le-Rideau to Loches

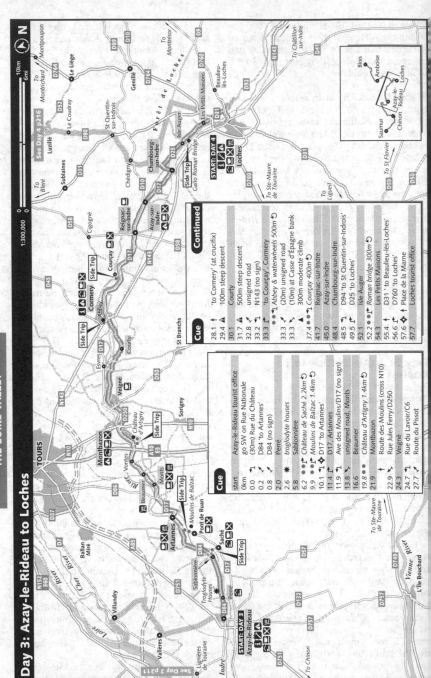

THE LOIRE VALLEY

Cue

start	Azay-le-Rideau tourist office
0km	go SW on Rue Nationale
0.0	(30m) Rue du Château
0.2	D84 to Artannes
0.8	D84 (no sign)
2.0	Perré
2.6	troglodyte houses
5.8	Sablonière
6.2	Château de Saché 2.2km ↻
9.9	Moulins de Balzac 1.4km ↻
10.1	D17 to Artannes
11.4	D17, Artannes
11.9	Ave des Moulins/D17 (no sign)
13.8	unsigned road, Monts
16.6	Beaumer
19.8	Château d'Artigny 1.4km ↻
21.9	Montbazon
22.9	Route des Moulins (cross N10)
24.3	Rue Jules Ferry/D250
24.7	Veigné
27.7	Rue du Lavoir/C6
27.7	Route du Pissot

Cue *Continued*

28.1	'to Cormery' (at crucifix)
29.4	100m steep descent
30.1	Courty
31.7	500m steep descent
32.8	unsigned road
33.2	N143 (no sign)
33.3	'to Courçay', Cormery
33.3	Abbey & waterwheels 500m ↻
33.3	(20m) unsigned road
33.3	(10m) at Casse d'Epagne bank
37.4	Courçay 400m ↻
41.7	Reignac-sur-Indre
45.0	Azay-sur-Indre
48.4	Chambourg-sur-Indre
48.5	D94 'to St Quentin-sur-Indrois'
49.5	D25 'to Loches'
52.1	Isle Auger
52.2	Roman bridge 300m ↻
54.3	Les Petits Maisons
55.4	D31 ' to Beaulieu-lès-Loches'
56.6	D760 'to Loches'
57.6	Place de la Marne
57.7	Loches tourist office

now replaced the drawbridges that once defended the city.

Loches

This well-preserved fortified town sits on the Indre, below a chateau complex on a rocky spur. Two intact sets of walls surround the hilltop complex, giving it an imposing appearance while, below, impressive fortified gates stud what's left of the wall surrounding the town. The narrow cobbled lanes of this medieval city echo with history and atmosphere.

Information The tourist office (☎ 02 47 91 82 82, fax 02 47 91 61 50, 🖳 www.lochesen touraine.com) is on place de la Marne (closes at 5.30 pm mid-September to June).

The Crédit Agricole is at 1bis rue de Tours. The post office is on rue Descartes.

The bike shop M Jourdain (☎ 02 47 59 02 15) is at 7 rue des Moulins; bike hire is available for 80FF a day (closed Sunday and, in winter, also on Monday).

Things to See & Do Walk up the steep rue du Château and through the Porte Royal to the **citadel**, protecting several elegant 17th- and 18th-century houses and the chateau. The **Logis Royal** (Royal Lodge; ☎/fax 02 47 59 01 32) is famous for the women who held court here – Joan of Arc; Agnès Sorel, Charles VI's powerful mistress; and Anne de Bretagne, wife of French Kings Charles VIII and Louis XII. At the other end of the promontory, over a drawbridge, is the 13th-century Norman **Donjon** (Keep; ☎/fax 02 47 59 07 86), which once housed gruesome torture chambers. Between the two is the **Église de St-Ours**, its porch adorned with imaginative Romanesque sculptures.

On the edge of the ramparts, **Maison Lansyer** (☎ 02 47 59 05 45), the former home of landscape painter E Lansyer (1835–93), displays his work and collection.

A free brochure from the tourist office describes a town **walking tour**; the best **view** of the chateau fortifications is from the public gardens. The municipal **pool** is by the camping ground.

Places to Stay The shady, riverside *Camping de la Citadelle* (☎ 02 47 59 05 91, fax 02 47 59 05 91, ave Aristide-Briand) charges 15FF per person and 40FF per site

in high season (open mid-March to mid-November). Entry to the pool next door is free for campers.

La Tour St Antoine (☎ 02 47 59 01 06, fax 02 47 59 13 80, 2 rue des Moulins) has older-style rooms from 130FF.

The two-star *Hôtel de France* (☎ 02 47 59 00 32, fax 02 47 59 28 66, 6 rue Picois) has rooms from 235FF; taking a *demi-pension* (half-board) is obligatory in July and August (closes Sunday night and Monday outside July and August). Three-star *Hôtel George Sand* (☎ 02 47 59 39 74, fax 02 47 91 55 75, 39 rue Quintefol) has lovely rooms in a 15th-century coach inn. Doubles with shower and toilet start from 250FF.

Places to Eat For fresh produce, *markets* are held on Wednesday and Saturday morning in place du Marché. An *ATAC* supermarket is on rue Descartes (closed Sunday afternoon).

As well as crepes, the very popular *Le Christyve* (☎ 02 47 59 25 59, 3 rue Picois) serves good-value meals such as paella and salads for 39FF (closed Thursday outside summer). *Pizzeria Sforza* (☎ 02 47 94 01 19, place de l'Hôtel de Ville) also comes highly recommended.

The restaurant in the *Hôtel George Sand* (see Places to Stay) serves elegant French food on a riverside terrace, with *menus* from 100FF to 240FF.

Day 4: Loches to Amboise

2¼–4½ hours, 45.6km

Visiting one of the jewels of the Loire Valley, lovely Château de Chenonceau, this route begins and ends in the remnants of feudal hunting forests, crossing farmland in between.

Start early to enjoy the fresh smells and wildlife in the 3586-hectare Fôret de Loches, once a royal forest. Retrace the route out of Loches to the busy D764, which has to be endured for a short distance before turning onto the forest's well-surfaced rollercoaster roads. At a crossroad, the **Pyramide de St-Quentin** (8.7km) is typical of the many pyramids built as meeting places for hunts in the 18th and 19th centuries.

Once out of the forest the route undulates to **Château de Chenonceau** (☎ 02 47 23 90 07), an oasis of Renaissance beauty spanning the river in five elegant arches. King

Day 4: Loches to Amboise

THE LOIRE VALLEY

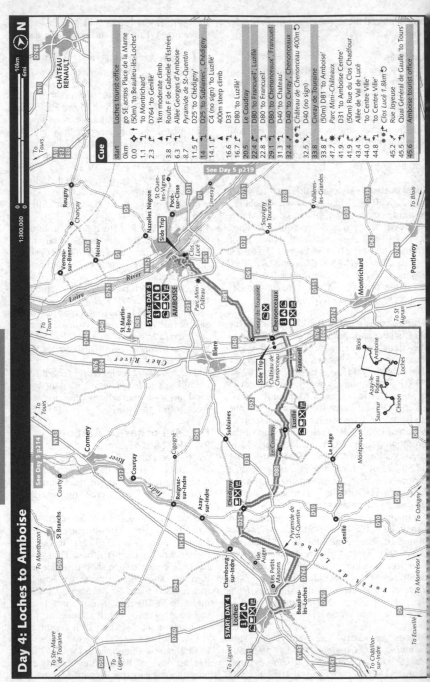

Cue	
start	Loches tourist office
0km	go SE across Place de la Marne
0.0	(50m) 'to Beaulieu-lès-Loches'
1.1	'to Montrichard'
2.3	D764 'to Genillé'
	1km moderate climb
3.8	Route F de Gabrielle d'Estrées
6.3	Allée Georges d'Amboise
8.7	Pyramide de St-Quentin
11.5	D25 'to Chédigny'
14	D25 'to Sublaines', 'Chédigny'
14.1	C4 (no sign) 'to Luzillé'
	400m steep climb
16.6	D31
16.7	D80 'to Luzillé'
20.5	Le Coudray
22.4	D80 'to Francueil', Luzillé
22.8	D80 'to Francueil'
29.1	D80 'to Chenonceaux', Francueil
31.3	D40 'to Château'
32.4	D40 to Civray', Chenonceaux
	Château de Chenonceau 400m ↻
32.5	D40 (no sign)
33.8	Civray de Touraine
33.8	(50m) D81 'to Amboise'
41.7	Parc Mini-Châteaux
41.9	D31 'to Amboise Centre'
41.9	(50m) Rue du Clos Chadfour
43.4	Allée de Val de Lucé
44.0	'to Centre Ville'
44.8	'to Centre Ville'
	Clos Lucé 1.8km ↻
45.2	Rue Joyeuse
45.5	Quai Général de Gaulle 'to Tours'
45.6	Amboise tourist office

Henri II left Chenonceau to his favourite mistress, Diane de Poitiers, but on the king's death de Poitiers was forced by the queen, Catherine de Médicis, to swap it for imposing Chaumont. Admission costs 45/35FF adults/children.

As the main access route to the extremely popular chateau, the road to Amboise is busy, but travels mostly through scenic woods. On the way, children might enjoy the **Parc Mini-Châteaux** (41.7km; ☎ 02 47 33 44 44), where 43 of the most famous Loire chateaux are recreated in miniature.

The route enters Amboise through the quieter suburbs; at 44.8km it's possible to turn right and follow the signs to **Le Clos Lucé** (☎ 02 47 57 62 88), where Leonardo da Vinci spent the last three years of his life. The painter came to Amboise in 1516 at the invitation of François I, reportedly bringing a certain painting of an enigmatically smiling lady. The house is at the top of a steep road (lined with troglodytic dwellings) on 2 rue du Clos Lucé. Visitors can tour several restored rooms and view scale models of Leonardo's marvellous inventions. Admission costs 32/18FF.

Amboise

The picturesque town of Amboise, nestling under its fortified chateau on the south bank of the Loire, reached its peak during the decades around 1500, when the luxury-loving King Charles VIII enlarged it and King François I held raucous parties there.

Information The staff at the tourist office (☎ 02 47 57 09 28, fax 02 47 57 14 35, ✉ www.amboise-valdeloire.com) make local hotel reservations for 2FF per phone call. Ask here for local hiking and cycling maps, including the 65km *Circuit des Trois Châteaux – Amboise, Chenonceaux et Chaumont* and the Vélotel pamphlet (closed Sunday afternoon outside July and August, and closed all day Sunday October to March).

The Crédit Agricole, BNP and Crédit Lyonnais are on rue Nationale. The post office is at 20 quai Général de Gaulle.

Cycles Richard (☎ 02 47 57 01 79) at 2 rue de Nazelles is well-stocked; bikes can be hired for 90/450FF a day/week (closed Sunday afternoon and Monday).

It's possible to email from telephone shop SARL IRACS at 111 rue Nationale.

Things to See & Do The rocky outcrop topped by the **Château d'Amboise** (☎ 02 47 57 00 98) has been fortified since Roman times. It houses a collection of Gothic and Renaissance furniture, two Empire salons and Léonardo da Vinci's tomb. The ramparts allow panoramic views. On summer evenings more than 400 locals star in a sound and light show.

Leonardo's Byke

Look around the gift shop at Leonardo's former home, Clos Lucé, and among the reproductions of Leonardo's sketches you'll see an allegedly early design for a 'byke'.

This 'Renaissance Bicycle', complete with chain and pedals, was found by scholar Augusto Marinoni on one of Leonardo's original manuscripts. It was drawn on the back of a sheet that had been glued to another in the *Codex Atlanticus*. He argued it was a student's reproduction of a drawing by the master. The Italians were ecstatic to have found 'proof' that the bicycle had been invented by a countryman.

However, that claim has been disputed by Hans-Erhard Lessing, who says art historian Carlo Pedretti had not seen the sketch when holding the manuscript up to the light in 1961. He suggests the sketch was forged during restoration of the manuscript.

Even if Leonardo didn't design the first bicycle, he did come up with blueprints that were well in advance of his time. The Clos Lucé museum includes reconstructions of just some of his inventions, including a proto-automobile, armoured tank, parachute and hydraulic turbine!

The sketch of a 'byke' once thought to have been drawn by Leonardo.

MARTIN HARRIS

THE LOIRE VALLEY

The **Maison Enchantée** museum (☎ 02 47 23 24 50), 7 rue du Général Foy, displays more than 300 *automates* (automation dolls). The **Musée de la Poste** (☎ 02 47 56 00 11), 6 rue Joyeuse, housed in the 16th-century Hôtel Joyeuse, has an interesting collection of postal service paraphernalia.

The flower-lined dike protecting Amboise from Loire floods is a fine place for a **riverside promenade**. Some of the best views of the town and its lacy chateau are from the bridge. Explore the **old town** with the tourist office's free English brochure.

To taste the region's wine, cheeses and meat products such as *foie gras* (fattened goose liver) visit the collective **Caveau de Dégustation** (☎ 02 47 57 23 69), opposite 14 rue Victor Hugo.

The 44m-high, seven-storey **Pagode de Chanteloup** is a pleasing 18th-century folly and all that remains of the grand Château de Chanteloup. It has an impressive view from the top, but the 2.5km ride out is along a busy road; go south on rue Bretonneau and follow the signs to 'La Pagode'.

The **swimming pool** is next to the camping ground.

Places to Stay The huge, two-star *Camping de l'Île d'Or* (☎ 02 47 57 23 37), on the Île d'Or (the island in the middle of the Loire, also known as Île Ste Jean), charges 15.60FF for a tent site plus 12.50FF per adult (open April to mid-October). A huge Alexander Calder stabile is out the front.

The *Centre Charles Péguy-Auberge de Jeunesse* (☎ 02 47 57 06 36, fax 02 47 23 15 80) is also on the island. Beds cost 50FF, and breakfast 15FF. Reception opens weekdays from 3 to 9 pm, and 6 to 8 pm on weekends.

An excellent bet is the rambling *La Brèche* (☎ 02 47 57 00 79, fax 02 47 57 65 49, 26 rue Jules Ferry) across the river. Basic singles start at 160FF and a double with bath costs 270FF; in high season, obligatory demi-pension costs 180FF.

The older *Hôtel de France et du Cheval Blanc* (☎ 02 47 57 02 44, fax 02 47 57 69 54, 6–7 quai Général de Gaulle) has large doubles from only 155FF.

The two-star *Hôtel Le Français* (☎ 02 47 57 11 38, fax 02 47 57 71 42, 1 place Chaptal) has comfortable, sound-proofed doubles with shower and toilet from 230FF.

Places to Eat On Friday and Sunday mornings a *food market* is held along the river.

A number of *food shops* line rue Nationale. Near the chateau entrance is a *SAP* grocery *(2 rue Victor Hugo)*, which is closed Sunday, and a *boulangerie (10 rue Victor Hugo)*, closed on Monday outside summer. The *Caveau de Dégustation* (see Things to See & Do) is another place to buy picnic ingredients.

Lots of touristy *fast-food outlets* are along rue Victor Hugo (below the chateau), rue Nationale and quai Général de Gaulle.

The informal *Restaurant de la Poste (☎ 02 47 23 16 16, 5 rue d'Orange)* serves *menus* of traditional French food for 60FF to 169FF (closed Tuesday outside mid-June to September). The food at *La Brèche* (see Places to Stay) is very good; regional *menus* cost from 79FF to 170FF.

Day 5: Amboise to Blois
2–4¼ hours, 43.4km

Sandwiched between impressive chateaux, this route passes the feudal-looking Château de Chaumont before discovering one of the most tranquil stretches of road along the Loire.

It's a busy few kilometres out of Amboise, but traffic decreases by Pocé-sur-Cisse. Between Limeray (8.4km) and Cangey the pretty route is lined with **wineries** offering tasting and sales. A **duck farm** (11.5km) sells foie gras.

After crossing the Loire outside Onzain (20.1km), it's a 500m detour to the steep driveway leading to the **Château de Chaumont** (22.8km; ☎ 02 54 51 26 26), on a bluff overlooking the Loire. This forbidding castle was forced on royal mistress Diane de Poitiers on the death of the king (see Château de Chenonceau; Day 4). Its most famous feature is the luxurious *écuries* (stables). Admission costs 32FF/21FF adults/children; entry to the chateau grounds is free. At the bottom of the driveway, the regional collective may be open for free **wine tasting**.

The wooded road to Candé-sur-Beuvron is busy at times, but once over the Beuvron River turn left immediately to travel through Candé (28.5km) and onto a quiet levee road.

The route leaves the river to weave through the outlying farms and suburbs of Blois. It reaches the water again at a spectacular vantage point of the medieval city

Day 5: Amboise to Blois

Cue		
start		Amboise tourist office
0km	←	go E along Quai G de Gaule
0.1	↑←	'to Nazelles'
0.5	←	over bridge
0.7	←	N152 'to Blois'
0.8	◇↗	D431 'to Pocé-sur-Cisse'
3.5	↗	'to Limeray'
4.0		Pocé-sur-Cisse
	↑←	D1 'to Limeray' (at church)
4.1	←	D1 (no sign)
4.3	↑	D1 (no sign)
8.4	←	D201 'to Cangey' Limeray
	↑←	(40m) D1 'to Cangey'
10.2	↑	D74, Cangey
10.2	↗	(80m) D71 'to Monteaux'

Cue			Continued
11.5	✳	duck farm
14.8	↗	'to Onzain'
15.0	←	Monteaux
15.2	↑	'to Onzain'
17.6		Meuves
20.1	←	'to Chouzy-sur-Cisse', Onzain
22.5	↗	D1F 'to Chaumont-sur-Loire'
20.8	←	'to Chaumont-sur-Loire'
22.8		Chaumont-sur-Loire
	↑←	D751 'to Candé-sur-Beuvron'
	•↝	Château de Chaumont 500m ↺
28.4	←	unsigned road (just after bridge)
28.5		Candé-sur-Beuvron
36.8	↑	D751 'to Challes'
37.0	←	Rue de la Bas Rivière
40.6	←	Rue de la Bas Rivière
40.8	◇↗	unsigned road
40.3	↗	Quai Aristide Briande
42.1		cross Pont Gabriel
42.1	•↝	Blois Area Chateaux 58km ↺
42.4	◇↗	Rue D'Papin 'to Office de Tourisme'
42.6	↑	Escalier Denis Papin
42.6	↗	Rue Gallois
42.5	⇡	follow (walk) route on inset map
43.4		Blois tourist office

THE LOIRE VALLEY

rising steeply up a hill. Unfortunately, the city's scenic attributes make it a bane to cyclists; Blois is a maze of steep, twisting one-way streets. To reach the tourist office it's necessary to negotiate a loop of town, climbing above the old town and dropping back into it. It's far easier on the legs and navigation skills to get off your bike at the traffic lights at the end of rue Porte Coté (42.9km) and follow the instructions on the inset map around place Victor Hugo and up the hill to the tourist office.

Blois

The medieval town of Blois (pronounced 'Blwah') was once the seat of the powerful counts of Blois, from whom France's Capetian kings were descended. From the 15th to the 17th century, the town was a centre of court intrigue, and during the 16th century it was virtually France's second capital. Many dramatic events took place inside the chateau.

The old city was seriously damaged by German attacks in 1940, but retains many charming buildings.

Information The tourist office (☎ 02 54 90 41 41, fax 02 54 90 41 49, e blois.tou rism@wanadoo.fr), 3 ave Dr Jean Laigret, is housed in the early-16th-century Pavillon Anne de Bretagne, a chateau outbuilding. The staff will phone around to find you a hotel room for no charge; reserving a room costs 12FF.

The Banque de France is near the train station at 4 ave Dr Jean Laigret. Several banks face the river along quai de la Saussaye near place de la Résistance. The tourist office also changes money.

The post office is near place Victor Hugo on rue Gallois.

Repairs and bike hire are available at Cycles Leblond (☎ 02 54 74 30 13, fax 02 54 74 6 07), 44 levée des Tuileries, 4km east of town along the river.

Things to See & Do The Château de Blois (☎ 02 54 74 16 06) has a compelling, bloody history and an extraordinary mixture of architectural styles: medieval (13th century); flamboyant Gothic (1498–1503) from the reign of Louis XII; very early Renaissance (1515–24) from the reign of François I; and classical (17th century). The Italianate François I wing includes a magnifi-

cent exterior spiral staircase. On summer evenings the chateau hosts a son et lumière show. The chateau houses an **archaeological museum** and the **Musée des Beaux-Arts**.

For something different, the **Maison de la Magie** (National Centre for the Art of Magic; ☎ 02 54 55 26 26), is across the square from the chateau. It has magic shows, interactive exhibits and displays of objects invented by the magician Jean-Eugène Robert-Houdin (1805–71), who was born in Blois, and after whom the great Houdini named himself.

Around the **old city**, brown signs explain tourist sights (in English).

Several of the most rewarding chateaux in the Loire Valley, including **Chambord** and **Cheverny**, are within 20km of Blois (see the 'Blois Area Chateaux' boxed text).

Places to Stay The two-star *Camping du Lac de Loire* (☎ 02 54 78 82 05, fax 02 54 78 62 03) is about 4km south of town, on route de Chambord in Vineuil. Two people with a tent are charged 49FF (open April to September).

The *Auberge de Jeunesse* (☎/fax 02 54 78 27 21, 18 rue de l'Hôtel Pasquier) is in Les Grouëts, 4.5km south-west of the train station. Dorm beds cost 60FF, and breakfast 19FF; kitchen facilities are available. Call before going there as it's often full.

Near the train station, the staff at the one-star *Hôtel St Jacques* (☎ 02 54 78 04 15, fax 02 54 78 33 05, 7 rue Ducoux) go out of their way to be friendly. Small, ordinary doubles with washbasin and bidet start at 125FF. Across the street, the family-run, two-star *Hôtel Le Savoie* (☎ 02 54 74 32 21, fax 02 54 74 29 58, 6 rue Ducoux) has neat, well-kept singles/doubles with shower, toilet and TV from 230/280FF.

The Vélotel *Anne de Bretagne* (☎ 02 54 43 94 04, fax 02 54 74 37 79, 31 ave Dr Jean Laigret), up from the tourist office, has rooms with shower and toilet for 295/335FF.

Places to Eat In the old city, a *food market* is held in place Louis XII on Tuesday, Thursday and Saturday until 1 pm. The *fromagerie* (cheese shop) and wine shop *Au Duc de Guise* (10 rue Porte Chartraine) keeps long hours (closed Sunday and Monday). Across from the train station on ave Gambetta is the giant, bakery-equipped *Intermarché* supermarket.

THE LOIRE VALLEY

Most restaurants and other eateries in Blois close for Sunday lunch. Several *cafe-rasseries* cluster around place de la Résistance. *La Tocade (☎ 02 54 78 07 78, 23 rue Denis Papin)* serves French food, with mains from 42FF; *menus* cost between 3FF and 135FF (closed Sunday night and on Monday outside June to August).

La Mesa (☎ 02 54 78 70 70, 11 rue Vauvert), a popular Franco-Italian joint with a courtyard, is an excellent place to stock up on carbohydrates. *Menus* cost 75FF and 130FF; vegetarians have a good choice (closed Sunday outside July to September).

Restaurant Le Maïdi (☎ 02 54 74 38 58, 42 rue St Lubin), in the old city, has excellent Moroccan *menus* from 65FF (closed Thursday except in July and August).

Au Rendez-Vous des Pêcheurs (☎ 02 54 74 67 48, 27 rue du Foix) specialises in fresh fish (88FF to 120FF). The *menus* start at 145FF (closed Sunday).

Blois Area Chateaux

Two of the Loire Valley's most stunning chateaux are near Blois: Chambord, to the east, is the region's largest and most spectacular, while Cheverney, to the south east, is the most magnificently furnished. Although it's possible to visit both on a 64km circuit, the tourist crowds make the access roads less-than-pleasant cycling.

The best way to see them may be to join a bus tour. From mid-May through August a bus travels from the Blois train station to the two chateaux, once a day in May and twice daily the other months. The tourist office sells tickets for the tour for 60/50FF adults/children (tour participants receive reduced tariffs on chateau admission fees).

If you're determined to see the chateaux by bike, leave Blois on the D765, turning left on the D33 through Vineuil and following the signs for Chambord. Leave early for the best chance of seeing wildlife in the Domaine de Chambord (13.4km), the 54 sq km hunting preserve that surrounds the vast **Château de Chambord** (16.5km; ☎ 02 54 50 50 02).

King François I began construction in 1519, employing 1800 construction workers and artisans for 15 years on its 440 rooms. It's suggested Leonardo da Vinci may have designed the famous double-helix staircase, in which two staircases wind around the same central axis but never meet. The entrance fee is 40FF/25FF adults/students. It's 45/30FF extra for the Spectacle d'Art Équestre (equestrian show), held once or twice daily between May and September. A *son et lumière* (sound and light show) is held nightly from mid April to mid-October.

From Chambord, take the D112 south through the forest to Bracieux, then turn onto the D102 and follow the signs to the neoclassical **Château de Cheverny** (34.6km; ☎ 02 54 79 96 29). Built between 1625 and 1634, the chateau's sumptuous rooms are outfitted with period furniture, paintings, tapestries, painted ceilings and walls covered with embossed Córdoba leather. Viscount Arnaud de Sigalas, whose family has owned Cheverny since it was built, displays his 80 hunting hounds at feeding time. His macabre trophy room is adorned with the antlers of almost 2000 stags hunted since the 1850s. The entry fee is 34/17FF adults/children.

While it is possible to leave Cheverny via back roads to follow the D77 along the Beuvron River, the roads bear little resemblance to those drawn on maps, and it's easiest to backtrack to Tour-en-Sologne. Turn left onto the D154, dogleg to the right over the D923 to the D117 and, at Huisseau-sur-Cosson, turn left and rejoin the D33 to Blois.

THE LOIRE VALLEY

Champagne

Champagne conjures up the image of endless vineyards producing grapes for the most celebrated drink in the world. One day's cycling through Champagne reveals that the area offers a lot more than vineyards and farmlands. Lakes and forests dot the region: the Montagne de Reims in the north, the Forêt d'Orient, the forests of the Aube to the south, the Ardennes to the north-east, the largest lake in France, Lac du Der Chantecoq, and gently flowing rivers such as the Marne. Three cities stand out: Reims, with its magnificent cathedral; Épernay, famed for its opulent champagne houses; and the medieval city of Troyes.

HISTORY

Champagne, known in Roman times as Campania (literally, 'Land of Plains'), is largely agricultural. Champagne's role in history goes back to 496 when Clovis I, the king of the Franks, was baptised in Reims, which then became the traditional site of French coronations.

In the Middle Ages the area was known for its trade fairs, and cities like Troyes flourished as centres of trade, learning and religion. The region was also known for its textile industry.

In the 18th and 19th centuries, after Dom Pérignon harnessed the bubbles in wine, the grape ruled the economy. However, only a tiny part of the region is devoted to growing champagne grapes. According to the AOC (Appellation d'Origine Contrôlée), only sparkling wine from the Marne and Aube regions can be labelled as champagne (see the 'North vs South' boxed text on the following page).

NATURAL HISTORY

Champagne is made up of two distinct regions. *Champagne crayeuse* refers to the deep, chalky soil – a remnant of an ancient seabed – instrumental to growing and storing champagne. The *Champagne humide,* with its damp soil, is an area of forests and pastures. Here the artificial Lac d'Orient and Lac du Der Chantecoq were created.

The forests of the region are made up primarily of oak with areas of pine, spruce

and fir. What can best be described as oversized bonsais are the dwarf beech trees found in the unique 'Faux de Verzy (see the 'Dwarf-Mutant Beech Trees boxed text later in this chapter). Wildlife such as deer and boar can be spotted in the forests.

The lakes of the area are heaven for bird-watchers. Thousands of birds – including cranes, herons, gulls, swans, eagles, ducks and wild geese – call the lakes home, using them as a stopover during the migratory months of October–November and March–April.

CLIMATE

This area benefits from temperate climates. Summer is pleasant with maximum temperatures generally 20°C to 30°C, although it sometimes rises to the mid-thirties. Rain is heaviest during winter; however, it is not unusual to be caught in a sudden downpour in spring and summer and occasionally in autumn.

Winds are strongest in winter, when the prevailing winds from the north and north-east bring chilly air.

INFORMATION
Maps & Books

Michelin map No 241 *Champagne, Ardennes* (1:200,000) is a good planning and touring map of the area. Covering Champagne and adjacent areas, the Michelin *Green Guide: Alsace, Lorraine, Champagne* provides good historical and sightseeing information.

For information on wine, Oz Clarke's Wine Companion to Champagne and Alsace has an A to Z of wine producers, well-presented touring information and a fold-out map.

The Fédération Française de Cyclotourisme (FFCT) publishes *La France à Vélo: Champagne-Ardenne* (118FF; see Books in the Facts for the Cyclist chapter).

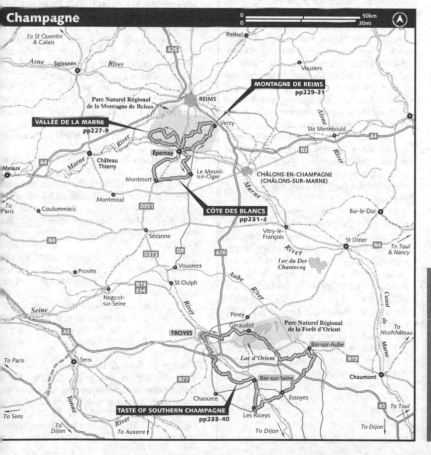

Information Sources

Both the *départements* (departments; administrative divisions) of Marne and Aube have their own tourist information centres: Tourisme de la Marne (☎ 03 26 68 37 52, fax 03 26 68 46 45), 13bis rue Carnot, Châlons-en-Champagne; and Tourisme de l'Aube (☎ 03 25 42 50 00, fax 03 25 42 50 88), 34 quai Dampierre, Troyes.

The Champagne Tourist Route

La Route Touristique du Champagne (The Champagne Tourist Route) is 600km of quiet back roads meandering through the region's most important wine growing areas: the

North vs South

To proudly display the label 'champagne' on a bottle anywhere in the world, the champagne must come from the departments of the Marne and Aube in Champagne. The biggest and most well-known champagne houses, such as Moët & Chandon, Mercier, Mumm, Taittinger and Veuve Cliquot, hail from the north in the Marne department. However, less familiar to many, the southern department of Aube boasts an excellent production.

Today the AOC (Appellation d'Origine Contrôlée) recognises champagne bottled in both the Marne and Aube as champagne, but in the early 20th century harmony did not exist between the north and the south.

In 1909, the Aube growers were excluded from the growing area of the AOC. To make matters worse, they were then not allowed to sell their grapes to their northern neighbours. This resulted in strikes and protests with continued struggle by the Aube growers to regain recognition by the AOC. It took 16 years until they were again allowed to display the prestigious AOC label on their bottles, but by then the northern producers dominated the market.

Past rivalries gone, and far from the elegant mansions of the north, the smaller Aube producers showcase their champagne in family-run cellars. Once again they can sell their grapes to the north and continue to be recognised in the world of champagne.

Montagne de Reims, between Reims an Épernay; the Vallée de la Marne, west c Épernay; the Côte des Blancs, south of Éper nay; and the Côte des Bar in the Aube regio just south of Troyes. Portions of several c the rides in this chapter follow the rout through vineyards, wine villages and forest:

A booklet explaining the route is avail able in tourist offices. In French and Eng lish, it lists most of the champagne house en route, their specialities, hours of opera tion, plus tour and tasting information.

GATEWAY CITIES
Reims

Reims (rhymes with the French pronuncia tion of 'prince') has been an important rel gious, political and artistic centre since th 5th century AD. After Clovis I was baptise here in AD 496, Reims became known a the 'Coronation City'.

As early as the 12th century, Reims pros pered from its cloth industry, later to be ou shone by champagne production, which i still one of the city's main industries.

In WWI more than 80% of the city wa destroyed. It was rebuilt with lots of wid boulevards and parks. On 7 May 1945, Ger many's unconditional surrender was signe here, effectively ending WWII in Europe.

Information The busy tourist office (☎ 0 26 77 45 25, fax 03 26 77 45 27, 🖳 www.tou isme.fr/reims) is across the street from th cathedral at 2 rue Guillaume de Machault. offers money exchange on weekends an public holidays. Several banks are on block north of the tourist office on ru Carnot.

The full-service bicycle shop Cycle Boulanger (☎ 03 26 47 47 59), 5 blvd Lundy is just a few minutes' ride from the train sta tion or the tourist office.

The cyber cafe Clique & Croque (☎ 0 26 86 93 92, 🄴 clique.croque@wanadoo.fr is in a tiny arcade, Passage du Commerce entered at 27 rue de Vesle.

Things to See & Do If time allows onl one stop, visit the magnificent Gothi **Cathédrale Notre Dame**, right across th road from the tourist office. The museur **Palais du Tau** (☎ 03 26 47 81 79), to th right of the cathedral, has tapestries, statue and ritual objects from the cathedral. Th stunning church, **Basilique St Rémi,** and the **Musée St Rémi** (☎ 03 26 85 23 36), housing 16th- to 19th-century weapons, are right next to each other on place St Rémi, about 1.5km south-east of the tourist office.

For champagne buffs, visit some of the Reims **champagne houses,** including Mumm (☎ 03 26 49 59 70), Taittinger (☎ 03 26 85 84 33) and Pommery (☎ 03 26 61 62 56).

Enjoy free **outdoor concerts** from the end of June through August during Les Flâneries Musicales d'Été.

Places to Stay & Eat The *Centre International de Séjour* youth hostel (☎ 03 26 40 52 60, fax 03 26 47 35 70, allée Polonceau), in Parc Léo Lagrange, is about 1km south of the train station across the canal. A dorm bed costs 68FF, and 89FF for a single.

For a selection of hotels look in the pedestrianised place Drouet d'Erlon. The small *Hôtel Monopole* (☎ 03 26 47 10 33, No 28) has doubles with shower from 150FF. The larger and very comfortable *Grand Hôtel du Nord* (☎ 03 26 47 39 03, fax 03 26 40 92 26, No 75) has doubles from 285FF. Off place Drouet d'Erlon is rue Thillois, where the budget *Hôtel Thillois* (☎ 03 26 40 65 65, No 17) has basic singles/doubles with hand basin from 120/140FF (more with shower and toilet). Opposite the train station, and also off place Drouet d'Erlon, is the lovely *Grand Hôtel de l'Univers* (☎ 03 26 88 68 08, fax 03 26 40 95 61, ☻ hotel-univers@ebc.net, 41 blvd Foch) with rooms from 320/360FF.

Markets are held daily in different parts of Reims from 6 am to 1 pm; the tourist office has a list. A *Monoprix* supermarket is at 1 rue Talleyrand. Place Drouet d'Erlon is lined with *restaurants* to suit all tastes and budgets. There is also a fine dining restaurant at the *Grand Hôtel de l'Univers*, plus some *eateries* on rue Thillois.

Getting There & Away Reims has direct trains to/from Paris' Gare de l'Est (140FF, 1½ hours, seven to 10 a day), none of which take bicycles except in a *housse* (bike bag); Épernay (33FF, 20 to 40 minutes, 10 to 15 a day, about six take bicycles); and Dijon (209FF, 3½ hours, three a day).

To reach Verdun – and do the Verdun Battlefields ride in the Alsace & Lorraine chapter – change trains in Châlons-en-

Champagne (141FF, 3½ hours, three a day). Only one midday train to Châlons takes bicycles without a bike bag and you must then wait five hours to connect to Verdun. Another option for getting to Paris' Gare de l'Est is via Meaux (140FF, 2½ to three hours, two a day, both take bicycles).

No trains run between Reims and Troyes but TransChampagne (☎ 03 26 65 17 07) runs two buses daily (109FF, 1½ hours) with a charge of 16FF per bike.

Around Épernay

Épernay lies in the heart of three of the major grape-growing areas of Champagne: the Montagne de Reims, the Vallée de la Marne and the Côte des Blancs. Set in the beautiful Marne River Valley and surrounded by vine-covered hills, it makes a great base for day trips to discover the land from where the grapes stem and sample the final effervescent product.

PLANNING
When to Ride
The best time is April to October; however, the rides can be done all year. Spring sees the vines budding, while the warm summer months are lovely for cycling. In August the grapes become plump on the vines and harvest occurs in September or October.

Maps
Michelin map No 241 *Champagne, Ardennes* (1:200,000) covers the entire region, but the area of the three rides is covered on the smaller Michelin map No 56 *Paris, Reims, Châlons-sur-Marne* (1:200,000).

GETTING TO/FROM THE RIDES
It's a 110km bike ride from Épernay to Troyes, the start of the Taste of Southern Champagne ride detailed later in this chapter.

The Verdun Battlefields ride is accessible by train from Épernay, as is Strasbourg, the start of the Alsatian Wine Route; both rides are in the Alsace & Lorraine chapter.

It's around a 100km ride from Épernay to Compiègne, the start of the Forêt de Compiègne and Île de France Diversity rides in the Paris & the Île de France chapter. However, train connections are easier through Paris.

Train

Direct trains run to/from Paris' Gare de l'Est (106FF, 1½ hours, about eight a day, none take bicycles), Reims (33FF, 20 to 40 minutes, 10 to 15 a day, six or seven take bicycles) and Strasbourg (235FF, four hours, two per day). To get to Verdun, change trains in Châlons-en-Champagne (129FF, three to four hours, three trains a day).

Méthode Champenoise

Champagne is made from using only three varieties of grapes: Chardonnay, Pinot Noir and Pinot Meunier. Each vine is vigorously pruned and trained to produce a small quantity of high quality grapes. To maintain exclusivity (and price), the amount of champagne that can be produced each year is limited to between 160 and 220 million bottles.

The process of making champagne – carried out by innumerable *maisons* (houses), both large and small – is a long one. There are two fermentation processes, the first in casks, and the second after the sugar and yeast is added, and the wine bottled.

During the two months that the bottles are aged in cellars and kept at 12°C, the wine turns effervescent. The sediment that forms in the bottle is removed by *remuage*, a painstakingly slow process in which each bottle – stored horizontally – is rotated slightly every day for weeks until the sludge works its way to the cork. Next comes *dégorgement*; the neck of the bottle is frozen, creating a blob of solidified champagne and sediment, which is then removed.

At this stage, the champagne's sweetness is determined by adding varying amounts of syrup dissolved in old champagne. If the final product is labelled *brut*, it is extra dry. *Extra-sec* means it is dry, but not as dry as brut, *sec* is dry, and *demi-sec* is slightly sweet. The sweetest champagne is labelled *doux*. A blend of red and white wine results in pink champagne, known as *rosé*.

Lastly, the bottles of young champagne are laid in the cellar. Ageing lasts between two and five years (and sometimes longer), depending on the *cuvée* (vintage).

Bicycle

To ride to Troyes on D roads, start on the Côte des Blancs day ride, continuing on the D9 after Le Mesnil-sur-Oger. At Vouarces, take the D51, then the D373 to St Oulph, cross the Seine River on the D178 and join the D20 along the Seine into Troyes.

To reach Reims from Épernay, begin on the day ride Montagne de Reims, then, shortly after Mailly-Champagne, take the busy D9 for about 15km to Reims.

ÉPERNAY

This town *is* 'champagne'; it was here that Moët & Chandon took Dom Pérignon's labour of love and made it into a huge industry. Épernay has the prestigious Avenue de Champagne, which is lined with opulent 19th-century mansions sitting above the 100km of *caves* (cellars) that house millions of bottles of 'bubbly'.

Information

The helpful tourist office (☎ 03 26 53 33 00, fax 03 26 51 95 22, e tourisme@epernay.net), 7 ave de Champagne, is open Monday to Saturday. From Easter to mid-October it opens on Sunday and holidays from 11 am to 4 pm. It sells a booklet of four bicycle rides, *Promenades en Vélo dans le Parc Naturel de la Montagne de Reims* (10FF); a *Topo-Guide VTT* (mountain bike) of the same region with five rides (40FF); and a book of 13 walks (50FF).

The Société Générale is at 4 rue Eugène Mercier and the Banque de France is on place de la République .

The best bike shop in town is Cycles Rémi Royer (03 26 55 29 61, fax 03 26 55 13 57), 10 place Hugues Plomb. They hire VTTs for 110/600FF a day/week.

L'Icone Café (☎ 03 26 55 73 93), 25 rue de l'Hôpital, has Internet access.

Things to See & Do

Touring the **champagne houses** and the endless rabbit warren of **underground cellars** is an experience not to be missed. Not only are the tours interesting and informative, but it is quite incredible to see the intricate network of *caves* filled with endless rows of bottles. The reward at the end is a *dégustation* (tasting).

The tourist office has information on cellar tours. Consider doing the traditional tou at **Moët & Chandon** (☎ 03 26 51 20 20), 18 ave de Champagne, or the slick, high-tech tour at **Mercier** (☎ 03 26 51 22 22), 70 ave de Champagne, where you are transported through the cellars on a laser-guided train. Take a jacket: it never reaches more than about 12°C in the cellars. Épernay also has a couple of interesting **museums** related to the champagne industry.

Places to Stay

The *Camping Municipal* (☎ 03 26 55 32 14, allée de Cumières) is on the banks of the Marne 2km north-west of the city centre. Adults pay 16FF each, plus 19FF for the site (open April to mid-September).

The *Foyer de Jeunes Travailleurs* (☎ 03 26 51 62 51, fax 03 26 54 15 60, 2 rue Pupin) is set up for people aged under 25 and working in town. Travellers can stay, space permitting, for 70FF. Call ahead to reserve. The closest *youth hostel* is in Verzy (☎ 03 26 97 90 10), 24km north-east of Épernay (Verzy is on the Montagne de Reims ride).

About 1km south of the centre is the charming *Hôtel St Pierre* (☎ 03 26 54 40 80, fax 03 26 57 88 68, 1 rue Jeanne d'Arc), in a 20th-century mansion. Singles/doubles start at 118/130FF, or from 153FF with shower and toilet. *Hôtel Le Progrès* (☎ 03 26 55 24 75, fax 03 26 54 32 60, 6 rue des Berceaux) has rooms with shower and toilet from 195FF.

Near the train station on the pleasant place Mendès-France are two good-value hotels offering rooms with shower from 180FF: *Hôtel de la Cloche* (☎ 03 26 55 15 15, fax 03 26 55 64 88, No 5) and *Hôtel Le Chapon Fin* (☎ 03 26 55 40 03, fax 03 26 54 94 17, No 2).

Places to Eat

The *covered market* (cnr rue St Thibault & rue St Gallice) comes alive at Halle St Thibault on Wednesday and Saturday morning. On Sunday morning an *open-air market* is held at place Auban-Moët. The *Marché Plus* supermarket (13 place Hugues Plomb) is open daily and *boulangeries* (bakeries) abound on the streets leading off the square.

For salads, sandwiches, pasta and a 68FF daily *menu* (set meal), try the busy *Le Progrès* (☎ 03 26 55 22 72, 5 place de la République). For excellent Champenois fare, head to *La Cave à Champagne* (☎ 03 2655 50 70, 16 rue Gambetta). This small and very popular restaurant has *menus* from 79FF to 140FF; it is wise to reserve (closed Tuesday in July, and all of August). The *Hôtel Le Chapon Fin* has good *menus* ranging from 72FF to 175FF. The slightly more upmarket restaurant at the *Hôtel de la Cloche* has *menus* from 75FF to 250FF.

All restaurants listed here open for lunch and dinner.

Vallée de la Marne

Duration	2½–4½ hours
Distance	46.3km
Difficulty	easy-moderate
Start/End	Épernay

This is a day of mostly gentle riding and panoramas, with only a few short, steep climbs. The scenery varies from the beautiful Marne River Valley to vineyards clinging to hillsides studded with wine villages. The route visits the villages of Hautvillers, home of Dom Pérignon, and Fleury-la-Rivière, which boasts a huge fresco, and provides many champagne-tasting opportunities.

After leaving Épernay the ride crosses the Canal Latéral à la Marne and enters the Montagne de Reims region. Vineyards line the road to Hautvillers, with markers reading like a who's who of champagne.

Hautvillers (5.6km) was home to the most famous cellar master of all time, Dom Pérignon (see the 'Merci, Dom Pérignon' boxed text later in the chapter). At his **Benedictine Abbey**, the church can be visited. Many doorways in the village bear beautiful wrought iron signs. The **wireless museum** (☎ 03 26 51 96 19) is at 95 rue des Buttes (closed Tuesday). The first steep climb is out of Hautvillers, to a **viewpoint** (6.4km) overlooking Épernay and the Marne River Valley.

Just outside Fleury-la-Rivière (14.6km), the enormous **fresco** on the Coopérative Vinicole wall depicts the region's history and is worth the detour; continue through the village on the D22 in the direction of Châtillon-sur-Marne. On the main route, there is another quick, steep climb out of town.

The 33m-high **statue of Pope Urbain II** dominates the town of Châtillon-sur-Marne,

CHAMPAGNE

CHAMPAGNE

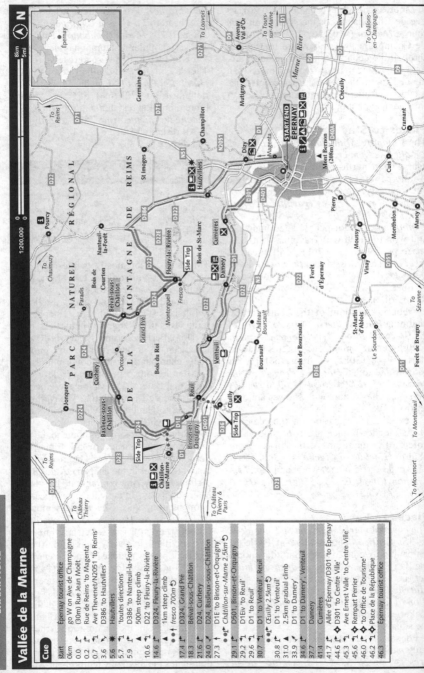

Vallée de la Marne

Cue		
start		Épernay tourist office
0km		go W on Ave de Champagne
0.0	↰	(30m) Rue Jean Moët
0.2	↱	Rue de Reims to Magenta'
0.7	↱	Ave Thevenet/N2051 'to Reims'
3.6		D386 'to Hautvillers'
5.6	✳	Hautvillers
5.7	↰	'toutes directions'
5.9	◂	D386 'to Nanteuil-la-Forêt'
		500m steep climb
10.6	◂	D22 'to Fleury-la-Rivière'
14.6	◂	D324, Fleury-la-Rivière
		1km steep climb
	↰	*fresco* 700m ↻
17.4	◂	D324, Grand Pré
18.3	◂	Belval-sous-Châtillon
21.6	↱	D24, Cuchery
24.0	↰	D24, Basileux-sous-Châtillon
27.3	↱	D1E 'to Binson-et-Orquigny'
	↰	*Châtillon-sur-Marne 2.5km* ↻
29.1	↱	D501, Binson-et-Orquigny
29.2	↱	D1Ev 'to Reuil'
29.6	◂	D1 'to Reuil'
30.7	↱	D1 'to Venteuil', Reuil
	↰	*Œuilly 2.5km* ↻
30.8	↰	D1 'to Venteuil'
31.0	◂	2.5km gradual climb
33.9	↱	D1 to Damery
34.6	↰	D1 'to Damery', Venteuil
37.7		Damery
41.4		Cumières
41.7	◆↱	Allée d'Épernay/D301 'to Épernay
44.6	↱◆	D301 'to Centre Ville'
45.3	◆↱	Ave Ernest Valle 'to Centre Ville'
45.6	◆↱	Rempart Perrier
46.0	◆◆↱	'to Office de Tourisme'
46.2	◆↱	Place de la République
46.3		Épernay tourist office

he destination of another side trip. To continue on the route, look for the small road marked D1E to Binson-et-Orquigny, where the route begins to follow the Marne.

Œuilly (30.7km) is a side trip across the Marne (D601). Its **Maison Champenoise** (☎ 03 26 57 10 30), cour des Maillets, shows the lifestyle of wine growers since the 18th century, complete with early-20th-century schoolroom; admission costs 35FF.

From Venteuil (34.6km) it's downhill all the way to Épernay with fabulous views over the Marne River Valley, Château Boursault and the vineyards.

Merci, Dom Pérignon

The pop of the cork. The clink of champagne flutes. Celebration!

It all began in the 17th century when the monk, Dom Pérignon, cellar master at the Benedictine Abbey of Hautvillers for 47 years, 'perfected' champagne. To speed up the slow process of wine making, he added a little yeast, resulting in bubbles and, unfortunately, exploding bottles. Soon he was to solve his problem. He put his product into strong English bottles better able to take the pressure than locally produced bottles. Then he capped them, thereby sealing in the bubbles with a new kind of bottle stopper – the cork, from Spain – which was forced into the mouth of the bottle under high pressure. Et voilà, Champagne was born! Merci, Dom Pérignon!

Champagne pays homage to Dom Perignon, master champagne maker.

Montagne de Reims

Duration	2½–5 hours
Distance	52.8km
Difficulty	easy-moderate
Start/End	Épernay

This ride reveals the nature of the Parc Naturel Régional de la Montagne de Reims, which covers 50,000 hectares, 68 villages and hamlets and a mix of forests and vineyards. The name Montagne (mountain) evokes images of a summit, but the park's high point, Mt Sinaï, is only 283m, the area being mostly gentle inclines.

The tourist office in Épernay can supply brochures detailing cycle routes (both on- and off-road), walks and events in the park, as can the Maison du Parc (☎ 03 26 59 44 44, fax 03 26 59 41 63) in Pourcy.

Skirting the forest to the north and south, the route passes many Grand Cru vineyards, offering lovely views and tasting opportunities. Other than a steady climb to a unique forest of dwarf beech trees and one short but steep climb, the terrain is undulating.

Just outside Épernay, a bike lane on the D201 leads to Ay, and its small Champenois museum, **Maison du Vin** (☎ 03 26 55 18 90), at 2 rue Roger Sondag. At 6.9km it is a short climb to the **Mutigny viewpoint** to the left.

The pretty town of Avenay Val d'Or has a **church** from the 13th and 16th centuries.

Built for one of Louis XIV's ministers, Louvois' **chateau** is now a private residence. After the hard left turn 400m after the chateau, begin the steady 4km climb through forest to enter the Forêt de Verzy (19.6km).

Continue past the Les Pins parking and picnic area to the entrance, Parking Les Faux (22km), turning right just before the small St Basle's church to reach the **Faux de Verzy**, and its dwarf beech trees (see the boxed text overleaf). Continue 300m after the right turn to the parking area, go through the far gate and continue 800m on the paved road. At the sign 'Zone de Vision de Faux' continue a further 400m until the information board. Walk about 100m to the fenced area of dwarf beech trees. Return to the D34 the same way, passing some dwarf trees that have been fenced off beside the road. For a view of the area, cross the D34 and walk the short trail to the **Mt Sinaï viewpoint**.

CHAMPAGNE

Montagne de Reims

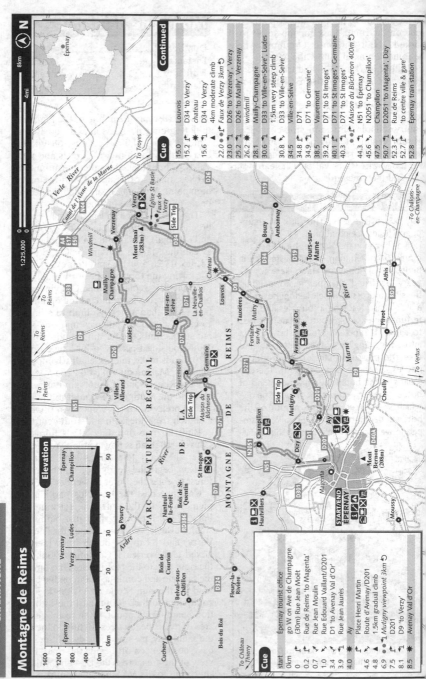

Elevation

1600
1200
800
400
0m

Épernay   Verzy   Verzay   LFudes   Verzenay   Champillon   Épernay

0km   10   20   30   40   50

Cue

start	Épernay tourist office
0km	go W on Ave de Champagne
	(30m) Rue Jean Moët
0	Rue de Reims 'to Magenta'
0.2	Rue Jean Moulin
0.7	Rue Edouard Vaillant/D201
1.0	D1 'to Avenay Val d'Or'
3.4	Rue Jean Jaurés
3.9	
4.0	✳ Ay
4.6	Place Henri Martin
4.8	Route d'Avenay/D201
	1.5km gradual climb
6.9	Mutigny viewpoint 3km ↻
7.5	D201
8.1	D9 'to Verzy'
8.5	✳ Avenay Val d'Or

Cue   Continued

15.0	Louvois
15.2	D34 'to Verzy'
	✳ chateau
15.6	D34 'to Verzy'
	▲ 4km moderate climb
22.0	●●↻ Faux de Verzy 3km ↻
23.0	D26 'to Verzenay', Verzy
25.2	D26 'to Mailly', Verzenay
26.2	✳ windmill
28.1	Mailly-Champagne
30.6	D33 'to Ville-en-Selve', Ludes
	1.5km very steep climb
30.8	D33 'to Ville-en-Selve'
34.5	Ville-en-Selve
34.8	D71
34.9	D71 'to Germaine'
38.5	Vauremont
39.2	D71 'to St Imoges'
40.1	D71 'to St Imoges', Germaine
40.3	D71 'to St Imoges'
	●●↻ Maison du Bûcheron 400m ↻
44.3	N51 'to Epernay'
45.6	N2051 'to Champillon'
47.5	Champillon
50.7	D205I 'to Magenta', Dizy
52.3	Rue de Reims
52.7	'to centre ville & gare'
52.8	Épernay train station

After Verzy (23km), enjoy stunning vineyard views and champagne-tasting opportunities. High atop Verzenay, a regal **windmill** has views towards Reims. The **lighthouse** to the east is to become a wine museum.

A very steep 1.5km climb (13% gradient) begins right in the village of Ludes. The next 10km are forested roads. Pass the tiny hamlet of Vauremont before climbing to Germaine. There is a short side trip to its forestry museum, **Maison du Bûcheron** (☎ 03 26 59 44 44), only open weekends and holidays from May to November.

At 44.3km join the busy N51 for 1km. Carefully change to the left lane for the exit (45.6km) to Champillon. From here it's fantastic vineyard and valley views as you descend 4km towards Épernay.

Côte des Blancs

Duration	3–5½ hours
Distance	57.5km
Difficulty	easy-moderate
Start/End	Épernay

The ride begins in the Côte des Blancs region, which is filled with vineyards overflowing with chardonnay grapes and dotted with appealing wine villages. It loops back to Épernay through shady forests on almost deserted roads, with a stop at the Château de Montmort. For an afternoon treat, a side trip visits a *chocolaterie* for a taste and tour.

The first part of the day sees open vineyards on hillsides and some of the prettiest villages in the vicinity, with only a couple of kilometres between each. The rest of the day is mostly forested, with a few quiet rural towns and easy ups and downs.

The ride leaves Épernay along one of the richest and most prestigious streets in France, the **Avenue de Champagne**, lined with big-name champagne houses.

In Chouilly (4.5km) look for the tiny rue des Charbonniers with a sign for the *Circuit Vignoble* (Wine Circuit) to Cuis. The vineyards are those of the Côte des Blancs, the premier area for growing Chardonnay grapes. The village of Cuis (9.1km), off to the right, has a 12th-century church perched on a hill. This is the first of several picturesque and very proud Côte des Blancs villages.

Dwarf-Mutant Beech Trees

No-one knows why the forests near Verzy are home to about 800 bizarrely malformed beech trees, but their presence has been documented since the 6th century AD. Scientists have determined that the phenomenon is genetic, but that hardly explains why so many of these so-called *faux* are found in the same small area. One thing is certain though: because their gnarled and contorted branches droop towards the ground to form an umbrella-shaped dome, faux struggle to compete for light with their non-mutant companions.

Some of the mutant trees, which grow slowly and live a very long time, can reproduce sexually, but to help nature along and ensure the survival of these botanical curiosities, experts from the University of Reims carry out in-vitro fertilisation of the trees.

Cramant is easily identified by its 8.6m-high **giant champagne bottle**. At 12km stop and turn around for a **view** of Cramant. The small, steep-streeted town of Avize (13.6km) is home to a wine school. At 15.3km, **Oger** is a *Ville Fleuri* (floral town) and home to the **Museum of Wedding Customs and Traditions** (☎ 03 26 57 50 89), at 1 rue d'Avize.

In Le Mesnil-sur-Oger (16.7km), the **Wine and Vineyard Museum** (☎ 03 26 57 50 15), 7 route d'Oger at Launois Père et Fils, also offers vineyards tours, held daily at 10 am and 3 pm. Climb through the village and past the Hôtel de Ville. The road climbs 1.6km and has spectacular views along the way.

It's easy riding through forests, farmlands and villages to Montmort (34.5km), with its impressive 16th-century **Renaissance chateau** (☎ 03 26 59 10 04), dominating the small town. From mid-July to mid-September, there are guided visits at 2.30 and 4.30 pm daily, except Monday. It's a tricky turn to the right to leave Montmort. The Hôtel de la Place is to the left as you descend on the D411.

St-Martin d'Ablois, with its striking **church steeple**, is where the vineyards begin again. Just before Pierry, the **Église de**

CHAMPAGNE

CHAMPAGNE

Côte des Blancs

Cue	
start	Épernay tourist office
0km	go SE on Ave de Champagne/D3
4.5 ↱	Rue des Charbonniers, Chouilly
4.6	C5 'to Cuis'
9.1 ↰	D10 'to Cramant', Cuis
11.2 ↙	D10
11.4	Cramant
13.6	Avize
13.7 ↰	D10
13.8 ↱	D10 to Oger'
15.3	Oger
16.7 ↰	Le Mesnil-sur-Oger
16.8 ↱	D238/Grande Rue 'to Montmort'
17.0	Rue Persault-Maheu
	1.6km moderate climb
21.2	D38, Gionges
24.5	D36/D38, Villers-aux-Bois
34.0	D18 'to Montmort'
34.4	Château de Montmort
34.5 ↰	D18 'to Le Baizil', Montmort
34.5 ↱	(30m) Rue du Fort Rocher/D411
34.5 ↰	(60m) D411 'to Lucy'
35.2	D411
35.5 ↱	D411 'to Lucy'
36.4	Lucy
36.6 ◀	2km gradual climb
40.3 ↰	D411 'to Épernay'
41.8 ↱	(50m) D211 'to Épernay', Le Baizil
48.0 ↱	D11 'to Épernay'
51.2 ↰	D951 'to Épernay'
51.8 ↱	'to Pierry'
52.0 ↰	'to Moussy'
54.4 ● ●	Chocolaterie 1km ↺
56.6 ↱	Rue de Sézanne
56.9 ↰	Rue des Archers
57.1 ↱	Rue Jean Chandon
57.4 ↰	Rue Fleuricourt
57.5 ↱	Place de la République
57.5 ◇	(30m) Épernay tourist office

Chavot (52.5km), dating from the 12th and 16th centuries, is high on the hill to the right.

In Pierry (54.4km) chocolate lovers should immediately turn right, then left onto allée de Maxenu to the **Chocolaterie Thibaut** (☎ 03 26 51 58 04). Open the door and inhale. Your taste buds will surely be tempted by this chocolate factory and shop. Continue the 3km on arterial roads to Épernay.

The South

The Aube department, of which Troyes is the capital, is a major producer of champagne (about 20 million bottles a year). However, historical disagreements that saw it barred from Champagne's Appellation Origine Contrôllée (AOC) region early in the 20th century mean that today it still misses out on the recognition accorded the Marne department and the big maisons around Reims and Épernay (see the 'North vs South' boxed text earlier in this chapter).

The region boasts the huge Forêt d'Orient which, with its three large artificial lakes – Lac d'Orient, Lac du Temple and Lac Amance – offers many outdoor activities.

Taste of Southern Champagne

Duration	3 days
Distance	173.8km
Difficulty	moderate
Start/End	Troyes

Water sports, birdwatching, hiking, champagne tasting and visiting Renoir's studio are some of the varied attractions on this ride. Spectacular vistas of the Côte des Bar area are at every turn, through forests, river valleys, hills and vineyards. Culture buffs can visit some unusual churches and museums.

PLANNING
When to Ride
It is possible to do this ride any time of the year. Summer is best for water sports at the lakes of the Forêt d'Orient; choose autumn if you are interested in the grape harvest and for birdwatchers, October and April offer good weather and sights of migratory birds.

Maps
Michelin map No 241 *Champagne, Ardennes* (1:200,000) covers the entire region, but the ride is covered on the smaller Michelin map No 61 *Paris, Troyes, Chaumont* (1:200,000).

GETTING TO/FROM THE RIDE
A bus connects Troyes with Auxerre, the start of the Classic Burgundy ride in the Burgundy chapter.

Trains connect with Strasbourg for the Alsatian Wine Route, and with the Verdun Battlefields ride (both in the Alsace & Lorraine chapter).

Épernay, the base for three rides detailed earlier in this chapter, is a 110km ride from Troyes.

Bus
TransChampagne (☎ 03 26 65 17 07) runs two buses daily to Troyes (109FF, plus 16FF per bike, 1½ hours). Les Rapides de Bourgogne (☎ 03 25 71 28 42) runs one bus a day to Auxerre, Monday to Thursday only (85FF, 2½ hours, bikes travel free).

Train
Direct trains serve Paris' Gare de l'Est (117FF, two hours, eight a day). Only the 7.28 am train from Paris and the 10.18 pm to Paris take bikes. To reach Verdun, change trains at Chaumont (183FF, three hours, one a day). Trains to Strasbourg (go via Mulhouse (280FF, four to five hours, six a day).

Bicycle
See Getting to/from the Rides in the Around Épernay section for information on cycling to Épernay.

THE RIDE
Troyes
Troyes owes its original glory to the counts of Champagne who, in the 10th century, made it into a prosperous city. From then the wealth continued with trade fairs and industries such as knitwear, which developed in the 16th century. Troyes has been well known as an artistic centre for centuries with a famous school of architecture, studios of sculptors and painters, and workshops creating the stained glass found in the numerous churches.

CHAMPAGNE

In 1524 fire spread through the city. Funds were not a problem and much was rebuilt with the half-timbered houses seen today.

Troyes didn't make its fortunes from the champagne trade alone. Although the city is affectionately known as the *bouchon de Champagne* (champagne cork), the nickname comes from the layout of its medieval core.

Information The main tourist office (☎ 03 25 82 62 70, fax 03 25 73 06 81, 🖳 www.ot-troyes.fr) is a block from the train station, at 16 blvd Carnot. Its annexe (☎ 03 25 73 36 88) is on rue Mignard, opposite Église St Jean. Both offices open Monday to Saturday. The annexe is also open on Sunday and holidays in July and August. The tourist office has *points d'acceuil* (information booths) at five city churches.

Several banks in Troyes offer exchange. Crédit Mutuel and Societé Géne are on place Alexandre Israël. The main post office is at 38 rue Louis Ulbach.

An excellent bike shop, Cycles Jaillant-Venon (☎ 03 25 73 30 87), is at 49 rue Georges Clémenceau; Cycles Bordier (☎ 03 25 73 0156) is at 42 rue Deschainets.

Things to See & Do The medieval city of Troyes is a cultural, architectural and historical feast. From mid-June to late August, the city comes alive with all types of **music** and free **concerts** on weekends.

Walk down tiny **Ruelle des Chats** (Alley of the Cats), which looks just as it did in medieval times, and wander through the city's many streets of well-maintained, 16th-century **half-timbered houses**. Visit one of the nine major churches, such as **Cathédrale St Pierre et St Paul** (place St Pierre), with its exceptional stained glass, and **Église Ste Madeleine** (rue de la Madeleine), which has an intricate 16th-century rood screen.

Troyes has several museums, including the **Musée d'Art Moderne** (☎ 03 25 76 26 80) at place St Pierre (next to the cathedral); **Musée de la Pharmacie** (☎ 03 25 80 98 97) on quai des Comtes de Champagne, with a collection of pharmacy equipment; and the **Musée de la Bonneterie** (Knitwear Museum; ☎ 03 25 42 33 33), covering the history of the industry in Troyes. If you have pannier space and enjoy shopping, Troyes is known for its **factory outlet stores**.

Places to Stay The *Camping Municipal* (☎ 03 25 81 02 64, 7 rue Roger Salengro) is about 3km north-east of the centre in the suburb of Pont Ste Marie. It is open from April to mid-October, charging 30FF for a tent site plus 25FF per adult.

The *Auberge de Jeunesse (☎ 03 25 82 00 65, fax 03 25 72 93 78, e troyes-rosiere.@fuaj.org, 2 rue Jules Ferry)* is about 5km south of the city. A bed costs 48FF per night, and breakfast 19FF.

The *Hôtel Les Comtes de Champagne (☎ 03 25 73 11 70, fax 03 25 73 06 02, 56 rue de la Monnaie)*, in a 12th-century house, is well situated and offers a warm reception. Singles/doubles without shower start at 120FF (180/200FF with shower and toilet). The *Hôtel du Cirque (☎/fax 03 25 76 15 42, 5 rue de Priez)* has plain rooms with shower and toilet for 165/185FF.

The charming *Hôtel Arlequin (☎ 03 25 83 12 70, fax 03 25 83 12 99, 50 rue Turenne)* has rooms from 175/200FF. The newly renovated *Hôtel Le Royal (☎ 03 25 73 19 99, fax 03 25 73 47 85, 22 blvd Carnot)*, run by friendly owners, has rooms with shower and toilet from 335/370FF.

Places to Eat The covered 19th-century market, *Les Halles (cnr rue Général de Gaulle & rue de la République)*, is open Monday to Saturday, but closed from 12.30 to 3 pm.

A small *Casino* supermarket is across from Les Halles; the large *Prisunic* supermarket is at 71 rue Émile Zola. There are several *boulangeries* on the same street. Chocoholics should make fast tracks to *Palais du Chocolat (2 rue de la Monnaie)*

Eateries abound along the pedestrian zone rue Champeaux to place Alexandre Is-raël, including *Grill St Jean* (French), *La Tourelle* (crepes) and *l'Alhambra* (North African). For salads, omelettes and fondue for lunch or dinner, try *Saladerie aux Délices de l'Escargot (☎ 03 25 73 02 27, 90 rue Urbain IV)*. It's closed all day Sunday and Monday evening. Salads start at 40FF and *menus* at 65FF. At No 82 is *Che Camille-La Galtouze (☎ 03 25 73 22 75)* serving French cuisine with *menus* from 65FF. *Restaurant Hôtel Le Royal* has excellent French cuisine with *menus* from 115FF (closed for Saturday lunch and on Sunday evening).

Day 1: Troyes to Bar-sur-Aube
3½–6 hours, 65.9km

Ride through the area known as the Champagne humide – the verdant, forested area of the huge Forêt d'Orient. Cycling is leisurely; for the first half of the day much of it is through gentle forest near the Lac d'Orient. Leaving the forest, it remains relatively flat until a drastic change from forest to vineyard, when the hills become more pronounced. The ride ends with an easy climb before dropping into the Aube valley.

Begin on rue Girardon, beside the Abbaye St Loup (adjacent to Cathédrale St Pierre et St Paul) in the north-east of the city. Leaving Troyes, the first several kilometres are on busy arterial roads and the N19. There are a few tricky intersections and several roundabouts (traffic circles) with multiple exits. Begin early before the traffic becomes heavy. At 8.2km, the route leaves the N19 and the rest of the day is peaceful cycling on idyllic country roads.

At Laubressel (11.2km) the road splits and the route continues straight, though veering right will also lead through the village to rejoin the route at 12.8km. The road is known as the **Route du Balcon du Parc** and has views of the Forêt d'Orient.

The **Parc Naturel Régional de la Forêt d'Orient** covers 70,000 hectares of forests, fields, lakes, rivers and small communities. Géraudot (23.2km) lies on the **Lac d'Orient**, the biggest of the park's three artificial lakes. It has an interesting **church** and makes a good base for spending time in the area, with a *chambre d'hôte* (B&B) and *camping grounds*. Activities include **hiking, cycling, water sports, birdwatching** (there's a side trip to a bird observatory at 27.2km) and **wildlife viewing**. The main park office, the **Maison du Parc** (☎ 03 25 43 81 90, fax 03 25 41 54 09), is in Piney, about 10km off the route. Another Maison du Parc (29.2km) on the route has park information and exhibits.

The chateau in Vendeuvre-sur-Barse was being restored at the time of writing. The pretty village of Les Puits has a **16th-century church** and Longpré-le-Sec has a **church** with sections from the 12th century, where the route turns left.

The route goes through the small Forêt de Bossican, emerging at 54km to an exhilarating 2km descent through vineyards into Meurville, and the first signs for the *Route Touristique du Champagne*. At Le Val Perdu (60.4km), a gentle ascent begins. The day concludes gliding 3km into Bar-sur-Aube.

Side Trip: Nigloland
½–1 hour, 18km

Nigloland (☎ 03 25 27 94 52) is one of the biggest family **amusement parks** in France. It offers attractions and rides in a 'green' setting. The park is best reached on the D46 on the left bank of the Aube River, rather than the busier N19. From Bar-sur-Aube cross the river, turn right after 100m onto the D46 in the direction of Proverville and Dolancourt. In Dolancourt, take the D44 to Nigloland. Adult entry costs 75FF; children under 12 pay 65FF and admission is free for children less than 1m tall.

Bar-sur-Aube

Nestled in a valley surrounded by wooded hillsides, this town is on the right bank of the Aube River. In medieval times, its strategic position at the crossroads of northern and southern Europe made it an important and prosperous trading centre, hosting an annual trade fair. Remnants of this rich past are obvious in the town's architecture and historical sites.

Although there are no champagne producers in the town, the vineyards are not far away. Bar-sur-Aube was instrumental in the Aube wine growers' fight to retain the AOC Champagne rating (see the 'North vs South' boxed text earlier in this chapter).

Information The tourist office (☎ 03 25 27 24 25, fax 03 25 27 40 02) is on place de l'Hôtel de Ville. It is open all year Monday to Saturday, and on Sunday from mid-June to mid-September.

Banque Populaire de Champagne and Banque Nationale de Paris are on place de l'Hôtel de Ville. Banque SNVB is at 87 rue Nationale.

The bike shop Cycles Yves François (☎ 03 25 27 05 68) is at 30 rue Nationale.

Things to See & Do The 12th-century **Église St Pierre** has a covered wooden gallery, probably used as a meeting place for traders during Champagne Fairs. Rue d'Aube has fine examples of **architecture** reminiscent of the prosperous Middle Ages, and for **timbered houses**, visit rue Thiers.

CHAMPAGNE

CHAMPAGNE

Day 1: Troyes to Bar-sur-Aube

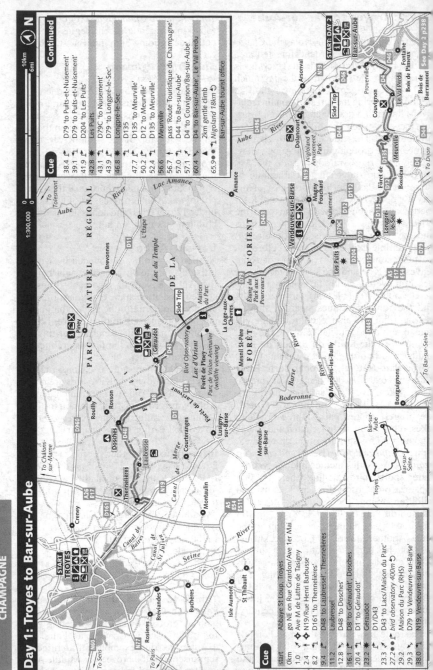

See Day 2 p238

Cue		
start		Abbaye St Loup, Troyes
0km		go NE on Rue Girardon/Ave 1er Mai
1.0	◇↑	Ave M de Lattre de Tasigny
2.4	◇↑	N19/Rue Henri Barbusse
8.2	↱	D161 to Thennelières'
9.4	↰	D48 'to Laubressel, Thennelières'
11.2		Laubressel
12.8	↰	D48 'to Dosches'
16.1	↱	D8 'to Géraudot', Dosches
20.4	↱	D1 'to Géraudot'
23.2		Géraudot
23.3	↰	D1/D43
23.3	↱	D43 'to Lacs/Maison du Parc'
27.2 ●●	↱	bird observatory 400m ⟳
29.2		Maison du Parc (RHS)
29.3	↰	D79 'to Vendeuvre-sur-Barse'
38.0	↱	N19, Vendeuvre-sur-Barse

Cue			Continued
38.4	↰		D79 'Puits-et-Nuisement'
39.1	↱		D79 'Puits-et-Nuisement'
41.9	↰		D204 'to Les Puits'
42.8	✳		Les Puits
43.1	↱		D79C 'to Nuisement'
43.9	↰		D79 'to Longpré-le-Sec'
46.8	✳		Longpré-le-Sec
			D135
47.7	↰		D135 'to Meuville'
50.2	↱		D12 'to Meuville'
52.4	↰		D135 'to Meuville'
56.6			Meuville
			pass 'Route Touristique du Champagne'
56.7	↱		D44 'to Bar-sur-Aube'
57.0	↱		D44 'to Bar-sur-Aube'
57.1	↰		D4 'to Couvignon/Bar-sur-Aube'
60.4	▲		D4 to Bar-sur-Aube', Le Val Perdu
			2km gentle climb
65.9 ●●	↱		Nigoland 18km ⟳
			Bar-sur-Aube tourist office

For those interested in **walks**, the tourist office has a free brochure, *Chemins et Sentiers du Barsuraubois,* with four circuits from the tourist office. North-west of Bar-sur-Aube, in Dolancourt, is the amusement park, **Nigloland** (see Side Trip).

Places to Stay Bar-sur-Aube has only two hotels, so reservations are advised.

The two-star *Camping Municipal La Gravière (☎ 03 25 27 12 94, ave du Parc)* charges 4FF per tent site and 6FF per adult (open April to mid-October).

The tiny but charming seven-roomed *Hôtel St Pierre (☎ 03 25 27 13 58, 5 rue St Pierre)* has singles/doubles without shower for 100/130FF and with shower and toilet from 140/180FF. The plain *Hôtel La Pomme d'Or (☎ 03 25 27 09 93, fax 03 25 27 18 61, 79 Faubourg de Belfort)* has doubles without/with a shower from 120FF/170FF.

Les Combelles (☎ 03 25 27 00 36, fax 03 25 27 78 80) is a *gîte d'étape* (lodging for walkers or cyclists) in Baroville, 7km along the Day 2 route. A dorm bed costs 60FF.

Places to Eat Saturday is *market* day. The *8 à Huit* supermarket is at 91 rue Nationale and the *Casino* supermarket is on place de l'Hôtel de Ville.

Several *eateries* are on rue Nationale. For salads and pizzas from 38FF try *L'Albatross (☎ 03 25 27 14 17, No 136)*, and for kebabs and *schwarma* (souvlaki) from 20FF, head to the *Ankara (No 3)*.

For regional cooking, two restaurants stand out, both with *menus* starting at 99FF: *La Toque Baralbine (☎ 03 25 27 20 34, 18 rue Nationale)* and *Le Cellier aux Moines (Monks' Vaults; ☎ 03 25 27 08 01, rue Général Vouillemont)*, an ambient place with 12th-century vaulted ceilings.

Day 2: Bar-sur-Aube to Bar-sur-Seine

3½–6 hours, 64.5km

Following portions of the *Route Touristique du Champagne*, the ride from Bar-sur-Aube to Bar-sur-Seine is in an area known as the Côte des Bar, blessed with the chalky soil needed for grape growing. But the ride takes in more than vineyards, wine villages and champagne-tasting houses: forests and rolling hills are the order of the day, interspersed with the occasional field of brilliant sunflowers.

Leaving Bar-sur-Aube the road quietly follows the Aube River. Baroville hosts the day's first champagne cellars. Immediately after leaving Baroville, there is a climb with fabulous views over the Aube valley. On the descent to Champignol-lez-Mondeville, it's a short side trip (16.2km) to the 12th-century **Chapelle Romaine** perched on a hill.

It's forested rolling hills and forests until Fontette where there are more champagne producers. From here it's a luxurious descent through vineyards for 4km to Essoyes, in a pretty setting on the Ource River.

Spend a little time in Essoyes (31.8km): Renoir did! In the town are the famous impressionist's studio, **Atelier Pierre-Auguste Renoir** (☎ 03 25 38 56 28), the **cemetery** where he is buried and a walk, **Chemin de Renoir**, to some of the spots where he painted. The **Maison de la Vigne** (Vineyard Museum; ☎ 03 25 29 64 64) is at 9 place de la Mairie.

After Essoyes, entering the Forêt Domaniale d'Essoyes, there is a steady 5km climb. A side trip (41.3km) to Courteron, 2km south on the D971, visits ancient **cadoles** (beehive-shaped shelters made from rocks to harbour workers in hot and cold weather). A pamphlet describing a walk to 12 cadoles, the 8km **Circuit de Cadoles**, is available in Courteron (☎ 03 25 38 20 94). The **Sentier de Crêtes**, a 30km trail passing through Gyé-sur-Seine and Courteron, can be done either on foot or VTT. Brochures are available from Gyé-sur-Seine (☎ 03 25 38 24 60). There are more cadoles around Les Riceys.

Back on the route, head into the attractive village of Gyé-sur-Seine and then wind past its many champagne houses.

The cluster of three small villages known as **Les Riceys** is famous for the unique rosé wine which can be tasted in the cellars or in town. Ride through these appealing villages and visit **Église St Pierre** at Ricey-Bas (51.2km). Leaving Ricey-Bas, the **Musée de Vieux Tacots** (Classic Car Museum; ☎ 03 25 29 31 53) is on the left (52km).

From Ricey-Bas to Bar-sur-Seine the route is fairly flat as it is close to both the Laignes and Seine Rivers. The last few kilometres before Bar-sur-Seine are on the busy N71.

Bar-sur-Seine

Bar-sur-Seine is on the banks of the Seine. As early as the 9th century AD it existed as a fortified town. By the 12th century the

CHAMPAGNE

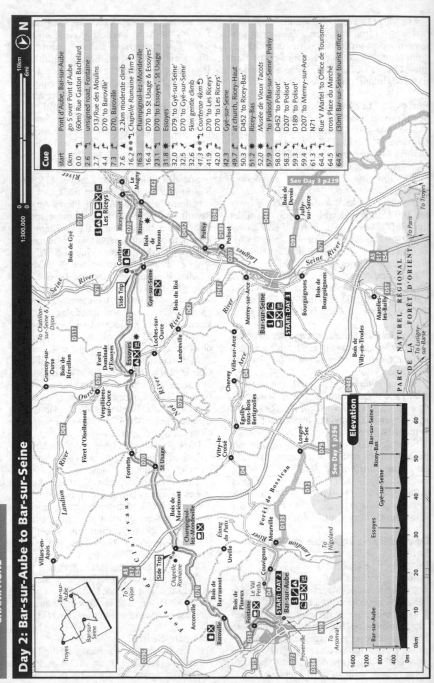

Day 2: Bar-sur-Aube to Bar-sur-Seine

CHAMPAGNE

Cue	
start	Pont d'Aube, Bar-sur-Aube
	go S over Pont d'Aube
0.0	(60m) Rue Gaston Bachelard
	unsigned road, Fontaine
2.6	D13/Rue des Moulins
2.7	D70 'to Baroville'
4.4	D70, Baroville
7.3	2.2km moderate climb
7.6	Chapelle Romaine 1km ↺
16.2	Champignol-lez-Mondeville
16.3	D70 'to St Usage & Essoyes'
16.4	D70 'to Essoyes', St Usage
23.1	Essoyes
31.8	D79 'to Gyé-sur-Seine'
32.0	D70 'to Gyé-sur-Seine'
32.5	5km gentle climb
32.6	Courteron 4km ↺
41.3	D70 'to Les Riceys'
41.9	D70 'to Les Riceys'
42.0	Gyé-sur-Seine
42.3	at church, Ricey-Haut
49.7	D452 'to Ricey-Bas'
50.3	Ricey-Bas
51.2	Musée de Vieux Tacots
52.0	to Polisot/Bar-sur-Seine', Polisy
57.9	D452 'to Polisot'
58.0	D207 'to Polisot'
58.3	D189 'to Polisot'
59.3	D207 'to Merrey-sur-Arce'
59.4	N71
61.3	Rue V Martel 'to Office de Tourisme'
64.4	cross Place du Marché
64.5	(30m) Bar-sur-Seine tourist office

Elevation

See Day 3 p239
See Day 1 p236

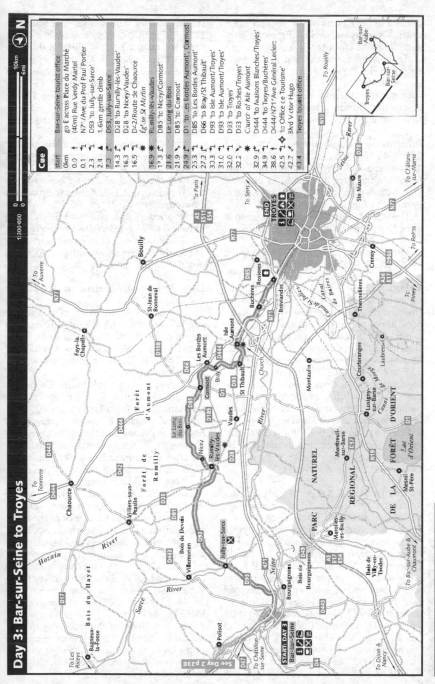

Day 3: Bar-sur-Seine to Troyes

Cue		
start		Bar-sur-Seine tourist office
0km		go E across Place du Marché
0.0	←	(40m) Rue Verdy Martel
0.1	↑	N7' /Ave du Prof Paul Portier
2.3	↑	D93 'to Jully-sur-Sarce'
2.4	⚠	1.6km gentle climb
7.3	↗	D53, 'Jully-sur-Sarce'
14.3	↗	D28 'to Rumilly-les-Vaudes'
16.3	↗	D28 'to Nicey/Vaudes'
16.5	↗	D-2/Route de Chaource
	✸	Eg!'se St Martin
16.9	✸	Rumilly-lès-Vaudes
17.3	↗	D85 'tc Nicey/Cormost'
21.6		Le Long du Bois
21.9	↘	D85 'tc Cormost'
24.9	↗	D1 'to..Eordes Aumont', Cormost
25.3	↗	D85 'to Les Bordes Aumont'
27.2	↗	D66 'to Bray/St Thibault'
30.3	↗	D93 'to Isle Aumont/Troyes'
31.0	↗	D93 'to Isle Aumont/Troyes'
32.0	↑	D33 'to Troyes'
32.2	↗	D33 'to Roches/Troyes'
	✸	Cnurcr of Rle Aumont
32.9	↑	D444 'to Maisons Blanches/Troyes'
34.9	↑	D444 'to Troyes/Buchères'
38.6	↑	D-444/N71 'Ave Général Leclerc'
42.5	✧↗	'to Office ce Tourisme'
42.7		Blvd V:ctor Hugo
‹3.4		Troyes tourist office

chateau of the Counts of Bar sat above the town, but today only ruins of the castle remain; only the clock tower is intact.

An important market town in the area, Bar-sur-Seine derived its wealth from commerce during the 16th and 17th centuries. Unfortunately, the town has seen its share of destruction during several wars and suffered during WWII.

Information The tourist office (☎ 03 25 29 94 43, fax 03 25 29 70 21, ☐ www .champagne-multimedia.com/otsi) at 33 rue Gambetta on place du Marché is open all year Monday to Saturday, and on Sunday morning in July and August.

The Banque Populaire de Champagne is at 86 Grande Rue and Banque Nationale de Paris is at 20 rue de la République.

The best bike shop is Cycles Vezien (☎ 03 25 29 71 52) at 83 Grande Rue.

Things to See & Do The lifeline of Bar-sur-Seine is Grande Rue de La Résistance (more commonly known as Grande Rue). Most shops and restaurants are found here, and a stroll down the street reveals lovely facades of 16th-century **half-timbered houses**. The narrow entrance between Nos 135 and 137 Chemin de la Tour de l'Horloge leads to the **clock tower**. From here there is a great view of the town and the Seine valley. To **walk** along the Seine head to Promenade du Croc Ferrand.

Église St Étienne, built in the 16th century, has some fine features, including interesting stained-glass windows and a mix of Gothic and Renaissance styles.

Places to Stay & Eat Although a thriving town, Bar-sur-Seine lacks accommodation options. It has only three hotels and no camping ground (though this may reopen).

The closest camping ground is in Les Riceys: *Camping Municipal Château St Louis* (☎ 03 25 29 30 32). It costs 13FF per adult and 7FF per site (open mid-May to mid-September). Another *camping ground* is en route, in Essoyes (open April to September). There is also a *Gîte d'Étape* (☎ 03 25 29 30 32) in Parc du Château St Louis in Les Riceys, which charges 50FF per adult.

The most central hotel is *Hôtel Du Commerce* (☎ 03 25 29 86 36, fax 03 25 29 64 87, 30 rue de la République), which has

singles/doubles with shower and toilet for 185/195FF. Just across the Seine, 400m from the town centre, is *Hôtel Barséquanais* (☎ 03 25 29 82 75, fax 03 25 29 70 01, 12 ave du Général Leclerc). All rooms have shower and toilet and begin at 200FF.

A lively *market* takes place on Friday morning at place du Marché. Several *boulangeries* can be found on Grande Rue. An *8 à Huit* supermarket is at No 125.

Several *eateries* can be found on Grande Rue. For crepes, try the intimate *Crêperie l'Amandine* (☎ 03 25 29 99 94, No 111), or *La Crêperie* (☎ 03 25 29 81 39, No 146) in a half-timbered house. Across the road, *La Chaloupe* (☎ 03 25 29 88 57, No 157) serves pizzas, salads and more. Both hotels have restaurants: *Hôtel Du Commerce* has a cosy dining room with *menus* starting at 53FF; *Hôtel Barséquanais* has indoor and outdoor dining and *menus* from 59FF.

Day 3: Bar-sur-Seine to Troyes
2–4 hours, 43.4km
Vineyards change to fields of wheat and sunflowers as the route proceeds and the pleasant forests of Champagne are interspersed with farmland for a good part of the ride. The only incline is within a few kilometres of the start.

The lovely village of Rumilly-lès-Vaudes has two sights dating from the 16th century. **Le Manoir des Tourelles** is a small, storybook castle flanked by turrets. The **Église St Martin** has many interesting features, including the sculpture-surrounded doorway, the altar, the turreted bell tower and, above all, some marvellous **gargoyles**. Open daily, there is an English information sheet inside.

Forests and fields line the roads to Isle Aumont with its extraordinary church (32.2km). Known as the **church of the three sanctuaries**, it is more like a museum, housing sarcophagi, paintings and statues. The church has three distinct styles, the oldest from the 10th century, added to in the 12th century and again in the 15th and 16th centuries. Entry is by appointment only (☎ 03 25 41 82 33, or call one of the numbers listed on the door).

The last 10km of the ride becomes increasingly busy towards Troyes. Be aware of the D444 changing to the N71 at 38.6km. It then continues straight for 4km, changing names several times.

Alsace & Lorraine

hese neighbouring frontier regions in rance's north-eastern corner share a bloody istory of conquest and battle. In this century alone, they have seen some of the worst ghting of both world wars. Worlds apart nguistically, culturally and geographically, Alsace is by far the more scenic, while the attlefields of Verdun are unforgettable.

Alsace

ucked between the Vosges mountains and ne Rhine, Alsace crams a diverse landscape nto a thin wedge, just 190km long and 0km wide. It is made up of only two *départements* (departments; administrative divisions): Bas-Rhin (Lower Rhine), which akes in the area north of Strasbourg, and Haut-Rhin (Upper-Rhine), which covers the outhern parts of the region.

Alsace is one of the most cycle-friendly egions in France. An extensive network of arless bike routes – often using quiet service oads and designated bikepaths – winds its ay through vineyards, orchards, forests and rmland. Half-timbered, Hansel-and-Gretel yle houses, bedecked with colourful geraiums, spill into quaint, cobblestoned streets. o the south, the stark and windswept *ballons* (balloons; smooth, round-topped hills) f the Parc Naturel Régional des Ballons des osges are, quite simply, stunning. The unulating Route des Vins d'Alsace (Alsatian Wine Route) is a great showcase for the, ostly white, wines produced in Alsace Gewürztraminer and Riesling).

Like Lorraine, many parts of Alsace are so highly industrialised, producing textiles, ars and railway engines. Fortunately for irsty cyclists, Alsace also produces more an half the beer in France (see Things to ee & Do under Strasbourg).

HISTORY

ince the Middle Ages, the borders of Alace have been fiercely disputed by kings, ilitary figures and religious leaders. *La Marseillaise*, that rousing call to French ride, was composed in Strasbourg in pril 1792, but the trouble over boundries continued.

In Brief

Highlights
- Verdun's battlefields
- the **Parc Naturel Régional des Ballons des Vosges**
- tasting Alsace's white wines

Terrain
Gently undulating in Alsace, although the Parc Naturel Régional des Ballons des Vosges can be quite hilly; the Verdun battlefields are mainly rolling hills and plains.

FFCT Contacts
- **Ligue Alsace**, 65 rue du Général-Leclerc, 67540 Otswald
- **Ligue Lorraine**, 21A rue Mangin, 57500 St Avold

Cycling Events
- **Le Trois Ballons Randonnée** (late June) starts in Luxeil-les-Bains, Alsace

Special Events
- **Fête de Musique de Strasbourg** (early June to early July)
- **Foire des Vins** (early August) Colmar
- **Grape Harvest Festival** (first Sunday in October) Barr
- **Armistice Day** (11 November) Verdun

Gourmet Specialities
- Alsace's *choucroute alsacienne* (sauerkraut served hot with pork, sausage and ham) or *baeckeoffe* (baker's oven; a stew of several kinds of meats and vegetables)
- at Alsatian bakeries, *flammeküche* (a thin layer pastry topped with cream, onion and bacon) and *kougelhopf* (ribbed, domed almond cake)
- *quiche lorraine* and *dragée* (sugared almonds)
- Alsace's white wines Gewürztraminer and Riesling; Lorraine's brandies and other *eaux de vie* made with mirabelle plums

Ceded to Germany in 1871, following France's humiliating defeat in the Franco-Prussian War, Alsace was then returned to France after Germany's defeat in WWI.

A government-run program to remove all traces of German influence (eg, by banning German-language newspapers) was swiftly quashed following Germany's second annexation of Alsace in 1940, when anyone caught speaking French was imprisoned. The Alsatian language, a dialect of German similar to those spoken in parts of Germany and Switzerland, was also banned.

Following WWII, Alsace was once again returned to France. In 1949, as a symbol of hope for Franco-German cooperation, Strasbourg was chosen as the seat of the Council of Europe, and later as the headquarters of the European Parliament. Alsace remair more German than French in both languag and manner.

The first excursion of the Tour de Franc outside of France was into Alsace in 190: which was then under German rule. Th first mountain climb of the Tour, up th super-steep Ballon d'Alsace, was intre duced the following year. The 215km 'Tro Ballons' randonnée, which takes place i late-June, includes the Ballon d'Alsace, a well as the Petit and Grand Ballons.

NATURAL HISTORY
Movement in the Hercynian period 600 mi lion years ago raised the Massif des Vosge Long eroded by water, wind and glacier the Vosges have smooth rounded top

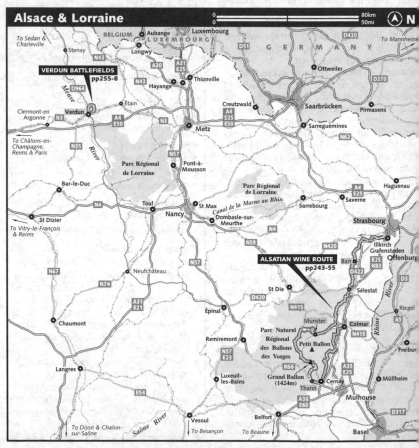

aped like balloons, which peak between 200m and 1424m.

Towering over thick forests of beech and ak, and dotted with lakes and rolling pas- ires, the Parc Naturel Régional des Ballons es Vosges, established in 1989, is home to eer, beavers and a small number of (intro- uced) lynx. Alsace is also home to the ma- estic *cigognes*, or white storks. While the raining of the marshes along the Rhine, as ell as heavy industry and several accidents ith high-tension cables, has seriously de- leted their numbers – in the early 1980s iere were only three pairs left in all of Al- ice – a vigorous reintroduction program as seen the numbers grow in recent years o more than 700 birds.

CLIMATE

efitting this region of contrasts, the tem- eratures in Alsace can vary greatly. Sum- ier temperatures are usually in the upper 0s, while winters are cold enough to keep now on the ground for weeks on end. Pre- ailing winds come from the west and outh-west, carrying rain and snow.

Temperature inversions sometimes drown ie valleys in a sea of cloud, while the luish peaks of the mountains are bathed in right sunlight.

In autumn the vineyards of the Route des ins d'Alsace glow golden as their leaves nange colour. The mountain passes in the arc Naturel Régional des Ballons des osges can be closed by snow until the end f May.

INFORMATION
Information Sources

lsace's Comité Régional du Tourisme ☎ 03 88 25 01 66, fax 03 88 52 28 29, e crt)tourisme.alsace.com, ⌨ www.tourisme-al ice.com/ang) is at Abbaye des Prémontrés, P 97, 54704 Pont-a-Mousson cedex.

The villages along the Route des Vins ' Alsace all have tourist offices, often lo- ited inside the *mairie* (town hall) or the ôtel de Ville. They can provide informa- on on wine tastings, accommodation and estaurants in the region.

As mountain passes can be closed until lay, information on access to the Grand allon and the Col de la Schlucht can be otained from the Maison du Parc (☎ 03 89 3 90 20, fax 03 89 77 90 30) in Munster.

Place Names

While it shouldn't pose any problems for reading city names on maps, bilingual French-Alsatian street signs, menus and the like are common throughout the region, particularly in Strasbourg.

Alsatian Wine Route

Duration	4 days
Distance	233.1km
Difficulty	moderate-hard
Start	Strasbourg
End	Colmar

Ride through a region of great charm and character. Using designated bikepaths for the most part, the ride winds through the heart of the undulating Route des Vins d'Alsace and some of the area's prettiest villages. It then heads for the hills, to the rugged beauty of the Vosges massif, includ- ing the magnificent ridge road the Route des Crêtes and the Grand Ballon. From this spectacular viewpoint the route drops to rejoin the southern end of the wine route.

PLANNING
When to Ride

Autumn and spring are the best seasons to cycle in Alsace; while autumn is cold, the turning colours of the vineyards are spec- tacular. The Massif des Vosges is particu- larly attractive in spring, when snow may still linger on the ballons.

July and August is the traditional holiday period and accommodation in Alsace, par- ticularly along the Route des Vins and in Strasbourg, can be hard to find.

Try to make this a mid-week ride; the D417 from Munster to the Col de la Schlucht and the Route des Crêtes (Day 3) are popu- lar weekend drag strips for xmotorcyclists.

Maps & Books

The Michelin map No 87 *Vosges, Alsace* (1:200,000) gives particularly good cover- age of the ride.

Most of the route on Days 1 and 2 is de- tailed on the *Carte de Parcours Cyclables en Bas-Rhin*. The free map is available in Strasbourg from the Agence de Dévelopment Touristique (☎ 03 88 15 45 80, ⌨ www .tourisme-alsace.com), 9 rue du Dôme.

What to Bring

Thick, full-length gloves and a windbreaker are necessary for the descent from the Grand Ballon, even in high summer.

The Route des Crêtes is a fairly remote stretch, with limited facilities. If planning on camping along the way, buy provisions for *two* days in Munster.

GETTING TO/FROM THE RIDE

Colmar is about 150km north-east of Besançon, the start town for The Jura ride in the French Alps & the Jura chapter.

Strasbourg

Air Strasbourg is served by an international airport (☎ 03 88 64 67 67), 12km southwest of the city centre. Unfortunately it is not yet linked to the *réseau cyclable* (network of bikepaths), although it lies close to the Wine Route.

Train The train station is about 400m west of the Grande Île.

Trains run from Paris' Gare de l'Est (240FF, four hours). Ascertaining which particular service takes bikes requires the patience of a saint. Check with the SNCF for bike-friendly timetables.

Internationally, trains run from Basel (110FF, 1½ hours), Frankfurt (215FF, three hours) and Amsterdam via Brussels (420FF, eight hours).

Colmar

Train Colmar train station is at place de la Gare, 1km from the town centre.

To get to Paris' Gare de l'Est, change trains at Strasbourg (242FF, six hours). Go to Besançon via Mulhouse and Belfort (130FF, three hours).

THE RIDE
Strasbourg

Meaning 'city of the roads' in German, Strasbourg has long served as a meeting point for the roadways and waterways which link the Mediterranean with the Rhineland.

Stylish, sophisticated, modern and 'green', Strasbourg is a vibrant, buzzing place. With its geranium-lined canals and pedestrianised streets, Strasbourg is a great place to explore on foot.

The town is also extremely cycle-friendly. A network of government-funded bikepaths makes getting around easier. Maps of th réseau cyclable are available at the touris office for 15FF.

Information The main tourist office (☎ 0 88 52 28 28, fax 03 88 52 28 29, @ ots @strasbourg.com, 🖳 www.strasbourg.com is at 17 place de la Cathédrale. A branch (☎ 0 88 32 51 49) is outside the train statio (closed Sunday from November to Easter

The Banque de France is at 3 plac Broglie. The CIC Banque CIAL exchang bureau in the train station charges a stee 25FF commission. The post office at th place de la Cathédrale will also chang money.

Log on at the Best Coffee Shop, 10 qu des Pêcheurs.

Veloxygen (☎ 03 88 32 59 48), 2 rue d Marais Vert, can provide topomaps of th region and spare parts.

A laundrette at 29 Grand Rue is ope daily from 8 am to 8 pm.

Things to See & Do Take a **walk** aroun town, particularly the areas around Grand Île and Petite France. Formerly home t fishermen, tanners and millers, **Petite Franc** still evokes a sense of a town within a tow where *winstubs* (traditional Alsatian eate ies) serve frighteningly large beers, an street performers entertain in place Klébe and place de la Cathédrale. The streets of th old city are especially enchanting at night.

The imposing Gothic **Cathédrale Notr Dame**, in the middle of the old city, wa begun in 1176 to replace a cathedral tha had burned down. Rebuilt using red san stone from the Vosges massif, the exterie is as stunning as the inside. Stained-gla windows, a *horloge astronomique* – astre nomical clock dating from 1838 – and viewing platform above the facade mak this much more than just another church tick off the list.

Strasbourg has a great collection of m seums. The **Musée d'Art Moderne et Cor temporain**, place Ste Marguerite, houses a impressive collection of works fro Monet, Manet, Chagall and Klimt. In group of 14th- and 16th-century building at 3 place du Château, the **Musée de l'Œu vre** contains a magnificent collection of R manesque, Gothic and Renaissanc sculpture. The telephone number for bot museums is ☎ 03 88 52 00 00. Check with the tourist office for a full list of museums.

The **Kronenbourg** (☎ 03 88 27 41 59) and **Heineken** (☎ 03 88 19 59 53) breweries offer tours (in French, German and English) of the production facilities and, importantly, tastings.

Places to Stay Finding accommodation in Strasbourg can be a nightmare from Monday to Thursday during the one week each month (except August) when the European Parliament is in session. Check with the tourist office for session times.

The shadeless *Camping de la Montagne Verte* (☎ 03 88 30 25 46, 2 rue Robert Forrer) charges 33FF per person. Next door, the *Auberge de Jeunesse René Casin* (☎ 03 88 30 26 46, fax 03 88 30 35 16, 9 rue de l'Auberge de Jeunesse) charges between 69FF and 149FF, depending on the number of people in the room (hostelling card required). Breakfast is included. Both the hostel and camping ground are accessible along a bikepath from the town centre; take the Day 1 route for 3.1km, then turn right and follow the signs.

The swish, central *CIARUS* hostel (☎ 03 88 15 27 88, fax 03 88 15 27 89, 7 rue Finkmatt) is the best deal in town. Charges range from 90FF in a dorm to 185FF for a single, including breakfast. No hostelling card is necessary but it's best to book ahead.

A (fairly long) stone's throw from the train station, *Hôtel Weber* (☎ 03 88 32 36 47, fax 03 88 32 19 08, e ficelles@wanadoo.fr, 22 blvd de Nancy) has doubles from 140FF (220FF with shower and toilet). On the Grande Île, *Hôtel Patricia* (☎ 03 88 32 14 60, fax 03 88 32 19 08, 1a rue du Pruits) occupies a former convent on a quiet back street. Doubles with shower and toilet cost 220FF. The two-star *Hôtel le Grillon* (☎ 03 88 32 71 88, fax 03 88 32 22 01, 2 rue Thiergarten) has single/doubles from 230/270FF with shower and toilet.

Places to Eat An all-day *food market* takes place each Wednesday and Friday at place Broglie. Other self-catering options include *Le Marché* supermarket (34 rue du 22 Novembre) in the Nouvelles Galleries department store. Near the train station is the *Coop* supermarket (19 rue du Faubourg National). Both close on Sunday.

Strasbourg's large immigrant population is reflected in its restaurants. Cambodian, Laotian and Turkish eateries are plentiful around the Petite France and Grand Île area. For all-Alsatian winstubs try *St Sépulchre* (☎ 03 88 32 39 97, 15 rue des Orfèvres), where dishes start from 75FF each, or *Winstub Le Clou* (☎ 03 88 32 11 67, 3 rue du Chaudron), a cosy place where diners share long tables. *Baeckeoffe* (a stew of several kinds of meats and vegetables; 97FF) and *choucroute* (sauerkraut; 78FF) are accompanied by a huge range of local wines.

Day 1: Strasbourg to Barr
2–4 hours, 47.6km

The route heads out of town along the dead-flat, car-free bikepath, before weaving through the villages and vineyards of the Route des Vin d'Alsace. Getting out of Strasbourg is a little tricky. Head through the streets of central Strasbourg, before crossing the Ill River to join a designated bikepath which travels along quai Kléber to behind the **Musée d'Art Moderne et Contemporain**. The bikepath at the museum is not always clearly marked, but heads across the paved area towards the canal, where it rejoins the bikepath, following signs to 'Montagne Verte/Lingolsheim'.

At rue de la Montagne Verte, the bikepath signs change to 'Lingolsheim/Eckbolsheim', then to 'Eckbolsheim/Molsheim'. Shortly after, the path crosses the Canal de Bruche, becoming the designated bikepath to Molsheim. From here it's almost a 20km, fairly straightforward run past the moated, medieval village of Dachstein and then into the village of Molsheim.

The ride skirts Molsheim's centre (25km). Follow signs into town to see its attractions, which include the 16th-century **Metzig** (town hall) and medieval **Porte des Forgerons** (blacksmith's gate).

Head along another bikepath running parallel with the D422, past an unattractive commercial centre. Here, the bikepath is difficult to follow; after crossing the train lines leading into Dorlisheim, turn left onto the street signposted 'Salle de Vélo Club'. Here (26.3km), pick up the next bikepath, signed to 'Rosheim/Obernai', the fixrst part of which runs through a residential area. It then follows a disused service road for several kilometres through farmland.

ALSACE & LORRAINE

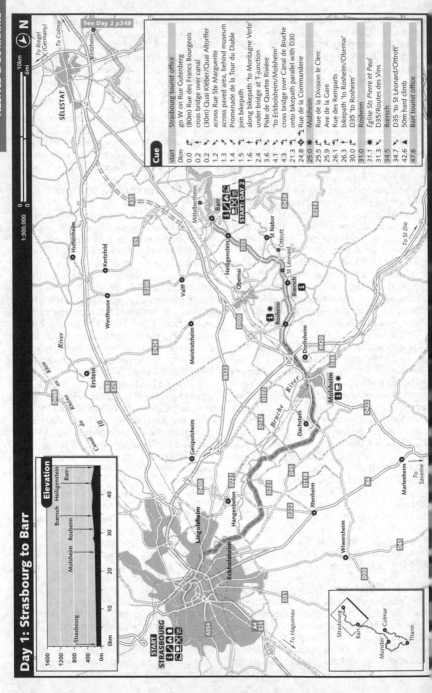

Day 1: Strasbourg to Barr

Elevation

Cue		
0km	start	Strasbourg tourist office
		go W on Rue Gutenberg
0.0		(80m) Rue des Francs Bourgeois
		cross bridge over canal
0.2		(30m) Quai Kléber/Quai Altorffer
0.2		across Rue Ste Marguerite
1.2		across paved area, behind museum
1.3		Promenade de la Tour du Diable
1.4		join bikepath
1.5		along bikepath 'to Montagne Verte'
1.6		under bridge at T-junction
2.4		Piste de Quartre Rivière
3.6		'to Eckbolsheim/Molsheim'
4.1		'to Eckbolsheim/Molsheim',
21.3		cross bridge over Canal de Bruche
4.3		onto bikepath parallel with D30
24.8		Rue de la Commanderie
25.0		Molsheim
25.5		Rue de la Division le Clerc
25.9		Ave de la Gare
26.1		Rue des Remparts
26.3		bikepath 'to Rosheim/Obernai'
30.0		D35 'to Rosheim'
31.0		Rosheim
31.1		Église Sts Pierre et Paul
31.3		D35/Routes des Vins
34.5		Bœrsch
34.7		D35 'to St Léonard/Ottrott'
42.6		50m hard climb
47.6		Barr tourist office

START
STRASBOURG

See Day 2 p249

N
1:300,000

To Riegel (Germany)
To Colmar

Kintzheim
SÉLESTAT

Huttenheim
Kertzfeld
Mittelbertheim
Barr
START: DAY 2

Westhouse
Valff
Heiligenstein
Obernai

Meistratzheim
Rosheim
St Nabor
Ottrott

Geispolsheim
Dorlisheim
St Léonard
Bœrsch

Ernstein

Dachstein
Molsheim

Ittenheim
Wiwersheim

Lingolsheim
Hangenbieten
Eckbolsheim

Marlenheim
To Saverne

STRASBOURG
To Haguenau

To St Die

Bruche River
Canal du Bruche
Ill River
Rhin au Rhône Canal

Strasbourg
Barr
Munster   Colmar
Thann

In Rosheim (31km) is the 12th-century Église Sts Pierre et Paul (Church of Sts Peter and Paul). The four corner ornaments atop the church represent a lion resting his paws on a person's shoulders. Symbolising humanity's enduring battle against the evils of the secular world, the lion is meant to guard the person from temptations of flesh and folly.

From here, follow the D35, the official start of the Route des Vins d'Alsace through the very pretty town of Bœrsch (34.5km) and into a riesling wonderland of vineyards and tiny villages. A short but tough climb leads to the village of Heiligenstein (43km), and a gorgeous, sprawling **view** of the region's many prized vineyards (see the boxed text below). From here, it is a 4km descent into the extremely photogenic town of Barr.

Barr

Originally inhabited by wine growers and tanners, Barr retains much of its traditional Alsatian charm. A hilly town, the upper part is dominated by the Hôtel de Ville, which occupies a spectacular Renaissance mansion. The infinitely 'strollable', pedestrianised lower part of town is home to most of Barr's shops and restaurants.

Barr also sits at the foot of the Kirchberg de Barr vineyard, listed as a winery producing *Grand Crus*, or great vintages, including the famous Gewürztraminer.

Information The helpful, multilingual tourist office (☎ 03 88 58 52 22, fax 03 88 58 52 20) is down the hill from place de l'Hôtel de Ville on rue des Bouchers.

The Société Général on Grand Rue has a currency exchange. Otherwise, the Bank

Alsatian Wines

In the 11th century, vineyards were introduced to Alsace along the left bank of the Rhine River. Protected from wet westerly winds by the Massif des Vosges, the vines here more than benefited from their sunny, south-easterly orientation. By the Middle Ages, the wines had earned a reputation as being among the best and most expensive in Europe, gracing the dinner tables of kings, queens, emperors and princes.

The 14th century was the golden age of Alsatian wine, and saw an expansive export industry flourish. Casks were taken by road to Sélestat, where they were shipped up the Ill River to Strasbourg. From there, they were transported along the Rhine to Switzerland and north into Cologne (Germany) and the Nordic countries.

During this period, abbeys and religious orders had an enormous influence on vineyard cultivation, to the point that the monks were nicknamed 'the fathers of the vine'. The highly-rated, *grand cru*-classified winery of Muenchberg, near Nothalten, is known as the 'Monk's Mountain'.

On the day of 'Wielada', the wine merchant used to come to buy the year's harvest. Excitement and apprehension mounted as he approached, heralded by the village bell. Although this tradition no longer exists, many other festivals and tastings continue along the Route des Vins.

Then came WWI, which ruined the soil and decimated a population. The industry has been steadily rebuilt since, and Alsatian wines are once more regarded as among the best in the country, their bouquets enhanced by their late-ripening in September.

Mainly whites, including Riesling and the exotically named Gewürztraminer, the wines of Alsace, unlike other French wines, are usually named according to the grapes from which they are made rather than their locality.

In 1962, the highly prized Appellation d'Origine Contrôlée (AOC) quality control system was applied to the wines of Alsace. Wineries must fulfil a strict set of criteria to be allowed to produce wines marked as Alsace, Grand Cru (the top quality wine; awarded in 1972) or Crémant d'Alsace (a sparkling wine; awarded in 1976). See 'The ABC of AOC' boxed text in the South-West France chapter for an explanation of this labelling system.

The phrase *vendanges tardives* (late harvest) and *selection de grains nobles* (selected from super-ripe – and therefore sweet – grapes) may complete the label on Alsace or Alsace Grand Cru wines. These designate exceptional wines produced according to some of the strictest of all French AOC standards.

CIAL, place du Pommes de Terre, has an ATM. Cycles Peugeot, 45 Grand Rue, can help with sales and repairs.

Things to See & Do Take a **stroll** through the streets of Barr, visit **Pagan's Wall** (an 11km-long megalithic enclosure) or go on a **guided tour** of the town cellars and tanneries (reserve at the tourist office for these tours). A **wine walking path**, signposted with tasting notes, winds through the vineyards of the Kirchberg de Barr.

Places to Stay In the centre of town, *Camping St Martin* (☎ 03 88 08 00 45) charges 28FF per person (open mid-June to mid-October). *Camping Municipale Ste Odile* (☎ 03 88 08 02 38), in a forest 3km from town, charges 38FF per person (open March to October).

Barr has several *chambres d'hôtes* (B&Bs). *Mme Martine Huber* (☎ 03 88 08 28 30, 11 rue de l'Altenberg) charges 120/150FF for a single/double (communal shower and toilet) and has a garage for bikes. Up the street, *M Gérard Ball* (☎/fax 03 88 08 10 20, 39 rue de l'Altenberg) charges 220FF for a double with shower and toilet.

Domaine Bachert (☎ 03 88 08 95 89, fax 03 88 08 43 06, ☻ nbachert@caramail .com, 35a rue Docteur Sulzer), one of the region's premier vineyards, offers doubles with shower and toilet for 200FF to 290FF. *Dégustations* (tastings) are possible.

Places to Eat A traditional *market* is on Saturday morning at the end of Grand Rue. The *mini-market* is on rue Taufflieb (closed Monday). Carbo-load at *Pizza Enzo* (☎ 03 88 08 04 07, 5 rue Taufflieb), where huge pizzas start at 40FF (takeaway only).

For a fairly extravagant feed, try *S'Barrer Stubber* (☎ 03 88 08 57 44, 5 place de l'Hôtel de Ville). The three-course *menu* (set meal), featuring regional dishes such as *gratin de munster* (creamy potato dish topped with munster cheese) and *jambonneau* (knuckle of ham), starts at 75FF. *À la carte* (off the *menu*) dishes range from 70FF to 200FF.

Day 2: Barr to Munster
3½–6½ hours, 65km

An undulating day with a side trip to the Château Haut-Kœnigsbourg, the route is along bikepaths beside the road for much of the trip. It leaves the wine route to finish in the lush Vallée de Munster, at the foot of the Massif des Vosges.

From the tourist office, head downhill across rue Bannscheid, veering left onto what appears to be a back alley. This is the start of the bikepath to Andlau. Both high on the hill above the path are the **Château de Haut Andlau**, built in 1337, and the **Château de Spesbourg**, built in 1247.

From Andlau, head to the gorgeous, hillside village of Itterswiller (7.3km), in the heart of the Route des Vins. The way is punctuated by a series of information boards detailing, in French and English, wine making processes and the characteristics of some of the region's best drops.

Continue along the bikepath/D35 through the traditional wine-making towns of Nothalten (10.0km) and Blienschwiller, then the fortified, flower-lined village of Dambach-la-Ville, past the impressive **Château Bernstein** (13.7km) on the hill, and into the town of Dieffenthal.

It's quite difficult to find the bikepath in Dieffenthal; look for a street marked by a cross (15.6km). Stay on the path/road, passing through Scherwiller and Châtenois (20.2km). Just before St Hippolyte, the road becomes the D1B and turns right. The **Château du Haut-Kœnigsbourg** (see Side Trip) is a 10km detour from town.

From St Hippolyte, continue along the D1B. After Rorschwihr climb steadily through the vineyards to Bergheim and the extremely touristy – and deservedly so – town of **Ribeauvillé** (35.4km). Dozens of half-timbered houses line cobblestone streets in this typically Alsatian town.

This stretch of the wine route attracts a large number of motorised tourists. Be prepared to dodge sports cars, motorcycles and tour coaches.

The bikepath reappears at the back of Ribeauvillé, where a very steep climb leads into Hunawihr, and the frisky white storks at the Stork Reintroduction Centre (Centre de Réintroduction des Cigognes; ☎ 03 89 73 72 62) at the eastern end of town.

Head through Riquewihr and Kientzheim to reach Sigolsheim (44.2km), where the bikepath disappears again. Cross the N415; the bikepath reappears soon after entering Turckheim.

Day 2: Barr to Munster

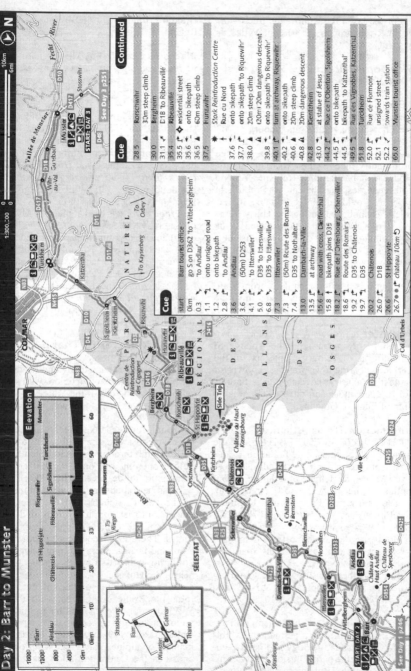

Elevation

Barr · Andlau · Châtenois · St-Hippolyte · Ribeauville · Riquewihr · Sigolsheim · Turckheim · Munster

Cue	
start	Barr tourist office
0km	go S on D362 'to Mittelbergheim'
0.3	'to Andlau'
1.1	onto unsigned road
1.2	onto bikepath
2.8	'to Andlau'
3.6	Andlau
3.6	(50m) D253
4.1	'to Ittersviller'
5.0	D35 to Ittersviller'
6.8	D35 to Ittersviller'
7.3	Ittersviller
7.3	(50m) Route des Romains
7.4	D35 to Nothalten'
13.0	Dambach-la-Ville
13.5	at archway
15.6	road with cross, Dieffenthal
15.8	bikepath joins D35
18.2	Rue de l'Ortenbourg, Scherwiller
18.6	Route des Romains
19.2	D35 to Châtenois
19.7	D35
20.2	Châtenois
26.0	D1B
26.6	St Hippolyte
26.7	château 10km

Continued	
28.5	Rorschwihr
	30m steep climb
30.0	Bergheim
31.1	D1B to Ribeauvillé
35.4	Ribeauvillé
35.5	residential street
35.6	onto bikepath
36.5	60m steep climb
37.5	Hunawihr
	Stork Reintroduction Centre
	Rue cu Nord
37.6	onto bikepath
37.7	onto bikepath to Riquewihr'
38.0	20m steep climb
	120m 20m dangerous descent
39.8	onto bikepath to Riquewihr'
40.2	turn at archway, Riquewihr
	onto bikepath
40.6	20m steep climb
40.8	20m dangerous descent
42.8	Kientzheim
43.0	at statue of Jesus
44.2	Rue ce l'Oberlion, Sigolsheim
44.5	onto bikepath
44.5	bikepath to Katzenthal'
49.5	Rue ces Vignobles, Katzenthal
51.8	Turckheim
52.0	Rue de Flormont
52.1	unsigned street
52.2	towards train station
65.0	Munster tourist office

See Day 1 p246
See Day 3 p251

1:300,000

N

For the last 13km follow the line of the Fecht River through the verdant Vallée de Munster.

Side Trip: Château du Haut-Kœnigsbourg

¾–1 hour, 10km

At St Hippolyte, turn right onto the D1Bi, where a reasonably steep 5km climb leads to the **Château du Haut-Kœnigsbourg** (☎ 03 88 82 50 60, fax 03 88 82 50 61). This impressive landmark sits high on a forested promontory above the Alsatian plains. Home to noble families from the 12th to 15th centuries, the chateau was rebuilt in 1479 to provide defences suitable for artillery. Demolished during the Thirty Years War (1618–48), it was reconstructed at the beginning of the 20th century to house collections of 15th- and 17th-century furniture and weapons.

Opening times change according to season, but it is usually open daily from 9 am to noon and 1 pm to 4 pm, later from June to September. Entry costs 40FF.

Munster

Munster grew up around the Abbaye St Grégoire, a 7th-century monastery. In the 18th century, the town was best known for its textile industry; nowadays, it is famous for its eponymous soft cheese. There is no sign of Eddy or Grandpa.

Information The tourist office (☎ 03 89 77 31 80, fax 03 89 77 07 17) is through the archway of the Maison de Prélat on 1 cour de l'Abbaye. It is closed Sunday, except from May to September and during school holidays, when its hours are 10 am to noon.

The Maison du Parc Naturel Régional des Ballons des Vosges (☎ 03 89 77 90 22, fax 03 89 77 90 30), which shares the same building as the tourist office, dispenses topomaps and can advise of any road closures through the park.

For all other facilities, head to Grand Rue. The Banque Populaire is at No 9, and Richard Stey Cycles is at No 10.

Things to See & Do The **Maison du Parc** (see Information) has a permanent exhibition of the history, geology and natural environment of the park. Outside are the ruins of the ancient Benedictine **Abbaye St Grégoire**, founded in 660 by monks from Ireland.

Places to Stay & Eat The riverside *municipal camping ground* (rue du Gunsbach) charges 25FF per person.

Hôtel des Vosges (☎ 03 89 77 31 41, fax 03 89 77 59 86, 58 Grand Rue) has roomy doubles from 190FF (260FF with shower and toilet). Hall showers cost 10FF. Reception is closed on Sunday afternoon and on Monday except during school holidays. The swish three-star *Hôtel Verte Vallée* (☎ 03 89 77 15 18, rue du Gunsbach) has doubles from 380/440FF low/high season. An extra bed costs 80FF.

A *food market* is held at place de Marché on Saturday. Otherwise, *boulangeries* (bakeries) and a *Coop* supermarket (closed Sunday) line Grand Rue. Towards the Col de la Schlucht, there is a larger *Super U* supermarket, also closed Sunday.

The *menu* at the fabulously authentic *Restaurant à l'Alsacienne* (☎ 03 89 77 4. 49, 1 rue du Dôme) is a delicious bargain at just 69FF.

Day 3: Munster to Thann

4–5½ hours, 65km

The ride changes pace today and heads for the hills. It is a *very* tough 65km, with some serious climbing out of the Vallée de Munster. If it proves to be too much, you can do it over two days.

From Munster, take the D417 out of town. At Stosswihr, the road begins a long steady climb through pine and beech forest before opening out onto the barren and panoramic **Col de la Schlucht** (18km).

It can be something of a circus at the top of the col, particularly on the weekend where motorists, motorcyclists and tour buses spoil the moment by spewing exhaust fumes. There are a couple of *restaurants* atop, and thrill seekers can rent a *luge* for 26FF for a heart-stopping descent from nearby Le Hohneck.

On the other side of the col the route joins the Route des Crêtes, built during WWI to supply French frontline troops. The undulating, well-surfaced road runs past L. **Collet Jardin** (19km), which houses all manner of alpine plants and wildflowers, and then the **Centre Initiation Nature**, an environmental education centre, 1km later

Day 3: Munster to Thann

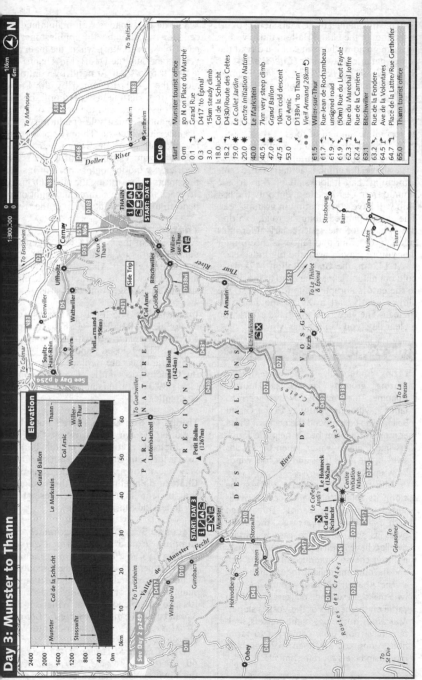

Elevation

Grand Ballon

Col Amic

Le Markstein

Col de la Schlucht

Thann

Willer-sur-Thur

Munster

Stosswihr

See Day 2 p249

Cue

start		Munster tourist office
0km		go N on Place du Marché
0.1		Grand Rue
0.3		D417 'to Épinal'
3.0		15km steady climb
18.0		Col de la Schlucht
18.2		D430/Route des Crêtes
19.0		Le Collet Jardin
20.0		Centre Initiation Nature
40.0		Le Markstein
40.5		7km very steep climb
47.0		Grand Ballon
47.5		10km cold descent
53.0		Col Amic
		D138bi 'to Thann'
		Vieil Armand 28km ↻
61.5		Willer-sur-Thur
61.7		Rue Jean de Rochambeau
61.9		unsigned road
61.9		(50m) Rue du Lieut Fayolle
62.3		Rue du Marechal Joffre
62.4		Rue de la Carrière
63.1		Bitschwiller
63.2		Rue de la Fonderie
64.5		Ave de la Volontares
64.7		Place de la Lattre/Rue Gerthoffer
65.0		Thann tourist office

N

10km
6m

To Belfort

To Mulhouse

Doller River

THANN

START: DAY 4

Cernay

Vieux Thann

Uffholtz

Wattwiller

Wuenheim

Soultz-Haut-Rhin

To Ensisheim

To Colmar

To Turckheim

Vallée de Munster

Wihr-au-Val

Gunsbach

Soultzeren

Hohrodberg

Orbey

To St Dié

D417

D10

D5B

D417

Munster

START: DAY 3

Stosswihr

See Day 4 p254

Col de la Schlucht

Le Collet Jardin

Le Hohneck (1362m)

Centre Initiation Nature

Routes des Crêtes

To Gérardmer

D430

Petit Ballon (1267m)

PARC NATUREL RÉGIONAL DES BALLONS DES VOSGES

Lantenbachell

To Gue-Swiller

Grand Ballon (1424m)

Col Amic

Goldbach

Bitschwiller

Willer-sur-Thur

Side Trip

Vieil Armand (956m)

Thur River

St Amarin

Le Markstein

Krth

Fecht River

Route des Crêtes

To Le Thillot & Épinal

To La Bresse

Strasbourg

Barr

Colmar

Munster

Thann

In the tiny hamlet of Le Markstein (40km) at the foot of the Grand Ballon, those whose legs can go no further can call it a day at the somewhat pricey, two-star *Hôtel Wolf* (☎ 03 89 82 61 80, fax 03 89 38 72 06). Named after the famous 'ballon bagger', Édouard Wolf, the chalet-style hotel has doubles with shower from 225FF, or 325FF for the *demi-pension* (half-board), which includes an incredible amount of food.

If pushing on to Thann, continue along the D431. While the Grand Ballon looms large above, the climb is actually far less intimidating than it looks. It is 7km to the summit from Le Markstein, but only the last 3km will have you grunting in granny gear. The graffiti painted along the road, exalting the exploits of the (particularly German) riders in the Tour de France, is a reminder that you're playing with the big kids.

At 1424m, the **Grand Ballon** (47km) is cold but magnificent. The drop to the plains to the east is abrupt, while to the west, the slopes gently fall away to the Lorraine Plateau. The views are worth the effort – on a clear day, you can see the Alps.

The Vosgian Cow

Lazing contentedly in the wide upland grazing grounds known as Hautes-Chaumes, the Vosgian cow will seem to taunt as you slog your way to the Grand Ballon. The bells around the necks of these enormous, indolent beasts help the farmers find them in winter, when the clouds swirl in, the grass thins and the cold winds blow up from the valleys.

With black patches and a white stripe along its spine, this hardy cow is well-suited to mountain rearing. Threatened with extinction 50 years ago, the breed owes its survival to the care mountain dwellers have given it. The extremely tasty munster cheese is produced from the rich and flavoursome milk of the Vosgian cow.

The Alsatian term *malker* means 'one who milks'. In summer, malkers graze their cattle on the heights of the Vosges slopes. *Marcairies*, rustic overnight malkers shelters, have now been converted to farm-house inns and are open to hikers and mountain bikers for refreshments.

The descent road is well maintained, except for two stretches of cobblestones jus past Col Amic (53km), where the main route veers right onto the D13Bvi to Thann. Take a side trip to **Vieil Armand** by continuing along the D431. Renamed by the French troops from Hartmannswillerkopf, this hill-top fortress witnessed the deaths of 30,000 French and German soldiers during WWI.

Once in Willer-sur-Thur (61.5km), take the bikepath along the Thur River into the back of Thann. Getting out of Willer is a little tricky; wind through a maze of residential streets before hitting the bikepath proper. To reach the Thann centre, turn right onto a pedestrian bridge/walkway over the river.

Thann

At the foot of the Grand Cru Rangen vineyard, Thann is the southern gateway to the Route des Vins d'Alsace. A fairly unremarkable town, its attractions lie in the surrounding Vosges and vineyards.

Information The tourist office (☎ 03 89 37 96 20, fax 03 89 37 04 58) is at 6 place Joffre and may have a map of the bikepath in Haut-Rhin (closed Sunday).

Several banks are in place Joffre and rue du Général de Gaulle. Cycles Kippeler (☎ 03 89 37 52 01) is at 62 rue du Général de Gaulle.

Things to See & Do There's not a lot to see or do in town. Check out the **Collégiale St Thiébaut**, a collegiate church built between the 13th and 16th centuries. On the way out of town, look for the ruins of the **Château d'Engelbourg** and the vestiges of the ancient **Tour des Sorcières et de** (Witches and Storks Tower).

Places to Stay & Eat The extremely basic camping ground *Halte pour Campeur* (☎ 03 89 37 96 20, ave du Blosen) charges 10FF per person. It's small and friendly, but shares showers and toilets with the municipal stadium next door (open July and August). It's also possible to camp at Willer-sur-Thur 3.5km before Thann; *Camping Le Long Pré* (☎ 03 89 82 32 96), on the run into Willer charges 24FF per person.

Gîte d'Étape St Thiébaut (☎ 03 89 37 5 60, fax 03 89 37 94 03, 22 rue Kléber), in the town centre, charges 50FF per person

reakfast 26FF). The two-star *Hôtel de
rance* (☎ *03 89 37 02 93, fax 03 89 37 47
9, 22 rue Général de Gaulle)* has doubles
om 240FF with shower and toilet.

Pick up road snacks at the *Coop super-
arket (place de la Lattre)*, closed Sunday.
he *health food store (6 rue Gerthoffer)* is
other good place for snacks and is open
esday to Saturday.

A collection of *brasseries*, *boulangeries*
d *pizzerias* can be found along rue du
énéral de Gaulle.

ay 4: Thann to Colmar
/2–4 hours, 55.5km

eave behind the Vosges to rejoin the south-
n end of the wine route, mostly travelling
bikepaths, not all of them easy to find.

From place Joffre, cross the Thur River,
cking up the bikepath to Vieux Thann.
estled between the steep vineyards of the
angen and the banks of the Thur, this sec-
on is very pretty.

Staying on the bikepath, head through Cer-
y (6.5km) and Uffholtz. Skirt Wattwiller,
here a long descent followed by a slight
imb (a piece of cake after the ballons) leads
the towns of Wuenheim, Soultz-Haut-Rhin
d then Guebwiller (19.5km) – another
eranium-filled gem of a place.

At Bergholtz, pick up the bikepath again
skirt Orschwihr. Here the route enters the
gion known as the 'noble valley'. Sitting
the shadows of the Grand and the Petit
allon, the region's dry, warm climate and
cture-perfect location has for centuries at-
acted aristocratic and noble families to set-
e. The bikepath is not clearly marked
ound Rouffach (34km), which is home to
any remarkable **Renaissance buildings**.
om here, head into Pfaffenheim (41.5km),
mous for its old **wine makers' houses**,
here you join the D1v, following signs to
ueberschwihr.

A very steep climb leads to Vœgtlin-
ofen, but the route then flattens out for the
n into Husseren-les-Châteaux, where high
the hill sit the vestiges of an old **chateau**.
's a sweeping descent into Eguisheim
9.5km) and then Colmar.

olmar
n the broad plains of the Rhine, Colmar
s prospered through the wine trade.
kened to the set of an operetta, the town

is outrageously picturesque. Full of brightly
coloured buildings in a maze of tiny lanes
and pedestrianised streets, it's is a great
place to kick back at the end of the ride.

For 10 days during the first half of August,
Colmar hosts the Foire Régionale des Vins
d'Alsace (Regional Wine Fair of Alsace).

Information The tourist office (☎ 03 89
20 68 92, fax 03 89 41 34 13, e accueil
@ot-colmar.fr) is at 4 rue des Unterlinden.
Its Sunday hours are 10 am to 2 pm.

The Banque de France is at 46 ave de la
République. The tourist office has a currency exchange service, but the rate is woe-
ful. The main post office, 36 ave de la
République, will also change money.

Cycles Geiswiller (☎ 03 89 41 30 59), 4–6
blvd du Champ de Mars, hires bikes for
100FF per day (closed Sunday and Monday).

Wash those knicks at Point Laverie, 1 rue
Rueset, open daily.

Things to See & Do Colmar is a wan-
derer's paradise, particularly around **rue de
Tanneurs**, which leads into **Little Venice** at
the southern edge of the old city, and the
quai de la Poisonnerie along the Lauch
River.

The **Maison des Têtes**, 19 rue des Têtes,
built in 1609, has a fantastic facade of no less
than 106 grotesque, grimacing stone faces.

Housed in a 13th-century monastery, the
Musée d'Unterlinden (☎ 03 89 20 15 50),
rue des Unterlinden, displays a collection of
predominantly religious art, including the
Rétable d'Issenhelm (Issenheim Altarpiece),
an extraordinary piece of work featuring several interlocking paintings.

Places to Stay & Eat In Horbourg-Wihr,
3km east of Colmar, *Camping de l'Ill* (☎ 03
89 41 15 94, route de Neuf Brisach)* charges
20FF for a site plus 17FF per adult (open
February to November).

The busy *Maison des Jeunes et de la Culture* (☎ *03 89 41 26 87, fax 03 89 23 20 16,
17 rue Camille Schlumberger)* is convenient
to the train station. It charges 50FF for a bed
(no breakfast) in a room of two or more. Call
ahead if arriving on Sunday afternoon.
Slightly further away, the *Auberge de Jeunesse Mittelhart* (☎ *03 89 80 57 39, fax 03 89
80 76 16, 2 rue Pasteur)* charges 70FF per
person. Breakfast is included.

ALSACE & LORRAINE

Day 4: Thann to Colmar

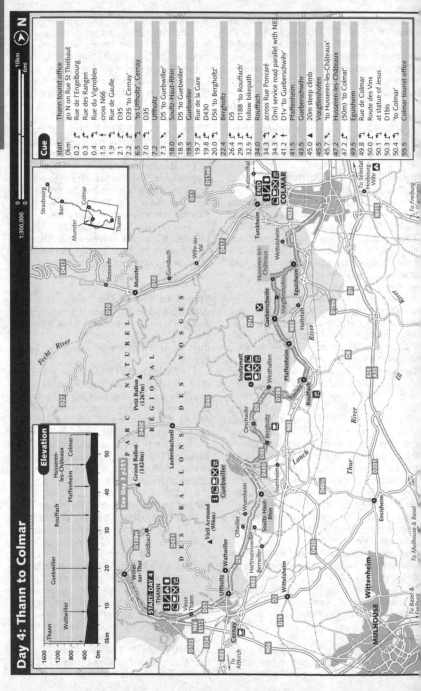

Cue	
start	Thann tourist office
0km	go N on Rue St Thiébaut
0.2	Rue de l'Engelbourg
0.3	Rue des Rangen
0.4	Rue du Vignobles
1.5	cross N66
1.9	Rue de Gaulle
2.1	D35
2.2	D35 'to Cernay'
6.5	'to Uffholtz', Cernay
7.0	D35
7.2	Uffholtz
7.3	D5 'to Guebwiller'
18.0	Soultz-Haut-Rhin
18.5	D5 'to Guebwiller'
19.5	Guebwiller
19.7	Rue de la Gare
19.8	D430
20.0	D5ii 'to Bergholtz'
22.4	Bergholtz
26.4	D5
29.3	D18B 'to Rouffach' follow bikepath
32.5	Rouffach
34.0	across Rue Poncaré (2m) service road parallel with N83
34.3	D1v 'to Gueberschwihr'
41.2	Pfaffenheim
41.5	Gueberschwihr
43.5	20m steep climb
45.0	Voegtlinshofen
45.5	'to Husseren-les-Châteaux'
45.7	Husseren-les-Châteaux
47.2	(50m) 'to Colmar'
49.5	Eguisheim
49.8	Rue de Colmar
50.0	Route des Vins
50.1	at statue of Jesus
50.3	D1bis
50.4	'to Colmar'
55.5	Colmar tourist office

Also near the train station, *Hôtel la* *haumiére* (☎ 03 89 41 08 99, 74 ave de la *‹publique)* has doubles with wash basin d bidet for 180FF. Singles/doubles with ower and toilet cost 220/240FF. Hall owers are free. Reception is closed on nday from 1 to 5 pm.

A *food market (rue des Écoles)* is held on ursday morning. The *Monoprix* super-arket is across the road from Musée Unterlinden (closed Sunday). The *restaur-ts* are on Place de l'Ancienne Douane.

Replace lost calories in *La Maison Rouge* ☎ 03 89 23 53 220, 9 rue des Écoles), where e two-course Alsatian *menu* costs 85FF.

orraine

s a prime steel production centre, Lorraine s gained a reputation as a lifeless indus-al wasteland – the girl-next-door to her autiful and stylish neighbour Alsace. owever, while the region lacks gorgeous untryside, chateaux and vineyards, ancy and Metz are vibrant, energetic cities at are well worth a stopover, while the le through the Verdun battlefields is both structive and unforgettable.

Lorraine is divided into four departments Haute-Marne and Vosges south of Nancy d, to the north, Moselle and Meurthe-oselle (home to the Verdun battlefields).

ISTORY

rraine is mainly famous as the birthplace 'Jeanne d'Arc (1412–31), at Vaucouleurs. n early 'girl power' exponent, Joan of Arc llied the French against the English during e Hundred Years War before being burned the stake for witchcraft and heresy in 31. She was declared a saint in 1920.

Annexed by Germany from 1871 to 913, Lorraine – with Alsace – has served a pawn in several games of nationalist g-of-war. More recently, the region has come synonymous with the horrors of ar. The battles of Verdun between Febru-y 1916 and August 1917 took the lives of ore than 800,000 soldiers on both sides. It not surprising President de Gaulle chose e double-barrelled cross of Lorraine as e emblem of the 'Free French' in WWII.

Notable cyclists from the region include e former champion of France, Henri

Anglade, who was born in Thionville. Metz – where Lance Armstrong rewrote Tour de France history in 1999 by overcoming tes-ticular cancer to win the testing time-trial stage – has hosted several stages of the race since 1907. In Bar-le-Duc, close to Verdun, the *vélocipède* (an early bicycle, also known as a bonshaker) was invented by father and son Pierre and Ernest Michaux in 1861 (see History of Cycling in France in the Facts about France chapter).

NATURAL HISTORY

While most of Lorraine is a mix of agricul-tural plains and great scars of heavy indus-try, the plateaux of the west are dotted with small lakes and plum orchards, the east has wine-growing slopes, and the thickly forested Vosges mountains dominate the topography of the south-west.

Much of the landscape is contorted from the battles of two world wars. In the area around Verdun alone, more than 207,600 hectares of land were churned to a depth of 2m to 3m by 60 million shells, leaving a lunar landscape strewn with unexploded bombs and military hardware, and drinking wells and springs clogged by toxic gases.

CLIMATE

It can be cold and wet in Lorraine when the rest of France is sunny and warm. Storms are common in June and July, so pack heavy-duty wet weather gear. Winters are bitterly cold. Prevailing winds come from the south and south-west.

INFORMATION

The Lorraine Comité Régional du Tourisme (☎ 03 87 37 02 16, fax 03 87 37 02 19, e crt@cr-lorraine.fr) is in Metz, place Gabriel Hocquard.

Verdun Battlefields

Duration	1½–3 hours
Distance	25km
Difficulty	easy
Start/End	Verdun

This ride includes all of the major battle sites and monuments north of Verdun, in-cluding the bomb-ravaged remains of the village of Fleury and the powerful Ossuaire de Douaumont (Douaumont Ossuary; a human burial chamber). If ever you needed confirmation of the sheer senselessness of war, this tour of the battlefields will do it.

PLANNING
When to Ride
June to September are best, although it is also worth braving the cold of autumn to visit the battlefields on Armistice Day (11 November), when a host of memorial celebrations take place in and around Verdun.

Maps & Books
The ride is well signposted from Verdun – follow the signs for the 'Champs de Bataille'. If maps are required, pick up the *Champs de Bataille* map (15FF) from the Verdun tourist office.

The excellent first-hand account of the horrors of Verdun in the 'France' volume of the *Travellers' Tales* series makes a harrowing read.

Memorial Etiquette
Total silence and sober dress are required inside the Ossuaire du Douaumont. Shorts are fine, but don't clatter through in your cleats.

GETTING TO/FROM THE RIDE
Verdun is about 120km from Épernay, the start of several rides in the Champagne chapter. The town is poorly serviced by trains from other cities in the region, except for Strasbourg, the start of the Alsatian Wine Route detailed earlier in this chapter.

Train
The Verdun train station is 700m north-west of the cathedral.

One of the easiest ways to approach Verdun is from the Champagne city of Reims (110FF, change at Châlons-en-Champagne, 1¼ hours, close to Épernay. Infrequent services also go from Paris (180FF, 3¼ hours) and convenient trains run from Strasbourg (170FF, 2½ hours with a change at Metz). Only one train per day to each destination takes bikes not packed in a bike bag. Check with the SNCF for bike-friendly timetables.

THE RIDE
Verdun
The horrific events which took place between February 1916 and August 1917 ensure that

the city of Verdun remains synonymous wi senseless slaughter. It is fitting that the ci has been chosen as a World Centre for Peac Liberty and Human Rights.

Central Verdun straddles the Meu River and its two canals, but the liveli part of town, the Ville Haute (Upper Towr is on the river's western bank.

Information The tourist office (☎ 03 2 86 14 18) is on the east bank of the Riv Meuse at place de la Nation (closed afte noons on Sunday and public holidays).

Money can be changed at the Banque France, 12 quai de la République, or Caisse d'Épargne on rue Mazel, opposite t Victory Monument. The main post office, ave de la Victoire, will also exchange mone

For bike repairs and rentals (100FF p day), Cycles Flavenot (☎ 03 29 86 12 4 is on the Rond Point des États-Unis. laundrette is on ave de la Victoire.

Things to See & Do Given its histor Verdun is a fairly grim place, and it is ea to be overwhelmed by the events of 191

The **Monument à la Victoire**, which to ers over rue Mazel, honours 'the victorio living and dead', particularly those w died in the Battle of Verdun. The **Citade Souterraine** (☎ 03 29 86 62 02), on ave 5e RAP, contains the remains of an und ground command centre where more th 10,000 men were housed while waiting be called to the front. Its facilities includ a bakery, a hospital and a petrol station, serviced by a narrow-gauge rail system. formative, half-hour tours are run; try visit before 10 am, and bring a jump (sweater) – the temperature below is 7°C

If you do nothing else in Verdun, visit t inspirational **Centre Mondial de la Pa** (☎ 03 29 86 55 00), in the Palais Épiscop up the hill next to the cathedral on pla Monseigneur Ginisty. It features a movi exhibition on peace and human rights.

Places to Stay & Eat Follow the sig from the train station to *Camping L Breuils* (☎ 03 29 86 15 31, allée d Breuils), 500m west of the Citadelle Soute raine (open April to mid-October). charges 15FF for a site and 23FF per adu The 69-bed *Auberge de Jeunesse* (☎/fax 29 86 28 88, place Monseigneur Ginist

Magnificent half-timbered houses line the streets in the old city of Troyes.

Street artist in Troyes' place Alexandre Israël.

Visit the Möet & Chandon winery, Épernay.

Get close to the bubbles in Champagne – go wine tasting.

INGRID RODDIS

See traditional Alsatian architecture in Riquewihr.

INGRID RODDIS

Enjoy spectacular views near Col de la Schlucht.

GREG ELMS

Try Alsace's famous white wines...

GREG ELMS

...or indulge in Alsatian beer, said to be the best in France.

INGRID RODDIS

Explore quiet roads among Riquewihr vineyards.

FRANCES LINZEE GORDON

Marvel at Strasbourg's Cathédrale Notre Dame.

up the hill behind the cathedral, charges 70FF for a bunk and breakfast.

Hôtel Verdunois (☎ 03 29 86 17 45, 13 ave Garibaldi), near the train station, has doubles for 160FF (220FF with shower). The upmarket *Hostellerie du Coq Hardi* (☎ 03 29 86 36 36, fax 03 29 86 09 21, 8 ave de la Victoire) has roomy singles/doubles from 350/500FF.

A *food market* (rue Victor Hugo) is held each Friday morning. Other self-catering options include the *Monoprix* supermarket (rue Mazel), which is closed Sunday. Carbo-load at *Pizzeria del Vicolo* (☎ 03 29 86 43 14, 33 rue Gros Degrés), where pizzas start at 35FF. Up the street, *Le Châtel* (☎ 03 29 86 20 14, 34 rue Gros Degrés) serves an inspired Lorraine-style *menu* from 98FF.

Verdun Battlefields

1¼–2½ hours, 25km

Although short and not physically difficult – with only one longish, easy climb at the start – this day can be draining as you struggle to comprehend the lives that were lost and the villages that were literally wiped from the map.

From Verdun, the ride heads north-east, climbing gently through forest to reach the **Monument Maginot** (7.5km), dedicated to André Maginot, the French minister of war (1929–31) who was largely responsible for the Maginot Line on the border with Belgium. Maginot was seriously injured on 9 November 1914, while trying to stop the German advance on Verdun, and the monument commemorates this act of bravery, rather than the blunder of the Maginot Line. The Maginot Line blunder was to build an underground defence network from the Franco-German border to the Swiss border. It was believed to be impenetrable, however, the Germans simply wandered around into France across the unprotected northern frontier in Belgium).

Soon after, the **Monument du Lion** marks the extent of the German advance on Verdun on 23 June 1916.

The **Fort de Vaux** makes a worthwhile side trip. It was here that, on 1 June 1916, German troops entered the fort's tunnel system and attacked the French defenders from inside their own ramparts. After six days of bloody hand-to-hand combat, the French troops, having been reduced to drinking

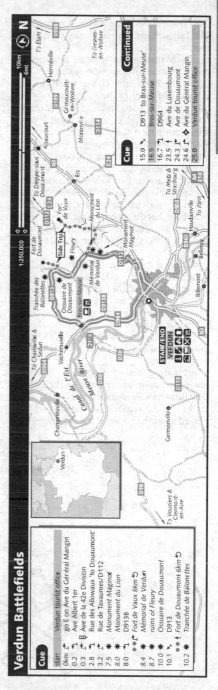

their own urine, were forced to surrender. The fort was recaptured by the French five months later.

The **Mémorial de Verdun** honours the many French soldiers who lost their lives. Less than 500m later sit the remains of the village of **Fleury** (8.7km), *détruite* (wiped off the map) during fighting. The contorted landscape of rubble now covered by soft moss can't hide the fact there were once 3000 peasants, craftspeople, shopkeepers and farmers living in and working the harsh Lorraine landscape. These people were displaced, evacuated or killed in the Battle of Verdun. It is particularly haunting to wander along walking paths bearing the names of streets that disappeared, past the remains of the wash house, the grocer, the town hall and the schoolyard where children once played.

Continue along the D913B to reach the compelling and moving **Ossuaire de Douaumont**. Designed as the ultimate symbol of war and peace – a bomb shell and a cross – the ossuary was built over a 10-year period beginning in 1922. Within the imposing structure, the bodies of 130,000 unidentified soldiers are interned in 46 separate tombs.

A hundred metres after the Ossuary you have the option to continue to the **Fort de Douaumont**. Given its location on the highest hill in the region, the fort should have played a strategic role in the fighting. How-

On the Nature of War

Life is nowhere more intense than at the front: hope, enthusiasm, anger, destruction, sacrifice – everything is condensed within this small interval of time and space.

Mao Teng

ever, in a serious error of judgment, the French high command disregarded warnings of an impending German offensive and when the Battle of Verdun began in 1916, the fort was left with an ineffectual, skeleton crew and captured after only four days of fighting.

Soon after, you'll reach the **Tranchée des Baïonettes** (Trench of the Bayonets) where, as popular mythology has it, the 137th infantry regiment was buried alive during a bombardment from the Germans, leaving only the tips of their bayonets protruding from the earth. Rusted tips poke from the graves of several unknown French soldiers; beneath the dirt lies a son, a brother, a husband, a lover or a father who did not return from the war.

From here, a sweeping descent drops into Bras-sur-Meuse (16.5km). The road here is part of the **Voie Sacrée** – the Sacred Way – a stretch of road which, during the heaviest fighting, saw more than 35,000 vehicles carrying soldiers and material pass over it each week. The very busy D964 returns to Verdun

Burgundy

The gentle rolling terrain of Burgundy makes the region a deservedly popular cycling destination. A patchwork of meadows and vine-covered hillsides, Burgundy is dotted with tiny villages, many of which time seems to have forgotten. Peaceful canals and stunning chateaux, quiet back roads and a rich architectural heritage all add to the indulgent charm of cycling in Burgundy. The good food and freely flowing wine might have something to do with it too. Burgundy makes some of the world's finest red wines and the finest of the finest can be found along the magical Côte d'Or.

Burgundy is not *all* gentle cycling and gastronomic indulgence, however. The vast forests and rocky escarpments of the Parc Régional du Morvan can be quite steep, making for some reasonably strenuous cycling in places.

HISTORY

Burgundy has been settled since ancient times. The Morvan is home to a number of Gaulish settlements dating to the 1st and 2nd centuries BC, and the former capital, Bibracte, is now a major archaeological site.

Formerly the independent Duchy of Burgundy, this historic *pays* (land) was ruled by a succession of dukes with names reflecting their quest for power and prestige: Phillip the Bold (1364–1404), John the Fearless (1404–19), Phillip the Good (1419–67) and Charles the Bold (1467–77).

Throughout the 14th and 15th centuries, Burgundy's prosperity attracted musicians, artists and architects from Holland, Luxembourg and much of what is now Belgium to the capital city, Dijon, where their artistic legacies live on in the city's museums and fine buildings.

Burgundy was returned to the French Crown in 1477, when Louis XI invaded neighbouring Franche-Comté and annexed Burgundy, consolidating it into a unified territory. Nowadays, Burgundy comprises the *départements* (departments; administrative divisions) of Côte d'Or, Nièvre, Saône-et-Loire and Yonne.

In the 18th and 19th centuries, the region served as a vital transport link between the north and south of France.

In Brief

Highlights
- World-Heritage-listed **Vézelay**
- the **Roman** ruins at **Bibracte**
- wine tasting on the **Route des Grands Crus**

Terrain
Mainly rolling hills and pastures, the Parc Régional du Morvan can be surprisingly steep in places.

FFCT Contact
Comité Régional de Bourgogne (☎ 03 85 86 17 34, fax 03 85 86 31 04) Cité de la Croix Vert – Bait 1, No 3, BP 90, 71403 Autun Cedex

Cycling Events
- **FFCT Challenge de Bourgogne** 180km cyclosportive (mid-June)
- **FFCT Les Grands Crus de Bourgogne** 100km cyclosportive (mid-September)

Special Events
- **Pilgrimage** (22 July) Vézelay
- **'Once upon a time in Augustodunum' festival** (August) Autun
- **Wine Auction** (3rd Sunday in November) Beaune

Gourmet Specialities
- *boeuf bourguignon* (beef slow-cooked in red wine with mushrooms, bacon and onions)
- *escargots à la bourguignon* (snails stuffed with garlic, parsley and butter)
- Dijon mustard
- Top-shelf red wines, such as Gevrey-Chambertin, Vougeot and Meursault
- Chablis dry white wines

NATURAL HISTORY

From Auxerre to the north-east, Burgundy is crossed by numerous limestone-walled valleys. Their sunny slopes lend themselves to the cultivation of predominantly white wines in the area around Chablis.

Straddling all four of the region's departments, the Parc Régional du Morvan was established in 1970. Its 137,000-hectare granite massif is thickly forested, hiding a network of rivers and hamlets. The limestone escarpments of the Côte d'Or rise where the Morvan meets the plains.

Burgundy has an abundance of water and waterways. Great canals such as the Canal de Bourgogne snake through the region, while the Yonne and the Seine Rivers both take their source in the Morvan. Several lakes, such as the gorgeous Lac des Settons near St Brisson, dot the countryside.

Like most agricultural regions, most of the animal life in Burgundy ends up on the table. The white Charolais cattle that graze on the many plains are also the succulent stuff of the emblematic regional dish, *boeuf bourguignon.*

The Morvan is comprised of extensive tracts of beech, oak, birch and coniferous forest, though much of it has been logged. Herbs are harvested for medicinal purposes. On the plains, cherry trees and poppy fields are common, while blackcurrants, strawberries and gooseberries can be found between the vines of the Côte d'Or.

CLIMATE

Burgundy's weather is a mixed bag. It does not attract the temperature extremes that the Alps do, with average temperatures hovering around 26°C in August and 6°C in January. Nor does it attract excessive rainfall, except for the Morvan, which can be sub-

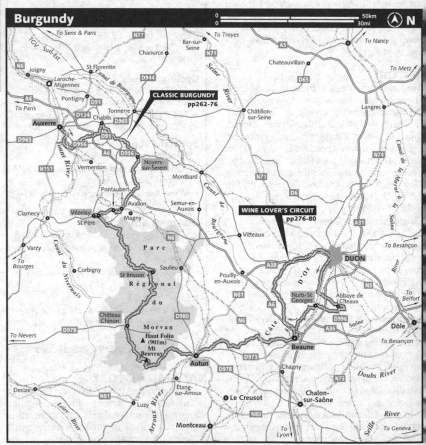

ect to heavy rain and snow. The storms that
o blow in tend to come from the west,
ropping their bundle on the area around
he Côte d'Or, prompting the saying 'it is
l winds and ill folk that come from the
Morvan'. The prevailing winds from the
outh, however, bring warmer, Mediter-
anean winds, necessary for healthy grape
ines.

INFORMATION
Maps & Books
Both rides in this chapter are covered by
Michelin maps No 65 *Montargis, Auxerre,
Dijon*, No 66 *Dijon, Besançon, Mulhouse*
and No 69 *Bourges, Nevers, Mâcon* (all
:200,000).

The Fédération Française de Cyclo-
ourisme (FFCT), through Éditions Franck
Mercier, publishes the regional cycling
uide *La France à Vélo: Bourgogne,
ranche-Comté* in French (118FF; see
Books in the Facts for the Cyclist chapter).

For general reading, pick up *Wonderful
Burgundy,* by Jean-François Bazin, from
ny tourist office or large newsagent in the
egion. The autobiographical *Long Ago in
rance*, by MFK Fisher, describes the slow
hythm of Burgundy life between the two
vorld wars when people simply ate, drank
nd gossiped.

Information Sources
The Comité Régional du Tourisme de Bour-
ogne (☎ 03 80 50 90 00, fax 03 80 30 59
5, ▭ www.burgundy-tourism.com) in
lace Darcy, Dijon, can provide information
n sightseeing, accommodation and wine
asting.

Mountain bikers can pick up a copy of *Le
Morvan en Vélo Tout Terrain*, a packet of
olour-coded map sheets detailing more
han 1400km of waymarked routes. It's
vailable from the tourist office in Dun-les-
laces or from the Parc Régional du Moran Maison du Parc in St Brisson (see Day
of the Classic Burgundy ride).

PLANNING
When to Ride
pring is the most attractive time to cycle in
Burgundy. While summer harvesting leaves
nattractive tracts of bare dirt in autumn,
estivals and celebrations are held year-
ound along the Côte d'Or.

GATEWAY CITIES
Dijon
Occupying a strategic place on the Celtic tin
merchants' route between Britain and the
Alps, the vibrant city of Dijon was at its
height of prosperity during the 14th and
15th centuries under the rule of the Dukes
of Burgundy. With infinitely strollable
streets, elegant buildings and many fine
restaurants, Dijon is the perfect place for
post-ride indulgence.

Information The tourist office (☎ 03 80
44 11 44, fax 03 80 42 18 83, ▭ www.ot-di
jon.fr) is on place Darcy. The Banque de
France is at 2 place de la Banque. The main
post office is at place Grangier.

Dijon has several bike shops. Try Cycles
Theurel (☎ 03 80 30 86 80), 81 rue Berbisey.
Check your email at Station Internet, inside
the train station opposite the bus ticket win-
dow. There are two laundrettes along rue
Berbisey.

Things to See & Do The impressive
Palais des Ducs et Des États de Bourgogne
(Palace of the Dukes and States General of
Burgundy) is the former palace of the Dukes
of Burgundy. The east wing, completed in
1852, also houses the **Musée des Beaux-
Arts** (Museum of Fine Arts; closed Tuesday). Dijon is a museum lover's paradise;
contact the tourist office for a full listing.

For an insight into the city's medieval
and Renaissance past, check out the **hôtels
particuliers** (aristocratic townhouses) along
rue Verrerie and rue des Forges, Dijon's
main street until the 18th century. The
Gothic **Hôtel Chambellan** at 34 rue des
Forges (now a branch of the tourist office)
is particularly impressive.

If you still have the legs for it, Dijon has
several **boîtes** (nightclubs) where you can
get down and boogie. Pick up a copy of
Dijon Nuit et Jour at the tourist office.

Places to Stay & Eat The *Camping du
Lac (☎ 03 80 43 54 72, blvd Chanoine Kir)*
is 1.4km west of the train station behind the
psychiatric hospital. Open from April to
mid-October, it charges 16FF per adult plus
12FF for a tent. The *Centre de Rencontres
Internationales et de Séjour de Dijon
(CRISD; ☎ 03 80 72 95 20, 03 80 70 00 61,
1 blvd Champollion)* is 2.5km north-west of

the centre. A dorm bed costs 75FF, including breakfast (8FF extra for each of the first four nights with no hostelling card). *Hôtel Monge* (☎ *03 80 30 55 41, fax 03 80 30 30 15, 20 rue Monge)* has doubles from 140FF (210FF with shower). Around the corner, the two-star *Hôtel Condorcet* (☎ *03 80 41 25 39, 35 rue Condorcet)* has clean, comfortable singles from 140FF and doubles with shower and television for 250FF.

Le Potimaron (☎ *03 80 43 38 07, 4 ave de l'Ouche)* serves vegetarian meals from 65FF (closed Sunday). *Le Verdi* (☎ *03 80 30 25 88, 24 place Émile Zola)* has excellent pizza and pasta dishes from 48FF. Crack open your piggy bank for the luxurious Burgundian feast on offer at the *Hostellerie du Chapeau Rouge* (☎ *03 80 30 28 10, fax 03 80 30 33 89, 5 rue Michelet)*, where *menus* (set meals) range from 160FF to 400FF.

Getting There & Away Dijon is accessible by plane, train or bus.

Air Dijon-Bourgogne airport (☎ 03 80 67 67 67) is 6km south-east of the city. The airport bus will carry bikes.

Train The Dijon train station is 300m west of the tourist office, on ave Maréchal Foch.

Destinations include Paris' Gare de Lyon (135FF, two hours), Avignon (290FF, four hours), Strasbourg (165FF, 2¾ hours), Auxerre (125FF 2¼ hours) and Nice (372FF, eight hours) and Besançon (77FF, one hour). Check with the SNCF for bike-friendly timetables.

Bus From Britain, the European Bike Express service (see Bus under Continental Europe in the Getting There & Away chapter) charges UK£149 (return) to take a passenger and bike to nearby Beaune.

Les Rapides de Bourgogne (☎ 03 86 94 95 00) runs several bike-friendly services connecting Dijon with Beaune (32FF, one hour, eight a day) and other destinations, including Auxerre (92FF, 1¼ hours). The bus station (☎ 03 80 42 11 00) is on ave Maréchal Foch (next to the train station).

Bicycle If catching the European Bike Express bus to Beaune, follow Day 3 of the Wine Lover's Circuit (detailed later in this chapter) to Dijon.

Classic Burgundy

Duration	7 days
Distance	360km
Difficulty	moderate
Start	Auxerre
End	Dijon

This ride has a bit of everything Burgundian. The route winds across the gentl limestone slopes of the Chablis vineyard and along the valley of the Serein to reac the picturesque medieval village of Noyers sur-Serein. From here, the ride heads t Avallon, where the peaceful Vallée d Cousin opens onto a patchwork of vine yards, pastures and sunflower fields. Th UNESCO World Heritage-listed village c Vézelay, perched high above the Burgund plains, is the highlight and end town of Da 2. The terrain becomes more challenging fo the next couple of days as the route climb through the thick forests of the Morvan t peak at the working archaeological dig ato Mont Beuvray. From here, the ride wind along the prized vineyards of the Côte d'O to finish via the Canal de Bourgogne.

PLANNING
What to Bring
The Parc Régional du Morvan has limite facilities. If camping along this stretch o the ride, provisions for *two* days should b bought in Noyers-sur-Serein or carried fron Auxerre.

GETTING TO/FROM THE RIDE
It is possible to adapt this ride to join wit the Wine Lover's Circuit (detailed later i this chapter), making a nine-day ride. Com plete up to Day 6 of this ride to start/end th Wine Lover's Circuit in Beaune.

Dijon is only about 75km from Be sançon, the start of The Jura ride in th French Alps & the Jura chapter.

Auxerre is connected by train to Troyes the start of another wine ride, Taste o Southern Champagne, in the Champagn chapter.

Auxerre
Bus From Europe, the European Bike Ex press service (see Bus under Continenta Europe in the Getting There & Away chapter

charges UK£154 to take a passenger and bike to Auxerre and pick them up from Dijon.

Les Rapides de Bourgogne (☎ 03 86 94 95 00) run bike-friendly buses from Dijon to Auxerre (92FF, 1¼ hours). The bus arrives at the Gare Routière in Auxerre, rue des Migraines.

Train The Auxerre–St Gervais train station, on the right bank of the Yonne on rue Paul Doumer, has 10 to 14 daily connections to Laroche-Migennes (20 minutes), where you will need to change if coming from Paris' Gare de Lyon (135FF, two hours). A direct train runs from Dijon (125FF 2¼ hours). Check with the SNCF for bike-friendly timetables.

Dijon
See the Gateway Cities section (p262) for information on getting from Dijon.

THE RIDE
Auxerre
Overlooking the Yonne, the hilly Auxerre once served as an important trade link on the great Roman highway between Lyon and Boulogne. Nowadays the town is a good base for cruising the waterways of Burgundy. An attractive town, Auxerre is graced by belfries, spires and half-timbered houses.

Most facilities are on the left bank of the Yonne, around the pedestrianised rue de l'Horloge and place Charles Surugue.

Information The bend-over-backwards helpful tourist office (☎ 03 86 52 09 19, ☎ 03 86 51 23 27, 🖳 www.ipoint.fr/auxerre) is at 1–2 quai de la République (closed Sunday afternoon, except from June to September). The Banque de France is at 1 rue de la Banque. The tourist office will also change money on Sunday and holidays. The post office and pharmacy are both on place Charles Surugue.

Run by the 1995 World Mountain Bike (VTT) Champion, Serge Oskwarek, Cycles Oskwarek (☎ 03 86 52 71 19) is at 22 rue de Preuilly and rents bikes for 100/150/300FF a day/weekend/week.

If you are desperate to use the Internet, L'Étaing Snack Bar (☎ 03 86 72 96 60) on allée de la Bahai, near Lycée Fournier, is a bit of a hike from the town centre. A laundrette is on ave Jean Jaurès, near the train station.

Things to See & Do There are great views of the city from **Pont Paul Bert**. The central, spire-topped **Tour de l'Horloge** (clock tower), first built in 1483, keeps track of the hours in a day as well as the days in the lunar month. The somewhat lopsided Gothic **Cathédrale St Étienne**, constructed between the 13th and 16th centuries on the site of a 5th-century religious sanctuary, has only one northern bell tower instead of two. The unusual frescoes in the crypt date from the 11th century.

Watch the top-class **football** and **rugby** teams train and play across the road from the camping ground.

Places to Stay Wake up to the birds at the *Camping Municipale (☎ 03 86 52 11 15, 8 route de Vaux)*. Open from April to September, it charges 28FF per adult. The *Foyeur des Jeunes Travailleurs (☎ 03 86 46 95 11, 16 ave de la Résistance)* is behind the train station. For women only, the *Foyeur des Jeune Travailleuses (☎ 03 86 52 45 38, 16 blvd Vaulabelle)* is a little less central. Both hostels charge 80FF for a single room, including breakfast. *Hôtel Morin (☎ 03 86 46 90 26, fax 03 86 46 73 57, 4 ave Gambetta)*, by the river, has singles/doubles with shower and toilet for 160/240FF. The quaint *Hôtel Le Seignelay (☎ 03 86 52 03 48, fax 03 86 52 32 39, 2 rue du Pont)* has 280/320FF doubles/triples with shower. A few rooms with washbasin cost 170FF.

Places to Eat A *food market* takes place on Tuesday, Friday and Saturday mornings at place de la Arquehuse. There is a *Monoprix* supermarket at place Charles Surugue. The *Atac* supermarket on rue de Preuilly is closer to the camping ground (closed Monday). *La Vie en Rose (☎ 03 86 46 90 26, 4 ave Gambetta)* serves pizzas from 39FF. Splash out at the restaurant in the *Hôtel de Seignelay*. The 98FF *menu* features delicious, authentic local cuisine (open 7 to 9 pm).

Day 1: Auxerre to Noyers-sur-Serein
3½–4½ hours, 57km
The route follows the line of the Yonne River before winding across rolling countryside, dotted with vineyards and medieval villages, to finish at the walled town of Noyers-sur-Serein. From the tourist office

BURGUNDY

Day 1: Auxerre to Noyers-sur-Serein

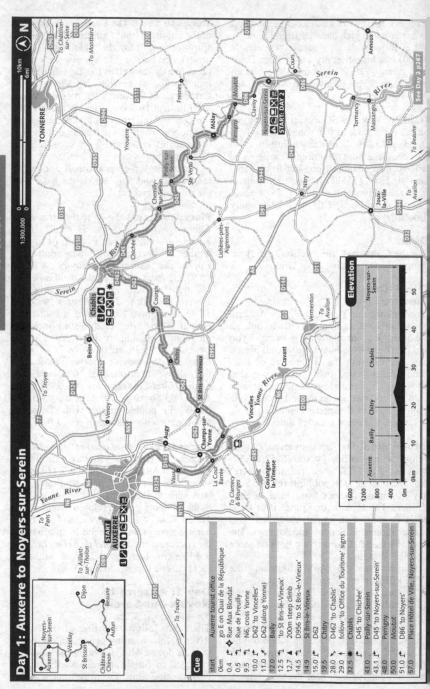

Elevation

Cue		
start		Auxerre tourist office
0km		go E on Quai de la République
0.4		Rue Max Blondat
0.5		Rue de Preuilly
9.5		N6, cross Yonne
10.0		D62 'to Vincelles'
11.0		D62 (along Yonne)
12.0		Bailly
12.5		'to St Bris-le-Vineux'
12.7		200m steep climb
14.5		D956 'to St Bris-le-Vineux'
14.9		St Bris-le-Vineux
15.0		D62
19.5		Chitry
28.0		D462 'to Chablis'
29.0		follow 'to Office du Tourisme' signs
32.5		Chablis
43.0		D45 'to Chichée'
43.1		Poilly-sur-Serein
48.0		D45 'to Noyers-sur-Serein'
50.0		Perrigny
51.0		Moutot
57.0		D86 'to Noyers'
57.0		Place Hôtel de Ville, Noyers-sur-Serein

See Day 2 p267

n Auxerre, head towards the Pont Paul Bert, crossing the river just out of La Cour Barrée (9km).

From here, the ride winds across the gentle slopes of the Chablis vineyards and into the town of the same name.

Chablis (32.5km) is known as 'the Golden Gate of Burgundy', after the great white wines produced in the region (see the Chablis Wine' boxed text). However, it's an over-priced place for a tipple. Give the tastings in town a miss and head for one of the many cellars on the route outside of town, or the wine cooperative *La Chablisienne* on blvd Pasteur, on your way to Noyers. Just look for the magic word *dégustations* (tastings).

Chablis does have several things to see and do that are not wine-related. A traditional Burgundian **market** is held Sunday morning. Check out the 13th-century **Église St Martin**, founded in the 9th century, the bastions of the **Porte Noël**, a set of medieval gates, or the remains of a centuries-old **synagogue**.

Head out of Chablis along the Serein valley, through the peaceful towns of Molay (46km) and Perrigny (48km), to finish in Noyers-sur-Serein.

Noyers-sur-Serein

The epitome of a charming medieval village, the half-timbered houses and cobbled streets of Noyers are contained within the loop of the Serein. The narrow streets are great for aimless wandering. Just watch out for the 'bottom bombs' from the birds nesting at the Hôtel de Ville.

There is no tourist office or bank in town. The closest bike shop is Ets Barbotte (☎ 03 86 82 81 72), just past Perrigny, on your way in to Noyers.

Things to See & Do A lovely **riverside walk** circles the ramparts of Noyers. The **Musée de Noyers** (☎ 03 86 82 89 09) houses a collection of Naïve art. Also known as 'Sunday artists', the Naïve painters had no formal training, coming from working-class backgrounds.

Places to Stay & Eat It's fairly basic at the riverside *Camping Municipale*. It charges 20FF for two people and a tent. If no-one comes to collect your money, settle up at the Hôtel de Ville.

Chablis Wine

Originally planted by the monks of Poligny in the 12th century, the vineyards of Chablis are now considered to be some of the most exclusive in the world. Producing dry white wines pressed only from chardonnay grapes which grow in the clay and limestone marl of the surrounding hills, the wine growing region of Chablis covers 240,000 hectares.

Unlike Bordeaux, where wine *appellations* (quality-controlled wine growing regions) take their name from *domaines* or specific vineyards, the *appellations* on Chablis bottles (like those elsewhere in Burgundy) refer to the *climats*, or climates in which the different *cépages* (grape varieties) are grown. This typically Burgundian way of classifying wine attributes each plot of land with its own properties (soil, subsoil, exposure etc), which reflect the nuances and 'personality' of the land and, therefore, the wine.

Chablis wine is divided into three orders. At the top, *Grand Cru* wines, distinguished by their rich golden colour, are produced from grapes grown in a tiny area spanning a mere 1520 hectares. The big daddy of the Chablis Grand Cru is Grenouille – it's unlikely you'll be able to afford to even sniff the cork. Next are the lighter and less full-bodied wines of the *Premier Cru*, which include appellations such as Mont de Milieu and Preuses. The remaining and vast proportion of the Chablis vineyards are given over to wines known as *Appellation Chablis Contrôllée*. Making up half of the production in Chablis, the appellations of these dry and pale wines refer to the method of their preparation as well as to their less reliable *climat*. All Chablis AOC wines cellar well.

There is only one hotel in town, but it's a beauty. With a 12th-century tower, peaceful gardens and great artwork on the walls, *Hôtel de la Vielle Tour* (☎ 03 86 82 87 82 69, fax 03 86 82 66 94, place du Granier à Sel) is the perfect place to pamper yourself. Doubles with shower cost 250FF. It has no credit card facilities.

A *supermarket* is just inside the southern gate (closed Wednesday afternoon). A *boulangerie* (bakery) and a *charcuterie* (delicatessen) can be found on place Hôtel de Ville. *Restaurant de la Porte Peinte* (☎/fax 03 86 82 81 07) has a regional *menu* for 95FF (closed Sunday and Monday nights). The only place to eat on Sunday night is the restaurant in the *Hôtel de la Vielle Tour*. Meals, using fresh local produce, cost 70FF.

Day 2: Noyers-sur-Serein to Vézelay

3–4 hours, 47.5km

The route winds through peaceful countryside, the once-fortified town of Avallon and the verdant Vallée du Cousin, to finish at the hilltop village of Vézelay. From Noyers, head through the southern gate under the clock tower. The road meanders over rolling countryside through the tiny villages of Tormancy (7.6km) and Massangis (8.5km). Expect to be either gawked at or greeted warmly as you head through this incredibly untouched part of Burgundy. Soon after, you'll reach the hamlet of Civry-sur-Serein (10.8km). On the banks of the Serein, this peaceful village is about as far away from the hustle and bustle of Paris as you can get. Check out the **church** with its intricate stained-glass windows and imposing entry pillars, and the **Roman baths** on your way out of the village.

Continue along the banks of the Serein, through the fairly unremarkable town of L'Isle-sur-Serein (14.5km), and along a quiet road which undulates through forest to reach Avallon (30.5km). On a rocky spur overlooking three valleys, Avallon has played an important military role from as far back as the 9th century. The **old city** is particularly deserving of a few hour's wandering.

From Avallon, a steep descent drops into the lush **Vallée du Cousin**. Considered by the locals to be a national treasure, it is definitely worth picking up some supplies in Avallon and heading to this forested, riverlined valley for lunch.

At Pontaubert (36.5km) the valley ends and the ride climbs steadily across some of the most beautiful countryside in Burgundy. From St Père (45.5km), the 2km to Vézelay is steep, but the views from the top are absolutely worth the effort.

Vézelay

Location, location, location! Perched high atop a hill, this UNESCO World Heritage listed village is sure to impress. Pillaged by the Huegenots and razed during the Revolution, it is now an important place for pilgrims (see the 'St Jacques de Compostelle Pilgrimage' boxed text in the Languedoc Rousillon chapter).

The tourist office (☎ 03 86 33 23 69, fax 03 86 33 34 00) is on rue St Pierre (closed Thursday), up the hill to the right from place du Champ de Foire.

Vézelay has no bank, but the post office has an ATM. The tourist office will also change money. There is no bike shop in town.

Things to See & Do Vézelay's main drag, **rue St Pierre**, has an interesting, somewhat esoteric collection of shops selling everything from jewellery to local wines to metaphysical literature.

The town's main drawcard, the **Basilique Ste Madeleine**, is magnificent. Universally considered to be a masterpiece of Romanesque art, a nave is offset by the large windows and arches of Gothic architecture. There is a great view over the Cure Valley from the gardens.

The **Foire Cantonale du Vézelian**, a traditional country fair, is held each spring in early June. The **Pilgrimage** on 22 July celebrates the feast day of St Mary Magdalene.

Places to Stay & Eat Sleep under the mulberry trees at the *camping ground* (☎/fax 03 86 33 24 18) behind the youth hostel, on the road to L'Étang. It charges 20FF per person and 5FF for the tent. The *Auberge de Jeunesse* (☎/fax 03 86 33 24 18) charges 45FF (52FF without a hostelling card) for a very basic dorm bed.

There are three *chambres d'hôtes* (B&Bs) on rue St Pierre. At *Atelier Van den Bossche* (☎/fax 03 86 33 32 16), doubles cost 270FF (320FF for a private bathroom). There are several hotels around place du Champ de Foire, including *Hôtel du Cheval Blanc* (☎ 03 86 33 22 12, fax 03 86 33 34 29), which has doubles from 200FF.

The *boulangerie* and *supermarket* are on rue St Pierre. Both are closed on Sunday. Rue St Pierre has a heap of *restaurants*, many of which are extortionately priced.

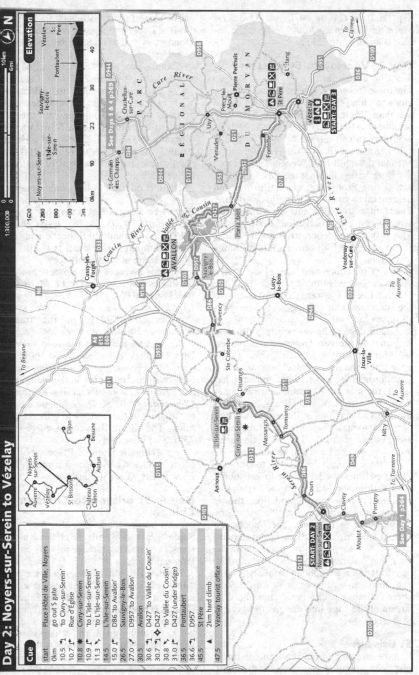

Day 2: Noyers-sur-Serein to Vézelay

Cue		
start		Place Hôtel de Ville, Noyers
0km	↰	go out S gate
10.5	↱	to Civry-sur-Serein'
10.7	↰	Rue d'Église
10.8	✳	Civry-sur-Serein
10.9	↱	'to L'Isle-sur-Serein'
11.3	↘	'to L'Isle-sur-Serein'
14.5		L'Isle-sur-Serein
15.0	↰	D86 'to Avallon'
26.5		Sauvigny-le-Bois
27.0	↙	D957 'to Avallon'
30.5		Avallon
30.6	↰	D427 'to Vallée du Cousin'
30.7	↰	D427
30.8	↰	'to Vallée du Cousin'
31.0	↰	D427 (under bridge)
36.5		Pontaubert
36.6	↰	D957
45.5		St Père
	▲	2km hard climb
47.5		Vézelay tourist office

Elevation

BURGUNDY

Try *La Dent Creuse* (☎ 03 86 33 36 33, *place du Champ de Foire*), where the regional *menu* costs 79FF.

Day 3: Vézelay to St Brisson
4–5¼ hours, 51.5km

The route leaves the vineyards and pasturelands to climb through the thick forests of the Parc Régional du Morvan. The *only* restaurant in St Brisson can close as early as 7.30 pm, so call ahead if you're not self-catering and are likely to arrive late.

Head downhill from Vézelay and across the Cure Valley through the tiny village of Usy (8km). From here, a beautiful forested descent takes you into Chastellux-sur-Cure. The impressive **Château de Chastellux** (18km) can only marvelled at from afar. The private residence of the Chastellux family since the 13th century, it is off limits to visitors.

From Chastellux-sur-Cure, a long stretch involving some climbing leads past the pleasant **Lac du Crescent** (23.5km) and up to the unremarkable village of Marigny-l'Église (25.5km).

A long descent brings you into the **Parc Régional du Morvan**. Quite steep in places, the Morvan derives its name from Celtic etymology and means 'black mountain'.

Unfortunately, the forestry industry has left its mark on the Morvan; the ride passes tracts of cleared land and piles of logs. Still, the Morvan remains sufficiently *bocager* (wooded) to make for some peaceful cycling along quiet back roads. The roads, however, are badly surfaced and can be slippery.

Continue through the Morvan to Dun-les-Places (41km), the last place to get tourist information (see St Brisson for details). If looking for *hotel* accommodation, this is the place to stop as well (see Places to Stay & Eat under St Brisson). The **Maison du Parc**, a side trip at 50.5km, is not accommodation. It supplies information about the park and has a museum and herbularium (see St Brisson for contact details).

From Dun-les-Places, a beautiful 7km stretch climbs steadily beside the tumbling stream of the Cure into the quiet village of St Brisson.

St Brisson
Remote and away from it all, this is really just a convenient place to stop for the night.

The closest tourist office (☎ 03 86 84 6. 05) is at Dun-les-Places. It is closed all da Monday, as well as on Saturday and Sunda mornings.

About 1.5km out of St Brisson, the Mai son du Parc (☎ 03 86 78 79 00, fax 03 8 78 74 22) sells topomaps and hiking an VTT guides (closed weekends). Th grounds of the Maison du Parc are als home to the **Musée de la Résistance e Morvan** (☎ 03 86 78 72 99) and a **Herbu larium**, which features more than 160 loca plant species, some of which are reportedl hallucinogenic.

There is no bank or bike shop in town.

Places to Stay & Eat A very basic *camp ing ground* (☎ 03 86 78 71 48) charge 11FF per adult and 10FF for the tent (ope Easter through September). It is also pos sible to camp at Dun-les-Places.

There is no hotel in St Brisson, but Dun les-Places has several. Try *Le Mont Velin* (☎ 03 86 84 63 04, fax 03 86 84 64 09, rout 19 Mars) in town, where doubles with showers cost 190FF, or the tranqui *L'Auberge Ensoleilée* (☎ 03 86 84 62 76) 1.5km out of town, on the road to Vieu Dun. Doubles with shower cost 160FF.

In St Brisson, the small *alimentatio générale* (general store) on the main squar has a limited range of supplies. *Restauran Clémendot* (☎ 03 86 78 72 75), on the roa to Gouloux, is the best – and only – deal i town. The filling four-course *menu* cost 75FF. Get there early.

If staying in Dun-les-Places, both L Mont Velin and L'Auberge Ensoleilée hav *restaurants* with 85FF *menus*.

Day 4: St Brisson to Château Chinon
2¼–3½ hours, 38km

Some great downhill stretches throug forests and past lakes make this day particu larly enjoyable.

From St Brisson, head south to the prett village of Gouloux (4.5km) and the surpris ingly interesting **Musée de la Saboteri** (Woodcarvers' Museum), which features collection of wood-carving tools and cra work. A 'living museum', it is possible t watch the *sabotiers* in action as they whit tle that fine Morvan forest into all manne of shapes. The local carvers hold the recor

N

1:300,000

0	10km
0	6ml

See Day 5 p271

BURGUNDY

Days 3 & 4: Vézelay – St Brisson – Château Chinon

Cue Day 3

start		Vézelay tourist office
0km		go E on D957 'to St Père' (downhill)
2.0		St Père
2.2	↰	D36 'to Usy'
8.0		Usy
14.0	↱ ◈	D44
18.0	✳	Château de Chastellux
18.2	↰	1.5km moderate climb
19.5		L'Huis Raquin
19.6	↰	'to Lac du Crescent'
19.7	↰	unsigned rd (at pétanque courts)
20.2	◀	1km steep climb
20.3	↘	D518 'to Marigny'
20.4	◀	500m steep descent
23.9	◀	1.5km steep climb
25.3	↰	D210
25.5	↰	D210, Marigny l'Église
34.0	↰	D286
39.0	↰	D6 'to Dun-les-Places'
41.0		Dun-les-Places
41.6	↰	D6
43.0	↰	D6
50.5	↰	D20
	● •	Maison du Parc 1km ↺
51.5		St Brisson town square

Cue Day 4

start		St Brisson town square
0km		go S past the bar, on road to Gouloux
2.0	↰	'to Montsauche/Lac des Settons'
4.0		D292 'to Gouloux'
4.5		Gouloux
4.6	✳	woodcarvers' museum
4.9	↱	D292 (no sign)
6.5	↰	'to Lac des Settons'
10.5		Lac des Settons
13.0	↱	D193
17.0	↰	Rive Gauche/D531
17.5	◀	D290 'to Panchez'
21.0	↱↱	D290 'to Panchez'
23.0		D37
		Planchez
33.0	◀	1km gradua climb
34.0	◀	1km very steep climb
35.5	◀	D944
38.0		Château Chinon tourist office

PARC RÉGIONAL

Maison du Parc

START DAY 4 St Brisson

Lac du St Agnan

Le Breuil Woodcarvers' Museum

Gouloux

Les Settons

Montsauche-
les-Settons

DU MORVAN

Dun-les-
Places

Brassy

To Corbigny

Vieux Dun

Vermot

Mazignien

Chalaux

Marigny l'Église

Château
de Chastellux

L'Huis-
Bobin

L'Huis Raquin

Chastellux-
sur-Cure

To St-Germain
des Champs

Lac du
Crescent

To Arnay-le-Duc

To Auxerre

Coulon River

Cure River

START DAY 5 Château
Chinon

Anost

Planchez

Coralay

Montbois

Ruisseau
Morin

Yonne River

To Nevers

La
Gutteleau

Chigny

Les Brankssos

Max-en-
Morvas

Saulieu

See Day 2 p267

Vézelay START DAY 3

St Père

Fontette

Ménades

Précy-
le-Moult

Usy

Pierre
Perthuis

To St-Germain
des Champs

To Corbigny

Cure River

Elevation

Day 4

Okm	10	20	30	

St Brisson — Gouloux — Planchez — Château-Chinon

Day 3

0km	10	20	30	40	50

2000
1600
1200
800
400
0m

Vézelay — St Père — L'Huis-Raquin — Château de Chastellux — Marigny-l'Église — L'Huis-Bobin — St Brisson

for the world's largest wood carving: a giant shoe, carved from a single piece of wood, measuring a startling 45m and weighing 18 tonnes.

From Gouloux, head through a mix of forest, farmland and sleepy agricultural hamlets along a very peaceful back road, where the only traffic you're likely to encounter is slow agricultural vehicles.

From here, a long descent drops to the gorgeous **Lac des Settons** (10.5km). Dawdle around the lake – it's too beautiful to rush – and onto the road to Planchez (23km). Climb slowly but steadily through pockets of forest and pasture, before a long descent through Planchez.

The road to Château Chinon is mainly downhill, although it is in desperate need of repair. A nasty final climb leads to the D944 turn-off into town.

Château Chinon

This nondescript town's main claim to fame is that François Mitterand was mayor before his election as President of France in 1981.

The tourist office (☎/fax 03 86 85 06 58) is at 2 place St Christophe (closed Sunday morning and Wednesday; closed mornings during school term). The Crédit Lyonnais bank is opposite the tourist office in the square. Peugeot Cycles (☎ 03 86 85 29 18) is on blvd de la République. It is possible to buy white gas (shellite) at Technicien du Sport, next to the bike shop.

Things to See & Do Check out the **fountain** at place François Mitterand. A Daliesque mechanised sculpture, this wacky collaboration between Niki de Ste Phallée and Jean Tingley features, among other things, a woman spurting water from her breasts.

The **Musée du Septennat** (☎ 03 86 85 19 23), at 6 rue du Chateau, displays a collection of official gifts presented to President Mitterand during his two *septennats* (seven-year terms).

Places to Stay & Eat The swish *Camping Municipale Perthuy d'Oiseaux* (☎ 03 86 85 08 17) costs 41FF per adult (open May through September). The *Hôtel Lion d'Or* (☎ 03 86 85 13 56, 10 rue des Fossés) has doubles from 160FF (200FF with shower and toilet). Reception is closed on Sunday and after 5 pm on Monday. Two-star *Hôtel Le Vieux Morvan* (☎ 03 86 85 05 01, fax 03 86 85 02 78, 8 place Gaudin) has doubles with shower and a view from 290FF.

There are two **supermarkets** on blvd de la République (both closed Wednesday).

La Vielle Pizzeria (rue des Fossés) serves big pizzas from 48FF and has a friendly bar downstairs (closed Monday). The **restaurant** at Hôtel Le Vieux Morvan is on the flash side. The cheapest *menu* starts at 95FF (not available on Saturday night).

Day 5: Château Chinon to Autun
3½–4½ hours, 54.5km
The route climbs through the southern Morvan, visiting significant Gallo-Roman and Roman settlements.

From Château Chinon, head south, where a reasonably long, but easy, climb leads through the Fôret de la Gravelle to the tiny hamlet of Les Buteaux (11km). The road climbs steadily for another 5km through more pristine forest, where it then descends through pockets of pasture and forest into the small village of Les Puits (19km).

A reasonably flat stretch of road affords incredible views of Mont Beuvray, then climbs slightly to reach the **Bibracte Museum** (24.5km). This houses a permanent exhibition of Celtic civilisation and Bibracte culture, displaying many of the findings of the excavations of Bibracte (see the 'Bibracte' boxed text overleaf), including ceramic vases, tools, jewellery and sculptures. The museum also has a *cafe* and boutique, and can provide general information about the Parc Régional du Morvan.

Limber up your climbing legs – the ascent to the **ruins** of Bibracte atop Mont Beuvray is cruel, to say the least! A *very* steep (up to 20%) climb through the twisted beeches of the Morvan forest leads to the top. It might be easier to walk to the summit, but it is worth the effort to cycle. (If the climb proves too steep, it is possible to stay on the D3, which is rejoined by the road down from Bibracte, leading to St Léger-sous-Beuvray.) The descent from Bibracte, over a very uneven, unstable road surface, can be extremely treacherous.

From St Léger-sous-Beuvray, the road runs gently downhill, following the line of the Méchet River through picturesque pasture land. At 50km take care turning onto the busy

Day 5: Château Chinon to Autun

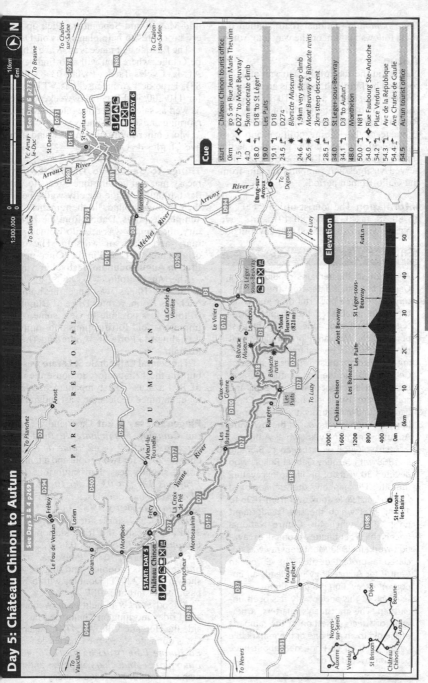

BURGUNDY

Cue		
start		Château Chinon tourist office
0km	↙	go S on Rue Jean Marie Theurin
1.5	◆ ↱	D27 'to Mont Beuvray'
4.0	↰	5km moderate climb
18.0	↱	D18 'to St Léger'
19.0		Les Puits
19.1	↱	D18
24.5	↰	D27ª
		Bibracte Museum
24.6	✱	1.9km very steep climb
26.5	✱	Mont Beuvray & Bibracte ruins
	◄	2km steep descent
28.5	↰	D3
34.0		St Léger-sous-Beuvray
34.1	↱	D3 'to Autun'
48.0		Monthelon
50.0	◆ ↗	N81
54.0	◆ ↗	Rue Faubourg Ste-Andoche
54.2		Place Verdun
54.3	↱	Ave de la République
54.4	↰	Ave Charles de Gaulle
54.5		Autun tourist office

route nationale (national road), which the route follows for 4km on the way into Autun.

Autun

Nestled at the foot of the Morvan and surrounded by farmland, Autun is an attractive town. First settled around 10 BC, Autun (then known as Augustodunum after the Roman Emperor Augustus) took over from Bibracte as the leading political and economic centre, where it was regarded as the 'sister and rival of Rome'. Several preserved vestiges and ramparts remain from the Gallo-Roman period.

Information The tourist office (☎ 03 85 86 80 38, fax 03 85 86 80 49) is at 2 ave Charles de Gaulle (closed Sunday outside

Bibracte

At 821m sit the remains of Bibracte, a Gaulish town that dates from the 1st century BC, when a powerful tribe known as the Aedui established their capital. Strategically built atop one of the highest points of the Morvan, Bibracte also sat at the crossroads of several trade routes linking the Mediterranean regions to those of Celtic Europe. In the 2nd century Bibracte became an important political, religious and crafts centre. However, in the early Christian era, under Augustus, the city's importance diminished in favour of the low-lying Augustodunum (now known as Autun).

Archaeological work began at Bibracte in 1868 with Jacques-Gabriel Bullot, who devoted 30 years of his life to excavating the site. His nephew, the archaeologist Joseph Déchelelle, took over from 1895 to 1904, after which the site lay dormant until 1984, when the Centre National Recherche Scientifique resumed excavation work. In 1988 Mont Beuvray was declared a protected site. The European Centre for Archaeology now leads an important excavation program there.

Much of this ancient city has been unearthed. The craftsmen's quarters, a network of streets, a section of the ramparts of the old town and one of the remarkable pincer gates of La Porte de Rebout have been uncovered to date.

mid-May to mid-September). Pick up winery brochures to help plan visits on Day 6

The Banque de France is at 38 ave Charles de Gaulle, where you will also find several ATMs. Cycles Tacnet (☎/fax 03 85 86 37 83), 1 rue de l'Arquebuse, has VTT rentals for 110/200/500FF per day/weekend/week as well as sales and service (closed Monday morning and all day Sunday).

Most other facilities can be found along ave Charles de Gaulle.

Things to See & Do The **old town** is a messy maze of cobblestone streets to wander through. Outside the city walls, behind the camping ground, lie the remains of the **Temple de Janus**. Dating from the 1st century, the temple was a Gallo-Roman sanctuary and place of worship. The city's origins are celebrated in the **'Once upon a time in Augustodunum' festival** in August.

The **Musée Rolin** (☎ 03 85 52 09 76) at 5 rue des Bancs was once the home of Nicholas Rolin, former Duke of Burgundy. In town it is possible to view some of the impressive old fortifications and ramparts, including the **Porte Ste André** and **Théâtre Romain**.

The central **Cathédrale St Lazare** was first built in the 12th century to house the relics of St Lazarus. The tympanum above the main entrance depicts the Last Judgment.

Places to Stay & Eat The friendly, family-run *Camping Municipale du Pont d'Arroux* (*☎ 03 85 52 10 82, route de Saulieu)* charges 23FF for two people and a tent. The noisy, slightly less than salubrious *Hôtel François 1er* (*☎ 03 85 86 10 11, 14 rue Mazagran)* has doubles for 150FF. *Hôtel Le Concorde* (*☎ 03 85 52 38 41, 1 rue de l'Horloge)* has singles/doubles from 150/200FF. Opposite the train station, *Hôtel Commerce et Touring* (*☎ 03 85 52 17 90, fax 03 85 52 37 63, 20 ave de la République)* has doubles and triples with shower from 220FF. Doubles with a washbasin only start at 140FF.

A food *market* is held each Wednesday and Friday morning on Champ de Mars, outside the Hôtel de Ville. An *ATAC* supermarket is opposite No 35 rue Charles de Gaulle. *La Bonne Pâte* (*☎ 03 85 52 11 76, 43 rue Faubourg St-Andoche)* has pizzas and pasta dishes from 40FF (closed Sunday).

Day 6: Autun to Beaune

WINE LOVER'S CIRCUIT p276-80

1:300,000

0 ____ 10km
0 ____ 6ml

(N)

Elevation

Cue	
start	Autun tourist office
0km	go NE on Ave Charles ce Gaulle
0.1	Ave de la République/D107
2.5	D107, St Pantaleon
2.6	D107
4.5	St Denis
4.6	D116 'to Curgy'
7.0	Curgy
7.1	V1 'to St Léger'
9.0	Vergoncey
9.1	D116
11.5	D26, St-Léger du Bois
13.8	D26 'to Sully'
15.5	Sully
	⊙ ● ☜ Château de Sully 3km
16.1	D241 'to Épinac'
18.6	D43 'to Épinac'
18.8	D43, Épinac

Cue	Continued
18.8	(2m) Rue Jean Bouver/Rue Jean Jaurès
20.0	D217, La Verrerie
20.5	'to La Garenne'
22.0	D217, La Garenne
25.0	D217
25.3	D14
27.0	Molinot
27.1	D33
27.2	D33E 'to Ivry-en-Montagne'
31.0	Ivry-en-Montagne
31.2	30m very steep climb
31.5	N6 to Chagny
33.0	D17 'to Beaune'
46.0	skirts Fommard
46.5	D973/N74
49.5	Beaune tourist office

The *restaurant* in the Hôtel Commerce et Touring has Burgundian *menus* for 65FF, 84FF and 140FF.

Day 6: Autun to Beaune

3–4 hours, 49.5km

Head across the flat Pays Nicholas Rolin, the stretch of valley between the Morvan and the wineries of the Côte d'Or, named after the Autun-born lawyer who established the celebrated Hospice de Beaune.

From Autun, cycle north-east across the countryside through the small towns of St Denis, Curgy and Sully (15.5km), where the impressive **Château de Sully** (☎ 03 85 82 01 08) makes an excellent place to detour for a refresher (35/15FF chateau/gardens-only entry).

From here, continue across the Pays Nicholas Rolin to Épinac, then onto Molinot. Look out for the interesting **chateau** on the outskirts of town. Even if you could swim the moat, it's still off-limits to visitors.

Continue to Ivry-en-Montagne (31km), where a very steep (but short) climb leads onto the escarpments of the Côte d'Or. A long descent twists along the Côte de Beaune and through some of the most beautiful countryside in Burgundy. Several **wineries** can be found off the main road – it's up to you where to tipple. The Autun and Beaune tourist offices have plenty of brochures.

From here, it's downhill into Beaune. The road can be very busy, particularly on weekends, when motorists zoom past on their way to quaff their next pinot noir. Nerves of steel are required for the streets of Beaune. The self-coined moniker 'Beaune, the courteous city', clearly does not extend to those behind the wheel.

Beaune

The capital of the Côte d'Or, Beaune is a working centre of wine production, making and selling some of Burgundy's finest. The pretty town centre is a maze of narrow cobblestone streets, and the magnificent Hôtel-Dieu hospital is unforgettable.

Information The well-equipped and helpful tourist office (☎ 03 80 26 21 30, fax 03 80 26 21 39, ⓔ otbeaune@hol.fr) is at 20 rue de l'Hôtel-Dieu (closed Sunday). It has the free *Circuits en Côte d'Or* brochure, which lists – in English – several itineraries

of wineries that could be visited on Day 6. A Banque de France is at 26 place Monge; an ATM is opposite the tourist office. The post office is at 7 blvd St Jacques. Try Cycles Tillot (☎ 03 80 24 70 08), 50 rue de Faubourg Madeleine, for sales and service.

Things to See & Do Beaune makes a great base for **wine tasting day trips** to the Côte de Beaune and Côte de Nuits. The tourist office can supply maps showing villages with cellars that offer tastings. Dégustations in the 18th-century cellar of **Reine Pédauque** (*☎ 03 80 22 23 11, rue de Lorraine)* include tastings of four wines and an informative guided tour, not always in English.

Beaune's most impressive attraction is the **Hôtel-Dieu des Hospices de Beaune** (☎ 03 80 24 45 00), a charity hospital founded by Chancellor Nicholas Rolin and his wife, Grigoire de Salins, in 1443. With its colourful mosaic roof, the great Hall of the Poor (a bed-lined chapel in which the frail and infirm could pray without leaving their beds), a display of painfully archaic surgical drills and the haunting polyptych of the Last Judgment, the incredible Hôtel-Dieu is not to be missed. The charity also owns more than 60 hectares of vineyards; its **wine auction** on the third Sunday of November attracts bidders from around the world.

Housed in the former mansion of the Dukes of Burgundy, the **Musée du Vin de Borgogne** (☎ 03 80 22 08 19) on rue d'Enfer has exhibits of everything you'll ever need to know about wine making.

Places to Stay & Eat The zoo-like *Camping Les Cent Vignes* (*☎ 03 80 22 03 91, 10 rue Auguste Dubois)* charges 16FF per adult and 23FF per site. *Hôtel Rousseau*, run by a friendly lady, has rooms like grandma used to make. Basic singles start at 135FF. Doubles with showers start at 180FF, including breakfast. You'll have to lock your bike in a courtyard somewhat exposed to the elements. *Hôtel au Grand St Jean (☎ 03 80 24 12 22, fax 03 80 24 15 43, 18 rue Faubourg Madeleine)* has doubles from 230FF.

For food, *market* day is Saturday morning, in place Carnot. A *Casino supermarket* is at 14 rue Monge (closed Tuesday and Sunday afternoons). Several upmarket food shops line rue Carnot, including *Le Tast' Fromage*, for all your cheesy needs.

Day 7: Beaune to Dijon (& Day 3 Wine Lover's Circuit)

Elevation

1600 / 1200 / 800 / 400 / 0m

Beaune — Savigny-lès-Beaune — Bouilland — Antheuil — Pont de Pany — Dijon

60m / 60

0km 10 20 30 40 50 60

Cue

start		Beaune tourist office
0km	↑	SW on Rue Maufroux
0.1	←	Rue Maufroux
0.2	→	Blvd Bretonnière
0.3	↖	follow ring road
1.5		N74
2.0	←	D18 to Savigny-lès-Beaune'
3.0	→	D2
5.3		Savigny-lès-Beaune
5.5	↖	'to Camping'
5.7	↗	D2 'to Bouilland'
16.0		Bouilland
16.3	◄	3km very steep climb
16.6	↗	D2
20.3	←	D115 'to Antheuil'
21.0	◄	500m very steep descent
23.0		Antheuil
24.0	↖	D33 'to Dijon'
27.0	✱	Abbaye de la Buissière
40.0	↘	D905, Pont de Pany
42.0	↓	under autoroute 'to Dijon'
49.0	←	over river, Velars-sur-Ouche
49.1	↓	onto canal bikepath
61.6	↓	end of bikepath
61.6		Rue de l'Hôpital 'to Hôpital CHS'
61.8	↖	Ave Albert 1er
61.9	←	Blvd de Sevigné
62.0		Dijon tourist office

WINE LOVER'S CIRCUIT p276-80

START DAY 7 BEAUNE

END DIJON

To Châtillon-sur-Seine
To Troyes
To Chalon-sur-Saône
To Besançon
To Vandenesse-en-Auxois & Paris
To Arnay-le-Duc

Mort Afrique (606m)

Ouche River • Rhoin River

Plombières-lès-Dijon
Pasques
Fleurey-sur-Ouche
Velars-sur-Ouche
Pont de Pany
Agey
Barbirey-sur-Ouche
Gissey-sur-Ouche
Auvillard
La Bussière-sur-Ouche
Abbaye de la Bussière
Veuvey-sur-Ouche
Pont d'Ouche
Bligny-sur-Ouche
Fixin
Gevrey-Chambertin
Musigny
Nuits-St Georges
Agencourt
Chaux
Magny-les-Villers
Pernand-Vergelesses
Savigny-lès-Beaune
Bouilland
Antheuil
Boulland
Cilly-les-Cîteaux
St Bernard
Ternant
Quemigny-Poisot

See Days 1 & 2 (Wine Lover's Circuit) p273
See Day 6 p274

Étangs de Rouey et Lacanche

BURGUNDY

N

1:300,000 0 10km / 6mi

Camping Les Cent Vignes has a surprisingly good *restaurant*, serving wines by the glass and *menus* for 68FF and 80FF. For traditional Burgundian fare, descend into the bat cave of *Caveau St Gilles* (☎ 03 80 24 70 67, 29 rue Carnot), where the *menu* costs 75FF. A number of *restaurants* can be found around place Carnot, petite place Carnot and place Félix Ziem.

Day 7: Beaune to Dijon
3½–4½ hours, 62km
The route weaves through several pretty wine growing villages before climbing over rolling hills and descending onto the banks of the Canal du Bourgogne, which provides a car-free entry to the delightful city of Dijon.

From Beaune, use the ring road to head north-west through the gorgeous wine growing village of Savigny-lès-Beaune (5.3km). The road climbs gently through the vineyards along the banks of the Rhoin before narrowing into a shady gorge.

Immediately after Bouilland (16km), a reasonably steady climb leads to a plateau

where a very steep descent drops to the sleepy town of Antheuil (23km). Continue alongside the Canal de Bourgogne; the only vehicle along this stretch is likely to be the mobile cheese van bringing *fromage* to the tiny villages in the region.

Just before the village of La Bussière-sur-Ouche (27.5km) is the **Abbaye de la Bussière**. Founded in the 12th century by the monks of the famous Abbaye de Cîteaux (see Day 1 of the Wine Lover's Circuit), it is now a diocesan retreat. The grounds are beautiful, but picnics are a no-no.

Continue along the D33, through several nondescript agricultural villages and into Pont de Pany (40km), where the route then follows the Ouche towards Dijon. Unfortunately, the route, on the D905, runs beside the autoroute for 8km or so, before meeting the beautiful, tulip-lined, shady bikepath along the Canal de Bourgogne to Dijon, the culinary capital of Burgundy (see 'The Burgundian Snail' boxed text).

Dijon
See Dijon (pp261–2) in the Gateway Cities section for information about accommodation and other services.

The Burgundian Snail

Helix pomatia – the Burgundian snail – is believed to be the incarnation of both the Burgundy land and the spirit of its people. Found fossilised in stone, incorporated into wrought iron works and sculpted in Romanesque and Gothic buildings (see the Hôtel Chambellan in Dijon), the spiral of the snail's shell evokes the universality of Burgundy.

Like the people of Burgundy, the snail is happy in its shell. If you upset it, you will get nothing out of it. If you win its confidence, it will be loyal.

Despite this reverence, Burgundians still find the snail delicious grilled with salt or sautéed with butter, garlic and parsley!

KELLI HAMBLET

Look for Burgundy's signature snail carved into the facade of Dijon's Hôtel Chambellan.

Wine Lover's Circuit

Duration	3 days
Distance	127km
Difficulty	easy
Start/End	Dijon

For the most part, this ride follows the Route des Grands Crus (see the 'Burgundy Wines – A Drinker's Guide' boxed text later in the chapter for an explanation of *Grands Crus*). Running from Dijon to Nuits-St Georges, this tourist route passes some of the region's most prestigious vineyards and winds through delightful villages known and revered by wine buffs around the world. With the opportunity to dine in restaurants boasting world-class chefs, and a gently undulating route, this ride makes for some wonderfully self-indulgent cycling. Just watch out for *crise de foie* – a 'crisis of the liver' brought about by eating too much rich food. The ride also includes the impressive Château du Clos de Vougeot and the historic Abbaye de Cîteaux.

HISTORY

Covering about 8000 hectares, the vineyards of the Côte d'Or have a rich and colourful history. Worked by Cistercian monks throughout the 12th and 13th centuries, barrels of wine from the region were popular gifts for important religious figures. In the 15th century the Dukes of Burgundy took to styling themselves as the 'lords of the best wines in Christendom', a claim some people still hold true to this day.

The 19th century brought several changes to vine growing in Burgundy. Phylloxera lice almost destroyed the French wine industry by attacking the roots of the vine plant. Prior to the devastating outbreak in the region in 1880, vines were grown without any attention to layout or planning. The neat, carefully planted rows of vines, which are characteristically 'Burgundian', are the result of an extensive replanting program using phylloxera-resistant rootstock imported from the USA, with which the Burgundy vines were grafted.

The 20th century saw several wine brotherhoods established, most famously the Confrérie des Chevaliers du Tastevin – the Brotherhood of the Tastevin Knights – established in the 1930s to promote the Côte wines (see 'The Brotherhood of the Tastevin Knights' boxed text overleaf).

NATURAL HISTORY

Described by the 19th-century French writer Stendhal as 'a little dry and ugly mountain', the nature of the Côte d'Or is perhaps more accurately reflected in its literal English translation, 'the golden hillside'. This refers to both the colour of the vines and the fact that they produce wines that are worth their weight in gold. The vineyards are planted on predominantly limestone marl along only the eastern side of the hill, which warms up quickly in the spring and is sheltered and oriented for maximum sunlight during the rest of the year. This exposure also makes the grapes very sweet, giving the wine a higher than average alcohol content.

GETTING TO/FROM THE RIDE

It is possible to adapt this ride to join up with the seven-day Classic Burgundy ride (detailed earlier in this chapter), making a nine-day ride. Complete up to Day 6 of the Classic Burgundy Ride to start/end the Wine Lover's Circuit in Beaune.

Dijon is only about 75km from Besançon, the start of The Jura ride in the French Alps & the Jura chapter.

Dijon

See the Gateway Cities section (pp262) for information on getting to/from Dijon.

Beaune

Beaune's train station, ave du 8 Septembre, is served by local trains on the Dijon-Lyon line.

The service to Dijon (38FF, 20 minutes, 14 to 20 a day) only takes bikes on some services. Check with the SNCF for bike-friendly trains. Beaune is linked to Paris' Gare de Lyon (220FF, two hours) by one or two direct TGVs a day.

From Britain, the European Bike Express service (see Bus under Continental Europe in the Getting There & Away chapter) charges UK£149 (return) to take a passenger and bike to Beaune.

THE RIDE
Dijon

See Dijon in the Gateway Cities section (pp261–2) for information on accommodation and other services.

Day 1: Dijon to Nuits-St Georges

3–4 hours, 43km

An easy day's pedalling, the route winds through the gorgeous, golden vineyards of the Côte d'Or. From Dijon, head south to Marsannay-la-Côte: the official start of the **Route des Grands Crus** and some of the most picturesque cycling in Burgundy. There are plenty of places to eat and drink along the route. Each village has an information board listing its wineries, *caves* (cellars) and restaurants.

The route is well signposted to Vougeot, where the worthwhile side trip to the **Château du Clos de Vougeot** (☎ 03 80 62 86 09) is also well signed. Dating from the 14th century, the chateau is a wine lover's heaven. An amazing cellar, stacked with bottles dating from the beginning of the century, awaits tasting by the famous Confrérie des Chevaliers du Tastevin (see 'The Brotherhood of the Tastevin Knights' boxed text overleaf).

BURGUNDY

BURGUNDY

The Brotherhood of the Tastevin Knights

Throughout the wine-growing regions of Burgundy, several wine brotherhoods have been established over the years. Operating as friendly societies, these brotherhoods offer mutual and reciprocal assistance to their members in time of need. If a wine grower is not able to harvest their wine either through accident or illness, they are helped by their 'brothers'.

Founded in 1934, the Confrérie des Chevaliers du Tastevins (the Brotherhood of the Tastevin Knights) is the oldest and most prestigious in Burgundy. Established as a promotional society, the brotherhood came into being during the 1930s Depression. At the time, wine, like most other luxuries, was not selling particularly well, so several inhabitants of Nuits St-Georges decided to get together to drink the wine that no-one would buy. To justify this extravagance, they invented a wine brotherhood.

The brothers wear the triple badge of Noah (the father of wine), St Vincent (the patron saint of wine growers) and Bacchus (the god of wine) on the shoulders of their red robes. They meet 20 times a year in the Clos de Vougeot chateau, which they acquired in 1994. At each chapter, its members – mainly Burgundy's business and political elite – anonymously taste test 'which wines one would like to offer to one's friends'. These wines are called tastevinées, which set the standards for the rest of Burgundy's wines.

From Vougeot the ride heads east, passing through the tiny village of Gilly-lès-Cîteaux (20km). It is worth detouring into the heart of town, where the medieval, moated **Château de Gilly** makes an impressive photo opportunity.

From Gilly, the route winds through pockets of forest to reach the **Abbaye de Cîteaux** (29km), in a vast oak wood. A Cistercian monastic order has met here since the 12th century. Guided tours are possible (☎ 03 80 61 11 53; closed Tuesday).

From the Abbaye the ride returns to the Côte d'Or, passing through the small towns of St Nicholas-lès-Cîteaux (34km) and Agencourt, to finish in Nuits-St Georges. This long, flat stretch of road is also something of a local drag strip.

Nuits-St Georges

Slap bang in the heart of the vineyards, Nuits-St Georges is the self-declared capital of the Côte de Nuits – the strip of vineyards running between this town and Dijon known as the 'Champs Élysées of the Côte d'Or'. The central square is dominated by a 17th-century belfry.

The tourist office (☎ 03 80 61 22 47, fax 03 80 61 30 98) is on rue Sonoys. The bank, the bike shop, the boulangerie, the post office and the pharmacy can all be found along place de la Libération.

Things to See & Do Nuits-St Georges' *raison d'être* is its **dégustations**. The tourist office can provide a full listing of which cellars offer tastings. The **Musée de Nuits-St Georges** (☎ 03 80 62 01 57) houses a collection of Gallo-Roman works and a display on the history of Cîteaux monks in the area.

Places to Stay & Eat The *Camping de Moulin de Prissey* (☎ 03 80 62 31 15) is 5km south at Prémeaux-Prissey along the N74. It charges 50FF for two people and a tent (open April through October).

Hotel accommodation is on the pricey side in Nuits-St Georges. The cheapest bed is at the *Hôtel de l'Étoile* (☎ 03 80 61 04 68, place de la Libération). Singles/doubles with shower cost 150/200FF. *Hostellerie St Vincent* (☎ 03 80 61 14 91, fax 03 80 61 24 65, rue Général de Gaulle) has doubles with shower from 360FF to 400FF (closed Monday).

Mme de Loisy runs a luxurious *chambre d'hôte,* (☎ 03 80 61 02 72, fax 03 80 61 36 14, 28 rue Général de Gaulle). Doubles/quads cost 650/950FF.

A *food market* takes place on Friday morning. A *Petit Casino* supermarket is on Grand Rue (closed Thursday morning).

Restaurant des Cultivateurs, (☎ 03 80 61 10 41, 12 rue Général de Gaulle) serves regional dishes from 50FF.

L'Alambic (☎ 03 80 61 35 00), attached to the Hostellerie St Vincent, has Burgundian *menus* for 85/120/150FF.

Days 1 & 2: Dijon – Nuits-St Georges – Beaune

BURGUNDY

N ⊕

1:300,000

Cue — Day 1

Cue	
start	Dijon tourist office
0km	go SW on rue Dr Chaussier
0.4	Rue de l'Hopital/NT4
0.7	onto ring road
0.8	D122 'to Marsannay-la-Côte'
7.5	Fixin
11.5	Gevrey-Chambertin
17.5	'to Clos de Vougeot' Vougeot
17.6	D122E
18.5	Clos de Vougeot 4km
20.0	Gilly-lès-Cîteaux
20.5	'to Abbaye de Cîteaux'
20.6	D109C 'to Abbaye de Cîteaux'
23.0	St Bernard
23.1	D116B 'to Abbaye de Cîteaux'
23.5	D109C
29.0	D996
	Abbaye de Cîteaux
30.0	D8 'to Nuits-St Georges'
34.0	St Nicholas-lès-Cîteaux
40.0	Agencourt
42.6	Rue Docteur Legrand
42.9	Rue Sonoys
43.0	Nuits-St Georges tourist office

Cue — Day 2

Cue	
start	Nuits-St Georges tourist office
0.1	go W on Rue Sonoys
	N74
0.2	'to Chaux'
0.4	D8 'to Chaux'
0.5	2×1r gradua climb
5.0	Chaux
5.5	C2 to Villers-la-Faye
8.0	Villers-la-Faye
8.1	cnb D115
8.2	D1 5C
9.0	Magny-lès-Villers
9.3	C5 'to Perrand-Vergelesses'
5.5	20m very steep climb
13.0	D18 'to Beaune'
15.5	D18
21.5	conco ring road
21.7	Blud Bretonière
20.8	Rue Maufoux
21.9	Flcce de la Hache
22.0	Beaune tourist office

Elevation: Day 1 — Dijon, Gevrey-Chambertin, Vougeot, Nuits-St Georges, St Nicholas-lès-Cîteaux (0km 10 20 30 40)

Day 2 — Nuits-St Georges, Chaux, Magny-les-Villers, Beaune (0km 10 20)

1600 1200 800 400 0m

See Day 3 p275
See Day 3 p275

Burgundy Wines – A Drinker's Guide

Believed to have been introduced to the region by the Romans, the wines of Burgundy are regarded as being among the best in the world. Having been extensively worked by the Cistercian monks from the 12th century onwards, the wine trade took off in the 18th century when commercial warehouses were established in Beaune, Nuits-St Georges and Dijon.

The *vignerons* (wine growers) generally have small vineyards (rarely more than 10 hectares), partly because the land is incredibly valuable, but largely because the Napoléonic Code insists every family member receive equal inheritance.

Burgundy does not produce any blended wines. Made almost exclusively with pinot noir – the 'aristocrat of grapes' – the wines of Burgundy are aged for between 10 and 20 years before bottling.

Burgundy uses a pyramid system to classify its wines. At the top are the *Grand Cru* wines, which are identified by the name of the vineyard only. Names to watch for include Corton, Corton Charlemagne, Chevallier Montrachet, Gevrey-Chambertin and Vougeot. Next down are the *Premier Cru* wines, which are first labelled with the name of the village and then with the name of the vineyard. Look for Beaune-Grièves, Volnay-Caillerets or Pommard-Rugiens. On the bottom tier are the *Appellation Communal*, or village wines, which are only named by their village. Names to look for include Beaune and Sauvigny-les-Beaune.

Wine tasting is something of an art form; see the 'Study, Swirl, Sniff, Sip, Swallow' boxed text in the Facts for the Cyclist chapter for a guide. If you want to really know what's passing your lips, the Tourist Office in Beaune sells tasting notes (in English and French). Try either *Les Vignobles de Bourgogne* (100FF) or *Les Vins de Bourgogne* (84FF).

Just remember: on a bike, *you* are the designated driver.

Day 2: Nuits-St Georges to Beaune
1¼–2 hours, 22km

A short day, this ride leaves plenty of time to quaff wine and wander the streets of beautiful Beaune. The ride travels through the heart of the Côte de Beaune and several *Première Cru* vineyards (see the boxed text above for details of this classification), where you can sample some of Burgundy's finest pinot noir.

From Nuits-St Georges, head through Chaux (5km) and onto the Côte de Beaune. The road winds through the vineyards and the villages of Villers-la-Faye and Magny-lès-Villers. A short grunt of a climb leads to the Première Cru vineyards of Pernand-Vergelesses and into the attractive town (12km).

Continue winding down through the vineyards to reach Beaune.

Beaune
See Beaune in the Classic Burgundy ride (pp274–6) for information on accommodation and other services.

Day 3: Beaune to Dijon
3½–4½ hours, 62km

See Day 7 (pp275-6) of the Classic Burgundy ride for a map and description of this day.

South-West France

With its magnificent beaches, expanses of pine forest, dense oak woods, famous wine-growing region, extraordinary food, and architecture and artefacts testifying to a rich history of human settlement, South-West France has something to offer every cycle tourist. Whether you're looking for a leisurely family holiday, an indulgent, wine-quaffing, gourmet B&B experience or a dip into an archaeological and architectural wonderland, you'll find it here.

In this chapter, South-West France incorporates the region of Aquitaine (along the Atlantic Coast and inland east of Bordeaux) and a little of Limousin et Périgord.

CLIMATE

South-West France is known for its mild climate. Around Bordeaux the wide Gironde Estuary carries the steady humidity and temperate climate of the Atlantic Ocean far inland, while the Landes forest to the south acts as a windbreak.

The Atlantic Coast is one of the sunniest places in France, receiving more than 2000 hours of sunshine a year – most of them between May and September. In these months, average daytime coastal temperatures are 20°C. While autumn on the coast is very wet, inland, around the wine-growing areas, the weather is delightful. The winter is short and snow rarely falls. Spring is usually mild and damp. Summer is hot, with occasional storms. The prevailing wind is from the west.

This mild, maritime climate extends inland to the Dordogne, which experiences weather influences from both the Atlantic Ocean and the mountains of the Massif Central. Here spring is cool and wet, and summer (June to September) long and hot. Winter is usually mild but can be cold and dry. Autumn is generally dry and sunny, with comfortable riding temperatures (17°C maximum).

INFORMATION
Maps & Books

Lonely Planet's *South-West France* covers this region in more detail.

The Michelin map No 3033 *Bordeaux* (1:150,000) covers 75km around Bordeaux and the Bordeaux Wine Explorer ride. It includes a Bordeaux city map and index.

The free *Gironde: Carte des Pistes Cyclables*, available from most tourist offices, shows 500km of bikepaths in the *département* (department; administrative division). Last published in 1998, it's losing accuracy; check with locals before taking the narrow orange routes, as some have been closed.

The Caves, Cuisine & Chateaux ride is covered by the Michelin map No 235 *Midi-Pyrénées* (1:200,000).

Information Sources

The Aquitaine region administers the departments of the Gironde, Dordogne, Lot-et-Garonne and, to the south, Landes and Pyrénées-Atlantiques. Its tourist office (☎ 05 56 01 70 00, fax 05 56 01 70 07, 🖳 www.cr-aquitaine.fr) is at 23 Parvis des Chartrons, Bordeaux. This chapter also extends into the Lot department of the Midi-Pyrénées region. See Information Sources under each subregion for departmental contact details.

The Gîtes de France office (see Accommodation in the Facts for the Cyclist chapter) has *gîte* (self-contained accommodation) and *chambre d'hôte* (B&B) guides for the Gironde, Dordogne and Lot.

The Gironde department's free walking guides (Plans-Guides Randonnées – VTT) detail paths suitable for mountain biking.

GATEWAY CITIES
Bordeaux

Bordeaux is known for its neoclassical architecture, wide avenues and well-tended public squares and parks, which give the city an 18th-century grandeur. Its excellent museums, ethnic diversity, lively university community and untouristed atmosphere make it more than just a convenient stop before beginning a ride.

Information The helpful tourist office (☎ 05 56 00 66 00, fax 05 56 00 66 01, 🖳 www.bordeaux-tourisme.com) is at 12 cours du XXX Juillet (closes at 4.30 pm on Sunday from October to April). Hotel reservations around Bordeaux are free. The office has an excellent free city map, *Bordeaux Plan Guide*.

For the Bordeaux city *Pistes Cyclable* (Bikepaths) map go to the Hôtel de Département (☎ 05 56 99 33 33) behind the Centre Mériadeck on rue Jean Fleuret.

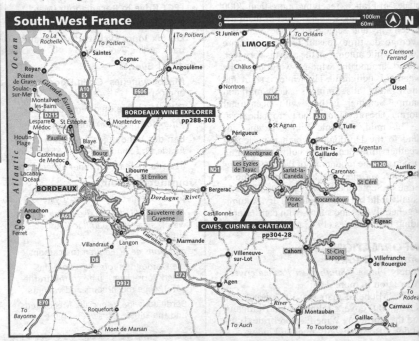

A Banque de France is around the corner from the tourist office at 15 rue Esprit des Lois. Other nearby banks are on cours de l'Intendance, rue Esprit des Lois and cours du Chapeau Rouge. The main post office is at rue du Château d'Eau.

Cycles Peugeot Pasteur (☎ 05 56 92 68 20, fax 05 56 94 22 27), 42 cours Pasteur (near place de la Victoire), is well stocked, though busy, so repairs can take a while. It rents mountain bikes (VTTs) for 70/250FF a day/week (closed Saturday afternoon in July and August).

Cyberstation (☎ 05 56 01 15 15) is at 23 cours Pasteur.

Things to See & Do Explore Bordeaux's beautiful gardens, squares, promenades and graceful buildings with the tourist office's free city map and **walking tour** itinerary.

The outstanding **Musée d'Aquitaine** (☎ 05 56 01 51 00), 20 cours Pasteur, illustrates the history and ethnography of the Bordeaux area from 25,000 years ago to the 19th century. The **Musée des Beaux-Arts** (☎ 05 56 10 16 93), 20 cours d'Albret, is in the 18th-century Hôtel de Ville complex. The museum has a large collection of paintings, including 17th-century Flemish, Dutch and Italian works. Nearby, the **Musée des Arts Décoratifs** (☎ 05 56 00 72 50), 39 rue Bouffard, specialises in faïence (earthenware), porcelain, silverwork, glasswork and furniture.

Entrepôts Lainé, built in 1824 as a warehouse for the rare and exotic products of France's colonies (coffee, vanilla etc), now houses the **Musée d'Art Contemporain** (☎ 05 56 00 81 50), whose entrance is opposite 16 rue Ferrère. The **Centre National Jean Moulin** (☎ 05 56 79 66 00), facing the north side of the cathedral, has exhibits on France during WWII.

In 1137, the future King Louis VII married Eleanor of Aquitaine in the **Cathédrale St André**. The exterior wall of the nave dates from 1096; most of church was built in the 13th and 14th centuries.

The main shopping area is east of place Gambetta along the pedestrianised **rue Porte Dijeaux**; the upscale, boutique-lined **cours de l'Intendance** and **rue Ste Catherine**.

For **wine activities** see Information Sources for the Bordeaux Wine Region, later in this chapter.

Places to Stay Bordeaux has lots of reasonably priced hotels. Avoid staying in the seedy train station area.

Both camping grounds are 10km out of town. *Camping Les Gravières* (☎ 05 56 87 00 36) is 10km south-east of the centre, at place de Courréjean in Villenave d'Ornon. It costs 22FF for a site and 19FF per adult. Follow the route du Toulouse out of Bordeaux and turn left at the Porte de la Maille.

The *Auberge de Jeunesse* (☎ 05 56 91 59 51, fax 05 56 94 02 98, 22 cours Barbey) was being renovated at the time of writing. Dorm beds cost 62FF.

One of Bordeaux's best cheapies is the two-star *Hôtel Touring* (☎ 05 56 81 56 73, fax 05 56 81 24 55, 16 rue Huguerie); its large singles/doubles cost 120/140FF. The *Hôtel de Famille* (☎ 05 56 52 11 28, fax 05 56 51 94 43, 76 cours Georges Clemenceau) has ordinary but homely rooms from 110/120FF. Hall showers are free.

The *Hôtel Bristol* (☎ 05 56 81 85 01, fax 05 56 51 24 06, e bristol@hotel-bordeaux.com, 4 rue Bouffard) has cheerful and comfortable doubles/triples with 4m-high ceilings, bathroom, toilet and small fridge from 210/290FF; avoid the small, hot and smelly top floor rooms. Bike storage, up the road, is a bit awkward. The *Hôtel de Sèze* (☎ 05 56 52 65 54, fax 05 56 44 31 83, 7 rue de Sèze) has older-style singles/doubles for 220/250FF; some rooms are noisy.

Places to Eat Halfway between the train station and place de la Victoire, the renovated *Marché des Capucins*, off cours de la Marne, opens Tuesday to Sunday mornings. Other fresh produce markets are held at different locations in Bordeaux daily; ask the tourist office for the list. A vast, cheap *Auchan* supermarket is in the Centre Mériadeck. The eastern entrance is opposite 58 rue du Château d'Eau (closed Sunday).

Close to place de Tourny, the cheese shop *Fromagerie Antonin* (6 rue de Fondaudège) is closed daily from 12.45 to 4 pm, on Monday morning and Sunday. Several other *food shops* are in the immediate vicinity.

The inexpensive cafes and restaurants around place de la Victoire are popular with students. They include the *Cassolette Café* (☎ 05 56 92 94 96, 20 place de la Victoire), which offers great-value, family-style French food for 12/36FF per small/large *cassolette* (terracotta plate). It opens for lunch and dinner (closed Sunday).

The richly ornamented *Restaurant Agadir (☎ 05 56 52 28 04, 14 rue du Palais Gallien)* has enormous serves of Moroccan couscous and tajines for 60FF to 80FF; *menus* (set meals) cost 60FF (lunch) to 150FF. A number of other restaurants line the street. Near the Musée d'Aquitaine, several *ethnic restaurants* (Vietnamese, Indian, Lebanese) are on rue du Hâ. *Chinese restaurants* line rue St Rémi, a block north of place du Parlement.

Popular *Chez Édouard (☎ 05 56 81 48 87, 16 place du Parlement)* offers French bistro-style meat and fish dishes. *Menus* cost from 57.50FF (weekday lunches) to 139.50FF. Several other *cafes* and *restaurants*, some with terraces, are nearby.

Getting There & Away Bordeaux is one of France's largest regional transport hubs.

Air Several larger international airlines fly direct to Bordeaux; see the Getting There & Away chapter for details. See the Getting Around chapter for details of domestic flights. Bordeaux airport (☎ 05 56 34 50 50) is 10km west of the city centre. The Jetbus shuttle (☎ 05 56 34 50 50) departs every 30 minutes from the airport and the city between 5.30 am and 10.45 pm. A one way/ return ticket costs 35/55FF; bikes free.

Train Bordeaux train station, Gare St Jean, is about 3km from the city centre and has showers (20FF); watch bikes carefully here. The least trafficked route into town is west along cours de la Marne then, at place de la Victoire, along the pedestrianised rue Ste Catherine. The information office annexe can provide a map and directions (closed Sunday between October and April).

As is usual in places serviced mostly by TGVs, few trains between Bordeaux and large regional hubs carry unbagged bikes. Destinations served include Bayonne (132FF, one hour, 12 to 15 a day), Clermont-Ferrand (286FF, six to seven hours, four to six a day), Nantes (237FF, four hours, four or five a day), Nice (441FF, eight hours, seven a day), Sarlat (118FF, two to three hours, five a day or two on Sunday, one or two take bikes) and Toulouse (163FF, two hours, 10 a day, one takes bikes). See the Getting to/from the Ride sections for regional destinations.

From Paris, take the TGV Atlantique from Gare Montparnasse (337FF to 387FF, three hours, at least 16 a day). Non-TGV trains, which all carry bikes unbagged, leave from Gare d'Austerlitz. In summer one train a day carries bikes in both directions.

Bus From the UK, the European Bike Express service (see Bus in the Getting There & Away chapter) charges £169 (return) to take a passenger and their bike to Bordeaux. Pick-up options are Bordeaux and Agen (which is closer to Cahors, the end town of the Caves, Cuisine & Chateaux ride).

Bordeaux Wine Region

The 113,000-hectare wine-growing area around the city of Bordeaux is the world's largest fine-wine-producing region. Think Haut-Brion, Mouton-Rothschild and Yquem and you have just a few of the prestigious wineries that crowd around Bordeaux. Most famously a region of great reds and painstakingly created dessert wines, Bordeaux also produces rosés, sweet and dry whites, and sparkling wines. The majority have earned the right to include the abbreviation AOC (Appellation d'Origine Contrôlée; also AC) on their labels. This indicates the contents have been grown, fermented and aged according to strict regulations (see 'The ABC of AOC' boxed text overleaf).

Bordeaux has more than 5000 *chateaux* (also known as *domaines, crus* or *clos*). Don't expect palatial residences – here the term refers to the properties where grapes are raised, picked, fermented and then matured as wine; the rest of the 12,500 wine growers in the region hand over wine production to the Gironde's 57 cooperatives. In 1997, the Bordeaux growers produced 855 million bottles of wine – more than a quarter of France's AOC wine production; in 1998, sales totalled 20,000 million francs.

HISTORY

Bordeaux has been producing wine for at least 700 years – the Latin poet Ausonius (circa AD 310–93) was the first known wine rower. In the 11th century demand for wine rew with economic expansion in Europe. Blaye, Bourg and the Graves had vineyards in the 12th century (most of the Médoc was so marshy until the late-17th century).

Fate kick-started Bordeaux's wine trade when, in 1152, Eleanor of Aquitaine married Henry Plantagenet, later the King of England, bringing with her a dowry of Gascony and a large chunk of western France. To keep on the good side of his new subjects, Eleanor's hubby waived the export tax on ships leaving Bordeaux, making the region's wine much cheaper than other imports in England. This trade continued even after the end of the Hundred Years' War (1337–1453), when Gascony reverted to French rule.

The Dutch drained the Médoc wetlands in the mid-17th century to allow successful grape growing, but Bordeaux's top drops only reached England in the early-18th century, after several shiploads were captured during the wars between the French and the British. Smuggling helped keep trade alive while the Brits imposed huge import taxes on things French. Official merchants eventually took over from the black market and developed a brisk trade – many of the original 18th-century firms still exist.

A series of plagues from 1852 decimated the region's vines. The early-20th century wasn't good for trade, with two world wars and Prohibition in the USA. However, in the late-1950s chateaux began reviving the quality that had characterised the region. Bordeaux led initiatives such as chateau bottling (instead of selling in bulk to merchants) and many appellations were classified to maintain stricter controls on quality.

NATURAL HISTORY

Bordeaux's maritime climate is extended inland by the Gironde Estuary at the confluence of the Garonne and the Dordogne rivers. Up to 12km wide and 75km in length, it is the largest estuary in Europe.

The poor, gravelly soil of the Médoc, in the tongue of land between the Atlantic Ocean and the Garonne River, produces exceptional wine; vines grow deep roots, protecting them from flood, drought and temperature extremes. Estates near the river have better drainage, which promotes deeper root growth and therefore better wine, hence the old Bordeaux saying that the best estates are those that 'see the water'. Closer to the river mouth, soil contains more clay, reducing drainage and changing the character of the wine.

Each commune's characteristics have been matched to grape varieties by trial and error over time, and today the ideal grape for each area is specified by the AOC system (see 'The ABC of AOC' boxed text overleaf).

INFORMATION
Information Sources

The Maison du Tourisme de la Gironde (☎ 05 56 52 61 40, fax 05 56 81 09 99, ☐ www .tourisme-gironde.cg33.fr) is at 21 cours de l'Intendance, Bordeaux (closed Sunday). Across the street, the Maison du Vin de Bordeaux (☎ 05 56 00 22 88, fax 05 56 00 22 82, ☐ www.vins-bordeaux.fr), 3 cours du 30 Juillet, runs free wine tastings and has a wealth of information on chateau visits (open weekdays and, from June to mid-October, Saturday until 4 pm). Its free map of production areas, *Vignoble de Bordeaux*, and the brochure *A Bordeaux Wine Tour* provide a good introduction to the region, as does the excellent Web site. Contact details and visiting hours of many chateaux, listed by *famille* (wine growing area), are contained in the brochure *Guide Vignobles et Chais en Bordelais*. Also ask for the *guides découvertes* for the major Bordeaux appellations.

Warnings

The same warnings about drinking and driving apply to drinking and cycling. Excess alcohol reduces judgement of distance and reaction time, which increases your chance of crashing. As a guide, the body metabolises one standard drink an hour – having more than that means it will take several hours for your blood alcohol concentration to fall to zero. Several tastings can add up to a standard drink, so keep tabs on the amount you drink at wineries. Carry a picnic so you can stop for a few hours or just buy wine to taste at the end of the day, once you're off your bike.

France's legal limit is 0.05%. Drivers – or cyclists – exceeding this amount face fines of up to 30,000FF and up to two years in jail.

SOUTH-WEST FRANCE

Local *maisons du vin* (tourist offices that deal mainly with winery visits) can provide information and advise on the best chateaux to visit; they also often sell wine at chateau prices and organise tastings.

Bordeaux's Musée du Vin (☎ 05 56 39 39 20), 12 cours du Médoc, traces the history of wine in the region and offers tastings and courses. A good way to get an overview of

the region is to join the Bordeaux tourist office's half-day chateaux bus tour (see the Gateway Cities section earlier in this chapter for contact details).

Gîtes Bacchus

The Gironde has a special category of Gîte Bacchus, in which the B&B owner is French resident and wine grower. They wi

---

The ABC of AOC

Appellation d'Origine Contrôlée (AOC or AC) is France's geographically based quality control system. The country is divided into *appellations*, or regions, to which strict manufacturing regulations apply. Developed originally for wine, the system has been adapted to prevent cheap imitations of cheese and other products.

In the wine industry, regulations cover *everything* about wine production: the plots deemed to be of suitable quality to grow grapes; the permitted grape varieties, and the proportions of each a wine may contain; the ripeness and alcoholic strength of harvested grapes; minimum vine age; and wine-making techniques. Wines are taste-tested annually before they can claim an AOC rating – 'failures' go to make brandy, at a considerable financial loss to the grower.

Drinking in the Bordeaux region can be confusing; it's divided into 57 appellations, each producing a different style of wine. For convenience, these are grouped into six *familles* (families):

Bordeaux and Bordeaux Supérieur These light reds can be great value and are meant to be drunk young.

Côtes de Bordeaux In this case, *côte* means hills; wines grown on the Bordeaux region's hills are light- to medium-bodied and mature quickly (includes the appellations Premières Côtes de Bordeaux, Premières Côtes de Blaye, Côtes de Bourg, Côtes de Castillon and Côtes de Francs).

Libournais This includes some of the most prestigious vineyards, in St Émilion and Pomerol. Merlot grapes predominate, producing soft, fruity wines. Although the medium- to full-bodied wines are drinkable young, the best appellations should be aged (also includes St Émilion Grand Cru, Lussac-St Émilion, Fronsac, and others).

Médoc and Graves Covering *the* big name chateaux, some of these wines cost thousands of dollars. Grown on the western bank of the Gironde (Médoc) and south of Bordeaux city (Graves), Cabernet Sauvignon is dominant. The wines are best aged, some for decades (also includes Haut Médoc, St Estèphe, Pauillac, St Julien, Listrac, Margaux and Pessac-Léognan).

Dry white wines The major appellation is Bordeaux, with light and crisp varieties or fuller-bodied and oak-aged whites (also includes Graves, Entre-Deux-Mers, Côtes de Blaye, Côtes de Bourg, Côtes de Francs and Pessac-Léognan).

Sweet white wines These are mostly produced with Sémillon, a grape susceptible to noble rot, which is used to produce sweet dessert wine. Sauternes is the most famous appellation (also includes Barsac, Loupiac, St-Croix du Mont, Cadillac and Cérons).

Quality Gradings

Quality classifications vary among appellations. Generally something labelled *Grand Cru* is a higher-quality wine than a *Premier Cru* (first growth), which is still one of the top drops.

The Bordeaux region's first classification system was introduced in the Médoc in 1855. Wine brokers drew up five gradings, with *Premiers Crus* at the top. The gradings continue downwards, with *Deuxièmes Crus* (second growths), *Troisième Crus*, *Quatrièmes Crus* and *Cinquièmes Crus*.

,ladly show guests around their vineyard nd wine making facilities, and can also ecommend regional wines and other growrs to visit.

Overseas Shipping

Touring the world's most famous wine region by bike is all very well, but what do ou do with that case of wine you just *had*

to buy? The best answer might be simply to drink it. Some wineries and wine merchants will organise shipment to anywhere in the world. However, this is an expensive option: you can expect to pay around 940FF per case to the USA, 910FF to Australia and 855FF to the UK.

Check your home country's import limits and duties first.

The ABC of AOC

The 61 Médoc chateaux eligible for these classifications are known as *Grand Crus Classés*. Today, 49% of wineries in the Médoc are classified as *Crus Bourgeois*, a lower grading.

Wines that don't qualify for an AOC rating carry a VDQS (*Vin Delimité de Qualité Supérieur*), Vin de Pays (a regional wine) or Vin de Table (table wine) classification. The VDQS label is seen as a stepping stone to AOC rating and is covered by similar strict laws. Vin de Pays, made according to certain specifications and taste tested, can be quite good. Vin de Table wines can specify only 'France' on the label and can be very ordinary.

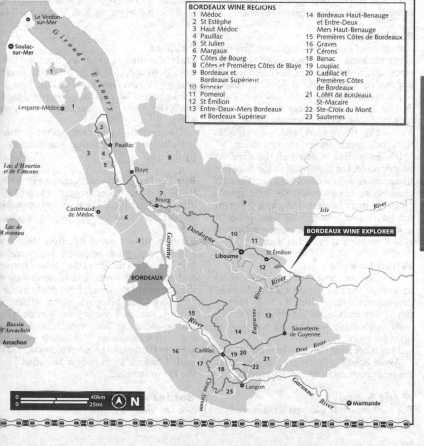

BORDEAUX WINE REGIONS
1 Médoc
2 St Estèphe
3 Haut Médoc
4 Pauillac
5 St Julien
6 Margaux
7 Côtes de Bourg
8 Côtes et Premières Côtes de Blaye
9 Bordeaux et Bordeaux Supérieur
10 Fronsac
11 Pomerol
12 St Émilion
13 Entre-Deux-Mers Bordeaux et Bordeaux Supérieur
14 Bordeaux Haut-Benauge et Entre-Deux Mers Haut-Benauge
15 Premières Côtes de Bordeaux
16 Graves
17 Cérons
18 Barsac
19 Loupiac
20 Cadillac et Premières Côtes de Bordeaux
21 Côtes de Bordeaux St-Macaire
22 Ste-Croix du Mont
23 Sauternes

BORDEAUX WINE EXPLORER

SOUTH-WEST FRANCE

Bordeaux Wine Explorer

Duration..7 days
Distance 294.4km
Difficulty ....easy-moderate
Start..Pauillac
End ....Bordeaux

Give me books, fruit, French wine and fine
weather…

John Keats

Explore the world's largest fine-wine producing region, passing more than 1000
wineries and sampling Bordeaux's six wine
regions. Visit big-name wineries such as Margaux, Latour and Mouton-Rothschild and
discover your own little gems. This scenic
route is lined with interesting museums, Romanesque churches and historic towns.

PLANNING
If your chief motivation for doing this ride
is to visit some prestigious wineries, or the
place that makes your favourite drop, it's
imperative to be organised. Many chateaux
require tour bookings days, weeks or even
months in advance. Others may only open
on weekends or in the afternoon (most close
for lunch). Book tours, and accommodation, for summer several months ahead.

It's impossible to detail all the wineries
on this route, but they're all in the booklets
listed under Information Sources. Contact
chateaux to request tours; the most prestigious are more interested in genuine potential buyers, so getting your wine seller at
home to make the request may win person-
alised attention at the cellar door.

When to Ride
Late September and October are ideal, to
appreciate the mild weather and colours of
the autumn countryside. It's also harvest
time ('vintage'), good for harvest festivals
– although many wineries are too busy to
open for tours.

May is cool and pleasant; June can be wet.
Avoid finishing the ride on Sunday, when
the bikepath into Bordeaux is crowded.

Maps & Books
See the Maps & Books section earlier in the
chapter. The Information Sources section

lists brochures which contain useful maps;
wineries are usually listed only under their
village name.

Mitchell Beazley's *Wine Atlas of France*
is an excellent planning resource for serious
wine explorers; copies of the atlas maps are
invaluable – better than road maps – for negotiating the unsigned back roads to estates
just off the route.

What to Bring
It would be a tragedy to forget the corkscrew;
pack a plastic wineglass and picnic utensils
for dining alfresco.

GETTING TO/FROM THE RIDE
Public transport links Hendaye, the end of
the Raid Pyrénéen, to Bordeaux. It's also
possible to cycle (around 300km – on
bikepaths) from Bayonne, near Hendaye, to
Soulac-sur-Mer; trains link Soulac-sur-Mer
to Pauillac.

Pauillac
Train Pauillac is about an hour by train
from Bordeaux (53FF). Several trains carry
unbagged bikes each weekday (less on
weekends). The special weekend *Médoc
Océan* morning train also carries unbagged
bikes.

The easiest – and most scenic – route
from the station to Pauillac tourist office is
by the quai.

Bus The No 705 Citram Aquitaine (☎ 05 56
99 57 83) bus takes bagged bikes (49FF
plus 20FF per bike, 1¼ hours, 10 on weekdays, 17 on Saturday and two on Sunday.

Bicycle Allow a day to ride from Bordeaux
and be prepared to negotiate heavy traffic
for the first 10km. Avoid the grubby, narrow
and busy D209. Instead, head north-west to
the boulevard ring road; from the tourist office, take the bikepath along allées de
Tourny, which becomes rue Fondaugège
and so on; at the boulevard, turn right and
then left into ave de Tivoli, following the
signs to Blanquefort. Travel along the D21
until Château Siran, where the road joins
the D2 to Pauillac.

Bordeaux
See the Gateway Cities section (p284) for
information on getting from Bordeaux.

It's said Burgundy produces the world's best unblended wines; vineyard views from Château Chinon.

Burgundy's colourful tiled roofs are unmistakeable.

Stock up on ewes milk cheese in Beaune.

The roof tiles are a particularly striking feature of the medieval Hôtel-Dieu des Hospices de Beaune.

SALLY DILLON

Cos d'Estournel winery mimics a Sultan's palace.

JULIA WILKINSON

Sarlat-la-Canéda's famous Saturday market.

SALLY DILLON

Spectacular riding on the St-Cirq Lapopie towpath.

SALLY DILLON

Even St Émilion's festivals pay homage to wine.

SALLY DILLON

One of the best views of the Dordogne River is from the walled town of Domme.

THE RIDE
Pauillac

The capital of the Grand Cru country of the Médoc, Pauillac is a charming town where the pace of life is as tranquil as the estuary it sits on. Here the Gironde stretches at least 3km across and, before it was dredged, made the town an important port. Although the centre of a multi-million-dollar wine industry, Pauillac hasn't turned all snobby – where else could you find a summer 'Wine, Gastronomy and Breeding Festival'? Still, touches of wine-industry style make Pauillac a great place to kick back and relax; find a bar by the water and watch the river turn to gold in the sunset.

Information The Office de Tourisme-Maison du Vin (☎ 05 56 59 03 08, fax 05 56 59 23 38, e tourismeetvindepauillac@wanadoo.fr), route de la Rivière, can help plan chateau tours; it hires VTTs for 70FF per day.

A Crédit Agricole is at 25 rue Ferdinand Buisson. Moto Médoc (☎ 05 56 59 11 74) at 6 place du Maréchal Foch sells and services bikes. Email at the innovative Internet bar and wine shop, le.com Bar à Vin (☎ 05 56 75 28 28), 2 quai Léon Perrier.

Things to See & Do In summer the Maison du Vin hosts free **wine-tasting** evenings run by local winemakers. It also runs **wine tours, tasting classes** and **bottling sessions**.

For fishing, ask at the tourist office to rent **carrelets**, the traditional fishing huts that line the banks of the Garonne.

The tourist office sells maps detailing (in French) four **bike circuits** of between 25km and 55km and brochures for **walking routes** of the town and surrounding vineyards.

Places to Stay The shaded, riverside **Camping Les Gabarreys** (☎ 05 56 59 16 61, fax 05 56 73 30 68, route de la Rivière) is 2.2km south of town. Tent sites cost 42/55FF for one/two people (open April to mid-October).

The **Hôtel de France et d'Angleterre** (☎ 05 56 59 01 20, fax 05 56 59 02 31, 3 quai Albert Pichon), on the water, has rooms with shower and toilet for 300FF (closed Christmas/New Year).

At Leyssac, 7km north of Pauillac on the Day 1 route, the elegant, three-star **Château Pomys** (☎ 05 56 59 32 26, fax 05 56 59 35

24) – classified Cru Bourgeois Supérieur – for once, does resemble a noble residence; it charges 370FF for pleasant doubles with shower and toilet, and 40FF for breakfast. Visits to the *chai* (cellar) can be arranged.

Clos de Puyzac (☎/fax 05 56 59 35 28, 8 route des Ormes de Pez) is a chambre d'hôte 11km north of Pauillac. Follow the Day 1 route for 10.1km, then turn left to Pez. The owners are winemakers and are happy to show you their chai. Sweet double rooms cost 230FF (shared bathroom) or 290FF with private bathroom and kitchen; the closest restaurants are in St Estèphe, 2km away.

Places to Eat A Saturday-morning **market** is held in the middle of Pauillac. The **Casino** supermarket is on rue de Vignes Oudides (closed Sunday afternoon). A **boulangerie-patisserie** is at 12 rue Jean Jaurès (closed Monday and on Sunday afternoon).

For take-away wine, the **Maison du Vin** offers chateau prices. The wine merchant **le.com Bar à Vin** (2 quai Léon Perrier) is a great place to kick back for wine, coffee, snacks and jazz; and for structured wine tastings. Next door, at **Enzo** (☎ 05 56 59 07 83), pizza *menus* start at 70FF (closed Sunday in winter, and December through January).

The **Hôtel de France et d'Angleterre** restaurant has a riverfront terrace and *menus* for 85FF to 220FF (closed Sunday night and Monday in the low season).

Day 1: Pauillac Circuit
1–2 hours, 21km

A simple, small loop, this ride could be done in an afternoon or stretched over a leisurely day to incorporate several pre-booked winery visits. It's pleasant cycling, with a few short hills, a flat riverside stretch and plenty of opportunities to visit wineries. The gently rolling hills support orderly rows of meticulously tended grape vines (mainly Cabernet Sauvignon) that produce some of the world's most sought-after red wines.

At 3.2km a side trip visits the famous **Château Mouton-Rothschild** (☎ 05 56 73 21 29, fax 05 56 73 21 28). Its **Musée du Vin dans l'Art** is a priceless collection of wine-related art spanning three millennia. The slick 20FF guided tour (by appointment only) visits the museum, the wine making facilities, the richly stocked store and the famous Grand Chai. Tours with tastings

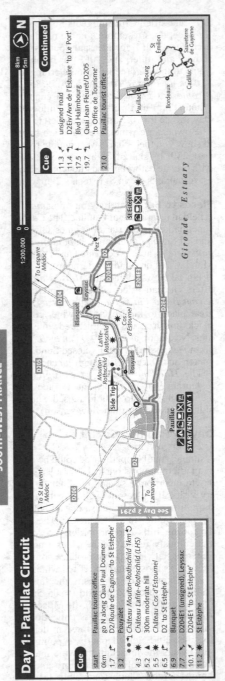

See Day 2 p291

SOUTH-WEST FRANCE

Day 1: Pauillac Circuit

Cue		
start		Pauillac tourist office
0km	⬆	go N along Quai Paul Doumer
1.7	⬅	D2/Route de Cagnon 'to St Estèphe'
3.2		Pouyalet
4.3	●●⬆	Château Mouton-Rothschild 1km ↰
5.2	✳ ⬅	Château Lafitte-Rothschild (LHS)
5.5		300m moderate hill
6.5	⬆	Château Cos d'Estournel
6.9	➘	Blanquet
7.7	➘	D204E1 (unsigned), Leyssac
10.1	➘	D204E1 to St Estèphe'
11.2	✳	St Estèphe

Cue		
11.3	➘	unsigned road
11.4	⬅	D2Eiv/Ave de l'Estuaire 'to Le Port'
17.5	⬅	Blvd Halimbourg
19.7	➘	Quai Jean Fleuret/D205 'to Office de Tourisme'
21.0		Pauillac tourist office

(weekdays only) cost 80FF (closed weekends from November through March).

The beautifully landscaped **Château Lafite Rothschild** (4.3km; ☎ 05 56 89 78 00) is one of the original four Premier Cru Classé chateaux. Only a round tower of the medieval chateau remains; the current building dates from the 18th century (open Tuesday to Thursday afternoons, by appointment).

At the top of the day's only real hill is the quirky, orient-inspired **Château Cos d'Estournel** (5.5km; ☎ 05 56 73 15 55, fax 05 56 59 72 59, e estournel@estournel.com) built in the late-19th century by Louis Gaspard d'Estournel. Reservations for the free one-hour tour and tasting must be made in writing at least 24 hours in advance.

The St Estèphe **Maison du Vin** (☎ 05 56 59 30 59, fax 05 56 59 73 72) is on place de l'Église. On summer weekdays it runs 30FF *dégustations* (tastings) from 11 am to 6 pm. Across the square, this tiny town's huge 18th-century **church** has visible 9th-century Romanesque foundations and a lavish interior.

From St Estèphe head down to the banks of the Gironde, where wooden *carrelets* support nets over the water. Chateaux peer over gently sloping vineyards; these are the lucky few which 'see the water'.

Day 2: Pauillac to Bourg
1¾–3½ hours, 35km

Another day for the 'no hills' enthusiast, the route sticks by the river, crossing the Garonne on a ferry (☎ 05 57 42 04 49) at Port de Lamarque (18FF, bikes 8FF; four to nine daily) – check sailing times with the Pauillac tourist office. East of the river, the route takes the small, mostly flat *corniche* (coast road) to Bourg. This avoids the area's rolling countryside, but also bypasses a lot of wineries – those with the thirst for more can take the hard detour from Plassac.

Up to 30km can be added to the day with alternative routes and side trips – the longest of which enters the Margaux appellation, home to some of Bordeaux's most celebrated vineyards.

The main road south of Pauillac is dotted with palatial wine-making estates. A pick of the best is the elegant **Château Pichon Longueville** (2.7km); across the road the **Château Comtesse de Lalande**, built and still run by a woman (a rarity in Bordeaux), and the extremely friendly **Château Latour**

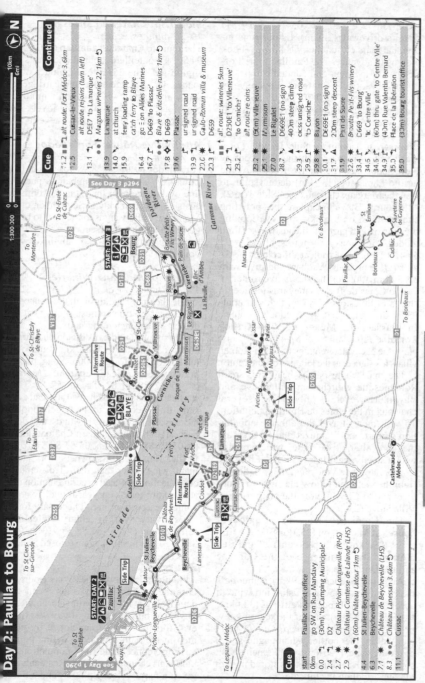

N

1:300 200 0
0

10km
6mi

SOUTH-WEST FRANCE

Cue | Continued

11.2 alt route: Fort Médoc 3.6km
12.5 Cussac-le-Vieux
        alt route rejoins (turn left)
13.1 D5E7 'to Lamarque'
13.9 Lamarque
        Margaux wineries 22.1km
14.0 at church
15.9 ferry loading ramp
        catch ferry to Blaye
16.4 gc c: on Allées Marines
16.7 D669 'to Plassac'
        Blaye & citadelle ruins 1km
17.8 D669
19.6 Plassac
19.9 unsigned road
20.0 unsigned road
        Gallo-Roman villa & museum
20.3 D659
21.7 alt route: wineries 5km
        D250E1 'to Villeneuve'
23.2 'to Corniche'
        alt route rejoins
23.2 (5km) Villeneuve
25.7 Marmisson
27.0 Le Rigalet
28.7 D669E1 (no sign)
        400m steep climb
29.3 cross unsigned road
29.5 'to Corniche'
29.8 Bayon
30.1 D669E1 (no sign)
31.7 220m steep descent
31.9 Pain de Sucre
        Broutte Pe it-Fils winery
32.6 C669 to Bourg
33.4 'tc Centre Ville'
34.5 (60m) thru gate 'to Centre Ville'
34.9 (4.0m) Rue Valentin Bernard
35.0 Place ce la Libération
35.0 (30m) Bourg tourist office

Cue

start	
0km	Pauillac tourist office
0.0	go SW on Rue Manday
2.4	(30m) 'to Camping Municipale'
2.7	D2
2.9	Château Pichon-Longueville (RHS)
	Château Comtesse de Lalande (LHS)
	(60m) Château Latour 1km
4.4	St-Julien-Beychevelle
6.3	Beychevelle
7.1	Château de Beychevelle (LHS)
8.3	Château Lanessan 3.6km
11.1	Cussac

(☎ 05 56 73 19 80, fax 05 56 73 19 81) down a driveway (2.9km). Latour runs individual tours on summer weekdays – book months in advance. The Pauillac tourist office has further tour and contact details.

The beautiful **Château Beychevelle** (7.1km; ☎ 05 56 73 20 70, fax 05 56 73 20 71, ⓔ beychevelle@beychevelle.com) allows weekday visits year-round.

Horse lovers should detour to **Château Lanessan** at 8.3km (see Side Trip 1). For a break from wineries, visit the 17th-century **Fort Médoc** (see Alternative Route). At the turn to Lamarque (13.1km) detour south to visit the Margaux chateaux (see Side Trip 2).

Detour to Blaye to explore the sprawling **citadel** ruins, on a rocky spur overlooking the narrowest part of the estuary. Book guided, 25FF tours at the tourist office (☎ 05 57 42 12 09). The **Syndicat Viticole** (☎ 05 57 42 91 19), on cours Vauban, can give winery information for the alternative route.

The Côtes de Blaye vineyards terrace up slopes of limestone clay soil that's dramatically different from the Médoc's pebbles. In Plassac, the **Musée et Villa Gallo-Romaine** (20.0km; ☎ 05 57 42 84 80) displays the excavated remains of Gallo-Roman villas (it's signed, to the left, just off the route).

The main route passes beautiful, small **Romanesque churches** at Villeneuve and Bayon. However, it only passes several chateaux in the Côtes de Bourg appellation. To visit more, travel through the appellation's heart, via Montuzet and St Ciers on the hard alternative route, which begins with a steep ascent from Plassac. From the Conservatoire de Vinicole (20.3km), dogleg right then left and follow the signs to Montuzet and St Ciers. Rejoin the main route at Villeneuve (23.2km).

The Corniche Fleuri has **troglodyte houses** at Marmisson (25.1km). At the iron cross (29.1km) is a panorama of the **Bec d'Ambès**, the confluence of the Garonne and the Dordogne.

At **Pain de Sucre** (31.9km) someone's likely to be selling fresh fish. Find wine to accompany it at **Brouette Petit-Fils** (32.6km; ☎ 05 57 68 42 09), one of the region's few producers of *méthode traditionelle* (fermented in the bottle, Champagne-style) sparkling wine. Free tours – in French – visit some of the 1.5 million bottles stored in 3km of caves riddling the hillside.

Side Trip: Château Lanessan
10–20 minutes, 3.6km

The route to **Château Lanessan** (☎ 05 56 58 94 80, ⓔ bouteiller@bouteiller.com) is well signposted. The 35FF tour includes a visi to the chai, the large horse-and-carriage museum and tasting. If you don't mind dir roads, ask for directions to the lovely back route along the levees to Beychevelle.

Alternative Route: Fort Médoc
¼–½ hour, 4.9km

Fort Médoc (☎ 05 56 58 98 40) was built by Louis XIV's architect Vauban as part of a line of defence over the estuary. Admission costs 12FF (open May to September, close Monday). Follow signs to the fort; to return go left at the first intersection. The D2E9 re joins the main route 1km south of where you left it.

Side Trip: Margaux Wineries
1¼–2¼ hours, 21.6km

While the only road through the area can be quite busy, no true enthusiast can visit Bor deaux and not reach Margaux.

The snobby **Syndicat Viticole de Margau** (☎ 05 57 88 70 82) is 8.7km south of the turn-off on the D2. Just 100m along, the cele brated neoclassical **Château Margau** (☎ 05 57 88 83 83, fax 05 57 88 31 32 ⓔ chateau-margaux@chateau-margaux.com runs free weekday tours which book u months ahead (no tours in August and durin harvest). The ultra-modern **Château Palme** (☎ 05 57 88 72 72, fax 05 57 88 37 16) is further 1km south. Its owners work hard t make wine better than their Troisième Cr classification and lead experimentation in th area. Daily tours run year-round. Except i winter, reservations aren't necessary for fre tours of the early-17th-century **Château d'Is san's winery** (☎ 05 x57 88 35 91, fax 05 5 88 74 24), 1km south again (closed Sunday

Bourg

Although still known locally as Bourg-su Gironde, shifting river sands mean thes days Bourg is flanked by the Dordogne. Th town was one of a chain of *bastides* (med eval fortified towns) developed by noble men in the 13th century to define politica territory, concentrate rural populations an kick-start economic growth. Residents wer given a narrow house plot around a marke

quare, plus land they could cultivate out-
ide the town.

Bourg retains some of the original
astide gates and fortifications, plus its
8th-century citadel. The quiet town is the
apital of the Côtes de Bourg appellation,
nd is a good place to just sit by the water
nd relax.

nformation The tourist office (☎ 05 57 68
1 76, fax 05 57 68 30 25) occupies one of
ne grandest houses on place du République.
: opens Tuesday to Sunday until at least
pm from Easter to September. In the other
nonths it's only open weekday afternoons,
) 7 pm.

The Maison du Vin (☎ 05 57 94 80 20,
ax 05 57 94 80 21, ⌨ bourg.cotes-bordea
x.alienor.fr) is at 1 place Epernon.

The Crédit Agricole is on the D669/ave F
)alcau. The post office is on rue du Château
'ieux.

Espace 2 Roues (☎ 05 57 68 40 48), 9 ave
'harles de Gaulle, does repairs and has
ental bikes.

hings to See & Do The tourist office
.ns **guided tours** of the heritage-listed
)wn and has several **walking/VTT route
naps** for the area.

The citadel's chateau has been recon-
tructed in the **Parc de la Citadelle**, where
ne balcony allows fine river views. Here,
ne **Musée Hippomobile au Temps des
alèches** (☎ 05 57 68 23 57) displays 40
eautiful, 19th-century horse carriages.

In a 16th-century house on rue E Couz
1et, the eclectic **Musée Maurice Poignant**
☎ 05 57 68 31 76), an interesting collec-
on, showcases local traditions, cinemato-
raphy and archaeology.

Watch fishermen at work in the port, or
ead west on rue Hoche to see the Gironde's
ldest (11th-century) **wash house**. Next to
ne camping ground, the **municipal pool** has
backdrop resorts would kill for.

laces to Stay The small, basic **Camping
/lunicipale la Citadelle** (☎ 05 57 68 40 06)
. at the foot of the bastide, by the river.
haded sites cost 10FF, plus 9.50FF per
erson (open May to September); check in
: the pool.

Hotel le St Christophe (☎ 05 57 68 22
6, place de la Libération) has a monopoly
on accommodation in Bourg. It charges
from 190FF for a double with shower.

At Pain de Sucre, 3.1km before Bourg,
the Guerin family offers **chambre d'hôte**
(☎/fax 05 57 68 23 42) in their riverside
home, with comfortable single/double rooms
for 220/250FF.

Two kilometres north of Bourg, the Gite
Bacchus **Château de la Grave** (☎ 05 57 68
41 49, fax 05 57 68 49 26) has rooms in a
Louis XVIII-style restored villa in the heart
of a vineyard. Doubles cost 300FF. To get
there, at the entry to Bourg, turn left off the
D669 onto the D251 (signposted to 'Berson/
St Trojan') 400m before the Champion
supermarket; take the second right on the
D251 and follow the signs.

Places to Eat Bourg's **market** is held on
Sunday morning in place de la Libération.
The **Boulangerie de Vieux Four** is on the
square (closed Monday and Sunday). The
large **Champion** supermarket is on the
D669 (closed Sunday afternoon).

Le Plaisance (☎ 05 57 68 45 34, 4 place
Eugène Marchal), near the harbour, is a
busy brasserie selling pizzas from 36FF to
54FF. **Le Troque Sel** (☎ 05 57 68 30 67,
1 place Jeantet), offers local dishes, specialising in fish, with menus from 65FF to
145FF and reasonably priced wine.

Day 3: Bourg to St Émilion
2¼–5½ hours, 54km
Travel across gently rolling countryside,
through several appellations, including exclusive Pomerol and St Émilion.

Exit Bourg downhill through the fortified
Porte de la Mer, inscribed with the dates of
the nine sieges in the town's history. For
prehistory, take the signed side trip to the
Grottes de Pair-non-Pair (5.5km; ☎ 05 57
68 33 40), named 'Even-Odd' after a village
that was lost by its owner in a game of
heads or tails. It's no Lascaux, but the simple cave and lack of tourist hype make for
a genuine feeling of discovery. The 15FF
guided tour of the 25,000-year-old cave engravings takes about 40 minutes (open May
to September).

The **Pierres de Graves quarry** (6.6km)
once supplied stone to build Bordeaux and
was used as the setting for Robert Hossein's
film Les Misérables. Some of the stone may
even have found its way into the elegant

SOUTH-WEST FRANCE

Day 3: Bourg to St Émilion

Cue

start		Bourg tourist office
0km		go E across square
0.0	↰	(50m) Rue Cahoreau
0.2	↱	Cours de l'Abbaye
2.9	↰	unsigned road
3.6	↱	D669 'La Lustre'
4.8	↱	D133 (no sign)
5.5	●●●	Grottes 600m ↺
6.6	✴	quarry
6.7	↱	D133 (no sign)
6.9	↱	D669 (no sign)
10.5	↰	D115, St Gervais
12.1	↱	D115 'to St-André de Cubzac'
12.6	↱	D115 'to Virsac'
13.1	●●●	Château de Bouilh 1.8km ↺
		cross N137 via service road
		(20m) Chemin de Virsac
14.3	↱	D115E1
15.4	↱	D115E2 'to St Antoine'
15.8		pass under N10 on service road
15.9	↱	D115E1 'to St Antoine'
16.4	↱	D10 'to Aubie-Espessas'
16.6		St Antoine

Cue (Continued)

17.3	↱	D10 (no sign)
18.4	↰	unsigned road, Espessas
20.4		Salignac
23.1	↰	D246 'to Mouillac'
23.8		Mouillac
27.2	↱	D138E4 'to Lugon', Les Gaussens
29.8	↱	D138E4 'to Lugon'
31.5		unsigned road at church, Lugon
31.5	↱	(50m) D138 'to Villegouge'
31.5	↱	(30m) D138E3 'to St Aignan'
33.9		Meyney
34.2	↱	'to Villegouge'
34.7	↰	D246 'to St Aignan'
37.0		Vincent

Cue (Continued)

39.4	↱	'to Port'
39.9	↰	D670 'to Libourne'
40.4	↱	D670 'to Libourne'
42.7	↱	'to Centre Ville'
43.6	✴	'to Office de Tourisme'
43.9		Libourne
44.0	↰	400m cobbled road
44.4		at museum, unsigned road
44.5	↱	D670 'to St Émilion'
44.6	◇	unsigned road/'to St Émilion'
44.9	◇	'to St Émilion'
45.0	◇	'to Pomerol'
45.2	↱	'to Pomerol'
47.5	■	alt route: Pomerol 2.8km
48.1	■	alt route rejoins (go left)
48.7	↰	D243 'to St Émilion' – Le Cros
50.7	↱	'to Office de Tourisme'
53.6	↰	'to Office de Tourisme'
53.9		Rue du Clocher
54.0		(30m) St Émilion tourist office

See Day 2 p291
See Day 4 p297
START: DAY 3
START: DAY 4

8th-century **Château du Bouilh** (☎ 05 57 3 01 45), a well-signed side trip at 12.6km. he chateau, in the centre of a large wine state, has a 500m rough driveway, unsuitble for road bikes. Tours and tastings cost 0FF (open Thursday to Sunday afternoons etween July and September).

After the mess of roads into St Antoine, he scenery gets better and better. Each vilage has a beautiful Romanesque church; nd early-morning cyclists may spot deer in voods among the vineyards.

Riverside scenery takes over towards Liourne (43.9km), a once busy port bastide ounded by the Black Prince – Edward,)uke of Aquitaine – in 1268. It retains the npressive 15th-century town hall and araded central square.

To ride through the heart of the most exensive wine real estate in the world, turn left efore Catusseau (see Alternative Route).

Alternative Route: Pomerol
.8km, 15 minutes

his tiny appellation measures only 3km by km but, as it produces some of France's nost distinctive wines, its land changes ands at a premium, with that cost reflected n its wine prices. The most expensive omes from the seven-hectare Château 'etrus, where a bottle of the 1996 was selling for around 5600FF at the time of writing.

Turn left off the main route onto small arm roads, following signs to Pomerol hrough two intersections. Turn right towards the church at the T-junction. To visit he **Syndicat Viticole** (☎ 05 57 25 06 88) nd some of the **wineries**, turn left after the hurch. Otherwise turn right, then left and ght at the following two T-junctions. At he third, turn left to rejoin the main route.

St Émilion

his medieval village is renowned for its ull-bodied, mellow red wines and its beauiful architecture. Built on two limestone ills overlooking the Dordogne River val-ey, the town takes on a luscious golden hue s the sun sets.

In the 8th century, a Benedictine monk amed Émilion moved into a cave fed by a pring. A monastery was later established, round which a walled city grew. During he Middle Ages, St Émilion was a staging ost for pilgrims heading to Santiago de Compostela (see the 'St Jacques de Compostelle Pilgrimage' boxed text in the Languedoc-Roussillon chapter). The town's 12th-century wine-growing traditions continue; the red-robed Jurade guild leads ceremonies for major events – which are celebrated with gusto – if you get the chance, join the festivities to experience French village life at its best.

Information The tourist office (☎ 05 57 55 28 28, fax 05 57 55 28 29, ℮ st-emilion .tourisme@wanadoo.fr), place des Créneaux, lists chateaux details in the *St-Émilion Guide* and may arrange visits; it rents bicycles for 90FF a day.

The Maison du Vin (☎ 05 57 55 50 55, fax 05 57 24 65 57) is around the corner at place Pierre Meyrat.

The Crédit Agricole on rue des Girondins has an ATM; the Caisse d'Épargne bank and post office are on rue Guadet.

Things to See & Do St Émilion's quaint streets and squares are lined with wine shops, most of which offer free **tasting** to serious buyers. Learn the art of wine tasting at the excellent **Initiations à la Dégustation** run by the Maison du Vin from mid-July to mid-September. At **Cloître des Cordeliers**, a ruined monastery on rue des Cordeliers, a century-old winery makes sparkling wine and offers cellar tours.

The town's most interesting historical sites can be visited only on the tourist office's guided **Église Monolithe Tour**, which includes the enormous underground church, cut from limestone between the 9th and 12th centuries; and sites such as the **Grotte de l'Ermitage**, the cave where Émilion lived.

Several of the city's medieval gates survive, including **Porte de la Cadène** off rue Guadet. Next door is **Maison de la Cadène**, a half-timbered early-16th-century house. The old town is most atmospheric at night.

Taste the town's famous **macaroons**, first made in the 17th century by Ursuline nuns.

Places to Stay About 2km north of St Émilion, the *Camping de la Barbanne* (☎ 05 57 24 75 80), on the D122, charges 40FF for a site and 25FF per person (open April to September). Two-bedroom cabins with shower and toilet cost 230/300FF in low/high season.

SOUTH-WEST FRANCE

Two *chambres d'hôtes* offer accommodation among the vines; the route into town passes both. At 52.7km, *Château Millaud Montlabert* (☎ 05 57 24 71 85, fax 05 57 24 62 78) produces Grand Cru wine and has doubles in a typical Girondine, 18th-century home for 300FF. At 54.2km, *La Gomerie* (☎/fax 05 57 24 68 85) has doubles for 260FF. The tourist office has a list of *B&Bs*.

The two-star *Auberge de la Commanderie* (☎ 05 57 24 70 19, fax 05 57 74 44 53, rue des Cordeliers) has spacious, flowery doubles from 280FF (350FF in June and most of September). The three-star *Logis des Remparts* (☎ 05 57 24 70 43, fax 05 57 74 47 44, rue Guadet) has a pool, and pleasant doubles from 350FF.

Places to Eat St Émilion has two *Spar Alimentation* groceries: north, on the D122; and south (closed Sunday morning) of town. The *boulangeries* are on rue Guadet and rue de la Grande Fontaine (both closed Monday afternoon from mid-October to June).

Pizzeria de la Tour (☎ 05 57 24 68 91, rue de la Grande Fontaine), below the Tour du Roi, has ordinary crepes and pizza (open Friday and weekends only in low season; closed November).

L'Huîtrier-Pie (☎ 05 57 24 69 71, 11 rue Porte Bouqueyre) serves excellent, large meals in a friendly atmosphere, with *menus* from 68FF to 170FF. Good Bordeaux wine costs 20/40FF per half-litre/litre.

L'Envers du Décor (☎ 05 57 74 48 31, rue du Clocher), a wine bistro, has *plats du jour* for 50FF, passable *menus* from 105FF and vintage wine by the glass (closed Sunday from November to June).

Day 4: St Émilion to Sauveterre de Guyenne

2¼–4½ hours, 44.9km

Leave the rich red wines and villages of the St Émilion jurisdiction for the dry white wines and fruity reds of the Entre-Deux-Mers region. This triangle between the Garonne and Dordogne rivers is a patchwork of woods, vineyards, farms and bastide towns, many of which retain traditional arcaded markets. Traversed by the pilgrim route to Santiago de Compostela, the region is dotted with picturesque churches.

The route climbs to St Hippolyte (6.3km) on the Ferrand plateau. The town is little more than a 14th- and 16th-century, wooden framed **church**, and a million-dollar **view** of the Dordogne Valley. Past the church, **Château de Ferrand winery** may have the doors open to its bottling line. Check your brakes before the steep, scenic descent out of St Hippolyte.

St-Étienne de Lisse (11.3km) is a pretty collection of historic buildings, including a 12th-century church and a ruined castle built by the English during the Hundred Years War. Hidden inside St Magne's 11th century church are several patches of Roman floor mosaics.

The English were finally expelled from France in Castillon-la-Bataille (17.3km), the site of the last battle in the Hundred Years War, in 1453.

The route also passes the **Maison du Vin de Castillon** (☎ 05 57 40 00 88).

It's a challenging climb to Pujols, where the enormous **church** (25.8km) packs tens of centuries of history into its walls. The view from the 16th-century **chateau ramparts** nearby is magnificent.

The **Moulin de Labarthe**, a rare 14th century fortified mill, is 500m off-route at 36.2km. Before Blasimon, detour to the ruins of a **Benedictine abbey**, alongside the 12th to 13th-century **Église St Nicolas**. The doorway suffered the fate of many religious structures in the Revolution, when the carved figures were beheaded.

Campers could stop in quiet Blasimon (37.8km), where the nearby *camping ground* is part of a lakeside centre offering a host of activities (☎ 05 56 71 55 62) and a *supermarket* and *snack bar* (all open mid June through September). From mid-June to mid-September, the tourist office (☎ 05 56 71 89 86) runs guided tours of the abbey and the bastide.

Sauveterre de Guyenne

A bastide created as Salva-Terra in 1281, Sauveterre de Guyenne once occupied a strategic position at the crossroads of major trade routes and changed hands 10 times during the Hundred Years War. Today it retains several half-timbered houses and fragments of its old wall.

Information The tourist office (☎ 05 56 71 53 45, fax 05 56 71 59 39) is on 2 rue St Romain.

SOUTH-WEST FRANCE

Day 4: St Emilion to Sauveterre de Guyenne

N | 0 — 10km
0 — 6mi

1:250,000

SOUTH-WEST FRANCE

See Day 5 p299

See Day 3 p294

Cue		
start	St Emilion tourist office	
0km	go W on Rue du Clocher	
0.0	(20m) Place Pierre Meyrat	
0.0	(70m) Ave de Verdun	
0.4	(2nd exit) D243 'to St Christophe'	
0.4	(60m) D243 (no sign)	
3.5	St-Christophe des Bardes	
3.7	D243 'to St-Genes ce Castillon'	
5.7	'Circuit Jurisdiction-de-St-Emilion'	
6.3	D243E2 'to St Hippciyte'	
6.9	'to St Hippolyte Church'	
7.9	'to Mairie'	
	'to Mairie', 'St Hippo yte'	
8.0	church & winery 800m ↻	
8.7	750m steep twisting descent	
	'to Château Capet-Cuillier'	
11.3	St-Etienne de Lisse	
11.7	D130 'to Castillon'	
14.5	St Magne	
16.1	D17 (no sign)	
16.3	unsigned road	
17.1	D936E3/Allée de la République	
17.3	Castillon-la-Bataille	
17.7	D130E3 (just over br dge)	
19.4	Route de la République	
20.3	D15 (no sign)	
20.5	just before Piquesègue	
21.0	Route de Bourresol	
23.0	D130 (no sign)	
23.6	D130 (no sign)	
24.4	D17 'to Blasimon'	
24.4	(45m) D232 'to Pujols'	
	1.7km moderate climb	
25.0	D232 (no sign)	
25.5	towards church	
26.1	Rue des Anciennes Écoles	
26.2	Pujols	
	D23D 'to Doulezon'	

Cue		
26.2	(10m) Place du Général de Gaulle	
26.3	Fue cu Stade	
26.8	120m steep descent	
28.0	D17 'to Blasimon'	
28.4	D232: 'to Ruch'	
29.0	900m steep climb	
29.4	D232: 'to Ruch'	
29.8	Ruch	
31.2	D232 (no sign)	
32.1	D232 (no sign)	
33.6	–17E3	
35.3	1.5km steep twistir g descent	
36.2	D17 'to Basimon'	
	Moulin de Labarthe 1km ↻	
37.1	D17 (no sign)	
	Blasimon Abbey 500m ↻	
37.6	C129/Rue Mercadier 'to Blas mon'	
37.8	Blasimon	
	across square onto 'ue Abbé Guédie'	
43.9	D670 'to Sauveterre'	
44.6	Rue Saubette to Centre Ville	
44.9	Place de la République	
44.9	(70m) across square	
44.9	(40m) Sauveterre tourist office	

Continued

Côte de St-Foy de la Grande

START: DAY 5

START: DAY 4

Sauveterre de Grande

Blasimon

Side Trip

Moulin de Blasimon Abbey Labarthe

Ruch

Vaure

Pujols

Castillon-la-Bataille

St Magne

St-Genes de Castillon

St-Etienne de Lisse

St-Christophe des Bardes

St Hippolyte

Side Trip

Raven

Branne

St-Jey d'Arners

St Georges

Le Cros

Mauriac

Douleson

Figueyrague

Moullets

Cramage

St Brice

Vignonet

Paulillac

Bourg

St Émilion

Bordeaux

Cadillac

Sauveterre de Guyenne

Dordogne

A few doors away, on the square, is the friendly Maison des Vins (☎ 05 56 71 61 28; closed Sunday and Monday).

A Caisse d'Épargne is on place de la République and a Crédit Agricole is on rue des Trois Bourdons.

Things to See & Do The **Maison des Vins** is great for tasting good-value wine; decent drops sell for as little as 22FF. A small **wine museum** is on place de la République.

Otherwise, Sauveterre is notable for the **Notre Dame de Sauveterre** church in place de la République. It has a beautifully frescoed chancel and intricate carvings. The tourist office runs **guided tours** of the town.

Places to Stay & Eat A new *camping ground* should be open in June 2001 – ask at the tourist office for details. The *gîte* near the *mairie* (town hall; ☎ 05 56 71 50 43) is sometimes available overnight for around 100FF.

The simple *Hôtel de Guyenne (☎ 05 56 71 54 92, Porte de Saubotte)* has doubles from 140FF; its restaurant serves *menus* from 48FF to 95FF.

La Croix Blanche (☎ 05 56 71 50 21, place de la République) has doubles from 150FF, and a restaurant serving *menus* from 58FF to 135FF.

A *market* is held Tuesday morning in place de la République. The *Super U* supermarket *(route de Libourne)* closes Sunday afternoon. The *bakery* next to the Maison des Vins must be one of the few places in France to sell whole-grain bread: stock up.

Day 5: Sauveterre de Guyenne to Cadillac

1¼–2½ hours, 25.2km

This easy route through the Entre-Deux-Mers wine region gives plenty of time to get to Cadillac early and visit the cellars and wineries around town. Forests make a change from the endless vines in this region, known mostly for its white wines.

Flowery Castelviel (6.9km) boasts the area's most beautiful example of Romanesque art in the doorway of its **12th-century church**. The pillars flanking the door are topped with carved capitals depicting sins and saints.

Although they look interesting, the imposing Château Benauge ruins, high on a

hill, are closed to the public, so save som energy for the last few hills into Cadillac The route passes the D120, where you ca turn right to the *Château de Broustare* B&B; see Places to Stay under Cadillac.

Cadillac

A bastide town founded in 1280, Cadilla hides behind its walls, a little oasis hemme in by busy roads. Inside, a network of cob bled streets leads to the grand chateau. Th overly ambitious first Duke of Epernon wa encouraged by King Henry IV to spend hi time building this lavish home a long wa from the capital, thus keeping his nose ou of the affairs of state.

Though the namesake American ca would hardly squeeze into Cadillac's mai square, it has a (tenuous) link with the tow It's said that General Motors stumbled ove the name when it merged with Cadillac, Detroit car maker, in the 1920s. That con pany had named itself after Detroit' founder, one Antoine Lamothe-Cadillac, Frenchman who left his home town nea Cadillac to seek his fortune in America.

Information The friendly, informativ staff at the tourist office (☎ 05 56 62 12 92 hire VTTs and accessories for 75/280FF day/week.

The Maison des Vins (☎ 05 57 98 19 2(fax 05 57 98 19 30, ☐ www.grainsnoble .com) is at 104 rue Cazeaux-Cazalet, on th way into town on Day 6.

The Caisse d'Épargne bank is on ru Cazeaux-Cazalet.

Natalie Christian's bike shop (☎ 05 56 6 67 76) is at 6 route de Branne, the mai street into town.

Things to See & Do At Easter, around 6 winemakers offer free tastings and tours f the **Portes Ouvertes** (Open Doors) weeken Locals show off their second love in th event's vintage car rally. Visit the **Maiso des Vins** to learn about the light, sweet whi wines of the tiny Cadillac appellation and th aromatic Premières Côtes de Bordeaux red

The 16th-century **Château des Du d'Epernon** (☎ 05 56 62 69 58) has a perm nent exhibition highlighting the building 'double life' as a stately home then a hars 19th-century women's prison. The **St Blais collegiate church** across the square no

Cue	
0km	Sauveterre tourist office
0.0	go SW on Rue Lafon 'to Langoï'
0.6	D230 to Gornac'
4.4	D230 (no sign)
6.5	D123 'to Castelviel'
6.9	Castelviel
7.4	unsigned road
8.9	D230 to Gornac'
9.7	unsigned road (at church)
9.8	unsigned road

Cue		Continued
9.8	230m D230 'to Cadillac', Gornac	
10.4	223C 'to Mourens'	
10.9	to St-Pierre de Bat	
11.5	Mourens	
14.9	St-Pierre de Bat	
15.0	to Arbis'	
16.4	C231 'to Escoussans', Arbis	
19.5	370m D231 'to Cadillac'	
20.4	pass B&B turn-off	
21.0	Le Bizoc	
25.0	Rue Porte de Benauges 'to Château'	
25.2	Rue cu General de Gaulle	
25.2	C0m1 Cadillac tourist office	

houses the elaborate funeral chapel of the Duke of Epernon.

The tourist office runs daily **guided tours** of the bastide and has an English brochure for a self-guided tour. Its free brochure 'Sentiers de Randonnées' details (in French) several walks.

Places to Stay The small, quiet *municipal camping ground* (☎ 05 57 98 02 10, rue du Port) has basic showers and toilets, and shady sites for 18FF plus 12FF per adult (open June to September).

The two-star *Hotel Détrée* (☎ 05 56 62 65 38, 22 ave de la Pont) is run by a friendly cyclist; clean, spacious doubles with a shower cost 160/200FF without/with toilet. Local workers frequent its basic *restaurant*, which offers 59/75FF lunch/dinner *menus*.

Despite its name, Cadillac's three-star *Hôtel du Château de la Tour* (☎ 05 56 76 92 00, fax 05 56 62 1159) is uninspiring with overpriced rooms (doubles from 490FF); only the pool has a chateau view.

The best choice is out of town: the three-star B&B *Château de Broustaret* (☎/fax 05 56 62 96 97), a beautiful 19th-century mansion with panoramic views and a two-star price. It's 5.5km north-east of Cadillac, on the D120 (Day 7 route). The rooms, with huge bathrooms, cost between 220FF and 250FF; there's a communal kitchen. The owner's son-in-law will show visitors around the vineyard and chai (open from Easter to October).

Places to Eat Cadillac's animated *market* is held Saturday morning in place du Château and place de la République. A *Petit Casino* is at 29 rue Cazeaux-Cazalet.

On a Sunday the *Pizzeria des Remparts* (☎ 05 56 76 90 77, 3 allées de Tassigny/the D10) is the only place to buy a meal in Cadillac, but the pizza (around 40FF) and pasta (from 31FF) is fairly ordinary (closed Wednesday). The nearest Sunday alternative is the excellent *Restaurant Braises & Gourmandises* (☎ 05 56 62 30 58), on the N113 in Preignac 7.5km away. It serves excellent regional dishes in a beautiful rustic setting.

L'Entrée Jardin (☎ 05 56 76 96 96, 22 rue de l'Oeuille) has excellent food and a pretty courtyard looking onto the chateau; the great-value 62FF lunch *menu* includes 250mL of wine.

SOUTH-WEST FRANCE

SOUTH-WEST FRANCE

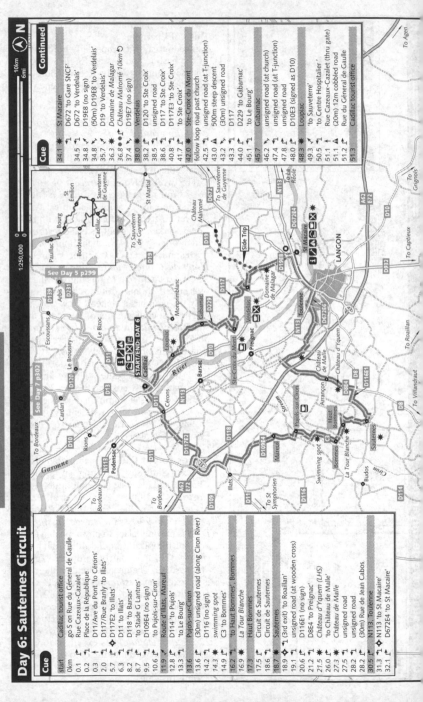

Day 6: Sauternes Circuit

Cue

start	Cadillac tourist office
0km	go S on Rue du Général de Gaulle
0.1	Rue Cazeaux–Cazalet
0.2	Place de la République
0.3	D11/Ave du Pont 'to Cérons'
2.0	D117/Rue Branly 'to Illats'
5.7	◇ D117E2 'to Illats'
6.3	D11 'to Illats'
8.2	D118 'to Barsac'
8.7	'to Stade G Lantres'
9.5	D109E4 (no sign)
10.6	'to Pujols-sur-Ciron'
11.9	Route d'Illats, Mareuil
12.8	D114 'to Pujols'
13.3	'to Le Bourg'
13.6	Pujols-sur-Ciron
13.6	(30m) unsigned road (along Ciron River)
14.2	D116 (no sign)
14.3	swimming spot
14.9	C3 'to Bommes'
16.2	'to Haut Bommes', Bommes
16.9	La Tour Blanche
17.3	Haut Bommes
17.5	Circuit de Sauternes
18.6	Circuit de Sauternes
18.7	Sauternes
18.9	◇ (3rd exit) 'to Roaillan'
19.1	unsigned road (at wooden cross)
20.6	D116E1 (no sign)
21.2	D8E4 'to Preignac'
21.5	Château d'Yquem (LHS)
26.0	'to Château de Malle'
27.3	Château de Malle
27.5	unsigned road
28.2	unsigned road
28.2	(30m) Rue de Jean Cabos
30.5	N113, Toulenne
31.3	◇ N113 'to St Macaire'
32.1	D672E4 'to St Macaire'

Cue — **Continued**

34.1	St Macaire
34.5	D672 'to Gare SNCF'
34.8	D672 'to Verdelais'
34.8	D198 (no sign)
35.7	(50m) D19E8 'to Verdelais'
36.3	D19 'to Verdelais'
36.8	Domaine de Malagar
36.8	Château Malromé 10km ↺
37.4	D19E7 (no sign)
38.0	Verdelais
38.2	D120 'to Ste Croix'
38.5	unsigned road
38.6	D117 'to Ste Croix'
40.8	D117E3 'to Ste Croix'
41.7	'to Ste Croix'
42.0	Ste-Croix du Mont
42.0	follow loop road past church
42.5	unsigned road (at T-junction)
43.0	500m steep descent
43.2	(30m) unsigned road
43.3	D117
44.0	D229 'to Gabarnac'
45.1	'to Le Bourg'
45.7	Gabarnac
46.2	unsigned road (at church)
47.4	unsigned road (at T-junction)
47.8	unsigned road
48.0	D10E3 (signed as D10)
48.3	Loupiac
49.3	'to Sauveterre'
50.5	'to Centre Hospitalier'
51.1	Rue Cazeaux-Cazalet (thru gate)
51.2	(20m) 12m cobbled road
51.2	Rue du Général de Gaulle
51.3	Cadillac tourist office

Day 6: Sauternes Circuit

2½–5 hours, 51.3km

Explore some of the oldest vineyards in the Bordelais on this circuit around the Garonne and discover the liquid gold of Sauternes wine. With only a swimming costume and a picnic in the panniers, the few hills are easily manageable.

The route travels along the shaded Ciron stream, which provides ideal **swimming spots**. Mist created when its cold water merges with the warmer Garonne aids the growth of the fungus *Botrytis cinera* (noble rot) on grapes, which concentrates their sugars for Sauternes wine.

The route passes many vineyards. **La Tour Blanche** (16.9km), a viticulture school, produces some of the region's best Premier Cru Classé and offers regular tours.

Find out winery visiting hours at Sauternes (18.7km). The tourist office (☎ 05 56 76 69 13, 🖳 www.ot-sauternes.com) closes Sunday and Monday in the low season. The wine centres are past the tourist office on place du Mairie – go to the friendly **Caveau du Sauternes** (☎ 05 56 76 62 17), next to the snooty Maison du Vin, for advice on wines and wineries, and free tastings to likely buyers.

The prestigious **Château d'Yquem** (21.5km) is the second large winery on the D8E4. Yquem carefully selects each grape, making only about a glass of wine from each vine. The wine is sold at stellar prices and then has to be cellared for at least a decade before drinking (no tours).

The **Château de Malle** (☎ 05 56 62 36 86) has fascinating tours (in French, with English brochure) of its winery and 17th-century chateau (open April to October).

St Macaire is a medieval trading centre well worth exploring (the route goes to the town gate). It's most famous for the remarkable arcaded **place du Mercadiou** (God's Marketplace) and **St Sauveur** church. The tourist office (☎ 05 56 63 03 64), past the gate, has maps.

Climb to **Domaine de Malagar** 05 57 98 7 17), a museum dedicated to 20th-century French writer François Mauriac.

Château Malromé (a signed side trip at 6.8km) was the summer home of painter Henri de Toulouse-Lautrec. Guided tours 30FF) visit the chais – Lautrec was fond of the bottle and used to tell his doctors, 'I'll drink milk when the cows start eating grapes' (closed in the low season except for Sunday afternoons).

Lautrec died in 1901 at 36, from the effects of alcoholism and syphilis, and is buried in the **cemetery** in Verdelais (38km); the neighbouring **stations of the cross** leads to a spectacular viewpoint. Verdelais is the Gironde's most important pilgrimage site; plaques fill its **Notre-Dame church**.

From the village of Ste-Croix du Mont, which stands on a bed of **fossilised oysters**, road signs are limited; some abbreviate the D10E3 to 'D10' – but most roads lead to Cadillac. In Loupiac (48.3km), visit the Domaine Portal Rouge winery's Gallo-Roman mosaics – **Via Mosaica** (☎ 05 56 62 93 82) – part of thermal baths built from the 2nd to 5th centuries.

Day 7: Cadillac to Bordeaux

3–6 hours, 63km

A relatively easy end to the tour, the route undulates through vineyards and woods, joining a flat, well-surfaced bikepath in the second half.

At the **Monatère de Broussey** (6.8km), brown-clad Carmelite brothers have been producing wine since 1841. At 188km, take the side trip to **Château le Haux** (☎ 05 57 34 51 11), a winery that dates from the Middle Ages. It offers guided tours and tastings.

The ruins of the Benedictine **Abbaye de la Sauve-Majeur** (26.5km; ☎ 05 56 23 01 55) remain grandiose despite a tragic history. Founded in 1079, the abbey was damaged by wars; its buildings were eventually pulled apart for building stone. The **Syndicat Viticole de l'Entre-Deux-Mers** (☎ 05 57 34 32 12) is next door.

After La Sauve, follow the bikepath signs to the converted railway line; the start (27.8km) is marked with green paint. Watch for cars as the route crosses many roads. It takes the flat route through the hilly area known as 'Little Switzerland', but skirts the wineries and towns; several are worth exploring briefly. **Créon** (32.7km), capital of the Entre-Deux-Mers region, has a 13th-century arcaded square. At Sadirac (37.8km), pottery using the local blue clay is a busy industry; see some at the small **Musée de Poterie** (☎ 05 56 30 60 03). Admission costs 10FF (open every afternoon from Tuesday to Sunday).

SOUTH-WEST FRANCE

SOUTH-WEST FRANCE

Day 7: Cadillac to Bordeaux

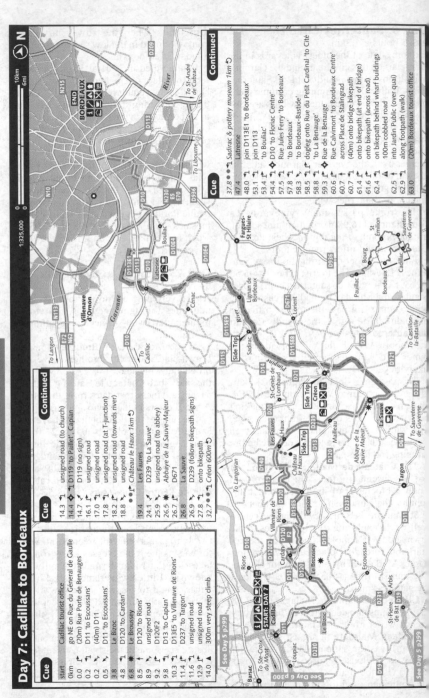

Cue

start		Cadillac tourist office
0km	↰	go NE on Rue du Géneral de Gaulle
0.0	↰	(20m) Rue Porte de Benauges
0.2	↱	D11 'to Escoussans'
0.2	↰	(40m) D11
0.5	↱	D11 'to Escoussans'
3.8	✳	Le Bizoc
4.8	↱	D120 'to Cardan'
6.8	✳	Le Broussey
6.8	●●↰	*Château le Haux 1km* ↻
8.5	↰	D120 'to Rions'
8.9	↱	unsigned road
9.2	↰	D120F2
9.8	↱	D13 'to Capian'
10.3	↰	D13E5 'to Villenave de Rions'
11.4	↱	D237 'to Targon'
11.6	↰	unsigned road
12.9	↰	unsigned road
14.0	◢	300m very steep climb

Cue — Continued

14.3	↰	unsigned road (to church)
14.4	◈	D119 'to Paillet', Capian
14.7	↰	D119 (no sign)
16.1	↱	unsigned road
17.0	↱	unsigned road (at T-junction)
17.8	↱	unsigned road (towards river)
18.2	↰	unsigned road
18.8	●●↰	*Château le Haux 1km* ↻
19.4	✳	Les Faures
24.1	↱	D239 'to La Sauve'
25.9	✳	unsigned road (to abbey)
26.5	✳	*Abbaye de la Sauve-Majeur*
26.7	↰	D671
26.8	↰	La Sauve
26.9	↱	D239 (follow bikepath signs)
27.8	↰	onto bikepath
32.7	●●↰	*Créon 600m* ↻

Cue — Continued

37.8	●●↰	*Sadirac & pottery museum 1km* ↻
47.4	↱	Latresne
48.0	↰	Join D113E1 'to Bordeaux'
53.1	↰	Join D113
53.4	↱	'to Bouliac'
54.4	↰	D10 'to Floriac Centre'
57.5	↲	Rue Jules Ferry 'to Bordeaux'
57.8	↱	'to Bordeaux'
58.3	↱	'to Bordeaux-Bastide'
58.5	↲	dogleg onto Rue du Petit Cardinal 'to Cité
58.8	↱	'to La Benauge'
59.3	↰	Rue de la Benauge
60.6	↰	Rue Calvimont 'to Bordeaux Centre'
60.7	↰	across Place de Stalingrad
60.7	↰	(40m) onto bridge bikepath
61.4	↰	onto bikepath (at end of bridge)
61.6	↲	onto bikepath (across road)
62.4	↲	on bikepath behind wharf buildings
		100m cobbled road
62.5	↰	into Jardin Public (over quai)
62.9	↰	along footpath (walk)
63.0		(20m) Bordeaux tourist office

See Day 5 p299

START DAY 7 Cadillac

See Day 5 p299

Out of Latresne the bikepath goes on road for 600m, then between the river and the D113 for 4.5km. The route then weaves through back streets, crossing the Pont de Pierre on a bikepath that then travels along the wharves and through the Esplanade des Quinconces gardens to the tourist office.

Bordeaux

See the Gateway Cities section (pp282–4) for information about accommodation and other services.

Périgord & Quercy

Imagine 'typical' French countryside and you're likely to conjure up something resembling Périgord and Quercy, the old names for the departments administered today as the Dordogne and the Lot. The regions' cliff-lined watercourses, fields of sunflowers and corn, oak and walnut woods, peaceful roads, tiny villages and colourful markets give them a heady appeal. Combine these with a laid-back lifestyle, superb cuisine and the world's richest collection of cave art and you have a part of France you could spend years exploring.

The Dordogne clamours for tourist attention, with languid rivers, close villages, thick vegetation and an established tourist network. The sparsely populated Lot is dominated by its bare, haunting *causses* (high limestone plains), deeply cut by winding rivers and dotted by isolated, quirky villages less touched by tourism. The two regions have many official 'Plus Beaux Villages de France' (Most Beautiful Villages of France). Below the surface are caves such as Lascaux and Pech Merle, which house galleries of sophisticated prehistoric art.

This tranquil region was racked by strife during the Middle Ages. Cliffs bristle with castles and bastides, a legacy of the bloody conflicts, first between the French and the English in the Hundred Years War, then between the Catholics and Protestants in the Wars of Religion.

NATURAL HISTORY

Between Paris and the Pyrenees, the mild Périgord is divided into four subregions, which take names (a little whimsically) from the colour of the countryside. In the north around Brantôme, Périgord vert (green) has verdant vegetation. Périgord blanc (white) crosses the centre of the department from east to west, taking in the Dordogne capital, Périgueux, and the chalky cliffs of the causses. The vineyards of Périgord pourpre (crimson) produce spectacular autumn colours and the famous deep red wine of the south-west, around Bergerac. Finally, Périgord noir (black), also known as the Sarladais, is an area of dense oak woods in the south-east around Sarlat, and home to the *truffe* (truffle), the 'black diamond' of Périgord. It has the densest concentration of interesting sites and is the focus of the tour in this section, along with the equally well-known department of the Lot, or Quercy – a warm, unmistakably southern region which lies south of Limousin and east of Périgord.

The west-flowing Dordogne, Lot, Vézère and Célé Rivers once provided the main means of communication and transport. Wood, wine and fruit were carried to Bordeaux on boats, which were then broken up for firewood. Heavier, flat-bottomed sailing boats, *gabarres*, then sailed back; replicas of these now carry tourists (see Day 4). Many chateaux, such as Montfort (Day 5), were built to control the river trade.

INFORMATION
Books

The coffee-table book *The Most Beautiful Villages of the Dordogne*, by James Bentley, with photographs by Hugh Palmer, features many of the villages visited on the route.

Cycle touring and off-road options are detailed in the French-language topoguides *Cyclotourisme en Quercy* (about 40FF); *Guide du Cyclotourisme dans le Lot* (about 40FF); *VTT 36 Circuits – Le Lot en Quercy* (50FF); and *Tour du Lot Équestre, Pédestre et VTT* (40FF). These are available from newsagents or departmental tourist offices.

Information Sources

The highly organised departmental tourist offices are the best sources of information:

Dordogne (☎ 05 53 35 50 24, fax 05 53 35 50 05, ▯ www.perigord.tm.fr) 25 rue Wilson, BP 2063, 24002 Périgueux Cedex

Lot (☎ 05 65 35 07 09, fax 05 65 23 92 76, ▯ www.quercy.net) 107 quai Eugène Cavaignac, Cahors (1st floor, open weekdays)

Both departments organise supported cycle tours. The Lot department, especially, is extremely bicycle friendly. It can supply *Countryside Sports in the Lot* (which details hire outlets, tour companies, plus *Rando Étapes* – accommodation with bike shelter). Most Quercy towns are linked to its Web site.

See also Information Sources at the start of the chapter.

Caves, Cuisine & Chateaux

Duration	9 days
Distance	454.8km
Difficulty	moderate
Start	Les Eyzies de Tayac
End	Cahors

Marvellous food, ancient cave art, grand chateaux and fabulous cycle touring – this ride has it all. Work off the rich *foie gras* (fattened goose liver; see 'The Golden Goose' boxed text later in this chapter) and wine by cycling through castle-studded gorges, riddled with prehistoric art galleries. Some of the world's finest cave art is on show at sites such as Lascaux and Pech Merle. Trace medieval history through the churches and chateaux lining the route.

Climbing from the rivers up to the *causses* requires a moderate level of fitness.

The Dordogne and Célé rivers have good swimming spots, but beware the current; ask locals if it's safe.

PLANNING
When to Ride
Early autumn (September) is most striking, when the forest colours are changing and the air is crisp and cool. The summer tourist influx is gone but accommodation is still open. Travelling in May and early June also avoids the crowds and heat.

Summer, the festival season, is still pleasant; most of the route is on quiet roads, but book accommodation in advance.

Cycling is possible in winter, though accommodation may be scarcer; this is when most of the region's food delicacies, including truffles, are sold (see the 'To Market, To Market' boxed text). To combine cycling with a regional cooking course, go between October and April.

Book as soon as possible to visit the Grotte de Font de Gaume (see Day 2).

GETTING TO/FROM THE RIDE
Trains link this ride with the Bordeaux Wine Explorer ride. Cahors is only 1½ hours by train from Toulouse, the gateway to several rides in the Pyrenees chapter.

Train
Les Eyzies de Tayac The train station is 1km west of town, off the D47; turn right out of the station and follow the road into town.

Trains travel to Les Eyzies from Bordeaux via Le Buisson (109FF, two to three hours, one takes bikes) or via Périgueux (118FF, two hours). Theoretically, only about three trains a day carry bikes as hand luggage between Périgueux and Les Eyzies, but the conductor may turn a blind eye for that tiny leg. No trains from Agen (87FF, 1¾ hours, three daily) take unbagged bikes.

Cahors The train station is on place Jouinot Gambetta (place de la Gare).

Cahors is on the main SNCF line between Paris' Gare d'Austerlitz (328FF, five hours during the day, five a day, none take unbagged bikes) and Limoges. To reach

To Market, To Market

Some of the huge, colourful markets on this route are among the best in France. Established in the Middle Ages through the granting of special privileges by overlords, the weekly or bi-weekly events remain the mainstay of the region's economy. In many small towns, the *halle*, or covered market, is one of the most impressive buildings.

They're great places to discover the region's specialities, so try to plan your trip to coincide with at least one of the largest: those in Sarlat, St Céré or Cahors. Sarlat's, in particular, is famous throughout France.

You'll find *foie gras* (fattened goose liver) on sale from November to March; mushrooms (including the tasty *cèpes*), chestnuts and walnuts in autumn; truffles from December to March; and strawberries between April and November.

Market days for each town visited on the route are listed under Places to Eat.

Bordeaux, change trains at Montauban (186FF, two to three hours). Two trains a day take bikes unbagged to Toulouse (87FF, 1½ hours, 16 a day).

Take the combined train/bus service to return to Les Eyzies (117FF, three to 4½ hours, two a day) or to reach Agen (117FF, 1½ to two hours, 14 a day); bagged bikes only.

A combined train/bus service runs to Agen (117FF, one to two hours, 14 a day, none take bikes).

Bus
From the UK, the European Bike Express service (see Bus in the Getting There & Away chapter) charges £169 (return) to take a passenger and their bike to Agen; trains connect Agen to Les Eyzies and Cahors.

THE RIDE
Les Eyzies de Tayac
Calling itself the 'World Capital of Prehistory', Les Eyzies is surrounded by prehistoric sites – many of the world's most significant are within 20km. Sandstone buildings huddle under the chalky cliff, from which the National Museum of Prehistory is carved.

Information The tourist office (☎ 05 53 06 97 05, fax 05 53 06 90 79) is on Les Eyzies' main street, the D47, by the square (closed weekends from November to mid-March). Currency exchange is only available here and at the post office, 200m south.

Bike repairs and spare parts are available at the mower and motorbike shop Motoculture de Plaisance (☎ 05 53 46 70 15), 2km east of the centre on the D47/route du Sarlat.

Things to See & Do The town's two museums provide an excellent introduction to the area's prehistoric human habitation. The **Musée National de la Préhistoire** (☎ 05 53 06 45 45), on the D47, offers some English explanations for displays of artefacts and fossilised skeletons. The **Abri Pataud** (☎ 05 53 06 92 46), 250m north-east along the cliff, is a Cro-Magnon shelter inhabited over a 15,000-year period; with displays of excavated bones and artefacts. The ibex carved into the ceiling is from about 19,000 BC.

Several other prehistoric sites are just a short ride from Les Eyzies, although they are along busy roads. The **Grotte du Grand Roc** (☎ 05 53 06 92 70), with masses of translucent stalactites and stalagmites, is 3km northwest along the D47. Nearby is the prehistoric site of **Laugerie Basse** and a still-inhabited troglodytic hamlet.

The cave at **Rouffignac** (☎ 05 53 05 41 71), 15km north along the D47 and the D3, the area's largest, has more than 100 engravings and paintings.

Places to Stay The verdant *La Rivière* camping ground (☎ 05 53 06 97 14, fax 05 53 35 20 85) is 1.3km west, across the Vézère on the C2. Riverside sites cost 38FF per site, plus 26FF per person (open April to mid-October).

Most hotels and restaurants are along the D47. The *Hôtel des Falaises* (☎ 05 53 06 97 35), across from the Abri Pataud, has basic doubles with shower from 170FF.

The two-star *Hôtel du Centre* (☎ 05 53 06 97 13, fax 05 53 06 91 63), next to the tourist office, has pleasant doubles with bath and toilet from 290FF (open February to October).

Places to Eat The Monday morning *market* is held by the river between April and October. The *grocery* across from the tourist office stocks bread (closed Sunday afternoon). Many shops sell foie gras and other goose products: *La Ferme aux Canards du Bois Bareirou*, has tastings and can explain how each is prepared.

La Milanaise (☎ 05 53 35 43 97), opposite the Abri Pataud, is a pizzeria with excellent pasta (from 45FF), salads and a temping 98FF *Menu Périgordian*.

The *Hôtel du Centre* restaurant offers fine dining; the 100FF *menu du terroir* offers a chance to try regional specialties (lunch only); at night *menus* start at 120FF.

For a splurge, the renowned *Hôtel du Centenaire* (☎ 05 53 06 68 68), at the eastern end of town, on the corner of the D706, is part of the Relais et Château chain and has food – and prices – to match: *menus* range from 325FF to 650FF; desserts start at 100FF (open April to October).

Day 1: Circuit via Cadouin Bike Museum
3¾–7½ hours, 76.6km
This day circuit plunges into Dordogne countryside at its finest: moss-lined lanes weave

SOUTH-WEST FRANCE

Day 1: Circuit via Cadouin Bike Museum

1:250,000

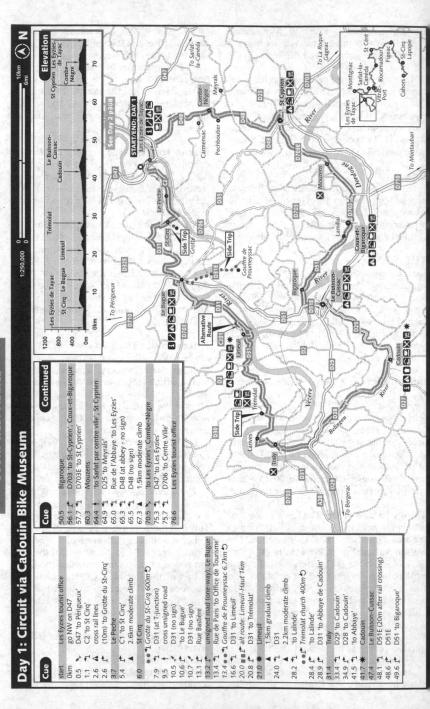

Cue	
start	Les Eyzies tourist office
0km	go NW on D47
0.5	D47 'to Périgueux'
1.1	C2 'to St Cirq'
2.6	cross rail lines
2.6	(10m) 'to Grotte du St-Cirq'
3.7	Le Peche
5.4	C1 'to St Cirq'
6.0	St Cirq
7.9	Grotte du St-Cirq 600m
7.9	D31 (at T-junction)
9.5	cross unsigned road
10.5	D31 (no sign)
10.6	'to Le Bugue'
10.7	D31 (no sign)
13.1	Rue Bastière
13.2	unsigned road (one-way), Le Bugue
13.4	Rue de Paris 'to Office de Tourisme'
13.4	Gouffre de Proumeyssac 6.7km
16.6	D31 'to Limeuil'
20.0	alt route: Limeuil-Haut 1km
20.8	D31 'to Trémolat'
21.0	Limeuil
21.0	1.5km gradual climb
24.0	D31
28.2	2.2km moderate climb
28.2	'to Lalinde'
28.4	Trémolat church 400m
28.4	'to Lalinde'
28.9	D31 'to Abbaye de Cadouin'
31.4	Traly
33.4	D29 'to Cadouin'
34.9	D28 'to Cadouin'
41.5	'to Abbaye'
41.7	Cadouin
47.4	Le Buisson-Cussac
48.1	D51E (20m after rail crossing)
48.6	D51E
49.6	D51 'to Bigaroque'

Cue	Continued
50.5	Bigaroque
56.1	D703 'to St-Cyprien', Coux-et-Bigaroque
57.7	D703E 'to St Cyprien'
60.3	Mouzens
64.4	C2 'to St Cirq'
64.9	D25 'to Meyrals'
65.0	'to Sarlat par centre ville', St Cyprien
65.3	Rue de l'Abbaye 'to Les Eyzies'
65.5	D48 (at abbey - no sign)
67.3	D48 (no sign)
70.5	'to Les Eyzies', Combe-Nègre
75.3	1.5km moderate climb
75.7	D47 'to Les Eyzies'
76.6	D706 'to Centre Ville'
	Les Eyzies tourist office

Elevation

Les Eyzies de Tayac		Le Bugue	Limeuil	Trémolat	Cadouin	Le Buisson-Cussac	St Cyprien	Les Eyzies de Tayac

Combe-Nègre

See Day 2 p308

START/END: DAY 1
Les Eyzies de Tayac

Side Trip — Grotte

Side Trip — Gouffre de Proumeyssac

Alternative Route

Side Trip

To Périgueux · To Sarlat-la-Canéda · To Montauban · To Bergerac

Dordogne · Vézère · River · Bélingou

Bigaroque · Coux-et-Bigaroque · Le Buisson-Cussac · Cadouin · Mouzens · Lamillal · St Cyprien · Meyrals · Carmensac · Pechboutier · Combe-Nègre · Le Peche · St Cirq · Limeuil · Trémolat · Larives · Traly

hrough thick oak groves, passing market gardens and ancient brown houses. The highlight s visiting Cadouin, home to France's largest cycle museum and a beautiful abbey.

Leave Les Eyzies with the cliff on the right. The first settlement, **Le Peche** (3.7km), provides an introduction to classic Dordogne architecture (see the 'Périgord & Quercy Architecture' boxed text later in this chapter). Detouring into the heart of St Cirq (6km) reveals housing dug into the rock, complete with hollowed dovecotes. The **Grotte du St-Cirq** (☎ 05 53 07 14 37), 300m off-route, is called the 'Sorcerer's Cave' for the engraving of a Magdalenian figure with a deer's body and masked face. Its **museum** s closed Sunday, and mornings outside June to mid-September.

Le Bugue (13.2km) is the gateway to the **Gouffre de Proumeyssac** (☎ 05 53 07 27 47), known as the 'Crystal Cathedral'. See its impressive domed chamber and stalactites on the slick guided tour. The side trip includes a 2km moderate climb; follow signs onto the D31E (closed January, plus February and November mornings).

The medieval bastide of **Limeuil** (a 'Plus Beaux' village) was once an important strategic defence at the junction of the Dordogne and Vézère Rivers. It's an energetic uphill walk into the town's cluster of flower-draped cottages. Mountain-bike tourers can ride into the bastide on the C201 alternative route; it's a steep climb and a steeper descent over cobbles.

Detour into Trémolat (28.2km), where all the religious architectural features of the Périgord are demonstrated in one building, the 12th-century Romanesque **church**. The entire village often sheltered within its fortifications.

Cadouin's **abbey** was an important pilgrimage centre (see the 'St Jacques de Compostelle Pilgrimage' boxed text in the Languedoc-Roussillon chapter) until its holy relic, believed to be a piece of Christ's head shroud, was revealed to be a fake in 1934. A **museum** is devoted to eight centuries of pilgrimage (☎ 05 53 63 36 28; closed January, and Tuesday outside July and August).

The **Musée du Vélocipède** (☎ 05 56 63 46 60) traces the evolution of the bicycle with a large collection of beautifully preserved original machines, from the 1817 *Draisienne* (wheeled hobbyhorse) to the

chain-driven *Bicyclette*. See the History of Cycling in France section in the Facts about France chapter.

At St Cyprien (64.4km), stay alert at the town exit for several quick left turns across busy roads.

Day 2: Les Eyzies to Montignac
1½–3½ hours, 33.2km

Take a trip back through time, with opportunities to see cave art, ancient cave dwellings and primitive tools. The route mostly meanders by the Vézère River, with hilly sections as it negotiates the cliffs or travels inland. There's time to visit several attractions and to reach Montignac in time to book tickets for Lascaux II (see Day 3).

Head out of town with the cliff to the left. At 0.8km, a side trip leads to the **Grotte de Font de Gaume** (☎ 05 53 06 90 80) with one of the most astounding collections of prehistoric art open to the public. Its painted figures were created 14,000 years ago. Only 200 visitors a day are allowed; reserve a 35FF, 40-minute tour (some in English) by visiting the cave or calling days ahead (a week ahead in July and August; closed Tuesday). The **Grotte des Combarelles**, also worth seeing are another 1.6km along (same conditions).

Gourmets may want to visit the goose farm, the **Élevage des Granges** (11.1km; ☎ 05 53 06 94 51). Opposite the field of downy goslings and geese, a shop sells the end result.

The Golden Goose

If truffles are this region's black diamonds, then livers – or more precisely, fattened livers – are its gold. One of this region's main products is *foie gras*, literally fat liver, the melt-in-your-mouth result of fattened geese *(oie)* or ducks *(canard)*.

The birds are force fed to enlarge their livers. In the force feeding *(gavage)*, a goose's neck is stroked to encourage swallowing, while ground meal and corn is poured into its gullet three times a day for several weeks. The process doubles or even triples the weight of the birds' livers. Some foreigners view this practice as rather barbaric, but most French people don't give it a second thought.

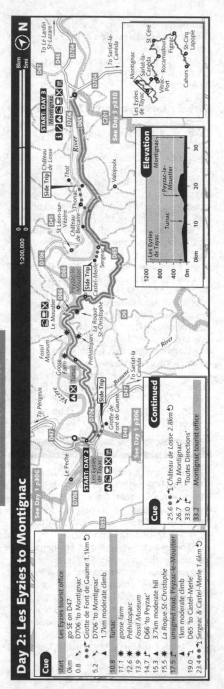

Day 2: Les Eyzies to Montignac

Cue		
start		Les Eyzies tourist office
0km		go SE on D47
0.8	•↑	D706 'to Montignac'
	•↑	Grotte de Font de Gaume 1.1km ↺
5.2	↑	D706 'to Montignac'
	▲	1.7km moderate climb
10.8	✱	Tursac
11.1	✱	goose farm
12.6	✱	Préhistoparc
13.9	✱	Fossil Museum
14.7	↱	D66 'to Peyzac'
15.3	▲	3.7km moderate hill
15.5	✱	La Roque St-Christophe
17.5	↱	unsigned road, Peyzac-le-Moustier
	▲	1km moderate climb
19.0	↱	D65 'to Castel-Merle'
23.4	•↑	1 Sergeac & Castel-Merle 1.6km ↺

Cue		
25.6	•↑	1 Château de Losse 2.8km ↺
26.7	↑	'to Montignac'
		'Toutes Directions'
33.0	↱	
33.2		Montignac tourist office

Continued See Day 1 p306

SOUTH-WEST FRANCE

The **Préhistoparc** (12.6km; ☎ 05 53 50 73 19) recreates scenes from the daily life of Mousterian (Neanderthal) hunters.

The tiny **Fossiles les Prehistoire Expo Musée** (13.9km; ☎ 05 53 50 81 02) has a large display of fossils.

A beautiful, tiny road winds between the overhanging cliff and the Vézère to **La Roque St-Christophe** (15.5km; ☎ 05 53 50 70 45). This 900m-long series of terraces and caves on a sheer cliff face has an extraordinary history as a natural bastion, from Mousterian people 50,000 years ago to Protestants in the late-16th century.

Detour left at the stone cross (23.4km) to visit picturesque **Sergeac**, with its fortified church, and **Castel-Merle** (☎ 05 53 50 79 70), with Magdalenian sculptures. Admission to Castel-Merle's small museum costs 25FF (open until 7 pm in July and August, 5.30 pm from Easter to September, when it's closed Wednesday).

At 25.6km it's a detour on busy roads to **Château de Losse** (☎/fax 05 53 50 90 08). Guided tours visit the medieval fortress, with its period tapestries and furniture. Admission costs 32FF (open Easter to September).

The back road to Montignac wends lazily along the Vézère, with a splendid view of the chateau and weirs.

Montignac

This relaxing town on the Vézère achieved sudden fame after the nearby Grotte de Lascaux (see Day 3) was discovered. The attractive old city and commercial centre are on the north side of the river, but tourist services are on the south, around place Tourny and along rue du Quatre Septembre.

Information The tourist office (☎ 05 53 51 82 60, fax 05 53 50 49 72), upstairs at 22 rue du Quatre Septembre (closed Sunday, except in July and August), is next to the 14th-century Église St-Georges le Prieuré. In July and August, tickets to Lascaux II (see Day 3) must be pre-purchased next door.

Banks are on the north side of the river. The post office down from the tourist office also exchanges money.

Didier Faure's bike shop (☎ 05 53 51 90 78) is in rue Joubert.

Things to See & Do In the tourist office, the **Musée Eugène le Roy** re-creates the room where Le Roy wrote *Jacquou le Cro-quant*, and displays ancient craft. The priory across the street hosts a daily **craft market**.

On the north bank, the beautiful **St-Pierre de Vézère** church has an unusual striped stone interior.

Little remains of the fortress once owned by the counts of Périgord, but it's pleasant to stroll through the **old town's** antique shops and riverside houses.

Places to Stay By the river, 500m south of the centre, *Camping Municipal de Bleufond* (☎ 05 53 51 83 95, *ave Aristide Briand*) charges 20FF per site plus 15FF per person (open April to mid-October).

The *Hôtel de la Grotte* (☎ 05 53 51 80 48, *fax 05 53 51 05 96, 63 rue du Quatre Septembre*), 200m east of the tourist office, has doubles from 165FF.

Further down the road, *Le Lascaux* (☎ 05 53 51 82 81, 109 ave Jean Jaurès) has neat doubles with shower and toilet for 220FF.

Places to Eat The main *market* is held Wednesday morning around the St-Pierre de Vézère church, a smaller one operates Saturday morning. The *Casino* supermarket (closed Sunday afternoon and Monday) is next to the post office on rue du Quatre Septembre. The *boucherie*, *charcuterie* and *patisserie* are on the same street.

Over the river, the waterside *Restaurant Pizzeria Les Pilotis* (☎ 05 53 50 88 15, 6 *rue Laffitte*) has salads, pizzas (from 35FF) and meat dishes. *Snack Bio* (☎ 05 53 50 18 51, 28 rue de Juillet) sells excellent vegetarian dishes to eat in or take away for 12FF per 100g.

The *Hôtel de la Grotte* restaurant has very good Périgord *menus* for 78FF to 195FF. The *Le Lascaux* restaurant serves regional *menus* starting from 70FF.

Day 3: Montignac to Sarlat-la-Canéda

2½–4½ hours, 44.2km
This route stretches the legs, cutting across country, in and out of river valleys.

The turn-off to Lascaux is 1.8km from Montignac; for a flatter route, follow signs to Bellevue instead of the signed vehicle route.

Stumbled on in 1940 by four teenagers searching for their dog, Lascaux is adorned with extraordinary prehistoric paintings.

The cave was closed in 1963, after paintings became damaged, and a precise replica was meticulously recreated a few hundred metres away, in **Lascaux II** (☎ 05 53 51 95 03); it's surprisingly evocative (open daily from April to October, otherwise closed Monday). Tickets (50FF) are sold at the entrance except in July and August, when they must be purchased in Montignac; phone reservations aren't accepted.

The route climbs out of the Vézère Valley to the pretty village of La Chapelle-Aubareil (10.1km), descending through woods into the Beune Valley. The energetic can take the signed side trip (18.5km) to colourful **Tamnies** – a Village Fleuri (Village in Bloom).

For more prehistoric art, turn right at 22.4km; go quickly left and follow the signs to the **Abri du Cap Blanc** (☎ 05 53 59 21 74). Here, in a natural shelter, artists created detailed relief figures more than 15,000 years ago. Guided tours have English explanatory sheets (open daily from April to October; 30FF).

Climb steadily past Marquay (25.4km), with its enormous **fortified church**, before the steep pinch to the **Cabanes du Breuil** (30.7km; ☎ 05 53 29 67 15), the largest collection of stone shepherds' huts, (also *bories*), in South-West France.

Several turns after the cabanes aren't marked on the map; follow the largest road and the cues.

It's worth negotiating the steep driveway to just look at the exterior of the fairytale **Château de Puymartin** (☎ 05 53 59 29 97). Tours cost 30FF (open April to November).

Avoiding the D47's traffic, the back road to Sarlat is mostly unsigned. As the centre of Sarlat is closed to traffic, it's easiest to follow the signposted *route piéton* (pedestrian route). After the police headquarters, walk across the road and through place de la Grande Rigaudie. A few steps lead into and out of the park; after crossing rue Jean-Joseph Escande ride along the old town's cobbled streets; follow signs to the tourist office.

Sarlat-la-Canéda

The beautiful, well-restored town of Sarlat, administratively twinned with nearby La Canéda, is the capital of Périgord noir. Established around a Benedictine abbey in the late-8th-century, it became prosperous in the

SOUTH-WEST FRANCE

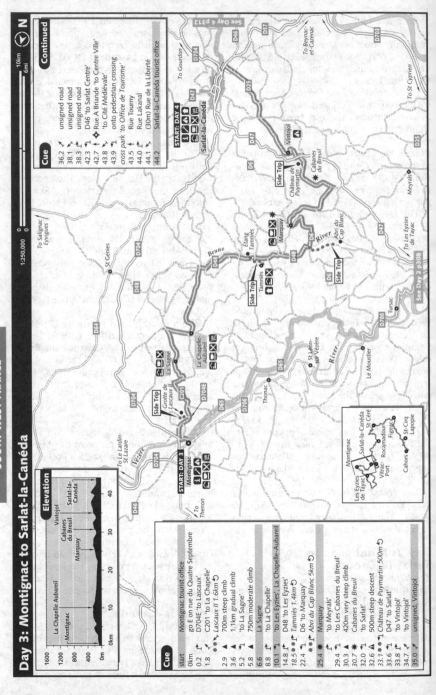

Day 3: Montignac to Sarlat-la-Canéda

1:250,000

Elevation

1600
1200
800
400
0m

0km   10   20   30   40

La Chapelle Aubareil · Montignac · Cabanes du Breuil · Marquay · Vintojol · Sarlat-la-Canéda

Cue

start	Montignac tourist office
0km	go E on rue du Quatre Septembre
0.2	D704E 'to Lascaux'
1.8	C201 'to La Chapelle'
	Lascaux II 1.6km
2.9	700m steep climb
3.6	1.1km gradual climb
5.2	'to La Sagne'
5.8	750m moderate climb
6.6	La Sagne
8.8	'to La Chapelle'
10.1	'to Les Eyzies'; La Chapelle-Aubareil
14.8	D48 'to Les Eyzies'
18.5	Tamniès 1.4km
22.4	D6 'to Marquay'
	Abri du Cap Blanc 5km
25.4	Marquay
	'to Meyrals'
29.4	'to Les Cabanes du Breuil'
30.3	420m very steep climb
30.7	Cabanes du Breuil
32.0	'to Sarlat'
32.6	500m steep descent
33.1	Château de Puymartin 500m
33.6	D47 'to Sarlat'
33.8	'to Vintojol'
34.7	'to Vintojol'
35.0	unsigned, Vintojol

Cue — Continued

36.2	unsigned road
38.1	unsigned road
38.3	unsigned road
42.3	D46 'to Sarlat Centre'
42.7	Rue A Briande 'to Centre Ville'
42.8	'to Cité Médiévale'
43.3	onto pedestrian crossing
	cross park 'to Office de Tourisme'
43.5	Rue Tourny
44.0	Rue Lakanal
44.1	(30m) Rue de la Liberté
44.2	Sarlat-la-Canéda tourist office

0   1:250,000   10km
0   6mil
N

To Gourdon

To Beynac-et-Cazenac

START DAY 4
Sarlat-la-Canéda

See Day 4 p312

To St Cyprien

To Les Eyzies de Tayac

Meyrals

Vintojol

Château de Puymartin

Cabanes du Breuil

Side Trip

Marquay

Étang Tamniès

Beune

St Genies

To Salignac Eyvigues

Abri du Cap Blanc

River

Side Trip

Tamniès

St Léon-sur-Vézère

River

Tursac

Le Moustier

Thonac

La Chapelle Aubareil

Side Trip
Grotte de Lascaux

La Sagne

START DAY 3
Montignac

To Le Lardin-St Lazare

Vézère

To Thenon

See Day 2 p308

Montignac
Les Eyzies de Tayac
Sarlat-la-Canéda · St Céré
Vitrac Port · Rocamadour
Cahors · St-Cirq Lapopie · Figeac

Middle Ages but was ravaged during the Hundred Years War (it was on the border between French and English territory) and the Wars of Religion. These days, Sarlat features more heritage-listed buildings per square kilometre than any other European city. The town attracts many tourists, especially for the year-round Saturday market.

Information The main tourist office (☎ 05 53 31 45 45, fax 05 53 59 19 44) on place de la Liberté occupies the beautiful Hôtel de Maleville (closed Sunday October to June).

Several banks are located along rue de la République. The main post office is on place du 14 Juillet.

The route into town passes Société Sarladaise de Cycles (☎ 05 53 28 51 87, fax 05 53 30 23 90) on 36 ave Thiers. It offers overnight repairs (drop off by 7 pm) and hires bikes for 70/250FF per day/five days.

Email services are available at G@moenet (☎ 05 53 31 45 91), on the roundabout (traffic circle) just before the railway line on rue L Dubois heading south of town (closed Monday).

Things to See & Do Sarlat is entirely lit by gas lamps; an evening stroll around the **medieval town** is a must. The tourist office's free map describes a walking tour of Sarlat's historic centre, which includes the **Cathédrale St Sacerdos**, once part of the Cluniac Abbey, and the ornate Renaissance **Maison de la Boétie**, birthplace of the writer Étienne de la Boétie (1530–63). The tourist office also runs guided tours. The quiet residential area west of rue de la République is worth exploring; rue Jean-Jacques Rousseau makes a good starting point.

The **Musée de l'Automobile** (☎ 05 53 31 62 81), 17 ave Thiers, displays vintage motor vehicles.

Places to Stay Sarlat has no really cheap hotels. In July and August, accommodation books out way in advance.

For camping, the four-star **Les Périères** (☎ 05 53 59 05 84, fax 05 53 28 57 51) is about 800m north-east of the medieval town along the D47 towards Ste Nathalène. It charges a whopping 144FF for two people in high season (open April to September).

More convenient is the simple **Auberge de Jeunesse** (☎ 05 53 59 47 59, 77 ave de *Selves*), which charges 27FF per person for tents pitched in the tiny back garden. Dorm beds cost 48FF (open mid-April to mid-November; reception opens only between 6 and 8 pm).

The tourist office has a complete list of **chambres d'hôtes**. About 1.2km north of Sarlat, **Chambres d'Hôtes Gransard** (☎ 05 53 59 35 20, Colline de Péchauriol) has extremely comfortable doubles for 200FF (open April to October).

The rustic, two-star **Hôtel Marcel** (☎ 05 53 59 21 98, fax 05 53 30 27 77, 50 ave de *Selves*) has doubles from 220FF with shower and toilet. The friendly two-star **Hôtel Les Récollets** (☎ 05 53 31 36 00, fax 05 53 30 32 62, 4 rue Jean-Jacques Rousseau) has quiet, comfortable singles/doubles with shower and toilet for 288/377FF (including breakfast).

For three-star comfort try the elegant **Hôtel de la Madeleine** (☎ 05 53 59 10 41, fax 05 53 31 03 62, 1 place de la Petite Rigaudie), which has spacious rooms with shower for 357/444FF, including breakfast (closed November to early February).

Places to Eat Long a driving force in the town's economy, Sarlat's **Saturday market** on place de la Liberté offers edibles in the morning and durables all day. Périgord delicacies on sale depend on the season (see the boxed text 'To Market, To Market' earlier). A smaller **fruit and vegetable market** operates on Wednesday morning. Many shops sell foie gras and other pricey regional specialities. The **Casino** supermarket is at 32 rue de la République (closed Monday).

Tourist-oriented restaurants line the streets north, north-west and south of the cathedral. **Chez Marc** (☎ 05 53 59 02 71, 4 rue Tourny) has friendly service and reasonably priced, good food; the 78FF *menu* offers extraordinary choice (closed Monday night and, in low season, on Sunday).

For upmarket Périgord-style cuisine, try the extremely popular **Auberge de Mirandol** (☎ 05 53 30 23 90, 7 rue des Consuls); make reservations or join a queue. The four-course 115FF option is loaded with regional specialties.

The elegant restaurant attached to the **Hôtel de la Madeleine** has *menus* from 115FF to 205FF (open from mid-March to November).

SOUTH-WEST FRANCE

SOUTH-WEST FRANCE

Day 4: Sarlat-la-Canéda to Vitrac-Port

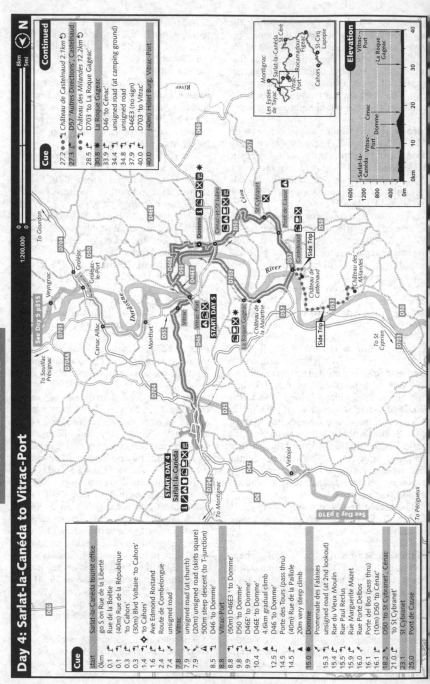

Cue

start	Sarlat-la-Canéda tourist office
0km	go S on Rue de la Liberté
0.1	Rue de la Boétie
0.1	(40m) Rue de la République 'to Cahors'
0.3	(30m) Blvd Voltaire 'to Cahors'
0.3	'to Cahors'
1.4	◊
1.6	Ave Edmond Rostand
2.4	Route de Combelongue
7.4	unsigned road
7.8	Vitrac
7.9	unsigned road (at church)
7.9	(20m) unsigned road (skirts square)
	500m steep descent (to T-junction)
8.5	D46 'to Domme'
8.8	Vitrac-Port
8.8	(50m) D46E3 'to Domme'
9.8	D50 'to Domme'
9.9	D46E 'to Domme'
10.4	D46E 'to Domme'
	4.6km gradual climb
12.5	D46 'to Domme'
14.5	Porte des Tours (pass thru)
14.5	(40m) Rue de la Paillole
	20m very steep climb
15.0	Domme
15.0	Promenade des Falaises
15.3	unsigned road (at 2nd lookout)
15.4	Rue du Vieux Moulin
15.4	Rue Paul Reclus
15.5	Rue Marguerite Mazet
16.0	Rue Porte Delbos
16.0	Porte del Bos (pass thru)
16.1	(10m) D50 'to Cénac'
16.1	D50 'to St Cybranet', Cénac
18.2	'to St Cybranet'
21.0	St Cybranet
23.1	Pont de Cause
25.0	Pont de Cause

Cue — Continued

27.2	Château de Castelnaud 2.1km ↻
27.3	D57 'Autres Directions' Castelnaud
27.3	Château des Milandes 12.2km ↻
28.5	La Roque Gageac
30.8	D703 'to La Roque Gageac'
33.9	D46 'to Cénac'
34.4	unsigned road (at camping ground)
34.8	unsigned road
37.9	D46E3 (no sign)
40.0	D703 'to Vitrac'
40.0	(40m) Hôtel Burg, Vitrac-Port

N

1:200,000

8km
5ml

Elevation

Day 4: Sarlat-la-Canéda to Vitrac-Port

2–4 hours, 40km

Delve into the best of the Dordogne Périgourdine, alongside the Dordogne River. A hotly disputed territory in the Hundred Years war, the area is dotted with heavily defended chateaux and bastides.

Vitrac-Port has limited services; stock up in Sarlat before setting off (head towards the cathedral).

Unload at Vitrac-Port (8.8km) before negotiating the remaining circuit; it includes two rewarding side trips, which, in total, add 14.3km.

Despite appearances, the climb to the immaculately restored bastide of Domme is, in fact, gradual. Enter through the beautiful **Porte des Tours** (14.5km), a gate in the near-intact 13th-century ramparts. The gate hides the **Prison des Templiers**, the prison of the Knights Templar. Held here in 1307, they scratched religious graffiti into the walls (guided tours by appointment; call the tourist office ☎ 05 53 31 71 00). Inside the village, the cliff-side **Belvédère de la Barre** has a stunning panorama of the Dordogne River.

The route leaves town via the Promenade des Falaises. A less interesting, but flat, alternative is to cross the square diagonally then turn left into rue Marguerite Mazet to rejoin the route.

At 27.2km it's worth detouring to the **Château de Castelnaud** (☎ 05 53 31 30 00), looming above medieval Castelnaud. It has everything you'd expect from a cliff-top castle: massive fortifications and a superb panorama. The self-guided tour brings it to life. Admission costs 35FF (open daily from March to mid-November; otherwise from 2 to 5 pm, Sunday to Friday).

At 27.3km, a signed side trip leads to the fairy-tale Renaissance **Château des Milandes** (☎ 05 53 07 16 38), the beloved home of African-American dancer and music-hall star Josephine Baker (who performed in a skirt of bananas in the 1920s). Falconry displays happen in fine weather (open March to October; entry is a steep 43FF).

The pretty hamlet of La Roque Gageac (30.8km) is of more interest for its tan houses clinging to the cliff than for its ancient cave dwellings, which aren't a patch on La Roque St-Christophe (see Day 2). From Easter through October, several operators run trips in a replica **gabarre**; Les Caminades (☎ 05 53 29 40 95) charges 45FF for one hour.

Vitrac-Port

On the Dordogne River, tranquil Vitrac-Port is little more than a few hotels with some camping grounds nearby; direct queries to the Sarlat tourist office.

Things to See & Do Vitrac's a great place to kick back, enjoy the cooler evening air or walk along the river. Both hotels have **pools**, and Canöc Soleil Plage (☎ 05 53 28 33 33) hires **canoes** from Plage de Caudon (the river beach beside the bridge).

Places to Stay & Eat Across the Dordogne and 1.8km along the D50 towards Cénac, the four-star *Camping Soleil Plage* (☎ 05 53 28 33 33, fax 05 53 29 36 87) has tennis courts, a pool, bar, restaurant and a shop, but charges 53FF per site plus 33FF per person (open April to mid-November). The two-star *Camping Clos Bernard* (☎ 05 53 28 33 44, Cingle de Montfort), 1.8km east, has shady sites for 19FF plus 19FF per person (open April through September).

The two-star *Hôtel Plaisance* (☎ 05 53 31 39 39, fax 05 53 31 39 38, the D46) charges 220/280FF for a double room with toilet and shower/bath. Its restaurant offers *menus* from 78FF, including a sumptuous, five-course regional *menu* for 112FF.

Across the road, the ivy-covered *Hôtel Burg* (☎ 05 53 31 52 52) has a restaurant with *menus* at similar prices. Its rooms, a few hundred metres west, cost 180/220FF a single/double.

Day 5: Vitrac-Port to Rocamadour

2¼–5½ hours, 56.8km

This is another hilly day, which passes more striking chateaux along the cliffs and winds through alluvial farmland by the Dordogne, before climbing into the dry causses towards Rocamadour. Entering the Lot department around 27km, grey chalky cliffs replace the golden sandstone of the Dordogne and housing styles change (see the boxed text 'Périgord & Quercy Architecture' overleaf).

Head along the Cingle de Montfort on a delightful tiny road hemmed between sandstone cliffs and the river. Montfort's 15th-century **chateau** (☎ 05 53 28 57 80), in a grandiose cliff-top setting, was rebuilt four times after being razed by attackers. The park and ramparts are open for tours.

A small **lookout** (4.4km) on the narrow, winding descent from Montfort has views towards the chateau. A well-surfaced bikepath escapes the busy stretch from Carsac-Aillac. It's marked with red-striped white posts.

Grubby, busy Souillac (33km) hides a gem: the blindingly white **Abbaye Ste Marie**. The imposing exterior of the 12th-century church is all that escaped the Wars of Religion (the abbey was rebuilt during the 17th century).

The **Château de Belcastel** (42.6km) defends a strategic position above the confluence of the Dordogne and Ouysse rivers. Watch the hairpin bend towards the valley floor. Detour to the **Grotte de Lacave** (43.7km; ☎ 05 65 37 87 03), where stalactites drip above underground lakes. The one-hour tour costs 42FF (open March to mid-November).

The steep climb from the caves turn-off passes the **Ferme du Berthou** (45.6km), where the geese could grow fat on the sumptuous view alone; the farm shop sells goose products. It's a steady climb to the barren limestone plateau, rewarded by spectacular views of Rocamadour from L'Hospitalet.

In L'Hospitalet, visit Rocamadour's chateau (see Things to See & Do under Rocamadour); it's signed from the route. The tourist office here (see Information under Rocamadour) is a good place to book accommodation before descending into the old town, known as the Cité. Enter Rocamadour through the Porte Salmon, one of eight remaining gates built to control the flow of pilgrims and for defence.

Rocamadour

Scattered over a 150m-high cliff face above the Alzou River, the old city was, from the 12th to 14th centuries, an important stop for pilgrims en route to Santiago de Compostela.

Périgord & Quercy Architecture

One of the greatest delights of touring in this region is passing clusters of distinctive, elegant rural houses, many of them half-timbered. Although many farmers have left the region, their centuries-old stone homes have been saved and restored as holiday houses.

In the Périgord noir, houses are usually built of golden limestone; their steeply pitched roofs of brown *lauzes* (flat tiles) are made of heavy limestone rather than the usual slate.

Quercy houses are more eccentric; towers and added features create a gingerbread-house look. They're built of white limestone and have either steeply pitched lauze, roofs or shallower, terracotta-tile roofs. Traditional houses may have a stable and storerooms built just below ground level, with the living quarters upstairs reached by an outside staircase.

Throughout the region, dovecotes play a significant part in determining the architectural style. Pigeons were kept for their droppings, which were used as fertiliser, medicine and even in baking, and were an important indicator of their owner's wealth. In the Périgord, dovecotes are small towers attached to the homes (look for the square openings under the roof). Quercy dovecotes are separate buildings, sometimes built on a porch or columns.

The region also contains a wealth of dry stone architecture; kilometres of dry shingle walls lace the plateau above Rocamadour, and small, rounded huts known as *cabanes* or *bories* are often by the road side. One large collection of cabanes is found at Breuil (see Day 3).

Romanesque churches abound; many of them retain original features thanks to their location in communities too poor to renovate their places of worship in Gothic or Renaissance styles.

KELLI HAMBLET

Quercynois houses have eccentric rooflines; spot the attached dovecotes by the small windows in the roof.

Day 5: Vitrac Port to Rocamadour

Cue		
start		Hôtel Burg, Vitrac-Port
0km		go E 'to Cingle de Montfort'
2.9	✳	Montfort
6.1	↰	D704 'to Cahors', Carsac-Aillac
6.1	↱	(40m) D704 'to Cahors'
6.2	↰	D704 'to Cahors'
6.5	↱	bikepath
6.5	↱	(30m) 'to Grolèjac plan d'eau'
7.7	↱	'to Grolèjac plan c'eau'
9.0	↱	unsigned farm road
9.5	↰	unsigned road at T-junction
9.7	↱	'to Carsac', Grolèjac-Le Port
10.0	↰	D50 'to Veyrignac'
15.9		Ste Mondane
19.2	↟	'to Mareuil', St-Julien de Lampon

Cue			Continued
29.9	↙	D255 'to Souillac'
30.1	↗	D255 'to Souillac'
32.3	↰	D703
32.9	↱	'to Centre Ville'
33.0	✳	Souillac
33.1	↰	N20 to Rocamadour
34.5	↱	D43 'to Grotte de Lacave'
39.0		Pinsac
40.2	△	300m single-lane bridge
42.6	✳	Belcastel
		'1km steep descent (with hairpin)
43.7	↱	'to Grotte de Lacave'
45.0	↰	D247 'to Rocamadour'
	●●●↱	Grottes de Lacave 400m ↺
45.5	▲	600m steep climb
	▲	5.3km moderate climb
		Ferme du Berthou
54.9	✳↱	D573 'to Maison du Toursme'
55.0		L'Hospitalet tourist office
55.5	△	50m tunnel
56.8		Rocamadour tourist office

Elevation

Map

SOUTH-WEST FRANCE

Named after St Amadour, who first built an altar to Mary on the site ('Amateur' meant servant of Mary), Roc-Amadour saw fewer pilgrims during the Hundred Years War.

Despite a turbulent history, pilgrimages continue, and the most important dates in Rocamadour today are Christmas and Easter, the 14th and 15th of August and Mariane week around the 8th of September. In winter you'll share the place only with the locals and the town has a magical charm at night, year-round, when most tourists have left.

Information It's wise to book a hotel from the L'Hospitalet tourist office (☎ 05 65 33 74 13, fax 05 65 33 74 14), before descending into the Cité. The Cité's Syndicat d'Initiative (☎ 05 65 33 62 59, 💻 www.ro camadour.com) closes mornings, and on Tuesday from November to March.

Both tourist offices will exchange money. ATMs are at Porte Salmon and the post office in the Cité and outside the L'Hospitalet tourist office. The service stations in L'Hospitalet might do basic bike repairs. Garage Sirieys (☎ 05 65 33 63 15) is on the road to the chateau, and Garage Larnaudie (☎ 05 65 33 42 45) on the route de Gramat.

The tourist office in L'Hospitalet has email.

Things to See & Do Rocamadour's holy sites, stepped into the hill above the Cité, are collectively called the *parvis*. Two cemeteries and five sanctuaries cluster around **Chapelle Notre Dame**. This chapel, the heart of the pilgrimage, houses a 12th-century black Madonna, said to have miraculous powers. From the parvis, guided tours of the **pilgrimage sites** access some of the closed chapels.

The excellent **Musée d'Art Sacré** (☎ 05 65 33 23 23) in the Abbot's Palace has a beautiful collection of sacred art and artefacts dating from the 12th century. The tourist office in the Cité has a display of **Jean Lurçat tapestries** (see the St Céré section for details on the artist). The **Musée du Jouet Ancien** (☎ 05 65 33 60 75) displays more than 100 children's pedal cars.

The Cité is connected to the chapels and L'Hospitalet by the **Grand Escalier** – a staircase once climbed by penitents on their knees as a punishment for sins – and a path marked with graphic **Stations of the Cross**. These days, an elevator provides an easier option (bikes not allowed). At the top, the ramparts of the 14th-century **chateau** are accessible at all hours for their view (13FF).

Places to Stay & Eat Unless otherwise detailed, opening times are from April to early November.

In L'Hospitalet, camping ground **Relais du Campeur** (☎ 05 65 33 73 50, place de l'Europe), charges 65FF for two people (closes late September).

In the middle of the Cité, the one-star **Hôtel du Globe** (☎ 05 65 33 67 73) gives a family welcome and has homely doubles with shower and toilet from 190FF. The *only* place to stay early in the year in the Cité is the one-star **Hôtel du Roc** (☎ 05 65 33 62 43, fax 05 6 33 62 11); small but adequate doubles with shower and toilet start at 180FF (open February to October).

The two-star **Le Panoramic** (☎ 05 65 33 63 06, fax 05 65 33 69 26) has a terrace pool overlooking Rocamadour. A double room with shower costs 250FF. Its *restaurant* serves regional *menus* from 78FF to 125FF (open from early February).

The only food store is the **Superette** *(place de l'Europe, L'Hospitalet)*. It sells fresh produce, bread and a range of basics (open April to September). The **bakery** is in the Cité near Porte Salmon.

At the eastern end of town, the shady **Jardins de la Louve** (☎ 05 65 33 62 93, place Hugon) sells pizza, salads and regional dishes, with *menus* from 68FF (closed January and on Monday between November and March).

Hôtel Ste-Marie (☎ 05 65 33 63 07, place des Senhals) at the foot of the parvis, has a panoramic terrace and *menus* from 74FF to 250FF; its food doesn't always match its reputation (closes mid-October). For gourmet regional dining, try the restaurant at the **Hôtel du Château** (☎ 05 65 33 62 22); dinner for two costs around 300FF.

Day 6: Rocamadour to St Céré
2½–5¼ hours, 52.2km

This day travels into the heart of Quercy, through a string of typical Quercynoise villages (many ranked among France's 'Plus Beaux') and past several castles. Start early to allow time to visit the Gouffre de Padirac; in summer queues for this spectacular attraction can snake around for an hour.

Day 6: Rocamadour to St Céré

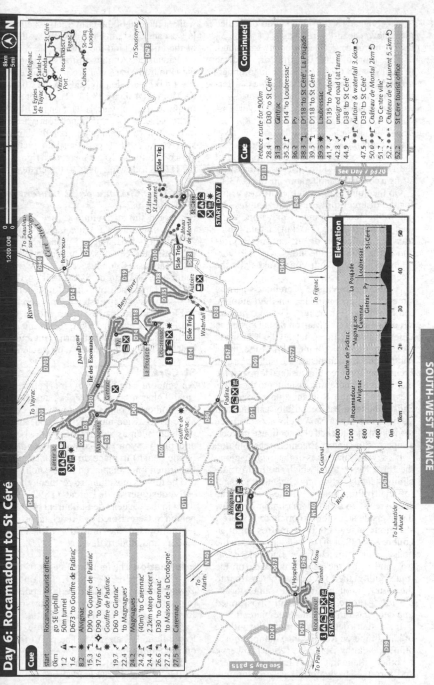

Cue

Start		Rocamadour tourist office
0km		go SE (uphill)
1.2	⚠	50m tunnel
1.6	←	D673 'to Gouffre de Padirac'
8.2	✳	Alvignac
15.3	↱	D90 to Gouffre de Padirac'
17.6	♦	D90 to Vayrac'
	✳	Gouffre de Padirac
19.7	↘	D60 'to Gintrac'
22.4	↗	'to Magnagues'
24.2		Magnagues
24.2	↱	(40m) 'to Carennac'
24.4	⚠	2.2km steep descent
26.6	↱	D30 'to Carennac'
27.2	↗	'to Maison de la Dordogne'
27.5	✳	Carennac

Cue Continued

		retrace route for 900m
28.4	←	D30 'to St Céré'
31.3		Gintrac
35.2	↱	D14 'to Loubressac'
36.2		Py
38.3	↰	D118 'to St Céré'. La Poujade
39.5	↱	D118 'to St Céré'
39.5		Loubressac
41.7	✳	D135 'to Autoire'
42.8	↘	'to Autoire'
44.9	↗	unsigned road (at farms)
47.5	↱	Autoire & waterfall 3.6km ↻
50.0	↱	D38 'to St Céré'
51.7	↘	Château de Montal 2km ↻
52.2		D30 'to St Céré'
52.2		'to Centre ville'
52.2		Château de St Laurent 5.2km ↻
52.2		St Céré tourist office

Elevation

SOUTH-WEST FRANCE

At Alvignac (8.2km) the studio of skilled **glassblower** Jean-Pierre Mateus (☎ 05 65 33 68 29), on rue des Écoles, is open year-round.

The tour of the **Gouffre de Padirac** (17.6km; ☎ 05 65 33 64 56), a huge underground chasm with giant stalactites, offers the closest thing – at least in *this* world – to a cruise to Hades across the Styx River. Discovered in 1889, the cave's river is 103m below ground level. The subterranean river cruises are unashamedly mass-market, but retain an innocence and style reminiscent of the 1930s, when the first lifts were installed. Bring a coat – the temperature inside is 13°C.

On the quiet road from the gouffre watch for the discreet turn-off to Magnagues. An oak wood laced with mossy dry-stone walls leads to **Magnagues** (24.2km), a totally untouristed collection of ancient farmhouses and barns. Admire the **view** over the Dordogne while checking your brakes for the steep descent.

A 'Plus Beaux Village', **Carennac**'s narrow streets are lined with brown-tiled houses, some from the 16th century. The cue sheet instructions stop at the **Maison de la Dordogne Quercynoise** in the Château de Carennac (☎ 05 65 10 91 56), a museum of the area's natural and human history. Displays are in French, but the three-dimensional topographic map gives an interesting insight into the route. Next door is the Romanesque priory: it's **Église St Pierre** has beautifully carving and stained glass. The restored cloisters are open to visitors; the attached chapter house protects a superb 15th-century Entombment sculpture.

It's several kilometres of flat cycling along the Bave River, after which the main route climbs steadily to two more beautiful villages (officially Plus Beaux Villages) and some great views. To avoid more climbing, follow the riverside signs for a shortcut to St Céré.

Detour a few hundred metres right at **Loubressac** (39.6km) to wander between the houses, study the church's elaborate doorway and enjoy the panorama. Back on the route, follow the road below the castle into the valley, through dairy and walnut farms, towards **Autoire**, magnificently positioned in a deep gash in the limestone plateau.

It's a short detour to explore the village of half-timbered Renaissance manor houses built by wealthy *vignerons* (wine growers); no other village in Quercy has more towers and turrets. The **waterfall** is a 10-minute

walk at the end of the farm track, Chemin d la Cascade, just after the church. At the to of the cliffs behind the village, the ruins o a Château des Anglais fortress dating fror the Hundred Years War are just visible.

At 44km, a side trip leads to the **Châtea de Montal** (☎ 05 65 38 13 72), rebuilt piece by-piece from private collections. Althoug fortress-like outside, its inner courtyard is monument to Renaissance beauty. Admis sion costs 30FF (open April to Octobe closed Saturday). To get there, turn right ont the D241, following signs to the chateau.

Side Trip: Château de St Laurent
½–¾ hour, 5.2km

It's worth the stiff climb to see artwork that revolutionised French tapestry in th 20th century. Artist Jean Lurçat has turne the walls and ceilings of his eclectic hom into 'canvasses' for his work. Now a mu seum, the **Château de St Laurent** (☎ 05 6 38 28 21) is open mid-July to Septembe plus two weeks at Easter; admission cost 15FF. Head north-west from the St Cér tourist office and turn right, following sign to the casino; after 500m turn right and fol low the signs to the museum up a steep hill

St Céré

An ancient Haut Quercy market centre small, charming St Céré is packed wit half-timbered houses. The town still come alive at its twice-monthly fair and, amon products such as superb local strawberrie and plums, you can still see the *taouil* (stone bench) in place du Mercadial wher fishermen once displayed their catch.

The town's most famous resident, the tap estry designer Jean Lurçat (1892–1966) lived in the Château de St Laurent on the hi behind St Céré. Bored by French tapestry, h revolutionised the industry with vibran colours and modern designs.

Information The tourist office (☎ 05 65 38 11 85, fax 05 65 38 38 71, e saint-cer @wanadoo.fr) is in place de la Républiqu (closed Sunday, except in the morning fo July and August) and is very helpful.

The Crédit Lyonnais at 11 rue de la République has an ATM. The post office i on rue Faidherbe.

The bike shop St Chamant (☎/fax 05 6 38 03 23) is at 45 rue Faidherbe.

Things to See & Do St Céré buzzes on **fair days**, the first and third Wednesday of the month, when business is strung out in around town. By the river off place de la République is the early-morning veal market, where sellers in berets and long black coats extol the virtues of their animals. At the square outside the church people queue for slabs of cheese. Find fresh produce at place du Mercadial: *charcuterie* (cured meats); dried fruit; olives; bread; and wonderful *pain épice* (fruit cake) carved from huge slabs. Clothes and household items are sold in place de la République.

The tourist office runs guided tours of the **medieval town** and has a free self-guided tour leaflet.

Don't miss Lurçat's mind-blowing, wall-sized tapestries. See them at the **Casino Gallery** (☎ 05 65 38 19 60; free entry), in rue Moussinac, or at the **Château de St Laurent**, above the town (see Side Trip under Day 6).

Since the late-8th century, worshippers have been visiting the **Église St Spérie**, dedicated to Spérie, who was beheaded for refusing to marry a local nobleman.

Places to Stay & Eat The quiet, riverside camping ground *Le Soulhol* (☎/fax 05 65 38 12 37, off quai Auguste Salesse) is beside the pool and tennis courts. Sites cost 17FF, plus 9FF per person (open April to September).

La Taverne de Gargantua (☎/fax 05 65 38 04 83, 21 ave Anatole de Monzie) is on a busy road. Clean, older-style doubles are 150FF (180FF with shower). Locals frequent the *restaurant* for its good-value 60FF and 100FF *menus* (closed February, Sunday nights, and Sunday lunch in low season).

Hôtel le Touring (☎ 05 65 38 30 08, fax 05 65 38 18 67, place de la République) has a bird's eye view of the markets, large rooms and a friendly welcome. Doubles cost 249FF.

In an old Quercynoise house by the canal, the two-star *Victor Hugo* (☎ 05 65 38 16 15, fax 05 65 38 39 91, 7 ave des Maquis) has doubles with shower and toilet for 240FF. Its *restaurant* is gourmet and charges for it: menus start at 87.50FF but hover between 135FF and 200FF (closed on Monday and for three weeks each in March and October).

For the twice-monthly *fair*, see Things to See & Do. A Saturday-morning *market* is held in place du Mercadial. The *Topco* supermarket *(5 place de la République)* closes Sunday afternoon.

Le Caprice (☎ 05 65 38 34 22, rue Pasteur) serves salads, pasta and pizzas, including vegetarian choices, for around 40FF; grills cost more (closed Monday and on weekend lunch times in low season). *Puymule* (☎ 05 65 10 59 10, 1 place de l'Église) serves pasta, pizza, salad and grills and has *menus* from 40FF to 90FF (closed Sunday and Monday night).

Day 7: St Céré to Figeac
2½–5 hours, 50.1km

This is another hard day, climbing out of the Beune and across smaller valleys en route to the Célé. The solid climb from town is rewarded with beautiful ridge-top riding, fabulous downhills and, towards the day's end, scenic Quercynoise villages.

Head towards the bridge over the Bave to begin. At Leyme (12.5km), the **church** has 'hypocrites' stalls, in which monks could sit through long services while appearing to be standing. Out of Leyme, cycle through a dense wood in a regional park.

In Lacapelle-Marival, the 13th- and 15th-century **chateau** (22.9km) is being restored, providing a stark reminder of the heritage lost since the Revolution. Remnants of the chateau and fort are scattered through the village, which was ruled from the 12th to 18th centuries by the Cardaillacs, one of Quercy's most powerful families.

From St Bressou, the cycling is fabulous, winding down through woods (watch the hairpin bends) before climbing comfortably to Cardaillac, another stronghold of the Cardaillacs, whose modest family motto was 'They were known in all the world'.

The town has shrunk since its heyday. Today its living **Musée Eclaté** (scattered museum; 35.8km) showcases village life. Exhibits include the school, old farming tools, and local crafts. Elderly locals run two-hour tours (in French); entry is by donation. It's open July and August afternoons (except Saturday), at 3 pm in September, otherwise by appointment; call M Mazembert (☎ 05 65 40 15 65).

It's easy to miss the turn-off to Doulan (39.3km) – fly past and you'll end up on the busy N140, which reaches Figeac in 5km but is best avoided. The small, steep road to Doulan travels past some of the most beautiful houses of the day, doglegs over the N140, then enters Figeac on the quietest route.

SOUTH-WEST FRANCE

Day 7: St Céré to Figeac

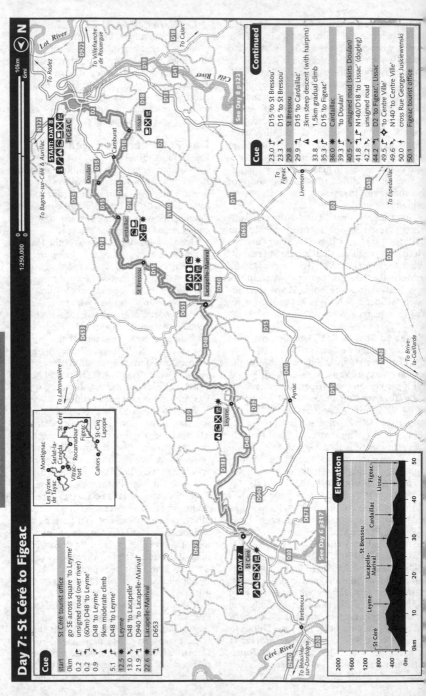

Cue

start		St Céré tourist office
0km		go SE across square 'to Leyme'
0.2	↱↰	unsigned road (over river)
0.2	↱←	(60m) D48 'to Leyme'
0.9	◀	D48 'to Leyme'
5.1	↱	9km moderate climb
		D48 'to Leyme'
12.5	✳	Leyme
13.0	↱	D48 'to Lacapelle'
21.9	↰	D940 'to Lacapelle-Marival'
22.6	✳ ↱	Lacapelle-Marival
		D653

Cue Continued

23.0	↱	D15 'to St Bressou'
23.3	↱	D15 'to St Bressou'
29.8		St Bressou
29.9	↱ ◀	D15 'to Cardaillac'
		3km steep descent (with hairpins)
33.8	◀	1.5km gradual climb
35.3	↱	D15 'to Figeac'
36.0	✳	Cardaillac
39.3	↱	'to Doulan'
40.5	↱	unsigned road (skirts Doulan)
41.8	↱↰	N140/D18 'to Lissac' (dogleg)
42.2	↱	unsigned road
44.2	↱	D2 'to Figeac' Lissac
49.5	◇ ↰	'to Centre Ville'
49.6		N140 'to Centre Ville'
50.0		cross Rue Georges Juskiewenski
50.1		Figeac tourist office

Elevation

Figeac

On the Célé River, Figeac has a picturesque old city, with many houses from the 12th to 18th century. Founded in the 9th century by Benedictine monks, it became a prosperous medieval market town, an important stop for pilgrims travelling to Santiago de Compostela and, later, a Protestant stronghold.

Information Service is brusque in the tourist office (☎ 05 65 34 06 25, fax 05 65 50 04 58, e figeac@wanadoo.fr) on place Vival (closes at 5.30 pm October to April and on Sunday afternoons outside July and August).

A Crédit Agricole is on the N122, on the route into town. Some banks are along ave Fernand Pezet; the post office is at No 6.

Cycles Lacoste (☎ 05 65 34 60 92), on rue St Martha, after the roundabout into town, is well stocked. Cybercafe l'Experience (☎ 05 65 34 00 57) is at 10 ave Émile Bouyssou.

Things to See & Do The tourist office is housed in a handsome 13th-century building, the **Oustal de la Mounédo**. Upstairs, the **Musée du Vieux Figeac** has a varied collection of antique clocks, coins and minerals.

Figeac's most illustrious son is the brilliant linguist and founder of Egyptology, Jean-François Champollion (1790–1832), who deciphered the written language of the pharaohs. His childhood home is now the **Musée Champollion** (☎ 05 65 50 31 08), on rue des Frères Champollion. In the neighbouring courtyard is an enormous copy of the Rosetta Stone, which Champollion studied to decipher the language.

North of the museum, **rue de Colomb** is lined with centuries-old mansions; many have a *soleilho*, an open attic below the roof. Near the river, on rue du Chapitre, the **Église St Sauveur**, built from the 12th to 14th centuries, features century-old stained glass.

The tourist office sells a topoguide, *Figeac et Son Pays*, which details short hikes in the area.

Places to Stay The *Les Rives du Célé* camping ground (☎ 05 65 34 59 00, fax 05 65 34 83 83), off the Capendac-Rodez road, 5km south, has a wave pool and waterslide. It charges 57/95FF in low/high season for two people (open April to September).

In the old city, two-star *Hôtel Champollion* (☎ 05 65 34 04 37, 3 place Champol-

lion) has double rooms with shower and toilet for 195FF.

Across the square from the train station, **Le Terminus** (☎ 05 65 34 00 43, fax 05 65 50 00 94, 27 ave Georges Clemenceau) has doubles with shower and toilet for 250FF. A few blocks west of the train station, the **Hôtel Le Toulouse** (☎ 05 65 34 22 95, 4 ave de Toulouse) has serviceable doubles with shower and toilet from 180FF.

Places to Eat Place Carnot hosts a *food market* on Saturday morning; the biggest is the last one each month.

A *Casino* supermarket is on the intersection of the N140 and the D2. *Fruits & Primeurs*, across from the tourist office, has good produce and regional gourmet delights (closed Sunday and Monday). Rue Gambetta is lined with *patisseries*.

Across Pont Gambetta from the town centre, **À l'Escargot** (☎ 05 65 34 23 84, 2 ave Jean Jaurès) has been run by the same family since 1950. *Menus* of family-style Quercy cuisine cost 85FF to 168FF; the *plat du jour* is 55FF (closed Monday night). **Restaurant Vimean Ekreuch** (☎ 05 65 34 79 65, 10 rue Baudel)* serves Chinese food, with *menus* for 85FF and 125FF (closed Monday).

Day 8: Figeac to St-Cirq Lapopie
3–6 hours, 60.8km
One of the most dramatic days on the tour, the route follows the spectacular narrow, winding D41 along the Célé between limestone cliffs. Much of the ride is on the Chemin de Puy, a route to Santiago de Compostela. It's worth detouring into the small villages tumbling down the cliffs, whose streets hide centuries-old houses.

It's only 1.5km of busy roads to the countryside; head first towards the fruit shop. At 7km watch for a small road to the right, signposted to Le Moulin. Past the old *moulin* (mill), it crosses the wooded river into the beautiful Célé Valley.

It's only a short detour to **Espagnac-Ste Eulalie** (21.7km), the most photographed town on the Célé. Across the stone bridge, see the remains of the **abbey** and the **church's** peeling interior. Enthusiastic, one-hour tours cost 7FF.

Dramatic St Sulpice (31.3km) has a 12th-century **castle** (rebuilt in the 14th and 15th centuries) guarding the town.

SOUTH-WEST FRANCE

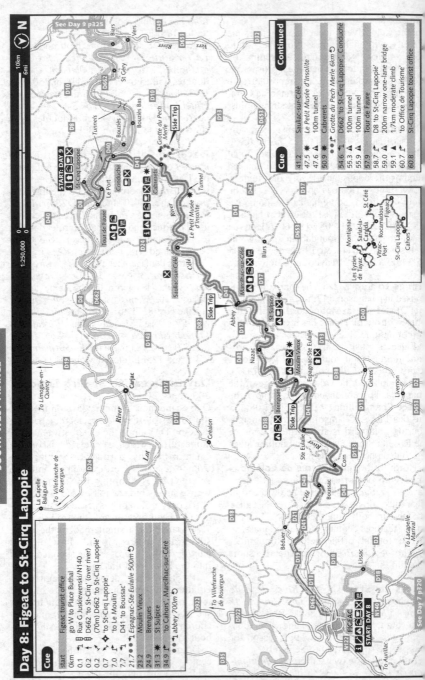

Day 8: Figeac to St-Cirq Lapopie

Cue

start	Figeac tourist office
0km	go W to Place Buthal
0.1	Rue G Juskiewenski/N140
0.2	D662 'to St-Cirq' (over river)
0.2	(70m) D662 'to St-Cirq Lapopie'
0.7	'to St-Cirq Lapopie'
7.0	'to Le Moulin'
7.7	D41 'to Boussac'
21.7	Espagnac-Ste Eulalie 500m ↻
23.2	Moulin Vieux
24.9	Brengues
31.3	St Sulpice
34.9	'to Cahors', Marcilhac-sur-Célé ↻
	abbey 700m ↻

Continued

Cue

41.2	Sauliac-sur-Célé
47.5	Le Petit Musée d'Insolite
47.6	100m tunnel
50.9	Cabrerets
	Grotte du Pech Merle 6km ↻
54.6	D662 'to St-Cirq Lapopie', Conduché
55.3	100m tunnel
55.9	100m tunnel
57.9	Tour de Faure
58.7	D8 'to St-Cirq Lapopie'
59.0	200m narrow one-lane bridge
59.1	1.7km moderate climb
60.7	'to Office de Tourisme'
60.8	St-Cirq Lapopie tourist office

See Day 9 p325

See Day 7 p320

1:250,000

0 10km / 6mi

N

Detour into picturesque Marcilhac-sur-Célé (34.9km), whose Benedictine monks must have kicked themselves when Rocamadour, which they'd practically abandoned, became a major pilgrimage destination. They had to accept a pay off by the monks who'd taken over the site. Their own **abbey** flourished until the Hundred Years War, when it was virtually destroyed. Guided tours (in French) cost 15FF.

Below the chateau ruins beyond lovely Sauliac-sur-Célé is an excellent **picnic spot** (42.6km). The cliffs are riddled with **fortified caves**, used for shelter during times of strife in the Middle Ages.

Sculptures made from old bicycles, farm machinery and wood spill onto the cliff at the **Petit Musée d'Insolite** (47.5km).

Near Cabrerets (50.9km) is the last chance to see cave art (see Side Trip). Cabrerets' dramatic Château des Anglais is known as the **Château du Diable** (in the Hundred Years War the English were often known as the evil, or *diable*).

The Célé River merges with the Lot at Conduché (54.6km). Take care in the tunnels through the Lot Valley. Tour de Faure (57.9km) is the last place for self-caterers to buy *food*, though don't rely on the shop being open. The only *camping ground* is just over the bridge (59km). It's a steep climb to St Cirq, but the sight of the prettiest town in Quercy atop sheer cliffs rewards the effort.

Side Trip: Grotte du Pech Merle
½–¾ hour, 6km

Visit the best collection still open to the public after Lascaux's closure by climbing steadily to the **Grotte du Pech Merle** (☎ 05 65 1 27 05); turn right onto the D13 and follow the signs. Or, it's a 1km walk uphill from Cabrerets. The 1200m of chambers and galleries feature animal paintings created 16,000 to 20,000 years ago; limestone formations; scratchings made with bear claws; and fossilised footprints of a mother and child.

Visitor numbers are limited; reserve in advance. From April to October, regular one-hour guided tours (English text available) run until 5 pm. Tickets cost 44FF.

St-Cirq Lapopie

Once the site of three castles, strategically positioned St-Cirq Lapopie was a busy little town in the 13th century. The castles were mostly destroyed in the Hundred Years War and the Wars of Religion, with the carved stone used in the sea of houses terracing up the hill.

The town takes its name from St Cirq, a child martyred in Asia Minor under Diocletian; it's believed his relics found their way here. Lapopie, a Celtic word referring to an elevated place, was the family name of the local lords during the Middle Ages.

Information The tourist office (☎/fax 05 65 31 29 06, e saint-cirq.lapopie@wanadoo.fr) has an English brochure on the village. St Cirq has no street names.

A Crédit Agricole opens in Tour de Faure on Thursday from 2 to 4 pm.

For basic bike repair, try Cap Liberté (☎ 05 65 35 97 05, fax 05 65 22 35 37), at the camping ground daily between mid-June and mid-September (try telephoning out of season).

Things to See & Do The entire **village** of St-Cirq Lapopie is classified as an historic monument; walk around the cobbled alleys lined with stone and half-timbered houses. Many shelter **artisans studios**. The tourist office runs guided tours in holiday season.

The **Maison de la Fourdonne** (☎/fax 05 65 31 21 51) showcases the town's woodturning heritage; it explains the history of the settlement and the area's geography. In summer the atmospheric **outdoor theatre** in the courtyard hosts plays, musical performances and films. The **Musée Rignault** (☎ 05 65 31 23 22) displays a collection of furniture and European and African art.

Climb the ruins of the 13th-century, hilltop **chateau** for a stunning panorama.

Cap Liberté (see Information) runs **VTT day trips** between April and September, hires out VTTs from mid-June to mid-September and arranges **canoe trips**.

The tourist office rents laser disks (in French) for a **walk** around the countryside.

Places to Stay & Eat Tour de Faure's riverside *Camping de la Plage* (☎ 05 65 30 29 51), at the bridge linking the D662 with the road to St Cirq-Lapopie, charges 30FF per person.

The *gîte d'étape* (lodging for cyclists and walkers) in the Maison de la Fourdonne (☎/fax 05 65 31 21 51) is the best option in town. It has 23 beds in five clean rooms with

SOUTH-WEST FRANCE

individual bathrooms, a map room and a dining room and kitchen. It costs 60FF per person and is popular, so book early.

The *Auberge du Sombral* (☎ 05 65 31 26 08, fax 05 65 30 26 37), across from the tourist office, has rooms for 260FF to 375FF; don't expect a warm welcome unless you eat all meals there. Its *restaurant* has a reputation for being overpriced: *menus* cost 100FF to 200FF (open from April to mid-November; the restaurant and reception close Wednesday, October to June).

The closest *grocery* and *bakery* are at Tour de Faure. In summer, a *dépôt de pain* is at the top of St Cirq.

Le Troubador (☎ 05 65 31 23 43), up the hill from the tourist office, serves excellent food in a room hung with local artwork. *Menus* cost from 70FF: the gourmet 125FF choice is a treat.

At the bottom of town, the *Restaurant l'Oustal* (☎/fax 05 65 31 27 60) serves good-quality, regional food, with evening *menus* from 95FF (closed November to January).

Day 9: St-Cirq Lapopie to Cahors

2–4 hours, 40.9km

The final day continues cutting through the causses of Quercy, now following the wide lower reaches of the Lot. Retrace the steps of gangs who pulled barges of salt, spices and dried fish from Bordeaux along the path cut into the cliffs, then travel along wide alluvial plains between wooded hills and dramatic cliffs. As traffic increases, the route turns inland to climb onto the plateau before dropping into Cahors.

From the tourist office backtrack onto the D8 and head downhill; after the first car park look for a sealed road leading left to the **Ganil towpath**. (If it's bucketing rain, consider following the Day 8 route to the Conduché junction, then turn left on the D662 towards Bouziès, where the towpath ends.) The towpath, dug between 1843 and 1847, now forms part of the GR36, passing a medieval mill and a 19th-century lock keepers' cottage and a **frieze** (4.7km) carved into the rock. Starting as a good bitumen road, it becomes well-packed gravel, then rough cobblestones – you'll probably have to walk for 300m.

Across the suspension bridge outside Bouziès is the **Défilé des Anglais** (6.3km), whose cave-like openings could be reached only by ladders (the weak were lifted up in baskets) in times of strife.

At Vers (19.6km), another ruined **chateau** clings to the cliffs above the confluence of the Vers and Lot rivers, where part of a Gallo-Roman **aqueduct** remains. The route climbs steadily above the cliffs into the forested rolling hills. At the crossroad at the top of the hill signage is a little confusing: go right, then veer left at each turn until the T-junction, then go right onto the D8 for a magnificent downhill into Galessie and Arcambal (28.6km).

It's another climb to a good **viewpoint** at St Cirice (35km). Few signs exist, but the locals happily help with directions. Take care on the steep descent. Once on the D22, navigation is simple; follow the signs for Cahors (Centre Ville).

Cahors

Cahors, the former capital of the Quercy region, is a quiet town with a relaxed atmosphere. Surrounded on three sides by a bend in the Lot River and circled by hills, its medieval bridge is famous throughout France.

In the Middle Ages, Cahors was a prosperous commercial and financial centre. Pope John XXII, a native of Cahors and the second of the Avignon popes, established a university here in 1331.

Cahors is near a route to Santiago de Compostela and had a pilgrim hospital as early as the 11th century.

Information The large, efficient tourist office (☎ 05 65 35 09 56, fax 05 65 23 98 66, e cahors@wanadoo.fr) is on place François Mitterrand (closed Sunday, except in the morning between May and August). Pick up the free brochure *Key to the Lot* (in English) for excellent practical information.

Banque de France is at 318 rue Président Wilson, and the main post office at No 257. Other banks are on blvd Léon Gambetta.

Cycles 7 (☎ 05 65 22 66 60) is at 417 quai de Regourd; it hires out VTTs for 80FF a day.

Things to See & Do Ask a French person to name the country's most beautiful bridge and they're likely to say **Pont Valentré**, a fortified medieval bridge spanning the Lot in six arches. With its three towers, it was built in the 14th century for defence rather than for traffic.

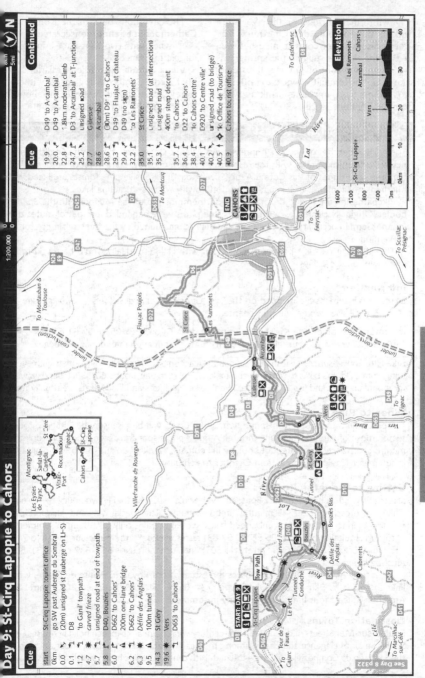

Day 9: St-Cirq Lapopie to Cahors

Cue

start		St-Cirq Lapopie tourist office
0km		go SW past Auberge du Sombral
0.0	↖	(20m) unsigned st (auberge on L↖-S)
0.1	↗	D8
1.2	↖	'to Ganil' towpath
4.7	* ☀ ◢	carved frieze
5.7		unsigned road at end of towpath
5.8	↖	D40, Bouziès
6.0	↖	D662 'to Cahors'
6.2	◢	200m one-lane bridge
6.3	↖	D662 'to Cahors'
9.5	◢	Défilé des Anglais
14.3		St Géry
19.6	*	Vers
	↖	D653 'to Cahors'

Cue — Continued

19.9	↖	D49 'to A'cambal'
20.0	↖	D49 'to A'cambal'
22.8	↗	'.8km moderate climb
24.7	↖	D3 'to Arcambal' at T-junction
25.2	↗	unsigned road
27.7		Galessie
28.6		Arcambal
28.6	↗	(30m) D9-1 'to Cahors'
29.3	↖	D49 'to Flujac' at chateau
29.4	↗	D49 (no sign)
32.2	↖	'to Les Ramonets'
35.0		St Circe
35.1		unsigned road (at intersection)
35.3	↖	unsigned road
	◢	400m steep descent
35.7	↗	'to Cahors
36.4	↖	'to Cahors centre'
38.4	↖	'to Cahors centre'
40.1	↗	D920 'to Centre ville'
40.2	↖	unsigned road (to bridge)
40.5	↖	D49 'to Office de Tourisme'
40.9	◈	'to Cahors tourist office

Elevation

St-Cirq Lapopie · Vers · Arcambal · Les Ramonets · Cahors

See Day 8 & 322

SOUTH-WEST FRANCE

Down from the bridge, on the river's left bank, is the **Fontaine des Chartreux**. The watery discovery of coins minted between 27 BC and AD 54 suggest the spring was used in the worship of Divona, the namesake of Gallo-Roman Cahors, two millennia ago. Cahors has pumped its drinking water from the Fontaine since 1880.

The cavernous nave of the Romanesqu Cathédrale St Étienne, consecrated in 111 is crowned with two 18m-wide cupolas (th largest in France).

Vieux Cahors, the medieval quarter east (blvd Léon Gambetta, is packed with fou storey houses linked by streets and alleyway so narrow you can almost touch both wall

Cycling the Atlantic Coast

The pristine beaches of France's unpretentious Atlantic Coast stretch from the English Channel to the Spanish frontier, with the resort of Arcachon midway, 60km west of Bordeaux. Behind the sand dunes of this Côte d'Azur (Silver Coast), extensive pine forests are laced with hundreds of kilometres of bikepaths and dotted with wildlife-attracting lakes.

Bikepaths link the Pointe de Grave, the northernmost tip of the Médoc, with the Spanish border. Originally cleared by resin tappers, the paths were expanded into patrol routes during the German occupation in WWII. Today they're maintained by the forestry service for fire prevention.

The Atlantic Coast is a perfect place to tour with children. Ideally, you'd base yourself in one town for a few days.

Information

Maps The bikepaths are mapped on the free *Gironde: Carte des Pistes Cyclables* – see the Maps & Books section early in this chapter.

Information Sources The Maison du Tourisme de la Gironde (☎ 05 56 52 61 40, fax 05 56 81 09 99, ✉ www.tourisme-gironde.cg33.fr) is at 21 cours de l'Intendance, Bordeaux.

Bike Hire Soulac-sur-Mer, Lacanau-Océan and Arcachon have large bike-hire outlets with everything from children's bikes to tandems and trailers. Expect to pay around 60/330FF per day/week for mountain bikes and 50/170FF for children's bikes. Helmets and kiddy seats are usually free.

When to Ride

The best time is the crisp, fresh spring, when the forests will be a sensory delight. The tourist season runs from around mid-June through August; prices soar and accommodation books out months in advance – regulars start booking in February. Weekly bookings are often mandatory in summer. Many places close from October to February.

Getting to/from the Beaches

SNCF trains and/or buses connect Bordeaux with Soulac-sur-Mer (82FF, two hours, five to eight daily) and Arcachon (52FF, 45 minutes, frequent trains). The special weekend *Médoc Océan* morning train to Soulac carries unbagged bikes; weekday trains only take them in summer.

Citram Aquitaine buses (☎ 05 56 99 57 83) also travel daily to Soulac-sur-Mer (No 713), Lacanau-Océan (No 702), Cap Ferret (No 601) and Arcachon (Nos 611, 612 and 613). Bikes must be bagged.

A car ferry (☎ 05 46 38 35 15) crosses the estuary from Royan to Pointe de Grave, which links to Soulac by 9km bikepath. A UBA ferry (☎ 05 56 54 60 32) connects Cap Ferret and Arcachon at least four times a day (hourly in summer).

Destination Towns

Soulac-sur-Mer Streets of distinctive 19th-century *villas balnéaires* (beach holiday houses) give Soulac an air of elegance and charm among the beachy batik and crowds. A important stop on the Santiago de Compostela trail since the mid-14th century, Soulac has a church famously saved

The tourist office brochure *Itineraires a Travers la Ville* comes with an English translation of the sights along a signed walking tour.

The **Musée Henri Martin** (☎ 05 65 30 15 13), 792 rue Émile Zola, also known as the Musee Municipal, has some archaeological artefacts and a collection of works by the Cahors-born pointillist painter Henri Martin

(1893–1972). The small **Musée de la Résistance** (☎ 05 65 22 14 25), on the north side of place Charles de Gaulle, has illustrated exhibits on the Resistance, the concentration camps and the liberation of France.

Walk to the top of the 264m-high, antenna-topped **Mont St Cyr**, across the river from Vieux Cahors, for excellent views – the trail

Cycling the Atlantic Coast

from the sand dunes; safe beaches; a museum of art and archaeology; and a great produce market. From nearby Pointe de Grave, boats visit the Phare du Cordouan (Cordouan Lighthouse).

The tourist office (☎ 05 56 09 86 61, fax 05 56 73 63 76) is at 68 rue de la Plage. The Crédit Agricole nearby has an ATM. Soulac has plenty of camping grounds and hotels. As well as the market, it has a supermarket and lots of cafes and restaurants, most specialising in seafood.

Montalivet-les-Bains This holiday village has a patrolled beach, cafes and restaurants. The town marks the start of the *naturist* (nudist) resorts, where thousands of families holiday in the raw. You don't have to strip off at every beach – plenty are designated *textiles*.

Hourtin-Plage This tiny resort town has a few cafes, restaurants, a camping ground and *meublés* (self-contained units) available in week blocks. Its main attraction is the beach. The tourist office at Hourtin (☎ 05 56 09 19 00, e hourtin.medoc@wanadoo.fr) handles bookings.

Maubuisson This pretty lakeside town is close to the Étang de Cousseau, home to a range of wildlife. The tourist office is in nearby Carcans (☎ 05 56 03 34 94, 🖳 www.tourisme.fr/carcans). Most accommodation is in *meublés*, or in the camping ground.

Lacanau-Océan Lacanau, with its surf beach, 2000-hectare lake and surrounding pine forest, bustles in summer. The town is like a large summer camp, offering just about any sport imaginable, plus several patrolled beaches. In August the world's big-name surfers roll in for the Lacanau Pro international competition.

The tourist office (☎ 05 56 03 21 01, fax 05 56 03 11 89, 🖳 www.lacanau.com) is on place de l'Europe. The rarely-open Crédit Agricole has an outside ATM; the post office also changes money. Lacanau has plenty of two-star hotels and two four-star camping grounds; the tourist office has a list of B&Bs. Cafes and restaurants abound and a market opens daily.

Cap Ferret This laid-back and charming town makes a great base for exploring the traditional *villages ostréicole* (oyster-farming villages) around the Bassin d'Arcachon. The tourist office (☎ 05 56 60 86 43, fax 05 56 60 94 54, 🖳 www.lege-capferret.com) can make bookings. Arcachon has plenty of hotels, a camping ground, and waterside cafes and restaurants.

Villages Ostréicole (Oyster Villages) L'Herbe is the bay's prettiest village ostréicole, but it's possible to ride (on roads) to several others from Cap Ferret. In L'Herbe, the tiny lanes and brightly painted wooden houses are much as they were at the turn of the 20th century.

Arcachon A quiet fishing village until the rail line from Bordeaux was extended in 1841, Arcachon gradually became populated with the seaside villas of wealthy Bordelais and is now a large resort town. The 3km-long, 114m-high Dune du Pyla, Europe's largest sand dune, is a short ride away. The Bassin d'Arcachon, a shallow, 250-sq-km tidal bay, is an ideal bird habitat; go to the Parc Ornithologique (☎ 05 56 22 80 93) at Le Teich to see some of Europe's rarest and most beautiful birds.

The Arcachon tourist office (☎ 05 57 52 97 97, fax 05 57 52 97 77, 🖳 www.arcachon.com) is at place Président Roosevelt. Arcachon has plenty of banks, plus restaurants and hotels in all price ranges; the closest camping grounds are at the Dune du Pyla, but they're pricey.

SOUTH-WEST FRANCE

begins near the south end of Pont Louis-Philippe. The GR36, GR65, and numerous marked **day walks** pass through Cahors.

The Centrale de Réservation Loisirs Accueil (☎ 05 65 53 20 90, fax 05 65 30 06 11), in the Chambre d'Agriculture du Lot in place François Mitterrand, can arrange canoe, bicycle and horse riding **excursions**, **cookery courses** and **boat rental** (open weekdays).

Places to Stay Rooms are hardest to come by in July and August. Many cheapies do not register new guests on Sunday unless it's arranged in advance.

The riverside, two-star **Camping St Georges** (*☎ 05 65 35 04 64, ave Anatole de Monzie*) is hemmed in by heavily trafficked roads. It charges 14FF per site, plus 14FF per adult. The office closes between 11.30 am and 4.30 pm (open March to October).

Foyer des Jeunes Travailleurs (*☎ 05 65 35 64 71, fax 05 65 35 95 92, 20 rue Frédéric Suisse*), serves as a hostel year-round. Beds cost 50FF. The office is staffed from 9 am to 6 pm.

Next to the Marché Couvert, the **Hôtel de la Paix** (*☎ 05 65 35 03 40, place des Halles/place St Maurice*) has basic but clean doubles from 150FF (190FF with shower). Hall showers are free. The reception is closed on Sunday and holidays.

The elegant three-star **Grand Hôtel Terminus** (*☎ 05 65 35 24 50, fax 05 65 22 06 40, 5 ave Charles de Freycinet*), one block up the hill from the train station, is a stained-glass-adorned place built around 1920. It has very comfortable doubles with shower from 350FF.

Places to Eat The **Marché Couvert** (also known as Les Halles), on place des Halles, is open morning and afternoon Tuesday to Saturday and Sunday afternoon. An **open-air market** is held around the Marché Couvert and on place de la Cathédrale on Wednesday and Saturday. **Food shops** can be found around place des Halles and along rue de la Préfecture; regional specialities include deep-red Cahors wine, foie gras, truffles and *cabécou* (a small, round goats cheese).

Near the tourist office, the **Champion** supermarket is across from 109 blvd Léon Gambetta (closed Sunday).

Most restaurants close on Sunday. At the friendly and unpretentious **Restaurant Le Troquet des Halles** (*☎ 05 65 22 15 81*), on tiny rue St Maurice near place des Halles, the *menu* costs only 55FF, including wine. From 7 to 10 am, the soup (16FF) comes with a glass of wine so you can *faire chabrol* (add the wine to the soup and drink it together). Buy a steak at the nearby Marché Couvert and the chef will cook it for an extra 9FF (closed for dinner outside June to September). The attractive, vegetarian **Restaurant L'Orangerie** (*☎ 05 65 22 59 06, 41 rue St James*) has salads from 20FF, main dishes from 42FF and *menus* for 68FF and 98FF (closed Monday and Sunday).

The best-known *haut cuisine* is served at the elegant **Restaurant Le Balandre** (*☎ 05 65 30 01 97*), attached to the Grand Hôtel Terminus. It serves creative cuisine based on traditional regional dishes and ingredients, including fish. Dinner *menus* cost from 150FF to 350FF (closed on Sunday night and Monday).

Massif Central

he striking mountain landscape of the Mas-
f Central, pocked with the cones of extinct
olcanoes, is unique in France. Blessed with
n abundance of mineral hot springs, the
ea is also known for its spa towns, among
em Vichy and Le Mont-Dore.

Except in the few small cities and the re-
ional capital, Clermont-Ferrand, life is pri-
arily rural and villages are few. The rich
olcanic soil supports maize, tobacco and
ineyards. At higher elevations, cows and
reep produce some of the country's most
opular (and affordable) cheeses (see 'The
emise of the Buronnier' boxed text later in
is chapter).

The region's two large regional parks, the
ramatic Parc Naturel Régional des Volcans
'Auvergne and its tamer eastern neighbour,
e Parc Naturel Régional du Livradois-
orez, together make up France's largest en-
ironmentally protected area.

The parks' rugged expanses make the re-
ion ideal for combining cycling with other
utdoor activities. The Massif Central is an
drenalin addict's paradise, offering moun-
in biking, hang-gliding and *parapent*
para-gliding) flights, rock climbing and
renuous walks. Thirteen Grande Randon-
ée (GR) tracks (including the GR4) cross
e region, along with hundreds of easier,
orter footpaths, many of which are suitable
r VTTs (mountain bikes). Many trailheads
re accessible only by car – or by bike.

The area's popularity with outdoor ad-
enturers means that it is spotted with *gîtes
'étape*, hostels for walkers, cyclists or
questrians. These often occupy rustic stone
uildings in stunning, quiet locations.

CLIMATE

he Massif Central receives most of its rain
n summer, usually as afternoon storms.
uring the storms, routes in the mountains
an cloud over and cold rain buffet unfor-
nate cyclists. The mountains usually es-
ape the heat extremes of lower places such
s Clermont-Ferrand, where summer tem-
eratures can reach the high 30s.

Winds tend to be from the north from
lay to August and from the south for the
est of the year, though the mountain ranges
reate their own unpredictable currents.

In Brief

Highlights
- reaching the summit of **Puy Mary**
- following the Tour route up the **Puy de Dôme**
- sleeping in a mountain **buron** (shepherds hut)

Terrain
Rolling hills dotted by volcanic puys in the north and divided by older, jagged mountain ranges in the south.

FFCT Contact
Ligue Auvergne, 1a rue Guérat, 03500 Saulcet

Cycling Events
- **Championnates de France de Cyclisme sur Route** road racing championships (June)
- **Les Vélovolcans cycling week** (June) Clermont-Ferrand

Special Events
- **Festival National et International du Court Métrage** short-film festival (January/February) Clermont-Ferrand

Gourmet Specialities
- cheese, such as cantal, st nectaire, bleu d'auvergne, fourme d'ambert and salers
- *fougasse* (brioche from the Cantal)
- *potée auvergnate* (stew of cabbage, potato, bacon, pork loin and sausages)
- mineral waters, such as Volvic and Mont-Dore

INFORMATION
The area known as the Massif Central covers roughly the area of Auvergne, an administrative region comprised of the *départements* (departments; administrative
divisions) of Allier, Puy de Dôme, Cantal
and Haute-Loire.

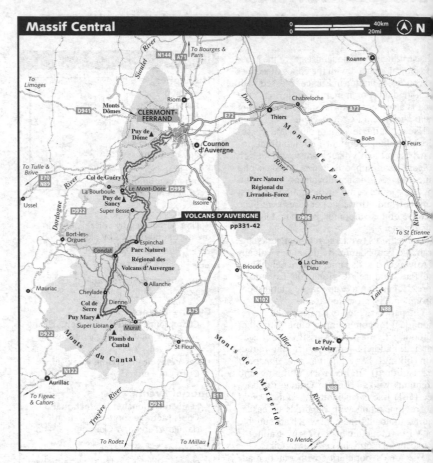

Maps

The Michelin map No 239 *Auvergne, Limousin* (1:200,000) covers the region. If you're combining walking or mountain biking with touring, IGN's Top 25 maps Nos 2531ET *Chaine des Puys*, 2432ET *Massif du Sancy*, 2534OT *Monts du Cézallier* and 2435OT *Monts du Cantal* (all 1:25,000) provide more detail.

Books

The Fédération Française de Cyclotourisme (FFCT) details more than 30 tours in the region in *La France à Vélo: Auvergne, Limousin* (see Books in the Facts for the Cyclist chapter).

Mountain bikers can tap into a plethora of resources, mostly available through book shops or tourist offices. The Office Nationa[l] des Fôrets publishes *Auvergne: Les Par[cours VTT Evasion* (see the 'Mountain Bik[ing' boxed text in the Facts for the Cycli[st] chapter). *Circuits Pedestres et VTT: Volcan[s] d'Auvergne* (98FF) describes 45 walking VTT routes in the region. Chamina (see In[formation Sources) publishes a series of re[gional topoguides and VTT guides.

Information Sources

The useful Comité Régional du Tourism[e] d'Auvergne (☎ 04 73 29 49 49, fax 04 73 3[11 11, 🖳 www.crt-auvergne.fr) is at 44 av[des États-Unis, Clermont-Ferrand. Ask f[or] a copy of *Auvergne: A Paradise of Space* an excellent two-part brochure (get both th[e 'Holiday Guide' and the 'Practical Guide

vith information on outdoor activities, in-
luding details of several fully supported
rganised tours run by the departmental
ourist offices.

Also in Clermont-Ferrand, details on
utdoor activities and related maps and
opoguides are available at the Espace Mas-
if Central (☎ 04 73 42 60 00, fax 04 73 42
0 90, ☐ www.centrefrance.com/tourisme
:mc), which occupies part of the Maison du
ourisme. Chamina (☎ 04 73 92 81 44, fax
4 73 91 62 24, ☐ www.chamina.com), 5
ie Pierre le Vénérable, sells topoguides and
iaps (open weekdays) and has information
n gîtes d'étape.

For brochures on gîtes and *chambres
'hôtes* (B&Bs), the Gîtes de France office
☎ 04 73 42 21 23, fax 04 73 93 14 41) is
1 the Hôtel du Département at 26 rue du St
sprit, Clermont-Ferrand. On weekdays, it
lso handles reservations for *gîtes ruraux*
rural lodgings). The Maison des Parcs
'Auvergne (☎ 04 73 55 11 63), rue Jean-
igot, 63500 Issoire, has information on
îtes d'étape and both regional parks.

The FFC, not to be confused with the
FCT, runs five Auvergne VTT centres; see
ie Facts for the Cyclist chapter for contact
etails.

Cycling Events

he annual Championnates de France de
'yclisme sur Route racing championship is
eld in the region in late June in conjunction
vith a week-long cycling festival, Les Vélo-
olcans. Contact the Comité Régional FFC
'Auvergne (☎ 04 73 37 95 15) for details.

Warning

Many *cols* (passes) in the area can be
closed by snow from October until late
May or even early June. Days 2 and 3 of
the Volcans d'Auvergne ride cross such
cols; outside June, July and August *always*
check if they're open before setting out.

Tourist offices should be able to tell you
which ones are open; French speakers can
find out the *état de la route* (condition of
the route) by calling a recorded information service:

Pas de Peyrol ☎ 04 71 45 53 00
Col de la Croix St-Robert ☎ 04 73 80 31 55

Volcans d'Auvergne

Duration	3 days
Distance	171km
Difficulty	hard
Start	Clermont-Ferrand
End	Murat

Travelling through the heart of the Parc
Naturel Régional des Volcans d'Auvergne,
this is a ride of dramatic and varied volcanic
landscapes. It's a big ride – the combination
of distances, climbing, breathtaking descents and challenging side trips give it a
hard grading. The weather can add to the
difficulty – at night and during storms, temperatures can plummet, even in summer –
and warm clothes and wet weather gear
should always be carried.

You could easily turn this into a 'moderate' ride by stretching it over six days, adding
nights at Orcival, Besse-en-Chandesse and
Le Claux, all charming towns with places to
stay and eat. It would be ideal to alternate
cycling with walking – the area is crisscrossed by hundreds of walking tracks
through fabulous countryside.

NATURAL HISTORY

Encompassing 3250 sq km, the Parc des
Volcans is the largest *parc naturel* (nature
park) in France. More than 90,000 people
live and work within its boundaries, which
is part of its charm; many buildings in the
150 towns and villages in this wild and
beautiful park are built of grey volcanic
stone. From the north, the park stretches for
120km from the Monts Dômes, the smooth,
cone-shaped *puys* (volcanic plugs; pronounced pwee) near Clermont-Ferrand, to
the spectacular Monts Dore, around Le
Mont-Dore, and to the older, more rugged
Monts du Cantal, farther south around the
Puy Mary and Murat.

The volcanic activity in this region
started about 20 million years ago, with the
last eruptions (in the Monts Dômes) peter-
ing out about 6000 years ago. The Monts du
Cantal are the remnants of France's largest
extinct volcano. During the Ice Age glaciers
shaved the tops off the cones and cut the
smooth slopes into corries (basins) and deep,
radiating valleys, creating the constantly undulating countryside that challenges cyclists

MASSIF CENTRAL

today. Meltwater eroded some volcanic plugs into the dramatic cliffs and chimneys that line the route.

Today, the area's thermal activity is harnessed in the hot springs of numerous spa towns. The volcanic soil also acts as a giant filter, producing spring water bottled under names such as Vichy and Volvic.

Some of France's great rivers originate in the Auvergne, including the Dordogne, Allier and Loire. Many of the area's lakes are volcanic craters that have filled with rainwater; others were created when lava flows created dams.

The region's vegetation varies according to soil type and altitude; the oakwoods on the hillsides give way to beeches and pines on the mountains. Above 1000m, mountain pastures feature abundant wildflowers, including gentians (used to make the local liqueur Gentiane). At 1500m and above, the subalpine vegetation includes myrtle and, around the high peaks, blue carnations. On the upland moors, carnivorous plants such as sundew are common.

In the mountains are mouflon (see the boxed text above), marmots, chamois and shy rock thrushes, with flame-like tails. The woods ring to the tapping of the green woodpecker, but the peregrine falcon is nearly extinct and is the subject of a regional breeding program.

PLANNING
When to Ride

The passage of this route over high passes means cycling is limited by the seasons (see the 'Warning' boxed text earlier in the chapter). The passes should open by June, a good month to cycle. Tourist crowds and traffic are worst in August. September and October can be pleasant, though it may be foggy.

Kings of the Mountains

Look out for *mouflon de Corse* (Corsican mouflon), a breed of mountain sheep often spotted sitting in the shade of the rocks, or grazing on fresh grass. About 150 live in the area though, as the name suggests, the animals aren't native to the area, but were introduced from the island of Corsica in 1956 by the local hunting association.

GETTING TO/FROM THE RIDE

For more remote hill country, connect this ride with the Upper Languedoc ride (in the Languedoc-Roussillon chapter), which starts in Nîmes. The train trip through the mountains to Nîmes is one of the most scenic in France; the route, which begins in Paris, is known as Le Cévenol.

Clermont-Ferrand

Clermont-Ferrand train station is on ave de l'Union Soviétique, 1km east of the cathedral in the city centre.

Only one service a day takes bikes outside a bike bag to Paris' Gare de Lyon (255FF, 3½ hours, six to eight a day) and Nîmes (184FF, 3¾ hours, two or three a day).

From the UK, the European Bike Express service (see Land in the Getting There & Away chapter) charges £159 (return) to take a passenger and bike to Clermont-Ferrand.

Murat

The train station (☎ 04 71 20 07 20) is on ave du Docteur Mallet at the bottom of town. Three or four trains a day to Clermont-Ferrand (91FF, 1¾ hours) take bikes.

THE RIDE
Clermont-Ferrand

The lively city of Clermont-Ferrand, by far the largest city in the Massif Central, is east of the Monts Dômes. The town centre, enlivened by a student population of about 34,000, sits on a long-extinct volcano.

Clermont-Ferrand was Christianised in the 3rd century. In 1095, it was the meeting place for the synod at which Pope Urban preached the First Crusade.

It was also the birthplace of Blaise Pascal (1623–62), the physicist, mathematician and philosopher who helped formulate the theory of probability.

These days, Clermont is the hub of France's rubber industry, better known to the rest of the world as the Michelin tyre empire. The company started life in 1830 manufacturing rubber balls. With the invention of the bicycle its main business became producing the brake block, 'The Silent' until 1891 when the company patented the invention that revolutionised cycling – a detachable bicycle tyre. Only a year later 10,000 cyclists were using it, and the technology was used in car tyres in 1895.

MASSIF CENTRAL

nformation The main tourist office (☎ 04
73 98 65 00, fax 04 73 90 04 11) is in the
Maison du Tourisme at place de la Victoire,
acing the cathedral (closed Sunday afternoon outside June to September).

The Banque de France is at 15 cours
Sablon, the Crédit Agricole at 3 ave de la
Libération and several other commercial
banks are at the northern end of place de
aude. The main post office is on rue Mau-
ice Busset. Cycles Géral (☎ 04 73 26 26
4) is at 267 rue de l'Oradou (closed Monday morning and Sunday).

Internet@Café (☎ 04 73 92 42 80) is at
2 rue Ballainvilliers.

Things to See & Do Explore the **old town**
with the tourist office's free historical walk-
ng guide *Welcome to Clermont-Ferrand* or
discover the city's many **fountains** with the
Tour of Fountains brochure.

Explore the quiet suburb of **Montferrand**,
.5km north-east of the cathedral, with its
many **Gothic and Renaissance houses** and
he **Musée des Beaux-Arts** (☎ 04 73 23 08
9) at place Louis Deteix.

In the town centre, Clermont's soaring
Gothic **Cathédrale Notre Dame** is built of
he region's dark grey volcanic stone; the
strong and light material has been used to
reate a vast, double-aisled nave held aloft
y particularly slender pillars and vaults.
The 12th-century **Basilique Notre Dame du
Port** is hidden in the north-east corner of the
ld city off rue du Port (go there via the
nteresting rue Blaise Pascal).

The **Musée Bargoin** (☎ 04 73 91 37 31),
5 rue Ballainvilliers, has an excellent pre-
istory section and colourful 18th- to 20th-
entury carpets.

Places to Stay The three-star *Le Chanset*
☎ 04 73 61 30 73) camping ground is about
km south-west in Ceyrat on a busy road.
Head out of Clermont-Ferrand on cours R
Poincaré; the camping ground is on ave
Jean Baptiste. Open all year, a tent site for
wo people costs 53FF from June to Sep-
ember (less the rest of the year).

The modern *Corum Saint Jean* (☎ 04 73
1 57 00, fax 04 73 31 59 99, 17 rue Gaultier
e Biauzat), also known as the Foyer des
eunes Travailleurs, accepts travellers year-
ound. A bed costs 80FF, including breakfast.
Check-in is possible 24 hours a day.

The cheery *Hôtel Foch* (☎ 04 73 93 48
40, fax 04 73 35 47 41, 22 rue Maréchal
Foch) has singles/doubles from 145/155FF.

Hôtel Régina (☎ 04 73 93 44 76, fax 04
73 35 04 63, 14 rue Bonnabaud) has tidy,
two-star rooms with shower from 220/
240FF.

Close to the train station, an excellent bet
is the old-fashioned *Hôtel Ravel* (☎ 04 73
91 51 33, fax 04 73 92 28 48, 8 rue de
Maringues) Rooms with shower start at
150/170FF.

Places to Eat The jumble of blue, yellow
and grey cubes that fills place St Pierre is
the city's *covered market*, open from 7 am
to 7.30 pm (closed Sunday). Nearby rue de
la Boucherie, one of the city's oldest streets,
is lined with *food shops*.

The *Nouvelles Galeries* department store
on place de Jaude has a basement supermarket. Near the train station, the *Éco Service* grocery is at 66 ave Charras.

Two blocks north of place de Jaude, rue
St Dominique and nearby alleys are home
to quite a few inexpensive *brasseries* and
ethnic restaurants (Tunisian, Indian, Viet
namese, Italian, Tex-Mex etc), where vegetarians might find it easier to find a meal.

A number of small restaurants can be
found along medieval, pedestrianised rue
des Chaussetiers. The cosy *Crêperie le
1513* (☎ 04 73 92 37 46) at No 3 has
savoury and sweet crepes (11FF to 60FF),
salads and other dishes.

In the old city, *Le Diablotin* (☎ 04 73 92
85 20, 8 rue Abbé Girard), a rustically elegant fish restaurant, has *menus* (set meals)
from 89FF. It opens for dinner only (closed
Sunday and Monday).

Near the train station, *La Crémaillère*
(☎ 04 73 90 89 25, 61 ave de l'Union, Soviétique) has *menus* of family-style Auvergnat cuisine for 50FF and 79FF (closed
Saturday evening and Sunday).

Day 1: Clermont-Ferrand to Le Mont-Dore
4½–6 hours, 57.4km
Much of this route involves climbing, starting with a steep ascent out of Clermont-
Ferrand into the undulating countryside of
the Parc des Volcans. The conical puys, lush
pastures, rugged cliffs and dark stone villages along the way are all postcard material.

MASSIF CENTRAL

Within a few kilometres of Clermont-Ferrand, the route winds through fields of cows and damp woods. From the tourist office, head west (with the cathedral to the right) to zigzag across place de la Victoire and head down place Sugny before hitting blvd Desaix, which circles the huge place de Jaude. Follow the signs across the *place* (square) to Puy de Dôme, then continue straight, following signs to Chamalières, Royat then Puy de Dôme.

For the first half of the day the 112 'recent' extinct volcanoes in the Chain of Puys add a dramatic backdrop to pastures scattered with wildflowers. Just after Fontanas (7.5km), a side trip goes to the most famous (and highest) of the puys, **Puy de Dôme**, though it's only possible to cycle to the summit on certain days (see the 'Puy de Dôme & Le Tour' boxed text overleaf).

Pretty Laschamp (16.1km) is a busy walking centre thanks to its location among rolling hills below Puy de Laschamp. After Pardon a trailhead in pine forest (25.2km) gives access to walks up **Puy de la Vache** and **Puy de Lassolas** (allow 2½ hours as the Puy de la Vache is the steepest in the chain, with a 28% gradient).

The route passes the park head office (26.7km) in the Château de Montlosier (☎ 04 73 65 64 00). Next door, the **Maison du Parc des Volcans d'Auvergne** has a good exhibit on volcanism and wildlife in the area (18FF, open daily from May to October); the *gîte* here has dorm accommodation.

The short stretch on the N89 is on a wide verge, and from Bessat (36.7km) the road travels along a spectacular ridge, from where the Chain of Puys look like a dragon's spine, with Puy de Dôme the horned head. At 40.7km, turn left on the D27 for the main route or right for the side trip to **Orcival** (follow the signs). This charming, slate-roofed village has a 12th-century, Auvergnat-Romanesque **basilica** – a massive structure built of dark volcanic blocks. Another 3km north, on the road signposted to Clermont-Ferrand, the 15th-century **Château de Cordes** (☎ 04 73 65 81 34), surrounded by ornamental gardens, is worth seeing for its remarkable volcanic stone exterior, though there's not much inside (20FF entry).

On the steady climb towards the cross-hatched, shattered rock cliffs of the Monts Dore range, two spectacular rock spikes come into sight. The **Roche de Tuilière** (1288m) is the cluster of prismatic trachyte columns and is the remains of a volcanic chimney; the other is the **Roche Sanadoire** (1286m). It's possible to walk to Sanadoire (trailhead at 46km, 1¾ hours return) – let out a few yells to find out why it's called the *pierre qui sonne* (the rock that rings). Otherwise, admire the view from the **look out** (47.5km).

The **Col de Guéry** (47.7km), at 1244m, is famous for its view over the forested Chausse corrie towards the roches. Near the col, the **Maison des Fleurs d'Auvergne** (☎/fax 04 73 65 20 09) opens as an information centre on the region's flowers from June to mid-September. Also nearby is the glacial **Lac de Guéry**, where there's a *hotel* and *restaurant*.

From the col it's a thoroughly delightful descent into Le Mont-Dore.

Le Mont-Dore

This lovely little spa town is a great place to spend a few extra days mountain biking, walking or trying some of the other adventurous activities on offer in the spectacular Puy de Sancy area. The town lies in a narrow, wooded valley along the Dordogne River, not far from its source.

Popular since Roman times for its curative waters, a thermal complex was built in the town in 1817 and was then enlarged and modernised at the end of the 19th century. Built from the dark local stone, the town bustles with walkers, hang-gliders and *curistes* attracted by the hot springs in cycling season, and with skiers in winter.

Information The tourist office (☎ 04 73 65 20 21, fax 04 73 65 05 71) is on ave de la Libération, in the indoor sport complex. The staff will make free hotel reservations (☎ 04 73 65 09 00) and sell topoguides for walking or mountain biking.

The Crédit Agricole is at 9 rue du Cap Chazotte (closed weekends). The main post office is on place Charles de Gaulle.

Bessac Sports (☎ 04 73 65 02 25), on rue de Maréchal Juin, has a good stock of spares and does repairs. It also hires full suspension VTTs for 200/1070FF a day/week (open daily from June to August and some days in September).

Day 1: Clermont-Ferrand to Le Mont-Dore

1:275,000

0 — 10km
0 — 6mi

N

Cue

Start		Clermont-Ferrand tourist office
0km		go W on Place de la Victoire
0.0	⤵	(5m) Place Sugny
0.2	⤴	(25m) Place Sugny
0.7	⤴	Rue Blatin 'to Chamalières'
3.3	▲	4.5km moderate climb
7.3		Fontanas
7.3	⤴	D90 'to Manson'
	••↺	Puy de Dôme 16.4km ↺
9.4	⤴	D90 'to Manson'
10.6		St Genès-sur-Charade
11.3	⤴	D90 'to Thèdes'
11.5	⤴	D767 'to Laschamp', Manson
16.1		Laschamp
16.2	⤴	D52 'to Beaune'
21.1	⤴	D5 'to Randanne', Parçon
21.3	▲	300m steep climb
25.2	✳	pays walks
26.7	✳	Maison du Parc
28.3		N89, Randanne
29.0	⤴	D561 'to Aurières-Vernines'
29.2	⤴	D561 'to Aurières-Vernines'
31.5	⤵	'to Vernines'
34.9		Vernines
36.7	⤴	D74 'to Orcival', Bessat
40.7	⤴	D27 'to Le Mont-Dore'
	••↺	Orcival and chateau 9.4km ↺
	▲	7km steady climb
41.8		Rouchaube
45.9	✳	D983 'to Col de Guéry'
46.0	✳	walk to Roche Sanadoire
47.7	✳	Col de Guéry, Maison des Fleurs
56.9	⤴	'to Centre Ville'
57.0	⤴	Rue Meynadier
57.2	⤴	Allée Georges Lagaye
57.3	⤴	Ave Jules Ferry
57.4		Le Mont-Dore tourist office

Set Day 2 p339

Elevation

2400
2000
1600
1200
800
400
0m

Clermont-Ferrand
Manson
Laschamp
Pardon
Randanne
Bessat
Col de Guéry (1268m)
Le Mont-Dore

0km   10   20   30   40   50

Map labels

COURNON D'AUVERGNE

START CLERMONT-FERRAND

ROYAT

Chamalières

St Genès-sur-Charade

Ceyrat

Thèdes

Manson

Fontanas

Font de l'Arbre

Laschamp

Puy de Dôme (1465m)

Puy de la Vache (1167m)

Puy de Lassolas

Beaune-le-Chaud

Pardon

Puy de Laschamp (1195m)

Maison du Parc

Puy de Charmont (1254m)

PARC NATUREL RÉGIONAL DES VOLCANS D'AUVERGNE

Monts Dômes

Lac d'Aydat

Randanne

Aurières

Vernines

Bessat

Orcival

Château de Cordès

St Pierre-Roche

Roche Sanadoire (1286m)

Roche Tuilière (1288m)

Lac de Guéry

Maison des Fleurs

Col de Guéry (1244m)

Rouchaube

Rochefort-Montagne

Sioule

Gorce River

River

Miouze River

LE MONT-DORE

START DAY 2

Chambon-sur-Lac

Murol

Lac Chambon

Puy de Besolle (1045m)

Le Verdier

Courbanges

Roche de l'Aigle

Moneaux

Col de la Croix St-Robert (1451m)

Besse-en-Chandesse

La Bourboule

To Issoire
To Riom
To Pontgibaud
To Ussel
To La Bourboule

MASSIF CENTRAL

Side Trip

Things to See & Do The **Établissement Thermal** (☎ 04 73 65 05 10), a huge hot springs complex on place du Panthéon, sits on the site of a Roman spa. Its waters are said to cure respiratory ailments and it offers a wide range of hydrotherapies from mid-May to late October. In summer there are guided tours of the cavernous, neo-Byzantine interior.

The forests, lakes, streams and peaks around the city are ideal for hiking and mountain biking. The tourist office has information on the many scenic **walks** in the area, including a free brochure with **cycling routes** near town. They also have a free **VTT trail** map *Circuits VTT: Le Mont-Dore Sancy*. Organise **paraskiing** with the École Ailes Libres (☎ 04 73 39 26 49 o ☎ 04 73 39 72 72, fax 04 73 69 40 27).

From ave René catch the **Funiculaire du Capucin** (☎ 04 73 65 01 25), a *belle époque* style funicular railway built in 1898, to th

Puy de Dôme & Le Tour

Looking like a Martian's balding pate, the transmitter-topped, steep-sided cone of Puy de Dôme rises starkly out of the landscape, offering a fantastic panorama of Clermont-Ferrand and the Chain of Puys from its 1465m summit.

The puy was a famous stage in the Tour de France during the 1950s and 60s, though the poor farming communities of central France haven't been able to attract the expensive race to the region for at least a decade. It was, most famously, the scene of a decisive battle between the two French cycling greats Jacques Anquetil and Raymond Poulidor in 1964. The pair slogged their way to the top, literally rubbing shoulders, neither able to expend the extra energy to shake the other off. Anquetil won the stage (and the Tour), while Poulidor won his way into French hearts by just missing out. He went on to be placed second in the Tour three times and third twice, but never cracked the big one, entering the French lexicon for his efforts: 'faire un Poulidor' means the same as the English expression 'the eternal bridesmaid'.

The other big Puy de Dôme moment was in 1959 when 'the Eagle of Toledo', Frederico Bahamontès, beat Henri Anglade, then champion of France, and the Luxembourg climbing legend Charly Gaul – the 'Angel of the Mountains' – to win the Tour.

These days it's essential to plan carefully to cycle to the summit. The corkscrew route is *only* open to bikes on Wednesday and Sunday mornings between May and September. Cyclists must start climbing between 7 and 8.30 am and be back at the bottom by 11 am (call ☎ 04 73 62 21 48 to check details); no exceptions are allowed. Allow 1½ hours to get to the base of the puy from Clermont-Ferrand. Thousands of cyclists also make a pilgrimage in late June for the annual FFCT Rallye du Puy de Dôme.

On other days it's possible to lock bikes at the bottom and catch the *navette* (minibus; 21FF) to the summit or walk up on the path that begins near the toll booth. The route to the puy is clearly signed from the intersection of the D68 and the D90. The private road spirals 7km to the top, gaining 595m in altitude. The first steep pinch (around 15%) just before the private road gives a taste of what's to come; the second quad-killing climb is about halfway to the top.

Jacques Anquetil (left) and Raymond Poulidor (right) jostle for position on the Puy de Dôme in the 1964 Tour.

MASSIF CENTRAL

Pic du Capucin. This 1270m-high wooded plateau above the town gives spectacular views. From the upper station, you can link up with the **GR30**, which wends its way southward to the Puy de Sancy, or walk back to town. Bikes travel free.

Explore the **Puy de Sancy**; see the side trip in Day 2 to ride to the base or, in July and August, catch a bus (no bikes allowed) from the tourist office.

Places to Stay Le Mont-Dore has lots of inexpensive accommodation. Book ahead in July and August. The two-star *Les Crouzets (☎ 04 73 65 21 60)* camping ground on ave des Crouzets is at the bottom end of town, across the river from the train station (open mid-May to September). It charges 14.50FF per adult and 13.50FF for a tent site.

Les Hautes Pierres (☎ 04 73 65 25 65), chemin des Vergnes, is a clean, friendly, modern gîte inside an old stone house. It has a communal kitchen and six-bed dorms with private bathrooms. A bed costs 65FF; call a day ahead to request *demi-pension* (half-board) at 155FF or full pension, with picnic lunch, for 190FF; the meals are excellent and include wine. Try to book ahead.

Hôtel Les Myosotis (☎ 04 73 65 01 35, 31 rue Louis Dabert) is one of the cheapest places in town, with basic rooms from 100FF.

The homey, 23-room *Hôtel Aux Champs d'Auvergne (☎ 04 73 65 00 37, 18 rue Favart)* has basic singles/doubles from 105/135FF.

Places to Eat The best place to purchase edibles is place de la République, where the *Petit Casino* and *ÉcoMag* groceries, the excellent *boulangerie* (bakery), the *charcuterie* (delicatessen) and the *marché couvert* (covered market) are open daily except on Sunday afternoon. Most places also close between 12.30 and 3 pm.

Pizzeria Le Tremplin (☎ 04 73 65 25 90) on ave Foch has pizzas for 39FF to 54FF (open evenings only, closed Monday in spring and autumn).

Many of Le Mont-Dore's hotels have restaurants with moderately priced *menus*. The *restaurant* in Hôtel Champs d'Auvergne specialises in Auvergnat cuisine such as *truffade* (potatoes prepared with

very young cantal cheese) and *fondue Auvergnate* (cantal cheese fondue). *Menus* cost between 58FF and 95FF, and takeaway dishes 35FF.

Le Boeuf dans l'Assiette (☎ 04 73 65 01 23, 9 place Charles de Gaulle) has hearty beef and mutton dishes for 58FF to 92FF; the *menus* cost 68FF and 89FF (closed Monday outside early July to September).

Fresh regional fare, including fish, is the speciality of *Le Louisiane (☎ 04 73 65 03 14, 2 rue Jean Moulin)*, which has *menus* from 85FF to 145FF and takeaway soup and *trouffade* for 39FF each (closed Wednesday outside summer).

Day 2: Le Mont-Dore to Condat
4½–6 hours, 61.3km

There are no pretensions about this stage: it starts the way it intends to continue, with a challenging ascent followed by a series of rolling hills. However, the scenery compensates. The road climbs out of wooded valleys and onto their open tops, travelling among jagged cliffs and rounded puys.

The day's steepest climb (15% gradient) is at the town exit, just past the bridge over the Dordogne. The highly recommended side trip to **Puy de Sancy** (1886m), Central France's highest peak, is much more gradual. From the Station du Mont-Dore the **Téléphérique du Sancy** (☎ 04 73 65 02 23) goes to 1780m, from where it's a 20-minute walk to the summit and its stunning panorama of the northern puys and the Monts du Cantal. The 30-minute service runs daily; one-way/return tickets cost 30/36FF. Given the walking opportunities around the Puy, it may be worth making this excursion a day trip.

The main route climbs steeply, giving heady views over Le Mont-Dore and passing the trailhead for the 1½ hour walk to the 30m **Grande Cascade**, the valley's largest waterfall. On the tops, between towering peaks, the woods give way to false heather and granite boulders. At the bare, rugged **Col de la Croix St-Robert** (7.4km, 1451m) check your bike's brakes before attempting the switchbacking road – it becomes a motor racing competition track in early August. Across expanses of pink willow-herb a spectacular landscape unfolds – a patchwork of fields and woods dotted with puys. In the distance is Chambon-sur-Lac, close to its eponymous lake and the remains of the 12th-century fortified Château de Murol.

The **Poterie de Moneaux** (12.9km) sells stylish raku pottery (open daily year-round). Nearby, in the beautiful, wooded glacial cirque of the Vallée de Chaudefour – a nature reserve and walking mecca – is the **Maison de Chaudefour** (15.8km, ☎ 04 73 88 68 80). It has interesting free displays on the landscape's volcanic and glacial origins, and an English brochure detailing a short **walk** to several waterfalls and lookouts; there's a *restaurant* across the road. On the climb out of the valley is the **Rocher de l'Aigle** (eagle's rock) cliff-top viewpoint (18km).

In the Allier valley, **Besse-en-Chandesse** (27.3km), with its medieval and Renaissance homes of volcanic stone and rounded shingle roofs, looks like a cluster of singed gingerbread houses. On the edge of the village are the remains of its ramparts and castle. Most of Besse is pedestrianised in summer; the tourist office (☎ 04 73 79 52 84) has a free brochure (in English) detailing a self-guided tour. The **Musée du Ski** (☎ 04 73 79 57 30) displays winter sport artefacts (open daily during school holidays; 15FF admission). Besse's *cafes* and *restaurants* make it a good place for a break; consider stocking up on regional products as Condat's dining options are limited. From the tourist office, leave towards the *Hôtel de Ville* (town hall), skirt it, continue along the Romanesque **Église St André** to a T-junction and turn right. Intersections are then clearly marked to Compains along the D36.

At 30.4km it's a 15-minute walk to the small **Cascade de Vaucoux** waterfall. On the long climb to **Lac de Bourdouze** (33.9km) the perfect cone of Puy de Montchal (1411m) rises to the right. From the Compains turn-off (38.2km), follow the D26 to Espinchal, climbing steadily along another very pretty glacial valley to the Col de Chaumoune (42.5km, 1155m).

The route enters the famous, cheese-producing Cantal department between Espinchal and Lavergne, where the D26 becomes the D305. Along the way farmers sell cheese from the dairy (see 'The Demise of the Buronnier' boxed text overleaf). After the Col de Chaumoune the route is mostly downhill and from Chanterelle (53.3km) it's a glorious descent through woods into the narrow Rhue River valley. From La

Chapelle the road is steep until the T-junction with the busier D678, so slow down towards the bottom. Follow the signs into Condat.

Condat

This small town is nestled in a lush basin, between the Mont-Dore range and the Cézallier Valley. Its slate-roofed houses cluster around one central street.

Information The lightly stocked tourist office (☎ 04 71 78 66 63), is at the entry to the village, down from the post office (closed Sunday afternoon in July and August; only open one day a week and on holidays the rest of the year – telephone for a recorded message detailing its hours).

The post office is on the corner of the D62 and Grand Rue, the main street that weaves through town. Next door is the Crédit Agricole, with an ATM.

Things to See & Do Condat is a good place for an early night. After a walk down the main street and a visit to the stone church, there's not much to do in town. But after the day's constantly rolling hills you're unlikely to be interested in a big night out.

Places to Stay & Eat The municipal *Camping de la Borie Basse* (☎ 04 71 78 52 85), 800m south of the town centre on the D678, has partly shaded, riverside sites for 10.50FF per person and 7.50FF for the site (open May to September).

The *gîte* (☎ 04 71 78 51 31) has basic beds with blankets in a barn-like dorm, but the showers are hot and the communal dining room has a blazing fire and a kitchen; a bed costs 40FF (open April to October). At the crossroads opposite the post office as you enter town, turn left up the hill and the gîte is 300m on the left; check in with Mme Martrout across the road.

At *Central Hôtel* (☎ 04 71 78 53 02, fax 04 71 78 53 02) on the main street, a double room with shower and toilet costs 280FF. The hotel *restaurant* across the road serves very ordinary *menus* from 60FF (lunch only) and 78FF to 200FF.

About 2km along the Day 3 route, on the D679, the *Hostellerie Le Lac des Moines* (☎/fax 04 71 78 65 96) is on the edge of a large lake where guests can pay to fish for trout. A double with bathroom costs 230FF

Day 2: Le Mont-Dore to Condat

MASSIF CENTRAL

N

10km
6mi

1:275,000

To St-Bonnett de Condat

See Day 3 p341

Cue

0km		Le Mont-Dore tourist office
		go SE on Ave de la Libération
0.1		'to Besse'
0.4		over bridge
0.5		unsigned road
		300m steep climb
0.3		'to Besse'
		Puy de Sancy 6km
0.8		(30m) 'to Besse'
0.9		Route de Besse/D36 'to Besse'
7.4		Col de la Croix St-Robert
		5km switchback descent
12.4		D36 'to Besse'
12.9		Moneaux
15.8		Maison de Chaudefour
17.1		D36 'to Besse'
19.5		Courbanges
21.3		300m steep climb
26.3		'to Centre Ville'
27.3		Besse-en-Chandesse
27.3		(30m) unnamed street
27.3		(10m) unnamed street
27.4		(40m) 'to Super Besse'
27.6		Rue des Écoles 'to Compains'
28.4		D36 'to Compains'
30.4		Cascade de Vaucoux walk
31.0		D36 'to Compains'
33.9		Lac de Bourdouze
38.2		D26 'to Col de Chaumoune'
42.5		Col de Chaumoune
46.3		Espinchal
48.0		D26 'to Condat'
53.3		Chanterelle
55.2		D678 'to Condat'
57.6		La Chapelle
		2.4km descent to busy road
60.0		'to Condat Centre'
61.2		Grand Rue (unsigned)
61.3		(100m) Condat tourist office

Clermont-Ferrand

Le Mont-Dore

Condat

Murat

Elevation

2400
2000
1600
1200
800
400
0m

Col de la Croix St-Robert (1451m)
Le Mont-Dore
Moneaux
Courbanges
Besse-en-Chandesse
Col de Chaumoune (1155m)
Chanterelle
Condat

0km 10 20 30 40 50 60

PARC NATUREL RÉGIONAL DES VOLCANS D'AUVERGNE

Valbeleix
La Godivelle
St Nectaire
Puy de Bessolles (1045m)
Murol
Chambon-sur-Lac
Lac Chambon
Rocher de l'Aigle
Le Verdier
Gorges de Courgoul
Cascade de Vaucoux
Anglards Bourdouz
Besse-en-Chandesse
Super Besse
Couze de Pavin
Lac de Montcineyre
Puy de Montchal (1411m)
Lac de Bourdouze
Compains
Col de Chaumoune (1155m)
Lac de Montchal
Rhue
Lac Chauvet
Picherande
Églisenave d'Entraigues
River
Espinchal
Lavergne
Chanterelle
D303
Lac des Moines
Condat
START: DAY 3
St Amandin
La Chapelle

La Tour d'Auvergne
La Bourboule
To Bort-les-Orgues
To Rochefort-Montagne
Dordogne River
Monts Dore
Col de la Croix St-Robert (1451m)
Chaudefour
Vallée
Courbanges
Moneaux
Maison de Chaudefour
Puy de Sancy (1886m)
Side Trip
La Grande Cascade
START: DAY 2
LE MONT-DORE

See Day 1 p335

D996 D203 D227 D5 D36 D619 D74 D30 D978 D149 D619 D2 D678 D679 D47 D3 D88 D645 D203 D922 D47 D45 (open May to September or October). Its *restaurant* opens for meals and serves snacks all day.

On the lower end of the main street is a *Petit Casino* (closed Sunday afternoon, and on Monday outside July and August) and a *patisserie*.

Book the morning before arriving to eat at *Domino (☎ 04 71 78 55 93)*, on the main street, which is reported to serve excellent food in large quantities; a *menu* costs 70FF.

The Demise of the Buronnier

The Auvergne – it's the name of a region and a cheese, the soft and elegant bleu d'auvergne. One of France's premier cattle rearing and cheese making regions due to its topography and climate, the Auvergne produces five of France's 34 Appellation d'Origine Contrôlée (AOC; a quality control system) cheeses. As well as the bleu d'auvergne, there's the slightly sour cantal, st nectaire, fourme d'ambert and salers, plus many other local varieties. Salers is still occasionally produced in a *buron*, a cow herder's hut where cheese is made during the summer.

It's possible to taste and buy all these cheeses along the way, because much of the route follows the Route des Fromages AOC d'Auvergne (map available from tourist offices, or ☎ 04 71 48 66 15). However, while it seems as if *everyone* is making and selling their own cheese, it's feared that traditional, small scale cheese production is a dying art in the area.

For centuries the mountains were dotted with burons, built of irregularly-shaped volcanic stone, with thick white grouting and roofs shingled with tiles of heavy volcanic stone. Come summer (around mid-May), herds of Salers red cows, adapted to the rigours of the region, were led up to the burons. There, several herdsmen, *buronniers*, would live for five months, making cheese of exceptional flavour, thanks to the cows' diets of tender summer grasses.

Today, however, most cheese is made in large dairies and only 10 burons remain active, while the 1000 or more burons used in the 19th century are falling into ruins.

Day 3: Condat to Murat

3½–5½ hours, 52.3km

This is a delightful way to end the tour, with valleys ringing with cow bells and the many ascents rewarded by gorgeous views. Start early if planning the side trip to the summit of Puy Mary.

Climbing out of Condat the route is along a tiny, traffic-free road cyclists dream about. It weaves up through deep woods, crossing moss-covered stone bridges and passing verges full of wildflowers. Stop in Lugarde (8.6km) for a look at its **church** with an exquisite mural on the altar. After leaving town under the multi-arched railway bridge the mountains beckon for the rest of the day.

After 16.1km the grey roofs of Riom-es-Montagnes come into sight across the valley to the west, near the striking ruins of the Château de Apchon on a rocky pinnacle. The narrow road becomes busier as it enters the **Vallée de Cheylade**; this route along the River Rhue is well known for its rich pastures, deciduous forests and pretty villages. From La Bastide (18km) it's easy to make out Puy Mary ahead, in a cluster of peaks known as the Monts du Cantal; an **information sign** 900m out of town labels (in French) the landforms in sight. The picturesque town of Cheylade (20.2km) boasts it has the Cantal's most beautiful **church** – its coffered ceiling is made of 17th-century painted oak tiles.

To split the day, stop in Le Claux (26.6km) – book accommodation through the Cheylade tourist office (☎ 04 71 78 90 67) – after which the valley closes in and the road climbs steadily through woods up the flank of Puy Mary. The view down the Cheylade valley from the **Col de Serre** (33km, 1364m) is a just reward for the long climb. It's well worth making the side trip to the **Pas de Peyrol** (1589m), to walk to the summit of the immense and majestic **Puy Mary** (1787m).

The main route continues on the gentle D680/Route des Crêtes down the gentle Santoire Valley. After Dienne (41.6km), the road climbs to the Col d'Entremont (45.2km, 1210m). The delightful descent into the Alagnon Valley circles the basalt crag known as the Rocher de Bonnevie (1070m), topped by a white statue of the Virgin.

Day 3: Condat to Murat

Cue

start		Condat tourist office
0km	↗	go S/W on Grand Rue (40m) at church
0.1	↗	at fountain
0.2	◇ ↑	D678 'to St Amandin'
0.5	↖	(70m) D678 (unsigned)
0.7	↖ ↑	D679 'to Lugarde'
1.1	◢	2.1km gradual climb
3.2	↖	D16 to Lugarde
4.6	↖	D62 'to Puy Mary'
8.5	✴	Lugarde
15.5	◢	550m steep climb
16.4	↖	D62 to Cheylade
18.0		information board
18.9	✴	Cheylade
20.2	✴	Cheylade
23.5		Curières
26.5		Le Claux
29.0	◢	4km steady climb b
29.7		La Maurinie
33.0	↑	D680 to Murat Col de Serre (1364m) ↻
	● ● ↗	Puy Mary 8.6km ↻
33.5	←	'Route des Crêtes'
35.9		Le Gardilhon
37.4		Lavigerie
41.6		Dienne
41.8	↖	D680 (unsigned)
41.9	↗	D680, e Peuch
44.0		Le Chaumeil
44.2	↗	D3 'to Murat'
45.2		Col d'Entremont
48.2		La Chevade
51.0	◇ ↖	D39 'to Murat Centre'
51.4	↖	Rue de Bonnevie 'to Centre Ville'
51.9	↖	Rue de Bonnevie 'to Centre Ville'
52.0	↖	(50m) Place du Planol
52.0	↖	(60m) Place/Rue de la Boucherie
52.1	↗	Rue des 12 et 24 Juin 1944
52.3	↑	'to Office de Tourisme'
52.3		(20m) Murat tourist office

Elevation

Navigation to the Murat tourist office is a little tricky. At place du Planol, turn right and ride in front of the fountain and the church, turning right again at the edge of the large, red covered market. Follow place de la Boucherie into rue de la Boucherie, turning left at rue des 12 et 24 Juin 1944. The street commemorates the events of those dates; Resistance members killed a Gestapo chief after the German occupation and reprisals followed, with 120 Murat citizens deported and 80 disappearing in the Death Camps.

Side Trip: Puy Mary
8.6km, 1–2 hours
The road towards the Pas de Peyrol heads along a ridge and then towards jagged cliffs rising out of a vast alpine pasture; look for mouflon on the rocks. Just before the Col d'Eylac (1460m), 2.6km after the Col de Serre, is an extremely steep pinch (around 15%), and the final bend before the pass has a 9% slope.

From the pass, the view of the Monts du Cantal is superb. In late summer the 30-minute **walk** to the Puy Mary summit is a pedestrian highway, but the panorama is astounding.

To spend the night in the mountains, stay at the *Gîte d'Étape* at the foot of the last haul up to the Pas de Peyrol. This *buron* (summer hut for shepherds) has been restored to a 15-bed dorm, with a hot shower, cosy kitchen with fireplace, and views to die for (37FF per person). Reserve through the office of Parc des Volcans-Aurillac (☎ 04 71 48 68 68) or try waiting for the warden to turn up at around 5 pm. Food is available at the *summit restaurant* or at small *cafes* around the gîte.

Murat
A fortified town in the 14th century, the town of Murat nestles in a natural amphitheatre at the foot of the Rocher de Bonnevie.

Information The tourist office (☎ 04 71 20 09 47, fax 04 71 20 21 94) is in the Hôtel de Ville at 2 rue Fauberg (closed Sunday, except from June to September).

A couple of banks are near the tourist office and the post office is across the street.

The very basic Peugeot shop, Cycle Escure (☎ 04 71 20 07 83) is at 3 place de la Boucherie (closed Sunday, and on Monday in low season). It hires VTTs (80/400FF a day/week) and the staff can help with maps.

Things to See & Do The **Maison de la Faune** (☎ 04 71 20 00 52), in the turreted stone building up the stairs across from the tourist office, is a better-than-average museum of stuffed and mounted wildlife set in re-creations of their habitat.

Explore **old Murat**, with some very beautiful 14th- to 19th-century houses, remains of the old city gates and ramparts, and the large Gothic church Notre-Dame-des-Oliviers. The tourist office has a free guided walk brochure, with an English translation.

Go **mountain biking**; the tourist office's free brochure *Circuits de Randonnée* details a four-hour tour departing from Albepierre-Bredons, 7km south-west of Murat.

You could easily spend extra time here **walking**; the GR4 and GR400 pass through town and several hiking destinations are only a few hours away.

Places to Stay The *Camping Municipal* (☎ 04 71 20 01 83), south of town on rue de la Stade, charges 9FF for a tent site and 9FF per adult (open June to September).

Auberge de Maitre Paul (☎ 04 71 20 14 66, fax 04 71 20 22 20, 14 place du Planol), in a charming old stone terrace, has bright, large singles/doubles with bathroom for 180/200FF.

The friendly *Hôtel du Stade* (☎ 04 71 20 04 73, 35 rue du Faubourg Notre Dame) has doubles from 120FF; hall showers are free. The two-star *Hôtel Les Messageries* (☎ 04 71 20 04 04, fax 04 71 20 02 81, 18 ave du Docteur Mallet) has rooms for 220/260FF.

Places to Eat Fresh food is sold around the church at the Friday morning *market*. The *Casino* supermarket is on place du Planol (closed Monday outside July and August). The *patisserie* across the road from the tourist office will heat snacks (closed Monday outside summer).

Auberge de Maitre Paul has an excellent reputation and offers pizzas from 37FF, and 65FF, 88FF and 95FF *menus* in its rustic dining room.

The next best choice is the *restaurant* at Hôtel Les Messageries, which has *menus* for 75FF to 180FF.

French Alps & the Jura

> It is by riding a bicycle that you learn the contours of a country best, since you have to sweat up the hills and coast down them. Thus you remember them as they actually are, while in a motor car only a high hill can impress you.
>
> **Ernest Hemingway**

Awesome, inspiring, tranquil, serene – superlatives rarely do justice to the spectacular alpine landscapes of the Alps and the Jura. Soaring, snow-topped peaks tower above verdant, forested valleys, alive with wild flowers. Mountain streams rush down from the massifs, carving out deep gorges on their way.

Known as *les cols du courage*, the mountains present a unique set of cycling challenges. The seemingly endless climbs and dizzy descents demand a reasonably high level of fitness, not to mention bike handling skills, but the sense of achievement on reaching the top more than compensates for the effort. Spending hours climbing a col (a ridge pass) knowing it will take a matter of minutes to descend is a thrill only cyclists can appreciate.

French Alps

HISTORY

The French Alps encompass two historical provinces: Savoie, which covers the northern portion of the region and culminates in Europe's highest peak, Mont Blanc (4807m); and Dauphiné, to the south, peaking in the vertiginous Hautes Alpes (High Alps), which stretch to the Italian border.

Historically important, the high cols of the Alps mark transport routes that for centuries have linked towns, villages, *départements* (departments; administrative divisions) and even countries. Col du Lautaret served as an important trade route between France and Italy before the Tunnel du Fréjus was built, while Col du Galibier marks the former frontier between what was then Savoie, and France.

Tourism in the Alps has largely been built around skiing, with the Vercors boasting several world-renowned cross-country trails. The International Olympic Committee chose

In Brief

Highlights
- conquering the **Alpe d'Huez**
- the **Gorges de la Bourne**
- climbing to the medieval fortified village of **Nozeroy**

Terrain
Extremely mountainous in the Alps, mainly undulating with some moderate hills in the Jura

FFCT Contacts
- Ligue Rhône Alpes, 310 rue de Bramefarine Villard Noir, 38530 Pontcharra
- Ligue Franche-Comté, 27 rue Jean-Jaurès, 39000 Lons le Saunier

Cycling Events
- **La Marmotte** (July) Le Bourg d'Oisans
- **Brevet de Randonneur des Alpes** (usually 17–18 July) Le Bourg d'Oisans
- **La Jurassique** (mid-July) Arbois
- **Le Galibier** (late-July) Valloire

Special Events
- **Transjurienne** cross-country skiing competition (late February) Montbéliard to Hauteville-Lompes
- **Fête du Terroir et de la Tradition** (17–18 July) Valloire
- **Goat Racing Festival** (late August) Méaudre
- **Fête du Biou** wine festival (first Sunday in September) Arbois

Gourmet Specialities
- the Alps' *raclette* (strongly flavoured melting cheese) and *gratin dauphinois* (baked layered potato and cream)
- the Jura's comté cheese, smoked ham, *saucisse de morteau* (smoked sausage)
- *vin jaune* (yellow wine) and *vin de paille* (straw wine) in the Jura; the Alps' Chartreuse liqueur and beers flavoured with grenadine and peach liqueurs

French Alps & the Jura

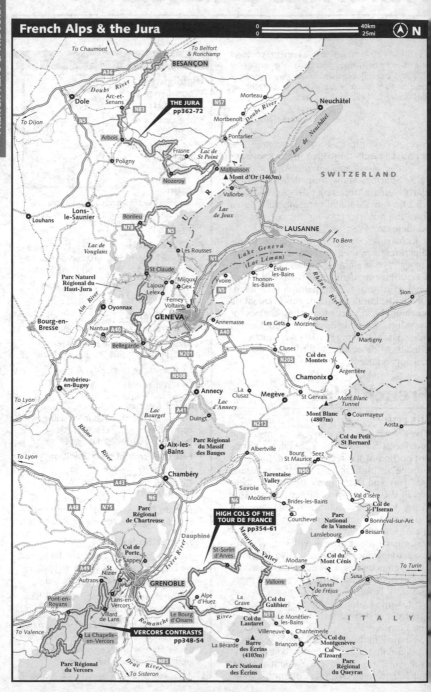

0	40km
0	25mi

N

To Chaumont

To Belfort & Ronchamp

BESANÇON

A36

Doubs River

Arc-et-Senans

Dole

To Dijon

N83

Morteau

Neuchâtel

Mortbenoît

Doubs River

N57

N5

Arbois

Frasne

Pontarlier

Lac de Neuchâtel

THE JURA
pp362-72

Poligny

Lac de St Point

Malbuisson

▲ Mont d'Or (1463m)

SWITZERLAND

Nozeroy

Vallorbe

Louhans

Lons-le-Saunier

Bonlieu

N78

N5

Lac de Joux

LAUSANNE

To Bern

Lac de Vouglans

Les Rousses

N1

Lake Geneva (Lac Léman)

Sion

St Claude

Mijoux

Gex

Yvoire

Evian-les-Bains

Thonon-les-Bains

Rhône River

Parc Naturel Régional du Haut-Jura

Lajoux

Lelex

Ferney Voltaire

N5

Ain River

Oyonnax

GENEVA

Annemasse

Les Gets

Avoriaz

Morzine

Martigny

Bourg-en-Bresse

Nantua

A40

Bellegarde

A40

Cluses

N205

Col des Montets

Argentière

Ambérieu-en-Bugey

N201

N508

Chamonix

To Lyon

Annecy

La Clusaz

Megève

St Gervais

Mont Blanc Tunnel

Lac Bourget

A41

Lac d'Annecy

N212

Mont Blanc (4807m)

Courmayeur

Duingt

Col du Petit St Bernard

Aosta

To Lyon

Aix-les-Bains

Parc Régional du Massif des Bauges

Albertville

Bourg St Maurice

Seez

A43

A48

N75

N6

Chambéry

Rhône River

A49

Parc Régional de Chartreuse

HIGH COLS OF THE TOUR DE FRANCE
pp354-61

Savoie

Moûtiers

N90

Val d'Isère

Col de l'Iseran

Brides-les-Bains

Courchevel

Parc National de la Vanoise

Bonneval-sur-Arc

Bessans

Dauphiné

Lanslebourg

Col de Porte

St-Sorlin d'Arves

Modane

Col du Mont Cénis

To Turin

Le Sappey

Maurienne Valley

St Nizier

Isère River

GRENOBLE

Valloire

Tunnel de Fréjus

Susa

Autrans

VERCORS CONTRASTS
pp348-54

Lans-en-Vercors

Alpe d'Huez

La Grave

Col du Galibier

ITALY

Pont-en-Royans

Villard de Lans

Le Bourg d'Oisans

Romanche River

La Grave

N91

Col du Lautaret

Le Monêtier-les-Bains

Chantemerle

To Valence

La Chapelle-en-Vercors

Villeneuve

Briançon

Col du Montgenèvre

Drac River

La Bérarde

▲ Barre des Écrins (4103m)

Col d'Izoard

Parc Régional du Vercors

N85

To Sisteron

Parc National des Écrins

Parc Régional du Queyras

Grenoble as the site of the Winter Games in 1968 and Albertville in 1992, when irreparable damage was done to the fragile alpine environment.

The history of cycling in the Alps is intimately linked to the Tour de France and the battles of the high cols have added to the majestic image of the race (see the boxed text 'Mountains of Magnitude – the High Cols of the Tour de France' overleaf).

NATURAL HISTORY

Stretching 370km from Lake Geneva (Lac Léman) to Provence in the south, the Alps are some of the most recently formed mountains in France and are still subject to change. Geological processes, such as frost-shattering and erosion, are responsible for the seemingly impenetrable limestone cliffs of the Vercors massif, which spans part of the western ramparts of the Alps.

Patterned by woodlands and pasture, the Vercors are in stark contrast to the rugged austerity of the Hautes Alpes (High Alps). Bounded by a natural mountain frontier, the High Alps lie in a sedimentary zone, which, in the Tertiary Age, formed and folded the mountains into a spectacular series of peaks and pinnacles.

The Alps have an abundance of plants and animals. Beech, oak, sycamore and chestnut trees all grow in the Vercors massif and the lower reaches of the region. Wild orchids, edelweiss and the yellow (poisonous) and purple (edible) gentian grow in the meadows of the Vercors and the protected Parc National des Écrins, while alpine asters and the beautiful purple saxifrage thrive at high altitude.

On the animal front, the Alps are home to marmot, whose characteristic whistle can be heard echoing around the mountains, as well as chamois, ibex, wild boar, roe deer and stag, which inhabit the region's higher reaches.

CLIMATE

Temperatures in the Alps tend to be higher than average in summer (maximum average: 27°C in July) and, not surprisingly, lower than elsewhere in France (maximum average: 3°C January) in winter. The Alps, particularly the Vercors massif, also tend to attract quite a bit of rain from September to November.

Conditions can change dramatically and rapidly in the mountains. Even in summer, it can be very cold on summits – expect a 1°C decrease in temperature for every 100m rise in elevation. The wind chill factor is of particular concern for cyclists – see What to Bring under Planning for each ride. Many of the high cols can be closed (look for col fermé signs on the approach road) as late as May or even June for those above 2500m.

INFORMATION
Maps

Michelin map No 77 Valence, Grenoble, Gap (1:200,000) covers both the Vercors Contrasts and the High Cols of the Tour de France rides.

Information Sources

For tourist information, contact the Comité Départemental du Tourisme de l'Isère (☎ 04 76 42 41 41, fax 04 76 50 28 69) in Grenoble, at 14 rue de la République, or the Comité Départemental du Tourisme des Hautes-Alpes (☎ 04 92 52 56 56, fax 04 92 52 56 57, ✉ www.tourisme.fr/gap/) in Gap, at 12 rue Faure du Serre BP 41.

For regional weather information, call the météo on ☎ 08 36 68 04 04.

GATEWAY CITIES
Grenoble

The region's largest city, Grenoble is spectacularly surrounded by three mountain ranges – the Vercors, the Chatreuse and the Belledonne. Former resident and writer Stenhal claimed 'at the end of every street there is a mountain'. The city has served as the capital of the Alps since the 14th century, when Louis XI designated the town a permanent parliamentary seat. At the converging point of the Drac and Isère rivers, Grenoble has, like elsewhere in the Alps, a sizeable hydroelectric industry.

However, Grenoble is still extraordinarily picturesque. Majestic buildings line the commercial district, while a series of pedestrianised streets gives a North African kasbah feel to the old town. With its mix of North African immigrants, student population and proximity to the mountains, Grenoble is an excellent, if eclectic, place to take a breather.

For a large city (pop 160,000), Grenoble is reasonably cycle friendly, with a series of bikepaths linking most of the city's sights.

Mountains of Magnitude – the High Cols of the Tour de France

In the imagery of the Tour de France, certain mountain passes are held to be *les lieux sacré* (sacred places), giving them an almost mythical status. Without exception, Le Puy du Dôme, the Col du Tourmalet, Mont Ventoux, the Col du Galibier and, of course, the legendary Alpe d'Huez intensify the drama of the race. They push the riders to their extremes and beyond. In short, they are where the heroes of the Tour are created and celebrated.

As a way of calculating the difficulty of a climb, and thus whether the col becomes a sacred place, each mountain pass is given a grade of one to four that indicates its degree of steepness, with one the steepest. The grade is calculated as the degree of rise per kilometre. In the High Alps, several cols are deemed to be *hors categorie* – so steep they are beyond classification.

The first alpine climb introduced to the Tour de France (in 1911) was the Col du Galibier. With an average gradient of 5.5%, this col has come to embody the ultimate toughness and harshness of the Tour de France. Its legend was consolidated in 1930, when a horrific high-speed crash nearly cost the race leader, André Leducq, his life and the yellow jersey.

Leading the *peloton* (literally 'bunch') over the Galibier, Leducq fell heavily at more than 90km/h. Semiconscious, Leducq remounted his bike, only to have a pedal fall off on the plunging descent. Crashing again, Leducq caused chasing rider Marcel Bidot to fall as well. 'This time I am really dead', Leducq told Bidot. 'Not yet...take my bike', the seriously injured Bidot replied. A journalist covering the race was standing roadside, leaning on his own bicycle. With a spanner and a pedal from the journalist's own bike, Bidot selflessly repaired Leducq's bike, who went on to win both the stage and the overall race.

The steep climb of the Col du Galibier is particularly impressive when the race comes in from the north. While the Galibier, the Lautaret and the Télégraphe are climbed regularly by the Tour, others such as the Col du Glandon or the Col d'Izoard (2361m) are less frequent inclusions. They are no less difficult; it is only their awkward geographic position that prevents them from becoming 'sacred places'. The Col du Glandon, for example, is a whopping 22km climb up from the Romanche Valley. Divided into three stages, with an overall height gain of 1200m and an average gradient of 5.5%, the degree of rise in the early first stage is a leg-shattering 10%.

Of course, the mountains mean nothing without the men who climb them. The lone *echapée* (break-away rider), dangling off the front of the peloton, is always an inspiring figure. Some of the greatest climbers in the history of the Tour include the Belgian Lucien Van Impe, who won the prestigious 'King of the Mountains' jersey no less than 10 times (and the race itself in 1976); the 'Angel of the Mountains', Luxembourg rider Charly Gaul (winner in 1958); the Italian *campionissimo*, Fausto Coppi (winner in 1949 and 1952); the 'Eagle of Toledo', Spaniard Frederico Bahamontès (who claimed victory in the Grand Prix de la Montagne a staggering six times, as well as the Tour de France in 1959); and, most recently, El Pirato, the Italian rider Marco Pantani, 1998 Tour winner.

While these 'goats' are dancing off the front of the peloton, the vast majority of riders are relegated to 'the bus'; the group of riders who work collectively to ensure they complete the mountain stages within the time limit set for each day's racing.

Wherever you ride in the Alps, you will find reminders of the great climbers in the Tour. Atop the Col d'Izoard, south of Briançon, is a statue commemorating the achievements of Fausto Coppi and Louisen Bobet, while a large marble monument near the summit of the Col du Galibier celebrates the achievements of Henri Desgranges, the man who first put the mountains into the Tour.

The toughest of the hors categorie climbs (a biased listing) are:

- **Col de la Croix de Fer** (2061m) – a 21km ascent at an average gradient of 6%
- **Col du Galibier** (2645m) – a 16km ascent (from the north) at an average gradient of 5.5%
- **Alpe d'Huez** (1860m) – a 13.8km ascent at an average gradient of 8.3%

Information The tourist office (☎ 04 76 42 41 41, fax 04 76 51 28 69) is on rue de la République and offers a free *Plan des Pistes Cyclables* outlining the city's bikepaths. From June to mid-September opening hours also include Sunday from 10 am to noon.

The Banque de France is on the corner of blvd Édouard Rey and ave Félix Viallet. ATMs abound along rue Félix Poulat. The main post office is somewhat out of the way, at 7 blvd Maréchal Lyautey.

Grenoble has several central bike shops. Tout Pour les Deux Roues (☎ 04 76 46 46 56), cours de la Libération, or Mountain Bike Grenoble (☎ 04 76 45 58 76), 6 quai de France, offer rentals (60/100FF for half-/one-day hire and 170FF for two-day rentals), plus sales and service. There are no bike shops on the Vercors Contrasts ride.

Le New Age Cyber Café (☎ 04 76 51 94 43) is opposite the Musée de Grenoble at 1 rue Frédéric Taulier.

The Club Alpin Français (CAF, ☎ 04 76 42 49 92), 1 rue Hauquelin, has information on VTT (mountain biking) trips.

Things to See & Do The old town is a treasure trove of **old book and clothing shops,** and is worth a day's wandering. Grenoble's bustling **music scene** is detailed in the *Guide DAHU,* available from the tourist office and newsagents. Quai St Laurent has several jazz and folk cafes.

No visitor to Grenoble can avoid taking the bubble-like **télépherique** from quai Stéphane Jay, between the Marius Gontard and St Laurent bridges, to the **Fort de la Bastille.** Built in the 16th century and strengthened in the 19th century, it protected Grenoble from enemy advances. Several **walking** trails lead from the disused chair lift (300m beyond the arch leading to the public toilets).

The **Musée de Grenoble** (☎ 04 76 63 44 44), 5 place de la Lavlette, has a world-renowned collection of paintings and sculptures from all historical periods. The **Musée Dauphinois** (☎ 04 76 85 19 01), 30 rue Maurice Gignoux, occupies a 17th-century former convent at the base of the hill leading to the Fort de la Bastille. It is best reached by the Pont St Laurent footbridge and has an insightful, informative display of mountain folklore and tradition.

Places to Stay & Eat Open all year, *Camping Les Trois Pucelles (☎ 04 76 96 45 73, 58 rue des Allobroges)* is one block west of the Drac River in the western suburb of Seyssins (32FF per person).

A bit of a hike from town, the Internet-equipped *Auberge de Jeunesse (☎ 04 76 09 33 52, fax 04 76 09 38 09, e grenoble.echi rolles@wanadoo.fr, 10 ave du Gresuvidian)* is 5km south of the train station along cours Jean Jaures; turn right when you see the Casino supermarket. It charges 70FF per person, including breakfast.

Hotels abound in Grenoble, but they can be busy (or closed) in August. In town, try the *Hôtel Beau Soleil (☎ 04 76 46 29 40, 9 rue des Bons Enfants),* off cours Berriat. Doubles with shower start at 180FF. *Hotel Lakanal (☎ 04 76 46 03 42, 26 rue des Bergers),* near place Condorcet, has singles/doubles with toilet and shower at 140/180FF.

A *food market* each Saturday morning is held in Les Halles St Claire, opposite the tourist office. The *Prisunic* supermarket *(cnr rue de la République & rue Lafayette)* has a basement food hall (closed Sunday).

Several excellent *North African restaurants* are in the old part of town along rue Chenoise and rue Renauldron. For more traditional *French fare,* try place Grenette. *Pizzerias* abound along quai Perriére. *Restaurant des Montagnes (☎ 04 76 15 20 72, 5 rue Brocherie)* serves enormous, gooey helpings of fondue and *raclette* (strongly flavoured melting cheese) from 45FF per person.

Getting There & Away Grenoble is well served by several airports and is a major train destination.

Air Domestic flights from Paris (around 400FF) land at Grenoble–St Geoirs airport (☎ 04 76 65 48 48), 45km north of Grenoble, from where a bus to Grenoble costs 70/100FF single/return (45 minutes). International flights operate to and from Lyon-Satolas airport (☎ 04 72 22 72 21), 95km from Grenoble. From Lyon-Satolas, the bus to Grenoble costs 135/200FF (65 minutes). Both bus services arrive and pick up in Grenoble at the *gare routière* (bus station), next to the train station. Boxed bikes can be taken on airport buses.

Train Grenoble's train station is on rue Émile Gueymard, 500m west of the town centre.

Destinations served include Bellegarde (90FF, two hours), Lyon (95FF, 1½ hours) and Avignon (220FF, 3½ hours) and Manosque (140FF, 3½ hours, three a day). Travelling from Paris' Gare de Lyon involves several changes (360FF). At least one bike-friendly train runs each day, although, depending on the destination, it might require several changes. Check with the SNCF for bike-friendly timetables.

International trains run to and from Geneva (120FF, two hours), Turin (215FF) and Milan (249FF). TGV conditions apply, except for the service to Geneva, which carries bikes without bike bags at least twice a day. The service to Milan requires a change at Chambery.

Bus From Britain, the European Bike Express service (see Bus under Continental Europe in the Getting There & Away chapter) charges UK£149 (return) to take a passenger and bike to Grenoble.

Vercors Contrasts

Duration	3 days
Distance	202km
Difficulty	hard
Start/End	Grenoble

Highlighting the dramatic contrasts of landscape in the mountains, this ride through the Vercors massif is a great introduction to the Alps. Craggy cliffs, desolate vistas, gruelling climbs, plunging gorges and long, flat stretches of meadowland are all found in this picturesque region.

From Grenoble, the route leads through a series of gorges and onto a long, flat plateau. It drops into the plunging Gorges de la Bourne, where meadow is interspersed with rural hamlets. From here, the going gets tough, as the route climbs four big cols, before sweeping past the dramatic Combe Laval to Pont-en-Royans, whose houses suspend precariously above the Bourne. The ride then swings past tranquil villages before descending once more into Grenoble.

The first VTT World Championships were held in the Vercors in 1987. See Maps & Books under Planning.

HISTORY

The natural fortress of the Vercors massif was put to use most notably in WWII by the Resistance movement. In one bloody battle on 23 July 1944, 700 soldiers and civilians were killed and several villages razed as the German SS moved through the steep, thickly wooded slopes of the Vercors. See the Day 2 ride description for details of two monuments to those who died.

NATURAL HISTORY

The Vercors is composed of two distinct areas. The area around the more accessible plateau *(lans)* near Villard de Lans is lush and cross-cut by a series of infant streams. Farther south, towards the Col de la Bataille, the terrain becomes much wilder (and steeper!). Since water tends to sink through the limestone rock of the Vercors, this part of the massif is largely devoid of vegetation.

PLANNING
When to Ride

The Col de la Bataille is officially closed from mid-November to mid-May. The best time to ride is spring (late May, June or early July). Outside of Grenoble, there are no bike shops on the ride.

Books

For information on VTT trails in the Vercors, the booklet *Drôme des Collines/Royans-Vercors* lists a series of 20 possible routes. It is available from tourist offices or from the Comité Départemental du Tourisme (☎ 04 75 82 19 26, fax 04 75 56 01 65). Pick up a free route description of the 150km waymarked La Grande Traversée du Vercors en VTT (The Great Cross Vercors Mountain Bike Ride) from tourist offices in Pont-en-Royans or La Chapelle-en-Vercors.

What to Bring

Long-fingered, thick gloves and a windproof jacket are essential to guard against wind chill on the descents. Bring a warm jacket for the caves on Days 2 and 3.

GETTING TO/FROM THE RIDE

Grenoble is also the start of the High Cols of the Tour de France ride detailed later in this chapter. Trains connect Grenoble with Bellegarde, the end of The Jura ride, also in this chapter.

It's about 170km to Forcalquier, the start of the challenging six-day ride The Luberon & Mont Ventoux; the closest rail connection to Forcalquier is Manosque. Trains also connect with Avignon for the Majesty of the Romans and The Luberon & Mont Ventoux rides (see the Provence & the Côte d'Azur chapter for all these rides).

See the Gateway Cities section (pp347–8) for information on getting to/from Grenoble.

THE RIDE
Day 1: Grenoble to La Chapelle-en-Vercors
5½ hours, 56.5km

The maze of one-way or pedestrianised streets makes leaving Grenoble a bit fiddly.

Head west from the tourist office, in the general direction of the train station towards the Vercors mountain range, until the satellite suburb of Fontaine. The route briefly hits the busy N532 through Sassenage (5km), famous for its stately home, the Château de Bérenge (☎ 04 76 27 54 44), and its *cuves* (subterranean rock pools). Reputed to be the home of Mélusine, a mermaid murdered by her husband, the cuves are believed to be the tears she cried when her life was cut short.

A long, steep but steady climb, with great views, heads out of the Vallée Grésuvidian, along the Gorges d'Engins and du Furon, skirting the tiny hamlet of Engins (19km) where the road flattens across the expansive central lans.

Continue until Villard de Lans (32km), a soothing, sleepy place to stop for a mid-ride refresher. From here, the D531 begins a welcome descent into the **Gorges de la Bourne**, first following the banks of the Bourne along the valley and through the hamlet of Les Jarrands before dropping steeply into the gorge proper.

At this point, spare a thought for the mules who, before the road was completed in 1872, would struggle through the gorge, heavily loaded with charcoal, the region's economic staple for many years.

Continue through the gorge over the **Pont de Valcherrière** (36.5km). With the river several hundred metres below, it is easy to see why the bridge is a popular spot with abseilers and speleologists.

At the Pont de la Goule Noire, continue straight ahead along the D103. An easy climb leads out of the gorge and onto a verdant, flower-lined lans leading into the hamlet of St Julien-en-Vercors (44.3km). From here, a long descent sweeps through the hamlets of St Martin-en-Vercors and Les Barraques-en-Vercors. The final 6km climbs steadily to reach La Chapelle-en-Vercors.

La Grande Moucherotte and La Peyrouse are the incredible limestone massifs that loom to the left.

La Chapelle-en-Vercors
La Chapelle-en-Vercors has been entirely rebuilt since July 1944, when the village was destroyed by German advances. Nowadays it is a popular winter base for cross-country skiing expeditions. It is also a caver's paradise, with many **natural wells** *(scialets)* in the surrounding countryside. A festival of caving films is held each year at the end of August.

The main street, ave Grands Goulets, houses the tourist office (☎ 04 75 48 22 54), the bank (last one until Grenoble), the pharmacy, a *boulangerie* (bakery), the post office and several restaurants and hotels.

Places to Stay & Eat At *Camping Les Bruyéres (☎ 04 75 48 21 46, fax 04 75 48 10 44)* it costs 34FF for a site for one or two adults. To get to the camping ground, follow the signs from the main road into town. The *Hôtel des Sports (☎ 04 75 48 20 39, ave Grands Goulets)* has doubles with shower from 200FF, while the two-star *Hôtel Bellier (☎ 04 75 48 22 36, ave Grands Goulets)* has rooms that vary in price according to the season. In July and August, expect to pay 370FF to 420FF for a double with shower and toilet, with discounts of up to 20% in other months.

A *Proximarché* supermarket is 50m from the camping ground. On ave Grands Goulets, *Le Thé à la Menthe* serves big (take-away) serves of couscous and kebabs; check out *La Toscana* for pizzas or *Bar du Nord* for steak and chips.

Day 2: La Chapelle-en-Vercors to Pont-en-Royans
4½–6 hours, 76.5km
Bring your climber's legs to bag the four big cols on this route.

From the tourist office, head south along the D178 towards Vassieux-en-Vercors. The

Day 1: Grenoble to La Chapelle-en-Vercors

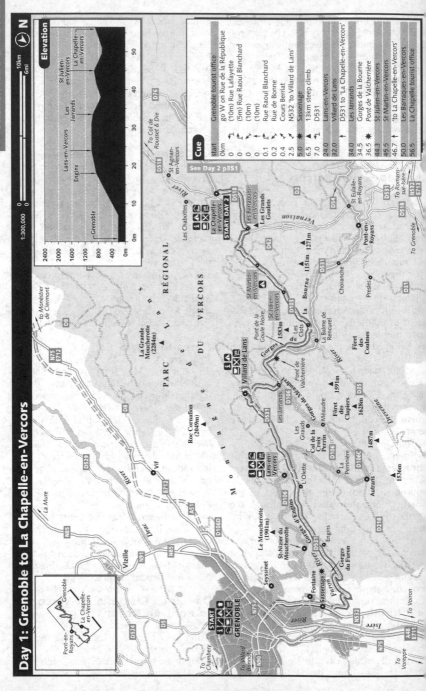

Elevation

Cue		
start		Grenoble tourist office
0km		go W on Rue de la République
0		(10m) Rue Lafayette
0		(5m) Rue Raoul Blanchard
0.1		(10m)
0.1		Rue Raoul Blanchard
0.2		Rue de Bonne
0.4		Cours Berriat
2.5		N532 'to Villard de Lans'
5.0	✳	Sassenage
6.5		13km steep climb
7.0		D531
24.0		Lans-en-Vercors
32.0		Villard de Lans
		D531 to 'La Chapelle-en-Vercors'
34.0		Les Jarrands
34.5		Gorges de la Bourne
36.5	✳	*Pont de Valcherrière*
44.3		St Julien-en-Vercors
45.5		St Martin-en-Vercors
46.7		'to La Chapelle-en-Vercors'
50.0		Les Barraques-en-Vercors
56.5		La Chapelle tourist office

See Day 2 p351

Day 2: La Chapelle-en-Vercors to Pont-en-Royans

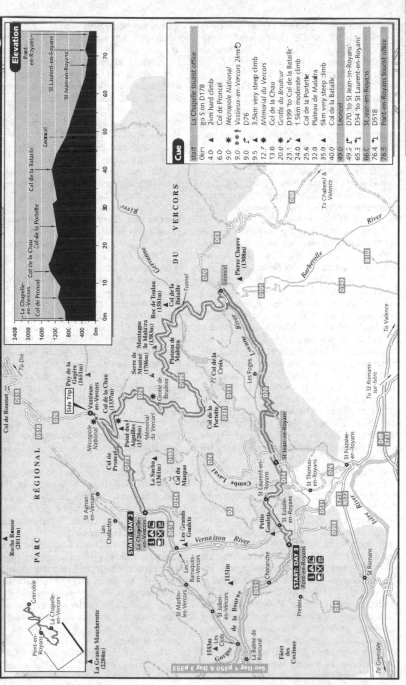

Cue		
start		La Chapelle tourist office
0km		go S on D178
4.0	▲	2km hard climb
6.0	▲	Col de Proncel
9.0	✳	Nécropole National
9.0	↱	Vassieux-en-Vercors 2km ⟳
9.0	▲	D76
9.5	▲	3.5km very steep climb
12.7	✳	Mémorial du Vercors
13.0	▲	Col de la Chau
20.0	✳	Grotte du Brudcur
23.1	↱	D199 'to Col de la Bataille'
24.0	▲	1.5km moderate climb
25.6	▲	Col de la Portette
32.0		Plateau de Malatra
35.0	▲	5km very steep climb
40.0	▲	Col de la Bataille
49.0		Léoncel
49.2	↱	D70 'to St Jean-en-Royans'
65.3	↱	D54 'to St Laurent-en-Royans'
66.0		St-Jear-en-Royans
74.4	↱	D518
76.5		Pont-en-Royans tourist office

Elevation

road dips slightly, before climbing slowly but steadily to the **Col de Proncel** (6km). The road along the Plateau de Vassieux is bordered to the east by a rocky ridge rising from thick forest and to the west by low hills covered with scrubby vegetation; it also passes some interesting rock formations.

From here, the road leads to one of the more tragic parts of the Vercors. The area around Vassieux-en-Vercors saw several hundred men, women and children slaughtered by the SS; the **Nécropole National** (9km) commemorates those who died.

It is worth the brief side trip to the village of Vassieux-en-Vercors, where the remains of several crashed German gliders remind of the events of July 1944.

A tough climb from the nécropole passes the **Mémorial du Vercors**, which commemorates the actions of the Resistance Movement, just before the **Col de la Chau**.

The road continues to climb through the Fôret de Lente before eventually flattening out several kilometres later. From here, a very long descent leads to the **Grotte du Brudour**, a huge underground cavern. Shortly after, the valley sweeps around the contours of a large natural amphitheatre which overlooks the Val de Bouvante.

A steady climb through beech and oak forest passes over the **Col de la Portette** (25.6km). The views are truly amazing.

The road begins to descend into the valley, then climbs to reach the **Plateau de Malatra**, where an extensive (and expensive) reforestation program is replacing the 150,000 trees felled in a violent storm nearly a decade ago.

From the plateau, the road climbs past the impressive **Roc de Toualu** to reach the **Col de la Bataille** (40km) – it is all downhill from here.

Continue through the tunnel and onto the long, long descent into Léoncel. A narrow, tree-lined gorge opens onto a relatively untouched valley before narrowing into another steep gorge. Offering great views across to the Combe Laval, the road reaches civilisation at St Jean-en-Royans, where the 18th-century tradition of **woodworking** continues to this day. Head through town, following the signs for Pont-en-Royans. Once in town, turn left and head along the D518 (the main street) for 100m to reach the tourist office.

Pont-en-Royans

Occupying a gorgeous setting at the mout of the Gorges de la Bourne, Pont-en-Royan is a convenient place to rest weary legs. Hal timbered houses hang high over the Bourne whose inviting pools make it a popular plac with the locals for a **swim** in summer.

The friendly tourist office (% 04 76 36 0 10, fax 04 76 36 09 24), Grand Rue, i closed Sunday. The staff have great loca knowledge and can suggest **hiking** and/o **VTT trips** in the Vercors massif.

The post office, the pharmacy, th boulangerie and several hotels and restaur ants are also in Grand Rue.

Places to Stay & Eat The municipa *camping ground* (☎ 04 76 36 06 30, fax 0 76 36 10 77) occupies a pretty location o the banks of the Bourne. Open from mic April through September, it charges 50FF fc a site for one or two adults. *Hôtel du Royan* (☎ 04 76 36 01 03, fax 04 76 36 13 46, Gran Rue)* has doubles with shower from 160FI *Hôtel Beau Rivage* (☎ 04 76 36 00 63, fa 04 76 36 00 11, Grand Rue)* has doubles wit shower from 190FF to 260FF. Both hotel also have fairly flash restaurants, servin *menus* (set meals) from 80FF to 200FF.

Both in Grand Rue are the *Petit Casin* supermarket and *La Galere Pizzeria*, whic serves crepes and grills as well as pizza from 40FF.

Day 3: Pont-en-Royans to Grenoble
4–6 hours, 69km

The route climbs back out of the Gorges d la Bourne via the picturesque **Site Natur des Coulmes**, where the Bourne rushe through the bottom of the gorge, while series of cirques carved by glacial move ments tower high above.

The ride is flat until Choranche (4.5km Here, the road begins its long climb throug the gorge back to the central plateau. Th turn-off to the incredible **Grotte d Choranche** is shortly after, where it is steep 3km climb to the spectacular under ground caves, famous for their needle-lik stalactites. It is freezing inside, so brin warm clothing.

The road through the gorge continue climbing to the hamlet of La Balme de Ren curel (12.6km), where the road flatten

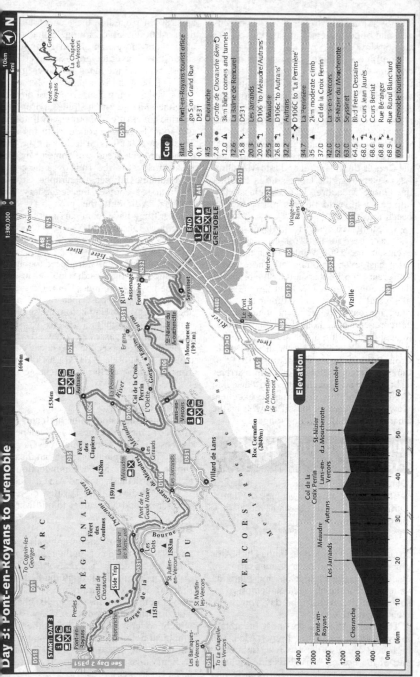

Day 3: Pont-en-Royans to Grenoble

1:300,000

N

10km
6mi

La Chapelle-en-Vercors
Grenoble
Pont-en-Royans

Cue

start		Pont-en-Royans tourist office
0km	↑	go S on Grand Rue
0.1	↰	D531
4.5		Choranche
7.8	●●	Grotte de Choranche 6km ⟳
12.0	⚠	3km blind corners and tunnels
12.6		La Balme de Remuzel
15.8	↰	D531
20.3		Les Jarrands
20.5	↑	D106 to Méaudre/Autrans'
25.5		Méaudre
26.8	↰	D106c to Autrans'
32.2		Autrans
	◆	D106C to 'La Perinière'
34.7		La Perinière
35	◣	2km moderate climb
37.0		Col de la Croix Perrin
42.0		La 's-en-Vercors
52.0		St-Nizier du Moucherotte
63.0		Seyssinet
64.5	↑↰↑	Blvd Frères Dessaires
68.0	↰↑↰	Ccurs Jean Jaurès
68.6	↱	Ccurs Berriat
68.8	↰ ↑	Rue Béranger
68.9	↱↰	Rue Raoul Blanchard
69.0		Grenoble tourist office

Elevation

St-Nizier du Moucherotte

Col de la Croix Perrin

Grenoble

Lans-en-Vercors

Méaudre   Autrans

Les Jarrands

Pont-en-Royans

Choranche

2400
2000
1600
1200
800
400
0m

0km   10   20   30   40   50   60

slightly. Along this stretch is a series of tunnels and blind corners. Cars are unlikely to stop or slow down.

Continue climbing through the gorge, crossing the Pont de la Goule Noire, where the route veers left on the D531 to rejoin the road used to descend into the gorge on Day 1. The remarkable Goule Noire is one of the points in the gorge where its underground streams surge to the surface.

Once back on the plateau at Les Jarrands, a delightful stretch of road passes through the **Gorges de Méaudret** and into Méaudre. Less severe than the Gorges de la Bourne, the Gorge Méaudret is more classically 'alpine', with wild flowers plus pine and beech forest.

A flat stretch leads to pretty **Autrans**. Used as a base for the cross-country skiing events in the 1968 Winter Olympics, the town has several monuments and statues. The great exposed scars left by the pistes on the surrounding hillsides, and the presence of several ski luges and summer toboggan runs, are reasons to either applaud shrewd entrepreneurs or bemoan the shameless ecological degradation of the area.

The ride then climbs over the **Col de la Croix Perrin** to reach the central village of Lans-en-Vercors before a final climb arrives at St-Nizier du Moucherotte and back into Grenoble. The steep descent gives excellent views of the Vercors massif as well as the Chartreuse and Belledonne ranges.

High Cols of the Tour de France

Duration	4 days
Distance	245km
Difficulty	hard–very hard
Start/End	Grenoble

It has been said that riding in the High Alps represents a magnificent dramatisation of cycling life. The high peaks and plunging valleys mirror the physical and emotion responses of the cyclist; one day you're up, the next you're down.

The High Alps are the most breathtakingly beautiful part of the French Alps. The high cols are also the most leg-shattering part of the French Alps. This ride includes five major alpine cols, each between 1500m and 2800m. Together, these cols total more than 14,000m of climbing. Some of the climbs are more than 15km from foot to summit, with average grades of over 7.5%. Those whose bike does not have granny gear will be wishing it had.

As well as being a superb test of physical toughness in a stunning alpine environment, the ride covers the five principal climbs that the Tour de France conquers in the Alps. This allows cyclists to follow in the footsteps – or cycle tread – of some of the very greatest riders in the Tour over the cols of the Lautaret, Galibier, Télégraphe, Croix de Fer and, of course, the legendary Alpe d'Huez. Although the pros may do it quicker, they have team cars and masseurs to help ease *their* pain!

HISTORY

The first alpine climb introduced to the Tour de France was the Col du Galibier in 1911, included by Tour founder Henri Desgrange. His decision was described as an 'act of adoration'. About 1km before the summit is a monument commemorating his work. The other mountain passes each have their own colourful history (see the boxed text 'Mountains of Magnitude – the High Cols of the Tour de France' earlier in this chapter).

PLANNING
When to Ride

The annual inclusion of the high cols in the Tour de France route means July can be both the best and the worst time to cycle in the Alps. The atmosphere is great, but the roads can be very busy, and accommodation hard to find, particularly around Alpe d'Huez.

The Col du Galibier is often closed by snow from mid-November to mid-May.

Books

A detailed set of topographical cycling guides to the main cols in the region, called *Atlas des Cols des Alpes du Nord* and *Alpes du Sud*, is available through the Fédération Française de Cyclotourisme (FFCT; see Books in the Facts for the Cyclist chapter). The informative book *Cols de France*, which covers elevation and other topographical details of *all* of the country's big climbs, can be obtained by emailing
e henry.dusseau@wanadoo.fr with a request (in French).

What to Bring

Long-fingered, thick gloves and a wind-proof jacket are essential to guard against wind chill on the long descents.

Good-quality lights are also recommended for the many tunnels. While most are short enough for the far end to be visible, the road through the Upper Romanche Valley is known as *le couloir de la peur* (the corridor of fear), on account of its many blind corners and potholed tunnels.

Information Sources

Information on access to the high passes can be obtained in Grenoble from Info-Montagne (☎ 04 76 42 45 90, fax 04 76 15 00 91), upstairs in the tourist office, or from the weather report posted out the front of the building.

For information on the major *cyclo-sportives/randonnées* (organised mass rides) in the Alps contact Top Club (☎ 04 76 00 01 54, fax 04 76 03 16 67, 🖳 www.sportcommunication.com/sportcom.htm).

Cyclotouristes Grenoblois (☎ 04 76 52 22 90, fax 06 80 67 05 80) organises the super-tough Brevet de Randonneur des Alpes.

Meet fellow 'col baggers' by joining the prestigious 100 Cols Club. Write to the *Col des Cent Cols*, Chainaz les Frases, Alby-sur-Chéran, F-74540 France.

GETTING TO/FROM THE RIDE

Grenoble is also the start of the Vercors Contrasts ride detailed later in this chapter. It's about 170km to Forcalquier, the start of the challenging six-day ride The Luberon & Mont Ventoux; the closest rail connection to Forcalquier is Manosque. Trains also connect with Avignon for the Majesty of the Romans and The Luberon & Mont Ventoux rides (see the Provence & the Côte d'Azur chapter for all these rides).

See the Gateway Cities section (pp347–8) for information on getting to/from Grenoble.

THE RIDE

Grenoble

See the Gateway Cities section (pp345–8) for information about accommodation and other services in Grenoble. The *Auberge de Jeun-esse* (see Places to Stay under Grenoble) is a convenient place to stay for the start and finish of this ride.

Day 1: Grenoble to Le Bourg d'Oisans

3½–4½ hours, 50.5km

Head out of Grenoble through the Romanche Valley, go east along the very busy N85, which becomes the N91. The only approach route to Alpe d'Huez from Grenoble, it can be a bit hairy in places. Around Vizille (15km) the bikepath disappears among the cars and motorbikes. This stretch of the ride is not exactly pleasant, although a visit to the Château de Vizille makes an interesting side trip. The views *do* get better closer to Le Bourg d'Oisans.

Built between 1602 and 1622 by Lesdiguières (France's last High Constable) as his country residence, the **Château de Vizille** earned notoriety as the meeting place for the Dauphiné Estates (the provincial parliament) in 1788. The meeting led to a resolution which protested the suppression of the National Parliament, from which developed a general cry of 'No Taxation without Representation'. This began a national movement which culminated in the French Revolution of 1789. Vizille prides itself on being 'the Cradle of the Revolution', and the chateau now houses a **Musée National de la Révolution**. The stunning grounds are a nice place for a picnic.

On the outskirts of Vizille, the road begins to climb steadily through the Lower Romanche Valley to cross the **Pont de la Véna** (42.5km), where there is a monument to the Resistance fighters of the Oisans region. Along this stretch, layers of sedimentary rock that were compressed and folded tens of thousands of years ago are particularly noticeable.

The road flattens slightly on the run into Le Bourg d'Oisans, the starting point of the side trip up Alpe d'Huez (see the boxed text 'Alpe d'Huez' overleaf). It is advisable to set up camp before contemplating the cruel climb. The 1998 Tour winner Marco Pantani climbed it in 32 minutes.

Le Bourg d'Oisans

Although one of the meccas of the Tour de France, this really is just a convenient place to stop over. In summer, and especially during Tour time, book a hotel in advance.

Information The tourist office (☎ 04 76 80 03 25), on rue Docteur Faure on the

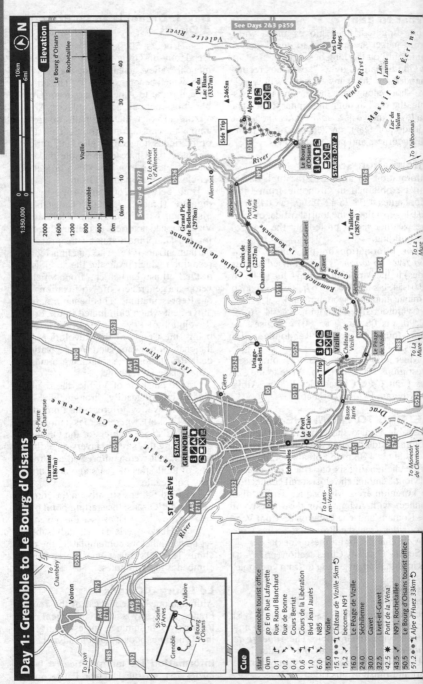

Day 1: Grenoble to Le Bourg d'Oisans

Elevation

Cue		
start		Grenoble tourist office
0km	↰	go E on Rue Lafayette
0.1	↱	Rue Raoul Blanchard
0.2	↰	Rue de Bonne
0.4	↰	Cours Berriat
0.6	↱	Cours de la Libération
1.0	↱	Blvd Jean Jaurès
6.0		N85
15.0		Vizille
15.1 ●●↰		Château de Vizille 5km ↺
15.2 ↗		becomes N91
16.0		Le Péage de Vizille
24.0		Séchilienne
30.0		Gavet
32.5		Livet-et-Gavet
42.5 ✴		Pont de la Véna
43.5 ↗		N91, Rochetaillée
50.5		Le Bourg d'Oisans tourist office
51.2 ●●↰		Alpe d'Huez 33km ↺

anks of the Romanche, is open daily dur-
ng summer. The Banque Rhône Alpes is
ext door to the post office, on ave de la
iare. An impressive array of state-of-the-
rt cycling exotica can be found at Cycles
t Sport, ave Général de Gaulle. Most other
icilities, including a pharmacy, can also be
ound on the pedestrianised ave Général de
aulle.

hings to See & Do During Tour time,
nd a bar with a television and share the

excitement of the race with the many other
cyclists who have made the pilgrimage.

Alpe d'Huez offers year-round **skiing**.
From the summit, chairlifts go to Pic du
Lac Blanc (3327m), which is also the starting point for several high-altitude **hikes**. In
the village of Huez, 4km from the summit,
La Maison de Patrimonie has a permanent
exhibition of traditional life in the Oisans

Places to Stay & Eat Le Bourg d'Oisans
has a staggering six camping grounds. *Le*

Alpe d'Huez

If mountains could talk, few would have better stories to tell than Alpe d'Huez, towering
above the Romanche Valley. The 13.8km lung-searing climb to the summit (1860m) has an
average grade of 8.5% and is ranked *hors catégorie* (above categorisation, ie, very steep) in
the Tour de France. The climb includes 21 numbered hairpin bends. The 'blue ribbon' stage
of the Tour – the stage finishing at the Alpe – has seen races won and lost, heroes made and
reputations shattered.

The Alpe's legend was born in the 1952 Tour (the first year of live television broadcasts),
when Italian rider Fausto Coppi won the stage there. Going on to take the overall victory by
nearly 27 minutes, the highest post-war winning margin, Coppi proclaimed 'it is by winning
at Alpe d'Huez that a rider knows he has become the *campionissimo* of the world'.

Despite this testimonial, the Alpe was dropped from the Tour's itinerary until 1976, when
Belgian rider Lucién van Impe claimed victory. Since then, it has been included in all but the
1980, 1985 and 1993 Tours. In 1979, to make up for its omission the following year, it was
climbed twice in consecutive days!

The day the Tour visits Alpe d'Huez is a grand celebration of people, colour and sounds.
Nearly 500,000 fans line the route. In most places, the crowd is within striking distance of the
riders, egging them on and sneaking in an unsolicited helping push – or sometimes hinder-
ing them. In 1986, an overzealous fan lobbed a handful of black pepper into the face of a
Belgian rider, while in 1999, the eventual stage winner, Guiseppi Guerini, had a few nervous
moments when he was knocked from his bike by a camera-wielding fan in the final metres.

Much of the magic of Alpe d'Huez lies in the fact aspiring amateurs can have a crack at the
climb themselves. On the day of the Tour, a snake of chrome and colour inches its way to the
summit as hundreds of riders painstakingly make their way to the top. Enthusiastic French spectators are usually on hand to dole out free samples of *pastis* (a liqueur) to kick riders along.

For those who require the moral support of several hundred fellow cyclists, a number of
randonnées, most notably La Marmotte, include the climb to Alpe d'Huez on their route (see
the Randonnées chapter).

A Dutch Mountain?

For a country lacking in mountains, the Netherlands has had remarkable success conquering
Alpe d'Huez, with riders such as Zoetemelk, Winnen, Breu, Rooks and Theunisse dominating
throughout the 1980s. Referred to as 'the southernmost tip in The Netherlands' and 'Holland's only mountain', Alpe d'Huez draws thousands of Dutch fans to the Tour.

On the day 'The Rembrandts', as the Dutch fans are fondly called, hang their national flag
from the trees and paint it on the road's surface, while everywhere a sea of faces are painted
bright orange. Rousing chants echo up the mountain and hulking men don plaits, clogs and
traditional Dutch dress as they beat drums and blow horns. It is a bizarre celebration of mountain climbing from this famous lowland.

Colporteur (☎ 04 76 79 11 44), off the N91, is the most central and charges 65FF for a site for one or two adults (open June through September). If the main camping ground is full during Tour time, pitch a tent on the soccer oval behind *Camping La Piscine* (☎ 04 76 80 02 41, fax 04 76 11 01 26) for 40FF per adult (open June through September). It's on the road to Alpe d'Huez.

The *Maison des Jeunes le Paradis* (☎ 04 76 80 01 76, 50 rue Thiers) charges 65FF for a bed in a 12-person dorm. The *Hôtel Beau Rivage* (☎ 04 76 80 03 19, fax 04 76 80 00 77, rue des Marquis de l'Oisans), behind the tourist office, has doubles from 190FF (260FF with TV, shower and toilet).

Saturday morning is *market* day, on ave Général de Gaulle. A *Petit Casino* is on ave Général de Gaulle and a big *Casino* is on the N91 towards the camping ground. *La Romanche* (☎ 04 76 80 01 52, rue Docteur Faure) serves big bowls of spaghetti bolognaise for 35FF. Other *eateries* can be found on ave Général de Gaulle.

Day 2: Le Bourg d'Oisans to Valloire
5–6 hours, 63.5km

Expect a hard day in the saddle, with 41km of climbing. Bring lights and nerves of steel for the series of tunnels. Until the Col du Lautaret, the ride skirts the border of the Parc National des Écrins. If the road is busy, the narrow valley can become fume choked.

Take the N91 from Le Bourg d'Oisans through the narrow, Upper Romanche Valley to reach the **Barrage du Chambon** (14km). Built between 1927 and 1936, the dam holds back the waters of the Lac de Chambon. From here to La Grave, the road runs very close to the Romanche River, where the glacial movements powder the rock, giving the water a blue-grey colour.

Head through the Combe de Malaval, where a dramatic waterfalls course down the hillsides; the **Saut de la Pucelle** (Maiden's Leap) is the most spectacular. Shortly after, the valley widens out onto the village of La Grave (25km) and the dramatic **Mer de Glace** (sea of ice) near La Meije glacier, which is accessible by chair lift from town in spring and summer (☎ 04 76 79 91 09); the route passes the chair lift operator. The scenery here is typically alpine; expansive green meadows dotted with wild flowers

are framed by the towering, glistening peaks of the Parc National des Écrins.

From La Grave, the road heads through yet another tunnel, rising steadily for about 10km to reach the **Col du Lautaret** (36km) with spectacular views. Formerly known as Collis de Altaureto, the Col du Lautaret takes its name from the small temple, or *altaretum*, built by the Romans to placate the deity of the mountains.

The approach to the imposing Col du Galibier passes the **Jardin Alpin**, which features more than 3000 varieties of high altitude plants. A long, leg-shattering climb then leads through several levels of vegetation to finish well above the tree line at the col. The **Souvenir du Henri Desgrange** monument is just before the top. The **Col du Galibier** affords panoramic views of the surrounding mountains, including Mont Blanc. Shake the lactic acid out of your legs before the dizzy descent into Valloire.

Valloire

It is remarkably easy to navigate the picturesque ski resort of Valloire; all facilities are either located on the road *in* to town or on the road *out* of town. There's not much to do in town outside winter.

The tourist office (☎ 04 79 59 03 96, fax 04 79 59 09 66, ☻ valloire@laposte.fr) and the Crédit Agricole bank are on the road out. Val d'Auréa Sport (☎ 04 79 59 09 12), on the road in, will do *basic* bike repairs.

Places to Stay & Eat On the way into town, *Camping de Ste Thécle* (☎ 04 79 59 03 90, fax 04 79 83 30 42) charges 28FF per adult (open mid-June to mid-September). *Hôtel Le Centre* (☎ 04 79 59 00 83, fax 04 79 59 06 87), behind the tourist office, has doubles from 160FF. The friendly *Hôtel Christiania* (☎ 04 79 59 00 57, fax 04 79 59 00 06) has swish doubles from 280FF.

Supermarkets can be found on both the roads. The *boulangerie* is on the road out of town. *Le Don Camillo* (☎ 04 79 59 08 21), on the road into town, serves pizza and pasta from 40FF.

Day 3: Valloire to St-Sorlin d'Arves
3½–4½ hours, 50km

This is the tour's toughest stage, with an unrelenting 20km climb through the Vallée

Days 2 & 3: Le Bourg d'Oisans – Valloire – St-Sorlin d'Arves

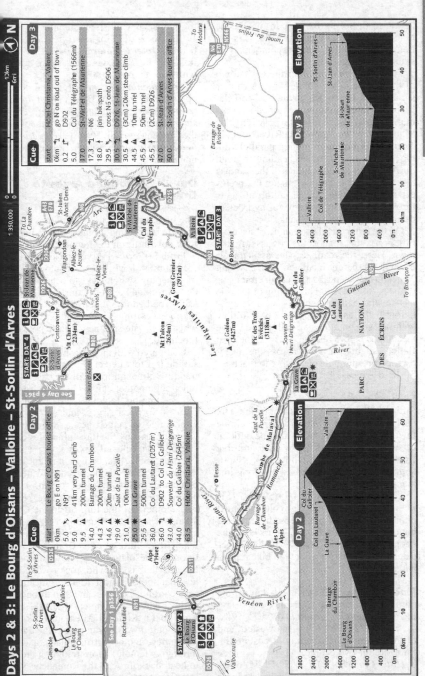

Cue

start		Le Bourg d'Oisans tourist office
0km		go E on N91
5.0	↖	N91
5.0	▲	41km very hard climb
9.5	▲	200m tunnel
14.0	▲	Barrage du Chambon
14.3	▲	200m tunnel
14.6	▲	20m tunnel
19.0	✳	Saut de la Pucelle
21.0	▲	100m tunnel
25.0	✳	La Grave
25.5	▲	500m tunnel
36.0	▲	Co du Lautaret (2057m)
36.0	↖	D902 to Col du Galibier'
43.0	✳	Souvenir du H'nri Desgrange
44.0	▲	Col du Galibier (2645m)'
63.5		Hôtel Christiaria, Valloire

Cue

start		Hôtel Christiania, Valloire
0km		go N on road out of town'
0.2	↖	D902
5.0	▲	Col du Télégraphe (1566m)'
17.0		St-Michel de Maurienne
17.3	↖	N6
18.0	↖	join bik-path
29.5	↖	cross N3 onto D506
30.5	↖	D926, St-Jean de Maurienne
		(3Cm) 2Okm steep climb
30.5	◀	10m tu nel
44.5	◀	50m tu nel
45.5	◀	(2Cm) D926
47.0		St-Jean d'Arves
50.0		St-Sorlin d'Arves tourist office

Arvan to St-Sorlin d'Arves. In places, the road gradient is as much as 13%. It is extremely hard going, but is accompanied by stunning views.

From Valloire, head over the easy climb of the **Col du Télégraphe** (5km). A former signal point, the col has an old Fort de Télégraphe at the top. A long descent on a well-maintained road leads into St-Michel de Maurienne. Cross the Arc River and, in 1km, join a bikepath running parallel with the very busy N6. When heading through the Arc Valley, the mountains of the Vanoise rise steeply on the right. It is not the prettiest valley to cycle in; an autoroute cuts through the middle and several hydroelectric plants line the Arc's banks.

On the outskirts of St-Jean de Maurienne (30.5km), the road splits, bypassing the town. Here, the road steepens as it travels through the barely inhabited Vallée Arvan. Majestic craggy peaks rear up on either side of the narrow valley. This section of the ride has several hairpin bends – and tunnels – before it flattens and dips briefly to follow an infant stream along the valley floor. Five kilometres before St-Jean d'Arves, the road flattens slightly, heading across the meadows, before climbing once more to reach St-Sorlin d'Arves.

St-Sorlin d'Arves

Sitting in the shadow of the Col de la Croix de Fer, St-Sorlin d'Arves typifies alpine town planning. The town had to be built on a 'sure place', accessible by road and free from avalanches and falling rock. Shops and houses are thus squeezed in a long line along a single main street.

The tourist office (☎ 04 79 59 71 77) is in this street. The Crédit Agricole bank next door has an ATM and keeps the enviable hours of 9 am to 12.30 pm, Thursday only. Technicien du Sport (☎ 04 79 59 70 83), beside the bank, can help out with bike repairs and some sales.

Places to Stay & Eat Knock 2km off the climb to the Col de la Croix de Fer by staying at the *camping ground* (☎ 04 79 59 78 42, fax 04 72 71 87 68) at the western end of town. Small and friendly, it costs 68FF for a site for two people.

Hôtel Clairvie (☎ 04 79 59 71 26) operates as a *gîte d'étape* (remote area lodging

for walkers or cyclists) in summer, charging 170FF to 200FF for *demi-pension* (half board). *Hôtel L'Entard* (☎ 04 79 59 71 25, fax 04 79 59 77 57, Grand Rue) has double with shower from 200FF.

An *alimentation general* (general store) is opposite the tourist office. A *depot du pai* (store selling bread) and another *genera store* can be found up the hill on the way to the camping ground. The usual *creperies* an *hotel/restaurants* are in the low end of the main street.

Day 4: St-Sorlin d'Arves to Grenoble

4½–5½ hours, 81km

The final section of this tour climbs throug still more stunning alpine scenery, before long downhill run to Grenoble.

From St-Sorlin d'Arves, head uphill. The road climbs slowly but surely along a series of sweeping switchbacks to peak at the Co de la Croix de Fer. It is a fairly nasty climb as the road gains 560m in 7.5km. Listen fo marmots calling to each other with lou whistles in late summer as they prepare t hibernate.

Compared with the other high passes, th **Col de la Croix de Fer** (7.5km) is relativel tranquil, although it is still the case of 'an other col, another cafe'. The view from th top is stunning, looking over several tarn onto St-Sorlin d'Arves, and across rang after range of jagged peaks, dominated t the south-east by the three pinnacles of Le Aiguilles (needles) d'Arves.

From the col, a bumpy descent drop through pristine alpine country. Waterfall crash off mountains and streams trickl across upland pastures. For those keen t bag another col, the turn-off to the Col d Glandon is about 2.5km down the descent

The road heads past the large artificia lake, the **Barrage de Grand Maison** through a desolate valley known as the Dé filé de Maupas – a wild, rocky-walled val ley that almost looks Mediterranean. The road continues to twist and turn through th valley, where an unpleasant little climb leads to Le Rivier d'Allemont (26km). A final, long downhill run passes the **Barrage du Verney**, another artificial lake, and goe through Allemont before rejoining the N9 to head back through the Romanche Valley into Grenoble.

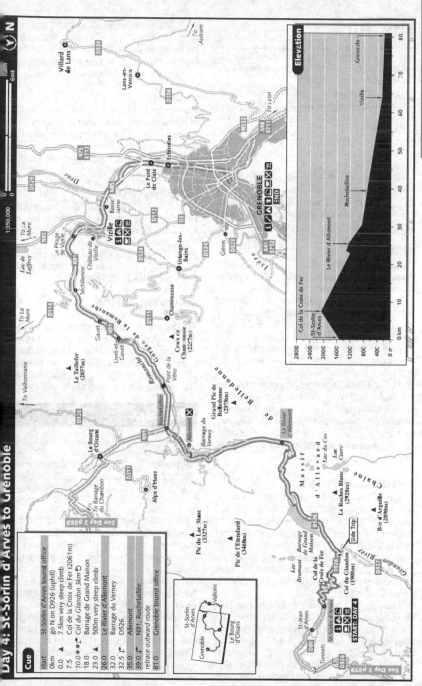

Day 4: St-Sorlin d'Arves to Grenoble

Cue		
start		St-Sorlin d'Arves tourist office
0km		go N on D926 (uphill)
0.0	▲	7.5km very steep climb
7.5		Col de la Croix de Fer (2061m)
10.0	●●↙	Col du Glandon 3km ↻
18.0	▲	Barrage de Grand Maison
23.0	▲	500m very steep climb
26.0	▲	Le Rivier d'Allemont
32.0	↱	Barrage du Verney
32.5	↳	D526
35.0		Allemont
39.0	↱	N91 Rochetaillée
		retrace outward route
81.0		Grenoble tourist office

Elevation

2800
2400
2000
1600
1200
800
400
0 m

0km   10   20   30   40   50   60   70   80

Col de la Croix de Fer
St-Sorlin d'Arves
Le Rivier d'Allemont
Rochetaillée
Vizille
Grenoble
END

The Jura

The area referred to as 'the Jura' corresponds roughly to the historical province known as Franche-Comté.

The landscape is extremely varied. Forests and meadows line the many gentle plateaux, while in the steeper, ridged sections, great rocky chasms and gorges cut through the cliff sides. Water is everywhere, spilling over spectacular falls and into more than 70 lakes.

Not quite as back-breakingly steep as the Alps, the terrain of the Jura is still physically challenging. The roads, however, are quieter, accommodation easier to find and the pace far slower.

HISTORY

Once part of the duchy of Burgundy, Franche-Comté was returned to the French crown in the 17th century.

The Jura has a long history of traditional industries such as woodworking, and pipe and cheese making (Comté, Bleu-de-Gex, Morbier). Industrialisation in the late 19th century transformed the region, with these time-honoured industries replaced by car and clock manufacturing.

About 40% of the Jura is covered by forest and forestry is still the region's economic mainstay. The Jura also produces several fine wine appellations. The distinctive *vin de paille* (straw wine), made near Arbois, uses an astonishing 100kg of grapes to produce 18L of wine.

NATURAL HISTORY

About 60 million years ago, huge chunks of limestone were folded into long parallel ridges and valleys in this region, leading to the term 'Jurassic' coming into geological usage. The pronounced south-west to north-east grain of these ridges means that cycling can either be extremely pleasant or very tough, depending on whether the grain is being followed or crossed.

The Jura is also home to beech, oak, fir, spruce and conifers; some of the trees are enormous. In spring, particularly, the upland meadows are full of wild flowers, including the dark blue spring gentian, the trumpet gentian, and the Boules d'Or, distinctive with their brilliant yellow flowers.

Wildlife is plentiful. Foxes and boar roam the lowlands, while red squirrels can be found in the High Jura above St Claude. On the lower plateaux, predatory birds such as hawks and kestrels can be found.

CLIMATE

Summer is usually warm, with average maximum temperatures in August hovering around 26.5°C. The average maximum temperature in January is an icy 4.8°C; prevailing winds blow from the west and rainfall are torrential.

INFORMATION

The Comité Régional du Tourisme de Franche-Comté (☎03 81 25 08 08, fax 03 81 83 35 82, e crt@franche-comte.org, ⌨ www.franche-comte.org) at Le Saint Pierre, rue de la République, 25044 Besançon Cedex can provide further information and itineraries for rides in the Jura.

GATEWAY CITIES
Dijon

The Jura is most easily accessed from Dijon which is only about 75km from Besançon, the start of The Jura ride following. See the Gateway Cities section in the Burgundy chapter (pp261–3) for all information on Dijon, including getting there and away.

The Jura

Duration	6 days
Distance	300.6km
Difficulty	moderate-hard
Start	Besançon
End	Bellegarde

This 'grand tour' of the Jura takes in the region's varied landscapes. Starting in the attractive countryside of 'le bon pays', the ride features some tough climbing to the spectacular Route des Sapins, then climbs through beautiful upland meadows and pastures towards Mont d'Or. It plunges through steep gorges which widen out onto the Lake District and climbs again through the peaceful Parc Naturel Régional du Haut-Jura. The ride follows part of the route used in the Grand Traversée du Jura, and a side trip provides the opportunity to cycle to Mont d'Or (see Side Trip under Day 3).

PLANNING
When to Ride
Spring and early summer are the best seasons to cycle.

Maps & Books
The detailed, topographical *Atlas des Cols es Vosges-Jura* is available through the FCT.

Michelin maps No 66 *Dijon, Besançon, Mulhouse,* No 70 *Beaune, Mâcon, Évian* and No 74 *Lyon, Chambery, Genève* (all :200,000) cover this ride.

What to Bring
The Jura can be very remote, with limited facilities. If camping at Bonlieu (the Lakes District) buy provisions for two days in Malbuisson. Cash-up in Besançon before heading off. After Arbois, there are no bike shops until Day 5.

GETTING TO/FROM THE RIDE
Besançon is about 75km from Dijon, start of the Wine Lover's Circuit and end of the Classic Burgundy ride, both in the Burgundy chapter.

It's also about 150km south-west of Colmar, the end of the Alsatian Wine Route in the Alsace & Lorraine chapter.

Trains connect Bellegarde with Grenoble, the start of the other rides in this chapter.

Check with the SNCF for bike-friendly timetables. At least one bike-friendly train per day runs between Besançon and Bellegarde in each direction, while several bike-friendly trains connect both towns with Lyon, Geneva and Colmar. Getting to places such as Nice will require a change at Lyon.

Besançon
Besançon's train station is 800m up the hill from the city centre.

Connections include Colmar (via Mulhouse and Belfort; 139FF, 2½ hours) and Dijon (77FF, one hour).

Trains run infrequently from Paris' Gare de Lyon (290FF, 2½ hours).

Bellegarde
The train station is in ave de la Gare.

Trains conveniently connect with several other cities, including Nice (320FF, four hours), Paris' Gare de Lyon (280FF, 3½ hours) and Geneva (90FF, 1½ hours).

Change at Lyon to go to Dijon (220FF, 3¾ to 4½ hours). A train taking bikes leaves for Grenoble at around 4 pm weekdays (72FF, 1¾ hours).

THE RIDE
Besançon
Almost fully enclosed by the Doubs River, Besançon is an attractive town. The capital of Franche-Comté, Besançon was first settled in Gallo-Roman times, later becoming an important stop on the early trade routes between Italy, the Alps and the Rhine.

Information The tourist office (☎ 03 81 80 92 55, fax 03 81 80 58 30, 🖳 www.besancon.com), 2 place de la Première Armée Française, is on the banks of the Doubs across the Pont de la République. The Banque de France is at 19 rue de la Préfecture. Grand Rue has several ATMs, and foreign currency can be exchanged at the train station information office.

The super-helpful Cycles de Griba, in rue du Breton, off Grand Rue, is closed Sunday and Monday morning; look for the cow in the window. Cycles Pardon (☎ 03 81 81 08 79) is at 31 rue d'Arenes. You can find a laundrette at 54 rue Bersot or log on at ROM Connection, rue du Lycée.

Things to See & Do Besançon is a lovely town for wandering. The historic **Battant quarter**, originally settled by wine makers, is a maze of shops; several 17th-century residences line the banks of the Doubs. The **Citadelle** sits high above the town and houses several museums and a zoo. It is a steep walk from the **Porte Noire**, which dates from the 2nd century.

The **Musée des Beaux Arts et d'Archéologie** (☎ 03 81 82 39 92), 1 place de la Révolution, has a display about clock-making in the Franche-Comté, as well as an impressive collection of mainly Renaissance paintings.

Places to Stay & Eat Open from May through September, *Camping de la Plage* (☎ 03 81 88 04 26) is 5km north-east of town on the N83 and costs 12FF per adult and 10FF for the tent site.

The sterile *Les Oiseaux* youth hostel (☎ 03 81 88 43 11, fax 03 81 80 77 97, 48 rue des Cras) is up the hill from the train station, off rue de Belfort. A bed and breakfast costs

80FF for the first night and 70FF for subsequent nights. *Hôtel de Paris (☎ 03 81 81 36 56, fax 03 81 61 94 90, 33 rue des Granges)* has doubles with toilet and shower/bath from 230/250FF. *Hôtel Gambetta (☎ 03 81 82 02 33, fax 03 81 82 31 16, 13 rue Gambetta)* has plain singles/doubles with shower from 225/255FF.

A *food market* takes place each Friday morning in place de la Révolution. *Pizzerias* abound along rue Bersot. The Battant quarter is also filled with *restaurants*.

Day 1: Besançon to Arbois
3–4 hours, 58.5km

The ride heads across the lush, undulating 'bon pays' of the Jura to finish in the quaint town of Arbois. From the tourist office, head across Pont de la République, dropping onto the bikepath along the Doubs and negotiating the small set of inconveniently placed steps. The path crosses the Doubs at Pont de Velotte and travels through fields of corn and maize to reach Avanne (10.4km) and Aveney. Shortly after is a lovely valley, where a quiet service road leads through Montferrand, crossing the Doubs soon after.

Head through Thoraise and follow the Doubs past the outskirts of Boussières and into Abbans-dessus. The slate-roofed, stone houses through these parts are characteristically Jurassienne.

Continue through the beautiful, gently sloping valley to skirt Byans-sur-Doubs. An undulating, forested stretch of road passes through Liesle and into Arc-et-Senans. Shortly after is the imposing, UNESCO Word Heritage-listed **Saline Royale** (40.2km; see the boxed text).

From the saltworks, the ride heads across the Loue, through the small villages of Cramans and Villers Farlay, before hitting a fantastic stretch of quiet forest into Arbois.

Arbois
An attractive, wine-producing town, Arbois is deservedly popular with travellers. This is where the scientist Louis Pasteur grew up.

The tourist office (☎ 03 84 66 55 50, fax 03 84 66 25 50, 🖳 www.arbois.com) is at the end of the main street, rue de l'Hôtel de Ville, at No 10. The main street has several banks. The motorbike shop Patrick Aviet (☎ 03 84 66 09 27), 1 rue de Bourgogne, is

the closest thing to a bike shop and does simple repairs – it is the last one until Day 5.

Things to See & Do The **Maison de Louis Pasteur** (☎ 03 84 66 11 72), 80 rue de Courcelles, is the house little Louis grew up in. It contains original furniture, as well as several items from Pasteur's laboratory.

Arbois is a pleasant place for a tipple. Try the superb **vin jaune** (yellow wine) and **vin de paille**. The locals have a saying: '*Du vin d'Arbois, Plus en boit, Plus on va droit*' ('The more you drink, the straighter you walk'). The Fête du Biou wine festival is on the first Sunday in September.

Places to Stay & Eat Next to the swimming pool on the road heading east to Mesnay, *Camping Les Vignes* (☎ 03 84 66 1 12, ave du Général Leclerc) charges 45FF per site. *Hotel Mephiso (☎ 03 84 66 06 49, 33 place Faramand)* has doubles with shower from 200FF.

The main street has a couple of *boulangeries* and a *Petit Casino*. A large *ATAC* supermarket is on the way into the town centre (closed Sunday). Most *restaurants* are in Grand Rue, although none are particularly cheap.

Day 2: Arbois to Nozeroy
4–5 hours, 59.5km

Some tough sections of climbing are well rewarded by beautiful scenery along the

Saline Royale

Designed by Claude-Nicholas Ledoux, an inspector at the saltworks and respected architect to boot, the saltworks of Arc-et-Senans are where classical architecture collides with the Industrial Age. Designed as an 'ideal city', Ledoux intended to build an entire town in concentric circles around the saltworks. Although Ledoux's dream was never fully realised – salt mining wasn't as economically viable as he hoped – his saltworks remain a showpiece of early Industrial Age town planning.

The buildings now house the International Centre for Studies of the Future, a salt museum (☎ 03 81 54 45 45) and a bookshop. Admission costs 38/30FF for adults/students.

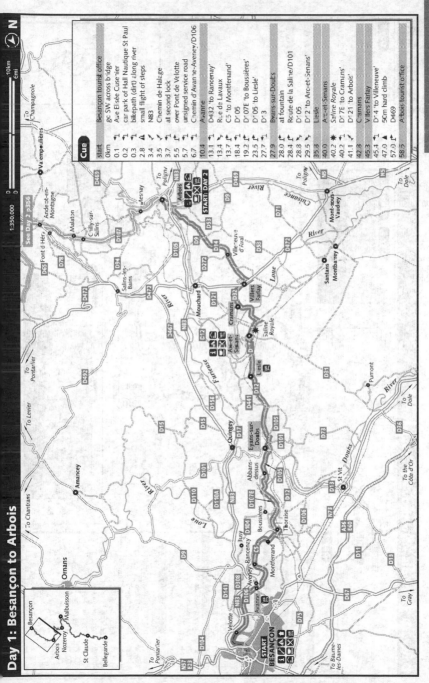

Day 1: Besançon to Arbois

Cue	
start	Besançon tourist office
0km	go SW across bridge
0.1	Av Elisée Cusenier
0.2	car park of Hall Nautique St Paul
0.3	bikepath (dirt) along river
2.8	small flight of steps
3.4	N83
3.5	Chemin de Halage
3.7	at second lock
5.5	over Pont de Velotte
5.7	unsigned service road
6.7	Chemin d'Avan'e-Aveney/D106
10.4	Avanne
13.1	D432 'to Rancenay'
13.4	R.e de Lavaux
13.7	C5 'to Montferrand'
18.4	D'05
19.2	D'07E 'to Boussières'
23.5	D'05 to Liesle'
27.7	D'3
27.9	Brans-sur-Doubs
28.0	at fountain
28.4	Route de la Saline/D101
28.8	D'05
29.5	D'2 'to Arc-et-senans'
35.8	Liesle
40.0	Arc-et-Senans
40.2	Saline Royale
40.2	D'7E to Cramans'
41.1	D'21 to Arbois'
42.3	Cramans
45.3	Villers Farlay
45.4	D'4 'to Villeneuve'
47.0	50m hard climb
57.0	D469
58.5	Arbois tourist office

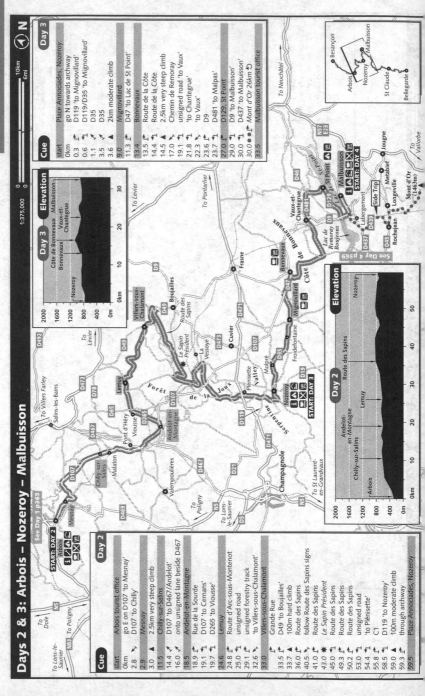

Days 2 & 3: Arbois – Nozeroy – Malbuisson

1:375,000

Day 3

Cue		
start	0km	Place Annociades, Nozeroy go N towards archway
	0.3	D119 'to Mignovillard'
	0.6	D119/D35 'to Mignovillard'
	1.1	D35
	3.5	D35
	3.6	2km moderate climb
	9.0	Mignovillard
	11.3	D47 'to Lac de St Point'
	13.4	Bonnevaux
	13.5	Route de la Côte
	14.4	Route de la Côte
	14.5	2.5km very steep climb
	17.0	Chemin de Remoray
	19.1	unsigned road 'to Vaux'
	21.8	'to Chantegrue'
	22.3	'to Vaux'
	23.6	D9
	23.7	D481 'to Malpas'
	27.0	D129, St Point
	29.0	D9 'to Malbuisson'
	30.0	D437 'to Malbuisson'
	30.0	Mont d'Or 26km
	33.5	Malbuisson tourist office

Day 3 Elevation

Côte de Bonnevaux / Bonnevaux / Vaux-et-Chantegrue / Malbuisson

Nozeroy

2000 1600 1200 800 400m

0km 10 20 30

Day 2

Cue		
start	0km	Arbois tourist office go E on D107 'to Mesnay'
	2.8	D107 'to Chilly'
	2.9	Mesnay
	3.0	2.5km very steep climb
	11.5	Chilly-sur-Salins
	14.4	D107 'to D467/Andelot'
	16.0	onto unsigned lane beside D467
	18.5	Andelot-en-Montagne
	18.9	Rue de la Sourde
	19.1	D107 'to Cernans'
	19.7	D265 'to Viousse'
	24.6	Lemuy
	24.8	Route d'Arc-sous-Montenot
	25.0	unsigned road
	29.1	unsigned forestry track
	32.6	'to Villers-sous-Chalamont'
	33.0	Villers-sous-Chalamont
	33.5	Grande Rue
	33.7	D49 'to Boujailles'
	36.0	100m hard climb
	40.5	Route des Sapins
	41.0	follow Route des Sapins signs
	43.0	Route des Sapins
	43.0	Le Sapin Président
	45.0	Route des Sapins
	49.3	Route des Sapins
	50.2	Route des Sapins
	53.0	unsigned road
	54.4	'to Plénisette'
	55.8	C1
	58.5	D119 'to Nozeroy'
	59.3	100m moderate climb
	59.3	through archway
	59.5	Place Annociades, Nozeroy

Day 2 Elevation

Arbois / Chilly-sur-Salins / Andelot-en-Montagne / Lemuy / Route des Sapins / Nozeroy

2000 1600 1200 800 400 0m

0km 10 20 30 40 50

0 10km
0 6mi

orgeous, tree-lined route Sapin, and a fin-sh in the medieval village of Nozeroy.
rom Arbois, head east to Mesnay, where, hortly after, a *very* tough climb heads hrough forest and onto a lush plateau, com-•lete with cows lazing in the meadows and awks soaring in the skies. A beautifully uiet, near-carless stretch passes through he hamlet of Chilly-sur-Salins (11.5km), vith its distinctive low stone farmhouses.

Undulating, sometimes poorly maintained oads wind across the wide lans through Andelot-en-Montagne and Lemuy (24.6km). Several kilometres out of Lemuy, the route •riefly follows a rough and bumpy forestry rack. Cyclists with very narrow tyres will eed to take it slowly, but the up side is the oad heads right into the heart of the tranquil ôret de la Joux.

Having rejoined the bitumen, head hrough Villers-sous-Chalamont (33km), vhere a big climb leads to the start of the nagnificent Route des Sapins, a beautiful Okm stretch of road that winds through hick fir forest; follow the Route des Sapins igns for 10km of turns in the forest. The vooded area covered by the ride is 10,000 ectares – an area the size of Paris. The for-st opens up periodically to give stunning iews of the valley through which you have ust ridden. Towards the end of the route is e Sapin Président (43km). This 200-year-ld 'King of the Forest' is more than 47m igh and measures a whopping 6m around ne base.

Once out of the forest, the route flattens hrough the wide Serpentine Valley, before a teep climb to the medieval fortified village f Nozeroy. The approach to the hill-top own rivals the one to Vézelay (see the Clas-ic Burgundy ride in the Burgundy chapter).

Nozeroy

The former home of the Chalons, the most owerful family in the Jura in the Middle Ages, Nozeroy's buildings were either built r razed by family members in fierce strug-les for the family riches. Once encircled by amparts, accessible only through a fortified ateway, Nozeroy maintains much of the tmosphere of its 14th-century origins.

Information The tourist office (☎ 03 84 1 19 15, fax 03 84 51 11 40), place Anno-iades, is closed on Saturday afternoon and

Sunday. The Crédit Agricole bank is in Grand Rue. The town has no bike shop.

The tourist office can provide a map in-dicating the various **historic buildings** on a walk of town and it will also organise guided tours.

The **Assaut des Remparts**, a medieval fair, takes place at the end of July.

Places to Stay & Eat The *camping ground* charges only 23FF per adult. Facili-ties are basic, but as it's perched above a beautiful, meadowed valley the view is out of this world; follow the signs from the square. If nobody comes to collect your money, pay at the tourist office. *Hôtel des Remparts* (☎ 03 84 51 18 69), signposted from the main square, has doubles/triples with shower from 200/250FF.

A *boulangerie* and a *Petit Casino* super-market can be found on Grand Rue. *Le Re-lais Médiéval* (☎ 03 84 51 16 81, place Annociades) serves several different kinds of fondue from 56FF. The *Menu Montagnard* (mountain *menu*) costs 92FF.

Day 3: Nozeroy to Malbuisson
2½–3½ hours, 33.5km
This short ride heads out of the Serpentine Valley through pockets of quiet forest, be-fore descending onto the picturesque Lac de St-Point and Malbuisson.

From Nozeroy, head east to Mignovillard (9km). Shortly after, the route climbs steeply to reach the Côte de Bonnevaux, where a fantastically quiet back road winds through the firs and ferns of the Bois de la Haute Joux. Head across the hill's crest, be-fore descending through the wild flowers into yet another gorgeous flower-filled val-ley. The last part of the ride is gently undu-lating for the most part, although it drops steeply onto Lac de St-Point before finish-ing in Malbuisson (see the boxed text 'The Legend of Lac de St-Point' overleaf).

Side Trip: Mont d'Or
1½–2½ hours, 26km
The highest peak in the region, Mont d'Or (1463m) was so named because it was thought to contain deposits of gold. The *or* in Mont d'Or, however, turned out to be fool's gold. An incredibly steep climb from Malbuisson heads through a narrow gorge and up to the summit where, on a clear day,

Mont Blanc can be seen. The steep ridges of the Jura are on perfect display at Mont d'Or where the mountain drops steeply away into Switzerland.

It is possible to turn off at the 30km mark and ride up the Mont as a part of Day 3. However, considering the difficulty of the side trip, it's a good idea to head into town first and allow an extra day to make the climb without panniers; this will add 7km total to the side trip. From the tourist office head west on the D437. One kilometre after you pass Labergement turn left onto the D439, following signs to Mont d'Or. Veer left onto the D45 at the 9km mark; the road up the Mont is on the right about 1km along – your legs will probably have blown by now, but it's another 3km of climbing to the summit. Return the way you came.

Malbuisson

Occupying a stunning position at the base of the Jura, Malbuisson sits on the more touristy bank of the lake. It is also the only place for miles with an ATM and a supermarket.

The tourist office is at the end of Grand Rue (closed Sunday afternoon). There is no bank, but the post office, on Grand Rue, has an ATM. There is no bike shop either.

All manner of **aquatic activities** are possible; ask at the tourist office. The office also sells topomaps for **VTT excursions** and **walks**. The French **VTT championships** are held each year at nearby Metabief.

The Legend of Lac de St-Point

An impressive body of water, Lac de St-Point is shrouded in legend. Story has it that one night a woman dressed in rags and carrying a small child asked for shelter in the thriving town of Damvaultier, on the river Doubs. The inhabitants of Damvaultier turned the woman down. Desperate, she prayed to the heavens for food and shelter. As if to answer her prayers, an elderly hermit appeared out of nowhere and put her up for the night. The next morning they awoke to discover a large lake – now Lac de St-Point – had engulfed the village of Damvaultier.

Places to Stay & Eat On the banks of the lake, **Les Fuvettes** camping ground (☎ 03 81 69 31 50, fax 03 81 69 70 46) charges 65FF (open April through October). The **camping ground** at St Point (☎ 03 81 69 61 64) charges 56FF for a site for two adults. Grand Rue has several hotels, including **La Fuvelle** (☎ 03 81 69 30 12) where doubles start at 220FF, and **Le Bon Accueil** (☎ 03 81 69 50 38), which charges 220FF for a double with shower. A gîte d'étape, **L'Auberge au Galop** (☎/fax 03 81 49 10 06, 27 rue du Vieux Village), is at Metabief. Open all year round, it charges between 70FF and 90FF for a dorm bed.

A **boulangerie** and **fromagerie** (cheese shop) can both be found in the main street. Grand Rue has a **supermarket** (closed Sunday afternoon and holidays). **Le Bon Accueil** has a reasonably priced restaurant and at **Le Troquet** (☎ 03 81 69 71 13), also in the main street, the sandwiches and salads are more than substantial.

Day 4: Malbuisson to Bonlieu

2½–4½ hours, 53km

The terrain on this lovely stage is mainly flat or downhill.

From Malbuisson, retrace the Day 3 route into town before turning left onto the D46. A great, flat stretch follows the valley of the Doubs past the **Remoray nature reserve**, home to several different sorts of aquatic and bird life, and then onto a wide valley. The ride passes through several tiny hamlets before reaching Chaux Neuve (22.5km) where budding Eddy-the-Eagles can try their luck at the **ski jump** on the slopes of Mont Noir.

From here, a long descent winds through a gorge, following the curve of the Saine. At the hamlet of Les Planches, the gorge feeds into the dizzying **Gorges de la Langouette** (37.5km). A slight climb out of the gorge and then a long 'false flat' passes the Lacs de Maclu, the official start of the beautiful **Region des Lacs**, an area particularly rich with folklore and culture. The ride then passes the lakes Narlay (45km) and Ilay to finish in Bonlieu.

Bonlieu

Bonlieu is really just a place to stop overnight. There is no tourist office, bank, bike shop or general food store.

Days 4 & 5: Malbuisson – Bonlieu – St Claude

Day 4

Cue		
start		Malbuisson tourist office
0km		go W on D437
3.5	⌐	D9
4.5	⌐	D46 'to Remoray'
5.0	✳	Remoray Nature Reserve
16.5		Les Pontents
22.5		Chaux Neuve
30.0	⌐	D127, Foncine-le-Bas
34.0	⌐	D127 'to Les Planches'
35.0		Les Planches-en-Montagne
36.0	↘	D127E 'to Gorges de la Languette'
39.0	↘	D16 'to Chaux des Crotenay'
41.0		Chaux des Crotenay
43.5	⌐	N5
43.5	⌐	(20m) D75 'to Le Frasnois'
47.5		Lacs de Maclu
48.0		Le Frasnois
50.5		Lac d'Ilay
51.0		Ilay
52.0	↗	N78
53.0		Bonlieu, opposite pizzeria

Day 5

Cue		
start		Bonlieu opposite pizzeria
0km		go W on N78
2.5	⌐	D67 'to St Maurice'
6.3		St Maurice
6.4	⌐	D23 'to Prénovel'
		6km steep climb
15.3	⌐	D28
18.4	⌐	D146 'to Chaux des Prés'
19.0	⌐	D28
21.0		Château des Prés
21.6	↙	D437
28.2		La Rixouse
29.0		'Roche Blanche/Noire Combe'
29.1	↘	1.5km very steep descent
31.2	⌐	1km moderate climb
33.0	⌐	'to St Claude'
34.7	⌐	'to St Claude'
38.9		D437
40.0	⌐	D437
41.0	⌐	cross the Bienne River
41.3	⌐	Blvd de République/Rue ce Pré
41.6		St Claude's tourist office

Elevation — Day 5

Bonlieu · Prénovel · Château des Prés · La Rixouse · St Claude

2000 / 1600 / 1200 / 800 / 400 / 0m

0km · 10 · 20 · 30 · 40

A series of waterfalls linked by a walking trail, the spectacular **Cascades du Hérisson** are particularly impressive after a downpour. For the brave, it is possible to walk behind the **Grand Saut**, where the water drops 60m from an overhanging cliff. It's a 4km return walk to the falls; follow the signs from the main street, the N78.

Places to Stay & Eat On the road into town, *L'Abbaye* camping ground charges 44FF a night. Run by M and Mme Grillet, the only *chambre d'hôte* (☎ *03 84 25 59 12)*, in town on the road to the cascades, costs 210FF for a single or double. They will also let you pitch a tent in their back yard. *La Poutre* (☎ *03 84 25 57 77, fax 03 84 25 51 61, 25 Grande Rue)* has classy, comfortable doubles with shower and television for 260FF.

Food options are thin on the ground in Bonlieu. The *camping ground* has a limited range of supplies and while there is no boulangerie as such, the *boulanger* does call each morning at the camping ground. Like an oasis in a food desert, *Les Cascades* (☎ *03 84 25 58 22)*, in the main street, serves enormous wood-fired pizzas from 50FF. Opposite the camping ground, *Au Châlet* (☎ *03 84 25 57 04)* serves excellent, expensive regional cuisine. The *plat du jour* costs 65FF; sharing a *fondue jurassienne* will set each person back 64FF.

Day 5: Bonlieu to St Claude
2½–3½ hours, 41.6km
This stage is reasonably easy, with the only climb of any note soon after Bonlieu. The ride takes in stunning views over several valleys through the Parc Naturel Régional du Haut-Jura.

From Bonlieu, climb through the quiet, carless Fôret de Prénovel, then descend through a wide, relatively untouched valley and into the **Parc Naturel Régional**.

Once in the park, a long sweeping descent affords amazing views into the spectacular **Gorges de la Bienne**. At La Rixouse (28.2km), the path drops into the gorge itself by way of a very steep, but stunningly beautiful descent. The road then crosses the river (31km) to climb back out of the gorge. The climb is not steep, but the road is in need of repair. From the top, it is all downhill into St Claude.

St Claude
Chosen 1500 years ago by two hermits as a monastic retreat, St Claude retains little of its original charm. It is now a high-testosterone town that some women may find intimidating. However, it is a convenient place to do washing and cash up.

The tourist office (☎ 03 84 45 34 24) is at the end of ave du Pré. The Banque Populaire is at 43 rue du Pré and Cycles Guy Burdet (☎ 03 84 45 22 46) is at 20 rue Rousset.

Things to See & Do The **Câthedrale St Pierre** on rue Gambetta, first built in the 14th century, sits on the site of the original monastery. The stalls, rebuilt after a fire in 1983, have been reconstructed to depict life in the 15th century. A former pipe-making powerhouse, St Claude has two museums. **Pipes Genod**, 13 rue Faubourg Marcel, is still a working factory, but visits are welcome. Just past the cathedral, the **Musée de la Pipe et du Diamant** brings together St Claude's two big industries – smoker's pipe making and precious stones.

Places to Stay & Eat The *camping ground* (☎ *03 84 45 00 40, rue du Martinet)* is at Le Martinet, 3km south of town. It charges 30FF per adult (closed from October through April). The slightly less than salubrious *Hôtel de la Poste* (☎ *03 84 45 52 34, 1 rue Reybert)*, near the post office, has doubles from 160FF. *Hôtel La Poyat* (☎ *03 84 45 49 81, 7 rue de la Poyat)*, off ave du Pré, has doubles with shower for 195FF.

Two small *supermarkets* and several *brasseries* are in rue de Pré. *Le Lagon Bleu* (☎ *03 84 45 71 22, 3 route de Gèneve)*, near the camping ground, serves Thai and Chinese dishes from 50FF.

Day 6: St Claude to Bellegarde
3½–4½ hours, 54.5km
Experience some of the nicest cycling in the Jura; peaceful roads afford stunning views of the surrounding mountains and valleys. From St Claude, a super-gruelling long climb heads out of town before dropping into a quiet valley. Another climb leads through the hamlet of Les Bouchoux, before opening onto a wide plateau. The white cliffs look almost Mediterranean and the views back across the valleys and ridges of the Jura are stunning.

Day 6: St Claude to Bellegarde

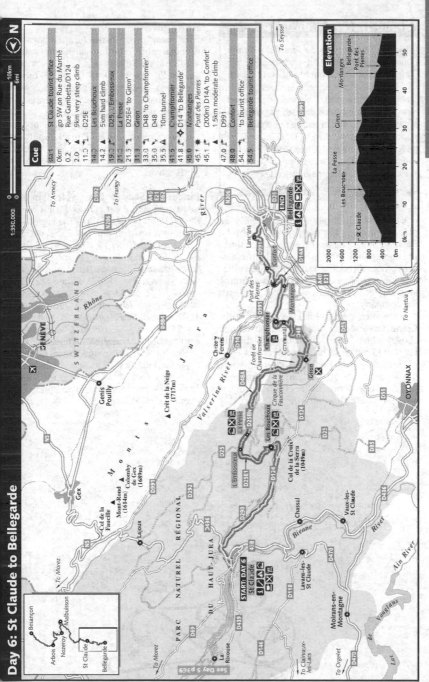

Cue			
sta.1			St Claude tourist office
0km		↙	go SW on Rue du Marché
0.2		↗	Rue Gambetta/D124
2.0		◄	9km very steep climb
11.0		◄	D25E
14.0			Les Bouchoux
14.2		◄	5km hard climb
19.0		⌐	D25, 'Embossieux'
21.0			La Pesse
21.5		⌐	D25E4 'to Giron'
31.3			Giron.
33.0		⌐	D48 'to Champfromier'
35.0		◄	D48
35.5		◄	10m tunnel
41.5			Champfromier
41.8		◇	D14 'to Bellegarde'
45.0			Montanges
45.1		✳	Pont des Pierres
45.1		⌐	(200m) D14A 'to Confort'
		◄	1.5km moderate climb
47.0		⌐	D991
48.0			Confort
54.		⌐	to tourist office
54.5			Bellegarde tourist office

Elevation

Grand Traversée du Jura

The Grand Traversée du Jura (GTJ; Grand Jura Crossing) is a 370km cross-country ski-ing track that runs from Montbéliard (north of Pontarlier) to Hauteville-Lompes (south-west of Bellegarde). This well-maintained and well-signed track through rugged, un-spoilt countryside can also be undertaken on foot or mountain bike (VTT). Contact GTJ-ENJ (☎ 03 84 52 58 10, fax 03 84 52 35 56, e gtj@wanadoo.fr), rue Baronne-Delort BP 132, F-39304, Champagnole cedex.

Continue climbing – quite steeply in places – to the picturesque village of La Pesse (21km). The payoff for all that climb-ing comes soon after, when a welcome des-cent passes through a beautiful, quiet valley. The air is fresh and the scenery is stunning along quiet back roads with only the birds for company.

Soon after, the route links with part of the **Grand Traversée du Jura** (see the boxed text above) which winds down through the vil-lages of Giron and Champfromier.

Head across the **Ponte des Pierres**, where the Valserine flows far below. From here, there is one more little climb before a sweeping descent into Bellegarde.

Bellegarde

Like most towns in the Jura, Bellegarde is unremarkable. The tourist office (☎ 04 50 48 48 68; on Sunday and holidays ☎ 04 50 56 56 25, fax 04 50 48 65 08, e otbelleg @cc-pays-de-gex.fr) is at 24 place Victor Be. The bank, post office and pharmacy are all in rue de la République.

Also in rue de la République, opposite the Stoc supermarket, Patrick Sport sells stove fuel. It is one of the few places in France that sells white gas (shellite) for MSR stoves.

Places to Stay & Eat Cycle 2km out of town to reach *Le Crête d'Eau Camping* (☎ 04 50 56 60 81); follow the signs on the route into town. It charges 33FF per adult. The *Touring Hôtel* (☎ 04 50 56 08 08, fax 04 50 48 50 62, 15 ave de la Gare) is 50m from the train station. It has quiet doubles with shower for 180FF. *Hôtel 1re Classe* (☎ 04 50 56 62 53, fax 04 50 48 62 88, ave de Lattre de Tassigny) has doubles from 160FF. *La Belle Époque* (☎ 04 50 48 14 46, fax 04 50 56 01 71, 10 place Gambetta) has somewhat pricey doubles from 300FF.

Rue de la République has a large *Stoc* supermarket, as well as several *brasseries. Pizzeria Capri* (☎ 04 50 56 08 09, 9 ave de la Gare) serves 40FF pasta and pizza (open evenings only).

Languedoc-Roussillon

The region of Languedoc-Roussillon, formed in the 1960s from two historic provinces, comprises the five *départements* (departments; administrative divisions) of Lozère, Gard, Hérault, Pyrénées-Orientales and Aude. It stretches in an arc along the coast from Provence to the Pyrenees, bordering the Massif Central in the north.

Roussillon, or French Catalonia, lies at the eastern end of the Pyrenees, bordering Spain. It retains many symbols of its time as part of the former Catalan autonomous region in the north-east of modern-day Spain.

HISTORY

Languedoc was settled as early as 450,000 BC. The name comes from *langue d'oc*, a language closely related to Catalan. Invasions by Phoenicians, Greeks, Romans, Visigoths and Moors preceded Frankish control in about the 8th century AD. The Albigensian Crusade, launched to suppress the heretical Cathars in 1208, led to Languedoc's annexation by the French kingdom.

Roussillon, also inhabited since prehistoric times and invaded by the same cast of characters as Languedoc, came under control of Catalonia-Aragon in 1172. When the Catalans revolted against Madrid in 1640, France's King Louis XIII and his infamous Cardinal Richelieu came to their 'aid'. In 1659 the Treaty of the Pyrenees defined the border between Spain and France, and Roussillon became French, no matter what the locals wanted.

NATURAL HISTORY

Languedoc has two distinct areas: the lower plains, known as *Bas Languedoc*, and the rugged, mountainous *Haut* (Upper) Languedoc to the north.

On the plains are the cities and agricultural heartland. Ancient, sunbaked Nîmes marks the eastern boundary with Provence. Away from the coast, ruined castles crown rocky outcrops and countless vineyards make Languedoc a prime wine region of France.

Upper Languedoc's isolation attracts visitors in search of the great outdoors. Lozère, France's most sparsely populated department, includes the Parc National des Cévennes, a

wild mountain area long the refuge of hermits, exiles and, nowadays, touring cyclists. The bare limestone plateaux of the Grands Causses (see the boxed text later in the chapter) rise above deep canyons and little towns dot the landscape like oases.

Roussillon is at the southern end of the plain of Bas Languedoc. West of Perpignan rises the mighty Pic du Canigou and all around are vineyards, olive and fig groves, and vegetables. The flat coastline ends abruptly with the rocky foothills of the Pyrenees meeting the Côte Vermeille, an area of red rocks and soil which inspired the most renowned Fauvist artists.

CLIMATE

'Mediterranean' sums up the climate of the region. Similar to Provence, the climate typically features warm to very hot, dry summers and mild, wetter winters. The region frequently experiences warm, drying north-westerly winds in summer. Wind chill makes it very cold in winter. When the bitter Mistral blows down the Rhône valley, its effects can be felt as far to the south-west as Carcassonne.

The King of Cheeses

France's most famous blue cheese is produced in, and named after, the Languedoc village of Roquefort. But the mouldy, blue-green-veined delicacy can be tasted all over the region.

The veins running through roquefort are the spores of microscopic mushrooms, gathered in the caves at Roquefort and then cultivated on leavened bread. During the cheese's ripening process – which takes place in the same natural caves – delicate draughts of air called *fleurines* cut through the caves, encouraging the blue *penicillium roqueforti* to eat through the white-cheese curds. The term fleurine is derived from the langue d'oc word *flarina*, meaning 'to blow'.

At around 100FF a kilogram, roquefort is one of France's priciest and most noble cheeses. In 1407 Charles VI granted exclusive roquefort-cheese-making rights to the villagers of Roquefort. In the 17th century, the Sovereign Court of the Parliament of Toulouse imposed severe penalties against fraudulent cheese makers trading under the Roquefort name.

INFORMATION
Information Sources

The Comité Régional du Tourisme du Languedoc-Roussillon (☎ 04 67 22 81 00, fax 04 67 58 06 10, ✉ contact.crtlr@sunfrance.com, 💻 www.cr-languedocroussillon .fr/tourisme) is in Montpellier, at 20 rue de la République.

Remote Cévennes

Duration	5 days
Distance	405.7km
Difficulty	moderate-hard
Start	Avignon
End	Nîmes

Have a taste of the Cévennes in two days (Avignon to Villefort; see Information under Villefort for details) or go the 'full *montée*' in five days. You'll ride from the Rhône valley on minor roads through fine-wine country and past the bizarre Chartreuse de Valbonne, then explore the thrilling Gorges de l'Ardèche. Heading into the romantic, remote Cévennes, follow the tracks of Robert Louis Stevenson, whose account of his *Travels with a Donkey in the Cévennes*, more than 120 years ago, put this hilly area on the world map (see the 'Travels with a Donkey' boxed text overleaf).

The highlight of the ride is the ascent past Causse Méjean to the 1565m summit of Mont Aigoual, where 360° views from the weather observatory leave you gasping. The following 45km (on Days 4 and 5) are all downhill. There is only one relatively low climb on Day 5 before continuing the descent to Nîmes.

NATURAL HISTORY

The Ardèche River cuts through the limestone plateau of Bas Vivarais. It separates the Plateau des Gras from the Plateau d'Orgnac with a spectacular series of gorges, some 30km long and often more than 200m deep. The southern climate's dry summers supports *garrigue* (fragrant, herbal scrub), olives and almonds, and vineyards.

The Parc National des Cévennes (PNC) to the west, created in 1970 to bring ecological stability to a region long disturbed by human activity, covers 910 sq km. Its granite peaks, including Mont Lozère, are covered with heather, peat bogs and rushing streams in summer, and snow and ice in winter.

Sweet chestnut trees *(châtaigniers)*, first planted in the Middle Ages, carpet the Park's central region of inaccessible ravines and jagged ridges.

The Park's high point, Mont Aigoual, and the neighbouring Montagne du Lingas region, are known for their searing winds and heavy winter snows. Beech trees thickly cover the slopes.

PLANNING
When to Ride

The riding season is limited by snow on Monts Lozère and Aigoual. Roads should be clear from May to October. If in doubt, call the meteorological station on Mont Aigoual (☎ 04 67 82 60 01). To cut the ride to two days, see Information under Villefort.

Maps

Michelin map No 80 *Albi, Rodez, Nîmes* (1:200,000) covers the route.

What to Bring

Camping equipment is recommended for flexibility in this remote region. However, camping grounds in this area, particularly the Gorges de l'Ardèche, are expensive and discriminate against solo travellers, especially cyclists. Fees are based on a *forfait* (fixed price – though it can be translated as a 'serious crime'!), a minimum fee for two people in a car with a large tent or caravan.

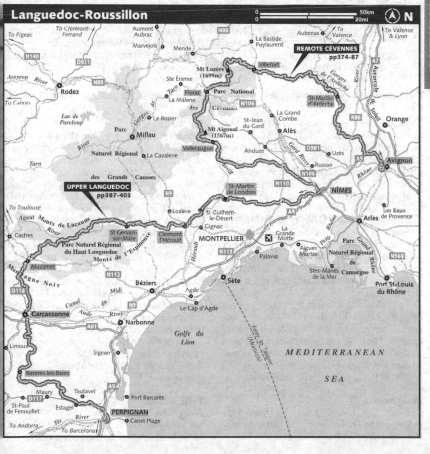

Travels with a Donkey

On tough days, when the decision to cycle across the wild, untamed Cévennes seems like the craziest idea you ever had, take heart – you are travelling in relative comfort. In October 1978, Scottish writer Robert Louis Stevenson chose to cross the mountain range with an *âne* (donkey).

'I was looked upon with contempt, like a man who should project a journey to the moon, but yet with a respectful interest, like one setting forth for the inclement Pole', Stevenson wrote in *Travels with a Donkey in the Cévennes,* published the following year.

Accompanied by the mouse-coloured Modestine, purchased at the market for 65FF and a glass of brandy, Stevenson took 12 days to travel the 220km on foot (Modestine carried his gear) from Le Monastier to St-Jean du Gard. Afterwards, he sold his ass – and wept.

The Stevenson Trail, first retraced and marked with the cross of St Andrew by a Scottish woman in 1978, today follows the GR70, crossing Mont du Goulet (1497m) and Mont Lozère (1699m) en route.

In case there's the temptation to trade in your bike, donkeys, which can be hired in Florac, carry 30kg to 50kg but can only cover 10km to 25km a day.

1897 woodcut frontspiece to the 1st edition of *Travels with a Donkey in the Cévennes.*

WALTER CRAN

LANGUEDOC-ROUSSILLON

Typically, this means a solo cyclist or couple with a small tent (and no car, of course) will be expected to pay upwards of 70FF in low season and 100FF in high season. Some camping grounds with pools and other facilities aimed at long-stay holiday-makers charge as much as 160FF a night.

GETTING TO/FROM THE RIDE

Avignon is the start of the Majesty of the Romans ride and the end of The Luberon & Mont Ventoux ride (both in the Provence & the Côte d'Azur chapter). Nîmes is the start of the Upper Languedoc ride described later in this chapter.

To explore the volcanic *puy* country of the Massif Central, link this ride with the Volcans d'Auvergne ride in the Massif Central chapter. The train trip through the mountains to the ride's start, Clermont-Ferrand, is one of the most scenic in France; the route, which begins in Paris, is known as Le Cévenol.

Avignon

See the Luberon & Mont Ventoux ride (p458) in the Provence chapter for information on getting to/from Avignon.

Nîmes

The train station is 1.4km from the tourist office. Go south across rue Général Perrier to place du Maison Carrée. Take blvd Victor Hugo, skirting around the Arènes and making a left onto rue de la République. Turn right at Square du 11 Novembre 1918 then left at ave Feuchères, which meets blvd Sgt Triaire opposite the entrance.

Head back to Avignon on one of the 10 trains – at least – per day (46FF, ½ hour, all carry bikes). Ten TGVs per day run to Paris (four hours, reservation is compulsory). Most have only 1st-class seats (598FF) but one or two have 2nd-class places (380FF to 444FF). Only one service a day to Clermont-Ferrand takes bikes unbagged (184FF, 3¾ hours, two or three a day).

About three non-TGVs run to Paris daily, carrying bikes (380F, nine hours). About five trains go to Nice via Marseille (229FF, four to six hours).

THE RIDE
Avignon

See Avignon (pp472–3) in the Luberon & Mont Ventoux ride in the Provence chapter for information about accommodation and other services.

Day 1: Avignon to St-Martin d'Ardèche

4–7½ hours, 75.7km

This is a mostly unstrenuous day – with only two notable climbs, and a maximum altitude of 288m at 47km – riding through wine country and extremely small, lightly trafficked roads.

Ride out through Villeneuve-lès-Avignon, turning left to Pujaut at a crossroads (from which Villeneuve's pleasant *Camping La Laune* is 300m to the right). Follow a quiet, mostly level *route des vins*, passing through little villages like Tavel (claiming France's *premier rosé*), Lirac (home of a famous Côtes du Rhône vintage wine), St-Laurent des Arbres (**12th-century church**) and Laudun (below the **Camp de César**, an important regional archaeological site).

After Tresques (36.1km), follow a maze of tiny roads climbing through vineyards to Sabran (47km) at 286m. A fine panorama rewards the climb to this village which features a **Romanesque church** and the ruins of a **medieval castle**.

Descend, cross the D6 and weave your way to La Roque-sur-Cèze (56km), enjoying its narrow, pedestrianised streets and the nearby 13th-century, stone-arched bridge. There are two camping grounds nearby – *Camping La Cascade*, 600m before the village, charges 80FF for a site for two people.

A moderate climb leads towards the ancient Carthusian abbey, the **Chartreuse de Valbonne** (☎ 04 66 90 41 24). The fortified monastery, founded in 1203, comprises a church and a group of houses which have been restored since being ravaged in the Wars of Religion. Wine is produced here under the Côtes du Rhône *appellation* (quality-controlled wine-growing region) and tastings are available. Accommodation is offered in the former monks quarters – 190FF a double with shower and toilet).

Ride down through the Forêt de Valbonne into the Ardèche valley.

St-Martin d'Ardèche

This village, attractively sited on the bank of the Ardèche River, serves as the eastern gateway to the Gorges de l'Ardèche. An Office de Tourisme (☎/fax 04 75 98 70 91) is

on place de l'Église. There is neither bank nor bike shop in town.

Things to See & Do Hire canoes at numerous locations in and around St-Martin d'Ardèche. Chez Raymond (☎ 04 75 98 84 28) is on the riverbank in the village. Camping La Revire also hires canoes.

Places to Stay & Eat At the north-western end of town, *Camping La Revire* (☎ 04 75 98 71 14, *route des Gorges*) charges 66.50FF (71.50FF in high season) for a site for one or two adults. A cheaper option is *Camping Les Oliviers* (☎ 04 66 82 14 13, *chemin de Tête Grosse*), which is signposted to the right off the D343 on Day 1 – about 1.8km after St-Paulet de Caisson. Tariffs start at 45FF for one in a small tent and it has a snack bar.

St-Martin offers a few indoor accommodation options, including the *Hôtel Les Mimosas* (☎ 04 75 04 62 79), on the D290, which has rooms from 200/320FF with toilet/ toilet and shower. *L'Auberge des Gorges* (☎ 04 75 98 79 03, *route des Gorges*) has doubles from 150FF

There are *bakeries* and an *alimentation générale* (grocery store) on the main street, but no supermarket.

The village's numerous cafes and restaurants include *Casa Pépé* (☎ 04 75 98 65 95) and the *Crêperie Le Crépuscule* (☎ 04 75 98 65 52), both on rue Andronne, which offer tasty, inexpensive dishes.

Day 2: St-Martin d'Ardèche to Villefort

4½–9 hours, 95.3km

Despite the distance, it's not a very hard day and the scenery will distract from any pain. There are some undulations in the first 30km through the gorges, reaching just above 300m, but only one long, moderately graded climb of 15.6km to the Col du Mas de l'Air (83.4km). Afterwards there's a 9km downhill freewheel.

Start early to enjoy the gorges in the cool, tourist-free morning. At 3.3km, a sign announces your entry to the **Gorges de l'Ardèche Réserve Naturelle**. Created in 1980, the reserve protects the 100 species of birds, reptiles and numerous small mammals which call the Gorge home. After another 4.6km, you can pay to visit the

LANGUEDOC-ROUSSILLON

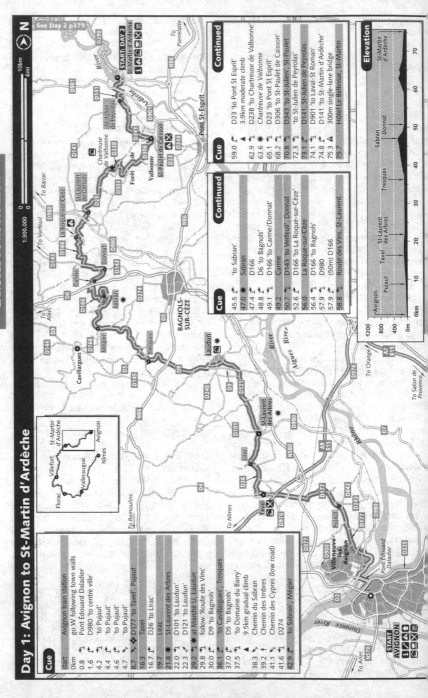

Day 1: Avignon to St-Martin d'Ardèche

Cue	
start	Avignon train station
	go W following town walls
0km	Pont Édouard Daladier
0.8	D980 'to centre ville'
1.6	'to Pujaut'
4.2	'to Pujaut'
4.4	'to Pujaut'
4.6	'to Pujaut'
4.7	'to Pujaut'
8.7	D177 'to Tavel', Pujaut
16.3	Tavel
16.7	D26 'to Lirac'
19.7	Lirac
21.8	St-Laurent des Arbres
22.0	D101 'to Laudun'
22.3	D121 'to Laudun'
29.2	at Marché U, Laudun
29.8	follow 'Route des Vins'
30.0	D9 'to Bagnols'
36.1	'to Cavillargues', Tresques
37.0	D5 'to Bagnols'
37.5	'to Domaine du Barry'
	9.5km gradual climb
38.3	Chemin du Sabran
39.2	Chemin des Imbres
41.1	Chemin des Cyprès (low road)
41.6	D274
42.9	'to Sabran', Mégier

Cue		Continued
45.5		'to Sabran'
47.0	※	Sabran
47.4		D166
48.8		D6 'to Bagnols'
49.1		D166 'to Carme/Donnat'
49.2		Carme
50.7		D143 'to Verfeuil', Donnat
52.6		D166 'to La Roque-sur-Cèze
56.0		La Roque-sur-Cèze
56.4		D166 'to Bagnols'
57.9		D980
57.9		(50m) D166
58.8		Route des Vins, St-Laurent

Cue		Continued
59.0		D23 'to Pont St Esprit'
		3.9km moderate climb
62.9	◀	D238 'to Chartreuse de Valbonne'
63.6	※	Chartreuse de Valbonne
65.1		D23 'to Pont St Esprit'
68.2		D306 'to St-Paulet de Caisson'
70.8		D343 'to St-Julien', St-Paulet
72.3		'to St-Julien de Peyrolas'
73.1		D141, St-Julien de Peyrolas
74.1		D901 'to Laval-St Roman'
74.8		D141 'to St-Martin d'Ardèche'
75.3	▲	300m single-lane bridge
75.7		Hôtel Le Bellevue, St-Martin

	Elevation
	St-Martin d'Ardèche

1200	
800	
400	
0m	Avignon Pujaut Tavel St-Laurent des Arbres Tresques Sabran Donnat
	0km 10 20 30 40 50 60 70

See Day 2 p379

START: DAY 2
St-Martin d'Ardèche

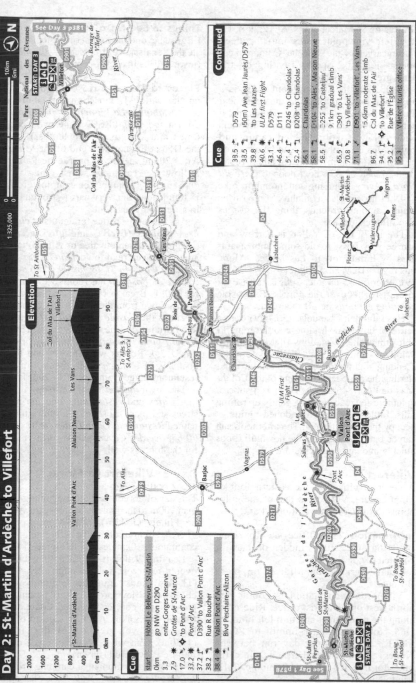

Day 2: St-Martin d'Ardèche to Villefort

Elevation

Cue

start		Hôtel Le Bellevue, St-Martin
0km		go NW on D290
3.3	✱	enter Gorges Reserve
7.9	✱	Grottes de St-Marcel
17.0	↖ ✧	'to Pont d'Arc
33.2		Pont d'Arc
37.2	↙	D390 to Vallon Pont d'Arc
38.2		Rue R Boucher
38.4	✱ ↑	Vallon Pont d'Arc
		Blvd Peschaire-Alizon

Continued

Cue

33.5	↖	D579
33.5	↖	(50m) Ave Jean Jaurès/D579
39.8	↖	'to Les Mazes'
40.6		ULM first Flight
43.1	↖	D579
46.4		D111
5˙.4	↖	D245 'to Chandolas'
52.4	↖	D208 'to Chandolas'
56.1		Chandolas
58.1	↖	D104 'to Alès' Maison Neuve
58.5	↖	D252 'to Casteljau'
65.5	↖	9.1km gradual climb
70.8	↖	D901 'to Les Vans'
71.1	↖	'to Villefort'
	◄	D901 'to Villefort' Les Vans
867		~5.6km moderate climb
94.1	↖	Col du Mas de l'Air
95.2	✧	'to Villefort'
95.3	↖	Rue de l'Église
		Villefort tourist office

LANGUEDOC-ROUSSILLON

Grottes de St-Marcel caves. At 12.2km, La Rouvière **viewpoint** looks into the deep chasm carved by the Ardèche. Colourful canoeists look like specks floating on the dark, greenish waters.

At 33.2km, the striking **Pont d'Arc** is a huge limestone arch astride the river near the town of Vallon Pont d'Arc. Hundreds, if not thousands, of canoeists and kayakers glide below it daily. **Guided canoe and kayak trips** down the river can be arranged in Vallon (38.4km) at Escapade Loisirs (☎ 04 75 88 07 87), next door to *Café du Nord*. Caving, climbing and mountain bike (VTT) trips are also available. Some of the many camping grounds along the gorges also offer canoe hire.

The D579 out of Vallon is narrow and can be very busy. Avoid some unpleasantness by turning off to Les Mazes. Along this road is **ULM First Flight** (☎ 04 75 36 85 79), offering 15-minute, 200FF, ultra-light aircraft flights over the gorges. Expensive *camping grounds* lie off this road.

Head through Chandolas (56.1km) onto a series of tiny roads leading into the remarkable limestone formations of the **Bois de Païolive**. Climb an easy 9.1km before descending slightly to Les Vans (71.1km) and starting the more serious ascent of the **Col du Mas de l'Air** (846m). The D901 is a superb, quiet forested road, winding gently up rolling hills. Little more than abandoned buildings occupy the top of the col. The afternoon sun can be ferocious here but the downhill drops quickly into laid-back Villefort.

Villefort

A peaceful village at the eastern foot of Mont Lozère, Villefort is one of the entry points to the Cévennes National Park.

Information The Office de Tourisme (☎ 04 66 46 87 30) is hidden on narrow, cobbled rue de l'Église.

Crédit Agricole du Midi is on place Bosquet.

Villefort's train station is about 1km north-west of the tourist office. Ride north along the main street and turn left onto the D66, following signs uphill to 'Gare SNCF'. Six trains per day run between Nîmes and Clermont-Ferrand; all carry bikes for free. It's about a 90-minute, 76FF trip to Nîmes.

Things to See & Do Wander along rue de l'Église beyond the tourist office to appreciate the **Renaissance streetscape** – the *mairie* (town hall) is in a 15th-century building.

Places to Stay & Eat Nestled discreetly up the valley 1.5km from the centre of town, *Camping La Vignette* (☎ 04 66 46 83 56) charges 24/40FF for one/two people (open mid-May to mid-September). Take the D66 at the northern end of the village. After 200m veer right on rue de Palhère. Follow the 'camping' signs, going right onto rue de la Lampe. The camping ground is 400m along this very narrow, rough track in a field on your right.

Ask the tourist office for details of *chambres d'hôtes* (B&Bs) and *gîtes d'étape* (lodgings in a remote area or village) in the area. In the centre of town, *Hôtel Chez Fernand* (☎ 04 66 46 81 38, fax 04 66 46 89 23, 9 place du Bosquet) has rooms with shower for 210FF. Breakfast/dinner costs 28/65FF.

Just down from the tourist office and adjacent to the *Casino supermarket* in place du Portalet is the FFCT-recommended *Hôtel Balme* (☎ 04 66 46 80 14, fax 04 66 46 85 26). Rooms with shower and toilet cost 295FF. *Menus* (set meals) in the restaurant range from 130FF to 200FF.

The town *market* is on Thursday morning. *Cafes* and *restaurants* line the main street and place Bosquet. The intriguingly named *Restaurant Chez Tintin* (☎ 04 66 46 90 83, ave des Cévennes) is worth visiting for the food as well.

Day 3: Villefort to Florac
3½–7 hours, 72km

This day offers constant thrills, gaining more than 900m to the granite-boulder-strewn Col de Finiels (1541m), near Mont Lozère. There's 24km of climbing before an almost continuous, 30km descent to Florac (542m).

Leaving Villefort, cross a long bridge over a reservoir, ride through tiny Altier (11.7km) and begin the relatively easy climb to Le Bleymard (30.1km), passing the picturesque, conifer-shrouded **Château du Champ** at 13.6km. Another 13.1km of uphill brings you to the **Col des Tribes** (1130m) from where you can coast down into Le Bleymard (1069m).

The village's municipal camping ground *La Gazelle* (☎ 04 66 48 60 48) is pleasantly

Day 3: Villefort to Florac

See Day 2 p379
See Day 4 p384

LANGUEDOC-ROUSSILLON

Elevation

Cue		
start		V'llefort tourist office
0km		go N on Rue de l'Église
0.1	↰	D901
0.7	↱	D901 'to Le Bleymard'
1.5	↱◆	D901 'to Le Bleymard'
11.7	◀	Altier
	▲✹	'5km gradual climb
13.6	✹	Château du Champ
26.7		Col des Tribes
29.4	↰	D20 to Centre Ville'
30.1		Le Bleymard

Cue		Continued
31.9	↖	D20 'to Mont Lozère'
	▲	9km moderate climb
36.8		Mont Lozère sk resort
41.9		Col de Finiels
51.4		D998 'to Pont ce Montvert'
52.0		D998 'to Florac: Pont de Montvert
65.9		Cocures
63.1		Bédoués
70.5	↰	N106 'to Florac'
71.6	↱	D16 'to Florac'
72.0		Florac tourist office

START: DAY 3 Villefort

START: DAY 4 Florac

located on the Lot River at the entrance to town. The fees are 14/22.50FF for one/two people; hot water costs extra. Nearby, there is a signposted, 11km **VTT trail** to *Les Sources du Lot* (the source of the Lot River). The circuit is one of 70 walks and bike trails described on a guide published by the Department of Lozère, available from tourist offices in the region. Le Bleymard is on the GR70 – *Le Chemin (Path) de Robert Louis Stevenson* (see the 'Travels with a Donkey' boxed text earlier in the chapter).

Climb steadily from Le Bleymard to the ski resort of Mont Lozère (1397m). **VTT hire** is available at the main chalet on the D20 – this is also a PNC information centre.

Continue up through a landscape of dwarf trees to **Col de Finiels** (40.9km) where weathering has created giant granite 'marbles' which lie amid fields of colourful wild flowers. There are panoramic views to distant hazy, rolling ranges. Walk in the fields next to the road and soak up the atmosphere.

The 700m-in-11km descent to Pont de Montvert (52km) is fantastic fun. The village celebrates the anniversary of Stevenson's donkey trip each June/July with displays, walks and theatre, and it has a PNC information booth beside the pretty Tarn River. After a brief easy climb out of Pont de Montvert – a 50m gain in 2km – the downhill to Florac goes on and on. It's one of those delightful French cycling routes which snakes along the edge of a river gorge, crossing crumbling stone bridges, meandering through shady oak, chestnut and pine forest, offering wonderful panoramas of curvaceous, rocky mountain ranges and distant green hills. Every time you stop, the sound of the tumbling Tarn replaces the rush of wind in your ears.

Florac

The first sight of Florac's drab, narrow, car-thronged main street, ave Jean Monestier, is decidedly uninspiring. The town's redeeming feature is its plane-tree-shaded square, Esplanade Marceau Farelle, the next street to the west. It's full of cafes and restaurants and is overlooked by the prominent buttresses of the Causse Méjean.

Information The tourist office (☎ 04 66 45 01 14, fax 04 66 45 25 80) is on ave Jean Monestier.

In the restored 17th-century Château de Florac on place du Palais is the PNC's Maison du Parc (☎ 04 66 49 53 01, fax 04 66 49 53 02, e pnc@bsi.fr). A detailed park guidebook (70FF) is available in English.

Banque Populaire du Midi is at 68 ave Jean Monestier.

VTTs can be hired from Cévennes Évasion (☎/fax 04 66 45 18 31, e cevennes .evasion@wanadoo.fr), 5 place Boyer, off Esplanade Farelle. Maps of PNC trails supplied, as is transport if required. While not a bike shop, it also has bike tools and may be able to help with emergency repairs. The company also organises caving and rock climbing expeditions for groups.

Things to See & Do Ask the tourist office for details on many **outdoor activities** – caving, canyoning, kayaking and canoeing. The Maison du Parc has **hiking** information.

Gliders take off from the Florac aerodrome (☎ 04 66 45 15 46, fax 04 66 45 67 89) on the Plaine Chanet in the centre of the Causse Méjean, about 17km south-west of Florac.

Places to Stay The two municipal camping grounds are each 1.5km from the town centre in opposite directions. Both charge around 40/55FF for one/two people. *Le Pont du Tarn* (☎ 04 66 45 18 26, fax 04 66 45 26 43) is off the N106 going north to Mende (open from April to mid-October). To the south, *La Tière* (☎ 04 66 45 00 53) is on the D907 (open from mid-June through August).

Florac has a couple of gîtes d'étape. *L'Ancien Presbytère* (☎ 04 66 45 24 54, 18 rue du Pêcheur) and the town-run central *gîte* (☎ 04 66 45 14 93, 1 rue du Four) charge around 50FF for a bed. Reservation is essential.

Hôtel Central et de la Poste (☎ 04 66 45 00 01, fax 04 66 45 14 04, 4 ave Maurice Tour), near place du Souvenir, charges from 170FF for rooms with shower. *Hôtel Les Gorges du Tarn* (☎ 04 66 45 00 63, fax 04 66 45 10 56, 48 rue du Pêcheur) has basic rooms from 180FF and doubles with shower for 250FF. Best value is *Grand Hôtel Central du Parc* (☎ 04 66 45 03 05, fax 04 66 45 11 81, 47 ave Jean Monestier, where spacious doubles with shower start from 240FF.

Places to Eat There's a *Champion* supermarket plus an *alimentation générale* on ave Jean Monestier and a *convenience store* at 13 rue La Croisette. Local foods – liqueurs, jams, cheese, chestnut concoctions – are available at the *Maison du Pays Cévenol (3 rue du Pêcher)*.

You can eat at most of Florac's hotels. *La Source du Pêcher* (☎ 04 66 45 03 01, *1 rue du Mémurei), near the town hall, has a lovely location on the Pêcher River. Don't budge the *Chapeau Rouge* (☎ 04 66 45 23 40, *4 rue Théophile Roussel)* by its shed-like cover. Excellent regional *menus* start at around 70FF.

Day 4: Florac to Valleraugue
3½–6½ hours, 66.6km

There's a lot of climbing early in the day, some of it steep. It's basically all up from Florac to Mont Aigoual, a gain of more than 020m in 38km. The best part? After that you don't need to turn a pedal for 28km. Start early and there'll be almost no traffic.

Leaving Florac (542m), the road undulates gently to little Fraissinet de Fourques (18.4km; 736m), where a moderate climb – it would be hard under a baking afternoon sun – begins to the slightly schizoid **Col de Perjuret**. Signs indicate the pass is at 1028m altitude when approached from one direction and 1031m from another. Take a break here to soak in the panorama of the PNC. Dramatic rock outcrops jut from the desolate Causse Méjean and virtually the only sounds are birdsong and distant peals of cow bells. It's a spiritually enriching environment.

The climb continues towards **Mont Aigoual** along a ridge through cool conifer forest with occasional picnic tables and views which improve all the time. After another 14.4km, and perhaps 90 minutes in low gears, veer right to reach the 1567m summit, where 360° views of receding lumpy forested ranges and bare plateaux unfold from the castle-like tower of the weather observatory. There's a *gîte d'étape* (☎ 04 67 82 62 78), *snack bar*, toilet and souvenir shop here.

When you can tear yourself away, ride 400m back to a junction and take the road to the right which begins the continuous downhill to Valleraugue. Descend through the Col de la Sereyrède (1300m) to L'Espérou (46.9km). *Shops* and *cafes* here make it a convenient lunch stop; otherwise, continue cruising downward towards Valleraugue (438m). Glance up occasionally to the summit of Aigoual where the now-diminutive observatory can still be spotted, perched on the edge of the precipice.

Valleraugue
This village in the steep-sided valley of the river Hérault was founded in the 12th century. Its Pont de la Confrérie is the only one in the valley to have survived the Hérault's floods for eight centuries.

The tourist office (☎ 04 67 82 25 10) is in Quartier Horts. A Crédit Agricole is in Quartier André Chamson. There is no bike shop in town.

Things to See & Do A track called the **4000 Steps** leads from Valleraugue to the Aigoual summit through heath and forests of chestnut and beech. It takes about five hours return with 1230m of climbing. There's an annual footrace up the track in June.

Les Grands Causses

West of the Cévennes lies the Parc Naturel Régional des Grands Causses (☐ www.parcs-naturels-regionaux.tm.fr). This 315,000-hectare area of harsh limestone plateaux, forming the southern rim of the ancient Massif Central. Scorched in summer and bitterly windswept in winter, their stony surfaces have allowed water to filter through, forming a labyrinth of subterranean caverns.

Rivers, such as the Tarn, have cut deep gorges which divide the plateaux into four distinct sections. Causse Méjean, averaging around 1000m, is the highest of these sections, as well as the most barren and isolated. It is accessible via the steep and tortuous D16 west of Florac or it can be surveyed from the Col de Perjuret on the D907 south of the town (see Day 4 of the Remote Cévennes ride). Occasional fertile depressions dot the poor pastures and streams disappear into the limestone through sinkholes, funnels and fissures. **Cévennes Évasion** (see Information for Florac) organises trips to the Grands Causses.

LANGUEDOC-ROUSSILLON

LANGUEDOC-ROUSSILLON

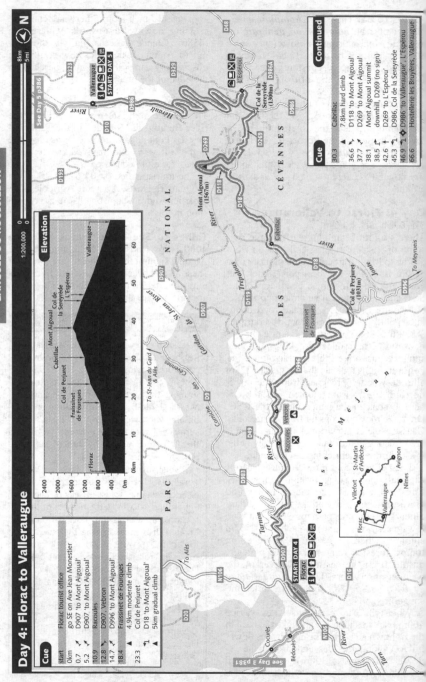

Day 4: Florac to Valleraugue

Cue

start		Florac tourist office
0km		go SE on Ave Jean Monestier
0.7	↗	D907 'to Mont Aigoual'
5.2	↗	D907 'to Mont Aigoual'
10.9		Racoules
12.8	↖	D907, Vebron
14.7	↗	D996 'to Mont Aigoual'
18.4		Fraissinet de Fourques
	▲	4.9km moderate climb
23.3	↰	D18 'to Mont Aigoual'
	▲	5km gradual climb

Cue — Continued

30.3		Cabrillac
	▲	7.8km hard climb
36.6	↰	D118 'to Mont Aigoual'
37.7	↱	D269 'to Mont Aigoual'
38.1		Mont Aigoual summit
38.5	↱	downhill, D269 (no sign)
42.6		D269 'to L'Espérou'
45.3	↱	D986, Col de la Sereyrède
46.9	◆	D986 'to Valleraugue', L'Espérou
56.6		Hostellerie les Bruyères, Valleraugue

Elevation

Florac — Fraissinet de Fourques — Col de Perjuret — Cabrillac — Mont Aigoual — Col de la Sereyrède — L'Espérou — Valleraugue

Places to Stay & Eat The camping ground, *Camping Le Pied d'Aigoual*, is about 2.5km before town on the D986. It charges 42/64FF for one/two people.

The FFCT-recommended *Hostellerie Les Bruyères* (☎ *04 67 82 20 06, D986)* has doubles with shower and toilet from 250FF. Breakfast costs 32FF and its restaurant has *menus* from 85FF to 140FF. Also FFCT-recommended and on the D986 at the top end of town, *Hôtel Le Petit Luxembourg* ☎ *04 67 82 20 44, fax 04 67 82 24 66)* charges from 220FF. Its restaurant is opposite and has *menus* from 85FF to 238FF. Breakfast costs 30FF.

The *Alimentation La Valleraugeroise* (6 *Quartier André Chamson)* supplies basic groceries. For a good coffee, try *Café du Jardin* (☎ *04 67 82 23 34)* on rue Luxembourg. *Pizzéria Restaurant Le Mourètou* ☎ *04 67 82 22 30, route Aigoual)* serves tasty takeaway pizza.

Day 5: Valleraugue to Nîmes
½–6½ hours, 96.1km

It's a long-distance day but, after 9.8km of moderate to very steep climbing early on, the trend is decidedly downhill.

Follow the river out of Valleraugue down to Pont de l'Hérault (15.4km), where you turn onto the fast-trafficked D999. Shortly after, pull off onto the D11 to climb to Lumène. After the village there is no water or services for a long 16km before La Cadière (38.1km). The hard 7.4km climb of the **Montagne de la Fage** is on the narrowest, most twisting road imaginable. Views reach back to Mont Aigoual's observatory. A dangerous descent follows on the single-lane road. Beware oncoming vehicles on the many blind bends. (The D999 from Pont de l'Hérault to La Cadière, though much less pleasant, could be a faster, easier alternative.)

St-Hippolyte du Fort (42.6km) – quaintly called 'St-Hippo' (pronounced ee-poh) by locals – has a big *Super U* supermarket but not much else to divert the cyclist. Its claim to fame is as the 'world capital of the safety footwear industry'. Cycles Bonnefoux (☎ 04 66 77 21 10) is on the corner of rue du Fort and rue du Fondeville, not far from Super U.

Towards Durfort (53.1km), an almost imperceptible rise briefly interrupts the downward trend. Back on tiny roads now, descend eastwards via Canaules-et-Argen-

tières (61.7km) and Savignargues (65.8km). There's more traffic on the D907 approaching Nîmes, but probably not too much until you cross the N106 and enter the built-up area outside the city. From 95km, follow the 'Office de Tourisme' signs to the finish.

Nîmes
Founded by Augustus Caesar as Nemausensis, the city reached its zenith in the 2nd century AD, receiving its water via an aqueduct system that included the triple-decked Pont du Gard, 23km north-east. Nowadays, Nîmes is graced by some of the most well-preserved Roman public buildings in Europe. Spanish influence is felt during the three annual *férias* (bullfighting festivals).

Information The main tourist office (☎ 04 66 67 29 11, fax 04 66 21 81 04, ▣ www .nimes.mnet.fr) is at 6 rue Auguste. It supplies a calendar of special events in Nîmes. The annexe (☎ 04 66 84 18 13) inside the train station is closed on winter weekends.

Commercial banks line blvds Victor Hugo and Amiral Courbet.

There are two email/Internet cafes. Le Vauban (☎ 04 66 76 09 71) is at 34ter rue Clérisseau. Le Pluggin (☎ 04 66 21 49 51; closed Sunday) is at 17 rue Porte d'Ales.

Bike shops include Cycles Rebour (☎ 04 66 76 24 92), 38 rue Hôtel Dieu, Cycles Ginet (☎/fax 04 66 84 16 03), 2040 ave Maréchal Juin, and Passieu Cycles (☎ 04 66 21 09 16, fax 04 66 21 69 19), 2 place Montcalm.

Things to See & Do In the centre of Nîmes is the Roman amphitheatre, **Les Arènes** (☎ 04 66 76 72 77), reminiscent of Rome's Colosseum. Built around AD 100 to seat 24,000 spectators, it is better preserved than any other such structure in France, retaining even its upper storey, unlike its Arles counterpart. Covered by a modern high-tech removable roof from October to April, it is used for theatre, music concerts and bullfights.

Near the main tourist office is the remarkably well-preserved, rectangular, Greek-style temple called the **Maison Carrée** (Square House; ☎ 04 66 36 26 76). It was built around AD 5 to honour Augustus' two nephews, and has been a meeting hall (in the Middle Ages), a private residence, a stables

LANGUEDOC-ROUSSILLON

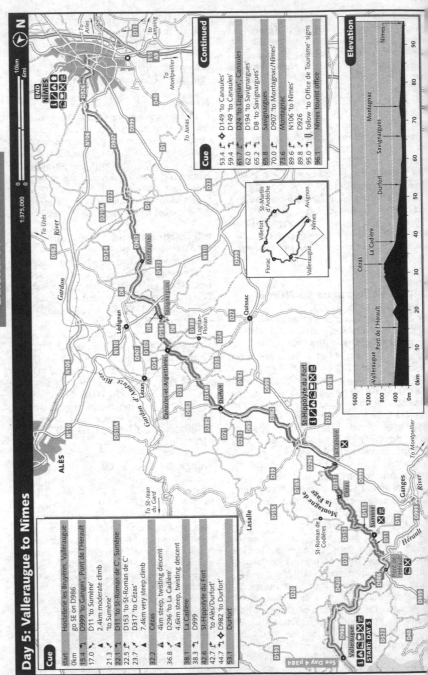

Day 5: Valleraugue to Nîmes

Cue

start		Hostellerie les Bruyères, Valleraugue
0km		go SE on D986
15.4	↰	D999 'to Ganges', Pont de l'Hérault
17.0	↰	D11 'to Sumène'
21.3	◣	2.4km moderate climb
		'to Sumène'
22.1	↰	D11 'to St-Roman de C', Sumène
22.5	↱	D153 'to St-Roman de C'
23.7	↱	D317 'to Cézas'
	◣	7.4km very steep climb
32.2		Cézas
	◢	4km steep, twisting descent
36.8	↱	D296 'to La Cadière'
	◢	4.6km steep, twisting descent
38.1		La Cadière
38.3	↰	D999
42.6		St-Hippolyte du Fort
44.7	↱	'to Alès/Durfort'
44.7	↱ ◇	D982 'to Durfort'
53.1		Durfort

Cue **Continued**

53.4	↰ ◇	D149 'to Canaules'
59.4	↱	D149 'to Canaules'
61.7	↰	D24 'to Logrian', Canaules
62.0	↱	D194 'to Savignargues'
65.2	↰	D8 'to Savignargues'
65.8		Savignargues
70.0	↱	D907 'to Montagnac/Nîmes'
73.6		Montagnac
89.6	↱	N106 'to Nîmes'
89.8	↱	D926
95.0	↱ ℹ	follow 'to Office de Tourisme' signs
96.1		Nîmes tourist office

Elevation

(in the 17th century), a church and, after the Revolution, an archive. Across the square to the west is the striking **Carrée d'Art** (Square of Art; ☎ 04 66 76 35 77), containing the municipal library and Musée d'Art Contemporain (Contemporary Art Museum).

The **Musée de Vieux Nîmes** (☎ 04 66 36 00 64) has historical exhibits in the episcopal palace 50m south of the **Cathédrale de St Castor** on place aux Herbes. Also interesting, the **Musée d'Archéologie** (☎ 04 66 67 12 57), 13 blvd de l'Amiral Courbet, houses Roman and pre-Roman relics unearthed around Nîmes.

Places to Stay The municipal camping ground *Domaine de la Bastide* (☎ 04 66 38 09 21, route de Générac) is about 4km south of town on the D13 heading towards Générac (on the Day 2 route in the Majesty of the Romans ride in the Provence & the Côte d'Azur chapter). It is open all year and charges 41/67FF for one/two people.

If you intend to do the Upper Languedoc ride, a more convenient camping ground may be *Les Chênes* (☎ 04 66 80 99 07), about 200m south of Junas and signposted from the D40, 25km south-west of Nîmes. It has a pool, is open Easter to mid-October and charges around 35/55FF.

The *Auberge de Jeunesse* (☎ 04 66 70 49 79 or 04 66 23 25 04, fax 04 66 23 84 27, chemin de la Cigale) is 2km north-west of the centre. Beds are 47FF a night; reservation is advisable in summer. VTTs are available for hire.

The Gîtes de France office (☎ 04 66 27 94 94, fax 04 66 27 94 95, place des Arènes), inside the Maison du Tourisme, arranges *rural accommodation* as well as *B&B* in town.

Many cheap, decent hotels are situated in the old city. *Hôtel Le Lisita* (☎ 04 66 67 66 00, fax 04 66 76 22 30, 2 blvd des Arènes) has dreary singles/doubles with shower from 100/180FF. *Hôtel de la Maison Carrée* (☎ 04 66 67 32 89, fax 04 66 76 22 57, 14 rue de la Maison Carrée) has small but clean doubles with shower, toilet and TV for around 240FF.

Slightly more upmarket *Hôtel de l'Amphithéâtre* (☎ 04 66 67 28 51, fax 04 66 67 07 79, 4 rue des Arènes) has doubles with shower and toilet from 170FF to 250FF, while colourful *Hôtel Central* (☎ 04 66 67 27 75, fax 04 66 21 77 79, 2 place du Château) charges about 230FF for doubles with bath and TV.

Places to Eat Nîmes is well endowed with hypermarkets, including a *Géant Casino* (54 rue Forez), plus supermarkets such as *Prisunic* (blvd de l'Amiral Courbet). *Fruits Pas Cher* (ave Bir Hakeim) sells just that – cheap fruit.

Street markets are on Thursday in the old city during July and August, while the covered food market, *Les Halles*, between rue Guizot and rue des Halles, is open daily until midday.

Place aux Herbes and place du Marché have big bustling *cafes* in summer, but cool locals patronise the *cafes* around the Maison Carrée.

For cheap snacks *La Casa Don Miguel* (☎ 04 66 76 07 09, 18 rue de l'Horloge) does a variety of Spanish tapas.

Les Olivades (☎ 04 66 21 71 78, 18 rue Jean Reboul) specialises in local wines and has *menus* from 85FF. Close to Église St Baudille is *Le Menestrel* (☎ 04 66 67 54 45, 6 rue le Bavarois Nîmois), which has *menus* from around 60FF from Monday evening to Saturday.

For North African cuisine, try *Lakayna* (☎ 04 66 21 10 96, 18 rue de l'Étoile), which specialises in Algerian couscous variations, or *La Kasbah* (☎ 04 66 29 68 69, 6 rue de Générac), a medium-priced Moroccan restaurant.

Upper Languedoc

Duration	7 days
Distance	458.8km
Difficulty	moderate-hard
Start	Nîmes
End	Perpignan

A journey into the remote *arrière pays* (back country) of Upper Languedoc is like going back in time. In the area covered by the Parc Naturel Régional du Haut Languedoc nestle small villages which seem to have hardly changed in a century. The untouristed Monts de Lacaune and de l'Espinouse and the Montagne Noire are superb cycle-touring locales. Quiet roads with generally easy to moderate gradients climb low cols amid

LANGUEDOC-ROUSSILLON

jagged limestone outcrops, skirt pretty lakes and squeeze through narrow defiles.

Short climbs on Days 1 to 3 take you no higher than 380m. Day 4 is a big ride in the mountains, with a 24.5km downhill to end the day. Day 5 has another long ascent to start with but then goes downhill to fairy-tale Carcassonne. The two subsequent days to Perpignan undulate through the foothills of the Pyrenees, past ruined castles, reaching maximum altitudes of 711m (Day 6) and 667m (Day 7).

PLANNING
Maps
The route is covered by Michelin maps No 83 *Carcassonne, Montpellier, Nîmes* and No 86 *Bagnères-de-Luchon, Andorre, Perpignan* (both 1:200,000).

What to Bring
Indoor accommodation is very limited in most towns en route. Bring camping equipment to take advantage of the many camping grounds.

There are not many supply points such as supermarkets between Sommières (Day 1) and Clermont l'Hérault (Day 2 destination) – carry some supplies with you or go off-route, say to Aniane (near St-Jean de Fos, Day 2) if in need.

GETTING TO/FROM THE RIDE
Nîmes is the end of the Remote Cévennes ride detailed earlier in this chapter. Perpignan is only about 37km from Cerbère, the start of the Raid Pyrénéen (see the Pyrenees chapter). A scenic back route links Perpignan to Foix, the start of two rides in the Pyrenees chapter.

Nîmes
See the Remote Cévennes ride (p376) for information on getting to/from Nîmes.

Perpignan
Train Perpignan's train station is about 1.5km south-west of the tourist office on ave du Général de Gaulle.

Up to five bike-carrying trains run daily to Nîmes (141FF, 2½ to 3½ hours) and one runs to Avignon (166FF, about three hours), the start of the Remote Cévennes ride. Numerous faster TGVs also serve these destinations but won't carry bikes unbagged.

Frequent trains travel to Cerbère (43FF, 45 minutes, all trains carry bikes). To link to Foix, go via Toulouse on the once daily non-TGV train that takes bikes (203FF, 4¼ hours).

Bus From Britain, the European Bike Express service (see Bus under Continental Europe in the Getting There & Away chapter) charges UK£169 (return) to take a passenger and bike to Perpignan.

Bicycle Riding to Cerbère is not recommended. The N114 is the only road you can use for the last 20km – it's busy and unpleasant a lot of the time, and hilly all the time. You have to use it in the other direction, anyway. Once will be enough.

To Foix, ride a superbly scenic route along the winding back roads via Ille-sur-Têt, Puilaurens, through the Défilé d'Able (D107) to Belfort, then to Bélesta and Lavelanet. All these towns are possible overnight stops on the two- to three-day ride (about 170km).

THE RIDE
Nîmes
See Nîmes (pp385–7) in the Remote Cévennes ride for information about accommodation and other services.

Day 1: Nîmes to St-Martin de Londres
3–6 hours, 63km
This easy day's ride leaves the busy Nîmes region via ancient Sommières. Further on amid craggy limestone outcrops, lie sleepy villages and the sun-drenched, ordered vineyards of the Pays d'Oc. There is only one notable climb, a gradual gain of about 180m over 7km, finishing at around the 55km mark.

The majority of the first 28km is on the dull, flat D40, which at least has a bike lane or shoulder most of the way.

Modern Sommières (28km) is carved up by nasty roads, but its old city is a pleasant, car-free haven with a central square surrounded by covered arched walkways. Plenty of *cafes* make it a nice place to relax.

Cycle on through the Pays d'Oc wine region. Shadeless vineyards dominate the scene along with views to distant silvery orange limestone massifs. A couple of these

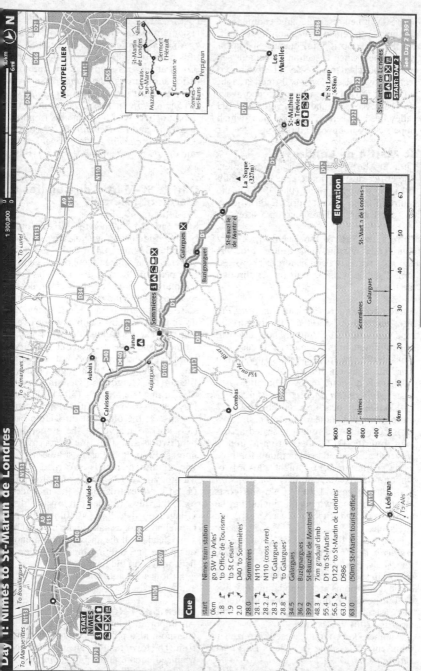

Day 1: Nîmes to St-Martin de Londres

LANGUEDOC-ROUSSILLON

Cue		
start	0km	Nîmes train station
	0km	go SW 'to Arles'
	1.8	'to Office de Tourisme'
	1.9	'to St Cesaire'
	2.0	D40 'to Sommières'
	28.0	Sommières
	28.1	N110
	28.2	N110 (cross river)
	28.3	'to Galargues'
	28.8	'to Galargues'
	34.5	Galargues
	36.2	Buzignargues
	39.9	St-Bauzille de Montmel
	48.3	7km gradual climb
	55.4	D1 'to St-Martin'
	56.5	D122 'to St-Martin de Londres'
	63.0	D986
	63.0	(50m) St-Martin tourist office

Elevation

near St-Mathieu resemble large canine teeth and one has a ruined chateau on its summit. The **Pic St Loup** (658m) outside St-Martin was formed when a section of ancient sea bed was punched into the sky. The two raised sections would once have formed a right angle but the join is missing, eroded away over eons. Now a rounded, garrigue-covered valley lies between the massive slabs which slope steeply in opposite directions.

St-Martin de Londres

Little St-Martin lies in the Lamalou valley. The Office de Tourisme (☎/fax 04 67 55 09 59) is on the main street (the D986) in the centre of town. Crédit Agricole du Midi is at 3 ave Littoral. There is no bike shop.

Things to See & Do The 11th-century church of **St Martin**, in the centre of the village, has recently been restored. The **GR60** long-distance walking trail passes through the town.

Places to Stay & Eat The *Camping Pic St Loup* (☎ 04 67 55 00 53) is along a side road from the D122, 400m before town. The minimum high season tariff is based on a forfait of 69FF for two people (open from April through September).

There is no hotel in town, but there is a hostel, *Auberge du Bayle* (☎/fax 04 67 55 72 16), 7km away near Frouzet (on the Day 2 route). Turn left at the 6.4km mark; the hostel is 700m along a rough, unsealed access road from the D122. Open from March to November, it has 30 beds in rooms for three to six people for 60FF a night, plus a two-person 'studio' for 250FF. *Demi-pension* (half-board) costs 160FF. Camping costs 40/60FF for one/two people, including the use of a shared kitchen. Reservations are advisable.

Nearby, in the centre of Frouzet, *Le Hameau de l'Étoile* (☎ 04 67 55 75 73, fax 04 67 55 09 10) can be reserved by groups in summer and is always booked out early. It has rooms accommodating one, two or four people. A double room with breakfast costs 350FF for two; with all meals the tariff is 320FF *per person*.

Another 7km en route, west of Frouzet, at minuscule Causse de la Selle is *Le Vieux Chêne* (☎ 04 67 73 11 00, fax 04 67 73 10 54), where doubles with shower and toilet

cost 320FF, demi-pension 380FF, and restaurant *menus* from 110FF to 210FF.

An *alimentation générale* is on St Martin's place de la Fontaine. *Café des Autobus* is at the bus stop opposite the tourist office and there is a *boulangerie* in town.

Restaurants include *Mas du Loup* (☎ 04 67 55 00 43), on the D986 south of the tourist office, which has menus from 65FF to 250FF; and *La Pastourelle* (☎ 04 67 5. 72 78, 350 chemin de la Prairie), a little out of town, with *menus* from 110FF to 270FF.

Day 2: St-Martin de Londres to Clermont l'Hérault
2½–5 hours, 49.5km

Start early to conquer the hills before the blazing midday sun sets in. After Causse de la Selle (244m, 15.4km), the gradient is easier but the route still continues gently up to a peak of 280m at 19.3km. Descend to the plains for a gentle idyll along deserted roads between vineyards.

To start, climb to Frouzet then coast down past the weir to a high bridge over the Hérault. There's **canoe hire** (☎ 04 67 73 1. 45) here, and a steep climb out to Causse de la Selle (15.4km). The reward is a delightful, wriggling descent through a shady defile and the Gorges de l'Hérault to tourist St Guilhem-le-Désert (30.1km), where Kayapuna (☎ 04 67 57 30 25) hires canoes.

Pause at the old **Pont du Diable** bridge (33.2km) to marvel at the stonemason's handiwork and the fine vista over the gorges. Enjoy the classic southern French wine country on mostly level roads between Montpeyroux (38.2km) and Jonquières (42km). Vineyards flank the meandering road, the rows of vines run towards distant villages on the slopes of limestone hills. Crenellated ridges bake under a hot summer sun. Cicadas fill the air with their monotonous noise and nothing much, besides cyclists, moves in the heat.

Follow signs into Clermont across a new autoroute.

Clermont l'Hérault

An important player in the wine industry, Clermont also produces olive oil and dried fruit. The town features an attractive pedestrianised square and a big *centre commercial*, off the N9, on the outskirts.

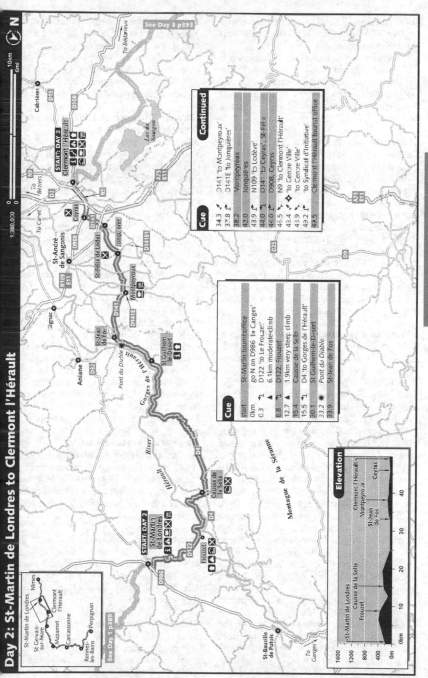

Day 2: St-Martin de Londres to Clermont l'Hérault

LANGUEDOC-ROUSSILLON

Cue

start		St-Martin tourist office
0km	↗	go N on D986 'to Ganges'
0.3	↱	D122 'to Le Frouzet'
	◀	6.1km moderate climb
8.8	◀	D122, Frouzet
12.7	◀	1.9km very steep climb
15.4		Causse de la Selle
15.5	↱	D4 'to Gorges de l'Hérault'
30.1		St Guilhem-le-Desert
33.2	✳	Pont du Diable
33.9		St-Jean de Fos

Cue — **Continued**

34.3	↗	D141 'to Montpeyroux'
37.8	↰	D141E 'to Jonquières'
38.2		Montpeyroux
42.0		Jonquières
43.9	↱	N109 'to Lodève'
44.0	↰	D141 'to Ceyras', St-Félix
46.0	↱	D908, Ceyras
45.5		N9 'to Clermont l'Hérault'
43.4	✦	'to Centre Ville'
43.9	↱	'to Centre Ville'
49.2	↰	'to Syndicat d'Initiative'
49.5		Clermont l'Hérault tourist office

Elevation

Information The Office de Tourisme (☎ 04 67 96 23 86, fax 04 67 96 98 58) is at 9 rue René Gosse.

Banks can be found on blvd Gambetta.

Cycles Respaud (☎ 04 67 96 00 98) is in the town centre at 37 blvd Gambetta. On the way to the Lac du Salagou is Ozone Bike Shop and VTT Hire (☎ 04 67 96 27 17), ave Maréchal Joffre.

Things to See & Do Buy olive oil at the factory on ave Wilson; tour the premises in December and January (only). An unusual variety of long, green olives is exclusively available in Clermont.

The town's landmark buildings are the ruined **feudal castle** above the village (reached via the narrowest of streets) and the fine Gothic **Église de St Paul** on 2 rue Jean Jacques Rousseau.

Eight **VTT circuits**, graded from very easy to difficult, are marked out around the artificial Lac du Salagou, 5.6km west of town; follow the Day 3 route and look for the 'to Lac/to camping' signs.

Places to Stay & Eat As well as the lake, the huge recreation area Base de Plein Air du Salagou (☎ 04 67 96 05 71) contains *Camping Municipal Le Salagou*, open all year. The tariff is 47/59FF for one/two people. Gîtes with four or five beds are available by the week only in July and August (2030FF) and for 290FF per night at other times.

The tourist office has a list of *farm stay*, *B&B* and other *gîte* accommodation in and around Clermont.

In town, the *Hôtel-Restaurant Le Terminus* (☎ 04 67 96 10 66 or ☎ 04 67 88 45 00, 11 allée Roger Salengro), 300m downhill from the tourist office, has doubles from 250FF, a 65FF lunch *menu* and dinner *menus* from 87FF to 146FF. On the way out towards Béziers (south), the *Hôtel-Restaurant Sarac* (☎ 04 67 96 06 81, fax 04 67 88 07 30, route de Nébian) offers doubles with bath/shower and toilet from 250FF. *Menus* cost 120FF and 150FF.

The *Hyper U* hypermarket is in the centre commercial towards Béziers on the N9.

Cafes and *restaurants* cluster around the central square. For takeaways and light meals try the snack bar *Le Novelty* (☎ 04 67 96 93 22, place Martyrs de la Résistance). *Pizzéria Pinocchio* (☎ 04 67 96 22 51) is at 22 rue Marché. Sample Asian flavours a *New Viet Nam* (☎ 04 67 88 17 60, 4 rue Viala). *La Mangeoire* (☎ 04 67 96 36 37, 24 blvd Ledru Rollin) specialises in delectable seafood dishes such as *coquilles St Jacques* (scallops) and *foie gras maison* (home-made pâté). Meals start from 60FF

Day 3: Clermont l'Hérault to St Gervais-sur-Mare

2½–5 hours, 50.9km

Traverse a lumpy landscape with red soils, lakes and rivers, finishing on the edge of the Parc Naturel Régional du Haut Languedoc The two notable hills both have moderate gradients.

Ride around the south side of the Lac du Salagou, its blue waters contrasting strikingly with the red earth of the surrounding hills. The area is, not surprisingly, called La Vallée Rouge. A **bizarre sight** about 1km past Liausson (9km) is the sandy, barren soil covered in hundreds of people's names spelled out in large and small rocks.

Ten kilometres further, on the ascent of the Col de la Merquière, is the **palaeontological site** of La Lieude. The tracks of early reptiles and mammals (around 255 million-years-old) have been uncovered below the ruins of the Château Malavieille

At the ancient fortified village of Bous sagues, there is a signposted **walking tour** Enter the Parc Naturel Régional du Hau Languedoc approaching St Gervais.

St Gervais-sur-Mare

As the seventh stop for pilgrims and randon neurs on the Chemin de Compostelle (see the 'St Jacques de Compostelle Pilgrimage boxed text overleaf), diminutive St Gervais has convenient accommodation and food services.

Information The tourist office (☎ 04 67 23 61 15) is in the central place de l'Église It's only open seasonally. If closed, the tow hall (☎ 04 67 23 60 65) has information Crédit Agricole du Midi is on rue Castres There is no bike shop.

Things to See & Do The village's narrow alleys (**les calades**), interconnected by arched passages, are worth exploring on foot

St Gervais is also near the **GR653** long distance walking trail in the Parc Nature

Day 3: Clermont l'Hérault to St Gervais-sur-Mare

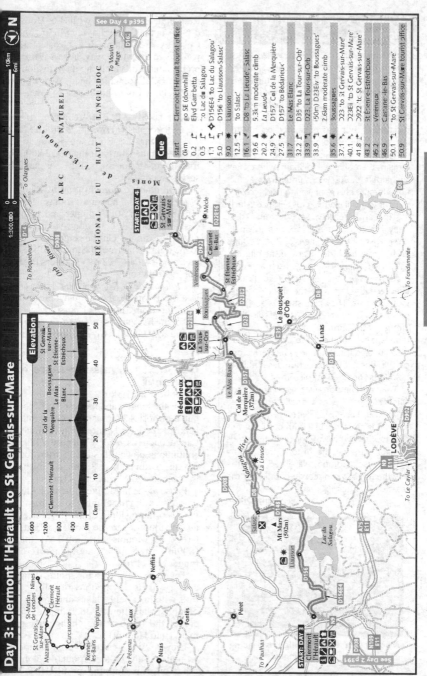

LANGUEDOC-ROUSSILLON

Cue

start		Clermont l'Hérault tourist office
0km		go SE (downhill)
0.2	⌐	Blvd Gambetta
0.5	⌐	'to Lac de Salagou'
1.1	✧	D156E4 'to Lac du Salagou'
5.0	⌐	D156 'to Liausson-Salasc'
9.0	✳	Liausson
12.5	✳	'to Salasc'
16.1	⌐	D8 'to La Lieude', Salasc
19.6	▲	5.3km moderate climb
20.2	✳	La Lieude
24.9	⌐	D157, Col de la Merquière
27.5	⌐	D157 'to Bédarieux'
31.7		Le Mas Blanc
32.2	⌐	D35 'to La Tour-sur-Orb'
33.9	⌐	D23, La Tour-sur-Orb
33.9	⌐	'(50m)' D23Eiv 'to Boussagues'
	▲	2.6km moderate climb
35.6	✳	Boussagues
37.1	⌐	D23 'to St Gervais-sur-Mare'
40.1	⌐	D23Eii 'to St Gervais-sur-Mare'
41.8	⌐	D922 'to St Gervais-sur-Mare'
43.2		St Etienne-Estréchoux
45.2		Vérenoux
46.9		Casane-le-Bas
50.1	⌐	'to St Gervais-sur-Mare'
50.9		St Gervais-sur-Mare tourist office

St Jacques de Compostelle Pilgrimage

For centuries pilgrims have travelled across France towards the Spanish city Santiago de Compostela (St Jacques de Compostelle in French) to pay homage to the Shrine of St James. It's said the Apostle James the Great came to Spain in AD 91 to spread the Gospel, but was beheaded on returning to Judaea, becoming the first Apostle matyred for his beliefs. Legend has it his remains were shipped to Spain, where they lay hidden for 800 years, until strange stars hovering over his grave led to its discovery.

Four 'official' routes cross France, starting in Paris, Vézelay, Le Puy and Arles. They merge at Puente la Reina in Spain after crossing the Pyrenees at Roncesvalles and Somport. At the height of the pilgrimage, towns along the way, such as Rocamadour (see the South-West France chapter), thrived with the influx of religious tourists. They built shelters and hospitals to house, feed and treat pilgrims, along with shrines and massive Romanesque churches. Ste Madeleine at Vézelay (see the Burgundy chapter) is one of the finest of these churches, built to hold large numbers of pilgrims.

The most important pilgrimage in the Middle Ages, it was virtually abandoned from the late-16th century. However, today it is again popular with both pilgrims and tourists, who walk or cycle hundreds of kilometres on the historic trail. Many aim to reach Compostela on 25 July, the day the tomb was discovered and now the feast of Santiago.

Sally Dillon

A hostel sign welcomes pilgrims heading for Santiago de Compostela.

Régional. This links with Le Bousquet d'Orb via the Col du Layrac (765m) and Col des Clares (600m). It's at least a full-day walk to go the whole way; access it from the pretty village of Mècle, about 4km along the narrow D22E16, which heads west from the D922 about 1.6km north-east of town.

Places to Stay & Eat A camping ground, *Le Clocher de Nayran* (☎/fax 04 67 23 64 16), is near the Bouissou River at Les Bouissounades; turn off the D922 800m before town. Its forfait is 48FF. A snack bar serves meals.

Auberge au Capucin (☎ 04 67 23 63 11, place de l'Église) has guest rooms or dormitory beds from 50FF; dinner and breakfast cost an extra 100FF. Its good-value *restaurant* offers dinner. On the route out of town to the right 800m from the tourist office, *Gîte de Cours* (☎ 04 67 23 69 49) offers B&B for 80FF per person.

Château de la Roche (☎ 04 67 23 60 87) is a B&B on the D922 just before town, charging from 100FF per person.

Town has an *alimentation générale* (1 rue Marianne), two *boulangeries* and a pleasant *cafe* (place de l'Église).

Day 4: St Gervais-sur-Mare to Mazamet

4½–9 hours, 91.3km

This is the longest and hardest day of the ride but the most scenic as you climb into the heart of the Parc Naturel Régional du Haut Languedoc. It's made easier by 24.5km of continuous downhill, starting from just before the 67km point at 833m and finishing at the entrance to Mazamet (241m).

Pause at the attractive village of Andabre before tackling the climb, facing the *versant nord* (northern slope) of the forested Mont de l'Espinouse, to Le Péras (8.1km) and Croix de Mounis (10.8km). At the top (809m), there is a panorama of rolling ranges and cliffs.

The route stays high for about 70km. The countryside is a symphony of rolling green hills with lush fields, lakes and forest, some of it pine plantation. At 38.3km, the D62 becomes the D150 at the change of department (into Hérault).

Eleven **VTT circuits** are signposted around La Salvetat-sur-Agout (44.5km), another pilgrim stopping point. Hire bikes

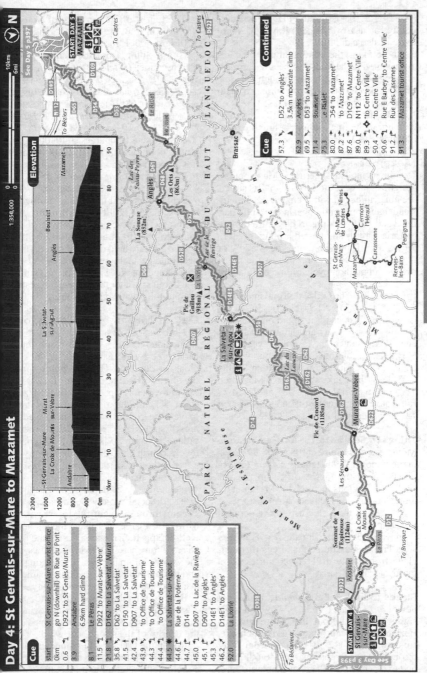

Day 4: St Gervais-sur-Mare to Mazamet

LANGUEDOC-ROUSSILLON

See Day 5 p397

See Day 3 p393

Cue

start		St Gervais-sur-Mare tourist office
0km	↑	go N (downhill) on Rue cu Pont
0.6	↑	D922 to St Geniès/Murat'
3.9	▲	Andabre
		6.9km hard climb
8.1	▲	Le Péras
11.5	↰	D922 to Murat-sur-Vèbre'
21.8	↰	D162 'to La Salvetat'
35.8	↱	D62 'to La Salvetat'
41.5	↰	D150 'to La Salvetat'
42.4	↰	D907 'to La Salvetat'
43.9	↱	'to Office de Tourisme'
44.3	↰	'to Office de Tourisme'
44.4	↱	'to Office de Tourisme'
44.5	✱	La Salvetat-sur-Agout
44.6	↰	Rue de la Poterne
44.7	↰	D14
45.0	↱	D907 'to Lac de la Raviège'
45.1	↱	D907 'to Angles'
45.3	↱	D14E1 'to Angles'
46.2	↰	D14E1 'to Angles'
52.0	↰	La Lixiné

Continued

Cue

57.3	↱	D52 'to Angles'
		3.5km moderate climb
62.9	▲	Angles
69.5	↰	D53 'to Mazamet'
71.4		Boissel
75.3		Le Ralet
80.0	↰	D54 'to Mazamet'
87.2	↱↰↰↱↱↱	'to 'Mazamet'
87.6	↰	D129 'to Mazamet'
89.0	↱	N112 'to Centre Ville'
89.3	◇	'to Centre Ville'
90.4	↱	'to Centre Ville'
90.6	↰↱	Rue E Barbey 'to Centre Ville'
91.2	↰	Rue des Casernes
91.3	↰	Mazamet tourist office

(☎ 04 67 97 65 13) at the Plage des Boul-douïres on nearby Lac de la Raviège, where there is also camping.

At 55.5km, the road number changes again, entering the Midi-Pyrénées department of Tarn and climbing gently through pine forest. This peaceful road gives glimpses back to the lake and the surrounding hills.

A 3.5km climb is followed by an easy, 2km hill to the final summit before the route plummets to Mazamet.

Mazamet

Despite its industrial heritage, Mazamet is a delightful place to stop overnight. Its streets are not gridlocked with frenzied traffic – instead, handsome buildings, large public gardens and parks feature in its centre and an historic walk is signposted around town. In the valley of the Thoré and the shadow of the Montagne Noire, Mazamet is the home town of champion cyclist Laurent Jalabert.

Information The Office de Tourisme (☎ 05 63 61 27 07, fax 05 63 98 24 16) is in rue des Casernes. It's open until 10 pm on Tuesdays but closed on Sunday afternoons in summer and all day Sunday the rest of the year.

Banks, including Crédit Lyonnais and BNP Paribas, cluster on cours René Reille.

At least three bike shops serve Mazamet. Try Gutkin Sports (☎ 05 63 61 44 02) at 27 rue Nouvela or Faury (☎ 05 63 98 87 74) at 127 ave Maréchal Foch.

Things to See & Do The Musée d'Histoire Mémoires de la Terre (☎ 05 63 98 99 76) is in the imposing 19th-century *maison Fuzier*, not far from the tourist office on rue des Casernes. Exhibits focus on the Mazamet region's human and archaeological history.

See Day 5 for a side trip to the perched village of **Hautpoul**.

In early July, the music fest **Fanfares sans Frontières** attracts hundreds of musicians from many different countries for a multi-day street party.

Places to Stay & Eat *Camping Municipal de la Lauze* (☎/fax 05 63 61 24 69) is a well-signposted 2km from the centre towards Béziers in the locality known as La Richarde, south of the N112. It is open from May through October and charges 46/68FF for one/two people. VTTs are available for hire.

The tourist office has a list of *chambres d'hôtes* in the area. Prices range from 170FF to 300FF for two people.

About 300m from the centre, toward Carcassonne, *Hôtel-Restaurant Le Boulevard* (☎ 05 63 61 16 08, fax 05 63 98 44 86, 24 blvd Soult) has doubles from 220FF and *menus* from 68FF to 145FF. Opposite the post office, *Hôtel-Restaurant Le Jourdon* (☎ 05 63 61 56 93, fax 05 63 61 83 38, 7 ave Albert-Rouvière) charges 260/300FF for a single/double with shower. Its restaurant has a good reputation and *menus* from 70FF to 230FF. *Le Grand Balcon* (☎ 05 63 61 0-87, fax 05 63 98 61 69, 5 Square Gaston Tournier), adjacent to the tourist office, has rooms for 250/320FF. Breakfast costs 40FF. Its brasserie serves reasonable meals with main courses from around 50FF to 90FF.

Markets are held on Tuesdays, Saturday and Sundays in the central square. A *Leader Price* supermarket is at 14 place Gambetta and about six other *food stores* are scattered around the town's business area.

Day 5: Mazamet to Carcassonne
2½–5 hours, 51.5km

Immediately there's a solid climb into the Montagne Noire, named for its thick dark cloak of conifers. The **viewpoint** opposite the tourist office annexe on the D118, 3.5km out of town, has a panorama over Mazamet.

At 4.1km, the tiny road to **Hautpoul** leaves the route. With its steep pedestrianised streets and great views, the perched village is worth a visit. It is a 3km, mostly level side trip on a very narrow country lane.

Near the top of the climb is a **rest area** with some shady picnic tables, after which you enter the Aude department. Leaving the D118, descend rapidly beside a cascading stream through beautiful forest. At little Miraval-Cabardès (21.9km) there's another well-equipped **picnic area** beside the Orbiel River. From here the road meanders along the valley bottom between interlocking spurs and through villages with similar names and a similar lack of commercial activity.

Beyond the village of Lastours (32.6km) a **wind farm's** 10 tall, twin-blade wind turbines thrust skywards on a ridge, harvesting the energy of the strong, hot wind.

Rejoin the D118 at a big roundabout (traffic circle; 44.3km), and follow signs on a convoluted route to the train station.

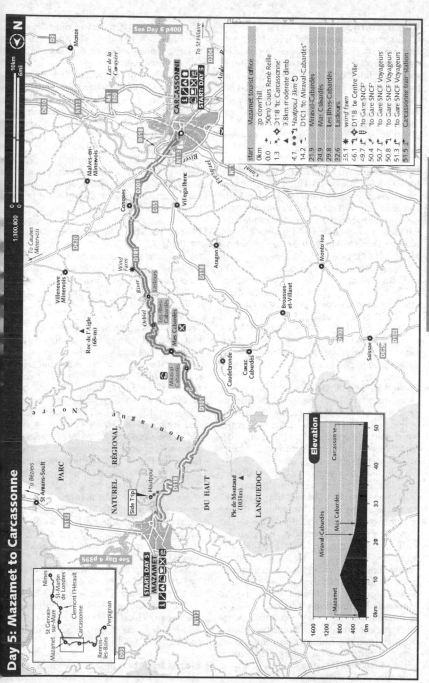

Day 5: Mazamet to Carcassonne

LANGUEDOC-ROUSSILLON

start	0km	Mazamet tourist office
		go cowrhill
	0.0	50m) Cours René Reille
	1.3	D118 'tc Carcassonne'
		9.8km moderate climb
	4.1	Hautpol 3km ↰
	14.2	D1C1 'tc Miraval-Cabardès'
	21.9	Miraval-Cabardès
	24.9	Mas Cabardès
	29.8	Les Ilhes-Cabardès
	32.6	Lastours
		wind farm
	35.1	
	46.1	D118 to Centre Ville'
	49.7	'to Gare SNCF'
	50.4	'to Gare SNCF'
	50.7	'to Gare SNCF Voyageurs'
	50.8	'to Gare SNCF Voyageurs'
	51.3	'to Gare SNCF Voyageurs'
	51.5	Carcassonne train station

Elevation

Miraval-Cabardès

Mas Cabardès

Carcassonne

Mazamet

Carcassonne

Cycling to Carcassonne's fairy-tale, car-free old city *(La Cité)* involves a battle of crusade proportions against the modern-day traffic nightmare in its Ville Basse. This lower town was established in the mid-13th century after the Cité, the fortified upper part of town, was seized by Simon de Montfort in the Albigensian Crusade. More than 200,000 visitors are lured to Carcassonne each July and August alone.

Information The main tourist office (☎ 04 68 10 24 30, fax 04 68 10 24 38, 💻 www .tourisme.fr/carcassonne) is in the Ville Basse at 15 blvd Camille Pelletan, about halfway between the train station and the Cité (closed Sunday). The Cité has a small tourist office (☎ 04 68 10 24 36, fax 04 68 10 24 37) in the Tour Narbonnaise.

Major banks centre on place Carnot in the Ville Basse.

The city has numerous two-wheeler dealers, including Claude Cyclos (☎ 04 68 71 68 60, 19 blvd Varsovie), Cycles Raynaud (☎ 04 68 25 19 27, 31 blvd Varsovie) and Cycles Marson (☎ 04 68 25 25 89, 13 allée Bezons). Bike spares are also available in the various hypermarkets.

Things to See & Do Walking or cycling along the towpaths of the **Canal du Midi** is pleasant, but the **Cité** is Carcassonne's only major sight. It is enclosed by two walls which constitute one of the largest city fortifications in Europe. There are 52 stone towers on the ramparts.

Only the lower sections of the walls are original. Everything else, including the anachronistic roofs shaped like witches' hats, was added in the 19th century. Cross the drawbridge over the dry moat to the massive **Porte Narbonnaise**. Wander the walkways and grassy fields between the inner and outer walls. Rue Cros Mayrevieille, full of souvenir shops, leads up to **place du Château** in the heart of the Cité. Nearby, on rue du Grand Puits, is the **Musée de l'Inquisition** (☎ 04 68 71 44 03, 📧 intermusee@aol.com), exhibiting various torture instruments and other gruesome trophies from the 13th to 18th centuries. A bizarre contrast is achieved by the location of the **Musée des Dessins Animés** (Cartoon Museum) in the same street.

The **Château Comtal** (Counts' Castle; ☎ 04 68 25 01 66), across another dry moat at 1 rue Viollet-le-Duc, is only accessible on an organised tour.

Falconry is demonstrated at 3 pm at **Les Aigles de la Cité** (☎ 04 68 47 88 89), 800m south of the Cité walls on the Colline de Pech Mary. *Aigles* (eagles), *faucons* (falcons) and *vautours* (vultures) are just some of the birds of prey on display.

On 14 July, Bastille Day **fireworks** light up the Cité. Classical music concerts are held on Sunday afternoons from June to September in the Basilique St Nazaire, as a part of the **Festivales d'Orgue de la Cité** (☎ 04 68 47 26 97).

Places to Stay The *Camping de la Cité* (☎ *04 68 25 11 77*) is on route de St-Hilaire, about 3.5km south of the main tourist office. It charges 56/99FF for one/two *randonneurs* (non-motorised travellers). It has a great view to the walls and towers in the setting sun.

The *Auberge de Jeunesse* (☎ *04 68 25 23 16, fax 04 68 71 14 84, rue du Vicomte Trencavel*) is in the heart of the Cité. Dorm beds cost 72FF a night, including breakfast. It has a snack bar.

Near the train station, the clean and attractive *Hôtel Astoria* (☎ *04 68 25 31 38, fax 04 68 71 34 14, 18 rue Tourtel*) offers doubles with washbasin/shower, toilet and TV from 130/180FF (10FF more in July and August). The *Hôtel Central* (☎ *04 68 25 03 84, fax 04 68 72 46 41, 27 blvd Jean Jaurès*), opposite the Palais de Justice in the Ville Basse, has spartan but adequate doubles with shower, toilet and TV for 220FF. Rooms at the back are quieter.

Near the Cité, room prices start from around 260FF. Inside the walls, prices are higher. *Hôtel des Remparts* (☎ *04 68 71 27 72, fax 04 68 72 73 26, 3 place du Grand Puits*) has gaudy modern doubles for around 350FF.

More upmarket, the *Hôtel du Donjon* (☎ *04 68 71 08 80, fax 04 68 25 06 60, 2 rue du Comte Roger*) is in a medieval building with doubles from 390FF. The ultimate, *La Barbacane Hôtel* (☎ *04 68 25 03 34, fax 04 68 71 50 15, place de l'Église*) has palatial rooms from 1000FF.

Places to Eat On place Carnot on Tuesday, Thursday and Saturday, *open-air markets* sell flowers, fruit and vegetables. *Les Halles* covered market on rue de Verdun sells fresh fish and meat daily except Sunday.

As befits a city of its size, Carcassonne has numerous supermarkets. Among others, there's *Intermarché* on rue Claude Chappe, *Monoprix* at 17 rue Georges Clemenceau and *Shopi* at 25 ave Henri Gout. Several hypermarkets, including *Géant*, *Leclerc* and another *Intermarché*, are in the outlying *zone industrielle* Pont Rouge and *centre commercial* Salvaza.

Cafes spill out into the Ville Basse's place Carnot in summer while, in the Cité, place Marcou is the coffee drinker's mecca. Popular local restaurants include *Au Bon Pasteur* (☎ 04 68 25 49 63, 29 rue Antoine Armagnac) in the Ville Basse, which serves seafood, *cassoulet* and foie gras and has *menus* from 75FF. In the Cité, *Auberge de Dame Carcas* (☎ 04 68 71 23 23, 3 place du Château) has a casual atmosphere and moderate prices, with high-quality regional *menus* from around 90FF.

Day 6: Carcassonne to Rennes-les-Bains

3–6½ hours, 65km

A hilly day offering views to rocky eastern Pyrenees peaks, four notable climbs will challenge cyclists. One is from Greffeil (220m, 28.8km), gaining 400m over 12.3km.

To avoid traffic, carefully make your way through pedestrianised streets south of the train station to blvd du Commandant Roumens and head left to the Cité on this busy street. You'll appreciate why the area you are leaving is known as the Ville Basse as you hit the hill to the Cité walls.

Pass near the camping ground on the way out of town and head onto quiet little roads towards the foothills of the romantic Pyrenees. Vineyards and patchwork fields dominate the scenery and a Catalan influence is evident in the style of houses – white cottages with curved red roof tiles – and the names on gravestones in village cemeteries.

Camping à la ferme (camping on the farm) is available after Ladern-sur-Lauquet in a pleasant location (24.7km) on the Alberte River. At the crest of a hill after Valmigère is a distant but fine view to the rocky Pic du Canigou, at 2784m the highest peak in the eastern Pyrénées and long a focus of myth and religious belief.

Descend 320m in 6km to Arques where there is an unusual French *grocery* – it's open *uninterrupted* all day, every day (9 am to 7 pm). The nearby *bakery*, closed daily from 12.30 to 4 pm, makes *le pain du pays cathare* (Cathar-country bread). There is a *camping ground* here (see Places to Stay & Eat under Rennes-les-Bains) and a picnic/recreation area around a small lake. Otherwise, ride another easy 9km to reach a hotel for the night.

Rennes-les-Bains

Not a lot happens in this sleepy village, which caters to the dwindling number of cure seekers who come to bathe in the town's spas. Rennes-les-Bains is *jumelé avec* (twinned with) a sister city of) Rennes-en-Bretagne, which explains the name of the town's central Place des Deux Rennes.

Town information is available from the Syndicat d'Initiative (☎ 04 68 69 88 04) in the main street, rue des Thermes/D14. There is neither bank nor bike shop.

Things to See & Do There are **Thermal baths** on rue des Thermes, downhill from the Hôtel de France on the right.

Places to Stay & Eat Resort-style camping is available at Arques, 9km before Rennes. At Rennes, *Camping Le Village du Lac* (☎ 04 68 69 88 30, fax 04 68 69 85 49) is 1.3km east of the centre. It charges 112FF for two or three people in July/August (47FF April to June). It has cabins, accommodating up to six people, available by the night from April to June for 230FF but by the week only in July/August (2541FF). It also has a snack bar for meals.

One kilometre beyond Rennes on the D14, the pleasant *Camping la Bernède* (☎ 04 68 69 86 49, fax 04 68 74 09 31) charges 36/53FF for one/two people.

Hôtel de France (☎ 04 68 69 87 03, fax 04 68 69 86 55, rue des Thermes/ D14) has doubles with shower and toilet from 160FF. Breakfast costs 25FF. Its restaurant has *menus* from 75FF to 220FF.

There are *grocery* and *bakery* shops in place des Deux Rennes, along with a *snack bar* and a *restaurant/pizzeria* (☎ 04 68 69 89 52).

Le Moulin d'Arques (☎ 04 68 69 80 61), an attractive restaurant, is right below the

LANGUEDOC-ROUSSILLON

Day 6: Carcassonne to Rennes-les-Bains

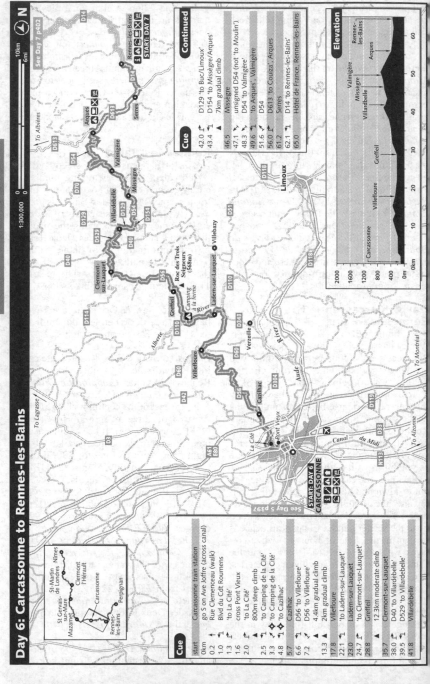

See Day 7 p402

START: DAY 7

See Day 5 p397

START: DAY 6
CARCASSONNE

Elevation

Cue | Continued

42.0 ↱	D129 'to Buc/Limoux'
43.4 ↱	D154 'to Missègre/Arques'
	7km gradual climb
46.5 ◀	Missègre
47.1 ↱	unsigned D54 (not 'to Moulin')
48.3 ↱	D54 'to Valmigère'
49.6 ↰	'to Arques', Valmigère
51.6 ◆	D54
56.0 ↰	D613 'to Couiza', Arques
61.2	Serres
62.1 ↱	D14 'to Rennes-les-Bains'
65.0	Hôtel de France, Rennes-les-Bains

Cue

start	Carcassonne train station
0km	go S on Ave Joffre (across canal)
0.2	Rue Clemenceau (walk)
1.0	Blvd du Cdt Roumens
1.3 ↱	'to La Cité'
1.6	cross Pont Vieux
2.0 ◀	'to La Cité'
	800m steep climb
2.5 ↰	'to Camping de la Cité'
3.3 ↱	'to Camping de la Cité'
4.8 ◆◆	'to Cazilhac'
5.7	Cazilhac
6.6 ↱	D56 'to Villefloure'
7.2 ◀	D56 'to Villefloure'
	4.4km gradual climb
13.3 ◀	2km gradual climb
17.8	Villefloure
22.1 ↱	'to Ladern-sur-Lauquet'
23.0	Ladern-sur-Lauquet
24.7 ↱	'to Clermont-sur-Lauquet'
28.8	Greffeil
	12.3km moderate climb
35.7	Clermont-sur-Lauquet
38.0 ↰	D40 'to Villardebelle'
39.5 ↱	D529 'to Villardebelle'
41.8	Villardebelle

N
1:300,000
0   10km
0   6m

To Lagrasse
To Albières
To Montréal
To Alzonne
To La Cité
Pont Vieux
Canal du Midi
Aude River
Alberte River

Rennes-les-Bains
Arques
Serres
Valmigère
Missègre
Villardebelle
Villebazy
Clermont-sur-Lauquet
Greffeil
Roc des Trois Seigneurs (568m)
Camping à la ferme
Ladern-sur-Lauquet
Verzeille
Villefloure
Cazilhac

D14
D613
D54
D70
D129
D329
D40
D114
D56
D110
D348
D50
D72
D3
D56
D104
D118
D110
D51
A61 E80
D118
D33
D6

(Inset map)
St-Martin de Londres
Nîmes
St Gervais sur-Mare
Clermont l'Hérault
Mazamet
Carcassonne
Perpignan
Rennes-les-Bains

chateau on the way out of Arques towards Rennes. It offers a *menu régional* (95FF), a *menu cassoulet* (99FF) and a *menu gastronomique* (150FF).

Day 7: Rennes-les-Bains to Perpignan

4–8½ hours, 87.6km

Start the day cycling in the remote, rocky hills of *Pays Cathare* (Cathar country), studded with the ruins of ridge-top chateau forts, and finish in the civilised, bourgeois city of Perpignan. The terrain is hilly but you'll score several cols, some of which are unknown to Michelin mapmakers, and get some great views.

Early on there's a solid climb around the Pic de Bugarach after which you bag **Col du Linas** (13.5km), somewhere between 667m (col sign) and 680m (Michelin map) above sea level. The next two cols are lower, easier and not on the Michelin map. They offer views along the valleys to limestone crags and ridges on which the Cathars built their castles, such as the Château de Peyrepertuse, with local stone. Thus camouflaged, the ruins look like extensions of the mountain tops.

You'll feel like you are really entering the mountains when, at the top of a strenuous climb to the **Grau de Maury**, a sign announces the Département of Pyrénées-Orientales.

After descending to the lowlands nearer Perpignan, watch out for a couple of dangerous railway level crossings, waiting to bring down the unsuspecting cyclist (at 67.7km after Maury and at 72.9km after Cases de Pène).

The last 25km into Perpignan is flat, fairly dull and quite complicated, but mostly well signposted.

Perpignan

More Catalan than French, Perpignan was the capital of the kingdom of Majorca, which stretched to Montpellier and included the Balearic Islands, from 1278 to 1344. Modern Perpignan, capital of Roussillon and home to 110,000 people, is an important commercial centre and the second-largest Catalan city after Barcelona.

The city centre is heavily trafficked but full of interesting architecture. The formal *platane* (plane-tree) shaded park near the tourist office is a good place to relax.

Information The tourist office (☎ 04 68 66 30 30, fax 04 68 66 30 26, ✉ www.little-france.com/perpignan) is in the Palais des Congrès, place Armand Lanoux, on the north-eastern edge of the Promenade des Platanes.

The Catalan Cultural Centre (☎ 04 68 34 11 70), 42 ave de Grande Bretagne, promotes Catalan language and culture.

The Banque de France is at 3 place Jean Payra and several other banks are on blvd Clemenceau to the north-east.

There's a number of bike shops. Try Cycles Mercier Roussillonais (☎ 04 68 85 02 71), 20 ave Gilbert Brutus, MBK (☎ 04 68 54 60 80), 1 ave Lycée Arago, or Véloland (☎ 04 68 08 19 99), 95 ave Maréchal Juin.

Things to See & Do The Casa Païral (☎ 04 68 35 42 05) is a museum of Roussillon and Catalan folklore in the 14th-century town gate called Le Castillet, on place de Verdun. From the terrace at the top there are great views of the old city and the citadel.

The 1276 Palace of the Kings of Majorca (☎ 04 68 34 48 29), on a small hill entered via rue des Archers to the south of the old city, can be inspected daily from May to September. Once surrounded by fig and olive groves, the grounds were lost when the palace was enclosed by the formidable walls of the Citadel.

Gloomy 14th- to 16th-century Cathédrale St Jean is crammed into place Gambetta. It has nice stained glass and splendid Catalan altar pieces.

For novelty value, check out the plaque and covered wagon outside the train station. Dedicated to Catalan surrealist painter Salvador Dali (1904–89) who was visiting Perpignan in 1965, they explain how he, on emerging here from a taxi, 'suddenly...found myself in the centre of the universe'. What *was* he on? Dali's painting of Perpignan's train station now hangs in a Düsseldorf (Germany) museum.

Places to Stay Dreary *Camping La Garrigole* (☎ 04 68 54 66 10, 2 rue Maurice-Lévy) is at the western edge of town. It's on a very small suburban plot discreetly tucked from view behind a hedge. The tariff is 39/62FF for one/two people. North of town is the better-equipped *Le Catalan* (☎ 04 68 63 16 92, route de Bompas). It charges

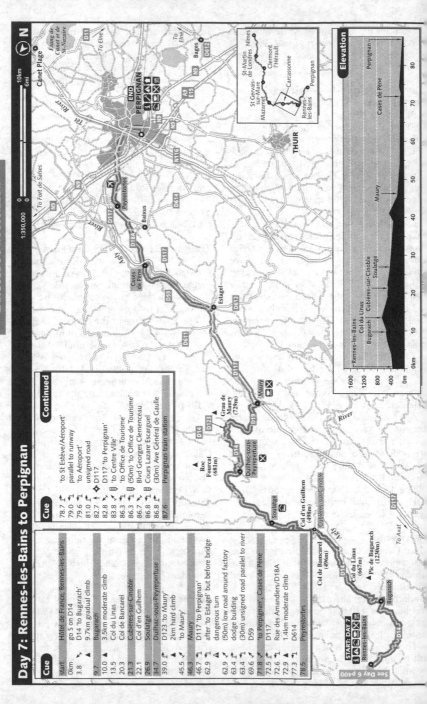

Day 7: Rennes-les-Bains to Perpignan

Cue

start		Hôtel de France, Rennes-les-Bains
0km		go S on D14
3.8		D14 'to Bugarach'
		9.7km gradual climb
9.7		Bugarach
10.0		3.5km moderate climb
13.5		Col du Linas
20.3		Col de Bancarel
21.3		Cubieres-sur-Cinoble
22.1		Col d'en Guilhem
26.9		Soulatgé
34.7		Duilhac-sous-Peyrepertuse
		2km hard climb
39.0		D123 'to Maury'
		'to Maury'
45.5		
46.3		Maury
46.7		D117 'to Perpignan'
62.9		after 'to Estagel' but before bridge
		dangerous turn
62.9		(50m) low road around factory
63.4		dodge building
		(30m) unsigned road parallel to river
69.6		D59
71.8		to Perpignan', Cases de Pène
72.5		D117
72.6		Rue des Amandiers/D18A
72.9		1.4km moderate climb
77.3		D614
78.5		Peyrestortes

Cue — Continued

78.7		'to St Estève/Aéroport'
		parallel to runway
79.0		D14 'to Bugarach'
79.6		'to Aéroport'
		unsigned road
81.0		D117
82.7		D117 'to Perpignan'
82.8		'to Centre Ville'
83.8		'to Office de Tourisme'
86.3		(50m) 'to Office de Tourisme'
86.7		Blvd Georges Clemenceau
86.8		Cours Lazare Escarguel
86.8		(30m) Ave Général de Gaulle
87.6		Perpignan train station

Elevation

round 40FF per person in low season and 5FF in July and August. It has a restaurant.

If you intend riding to Foix, conveniently located 17km west of Perpignan is shady *Camping Municipal Millas*, which charges a mere 21FF per person – but oh, the bells, the bells!

The *Auberge de Jeunesse* (☎ 04 68 34 63 2, fax 04 68 51 16 02, ave de Grande Bre- agne), in the Parc de la Pépinière, charges 70FF a night, including breakfast.

There's a string of hotels along ave du Général de Gaulle towards the train station. *Hôtel L'Express* (☎ 04 68 34 89 96) at No has small but adequate rooms for two without/with shower for around 95/115FF.

The clean, one-star *Hôtel Avenir* (☎ 04 68 34 20 30, 11 rue de l'Avenir) has basic single rooms for 90FF and doubles with shower from 120FF. The more upmarket *Hôtel de la Loge* (☎ 04 68 34 41 02, fax 04 68 34 25 13, 2 rue des Fabriques d'En Nabot) has rustic doubles with shower/bath for 285/330FF.

Places to Eat Perpignan is well served with a number of hypermarkets, including *Auchan* on ave d'Espagne and two *Leclercs*, one to the north of the *city (2130 ave de Languedoc)*, the other to the *south (70 ave Victor Dalbiez)*. Supermarkets include a *Champion (21 blvd Desnoyés)* and an *Intermarché (955 ave Julien Panchot)*.

Food markets are held every morning on place des Poilus, and in the covered market on place de la République (closed Monday).

Bars and *cafes* cluster in place de la République, along ave du Général de Gaulle and near the station. For takeaways and snacks, try *Hopi Cafétéria* (☎ 04 68 61 56 72) at 314 ave de Languedoc.

Popular, low-cost restaurants in the town centre include the Catalan *Casa Sansa* (☎ 04 68 34 21 84, 2 rue des Fabriques Nadal) and *La Bodega du Castillet* (☎ 04 68 34 88 98, rue des Fabriques Couvertes). A good place for regional specialities is the *Opéra Bouffe* (☎ 04 68 34 83 83, Impasse de la Division), south-west of place Jean Jaurès, which has *menus* starting at 70FF. Excellent value is *Le Caneton (12 rue Victor Hugo)*, a tiny place in a private house, with huge servings and a three-course *menu* from around 30FF.

The Pyrenees

Stretching for 430km in a line from the Bay of Biscay on the Atlantic Coast to the Mediterranean Sea, the Pyrenees form a natural boundary between France and Spain, with the border mostly following the watershed. The mountain chain links the Basque Country (*Euskadi* in Basque) in the western *département* (department; administrative division) of Pyrénées-Atlantiques, through the long, narrow Parc National des Pyrénées in the middle, to the Catalan region of the Pyrénées-Orientales. It's all spectacular cycling country.

HISTORY

The western end of the Pyrenees is populated by the Basques who, like the Catalan people (see the Languedoc-Roussillon chapter), live in an area straddling the French-Spanish border. Their early history is largely unknown, although the Romans recorded a tribe called the Vascones living in the area. The Basques took over what is now southwestern France in the 6th century. They were converted to Christianity in the 10th century and are still known for their strong devotion to Catholicism.

Basque nationalism flourished immediately before and during the Spanish Civil War (1936–39), when Franco's fascists destroyed the city of Guernica, symbol of the Basque nation and centre of nationalist activity. Some Basques still dream of an independent Euskadi state carved from France and Spain – the terrorist organisation, ETA (*Euskadi ta Azkatasuna*; Basque Nation and Liberty), still carries out bombings and other violent acts.

NATURAL HISTORY

The Pyrenees are of a similar age to the Alps (Tertiary era) but, being lower and more southerly, are less affected by glaciation, though landforms created by small glaciers dot the area. Exposed crystalline rock forms the uplands, while folded limestone makes up the lower slopes. Of the three main ranges, the central one is the highest, culminating in Pic d'Aneto (3404m), on the Spanish side south of Bagnères de Luchon.

The French side of the Pyrenees is steeper. Among its characteristic features

In Brief

Highlights
- the thrilling descent from **Col de Marie-Blanque**
- climbing to the **Col du Tourmalet** and **Col Bagargui**
- the lively Basque town of **St Jean-Pied de Port**
- completing the **Raid Pyrénéen**

Terrain
Extremely mountainous, with winding, narrow climbs (and descents) as long as 30km.

Cycling Contact
Ligue Pyrénées, 4 Impasse des Monts de la Margeride, 31240 l'Union

Cycling Events
- **Fabio Casartelli Memorial rides** (☎ 06 80 21 43 41, mid-July) St Girons

Special Events
- **Fêtes de Bayonne** Basque music and 'running with the bulls' (five days every August) Bayonne
- **La Fête du Thon** tuna and traditional Basque music festival (first Saturday after 1 July) St-Jean de Luz
- **Saint's Day of St John the Baptist** bonfires, music and dance (weekend before 24 June) St-Jean de Luz

Gourmet Specialities
- *confit d'oie* (goose cooked and stored in its own fat)
- *garbure* (cabbage and bean soup) or *ttoro* (fish stew)
- *fromage de brebis* (ewes cheese) and *fromage de chêvre* (goats cheese)

are *gaves* (torrents), where water descend in cascades, and natural amphitheatres most notably the Cirque de Gavarnie sout of Luz St-Sauveur.

While the passes are high and difficult, the range has never been an impenetrable barrier to humans with the Basques and Catalans populating both sides at opposite ends. However, travel along the ranges is made more difficult by the transverse river valleys. Until recent times the population was isolated, dependent on a subsistence economy based on sheep and cattle raising, wool growing, and the exploitation of forests and minerals. Mines extract bauxite, talc and zinc.

CLIMATE

The Pyrenees are subject to a Mediterranean climate of hot summers and mild winters. Frost is rare, spring and autumn downpours are sudden but brief, and summer is virtually without rain, except at the western end, where westerly winds off the Atlantic bring higher humidity and frequent rain storms. Except in the west, prevailing winds are light – their direction isn't very critical as riders on mountain passes make frequent changes of direction.

For weather information in the department of Hautes-Pyrénées, call the *météo* (weather bureau) on ☎ 08 36 68 02 65. The météo number for Pyrénées-Atlantiques is ☎ 08 36 68 02 64.

INFORMATION
Information Sources

Information is available in Paris at the Maison des Pyrénées (☎ 01 42 86 51 86, 15 rue St Augustin, metro Quatre Septembre). Pyrenean regions and individual departments have Web sites with useful information.

Warning

Descents in the Pyrenees are dangerous. Gradients are often steep, roads are narrow, bends are sharp and sudden, sightlines often poor. Watch for gravillons (ball-bearing-like gravel used in road repair), especially on the bends.

You are sharing a skinny strip of bitumen with cars and even tourist coaches, which can appear from nowhere. Keep your speed under control and never cross the centre of the road.

Ensure your brakes stop effectively and check the cables are in perfect condition before riding.

The Comité Régional du Tourisme (CRDT) du Languedoc-Roussillon (☎ 04 67 22 81 00, fax 04 67 58 06 10, ✉ www.cr-languedocroussillon.fr/tourisme) covers the eastern end of the Pyrenees. It is at 20 rue de la République, 34000 Montpellier.

The CRDT de Midi-Pyrénées (☎ 05 61 13 55 55, fax 05 61 47 17 16, ✉ midi-pyrenees@crtmp.com) is at 54 blvd de l'Embouchure, BP 2166, 31022 Toulouse Cedex 2. Useful sites for the central Pyrenees include ✉ www.mipnet.fr, ✉ www.cg65.fr (for Hautes-Pyrénées department), ✉ www.cg31.fr (for Haute-Garonne department), or ✉ www.cr-aquitaine.fr, which covers the south-western department of Pyrénées-Atlantiques.

The Ariège department's Web site ✉ www.ariege.com has a cycling section; click on 'what to do', then 'cycling'.

GATEWAY CITIES
Toulouse

France's fourth-largest city, Toulouse is renowned for its high-tech industries, particularly its aerospace facilities. It is also a major education centre. Much of the city is built of rose-red brick, and its centre has a laid-back charm.

Getting There & Away Toulouse has international air connections and is one of south's major rail hubs.

Air Air Toulouse-Blagnac international airport (☎ 05 61 42 44 00) is 8km north-west of the city centre. Air France and Air Liberté between them have over 30 flights a day to/from Paris (mainly Orly). There are also daily or almost-daily flights from many other cities in France and Europe.

Train Toulouse's train station, Gare Matabiau, is on blvd Pierre Sémard, about 1km north-east of the city centre.

Local destinations served by many daily direct trains include Bayonne (196FF, 3¾ hours), Bordeaux (165FF, 2½ hours), Cahors (87FF, 1½ hours), Carcassonne (74FF, one hour), Foix (69FF, 1¼ hours) and Perpignan (183FF, four hours).

The fare to Paris is 356FF by Corail (6½ hours, Gare d'Austerlitz) and 447FF by TGV (5½ hours, Gare Montparnasse via Bordeaux).

Bus From Britain, the European Bike Express service (see Bus under Continental Europe in the Getting There & Away chapter) charges UK£169 (return) to take a passenger and bike to Toulouse.

Foix Circuits

INTRODUCTION TO THE PYRENEES
Duration	3½–7½ hours
Distance	75.7km
Difficulty	moderate
Start/End	Foix

PYRENEAN FOOTHILLS
Duration	2 days
Distance	92.8km
Difficulty	hard
Start/End	Foix

The attractive city of Foix is a convenient base for these circuits. The Introduction to the Pyrenees is of moderate difficulty only due to its length, as it follows the valleys and hills of the Montagnes du Plantaurel. The Pyrenean Foothills is a hard two-day trek over some of the cols (mountain passes) of the Massif de l'Arize to Massat and back via Tarascon-sur-Ariège.

PLANNING
When to Ride
The roads will be passable most of the year, but the limited opening dates of camping grounds and tourist attractions make Easter through September the best time to ride, particularly from June to mid-July when the weather is warm and the tourists are few.

Maps
Michelin map No 86 *Luchon, Andorre, Perpignan* (1:200,000) covers both rides.

GETTING TO/FROM THE RIDES
A scenic back route links Foix to Perpignan, the end of the Upper Languedoc ride in the Languedoc-Roussillon chapter. Foix is close to Tarascon-sur-Ariège, where Day 1 of the Raid Pyrénéen, described later in this chapter, starts.

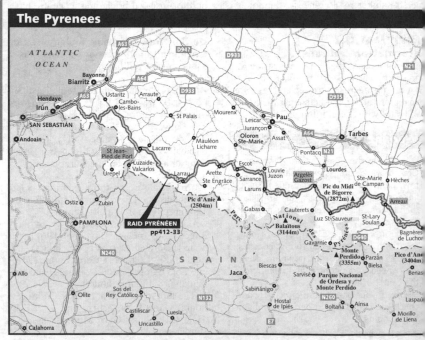

The Pyrenees

Train

The Foix train station is on rue Pierre Se-
mard, east of the river and north of the business area.

Foix is on the line from Toulouse (70FF,
one hour, seven trains a day) and is 15 minutes from Tarascon-sur-Ariège (19FF, five a
day). The daily train to/from Perpignan carries bikes unbagged (200FF, 4¼ hours).

Bicycle

The Pyrenean Foothills route links with the
Raid Pyrénéen at Tarascon. Ride to/from
Perpignan via the route described for the
Upper Languedoc ride (p388) in the
Languedoc-Roussillon chapter.

THE RIDES

Foix

Foix (population 10,000) is in the foothills
of the Pyrenees at an altitude of 380m. Distinguished by its castle, 11th-century church
and ancient streets lined with medieval,
half-timbered houses, it is the main town of
the Ariège department.

The new bypass tunnel beneath the Plantaurel Mountains takes passing traffic away
from the centre of Foix, making it far more
attractive to cyclists.

Information The tourist office (☎ 05 61
65 12 12, fax 05 61 65 64 63; closed Sunday) is at 45 cours Gabriel Fauré, in front of
the impressive *mairie* (town hall).

A Banque de France is at 3 rue Lieutenant Paul Delpech.

The bike shop, Les Cyclos Fuxeens
05 61 05 29 98; closed Sunday and Monday), 16 rue de Labistour, does repairs but
does not hire bikes. For that, call Intersport
(☎ 05 61 65 00 41).

Things to See & Do The imposing, triple-
towered **Château des Comtes de Foix**
stands guard over the town. Built in the 10th
century as a stronghold for the Counts of
Foix, it was used as a prison from the 16th
century onwards and prisoners' graffiti can
still be seen engraved on the stones. Today
it houses the Ariège museum's collection
of Prehistoric, Gallo-Roman and Medieval
archaeology.

A **market** on place St Volusien each Friday sells food and goods.

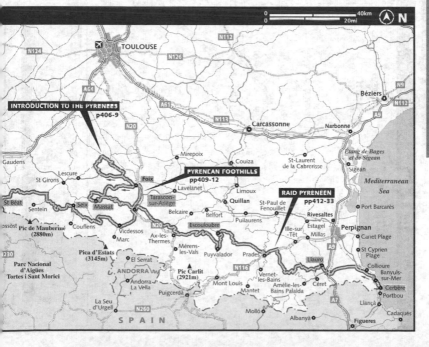

PYRENEES

Introduction to the Pyrenees

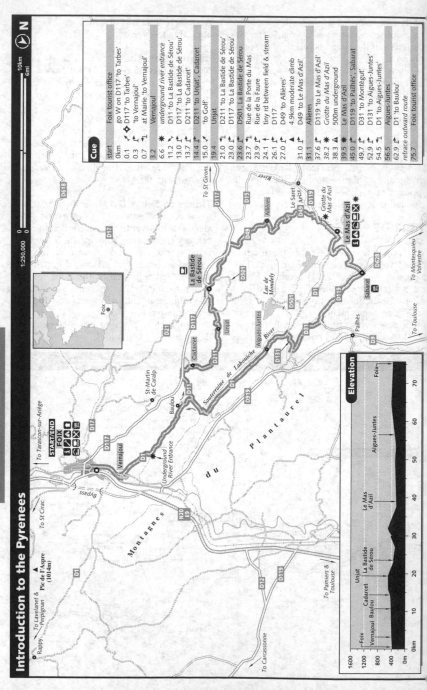

Cue

start	Foix tourist office
0km	go W on D117 'to Tarbes'
0.1	D117 'to Tarbes'
0.3	'to Vernajoul'
0.7	at Mairie 'to Vernajoul'
3.2	Vernajoul
6.6	*underground river entrance*
11.2	D11 'to La Bastide de Sérou'
13.0	D117 'to La Bastide de Sérou'
13.7	D211 'to Cadarcet'
14.4	D211 'to Unjat', Cadarcet
15.0	'to Golf'
19.4	Unjat
21.0	D211 'to La Bastide de Sérou'
23.0	D117 'to La Bastide de Sérou'
23.6	D501 'La Bastide de Sérou
23.7	Rue de la Porte du Mas
23.9	Rue de la Faure
24.1	tiny rd between field & stream
26.1	D117
27.0	D49 'to Allières'
	4.9km moderate climb
31.0	D49 'to Le Mas d'Azil'
31.1	Allières
37.6	D119 'to Le Mas d'Azil'
38.2	Grotte du Mas d'Azil
38.3	500m underground
39.5	Le Mas d'Azil
45.0	D119 'to Palhès' Sabarat
49.7	D31 'to Montégut'
52.9	D131 'to Aigues-Juntes'
54.5	D1 'to Aigues-Juntes'
56.5	Aigues-Juntes
62.9	D1 'to Baulou'
	retrace outward route
75.7	Foix tourist office

Places to Stay The noisy *Camping du Lac de Labarre* (☎ 05 61 65 11 58, fax 05 61 06 52 62) is on the N20, just north of town. The tariff is around 60/75FF for one/two.

Hostel-style accommodation is available at the *Auberge Léo Lagrange* (☎ 05 61 65 09 04, 16 rue Noël Peyrevidal) in the middle of the old part of town. Beds in rooms for one, two or four people cost 80FF per night. *Demi-pension* (half-board) is also available.

Of four hotels in central Foix, two provide the best value. They are *Hôtel Audoyeons* (☎ 05 61 65 52 44, fax 05 61 02 68 18, place Dutilh) where rooms with shower cost around 260FF and *menus* (set meals) range from 75FF to 125FF; and the more modest *Hostellerie La Barbacane du Château* (☎ 05 61 65 50 44, fax 05 61 02 74 33, 1 ave de Lérida), right below the château, which charges from 195FF for doubles.

Places to Eat A large *supermarket* is south of the main cours Gabriel Fauré – ride along ave Général de Gaulle and it is across the car park (closed Sunday afternoon). See the Things to See & Do section for the town market.

Vanille Chocolat (☎ 05 61 65 36 90, 19 rue des Marchands) serves good-value salads and grills (closed Sunday). *La Bodega* (☎ 05 61 02 91 26, 7 rue Lafaurie) specialises in tapas and paella (open daily). *Self-Service Gros* (☎ 05 61 65 00 07, 27 cours Gabriel Fauré) has self-service steak, salad and chips from around 50FF.

Introduction to the Pyrenees
½–7½ hours, 75.7km

This route is a good introduction to the Pyrenees, with a visit to a subterranean river plus some subterranean cycling. Also on the itinerary are fascinating small villages, tiny roads and beautiful pastoral scenes, with only one real hill.

Head out of town around the chateau and climb gently through the village of Vernajoul. About 3km further on is the entrance to the **Rivière Souterraine de Labouiche** (5.6km). Tours (75 minutes) of the underground realm are available daily; the ticket office (☎ 05 61 65 04 11) is on the left. The cavern system consists of galleries on five levels linked by cascades, wells and syphons.

Travel by boat an amazing 1.5km along the underground river, the longest such trip in Europe.

Continue on quiet roads up a gentle hill past what is a mercifully rare sight in France, a golf course, near Unjat.

Take a break for morning tea or lunch at La Bastide de Sérou (23.6km) to prepare for a near-5km climb. While steep in parts, it only rises about 200m in that distance and has good views of the lush valley below.

The following downhill leads to the next fascinating point of interest, the **Grotte du Mas d'Azil** (38.2km), where the road is literally swallowed up and disappears underground. The huge cavern is one of the region's most important prehistoric sites and is the only drivable (or cyclable) cave in Europe.

The rushing river, Arize, which has carved out a portal 65m high and 50m wide, fills the void with noise amplified by echoes. Humans used the grotto for shelter from 30,000 BC until the Middle Ages. Cathars and Huguenots have also called the cave home. Relics of human and animal occupation are displayed. Call ☎ 05 61 69 97 22 for information about guided tours or bring a torch (flashlight) to inspect the cave on your own.

The village of Le Mas d'Azil, just beyond the cavern, has a **Musée de la Préhistoire** (☎ 05 61 69 97 22). **Dolmens** (standing stones) up the hill are visible from the township; follow the signs to the two signposted walks around the sights. A municipal *camping ground* (☎ 05 61 69 79 70) is 1.7km along the D119 (22/37FF for one/two people).

Swinging back towards Foix, the delightfully quiet D1 undulates through fields harbouring deer as well as domestic stock, and climbs gently onto the side of the Montagnes du Plantaurel. Limestone scarps reach above the forest seemingly to scrape the sky.

Follow signs back to Baulou (65.1km) and then rejoin the outward route to Foix.

Pyrenean Foothills
2 days, 92.8km

See magnificent mountain scenery in terrain to challenge *grimpeurs* (climbers). This sampler of Pyrenean cols is not for the faint-hearted.

PYRENEES

Day 1: Foix to Massat
3–5 hours, 45.8km
Take care leaving the traffic melee of Foix at the tricky left turn towards St-Pierre de Rivière as fast, overtaking traffic does not slow on the bend.

The road climbs continuously for 30km, at first through beech, pine and fir forest, steepening significantly after Burret (13.5km). Glimpses to bare Pyrenean peaks are occasionally beyond the trees. It can be a very hot ride but a few villages have shops and/or water. There is a **spring** at 13.6km – to operate the tap, press down on the handle, don't try to turn it.

At the Col des Marrous (18.6km) is a *hotel/bar/restaurant* and just beyond is the start of a marked mountain bike (VTT) trail descending through the forest. (Ask for a map at Foix tourist office.)

After the unsigned Col de Jouels (1250m) the gradient eases slightly. Col de Péguère (1389m, but still not the top of the climb) at 27.1km has a view to the valley. Massat is visible a long, long way down.

A 'shortcut' is signposted to Massat from here but it's not recommended. The downhill is so extremely steep (18% according to the road signs), twisting and narrow that it would be difficult to control a loaded bike and the rims might overheat, causing a blowout.

Continue past the orientation table on the upper road to reach the Col de Portel (30.6km), at 1465m the highest point on this leg. The Sommet de Portel, the col's peak, is at 1485m.

The steep descent (averaging 7.5%) from Col de la Crouzette (34.3km, 1245m) finishes at Biert, which has *food* and *accommodation* and is only 2.8km, with a gentle climb, from Massat.

Massat
The pretty mountain village of Massat used to be bigger. Now home to about 250 people, it nestles in the valley of the Arac below Massif de l'Arize. It is the centre of Le Pays Massatois, an area popular for walking, horse riding and mountain biking.

Information The Office du Tourisme (☎ 05 61 96 92 76), 6 rue des Prêtres, can advise of the best routes for exploring Le Pays Massatois.

Things to See & Do On the D618 at the edge of town in the direction of Day 2, L Musée du Vieux Moulin preserves relics of the era when the mill supplied the town electricity. Go horse riding at the town Centre Équestre Boutou (☎ 05 61 96 98 77

There are numerous marked and un marked **trails** around nearby Biert. Guests the Pyrenean Pursuits Guesthouse (Se Places to Stay) can hire VTTs.

Places to Stay Pleasant, quiet *Campin Le Pouech* (☎ 05 61 04 95 22), uphill on th south side of town, charges 12FF for a te site and 11FF per adult.

The most bicycle-friendly place to stay on the north side of the D618, 1km south east of Biert, in the cyclists-only *Pyrenea Pursuits Guesthouse* (☎ 05 61 04 90 61 o 05 61 04 91 10, ✉ ppflan@club-internet.fr It's run by a couple of expatriate Englis cyclists. A room, evening meal with aper tif and wine, and a 'sporting' breakfast cos 200FF per person per night.

Hôtel Coutanceau (☎ 05 61 96 95 56) o rue des Prêtres charges from 180FF for room with shower to 240FF with showe and toilet. Breakfast costs 38FF.

Hostellerie des Trois Seigneurs (☎ 0 61 96 95 89), at the western end of towr has rooms with shower and toilet fron 185FF or charges 255FF per person fc demi-pension. Its restaurant has *menu* from 70FF.

Little *Hôtel Le Globe* (☎ 05 61 96 96 66 in the town centre, charges 240FF per pe son for demi-pension.

Places to Eat A *Petit Casino* supermarke is on Massat's main street.

Café du Globe (☎ 05 61 96 90 61), unde the hotel, serves snacks costing from 18F to 45FF.

Auberge du Gypaète Barbu (☎ 05 61 0 89 92, place de l'Église), in Biert, is run b the son of the Hôtel Coutanceau proprieto The cuisine is renowned and *menus* rang from 70FF to 155FF.

Day 2: Massat to Foix
3–5 hours, 47km
The day's ride continues the Pyrenean idy with forested climbs to two cols, neithe very hard but the second very scenic an more than 1200m high.

Pyrenean Foothills

1:300,000

0 — 10km / 6mi

N

Day 1

Cue		
start	0km	Foix tourist office
	0.1	go N on D117 'to Tarbes'
	0.3	D117 'to Tarbes'
		'to St-Pierre de Rivière'
		dangerous intersection
	0.6	'to St-Pierre de Rivière'
		30km moderate climb
	4.6	St-Pierre de Rivière
	7.5	La Coupière
	8.7	Buret
	~3.6	spring
	~8.5	Col des Marrous
	27.1	D72 'to Tour Laffont'
	30.6	Col de Péguère
	34.3	D18 'to Biert'
		D18 to la Crouzette
	43.0	D518 'to Massat', Biert
	45.8	Avassat tourist office

Day 2

Cue		
start	0km	Massat tourist office
	0.5	go N on D618
		12.1km moderate climb
	2.7	Espies
	5.7	Col des Caougnous
	12.6	Col de Port
	29.2	Lacombe & cave at 3.6km
	30.2	D8 'to Foix' Aignac
	32.6	D8 'to Foix' Aignac
	34.9	D8 'to Foix'
	36.2	Amplang
	39.4	'to Foix'
	41.8	Pravols
	43.9	Ferrières
	46.4	Cours Gabriel Fauré
	47.0	Foix tourist office

Elevation

Day 1

Day 2

PYRENEES

The first, Col des Caougnous (5.7km; 947m) is at the junction of the D618 and the road which plummets from Col de Péguère, overlooking Massat. The route continues climbing fairly easily to **Col de Port** (12.6km, 1249m) for a panoramic view along the valley of the Saurat River. The route mostly descends from here. Hungry cyclists may have to go off route in this area. Saurat, a short detour at 22.4km, has a *bakery*, a *grocery store* and a *gîte*. The centre of Tarascon-sur-Ariège is another detour later.

A side trip at 29.2km leads to Lacombe, where **Le Parc Pyrénéen de l'Art Préhistorique** (☎ 05 61 05 10 10) is a series of 13 caves adorned with rock paintings thousands of years old (open April to mid-November). It's on route de Banat; follow the signs.

Without actually entering Tarascon proper, the route traverses a huge roundabout (crossing the busy N20), then swings north at the next roundabout to parallel the N20. At a third roundabout (34.9km) is a large grassy *picnic area* without tables. One short, briefly steep hill follows before the road descends all the way to Foix.

The village of Ferrières (43.9km) has a small *store*.

Raid Pyrénéen

Duration	10 days
Distance	827km
Difficulty	very hard
Start	Cerbère
End	Hendaye

While the peaks of the Pyrenees are generally lower than those of the Alps, the passes are often higher, steeper and – mountain-cycling enthusiasts would say – more romantic. These ideal factors set the stage for a true challenge to cycle tourists, a traverse of the legendary range from the Mediterranean Sea to the Atlantic Ocean.

This classic, unforgettable ride combines long distances with steep slopes, summer heat, isolated villages and stupendous mountain scenery. It's only for those who really like hills, hills and more hills, 10 days in a row. Although we've classed it as 'very hard', it's officially classified as *hors categorie*, meaning it is so difficult it is beyond classification.

Starting and finishing at sea level, the *raid* (long-distance ride) takes cyclists up 28 significant climbs and innumerable other hills as high as 2115m (Col du Tourmalet). There is 16,000m of climbing in roughly 800km. Riders who preregister with the Cyclo Club Béarnais (see Planning), obtain the *brevet* (route card) and have it stamped at nominated *contrôles* (checkpoints) while riding the route within 10 consecutive days qualify for an attractive medallion.

An entertaining feature of some of the passes is the series of roadside signs with information about the climb, including the average gradient for each kilometre. At the top and bottom of these passes a sign summarises the distance covered and altitude gained, plus average and maximum gradients en route.

PLANNING

Request a Raid Pyrénéen application form some time in advance (three months before leaving home would be good) by sending an international reply coupon (available at post offices) to Cyclo Club Béarnais Cyclotourisme, 59 ave Louis Sallenave, 64000 Pau. After sending the completed form with the entry fee (50FF), you will receive a route card and *plaque* (numbered identification sign for your bike).

Slow Beginning for a Big Ride

Originally the dream of Cyclo Club Béarnais leading light, Maurice Bugard, in 1912, a definitive route for Raid Pyrénéen and a successful attempt on it had to wait until 1950. In June that year, Paul Mathis left Cerbère with companion, Mademoiselle Betbeder, to ride to Hendaye and establish a maximum time to challenge other *randonneurs* (long-distance cyclists). That time was set at 100 hours for a 710km route over 18 passes.

Later, a *version touriste* more suitable for unsupported riders was developed. That longer route, over 10 more passes, in 10 days, is the one described in this section.

From its tentative start, the popularity of the challenge has increased to several hundred riders on each version every year. (Each can be ridden in either direction.)

The break-up of these ride directions is
based on the availability of scarce indoor accommodation, which *must* be booked beforehand. Bringing camping gear means you
are much more flexible (see What to Bring).

Banks can be hard to find on this route,
which follows remote roads through tiny
villages. Take enough money to last between the larger towns. Most hotels accept
credit cards and FF travellers cheques.

When to Ride

The route is officially open from June
through September. June and September are
best for riding; avoid the heat and crowds of
the height of summer. Tour de France fans
may care to ride when the Tour visits the region in July, but be aware that some roads
may be closed and accommodation full.

Maps

Use Michelin maps No 85 *Biarritz, Lourdes,
Luchon* and No 86 *Bagnères de Luchon, Andorre, Perpignan* (both 1:200,000).

What to Bring

Camping gear is recommended in case unpredictable mountain weather prevents you
from reaching a planned stopover. In addition, you are much more flexible and able
to ride longer distances early on if possible,
breaking the journey at camping grounds in
Prades, Ascou, Aulus-les-Bains, St Béat,
Arreau, Argelès Gazost, Arette and St Jean-
Pied de Port. This 'saves' a day, which may
be handy if things go wrong.

GETTING TO/FROM THE RIDE

The Raid Pyrénéen starts about 37km from
Perpignan, the end of the Upper Languedoc
ride in the Languedoc-Roussillon chapter.
Head up the coast from Hendaye to Bor-
deaux for the Bordeaux Wine Explorer ride
(South-West France chapter).

Cerbère

From Toulouse, head to Perpignan and connect to Cerbère. Only the 6.30 pm train from
Toulouse to Perpignan is direct and will take
bikes (143FF, 2½hours); the two other bike-
carrying trains require a change at Narbonne.
To Cerbére from Perpignan, all the frequent
trains carry bikes (43FF, 45 minutes).

From Britain, the European Bike Express
service (see Bus under Continental Europe in

the Getting There & Away chapter) charges
UK£169 (return) to take a passenger and bike
to Perpignan, and to pick up from Bayonne.

Hendaye

All transport from Hendaye heads to Bayonne, on the Atlantic Coast, for onward travel.

Air Catch a bus or train to Bayonne to fly
to other destinations within France. Bayonne's domestic airport (☎ 05 59 43 83 83)
is 5km south-west of the centre.

Bus A bus to Bayonne runs 10 times a day
Monday to Saturday (30.50FF, 1½ hours).
Call ATCRB (☎ 05 59 26 06 99) for bus sta-
tion directions and bike-carriage conditions.
See the Cerbère section for an ideal pick-up
service from Britain.

Train Hendaye train station, blvd du Général
de Gaulle, is signposted from near the beach.

Catch a train to Bayonne (46FF, 35 minutes, about one an hour) for connections to
Toulouse (190FF, about four hours, at least
five direct trains daily) or Bordeaux (142FF,

PYRENEES

1½ hours by TGV, bike-carrying trains take longer, about two a day carry bikes). Check with the SNCF for bike-friendly timetables.

From Bayonne, TGVs run to Paris' Gare Montparnasse (413FF, five hours), plus two daily bike-carrying trains travel overnight to Paris' Gare d'Austerlitz (371FF, about eight hours).

THE RIDE
Cerbère

A town with a distinct frontier feel, Cerbère is just 4km from Spain. It has huge railway yards around its 'international' train station, perched above the town centre. Its grey, pebbly beach has no shortage of sun-worshippers in summer and water sports are popular. But if it weren't for the start/finish point for the Raid Pyrénéen, it is doubtful any cycle tourist would bother visiting, unless they were heading south over the border. Get the first stamp on your route card before leaving.

Information The tourist office (☎ 04 68 88 42 36, fax 04 68 88 48 62) is behind the beach on the main drag, the N114.

The Crédit Agricole is on rue Larousse. There is no bike shop.

Things to See & Do The crumbling 1925 Hôtel Le Belvédère du Rayon Vert, up the hill near the train station, is the town's architectural curiosity, shaped like a huge boat.

A **scuba diving** club (☎ 04 68 88 41 00) can assist in discovering the nearby marine reserve. Hire a **kayak** (☎ 06 09 58 29 36) or watch **petanque (bowls) tournaments**. Otherwise, ride out of town – **Spain**, with its mirror-image town of Portbou, is just over the hill (via the 170m-high Col des Balitres) and a good **viewpoint** is on the way at the lighthouse on Cap Cerbère.

Places to Stay & Eat Crowded, barren *Camping Peyrefitte* (☎ 04 68 88 41 17) is 3km north of town off the N114. It has a good sea view but run-down facilities and charges 38/58FF for one/two people. *Camping L'Atlantis* (☎ 04 68 88 42 99, route d'Espagne), at Plage del Saurell to the south of town, charges 41/62FF and has rooms from 180FF per night.

Ask the tourist office about *chambres d'hôtes* (B&Bs).

Hôtel-Restaurant La Dorade (☎/fax 04 68 88 41 93, ave Général du Gaulle) ha reasonable singles/doubles with shower an toilet in a quiet annexe in the village fo 165/260FF. In the main part of the hote similar rooms cost 205/255FF (more for se view). *Menus* range from 82FF to 115FF.

La Vigie (☎ 04 68 88 41 84, fax 04 68 8 48 87, route d'Espagne) up the hill south o town, has rooms with shower, toilet and se view from 260FF for one or two, 275F with balcony. *Menus* range from 80FF t 135FF.

A small *Casino* supermarket faces centra place de la République; a choice of *bou langeries* and *cafes* are on the square.

Day 1: Cerbère to Llauro
3½–6 hours, 60.4km

This relatively short day reaches the low slopes of the eastern Pyrenees where se vices are extremely limited. Llauro's onl form of accommodation is a camping groun with tent sites. The closest beds are in hotel at Le Boulou, about 1km north of the rou along N9 at 48km. Riders who want to p in a big day will find hotels and camping Prades (see Day 2).

An early morning start will ensure littl traffic on the usually busy N114, whic wiggles northwards along the scenic Côt Vermeille (ruby coast) towards Argelès-su Mer. Collioure (18.4km), a port that in spired the artist Matisse, is worth a pause its southern entry for a photograph.

Laroque des Albères (35.3km) has a bik shop in its *centre commercial*, Cycles de Albères (☎ 04 68 89 89 60).

The turn onto the D13 at 52.3km mark the departure from the busy roads of the rel atively populated coastal lowlands, heraldin the first real climb of the Pyrenees. Abou 5.2km of moderate uphill along foreste minor roads leads to the day's finish.

Llauro

This quiet mountain village lies at abou 300m altitude amid cork forest, 1.5km be fore the col of the same name. The town' only services for cyclists is a campin ground and a food store. There is little to d other than explore the village streets an wander in the scenic surrounding forests.

The Mas Cantuern *chambre d'hôte*, 7km beyond Llauro, no longer operates. It is liste

Day 1: Cerbère to Llauro

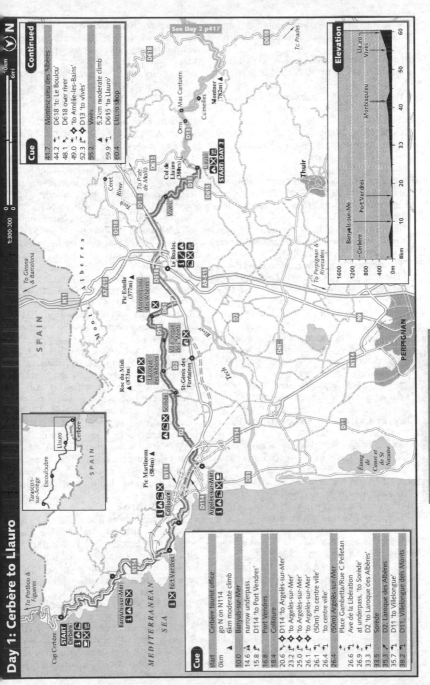

PYRENEES

Cue (Continued)

41.7		Montesquieu des Albères
44.2	↰	D618 'to Le Boulou'
48.1	↱	D618 over river
49.0	◇↰	'to Amélie-les-Bains'
52.3	↰	D13 'to Vivès'
55.2		Vivès
	▲	5.2cm moderate climb
59.9	↰	D615 'to Llauro'
60.4		Llauro ◆shop

See Day 2 p417

Col de Llauro (386m) ▲

Llauro ◆ **START: DAY 2**

Elevation

Banyuls-sur-Mer — Port-Vendres — Montesquieu — Vivès / Llauro

Cue

start		Cerbère tourist office
0km		go N on N114
	▲	6km moderate climb
10.0		Banyuls-sur-Mer
14.6	⚠	narrow underpass
15.8	↱	D114 'to Port Vendres'
16.8		Port Vendres
18.4		Collioure
20.6	◇↱	D114 'to Argelès-sur-Mer'
23.2	↱	'to Argelès-sur-Mer'
25.0	◇◇◇	'to Argelès-sur-Mer'
26.1	↰↱	(50m) 'to centre ville'
26.4	↱	'to centre ville'
26.4		(50m) Argelès-sur-Mer
		Place Gambetta/Rue C Pelletan
26.6	↱↰	Ave de la Libération
26.9	↰	at underpass, 'to Sorède'
33.3	↱	D2 'to Laroque des Albères'
33.5		Sorède
35.3	↱	D2 Laroque des Albères
35.7	↰	D11 'to Villelongue'
38.2	↱	D11, Villelongue dels Monts

as a Raid Pyrénéen contrôle point, so it may be best to get a route card stamp at Llauro.

Information Le Boulou has a Syndicat d'Initiative (☎ 04 68 87 50 95) at 1 rue du Château.

Banks, also in Le Boulou, include a Crédit Agricole at 12 ave Général de Gaulle and others along rue de la République.

Générations Motos (☎ 04 68 87 02 32, 9 ave de Lattre de Tassigny, Le Boulou) can assist with bike repairs.

Places to Stay & Eat In Llauro, *Camping Communal* (☎ 04 68 39 42 08) has a bar which serves snacks. Tent sites cost 20FF per person.

The only other place in town to buy food is the *alimentation générale* (general store) at 14 route des Cerisiers/D615.

The nearest indoor accommodation is at Le Boulou. The classy 3-star *Le Relais des Chartreuses* (☎ 04 68 83 15 88, fax 04 68 83 26 62, 106 ave d'En Carbonner) charges from 430FF to 720FF for a double room with breakfast.

Le Boulou has *supermarkets*, a *general store*, plus *cafes*, *restaurants* and *boulangeries* in its commercial area and on its main street (the N9). For reasonably priced, wholesome fare, try *Relais de la Gare* (☎ 04 68 83 11 65, 44 av Général Joseph Santraille).

Day 2: Llauro to Escouloubre

6½–11½ hours, 115.2km
Next is a harder ride. Bag three early cols, Llauro ((380m), Fourtou (655m) and Xatard (752m), before a brief descent. Then begin the serious ascent of Col de Palomère (30.2km), which takes you above 1000m for the first time, cresting at 1036m.

The next 23km is not very taxing – it's downhill to Marquixanes (56.6km) at 265m. The bad news is, this makes the nearly 20km climb to the 1506m Col de Jau quite steep but, take heart, it's through lovely beech forest and on a quiet road. Take a break from climbing at a picnic table under a talc mine's conveyor (82.7km).

Prades (62.9km) has a bike shop, camping ground, hotels and numerous eateries. Cycles Cerda (☎ 04 68 96 54 51) is at 114 ave du Général de Gaulle (closed Monday morning and all day Sunday); it's the last on the route until Tarascon-sur-Ariège on Day 3.

Camping Bellevue (☎ 04 68 96 48 96 on Ria Sirach near the northern edge o town, charges 56FF for two people and tent.

Pradotel (☎ 04 68 05 22 66, fax 04 68 0 23 22, 17 ave du Festival, La Rocade), 4k from the train station, charges from 305F to 355FF for clean doubles. Of a simila standard, *Interhexagone* (☎ 04 68 05 31 3, fax 04 68 05 24 89, Plaine St Martin/th N116) charges from 330FF to 460FF fo doubles with breakfast. Each has restau ants with *menus* from around 100FF.

Cafes and *bars* around place de l République include the *Brasserie de l'Eu rope* (☎ 04 68 05 37 07) at No 15, wit good-value snacks. For Catalan specialitie try *L'Hostal de Nogarols* (☎ 04 68 96 2 57) on the D27 at the southern edge o town. *Menus* start from 100FF (close Tuesday night and all day Wednesday).

Uphill at Molitg-les-Bains (74.1km 610m), the one-star *St Joseph* (☎ 04 68 0 00 92, fax 04 68 05 01 62) on the D14 offer double rooms with breakfast from 203FF t 228FF. Guests are welcome to use the the mal baths.

About 3km along a gravel road leadin from Jau's summit is the *Refuge du Calla* (☎ 04 68 05 00 06). Follow the signs to th left, off the route. The refuge is open fro late June to late September and all scho holidays. A dorm bed costs 45FF. Meals, in cluding breakfast, *pique niques* (takeawa lunches) and dinner, start at 60FF.

Another all-too-quick downhill is ove after 11km and the relatively easy ascent o the 1256m-high Col du Garavel (109.8km begins. Descend slightly to Escouloubre.

Escouloubre

One of many towns in the eastern Pyrenee which has suffered rural decline and de population, Escouloubre now offers virtu ally no services except accommodatio Explore its quiet, winding streets lined wit decaying stone buildings.

Places to Stay & Eat The sole place t stay and eat is the *gîte d'étape* (☎ 04 68 2 44 02) in the very centre of the tiny village A bed in the 14-person dorm costs 65F Double rooms cost 260FF for two, includ ing breakfast. Dinner starts from 90FF pe person. Cooking facilities are available.

Summer in the Massif Central means wildflowers.

Besse-en-Chandesse's dark volcanic-stone church.

The Alps always inspire feats of daring in the Tour de France peloton – try some of the cols yourself.

Cycling up the Col de Jouels in the fog.

Arreau sits on the confluence of two rivers.

Canoeing is popular in the Gorges de l'Ardèche.

You can cycle across the Pont du Gard in Nîmes, one of France's most important Roman structures.

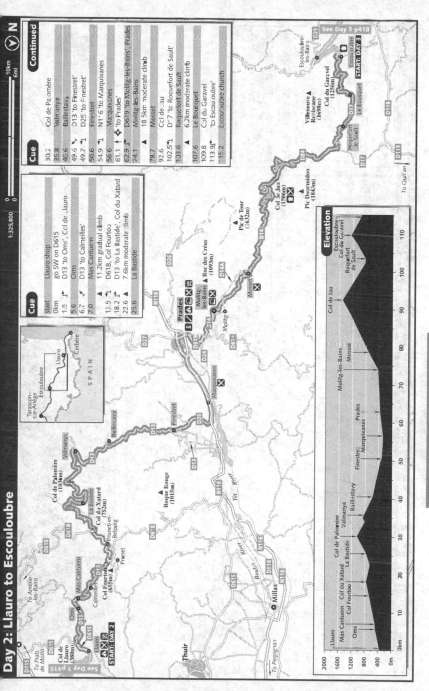

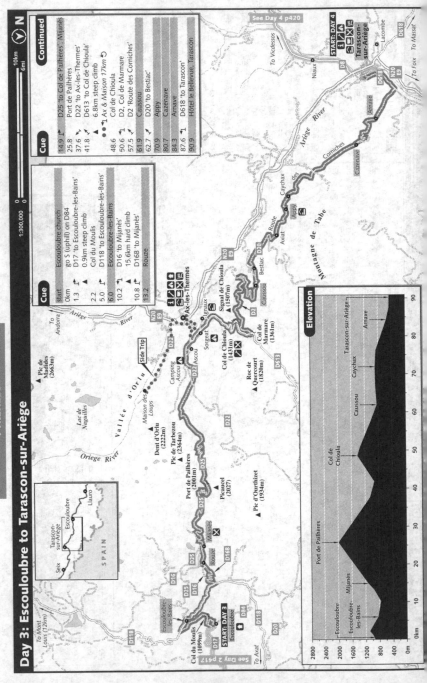

Day 3: Escouloubre to Tarascon-sur-Ariège

Continued

Cue

14.9	D25 'to Col de Pailhères', 'Mijanès'
25.8	Port de Pailhères
37.6	D22 'to Ax-les-Thermes'
41.8	D613 'to Col de Chioula'
	6.8km steep climb
48.6	Ax & Maison 17km ↻
50.6	Col de Chioula
57.5	D2, Col de Marmare
61.9	D2 'Route des Corniches'
62.7	Caussou
70.9	D20 'to Bestiac'
80.7	Appy
84.3	Cazenave
87.6	Arnave
90.9	D618 'to Tarascon'
	Hôtel le Bellevue, Tarascon

Cue

Start	Escouloubre church go S (uphill) on D84
1.3	D17 'to Escouloubre-les-Bains'
	0.9km steep climb
2.2	Col du Moulis
5.0	D118 'to Escouloubre-les-Bains'
6.0	Escouloubre-les-Bains
	D16 'to Mijanès'
	15.6km hard climb
10.8	D16B 'to Mijanès'
13.2	Rouze

Elevation

Day 3: Escouloubre to Tarascon-sur-Ariège

4½–9 hours, 90.9km

Descend to near-deserted Escouloubre-les-Bains (6km) and, if possible, obtain a stamp for your route card. (Mijanès, 8.9km farther on, is an alternate contrôle).

The long, hard climb to Port de Pailhères takes the route to the second-highest altitude for the Raid, 2001m, followed by a steep, hairpinned descent towards Ascou.

Pass *Camping Ascou* (☎ 05 61 64 60 03), on the left at 38.4km, which charges 38/58FF for one/two. At 41.8km, it's worth visiting Ax-les-Thermes and the Maison des Loups if you have time (see Side Trip).

To continue, turn up the road to the Col de Chioula (48.6km), a steady 7km ascent with a few switchbacks near the top. The 1431m summit offers a superb **view**, clouds permitting, of the Pyrenean summits along the Spanish border south of Ax. The chalet here has a *restaurant* (☎ 05 61 05 40 40) and VTT hire (☎ 05 61 64 20 00). Ten VTT circuits totalling 160km are signposted on the surrounding mountainside, suitable for all levels of rider. A map is free.

Descend to the Col de Marmare (1361m) and turn onto an extremely minor road, the scenic Route des Corniches. Wind down along the mountainside, through villages with virtually no services, to Tarascon.

Side Trip: Ax-les-Thermes & Maison des Loups

1–2 hours, 17km

Along the beautiful Vallée d'Orlu, south-east of Ax-les-Thermes, is the **Maison des Loups** (☎ 05 61 64 02 66), where European and North American wolves are displayed in natural surroundings, with information on the species and the program to save them (entry is 32FF).

The 3.5km to Ax is all downhill on the fairly quiet D613, but there's plenty of time to enjoy the forest scenery on the climb back.

Accommodation options in Ax include *Camping Malazéou* (☎ 05 61 64 69 14), where you can camp on 'the hill' for 31/40FF for one/two people in high season; and the *Hôtel le Breilh* (☎ 05 61 64 24 29), in the centre next to the tourist office, with rooms from 180FF.

To the maison, it's a short climb out of Ax on the busy N20 before an idyllic, easy

4km on the D22; the Maison is just past Forge d'Orlu. Return to Ax and then back to the route the same way.

Tarascon-sur-Ariège

One of the largest towns on the Raid Pyrénéen route, Tarascon has most services, the main attraction being the many caves in the area. At nearby Lacombe, on route de Banat, is **Le Parc Pyrénéen de l'Art Préhistorique** (☎ 05 61 05 10 10), a series of 13 caves decorated with rock paintings.

Information The tourist office (☎ 05 61 05 94 94) is in the Centre Multimédia on ave des Pyrénées.

Crédit Agricole is on ave Ayroule. Many banks, including Banque Populaire at No 12, are on ave Victor Pilnes.

The bike shop, Daniel 2-Roues (☎ 05 61 05 90 76), 6 place de la République, does repairs but has no bike hire (closed Sunday and Monday).

Places to Stay & Eat Signposted to the left off the route, 1.7km from the centre of Tarascon towards Niaux, *Camping le Pré Lombard* (☎ 05 61 05 61 90) charges 60FF for two campers.

Hôtel Confort (☎ 05 61 05 61 90, 3 quai Armand Sylvestre) is beside the Ariège River and has rooms from 150FF to 250FF and *menus* featuring regional dishes from 70FF to 120FF.

The unfriendly *Hostellerie de la Poste* (☎ 05 61 66 86 33), on the main ave Victor Pilhes, has rooms with washbasin from 160FF, with shower and toilet from 235FF.

The hotel-pizzeria-creperie *Le Bellevue* (☎ 05 61 05 60 45) is the main eatery in the centre of town. Several *boulangeries*, small *supermarkets* and other *shops* are nearby for supplies.

Day 4: Tarascon-sur-Ariège to Seix

4–7 hours, 70.8km

This ride is tough with almost 32km of climbing. It starts pretty flat for the short distance to Niaux, 5.1km south-west of town. Stop here for the folk museum **Le Musée Pyrénéen de Niaux** (☎ 05 61 05 88 36).

Niaux is also the point of access for **La Grotte de Niaux** (☎ 05 61 05 88 37), one of Europe's most important cave painting

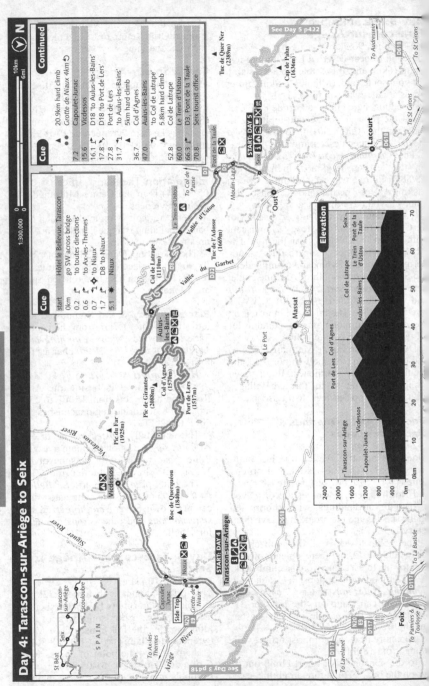

Day 4: Tarascon-sur-Ariège to Seix

PYRENEES

1:300,000

N

10km
6mi

Cue

start	Hôtel le Bellevue, Tarascon
0km	go SW across bridge
0.2	'to toutes directions'
0.6	'to Ax-les-Thermes'
0.7	'to Niaux'
1.7	D8 'to Niaux'
5.1	Niaux

Cue Continued

	20.9km hard climb
	Grotte de Niaux 4km
7.2	Capoulet-Junac
15.6	Vicdessos
16.1	D18 'to Aulus-les-Bains'
17.8	D18 'to Port de Lers'
27.8	Port de Lers
31.7	'to Aulus-les-Bains'
	5km hard climb
36.7	Col d'Agnes
47.0	Aulus-les-Bains
	'to Col de Latrape'
	5.8km hard climb
52.8	Col de Latrape
60.0	Le Trein d'Ustou
66.3	D3, Pont de la Taule
70.8	Seix tourist office

See Day 5 p422

START DAY 5
Seix

START DAY 4
Tarascon-sur-Ariège

Side Trip
Grotte de Niaux

Niaux

Vicdessos

Capoulet-Junac

Roc de Querquéou (1840m)

Pic du Far (1925m)

Pic de Gérantes (2088m)

Col d'Agnes (1570m)

Port de Lers (1517m)

Aulus-les-Bains

Col de Latrape (1110m)

Tuc de l'Adosse (1669m)

Vallée du Garbet

Vallée d'Ustou

Le Trein d'Ustou

To Col de Pause

Moulin-Lauzé

Pont de la Taule

Oust

Massat

Le Port

Tuc de Quer Ner (2389m)

Cap de Pahts (1630m)

Lacourt

To Audressein
To St Girons
To St Girons

To Pamiers & Toulouse

Foix

To Lavelanet

To La Bastide

D618
D618
D618
D3
D8
D32
D8
D18
D3
N20
D117
D117
D111

See Day 3 p418

Ariège River
Signet River
Vicdessos River

SPAIN

St Béat
Seix
Tarascon-sur-Ariège
Ecouloubre

To Ax-les-Thermes

Elevation

Tarascon-sur-Ariège
Capoulet-Junac
Vicdessos
Port de Lers
Col d'Agnes
Aulus-les-Bains
Col de Latrape
Le Trein d'Ustou
Pont de la Taule
Seix

2400
2000
1600
1200
800
400
0m

0km   10   20   30   40   50   60   70

ites, dating from 12,000 BC. It's open for inspections from July through September; bookings essential. Take a left turn out of Niaux and follow signs up the winding mountain road. The 4km round trip takes 30 to 40 minutes and is uphill all the way there.

From Niaux a long climb starts towards Port de Lers (27.8km, 1517m), passing picnic tables at 16.4km. A short descent allows some recovery before the steep 5km up to Col d'Agnes (36.7km).

From 1570m the route plummets 850m in 10km into Aulus-les-Bains (47km). Here are a number of *food shops*, plus *Camping Le Couledous* (☎ 05 61 96 02 26), about 100m north-west of the town centre, which charges 38/56FF for one/two people, and three hotels. *Hôtel France* (☎ 05 61 96 00 90, fax 05 61 96 03 29) asks 180FF for a double with shower and toilet, while the *Beauséjour* (☎ 05 61 96 00 06) and the *Terasse* (☎ 05 61 96 00 98, fax 05 61 96 01 12) each charge 280FF for a double with shower and toilet.

To continue, hit the hill out of Aulus and climb 400m in 5.8km to the 1110m-high Col de Latrape (52.8km). A great downhill leads to Seix.

Seix

This picturesque, lively little village of the Ariège department perches astride the Salat River at 500m altitude. It is 25km from the ski resort of Guzet-Neige (to the south-east) and 120km from Toulouse (north-west).

Information The tourist office (☎ 05 61 96 52 90, @ otsiseix@ifrance.com) in place Champ de Mars is open every day. It (or most other businesses in town) can supply a stamp for the Raid Pyrénéen.

Crédit Agricole has a branch on route de Salau and there is an ATM at the post office. There is no bike shop.

Things to See & Do Seix village is dominated by its 15th-century royal **castle** and an elaborately decorated **church**.

The **long-distance walking** route, the GR10, leaves the road south of town at Moulin-Laga, heading toward the Spanish border, but undertaking it would require an overnight hike.

The superb viewpoint of the **Col de Pause** (1527m) is accessible by bicycle,

20.5km south then west via the D3, and steeply up the skinny, sinuous D703.

Details on a variety of **activities**, including hiking, tennis, whitewater sports and horse riding, are available from the tourist office.

Places to Stay & Eat The *Camping Municipal La Cote* (☎ 05 61 96 50 53) is on the bank of the Salat River, 2.5km north along the D3 towards Oust. It charges 20/28FF for one/two.

At Pont de la Taule, 4.5km before Seix, the *Auberge des Deux Rivières* (☎ 05 61 66 83 57, route de Guzet-Neige/D8) has good-value doubles with toilet and bath from 195FF and excellent regional *menus* from 78FF to 145FF.

In Seix village, the *Auberge du Haut Salat* (☎ 05 61 66 88 03) charges from 180FF to 240FF, while the *Hostellerie de la Poste* (☎ 05 61 66 86 33), about 2km away in Oust, charges from 160FF to 380FF.

The town square hosts *markets* on the first and second Thursdays each month. There is a small *Casino* supermarket in place Joffre. An excellent bakery, *Le Petrin Gourmand*, is tucked around a kink in the road in the village centre.

Hôtel/Restaurant du Mont Vallier (☎ 05 61 66 83 68) on the town square has *menus* featuring regional specialities from 100FF.

Day 5: Seix to St Béat
4–7½ hours, 76.8km

Start the day with a visit to Seix's excellent bakery, *Le Pétrin Gourmand*, then gain nearly 900m on the 13.2km climb up Col de la Core (1395m). Lose most of the height gained on the run down to Castillon-en-Couserans (30km), a good place for lunch with its *alimentation* and *cafes* on ave Noël Peyrevidal.

Two more major climbs come before the day's end: the infamous Col de Portet d'Aspet (49.7km, 1069m), scene of Fabio Casartelli's death in the 1995 Tour de France (see the 'Mort Pour Le Tour' boxed text in the Provence & the Côte d'Azur chapter); and the seemingly endless Col de Menté (65.7km, 1349m). A *restaurant* is at the top of Portet d'Aspet.

Between the two the route descends past the Casartelli memorial (53.3km) to 635m, giving only a brief respite while pedalling along the Ger River valley.

Day 5: Seix to St Béat

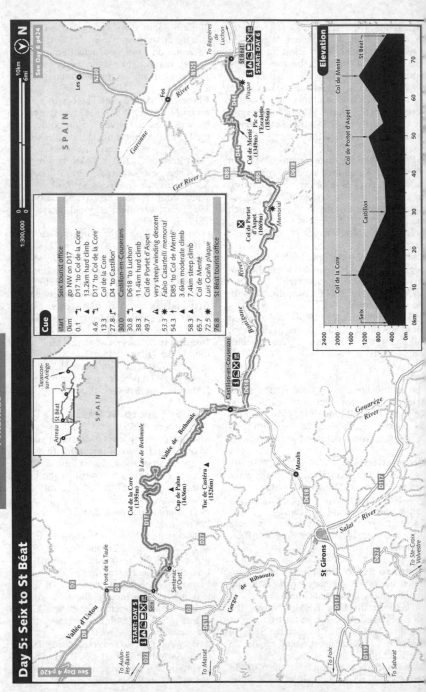

Cue

start		Seix tourist office
0km	↰	go NW on D17
0.1	▲	D17 'to Col de la Core'
4.6	↰	13.2km hard climb
13.3		D17 'to Col de la Core'
27.8	↱	Col de la Core
30.0		D4 'to Castillon'
		Castillon-en-Couserans
30.8	↰	D618 'to Luchon'
38.3	▲	11.4km hard climb
49.7		Col de Portet d'Aspet
53.3	⚠ ✳	very steep/winding descent
		Fabio Casartelli memorial
54.1	▲ ↰	D85 'to Col de Menté'
58.3	▲	3.6km moderate climb
65.7	▲	7.4km steep climb
72.5	✳	Col de Menté
		Luis Ocaña plaque
76.8		St Béat tourist office

Elevation

PYRENEES

The Col de Menté climb is mostly through forest, starting out very steeply, with some sections in excess of 9% gradient. Near the bottom of the descent, look for the small **plaque** (72.5km) commemorating Spaniard Luis Ocaña's fall in the rain (and a mudslide) while leading the 1971 Tour. Forced to withdraw, he had to wait until 1973 for victory, ending Belgian Eddy Merckx's streak of four straight wins.

Land in St Béat after a wonderful, exhilirating descent.

St Béat

St Béat is a bottleneck which sees a huge amount of traffic heading to and from Spain on the N125. Trucks and cars jam the centre of this otherwise pleasant village, making it noisy and dangerous.

The Office du Tourisme (☎ 05 61 79 77 00) is on ave Général Gallieni near the corner of the D44 (open daily in high season). Crédit Agricole is in the town centre on ave Général Gallieni. There is no bike shop.

If the hectic main street is too much, stock up and head south for Fos (6km), where there's a hotel-restaurant.

Places to Stay & Eat St Béat has two camping grounds, both surprisingly quiet given the proximity of busy roads. *Thei la Garonnette* (☎ 05 61 79 41 36) is beside the Garonne River, near the intersection of the N125 and the D44. It charges 29/46FF for one/two people, including hot showers. The similarly-priced *municipal camping ground* (☎ 05 61 94 35 39) is just south of the town centre.

Hôtel-Restaurant du Pont (☎ 05 61 79 40 22) is at the north end of town, set back off the N125. It has doubles with washbasin from 120FF, or with toilet from 140FF. *Menus* start from 95FF.

St Béat has most services, including three *bakeries*, a small *Casino* supermarket and *cafes*.

Hôtel-Restaurant Fos (☎ 05 61 79 29 00), 6km south, has good rooms for 140/170FF for one/two people and *menus* starting at 100FF.

Day 6: St Béat to Arreau
4–7 hours, 71km

Another shortish day, with a blessedly easy start and picnic areas at 34km, 43.8km and 56.8km. The route follows the Garonne River gently upstream and out of the country. The Spanish leg is less than 18km through the thriving town of Bossòst and up the steep road to the Col du Portillon (27.8km, 1320m), where the route re-enters France.

The climb has an average gradient of about 7% but is considerably steeper in places. A smooth 'hot-mix' surface replaced the original rough aggregate on the Spanish side just in time for the passage of the 1999 Tour de France over Portillon. Enjoy fine views of the Garonne River valley on the way to the forest-shrouded summit. The descent is something else – long, steep straights tempt riders to alarming velocity while hairpins require heavy braking and slow-cornering speeds.

At the bottom is Bagnères de Luchon (38.4km), a spa town with an attractive broad central boulevard and a wide range of shops. There are a couple of bike shops – MBK Cycles (☎ 05 61 79 12 87), 82 ave Maréchal Foch/D125, does repairs (closed Monday).

The long ascent of the Col de Peyresourde starts just out of town and is particularly hard – straight after lunch in the shadeless heat of the afternoon. With the grade averaging around 7% for 13km, ample water supplies are essential. Everpresent is the dull clang of cowbells – which are sometimes even attached to goats or horses. The route is nearing the col (52.7km) when the road begins a series of four switchbacks, each 500m long. A *cafe–snack bar* is at the otherwise dull summit – the best views are about 500m before the top.

The route sweeps down to Arreau on the valley floor, with panoramic views en route.

Arreau

A pleasant mountain town at the meeting of four valleys, Arreau's historic narrow streets lack footpaths and harbour some exceptionally rude and aggressive drivers. Fortunately the car-free *ruelles* (alleyways) west of the centre provide respite and beg exploration.

Information The tourist office (☎ 05 62 98 63 15), 1 rue St Exupère, is across the river in Château des Nestes (closed Sunday afternoon). Follow signs from the centre.

Day 6: St Béat to Arreau

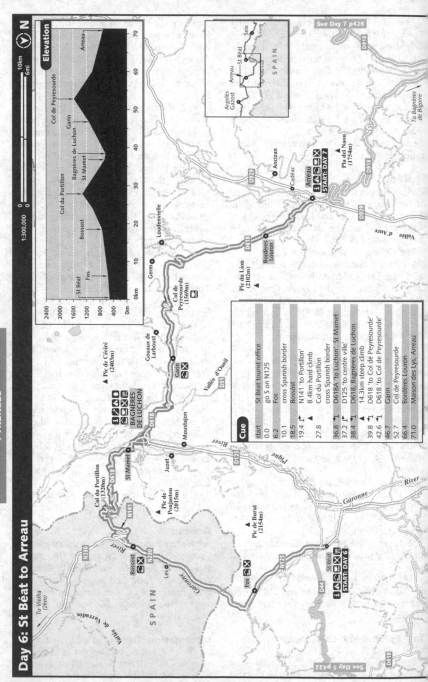

Elevation

1:300,000

Cue

start	St Béat tourist office
0.0	go S on N125
6.2	Fos
10.1	cross Spanish border
18.5	Bossòst
19.4	N141 'to Portillon'
27.8	Col du Portillon
	cross Spanish border
36.8	D618A 'to Luchon', St Mamet
37.2	D125 'to centre ville'
38.4	D618, Bagnères de Luchon
	14.3km steep climb
39.8	D618 'to Col de Peyresourde'
42.6	D618 'to Col de Peyresourde'
46.7	Garin
52.7	Col de Peyresourde
66.4	Bordères Louron
71.0	Maison des Lys, Arreau

See Day 7 p426

See Day 5 p422

PYRENEES

The Banque Populaire is at 8 quai Neste. Crédit Agricole is at 25 place de la Mairie. There is no bike shop.

Things to See & Do The village is known for its **craft shops** and a sticky cake called **gâteau à la broche** brought to the Pyrenees from the Balkans by Napoleon's armies. Along with the tourist office (with the same hours and phone number) in Château des Nestes is a **museum** of Pyrenean craft work (entry free).

Arreau's most attractive buildings are the Renaissance **Maison des Lys**, on Grande Rue in the centre of town, covered in fleurs-de-lys timberwork, and the Romanesque **Église St Exupère**, across the river from the Maison.

Kayaking and **rafting** on the town's white-water streams are popular. Adréna-ine Rafting (☎ 05 62 40 04 04) is on route de Luchon in the centre of the village.

If you're staying a while in the region, ask at the tourist office for the *Passeport Vélo*, a special **route card** produced by the Conseil Général des Hautes-Pyrénées. Get it stamped at various locations, after cycling up a series of climbs in the department, to earn a certificate.

Places to Stay & Eat Tucked away on the bank of the rushing Neste d'Aure off the D19 just south of the centre is *Camping Municipal Arreau* (☎ 05 62 98 65 56, fax 05 62 98 68 78). It charges 32/49FF for one/two people (closed in October).

Beside the Neste d'Aure 5km south (off-route) along the D929 at Cadéac, the *Hostellerie du Val d'Aure* (☎ 05 62 98 60 63, fax 05 62 98 68 99) has a park-like lo-cation and rooms with toilet and a shower or bath from 215FF to 270FF. (Demi-pension costs 230FF to 285FF per head and is obligatory in high season.)

The *Hôtel d'Angleterre* (☎ 05 62 98 63 30, fax 05 62 98 69 66, route de Luchon) is in the centre of town. Doubles with toilet and shower range from 230FF to 340FF. *Menus* start at 78FF and go up to 200FF.

The town *marché* (market) takes place on Thursday.

Day 7: Arreau to Argelès Gazost
4–8 hours, 84.1km

This is the day you have been waiting for! Start fresh on the beautiful 90-minute climb to the most attractive col, Aspin (1489m) at 13 4km. With herds of pale orange cows wandering across the road in search of handouts, superb **views** to the Pic du Midi de Bigorre (2872m; near the top of Col du Tourmalet) and cool forest on the western side, Aspin is a dream.

The descent to Ste-Marie de Campan (26.6km) is also a dream run. A *bakery* or *cafe* stop in the town centre is a must before joining the many other cyclists beginning the assault on the big one – Col du Tour-malet. It's 17km away and 1258m above the town. Ste-Marie de Campan is another con-trôle where the route card must be stamped – the *Bar-Brasserie des Deux Vallées* should be happy to do this.

Take the Tourmalet climb steadily and the distance will just drop away. The gradient starts gently but gradually increases towards the top. The ski village of La Mongie, 4.5km from the summit, has *accommodation* and *refreshment* facilities. At the summit, which should take about two solid hours of pedal-ling to reach, is a *restaurant*, souvenir shop and a larger-than-life statue of a mounted cyclist, commemorating the Tour de France crossings of Tourmalet (see the 'Pilgrims in the Pyrenees' boxed text).

Once over the top about 41km of down-hill awaits and, psychologically, a weight has lifted – the Atlantic goal is almost in sight…only eight passes and 300km to go!

Barèges (58.3km), the first sizeable town since Arreau, is 15km down the green grassy mountain. Keep going down through Esterre (65.2km), with two *camping grounds*, to busy Luz St-Sauveur (66.1km), with *super-markets*, *bakeries* and plenty of excuses for a break. (This is the junction with the road to the amazing Cirque de Gavarnie –about 30km south – a gigantic amphitheatre-like formation of rock, more than 4km wide at its base and 14km around the crest line.) From here, another 250m in height waits to be washed off in the next 18km to Argelès Gazost.

Argelès Gazost
A town at the junction of several mountain valleys, Argelès Gazost has a modern com-mercial area surrounding an older village centre. Here, narrow alleyways are lined with attractive 16th- and 17th-century buildings.

PYRENEES

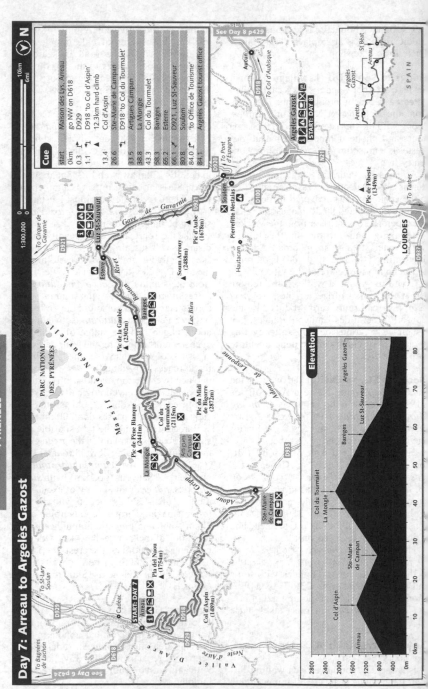

PYRENEES

Day 7: Arreau to Argelès Gazost

See Day 6 p424

See Day 8 p429

Cue

start	Maison des Lys, Arreau
0km	go NW on D618
0.3	D929
1.1	D918 'to Col d'Aspin'
	12.3km hard climb
13.4	Col d'Aspin
26.6	Ste-Marie de Campan
	D918 'to Col du Tourmalet'
33.5	Artigues Campan
38.8	La Mongie
43.3	Col du Tourmalet
58.3	Barèges
65.2	Esterre
66.1	D921, Luz St-Sauveur
80.8	Soulom
84.0	'to Office de Tourisme'
84.1	Argelès Gazost tourist office

Elevation

Pilgrims in the Pyrenees

Pilgrim routes crisscross the Pyrenees on the way to Santiago de Compostela in Spain and to Lourdes, near Pau. Another type of Pyrenean pilgrim, perhaps even more numerous, is the cyclist who follows the routes of the Tour de France up the passes of this famous mountain range.

Such routes are usually marked by names of Tour greats scrawled semi-permanently on the road surface. Recently signs erected by Hautes-Pyrénées authorities have begun to cater for these 'pilgrims' by giving altitude, gradient and distance information at each kilometre point on selected cols – some famous, others nearly unknown.

After the Alpe d'Huez in the Alps, probably the best-known Tour de France climb is the Pyrenees' Col du Tourmalet. One of the highest road passes in the range, the 2115m col was first used in the 1910 Tour. On 21 July, Octave Lapize was the first rider to conquer the then unsealed climb. He went on to win the 326km stage from Bagnères de Luchon to Bayonne in a time of 14 hours 10 minutes.

Nowadays the 1258m ascent of the eastern face from Ste-Marie de Campan is over a distance of 17km, all on sealed road. The average gradient is 8%. Heading east from Luz St Sauveur the height gain is 1404m in about 22km at an overall average of 7.5%. But the last kilometre is the steepest, averaging a punishing 10%.

Usually on the Tour route immediately before or straight after the climb of Tourmalet, pretty Col d'Aspin is lower and somewhat easier. Heading west it's a 12km climb from just outside Arreau. The road snakes its way from 690m to 1489m, averaging an innocuous sounding 6.7%. The first kilometre, though, is at a mere 4% gradient. In the middle, the numbers reach 9.5% for a couple of grinding kilometres. In 1999 the Tour made its 65th ascent of Col d'Aspin.

The Pyrenean passes of Portillon, Peyresourde and Portet d'Aspet are long, hard climbs, among many others, where you are sure to be spurred on by your favourite rider from recent, or not so recent, years. Imagine yourself to be Lance (Armstrong), Vivi (Richard Virenque) or Jaja (Laurent Jalabert), (Marco) Pantani or (Bjarne) Riis, even (Miguel) Indurain, (Greg) LeMond or (Bernard) Hinault as you struggle upwards. The big names are all climbing with you, inscribed in flaking white paint on bitumen if not actually appearing in the flesh. *Allez!* (Go!)

An unusual Pyrenean pilgrimage site is the chapel of Notre Dame des Cyclistes (Michelin map No 79 *Bordeaux, Agen, Montauban*, southern part of fold 12). Set in a rural location off the D626, 2.5km southeast of Labastide d'Armagnac, this tiny 12th-century church is filled with cycling memorabilia. Entrance to the grounds is through gates made from bicycle parts. Jerseys belonging to famous cyclists like Merckx, Bobet, Hinault, LeMond and many others create frescoes on the walls, while one of the bicycles from the first Tour de France (1903) is on display. Luis Ocaña was married here.

The 1989 Tour stage from Bordeaux to Pau visited Notre Dame des Cyclistes to commemorate the church's 30th anniversary. (Just to show the French are fervent about things other than cycling, only 30km away near Grenade-sur-l'Adour, is a pilgrimage site of an entirely different nature – the chapel of Notre Dame du Rugby, decorated, of course, with rugby jerseys.)

Signs and even statues mark many of the cols along the Raid Pyrénéen.

Information The tourist office (☎ 05 62 97 00 25 , fax 05 62 97 50 60) is in place de la Mairie (closed all day Sunday except in high season, when it's open until noon).

Argelès Gazost is blessed with three bank branches, including Crédit Lyonnais in place du Foirail.

Sports Loisirs Diffusion (☎ 05 62 97 55 78) at 1 ave Charles de Gaulle does repairs.

Things to See & Do On the N21 at the northern edge of town, **Le Musée de la Faune Sauvage** (☎ 05 62 97 91 07) has displays on European animals.

For mountain goats, it's a 15km – including a 12km steep climb – **ride** to the ski resort of Hautacam – scene of a dramatic 1994 Tour de France stage finish between Miguel Indurain and French champion Luc Leblanc (Leblanc won the stage, Indurain the Tour). Take the D100.

Ask the tourist office about the map *VTT des 7 Vallées* – 10 **VTT rides** of up to 30km in length, with as much as 1120m of climbing.

Places to Stay & Eat Peaceful *Camping La Prairie (☎ 05 62 97 11 87)* is at Lau Balagnas, just south of Argelès on the D921. The tariff is 34/51FF for one/two people.

Le Bon Repos (☎ 05 62 97 01 49, fax 05 62 97 03 97, 13 route du Hautacam) is 1km east from the centre. Doubles start at 150FF, rising to 220FF according to proximity to the garden.

Hôtel Beau Site (☎ 05 62 97 08 63, fax 05 62 97 06 01, 10 rue du Capitaine Digoy) has pleasant rooms from 230FF and an 80FF *menu du jour* (set meal of the day).

The Tuesday morning *market* in front of the church is a 200-year-old tradition in Argelès. There are a couple of *supermarkets* and the usual choice of *bakeries* for a town of this size.

Try the 49FF *assiette du randonneur* (randonneur's platter) at *Restaurant La Grange (☎ 05 62 97 26 52)* in rue de Verdun, the narrow street uphill from Hôtel Beau Site. Open for lunch and dinner, it has *menus* for 75FF and 95FF.

Day 8: Argelès Gazost to Arette
5–10 hours, 100.1km
This day challenges yesterday in the beauty of its scenery. The tiny road over the 1156m Col des Bordères (14.5km) drops into Arrens

Marsous, where an information centre (☎ 05 62 97 49 49; closed Sunday outside school holidays) for the **Parc National des Pyrénées** has interesting exhibits on its wildlife.

Arrens is at the foot of Col du Soulo (26.4km, 1474m). The climb is taxing – very steep in places and exposed to blazing sun – but has a welcome **picnic area** at 24.2km. Feral ponies demand handouts at the top. Although easily avoided, feed or tease them and they will bite. There is a *cafe/snack-bar* and, usually, *stalls* selling local produce.

The narrow road then follows the contour along the side of a sheer mountain face through some short tunnels, finally climbing steeply to reach the summit of Col d'Aubisque (36.3km, 1709m). The *restaurant* here is an excellent lunch venue, offering inexpensive, tasty dishes with a multi-million-franc **view** from the terrace of 2613m Pic de Ger thrown in for free. Get your route card stamped.

Another magical descent follows – drop 27km and nearly 1200m to reach Bielle (63.2km). Don't let your legs stiffen up there is another 540m climb to come – the Col de Marie Blanque (75km, 1073m), another pass popular with designers of Tour de France courses. Fortunately, the eastern face is far less steep than the western. The descent plummets in almost a straight line to little Escot (84.3km), making this probably the fastest downhill on the Raid route. Take care.

A brief sojourn on a *route nationale* (major road) leads to the quieter D918 for a final brief climb (gain about 100m) in a series of wiggles into Arette.

Arette
This tiny village occupies a little-visited corner of the Basque region called La Soule. In August 1967 it was shaken by a severe earthquake, a rarity in France, and almost totally destroyed.

The tourist office (☎ 05 59 88 95 38, fax 05 59 88 95 41) is in the town centre or place de l'Église (closed Sunday).

Crédit Agricole is at 14 place de l'Église. There is no bike shop.

Things to See & Do All details for these things to see and do are available from the tourist office.

In the town centre, **La Maison du Barétous** displays the food and cuisine of former

Day 8: Argelès Gazost to Arette

1:325,000

N

0 ____ 10km
0 ____ 6mi

Cue

start		Argelès Gazost Tourist office
0km		go W to Ave des Pyrénée
0.1	↰	Ave des Pyrénées
0.2	↰	Place du Forail
0.4	↰	D918 'to Arens'
3.3	↰	2.9km moderate climb
3.3		D103 'to Arcizans Avant'
3.5		Arras-en-Lavedan
5.9	↱	'to Sireix'
11.8	↰	D105 'to Arre.s', Estaing
14.5		8.6km moderate climb
14.5	↱	Col des Bordères
17.4	↱	'to Arrens'
18.3	↰	D105 'to Arrens'

Cue — Continued

18.3	✳	Arrens
	◀	D918 'to Col du Sou'lor'
	◀	7.6km hard climb
26.4	◀	Col du Soulor
30.0	◀	200m unlit wet tunnel
	◀	6.3km moderate climb
36.3	◀	Col d'Aubisque
40.8		Gourette
49.0		D918 'to Pau', Eaux Bonnes
53.2	↰	D934 'to Laruns'
54.9		Laruns
61.0	✧	D934B 'to Bielle'
63.2		Bielle
63.5	◀	D294 'tc Col de Marie Blanque
		11.5km steep climb
75.0		Col de Marie Blanque
84.3	↱	D238 'ts Sarrance' Escot
85.0	↱	N134
89.9	↱	D918 'to Arette'
100.1		Arette tourist office

See Day 9 p431

See Day 9 p431

Elevation

PYRENEES

times, showing the development of the lifestyle of the Barétous valley.

On the north-western edge of the village, in the forest, is an **arboretum** and sign-posted thematic walk revealing the ecological diversity of the area.

Beside the tourist office, the **Seismological Centre** researches earthquakes in the local area and beyond. Inspections of seismological equipment and displays on the 1967 quake can be arranged.

VTT routes are signposted in the area and bikes can be hired at the service station (☎ 05 59 88 90 61, fax 05 59 88 95 75). Guide maps are available at the tourist office.

Places to Stay & Eat The small *Camping Municipal*, a couple of hundred metres from the centre of town, has attractive sites (but rather too many large slugs, which crawl into and over everything exposed). The tariff is 16FF per person.

Hôtel-Restaurant Salies (☎ 05 59 88 90 78, fax 05 59 88 94 37, place de l'Église) has doubles with bath/shower for 200FF. Its *menus* range from 60FF to 135FF.

A couple of thinly stocked *grocery stores* serve the town.

Day 9: Arette to St Jean-Pied de Port

3½–7½ hours, 76.4km

Think the pain is almost over?…well, sorry, you ain't seen nothin' yet. Col Bagargui awaits and those who struggle to its summit have been known to call it something else.

Fairly easy riding leads past Licq, after which a 10km gentle climb provides a good warm-up. From Larrau (32.5km), another contrôle, descend 120m and swing onto a road too narrow to share with motorised traffic. The next 10km gains 800m as the road switches back and forth and heaves itself towards the sky. The average totally belies the steepness of this climb – it is undoubtedly the worst on the westbound Raid – and it is utterly shadeless.

At the top is blessed relief with shady trees and a *restaurant*, but keep up a regular food and fluid intake on the way up to prevent complete exhaustion.

Score a bonus 'secret' col, Hegui Xouri (to pronounce, try 'eggy choory'), on the descent. Pass the bar/restaurant/hotel, *Chalet de Cize*, then cruise up to bag the Col de

Burdincurutcheta (53.6km), a mere 6.5% average which will feel like downhill after Bagargui. From here, at 1135m, it's 104km to 'home' with two passes to climb. The higher one is 176m – feel good? On the 23km descent to St Jean, imagine what those poor souls doing the Raid west-east would dub the unpronounceable Burdincurutcheta

St Jean-Pied de Port

A lively Basque town with a fine medieval centre, St Jean is 8km from Spain and 42km as the *corbeau* flies, from the Atlantic.

Information The tourist office (☎ 05 59 37 03 57, fax 05 59 37 34 91) is at 14 place du Général de Gaulle, below the town walls (closed Sunday from October to June).

A BNP agency is at 5 rue Zuharpéta. Crédit Agricole and Sociéte Générale have branches in place du Marché.

To hire a VTT call ☎ 05 59 37 21 79, but there are no repair services.

Things to See & Do Wander around **place du Général de Gaulle**, with elegant buildings and **Porte de Navarre**, the gate to the old town, which begs to be explored on foot.

The tourist office sells a 10FF folder of rudimentary maps for five circular back road walks, up to 16km long, around St Jean. The routes are ideal for mountain biking.

Places to Stay Signposted up the hill from place du Général de Gaulle is the cramped *Camping Municipal Plaza-Berri (☎ 05 59 37 11 19)*. It charges 22/36FF for one/two people (open late May to late September).

Hôtel des Remparts (☎ 05 59 37 13 79, fax 05 59 37 33 44, 16 place Floquet) is on the way out of town towards Bayonne. It's about the cheapest in town. Doubles with shower cost 200FF to 250FF.

Nearby *Hôtel Etche-Ona (☎ 05 59 37 01 14, 15 place Floquet)* charges 290FF for clean doubles.

More expensive is the *Hôtel le Central (☎ 05 59 37 00 22, fax 05 59 37 27 79, 1 place du Général de Gaulle)* where luxurious doubles with shower start at 320FF.

Splurge at the classy *Hôtel-Restaurant Les Pyrénées (☎ 05 59 37 01 01, fax 05 59 37 18 97, 19 place du Général de Gaulle)* where superb doubles cost from 550FF to 900FF and there is a pool.

Day 9: Arette to St Jean-Pied de Port

PYRENEES

Cue

Start		Arette tourist office
0km	⤴	go E to D133
0.1	⤵	D133 'to Aramits'
3.5	⤴	D919 'to Lanne-/Aramits'
4.3	⤴	D9 'B to La ine'
6.9		La ine
12.6		Montory
15.3	⤴	D25 'to Larau'
23.8	⤴	D26 'to Larrau'
30.0	▲	2-km steep climb
32.5		La rau
32.9	⤴	C 9 'to Iraty'
34.5	▲	1C.2km very steep climb
44.7		Col Bagargui
45.5		Col Hegui Xouri
51.3	⤴	D18 'to St Jean-Pied de Port'
51.5		Chalet de Cize
	▲	2-1km ge-itle climb
55.6		Col ce Bu-dincurutcheta
73.5	⤴	D933 'to St Jean-Ped de Port'
76.4		St Jean-Ped de Port tourist office

Elevation

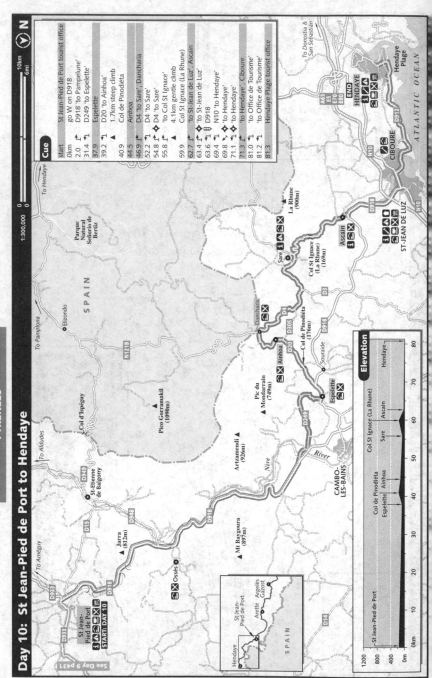

Day 10: St Jean-Pied de Port to Hendaye

Cue

start		St Jean-Pied de Port tourist office
0km	↰	go W on D918
2.0	↰	D918 'to Pampelune'
31.4	↱	D249 'to Espelette'
37.9		Espelette
39.2	◀	D20 'to Ainhoa'
		1.7km steep climb
40.9		Col de Pinodiéta
44.5		Ainhoa
46.9	↱	D4 'to Sare', Dancharia
52.2	↰	D4 'to Sare'
54.8	◇↱	D4 'to Sare'
55.8	↱	to Col St Ignace
	◀	4.1km gentle climb
59.9		Col St Ignace (La Rhune)
62.7	↱	'to St-Jean de Luz', Ascain
63.4	◇↱	to St-Jean de Luz
63.6	↰	D918
69.4	◇	N10 'to Hendaye'
69.8	↱	to Hendaye'
71.1	◇	to Hendaye'
71.3	↰	to Hendaye', Ciboure
81.0	↱	'to Office de Tourisme'
81.2	↱	'to Office de Tourisme'
81.3		Hendaye Plage tourist office

Elevation

PYRENEES

See Day 9 p431

Places to Eat The Monday *markets* are in place du Général de Gaulle. A big *Intermarché* is on the way into town from the east; *bakeries* and other *food stores* are spread randomly.

Café de la Paix (☎ 05 59 37 00 99, *4 place Floquet*) does pizza, paella and salads and has *menus* from around 65FF.

In the *Hôtel des Remparts* the downstairs bar/restaurant has a daily 60FF *menu*. The *Hôtel Etche-Ona* serves good-quality *menus* from 110FF to 260FF. At the *Hôtel le Central menus* range from 98FF to 210FF. The *Hôtel-Restaurant Les Pyrénées* offers gourmet *menus* from 240FF to 520FF.

Day 10: St Jean-Pied de Port to Hendaye
4–8 hours, 81.3km

Despite the mere 176m and 169m heights of Cols Pinodiéta and St Ignace respectively, the day is made harder by the increased traffic as the route re-enters 'civilisation'.

Espelette (37.9km), the last contrôle before Hendaye, is an interesting place for a break before tackling the last climbs. Its buildings are bedecked with red peppers, local produce much used in Basque cuisine. Etcheverry Cycles (☎ 05 59 93 86 13; closed Sunday and Monday), on the main square, hires VTTs.

Col Pinodiéta (40.9km) also has a kick to it – most will need their lowest gears, though only briefly. Fortunately the route *doesn't* approach the climb via the road from Souraide – that ascent has a 21% grade, according to the Michelin map.

A picnic area at 48km is perfect for lunch before climbing Col St Ignace (also known as Col La Rhune).

Largely due to the frequency of rain on the west coast, the first good view of the Atlantic probably won't come before reaching Ciboure (71.3km). The road, very heavily trafficked from here, hugs the undulating coastline south to an anticlimactic finish at Hendaye.

Hendaye
A seaside resort sitting right near the Spanish border, Hendaye is neither particularly characterful nor cheap. Its train station was the venue of a 1940 meeting between Hitler and Spain's dictator Franco, at which Franco declined to side with Germany in WWII.

Information The tourist office (☎ 05 59 20 00 34, fax 05 59 20 79 17) is at 12 rue des Aubépines, behind the *plage* (beach). Follow signs off the ocean-side road. Don't forget to ask for the crucial final route card stamp.

Banks cluster along blvd Général de Gaulle, including one branch in the train station. A BNP agency is at 5 ave Allées.

The nearest bike shop is Cycles Morisson (☎ 05 59 47 00 49) at 46 ave Jean Jaurès Gibourne.

Things to See & Do As expected, activities are centred on the **beach** and the **ocean**. Swimming and lying on the sandy beach are popular. **Cruises** and **fishing trips** on the boat Arguia (☎ 05 58 43 94 81) cost 150FF for half a day.

Places to Stay A dozen or more camping grounds are located around Hendaye. Most charge upwards of 90FF for two people in high season. Try *Camping Les Acacias* (☎/fax 05 59 20 78 76, *route de la Glacière /D658*), five minutes from the beach.

Hôtel Bellevue (☎ 05 59 20 00 26, fax 05 59 48 15 79, *36 blvd Leclerc*) is a slightly old-fashioned Basque building on a busy road near the beach with a view over the Baie de Chingudy. Doubles with shower and toilet cost from 200FF. Demi-pension, from 250FF to 300FF, is obligatory from June to September.

Hôtel de la Gare (☎ 05 59 20 81 90, fax 05 59 48 18 28, *1 rue des Déportés*), near the train station, has doubles from 270FF. Breakfast costs 35FF.

Right opposite the beach, *Hôtel Lafon* (☎ 05 59 20 04 67, fax 05 59 48 06 85, *99 blvd de la Mer*) is a big establishment charging around 340FF for a double.

Places to Eat Check out the selection of *eateries* in the commercial area one street back from the beach. A good *supermarket* is on the western side of this street.

Worth a visit is the fish restaurant *La Petite Marée* (☎ 05 59 20 77 96, *2 ave des Mimosas*), with *menus* from 60FF to about 100FF.

For real Basque flavour, try *Ikaztegia* (☎ 05 59 20 16 29, *17 rue d'Irandatz*), where meals start at around 150FF (closed Monday and Tuesday in low season).

PYRENEES

Provence & the Côte d'Azur

Provence and the Côte d'Azur occupies the south-eastern corner of mainland France. It is the country's most varied area. Cosmopolitan coastal cities such as Marseille and Nice, with their noisy streets, contrast with the cycling paradise just inland, where tiny villages are linked by deserted mountain roads.

The terrain is varied too. From the Alps of Haute-Provence (Upper Provence) the land falls southwards to the Mediterranean – you can cycle continuously downhill for a hundred kilometres or more – but deep, steep-sided valleys create a barrier to east-west riding. The Rhône delta area, known as the Camargue, is a flat, windswept extravaganza of bird life, ideally explored by bike. The hilly, sunburnt Luberon is a mix of manicured vineyards and ancient villages tumbling haphazardly down rocky slopes. Legendary Mont Ventoux lurks in the hinterland, silently luring cyclist-pilgrims.

Sites of historic interest abound, with relics dating from prehistoric to Roman times alongside ruined and restored chateaux of the Middle Ages.

You can hire a *vélo tout terrain* (VTT, or mountain bike) in most towns. Some Grande Randonnée (long-distance walking) trails are open to VTTs.

There is something in Provence for every cyclist, from the avid mountain goat to the casual day-tripper. You'll get a taste of it all in the rides in this chapter, which can be easily strung together starting in the east and working towards the west.

HISTORY

Provence has been inhabited for an exceptionally long time. Million-year-old rock scratchings in Monaco's Grotte de l'Observatoire are among the world's most ancient. Modern civilisations have lived here since 30,000 BC and wall paintings of bisons, seals, ibex and other animals inside the Grotte Cosquer, south of Marseille, date from 20,000 BC. The first dwellings to be built, around 3500 BC, were *bories*, evident in Gordes. These one- or two-storey beehive-shaped huts, constructed of thin wedges of limestone without mortar, were inhabited as late as the 18th century.

In Brief

Highlights
- bird's-eye views on the **Grande Corniche**
- Provence's **perched villages**
- the huge **Gorges du Verdon**
- the Roman **Pont du Gard**

Terrain
Relatively flat along the coast and hilly to mountainous inland

FFCT Contacts
- **Ligue Côte d'Azur**, 211 ave de Lattre de Tassigny, 83250 La Londe
- **Ligue Provence-Alpes**, 4 chemin des Passadoires, 84420 Piolenc

Cycling Events
- **The Race to the Sun** (mid-February) professional race from Paris to Nice
- **La Lazarides Étoile Sportive** (early May) Cannes
- **Les Boucles du Verdon** (late May) Gréoux-les-Bains

Special Events
- **Carnaval de Nice** (mid-February) Nice
- **Fête des Gardians** bullfighting parade (1 May) Arles
- **Cannes International Film Festival** (mid-May) Cannes
- **Festival d'Avignon** theatre festival (mid-July to early August) Avignon

Gourmet Specialities
- famous fishy *bouillabaisse*
- *ratatouille* (eggplant, tomato and zucchini stew)
- dishes *à la provençale* (with garlic-seasoned tomatoes)
- *aïoli*, the strong garlic sauce used on fish

The Mediterranean coast around modern-day Marseille was colonised around 600 BC by the Greeks. Massilia became an important trading post, along with Nikaia (Nice), Monoïkos (Monaco) and Glanum (near St Rémy de Provence), at the same time as the Celts were penetrating the northern part of the region, mingling with the ancient, 'native' Ligurians.

The Romans helped the Greeks defend Massilia against invasion by the Celto-Ligurians in 125 BC, leading to the creation of Provincia Gallia Transalpina, the first Roman province (hence the name Provence). Under Caesar Augustus, amphitheatres seating 10,000 or more spectators were built to host gladiator combats at Arelate (Arles), Nemausus (Nîmes) and Vasio Vocontiorum (Vaison-la-Romaine), along with triumphal arches at Aurasio (Orange), Cabelio (Cavaillon) and Glanum. Aqueducts such as the massive Pont du Gard formed complex water supply systems for the Roman cities. In 6 BC Augustus also built a trophy monument at La Turbie, behind Monaco, to celebrate his victory over the Ligurians. Most of these sites can still be visited by cyclists.

After the collapse of the Roman empire in AD 476, Provence eventually came under the control of the Franks. In the 9th century, attacks by Muslim Saracens forced many villagers along the Maures coast, the Niçois hinterland and the more northern Alps to take refuge in the hills (see the 'Provence's Perched Villages' boxed text later in this chapter). However, the invaders also showed the populace how to exploit cork-tree bark.

Provence became a papal realm in 1274 and French-born Pope Clement V moved his headquarters from Rome to Avignon in 1309, beginning the city's most resplendent period.

Most of Provence was ceded to Louis XI of France in 1481 but the *Comté* (County) of Nice, mostly today's Alpes-Maritimes *département* (department; administrative division), did not become part of French Provence until 1860.

NATURAL HISTORY

Provence and the Côte d'Azur cover an area of almost 26,000 sq km shaped like an elongated oval. The region is bordered to the north-east by the Alps du Sud (Southern Alps), which form a natural frontier with Italy. Its western border, from near Orange through Arles, west of Marseille, is delineated by the Rhône, while the Mediterranean Sea laps Provence's southern edge.

Features include the flat Camargue salt marshes – home to water birds including flamingos – in the Rhône delta, and mountain ranges such as the red volcanic Massif de l'Esterel, the limestone Massif des Maures and the foothills of the Alps. The interior is dominated by hills and mountains which become higher towards the north. They culminate in the cycling mecca of Mont Ventoux (1912m), north-east of Avignon, and the Southern Alps, which include the wild, uninhabited Parc National du Mercantour, behind Nice.

Lower ranges include the lovely little Alpilles and the rocky Luberon.

Inland, west of Nice, lie the Gorges du Verdon, Europe's largest, most spectacular canyon. North-west of here, on the right bank of the Durance, is the Plateau de Valensole, Provence's lavender kingdom. On the left bank of the Durance is the Plateau d'Albion, a vast, uninhabited *causse* (bare limestone plateau).

Provence is still heavily forested, with about 38% of its land – 1.2 million hectares – under trees. The thickest forest, predominantly *chêne* (oak) or *pin* (pine), is in north-eastern Provence and the central Var department. *Chêne liège* (cork oak) and *châtaignier* (chestnut) are dominant in the Massif des Maures. *Maquis*, a common form of low, dense, shrubby vegetation, provides many Provençal cooking spices.

Fires are a threat to Provence's forests and the animals that depend on them – the population of Hermann tortoise, once found all over Mediterranean Europe, but now found only in the maquis of the Massif des Maures (and Corsica) was severely reduced by fire in 1990. Evidence of the ravages of recent fires can be seen around Vence.

Provence is home to a variety of France's many species of mammals (the most in Europe), amphibians, reptiles and fish. The 68,500-hectare Parc National du Mercantour, created in 1979, protects threatened species such as the vulture, the wolf, the chamois and the bouquetin (a wild goat) in the Alpes-Maritimes. A marine park, the Parc National de Port-Cros, covers the Île de Port-Cros and surrounding waters near Toulon. Geological wonders, including a 185 million-year-old fossilised ichthyosaurus skeleton and fossils from the tropical forests of 300 million years ago, are preserved in the 190,000-hectare

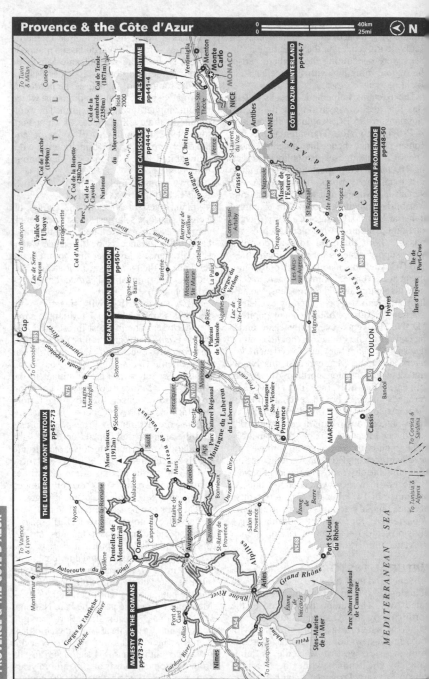

Provence & the Côte d'Azur

0   40km
0   25mi

N

ALPES MARITIME pp441-4

To Turin & Milan

Cuneo

I T A L Y

To Briançon

Col de Larche (1990m)

Col de la Bonette (2802m)

Col de la Cayolle

Col d'Allos

Barcelonnette

Vallée de l'Ubaye

Lac de Serre Ponçon

To Valence & Lyon

Montélimar

N86

Gorges de l'Ardèche

Ardèche River

Gardon River

A7

Autoroute du Soleil

Bollène

Orange

Carpentras

Nyons

Sault

THE LUBERON & MONT VENTOUX pp457-73

Mont Ventoux (1912m)

Malaucène

Vaison-la-Romaine

Dentelles de Montmirail

Sédéron

Laragne Montéglin

Sisteron

To Grenoble

Gap

N85

Route Napoléon

Durance River

Digne-les-Bains

Barrême

GRAND CANYON DU VERDON pp450-7

Riez

Moustiers-Ste-Marie

La Palud

Gorges du Verdon

Castellane

Comps-sur-Artuby

Barrage de Castillon

Verdon River

Isola 2000

Col de la Lombarde (2350m)

Col de Tende (1871m)

Parc National du Mercantour

Montagne du Cheiron

PLATEAU DE CAUSSOLS pp444-6

Vence

St-Laurent du Var

Peillon-Ste-Thècle

Ventimiglia

Menton

Monte Carlo

MONACO

NICE

Antibes

Grasse

CANNES

La Napoule

Massif de l'Estérel

St-Raphaël

CÔTE D'AZUR HINTERLAND pp444-7

MEDITERRANEAN PROMENADE pp448-50

Ste-Maxime

St-Tropez

Gr imaud

Massif des Maures

Draguignan

Les Arcs-sur-Argens

Brignoles

N7

N98

Île de Port-Cros

Îles d'Hyères

Hyères

TOULON

Bandol

Cassis

MARSEILLE

To Corsica & Sardinia

To Tunisia & Algeria

M E D I T E R R A N E A N   S E A

Aix-en-Provence

Montagne Ste-Victoire

Canal de Provence

Étang de Berre

A7

A8

A50

A52

A54

Port St-Louis du Rhône

Grand Rhône

Petit Rhône

Étang de Vaccarès

Parc Naturel Régional de Camargue

Stes-Maries de la Mer

St-Gilles

Nîmes

To Montpellier

Collias

Pont du Gard

MAJESTY OF THE ROMANS pp473-79

Rhône River

Arles

Albilles

Salon de Provence

St-Rémy de Provence

Cavaillon

Avignon

Durance River

Bonnieux

Gordes

Fontaine de Vaucluse

Parc Naturel Régional du Luberon

Montagne du Luberon

Apt

Céreste

Forcalquier

Manosque

Plateau de Valensole

Valensole

Lac de Ste-Croix

Aiguines

Plateau de Vaucluse

Murs

Plateau de

N100

D31

N85

N96

N202

D952

N7

A8

Réserve Géologique de Haute-Provence (Upper Provence Geological Reserve) around Digne-les-Bains. This extends over the Grand Canyon du Verdon.

CLIMATE

Sunny Provence is famed for its extraordinary light, which inspired painters such as van Gogh, Cézanne and Picasso. More than 2500 hours of sunshine bathe the region each year, an average of almost seven hours every day. The region's annual average temperature ranges from 15°C on the Côte d'Azur to 5°C in the north-east.

While prolonged rain periods are rare in summer, thunderstorms are relatively common in the late afternoon and evening. Though usually brief, they can be violent, but the roads generally dry overnight.

The infamous Mistral, a cold, dry, north-westerly wind, can be a trial for cyclists. Whipping across Provence for several days at a time with gusts reaching more than 100km/h, it is not a wind to ride into. The Mistral is generated by a high-pressure system over central France feeding air towards a low over the Mediterranean. It can cause sudden, dramatic temperature drops. These effects are worst in late autumn, winter and early spring – fortunately outside the main cycling season.

PLANNING
When to Go

For touring cyclists, particularly, the danger of sunburn is high. With summer temperatures soaring into the high 30s daily, an early morning start and an afternoon siesta in the shade of a tree is sensible.

If possible avoid touring in July and August when horrendous traffic near the coast, combined with the heat, makes cycling unattractive. Quieter May and June – when the temperature generally stays in the 20s – followed by September and October – when you can expect low 20s – are the best times.

What to Bring

For the occasional tunnel, a tail light will make you more visible to overtaking traffic.

INFORMATION
Books & Maps

Lonely Planet's *Provence & the Côte d'Azur* covers the area comprehensively with lots of practical information plus a guide to Provençal food and wine.

Essential background reading, and entertainment, is Peter Mayle's series of books, beginning with *A Year in Provence*, which deals with the idiosyncrasies of life in the Luberon and its inhabitants. You can see the house in which Mayle lived on the Luberon and Mont Ventoux ride.

Didier-Richard publishes *Les Guides VTT*, a series of mountain bikers' topoguides (in French). Each department publishes guides for cycle tourists, detailing numerous trails (also in French). Many tourist offices sell cycling itineraries (some in English), often compiled by the local cycling club.

INFORMATION SOURCES

The Comité Régional du Tourisme Provence-Alpes–Côte d'Azur (☎ 04 91 39 38 00, fax 04 91 56 66 61, ✉ www.cr-paca.fr) is in Marseille at Espace Colbert, 14 rue Ste Barbe.

FESTIVALS

Provence is mad on festivals. From prestigious film, theatre and music events to harvest celebrations and gyps pilgrimages, there's something happening year-round. Get the free listing *Terre de Festivals* from the regional tourist office.

GATEWAY CITIES
Nice

The fashionable but relaxed and fun capital of the Riviera, Nice makes a great base from which to explore the rest of the Côte d'Azur and into the Alpes Maritime.

Information The main tourist office (☎ 04 93 87 07 07, fax 04 93 16 85 16, ✉ www .nice-coteazur.org) is next to the train station on ave Thiers. Other information desks in town are the tourist office annexe (☎ 04 92 14 48 00) at 5 Promenade des Anglais (closed Sunday); the Nice Ferber branch office (☎ 04 93 83 32 64) on Promenade des Anglais, towards town from the airport; and inside the airport at Terminal 1 (☎ 04 93 21 44 11).

Banque de France is at 14 ave Félix Faure and Banque Populaire de la Côte d'Azur has branches at 92 blvd Gambetta and 457 Promenade des Anglais, near the airport

Cycles Arnaud (☎ 04 93 87 88 55), rue François 1er, off rue Grimaldi, is a helpful bike shop not far from the tourist office annexe. VTTs can be hired for around 100/180FF per day/weekend (2000FF deposit required). Nicea Location Rent (☎ 04 93 82 42 71, fax 04 93 87 76 36), 12 rue Belgique, has VTTs for hire from around 80FF a day.

The main post office is at 23 ave Thiers, a block south-west of the train station. Email and Internet access is available at The Web Store (☎ 04 93 87 87 99), 12 rue de Russie. For a drink while you surf, log in at La Douche Cybercafé (☎ 04 93 62 81 31), 32 cours Saleya.

Things to See & Do The palm-lined **Promenade des Anglais**, or 'English Promenade', provides a fine shoreside walking/cycling path out of the constant traffic. See the facade of the Art Deco **Palais de la Méditerranée**, crumbling in all its magnificence at 13–17 Promenade des Anglais. This 1930s casino was owned by American millionaire Frank Jay Gould and was France's top-earning casino until the 1970s when, ironically, Gould's luck turned and it was closed.

Vieux Nice is the area of narrow, winding streets between quai des États-Unis and the Musée d'Art Contemporain. At the eastern end of quai des États-Unis, atop a 92m hill, is the shady **Parc du Château**. It is popular for strolling and admiring the views of the city and the Baie des Anges or to visit the Cascade Donjon, an artificial waterfall. Open-air evening concerts are often held in summer.

Another nice place for a walk is the **Jardin Maréchal Juin**, a modernist red concrete garden on the east side of the Musée d'Art Moderne et d'Art Contemporain, ave St Jean Baptiste.

The **Matisse Museum** (☎ 04 93 81 08 08), 164 ave des Arènes de Cimiez, houses a fine collection of works by Henri Matisse. Matisse is buried in the cemetery of the 16th-century **Monastère Notre Dame de Cimiez** (Cimiez Monastery). His grave is signposted *sépulture Henri Matisse* from the graveyard's main entrance (beside the monastery's Église Notre Dame on ave Bellanda).

Nice's **beach** is pebbly and sections of it are private concessions where you have to pay for a chair or mattress. For **water sports**, various hire places offer sailboards, jet skis, parasailing and water-skiing.

For **scuba diving**, go to Water World (☎ 06 11 33 42 53) at the east end of quai des États-Unis in the private beach Castel Plage, opposite Tour Bellanda. **Glass-bottomed boat trips** are offered by Trans Côte d'Azur (☎ 04 92 00 42 30).

Details of **VTT trails** in the region are available from the Parc National du Mercantour office (☎ 04 93 16 78 88, fax 04 93 88 79 05), 23 rue d'Italie. The free *Les Guides Randoxygène* describes 40 park trails.

Places to Stay Nice has plenty of reasonably priced accommodation, which is easiest to find outside the Easter and July-August holiday periods when it fills by late morning.

The bus station information desk (☎ 04 93 85 61 81, 5 blvd Jean Jaurès) has details of Logis de France hotels and other idyllic properties in the region. For information on *gîtes* (self-contained accommodation) in and around Nice, contact Gîtes de France des Alpes-Maritimes (☎ 04 92 15 21 30, fax 04 93 86 01 06), 55 Promenade des Anglais).

The *Auberge de Jeunesse (☎ 04 93 89 23 64, fax 04 92 04 03 10, route Forestière de Mont Alban)* is 5km east of the train station. B&B costs around 70FF.

The *Hôtel Belle Meunière (☎ 04 93 88 66 15, 21 ave Durante)*, 100m from the train station, has non-bunk dorm beds from around 80FF, which includes breakfast. Doubles start from about 200FF with shower and toilet. The hotel has a pleasant garden.

Nearly opposite is the rambling *Hôtel Les Orangers (☎/fax 04 93 87 51 41, 10bis ave Durante)* in a turn-of-the-20th-century townhouse. A bed in a snug dorm with shower and huge windows costs around 85FF and the cheerful owner speaks excellent English. Doubles and triples with shower and balcony cost from 210FF.

Party animals should head to the *Backpackers' Hôtel (☎ 04 93 80 30 72, 32 rue Pertinax)*, where a dorm bed costs from 70FF a night and there's no curfew. It's above the Faubourg Montmartre restaurant.

Near the train station, the *Hôtel Les Cigales (☎ 04 93 88 33 75, 15 rue Dalpozzo)* has simple singles/doubles with shower from 165/185FF.

In Vieux Nice, *Hôtel Au Picardy (☎ 04 93 85 75 51, 10 blvd Jean Jaurès)* has rooms from 120/140FF. Hall showers cost 10FF.

More upmarket hotels include the homely **Hôtel Cronstadt** (☎ 04 93 82 00 30, 3 rue Cronstadt). Quiet, graceful rooms cost from 280/320FF, including breakfast.

The small, family-run **Hôtel le Floride** (☎ 04 93 53 11 02, fax 04 93 81 57 46, 52 blvd de Cimiez) has comfortable rooms with shower, toilet and views of the area's opulent mansions from 190/215FF.

The **Hôtel Campanile** (☎ 04 93 21 20 20, fax 04 93 83 83 96, 459 Promenade des Anglais) is across the road from the airport terminal – a shuttle service can take you there or it is a short walk. Comfortable, sound-proofed, air-conditioned doubles with shower and toilet cost 395FF.

A top-end place, the black-glass-walled **Melia Élysée Palace** (☎ 04 93 86 06 06, fax 04 93 97 03 36, 59 Promenade des Anglais) has singles from 800FF from July to September (rooms with views cost more). Add 150FF to prices for a double.

Places to Eat For self-caterers, a fruit and vegetable *market* is held daily except Monday in front of the prefecture, on cours Saleya, and a *fresh fish market* is held every morning on place St François. The no-name *boulangerie* (bakery) at the south end of rue du Marché is a great place for cheap sandwiches, pizza slices, traditional *michettes* (savoury bread stuffed with cheese, olives, anchovies and onions) and other local breads.

Large **Intermarché** and **Casino** supermarkets are on blvd Gambetta, while smaller **Prisunic** supermarkets are on ave Jean Médécin, opposite No 33, and on place Garibaldi.

Very cheap eating places cluster near the train station. Try **Flunch Cafétéria** (☎ 04 93 88 41 35), to the left of the station building exit.

Corsican food (plus music and song on Thursday, Friday and Saturday evenings) is on offer at **L'Allegria** (☎ 04 93 87 42 00, 7 rue d'Italie). Next door, the friendly, unpretentious **Restaurant au Soleil** (☎ 04 93 88 77 74) offers local cuisine at good prices, including an all-day omelette breakfast for 35FF. Another cheap favourite is the bustling **Restaurant de Paris** (☎ 04 93 88 99 88, 28 rue d'Angleterre) which has a bargain *menu* (set meal). Hungry backpackers flock to the cheap and cheerful **Le**

Faubourg Montmartre (☎ 04 93 62 55 03, 32 rue Pertinax). The house speciality is bouillabaisse (120FF for two).

In the city centre, good-value pizza can be found at **La Trattoria** (☎ 04 93 88 20 07, 37 rue de France). The nearby small, homely **Le Moulin à Poivre** (☎ 04 93 87 65 02, 22 rue de France) has plenty of homemade pasta dishes.

Near the port, **L'Olivier** (☎ 04 93 26 89 09, 2 place Garibaldi) will fill you up for around 100FF (closed Wednesday evening, Sunday and in August).

La Nissarda (☎ 04 93 85 26 29, 17 rue Gubernatis) serves reasonably priced specialities of Nice and Normandy.

For a mind- and budget-blowing traditional French meal in a luxurious setting, try the **Chantecler** (☎ 04 93 88 39 51, 37 Promenade des Anglais), inside the Hôtel Négresco, where you'll pay at least 500FF per head.

Getting There & Away With its international airport and good train access from Paris, Bordeaux and Italy, Nice is an excellent place to start a tour of Provence and the Côte d'Azur. Aéroport International Nice-Côte d'Azur (☎ 04 93 21 30 30, 🖳 www .nice.aeroport.fr) is 6km south-west of the city centre. The nearest train station is 500m to the north-east. Some hotels (the Hôtel Campanile, for example) offer free shuttles for guests. It is possible to ride to the airport: take Promenade des Anglais from the centre of Nice. It has a beachside bikepath for part of the way; continue on the track or the nature strip to the airport entrance on the left.

Bicycles can be carried free on most of the frequent non-TGV services around Provence – speak to the train's *contrôleur* (guard). Nice's main train station, Gare Nice Ville, also called Gare Thiers (☎ 04 36 35 35 35), on ave Thiers, is 1.2km north of the beach. Luggage can be left in lockers in the ticket hall between 7 am and 10 pm, for a maximum of 72 hours. It costs around 15/30FF for a small/large locker.

Up to 40 trains a day serve towns along the coast in each direction between St Raphaël and Ventimiglia (Vintimille), across the Italian border. The five TGVs a day between Nice and Paris' Gare de Lyon are 1st-class only (716FF), except for one 2nd-class

Provence's Perched Villages

The hill-top villages of Provence have their origins in the Dark Ages. In the 10th century villagers from the plains built new fortified settlements on top of rocky crags for defence against Saracen attacks. Many moved back to the plains only as recently as the 19th and 20th centuries.

Many of these high villages, now restored by an influx of craftspeople and holiday-makers, are remarkably well preserved. Their car-free streets are often barely wide enough for two pedestrians to pass. Houses arch over the alleyways, forming tunnels that both support the buildings and give shelter from the elements. These winding routes, up and down steps, draw the visitor on to see what is around the corner while at the same time making them feel uncomfortably like they are infringing on the privacy of the inhabitants.

Some of the most celebrated perched villages are Peille, Peillon and Roquebrune, on the Côte d'Azur; Gordes and Bonnieux, which tumble down the Luberon hillsides; and Les Baux de Provence, site of the Grimaldi's ruined feudal castle, in the Alpilles. If the tag 'the highest...' is a red rag to you, you will want to visit isolated Bargème, 'the highest perched village in the Var' (see Side Trip under Day 1 in the Grand Canyon du Verdon ride later in the chapter), now a permanent home to just a handful of people.

Originally constructed around castle keeps (donjons) and enclosed by solid walls, perched villages were entered by narrow main gates that could be easily defended. Side gates opened onto tortuous laneways, which often featured further gates and sharp turns to aid defence and confuse invaders.

A focal point of each perched village was the fountain, sometimes elaborately decorated and usually the only source of water for the villagers. Beautiful examples exist at Vaugines, in the Luberon, and at Vence, near Nice. The church, source of spiritual health, was fortified against attack and its bells warned of imminent danger.

(539FF, seven hours) service. Three night trains also run (510FF, 11½ hours,) but it may be cheaper or more convenient to go via Marseille. Eight trains connect Nice and Marseille each day (169FF, 2¾ hours, all take bikes).

Nice is also a port for ferries to/from Corsica. The SNCM ferries office (☎ 04 93 13 66 99 or 04 93 13 66 66, 🖳 www.sncm.fr) at the terminal, quai du Commerce, issues tickets and is open from 8 am to 7 pm (11.45 am Saturday) and, on Sunday, two hours before a scheduled departure only. Travel agents in town also sell tickets.

Marseille

Getting There & Away The Marseille-Provence airport (☎ 04 42 14 14 14), also called Marseille-Marignane airport, is 28km north-west of the city in Marignane.

Marseille's passenger-train station, served by both metro lines, is Gare St Charles (☎ 04 91 50 00 00). Direct trains carrying unbagged bikes serve Arles (91FF, 45 minutes to an hour, at least nine a day), Avignon (92FF, one to two hours, at least 11 a day) Nice (169FF, 2¾ hours, eight a day) and Nîmes (114FF, 1¼ hours).

The TGV service to/from Paris (379FF, 4¼ hours) runs about 10 times a day; travel times are expected to be cut by an hour when the TGV track extension to Marseille opens in 2001.

From mid-April to September, the SNCM (☎ 04 95 29 66 99, fax 04 95 26 66 77, 🖳 www.sncm.fr) runs a ferry service from Marseille to Porto Torres on the Italian island of Sardinia.

Milan

Getting There & Away The Italian city's new airport, Malpensa, is well placed at France's back door.

Several potential routes beckon cyclists into Provence from here. The tunnel-bypassed 1870m Col de Tende is one international gateway, while the 1990m Col de Larche (Colle della Maddalena) leads from Italy into the Vallée de l'Ubaye near Barcelonnette and then to Haute-Provence via either the Col d'Allos, the Col de la Cayolle or Col de la Bonette, the latter the highest in Europe at 2802m. The Col de la Lombarde (2350m), however, is the most pleasant, direct pass into upper Provence.

Alpes Maritime

Duration...2 days
Distance 69.5km
Difficulty ....moderate
Start...............................Peillon-Ste Thècle
End...Nice

Ride tiny, wiggly roads in the *arrière pays
Niçois* (Nice hinterland), visiting perched villages and gaining stunning panoramas of the
Côte d'Azur. Climb the scenic upper coast
road, the Grande Corniche, to look down on
the playground of the rich, Monte Carlo.

PLANNING
When to Ride
The route should be passable year-round,
but avoid the July-August traffic peak.

GETTING TO/FROM THE RIDE
The Côte d'Azur Hinterland and Plateau de
Caussols rides around Vence, and the
Mediterranean Promenade ride (all later in
this chapter), are also easily accessed from
Nice. Nice is a gateway city to Corsica, for
which two rides are detailed in this book.

Peillon-Ste Thècle
Peillon-Ste Thècle train station is a 20-
minute trip (15FF, four direct a day, all take
bikes) from Nice on the line to Sospel and
Breil-sur-Roya.

Nice
Avoid horrendous traffic by taking a train
from Nice the short distance to St-Laurent
du Var (11FF, 10 mins, two an hour, all take
bikes) to link with Vence. See the Gateway
Cities section (p439) for more information
on getting to/from Nice.

THE RIDE
Peillon-Ste Thècle
At 456m altitude, Peillon is known for its
precarious *nid d'aigle* (eagle's nest) location. The ride actually starts from the train
station, 3km down the hill from the town.

From the village car park, a footpath leads
to the **Chapelle des Pénitents** Blancs, note-
worthy for its set of 15th-century frescoes.
Longer **trails** lead to Peille (two hours on an
old Roman road), La Turbie (two hours) and
the Chapelle St Martin (1½ hours).

The three-star *Auberge de la Madone*
(☎ 04 93 79 91 17) has rooms starting from
550FF in the high season. Its *restaurant*
specialises in local cuisine (closed Wednesday). Book in advance.

Day 1: Peillon-Ste Thècle to Menton
2½–3½ hours, 33.2km
The ride starts with a steep climb to Peille
(alt 630m; 9km), a quaintly restored perched
village, little touched by tourism despite
being hyped as one of the Nice hinterland's
best. It houses the 12th-century **Chapelle St
Roch** on place Jean Mioul and features a
maze of streets too narrow for cars.

The road towards Ste Agnès (billed as
Europe's highest coastal village at 780m,
despite its inland position) clings dramatically to the edge of the precipitous mountainside, traversing numerous unlit tunnels
and the Col de Madone.

Follow the side trip to touristy Ste Agnès,
one of the *Plus Beaux* (Most Beautiful) villages of France and a good place for lunch.
It has a number of *restaurants* off the narrow alleyway leading to the **spectacular
lookout**. The road rejoins the D22 before
plunging into the centre of Menton.

Menton
Reputedly the warmest spot on the Côte
d'Azur, particularly in winter, Menton is
only a few kilometres from the Italian border. It is popular with older holiday-makers,
whose way of life has made the town more
tranquil and less pretentious than other hot
spots along the coast.

Menton was under Grimaldi rule, as
Monaco is still, until 1848, when it was sold
to Napoleon III for four million Francs.
Today it's known for cultivating lemons and
has a two-week lemon festival in February.

Ave Edouard VII links the train station
with the beach about 500m away; ave
Boyer, where the tourist office is, is 350m
to the east.

Information The tourist office (☎ 04 93
57 57 00, fax 04 93 57 51 00) is inside the
Palais de l'Europe, a contemporary art
gallery at 8 ave Boyer. In summer, free city
maps and information brochures are available from the open-air stall opposite Les
Halles, on quai de Monléon.

PROVENCE & THE CÔTE D'AZUR

PROVENCE & THE CÔTE D'AZUR

Alpes Maritime

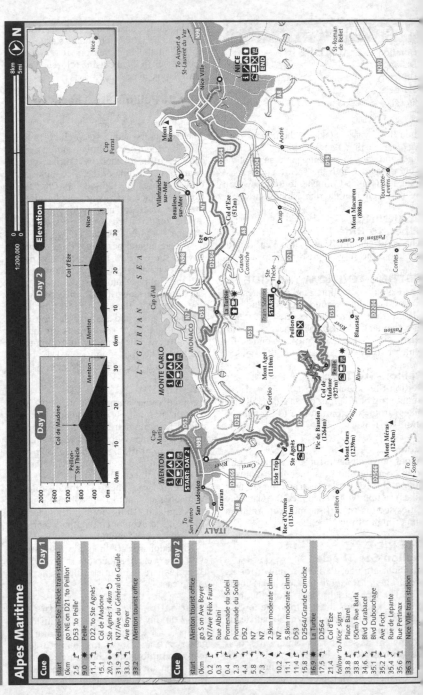

Cue	Day 1	
start		Peillon–Ste Thècle train station
0km		go NE on D21 'to Peillon'
2.5	↙	D53 'to Peille'
9.0	✱	Peille
11.4	↰	D22 'to Ste Agnès'
15.1		Col de Madone
20.5	●● ↰	Ste Agnès 1.4km ↻
31.9	↱	N7/Ave du Général de Gaulle
33.0	↱	Ave Boyer
33.2		Menton tourist office

Cue	Day 2	
start		Menton tourist office
0km		go S on Ave Boyer
0.2	↰	N7/Ave Félix Faure
0.3	↱	Rue Albini
0.4	↱	Promenade du Soleil
2.3	↰	Promenade du Soleil
4.4	↱	D52
5.8	↱	N7
7.3	↱	N7
10.2	◀	2.9km moderate climb
11.1	◀	5.8km moderate climb
11.4	↰	D53
15.8		D2564/Grande Corniche
16.9	✱	La Turbie
17.5		D2564
21.4		Col d'Eze
		follow 'to Nice' signs
33.8	↰	Place Barel
33.8	↱	(50m) Rue Barla
34.6	↰	Blvd Carabacel
35.1	↱	Blvd Dubouchage
35.2	↱	Ave Foch
35.4	↱	Rue de Lepante
35.6	↱	Rue Pertinax
36.3		Nice Ville train station

Barclays Bank is at 39 ave Félix Faure, while Crédit Lyonnais is two doors down ave Boyer from the tourist office. Other banks cluster along rue Partouneaux. The post office is in cours George V.

The bike shop, Michel Cycles Motos (☎ 04 93 57 65 71), is on 3 rue Guyau.

Things to See & Do Walk around the port area and old town, visiting a small 17th-century **fort** on the tip of land between Menton's two bays. Used successively as a salt cellar, prison and lighthouse, today it houses the **Musée Jean Cocteau** (☎ 04 93 57 72 30), which displays drawings, tapestries and ceramics by the French artist. In the old town, the Italianate **Église St Michel** is considered the grandest baroque church in southern France. Up the hill, via the Monté du Souvenir, is the **Cimetière du Vieux Château**. Further up, the **Cimetière du Trabuquet** has 'Commonwealth War Graves' mixed in with those of others who 'died for France' in campaigns in both Asia and Africa. Both cemeteries have spectacular views.

Play **boules** at the Pétanque Club du Marché (☎ 04 93 57 17 13), opposite Les Halles on quai de Monléon.

The best **beach** in the area is the sandy Plage des Sablettes, north-east of the Vieux Port. Hire **kayaks/sail boats** at the Base Nautique (☎ 04 93 35 49 70, fax 04 93 35 77 05), in Promenade de la Mer. **Boat trips** to Monaco and the Italian Riviera are offered by the Compagnie de Navigation et de Tourisme de Menton (☎ 04 93 35 51 72), at the Vieux Port.

Places to Stay The two-star *Camping Municipal St Michel* (☎ 04 93 35 81 23, route des Ciappes), 1km from the train station, accessed by a steep climb to the Plateau St Michel, has a great view. Tariffs are 42/62FF for one/two people (cheaper in low season).

The *Auberge de Jeunesse* (☎ 04 93 35 93 14, fax 04 93 35 93 07, Plateau St Michel) is a short distance from the camping ground. B&B costs around 70FF. It's closed from 10 am to 5 pm; the curfew is midnight.

Opposite the train station, *Hôtel le Terminus* (☎/fax 04 93 35 77 00, place de la Gare) has a few singles/doubles with hall showers from 140/160FF. If reception is closed, find staff in the bar or restaurant.

Towards the water, *Hôtel Claridges* (☎ 04 93 35 72 53, cnr ave de la Gare & ave de Verdun) has comfortable rooms from around 160/220FF while, in town, the *Hôtel des Arcades* (☎ 04 93 35 70 62, fax 04 93 35 35 97, 411 ave Félix Faure) charges from 180/220FF in the low season, rising to around 260FF in high season. For sea views, try *Le Grand Bleu* (☎ 04 93 57 46 33, 1684 Promenade du Soleil), where rooms start from 250/350FF in summer.

Places to Eat For self-catering, the *Marché Municipal*, on quai de Monléon in the old town, sells fresh food. It's open from 5 am to 1 pm (closed Monday). The *Marché U* supermarket is at 38 rue Partouneaux.

Cheaper places, including *pizzerias*, line quai de Monléon in the old town.

Ave Félix Faure and its pedestrianised continuation, *rue St Michel* are lined with places to eat, at any time of day. Along rue St Michel, takeaway crepes or *gauffres* (waffles) are available from around 12FF. *Place Clémenceau* and *place aux Herbes* in the old town are also full of restaurants. More pricey restaurants range along the breezy *Promenade du Soleil*.

Try *Le Chaudron* (☎ 04 93 35 90 25, 28 rue St Michel) for filling salads from around 40FF to 65FF and *menus* from 95FF. Italian-run *L'Ulivo* (☎ 04 93 35 45 65, place du Cap) specialises in mussel dishes, with nearly a dozen different types from around 50FF. Its pasta and huge salads are also good value.

Day 2: Menton to Nice

2½–3 hours, 36.3km

Menton's lively waterfront boulevard, the Promenade du Soleil, popular with cyclists, motorcyclists and motorists, but fortunately not with many trucks, stays close to sea level for 3.2km. It swings south-east onto Cap Martin, where spectacular coastal views unfold behind to Italy and there is little traffic until the N7. Climb past glorious homes, glimpsing how the top 2% live – in multi-million-franc mansions secluded behind high fences and hedges with locked gates and surveillance cameras.

From the D52 junction with the N7, there are great **views** over Monaco and Monte Carlo – it's clear why it is referred to as 'the Hong Kong of Europe'. Climbing steeply past frequently stalled traffic, you soon turn off onto the quieter D53. Laced with hairpin bends, it wriggles upwards above the Grimaldi's castle to the Grande Corniche at nearly 500m altitude. From here the climb to the **Col d'Eze** (21.4km) is almost imperceptible and the views superb. Pause at La Turbie's *boulangeries* and *food shops* for lunch supplies. Above the town towers the Roman **Trophée des Alpes**, open daily from April to September. Enter from place Théodore de Bamville.

A fast descent on a twisting, increasingly busy road ends the idyll, dumping you in central Nice, with its whirlpool of traffic.

Nice

See Nice (pp437–40) in the Gateway Cities section for information about accommodation and other services.

Vence Circuits

PLATEAU DE CAUSSOLS

Duration	5–10 hours
Distance	102.2km
Difficulty	hard
Start/End	Vence

CÔTE D'AZUR HINTERLAND

Duration	3½–7 hours
Distance	74.7km
Difficulty	moderate-hard
Start/End	Vence

The attractive but touristy inland town of Vence makes a good base for day rides on exceptionally tiny, near-deserted roads in the Côte d'Azur hinterland. The area is hilly – even mountainous – but offers numerous opportunities to visit picturesque perched villages, conquer little-known cols and escape the madding crowds. The two circuits could be combined into a very long, very hard one-day ride, but this is not recommended as it does not leave any time for side trips or sight-seeing.

PLANNING
When to Ride

Because both circuits use roads above 1000m, ice and snow can be a problem in colder months. Check with the tourist office in Vence if intending to ride outside May to October. Thunderstorms can be a summer hazard, particularly in the late afternoon.

GETTING TO/FROM THE RIDES

The Alpes Maritime ride, earlier in this chapter, and the Mediterranean Promenade ride, later, are both easily accessed from Nice.

These rides could easily precede or follow the rides in the Corsica chapter, with connections from Nice to any of the Corsica gateway cities.

Vence is not on a train line but is easily reached from Nice and other Côte d'Azur centres. Take a train from Nice to the St-Laurent du Var train station (11FF, 10 mins, two an hour); it's a short ride to Vence from there. Take ave Charles de Gaulle north for 1.7km, turning left onto the D118. This climbs steadily from sea level to 300m over 10km. At 11.1km veer right onto the D18 and, at 12.7km, go left onto the D2210. You reach the centre of Vence at about 19km.

THE RIDES
Vence

Information The Vence tourist office (☎ 04 93 58 06 38, fax 04 93 58 91 81) is in place du Grand Jardin (closed Sunday).

Banque Nationale de Paris is at place du Grand Jardin; Lyonnaise de Banque is at 4 place Maréchal Juin; and Banque Populaire is at 14bis ave de la Résistance.

Bike repairs and spare parts are available at Atelier Chromo (☎ 04 93 58 94 05, 247 route de Cagnes) or Vence Motors (☎ 04 93 58 56 00, 6 ave Poilus).

Things to See & Do The striking **Chapelle du Rosaire** (Chapel of the Rosary; ☎ 04 93 58 03 26), 468 ave Henri Matisse (the D2210), is on the left approaching town from the north-east. Matisse was 81 when he designed the project in 1951, having moved from war-torn Nice to Vence in 1943. Matisse's former villa, **Le Rêve**, is nearby. Follow the sign to 'Résidence Altitude 350'. **Art workshops** are held here; contact the Vence Station Touristique (☎ 04 93 58 40 10) in Villa Alexandrine, place du Grand Jardin.

Porte du Peyra, the main gate through the 13th-century wall encircling the old town, leads to pretty place du Peyra, which has a 16th-century fountain. Across the square, the mposing **Château de Villeneuve** and its 2th century watchtower house the **Fondaion Émile Hughes** (☎ 04 93 24 24 23), a culural centre specialising in 20th-century art xhibitions.

The tourist office issues free maps of a 5-minute, **self-guided tour** of the town

Places to Stay & Eat The camping ground s about 4km west of town. Follow signs to he shady *Camping Domaine de la Bergerie* ☎ 04 93 58 09 36, route de la Sine). It harges 43/76FF for one/two people.

The Dominican nuns offer beds in the *Maison Lacordaire* (☎ 04 93 58 03 26, fax 4 93 58 21 10, 466 ave Henri Matisse) adoining the Chapelle du Rosaire. Accomodation costs around 200FF a night and ooms must be reserved in advance.

More mundane is the *Hôtel la Lubane* ☎ 04 93 58 01 10, fax 04 93 58 84 44, 10 ve Joffre) with basic singles/doubles from 80/215FF. *Hôtel Victoire* (☎ 04 93 58 61 0, fax 04 93 58 74 68, place du Grand ardin) has rooms with shower/bath from 50/180FF above a noisy bar.

A fruit and vegetable *market* is held every norning except Monday on place du Grand ardin. For supermarkets, try the *Leclerc* 288 ave Émile Hugues) or *Prisunic (41 ave Henri Isnard).*

Rue du Marché, off place du Peyra, is rammed with delectable *food shops*. In the eart of the old town, *Le P'tit Provençal* ☎ 04 93 58 50 64, 4 place Clemenceau) erves delicious local dishes for moderate rices on its pavement terrace. Try also *Le Pigeonnier (☎ 04 93 58 03 00, 3 place du Peyra)*, in a 16th-century house. Its specialies are salmon ravioli and fresh pastries.

Plateau de Caussols
–10 hours, 102.2km

his circuit starts with a short climb west rom Vence (325m) then a descent to the tart of the **Gorges du Loup**. It's a long, cenic climb to the tourist honey pot of iourdon (758m). Its **13th-century castle** an be toured and there's an excellent view the coast; tacky souvenir shops and high rices detract from the experience.

The ascent to the limestone **Plateau de Caussols** (1100m) is on an almost deserted oad. From here the route stays at or above 000m for the next 30km. There are

panoramic views of the mountains and valleys from the road, which hugs the edge of a precipice for many kilometres.

A delightful sweeping descent through four short tunnels leads to Gréolières. After this village, take a very narrow road, with fairly gentle gradients, that winds from one side of the valley to the other through farming country and up to Cipières.

After about 7km downhill, a left turn rejoins the outward route to Vence.

Côte d'Azur Hinterland
3½–7 hours, 74.7km

This circuit uses the same route as the Plateau de Caussols ride as far as the northern end of the **Gorges du** Loup; it then turns north, instead of south, on the D3. A side trip from Vence could be done at the start or end of the day, or as a separate trip.

After a right turn onto the D2, the route climbs from about 650m to 1020m at Coursegoules (34.1km), a typical Provençal perched village with **11th-century castle ruins** and fortifications.

From here it is virtually all downhill for 40km back to Vence. The quiet, narrow road wiggles across the landscape, high above valleys and gorges and through desolate, fire-ravaged country, emerging to give views over the Var River, near Gattières. Here, civilisation and traffic reassert themselves and you have company on the road again.

Side Trip: Col de Vence
1½–2½ hours, 21km

If desired, this ride could be a separate half-day trip.

Ride up to the 963m **Col de Vence** via the D2 from the north side of town. The climb is constant and relatively steep in places but not especially hard on an unladen bike. It would best be done before the sun is high because of the lack of shade before the top.

A *restaurant* near the summit is popular with cyclists and there is also a pleasant treed area at the col itself where you can picnic. The road has only a few hairpins and mostly winds in and out of gullies and across the face of the mountain, offering good views to the south.

You can use the Col de Vence as a 'shortcut' home. The D2 heads south-east from near Coursegoules, climbing gently for 6km to the col then descending to Vence.

PROVENCE & THE CÔTE D'AZUR

Plateau de Caussols

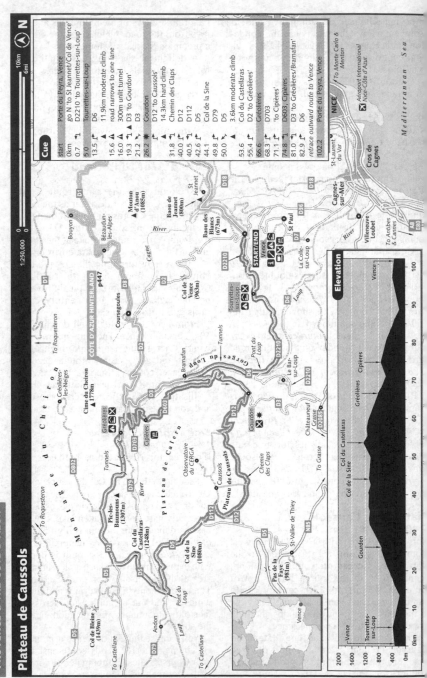

Cue

start		Porte du Peyra, Vence	D6
0km	↑	go N 'to St Jeannet/Col de Vence'	
0.7	←	D2210 'to Tourrettes-sur-Loup'	
5.0	←	Tourrettes-sur-Loup	
13.5	←	D6	
		11.9km moderate climb	
15.6	◄	road narrows to one lane	
16.0	◄	300m unlit tunnel	
19.3	↱	D3 'to Gourdon'	
21.2	↰	D3	
26.2	✱	Gourdon	
	↰	D12 'to Caussols'	
31.8		14.3km hard climb	
40.0	↰	Chemin des Claps	
40.5	↰	D12	
42.6	↱	D5	
44.1		Col de la Sine	
49.8	↰	D79	
50.0	◄	D5	
		3.6km moderate climb	
53.6		Col du Castellaras	
55.4	↱	D2 'to Gréolières'	
66.6		Gréolières	
68.3	↰	D703	
71.1	↱	'to Cipières'	
74.8	↰	D603, Cipières	
81.0	↱	D3 'to Gréolières/Bramafan'	
82.9	↰	D6	
		retrace outward route to Vence	
102.2		Porte du Peyra, Vence	

Elevation

Côte d'Azur Hinterland

⊕ N

1:250,000

0   10km
0   4ml

Vence

Elevation

1600						
1200						
800						
400						
0m						

0km   10   20   30   40   50   60   70

Vence   Tourrettes-sur-Loup   Coursegoules   Bouyon   Le Broc   Carros Village   Gattières   Vence

To St Aubin

To Castellane

To Draguignan

To Roquesteron &
Puget Théniers

To Puget Théniers

To Nice

To Monte Carlo
& Monaco

NICE

Aéroport
International
Nice-Côte d'Azur

Mediterranean
Sea

Levens

St-Martin
du Var

Carros

Carros
Village

Gattières

St-Laurent
du Var

Cros de
Cagnes

Cagnes-
sur-Mer

St Jeannet

St Paul

La Colle-
sur-Loup

Villeneuve-
Loubet

To Antibes
& Cannes

Vence
START/END

Tourrettes-
sur-Loup

Rocquefort-
les-Pins

Pont du
Loup

Gorges du Loup

Tunnels

Gourdon

Valbonne

To Antibes
& Cannes

Châteauneuf
Grasse

GRASSE

Plateau de Caussols

Caussols

Les Claps

Plateau de Calern

Cipières

Gréolières

Bramafan

St Barnabé

Col de
Vence
(963m)

Sice Trip

Baou des
Blancs
(673m)

Baou de
Jeannet
(800m)

Mouton d'Anou
(1085m)

Bézaudun-
les-Alpes

Bouyon

Les Ferres

Pierrefeu

Gilette

Coursegoules

Col de la
Sine
(1080m)

Pic-les-
Baumouni
(1307m)

Le Var

Var River

Cagne River

Esteron River

PLATEAU DE CAUSSOLS
p446

Cue

0km		Porte du Peyra, Vence
0.7	↰	go N 'to St Jeannet/Col de Vence'
5.0	↑	Tourrettes-sur-Loup'
13.5	↑	D6
	◭	11.9km moderate climb
15.6	◭	road narrows to one lane
16.0	◭	300m unlit tunnel
19.3	↰	D3 to Bramafan'
24.4	↰	D2 to Coursegoules'
	◭	6.6km moderate climb
32.5	◭	D8 to Coursegoules'
	◭	1.6km hard climb
34.1		Coursegoules
34.8	↖	D8 'to Bouyon/Bézaudun'
46.2		Bouyon
46.5	↰	D1 'to Carros/Le Broc'
54.4		Le Broc
57.9	↱	Carros Village
58.4	↰	D2209
63.6		Gattières
63.7	↗	D2210 'to Vence'
74.0	↰	to Vence 'centre ville' ↩ Col de Vence 21km
74.7		Porte du Peyra, Vence

PROVENCE & THE CÔTE D'AZUR

Mediterranean Promenade

Duration ....1¾–3½ hours
Distance 32.5km
Difficulty ....easy
Start..St Raphaël
End ....La Napoule

This easy jaunt on the Corniche d'Or passes plenty of coves to lure you off your bike and into the azure Mediterranean. With stunning views of the red rock Massif de l'Esterel, the offshore Îles de Lérins and trendy Cannes, the road has a shoulder for cyclists for much of the way. Numerous *buvettes* (refreshment terraces) are scattered along the roadside.

PLANNING
When to Ride
This year-round ride would be most pleasant when air and water temperatures are suitable for swimming – from June to August – but traffic would be considerably less outside that period.

You can ride in either direction, but from St Raphaël to La Napoule you ride on the side of the road directly adjacent to the beach. The views are 'in your face' and you don't have to cross traffic lanes to best appreciate them.

GETTING TO/FROM THE RIDE
The Alpes Maritime, Côte d'Azur Hinterland and Plateau de Caussols rides earlier in this chapter are all easily accessed from Nice. St Raphaël and La Napoule are on the rail line to Les Arcs-sur-Argens, the start of the Grand Canyon du Verdon ride later in this chapter.

The rides detailed in the Corsica chapter are also easily accessed from Nice.

St Raphaël
Train St Raphaël is served by frequent TER trains, which all take bikes for free, on the railway line between Nice (56FF, one hour, two an hour) and Marseille (135FF, 1¾ hours, 10 a day).

Bicycle St Raphaël is a full day's ride from Vence via the N7, the hilly inland route through the Massif de l'Esterel. If cycling from the east, it may be more time-efficient to do the ride in reverse, starting from La

Napoule, which is only 3km from the junction of the N7 and the coastal N98.

La Napoule is about a half-day ride from Vence via a complex network of roads which, though minor, still carry plenty of traffic from June to August. Navigate through St Paul, La Colle-sur-Loup, Roquefort-les-Pins, Valbonne, Plascassier, Mouans-Sartoux and Pégomas-le-Logis onto the D109. Head south to, and beyond, Mandelieu-la-Napoule.

La Napoule
Train Trains connect La Napoule with towns along the whole Côte d'Azur from Marseille (149FF, two hours, at least two a day carry bikes) to beyond Nice (41FF, 5 minutes, at least 10 a day carry bikes).

At least six trains a day to Les Arcs-sur-Argens take bikes (47FF, 1¾ hours).

Bicycle Ride to Les Arcs-sur-Argens via the N7 to Fréjus (passing a memorial plaque not far from La Napoule, to champion Niçois cyclist Adrien Buttafochi, 'who fell mortally wounded' on this road on 27 June 1937). Continue south-west on the coastal N98 and, beyond Ste Maxime, turn onto the D14 to Grimaud. Climb through the beautiful forest of the Massif des Maures to La Garde-Freinet, where there is a good-value camping ground, and follow the D558, turning onto the D48. Turn right onto the N7 at Vidauban, from where it's 8km to Les Arcs.

THE RIDE
St-Raphaël
St-Raphaël is the port where Napoleon Bonaparte landed on returning from Egypt in 1799 and from where he left for exile in Elba in 1814. The resort, 3km from Fréjus but now joined to it by development, was also one of the landing bases for Allied troops in August 1944.

Information The tourist office (☎ 04 94 19 52 52, fax 04 94 83 85 40, 🖳 www.saint-raphael.com) is opposite the train station on rue Waldeck Rousseau (closed Sunday).

Banque Populaire de la Côte d'Azur is at 11 rue A Baux. Cycles Thierry (☎ 04 94 95 48 46) is at 53 ave Alphonse Karr.

Things to See & Do Excellent sandy beaches nearby include the main **Plage de Veillat**. Eastwards, **Plage Beaurivage** is

White pebbles form a year-round impression of snow around the cycling mecca of Mont Ventoux.

In summer, Provence fields are awash with lavender glory.

Roadside stalls provide local treats.

The famous, 900m-long Pont St Bénézet spans the Rhône at Avignon.

The rugged cliffs of E Calenche near Porto are one of Corsica's most beautiful sights at sunset.

Charcuterie (salami), washed down by red wine, is typically Corsican.

The ruins of Terra Mozza.

Porte de Gênes, Bonifacio.

Cool, man! Ancient water fountains line the roads in Corsica.

ebbly. **Parachuting** and **wave riding** activities are available.

Further east, at the water-sports hub of **Port Santa Lucia**, the Centre Nautique Municipal (☎ 04 94 83 84 50, @ cnsr@comx.fr), on blvd Général de Gaulle, offers sailing, kayaking and guided expeditions.

Les Bateaux de St-Raphaël (☎ 04 94 95 7 46, fax 04 94 82 71 45), Gare Maritime, organises daily **boat excursions** in summer to the Îles de Lérins.

The fishing community honours its patron, St Peter, with the two-day **Fête de la St Pierre des Pêcheurs** each August.

Places to Stay & Eat Accommodation is not especially cheap in St Raphaël.

The *Auberge de Jeunesse Fréjus-St Raphaël (☎ 04 94 53 18 75, fax 04 94 53 25 76, chemin du Counillier)*, near Fréjus, allows camping for 32FF a night. Dorm beds cost from 66FF, including breakfast. Check in between 8 and 10 am or 6 and 8 pm.

The comfortable *Centre International du Manoir (☎ 04 94 95 20 58, fax 04 94 83 85 76, chemin de l'Escale)* is 5km east along the coast in Boulouris. It charges from 110FF for a dorm bed in low season and from 115FF in high season, when it is reserved for young travellers (18–35 years; mid-June to August).

The two-star *Hôtel Bellevue (☎ 04 94 19 90 10, fax 04 94 19 90 11, 24 blvd Félix Martin)* has good-value singles/doubles from 150/180FF. *Hôtel Le Thimothée (☎ 04 94 40 49 49, fax 04 94 19 41 92, 375 blvd Christian Lafon)* is in a quiet street. It has rooms from 290FF to 420FF in high season.

Get fresh fruit and vegies in the *old town square (junction rue de la République & rue du Peyron)* or buy fish at the jetty of the *Vieux Port*, at daily morning *markets*. Visit the supermarkets *Monoprix (58 blvd Félix Martin)* or *Champion (ave Général Leclerc)*.

For restaurant meals, try *The Loch Ness (5 ave de Valescure)*, a tavern serving traditional 'Scottish' fare such as Mexican steaks and Texas ribs. Eat with more local flavour at *La Sarriette (☎ 04 94 19 28 13, 45 rue de la République; closed Wednesday)*.

St Raphaël to La Napoule

½–3½ hours, 32.5km

Be cautious negotiating the wall-to-wall traffic out of the centre of St Raphaël. Once on the coast, navigation could not be simpler

– the N98 (the Corniche d'Or/Corniche de l'Estérel) leads directly to La Napoule with few serious climbs.

Past Boulouris there are views to the pretty **Cap du Dramont**, crowned by a military semaphore.

The village resort of Agay (10km) offers fine views of its perfectly horseshoe-shaped bay, encircled by sandy beaches backed by pine forest.

Beyond Anthéor, the awesome, red **Pic du Cap Roux** (453m) dominates the scene, reflected in the azure waters on a calm day. Take time to pause at one of the *buvettes* on this stretch of coast and relax, enjoying the view, a drink and lunch.

The highest point of the corniche is at Le Trayas (150m), 2km north of which is the large beach at the Anse (cove) de la Figueirette.

The resort of Théoule-sur-Mer features the restored, privately owned **Château de la Théoule**, which served as a soap factory during the 18th century.

Descending gently into La Napoule, watch out for conflicts at the roundabout (traffic circle) before turning down the street to the station.

La Napoule

At the south-western end of the Golfe de la Napoule, this attractive summer resort features a marina for pleasure boats and a restored castle.

Many services are in the adjacent town of Mandelieu, about 3km north. La Napoule's train station offers a convenient escape route from the traffic near Cannes.

Information The tourist office (☎ 04 93 49 95 31), ave Henry Clews, closes on weekends from December to February.

Two banks serve the combined villages of Mandelieu-La Napoule. Lyonnaise de Banque is on blvd des Écureuils and the Banque Populaire de la Côte d'Azur is on ave de Cannes.

There is no bike shop.

Things to See & Do Dominating the town is the 14th-century **Château de la Napoule** (☎ 04 93 49 95 05). The sea-facing Saracen tower was rebuilt early in the 20th century by Americans, Henry and Marie Clews. Afternoon tours depart the main entrance,

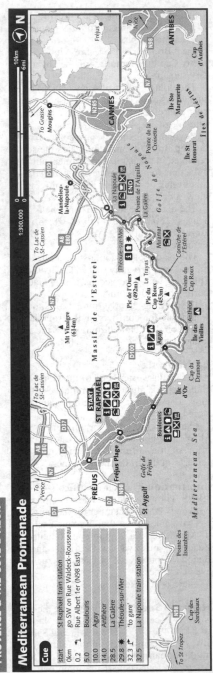

Mediterranean Promenade

Cue		
start		St Raphaël train station
0km		go SW on Rue Waldeck-Rousseau
0.2	↰	Rue Albert 1er (N98 East)
5.0		Boulouris
10.0		Agay
14.0		Anthéor
28.5		La Galère
29.8	✳	Théoule-sur-Mer
32.3	↲	'to gare'
32.5		La Napoule train station

on ave Henry Clews, from March to October (closed Tuesday).

Places to Stay & Eat The two-star *Hôtel La Calanque* (☎ 04 93 49 95 11, fax 04 9 49 67 44, ave Henry Clews), opposite th Château de la Napoule, has singles/double from 195/330FF. At the north end of tow is the pricey four-star *Hôtel Royal Casin* (☎ 04 92 97 70 00, fax 04 93 49 51 50, 60 ave du Général de Gaulle), with double from 690FF to 1650FF a night.

Mandelieu-La Napoule's supermarket include *Coccinelle* (822 ave Janvie Passero) and *Spar* (312 blvd des Écureuils)

Bars and *cafes* line ave de Cannes. Fo takeaway, try *Quick Restaurant* (☎ 04 93 4 24 20, allée Louis Blériot).

Restaurant Le Rioul (☎ 04 92 9769 0.' ave Henry Clews), near the castle, an *Restaurant des Amis* (☎ 04 93 49 42 81, 22 ave de Cannes) have *menus* from aroun 100FF. For seafood, visit the pricey *Le Bou canier* (☎ 04 93 49 80 51) on the water Mandelieu.

Grand Canyon du Verdon

Duration	3 days
Distance	159km
Difficulty	moderate-hard
Start	Les Arcs-sur-Argens
End	Manosque

This sometimes challenging but not over difficult trek travels from Les Arcs to th 'Grand Canyon of Europe' and into th Luberon. Add a day to explore the perche villages and quiet roads around Comps-su Artuby (see Side Trip under Day 1).

NATURAL HISTORY
Slicing through the limestone plateau on th southern fringe of Haute-Provence fo 25km between Moustiers-Ste Marie an Comps-sur-Artuby, the greenish, fluorin rich waters of the Verdon River hav formed the largest canyon in Europe – th Gorges du Verdon (or Grand Canyon d Verdon). Since 1997 the Parc Naturel R gional du Verdon has protected the 250m to 700m-deep gorges. From a mere 8m 90m wide at the bottom, the gorge rises rims separated by between 200m an

500m. The bottom of the canyon was first explored in its entirety only in 1905. Now it is also part of the Réserve Géologique de Haute-Provence, making it illegal to remove rocks, minerals and fossils.

PLANNING

When to Ride

Weather is most favourable from May to September, but tourist hordes descend on the Gorges du Verdon from mid-June to August, clogging the roads and lookouts from late morning to late afternoon. In these months, beat most of the tourists and the heat by aiming to reach Moustiers by about lunch time.

GETTING TO/FROM THE RIDE

The Luberon & Mont Ventoux ride detailed later in this chapter begins in Forcalquier, a short ride from Manosque.

Les Arcs-sur-Argens

Train At least six trains a day head to Les Arcs from Nice (70FF, 1¾ hours) and at least seven travel from Marseille (98FF, two hours); all take bikes.

Bicycle See the Mediterranean Promenade ride (p448) for information on cycling to Les Arcs from La Napoule.

Manosque

Train The train station, place Frédéric Mistral, is 2km south of the town centre. Manosque is served by at least four daily, bike-carrying trains from Marseille (83FF, 1¼ hours).

Bicycle To reach Forcalquier, exit the Manosque town centre by the north gate, following signs to Dauphin. Climb steadily on a winding, tree-lined road. After 5.6km and a 200m gain, the Col de la Mort d'Imbert offers views of the Observatoire de Haute-Provence. At 11.8km veer right onto chemin de St-Jean which becomes route de la Bastide Neuve. Turn left at the village (13.1km) and follow the white-arrowed Luberon Bike Route signs up into Forcalquier.

THE RIDE

Les Arcs-sur-Argens

The two drawcards to Les Arcs are its perfectly restored medieval old town, perched on a hillock above the modern village, and its Maison des Vins, where you can buy, taste and learn more than you ever wanted to know about the local wines. The tourist office (☎ 04 94 73 37 30, fax 04 94 47 47 94), place de Général de Gaulle, is at the foot of the medieval village.

Things to See & Do A market fills the central square on Tuesday and Thursday mornings. Wine tastings are available at the Maison des Vins Côtes de Provence (☎ 04 94 99 50 20, fax 04 94 99 50 29), 2km south of the village on the N7.

Places to Stay & Eat A popular camping ground, *L'Eau Vive* (☎ 04 94 47 40 66, fax 04 94 47 43 27) is on the riverbank, 1.2km south of the train station in the Quartier Point d'Argens. Cross the N7 and continue straight ahead for 100m. It charges 30FF per person and is open from March to October.

Crowning the old town, an 11th-century castle houses the elegant *Logis du Guetteur* (☎ 04 94 73 30 82, fax 04 94 73 39 95, place du Château), which has doubles from 350FF (600FF in July and August) and mouth watering *menus* from 150FF.

A *Champion* supermarket is in route Taradeau. See Things to See & Do for *market* details.

Several *cafes* line blvd Gambetta. The town has several attractive restaurants, including *L'Avenir* (☎ 04 94 73 30 58, route de la Gare). Sample local wines and culinary delights at *Le Bacchus Gourmand* (☎ 04 94 47 48 47), adjoining the Maison des Vins, from Tuesday to Saturday.

Day 1: Les Arcs-sur-Argens to Comps-sur-Artuby

3½–5 hours, 54.4km

This route involves some significant climbs – the morning's ride takes you above 600m at the Col de la Grange. After a brief descent, climbing resumes, reaching 920m at Comps.

The ride starts at the train station, 700m south-east of the centre of Les Arcs. Follow the D57 north-west towards Le Flayosquet, turning off at the edge of that village to climb to Ampus. The 9km climb to conquer the Col de la Grange (616m) is rewarded by magnificent views.

Roll down to quietly attractive Ampus. Its central square offers shade from the midday sun plus a fountain, *bar*, restaurant

Day 1: Les Arcs-sur-Argens to Comps-sur-Artuby

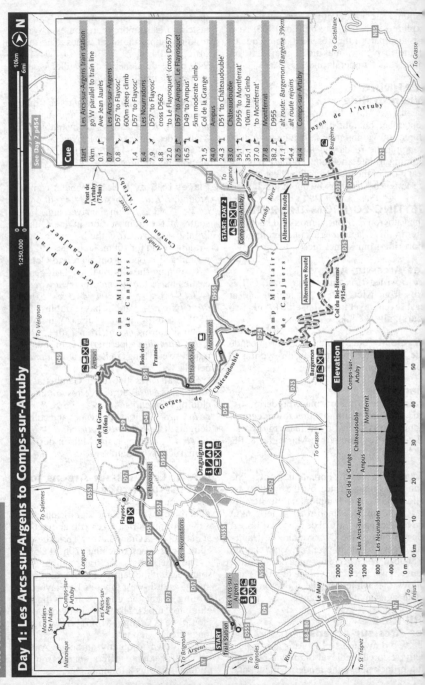

Cue

start	Les Arcs-sur-Argens train station
0km	go W parallel to train line
0.1	Ave Jean Jaurès
0.7	Les Arcs-sur-Argens
0.8	D57 'to Flayosc'
	600m steep climb
1.4	D57 'to Flayosc'
6.4	Les Nourradons
7.9	D57 'to Flayosc'
8.8	cross D562
12.0	'to Le Flayosquet' (cross D557)
12.5	D57 'to Ampus', Le Flayosquet
16.5	D49 'to Ampus'
	5km moderate climb
21.5	Col de la Grange
24.0	Ampus
24.3	D51 'to Châteaudouble'
33.0	Châteaudouble
35.1	D955 'to Montferrat'
	10km hard climb
37.0	'to Montferrat'
37.8	Montferrat
38.2	D955
41.1	alt route: Bargemon/Bargème 39km
	alt route rejoins
54.4	Comps-sur-Artuby

Elevation

La Fontaine (☎ 04 94 70 98 08; reservation essential), an *épicerie* (small grocery store) and boulangerie. Half a kilometre down the hill, the hotel/restaurant *La Bonne Auberge* serves lunch, with *menus* of 92FF and 35FF. Settle lunch with a stroll to the hill-top cross above the 11th-century **Romanesque church**. Mosaics along the path depict each stage of Christ's walk to his crucifixion.

It's a superb run along the narrow and sinuous D51. Mostly level or slightly up or down, the deserted road snakes through the badly fire-ravaged Bois des Prannes, with a curve every 100m or so adding an air of mystery. There's an impressive view approaching perched Châteaudouble (33km), above the gorge of the same name. Ride through the village's narrow alleys and archways to a *belvédère* (viewpoint) over the gorge.

The wide D955 runs through the gorge and climbs through dramatic bare limestone hills, another legacy of fires, emerging high above the Artuby river. Despite its 'red' (busy) indication on Michelin maps, it doesn't carry all that much traffic – a good proportion is army trucks associated with the nearby military base – and the majority is southbound. It's quite a long but gentle climb – a 420m altitude gain over 10.5km – to the Camp Militaire du Canjuers' tank-parking compound, after which the route loses 90m to cross the Artuby then gains another 120m or so over 5km to reach Comps.

Alternative Route: Bargemon & Bargème
2½–4 hours, 39km

It's worth sparing a day to take the described route to Comps and then make this into a moderate-hard circuit at a reasonable pace. To do this, from Comps, head south on the D955 back to the D19 junction. For a really tough, 80.1km day, it is possible to use this as an alternative route to Comps (turn right onto the D19 about 3.3km after Montferrat).

Follow the winding D19 eastwards, down to the right-hand turn-off (the D25) to Bargemon. Its **medieval churches** – Notre Dame de Montaigu, long an important pilgrim destination, and St Étienne – are worth visiting.

Take the D25 back out of town (uphill) to the 915m Col du Bel-Homme, gaining panoramic views to the south with every switchback. It's a tough, sun-exposed climb, with a gain of 440m in less than 8km, but it

levels out on the Grand Plan de Canjuers. This wild, rugged, inhospitable country is used by the army as a training ground and there are constant warnings not to leave the narrow road due to *danger du mort* (death) from unexploded ordnance. Periodically along the road there are special tank-crossing points. Distant limestone massifs create a spectacular backdrop to the north.

After 16km from Bargemon, veer left onto the tiny D37 which leads straight to **Bargème** – steeply and through pine forest for much of the last 2km. This restored village, its permanent population now less than 10, is the highest in the Var region at 1094m. Guided tours are available in July and August. Its main feature is the ruined **Château de Pontevès**, with open views of the Canjuers plateau and the foothills of the Alps. Return to Comps via the fast, direct D21.

Comps-sur-Artuby
Sleepy little Comps, the least touristy 'gateway' town to the Gorges du Verdon, is a great place to just relax. Information is available from the Commune de Comps-sur-Artuby (☎ 04 94 85 66 54), place de République.

Places to Stay & Eat *Camping Municipal du Pontet* (☎ 04 94 76 91 40) sprawls on the hillside 100m off the D71, 1km outside town. It charges a mere 20FF per person.

Near the town centre, the family-run *Grand Hôtel Bain* (☎ 04 94 76 90 06, fax 04 94 76 92 24) has been serving travellers since 1737. Rooms cost from 250FF to 370FF and meals are available in its *restaurant*.

Thirteen kilometres away (10km along the D955 to the north-west and 3km up the wiggly D90), in the perched village of Trigance, is the pricey *Château de Trigance* (☎ 04 94 76 91 18, fax 04 94 85 68 99). Rooms in the restored 10th-century castle start at 600FF. Tables in the upmarket *restaurant*, with sumptuous *menus* from 210FF, have to be reserved.

Comps has a *bakery* and a good *self-service store* which sells every basic necessity for a hungry cyclist.

Day 2: Comps-sur-Artuby to Moustiers-Ste Marie
3½–5 hours, 55km

The earliest possible start on this route is advisable during tourist season – 6.30 am is

Day 2: Comps-sur-Artuby to Moustiers-Ste Marie

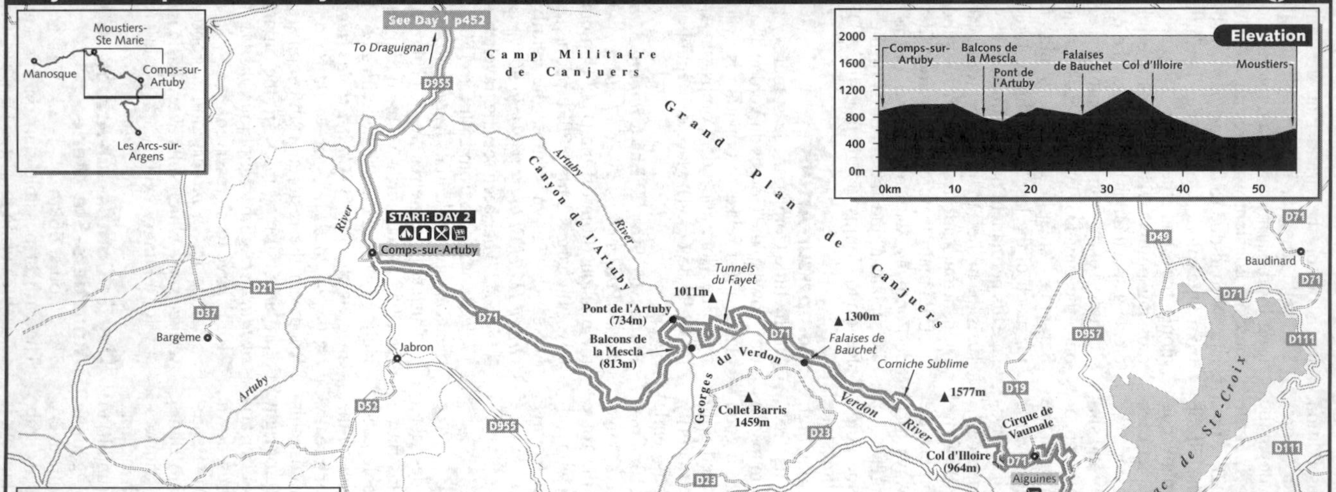

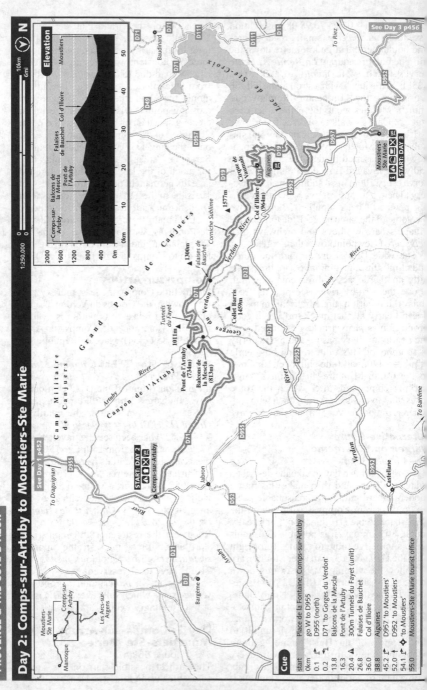

Cue

start		Place de la Fontaine, Comps-sur-Artuby
0km		go W to D955
0.1	↱	D955 (north)
0.2	↰	D71 'to Gorges du Verdon'
13.8		Balcons de la Mescla
16.3		Pont de l'Artuby
20.4	▲	300m Tunnels du Fayet (unlit)
26.8		Falaises de Bauchet
36.0		Col d'Illoire
38.8		Aiguines
45.2	↱	D957 'to Moustiers'
52.0	↑	D952 'to Moustiers'
54.1	↱ ✥	'to Moustiers'
55.0		Moustiers-Ste Marie tourist office

not too early – if you want to ride on a quiet road. Traffic on the recommended D71 (or Corniche Sublime) picks up significantly after 10 am but, until then, cyclists have it virtually to themselves. On leaving Comps, there are no shops until Aiguines (38.8km).

For the first 10km from Comps, the route ascends gently, gaining 100m to top 1000m. On a sweeping descent it loses 200m over 4km. Enjoy the speed rush but at 13.8km, as you rocket around a bend, be ready for the sign announcing the Balcons de la Mescla. Otherwise, by the time you have braked a heavy touring bike to a halt on the slope, you'll be way downhill of the short walk-way to the spectacular viewpoint. This ter-race of limestone rises from the Verdon's confluence with the Artuby river.

Continue rapidly down past the cafe-bar, *Relais de la Mescla*, gasping at the views. Cross the concrete arch of the Pont de l'Ar-tuby, a popular bungee-jumping venue 180m above the river and, at 734m altitude, the highest bridge in Europe. Continue along the rim of the gorge, passing under rocky over-hangs topped by loose boulders, seemingly only restrained from falling by haphazardly placed wire mesh. Shudder!

Shortly after, the unlit Tunnels du Fayet (20.4km) offer a dizzying vantage point over the gorge. The nearby *Hôtel du Grand Canyon du Verdon* (☎ 04 94 76 91 31, fax 04 94 76 92 29) has rooms from 300FF, and *menus* from 85FF to 150FF in a *restaurant* balanced on the very edge of the canyon.

The Falaises de Bauchet (26.8km) mark the narrowest point of the gorges and the road climbs from here to the Cirque de Vau-nale, a 1201m viewpoint, overlooking the Plateau de Valensole beyond Lac de Ste-Croix. In the next 3km it plunges nearly 350m to the Col d'Illoire, with a last look down into the stunning canyon.

The road continues steeply down to the attractively located, touristy village of Ai-guines and descends again to the Lac de Ste-Croix, boundary between the departments of Var and Alpes de Haute-Provence. Here, 8km from Moustiers, boating and *camping* are extensively catered for – you can paddle or pedal little boats upriver into the gorge.

Moustiers-Ste Marie

Pretty Moustiers (pop 580) was founded by monks in AD 433. It nestles on a rock shelf beneath a backdrop of two towering orange-hued cliffs. A 220m-long gold chain bearing a star hangs between the cliffs and the 12th-century Chapelle Notre Dame de Beauvoir perches on a ledge with a waterfall tum-bling past. The Ravin de Notre Dame flows through the village, crossed by several char-acterful stone bridges.

Information The tourist office (☎ 04 92 74 67 84, fax 04 92 74 60 65, 🖳 www.ville-mou stiers-sainte-marie.fr) is on rue Bourgade. It has English-language guides on the Parc Naturel Régional du Verdon (☎ 04 92 74 63 95, fax 04 92 74 63 94), BP 14, 04360 Moustiers Ste-Marie.

A Crédit Agricole is on rue Orville.

Things to See & Do Moustiers has re-vived its tradition of Provençal *faïence* (earthenware) largely for the tourist mar-ket. The Musée de la Faïence (☎ 04 92 74 61 64), rue Bourgade, has an excellent col-lection of local pieces.

Take an hour-long walk to the Chapelle Notre Dame de Beauvoir, up a steep trail with many steps from rue Bourgade. Fit-tingly, there are breathtaking views from the top. Another rough path to the west of the village is flanked by dozens of tongue-in-cheek novelty artworks which lead to a fine viewpoint of the town itself.

Places to Stay & Eat The *Camping St Jean*, 1.2km west of the town centre, off the D952, is open from 1 May to around 20 September. It charges 43/63FF for one/two people.

Moustiers' three hotels fill up fast. *La Bonne Auberge* (☎ 04 92 74 66 18, fax 04 92 74 65 11, route de Castellane), *Le Belvédère* (☎ 04 92 74 66 04, fax 04 92 74 62 31, ave de Lérins) and *Le Relais* (☎ 04 92 74 66 10, fax 04 92 74 60 47, place du Couvent) all have rooms from 250FF.

At the foot of the village is the upmarket *La Bastide de Moustiers* (☎ 04 92 70 47 47, fax 04 92 70 47 48, 🖳 www.bastide-mou stiers.i2m.fr, chemin de Quinson), run by acclaimed French chef Alain Ducasse. It is a 17th-century country house with rooms from 950FF to 1700FF in high season. Guests can have a gourmet picnic hamper for 150FF each or cooking lessons for 450FF each.

PROVENCE & THE CÔTE D'AZUR

Day 3: Moustiers-Ste Marie to Manosque

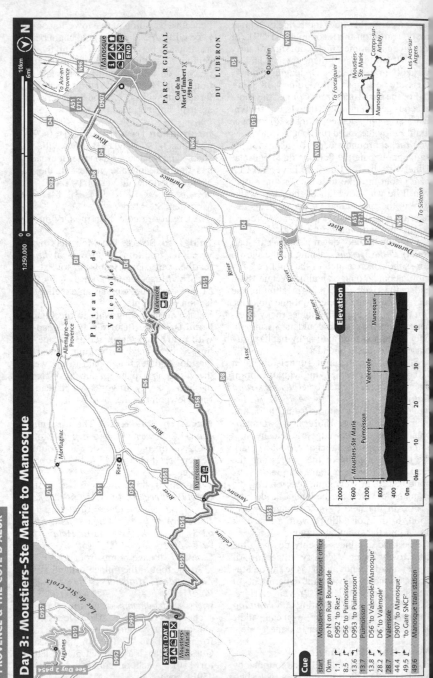

Cue		
start		
0km		Moustiers-Ste Marie tourist office
		go N on Rue Bourgade
1.1	↱	D952 'to Riez'
8.5	↱	D56 'to Puimoisson'
13.6	↱	D953 'to Puimoisson'
13.7		Puimoisson
13.8	↰	D56 'to Valensole/Manosque'
28.2	↱	D6 'to Valensole'
28.7		Valensole
44.4	↱	D907 'to Manosque'
49.5	↱	'to Gare SNCF'
49.6		Manosque train station

There's an *alimentation* (grocery store) on rue Diane and a *bakery* on place Couvert. *La Treille Muscate* (☎ 04 92 74 64 31, place de l'Église) offers simple, flavourful cuisine in a 160FF *menu*.

Day 3: Moustiers-Ste Marie to Manosque
3–4½ hours, 49.6km

Enjoy this gentle, mostly downhill jaunt through fields of waving wheat and fragrant lavender, passing farms with lavender products for sale. Towns on the way are small rural centres without tourist services. A long bridge crosses the Durance into lively Manosque.

Manosque

Manosque is the birthplace of Provençal writer Jean Giono (1895–1970) and an arts centre here has been dedicated to his memory. Accommodation in Manosque is substantially cheaper than in other towns on the route, making it a good base for exploration of the Luberon and the Gorges du Verdon.

Information The tourist office (☎ 04 92 72 16 00, fax 04 92 72 58 98), in place du Docteur P Joubert, is open Monday to Saturday, plus Sunday mornings in summer.

A Banque Populaire is at 29 blvd Elémir Bourges.

There are two bike dealers on blvd de la Plaine: Cycles Alègre (☎ 04 92 72 29 04) at No 14 and Cycles Bachelas (☎ 04 92 72 15 84) at No 24.

Things to See & Do Explore the attractive **pedestrianised centre** of town. Art exhibitions frequent the **Centre Jean Giono** (☎ 04 92 70 54 54), blvd Elémir Bourges. Giono's lifelong home, a cottage on the corner of Grande Rue and rue Torte, still stands. Frescoes by Armenian-born Jean Carzou cover 670 sq metres of wall inside the 19th-century **Chapelle de la Congrégation**, 7 blvd Elémir Bourges, and paint a frightening picture of the year 2000.

Places to Stay & Eat Of numerous camping grounds, the cheapest is the noisy *Camping Municipal Les Ubacs* (☎ 04 92 72 28 08, ave de la Repasse), 3km from the train station – follow the signs. It charges 40/56FF for one/two people.

The *Auberge de Jeunesse* (☎ 04 92 87 57 44, fax 04 92 72 43 91, ave de l'Argile, in Parc de la Rochette) charges around 92FF, including breakfast.

The friendly *Hôtel François 1er* (☎ 04 92 72 07 99, fax 04 92 87 54 85, 18 rue Guilhempierre) has rooms from about 160FF to 260FF, while the two-star *Grand Hôtel de Versailles* (☎ 04 92 72 12 10, fax 04 92 72 62 57, 17 ave Jean Giono) charges from around 130/170FF for doubles with washbasin/shower.

Organically-grown fruit and vegetables are available at the co-op *Le Blé en Herbe* (7 rue des Marchands). *Aux Mille Pâtes* (43 Grande Rue) sells homemade pasta.

Eat down-to-earth, hearty cuisine at *Le Petit Pascal* (☎ 04 92 87 62 01, 17 Promenade Aubert Millot) where *menus* start at around 60FF. *Le Lubéron* (☎ 04 92 72 03 09, 21bis place du Terreau) is rustic and recommended. Weekday *menus* start at around 82FF, ranging up to 300FF.

The Luberon & Mont Ventoux

Duration	6 days
Distance	339.8km
Difficulty	moderate-hard
Start	Forcalquier
End	Avignon

This is a challenging ride, especially in the hilly Luberon with a touring load, but it's very enjoyable. There are several possible side trips. Consider staying an extra night in Gordes to ride the Roussillon side trip (see Side Trip 2 under Day 3) at a relaxing pace.

Cyclists can explore the 1200-sq-km Parc Naturel Régional du Luberon on a 100km signposted cycle route that uses quiet roads and passes through many beautiful perched villages, some of which feature in Peter Mayle's bestselling book *A Year in Provence*. The westbound direction is recommended because it starts high and trends generally downwards. Many welcoming camping grounds and other accommodation on the cycle route can break the journey into even shorter sections.

The ride features an ascent of that cycling mecca, 1912m Mont Ventoux; the 22km downhill from the summit to is a real blast!

PROVENCE & THE CÔTE D'AZUR

It includes opportunities to visit Roman ruins at Vaison-la-Romaine and Orange and the chance to sample some of the ambrosial wines of Châteneuf-de-Pape.

PLANNING
When to Ride
Mont Ventoux is usually snow-covered above the 1300m level from December until May. The summit road is accessible only during the summer months.

GETTING TO/FROM THE RIDE
Avignon is the start of the Majesty of the Romans ride detailed later in this chapter. It's also a good base for the two rides in the Languedoc-Roussillon chapter: it's the start of the Remote Cévennes ride and is a short bike ride to Nîmes, the start of the Upper Languedoc ride.

Forcalquier
Forcalquier is not on a railway line but it's an easy ride from Manosque. See the Grand Canyon du Verdon ride (p451) for directions.

Avignon
Train The train station is across blvd St Roch from Porte de la République.

Avignon has frequent connections – all carry bikes – to/from Marseille (92FF, 1½ to 2½ hours, at least nine a day), Nice (226FF, four hours, at least two a day) and Nîmes (46FF, 30 minutes, at least 10 a day).

Avignon is linked to Paris by TGV (3½ hours, about 12 per day). Reservation is *obligatoire* and some have only 1st-class seats (593FF) but at least seven have 2nd-class seats (370FF). A 'night train' also runs to Paris most nights (7½ hours, 387FF).

TGVs also run daily to Lyon (192FF, 1½ hours, up to 15 per day), which has an international airport. Up to four TER trains, which all carry bikes free, run per day to Lyon (2½ to 3 hours, 152FF).

Bicycle For a short cut to Nîmes from Avignon, follow Day 3 of the Majesty of the Romans ride (pp473–9) in reverse.

THE RIDE
Forcalquier
Perched on a rocky hill 550m above sea level and surrounded by fields of sunflowers, Forcalquier is at the eastern end of the Luberon Bike Route. Its name comes from *Font Calquier*, meaning 'fountain on limestone rock'. Steep steps lead to the citadel at the top of the village where carillon concerts are held on Sundays in summer.

Information The tourist office (☎ 04 92 75 10 02) in place du Bourget overlooks the Gothic Église Notre Dame. It's open daily in summer and has free English-language brochures on the Luberon Bike Route.

The nearest bank is at Manosque.

Vélo Loisir en Luberon (☎ 04 92 79 05 82), BP 14, 04280 Céreste, helps cyclists with information on accommodation, bicycle rental and technical support along the Bike Route. Moto Culture (☎ 04 92 75 12 47), 5 blvd de République, does repairs.

Things to See & Do The town **cemetery**, 1km north of the centre on place du Souvenir Français, is the only *cimitière classé* (listed cemetery) in France.

Near Forcalquier, on the D308 (off the ride route in St Michel) is the **Observatoire de Haute-Provence** (☎ 04 92 70 64 00, ☐ www .obs-hp.fr), a national research centre.

Places to Stay & Eat *Camping Municipal St Promasse* (☎ 04 92 75 27 94), open April to October, is 600m from place du Bourguet (follow the signs). It charges 38/58FF for one/two people.

Le Grand Hôtel (☎ 04 92 55 00 35, fax 04 92 75 06 32, 10 blvd Latourette) has large rooms from 150FF.

The pricey *Hostellerie de Deux-Lions* (☎ 04 92 75 25 30, fax 04 92 75 06 41, 11 place du Bourguet) is booked out three months ahead in summer. Its rooms start from 300FF and its *restaurant* has *menus* from 98FF (lunch only) to 350FF.

A *Casino* supérette (small supermarket) is at blvd Latourette and an *épicerie* is at 15 blvd Berlue Perrussi, two doors from a good *bakery*.

Attractive *cafes* line place Bourguet. A la carte meals at little *Lapin Tant Pis* (☎ 04 92 75 38 88, place Vieille) cost around 180FF.

Day 1: Forcalquier to Apt
4–6 hours, 63km
Follow the Luberon Bike Route (LBR) all day. It is well marked with white arrows (east-bound) and orange-ochre arrows

(west-bound) on signs sporting a stylised bicycle design, and takes a convoluted route on some of the most obscure roads imaginable. Roads are frequently unnamed and unsignposted, except for the route markers. Alongside the LBR, colourful information boards provide details on accommodation, places to eat and sights.

Leaving Forcalquier, the LBR plunges into the valley of the Durance tributary, the Largue, and uses a section of former railway line. This stretch is exposed and waterless but there are great views north to the Montagne de Lure. The fields slope steeply at the angle of the underlying limestone strata.

After Reillanne (30.6km), the forested Luberon massif dominates the view ahead. On the lower slopes, a patchwork of fields sprout various colourful crops, including sunflowers, lupins and wheat. Oak forest dominates the ridges, occasionally descending into the valleys. The road to the **Prieuré de Carluc** – the ruin of an ancient priory with an attractive picnic spot by a stream – is so tiny it has grass growing down the middle.

Cross a Roman bridge to reach Céreste and take a road parallel to the N100 to La Viguière, where the ***Camping Le Bois de Sibourg*** charges just 27/40FF for one/two people. Weaving erratically, the LBR finds another retired railway line after Le Boisset. At 58.2km, an isolated **old train-station building** is identified as Baignes. Numerous roads cross this section, and as they have priority over the cycle route, they tediously slow progress every few hundred metres.

Apt

Apt is known for its grapes, cherries and *fleurions* (candied or crystallised fruit). In May it celebrates a **Fête de la Cerise** (Cherry Festival) and a **jazz festival** (☎ 04 90 75 54 27, 🖳 www.luberon.net/).

Information The tourist office (☎ 04 90 74 03 18, fax 04 90 04 64 30, 🖲 tourisme .apt@avignon.pacwan.net), 20 ave Philippe de Girard, opposite place de la Bouquerie near the N100 bridge over the Calavon River, is open Monday to Saturday. In July and August, it also opens from 9 am to noon on Sunday.

Information on the Parc Naturel Régional du Luberon and its two dozen *gîtes d'étape* (lodgings for walkers or cyclists) is available

from the Maison du Parc (☎ 04 90 04 42 00, fax 04 90 04 81 15, 🖲 pnr@wanadoo.fr), 60 place Jean Jaurès.

Apt has several banks, including Crédit Lyonnais on place Bouquerie and Société Générale at 2 place Carnot.

A bike shop, Cycles Agnel (☎ 04 90 74 17 16), is on quai de la Liberté/the N100, near the corner of rue Pasteur.

Things to See & Do Buy **Côtes du Luberon wine** at the rustic Vin du Pays, 70 rue du Docteur Gros. Locally produced **honey** and **candles** are available at La Bonbonnière, 47 rue de la Sous-Préfecture, while L'O à la Bouche, 98 rue St Pierre, sells **truffles** in season. Also in rue St Pierre is a **flea market** every Tuesday.

The **Musée de Paléontologie** (Palaeontology Museum), in the Luberon Park Office, focuses on prehistory plants and animals.

Places to Stay & Eat The *Camping les Cèdres* (☎/fax 04 90 74 14 61, route de Rustrel), open mid-February to mid-November, is beside the LBR to its north. Exit at a sign to 'Aire Cyclotouristique' (a well-appointed picnic area 100m north along the road the LBR overpasses). The entry road to the camping ground is next to the overpass. It charges 19/30FF for one/two people and a hot shower costs 3.40FF.

An *Auberge de Jeunesse* (☎ 04 90 74 39 34), 6km south-east of Apt in Saignon, charges around 80FF for B&B. Turn off the LBR south across the N100 near the former Baignes station building and climb on the D174 to the village.

Accommodation in Apt includes the *Hôtel du Palais* (☎/fax 04 90 04 89 32, place Gabriel Péri), which has basic doubles from 160FF and *menus* in its streetside *restaurant* starting from 90FF. *Hôtel L'Aptois* (☎ 04 90 74 02 02, fax 04 90 74 64 79, 289 cours Lauze de Perret), at the eastern edge of town, has doubles from 170FF and is open from mid-March to mid-February. *Auberge du Lubéron* (☎ 04 90 74 12 50, fax 04 90 04 79 49, 8 place du Faubourg du Ballet), north of the river near the pedestrian bridge, has comfortable doubles from 290FF (420FF in July and August).

Place de la Bouquerie is full of open-air cafes and restaurants when the sun shines. *Rue St Pierre* (down rue Pasteur beside the

PROVENCE & THE CÔTE D'AZUR

Day 1: Forcalquier to Apt

Cue		
start		Forcalquier tourist office
0km	↰	go W to Blvd Latourette
0.0	↰	(20m) Blvd Latourette
0.3	↱	Blvd Bouche
6.9	↱	(10m) Chemin de Blabaux 'to Apt'
8.6	↰	'to Apt'
11.0	↱	N100 onto bikepath
11.3	↱	D5 'to St Michel'
14.2	◀	4.8km moderate climb
		St Michel
17.1	↱	unsigned tiny road downhill
23.2	↱	'to Apt'
30.6	↱	Cours d'Argenlieu, Reillanne
30.7	↱	at town square war memorial
30.8	↱	Blvd de Salve
31.1	↱	'to Prieuré de Carluc'
35.8	✳	Prieuré de Carluc
36.1	↱	GR4
36.9	↱	GR4
38.4		unsigned road
39.1	↱	cross Pont Romain
39.4	↱	lane parallel to N100
39.5		unsigned road
39.5	↱	(50m) N100, Céreste
39.6	↱	V3B 'to Vitrolles'
40.0	↱	Ave des Plantiers
42.7	↱	'to La Viguière'
44.0	↱	unsigned road
44.8	↱	unsigned road
44.9	↱	unsigned road
45.1	↱	unsigned road
45.8	↱	unsigned road
46.5	↱	unsigned road
47.2	↱	D223
48.4		unsigned road
48.7		Le Boisset

Continued

Cue		
51.6	↱	D48 'to N100'
52.4	↰	bikepath parallel to N100
54.8		cross N100 to bikepath
58.2	✳	Baignes old train-station building
62.6		unsigned road
62.7		Chemin de l'Oratoire
62.8	↰	Rue du Ballet
62.8		(50m) Place du Ballet
62.9		cross pedestrian bridge
62.9	↱	(50m) Quai de la Liberté
63.0		Apt tourist office

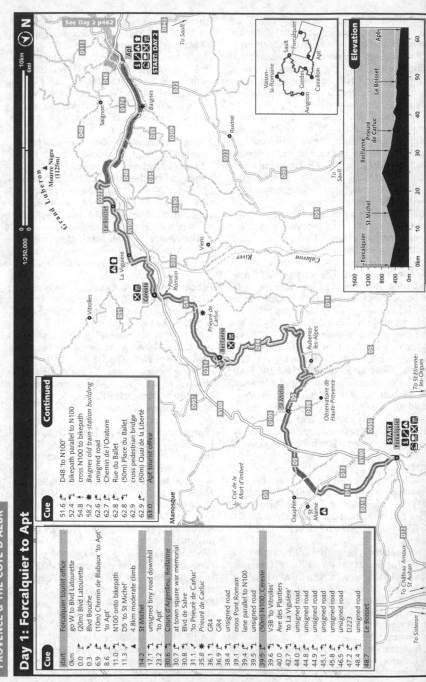

bike shop on the N100) has more bars, shops and places to eat. Try **Le Chant de l'Heure** (☎ *04 90 74 08 38, 23 rue St Pierre*), a creperie with *menus* from 65FF.

Little *Au Petit St Martin* (☎ *04 90 74 10 13, 24 rue St Martin*), hidden in the back streets (look for the big wooden spoon and fork hanging outside), has *menus* from around 50FF to 120FF.

Day 2: Apt to Cavaillon
3–5 hours, 48km

Below the forested slopes around Apt is a rich manicured patchwork of vineyard, olive groves and fruit farms dotted with *bories*, archaic dry-stone huts. High points allow glimpses of red ochre outcrops which give the Luberon soil its distinctive colour. The nearby **Château de Mille** vineyard has been producing some of the Luberon's best wines since the 12th century. Make a side trip for a tasting; the steep uphill on the return to the D3 is briefly taxing.

At Bonnieux (12km) there is a superb panorama to the north and west – the Marquis de Sade's ruined castle above Lacoste features prominently. The side trip to Lourmarin begins here (see Side Trip 1).

The LBR takes a very indirect, switchbacking route via Lacoste towards Ménerbes, where there's a short detour to author Peter Mayle's former *mas* (cottage), which featured in his book *A Year in Provence* (see Side Trip 2).

Ménerbes is a pretty perched village which boasts, of all things, a **corkscrew museum** (☎ *04 90 72 41 58*) in the chateau of the Domaine de la Citadelle (on the D3 to Cavaillon at the western foot of town). Try the pizzeria *La Bouche à Feu* (☎ *04 90 72 30 17, rue Klébert Guendon*) for lunch. It's renowned for delicious, giant salads.

The LBR uses a series of very tiny, often steep, roads winding through villages and agricultural land towards Cavaillon. Limestone outcrops provide dramatic relief. On reaching chemin de Dorio (43.8km), cut out more than 800m of unnecessary riding (400m up to a level crossing and 400m back) on unpleasant road by crossing the disused railway line opposite via a well-worn walking track and turning left onto the VC32.

Flat roads lead into busy Cavaillon; follow both the 'Centre Ville' and the 'Office de Tourisme' signs.

Side Trip: Lourmarin & Vaugine
2–3 hours, 34km

From the D3A at Bonnieux, veer left onto the D36 towards Lourmarin. After a gentle 75m climb to 466m the twisty road descends into the spectacular deep gorge (Combe de Lourmarin) between the massifs of the Grand and Petit Luberon. Boulders overhang the narrow road, used by tour coaches that often occupy both lanes on blind bends. Beware!

Little Lourmarin (alt 220m) has a Renaissance **chateau**, which can be toured, and a cemetery, off the D27, in which Provençal writer **Albert Camus** (1913–1960) is buried beside his wife. All who struggled through *L'Étranger* in French classes should come to pay their respects.

From Lourmarin ride a short loop – on the D27, the D45 and the D56 – to charming **Vaugines**, where parts of the popular films *Manon des Sources* and *Jean de Florette* (1986) were shot. See the giant horsechestnut tree and the fabulous moss-covered fountain that fills central place de la Fontaine. Return directly to Lourmarin westbound on the D56 and retrace the route up the gorge to Bonnieux.

Side Trip: Mayle's Mas
15–20 minutes, 3.2km

Peter Mayle's former house is an undistinguished looking cottage on the hillside at the end of a long driveway off the D3 near Ménerbes. (It is privately owned and not open for inspection – look at it from the road.) From the junction of the D3 and the road 'to Oppède/Cavaillon, ride 1.6km gently uphill to the start of the driveway on the left. (From the opposite direction, it's the second house on the right after the football field.) Return the same way.

Cavaillon

The market town of Cavaillon is at the western end of the Luberon. It is best known for its sweet melons, sold at the Monday morning melon market from May to September. There is a Fête du Melon in August.

Information The tourist office (☎ 04 90 71 32 01, fax 04 90 71 42 99; closed Sunday afternoon) is in place François Tourel at the west end of cours Bournissac.

Banks include the Crédit Lyonnaise and Banque Chaix on cours Bournissac.

Day 2: Apt to Cavaillon

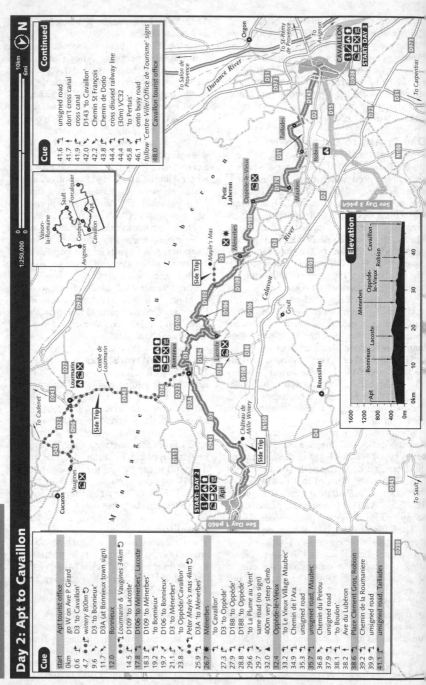

Cue

start	Apt tourist office
0km	go W on Ave P Girard
0.6	D3 'to Cavaillon'
4.7	winery 800m ↻
9.6	D3 'to Bonnieux'
11.7	D3A (at Bonnieux town sign)
12.0	Bonnieux
	← Lourmarin & Vaugines 34km ↻
14.5	D109 'to Lacoste'
17.8	D106 'to Ménerbes', Lacoste
18.3	D109 'to Ménerbes'
19.2	'to Bonnieux'
19.7	D106 'to Bonnieux'
21.1	D3 'to Ménerbes'
23.8	'to Oppède/Cavaillon'
	● Peter Mayle's mas 4km ↻
25.9	D3A 'to Ménerbes'
26.7	✳ Ménerbes
27.3	'to Cavaillon'
27.9	D188 'to Oppède'
28.8	D188 'to Oppède'
29.6	'to La Plume au Vent'
29.7	same road (no sign)
32.0	▲ 400m very steep climb
32.4	Oppède-le-Vieux
33.2	'to Le Vieux Village Maubec'
34.9	Chemin de l'Ara
35.3	unsigned road
35.7	unsigned road, Maubec
36.8	Chemin du Peirou
37.9	unsigned road
38.1	'to Boulon'
38.2	Ave du Lubéron
38.6	Place Clement Gros, Robion
39.2	Chemin de la Roumaniere
39.9	unsigned road
41.1	unsigned road, Taillades

Continued

Cue

41.6	unsigned road
41.7	don't cross canal
41.9	cross canal
42.0	D143 'to Cavaillon'
42.2	Chemin St François
43.8	Chemin de Dorio
44.4	cross disused railway line (30m) VC32
44.4	'to Pertuis'
45.8	onto busy road
46.1	follow 'Centre Ville/Office de Tourisme' signs
48.0	Cavaillon tourist office

Cyclix Cavaillon (☎ 04 90 78 07 96, ✉ cyclix@wanadoo.fr), 166 cours Gambetta, and Cycles Rieu (☎ 04 90 71 45 55; closed Tuesday), 25 ave Maréchal Joffre, off ave Gabriel Péri towards the train station, hire out bikes.

Things to See & Do Walk up the hill from the 1st-century BC Roman **Arc de Triomphe** next to the tourist office to **Chapelle de St Jacques**. Information boards next to the trail explain significant features and the orientation table at the top identifies all significant features in a 270° arc – the Alpilles, Mont Ventoux, the Route des Crêtes and villages you have passed.

Three blocks north is the 12th-century **Cathédrale St Véran**, with a fine Roman cloister. The city's 18th-century **synagogue** and adjoining **Jewish museum**, on rue Hébraïque, are also worth visiting.

At the tourist office, you can book various **guided tours** in July and August, including a three-hour cycling tour in the countryside and a tasting session of melons, melon liqueur and melon-filled chocolates.

Places to Stay & Eat Noisy *Camping de la Durance* (☎ 04 90 71 11 78, fax 04 90 71 98 77, Digue des Grands Jardins) is poorly signposted from the centre. From the tourist office it's 2.4km away – ride along cours Bournissac, turn right onto ave Gabriel Péri to a big roundabout, follow the signs to the left from there. It charges 38/65FF for one/two people (open April to October).

The tourist office has details of *gîtes ruraux* (country cottages) and *chambres d'hôtes* (B&Bs).

Central hotels include *Hôtel La Provence* (☎ 04 90 78 03 38, cours Bournissac), with rooms starting from 110FF, and *Hôtel Le Forum* (☎ 04 90 78 37 55, 60 place du Clos), with rooms from around 130FF up to 300FF.

For self-catering, there is a huge *Auchan* hypermarket beside the LBR at the entrance to town. For *market* details, see under Cavaillon, earlier.

Auzet Cavaillon (☎ 04 90 78 06 54, 61 cours Bournissac) is a bakery-cafe which makes more than 30 types of bread.

La Fin du Siècle (☎ 04 90 71 28 85, 42 place du Clos) is a popular brasserie with *menus* from around 70FF.

Day 3: Cavaillon to Gordes
1½–2½hours, 23.4km

This short stage allows time for a couple of interesting side trips (including one at the end of the day) and exploration.

The early part of the route out of Cavaillon is unavoidably traffic-infested, flat and dull but the riding improves after crossing Le Coulon, a pretty little stream a few kilometres out of town.

Ride through the yellow-stone village of Lagnes, with its cobbled streets and **art exhibitions**, held in the old wash-house off place de la Fontaine. There's a steep climb to the turn-off to Fontaine de Vaucluse (see Side Trip 1). At 13.7km, the Luberon's Resistance fighters are remembered by a **memorial** on the left.

Cabrières d'Avignon (15.5km), set in beautiful pine and cedar forest crisscrossed with walking paths, is the location of Peter Mayle's favoured *Le Bistrot à Michel* (☎/fax 04 90 76 82 08), which serves truffle omelettes (November to March) and other memorable meals. The *plat du jour* (dish of the day) costs around 90FF and there is a 100FF lunch *menu*.

After Les Imberts (17.2km) the D2 is narrow and unpleasant until a bike lane is marked. On the steepest section of the climb it becomes a separate bikepath. Soon there are stunning views to Gordes, perched on its hillside, and down the valley back to Bonnieux and the Luberon massif.

Side Trip: Fontaine de Vaucluse
½–1 hour, 9.5km

Outside Lagnes take the D100A, which suddenly loses 100m altitude through a series of hairpin bends, hurling you into the touristy little village of Fontaine de Vaucluse.

Follow signs to the right, on the D24, and reach a Promenade to where the Sorgue River ends its subterranean course and gushes to the surface. During the spring melt, up to 200 cubic metres of water per second spill forth from the base of the cliff, making it one of the world's most powerful springs. At other times the reduced flow seeps out downstream from the cliff and the spring is little more than a still, very deep (315m) pond. About 1.5 million tourists visit it each year and flock into restaurants and souvenir stalls along chemin de la Fontaine.

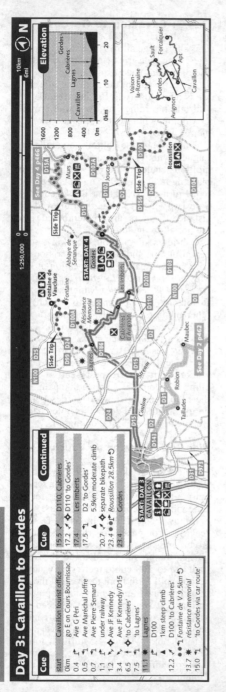

Day 3: Cavaillon to Gordes

Cue		
start		Cavaillon tourist office
0km		go E on Cours Bournissac
0.4		Ave G Péri
0.5		Ave Maréchal Joffre
0.7		Ave Pierre Semard
1.1		under railway
1.2		Ave JF Kennedy
3.4		Ave JF Kennedy/D15
6.5		'to Cabrières'
7.5		'to Lagnes'
11.1		Lagnes
		D100
12.2		1km steep climb
		D100 'to Cabrières'
13.7		'Fontaine de V 9.5km' résistance memorial
15.0		'to Gordes via car route'

Cue		Continued
15.5		D110, Cabrières
17.2		D110 'to Gordes'
17.4		Les Imberts
17.5		D2' to Gordes'
20.7		separate bikepath
23.4		Roussillon 28.5km
23.4		Gordes

START: DAY 3
CAVAILLON

START: DAY 4

Here also are **museums** dealing with the history of the WWII Resistance movement; justice and punishment; stalactites and speleology; and the work of Italian Renaissance poet Petrarch, who lived in the village from 1337 to 1353.

Return to the intersection of the D100A and the D24, continue west on the D24 and left onto the D99 to loop back to Lagnes.

Climb out of the village again and turn right onto the D100 to continue the original route. Avoid doing this steep climb twice by taking the D99 and the D24 to and from the fontaine.

Side Trip: Roussillon

1½–3 hours, 28.5km

Speedy riders could complete this side trip at the end of the day's ride. For a more leisurely ride, allow an extra day.

From the centre of Gordes, follow the D102 east towards Roussillon, descending and turning left after 2.5km onto the D2. After a further 3.5km turn right onto the D102, climbing into red **Roussillon** (alt 360m) at about the 9km mark.

The whole village is built with stone the colour of the distinctive ochre earth outcrop on which it perches. This contrasts with the bare surrounding area and the green of the conifers dotted around. The Romans used this soil to make pottery glazes 2000 years ago.

Walk along the 1km **Sentier des Ocres** (ochre trail), which begins about 100m north of the village centre. It leads through groves of chestnuts and maritime pines to bizarre ochre formations created by centuries of erosion.

Descend from Roussillon to the D2 then take the quiet D102 north past Joucas and upward on the D102A and the D4 to Murs (20km). The **views** are beautiful and, early on still mornings, you can watch hot air balloons rise from the valley floor.

From Murs, there is a scenic 8.5km downhill back to Gordes on the D15.

Gordes

In a stunning location on the rocky southern face of the Vaucluse plateau, this tiered village forms an amphitheatre overlooking the Sorgue and Calavon rivers. Atop its hill is a sturdy chateau dating from 1025 and rebuilt in the 16th century. Gordes is *very* popular with tourists in summer.

Information The tourist office (☎ 04 90 72 02 75, fax 04 90 72 04 39) is in the Salle des Gardes (Guards' Hall), place du Château. The town has no bank nor any bike shop.

Things to See & Do About 4km north-west of Gordes, off the D177, is the 12th-century Cistercian **Abbaye de Sénanque** (alt 510m). Still inhabited by monks, in summer it is framed by fields of lavender.

See also **Side Trip 2** for a scenic ride to the ochre village of Roussillon.

Places to Stay & Eat Off the route de Murs, *Camping Les Sources* (☎ 04 90 72 12 48, fax 04 90 72 09 43) is a large camping ground open from March to October. It charges 45/65FF for one/two people (58/ 84FF in July and August). Eleven kilometres away, near Murs, the more pleasant *Camping des Charlottes* (☎ 04 90 72 60 84) charges 38/54FF.

Ask at the tourist office about *B&Bs* in the area.

Le Provencal (☎ 04 90 72 04 20, place du Château), has rooms from 280FF. Its *restaurant* offers good takeaway pizza and snacks. *Chez Tante Yvonne* (☎ 04 90 72 02 54, place Genty-Pantaly) has rooms with shower and toilet for 300FF and a *restaurant* with *menus* from 120FF. *Auberge de Carcarille* (☎ 04 90 72 02 63, fax 04 90 72 05 74, D2) is 2.5km out and charges from 330FF per double. Its *restaurant* has *menus* from around 100FF. *Hôtel Le Gordos* (☎ 04 90 72 00 75, fax 04 90 72 07 00, D15), 1.5km before town, is pricey in high season (from 560FF for a room with shower, toilet and TV) and does not have a restaurant. Breakfast costs 65FF per person.

In Murs (see Side Trip 2), *Le Crillon* (☎ 04 90 72 60 31, fax 04 90 72 63 12) has double rooms with shower and toilet from 265FF and evening *menus* from 100FF.

Food is available at *Gordes Alimentation* in the town square. Murs has a small grocery store, the *Épicerie de Murs*, in its centre.

Day 4: Gordes to Sault
4–7 hours, 72km

Take the scenic D15 to Murs and continue climbing on the D4 over the **Col de Murs**. Tour de France graffiti is scrawled across the road near the 627m summit. There are picnic tables in three locations on the twisting

descent through thick oak Forêt de Vénasque and into a grey limestone-walled gorge.

At 24.6km is the turn-off to Vénasque, listed as one of France's most beautiful villages. Here you can visit a 5th-century **baptistry**, built on the site of a Roman temple, which is one of France's oldest edifices. Return down the hill to rejoin the ride route.

The next town, Malemort du Comtat (28.9km), has a cherry festival at the end of June. Climb into the hills past a huge quarry, getting your first view to the bare white summit of **Mont Ventoux** as you enter the Côtes du Ventoux wine region.

The unremarkable village of Villes-sur-Auzon (41.7km), with its two *camping grounds*, is the gateway to the very remarkable **Gorges de la Nesque**. While this huge diagonal slash across the landscape is not instantly awe-inspiring like the Grand Canyon du Verdon, it is in wild, remote and spectacular surroundings. The view from a bicycle saddle is thrilling as the road winds high on the steep, forested slopes, meandering upwards towards Sault through short tunnels and beneath overhangs of grey and reddish limestone. Best of all, the D942 is not overrun by tourists and traffic, especially in the morning. The only commercial activity in the 23km between Villes and Monieux is a cherry stall at a lookout point.

There's a **picnic area** about 3km past Villes and good views across to Blauvac. Olive trees on the roadside have been shaped by some keen worker into a near continuous hedge for tens of kilometres.

A fast downhill precedes a final 100m climb after Monieux into pretty Sault – at 765m the gateway to Mont Ventoux.

Sault
Lying 26km from the summit, Sault is the highest of three staging posts for the assault on Mont Ventoux. (The others are Malaucène – 377m, 21km away – and Bédoin – 275m, 21km away. Keen cyclists have been known to attempt ascents from all three places in one day!) It is a lively village with a view from its park across the valley of the Croc River to the Plateau de Vaucluse.

Ventoux's summit is considerably cooler than the surrounding plains – there can be a difference of up to 20°C – and receives twice as much precipitation. Bring warm clothes and rain gear.

PROVENCE & THE CÔTE D'AZUR

Day 4: Gordes to Sault

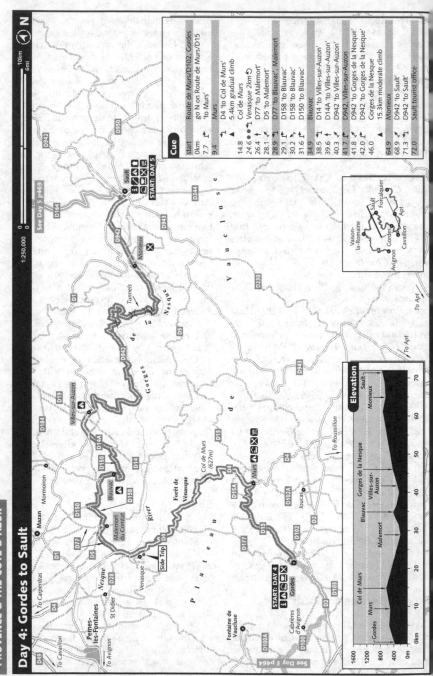

Cue		
start		Route de Murs/D102, Gordes
0km	⬑	go N on Route de Murs/D15
7.7	⬏	'to Murs'
9.4	◀	Murs
		D4 to Col de Murs'
14.8		5.4km gradual climb
24.6	●●↻	Venasque 2km ↻
26.4	⬏	D77 'to Malemort'
28.1	⬑	D5 'to Malemort'
28.9	⬏	D77 'to Blauvac', Malemort
29.1	⬑	D158 'to Blauvac'
30.2	⬏	D158 'to Blauvac'
31.6	⬑	D150 'to Blauvac'
34.9		Blauvac
38.5	⬑	D14 'to Villes-sur-Auzon'
39.6	⬏	D14A 'to Villes-sur-Auzon'
40.3	⬏	D942 'to Villes-sur-Auzon'
41.7	⬑	D942, Villes-sur-Auzon
41.8	⬏	D942 'to Gorges de la Nesque'
42.0	⬑	D942 'to Gorges de la Nesque'
		Gorges de la Nesque
46.0	◀	15.3km moderate climb
64.9		Monieux
68.9	⬑	D942 'to Sault'
71.3	⬏	D942 'to Sault'
72.0		Sault tourist office

Elevation

Information The tourist office (☎ 04 90 64 01 21, fax 04 90 64 15 03), opposite the park on ave de la Promenade, is open from April to September.

Crédit Agricole is on ave de l'Oratoire.

Albion Cycles (☎/fax 04 90 64 09 32), next to the Écomarché supermarket on route de St-Trinit towards the camping ground, hires rigid/full suspension VTTs for 70/150FF a day.

Things to See & Do The village houses a **museum** of natural history and has a fine **church** with a 12th-century nave.

The tourist office and town bookshops sell guides for **VTT routes** to the Ventoux area.

Places to Stay & Eat Shady *Camping Municipal du Defends* (☎ 04 90 64 07 18, fax 04 90 64 08 59, route de St-Trinit) is 2.2km from the centre, uphill. It charges 27/42FF for one/two people.

The *gîte d'étape Élevage de la Louche* (☎ 04 90 67 17 22, D164) is 1.8km out of town. The tourist office has a list of *chambres d'hôtes'* phone numbers in its window.

The FFCT recommended *Hôtel Signoret* (☎/fax 04 90 64 11 44, ave de l'Oratoire), has rooms from 150FF. Its restaurant offers traditional cuisine in *menus* from 85FF. The two-star *Hôtel d'Albion* (☎ 04 90 64 06 22, route de St-Trinit) charges 290/306FF for a single/double. Its *restaurant* has a vegetarian menu. For high rollers *Hostellerie du Val de Sault* (☎ 04 90 64 01 41, fax 04 90 64 12 74, Ancien Chemin d'Aurel) has doubles from 510FF in low season (560FF in July and August) and dinner *menus* from 150FF.

There's a couple of delectable *bakeries* at Porte des Aires and *Écomarché* supermarkets near the camping ground and next to the bike shop.

Day 5: Sault to Vaison-la-Romaine
4–6½ hours, 63km

The day starts with a short descent then a sustained climb from 700m to the 1912m summit of Mont Ventoux. Altitudes are shown on each kilometre marker by the roadside.

The 26km ride to the top should take at least 2½ hours and an early start is advisable. It is unlikely to be a solitary cycling experience. Dozens of cyclists on racing bikes make the climb every day of the week from each start point while others, perhaps more pressed for time, drive to *Le Chalet Reynard* (1415m) and ride the last 6km up from there.

For a while after leaving Sault, Mont Ventoux is invisible, lurking in wait behind a low, pine-forested hill. The summit, with its capping of broken whitish stones called *lauzes*, reappears after about 15km, bristling with striped antennas. At numerous points there are picnic tables and shelter sheds. At 13.9km, a viewpoint (altitude 1288m) has **plaques** with historical details about the Albion plateau and its prehistoric inhabitants, the Albici.

Five kilometres up from Le Chalet Reynard is the **Tom Simpson memorial** (see the 'Mort Pour Le Tour' boxed text overleaf).

The last kilometre of the climb is the steepest, but finally it's over and the immense panorama of Provence and the southern Alps takes away whatever breath you have left.

Mont Ventoux is the sole habitat of several species, including the snake eagle, numerous spiders and a variety of butterflies. Its forests, felled 400 years ago for shipbuilding, have been replanted in some areas since 1860 with a variety of species, including the majestic cedar of Lebanon. The mix of deciduous trees makes the mountain especially colourful in autumn.

The descent is on a very steep, narrow road for the first 6.3km. It switches back and forth across the face of the mountain before entering forest. The grade eases and the road widens for the rest of the descent. Suddenly, you'll be in the lively centre of Malaucène (48.1km), having hardly turned a pedal for more than 20km.

The town is a good place to get lunch. A *supermarket* is opposite the tourist office (☎/fax 04 90 65 22 59) in cours des Isnards and there are plenty of *cafes* nearby. A bike shop, ACS Cycles (☎ 04 90 65 15 42) is on ave de Verdun, on the corner of the D974 and the D938 as you enter town.

The rest of the day may seem an anticlimax after the drama of the Mont. At least it is easier, riding along gentle, shady byways through little villages such as Entrechaux (53.1km), with its imposing **ruined chateau**, across quaint old stone bridges and along part of a signposted *circuit cyclotouristique*. Ahead rise the limestone ridges of the Dentelles de Montmirail, just beyond Vaison-la-Romaine.

Mort Pour Le Tour

Almost every French village has a memorial to its *enfants, morts pour la patrie* (citizens killed in the world's great conflicts – WWI, WWII and other wars). The French also commemorate those who've died in the world's greatest cycle race, the Tour de France, with elaborate monuments.

Tommy Simpson, a champion British cyclist, died of exhaustion and heart failure near the summit of Mont Ventoux in the 1967 Tour. It was 13 July and he had been challenging for the leader's jersey. Later, amphetamines were found in his bloodstream. Ever since, the mountain and the large memorial to Simpson, on the eastern approach to the 1912m summit, have been a pilgrimage site for French and international cyclists.

The polished-marble surface of the monument superimposes Simpson's silhouette on the reflection of the summit. Innumerable caps, bidons and other cycling memorabilia left in tribute by passing cyclists surround its base. The epitaph, dedicated by Simpson's daughters, reads 'There is no mountain too high'. Simpson's last words were reportedly: 'Put me back on my bike.'

On 18 July during the 15th stage of the 1995 Tour, Barcelona Olympic champion Fabio Casartelli, 24, was killed in a fall while descending the steep Col de Portet d'Aspet in the Pyrenees. The spot, now marked by a huge sculpture of a winged wheel encircled by engraved stone tablets, flowers, cycling caps and water bottles, is visited by the Tour de France *peloton* (literally, bunch), which pauses to honour a fallen comrade. Each year since his death, Fabio's memory has been honoured with a multi-day program of rides, timed to coincide with the date of his tragic death, from the Pyrenean town of St Girons.

The Fabio Casartelli memorial, one of France's shrines to fallen cyclists.

Vaison-la-Romaine

Touristy Vaison has a wealth of Roman ruins and a picturesque medieval old town. Founded as a Celtic settlement, it was conquered by the Romans in the 2nd century BC and renamed Vasio Vocontiorum. Remains include mosaic-decorated villas, colonnaded streets, public baths, a theatre and an aqueduct which once brought water from Mont Ventoux.

Information The tourist office (☎ 04 90 36 02 11, fax 04 90 28 76 04) is on place du Chanoine Sautel off ave du Général de Gaulle.

Several banks include a BNP at 22 ave Jules Ferry and a Crédit Lyonnais at 67 Grand Rue.

Cycles Peugeot (☎ 04 90 36 03 29) is at 17 ave Jules Ferry.

Things to See & Do A grand marché Provençal fills place François Cevert or Tuesday morning and there are smaller markets on Thursday and Saturday mornings. Touristy Sunday markets take place in the Haute Ville during July and August.

The region's wines and foods can be tasted and bought at the **Maison des Vins**, in the basement of the tourist office.

Visit the medieval **Haute Ville** on the south bank of the Ouvèze across the **Pont Romain**. Narrow cobblestone alleys lead up past restored houses. At the summit is the imposing 12th-century **chateau**, modernised in the 15th century only to be later abandoned.

Gallo-Roman ruins can be visited at two sites: **Fouilles de Puymin**, on the east side of ave du Général de Gaulle, and **Fouilles de la Villasse**, to the west of the same road. The **Musée Archéologique** displays the silver

Day 5: Sault to Vaison-la-Romaine

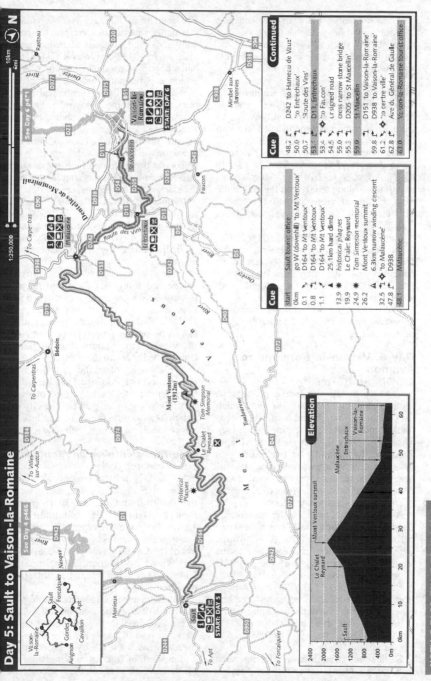

1:250,000

Cue

start	Sault tourist office
0km	go W (downhill) to Mt Ventoux'
0.1	D164 'to Mt Ventoux'
0.8	D164 'to Mt Ventoux'
1.1	D164 'to Mt Ventoux'
	25.1km hard climb
13.9	historical plaques
19.9	Le Chalet Reynard
24.9	Tom Simpson memorial
26.2	Mont Ventoux summit
	6.3km narrow winding cescent
32.5	'to Malaucène'
47.8	D938
48.1	Malaucène

Cue   **Continued**

48.4	D242 'to Hameau de Veux'
50.0	'to Entrechaux'
50.7	'Route des Vins'
53.1	D13, Entrechaux
53.4	'to Faucon'
54.5	Lt signed road
	cross narrow stone bridge
55.0	D205 'to St Marcellin'
55.3	St Marcellin
59.0	D151 'to Vaison-la-Romaine'
59.8	D938 'to Vaison-la-Romaine'
61.2	'to centre ville'
62.8	Ave du Général de Gaulle
63.0	Vaison-la-Romaine tourist office

Elevation

PROVENCE & THE CÔTE D'AZUR

bust of a 3rd-century patrician and likenesses of Hadrian and his wife Sabina. At Fouilles de la Villasse you can visit the mosaic- and fresco-decorated house in which the bust was discovered.

Places to Stay & Eat The *Camping du Théâtre Romain* (☎ 04 90 28 78 66, chemin de Brusquet) is open from mid-March to October and charges around 80FF for two in the high season.

The quiet but expensive hostel *Centre à Cœur Joie* (☎ 04 90 36 00 78, fax 04 90 36 09 89, ave César Geoffray), 500m south-east of town along the river at the end of the road, has great views of Mont Ventoux. Singles/doubles with breakfast cost from 220/280FF.

Hôtel Le Burrhus (☎ 04 90 36 00 11, fax 04 90 36 39 05, 2 place Montfort) and the *Hôtel des Lis* (same ☎/fax, 20 cours Henri Fabre), almost adjacent, charge from 240FF and 350FF respectively for a double with shower and toilet.

Ave du Général de Gaulle is lined with *pavement cafes*; there is a *Super U* super-market on ave Choralies.

Day 6: Vaison-la-Romaine to Avignon
4½–7 hours, 70.4km

Start a longish day with another picturesque section of *circuit cyclotouristique*, which uses a narrow, rough and somewhat steep track through forest, emerging at Séguret. The town's **Ville Fortifée** (fortified village; 7.9km) earns it the title of 'one of France's most beautiful villages'; walk along its narrow, cobbled streets. From the elevated road there are distant western views of a *centrale nucléaire* (nuclear-power station).

A short detour takes in the remarkable **Dentelles de Montmirail** (see Side Trip) before flat roads lead through vineyards, with the opportunity for *dégustation* (wine tasting) of the products of the *pays de Gigondas* at every turn.

Bustling Orange (31.9km) has a huge **Roman theatre** which is being restored and a huge but grubby **Arc de Triomphe** which is not. There are three bike shops in town. Try Cycles Picca (☎ 04 90 51 69 53) at 544 ave de Verdun.

Head south through more wineries, such as **Château Mont Redon**, in the famous

Châteauneuf du Pape region. The village of this name was originally a humble mining hamlet, called Calcernier after its limestone quarries. In 1317 Pope John XXII (1316–34) had a pontifical residence built here, around which a papal vineyard was established. Nowadays the village, surrounded by 3200 hectares of stony vineyards, is world-renowned for its rich, full-bodied red wine which boast a minimum alcohol strength of 12.5% (the highest in France). **Fête de la Véraison** on the first weekend of August celebrates the ripening of the grapes and the mid-September **Fête des Vendanges** marks the start of the harvest.

Inquire at the Châteauneuf du Pape tourist office (☎ 04 90 83 71 08, 🖳 www .chato9pape.enprovence.com) in place du Portail for a list of *domaines* (wine-producing estates) where you can taste and buy wine.

Weave around the wineries, cross the Rhône and follow its course on flat roads through Roquemaure and Villeneuve to the Pont Édouard Daladier into Avignon. The bridge's shared cycle-pedestrian paths on each side permit you to pause and take in the view of the famous **Pont St Bénézet** (Pont d'Avignon) to the north.

There's a lot of traffic to negotiate be-tween the Pont Édouard Daladier and the train station. It's easiest to go off-road – just follow the outer walls of the city in an anticlockwise direction. The station is op-posite the Porte de la République.

Side Trip: Dentelles de Montmirail
20–45 minutes, 6.4km

Take the D79 left 'to Gigondas'. Visit the village, 1.5km off the D7, and its *cafes*, then return from the centre 300m to make a right 'to Dentelles de Montmirail'. After 1.6km the road becomes steep and un-sealed. Park your bike and walk 400m to the top of the **Col du Cayron** (alt 400m) for su-perb views of the toothy, limestone Den-telles. The walking tracks below beg to be explored.

Return towards Gigondas, turning right (downhill) at the road from the village. After a few hundred metres, continue straight ahead instead of taking the D79 to the right. You will reach the D7 by a different road 1.2km south of where you originally turned off it. Turn left to rejoin the ride route.

Day 6: Vaison-la-Romaine to Avignon

Cue		
start		Vaison tourist office
0km	←	go E on Ave du G de Gaulle
0.2	←	Zone semi-piétonne
0.5	⌐	Roman bridge 'to Avignon'
1.1	↙	D977 'to Avignon'
2.1	↗	to 'Circuit cyclotouristique
2.5	◄	3.5km hard climb
		very rough surface
3.6	↘	unsigned road
3.9	↗	unsigned road
5.5	↗	unsigned road
6.1	↗	'to Séguret'
7.3	↗	unsigned road
7.7	↗	unsigned road
7.9	✳	Séguret ville fortifiée
8.4	✳	Séguret

Elevation

Cue		Continued
8.5	⌐	D23 'to Sablet'
10.4	◈	D7 'to Gigondas'
10.9	⌐	D7
13.4	●✳↩	Dentelles: 6.3km ↩
15.1	↗	D80 'to Orange'
16.4	⌐	D8
17.7	⌐	D977
19.1	◈	D67 'to Camaret', Violès
23.9	⌐	'to Orange'
25.7		Camaret-sur-Aigues
25.9	↗	'to Orange'
26.0	↗	D975 'to Orange'
31.3	◈	'to Centre Ville'
31.9	✳	Orange
32.0	↗	Rue Caristie
		Place des Frères Mounet
32.3	◈	'to Montélimar/Arc de Triphe'
32.4	◈	'to A7–A9', tourist office
32.5		Ave de Thermes to Nîmes
32.9	↗	Rue St Clément
34.4	◄	'to Le Grès'
37.4		Chemin de Maucoil
		5.8km moderate climb
39.6	◄✳	Château Mont Redon
41.4	↗	unsigned road
44.8		Châteauneuf du Pape
44.9	↗	D17 'to Roquemaure'
45.0	↗	D17 'to Roquemaure'
50.8	↗	D976 'to Roquemaure'
54.1	↗	D976 'to Roquemaure'
54.7		Roquemaure
55.1	↗	D980 'to Sauveterre'
57.8	◈	D980 'to Sauveterre'
58.2		D980 Sauveterre
65.0	↗	'to Villeneuve'
66.5	↗	'to Avignon'
67.6	⌐⊞	'to Avignon'
67.8	↗	'to Pont Édouard Daladier'
68.8	⌐	follow town wall
70.3	⌐	at Porte de la République?
70.4		Avignon train station

PROVENCE & THE CÔTE D'AZUR

Avignon

Avignon, as the seat of the Pope from 1309 to 1377, acquired its ramparts and reputation as a city of art and culture in that era. Today it continues its role as patron of the arts, notably through its annual performing arts festival. Other attractions include the region's Côtes du Rhône wine and its ruined 12th-century bridge.

Information The tourist office (☎ 04 90 82 65 11, fax 04 90 82 95 03, 🖳 www.ot-av ignon.fr), 41 cours Jean Jaurès, is 300m north of the train station. An annexe (☎ 04 90 85 60 16) is at the Pont St Bénézet, 400m north of the Daladier bridge.

Banque de France is in place de l'Horloge.

Cycles Robert (☎ 04 90 86 62 72) is outside the walls, 200m south of Porte St Michel, at 13 blvd Sixte Isnard. Cycles Peugeot (☎ 04 90 86 32 49), in the Quartier des Teinturiers at 80 rue Guillaume Puy, hires out bikes.

Log on at Cyberdrôme (☎ 04 90 16 05 15), 68 rue Guillaume Puy.

Things to See & Do The **Pont St Bénézet** (St Benedict's Bridge) is Avignon's most celebrated site/sight. Originally made of wood in the 12th century and rebuilt in stone by Pope Clement VI around 1350, all but four of 22 spans were washed away by floods in 1669. Walk onto the bridge (15FF) from cours Châtelet.

Within the restored ramparts is the cavernous, but largely empty, Gothic **Palace of the Popes** (☎ 04 90 27 50 74, 🖳 www.pala is-des-papes.com), place du Palais, built as a fortified pontifical court. The best view is from across the river in Villeneuve-lès-Avignon. The palace's main courtyard has played host to the Avignon theatre festival since 1947.

Walk 200m up the hill from the Cathédrale Notre Dame des Doms to **Rocher des Doms**, a lovely bluff-top park with great views reaching beyond the Alpilles. An orientation table explains what you should be able to see.

Numerous **museums** can be visited for free or at a nominal cost, displaying collections on archaeological history (Musée Calvet; ☎ 04 90 82 43 51, 67 rue Joseph Vernet); natural history (Musée Requien; ☎ 04 90 86 33 84, 65 rue Joseph Vernet); statuary (Musée Lapidaire; ☎ 04 90 85 75 38, 27 rue de l République); and 17th-century decorativ art, including earthenware and furnitur (Musée Louis Voland; ☎ 04 90 86 03 79, 1' rue Victor Hugo).

Places to Stay The *Camping Bagatell* *(☎ 04 90 85 78 45)* is an attractive, shad, camping ground north of the Daladie bridge on Île de la Barthelasse. It charge 39/56FF for one/two people. *Camping Mu nicipal St Bénézet (☎ 04 90 82 63 50, Île d la Barthelasse, chemin de la Barthelasse)* i a little further north. It charges 36/54F (47/75FF in high season).

The 210-bed *Auberge Bagatelle (☎ 0 90 85 78 45, fax 04 90 27 16 23)* is in th same park-like area as Camping Bagatelle Dorm beds cost 59FF per person.

There are plenty of hotels within and out side the town walls and across the river i Villeneuve-lès-Avignon. Reservations ar essential in July and August, when the tow is packed for its arts festival.

Within the walls is *Hôtel Splendid (☎ 0 90 86 14 46, fax 04 90 85 38 55, 17 rue Agri col Perdiguier)* with singles/ doubles wit shower from 130/200FF. Central *Hôte Mignon (☎ 04 90 82 17 30, fax 04 90 85 7 46, 12 rue Joseph Vernet)* has bright, sound proofed doubles with shower, toilet an cable TV from around 230FF. Nearby, smal *Hôtel Innova (☎ 04 90 82 54 10, fax 04 9 82 52 39, 100 rue Joseph Vernet)* has a court yard for parking bicycles, and rooms fron 160FF with shower, toilet and TV.

Outside the walls, *Hôtel St Roch (☎ 0 90 82 18 63, fax 04 90 82 78 30, 9 rue Pau Mérindol)* has well-equipped doubles start ing from 250FF.

In Villeneuve, bargain rooms are avail able in *Hôtel Beauséjour (☎ 04 90 25 2 56, 61 ave Gabriel Péri)* without/with shower from 130/160FF. More upmarket the beautifully-located *Hôtel L'Atelie (☎ 04 90 25 01 84, fax 04 90 25 80 06, 5 ru de la Foire)* has doubles from 270FF t 460FF, depending on the season.

Places to Eat A *food market* opens from 7 am to 1 pm in Les Halles on place Pi (closed Monday). The *Codec* and *Monopri* supermarkets are on rue de la République.

Near place de l'Horloge, the atmospheri *Natural Café (☎ 04 90 85 90 82, 17 ru*

Racine) serves hearty food in a rustic setting. Adjacent **La Fourchette** (☎ 04 90 85 20 93) has *menus* from 150FF. Reservations are essential and it's closed on weekends and for three weeks in August. **Le Brantes** (☎ 04 90 86 35 14, 22 rue Petite Fusterie) is a large pizza-grill place with excellent value 69FF *menus*.

Pleasant bohemian restaurants and bistros include the small **Sindabad** (☎ 04 90 14 69 45, 53 rue des Teinturiers), which offers good Tunisian, oriental and Provençal home cooking. **Le Bistro Russe** (☎ 04 90 85 64 45, 13 rue des Teinturiers) specialises in Russian vodka-fuelled drinks and dishes. At Monty Python-inspired **Woolloomooloo** (☎ 04 90 85 28 44, 16 rue des Teinturiers) microwave cookery is the speciality; it caters to vegetarians.

The refined **Restaurant Au 19ème** (☎ 04 90 27 16 00, 75 rue Guillaume Puy) is in the 9th-century home of absinthe inventor Jules Pernod. Hear harp recitals and live jazz while partaking of *menus* from 120FF.

Majesty of the Romans

Duration	3 days
Distance	206.9km
Difficulty	moderate
Start/End	Avignon

Wildlife and history buffs will revel in this cruise along mostly flat roads. The route takes in a feast of ancient Roman relics. The bird life in the Camargue, after Arles, is prolific. The ride crosses two miniature mountain ranges – the higher one, the Alpilles, reaches a dizzying 280m.

PLANNING
Maps

Four of Michelin's small sheet, 1:200,000 scale maps cover this route: No 80 *Albi, Rodez, Nîmes*, No 81 *Montélimar, Avignon, Digne*, No 83 *Carcassonne, Montpellier, Nîmes* and No 84 *Marseille, Toulon, Nice*. The larger sheet, No 245 *Provence, Côte d'Azur* (1:200,000), covers the entire route.

Information

A list of cycling routes through the Camargue, with detailed route explanations in English, is available from Le Vélo Saintois

(☎/fax 04 90 97 74 56), 19 ave de la République, Stes-Maries. VTT hire is also available.

What to Bring

A pair of binoculars will be useful for bird-watching in the Camargue; bring some insect repellent, too.

GETTING TO/FROM THE RIDE

Avignon is the end of The Luberon & Mont Ventoux ride detailed earlier in this chapter; see that ride (p458) for information on getting to/from Avignon. It's also the start of the Remote Cévennes ride in the Languedoc-Roussillon chapter.

THE RIDE
Avignon

See Avignon (pp472–3) in the Luberon & Mont Ventoux ride for information about accommodation and other services.

Day 1: Avignon to Arles
4½–7 hours, 71.3km

Follow the city walls clockwise from the station. Once across the Édouard Daladier bridge and heading south on the wide D2, traffic is less frenetic.

After Barbentane, with its fine 17th-century **chateau**, the gentle climb of La Montagnette past the **Abbaye St-Michel de Frigolet** is on a very quiet, forested road, virtually lined with picnic tables. The abbey (*frigolet* is the Provençal word for 'thyme') has a massive 12th-century, Roman-style cloister.

Ride via Graveson, with its **perfume museum** and Friday-afternoon **country market**, to unmomentous Maillane where there's a Frédéric Mistral **museum** in the house inhabited by the poet (1830–1914) from 1876. He is buried in the village cemetery.

Prettily located St-Rémy de Provence (35.5km) is the next interesting village. The birthplace of Nostradamus (1503–1566) and where Van Gogh spent his last years, the ancient village lies at the foot of the Alpilles. At its southern edge is the **Glanum archaeological site**, where remains of Greek and Roman settlement have been unearthed. *Accommodation* (including camping) is quite expensive.

Climb steadily to the Alpilles' summit (280m) and then freewheel down through

PROVENCE & THE CÔTE D'AZUR

Day 1: Avignon to Arles

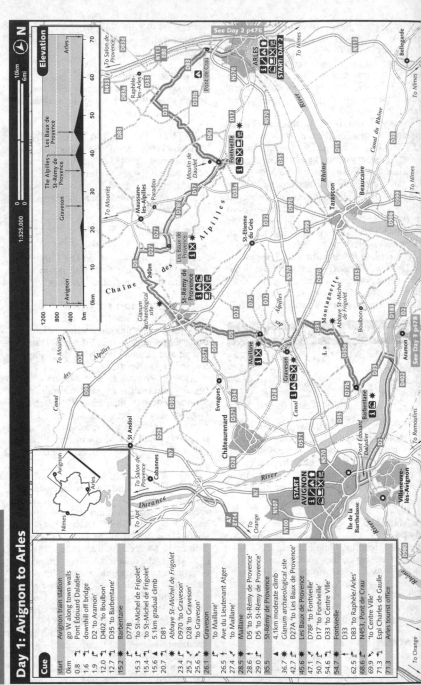

Cue	
start	Avignon train station
0km	go W along town walls
0.8	Pont Édouard Daladier
1.6	downhill off bridge
1.9	D2 'to Aramon'
12.0	D402 'to Boulbon'
12.7	D35 'to Barbentane'
15.2	Barbentane
	D77B
15.3	'to St-Michel de Frigolet'
15.4	'to St-Michel de Frigolet'
15.6	5.1km gradual climb
20.7	D81
23.4	Abbaye St-Michel de Frigolet
25.2	D970 'to Graveson'
25.6	D28 'to Graveson'
	'to Graveson'
26.1	Graveson
	Ave du Lieutenant Atger
26.5	'to Maillane'
27.4	'to Maillane'
28.5	Maillane
28.6	D5 'to St-Rémy de Provence'
29.0	D5 'to St-Rémy de Provence'
35.5	St-Rémy de Provence
	4.1km moderate climb
36.7	Glanum archaeological site
42.7	D27A 'to Les Baux de Provence'
45.6	Les Baux de Provence
47.1	D78F 'to Fontvieille'
50.7	D17 'to Fontvieille'
54.6	D33 'to Centre Ville'
54.7	Fontvieille
	D33
62.5	D83 'to Raphèle/Arles'
68.6	N453, Pont de Crau
69.9	'to Centre Ville'
71.3	Espl Charles de Gaulle
71.3	Arles tourist office

ranquil aromatic forest. The landscape be-
omes rugged and rocky with orange-grey
imestone outcrops.

Ten kilometres from St-Rémy, perched
n an isolated ridge offering a superb
anorama of the countryside, is pedestri-
nised Les Baux de Provence. Dominated
y its ruined **citadel**, former feudal home of
Monaco's Grimaldi family, it is daily over-
un by innumerable coach loads of tourists.

Fontvieille, a further 10km from St-
Rémy, is famed for the *moulin* (windmill)
immortalised by Alphonse Daudet in his
869 collection of short stories *Lettres de
mon Moulin* (Letters from my Windmill). In
eality, the 1814 *moulin de Daudet* housing
he **Musée de Daudet**, left of the route on
eaving the village, is not the one where the
vriter spent hours sunk deep in literary
hought. A trail leads past ruined Moulin
Ramet to **Moulin Tissot**, his true haunt.
Views extend across the Alpilles' plain.

Arles

This bustling city of 52,000 people lies at the
orthern tip of the Camargue alluvial plain
n the Grand Rhône. Arles boasts a historic
entre with a 20,000-seat Roman amphi-
heatre and a 12,000-seat restored Roman
heatre, both of which are used today for culural events and Camarguaise bullfights.

Vincent van Gogh lived here for a year in
888, immortalising many of the city's streets
nd surrounding rural areas on canvas.

Information The tourist office (☎ 04 90
8 41 20, fax 04 90 18 41 29) on esplanade
Charles de Gaulle, near blvd des Lices,
pens normal hours except Sunday (9 am to
pm from April to September; 10 am to
oon the rest of the year). The tourist office
☎ 04 90 49 36 90) next to the train station
loses at 5 or 6 pm and is not open Sunday.

Banks cluster on place de la République.

Bike shops Cycles Peugeot (☎ 04 90 96
3 77), 15 rue du Pont, and L'Arène du
Cycle (☎ 04 90 96 46 83), 10 rue Portagnel,
ire out bikes.

Things to See & Do Self-guided tours of
he amphitheatre **Les Arènes** (☎ 04 96 03
0) and the Roman **Théâtre Antique** (☎ 04
0 96 93 30) can be made outside perfor-
nance times (15FF; closes early at 4.30 pm
utside of April to September).

The austere **Église St Trophime** – its
richly decorated western portal faces place
de la République – was probably built
largely with stone cut from the Théâtre Antique in the late 11th and early 12th centuries. Inspect the serene **Cloître St
Trophime** (☎ 04 90 49 36 36), surrounded
by superbly sculptured columns.

Fourth-century Roman baths, the recently-
restored **Thermes de Constantin**, are near
the river on rue du Grand Prieuré.

Museums include the **Musée d'Archéologie d'Arles** (or Musée de l'Arles Antique;
☎ 04 90 18 88 88), with Roman and early
Christian relics; the **Museon Arlaten** (☎ 04
90 96 08 23), displaying articles related to
traditional Provençal life; and the **Musée
Réattu** (☎ 04 90 96 37 68), displaying
works by the world's finest photographers,

Vincent van Gogh

When Vincent van Gogh (1853–90) arrived in Provence in 1888, the quality of
light and the colours were a great revela-
tion to him. He spent an intensely productive year at Arles, during which he painted
all sorts of local scenes, among them the
Pont de Langlois, a little bridge that has
been rebuilt 3km south of Arles (from
town, take bus No 1 to the Pont van Gogh
terminus). Now famous, *The Bridge at
Arles* is displayed in the Kröller-Müller National Museum in the Netherlands.

In 1888, van Gogh's friend and fellow
artist Gauguin came to stay with him for
several months. But different temperaments
and approaches to art led to a quarrel and
van Gogh, overcome with despair, chopped
off part of his left ear. In May 1889, because of recurrent bouts of madness, he
voluntarily retreated to an asylum in Saint
Rémy (25km north-east of Arles over the
Alpilles), staying there for a year. In 1890,
while staying in Auvers-sur-Oise (just north
of Paris), van Gogh, lonely to the point of
desperation and afraid that his madness
was incurable, shot and killed himself.

Today, there are few tangible remains
of van Gogh's stay in Arles. All traces of his
rented yellow house and the nearby cafe
on place Lamartine, both of which appear
in his paintings, were wiped out in WWII.

PROVENCE & THE CÔTE D'AZUR

Day 2: Arles to Nîmes

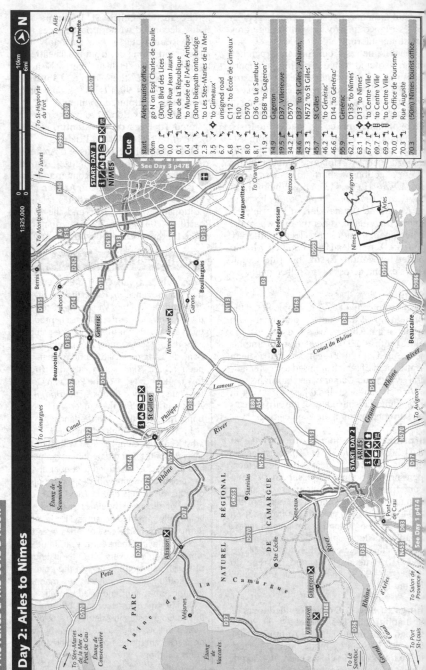

Cue

start	Arles tourist office
0km	go N on Espl Charles de Gaulle
0.0	(30m) Blvd des Lices
0.0	(40m) Rue Jean Jaurès
0.1	Rue de la République
0.4	'to Musée de l'Arles Antique'
0.4	(30m) bikepath onto bridge
2.3	'to Les Stes-Maries de la Mer'
3.5	'to Gimeaux'
6.7	unsigned road
6.8	C112 'to École de Gimeaux'
7.1	R10
8.0	D570
8.1	D36 'to Le Sambuc'
11.9	D36B 'to Gageron'
14.9	Gageron
19.5	D37, Villeneuve
34.2	D570
34.6	D37 'to St Gilles', Albaron,
42.3	N572 'to St Gilles'
45.7	St Gilles
46.2	'to Générac'
46.6	D14 'to Générac'
55.9	Générac
62.1	D135 'to Nîmes'
63.1	D13 'to Nîmes'
67.7	'to Centre Ville'
69.7	'to Centre Ville'
69.9	'to Office de Tourisme'
70.0	Rue Auguste
70.3	(50m) Nîmes tourist office

1:325,000

START: DAY 3
NÎMES
See Day 3 p478

START: DAY 2
ARLES
See Day 1 p414

aintings by Provençal artists from the 18th-
nd 19th-century and 57 Picasso drawings
ketched in 1970–71.

The **Fondation Vincent van Gogh** (☎ 04
90 49 94 04), inside the Palais de Luppé at
24bis Rond Point des Arènes, displays
paintings by other artists inspired by Arles'
most famous resident.

Early in July an **international photography
festival** draws people from around the world.
The two-week **Fêtes d'Arles** at the end of
June features poetry readings dance, theatre,
and music. The Festiv'Arles office (☎ 04 90
96 47 00) is at 35 place de la République.

The **bullfighting** season at the Arènes
runs from Easter to September.

Places to Stay & Eat Reasonably priced
accommodation is readily available.

Noisy, mosquito-thronged *Camping City*
(☎ 04 90 93 08 86, 67 route de Crau), on
the way into town from Pont de Crau, is
open from March to October and charges
36/69 for one/two people.

The *Auberge de Jeunesse* (☎ 04 90 96 18
25, fax 04 90 96 31 26, 20 ave Maréchal
Foch) has 100 beds and charges around
75FF, including breakfast. Its *restaurant*
serves meals from 47FF.

Hôtel de France et de la Gare (☎ 04 90
96 01 24, fax 04 90 96 90 87, 1 place Lamar-
ine) has rooms with shower and toilet from
185FF. Next door, *Hôtel Terminus et Van
Gogh* (☎/fax 04 90 96 12 32) has similar
rooms with washbasin from 140FF.

Mid-range *Hôtel Gauguin* (☎ 04 90 96
14 35, fax 04 90 18 98 87, 5 place Voltaire)
has doubles with shower for around 210FF,
while the pleasant *Hôtel du Musée* (☎ 04 90
93 88 88, fax 04 90 49 98 15, 11 rue du
Grand Prieuré), opposite Musée Réattu near
the Rhône, charges from 280FF a double.

Markets are held on Wednesday, on blvd
Émile Combe outside the city walls, and
Saturday morning, on blvd des Lices. Numerous supermarkets include a big *Leclerc*
(chemin de Moines) and two *Intermarchés*
(rue Gérard Gadiot and 1 rue Verrerie).

Place du Forum is a big outdoor restaurant area. Good-value salads and *plats du
jour* are available at *Le Bistrot Arlésien*
(☎ 04 90 96 07 22) for around 60FF. Try
also the *Restaurant van Gogh* (☎ 04 90 93
59 79, 28 rue Voltaire) where *menus* range
from 80FF to 100FF.

Day 2: Arles to Nîmes
4–7 hours, 70.3km

Leave Arles, crossing the Grand Rhône via
a cycleway in the bowels of the Pont de
Trinquetaille, from which you can see nothing, and follow flat, windswept roads into
the Camargue, the 780-sq-km delta of the
Rhône.

Watch for flamingos and other birds, as
well as mosquitoes, near the shore of **Étang
de Vaccarès**, part of the Parc Naturel Régional de Camargue. There's an elevated
viewing platform at 26.6km.

The information centre (☎ 04 90 97 86
32, fax 04 90 97 70 82, ☐ www.parcs-na
turels-regionaux.tm.fr/lesparcs/camab.html)
is at Pont de Gau, 19km off the route on the
D570 towards Stes-Maries de la Mer.

You may also see herds of cream-
coloured *chevaux* (horses) and black *tau-
reaux* (bulls) which roam under the
watchful eyes of mounted *gardians* (Camarguaise cowboys). Most bulls are raised
for fighting. Horse rides are available.

Just one small hill, before Générac
(55.9km), lies on the route to Nîmes. From
the top, at about 100m altitude, you'll be
able to see views of tall apartment blocks in
the city.

Bulls & Cowboys

Not all bullfighting ends with a dead bull.
In a *course Camarguaise* (Camargue-style
bullfight), white-clad *raseteurs* try to remove ribbons or *attributs* (rosettes) tied to
the bull's horns with hooks (known as *cro-
chets*) held between their fingers. Its origins date to the 15th century when dogs,
lions and bears were let loose in a ring to
chase a bull. The merry circus was finally
slammed as cruel in the 19th century and
the other animals banished from the ring,
leaving man alone to pit his wits against
the *taureau*.

Out of the limelight, bulls are bred, fed
and tended by *gardians*, Camargue cowboys who herd the region's cattle. These
mounted herdsmen are honoured by the
Fête des Gardians in Arles in May, during
which they parade through town on
horseback – clad in leather hats, chequered
shirts and dusty boots.

PROVENCE & THE CÔTE D'AZUR

PROVENCE & THE CÔTE D'AZUR

Day 3: Nîmes to Avignon

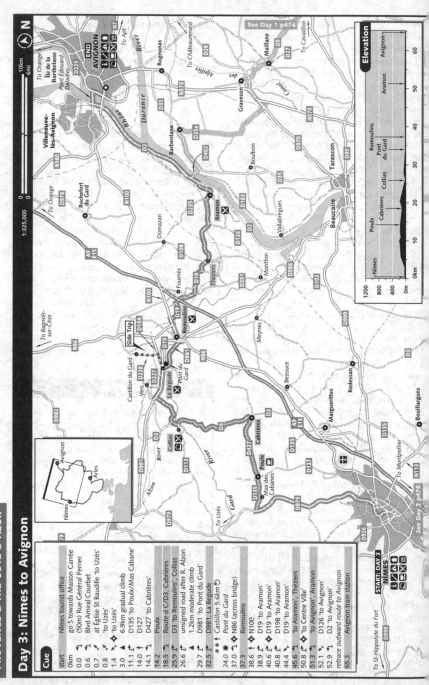

Cue		
start		Nîmes tourist office
0km		go S towards Maison Carrée
0.0	↰	(50m) Rue Général Perrier
0.6	↱	Blvd Amiral Courbet
0.7	↰	at Église St Baudille 'to Uzès'
0.8	↱	'to Uzès'
1.4	◇↱	'to Uzès'
3.0		6.9km gradual climb
11.1	↰	D135 'to Poulx/Mas Cabane'
14.0	↰	D127
14.1	↰	D427 'to Cabrières'
14.2		Poulx
18.5	↰	Route d C/D3, Cabrières
25.9	↰	D3 'to Remoulins', Collias
26.6		unsigned road after R. Alzon
		1.2km moderate climb
29.7	↱	D981 'to Pont du Gard'
32.5		D981, La Bégude
34.0	••••	Castillon 5.6km ↻
37.0	✳	N86 (across bridge)
37.3		Remoulins
38.6	◇↱	N100
38.9	↰	D19 'to Aramon'
40.6	↰	D19 'to Aramon'
40.8	↱	D19B 'to Aramon'
44.4	↰	D19 'to Aramon'
45.6	↱	'to Aramon', Théziers
50.8	◇↱	'to Centre Ville'
51.3	↱	to Avignon', Aramon
52.1	↰	D126 'to Avignon'
52.9	↱	D2 'to Avignon'
		retrace outward route to Avignon
65.3		Avignon train station

Nîmes

See Nîmes (pp385–7) in the Remote Cévennes ride in the Languedoc-Roussillon chapter for information about accommodation and other services.

Day 3: Nîmes to Avignon

½–5 hours, 65.3km

Follow a gently undulating course through several small villages to reach the massive **Pont du Gard** aqueduct (34km). This was once part of a 50km system of canals built around 19 BC by Emperor Augustus' powerful deputy and son-in-law Agrippa, to bring water from near Uzès to Nîmes.

The 35 small arches of the 275m upper tier, rising 49m above the Gard River, carry a 1.2m by 1.75m watercourse designed to carry 20,000 cubic metres of water a day. Stone came from the nearby Vers quarry, the largest boulders weighing more than five tonnes.

You can cycle across the road bridge, built in 1743 alongside the aqueduct's lower tier and, when renovations are completed, two million-plus visitors a year will be able to amble along the aqueduct's middle and (perhaps) top tier as well. The best view of the Pont du Gard is from the hill on the northern side (left bank) about 200m from the aqueduct (signposted 'Panorama'). Hire canoes to paddle under the aqueduct from Kayak Vert Gardon (☎ 04 66 22 84 83, fax 04 66 22 88 78), based upstream in Collias.

After the hustle of Remoulins, return to tiny, quiet roads going across country to the busy but wide D2, retracing the outward route from Day 1 of the ride. The route passes under two huge new viaducts for the TGV Mediterranean, rivalling the Pont du Gard in size if not in spectacle.

Side Trip: Castillon du Gard

20–30 minutes, 5.6km

North-east of the Pont du Gard, via the D19, D19A and uphill on the D228, is Castillon du Gard. Its **Musée du Vélo et de la Moto** (☎ 04 66 37 30 64) features historic machines from the 19th and 20th century, including bicycles of past hour-record holders Tony Rominger and Chris Boardman.

Castillon is worth a visit in its own right, with great views and a superb medieval atmosphere. Below the village, the attractively restored **Chapelle St Caprais** is surrounded by vineyards. Return to the route by the same roads.

Corsica

Corsica (Corse in French) is the most mountainous and geographically diverse of the Mediterranean islands, earning it the justified title of L'Île de Beauté (Island of Beauty). Although it covers only 8720 sq km, Corsica in many ways resembles a miniature continent, offering cyclists an unrivalled variety of terrain and scenery. Dramatic roads wind around the island's 1000km of rugged coastline and plunge between soaring granite peaks that stay snow-capped until July. Azure seas and icy mountain streams provide places to cool off, while the *maquis* (low, dense aromatic scrub that covers much of the coast) contributes to the sensory overload. The island's rich history, distinctive food and passionate people make Corsica an unforgettable touring destination.

HISTORY

Corsica's history is long and turbulent. The island's strategic position attracted the often unwelcome attentions of the major European and Mediterranean powers. Pisa, Genoa, France, Spain and Britain, not to mention the Moors and the armies of the Roman and Holy Roman Empires, have all fought on Corsican soil. These struggles have been matched by the Corsicans' own struggle for recognition by their rulers, who were rarely mindful of the islanders' needs.

It's believed the island has been inhabited since the Palaeolithic era, with artefacts like menhirs and dolmens providing evidence of megalithic era settlement. The Italian city-state of Pisa ruled from the 11th to 13th century, leaving a legacy of Romanesque churches; its rival Genoa took over in 1284, imposing brutal colonial rule. In the mid-15th century the Genoese handed the governing of Corsica – beset at the time by near anarchy, in part because of Muslim raids on coastal areas – to the Office de St Georges, a powerful financial organisation with its own army. To prevent seaborne raids from North Africa, the office built a massive defence system that included several citadels and a string of coastal hilltop watchtowers *(tours)*, many of which can be seen to this day.

In 1755, after 25 years of intermittent warfare against the Genoese, the Corsicans

In Brief

Highlights
- the cliffs of **E Calenche** at sunset
- a refreshing dip at the **Gorges de la Restonica**
- arriving in **Bonifacio**

Terrain
High mountains plunge to a rugged, hilly coastline in the west and drop to a narrow coastal plain in the east.

FFCT Contact
Ligue Côte d'Azur, 211 ave de Lattre de Tassigny, 83250 La Londe (mainland France)

Cycling Events
- **FFCT Corse Maritime** (mid-May) 10-day circuit from Ajaccio
- **Route du Sud** (early May) three-day race from Ajaccio to Porto Vecchio
- **FFCT Tour de l'Île de Beauté** (late May) 10-day tour from Ajaccio
- **FFCT Les Six Jours de l'Île de Beauté** (September) six-day tour in the north or south

Special Events
- **Catenacciu Procession** (Good Friday eve) Sartène
- **Fête de St Jean** (15 June) bonfires & Corsican chants held in most towns
- **Calvi Jazz Festival** (mid-June) Calvi
- **Napoleon's birthday celebrations** (15 August) Ajaccio
- **Rencontres des Chants Polyphoniques** (mid-September) Calvi

Gourmet Specialities
- home-made *charcuterie* (cured pork and salami)
- soft, fresh *brocciu* (sheeps cheese)
- wild olives
- chestnut beer or Cap Corse apéritif

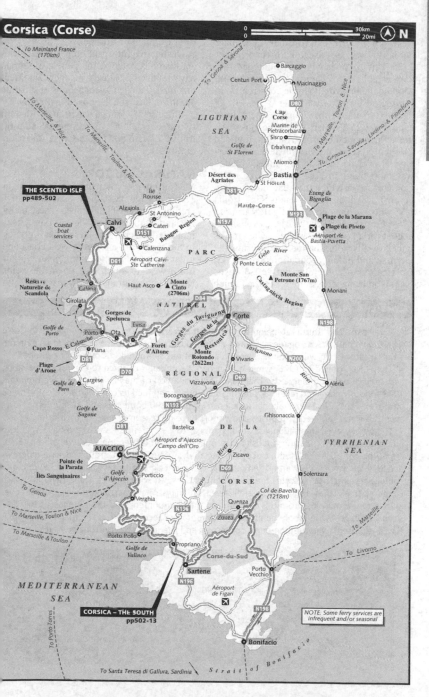

Corsica (Corse)

THE SCENTED ISLE
pp489–502

CORSICA – THE SOUTH
pp502–13

NOTE: Some ferry services are infrequent and/or seasonal

To Mainland France (170km)

To Genoa & Savona

To Marseille, Toulon & Nice

To Marseille, Toulon & Nice

To Genoa, Savona, Livorno & Piombino

To Marseille, Toulon & Nice

To Genoa

To Marseille, Toulon & Nice

To Marseille & Toulon

To Marseille

To Livorno

To Porto Torres

To Santa Teresa di Gallura, Sardinia

Barcaggio

Centuri Port

Macinaggio

Cap Corse

D80

Marine de Pietracorbara

Sisro

Erbalunga

Miomo

Bastia

LIGURIAN SEA

Golfe de St Florent

Désert des Agriates

D81

St Florent

Haute-Corse

Étang de Biguglia

N193

Plage de la Marana

Plage de Pineto

Aéroport de Bastia-Poretta

Île Rousse

Algajola

St Antonino

Cateri

Calvi

D151

Calenzana

Balagne Region

N197

PARC

Aéroport Calvi-Ste Catherine

D81

Golo River

Ponte Leccia

Monte San Petrone (1767m)

Castagniccia Region

Moriani

Réserve Naturelle de Scandola

Galéria

Girolata

Haut Asco

Monte Cinto (2706m)

NATUREL

D84

Gorges du Tavignano

Corte

Gorges de Spelunca

Evisa

Ota

Forêt d'Aïtone

Gorges de la Restonica

Monte Rotondo (2622m)

Vivario

Tavignano

N200

River

Golfe de Porto

Porto

E Calanche

Piana

Capo Rosso

D81

Plage d'Arone

D70

Cargèse

Golfe de Poro

RÉGIONAL

Vizzavona

D69

Ghisoni

D344

Aléria

N198

Golfe de Sagone

Bocognano

N193

Ghisonaccia

D81

Bastelica

DE LA

TYRRHENIAN SEA

AJACCIO

Aéroport d'Ajaccio-Campo dell'Oro

River

Zicavo

Pointe de la Parata

Îles Sanguinaires

Golfe d'Ajaccio

Porticcio

D69

CORSE

Solenzara

Verghia

N196

Col de Bavella (1218m)

Quenza

Zonza

Porto Pollo

Propriano

Golfe de Valinco

Corse-du-Sud

Porto Vecchio

MEDITERRANEAN SEA

Sartène

N196

Aéroport de Figari

N198

Bonifacio

Strait of Bonifacio

0   30km
0   20mi

N

CORSICA

declared their island independent. They were led by the extraordinary Pasquale Paoli (known as Pascal Paoli in French; 1725–1807), under whose enlightened rule they established a National Assembly and adopted the most democratic constitution in Europe.

The Corsicans chose inland Corte as their capital, set up a system of justice to replace the vendetta method of retribution, founded a school system and established a university. However, the island's independence was short-lived: in 1768 the Genoese ceded Corsica – over which they had no effective control – to their ally, French King Louis XV, whose troops defeated Paoli's army in 1769. France has ruled the island ever since, except for a period in 1794–96 when it was under English domination, and during the German and Italian occupation of 1940–43. Corsica's most famous native son was Napoleon Bonaparte, emperor of the French

and, in the early years of the 19th century ruler of much of Europe.

Despite having spent only 14 years as a autonomous country, the people of Corsic have retained a fiercely independent strea manifested in the violent actions of separati organisations (see the boxed text below).

Since 1975 Corsica has been divided in two *départements* (departments; adminis trative divisions): Haute-Corse and Cors du Sud.

NATURAL HISTORY

Measuring only 75km at its widest point, ar 180km in length, Corsica packs in an ir credible variety of landscapes. These incluc flatland marshes along the east coast, an ur inhabited desert – the Désert des Agriates in the top north, a tortured west coast and great spine of a mountain range runnir north-west to south-east down the centr Minor chains branch from the main spir

---

Corsican Nationalism

All over the island, the spray-painted initials of the Front de Libération Nationale de la Corse (FLNC) and nationalist slogans appear on walls and cliffs. These groups reflect – at an extreme – the dissatisfaction with external government that has simmered in Corsica for centuries.

The FLNC formed in 1976, when it launched a campaign of force to convey its message, with at least one bombing a day that year. The dissolution of the FLNC by the government in 1983 seriously damaged relations, but the movement continued its campaigns under the name of the 'ex-FLNC'. In 1997, nationalist violence included 290 bombings and 22 murders. (However, this is *not* targeted at tourists, and visitors have no reason to fear for their safety.)

Today, however, the nationalist groups appear to be suffering a crisis and have split into numerous factions, often in opposition to one another and seemingly outweighed by their armed branches. An indefinite truce was declared by four terrorist groups seeking independence in December 1999 after the French government agreed to talks. Yet, the movement's continuing existence indicates the discontent in Corsican society with a 'motherland' which is often perceived as distant and assimilative. Nationalists have adopted principles that cover a wide range of fields, from the economy to the environment and the defence of the Corsican language. (One theory behind the choice of the Moor's Head as the island's emblem is that it represents vanquishing one's oppressors and the ability to confront one's destiny).

SALLY DILLON

nd one group stands separate in the east; together, Corsica has more than 20 peaks bove 2000m. The highest is Monte Cinto, t 2706m.

Much of the alpine and rugged interior is ninhabited except by seasonal shepherds nd is protected within the large Parc Naurel Régional de la Corse (PNRC). Here *ergers* (shepherds) continue the age-old ractice of transhumance (see the 'Bergers f Corsica' boxed text later in the chapter). his region is home to the Laricio pine, the argest species in Europe; they grow up to 0m tall and some Corsican specimens are 000 years old. Their long straight trunks vere much prized as boat masts and the ees have been extensively logged over the enturies.

Corsica's isolation from the mainland nakes it home to many endemic species; of s 2000 plant species, 8% grow nowhere se. In the mountains, nearly half of all the nown species are endemic. Bird life on orsica is also very rich, including the now are peregrine falcon and the osprey.

The coastal fringe is covered by the naquis, where arbutus (strawberry trees), nastics, myrtle, cistus and heather grow nong a dense carpet of aromatic wild erbs such as thyme, lavender, mint, rose-nary and sage. The maquis is home to the ery rare leaf-toed gecko, though cyclists e more likely to see the lime-green Italian all lizard darting about on the rocks.

Olives, force-planted by the Genoese cenuries ago, have largely been left to grow ild, though new interest in the oil has ignited production in some areas. Large oves of chestnut trees (see the 'Wild Food f Corsica' boxed text later in the chapter) ow above 600m and below that grow cork es. Eucalypts were extensively planted st century to drain the malaria infested astal swamps. Fire is a major threat to the land's forests and maquis, one of the reans wild camping *(camping sauvage)* is ohibited.

LIMATE

orsica has a mild Mediterranean climate, ceiving more days of sunshine than anyhere in France. Summer (July and August) n be extremely dry and hot, with temperares reaching over 30°C; the north is usually tter than the south, and temperatures in the mountains of the interior are generally lower than on the coast. Some snow remains above 1600m between October and June.

Spring and autumn are both fine, with average maximum temperatures of around 15°C. Rain falls mostly in winter in frequent, short showers. The prevailing winds are the dry, gentle south-westerly *libeccio*, found especially in Haute-Corse in summer, and the *tramontane*, which comes down from the north in winter.

INFORMATION
Maps & Books

The Michelin map No 90 *Corse* (1:200,000) covers the entire island.

The FFCT *Corse* guide details (in French) 90 rides, ranging from 31km to 175km. Mountain bike (VTT) enthusiasts should look at Didier Richard's maps No 20 *Corse du Nord* (1:50,000) and No 23 *Corse du Sud* (1:50,000).

Dorothy Carrington's atmospheric travelogue *Granite Island* gives an excellent background to Corsica's history and culture.

For a more detailed description of diving and walking opportunities in Corsica, see Lonely Planet's *Corsica* guide.

Several excellent books detail Corsica's distinctive animal and plant life, but are only available in French. *La Corse* by Bournérias et al, in the Guides Naturalistes des Côtes de France series, is very thorough and is illustrated with drawings and photographs.

Information Sources

The Agence du Tourisme de la Corse (☎ 04 95 21 56 56, fax 04 95 51 14 40, 🖳 www .sitec.fr), 17 blvd Roi-Jérôme, Ajaccio, can supply several brochures on camping, festivals and hotels. Its brochure 'Tourisme Vert, Gîtes Ruraux' (Green Tourism, Rural Gîtes) may be useful for an extended holiday – it lists *gîtes d'étapes* (walkers hostels or self-contained accommodation), *fermes auberges* (farm, home-style restaurants) and details of winemakers, food producers, artists and activities by region.

The PNRC head office (☎ 04 95 51 79 00, fax 04 95 21 88 17, 🖳 www.parc-naturel-co rse.com) is at 2 rue Sergent Casalonga, Ajaccio. It can provide information on Corsica's parks and walking tracks, including a full list of gîtes in remote villages.

CORSICA

A Language Apart

Corsica remains fiercely patriotic and takes pride in keeping its distinctive language alive. The language has its roots in Italian, but also contains elements of Iberian, Ligurian and Genoese. French was then grafted onto this, particularly after it became compulsory for Corsicans to learn it at the end of the 19th century.

For years it was an offence to speak Corsican, just as the inhabitants of Brittany were forbidden to speak Breton. However, the language was officially accepted into the French lexicon in 1974. Many older people speak mainly Corsican and newspapers, popular music and literature keep the tradition alive. Learning a few simple greetings is guaranteed to encourage smiles:

Hello/Good day	*Bunghjornu* (boon-dyornoo)
Goodbye	*A venicci* (a ve-nichee)
Thank you	*Grazie* (gra-tsye)
Cheers!/Good health!	*A salute!* (a salooteh)
Best wishes!	*Pace i salute!* (pa-cheh ee salooteh)

Place Names

Two names exist for most places in Corsica – the original, Genoese-based Corsican names, which often end in 'u', and the 'Frenchified' names, where the 'u' translates to 'o'. Some road signs will carry both names, others just the Corsican; the French version may be crossed out or even bullet riddled. This guide uses the form adopted by Michelin in its maps (usually French), though cue sheets will show the version used on directional signs if they only carry the Corsican version. Corsican names are listed in parenthesis in the text. Words encountered on maps (the French follows in parenthesis) include:

bocca	*(col)*	pass
punta	*(pointe)*	headland, point
capu	*(cap)*	cape
caminu	*(chemin)*	path

Gîtes de France Corse (☎ 04 95 51 72 82 fax 04 95 51 72 89, ℮ Corsica.gites.d .France@wanadoo.fr), 9 rue Général Fior ella, Ajaccio, can provide information o the B&Bs and gîtes on the island.

As well as running several annual rides o the island (see Organised Rides, following the Fédération Française de Cyclotourism (FFCT) has a permanent mapped *randon née*, the 1000km Tour de Corse, which in volves 14,600m of climbing. Another is sti being ratified and will ultimately climb be tween 174 and 212 passes!

The Web site ▢ www.corsica-guide.cor has good background on Corsica, in Frencl

Organised Rides

Every year, the Fédération Française d Cyclotourisme (FFCT) runs four popula supported rides in Corsica, including th difficult 500km 'Les Six Jours de l'Île d Beauté', with north and south options th; climb all the island's popular high points i six days; each tour involves 5900m c climbing. See the Useful Organisations sec tion in the Facts for the Cyclist chapter fc FFCT contact details.

The Audax Club Parisien runs the Tou de Corse; see the Randonnées chapter.

GETTING TO/FROM CORSICA
Air
Corsica's four main airports are at Ajacci Bastia, Figari (near Bonifacio) and Calv The standard fare from Paris to any Co sican city is usually around 2000FF retur regardless of the season (1200FF if boug] two weeks in advance, student fa 1100FF). However, airlines offer variou discounts. Check the airport tax and th 40FF Corsica departure tax is included the ticket price. From April to Septemb flights go from many of the larger Fren cities. From April to October, and partic larly during summer, charter flights me the increase in passenger demand.

Several European airlines have conne tions to Corsica (see Sea in the Gettir There & Away chapter).

Boat
Details on ferry services are available fro many French travel agents. From mainlar France, ferries go to Bastia from Nice (tl closest port, 3½ hours by NGV), Toulon ar

Marseille all year, though from October to May the number of services plunges. The newer NGV services have halved the journey time between the Continent and Corsica; however, these services, which reach speeds of nearly 70km/h, cannot sail if the waves are over 4m high. The traditional car ferries take around six hours from Nice.

Fares are based on four periods. While passenger fares remain fairly consistent year-round, ferry tickets for cars can increase threefold in high season (July and August). Children aged four to 11 can get a 50% discount. Student, family and senior fares are also available. All passengers are charged a FF Corsican arrival and departure tax, plus variable port tax (eg, 30FF per person from Nice to Bastia; 42FF from Nice to Ajaccio). Prices quoted in this section are for passengers only and don't include taxes.

Corsica Ferries (in Nice ☎ 04 92 00 43 76, fax 04 92 00 43 77, ☐ www.corsicaferries.com) carries bikes for free. It runs NGVs from Nice (114FF to 180FF) from mid-March to October, with services every second day over Easter, several times a week in April and May, one daily from June to September and one a week (Friday) in October. Add 91FF per bike and a per-kilogram tariff for trailers for all tickets with Ferryrrranée (☎ 04 93 13 66 99, fax 04 93 13 66 in Nice, ☐ www.sncm.fr). It runs NGV services from Nice (from 210FF, similar schedule to Corsica Ferries) and car ferries from Toulon (from 256FF, 10½ hours, one to two a week in July and August only) and Marseille (from 256FF, 10 hours, every second day in June and November, more from ly to mid-October).

Ferries sail to Ajaccio from Marseille, Toulon, Nice – and Porto Torres (Sardinia). Boats also travel to Corsica from Porto Torres (Sardinia), Savona, Livorno, Genoa and Piombino in Italy; see Sea in the Getting There & Away chapter for details.

ETTING AROUND CORSICA
ain

This is the most interesting, fun and comfortable way to get between tours or to and from departure points. Despite – or perhaps because of – Corsica's metre-gauge, single-track rail system being a good century behind the TGV, travelling by train in Corsica an experience not to be missed. The trains

search and crawl their way through the stunning mountain scenery of the interior, stopping at tiny rural stations and, when necessary, for sheep, goats and cows. Bikes are happily carried for 74FF each (no matter how long the trip). Fewer trains usually run on Sunday. Relevant services include:

to	frequency	fare	hours
to/from Bastia			
Calvi	2	93FF	3
Corte	5	58FF	1½
to/from Ajaccio			
Bastia	4	122FF	3¾
Corte	4	65FF	2
Calvi	2	141FF	4½
to/from Corte			
Calvi	2	78FF	2½

Bus

Bus transport around Corsica is slow, infrequent, seasonal, relatively expensive and handled by a network of independent companies, with different rules on carrying bikes. Only the services between Ajaccio and Bonifacio, and Bonifacio and Bastia, carry bikes. See the Gateway Cities and Getting to/from the Ride sections for details of individual carriers and services.

GATEWAY CITIES
Bastia

Bastia is Corsica's economic centre and has the fourth most important port in France. Although not a tourist hub, Bastia has a lively and busy town centre, a pretty port, long beaches and a rich cultural life.

Bastia was officially founded in 1372, when the Genoese governor built a fortress (or *bastiglia*, hence Bastia) on the rocky headland. In 1452 the fortress became the provincial capital of Corsica under Genoese rule, and the seat of the governors. In 1811 Bastia lost its status as capital to Ajaccio. Since WWII Bastia's port and commerce has contributed to its return as the island's economic capital.

Information On the northern side of place St Nicolas is the small tourist office (☎ 04 95 55 96 96, fax 04 95 55 96 00). In the low season it closes for lunch and on Sunday afternoon.

The several banks on place St Nicolas include Banque Nationale de Paris and Société Générale (both with ATM and *bureau de change;* exchange bureau). Bastia's main post office is on ave Maréchal Sébastiani.

Sprint Orsini (☎ 04 95 32 39 00), 35 ave Émile Sari, is part of the BoutiCycle chain and is well stocked for cycle tourists (closed Sunday). For bike hire, go to Objectif Nature (☎/fax 04 95 32 54 34, mobile ☎ 06 12 28 52 84), 3 rue Notre Dame de Lourdes. The friendly owner stocks a selection of bikes (100/500FF per day/week) and can recommend routes.

Le Cyber bar and cafe (☎ 04 95 34 30 34), 2 rue du Castagne, offers email services.

Things to See & Do The palms and pastel-coloured buildings around the long, 19th-century **place St Nicolas** give it a tropical air, and the bars and cafes on its western side have a relaxing atmosphere. A statue of Napoleon, in a Roman emperor's tunic, watches over the square.

In summer the tourist office organises **guided tours** around the town, some in English. Sites in the Terra Vecchia, the oldest part of the town (south of place St Nicolas), include the famous **Église St Jean Baptiste**, recognisable by its twin bell-towers. From here, interesting little streets wind their way between tall houses to the old harbour and quai des Martyrs de la Libération. Across the water is the **Citadelle** and Terra Nova (the Genoese quarter). In the Citadelle, the **Palais des Gouverneurs** (Governors' Palace) now houses the **Musée d'Ethnographie Corse** (Museum of Corsican Ethnography; closed until at least 2001). Nearby is the **Église Ste Croix**, famous for its **black crucifix** and red velvet walls.

Objectif Nature (see Information) lists groups offering **activities** such as canyoning, diving, horse riding and parapenting.

The 11km-long, 2km-wide **Étang de Biguglia** is Corsica's largest lake. This nature reserve is an important staging post for birds migrating between Europe and Africa, and more than 100 rare species of bird can be seen here. A popular **cycle track** borders the lake's eastern side, but it's a 5km, busy ride south to get there.

Dive trips are run by Thalassa Immersion (☎ 04 95 31 78 90) at 2 rue St Jean (near the old port) and Club Plongée Bastiais (☎ 04

95 33 31 28), which operates from a boat the old port.

Places to Stay Book ahead, especially i summer; many places fill by noon ye round.

Camping du Bois de San Damian (☎ 04 95 33 68 02, fax 04 95 30 84 10) by the sea at Lido de la Marana (betwee the airport and Bastia) and comes comple with a waterpark. It costs 32FF per perso plus 12FF per site.

Hôtel de l'Univers (☎ 04 95 31 03 38, f 04 95 31 19 91, 3 ave Maréchal Sébastian virtually opposite the post office, has basi old doubles (shower and toilet upstairs) f 190FF and more comfortable, refurbishe rooms with all the mod cons for 310F Bikes can be parked in the garage.

The *Hôtel Central* (☎ 04 95 31 71 1 fax 04 95 31 82 40, 3 rue Miot) has som of the town's most comfortable rooms, wi shower, washbasin and toilet; some have small balcony. A basic double in low/hig season costs 200/260FF.

Hôtel des Voyageurs (☎ 04 95 34 90 8 fax 04 95 34 00 65, 9 ave Maréchal Séba tiani) is another first-rate hotel with a chee ful welcome. A single/double costs 25 280FF in low season and 300/350FF in hig season. It also has family rooms.

Hôtel Posta Vecchia (☎ 04 95 32 32 2 fax 04 95 32 14 05, quai des Martyrs de Libération) is the only hotel offering se views in Terra Vecchia. Smaller double cost 240/260FF, and larger rooms 36 400FF (higher tariffs are for summer).

Places to Eat A *market* is held from abo 8 am in place de l'Hôtel de Ville (als known as place du Marché) Tuesday to Su day. Local traders and producers sell hone fruit and veg, *charcuterie* (home-cured po sausages), wine and *feuilleté au brucc* (brocciu pastry). For regional specialiti outside market hours, try *U Muntagno* (☎ 04 95 32 78 04, 15 rue César Camp inchi); it's closed Sunday.

La Voûte (☎ 04 95 32 27 82, 6 rue Luc de Casabianca) is in a quiet street behin the harbour. It's worth making a detour f its rich and varied menu. Excellent pizza cooked over a wood fire cost 45FF to 50F

Brasserie du Marché (☎ 04 95 34 27 1 is one of a handful of restaurants situate around the old harbour. The seafood platter 128FF for the standard size) prepared in front of the customer is excellent; daily specials mainly consist of fish, or try a *menu* (set meal). Opposite, the first-rate *Restaurant U Murinuri* (☎ 04 95 32 45 99) offers three regional *menus* at 80FF, 100FF and 155FF.

Bistrot du Port (☎ 04 95 32 19 83), opposite the entrance to Hôtel Posta Vecchia, is an intimate, excellent restaurant with a wide range of imaginative a la carte dishes from about 42FF; fish is sold by weight 28FF per 100g for all varieties).

Jo la Braise (☎ 04 95 31 36 97, 7 blvd Hyacinthe de Montera) is a small, popular restaurant close to the Palais de Justice. It is rather plain from the outside but serves delicious food, with tasty pizzas for around 35FF to 40FF.

Getting There & Away Bastia-Poretta airport (☎ 04 95 54 54 54) is 24km south of the town. A shuttle bus runs frequently 50FF); your bike travels for free in the luggage compartment.

To ride from the airport, take the small road to the south, then head east on the D10 to la Canonica. At the beach, turn north to travel along the coast on the D107 or the bikepath that runs for most of the road's length. This leaves only 5km of riding along the very busy – and shoulderless – N193.

Bastia's ferry terminal is at the end of ave Pietri. Inside, tickets are sold for same-day travel; ticket offices open a few hours before ships arrive. Only the carriers' offices in town sell tickets for travel on a different day (all close Saturday afternoon and Sunday). See the Getting to/from Corsica section earlier for ferry details.

The train station (☎ 04 95 32 80 61) is at the western end of ave Maréchal Sébastiani. See the Getting Around Corsica section earlier for schedule details.

The bus station is virtually opposite the tourist office at the end of rue du Nouveau Port. Some buses leave from the train station, ave Maréchal Sébastiani or ave Pietri the airport shuttle stops at both). Buses generally travel once a day to Calvi, Porto Vecchio, Ajaccio and Bonifacio. Bikes can only be carried on the bus from Bastia to Bonifacio, via Porto Vecchio (see the Getting to/from the Ride section for the Corsica - the South ride).

Ajaccio (Aiacciu)

The port city of Ajaccio, the birthplace of Napoleon Bonaparte (1769–1821), is a pleasant enough place, despite having some very busy roads and rather unattractive parts. The provincial capital of Corse du Sud, the port of Ajaccio is the largest town on the island.

Spending some time here can also be educational: Ajaccio's several museums and many statues dedicated to Napoleon (who, local people will neglect to mention, never came back to visit after becoming emperor) speak volumes, not about Napoleon himself, but about how the people of his native town prefer to think of him. In June the Napoleonic era is celebrated in Les Journées Napoléoniennes, with parades, torchlight processions and fireworks.

Information The staff at the tourist office (☎ 04 95 51 53 03, fax 04 95 51 53 01), 1 place Foch, speak English and have a range of brochures and information on the town. The office opens from 8 am to 8 pm Monday to Saturday and Sunday morning in July and August, and until 6 pm weekdays or 5 pm Saturday the rest of the year.

The Maison d'Informations Randonnées du PNRC (☎ 04 95 51 79 10, fax 04 95 21 88 17), 2 rue Sergent Casalonga, can provide useful information on walking in Corsica (open until 6 pm weekdays from June to October).

The Banque de France is at 8 rue Sergent Casalonga. Crédit Lyonnais is at 59 cours Napoléon. Ajaccio has lots of ATMs. The main post office is at 13 cours Napoléon.

The excellent BoutiCycle Rout'Évasion (☎ 04 95 22 72 87), 8 ave du Docteur Noel Francini, is 2km north of town, but is well stocked for cycle tourists (closed Sunday and Monday). It's one of the few places in Corsica selling energy drinks. Locacorse (☎ 04 95 20 71 20, fax 04 95 20 44 52), 10 ave Beverini Vico, hires VTTs for 70/370FF a day/week (closed Sunday).

La Marge bookshop on rue Emmanuel Aréna, running off place Foch, offers Internet services.

Things to See & Do The Musée Fesch (☎ 04 95 21 48 17), 50 rue du Cardinal Fesch, houses an important art collection donated by Cardinal Fesch, Napoleon's maternal uncle, in 1839. It has some outstanding 14th- and 19th-century Italian paintings by Titian, Fra Bartolomeo, Veronese, Botticelli and Bellini. Next door, the **Imperial Chapel** houses the tombs of several members of the imperial family.

Ajaccio's gem, the **Municipal Library**, is next door. A visit will send a chill down the spine of any book lover. Its vast reading room is lined by 4m-high walnut shelves groaning under the weight of France's largest collection of rare books outside Paris, the oldest dating from 1475. The librarians are happy to show you the 16th-century leatherbound encyclopedias filled with intricate engravings.

The interesting **Musée A Bandera** (flag museum; ☎ 04 95 51 07 34), tucked away in rue du Général Lévie, provides an overview of Corsican history from its origins until WWII, through documents, artefacts and dioramas.

To see where Bonaparte lived his early years, visit his house in the **Musée National de la Maison Bonaparte** (☎ 04 95 21 43 89) on rue St Charles. The **Salon Napoléonien** (☎ 04 95 51 52 62) on the first floor of the town hall, has two rooms of Napoleonic mementos.

The private **Musée du Capitellu** (☎ 04 95 21 50 57), 18 blvd Danièle Casanova (a famous member of the Corsican resistance), provides a fascinating glimpse of the town's history.

The Venetian-style **cathedral** was built in the second half of the 16th century, in the old town at the corner of rue Forcioli Conti and rue St Charles. Inside is the font used to baptise Napoleon and the *Vierge au Sacré-Coeur* by Delacroix.

Activities available include **boat trips**, beach **swimming** and **diving**. Inquire at the tourist office.

Places to Stay It is difficult to find cheap accommodation in Ajaccio, although several two-star hotels are reasonably priced. Book ahead in summer.

Camping de Barbicaja (☎ 04 95 52 01 17) is next to a beach on the route des Sanguinaires about 4.5km west of the town centre. Fees are 40FF per person and 12FF for the site (open April to September).

The cheapest place to stay in town is *Hotel la Pergola* (☎ 04 95 23 36 44, 25 ave

Colonel Colonna d'Ornano). Its rooms a have hall toilets, and cost 170FF per doubl with hall shower, or 200FF with shower.

In the two-star category, *Hôtel Kallist* (☎ 04 95 51 34 45, fax 04 95 21 79 00, 5 cours Napoléon) is a favourite haunt of in dependent travellers. It offers money chang facilities, car, motorbike and VTT hire an locked bike parking. Its large, renovate rooms are clean and have bathroom, satel lite TV and telephone; many are nonsmok ing. Doubles cost 250FF October to June 275FF July to September and 340FF in Au gust. An extra charge of 50FF applies fo rooms with air-con or a kitchenette.

Friendly, central *Hôtel Bonaparte* (☎ 0 95 21 44 19, 1 rue Étienne Conti) has sma and jaded rooms, but they have good ha bour views and cost 320FF for a doubl (open April to October).

Places to Eat An excellent *market* is hel in place Campinchi every morning. Ajacci has plenty of supermarkets; the enormou *Monoprix* in cours Napoléon has a baker (closed Sunday).

Fast-Food Asiatique (☎ 04 95 21 23 3 1 rue Maréchal Ornano) offers unbeatabl prices for decent food: fried noodles cos 22FF and the daily special 30FF (open dail for lunch and dinner). For a real treat, vis the superb *Soleo* ice-cream parlour at th top end of place Foch, on ave de Paris (ope afternoons only, until midnight in summer

Several restaurants and pizzerias alon rue des Anciens Fossés, a narrow street i the old town, provide cheap food in a pleas ant setting; *U Borgu* (☎ 04 95 21 17 47) ha pasta starting at 37FF, good pizzas fror 44FF to 55FF, salads for around 40FF an *menus* from 65FF (open daily for lunch an dinner).

Le Restaurant de France, Chez Pietr (☎ 04 95 21 11 00, 59 rue du Cardina Fesch) is charming but rather old-fashionec It has a 95FF *menu* with a few Corsica specialities (open for lunch and dinne Monday to Saturday).

L'Estaminet (☎ 04 95 50 10 42, 6 rue d Roi de Rome) has a pretty dining room an terrace in the heart of the old town, but is ver pricey. It serves French haut cuisine rathe than Corsican specialities; good mains hove around 90FF (closed Sunday and at Monda lunchtime). Credit cards aren't accepted.

Getting There & Away Ajaccio's Campo dell'Oro airport (☎ 04 95 23 56 56) Is 8km outh-east of town. The hourly airport bus 20FF) will take bikes if there's room (6.30 am to 10 pm).

Ferries leave from Ajaccio's shipping and freight terminal (☎ 04 95 51 55 45) on quai 'Herminier. The SNCM Ferryterranée ☎ 04 95 29 66 99) office next to the CMN sells tickets for same-day travel. Reservations have to be made at the other offices.

From mid-April to October, Compagnie les Promenades en Mer (☎ 04 95 51 31 31, ax 04 95 23 23 27) runs boats from Ajaccio's Vieux Port to Bonifacio on Thursday 195FF one-way).

The ferry terminal also serves as a coach station. Services run to most parts of the island, but only those to Bonifacio take bikes. At least four buses a day go to Bonifacio in summer (two on Sunday and public holidays); only the 8 am service will carry bikes.

Ajaccio's train station (☎ 04 95 23 11 03) is on blvd Sampiero (place de la Gare). The left-luggage facility in the station costs 10FF for the first day. See the Getting Around Corsica section for train services.

The Scented Isle

Duration	5 days
Distance	222.9km
Difficulty	hard
Start	Calvi
End	Corte

Immerse yourself in the vibrant colours, heady scents and rugged scenery of Corsica on a tour that visits some of the island's most beautiful places. This ride works its way along the island's remote west coast, travelling through the shattered heart of the famous E Calanche rockscape before turning inland to climb into the mountains. An alpine pass on the island's highest road leads to the dramatic Scala di Santa Regina gorge before dropping into the Corsican capital, Corte, gateway to the Gorges de la Restonica.

PLANNING
When to Ride
May or early June are the best times to go; the weather is warm enough to swim, but not too hot to ride. However, avoid the

French World Rally Championship that tears around the island in early May. After mid-June prices begin to go up and it gets unpleasantly hot (30°C plus). July and August, especially, are unpleasant, for the heat and the enormous influx of tourists.

You're more likely to get a taste of Corsican life outside the tourist season; September would be another reasonable month.

What to Bring
It's essential to carry spare parts in Corsica, where it may be several days between bike shops. Specialist parts for tandems or high-end bikes are likely to be unavailable, even in Ajaccio. Having said that, pack light for the hills – many days in this tour feature more than 1000m of climbing.

Come prepared for glaring sunshine and swimming opportunities (sunscreen is expensive here). Walking shoes and a day pack are also recommended, as well as rain gear and warm clothes for Day 5.

On the bike, carry plenty of water. Water from the fountains on the side of the road is safe unless signed 'Eau non potable'.

Credit cards are not as widely accepted in Corsica as they are on mainland France and exchange rates are less competitive; the larger cities are the best places to get cash. Some towns don't have places to change money.

Corsica is spectacularly photogenic; carry plenty of film or budget to pay up to double the usual price.

GETTING TO/FROM THE RIDE
Ideally, combine this ride with some in the Provence & Côte d'Azur chapter, such as the Alpes Maritime, Plateau de Caussols or Côte d'Azur Hinterland rides, which all leave from near Nice.

To do this ride before the Corsica – The South ride, later in this chapter, catch a train between Corte and Ajaccio; to do this ride last (a more complicated option), link from Bonifacio to Ajaccio by bus, then take a train to Calvi.

Calvi
Air Calvi's Ste Catherine airport (☎ 04 95 65 88 88) is 7km south-east of the city centre. The runways are so close to the mountains that flights are often redirected to Bastia in high winds. You have to ride into town or catch a cab. Air France flies to Calvi.

Train Train is the best way to get there; see the Getting Around Corsica section earlier for details. The train station (☎ 04 95 65 00 61) is on ave de la République.

Bus Les Beaux Voyages (☎ 04 95 65 15 02) travels from Bastia (80FF, 2¼ hours) Monday to Saturday year-round, but they don't carry bikes. Travelling from Ajaccio by bus requires an overnight stop in Porto; SAIB (☎ 04 95 22 41 99) operates between the three cities. It has one service a day from Porto to Calvi (100FF plus 50FF for the bike, three hours, mid-May to mid-October only) and two daily (one on Saturday, none on Sunday) between Ajaccio and Porto (170FF plus 50FF per bike, 2¼ hours, year-round).

Corte

Train Trains from Corte go to Bastia, Ajaccio and Calvi; see the Getting Around Corsica section earlier for details.

Bus Corte is on the Bastia-Ajaccio bus route operated by Eurocorse (☎ 04 95 31 73 76). Buses from Corte leave from Le Grand Cafe du Bar Colonna daily. A single to Bastia costs 50FF, and to Ajaccio 65FF. A bike costs 30FF (only one or two carried per day).

From mid-April to mid-September, Autocars Cortenais (☎ 04 95 46 02 12) runs buses between Corte and Bastia via Ponte Leccia on Monday, Wednesday and Friday (50FF, 1¼ hours). The bus leaves from the Corte Voyages agency at 19 cours Paoli. It doesn't carry bikes.

THE RIDE
Calvi

Calvi is a thriving little town stretched along its bay under the Citadelle and Monte Cinto. The closest town to France, Calvi was once a Genoese stronghold. In 1794, a British expeditionary fleet assisting Pasquale Paoli's Corsican nationalist forces (see the History section earlier) besieged and bombarded Calvi. In the course of the battle the famous British naval commander Horatio Nelson was wounded by rock splinters and lost the use of his right eye.

Calvi hosts a very popular week-long jazz festival in mid-June.

Information The tourist office (☎ 04 95 65 16 67, fax 04 95 65 14 09, e omt.calvi @wanadoo.fr) is in the marina, above th harbour master's office *(capitainerie)*. It ca provide a variety of brochures and informa tion about the town (open daily until 7 pn June to October; in the other months it close at 5.30 pm weekdays and on Saturday after noon and Sunday).

A branch of Société Générale is on blv Wilson. The Crédit Agricole is at 8 ave de l République, opposite the council offices The post office, on blvd Wilson, has an ATM

Garage Ambrosini (☎ 04 95 65 02 13) o ave de l'Uruguay, near place Christoph Colomb, has basic spare parts and can d repairs. It also hires VTTs for 100/530F per day/week (closed weekends in winter)

Cyberc@fe: Cafe de l'Orient (☎ 04 95 6 00 19) is on quai Landry (open from 4 t 10 pm daily).

Things to See & Do Built at the end o the 15th century by the Genoese, Calvi' **Citadelle** towers over the town from it rocky promontory. It's definitely worth vis iting for the peculiar atmosphere. Th tourist office organises guided tours.

In the Citadelle, the 13th-century **Églis St Jean Baptiste** has a splendid dome an the *Christ des Miracles*, an ebony statu said to have repelled besieging forces i 1553. Just off place d'Armes is the **Oratoir de la Confrérie St Antoine**. Behind th building's ornate facade are frescoes fron the 15th and 16th centuries. The Citadell has five **bastions**, which provide wonderfu views. Near the Bastion Celle, to the north west, is a plaque marking the alleged birth place of Christopher Columbus.

Behind the pink exterior of the Baroqu **Église Ste Marie Majeure**, in the heart of th lower town, is an impressive dome. Th church houses 16th- and 18th-century can vasses and a statue of the Assumption.

Activities include beach **swimming** glass-bottomed **boat trips** and **diving** Check at the tourist office or the marina.

Look out for the excellent local poly phonic chanting group **Focu du San Ghjuva** who perform at festivals and special events

Places to Stay Near the beach about 1.5kr south of the centre is *Camping La Pinède (☎ 04 95 65 17 80, fax 04 95 65 19 60)*. It ha shaded, quiet sites, a *restaurant*, bar, laun drette, *supermarket* and recreation facilities.

t costs 36FF per person and 12FF per site open April to mid-October). Almost opposite, on ave Christophe Colomb, is *Camping Paduella* (☎ 04 95 65 06 16), which is less pleasant but cheaper, at 29FF per person and 2FF for the site (open May to October).

The welcoming *Auberge de Jeunesse BVJ Corsotel* (☎ 04 95 65 14 15, fax 04 95 65 33 72, ave de la République) is practically opposite the train station. A bed in a lean room (with bathroom) for two to eight people costs 120FF, including a generous breakfast. Evening meals cost 60FF. You don't have to belong to the hostel network open March to November).

Outside peak season, couples will probably find better value in a hotel. *Hôtel du Centre* (☎ 04 95 65 02 01, 14 rue Alsace Lorraine) has decent doubles with basin for 60FF (230FF in August). Rooms with shower cost 180FF to 250FF, depending on the season. Credit cards aren't accepted open June to September).

Hôtel Belvédère (☎ 04 95 65 01 25, fax 04 95 65 33 20, place Christophe Colomb), open year-round, has pleasant doubles with bathroom and TV for 230FF in the low season, 280FF in late June, July and September and 380FF in August. The reception is gruff and the secure balcony for bikes is up the stairs.

Places to Eat A *market* is held every morning in summer (thrice weekly in winter) in place du Marché Couvert from around 8 am. The large, bakery-equipped *Super U* supermarket is at the southern end of ave Christophe Colomb (closed Sunday afternoon in summer and all Sunday in winter). *Annie Traiteur* at 5 rue Clémenceau sells outstanding fruit and vegetables and Corsican delicatessen specialities.

Away from the sometimes tacky harbour restaurants, beyond the Tour du Sel on the ferry quay, is *Le Chalet du Port* (☎ 04 95 65 46 30), a pleasant bar open long hours in the high season. The food is simple, good and affordable: grilled pizzas (35FF), kebabs (30FF) or a plate of charcuterie (48FF).

La Voûte (☎ 04 95 65 12 83) is in a little room under the old courtrooms in the Citadelle, where criminals condemned to death would have spent their last moments. The welcome is now warmer and the two 100FF *menus* are good value (open for dinner June to September).

Tao (☎ 04 95 65 00 73) was set up by Tao Kanbey de Kerekoff. In 1935 he opened Corsica's first cabaret in what was the palace of the bishops of Sagone, in the Citadelle. Excellent food – mains from 95FF to 140FF – come with a wonderful bay view.

Day 1: Calvi to Galéria
2–4 hours, 39.4km

Explore one of Corsica's most remote areas, in a hard day's riding over the spurs of the crumpled north-west coast. Giant ochre boulders stand sentry by the route, where only a low dry-stone wall at times separates the road from a plunge into the ocean's clear depths. Dark green maquis seasons the air with an aroma of wild herbs. Few settlements punctuate the route, a legacy of Muslim pirate slave raids in the 14th and 15th century, and of plagues and the war of independence against the Genoese.

Start early to escape the heat and the traffic, both of which pick up after about 10 am.

Leave the Calvi tourist office by heading up the small side street past the taxi rank and the Beaux Voyages office to ave de la République, which becomes blvd de la Wilson. On the outskirts of town stay on the main road, despite a sign that appears to point to the right to Porto.

At the junction 3.9km out of Calvi, a steep road leads left to the **Notre Dame de la Serra**, commanding a windswept hilltop studded by pink granite boulders. The church was built in the 1860s on the site of a 15th century sanctuary; today the main attraction is its magnificent view. On the main route, the road stays in the hills, tracing a series of bays.

Behind the headland of Capo a u Cavallo and Capo di a Morsetta, stunted olive trees and eucalypts provide occasional shade and shepherds footpaths riddle the scrub. A rough path leads to the imposing ruins of **Terra Mozza** (20km), once the hunting residence of Napoleon's nephew. The vista through the massive stone window frames is superb.

The route finally drops down to the coast at 22.9km, where a track leads to a crescent of **pebble beach** sloping into the refreshing, clear waters of the Baie de Crovani. Swimmers take care, although this is one of the day's rare chances to swim, the beach's slope and the swell can make it difficult to return to shore.

CORSICA

Days 1, 2 & 3: Calvi – Galéria – Porto – Evisa

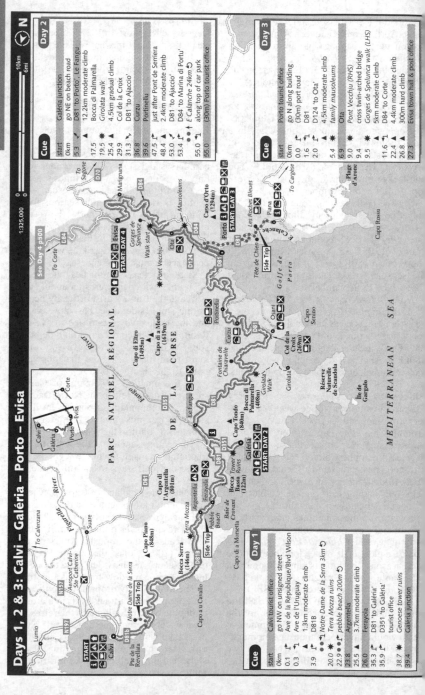

1:1,325,000

Cue — Day 1

0km	Calvi tourist office
0.1	go NW on unsigned street
0.3	Ave de la République/Blvd Wilson
	Ave de l'Uruguay
3.9	1.3km moderate climb
	D818
20.0	Notre Dame de la Serra 3km ↺
	Terra Mozza ruins
22.9	pebble beach 200m ↺
23.8	Argentella
25.5	3.7km moderate climb
26.0	Ferayola
35.3	D81 'to Galéria'
35.9	D351 'to Galéria'
	tourist office
38.7	Genoese tower ruins
39.4	Galéria junction

Cue — Day 2

0km	Galéria junction
5.3	go NE on beach road
	D81 'to Porto', Le Fangu
17.5	12.2km moderate climb
19.5	Bocca di Palmarella
25.4	Girolata walk
29.9	4.5km gradual climb
	Col de la Croix
31.3	D81 'to Ajaccio'
36.8	Curzu
39.6	Portinellu
47.5	just after Pont de Serriera
48.4	2.4km moderate climb
53.0	D81 'to Ajaccio'
53.4	D84 'to Marina di Portu'
	E Calanche 24km ↺
55.0	along top of car park
55.0	(30m) Porto tourist office

Cue — Day 3

0km	Porto tourist office
0.0	go N along building
	(30m) port road
1.6	D81
2.0	D124 'to Ota'
5.4	4.5km moderate climb
	family mausoleums
6.9	Ota
9.0	Pont Vecchju (RHS)
9.4	cross twin-arched bridge
9.5	Gorges de Spelunca walk (LHS)
11.6	5km moderate climb
	D84 'to Corte'
22.4	4.4km moderate climb
26.8	300m hard climb
27.3	Evisa town hall & post office

The hamlet of Argentella (23.8km) was once the base for a silver mine. Ferraghjola (26km, Ferayola) was also a mining community – iron ore was extracted nearby.

Galéria comes temptingly into sight at around 32km, before the road sweeps downhill and inland to skirt the Fangu delta. The syndicat d'initiative (tourist office; 35.9km) is in a little booth just across the five-arched bridge.

On the long, dry rise on the final approach to Galéria, one of Corsica's 90 Genoese coastal towers stands in ruins at the head of a crescent bay. The ride finishes at the junction of Galéria's two streets.

Galéria

This tiny, sleepy fishing village is the only settlement of any size on its stretch of coastline. Galéria is believed to have been first settled by the Phoenicians in the 6th century BC, and Roman artefacts suggest it was later the site of the important port. In the mid-15th century, Feudal wars and the Genoan occupation sent Corsicans into the hills. The area was deserted until the early 18th century, when families returned and staked contentious land claims based on occupation 'since time immemorial'.

Galéria is adjacent to the Fangu delta, protected as a nature reserve.

Information The tiny tourist office (☎ 04 95 62 02 27) is 3km from town, at the intersection of the D351 and the D81B. Galéria can fill up, so let the friendly staff here book accommodation (free service; closed noon to 4pm and all Sunday). Alternative accommodation is available in Le Fangu, on the Day 2 route.

Galéria has two streets, which are unnamed, but are known as rue de la village (the village road) and rue de la plage (the beach road). The post office (on the village road) and Ideal Camping (see Places to Stay) change money. Basic bike repairs might be possible at the camping ground, which hires VTTs for 120FF a day.

Things to See & Do Several paths lead down the cliff to Galéria's sandy beach; 500m out of town, below the tower, is the red pebble Plage de Ricinccia, the nudist haunt. Galéria's wild atmosphere and unique dive sites make it irresistible to divers, and

the tiny village boasts Corsica's largest dive centre, L'Incantu (☎ 04 95 62 03 65, fax 04 95 62 03 66), a friendly place in the hotel of the same name behind the church.

Tra Mare e Monti (☎ 04 95 65 21 26) hires inflatable motor dinghies for trips around the bay (including to Girolata).

Several walks leave from Galéria, including a 6½-hour trip across the peninsula to Girolata (accessible only on foot or by boat). The tourist office has details of other walks, including a 2½-hour walk in the Fangu delta. Here an alder wood creates an environment unique on Corsica; with its marshy environment, ferns, lianas and hops, it is more like cold European forest than the usual Mediterranean scrub, and it teems with rare wildlife.

Places to Stay & Eat The *Ideal Camping* (☎ 04 95 62 01 46, fax 04 95 62 07 46), on the river on the beach road, has lovely shaded sites. It charges 27FF per person and 13FF per site. It has the only public washing machines in town. If it's full, try the *Deux Torrents* camping ground (☎ 04 95 62 00 67, fax 04 95 62 03 32) 3.5km north of town, on the D81, across the river from the tourist office (open June to September).

The 30-bed gîte d'étape *L'Étape Marine* (☎ 04 95 62 00 46), about 1km up the Calca road (leading off the village road), recommends booking a month in advance. A bed in a clean, simple four-bed room costs 70FF. Its *restaurant's* filling *menu* costs around 80FF (open late-March to early November). *Demi-pension* (half-board) costs 140FF.

The *Auberge Galéris* (☎ 04 95 62 02 89), close to the water, up a long driveway beside the Hôtel le Filormosa, charges 170FF for a plain but airy double with shower, toilet, bidet and ocean view. Breakfast costs 25FF.

L'Auberge (☎ 04 95 62 00 15), opposite the church on the village road, has small, older doubles with shower and toilet for 280/330FF (low season/July), including breakfast. Its *restaurant* serves excellent, home-style Corsican meals (the best fish soup on the island!); the *menu* costs 90FF.

The two-star *Hôtel le Filormosa* (☎ 04 95 62 00 02, fax 04 95 62 03 44), across from the beach, has doubles with bath or shower and big balconies overlooking the ocean for 250FF (375FF for a triple). Its *restaurant* has *menus* from 85FF.

The basic **Supermarché Galéria** (☎ 04 95 62 00 04), 150m up the village road, is closed Sunday afternoon outside July and August.

Several waterside **restaurants** serve cheap pizzas and sandwiches. **A Sulana bar-glacier** is popular; sandwiches cost from 25FF, and salads, crepes, fish and pizzas 38FF to 53FF.

In a small wooden building with a balcony over the water, the **Loup de Mer** (☎ 04 95 62 04 15) is popular for upmarket dining, specialising in *langoustine* (crayfish); expect to pay around 55FF per 100g, with a minimum order of 300g. *Menus* start at 140FF.

Day 2: Galéria to Porto
2¾–5½ hours, 55km

A day with scenery defying superlatives, the wild coastline becomes even more rugged as the route drops into the shattered red granite landscape of the Golfe de Porto. It's not an easy day, though the main climb to the Bocca di Palmarella, followed by the Col de la Croix (Bocca di A Croce), is more steady than the rollercoaster route of Day 1. Both passes provide spectacular viewpoints; allow extra time to enjoy them. The route travels through only three small towns, although in tourist season a cafe is likely to set up in a shack at either of the passes.

Bus horns echo through the hills as traffic negotiates the sinuous coast road from the south – at several corners there is room for only one vehicle, meaning buses have to reverse to passing bays. As usual, drivers are courteous to cyclists. Cyclists are likely to travel faster than the vehicles downhill, so avoid getting stuck behind a tour bus.

Backtrack out of town, continuing straight ahead at the tourist office towards the jagged peaks of the Capo Tondo range. Le Fangu (Fango; 5.3km) marks the start of the hills, with the route clinging to the side of a deep river valley as it twists steadily towards the **Bocca di Palmarella** (408m; 17.5km). It gives a sweeping vista towards the rugged, forested Réserve Naturelle de Scandola and the town of Girolata, where the Mediterranean Ocean is so clear it's possible to see the bottom from the lookout. The **walk** to Girolata can be accessed at 19.5km. The ride passes a pretty, typical Corsican fountain, the **Fontaine de Chiaravelle** at 23.8km, providing a welcome place for a drink.

At the **Col de la Croix** (29.9km; 269m), it's a five-minute walk to the col's namesake crucifix and expansive coastal vistas to the north and south. On the descent shepherds dry-stone huts cling to the plunging hillside; look out for what must be the steepest set of herding yards in the world.

At Curzu (36.8km) the plain, multi-storey houses built from the local red granite defy attempts at guessing their age – they could be three years old or 300. Livestock is likely to wander onto the route on the long downhill 4km past Portinellu (39.6km).

All that height lost has to be regained on the last hard climb for the day, through stunning surroundings. Here the road is chiselled out of the crimson rock, forming a narrow, walled strip between the jagged cliff face and the precipice.

Consider your accommodation options before dropping into Porto – the town is scattered over the hillside, with the hotels by the port commanding higher prices. Some good hotels on the entry to town are ideally located for Day 3.

Side Trip: Piana & E Calenche
1–2 hours, 24km

The towering red granite pillars of E Calenche (rocky towers; in French Les Calanques) rise up to 300m from the sea, carved into a menagerie of forms by water and wind. Corsican legend says the Calenche is the work of the Devil: piqued by a shepherdess rejecting his advances, he created an eerie rockscape of his enemies, including representations of the shepherdess and her fiance.

The Calenche is best seen at sunset, when it combusts from ochre to blood red. Ideally this side trip would be stretched over an extra day, to allow time for some of the walking paths. However, cycling along the road that twists through this UNESCO-protected site is not to be missed, and could be tacked onto the end of Day 2 or the start of Day 3. Leave your panniers in Porto if possible, as it's a 400m climb.

At the intersection of the Marine road and the D84, stay on the D84 then follow the signs onto the D81 to the Calanche. The magic starts at the **Tête de Chien** (Dog's Head), a distinctively shaped boulder sign-posted on a large bend (7km). Here a walking track leads in 20 to 30 minutes to the Château Fort (Fortress), a natural platform with stunning views over the Golfe de Porto and the deep rocky inlets of E Calenche.

Don't finish the side trip here, however, as he rock crowds the road from this point to create 2.5km of dramatic cycling country.

The Calenche ends 2km before **Piana**, but it's worth continuing to this village to explore its narrow streets and visit its 18th-century church. One of the area's best beaches is another 1.5km south: the pebble **Plage d'Arone** is in a small cove carved out of the plunging cliffs. However, it's a 4km ride down and a masochist's climb back, with several sections of 16% grade and an average gradient of 9%.

Backtrack to Porto on the same route.

Porto (Portu)

Among the eucalypts at the edge of a wild bay, Porto sits on a small cove. The maquis-covered granite peaks encircling the town are dominated by the gargantuan massif of Capo d'Orto. Once just the port for the mountain village of Ota, today Porto attracts tourists drawn to its striking scenery and proximity to the stunning E Calenche and Scandola. In summer it becomes extremely busy. The harbour – La Marine – is divided from the upper town by Vaïta, or Porto-le-Haut. La Marine is cut in two by the Porto River.

Information Most of the staff at the friendly tourist office (☎ 04 95 26 10 55, e ot-porto@sitec.fr) in Porto Marine's car park speak English and can provide information on activities and walks (closed weekends outside July and August). The PNRC information office (☎ 04 95 26 15 14) is also in Porto Marine.

The only ATM is on the D84 in Vaïta. It takes all major credit cards. A bureau de change operates next to the pharmacy (closed weekends outside July and August). The small post office is on the D84 in Vaïta.

The bike hire outlet, Porto Location (☎/fax 04 95 26 10 13), opposite supermarket Banco on the D81, may be able to help with repairs. VTT hire costs 90/400FF a day/week. The shop also hires scooters and cars, but opens only for the tourist season, until 9 pm daily.

Things to See & Do Standing guard over the entrance to the fishing harbour, Porto's **Genoese tower** is an ideal place to watch the sun set over the gulf. The square tower, built in 1549, is on the UNESCO world heritage list and was restored in 1993.

Two companies arrange **boat trips** from Porto to the Réserve Naturelle de Scandola between April and October: Nave Va (information from Hôtel Le Cyrnée, ☎ 04 95 26 15 16) and Porto Linea (tickets and information from Hôtel Monte Rosso; see Places to Stay). To explore the Golfe de Porto on your own, hire **inflatable motor dinghies** from the crazy golf course in Porto Marine.

The Golfe de Porto is Corsica's **diving** gem. Granite plunges towards deep abyss' in the middle of the gulf. While the Réserve Naturelle de Scandola to the south is off-limits to divers, between Easter and October operators arrange dives around its boundary, where an abundance of marine life can be found. The Centre de Plongée du Golfe de Porto (☎/fax 04 95 26 10 29) is just after the bridge over the Porto River, opposite Les Oliviers camping ground. Génération Bleue (☎/fax 04 95 26 24 88) is right on the marina, next to the gangway on the right-hand side.

The **open-air cinema**, Cinesia, screens films in the eucalyptus forest in Porto Marine in summer.

Days 2 & 3: Galéria – Porto – Evisa

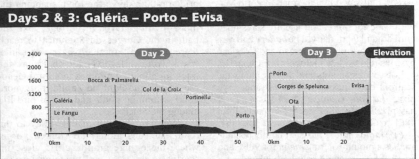

CORSICA

Places to Stay The friendly *Camping Sole Vista* (☎ *04 95 26 15 71, fax 04 95 26 10 79*) is the most convenient camping ground, as it's at the high end of town, on the D81 (south of the supermarkets). It has shady, secluded sites and clean bathroom facilities, charging 29FF per person and 10FF for the site. The *Camping Municipal* (☎ *04 95 26 17 76*), across the river from the marina, has less shade and basic facilities. Fees are 28FF per person and 10FF for the site (open June to September).

Although Porto has lots of hotels, the town virtually shuts at the end of summer. *Le Maquis* (☎ *04 95 26 12 19, fax 04 95 26 12 77*) is about 2km before the tourist office at the intersection of the D81 and the road to Ota (Day 3 route). This pleasant hotel offers five very basic doubles. Those with outside toilets cost 120FF or 150FF depending on the season. Demi-pension (from 200FF per person) is compulsory in August (closed for a few weeks in November/December and January/February).

Hotel le Colombo (☎ *04 95 26 10 14, fax 04 95 26 19 90*) is on the route into town and has breezy, beachy rooms. Tariffs include a copious breakfast, with freshly made jams (fig and walnut, Corsican preserved lemon, fresh mulberry – mmm). A double costs 300FF in June and September and 350/400FF in July/August (one person pays 40FF less). Prices are negotiable in the low season (closed December).

Places to Eat The *Banco* supermarket on the D81, near the pharmacy, has a bakery and is well stocked (closed Sunday afternoon, only open from April to October). *Timy* supermarket is next door. The Corsican products shop *Hibiscus* (☎ *04 95 26 16 05*), halfway down the road to Porto Marine, offers plates of Corsican specialities, with wine for 60FF, and usually stays open until around 9 pm daily. The *bakery* halfway down the port road sells bread and Corsican pastries (closed late October to Easter).

Lots of restaurants and hotels along the seafront have inexpensive *menus* and serve pizza. *La Tour Génoise* (☎ *04 95 26 17 11*) has pizza from 38FF to 55FF, pasta from 48FF to 60FF and a Corsican *menu* for 85FF. *Le Maquis* hotel's pleasant family restaurant has a mouthwatering *menu* for 90FF and an 140FF Corsican *menu*; book ahead.

La Mer (☎ *04 95 26 11 27*) in Porto Marine serves good seafood on its shaded terrace overlooking the gulf. It has excellent reasonably priced *menus* at 99FF and 138FF (open March to November).

Day 3: Porto to Evisa
1¼–2¾ hours, 27.3km

Climb into the cool of the interior, travelling high above the rugged Gorges de Spelunca and eventually leaving the maquis behind for dark groves of cork trees and chestnuts. Abandoned olive groves lie gnarled and overgrown by the road, and deserted cottages fall stone by stone into the gorges. Only a short day, it can easily be combined with the side trip to the E Calanche (see Day 2 Side Trip). There are opportunities to swim in icy streams and take time off the bike to walk to centuries-old Genoese stone bridges. Most families in the hills own a few pigs, which wander semi-wild before ending up as charcuterie (see the 'Wild Food of Corsica' boxed text overleaf). They are likely to amble out from the shadows to snuffle at your panniers – don't pet them, as they bite.

The little used Ota road is dominated by the Capo d'Orto massif to the south, though the spectacular views are mostly for the benefit of stone shepherds huts and elaborate **family mausoleums** (5.4km); it's said that in Corsica the best real estate is devoted to the dead. About 2km beyond tranquil Ota, after a hurtling descent past ancient olive trees, is the first of two Genoese bridges. The first, the graceful **Pont Veccjhu** (also known as the Pont de Pianella) is a perfect arch off the road to the right (9km). Scramble down the bank to see the bridge reflected in the pool at its base. It's possible to swim here. The pools near the next bridge (400m down the road, spanning the Aïtone and Tavulella Rivers) are much more inviting. Over the bridge, take the path to the **Gorges de Spelunca** to reach these pools, in a tumble of carved granite. It's a worthwhile diversion to follow the track for about 20 minutes to a third Genoese bridge, the **Pont de Zaglia**, plus more good swimming pools and lots of bird life among the alders.

It's a 2km slog out of the valley to the road that runs along the rugged gorge, where the orange granite cliffs close in, soaring to the right and plunging into the turbulent confluence of five rivers on the left. The climbing continues. At the turn-off to the hill-perched village of Marignana is a typical Corsican water fountain, **Fontaine d'Araghiu**. It's a good place to soak your shirt for the last dry, exposed section to Evisa.

Evisa

The peaceful mountain village of Evisa is popular with walkers in summer because it is where the Mare a Mare (Ocean to Ocean) and Mare e Monti (Ocean to Mountain) paths meet. A chestnut fair is held here every November.

Evisa has no information office; the post office and camping ground (see Places to Stay & Eat) will change money. The post office is below street level, on the right, in the middle of the village.

After you've sampled some of the Corsican delicacies at one of the shops in the main street, there's little to do in Evisa, but relax and enjoy the view. The **Casa di l'Artigiani** (Artisans Centre; ☎ 04 95 26 22 24) on the main street might be open.

Places to Stay & Eat The *Camping l'Acciola* (☎ 04 95 26 23 01, fax 04 95 26 20 29) is 2.4km (and 65m of climbing) out of town; turn right at the junction of the D70 and the D84, following signs to Ajaccio, and travel for 400m (although the sign at the turn-off says only 150m). Its *restaurant* serves 100FF and 130FF *menus* and snacks at all hours. Charges are 27FF per person and 12FF for the site (open June to September).

The *Gîte d'Étape d'Evisa* (☎ 04 95 26 21 88), near the post office at the end of a narrow street – turn right 300m after the Châtaignerie hotel – is prized among walkers for its warm reception. It charges 60FF per night in a pleasant, clean dormitory, or 160FF for generous demi-pension (open April to October).

La Châtaignerie (☎ 04 95 26 24 47) at the entrance to the village is the best place to stay. Its lovely doubles with shower cost 180FF in low season, 200FF mid-May to mid-July and 250FF mid-July to mid-September. Its *restaurant* has an excellent reputation, with an appetising 80FF summer lunch *menu* and a 95FF dinner *menu*. The wines are reasonably priced and credit cards are accepted (open March to October). Bikes have to be locked outside.

L'Aïtone (☎ 04 95 26 20 04, fax 04 95 26 24 18), 600m past the *mairie* (town hall), has pleasant doubles with a terrace, although these are expensive (from 420FF to 600FF). Cheaper rooms cost 200FF, according to the time of year. Open from May to September, it has a panoramic view and a swimming pool. Its *restaurant* offers *menus* from 95FF to 130FF. It has a garage for bikes.

Ceccaldi supermarket is on the right in the lower end of town (it has a long Sunday lunch break).

Several cafes in the village serve snacks; *Restaurant u Caracutu*, with a vine shaded outdoor eating area, is very friendly. It's on the left past the post office.

Day 4: Evisa to Corte
3½–6¾ hours, 67km

This spectacular route takes Corsica's highest road, passing through a medley of landscapes. Climb steadily from Evisa through the fragrant pinewood of the Fôret d'Aïtone, cross the alpine meadows and bald rock forms of the Col de Vergio, then wind through a clatter of shattered grey granite in the Scala di Santa Regina gorge. Most of the last 13km into Corte is a challenging climb through barren country. Start early to beat the heat and take advantage of the walking opportunities. Drink up at the several water fountains along the route (at 1.8km, 11km, 23.1km, 27.9km, 34.5km and 36.6km).

In the **Fôret d'Aïtone** thousands of Laricio pines soar up to 50m tall. The 1670-hectare forest also has significant numbers of beech, maritime pine, fir and larch, providing the base for a famous plant extract industry. Look for signposts to the left for the trail to the **piscine naturelle d'Aïtone** (4.4km), where the remains of three chestnut mills return to nature after a century of disuse, their enormous granite grinding stones, slowly breaking into pieces (see the 'Wild Food of Corsica' boxed text overleaf). Nearby a small waterfall feeds a natural pool.

On the left (6.9km), the short **Sentier de la Sittelle** (Nuthatch Path; the Corsican nuthatch is a bird endemic to the island), signposted by the Office Nationale des Fôrets (ONF), offers the chance to explore the forest. Climb to the rock platform behind the trees for a great view down the valley.

The forest thins to a low alpine meadow towards the **Col de Vergio** (1467m). The

CORSICA

pass is dominated by a large statue of Christ by Bonardi. A one-hour hike to the **Bergeries de Radule** (a shepherd's summer mountain dwelling) departs from behind the tourist cafe shack at the pass. It crosses swathes of aromatic mountain heath and drops into a crystalline alpine stream. Another 30 minutes past the bergerie is a waterfall. A map is plastered to the wall of the *cafe* where food is very reasonably priced (5FF coffee, 10FF chestnut cake, and 10FF for ¼L of good red wine).

The descent into the Forêt de Valdu-Niellu is fun; take care on the hairpin bend 4km down. The Laricio pines here are all that remains of the once vast forest that cloaked the region known as the Niolo. Taken from the Corsican for 'afflicted' *(niellu)* the region's name is even more ap-

propriate now most of it has been reduced to bare granite by fire. Plenty of picnic tables dot the route, along with the fountains mentioned earlier. The route crosses the Calasima River on a new bridge that has replaced the steeply arched Genoese **Pont Altu** (33.3km). The clear pools below are popular **swimming spots**. After Calacuccia (39.1km) and its large dam, the road plunges into the jaws of the Scala de Santa Regina, a tight valley with cliffs crashing into the river below. Until the tightly winding road was built in the 19th century, shepherds travelled along the valley walls on vertiginous mule tracks *(scala)*. Today bridges such as the stunning **Pont de l'Accia** (45.9km) carry the road around the cliffs.

A little after the bridge at the one-house hamlet of Santa Regina, look carefully

Wild Food of Corsica

Like its rugged coastline and wild mountains, Corsican food has a raw character, with intense flavours and farm-made products.

The island is not an easy place for vegetarians, who may have to settle for *omelette au brocciu* (cheese omelette) or stuffed eggplant. But omnivores can make the most of a kilojoule-burning cycle tour to sample Corsica's culinary delights.

Perhaps best known is the island's *charcuterie* (cured meats) made from semi-wild pigs fattened on *châtaigne* (chestnuts). Most products are still made in the farmhouse, with *prisuttu* (ham) being the true test of the maker's skill. Lower-quality hams are made into *salamu*, while other preserved meats include *coppa*, from the back of the pig, and *figatellu*, from the liver and innards. The ham is taken into mountain huts to dry, and is protected from heat in a basement, curing for up to two years. The meat of wild pig, *sanglier*, is also very popular, appearing in dishes like *civet de sanglier aux myrtes sauvage* (stew of boar with wild myrtle).

Until the last quarter of the 20th century chestnuts formed the staple diet of the island's human inhabitants, and the tree was known as *l'arbre à pain* (bread tree). The nut was dried, ground into flour and traded for olive oil, cheese and wine. Today chestnut flour still plays an important part in Corsican cooking, used in *castagnacciu*, a moist chestnut cake, and *fritelli*, deep-fried pastries, among other things.

The *maquis*, the dense shrubs and wild herbs that cloak Corsica's coastal areas, imparts distinct characteristics to many island specialities. Maquis herbs are used to flavour omelettes and to coat charcuterie, and its plants contribute to Corsica's diverse range of honeys (the first honey in France to receive an Appellation Originé Control quality-control rating). The best-known fruit of the maquis is the clementine, the island's symbol and the only Corsican fruit to be awarded an appellation. This citrus can only be sold with a few leaves attached, providing an instant freshness indicator.

Although the Genoese occupation of the coast ensured seafood didn't become an integral part of the Corsican diet, products of the sea feature heavily on menus today. Try the thick fish soup *(soupe au poisson)*, served with croutons smeared with mayonnaise and grated cheese.

Wine making has also improved in recent years, though vines were introduced to Corsica by the Greeks and Romans before the Christian era. A post-WWII program of subsidies to produce quality wines has paid off and Corsica now produces a few excellent wines, most of which should be drunk young.

among the boulders on either side of the road 50.2km) for **cave dwellings** used by shepherds on their route between the mountains and the coast. Walk behind the large boulders on the right to discover several rooms ingeniously created in natural shelters.

Stock up on water before crossing the Pont de Castirla (53.8km) and turning onto the D18. After the **cork grove** (55km) near Castirla, the monotony of the last 10km make it a long, hot climb to Collo di Quilico (654m) and onto Corte. The route enters the town on the main street, cours Paoli, which divides Ville Haute (High Town) and the Citadelle to the west, and the Ville Basse (Low Town) and the new quarter to the east. The tourist office is in the Citadelle, but several accommodation options are off this main street.

Corte (Corti)

The capital of Corsica, Corte is a hardy mountain town seemingly growing out of the rock on which its Citadelle is built. Although today home to the national university, Corte retains its rough edges, and street cafes host burly men smoking fat cigars and drinking Ricard with their morning short blacks. The town's peeling facades and unimposing buildings hardly do justice to its significant place in the island's history, or its efforts to remain a centre of Corsican culture.

Founded in 1419 by the Corsican viceroy Vincentello d'Istria, Corte was the only fortified town in central Corsica. Its strategic position – halfway between Bastia and Ajaccio – meant the town witnessed all of the battles against Genoese rule. It was the home of Pascal Paoli's first independent Corsican government between 1755 and 1769; he established the university here in 1765 (the university was reopened in 1981 to satisfy the nationalists' demands).

From Paoli's 1769 defeat, Corte was a French garrison town, and was even used as a base by the French Foreign Legion when it left North Africa in 1962.

Information The Maison du Tourisme et de la Culture (☎ 04 95 46 26 70, fax 04 95 46 34 05, e corte.tourisme@wanadoo.fr) is in the Caserne Padoue, formerly a prison and barracks, on the right of the Citadelle entrance off place du Poilu. The staff can supply a small town map and a list of places to stay; they can tell you which hotels have

places but won't make bookings (open Monday to Saturday until 6 pm in summer, and until 3 pm, with a lunch break, the rest of the year).

The PNRC Office (☎ 04 95 46 27 44) is next door; it supplies walking brochures and advice on itineraries (open daily in summer and autumn).

Several banks are on the north side of cours Paoli, including Crédit Lyonnais and Crédit Agricole, which both have ATMs. The main post office is on ave du Baron Mariani.

Kick Moto (☎ 04 95 46 29 83), 19 bis cours Paoli (actually up the small lane across from place Padoue), will do basic bike repairs and sells spare parts.

Things to See & Do The 'Parcours Patrimonial' pamphlet listing the town's **historic sites** is available from the tourist office.

It's well worth exploring the Citadelle. To its south, at the top of steps cut into the Restonica marble, is the old **chateau**. Prettily restored, this small fortified building was built in 1419 and extended by the French in the 18th and 19th centuries. Head to the rock **lookout** south of the Citadelle at sunset for a spectacular view of the orange-bathed battlements.

The FRAC (Fonds Régional d'Art Contemporain, ☎ 04 95 46 22 18), in the same building as the tourist office, often exhibits **Corsican artists**. Signs all around town point towards the studios of several **potters**, making unusual green- and blue-glazed terracotta pieces.

The **Musée de la Corse** (☎ 04 95 45 25 45) includes a floor of traditional Corsican objects and another of contemporary subjects, plus temporary exhibitions.

The **Palazzu Naziunale** (National Palace), the large rectangular building on the left before the Citadelle entry, used to be the palace of the Genoese lieutenant, and housed Paoli's government. Paoli lived in the palace, which was also the site of his groundbreaking university. The Palace still houses the library of the **Centre de Recherches Corses**, which contains everything ever written on Corsica and the area around Corte, and keeps copies of the nationalist press.

Altipani (☎ 04 95 61 09 88, e Altipani @infonie.fr) runs daily **walking tours** and evening strolls from late June until early September.

CORSICA

Days 4 & 5: Evisa – Corte – Gorges de la Restonica – Corte

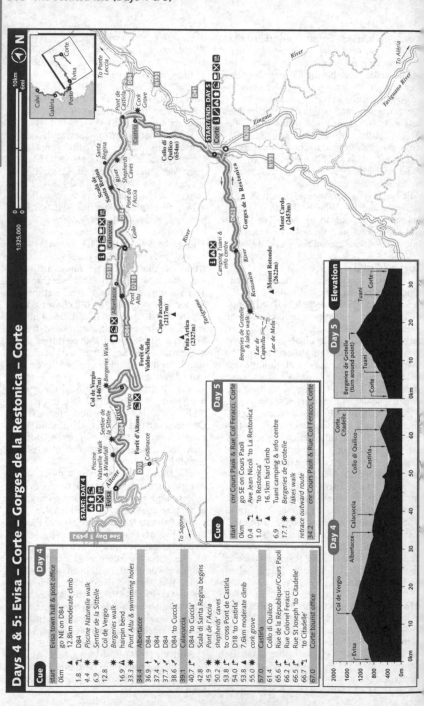

Cue — Day 4

start		Evisa town hall & post office
		go NE on D84
		12.8km moderate climb
1.8		D84
4.4	✱	Piscine Naturelle walk
6.9	✱	Sentier de la Sittelle
12.8		Col de Vergio
	✱	Bergeries walk
16.9		hairpin bend
33.3	✱	Pont Altu & swimming holes
34.4		Albertacce
36.9		D84
37.4		D84
37.7		D84
38.6		D84 'to Cuccia'
39.1		Calacuccia
40.7		D84 'to Cuccia'
42.8		Scala di Santa Regina begins
45.9		Pont de l'Accia
50.2	✱	shepherds' caves
53.8		D18 'to Castirla'
54.0		7.6km moderate climb
55.0	✱	cork grove
57.0		Castirla
61.4		Collo di Quilico
65.6		Rue de la République/Cours Paoli
66.5		Rue Colonel Feracci
66.5		Rue St Joseph 'to Citadelle'
66.7		'to Citadelle'
67.0		Corte tourist office

Cue — Day 5

start		cnr Cours Paoli & Rue Col Feracci, Corte
0km		go SE on Cours Paoli
0.4		Ave Jean Nicoli 'to La Restonica'
1.0		'to Restonica'
		16.1km hard climb
6.9		Tuani camping & info centre
17.1	✱	Bergeries de Grotelle
	✱	lakes walk
		retrace outward route
34.2		cnr Cours Paoli & Rue Col Feracci, Corte

Places to Stay At the bottom of town, *Camping Alivetu* (☎ 04 95 46 11 09, *allée du 9 Septembre*) is 1km along the road to Restonica. It charges 30FF per adult and 15FF for the site (open mid-April to early October).

More climbing is involved to reach the *Gîte d'Étape-Camping U Tavignanu* (☎ 04 95 46 16 85, fax 04 95 61 14 01), 1.5km from the centre. It charges 22FF per adult and 10FF per site. To get there, head west along chemin de Baliri on the west side of the Citadelle and look for signs to the camping ground, which is at the end of a narrow road 500m after the bridge (open Easter to October). It also has dorm beds (80FF including breakfast), available year-round.

Hôtel de la Poste (☎ 04 95 46 01 37, 2 place du Duc de Padoue) has basic, comfortable rooms (with shower and hall toilet) in a charming old building. Doubles cost 190FF (10FF more in high season). A warm welcome is guaranteed.

Hôtel HR (☎ 04 95 45 11 11, fax 04 95 61 02 85, 6 allée du 9 Septembre) is the largest hotel in Corte and also one of the cheapest. However, it is a little inconvenient for cyclists, at the bottom end of town. The rooms are pleasant; doubles start at 145FF. Book ahead.

Hôtel du Nord et de l'Europe (☎ 04 95 46 00 68, 22 cours Paoli) is excellent. All rooms have showers and some are studio size. Doubles cost 200FF (240FF with toilet). Outdoor adventurers are welcomed.

Places to Eat The small *SPAR* supermarket is on ave Xavier Luciani (closed Sunday). The general store *Alimentation Bagnoli* (☎ 95 46 02 02), on cours Paoli, has better fruit and vegetables and is open daily.

The shaded outdoor tables at the friendly *Café de France* on place Padoue are always busy with locals and tourists; it opens early for croissants and coffee – and even kickstarting pastis! – and closes late.

Baghioni (☎ 04 95 46 02 67, 7 cours Paoli) is a little bakery selling delicious, freshly baked sweet and savoury pastries. Try the *gâteau aux châtaignes* (chestnut cake) in season.

At night, two caravans with wood fired ovens inside (!) sell *pizzas* for between 30FF and 45FF; the one at the corner of ave Xavier Luciani and cours Paoli is very good; the other is in place du Duc de Padoue.

U Museu (☎ 04 95 61 08 36, rampe Ribanelle) is the best place to eat out. In the Ville Haute, it's on the right before the Citadelle. The atmosphere and service are excellent, the prices reasonable and it serves good Corsican specialities. The *menus* are good value – the 89FF one includes fish soup, trout in peveronatta (pepper, wine and tomato) sauce, cheese and dessert (open daily in summer but closed on Sunday and during the school holidays out of season).

Au Plat d'Or (☎ 04 95 46 27 16, 1 place Paoli) is a small, upmarket restaurant. Food is a la carte and imaginative; starters cost around 49FF, and mains from around 100FF.

Day 5: Gorges de la Restonica Circuit

1¾–3½ hours, 34.2km

After the desolate landscape on the approach to Corte on Day 4, it's hard to believe a gem such as the glacial-carved Gorges de la Restonica exists nearby. A road climbs steeply up this spectacular granite gorge, where the snow-fed Restonica River rushes over worn boulders. It's well worth the effort to go to the road end, where walking tracks lead into the mountains. However, for a relaxing day, just ride the fairly easy first 3km out of Corte, where some beautiful rock pools are screened from the road by pine trees. After this point, the road is often too high above the river to allow easy access to the water.

Bear in mind the mountains are often still snowcapped in May; strong winds sweep through the gorge and you should carry raingear and warm clothes. Pack walking shoes if planning a hike.

The day begins at the junction of cours Paoli and rue Colonel Feracci. The route to the gorge is well signed from Corte and though the road is extremely steep in places, many viewpoints provide places to stop and catch your breath. The lovely *Auberge de la Restonica* (☎ 04 95 45 25 25, fax 04 95 61 15 79), 2km from Corte, and the *Camping Tuani* (6.9km, ☎ 04 95 46 11 65) could be alternatives to staying in Corte. An information point (☎ 04 95 46 33 92) is open at Tuani until 8 pm daily from mid-June to mid-September. Look out for *mouflons* (mountain sheep), royal eagles and peregrine falcons.

A water fountain at 14.6km breaks the climb. At the top of the gorge is a hamlet of shepherds stone huts, the **Bergeries de Grotelle**, where the shepherds have made some concessions to tourism by installing cafe tables outside their homes. The best views are to be had at *Chez Felix*, run by its namesake *berger* (shepherd), who has a prime, isolated position about 15 minutes along the highly recommended **lakes walk**. Felix makes his own soft, fresh, delectable sheep's cheese *(fromage de brebis)* and sells huge rounds of it for 35FF; he also makes sandwiches with a friend's home-cured charcuterie and sells good wine for 5FF a glass.

The walk to **Lac de Melu** (1711m) and **Lac de Capitellu** (1930m) takes about 1¾ hours (one hour to the first lake). The path is signposted in yellow from the car park. The path to Lac de Melu follows the right bank of the Restonica for most of the way, before branching into two tracks. The track that continues

Bergers of Corsica

A shepherd sits on a stone wall beside his windswept cottage, carving knobbly, dark salami with a thick knife and tearing at a loaf of bread. The scene could be hundreds of years old, but exists today in the high mountains of Corsica. Here, more than 900 *bergers* (shepherds) and goatherds continue the practice of transhumance, moving their flocks to mountain pastures in summer, and back to the warmer coast in winter; their *bergeries* (stone huts) dot the mountains and sheep's bells ring out across the valleys.

The part of the day that isn't spent scrambling into the mountains to herd their flock home for the evening is spent milking and making cheese. The most famous is the Corsican *brocciu* (*broccio* in French), made by heating the whey left over from the regular cheese-making process. This soft, delicate product is eaten within three days of production, often appearing on menus in *omelette au brocciu* or, more challengingly, *brocciu à l'eau de vie*. For this dessert, brocciu is sprinkled with sugar and doused in rough Corsican brandy *(eau de vie)*.

Other cheeses are left to ripen over several months, intensifying their flavour; it's said they're like Corsicans, as their rough appearance disguises a soft heart.

along the bank is harder but is less likely to have snow on it in winter and spring.

Take care cycling the descent, which is seriously steep in places.

Corsica – the South

Duration	5 days
Distance	226km
Difficulty	hard
Start	Ajaccio
End	Bonifacio

Discover Corsica's most significant prehistoric sites on a tour that rollercoasts around the coast before climbing inland into the island's mysterious centre, where the tradition of the vendetta lives on. Climb through the ancient region of the Alta Roca to the popular hiking centre of Zonza, the departure point for a stage to the beautiful Col de Bavella. End the tour in Bonifacio, the jewel of Corsican cities.

PLANNING
See Planning under The Scented Isle ride earlier.

GETTING TO/FROM THE RIDE
Ideally, combine this ride with some in the Provence & Côte d'Azur chapter, such as the Alpes Maritime, Plateau de Caussols or Côte d'Azur Hinterland rides, which all leave from near Nice.

To do this ride after The Scented Isle ride, earlier in this chapter, catch a train between Corte and Ajaccio; to do this ride first, link from Bonifacio to Ajaccio by bus, then take a train to Calvi.

Ajaccio
See the Gateway Cities section (p489) for information on getting to/from Ajaccio.

Bonifacio
Air The nearest airport to Bonifacio is in Figari (☎ 04 95 71 10 10), 21km to the north. Air Liberté and Corse Air fly there.

Transports Rossi (☎ 04 95 71 00 11) connects with flights to provide a shuttle service to Bonifacio's harbour car park (50FF, 30 minutes) from late June to early September. It doesn't take bikes unless they're in a *housse* (bike bag). The trip from the airport to the centre of Bonifacio costs about 185FF in a taxi (station wagons will take bikes). Add 50% on Sunday, public holidays or at night.

Boat Boats leave Bonifacio only for Santa Teresa di Gallura in Sardinia (Italy). Booking offices are at the ferry terminal. See Italy under Sea in the Getting There & Away chapter for more detail.

Bus Eurocorse (☎ 04 95 70 13 79), with offices by the harbour, operates a Bonifacio to Ajaccio service, stopping at Porto Vecchio and several other places (110FF plus 50FF per bike, 3½ hours, only the first bus of the day takes bikes). Up to four buses depart daily during high season (two on Sunday and public holidays), and two daily in the low season (none on Sunday and public holidays).

The service to Porto Vecchio (40FF plus 25FF per bike, 30 minutes) connects with the Rapides Bleus bus (☎ 04 95 31 03 79) to Bastia, which also takes bikes on its morning service (115FF per person, 55FF per bike, three hours). From Bonifacio, buses leave at the small office opposite the harbour car park on ave Sylvère Bohn (the N196).

THE RIDE

Ajaccio

See Ajaccio (pp487–9) under Gateway Cities earlier in the chapter for information about accommodation and other services.

Day 1: Ajaccio to Porto Pollo

3¼–6½ hours, 63.9km

Be prepared for a long, hard day cycling the rollercoaster road around the Golfe d'Ajaccio and the Golfe de Valinco. In between are golden beaches and Genoese towers are lots of hills, some of them very, very steep (but short). It's a busy 12km to get out of Ajaccio's sprawl, but the hills don't start for another 18km, allowing time to enjoy some of the pleasant *plages* (beaches). This strip of coast has been extensively developed and in summer the beaches are dotted with restaurants, cafes and camping grounds.

From the Ajaccio tourist office, face the ocean and turn left onto quai l'Herminier/N193. Go straight, following signs to Bastia until the sixth roundabout (7.6km), where you turn right (following signs to Propriano). The **Tour de Capitello** appears above the marshes surrounding the airport.

Porticcio (Portichju; 16.2km) has a lovely **beach**, the last easily accessible water for 9km. To see a well-restored Genoese tower, take the short side trip to the **Tour de Isulella** (23.8km). Although the route passes several other towers, this is the easiest to get to. Travel 600m along the road towards the tower and look for a road discreetly signed to the *tour* (tower); a steep, short hill leads to 'Chemin de la Tour', which loops around the headland. Opposite the intersection, in the maquis on the left, a footpath climbs about 500m to the tower. Continue cycling around the loop for 1.8km to reach a road that drops down to the ocean, where granite boulders provide great swimming platforms.

More beaches are accessible at **U Ruppione** (25km), **Pietrocella** (28.8km) and **Verghja** (29.4km). At an intersection out of Verghja the road name changes to the D155 and the serious climbing begins. The first hill has an equally steep and twisting descent; halfway down is a **potter's studio** turning out pieces made in Provence-style designs that seem to be popular in the south. After the Portigliolo **beach** (34km) resist the temptation to go to the Castagna tower; after cycling a steep 2.4km guard dogs meet you at the locked gate.

The next extremely steep 1.3km averages a 10% grade, with a 13% section at the start. The very steep descent is followed by another hard climb, and the first 1.4km of 10% grade allows no time to catch your breath. From Acqua Doria it's a steady climb to the **Bocca di Canniccio** (43.6km), a good viewpoint. A long descent is followed by two more hills, with the second another very steep climb for the first 500m.

Serra di Ferro (58.5km) provides a welcome chance for a break; a stopover on the Mare e Monti (Ocean to Sea) walk, it's the only place to change money before Propriano (Day 2). A **knife maker** crafts beautiful pieces with timber and horn handles inset with precious metals (they start at around 1400FF). It's then downhill into Porto Pollo.

Porto Pollo (Porti Poddu)

Sweet little Porto Pollo is a cluster of houses along a few beaches. Although tourism is slowly encroaching, the Conservatoire du Littorale (Littoral Conservancy) has bought a chunk of land to try to preserve the unspoiled habitat.

Days 1 & 2: Ajaccio – Porto Pollo – Sartène

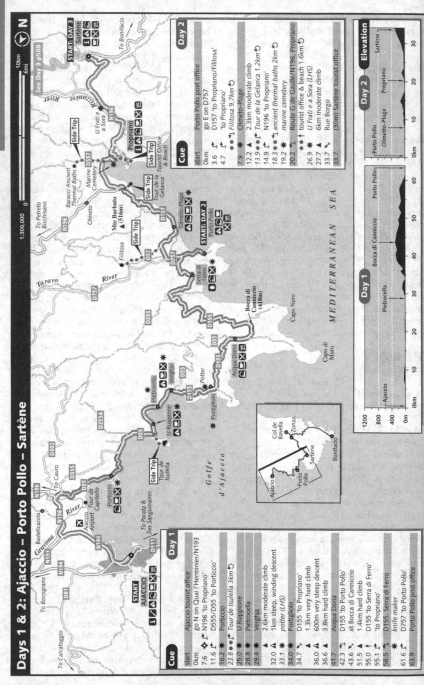

10km **6mi**
1:300,000

N

Cue — Day 1

0km	Ajaccio tourist office
	go N on Quai l'Herminier/N193
7.6	N196 'to Propriano'
11.6	D555/D55 'to Porticcio'
16.2	Porticcio
23.8	*Tour de Isulella 3km* ↩
25.0	U Ruppione
28.8	Pietrocella
29.4	Verghia
	2.6km moderate climb
32.0	1km steep, winding descent
	potter (LHS)
33.1	Portigliolo
34.7	D155 'to Propriano'
	1.3km very hard climb
36.0	600m very steep descent
36.6	3.8km hard climb
41.7	Acqua Doria
42.3	D155 'to Porto Pollo'
43.6	at Bocca di Canniccio
51.5	1.4km hard climb
55.0	D155 'to Serra di Ferro'
55.1	'to Propriano'
58.5	D155, Serra di Ferro
	knife maker
61.6	D757 'to Porto Pollo'
63.9	Porto Pollo post office

Cue — Day 2

start	Porto Pollo post office
0km	go E on D757
3.6	D157 'to Propriano/Filitosa'
4.7	'to Propriano'
	↑ Filitosa 9.7km ↩
7.9	Olmeto-Plage
12.2	2.3km moderate climb
13.9	*Tour de la Gelanca 1.2km* ↩
14.9	N196 'to Propriano'
18.3	*ancient thermal baths 2km* ↩
19.2	marine cemetery
20.2	Route G. de Gaulle/N196, Propriano
	tourist office & beach 1.6km (LHS)
26.9	*U Frati e a Sora (LHS)*
27.7	6km moderate climb
33.7	Rue Borgo
33.7	(30m) Sartène tourist office

Elevation

Day 1

Day 2

The town has no information centre, banking facilities or bike shop; its post office opens only from mid-July through August. The nearest place to change money is at Serra di Ferro (on the Day 1 route).

This is an excellent place to relax; laze on the **beach** and swim in the clear water. For more adventurous underwater exploration, talk to the **dive shops** near the *tabac* (tobacconist) and bakery.

Places to Stay & Eat The large *Camping U Caseddu* (☎ 04 95 74 01 80), at the entry to town, has little shade, but still tends to fill in summer. It has clean facilities, washing machines and a restaurant; charges are 31FF per person and 12FF per site (open May to early October).

Hôtel du Golfe (☎ 04 95 74 01 66), at the end of the village, is the cheapest hotel. Basic but clean doubles cost 200FF. Reception is generally at the pizzeria of the same name, by the harbour.

Hôtel Kallisté (☎ 04 95 74 02 38, fax 04 95 74 06 26) has comfortable, spotless rooms with telephone and bathroom and is the best option in Porto Pollo. Allow 280/310FF for a double room in the low season (maquis/sea view), 300/350FF in July. Demi-pension is available in July (350FF per person) and obligatory in August (400FF). Its *restaurant* has *menus* for 125FF and 140FF (open April to mid-October).

The *SETA Supermarché de la Plage* is by the beach, 500m past the camping ground (closed Sunday afternoon; may close seasonally).

At the harbour end of town, *La Bruscotta* bakery next to the tabac makes magnificent bread (open April to September).

L'Oasis, near the post office, serves pizzas, salads, crepes, omelettes and sandwiches starting from 20FF (open from 10 am until late daily).

Les Eucalyptus (☎ 04 95 74 01 52, fax 04 95 74 06 56), north of the supermarket, serves meals on its balcony, with *menus* from around 80FF.

Day 2: Porto Pollo to Sartène
1¾–3½ hours, 33.7km
Visit Corsica's most significant prehistoric site, Filitosa (allow an extra two hours), before the route turns inland to climb to Sartène, known as the most Corsican of the

island's towns. Another popular tourist strip, this section is peppered with campsites. Although the route takes a national road to Sartène, the traffic is not too heavy, even in high season.

From Porto Pollo, backtrack to the junction of the D757 and D155, continuing straight ahead. At 4.7km turn left for the side trip to climb to **Filitosa** (☎ 04 95 74 00 91). Inhabited from 5850 BC until the Roman period, the site's fortifications, buildings, megaliths and statue-menhirs – armed with swords and daggers – have been intensively studied since their accidental discovery in 1946. The hilltop site, shaded by olive trees (some up to a thousand years old), and the small **museum** are open daily from 8 am until sunset. Admission costs 22FF.

Olmeto-Plage (7.9km) is the start of a long strip of swimming beaches...and the start of the hills. The climbing is mostly gentle until the turn-off for the side trip to the **Tour de la Gelanca** (13.9km), a prettily restored tower at the bottom of a very steep hill. The detour is worth the return climb. After the next steep pinch it's downhill to Propriano, with the opportunity at 18.3km to detour on the D557 to the hot springs at the **Anciennes sources thermales de Baracci** (☎ 04 95 76 30 40). Once an elegant thermal resort, the main building is now closed, but it's still possible to bathe in the hot springs (admission 25FF, open from 9 am to 1 pm and 3 to 9 pm).

A sailor couldn't wish for a better burial place than the **marine cemetery** (*cimetière marin*; 19.2km) on a rise at the entrance to Propriano (Prupria). A busy timber port in the early 20th century, the town is now a summer holiday destination. At route Général de Gaulle, continue straight for 100m to reach the side street that leads to the tourist office and small harbour, where the waterside park has several taps to refill bottles and makes a good picnic spot. To reach a patrolled **beach**, continue for 600m along ave Napoléon.

After the climb out of town it's a gentle ride for 6km along the Rizzanèse Valley, where the sea breeze is likely to give gentle assistance and the kingfishers colourful company. A 2.5m-high *menhir* (standing stone) leans in the field to the left of the road at 26.9km, while its partner has fallen over. The pair, known as **U Frati e a Sora**, are said to have been a priest and a nun who ran away from Sartène for a dirty weekend and were turned into stone as God's punishment.

It's a steady climb past groves of cork trees into Sartène. The best hotels are 1.5km before the town; drop your bags if you want to explore.

Sartène (Sartè)

'The whole place breathes war and vengeance', poet Paul Valéry said about Sartène. This shadowy town seems to glare over the Rizzanèze Valley from its high granite walls. It was a bastion for large families of noblemen who didn't want anyone meddling in their business. The town has long been suspicious of outsiders, and for good reason. In 1583, pirates from Algiers carried 400 people into slavery in North Africa; such raids did not end until the 18th century. Sartène was long notorious for its banditry and bloody vendettas, and in the early 19th century a violent struggle between rival landowners deteriorated into house-to-house fighting, forcing most of the population to flee.

For a long time isolated and introverted, the town is now effectively the guardian of the island's traditions. Good Friday eve's Procession du Catenacciu, in which a shackled penitent carries a crucifix through the town, has been followed since the Middle Ages.

Information The syndicat d'initiative (☎ 04 95 77 15 40) is at 6 rue Borgo, a small lane running off place de la Libération (open weekdays from May to September).

The Crédit Lyonnais is on cours Général de Gaulle; the only ATM is outside the Crédit Agricole, at the bottom of cours Sœur Amélie near the petrol station.

The post office is on rue du Marché, not far from place de la Libération.

Sartène has no bike shop.

Things to See & Do The **old town** is a stone maze of steps and little streets, some of which are so narrow that a person can hardly pass through them. Don't miss the part that hasn't been turned into tourist shops, behind the museum.

Église Ste Marie, built in 1766, overlooks place de la Libération. It boasts a superb altarpiece. It also displays the chains and cross carried during the annual Catenacciu procession.

Go through the gateway below the town hall to reach the best of the old town, the **Santa Anna quarter** and its narrow streets.

The **Corsican Prehistory Centre** (☎ 04 95 77 01 09) is housed in a former prison. The cells display a collection of items of diverse origins and various ages, ranging back to the Neolithic era. Follow the steps off rue Antoine Crocce, which runs to the right behind place de la Libération.

Places to Stay The route into town is lined with several camping grounds. Small **U Farrandu** (☎ 04 95 73 41 69) is the closest, 2.5km before town; it's on the left of the N196 just before a bend. The facilities are clean, the service is friendly and the sites private and shady. Allow 33FF (total) for the first night and 30FF for subsequent nights (open from April to October).

Hôtel des Roches (☎ 04 95 77 07 61, fax 04 95 77 19 93), at the bottom of ave Jean Jaurès, is the only hotel in the centre of Sartène. The reception is chilly and its simple, old rooms are only worth the money if you can get one with the spectacular valley view. Doubles with bathroom cost 285 305FF (town/valley view). Its *restaurant* serves *menus* from 110FF.

The **Hôtel Rossi – Fior di Riba** (☎ 04 95 77 01 80, fax 04 95 77 09 58) is the best option. Its swimming pool is bliss after the long climb and the place has a warm, family atmosphere. Spotless and comfortable doubles cost 230/340FF low/high season. It's 1.5km and some climbing short of Sartène (open mid-March to mid-October). The posher **La Villa Piana** (☎ 04 95 77 07 04, fax 04 95 7. 45 65), next door, also has good, comfortable doubles ranging from 250/330FF (hall toilet) to 370/410FF (with balcony) in low/high season (open April to September).

Places to Eat The **market** is held on Saturday morning in the old town. Several **boulangers** and **fruit shops** line rue du Purgatoire. The **Super U** supermarket is at the bottom end of cours Sœur Amélie near the petrol station (closed Sunday).

The *cafes* surrounding place de la Libération serve light snacks and are great places for people watching.

U Passaghju (☎ 04 95 77 21 84), at the northern end of rue des Frères Bartoli, has a pleasant setting in the old town. It serves good *menus* for 60FF (lunch), 75FF and 95FF (open daily for lunch and dinner between April/May and September).

A Caramamu (☎ 04 95 77 07 84) is also in the old town; turn left after going go through the gateway by the town hall. With tables in the street and a wide range of *menus* until late, good pizzas cost 38FF to 52FF (open from late May to mid-October).

Day 3: Sartène to Zonza
2–4 hours, 39.9km

Cycle along the high sides of the Rizzanèse Valley, climbing deeper into the rugged heart of Corsica. In this region of the Alta Rocca the thick sounds of Corsican are likely to be overheard in villages that have changed little for hundreds of years. After the first 13km of mostly downhill, it's a steady, scenic climb to Zonza.

Out of Sartène the route follows the high road, passing through mountain hamlets and dark groves of cork trees. In the Granace intersection, marked by a well-tended water fountain (8.4km), rather than going sharp right, take the turn signed for Levie.

Just before crossing the bridge (13.4km) over the Fiumicicoli River, detour right to the quirky **Bains de Caldane** (☎ 04 95 77 00 34), where a hot spring feeds a small pool with 40°C water. Admission costs 20FF (open daily, 8 am to 8.30 pm).

From the bridge, the road climbs for the rest of the day, merging into the D268 at 15.1km and switching from the Fiumicicoli Valley into the Rizzanèse. Another water fountain is at 16.1km.

Once the stronghold of Rinuccio della Rocca, a fearsome warlord assassinated by the Genoese in 1511, **Ste-Lucie de Tallano** (Santa Lucia di Talla; 21.1km) remains prosperous. It retains many tall, grand 16th-century granite houses. Elm trees shade the Piazza di l'Ulmu and its large, elaborate **fountain**. In the square below, the **war memorial** features the famous – and extremely rare – rock quarried nearby, diorite oriculaire, known as Petra Uccjata (eye stone) in Corsican.

The town's Baroque **Église Paroissale** took on its present form in the 17th century, but dates to Roman times; inside is a finely worked bas relief of the Virgin and Child. The bar opposite has the church keys. The formidable **Casa Turra** fortified house behind

the church was built over the 15th and 16th centuries to harbour the town's residents in times of strife. The town post office may change money.

Follow the signs to the 18th-century **U Fragonu olive mill** (open 10 am to noon and 4 to 7 pm daily except Sunday), one of the oldest in the area and now converted to a museum. For tours ask at the mairie or the tourist office (☎ 04 95 78 41 95) across from the fountain.

On leaving, take care not to follow signs to Zoza, an entirely different town to Zonza. At the exit from town is the **Couvent St François** (21.5km), founded by Rinuccio in 1492 and currently being restored; the convent's main church might be open. Farther on, opposite the graveyard, the small, whitewashed **St Roch chapel** (22.7km) houses processional statues and is beautiful in its simplicity. Another **graveyard** at 25km makes for interesting exploring, and houses the ruins of the 9th- and 10th-century **chapel of Santa Maria Assunta**.

Prehistory fans might want to take the energetic detour to the Pianu de Levie (26.8km), where the **Casteddu di Cucuruzzu** (☎ 04 95 78 48 21) is Corsica's second most important prehistoric site after Filitosa. This Bronze Age (1400 BC) Torréen stone habitation retains several rooms. The mossy ruins are dominated by a *torri* (round tower) and surrounded by a large wall. From the D268, signs point left to a road that climbs fairly steeply for 1km before flattening out to climb to the plateau *(pianu)* and entrance. The 25FF admission includes a good recorded commentary in several languages (open daily 9 am to 7 pm between April and mid-October).

Levie (Livia; 30.1km), the capital of the Alta Rocca in the 18th century when it was larger than Sartène, is today a dusty village. The post office is the last place to change money until Day 5. The **Alta Rocca Museum** (☎ 04 95 78 47 98) showcases local artefacts, most significantly, the Dame de Bonifacio (Bonifacio Woman), the skeleton of a woman who died around 6570 BC, the oldest remains in Corsica (open Tuesday to Saturday between October and April, Monday to Saturday in May and June and daily from 10 am to 6 pm in high season).

Look out for the innovative, bike inspired gates (33.7km) at the entrance to San

CORSICA

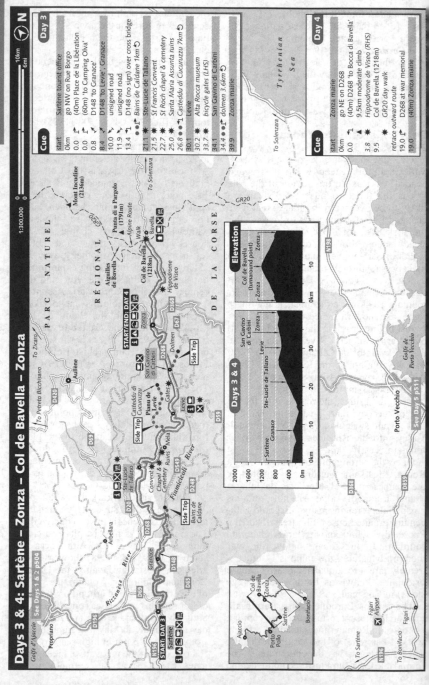

Days 3 & 4: Sartène – Zonza – Col de Bavella – Zonza

1:300,000

Day 3

Cue	
start	Sartène tourist office
0km	go NW on Rue Borgo
0.0	(40m) Place de la Libération
0.0	(60m) to Camping Olva'
0.8	D148 'to Granace'
8.4	D148 'to Levie ' Granace
10.0	unsigned road
11.9	unsigned road
13.4	D148 (no sign) over cross bridge
	Bains de Caldane 1km ↻
21.1	Ste-Lucie de Tallano
21.7	St Francis Convent
22.7	St Roch chapel & cemetery
25.0	Santa Maria Assunta ruins
26.8	↻ Casteddu di Cucuruzzu 7km ↻
30.1	Levie
30.2	Alta Rocca museum
33.7	bicycle gates (LHS)
34.1	San Gavino di Carbini
34.4	dolmen 3.6km ↻
39.9	Zonza mairie

Day 4

Cue	
start	Zonza mairie
0km	go NE on D268
0.0	(40m) D268 'to Bocca di Bavella'
3.8	9.5km moderate climb
9.5	Hippodrome de Viseo (RHS)
	Col de Bavella (1218m)
	GR20 day walk
	retrace outward route
19.0	D268 at war memorial
19.0	(40m) Zonza mairie

Elevation

Col de Bavella
(turnaround point)

Days 3 & 4

See Day 5 p511

Gavino di Carbini. Just after the water fountain (34.2km), a road leads to the right to several prehistoric sites. The best - but totally unsigned – is a magnificent **dolmen** hidden by a grove of trees. The detour involves climbing each way, but is well worthwhile. Take the turn signposted, strangely, with a historical marker to a menhir nearby. At 1.8km look for a small stone hut with a terracotta tiled roof (held down with rocks) to the right. Clamber over the stone wall opposite and follow an overgrown path into the trees. Among the cluster of large granite boulders is a moss-covered dolmen at least 2m tall. Another 300m along the road are the signposted standing stones, in a cleared field devoid of atmosphere.

After San Gavino the route enters chestnut forest and climbs past inspiring views of the stone 'needles' of the Aiguilles de Bavella before one last climb.

Zonza

This mountain village was briefly home to the exiled Mohammed V of Morocco in 1953 before he moved to Île Rousse. Now frequented by walkers and tourists heading for the famous peaks of Aiguilles de Bavella, the tiny town has amazing hotel resources.

The mairie (☎ 04 95 78 66 87), on the left at the entry to town, can supply basic tourist information (open until 5 pm weekdays). The nearest place to change money is at the post office in Levie (on the Day 3 route). The Zonza post office is on the D368. The nearest bike shop is in Porto Vecchio (Day 5).

Zonza is primarily a place of rest; find a cafe and enjoy the fabulous **views** of the Aiguilles de Bavella changing colour from ochre to golden with the passage of the sun. Stroll up the D368 to see the town's **older houses**, many of which are centuries old, and the church, which is sometimes open. Half a kilometre past the church is the **cemetery**, crowded with large family mausoleums.

Places to Stay & Eat The *Camping Municipal de Zonza* (☎ 04 95 78 62 74), on the banks of the Rizzanèse River, is a haven of tranquillity in the depths of the forest. It's on the D368 3km east of the village and charges 20FF per person and 14FF for the site (open mid-May to September).

Hôtel-Restaurant de la Terrasse (☎ 04 95 78 67 69) is the least expensive hotel in Zonza, and the family running it is extremely friendly. Doubles with bathrooms cost 220FF to 270FF. Its *restaurant* serves excellent food, including its own homemade charcuterie; the *menu* costs 90FF (open April to October). Bikes can be locked in the garage.

Hôtel-Restaurant le Tourisme (☎ 04 95 78 67 72) is a good choice. Doubles with TV, telephone and balcony cost 250/280FF to 320/360FF in low/high season (open May to October). It has a garage for bikes.

L'Aiglon (☎ 04 95 78 67 79) has a few beautiful doubles individually decorated by the proprietress. Each has a small bathroom and costs 300FF. The *restaurant* serves good local cuisine, with sophisticated *menus* for 90FF and 115FF.

The only bakery in town, *Boulangerie Zézé* sells out early – be there by about 8 am (closed on Wednesday outside July and August). The *Depot de Pain, Fruits et Legumes* supermarket opposite the D268/D368 junction is open daily from May to October.

Day 4: Col de Bavella
1–2 hours, 19km
Climb to Corsica's most beautiful pass, the hub of some excellent day walks. The climbing is steady, but start early to avoid the heat and allow time for a long walk. Much of the day is spent in sight of the imposing silhouette of the Aiguilles de Bavella.

From Zonza, the chestnut trees soon give way to a forest of Laricio pines, which in turn thins to subalpine meadow. Apart from the astounding views, the only feature of the route is the **Hippodrome de Viseo** (3.8km), notable as the highest horseracing track in Europe. Several stunning **lookout points** are worth stopping for, including those at 6.3km and 7.7km.

The Col de Bavella (Foci di Bavedda; 1218m) is marked by the statue of Notre Dame (or Madone) des Neiges. Look farther into the Bavella massif to spot the horns of mouflons that frequent the area. About 500m down past the col, the village of Bavella has several *gîtes d'étape* and excellent *restaurants* catering to walkers doing the GR20 walk. This famous long-distance route runs through the centre of the island.

It's possible to do one of the GR20's most beautiful – but strenuous – sections from the col. Alternatively, many of the paths in the area can be rewardingly wandered for an hour or two.

At the pass, the GR20 splits into two for several kilometres to the north-west. Joining the two options into a loop creates a long **day walk** (allow eight hours). Carry plenty of water as there are no water points for the first half of the walk. Start on the alpine route (flagged with yellow paint splashes) from near the *cafe* and head through the pines into the heart of the massif. The route scrambles through the pink granite used to teach rock climbing, crossing a stone slab with the aid of a chain. This could be very slippery in the wet, but normally isn't too bad if you're not carrying a big pack; perhaps reconsider if you suffer vertigo. The track climbs to the Bocca di u Pargulu (1662m), which has panoramic views to the ocean. The track drops to rejoin the main route (marked with red-and-white stripes) at a right angle, about four hours after starting. The GR20 then skirts the massif to the south-west to reach the col.

The return ride to Zonza is a downhill run to be savoured.

Day 5: Zonza to Bonifacio
3½–7 hours, 69.5km

Although the climbing isn't over completely, one-third of this day is downhill, reaching the coast at Porto Vecchio and then following the fairly flat, if dull, route into stunning Bonifacio.

An 11.7km hill climbs steadily out of Zonza, with only a few small dips, passing the **cemetery** and cutting through the tranquil pine trees of the Fôret Domaniale de Zonza. The view of the Aiguilles de Bavella is replaced by rounded granite boulders towards the **Bocca di Pelza** (874m; 6.8km). Fire has swept through the area several times in recent decades.

At the **Bocca d'Illarata** (991m) a fabulous granite landscape of rocks weathered into whimsical forms (*tafoni* in Corsican) invites exploration. The pyramid shape of the granite massif Punta di u Diamante (1198m) dominates the horizon to the south-west.

The **Cascades de Piscia di Gallo** (17.1km), which translates delightfully as Chicken's Piss Waterfall, is a tourist trap in summer. The cascades are as the name would suggest, but the walk is through pleasant forest and maquis and has some good viewpoints.

Much more inviting is the lake formed by the **Barrage de l'Ospedale** (Ospedale Dam, 18km), which has refreshing swimming spots in shallow water. Soon after the dam the long descent begins, passing a **lookout** (20.2km) over the flat coastal plain leading to Porto Vecchio. L'Ospedale (20.8km) has long been synonymous with peace and coolness away from the heat of the coast (it has a water fountain, too). Check your brakes here for the long downhill; it's steady, but has several hairpin bends.

As the altitude drops, the route re-enters the maquis and the warm coastal plain. At the roundabout (37.8km) at the entry to Porto Vecchio (Porti-Vechju) you're not missing anything by skipping the port, a characterless strip of tourist shops.

If you need a bike shop, a Peugot distributor is a few hundred metres past the turn off to the Citadelle (instead of turning right at the second roundabout, continue on the port road; the bike shop is on the right at the next roundabout). The *Hyper U* supermarket (38.6km; closed Sunday), on the left at the Citadelle turn-off, stocks a decent range of home-brand spare parts. In high season, it's also a good place to stock up on supplies before hitting the inflated prices of Bonifacio.

Porto Vecchio's **Citadelle** is fun to explore; founded in 1539 by the Genoese as a strategic east coast port, the inhabitants of the walled city survived attack by humans but were decimated by malaria. It wasn't until the marshes were drained that the city thrived. The beautiful rue Borgo gives an impression of what the city was once like, as does the Porte Génoise. The knife makers in the Citadelle are particularly entertaining.

The last 30km to Bonifacio is fairly dull but does give access to the string of golden beaches that lines the coast. The most famous is the **Plage de Palombaggia**, which is reached by a 10.5km road leaving the route at 45.5km. It's a long side trip, but camping and hotels are available year-round. More accessible, but with only holiday village accommodation (generally week-long bookings), is the beach at **Santa Giulia**. The turn-off at 47.1km leads 1km down a steep hill; take any left turn signed 'Access Plage' to reach a very touristed, but pretty, bush-fringed white-sand beach.

Several small passes inject some last challenges into the tour and the *fruit stalls*

CORSICA

1:300,000

10km / 6mi

N

Day 5: Zonza to Bonifacio

Cue

start		Zonza mairie
0km	↰	go N on D268
0.0	↱	(40m) D368 at war memorial
6.8	↱	'to Porto Vecchio'
11.7	✳	Bocca d'Illarata
17.1	✳	Cascades de 'Piscia di Gallo walk
18.0		Barrage de l'Ospedale
19.2	↱	D368 'to Pc to Vecchio'
		18.6km twisting descent
20.8		L'Ospedale
34.9		Palavesa
37.8	◆↱	D368 'to Centre Ville'
38.6	◆↱	'to Citadelle'
38.9	◆↱	Rue du G Leclerc
39.1	↱	'to Bonifacio', Porto Vecchio
	•↰⌐↰	Citade e 500m ↰
40.2	↱	unsigned road
40.7	↰	unsigned road
40.7	◆↱	(30m) 'to Bonifacio'
41.8	◆↱	N198 'to Bonifacio'
45.5	•↰	Plage de Palombaggia 21km ↰
47.1	•↰	Plage de Santa Giulia 2.2km ↰
52.8	↱	Bocca d'Arésia
65.0	↱	D58
66.3	◆↱	'to Bonifacio'
68.7	↱	Ave Charles de Gaulle
68.8	↱	into tunnel
69.0		short cut to tourist office (LHS)
69.2	↱↱	towards monument
69.4	↱	Rue Scamaroni
69.5	↱	Bonifacio tourist office

TYRRHENIAN SEA

Pointe de la Chiappe

Golfe de Porto Vecchio

Pointe de Capiciola

Plage de Palombaggia

Plage de Santa Giulia

Side Trip

Side Trip

Punta di u Cherchio (323m)

Cal Rossa

Porto Vecchio

Palavesa

D368

L'Ospedale

Barrage de l'Ospedale

Punta Fenaggia (1069m)

Punta di u Diamante (1198m)

Cascades de Piscia di Gallo

Bocca d'Illarata

Bocca di Pelza

Zonzat

START: DAY 5

PARC NATUREL RÉGIONAL DE LA CORSE

See Days 3 & 4 p508

Levie

D59

D859

Suartone

Bocca d'Arésia (69m)

Col de Pertusile

D191

D859

Figari Airport

Sotte

Figari

Golfe de santa Manza

To Sartène

N198

To Solenzara

To Col de Bavella

Inset map: Ajaccio — Porto Pollo — Sartène — Col de Bavella — Zonza — Bonifacio

Elevation

Zonza — Bocca di Pelza — Bocca d'Illarata — L'Ospedale — Palavesa — Porto Vecchio — Bonifacio

Vertical axis: 0m, 400, 800, 1200, 1600, 2000, 2400

Horizontal axis: 0km, 10, 20, 30, 40, 50, 60

at 63.2km may provide a much needed energy boost – **L'Ellara** also sells wine from the barrel for around 9.5FF/L.

It wouldn't be a cycle tour in Corsica without a final challenging climb and the Citadelle of Bonifacio certainly provides it, with the only cyclable road leading steeply through a tunnel and then even more steeply towards the old walled city. For a short cut, outside the tunnel a flight of stairs leads to the tourist office.

Bonifacio (Bonifaziu)

Standing atop chalky cliffs, watched over by its Citadelle, Bonifacio is a wonderful place – alone worth the trip to Corsica. The town owes a great deal of its beauty to its extraordinary coastal location: imagine a fjord about 100m wide plunging 1.5km into cliffs of white sculpted rock. Then imagine a Citadelle perched on top of these cliffs, dominating the turquoise depths of the Bouches de Bonifacio from a height of almost 70m.

This 'Corsican Gibraltar' is separated from Sardinia by only 12km of water.

Information The tourist office (☎ 04 95 73 11 88, fax 04 95 73 14 97) is at 2 rue F Scamaroni, very close to the Porte de France (closed weekends outside summer).

The Société Générale, at 7 rue St Érasme, on the southern side of the harbour, is the only bank in Bonifacio (closed weekends); it also has the town's only ATM. The bureau de change inside the ferry terminal has a terrible exchange rate and high charges. The post office is hidden in place Carrega in the Citadelle.

Tam-Tam windsurfer and cycle shop (☎ 04 95 73 11 59) is on route de Santa-Manza (the D58) east from the port; it stocks basic parts, does repairs and hires basic VTTs for 75/450FF per day/week.

Things to See & Do Of the two sets of steps that connect the harbour to the Citadelle, the **Montée St Roch** provides the most spectacular vistas. To the north is the Bastion de l'Étendard, a remnant of the fortifications built as a result of a siege in 1553. It is home to the **Mémorial du Passé Bonifacien** (Memorial to Bonifacio's Past), where various episodes in the town's history have been recreated. The nearby squares have fabulous ocean views.

Église Ste Marie Majeure was built b the Pisans and completed in the 14th cer tury. It retains its main feature: the **loggia** under the arches of which the notables the town used to gather. Opposite is the o **communal tank**, once used to collect rair water gathered by the many aqueducts rur ning above the streets.

The **Escalier du Roi d'Aragon** is also a re sult of the difficulties of supplying water t the town. Legend has it the 187 steps fror the south-western corner of the Citadelle t the sea were carved in one night by th King of Aragon's troops during the 142 siege. It is more likely that this impressiv scar down the cliff was carved to allow ac cess to a spring.

To the west of the Citadelle is **Église S Dominique**, one of Corsica's few Gothic re ligious buildings. Its altarpiece of poly chrome marble dates to the mid-18t century, and the reliquaries carried in pro cessions through the town during religiou festivals are fascinating.

The **marine cemetery**, with its immacu late lines of tombs, stretches out to the se on the eastern point. Although surrounde by ugly, neglected buildings, the tombs are fascinating and the view to the Sardinia coast, about 12km away, spectacular.

Ask the tourist office how to access sev eral nearby swimming **beaches**.

Sightseeing boat trips give one of the best views of the Citadelle and curiositie such as the Escalier du Roi d'Aragon, the Gouvernail de la Corse and the Grain d Sable (Grain of Sand; a stone pillar off the coast that seems to have escaped erosion) Numerous proprietors tout vigorously fo business along the quays.

At the foot of the Montée St Roch a sigr describes the **walks** in the area. Walk o cycle the spectacular one (one to two hours that travels along the cliffs past old military bunkers to the Pertusato Lighthouse.

Bonifacio offers many **diving** opportuni ties, although on unsettled days most sites are exposed to winds and strong currents The Atoll dive centre (☎ 04 95 73 02 83, fax 04 95 73 17 72) has an office on the harbour, next to the ferry terminal.

Places to Stay The majority of the hotels in Bonifacio have three stars, though some reasonable accommodation options do exist.

Camping l'Araguina (☎ 04 95 73 02 96, ave Sylvère Bohn), on the way into town, has tightly packed sites, but is only a few hundred metres from the harbour. It is quite shady, with clean facilities and a laundrette. Allow 33FF per person and 11FF per tent open April to October).

Hôtel des Étrangers (☎ 04 95 73 01 09, fax 04 95 73 16 99, ave Sylvère Bohn) is a few hundred metres north of the marina, on the western side of the road. This bike-friendly hotel is Bonifacio's only budget option. Its basic rooms all have bathrooms; prices vary according to the season, the room's size and position. Doubles overlooking the busy road, with no air-con or TV, cost 200FF (236FF in July and August). Prices include a good breakfast (open April to October).

Hôtel Le Royal (☎ 04 95 73 00 51, fax 04 95 73 04 68) is an excellent choice in the heart of the Citadelle. Its huge rooms (with air-con, TV and bathroom) sleep up to three people and cost 450FF in July, 600FF in August and 280FF to 350FF in the low season. Bikes are welcome in the rooms.

Places to Eat The many *shops* and *cafes* by the harbour serve sandwiches, pizzas and panini.

The *Timy* SPAR supermarket and several other small stores are on rue Doria (closed Sunday afternoon). The *Simoni* supermarket is on the southern side of the marina (closed Sunday afternoon in winter).

La Grillade (☎ 04 95 73 55 50), on the northern side of the marina, serves good-value food such as salads (30FF) and barbequed meat (from 70FF) under an arbour of Virginia creeper (closes for lunch in low season).

Les Terrasses d'Aragon (☎ 04 95 73 51 07, place Carrega) is one of Bonifacio's many pizzerias. In the Citadelle, opposite the post office, it has a terrace with a wonderful view and serves pizzas (from 40FF to 65FF) and *menus* (closed January).

Nearby, *U Castille* (☎ 04 95 73 04 99, rue Simon Varsi) is in a lovely stone room. Dishes include fish and meat (from 90FF to 120FF). It has *menus* for 80FF and 120FF.

Cantina Doria (☎ 04 95 73 50 49, 27 rue Doria) is an atmospheric, rustic little restaurant that has brought traditional Corsican mountain cuisine down into the Citadelle. The 70FF evening *menu* is deservedly popular and includes 250mL of wine (closed January and on Sunday and Tuesday evening in winter).

Les 4 Vents (☎ 04 95 73 07 50, quai Banda del Ferro), near the ferry quay, is popular for its fish in summer and its Alsace specialities in winter. Its *menus* start at 90FF (closed Tuesday in low season).

Randonnées

The French passion for organising (and bureaucratising) everything is as evident in the field of cycling as elsewhere. For instance, the cycle racing control body, Union Cycliste Internationale (UCI), was founded in Paris in 1900. (It is now based in Lausanne, a French-speaking part of Switzerland.)

The French are also keen organisers of many aspects of recreational cycling. The Fédération Française de Cyclotourisme (FFCT; see Useful Organisations in the Facts for the Cyclist chapter) has hundreds of affiliated clubs in cities and regions across France, which, among other events, run regular long-distance *randonnées* (rides), and maintain route notes for permanent tourist randonnées. The Audax Club Parisien also has dozens of affiliated clubs which run randonnées within set time limits and with commemorative medals as rewards. See the 'Types of Randonnée' boxed text for distinctions between these clubs' rides.

In this chapter we look at some of the more popular randonnées, including the Paris-Brest-Paris, Tour de Corse, Flèches de France, Memorial Fabio Casartelli and Raid Pyrénéen. Some of these randonnées have set time limits based on average speeds, while some, such as the Tour de Corse and the Randonnée Alpine, allow cyclists to complete the course at their own pace. There are too many scheduled randonnées to describe all of them here — contact the various organisers for calendars etc (see Information, following).

HISTORY

Cycle racing and randonnées in France share common roots. In 1904, Henri Desgrange, 'father' of the Tour de France, developed a style of cycling called 'Audax'. (The word comes from the Latin for 'bold' or 'courageous'.) Desgrange had been inspired by a group of Italian cyclists who, in 1897, had ridden 200km between sunrise and sunset, becoming known as 'les Audacieux'.

The Audax formula had a team of cyclists, under the control of a 'captain', riding long-distance routes together, at an average speed of 22.5km/h. While this style still exists in Europe, it is less popular than the style developed in 1921 by the Audax Club Parisien (ACP).

The ACP invented bicycle randonnées *allure libre* (at a free pace) over 300km, 400km, 600km and 1000km. Rather than staying in a group, riders could ride at their own pace, as long as they maintained an overall average speed of 15km/h for distances up to and including 600km, and 13.3km/hr for 1000km and over. These testing rides were called Brevets Randonneur Français. These brevets required a rider's achievement to be certified by checkpoint stamps and the approval of the ACP as the supervising authority.

ACP has successfully exported its long distance, non-competitive riding style to many other countries. The clubs that run the events are connected by an international organisation called Les Randonneurs Mondiaux (Worldwide Randonneurs). Brevets Randonneurs Français are now known as Brevets Randonneurs Mondiaux.

INFORMATION

The ACP Web site (💻 www.audax-club-parisien.com) maintains a listing of the volunteer contact people for some of the permanent and scheduled randonnées.

Clubs in numerous other countries also supervise rides in France. Audax United Kingdom (💻 www.aukhawk.demon.co.uk) oversees a series of PROFS (Permanent Rides on Foreign Soil), such as the 200km Tour of La Suisse Normande, which travels along the coast of Normandy and inland roughly in a circle around Caen.

The FFCT Web site 💻 www.ffct.org allows you to search for its scheduled and permanent randonnées by region and list ride details and the organiser's contact address. Also visit 💻 www.cyclopedie.com /cyclopassion/depart.html for a comprehensive calendar of long-distance rides.

Maps & Books

Many permanent randonnées are listed on the IGN map *France VTT & Randonnée Cyclos*; see the 'Cycle-Touring Map' boxed text in the Facts for the Cyclist chapter.

Out of print, but perhaps lurking on a library shelf or in some second-hand book shop, is *Les 100 Plus Belles Randonnées du Cyclotourisme*, by Jean Durry & Jacques

Seray (1984), a lavishly illustrated coffee table book, in French. Seventy-nine of the 'most beautiful' rides are in France.

Organised Tours

The UK-based Graham Baxter Sporting Tours (☎ 0113-284 3617, fax 284 3588, 🖳 www.sportingtours.co.uk), 21 Manor Gardens, Pool-in-Wharfedale, Otley, West Yorkshire, LS21 1NB, organises tour groups to some of the randonnées described in this chapter.

Scheduled Brevets

Of the hundreds of scheduled brevets held throughout France each year, this section lists our personal selection of some of the best.

PARIS-BREST-PARIS

The PBP, as it is affectionately known, is the most prestigious event in the world of non-competitive long-distance cycling. The 1200km event is held every four years (most recently in 1999) in the last week of August and is organised by the ACP. It attracts around 3500 riders from all over the world. While the largest number of participants come from France (1973 in 1999), significant numbers come from the USA (397), the UK (335), Australia (69) and countries bordering France. In the 1999 event countries such as Finland, Russia, the Ukraine, Ireland and Costa Rica were also represented.

Participants are required to finish the course within a total elapsed time of 90 hours. This means they need to average at least 13.3km/h.

Types of Randonnée

In French, the word randonnée can refer to a ride, walk or drive. So, for a cycle club, a randonnée refers to any bike ride. However, in English-speaking cycling circles, the term randonnée is used to describe long-distance rides over a set distance, usually timed. The French terms for different types of long-distance rides are explained here.

Brevets

The Audax Club Parisien uses the term Brevets Randonneurs, and the FFCT Brevets Sportifs to describe set, usually timed long-distance rides. These rides are open to all cycle tourists riding machines propelled solely by muscular effort, and can be either scheduled or permanent.

Scheduled Brevets These include mass-participation rides such as the Brevet de Randonneur des Alpes, and are scheduled for a specific date on the cycling calendar. In such events there is commonly a choice of routes to suit riders of varying fitness. The rides start early in the morning and a fee usually has to be paid before the day of the event. At the start riders are issued with route instructions and a brevet (certificate) that must be stamped at designated points along the route. Participants can ride at their own speed and with whomever they like, but usually must finish within a time limit, based on a 15km/h riding time.

Permanent Brevets These rides are over a set course, usually with a time limit, and can be tackled at any time by individuals or groups. The organising group provides route instructions, and riders must ensure the supplied brevet cards are signed and stamped at designated towns in, say, a cafe, hotel or other business. An excellent example of a permanent randonnée is the Raid Pyrénéen (see the section on the ride in this chapter). The term raid is used to indicate an extremely long – and therefore challenging – ride.

Randonnée Permanent

The FFCT has formulated 350 permanent tourist randonnées which take in an area's major attractions over several days. These are listed on their web site (see the Information section later). These have no time limit and can be done at any time by obtaining the route notes from the club listed as the contact.

History

The PBP began in 1891 as a single-stage race over approximately 1200km from Paris to Brest (on the Atlantic coast of Brittany) and back. The first victor was Frenchman Charles Terront. The event was deemed so extremely difficult that it was held only every 10 years until 1931. WWII interrupted the series, delaying the next event until 1948.

Of the seven editions up to and including 1951, six were won by either a Frenchman or a Belgian. The exception was the legendary Australian cyclist Hubert (Oppy) Opperman (1904–96), who prevailed in 1931 in a then course-record time of 49 hours, 21 minutes. Since 1951, the PBP has been run only for noncompetitive cyclists. However, competition for the fastest time is still intense: see the boxed text below.

Information

Entry can be arranged through a club in your country that is affiliated with Les Randonneurs Mondiaux, or by contacting the ACP organiser (fax 01 45 09 40 78), 7 ave de Normandie, 93220 Gagny. Affiliated clubs exist in many countries, including Britain, Australia, the USA and Canada. Entry costs about 600FF per rider.

PBP Rules

Prospective participants must qualify by completing a series of ACP-sanctioned lead-up rides involving randonnées of 200km, 300km, 400km and 600km in the year before PBP. These must be ridden within time limits based on an average speed of 15km/h. These qualifiers can be ridden in countries where Les Randonneurs Mondiaux clubs are active.

The Paris-Brest-Paris Experience

You really have to love cycling even to contemplate riding the 1200km Paris-Brest-Paris (PBP) randonnée. It also helps to have a high pain threshold and to be young, though the latter is not essential. I am amazed at the performances of some riders aged in their 50s and 60s. Most impressive to me was a French rider I met named Guy Lamaison, from a town near Lourdes. He was 59 when he finished the event in under 58 hours. There *must* be something in the water. (Though 20 years his junior and fitter than I had ever been, I could only manage 63 hours.)

Riding such a long distance in under four days with little sleep does funny things to your head. How else can I explain why I went back for a second and even a third time?

While the event is not a race, there is much prestige associated with fast times and fierce competition to finish first. US cyclist and triathlete Scott Dickson has taken line honours in each edition since the early 1980s (coming in at around 43 hours – an average of around 29km/h). In the 1995 PBP, Dickson finished in equal fastest time with eight other riders, including six Frenchmen, who had 'attacked' him for almost the entire 43 hours, 20 minutes of their ride. They struck a truce in the final kilometres and, in the non-competitive spirit of the event, crossed the line together. The first woman to finish, France's Brigitte Kerlouet, was less than two hours behind.

MUSÉE DE LA PUBLICITÉ, PARIS

PARIS - BREST - PARIS
1200 K"

GARIN 1er   en 52h 11' ½

STE
LA FRANÇAISE

MARQUE ✦ DIAMANT
e Brunel PARIS

A 1901 poster advertises the brand of bike that won that year's PBP. (Charles Brun)

PBP rules permit riders to use recumbents, tricycles and other non-standard machines but tri-bars and similar UCI-illegal equipment are banned. Strict rules govern the use of lighting and reflective equipment because PBP riders are on the road all day and, often, all night. Helmets are strongly recommended, though not (yet) compulsory.

The Randonnée

Since its centenary in 1991, the PBP route has started at St Quentin-en-Yvelines, near Versailles, south-west of Paris. It meanders west through Normandy and Brittany on a convoluted series of tiny, hilly roads, mostly travelling through crop lands and via a number of contrôle (checkpoint) towns – Villaines-la-Juhel (221km & 997km), Fougères (304km & 914km), Tinteniac (360km & 858km), Loudéac (445km & 773km), Carhaix (522km & 696km) and Brest (613km). On the return there is an extra checkpoint at Mortagne-au-Perche (1077km). As well as the advertised contrôles, there are three or four 'secret' checkpoints.

Because of the huge number of participants, start times are staggered. The first at 8 pm, for the fastest riders, allows them a maximum of 80 hours. Two hours later, the popular 10 pm start allows riders the full 90 hours to complete the distance. Often this mass of riders is broken up into smaller groups, which start at half-hour intervals. The third and final starting time, 5 am the following day, gives riders 84 hours to finish.

Cyclists ride for much of the day and night. The resulting sleep deprivation is a major hazard and a reason for many abandonments.

The Paris-Brest-Paris Experience

What could possibly attract cyclists to so much suffering? The answer, undoubtedly, is the atmosphere. Riding in such an international mix of thousands of experienced cyclists, at all hours of the day and night, for nearly four days, in a country where cycling is revered is an incredible experience. The people of the towns and villages turn out to watch, cheer and support. In the middle of a cold, black night, apparently kilometres from nowhere, you come upon a roadside stall where locals are serving free coffee and cake by the light of camping lanterns. Others stand at unlit intersections at 3 am to guide riders. The welcome at the finish is unforgettable.

The distances you can ride and speeds you can maintain among this fit, determined bunch are likely to be your greatest ever. As I said, though, it messes with your head...

In 1995 my wife, Alethea, and I clung desperately to the 40km/h peloton (bunch) as it charged from the start along empty pre-dawn roads. As the sun rose and the distance mounted, we found ourselves knocking off our fastest ever 100km, 200km, 300km...with only the shortest of breaks at contrôles (checkpoints). After 23 hours of near-continuous cycling, we were at Carhaix, deep in Brittany, with 517km under our wheels – on schedule for our dreamed-of sub-60-hour time.

After a brief sleep we rose to a new day, for the sprint to Brest then back to Fougères, the 900km mark, before another sleep. Near 3 am the next day, as we rolled into the contrôle, I was feeling strong. With 'only' 300km to the finish, I was tempted to ride on and set a fantastic time – against my cardinal rule of not riding in the two or three hours before dawn.

After a half-hour break, we left with Steve, another Australian, but the pace he set was uncomfortable. I had to sleep. Where? The next contrôle was 70km ahead. We came upon an attractive lawn in a village square. Telling Alethea I was going to lie there, I asked for the groundsheet from her front pannier. Unfortunately, she didn't have the groundsheet. Nor a front pannier. Neither of our bikes had a pannier, nor even a rack to carry one – I was hallucinating.

Instructing her to lie down next to me – as a windbreak – I instantly fell asleep. When I awoke at dawn, as stiff as a board, I could barely mount my bike. Alethea, nearly frozen, said she had not slept at all. We struggled on, only to be brought to a halt by a puncture in my rear tyre. It was my first flat in any PBP. It was followed, only an hour later, by the second. Both took an age to repair as my disoriented mind refused to help me. Our hopes of a stunning time evaporated. All because my brain played tricks due to sleep deprivation.

Neil Irvine

Riders have been known to fall asleep in daylight, crash and be unable to continue.

The large bunches charge off the starting line as if in a short time trial. Despite using roads open to normal traffic, the *peloton* (bunch) often forms an echelon occupying the full width of the carriageway. If traffic appears from the opposite direction, the whole bunch suddenly squeezes onto the right-hand side, where riders on the outside can be squeezed off the bitumen, ending up ignominiously in a muddy ditch.

At each contrôle, faster riders rush to have their route cards stamped and to resupply from support vehicles parked nearby. Others, without support crews, feed in the contrôle restaurant, usually set up in a school or town hall. Some riders, though, treat the event in a more casual way and take breaks at cafes along the route – a few relax with a glass of red wine and a cigarette or two!

Volunteers staff the contrôle restaurant, which is never short of wholesome food and drinks. Dormitory cots are often set up nearby and riders can specify a time to be woken.

The contrôle towns' populations are keen to be involved in the PBP, which has an atmosphere not unlike the Tour de France. They turn out to watch, cheer or set up unofficial wayside feeding stations. It's this fantastic support that makes the ride memorable for most participants.

MEMORIAL FABIO CASARTELLI

This is the second major *cyclosportive* (mass ride) event in the Pyrenean *département* (department; administrative division) of Ariège. Inaugurated in 1997, this annual cyclosportive takes place around 18 July, the anniversary of the Barcelona Olympic cycling champion's death. It is centred on St Girons, the starting point for the 1995 Tour de France stage over the Col de Portet d'Aspet, the scene of Casartelli's fatal crash.

Money raised from the event supports a fund established by the Casartelli family to aid professional cyclists injured in falls. Cycling personalities who have turned out to support previous events include Bernard Hinault and Claudio Chiappucci.

Before 2000 the event was held over a week or four days, a format difficult for participants. However, it is now scheduled on a weekend and organisers expect more than 800 participants.

Information

The event is organised with the support of the town of St Girons. To join the ride, write to Roue Libre, Mairie BP110, 09200 St Girons; or contact the organisers (☎ 05 61 04 03 20, ext 326, fax 05 61 66 38 95 ▣ www.ariege.com). The event brochure and entry form usually come out in March

The cost for the first day cyclosportive ride is 160FF. For the second day *cyclotouriste* ride it is 80/60FF for nonlicensed/ licensed riders (any form of cycling licence)

Participants receive a memorial jersey have a chance at prizes and awards and can pay extra for a hot meal at the end of each day. During the rides, refreshments are served by the local cycling clubs.

The Randonnée

All the rides are ridden within a time limit and start and finish at St Girons. Day 1 offers a choice of a 'small' 102km circuit or a 130km (approximately) route visiting Col de la Core (1395m), Col de Latrape (1110m) and Col d'Agnes (1570m).

Day 2 is a 95km route with a stop at the memorial to Fabio Casartelli, near the bottom of the Col de Portet d'Aspet (1069m).

PARIS-ROUBAIX RANDONNÉE

Since 1974, masochists have had the opportunity to test their endurance and skills on a 'tourist' version of the gruelling professional Paris-Roubaix classic. In June each year participants endure cobblestones over a choice of four distances, from 275km down to a mere 50km. In April, a mountain bike (VTT) version of the event is held, starting at Raismes. These rides are open to all cyclists, whether members of the FFCT or not.

See the 'Paris-Roubaix: Mud, Mayhem and Cobblestones' boxed text in the Paris & the Île de France chapter for details of the competitive ancestor of this randonnée.

Information

The event is organised by the Vélo Club de Roubaix Cyclotourisme (fax 03 20 45 14 84, ▣ asso.nordnet.fr/veloclubroubaix/Cy cloPRx.html), Paris-Roubaix Cyclo, BP15, 59390 Lannoy.

Entry costs 100FF for the 276km route, which starts at Cambronne-lès-Ribecourt, near Compiègne, between 4 and 7 am. Fees for shorter distances are lower – the 120km route from Raismes costs 40FF, the 75km from Beuvry 30FF, and the 50km route from Attiches 20FF. The shorter rides all start between 7 and 10 am. All rides have a time limit.

The Randonnée

Pavé (cobblestone) road is something of an endangered species these days, but the Paris-Roubaix randonnée, like the classic race, is helping to ensure this historic relic is preserved. Only about 56km of the ride is on genuine pavé, but that should be enough for even the most determined masochist, who will have to endure a coating of mud in wet weather, possibly a crash or almost certainly a puncture on a skinny-tyred bike. The route is well marked and all cobbled sections are closed to motor vehicles. Food is available at contrôle points en route.

LA MARMOTTE

Named after the hibernating alpine rodent, this early-July event is one of three classic rides making up the Trophée de l'Oisans, based in Le Bourg d'Oisans at the base of Alpe d'Huez, about 45km south-east of Grenoble. (The others – Grimpe de l'Alpe, a 13km mass-start ride up Alpe d'Huez, and Le Prix des Grandes Rousses, a 40km climb up the Alpe and on to the ski station of Vaujany (1250m) – are usually held within a week of La Marmotte.)

La Marmotte is a gruelling kick-start to summer for about 4000 cyclists who, in a day, ride 174km with 5000m of climbing, including the infamous crawl up the Alpe d'Huez (see the 'Alpe d'Huez' boxed text in the French Alps & the Jura chapter).

Information

Contact Sport Communication, BP 61, 38242 Meylan Cedex (fax 04 76 03 16 67, ✉ www.sportcommunication.com/bulletin .htm). The entry fee is 170FF.

The Randonnée

Starting in Le Bourg d'Oisans, riders first tackle the Col de la Croix de Fer (2068m), a 1350m gain that includes a short pinch at 12%. The Col du Télégraphe (1570m) is the halfway point on the climb of the dizzying Col du Galibier (2645m), from which the route winds precariously down through hairpins on steep gradients to Col du Lautaret

(2057m). The *coup de grâce* is the climb of Alpe d'Huez (1860m), with 21-hairpin bends.

Riders receive a classification for each individual event in the Trophée de l'Oisans and the time for the three events is compiled to give an overall classification. There are both scratch and age group classifications.

BREVET DE RANDONNEUR DES ALPES

The extremely difficult Brevet de Randonneur des Alpes (BRA) is based in the alpine city of Grenoble. Thousands of cyclists ride one of several courses, visiting some of the highest passes in the Alps. The ride celebrated its 40th edition in 1999.

Information

Contact Cyclotouristes Grenoblois, BP 181, 38004 Grenoble Cedex 1, for details or entry. The BRA is held biennially on a weekend in mid-July. Entry costs 60FF or 90FF.

The Randonnée

The BRA offers three route options of 300km, 260km or 252km with 5400m, 4950m or 4650m of climbing respectively.

Big-name climbs that feature in this ride, and also in the Tour de France, include Col du Galibier (2645m), where there's a monument to Tour creator Henri Desgrange; Col du Télégraphe (1570m); Col de la Croix de Fer (2068m); and, of course, Alpe d'Huez (1860m).

Permanent Brevets

FLÈCHES DE FRANCE

Since 1954, the Flèches de France, all starting from Paris (*flèche* means arrow), have become the most popular permanent randonnées on mainland France, with more than 34,000 completions.

The full series of 20 Flèche rides totals a distance of nearly 11,000km and qualifies the successful randonneur for a special *plaquette* (plaque). More than 500 *cyclotouristes* have finished the series.

Information

The contact for this ride is another ACP organiser, 16 rue des Prés, 95260 Mours. It costs 25FF to enter and an extra 40FF for a medallion.

RANDONNÉES

The Randonnées

These rides radiate from Paris to all corners of the 'Hexagon' of France:

Paris to...	distance
Calais	301km
Lille	275km
Charleville	245km
Strasbourg	497km
Montbéliard	449km
Belgarde	573km
Briançon	746km
Nice	958km
Marseille	908km
Perpignan	988km
Luchon	864km
Hendaye	904km
Bordeaux	584km
La Rochelle	465km
Nantes	419km
Brest	607km
Mont St Michel	326km
Cherbourg	388km
Le Havre	218km
Dieppe	175km

Riders must have a brevet card stamped in designated contrôle towns and can choose from three achievement categories:

Gold Must average 20km to 25km/h, depending on the distance covered
Silver Must average 15km to 20km/h, depending on the distance covered
Bronze Must cycle a minimum of 80km/day

DIAGONALES DE FRANCE

These rides crisscross France, creating a six-pointed star shape on the map. They link six axis points, each representing a corner of the French 'Hexagon': Dunkerque, Strasbourg, Menton, Perpignan, Hendaye and Brest.

Like the other permanent randonnées and raids, riders carry a numbered plaque on their bicycle and must stamp a route card at specified contrôles. People riding these randonnées are known as *diagonalistes*; it is a great honour to complete all nine *diagonales*.

Information

Contact Amicale des Diagonalistes de France (fax 05 56 52 18 91), 41 rue Fondaudège, 33000 Bordeaux.

The Randonnées

The *diagonales* and their time limits are:

route	distance	hours
Brest-Menton	1400km	116
Dunkerque-Perpignan	1190km	100
Strasbourg-Hendaye	1190km	100
Dunkerque-Menton	1190km	100
Brest-Perpignan	1060km	89
Brest-Strasbourg	1050km	88
Dunkerque-Hendaye	1050km	88
Hendaye-Menton	940km	78
Strasbourg-Perpignan	940km	78

RAID PYRÉNÉEN

Inaugurated in 1951, this randonnée along the length of the Pyrenees now has two versions. The original version, referred to as the Randonneur route, is 710km over 18 passes, with a time limit of 100 hours. The second, the Touriste version, officially listed as 790km, climbs 28 passes, and allows 240 hours (10 consecutive days) for the journey. The Touriste version is described in the Pyrenees chapter (see the Raid Pyrénéen ride, pp412–33), the other in this section.

Both start or finish in either Hendaye, on the Bay of Biscay, and Cerbère, on the Mediterranean.

Information

The Cyclo Club Béarnais Cyclotourisme, 59 ave Louis Sallenave, 64000 Pau, oversees both versions of this testing ride. Entry costs 50FF, a medallion 35FF more.

The Randonnée

The route of the Raid Pyrénéen Randonneur crosses only some of the passes of the longer Touriste version. Col d'Osquich (392m), Col de Port (1249m) and Col du Puymorens (1915m) are three passes exclusive to the Randonneur version. Part of the Randonneur version, including the Col de Port, is on the Pyrenean Foothills ride through Massat (near St Girons) and the Ariège department's Tarascon-sur-Ariège.

RANDONNÉES ALPINES

Siblings of the Raid Pyrénéen, these permanent randonnées exist in four variants: two with routes from Antibes on the Côte d'Azur via the French Alps to Thonon les Bains on

Lac Léman (Lake Geneva); the others begin either in Venice or Trieste, traversing Italy and Switzerland to reach Thonon.

The 740km Randonnée Alpine incorporates 43 cols and 18,187m of climbing while its longer sister, the 894km Randonnée Préalpine, requires just 17,962m of climbing to cross 48 cols.

Like the Raid Pyrénéen, the routes cross many passes which feature regularly in the Tour de France.

Information
All Randonnées Alpines are organised by Cyclos Randonneurs Thononais (☎/fax 04 50 26 59 85, ℮ georges.rossini@wanadoo .fr), route de Publier, Moruel-Marin, 74200 Thonon-les-Bains.

Michelin maps Nos 70, 74, 77, 81 and 84 (1:200,000; about 14FF each) or the larger sheet (same scale) Nos 244 and 245 (plus No 243 for the final 5km; about 32FF each) cover the routes.

The cost for the Préalpine and Alpine Randonnées is 30FF (35FF if registering from foreign countries), plus 145FF for each medallion (which includes a deluxe presentation box).

Graham Baxter Sporting Tours offers a supported attack on the 43-col Alpine ride. Riders start on a Sunday, aiming to complete the randonnée in seven days (averaging just over 100km per day). Cost of £589.00 includes10 nights bed and breakfast, eight evening meals, return coach travel from UK (with bike), entry fees and maps, ferry fares and port taxes.

The Randonnées
The Alpine route features a loop from Briançon into Italy across the infamous Col de Sestriere (2035m), returning to France via Susa. The highlight of the route is the crossing of the stark Col de la Bonette (2715m) on the highest tarmac road in Europe, which reaches 2802m 2km off-route at the Cime de la Bonette. Other well known Tour cols en route include Col de l'Iseran (2762m), Col du Galibier (2645m), Col d'Izoard (2361m), and the location of a monument to Tour greats Fausto Coppi and Louison Bobet), Col de la Cayolle (2327m) and Col de Vars (2111m).

Veterans rate the Randonnée Préalpine through the foothills of the Alps the tougher route – it follows roads which rise and fall

all the time and are not always as easily graded as on the major cols. It takes a lower and generally more westerly course than the Alpine but still rises over 2000m within the first 170km at the Col des Champs (2093m). The highest pass is Col d'Allos (2244m) at the 202km mark.

The organiser recommends no-one undertake these randonnées without utmost care in physical preparation and equipment and gearing selection.

TOUR DE CORSE
This randonnée is held on France's beautiful Mediterranean island of Corsica (Corse in French). Inaugurated in 1956, this randonnée is essentially 'touristic' and has no time limit, nor even a maximum distance. It can be ridden over several years, which need not even be consecutive.

Information
It is run by the ACP; contact the organiser, 32 rue Moissan, 93130 Noisy-le-Sec.

Riders must enter at least four weeks before the proposed departure. It costs 25FF (under 18s free); a medallion is 50FF extra.

The Randonnée
Each participant can choose their starting point, the order of their itinerary and the direction of travel, with the proviso that they must have a route card stamped at 16 different localities – Bastia, Macinaggio, Nonza, Calvi, Piana, Calacuccia, Corte, Ghisoni, Zicavo, Bastelica, Ajaccio, Propriano, Bonifacio, Zonza, Aleria and Piedicroce.

RANDONNÉE DES COLS CORSES
Cyclos Randonneurs Thononais (see Information under Randonnées Alpines) also runs this randonnée. This 1504km tour of Corsica, without a time limit, features 154 cols and 26,353m of climbing.

Information
Registration costs 30FF, a medallion a further 125FF (including presentation box). Michelin map No 90 *Corse* (1:200,000) covers the route.

The Randonnée
This ride, aimed at only the keenest cycle-mountaineers, visits virtually every pass on

Corsica's roads. It starts and finishes at Bastia, the island's largest town, near the northern tip. It traverses busy towns, wild countryside and varied, geologically fascinating terrain, it connects most of the island's extremities – Cap Corse in the north, Bonifacio in the south, Cargèse in the west. Its highest pass is the Col de Bavella (1218m), in the south-eastern quarter.

BREVET DES SEPT COLS UBAYENS

This ride takes you over seven major cols in a series of loop rides from Barcelonnette, near the Italian border, to some of the highest passes in the Alps. This permanent randonnée has no time limit.

Information

Contact the Maison de la Vallée de l'Ubaye (☎ 04 92 81 03 68, fax 04 92 81 15 26, 🖳 www.ubaye.com), 4 ave des Trois Frères Arnaud, 04400 Barcelonnette, for details. It costs 40FF to register for the medallion and ride guide.

The Randonnée

The 1991m Col de Larche (Colle della Maddalena) leads into Italy from the Vallée de l'Ubaye, near Barcelonnette. The Col d'Allos (2250m), the Col de la Cayolle (2326m) and the Col de la Bonette (2800m; the highest pass in Europe) link the valley to Haute-Provence.

Three more cols link the valley to other parts of the outside world. Cyclists keen enough to conquer all seven can earn a medal.

Special card punches have been installed at the top of the passes to enable cyclists to validate their route card. Unfortunately, vandalism and wear and tear may mean they don't all work properly all the time.

Language

While the French rightly or wrongly have a reputation for assuming that all human beings should speak French – until WWI it was the international language of culture and diplomacy – you'll find that any attempt to communicate in French will be much appreciated. Probably your best bet is always to approach people politely in French, even if the only sentence you know is *Pardon, madame/monsieur/mademoiselle, parlez-vous anglais?* (Excuse me, madam/ sir/miss, do you speak English?).

An important distinction is made in French between *tu* and *vous*, which both mean 'you'. *Tu* is only used when addressing people you know well, children or animals. When addressing an adult who is not a personal friend, *vous* should be used unless the person invites you to use *tu*. In general, younger people insist less on this distinction, and they may use *tu* from the beginning of an acquaintance. In this guide the polite form is used in most cases; where

both forms are given they are noted by the abbreviations 'pol' and 'inf' respectively.

All nouns in French are either masculine or feminine and adjectives reflect the gender of the noun they modify. The feminine form of many nouns and adjectives is indicated by a silent *e* added to the masculine form, as in *étudiant/étudiante*, the masculine and feminine for 'student'. In the following phrases we have indicated both masculine and feminine forms where necessary (separated by a slash, with the masculine form first). The gender of a noun is often indicated by a preceding article: 'the/a/some', *le/un/du* (m), *la/une/de la* (f); or a possessive adjective, 'my/your/his/her', *mon/ton/son* (m), *ma/ta/ sa* (f). With French, unlike English, the possessive adjective agrees in number and gender with the thing possessed, eg, *sa mère* (his/her mother).

For a more comprehensive guide to the French language, get hold of Lonely Planet's *French phrasebook*.

Cultural Savvy

Cyclists touring in France are generally warmly received, and the French are helpful in giving directions and offering other advice.

Be aware of cultural differences, follow some simple guidelines, and you will usually be able to win people over and avoid offending anyone.

- When you enter a shop, hotel, restaurant or tourist office, or need to ask a question or directions, begin with *bonjour* or *bonsoir* and always address people as *Monsieur* (Mr/Sir), *Madame* (Mrs) and *Mademoiselle* (Miss – when in doubt use *Madame*). Thank someone with *merci* or *merci beaucoup* and say *au revoir* when you leave.
- If invited to someone's home or a party, always bring some sort of gift, such as good wine (not some 10FF *vin de table*). Flowers are another good stand-by, but chrysanthemums are only brought to cemeteries.
- Never address a waiter or bartender as *garçon* (boy); use *s'il vous plaît* (please).
- When buying fruit, vegetables or flowers anywhere except at supermarkets, do not touch the produce or blossoms unless invited to do so. Show the shopkeeper what you want and he or she will choose for you.
- When being served cheese, never cut off the tip of pie-shaped soft cheeses (eg, camembert); always cut those cheeses where the middle is the best part (eg, blue cheese) so you take your share of the crust.
- Money, particularly income, is simply not discussed in France.
- Keep off manicured French lawns. Watch for *pelouse interdite* (Keep off the grass) signs in some parks and gardens.

Pronunciation

Most letters in French are pronounced more or less the same as their English equivalents. A few which may cause confusion are:

j as the 's' in 'leisure', eg, *jour* (day).

c before **e** and **i**, as the 's' in 'sit'; before **a**, **o** and **u**, as English 'k'. When underscored with a 'cedilla' (ç) it's always pronounced as the 's' in 'sit'.

French has a number of sounds that are difficult for Anglophones to produce. These include:

- The distinction between the 'u' sound (as in *tu*) and 'oo' sound (as in *tout*). For both sounds, the lips are rounded and projected forward, but for the 'u' the tongue is towards the front of the mouth, its tip against the lower front teeth, whereas for the 'oo' the tongue is towards the back of the mouth, its tip behind the gums of the lower front teeth.

- The nasal vowels. With nasal vowels the breath escapes partly through the nose and partly through the mouth. There are no nasal vowels in English; in French there are three, as in *bon vin blanc*, (good white wine). These sounds occur where a syllable ends in a single **n** or **m**; the **n** or **m** is silent but indicates the nasalisation of the preceding vowel.

- The **r**. The standard **r** of Parisian French is produced by moving the bulk of the tongue backwards to constrict the air flow in the pharynx while the tip of the tongue rests behind the lower front teeth. It's similar to the noise made by some people before spitting, but with much less friction.

Greetings & Civilities

Hello/Good morning.	*Bonjour.*
Good evening.	*Bonsoir.*
Good night.	*Bonne nuit.*
Goodbye.	*Au revoir.*
Please.	*S'il vous plaît.*
Thank you.	*Merci.*
You're welcome.	*Je vous en prie.*
Excuse me.	*Excusez-moi.*
Sorry/Forgive me.	*Pardon.*
Yes.	*Oui.*
No.	*Non.*
Maybe.	*Peut-être.*

Small Talk

How are you?	*Comment allez-vous?* (pol) *Comment vas-tu/ Comment ça va?* (inf)
Fine, thanks.	*Bien, merci.*
I'm tired.	*Je suis fatigué/e.* (m/f)
Where have you ridden from?	*Vous êtes parti d'où?*
Where are you riding to (today)?	*Où allez-vous aujourd'hui?*
I'm going from ... to ...	*Je vais de ... à ...*
Would you like to ride together?	*Voulez-vous rouler ensemble?*
What's your name?	*Comment vous appelez-vous?* (pol) *Tu t'appelle comment?* (inf)
My name is ...	*Je m'appelle ...*
I'm pleased to meet you.	*Enchanté* (m)/ *Enchantée.* (f)
How old are you?	*Quel âge avez-vous?*
I'm ... years old.	*J'ai ... ans.*
Do you like ...?	*Aimez-vous ...?*
What country are you from?	*De quel pays êtes-vous?*
I'm from ...	*Je viens ...*

Language Difficulties

I understand.	*Je comprends.*
I don't understand.	*Je ne comprends pas.*
Do you speak English?	*Parlez-vous anglais?*
Could you please write it down?	*Est-ce que vous pouvez l'écrire?*

Getting Around

| I want to go to ... | *Je voudrais aller à ...* |
| I'd like to book a seat to ... | *Je voudrais réserver une place pour ...* |

What time does the ... leave/arrive?	*À quelle heure part/arrive ...?*
aeroplane	*l'avion*
bus (city)	*l'autobus*
bus (intercity)	*l'autocar*
ferry	*le ferry(-boat)*
train	*le train*

Where is ...?	*Où est ...?*
the bus station	*la gare routière*
the bus stop	*l'arrêt d'autobus*
the metro station	*la station de métro*
the train station	*la gare*
the ticket office	*le guichet*

Signs

Entrée	Entrance
Sortie	Exit
Complet	No Vacancies
Renseignements	Information
Ouvert/Fermé	Open/Closed
Interdit	Prohibited
(Commissariat de) Police	Police Station
Chambres Libres	Rooms Available
Toilettes, WC	Toilets
Hommes	Men
Femmes	Women

I'd like a ... ticket.	Je voudrais un billet ...
one-way	aller-simple
return	aller-retour
1st class	première classe
2nd class	deuxième classe
How long does the trip take?	Combien de temps dure le trajet?
Do I need to ...?	Est-ce que je dois ...?
change trains	changer de train
change platform	changer de quai
left-luggage office	consigne manuelle
left-luggage locker	consigne automatique
platform	quai
timetable	horaire

Getting Around With a Bike

Does the bus/ferry/train carry bikes?	Est-ce que l'autobus/le ferry/le train transporte les vélos?
When is the next train allowing bikes as hand luggage?	Quand est le prochain train où on permet les vélos commes bagage à main?
The bike must be in a bag.	Le vélo doit être dans une housse.
You must remove the pedals/turn the handlebars.	Il faut demonter les pédales/tourner les guidons.
Where is the luggage carriage?	Où est le fourgon à bagages?
I'd like to send my bike to ...	Je voudrais envoyer mon vélo à ...
Will it be on the same train as me?	Est-ce qu'il sera dans le meme train que moi?
When will it arrive?	À quelle heure arrivera-t-il?

Where do I collect it from?	Où-est que je le reprends?
Where can I hire a car.	Où est-ce que je peux louer une voiture.

Around Town

I'm looking for ...	Je cherche ...
a bank/exchange office	une banque/un bureau de change
a bike-touring club	un club de cyclo-tourisme
the city centre	le centre-ville
the ... embassy	l'ambassade de ...
the hospital	l'hôpital
my hotel	mon hôtel
the market	le marché
the police	la police
the post office	le bureau de poste/la poste
a public phone	une cabine téléphonique
a public toilet	les toilettes
the tourist office	l'office de tourisme
Where is ...?	Où est ...?
the beach	la plage
the bridge	le pont
the castle/mansion	le château
the church	l'église
the island	l'île
the lake	le lac

Road Signs

Attention!	Danger!
Autres Directions	Other Destinations
Chaussée Deformée	Rough Surface
Chaussée Glissante	Slippery Surface
Col Fermé	(Road Over) Pass Closed
Fin de Travaux	End Roadwork
Gravillons	Gravel
(...) Obligatoire	(...) Compulsory
Priorité à Droite	Give Way to Right
Route Barrée	Road Closed
Sauf Riverains	Local Traffic Only
Sens Unique	One Way
Sortie de Camions	Trucks Entering
Stationnement Interdit	No Parking
Toutes Directions	All Directions
Travaux	Roadworks
Verglas	Ice
Virage	Winding Road

the (main) square	*la place (centrale)*
the old city (town)	*la vieille ville*
the ruins	*les ruines*
the tower	*la tour*

| What time does it open/close? | *Quelle est l'heure d'ouverture/ de fermeture?* |
| I'd like to make a telephone call. | *Je voudrais téléphoner.* |

I'd like to change ...	*Je voudrais changer ...*
some money	*de l'argent*
travellers cheques	*des chèques de voyage*

Shopping

bike shop	*le magasin de vélo*
bookshop	*la librairie*
chemist/pharmacy	*la pharmacie*

laundry/laundrette	*la laverie*
market	*le marché*
newsagency	*l'agence de presse*
supermarket	*le supermarché*

I'm just looking.	*Je ne fais que regarder.*
How much is it?	*C'est combien?*
It's too expensive.	*C'est trop cher.*
It's cheap.	*C'est bon marché.*
It's too big/small.	*C'est trop grand/petit.*
more/less	*plus/moins*

At the Bike Shop

Where can I find a bike repair shop?	*Où y a-t-il un réparateur de vélos?*
I have a flat tyre.	*J'ai un plat/une crevaison.*
I have a broken spoke.	*J'ai un rayon cassé.*

1	*moyeu* (hub)
2	*pignons* (cogs)
3	*roue libre* (freewheel)
4	*dérailleur arrière* (rear derailleur)
5	*chaîne* (chain)
6	*dérailleur avant* (front derailleur)
7	*boitier de pédalier* (bottom bracket)
8	*plateau* (chainring)
9	*manivelle* (crank)
10	*pédale automatique* (clipless pedal)
11	*valve ...* (... valve) *à la francais* (presta) *à l'anglaise* (Schrader)
12	*jante* (rim)
13	*pneu* (tyre)
14	*rayon* (spoke)
15	*sacoche* (pannier)
16	*porte-bagages* (pannier rack)
17	*fourche* (fork)
18	*jeu de direction* (headset)
19	*sac de guidon* (handlebar bag)
20	*guidons* (handlebars)
21	*câble* (cable)
22	*bidon* (water bottle)
23	*port bidon* (bottle cage)
24	*selle* (saddle)
25	*serrage de selle* (seat-post bolt)
26	*frein* (brake)

Could you ... ?	Pourriez-vous ... ?
adjust the gears	régler le dérailleur
adjust the saddle	ajuster la selle
inflate the tyres	(re)gonfler les pneus
true the (front/ rear) wheel	redresser la roue (avant/arrière)
'd like to hire ...	Je voudrais louer ...
a bicycle	un vélo
a mountain bike	un vélo tout-terrain/ VTT (pronounced 'vay tay tay')
a trailer	une remorque
a child's seat	une selle d'enfant
'd like to buy ...	Je voudrais acheter ...
some gloves	des gants
a helmet	un casque
some knicks	des cuissards
a jersey	un maillot

Allen/hex key	une clé allen
Allen bolt	une vis à six pans
battery	une pile
brake pad/block	un patin de frein
chain breaker	un dérive chaîne
chain lubricant	le lubrifiant de chaîne
cycle computer	un compteur de vitesse électronique
dynamo	une dynamo
elastic (ocky) strap	un sandow
(some) glue	(de) la colle
grease	la graisse
handlebar tape	le ruban de guidon
light bulb	une ampoule
lock	un antivol
mudguard	garde boue
nut	un écrou
patch (for tube)	une rustine
pump	une pompe
rim tape	un fond de jante
screw	une vis
spoke wrench	une clé à rayon
tube	une chambre à air

For more bike parts in French, see 🖳 www .sheldonbrown.com/eng-fren.html.

Directions & Road Conditions

How do I get to ...?	Comment dois-je faire pour arriver à ...?
Is it near?	Est-que c'est près?
Is it far?	Est-que c'est loin?
How many kilometres to ...?	Combien de kilomètres à ...?

Is it hilly?	Est-ce que c'est vallonné?
Is it steep?	Est-ce que c'est raide/escarpé?
The road climbs.	La route monte.
The road drops.	La route descend.
There are lots of hills.	Il y a beaucoup de collines.
Is there a lot of traffic?	Est-ce qu'il y a beaucoup de circulation?
Is there a bikepath near here?	Y a-t'il une piste cyclable près d'ici?
Is there a shortcut?	Est-ce qu'il y a un raccourci?
Can you show me on the map/ city map?	Est-ce que vous pouvez me le montrer sur la carte/le plan?
Is this road OK for bikes?	Est-ce qu'on peut rouler à vélo ici?

'Pedal Talk'

The following words and phrases will come in handy when you want to shoot the breeze with French cyclists you meet on your travels:

avoir les sorquettes légères – literally 'to have light socks', meaning to have good form on the bike, eg, *J'avais la socquette légère aujourd'hui* (I had a good day on the bike today).

une bécane – slang term for bicycle

chatouiller les pédales – literally 'to tickle the pedals'; an optimist's suggested method for climbing hills

une classique or trois vitesse – three-speed bicycle

un domestique – racing team rider who works selflessly for the team leader

échappé/e (m/f) – breakaway rider in a race

l'Enfer du Nord or *la Pascale* – popular name for the Paris-Roubaix race

la fringale – the arrival of *la fringale* is a variation on *l'homme au marteau* (see below)

la Grande Boucle – literally 'the big loop'; popular name for the Tour de France

(rencontrer) l'homme au marteau – literally '(to meet) the man with the hammer'; the French cyclist's equivalent of hitting the wall

un palmarès – record of victories

peloton – main group of riders in a race

la petite riene – literally 'the little queen'; reverential name for a bicycle

prendre la roue – to draft off another rider

un riseau cyclable – bikepath network

Go straight ahead.	*Continuez tout droit.*
Turn left.	*Tournez à gauche.*
Turn right.	*Tournez à droite.*
at the traffic lights	*aux feux*
at the next corner	*au prochain coin*
via ...	*en passant par ...*
behind	*derrière*
in front of	*devant*
opposite	*en face de*
to cycle	*faire du vélo*
to stop off at ...	*faire (une) étape à ...*
north/south	*nord/sud*
east/west	*est/ouest*
bitumen road	*une route goudronnée*
gravel road	*une route de gravier*
in good condition	*en bon état*
potholes	*nids de poule*
headwind	*vent de front/vent frontal*
tailwind	*vent arrière*

Accommodation

I'm looking for ...	*Je cherche ...*
the youth hostel	*l'auberge de jeunesse*
the camping ground	*le camping*
a hotel	*un hôtel*
a B&B	*une chambre d'hôte*
Where can I find a cheap hotel?	*Où est-ce que je peux trouver un hôtel bon marché?*
I'm looking for a good hotel with a garage (for my bike).	*Je cherche un bon hôtel avec un garage (pour mon vélo).*
What's the address?	*Quelle est l'adresse?*
Could you write it down, please?	*Est-ce que vous pourriez l'écrire, s'il vous plaît?*
Do you have any rooms available?	*Est-ce que vous avez des chambres libres?*
I'd like to book ...	*Je voudrais réserver ...*
a bed	*un lit*
a single room	*une chambre pour une personne*
a double room	*une chambre double*
a room with a shower/bath and toilet	*une chambre avec douche/bain et WC*

I'd like to stay in a dormitory.	*Je voudrais coucher dans un dortoir.*
How much is it ...?	*Quel est le prix ...?*
per night	*par nuit*
per person	*par personne*
Is breakfast included?	*Est-ce que le petit déjeuner est compris?*
May I see the room?	*Est-ce que je peux voir la chambre?*
Where can I leave my bike?	*Où puis-je laisser mon vélo?*
Can I take it to my room?	*Puis-je le mettre dans ma chambre?*
Do you have a garage?	*Avez vous un garage?*
Where is ...?	*Où est ...?*
the bathroom	*la salle de bains*
the shower	*la douche*
Where is the toilet?	*Où sont les toilettes?*
I'm going to stay ...	*Je resterai ...*
one day	*un jour*
a week	*une semaine*

Food

breakfast	*le petit déjeuner*
lunch	*le déjeuner*
dinner	*le dîner*
a bakery	*une boulangerie*
a cake/pastry shop	*une pâtisserie*
a delicatessen	*une charcuterie*
a grocery store	*une épicerie*
I'm a vegetarian.	*Je suis végétarien/ végétarienne.*
I don't eat meat.	*Je ne mange pas de viande.*
I'd like the set menu.	*Je prends le menu.*
I'd like pasta/rice.	*Je voudrais du riz/ des pâtes.*

See the Food and Drinks sections in the Facts for the Cyclist chapter for more words and phrases in French to keep you fuelled.

Health

I'm sick.	*Je suis malade.*
I need a doctor.	*Il me faut un médecin.*
Where is the hospital?	*Où est l'hôpital?*
I have diarrhoea.	*J'ai la diarrhée.*
I'm pregnant.	*Je suis enceinte.*

Emergencies

Help!	Au secours!
Call a doctor!	Appelez un médecin!
Call the police!	Appelez la police!
I've had a crash.	J'ai eu un accident.
I've been robbed.	On m'a volé.
I've been raped.	On m'a violée.
I'm lost.	Je me suis égaré/ égarée. (m/f)
Leave me alone!	Fichez-moi la paix!

I have sore knees.	*J'ai mal aux genoux.*
I have saddle sores.	*J'ai mal aux fesses.*
I have thrush.	*J'ai le muguet.*

I'm ...	*Je suis ...*
diabetic	*diabétique*
epileptic	*épileptique*
asthmatic	*asthmatique*
anaemic	*anémique*
I'm allergic ...	*Je suis allergique ...*
to antibiotics	*aux antibiotiques*
to penicillin	*à la pénicilline*
to bees	*aux abeilles*

anaesthetic cream	*crème anesthésique*
antiseptic	*antiseptique*
aspirin	*aspirine*
condoms	*préservatifs*
contraceptive	*contraceptif*
medicine	*médicament*
nausea	*nausée*
sunblock cream	*crème solaire haute protection*
tampons	*tampons hygiéniques*

Time, Dates & Numbers

What time is it?	*Quelle heure est-il?*
It's (two) o'clock.	*Il est (deux) heures.*
When?	*Quand?*
today	*aujourd'hui*
tonight	*ce soir*
tomorrow	*demain*
day after tomorrow	*après-demain*

yesterday	*hier*
all day	*toute la journée*
in the morning	*du matin*
in the afternoon	*de l'après-midi*
in the evening	*du soir*

Monday	*lundi*
Tuesday	*mardi*
Wednesday	*mercredi*
Thursday	*jeudi*
Friday	*vendredi*
Saturday	*samedi*
Sunday	*dimanche*
January	*janvier*
February	*février*
March	*mars*
April	*avril*
May	*mai*
June	*juin*
July	*juillet*
August	*août*
September	*septembre*
October	*octobre*
November	*novembre*
December	*décembre*

1	*un*
2	*deux*
3	*trois*
4	*quatre*
5	*cinq*
6	*six*
7	*sept*
8	*huit*
9	*neuf*
10	*dix*
11	*onze*
12	*douze*
13	*treize*
14	*quatorze*
15	*quinze*
16	*seize*
17	*dix-sept*
20	*vingt*
100	*cent*
1000	*mille*

one million	*un million*

Glossary

(m) indicates masculine gender, (f) feminine gender and (pl) plural

abbaye (f) – abbey
alimentation (f) – grocery store
appellation (f) – region/area that follows strict quality controls to produce wine or food specialities
arrondissement (m) – administrative division of a large city
auberge (f) – inn
auberge de jeunesse (f) – (youth) hostel
autres directions – other directions

baie (f) – bay
balisé – marked (such as sentiers balisés – marked paths)
ballons (m pl) – literally 'balloons', the rounded Massif des Vosges mountains
banlieue (f) – suburbs
bastide (f) – medieval fortified town
billet (m) – ticket
bocage (m) – wooded area
bois (m) – woods or forest
boulangerie (f) – bakery or bread shop
boules (f pl) – type of bowls played with metal balls on a sandy pitch; also called *pétanque*
bourg (m) – small village
brasserie (f) – restaurant usually serving food all day (original meaning: brewery)
break (m) – station wagon
bureau de change (m) – exchange bureau

calvaire (m) – calvary (monument representing Christ's crucifixion)
camping à la ferme – farm camping ground
carrefour (m) – crossroad
carte (f) – card, menu or map
cave (f) – wine cellar
causse (m) – limestone plateau (in south-central France)
chambre (f) – room
chambre d'hôte (f) – B&B
charcuterie (f) – delicatessen, pork butcher's shop or assorted cured meats and sausages
chocolaterie (f) – chocolate shop or maker
cirque –an alpine basin carved by a glacier, usually at the head of a valley
citadelle (f) – fortified city
cluse (f) – transverse valley in the Jura
col (m) – mountain pass
contrôle – checkpoint for raid ride

côte (f) – slope (hill) or coastline
cour (f) – courtyard
crête (f) – ridge (used to describe a road)
cyclosportive (m) – informal mass ride

dégustation (f) – tasting
demi-pension (f) – half-board (B&B with breakfast and either lunch or dinner)
département (m) – department (administrative division of France)
dépôt de pain – shop that sells bread
douane (f) – Customs

école (f) – school
écluse (f) – (canal) lock
écurie (f) – stables
église (f) – church
épicerie (f) – small grocery store (literally 'spice shop')
étang (m) – pond or pool

ferme (f) – farm
fermé – closed
fête (f) – festival
forêt (f) – forest
forêt domaniale (f) – national forest
foyer (m) – worker or student hostel
fromagerie (f) – cheese shop

gare (SNCF) (f) – train station
gare maritime (f) – ferry terminal
gare routière (f) – bus station
gendarmerie (f) – police station/force
gîte d'étape (m) – lodging usually in a village or a remote mountain area
Grand Cru (m) – French classification of exceptional, high-quality vineyards
gîte rural (m) – country cottage
glacier (m) – ice-cream maker or vendor

halage (m) – towpath (along a canal)
halles (f pl) – covered market or central food market
horloge (f) – clock
hôtel de ville (m) – city or town hall
housse (f) – bike bag

jardin (m) – garden
jours fériés (m pl) – public holidays

lac (m) – lake
laverie (f) – laundrette

ACRONYMS

French love acronyms as much as the British and Americans do. Many transport companies are known by acronyms whose derivations are entirely unknown by the average person.

AOC – Appellation d'Origine Contrôlée (officially controlled wine growing area; also used for cheese and some food products)
DAB – distributeurs automatiques de billets, or ATMs
FFC – Fédération Française de Cyclisme (French Cycling Federation)
FFCT – Fédération Française de Cyclo-tourisme (French Cycle Touring Federation)
FUAJ – Fédération Unie des Auberges de Jeunesse (French Hostel Association)
GR – Grande Randonnée (long-distance walking trail)
IGN – Institut Géographique Nationale (National Institute of Geography)
ONF – Office Nationale des Forêts (National Forests Office)
RF – Route Forestière (forest road)
SERNAM – SNCF's official freight service
SNCF –Société Nationale des Chemins de Fer (French Railways)
TER – Transport Express Régional (Regional Express Transport)
TGV – Train à Grande Vitesse (high-speed train)
VTC – vélo tout chemin (hybrid bike)
VTT – vélo tout terrain (mountain bike)

⊷⊶⊷⊶⊷⊶⊷⊶⊷⊶⊷⊶⊷

mairie (f) – city or town hall
maison (f) – house
maison de la presse (f) – newsagent
maison du parc (f) – national or regional park headquarters and/or visitors centre
manoir (m) – manor house
marcerie (f) – high mountain farm inn
marché (m) – market
marché couvert (m) – covered market
menu (m) – fixed-price meal with two or more courses
Mistral – incessant north wind in southern France that is said to drive people crazy
montagne (f) – mountain
moulin (m) – mill
musée (m) – museum

navette (f) – shuttle bus, train or boat

parapent (m) – paragliding
parc (m) – park
parc régional (m) – regional park
pâtisserie (f) – cake and pastry shop
pavé (m) – cobblestone
pays (m) – country or land
pétanque (f) – type of bowls played with metal balls on a sandy pitch; also called *boules*
piste cyclable (f) – bikepath
place (f) – square or plaza
plage (f) – beach
pont (m) – bridge
port (m) – harbour or port
porte (f) – gate in a city wall or door
poste/bureau de poste (f/m) – post office

quai (m) – quay or railway platform
quartier (m) – quarter or district

raid (m) – extremely long and challenging ride/randonnée
randonnée (f) – a drive, ride or walk; in French cycling circles, generally refers to a set course to be completed within a time limit
refuge (m) – mountain hut or shelter
réseau cyclable (m) – network of bikepaths
rive (f) – river bank (*rive droite* – right bank, *rive gauche* – left bank)
rivière (f) – river
rond-point (m) – roundabout or traffic circle
roundabout – traffic circle

sentier (m) – trail or path
son et lumière (m) – sound and light show
syndicat d'initiative (m) – tourist office

tabac (m) – tobacconist (also sells phonecards)
taxe de séjour (f) – tax on accommodation
télécarte (f) – phonecard
téléphérique (m) – cable car
toutes directions – all directions
tour (f) – tower or circuit
tuffeau – tufa stone, or limestone, found in the Saumur region of the Loire Valley

vedette (f) – boat (motorised)
vélo (m) – bicycle
vélo de ville (m) – city bike
vendange (f) – grape harvest
vielle ville (f) – old town or old city
vignoble (m) – vineyard
vitesse (f) – speed
voie (f) – train platform

This Book

Katherine Widing was the coordinating author of *Cycling France*; she wrote the introductory chapters as well as the Paris & the Île de France, Normandy & Brittany and Champagne chapters. Sally Dillon wrote the Loire Valley, South-West France, Massif Central and Corsica chapters. Catherine Palmer wrote the Alsace & Lorraine, Tour de France, Burgundy and French Alps & the Jura chapters; and Neil Irvine wrote the Pyrenees, Languedoc & Roussillon, Provence & the Côte d'Azur and Randonnées chapters.

The Your Bicycle chapter was written by Darren Elder with contributions by Nicola Wells, Neil Irvine and Sally Dillon. The Health & Safety chapter was written by Katherine Widing, Dr Isabelle Young, and Kevin Tabotta. Material from the 3rd edition of Lonely Planet's *France* and the 1st editions of *Corsica*, *The Loire*, *Provence & the Côte d'Azur* and *Europe* were used for parts of this book.

FROM THE PUBLISHER

Cycling France, the second in Lonely Planet's new series of cycling guides, has been a long time in the making. The series was developed by a team from Lonely Planet's Outdoor Activities Unit in Melbourne including Emily Coles, Sally Dillon, Teresa Donnellan, Chris Klep, Andrew Smith, Nick Tapp and series editor Darren Elder, assisted by Paul Clifton and Nicola Wells. The cover design for the series was developed by Jamieson Gross, who also designed this book's cover.

Sally Dillon and Helen Rowley coordinated the editing and mapping/design, respectively, of this book. Editorially, Sally was assisted by Angie Phelan, Thalia Kalkipsakis, Nicola Wells, Adam Ford, Evan Jones and Janet Brunckhorst; and Quentin Frayne organised the language chapter. In mapping, Helen was assisted by Sonya Brooke, Glenn van der Knijff, Jacqui Saunders, Andrew Smith and Simon Tillema; in design, by Mathew Burfoot, Lisa Borg and Andrew Tudor; and guidance came from Michael Blore and Teresa Donnellan.

Thanks go to Ron Shepherd and Paul Farren for invaluable historical input and the loan of precious archival material; Alex Landragin for wine advice; Leonie Mugavin for extra research; Adrienne Costanzo; Paul Bloomfield in the UK office; the staff of the Paris office, particularly Soph Riviore and Didier Buroc; Vincent Vallet and Ali Basa for all manner of French language queries; Kim Travers and Derek McKean for lending us the Audax medallions.

Geoff Rasmussen wrote computer programs to automate our processes. The staff of LPI, in particular Fiona Croyden, Brett Pascoe, Annie Horner and Matt King, also lent valuable assistance.

Jeff Crowe from Sport: The Library shot the photographs used in the Your Bicycle chapter. A crew from Cannondale USA and Cannondale Australia provided the bicycles for the Your Bicycle chapter; thanks to Nick Goljanin, Bill Conradt, Tom Armstrong and Matt Moon. Christie Cycles, Hawthorn, and Swim Bike Run, St Kilda, assembled the bicycles and provided technical assistance; thanks to Ian and Richard, in particular.

LONELY PLANET

You already know that Lonely Planet produces more than this one guidebook, but you might not be aware of the other products we have on this region. Here is a selection of titles that you may want to check out as well:

Walking in France
ISBN 0 86442 601 1

French phrasebook
ISBN 0 86442 450 7

World Food France
ISBN 1 86450 021 2

France
ISBN 1 86450 151 0

South-West France
ISBN 0 86442 794 8

Paris
ISBN 1 86450 125 1

The Loire
ISBN 1 86450 097 2

Europe on a shoestring
ISBN 1 86450 150 2

Corsica
ISBN 0 86442 792 1

Western Europe
ISBN 1 86450 163 4

Paris City Map
ISBN 1 86450 011 5

Read this First: Europe
ISBN 1 86450 136 7

Paris Condensed
ISBN 1 86450 044 1

Cycling Britain
ISBN 1 86450 037 9

Cycling New Zealand
ISBN 1 86450 031 X

Available wherever books are sold

LONELY PLANET

Guides by Region

Lonely Planet is known worldwide for publishing practical, reliable and no-nonsense travel information in our guides and on our Web site. The Lonely Planet list covers just about every accessible part of the world. Currently there are 16 series: Travel guides, Shoestring guides, Condensed guides, Phrasebooks, Read This First, Healthy Travel, Walking guides, Cycling guides, Watching Wildlife guides, Pisces Diving & Snorkeling guides, City Maps, Road Atlases, Out to Eat, World Food, Journeys travel literature and Pictorials.

AFRICA Africa on a shoestring • Cairo • Cape Town • Cape Town City Map • East Africa • Egypt • Egyptian Arabic phrasebook • Ethiopia, Eritrea & Djibouti • Ethiopian (Amharic) phrasebook • The Gambia & Senegal • Healthy Travel Africa • Kenya • Malawi • Morocco • Moroccan Arabic phrasebook • Mozambique • Read This First: Africa • South Africa, Lesotho & Swaziland • Southern Africa • Southern Africa Road Atlas • Swahili phrasebook • Tanzania, Zanzibar & Pemba • Trekking in East Africa • Tunisia • Watching Wildlife East Africa • Watching Wildlife Southern Africa • West Africa • World Food Morocco • Zimbabwe, Botswana & Namibia
Travel Literature: Mali Blues: Traveling to an African Beat • The Rainbird: A Central African Journey • Songs to an African Sunset: A Zimbabwean Story

AUSTRALIA & THE PACIFIC Auckland • Australia • Australian phrasebook • Australia Road Atlas • Bushwalking in Australia •Cycling New Zealand • Fiji • Fijian phrasebook • Healthy Travel Australia, NZ and the Pacific • Islands of Australia's Great Barrier Reef • Melbourne • Melbourne City Map • Micronesia • New Caledonia • New South Wales & the ACT • New Zealand • Northern Territory • Outback Australia • Out to Eat – Melbourne • Out to Eat – Sydney • Papua New Guinea • Pidgin phrasebook • Queensland • Rarotonga & the Cook Islands • Samoa • Solomon Islands • South Australia • South Pacific • South Pacific phrasebook • Sydney • Sydney City Map • Sydney Condensed • Tahiti & French Polynesia • Tasmania • Tonga • Tramping in New Zealand • Vanuatu • Victoria • Walking in Australia • Watching Wildlife Australia • Western Australia
Travel Literature: Islands in the Clouds: Travels in the Highlands of New Guinea • Kiwi Tracks: A New Zealand Journey • Sean & David's Long Drive

CENTRAL AMERICA & THE CARIBBEAN Bahamas, Turks & Caicos • Baja California • Bermuda • Central America on a shoestring • Costa Rica • Costa Rica Spanish phrasebook • Cuba • Dominican Republic & Haiti • Eastern Caribbean • Guatemala • Guatemala, Belize & Yucatán: La Ruta Maya • Healthy Travel Central & South America • Jamaica • Mexico • Mexico City • Panama • Puerto Rico • Read This First: Central & South America • World Food Mexico • Yucatán
Travel Literature: Green Dreams: Travels in Central America

EUROPE Amsterdam • Amsterdam City Map • Amsterdam Condensed • Andalucía • Austria • Baltic States phrasebook • Barcelona • Barcelona City Map • Berlin • Berlin City Map • Britain • British phrasebook • Brussels, Bruges & Antwerp • Brussels City Map • Budapest • Budapest City Map • Canary Islands • Central Europe • Central Europe phrasebook • Corfu & the Ionians • Corsica • Crete • Crete Condensed • Croatia • Cycling Britain • Cycling France • Cyprus • Czech & Slovak Republics • Denmark • Dublin • Dublin City Map • Eastern Europe • Eastern Europe phrasebook • Edinburgh • Estonia, Latvia & Lithuania • Europe on a shoestring • Finland • Florence • France • Frankfurt Condensed • French phrasebook • Georgia, Armenia & Azerbaijan • Germany • German phrasebook • Greece • Greek Islands • Greek phrasebook • Hungary • Iceland, Greenland & the Faroe Islands • Ireland • Istanbul • Italian phrasebook • Italy • Krakow • Lisbon • The Loire • London • London City Map • London Condensed • Madrid • Malta • Mediterranean Europe • Mediterranean Europe phrasebook • Moscow • Munich • the Netherlands • Norway • Out to Eat – London • Paris • Paris City Map • Paris Condensed • Poland • Portugal • Portuguese phrasebook • Prague • Prague City Map • Provence & the Côte d'Azur • Read This First: Europe • Romania & Moldova • Rome • Rome City Map • Russia, Ukraine & Belarus • Russian phrasebook • Scandinavian & Baltic Europe • Scandinavian Europe phrasebook • Scotland • Sicily • Slovenia • South-West France • Spain • Spanish phrasebook • St Petersburg • St Petersburg City Map • Sweden • Switzerland • Trekking in Spain • Tuscany • Ukrainian phrasebook • Venice • Vienna • Walking in Britain • Walking in France • Walking in Ireland • Walking in Italy • Walking in Spain • Walking in Switzerland • Western Europe • Western Europe phrasebook • World Food France • World Food Ireland • World Food Italy • World Food Spain
Travel Literature: Love and War in the Apennines • The Olive Grove: Travels in Greece • On the Shores of the Mediterranean • Round Ireland in Low Gear • A Small Place in Italy • After Yugoslavia

Index

Text
For a listing of rides, see the Table of Rides (pp4–5)

Bold indicates maps.

Boxed Text

ABOUT LONELY PLANET GUIDEBOOKS

Lonely Planet published its first book in 1973 in response to the numerous 'How did you do it?' questions Maureen and Tony Wheeler were asked after driving, busing, hitching, sailing and railing their way from England to Australia.

Written at a kitchen table and hand collated, trimmed and stapled, *Across Asia on the Cheap* became an instant local bestseller, inspiring thoughts of another book.

Eighteen months in South-East Asia resulted in their second guide, *South-East Asia on a shoestring*, which they put together in a backstreet Chinese hotel in Singapore in 1975. The 'yellow bible', as it quickly became known to backpackers around the world, soon became the guide to the region. It has sold well over half a million copies and is now in its 10th edition.

Today an international company with offices in Melbourne (Australia), Oakland (USA), London (UK) and Paris (France), Lonely Planet has an ever-growing list of books and other products, including: travel guides, walking guides, city maps, travel atlases, phrasebooks, diving guides, wildlife guides, healthy travel guides, restaurant guides, world food guides, first time travel guides, condensed guides, travel literature, pictorial books and, of course, cycling guides. Many of these are also published in French and various other languages.

In addition to the books, there are also videos and Lonely Planet's award winning Web site.

Some things haven't changed. The main aim is still to help make it possible for adventurous travellers to get out there – to explore and better understand the world.

At Lonely Planet we believe travellers can make a positive contribution to the countries they visit – if they respect their host communities and spend their money wisely. Since 1986 a percentage of the income from each book has been donated to aid projects and human rights campaigns.

> **Lonely Planet gathers information for everyone who's curious about the planet – and especially for those who explore it first-hand. Through guidebooks, phrasebooks, activity guides, maps, literature, newsletters, image library, TV series and Web site we act as an information exchange for a worldwide community of travellers.**

LONELY PLANET OFFICES

Australia
Locked Bag 1, Footscray, Victoria 3011
☎ 03 9689 4666 fax 03 9689 6833
✉ talk2us@lonelyplanet.com.au

UK
10a Spring Place, London NW5 3BH
☎ 020 7428 4800 fax 020 7428 4828
✉ go@lonelyplanet.co.uk

USA
150 Linden St, Oakland, CA 94607
☎ 510 893 8555 or ☎ 800 275 8555 (toll free)
fax 510 893 8572
✉ info@lonelyplanet.com

France
1 rue du Dahomey, 75011 Paris
☎ 01 55 25 33 00 fax 01 55 25 33 01
✉ bip@lonelyplanet.fr
🖥 www.lonelyplanet.fr

World Wide Web: 🖥 **www.lonelyplanet.com** *or* **AOL keyword: lp**
Lonely Planet Images: ✉ **lpi@lonelyplanet.com.au**